Global Marketing

Foreign Entry, Local Marketing, & Global Management

Fifth Edition

Johny K. Johansson
Georgetown University

McGraw Hill

Boston   Burr Ridge, IL   Dubuque, IA   Madison, WI   New York   San Francisco   St. Louis
Bangkok   Bogotá   Caracas   Kuala Lumpur   Lisbon   London   Madrid   Mexico City
Milan   Montreal   New Delhi   Santiago   Seoul   Singapore   Sydney   Taipei   Toronto

The McGraw·Hill Companies

GLOBAL MARKETING:
FOREIGN ENTRY, LOCAL MARKETING, AND GLOBAL MANAGEMENT
International Edition 2009

10 09 08 07 06 05 04 03 02 01
20 09
CTF   BJE

When ordering this title, use ISBN 978-007-126362-7 or MHID 007-126362-4

Printed in Singapore

www.mhhe.com

To my parents,
Ruth and Nils Johansson

About the Author

Johny K. Johansson is the McCrane/Shaker Chairholder in International Business and Marketing in the McDonough School of Business at Georgetown University. An expert in the areas of international marketing strategy and consumer decision making, especially as applied to Japanese and European companies and markets, Johansson has published over 70 academic articles and chapters in books. He is the author of *In Your face: How American Marketing Excess Fuels Anti-Americanism,* Financial Times/Prentice Hall, 2004, and (with Ikujiro Nonaka) of *Relentless: The Japanese Way of Marketing,* HarperBusiness, 1996. He has conducted numerous executive seminars in many countries, including Japan, Germany, Sweden, Hong Kong, Thailand, and India. He has also been a consultant to companies in many countries, including General Electric, Marriott, and Xerox in the United States; Beiersdorft and Ford Werke AG in Germany; Volvo and Electrolux in Sweden; and Honda, Dentsu, and Fuji Film in Japan.

Before joining Georgetown's faculty, Professor Johansson held faculty positions at the University of Washington and the University of Illinois. He also has held many visiting appointments in several countries. He was the first Isetan Distinguished Visiting Professor at Keio Business School (Japan) and the first Ford Distinguished Visiting Professor at University of Cologne in Germany. He also has been a visiting professor at New York University, Dalhousie University (Canada), Stockholm School of Economics, the Catholic University of Leuven (Belgium), the National Defense Academy (Japan), and the International University of Japan. In 1988 he was a Phelps scholar at the University of Michigan.

Professor Johansson earned Ph.D. and M.B.A. degrees from the University of California, Berkeley, and his undergraduate degree (Civilekonom) from the Stockholm School of Economics. A Swedish citizen, he lives in Georgetown, Washington, DC, with his wife, Tamiko, and their two daughters, Anna and Sonja.

Preface

Global marketing is one of the most exciting fields of business. With the emergence of China, India, Vietnam, Dubai, and other unlikely candidates for global pre-eminence, many people and many companies around the globe now believe in the basic soundness of globalization and free trade. Of course, there are clearly countries, companies, and people who have been shortchanged by the globalization process and who, not surprisingly, demand redress. While terrorism cannot—and, fortunately, is not—condoned by anybody sane, at least the antiglobalization activists are raising issues that the global marketer needs to pay attention to.

But there are other challenges as well. Global marketing is very demanding professionally. This goes for managing it or learning about it, and also for teaching it. It requires not only a good grasp of marketing principles and an understanding of the global environment, but also how the two interact—that is, how the environment impacts the applicability of the marketing principles. Good marketing might be good marketing everywhere—but this does not mean it is necessarily the same.

The challenge when writing a text in global marketing is how to avoid being overwhelmed by all the curious and amazing differences in the marketing environment in foreign countries. These differences make things fun and enjoyable—but also frustrating, since after a while it is difficult to see if any progress has been made. It is hard to see the forest for the trees. The key is to focus on the marketing decisions that have to be made—and then deal with those environmental factors that directly impact those decisions. This is the approach taken in this text. It discusses the complexities of global marketing and clarifies the managerial roles involved, without getting bogged down by the many environmental issues that are only marginally relevant.

Key Features

When compared to other texts on the subject, *Global Marketing* still has three main distinguishing features:

1. There are no introductory chapters on "the international environment" of politics, finance, legal issues, and economic regions. With the exception of culture, the book covers the environmental variables on an "as needed" basis, in the various chapters.
2. As opposed to the traditional view of one "marketing manager," the typical global marketing manager's job consists of three separate tasks: foreign entry, local marketing, and global management. Each requires different skills, as we will see. Our metaphor is that the marketer wears "three hats," sometimes successively. In foreign entry, in global management, and to a large extent even as a local marketer in a foreign country, the global marketer needs skills that the home market experience—or the standard marketing text—has rarely taught. The recognition of the three roles helps dispel the notion that "there is no such thing as international or global marketing, only marketing." This sentiment has some truth to it, but mainly in the local marketing portion of the job.
3. The material is based on a foundation of strategy and the theory of the multinational firm—for the most practical of reasons, because the theory helps the marketing manager understand what drives the company expansion abroad and how and when to adapt the various marketing functions involved to local conditions.

At the same time, much of the excellent research and tried-and-true teaching material that global marketers in business and academe have contributed over the years is reflected in the chapters and in the several cases that can be found at the end of each major section. My intent has been to retain and update much of the teaching and instructional material that has made global marketing such an exciting class in many business schools—and made for the start of an exciting managerial career—and to fit the material into a structure that reflects the global marketing management tasks. I have focused on material that is timely and up-to-date, and relevant to the global context.

Target Audience and Possible Courses

Global Marketing is aimed at the executive, the MBA student, or the senior undergraduate, none of whom is completely new to marketing or to the global environment. I have in mind a reader who is familiar with the basic marketing principles, and who has had some exposure to the international environment and the thrust toward a global economy. I have avoided unnecessarily complicated jargon—the global marketing job is inherently complex, and any opportunity to "keep it simple" has been capitalized on.

The three-way partition of the book makes it possible to construct several alternative course outlines from the book.

- A complete course on "Global Marketing," possibly using additional cases, is the "full-course" treatment.
- A shorter "Global Marketing Management" course, perhaps for executives, could go straight from the fundamentals in the first three chapters to Part Four, "Global Management," starting with Chapter 11. This is one approach I have used at Georgetown.
- An "International Marketing" course could focus on local marketing and global management, Parts Three and Four.
- An "Export Marketing" course could select the foreign entry chapters from Part Two, and then do the local marketing chapters in Part Three plus the pricing and distribution chapters in Part Four, "Global Management."
- At Georgetown I have also used the text in a second-year MBA class titled "Foreign Market Development," for which I assign Parts Two and Three on foreign entry and local marketing, and then only the first three chapters of Part Four, "Global Management."

New to the Fifth Edition

The fifth edition keeps the original structure (Foreign Entry, Local Marketing, Global Management) that has proved successful and popular among users. But based upon user and reviewer feedback, several changes have been introduced in order to make the text more relevant, useful, and up-to-date.

The five major changes are:

1. There is a new chapter on "Global Branding" (Chapter 13). This chapter extends the branding discussion in the previous edition, and adds new material on brand equity and on the added value that "globality" confers upon a brand. It also introduces the concept of country branding.
2. The "Global Marketing Strategy" chapter (Chapter 11), leading off Part Four on "Global Management," is a revised and updated version of the "Global Segmentation and Positioning" chapter in the fourth edition. The chapter still covers new research on global segmentation and positioning, but adds new material on resource allocation across products and markets.
3. The "Global Product" and "Global Services" chapters have been consolidated into Chapter 12, made possible by breaking out "Global Brands" into its own chapter. This means the fifth edition has the same number of chapters as the fourth.
4. The region-specific chapters in Part Three on "Local Marketing"—mature markets in Chapter 8, new growth markets in Chapter 9, and emerging markets in Chapter 10—have been updated, taking into account not only economic developments such as China's and India's emergence as major players, but also the new Russia, Vietnam, and the Middle East.

5. The e-commerce material in Chapter 17 has been updated, revised, and extended, recognizing the amazing developments after the emergence of Web 2.0.

There are also several other changes that serve to improve the coverage and incorporate new thoughts and research findings in global marketing. The local market research discussion in Chapter 7 has been expanded to incorporate more of the measurement and sampling difficulties in various countries that jeopardize comparability across markets. And, of course, many of the illustrations of global marketing practice in the "Getting the Picture" boxes have been updated or newly written.

Even with these changes, the basic structure of the text is the same as before. The sequence of an initial "Fundamentals" part followed by the three tasks involved in global marketing—foreign entry, local marketing, and global management—has proven resilient. According to instructor and student feedback, the structure facilitates both learning and teaching because it clarifies naturally the sometimes complex responsibilities and relationships that have to be managed in global marketing.

Supplements

Teaching a global marketing course requires more supplementary material than usual because of the amount of information about foreign countries that has to be provided. No one can master it all. I am pleased to say that the editorial staff at McGraw-Hill/Irwin has helped me put together what I think is a very strong resource package.

The supplements are especially designed by marketing professors, colleagues of mine, to help teachers of this course be more effective. We have taken care to offer the best supplements we could make available.

Online Learning Center www.mhhe.com/johansson5e

This supplement contains our Instructor's Manual that is designed to assist instructors in meeting the varied curricular and pedagogical challenges inherent in teaching an International or Global Marketing course. The manual is particularly sensitive to the needs of various kinds of global marketing classroom situations and includes syllabus construction, pacing of topic coverage and other teaching suggestions, lecture outlines, discussion of end-of-chapter questions and supplemental readings based on the varying perspectives and needs of the instructor. Included in this supplement are discussions of the PowerPoint slides and readings.

The Test Bank consists of more than 1,400 questions designed to thoroughly test the comprehension of basic terminology and concepts as well as the student's ability to apply those concepts. The material in each of the text's 18 chapters is tested by a battery of 60 multiple-choice, 10 short-answer, and 10 essay questions.

Also included is a comprehensive set of PowerPoint slides, many new to this edition, including both in-text and out-of-text graphics.

Acknowledgements

As in the previous editions, I have tried to make the text as fun and interesting to read as possible! You will, of course, judge for yourself whether I have succeeded. Many people have helped.

The fifth edition has built upon the contributions and inspiration of many people. First and foremost are my colleagues Claudiu Dimofte and Ilkka Ronkainen, who have been very instrumental in the work on global branding, in research, and for the text. Gary Bamossy, now a valued colleague here at Georgetown, was also very helpful not only with suggestions and reviews, but especially with the new material on the Web 2.0 development. And I want to thank Masoud Kavoossi at Howard University for his help with the new Middle East section, as well as general feedback on the text.

My former assistant, Cipriano de Leon, provided independent ideas and views. I am also grateful to Raul Alvarez of Comcast, an international executive who helped revise, update, and improve the text. I also must thank a former student, Nick Matthews, now with KPMG in Melbourne, whose material and summaries on transfer pricing were invaluable in the pricing chapter.

The environment at Georgetown's School of Business is still ideal, with its emphasis on "international" as a school theme, the support of the Dean, and the resources made available through the McCrane/Shaker chair, including a reduced teaching load and secretarial assistance. Friends and colleagues like Michael Czinkota, Paul Almeida, Stan Nollen, Rob Grant, Kasra Ferdows, Tom Brewer, Dennis Quinn, and others in marketing and international business always provide a stimulating environment for global work.

The fifth edition owes much to travel, conferences, and colleagues at other academic institutions as well. One conference in particular stands out. In May 2003, I took part in a Harvard symposium organized to celebrate the 30 years since Ted Levitt's *The Globalization of Markets* was published. As for travel, the integrative field trips with the Georgetown MBAs to Shanghai in 2006 and Ho Chi Minh City in 2007 were very helpful with new and interesting insights from both academicians and practitioners. In the Middle East, Sheikh Dr. Mohammed Saleh Al-Sharqi, the Chairman of the Emirates Educational Services in Fujairah, and Dean Michael Owen at Zayed University in Dubai were very helpful and insightful. So was Per Johansson, my nephew, who is General Manager of Orica Mining Services and runs its venture in Dubai. Teaching executive seminars in St. Petersburg also showed what is at stake when shifting a central command economy into a market-oriented society.

Among international scholars, Jean-Claude Larreche and Philippe Lasserre at Insead, Pankaj Ghemawat at Harvard, Alan Rugman and Hans Thorelli at Indiana, Nick Papadopoulos at Carleton, Tamer Cavusgil at Georgia State, Gary Knight at Florida State, David Tse at University of Hong Kong, Gert Assmus at Tuck, Bodo Schlegelmilch in Vienna, Craig Smith at London Business School, Jagdish Sheth at Emory, John Farley at Tuck, Tage Madsen at Odense, and Masaaki Kotabe and Preet Aulakh at Temple have had a strong impact on my thinking. So have Jean-Claude Usunier at Universite Louis Pasteur in Strasbourg; Christian Homburg at Mannheim University; Masaaki Hirano at Waseda; Saeed Samie at Tulsa; Tomas Hult at Michigan State; Jens Laage-Hellman at Chalmers in Gothenburg; Mosad Zineldin at Vaxjo University; Israel Nebenzahl at Bar-Ilan University; Bernard Simonin, now at Tutts; and Carlos Garcia-Pont at IESE, Barcelona. Tyler Cowen at George Mason University was very insightful in analyzing popular music in the Caribbean.

When it comes to global strategy, I have been greatly influenced by George Yip, now Dean at Rotterdam School of Management, Erasmus University, and Ikujiro Nonaka at Hitotsubashi University, both good friends and co-authors; Nick Binedell in Johannesburg; and Tadao Kagono at Kobe University. In global branding, the conference held at Georgetown in May 2001 helped my thinking a great deal. Special thanks go to the practitioners who presented their companies' branding philosophy, especially Hikoh Okuda and Gary Podorowsky of Sony, Dan Bonawitz of Honda, and Allen Adamson at Landor. I also learned much from Rajeev Batra at Michigan; Erich Joachimsthaler, Head of Vivaldi Partners; and Kevin Keller at Tuck. I have benefited from discussions with Pradeep Rau and Sanal Mazvancheryl at George Washington University, Monty Graham at the Institute of International Economics (IIE) in Washington, Susan Douglas at New York University, Chris Macrae of the World Class Branding Network in London, Hiroshi Tanaka at Hosei University in Tokyo, Shigeo Kobayashi of Honda's Future Research group, and Lia Nikopoulos of Landor Associates.

In electronic commerce, I have learned a great deal from Bill McHenry at Georgetown, Eric Boyd now at James Madison University, and Mikael Karlsson at Reson AB in Stockholm. Among marketing colleagues, I want to single out David Montgomery, now at Singapore Management University; Claes Fornell at Michigan; Philip Kotler at Northwestern; Dominique Hanssens at UCLA; Evert Gummesson at the University of Stockholm; and John Graham at Irvine, who all have helped bridge the gap between international and noninternational research in marketing.

Some of the practitioners I have had the good fortune to meet and learn from should also be thanked. Eddie Mak, the Director General of Hong Kong Economic and Trade Office was very persuasive about the opportunities in Asia. Paul Stiles with his background on Wall Street and disenchantment with free markets has also influenced my thinking a great deal. Trevor Gunn at Medtronic, Nicholas Lugansky at Bechtel, and James R. Millar at George Washington University provided incisive information about Russian developments. Flip de Jager at Volvo, Chong Lee at LG Korea, Bruce Wolff at Marriott, and John Stabb at Microlog also stand out. So do Saburo Kobayashi; Osamu Iida and Takanori Sonoda at Honda; Masumi Natsusaka at Kao in Tokyo; Masaaki Eguchi also at Kao; Per Surtevall at SIFO, Stockholm; Hermawan Kartajaya of Mark-Plus in Jakarta; Ulf Södergren and Lars-Göran Johansson at Electrolux; Casey Shimamoto, formerly of ExecNet, Tokyo; and Jan Segerfeldt of Segerfeldt & Partners in Stockholm. Several of my present and former students provided valuable input of one kind or another, especially Paul Lewis and Mitchell Murata at Georgetown.

I am especially grateful to the many people who have given me constructive feedback on the previous editions of the book. In particular, I want to thank Martin Cody of AIM International and Larry Cunningham at the University of Colorado in Denver. Nikolai Ostapenko at the University of Maryland and Georgetown was particularly helpful with the Russian material and with an overall review.

Special thanks are due to the case writers who graciously allowed me to use their work in the book: Tamer Cavusgil, now at Georgia State; Per Jenster at Copenhagen Business School; Pamela Adams at Bocconi; Richard Köhler and Wolfgang Breuer at Cologne University; Dave Montgomery at Stanford; Kasra Ferdows at Georgetown; Christian Pinson and Vikas Tibrewala at INSEAD; Sandra Vandermerwe at Imperial College, London; George Yip at London Business School; Chei Hwee Chua, Peter Williamson, and Arnoud de Meyer at Insead; and Eddie Yu and Anthony Ko at City University of Hong Kong.

The editorial staff at McGraw-Hill/Irwin deserves a great deal of credit. Laura Spell and Lori Bradshaw were great to work with, encouraging but also prompting me to get on with it. Michael Hruby behind the photos made it clear that there is more to a book than just the writing of it. I also wish to express my appreciation to the following individuals for reviewing the fifth edition: Prema Nakra, Maris College; Jacqueline M. Stravos, Lawrence Technological University; Trini Callava, Miami Dade College; Fred L. Miller, Murray State University; and Roberto Sanchez, Oregon State University.

Finally, I want to acknowledge the debt to my family. Tamiko, my Japanese wife, and Anna and Sonja, our two daughters with U.S. passports, faced firsthand the daily challenges of living in a multicultural and globalized city.

To all these people I say thank you. I think all of us hope that the new millennium will deliver on the glowing promises of globalization despite a less than fortunate beginning.

Washington, DC, July 2008
Johny K. Johansson

Brief Contents

Contents

PART THREE
LOCAL MARKETING   205

Chapter 7
Understanding Local Customers   207

Chapter 8
Local Marketing in Mature Markets   237

Chapter 9
Local Marketing in New Growth Markets   271

Part 1

Fundamentals

The globalization of today's marketplace makes many new demands on a marketer. Not only are there important decisions to be made about which countries' markets and segments to participate in and what modes of entry to use, but a marketer must also help formulate the marketing strategies in these countries and coordinate their implementation. He or she must speak for the local markets at headquarters but also explain the need for global standardization to local representatives. It is a job in which proven marketing techniques and face-to-face contacts are invaluable and one that requires a thorough grasp of marketing fundamentals and use of global communications.

Part One of this book shows how meeting these complex demands forces the marketing manager and his or her organization to reevaluate their marketing strategies. The desire to expand abroad needs to be tempered by a clear understanding of the firm's strengths and weaknesses. This analysis involves an in-depth reassessment of what makes the company successful at home and whether competitive advantages can be successfully transferred to foreign markets. It also requires an astute appraisal of how the company can best operate in a new cultural environment. It is not surprising that one primary concern, for both the small firm marketing abroad for the first time and the large multinational corporation trying to implement a global strategy, is the feasibility of a global marketing plan. As always, a critical issue for management is knowing not only what the company should do, but what it *can* do. This is never more relevant than in global marketing with its new and unfamiliar challenges, including the rise of China and India and the challenges from the recent global turmoil.

Chapter 1

The Global Marketing Task

"Brave new millennium"

After reading this chapter, you will be able to:

1. Explain why the opening of previously closed economies has led to greater global market opportunities but also to the threat of disruptions by terrorism and antiglobalization forces.
2. Judge whether an industry and company is ready for global strategies and should start thinking about standardizing the various marketing mix tools.
3. Identify the many reasons for going abroad, not just sales and profits. A company might enter a foreign market to challenge a competitor, to learn from lead customers, or to diversify its demand base.
4. Understand why global marketing involves new marketing skills, for example how to enter markets and how to manage the marketing effort in the local foreign market.
5. Separate the job (and career path) of the global marketing manager into three quite different tasks: foreign entry, local marketing abroad, and global management.

Chapter 1 describes the reality facing the marketing manager in today's global firm. As trade barriers are lowered, new growth opportunities in foreign markets open up and new markets are ready to be entered. At the same time, antiglobalization sentiments are kindled, leading to demands for concessions to local conditions. Foreign competitors enter local markets and previously unchallenged market positions need to be defended. The firm whose managers have a narrow view of its capabilities and its market will fall short. The purely domestic company often does not have enough managerial skill, imagination, and competence to respond to the opportunities or the threats of a global marketplace. Only by taking the leap and going abroad into competitive markets will a company stretch its resources and build the capability of its managers to a competitive level.

Chapter 1 illustrates how open markets and free competition have changed marketing and how the global marketer is forced by antiglobalization demands to become more than a functional specialist. Today's marketers must develop skills that help to determine the overall strategic direction of the firm and its place in the local economy. This chapter describes the three main tasks of the complex new global marketing endeavor—foreign entry, local marketing abroad, and global management, each an important component of the strategic capability of the manager and the firm.

Globalizing the iPod

The iPod, Apple Computer's breakthrough music player that can store and play thousands of songs (the latest figure is a mind-boggling 40,000) from a handheld computer no bigger than a cigarette pack, provides a striking illustration of what global marketing is all about.

When Steve Jobs, CEO of Apple Inc., first introduced the iPod in October 2001, it was received with skepticism. The digital music player was considered only marketable to a small, tech-savvy group of individuals, and the high price (starting at $399) made failure seem inevitable. The downloading of songs to the hard disk of a computer required a Mac computer, and the iPod was not usable on a standard PC.

But Steve Jobs proved critics wrong. Now, years later, iPod's success has been unmatched by any other digital music product in the world. Millions have been sold internationally at premium prices and it has shot Apple Inc. back into the mainstream market, long dominated by Microsoft's Windows.

The iPod has changed the market for digital music and the consumer demographics. The iPod gives consumers the freedom to control their environment and choose music that fits their mood. Digital music is cool not "geeky," and the iPod perpetuates the stylishness with its sleek design. These seemingly unimportant features make it the same kind of breakthrough that Sony's Walkman became back in 1979.

With its success in the United States, Apple did not lose time capitalizing on overseas potential. Introducing the iPod in Europe through its existing Mac dealerships, the sales rapidly rose despite the high price tags. Japan was also penetrated through the strong dealers already available. The one problem was capacity constraints—the success at home in the United States placed a strain on overseas expansion. But as early as March 2004, international sales of the iPod amounted to 43 percent of revenues, and the company posted a quarterly profit of 46 million U.S. dollars on iPod sales, tripling profits from the year before.

Steve Jobs and Apple were not standing still. Pressured by technological development and competitive imitation, the iPod was continuously upgraded with increased capability of storing songs, adding video and photo storage capability. Simultaneously, prices for the original units were coming down. Targeting the huge Windows market, and also to preempt competition, in 2003 Apple developed a model that would work with PCs. Nevertheless, by 2004 Dell and other computer makers offered their own versions of the iPod.

Typical of the high-tech industry, Apple also began releasing new models, including the Mini iPod, which was about as small as a credit card and initially held "only" about 1,000 songs. To overcome the copyright infringement problems of downloading songs the company launched the iTunes Music Store, which allows people to legally download one song at a time off the Internet for $0.99. If younger users do not have a credit card to pay with, parents usually do. Apple has also launched promotional alliances offering free downloads—such as Sprite buyers getting a number code for one free song. Since its opening, the online store has sold more that 100 million songs. Apple has also offered its iPod customers a wide range of subproducts that can be used with the iPod, including speakers and designer cases. And since July 2004, BMW drivers have been able to integrate their iPod stylishly into their car's sound system with a simple plug-in adapter.

By 2004, Apple was ready for the huge China market and struck up an alliance with Founder, China's largest PC distributor. Founder includes the Apple iTunes software (necessary for iPod use) in all of their computers. Wei Xin, chairman of Founder Group and Founder Technology, says, "Digital music is becoming very important to the Chinese PC market, and Apple's iTunes is the runaway market leader. As the first Chinese company to bundle this innovative software with our PCs, we are excited to provide our customers with the world's best digital music experience." As Rob Schoeben, Apple's vice president of applications product marketing, says, "Around the world, the iPod has revolutionized the way people manage and listen to their digital music. We are teaming up with Founder to deliver an easy-to-use, seamless music experience to millions of Chinese customers."

Several features of the iPod story illustrate concepts that will be important throughout this book. A high-tech product naturally has what is called a global market. The product is often developed in what we call a leading market. To stay competitive, innovation and new product development need to be continuous. Because of global competition, it becomes important to expand quickly into international markets. Local markets are easier to penetrate where existing dealers are available; where they are not available and where entry barriers are high, new alliances with existing firms are necessary. Imaginative innovation is also important to overcome regulatory obstacles in different countries. And the speed of penetration of any local market depends on having sufficient resources not used elsewhere.

As for new threats: When cell phones started to add music-playing features, Apple responded in kind—introducing its iPhone in 2007. By mid-2008 newspapers reported long queues of eager customers in cities around the world, from Stockholm to Sydney, as the iPhone was introduced globally. Global marketing is not simple and straightforward. It is exciting and challenging—and fun!

Sources: "Apple Strategy," *Brand Strategy,* May 14, 2004, p. 6; "Founder & Apple to Deliver World's Best Musical Experience to Chinese Customers," *PR Newswire,* May 18, 2004, p. 1; Steven Levy, "iPod Nation," *Newsweek,* July 26, 2004, pp. 42–50; www.apple.com; "Lines Form for New iPhone in Japan, Australia," *Associated Press*, Thursday, July 10, 2008.

Going Global

A lot of businesses are going global today. Ten or 15 years ago global business was mainly in the hands of a select number of multinational giants. Small and medium-sized businesses concentrated on their home markets and perhaps one or two neighboring countries. Not so any longer. Even the smallest businesses have realized that they have something to market in faraway countries, many of which have recently opened to foreign competition. Today, companies of all sizes in various industries from many countries are actively competing in the world's markets.

As long as world markets remain open, and terrorism and antiglobalization forces are under control, there is no stopping the spread of global competition. No markets are immune, as even government procurement business is opened to foreign suppliers. Deregulation and privatization confront sleepy public utilities with new and vigorous competitors, sometimes from countries in the same trading bloc.[1] Efficient foreign competitors from leading countries enter previously protected country markets and flush local companies out of comfortable market pockets. The lesson for all is that no market position is secure without attention to customer satisfaction and constant innovation.

Behind the development toward a more global marketplace lies a revolution in **global communications.** Satellite television broadcasts have eliminated national borders in mass media. Fax machines and other advances in electronic telecommunications have made it possible to develop company information networks that rival government intelligence operations. Online messaging via the Internet makes global communication instant and virtually cost-free. Today it is possible for headquarters to participate directly in decision making in any subsidiary. Managers can direct operations any place on earth from airplanes and automobiles; even when they're on vacation they can be seen on the beach talking on their mobile phones.[2]

Prominent movers in this raising of the competitive stakes in the 1980s were the Japanese; since then companies from many other countries have risen to the challenge. European companies, aided by the European integration (EU), have consolidated and rationalized to protect themselves and have in many cases become hunters on their own. Germany's BMW, Bosch, and Beiersdorf; France's Thomson and Alcatel; Ciba-Geigy and Nestlé in Switzerland; Italy's Benetton; and Finland's Nokia are some of the success stories. Others, like Volkswagen, General Motors' Opel, Electrolux, Fiat, Olivetti, ABB, and Volvo Trucks, have had their ups and downs. Operating in the new global environment requires skills not easily mastered, especially when the traditional position was bolstered by trade barriers and government protection.

Many Japanese companies have not fared well against international competition. Japanese markets were long protected by various tariff barriers, now removed, and also by nontariff barriers, some of which still remain. As standard economic theory suggests, such barriers often have the effect of supporting inefficient companies.[3] While Japanese automakers and electronics companies are generally very competitive worldwide, this is not the case in chemicals, pharmaceuticals, paper, medical machinery, and other industries. While rivalry among Japanese auto companies and electronics companies is fierce, companies in less successful Japanese industries have been content with covert collusion not to compete.

The lesson is that intense competition at home and abroad forces a company to be internationally competitive. Today's global marketing manager must understand and learn from foreign competitors and from foreign customers.

This chapter will first discuss recent developments in globalization and global marketing. Then the discussion will shift to some needed definitions of what global marketing involves and the distinction between global products and global brands. We then describe five main underlying forces of globalization, including the Internet, and how they create a need for (or constrain the potential of) global strategies. In the following section we show how managers can learn and develop knowledge assets from marketing abroad, assets that can be put to good use elsewhere. Finally, the chapter presents the three roles that a global marketing manager plays during his or her career and which make up the topics of Parts Two, Three, and Four of this book: Foreign Entry, Local Marketing, and Global Management.

The New Global Environment

Several new developments have helped change the environment for global marketing in the last few years.

Antiglobalization and Terrorism

At the beginning of the new millennium, strong **antiglobalization** voices were heard in many places around the world. Several smaller incidents protesting multinationals had taken place in the late 1990s. Dissidents trashed a KFC store in India for undermining local businesses, German environmentalists forced McDonald's to change their styrofoam packaging, and China outlawed door-to-door selling as akin to pyramid schemes. The movement gained momentum with news reports of Coca-Cola's bottling problems in Belgium, when several school children fell mysteriously ill after drinking Coke. A French farmer became famous for being jailed after attacking a McDonald's restaurant in France. The defining moment came in December 1999 when antiglobalization demonstrators from many countries managed to derail the World Trade Organization (WTO) Millennium Round of trade negotiations in Seattle. Antiglobalization forces gained steam throughout the year 2000, with continued questioning of the economic and social benefits of globalization. Demonstrators disrupted the World Bank/IMF meeting in Washington, DC, in September 2000 and forced the WTO to change the venues for other meetings. However, after the September 11, 2001, terrorist attacks on the World Trade Center in New York City, the antiglobalization movement lost impetus.

The relationship between antiglobalization and terrorism is complicated. At one level, terrorists are the ultimate antiglobalizers. Terrorists are willing to use violent means to disrupt any ordered interchange between countries. But the non-governmental organizations (NGOs) and other organizations making up the core of antiglobalization forces take a largely negative view of terrorism. Antiglobalizers are not typically against

Getting the Picture

"BAD ALL THE WAY AROUND"

Naomi Klein's *No Logo* book has obtained the elevated status of one of the antiglobalization movement's "Bibles." Klein's argument deals mainly with the dangers posed by global brands. Perhaps surprisingly, she argues that there is much damage from globalization in the developed world, not only in developing countries. We may usefully separate Klein's antiglobalization arguments into those related to developed countries and those related to developing countries.

According to Klein, antiglobalization has caused the following:

In Developed Countries	In Developing Countries
No space	Inequality
No choice	Poverty
No jobs	Exploitation
No logo	No local control

The effects in the two areas to some extent mirror one another. "No space" refers to the notion that brands are ubiquitous and that especially the younger generations in the developed world are dominated by the need for peer approval induced by powerful global branding. That can be compared with the "inequality" that has arisen in developing countries as only a minor percentage of the population shares in the rising affluence from globalization and thus can obtain the attractive global brands.

"No choice" suggests that the choices offered by global brands are in fact no choices at all. All diversity is gone; the brands are basically all the same except for their brand names. The counterpart in the developing markets is "poverty" that limits the choices realistically available in those countries as well. The "no jobs" effect in developed markets is directly reflected in the "exploitation" of local labor in developing countries. As jobs are shifted from the high-cost developed world to low-cost countries, part of the savings is made possible by pitiful working conditions.

Finally, the "no logo" effect in developed markets is Klein's contention that global brands become emblematic of individual identity, displacing local culture as expressed in local brands. By the same token, the multinational assembly plant in a developing country is controlled from far away, with little or no concern for local traditions and culture.

Each of these arguments contains a kernel of truth. However, for developing countries, most economic data show overall improvement in living and working conditions when multinationals enter, although *relative* differentials may become greater. As for the developed world, it is difficult to feel sorry for consumers. As successful brands incorporate the latest technology they naturally become similar. As the older generation argues, as it tends to do in Japan, that "we have enough gadgets," they still consider the products from their youth necessities. Even though the temporary job loss hurts, when jobs are moved overseas, others are created in more viable industries—as has been true throughout history and certainly is in the new millennium.

Sources: Graham, 2000; Klein, 2000.

---

economic exchange and trade—they are mainly against the alleged exploitation of poorer countries by advanced economies with great advantages. They tend to support local business and programs for equal sharing of benefits. The terrorists attack the whole world order and its political, military, economic, social, and religious basis. How to deal with terrorism raises a host of issues that we cannot cover here. Antiglobalizers are of more relevance for us here, since they do attempt to directly affect what is going on in the global marketplace.

Some new trade rules adopted by the WTO do reflect concerns of the antiglobalization movement. For example, third-world countries are allowed some relief from patent protection for important drugs such as anti-AIDS medication. The multinational drug companies are allowed to charge higher prices in developed countries to recoup R&D expenses, and then offer the same drugs in third-world countries at reduced prices.

The antiglobalization arguments involve a mix of economic, political, and social issues (see box, "Bad All the Way Around"). Foreign investment in poorer countries is said to exploit workers, imposing long working hours and substandard conditions. A critique that relates directly to marketing is that globalization has provided information about consumer choices to people who have no ability to pay for the products. Pent-up feelings of inferiority, envy, and rage can sometimes suddenly explode.[4]

To most professional economists and many other observers, the antiglobalization advocates do not have their facts right. By and large, the economic data supports the idea that globalization has increased the wealth of most peoples. Even in countries where working hours are long and conditions are hard, multinationals have increased the number of jobs available, and they also tend to pay higher wages than the going local average. As for frustrations caused by an array of new choices, economists accept the charge but argue that the solution is hardly to close the country from global influences but rather to attempt to increase local productivity and thus wages.[5]

At the management level, the path of globalization has to be followed with careful attention to disruptions caused to traditions and past practices. As will be stressed throughout this text, it is important for the global marketer to realize that as global strategies are pursued, the short-run effect can be very discomforting not only for the people in the local market but also for the employees inside the local subsidiary.

Anti-Americanism

After the American attack on Iraq in March 2003, strong expressions of anti-Americanism erupted in many places around the globe. Even in a country such as the United Kingdom, which joined the "coalition of the willing" and sent troops into Iraq, public opinion turned decisively against America. This development is relevant here not only because of the potential impact on the many global brands from the United States, but also because of the threat against the whole globalization process and the way the war has tended to isolate the United States from its allies.

According to opinion research, the percentage of people abroad with a favorable attitude toward the United States dropped precipitously as the war progressed. By the same token, the percentage of Americans who viewed other countries favorably also declined. Exhibit 1.1 shows some selected figures. However, the trend was reversed by 2005, as the figures show.

One question for global marketers is to what extent these kinds of negative sentiments translate into a rejection of American and other global brands. A 2004 global survey showed some negative brand effects.[6] For example, 15 global American brands showed a 2004 drop in "usage" from 30 percent to 27 percent, and the percentage for "honest" dropped from 18 percent to 15 percent. These figures might seem small, but if they represent a trend the news is not good for American marketers or, for that matter, any global marketers. The new opinion data, however, suggest that American brands might be less exposed in the future.

Fair Trade

One of the new developments in international markets partly spawned by antiglobalizers is the emergence of fair trade practices. **Fair trade** can be described as international trade that ensures that producers in poor nations get a fair share of the gains from trade. Fair trade products include some of the basic commodities from third-world nations such as coffee, bananas, and chocolate, but also crafts, clothing, and jewelry. The driving motivation is that world market prices for coffee, rice, and other commodities are highly volatile and often below the costs of production. A stable price, which covers at least production and living costs, is an essential requirement for farmers to escape from poverty and provide themselves and their families with a decent standard of living.

EXHIBIT 1.1
Anti-American Opinions

Source: Data from the Pew Research Center for the People & the Press.

Percent favorable toward the U.S.

Country	2002	2003	2005
Britain	75%	48%	55%
France	63	31	43
Germany	61	25	41
Spain	50	14	41
Poland	79	50	62
Russia	61	28	52

Percent of Americans favorable toward other countries

Country	2002	2003	2005
France	79%	29%	46%
Germany	83	44	60

Fair trade is an alternative way to doing business that promotes equal, sustainable relationships between consumers and producers. This includes paying fair wages in local communities, engaging in environmentally sustainable practices, and promoting healthy working conditions. The Body Shop, under the late Anita Roddick, was one of the Western firms in the vanguard of the movement, but others have joined, including Starbucks, the coffee chain. As fair trade standards have come to be accepted in the markets around the world, more and more consumers demand that companies sell certified products. As always in free markets, this means the companies sooner or later come to realize the advantages of doing just that.

The original proponents of fair trade were NGOs upset about the relatively low percentage of the final product price that went to the original producer. These NGOs included a wide array of social and environmental organizations such as Oxfam, Amnesty International, and Caritas International. The flag bearer today is FLO, the Fairtrade Labelling Organizations International. FLO International is a nonprofit, multistakeholder association involving 23 member organizations, traders, and external experts. The organization develops and reviews fair trade standards, assists producers in gaining and maintaining fair trade certification, and helps producers capitalize on market opportunities.

The basic weapon in forcing multinationals to adopt fair trade has been the development of a formal certification program for fair trade businesses. The most basic requirement for fair trade certification is a guarantee on the part of the multinational buyer to pay a reasonable price for the supplies from a producer. FLO certification standards for small farmers' organizations also include requirements for democratic decision making, ensuring that producers have a say in how the fair trade premiums are invested, and so on. Fair trade standards for hired labor situations ensure that workers receive decent wages and enjoy the freedom to join unions and bargain collectively. Fair trade certified plantations must also ensure that there is no forced or child labor and that health and safety requirements are met. The certified fair trade business is given the right to advertise that its products meet fair trade standards.

Fair trade is still small in magnitude, but growing fast. In 2006, fair trade certified sales amounted to approximately $2.3 billion worldwide, a 41 percent year-to-year increase. Fair trade products generally account for less than 5 percent of all sales in their product categories in Europe and North America. In October 2006, over 1.5 million disadvantaged producers worldwide were directly benefiting from fair trade while an additional 5 million benefited from fair trade funded infrastructure and community development projects.[7]

Like most developmental efforts, fair trade has proven controversial and has drawn criticism from both ends of the political spectrum. Free-market economists abhor fixed and set prices for producers, since prices serve as a signal as to what should (and what should not) be produced by free entrepreneurs. The counter-point is that since many agricultural commodities in advanced countries also have price guarantees, the argument is hypocritical and unrealistic, especially since many of these poor producers have no viable alternative occupation. More left-leaning economists argue that fair trade does not adequately challenge the current trading system because, as long as advanced nations protect their workers, poorer countries need more help than just stable prices. The counter-point to this is that globalization and free markets can be of benefit to all, and the WTO is attempting to reduce protective tariffs among advanced nations.

In the end, it seems quite likely that fair trade is here to stay. As it becomes a marketing advantage to be a fair trade business, multinationals will change their practices to become certified fair traders.

Global Warming and Green Trade

Two factors that have recently become issues in international trade are global warming and green trade. **Global warming** refers to the increased temperatures around the world, due to the weakening of the ozone layer in the earth's upper atmosphere. Although the precise reasons for this are still debated, the evidence suggests that deforestation and pollution are two main culprits. **Green trade** comprises the trade in organic products, a fast-rising trade category that is closely related to fair trade.

The global warming problem is being attacked with increasing intensity. It looks quite clear that the deforestation in many poor countries (including the Amazonas regions in South America) will slow down as incentives are being developed to maintain and not harvest existing forest stands. This leads to the argument that existing measures of gross domestic product (GDP) have to be adjusted to compute a sustainable GDP growth rate.[8] The likely outcome is less availability of certain materials on world markets, less foreign trade in these commodities, and an increase in the use of substitute materials. The antipollution measures include higher oil prices, with the expectation that higher prices will induce consumers and manufacturers to use less oil. The new outcome is likely to be an increase in local enterprise focusing on more organic products, and thus an increase in green trade.

Related to this development is the emergence of a new consciousness of the "carbon footprints" of various products shipped long distances around the world. The energy expended on shipping products such as water bottles from faraway destinations to consumer markets around the world has gained attention in this respect. Not only does the use of plastic bottles involve a considerable energy cost, the viability of shipping water from abroad into perfectly well-served local markets is now questioned. As long as no charge is leveled on carbon footprints and the externality costs of global warming, such shipments can be very profitable—we might all prefer to drink Evian. However, as global warming anxieties increase and get media attention, consumers around the world will pay more and more attention; then, firms will find it more profitable to avoid transportation, lower their carbon footprints, and stress their local organic roots.

It seems quite clear that global warming will have an increasing impact on international trade, including company outsourcing and close-to-market production. Very soon one of the most compelling reasons for a multinational firm to avoid outsourcing will be to limit the costs involved in justifying its large carbon footprint.

The Flat World

In 2005, *New York Times* columnist Thomas Friedman published a book entitled *The World Is Flat*. The book became a best-seller and received an award as the Best Business Book of the Year.[9] Friedman's notion is that a number of forces have come together to create a "level playing field" for all countries and competitors, allowing smaller firms and firms in less-developed countries to compete effectively around the world. Although his **flat world** thesis has been challenged by other observers as a vision that is not yet a reality, some of the factors that Friedman points to are useful for us to review here.

First, Friedman identifies 10 "flatteners" that have helped making the global world flat.

1. Collapse of Berlin Wall in 1989.
2. Netscape and the Web.
3. Workflow software, enabling machines to talk to other machines.
4. Open source software, blogs, and Wikipedia.
5. Outsourcing—subcontracting less critical activities.
6. Offshoring—outsourcing to foreign shores—IPods are assembled in Asia.
7. Supply chains—Wal-Mart's automatic re-ordering system is a good example.
8. Insourcing—UPS serves a client such as Toshiba with customer repair service.
9. In-forming—Google and other search engines make information easily available.
10. Personal digital devices—empowering individuals "on-the-go."

To Friedman, these factors all converged in the last few years to flatten the earth. Reinforcing each other, they created a need for companies to shift from a top-down organization to a horizontal collaborative framework. This was accompanied by a shift to "knowledge" as the basic resource and raw material of successful businesses. The 10 flatterners all helped to make knowledge transfer easier and quicker. A premium was put on competitive flexibility and mobility, and the successful company was one that could capitalize on often temporary opportunities in arbitrage between countries. At this game, even smaller players could excel.

There are two basic criticisms against Friedman. One is that large and established Western multinationals still carry a lot of weight. The second is that even though the world has been globalized, most business activity is still local and regional.[10] This is not the place to argue for-or-against Friedman, but it is important to recognize that the factors he has recognized do have—and will continue to have—an impact on how the world will shape up in the future. The criticism is, as one can see, that the world is not yet there. But given the developments so far, the direction seems clear. One example is the emergence of several new nations as major players in world markets. The so-called BRIC countries (Brazil, Russia, India, and China) are representative of the new global situation—these countries have now become important and powerful players in today's world business. They need to be taken seriously, and we will do that in detail in Part Three of this text.

The Dubai Phenomenon

One of the most striking globalization developments in recent times has been the emergence of Dubai (and, more recently, neighboring Arab countries) as new commercial centers of global economic activity. The development has involved huge investments in infrastructure, including gigantic office and residential complexes, up-to-date global communication and transportation networks, and hotel and leisure amenities to rival Las Vegas. The target market has been financial businesses and corporate headquarters, and wealthy individuals who can afford a luxurious lifestyle. In recent years the sheiks have decided to diversify their economies and not rely solely on oil. Supported by rising oil prices, the strategy has recently been adopted not just by Dubai, but also Abu Dhabi of the United Arab Emirates, as well as Saudi Arabia.

The Sheikh Zayed road in Dubai. A center of business and after-business activities, it features skyscrapers like the Emirates Towers and the Burj Dubai, and connects other new developments such as the Palm Jumeirah and the Dubai Marina. © Alasdair Drysdale/DAL

The Dubai development is stunning in the sheer scale of its imagination and ambition. Dubai is home to the tallest building in the world, the Burj Dubai. It features the world's first seven-star hotel, the Burj Al-Arab, and perhaps its most beautiful hotel, the Jumeirah Beach Hotel, shaped like an ocean wave. Its skyline rivals that of New York. It is creating new islands in the water off its shoreline, including a group of more than a hundred islets called "The World," depicting the countries of the world, each available for purchase. Sir Richard Branson has already bought England, and Brad Pitt is reported to have bought Ethiopia. Extensions from shore into ocean waters are developed where new luxury housing and office buildings are rising to great heights. Two new developments, Palm Jumeirah and Palm Deira, laid out as huge palm-trees jutting into the water, offer private shoreline to most of its owners. New (part-time) residents include British footballer David Beckham and Swiss tennis great Roger Federer.

Dubai is not particularly well situated to attract visitors from the United States or Japan or even Europe—Germany can be a good five hours away from Dubai by air, with a jet-lagging three hour shift in time. But the region has closer neighbors with surprisingly deep pockets, in Iran, India, and Pakistan. The country is also rapidly improving airports, establishing new airlines, and adding routes to provide easier access. Still, the economic logic behind the huge investments to attract businesses and wealthy tourists defies easy analysis.

These countries are basically Muslim, limiting female participation, banning alcohol, and restraining gambling in public places. Dubai has somewhat more liberal rules, making it a destination for visitors from more-restrictive countries such as Saudi Arabia. With a population of only 1.3 million, Dubai workers come mainly from other countries—taxi drivers are from Pakistan; restaurant waitresses from the Philippines; and many of the office workers who need to speak Arabic fluently are from other Arab countries such as Syria, Egypt, and Kuwait. Indians and Iranians have also flocked to Dubai, many working for the new foreign companies entering after Dubai lifted the restrictions on foreign direct investment (FDI) in the beginning of the new millennium. Adding to the puzzle is the fact that Dubai itself has very little oil, although it shares oil revenues with Abu Dhabi, the United Arab Emirates leader, with one of the largest oil reserves in the world.

The great advantage of Dubai seems to be its location. Situated on the northeastern spit of the Arabian peninsula, with a history going back to the days of the China silk road, it has historically served as an Arab transportation hub, within easy reach of Iraq, Iran, Pakistan, and India. It has gained by the rise in the price of oil, allowing its Arab neighbors to spend easy money in Dubai. It has, surprisingly, gained by the conflict in Iraq, in close proximity but still protected—the large American defense contractor Halliburton has moved its headquarters to Dubai. Dubai has also gained by the liquidity in the world's financial markets, including the vast financial reserves accumulated by China and Russia. When money is plentiful, easily available, and flows unhindered internationally, serving as a conveniently located financial and commercial hub is clearly profitable. But the risks are also clear: Military conflict, terrorism, nationalism, political protectionism, or a financial meltdown could all bring the house down.

But Dubai leaders are of course aware of these risks. When you speak to them they seem quite aware of the downside but also of the opportunities. Michael Owen, Dean of Zayed University's College of Business Sciences, is American born and educated. He says: "When I came here eight years ago, I expected it would be a short-term appointment. But the economy has diversified and grown successfully, new investments keep coming in, new buildings go up. One key successful strategic move has been to start attracting a larger number of tourists, with much expanded flight schedules, outstanding hotels, and expanded leisure activities. We have great beaches and golf courses, but also scuba-diving, jet-skiing and sandboarding, and even an indoor ski slope. It has expanded the market for tourists—even younger, active, and less-affluent people are now attracted to Dubai."

It remains to be seen whether Dubai can become the new Las Vegas, the new New York, and the new Cancun combined. The start is clearly auspicious.

Regionalization

Although in this book we will treat globalization and regionalization as relatively similar, there is growing awareness among marketers that regionalization is much more common than complete globalization. **Regionalization** means treating regions of the world as the new standardization unit. While domestic or national marketing strategies are adapted to the particular country market, and global strategies are standardized and implemented for the global market as a whole, regionalization means that similar marketing strategies are applied for regions—such as pan-European, North American or Asian strategies.

Many multinational companies have long organized along regional lines. As a typical example, the Hewlett-Packard Company breaks down its global organization into three regional sectors: Europe, Asia-Pacific, and the Americas. Similar structures can be found for Japanese companies such as Honda, Korean companies such as Samsung, and European companies such as Dutch Philips. A completely globalized organizational design is simply too unwieldy to manage, and customer needs and preferences sometimes differ markedly between regions.

A new factor that has encouraged regionalization is the insight that even in the age of the Internet and global communications, distance still matters. Understanding customers in different parts of the world requires some face-to-face contacts and personal experience. The same is true for managing employees and dealing with local subsidiary managers. These and related distance factors have been categorized by Ghemawat (2007b) as the four dimensions of a CAGE concept:[11]

1. Cultural distance—religious and language differences are still barriers.
2. Administrative distance—regulatory differences between countries pose problems.
3. Geographic distance—faraway markets are difficult to manage from home.
4. Economic distance—low development means weak infrastructure, payment ability, and so on.

Ghemawat develops the strategic concept of "semi-globalization" which is akin to regionalization. He argues that the multinational firm can adopt a semi-globalized strategy by adapting to each region and standardizing within each region. He then suggests that the firm deals with the differences between regions by "arbitrage," that is, exploiting differences between regions to moving operations to where they are best performed.

The regionalization strategy is also supported by empirical findings that show how unevenly the multinational firms' sales are spread over the world markets. By far the majority of sales for any multinational are in one or two regions, often close to home. An analysis by Rugman of the largest multinationals in the world ("The Fortune Global 500") finds that 64 percent of the firms derive more than 50 percent of their sales from their home region, close to 10 percent of the firms draw most sales from only two regions, and only nine multinationals are truly global with significant sales from three regions or more.[12] Three of these global firms are American (IBM, Intel, and Coca-Cola), three are Asian (Sony, Canon, and Flextronics, an electronics manufacturer headquartered in Singapore), and three are European (Finnish Nokia, Dutch electronics maker Philips, and LVMH, the French luxury goods company, whose brands include Louis Vuitton and Dior).

Rugman and Ghemawat both propose that corporate strategies be conceived in terms of regions rather than worldwide. Their analysis shows that, in fact, this what companies already do. It means that blind assumptions that all countries can be treated the same way and that distance between countries does not matter are in fact erroneous. It also means that when competitive advantages are analyzed, the proper market to look at might well be the region, not the country or the world. We will get back to this in Chapter 2, which deals with the strategic underpinnings of global marketing.

For many of the principles of global marketing discussed in this book, however, the distinction between regions and worldwide is less of a concern. The validity of the principles is not a matter of kind, but of degree. Just like globalization, regionalization still needs an analysis across countries that tells whether customers are similar or not, cultures are similar or not, and business is similar not. The standardization of marketing within a region can run into the same problems as standardizing across several regions. Yes, the chances are less, and the problems might be easier to spot, but the principles and the problems are the same. The big question, as we will see over and over again, is the degree to which the marketing can be adapted and fine-tuned to the local consumer, or whether standardization and offering the same as elsewhere is good enough.

Key Concepts

There are several key concepts we need to define clearly before going further.

Global Marketing

Global marketing refers to marketing activities coordinated and integrated across multiple country markets. The integration can involve **standardized products,** uniform packaging, identical brand names, synchronized product introductions, similar advertising messages, or coordinated sales campaigns across markets in several countries. Despite the term "global," it is not necessary that all or most of the countries of the world be included. Even regional marketing efforts, such as pan-European operations, can be viewed as examples of global marketing. The point is an integrated effort across several countries—and the principles are roughly similar whether one talks about 10 or 50 countries.

Multidomestic Markets

It is clear to any observer that consumers in different countries think, speak, and behave differently in many ways. The salient product beliefs, attitudes, and social norms vary considerably between markets. The extent to which quality concerns are important, the attitudes toward foreign products, and the degree to which individuals comply with social norms all affect consumers' decision making differently across countries. For example, if a Japanese shopper is often fastidious and examines a product carefully in the store, an American consumer may be more impulsive and respond to in-store promotions of new brands. More often than not, global marketing will challenge our preconceived way of looking at the world (see box "Mercedes' Old-Fashioned Cars").

Multidomestic markets are defined as product markets in which local consumers have preferences and functional requirements widely different from one another's and others' elsewhere.[13] The typical market categories include products and services such as foods, drinks, clothing, and entertainment, which tend to vary considerably between countries and in which many consumers prefer the local variants.

The firm selling into multidomestic markets needs to localize and adapt its products and services to the different requirements and preferences in the several markets. Levels of salt and sugar in food products might need to change, and color patterns and sizes of packaging might be redesigned for attractiveness and taste. Drinks need to be taste-tested and perhaps given strong communication support, educating the local consumers and trying to change their preferences, as Seven-Up has tried to do in the United States. In clothing, redesigning jeans to fit the different bodies of Asian people, widening the shoes, and shortening the sleeves, are necessary steps, but the multidomestic marketer may also have to create new colors, different styles, and alternative materials. Before globalization, firms were generally multinational for a reason: The products had to be adapted to each country's preferences. Marketing could not be uniform.

Global Markets

Global markets are defined as those markets in which buyer preferences are similar across countries. Within each country, several segments with differing preferences may exist, but the country's borders are not important segment limits. In some cases the "global" market is more like a "regional" market, encompassing a trade area such as

Getting the Picture

MERCEDES' OLD-FASHIONED CARS

Although Mercedes-Benz, the German carmaker, prides itself on the up-to-date technology it uses in its cars in the West, in other markets it is decidedly old-fashioned. Why? Because it has gone back to basics and become customer oriented.

In Saudi Arabia, auto engines are plagued by sand entering the cylinder blocks, gradually building up deposits until the engine cracks. But not in Mercedes cars. Most new cars use light aluminum alloys in their engines because their hardness increases engine performance and is fuel efficient. By using older-style softer steel alloys, Mercedes cars lose the efficiency race, but keep running when the sand filters in. The hard silicon in the sand simply gets buried inside the softer metal of the cylinder heads.

In Poland, Mercedes' market share was long on par with the Japanese cars' combined. Reason? The Poles are as rich as the oil sheiks? No, not yet. But for some models Mercedes has gone back to the old way of building cars from simple parts instead of using the integrated components and subassemblies that have served so effectively to increase Japanese manufacturing productivity. The problem with the modern techniques is that doing your own repairs is almost impossible, and repair costs rise since, when something breaks, whole assemblies are needed to replace a broken part. This matters less in Western countries where a big part of repair costs comes from the high cost of labor, and the new subassembly can be replaced quickly. But in Poland, labor is cheap. Mercedes sells well because spare parts are simple and inexpensive, and its cars can be fixed by the owner who can take his time to repair the car the do-it-yourself way or have a mechanic who is affordable fix it. And the same strategy is likely to work in many emerging countries elsewhere, as Prahalad has demonstrated for India.

Moral: "Back-to-basics" marketing requires imagination and an understanding of usage situations.

Sources: M. Wolongiewicz, student report, International University of Japan, June 1994; C.K. Prahalad, *The Fortune at the Bottom of the Pyramid* (Philadelphia: The Wharton School Publishing, 1996).

the EU, NAFTA, or Mercosur. Since the principal features of global marketing apply equally to regional and to truly global markets, this book will not make much of this distinction. However, it should be recognized that much of international trade takes place within such regions.

The typical characteristics of a global market have both customer and competitive aspects. The major global features to look for are the following:[14]

In Customers:

Increasingly common consumer requirements and preferences as gaps in lifestyles, tastes, and behavior narrow.

Global networks with a centralized purchasing function among business customers.

Disappearing national boundaries as customers travel across borders to buy wherever the best products and/or prices are found.

Increasing agreement among customers across the globe about how to evaluate products and services and recognition of which brands are the best.

In Competitors:

Competition among the same world-class players in every major national market.

Declining numbers of competitors in the core of the market as domestic companies defend their turf by specialization or merge with larger firms.

Increasing use of national markets as a strategic tool for the benefit of the firm's global network.

With global communications and spreading affluence, many previously multidomestic markets are becoming more susceptible to globalization. People all around the world now know and like ethnic foods, such as Middle-Eastern hummus, Spanish paella, and Beijing duck. Stylish clothes from Armani, Levi's, and Benetton are bought in many countries. Japanese sake, German beer, and French wine compete directly as a dinner drink in many local places. Larry King broadcasts his TV talk show from Hong Kong to a worldwide audience. As multidomestic markets open up and become more global, the rest of the world is able to pick and choose among the best that the multidomestic markets offer. Increasing affluence generates a desire for variety and creates opportunities for local specialties from foreign countries in leading countries.

EXHIBIT 1.2
Multidomestic versus Global Markets: Key Differences

Source: Reproduced from *Managing Global Marketing,* by Kamran Kashani with the permission of South Western College Publishing. Copyright © 1992 PWS-Kent Publishing Company. All rights reserved.

	Multidomestic Markets	**Global Markets**
Market boundaries	Markets are defined within country borders. Customers and competitors are of local region.	Markets transcended country borders. Customers and/or competitors cross frontiers to buy and to sell.
Customers	Significant differences exist among customers from different countries; segments are defined locally.	Significant similarities exist among customers from different countries; segments Cut across geographic frontiers.
Competition	Competition takes place among primarily local firms; even international companies compete on a country-by-county basis.	Competitors are few and present in every major market. Rivalry takes on regional or global scope.
Interdependence	Each local market operates in isolation from the rest. Competitive actions in one market have no impact elsewhere.	Local markets operate interdependently. Competitive actions in one market impact other markets.
Strategies	Strategies are locally based. Little advantage exists in coordinating activities among markets.	Strategies are regional or global in scope. Great advantage exists in coordinating activities within regions or worldwide.

The main differences between multidomestic and global markets are highlighted in Exhibit 1.2.[15] As can be seen, most marketing parameters in the multidomestic case are determined by national borders, as opposed to the global markets, in which borders matter much less.

Global Products

Although local preferences have sometimes demanded product adaptation, there have been many surprising successes for firms with standardized **global products.** Markets once thought to be very different across countries have been impacted by global brands. Consumer goods such as beer, food, and apparel and service providers such as accountants, lawyers, and even retailers are some of the categories in which global firms have been successful against locals in many countries. Add to this the typically global markets in many industrial products, high-tech products, and consumer durables such as cameras, watches, and VCRs, and in some ways the markets seem to grow more and more homogeneous. Increasing similarity of preferences has led to the success of global products, which in turn has fostered further homogeneity of markets. Hamel and Prahalad argue that in many cases new products lead and change preferences, so that the global firm should introduce many alternative new products, innovating and creating new market niches instead of trying to precisely target an existing segment.[16]

The key to success of the globally standardized products is not that they are especially cheap or that every consumer wants the same thing as everyone else. They are often the best-value products because they offer higher quality and more advanced features at better prices. They also tend to be stronger on the intangible extras such as status and brand image. But mostly they embody the best in technology with designs from leading markets and are manufactured to the highest standards. As much as they satisfy customers, they as often create new desires. In terms of the product life cycle, global products will often generate new growth in mature markets, as customers return sooner for upgrades and more modern features.

In global product markets, the firm needs to develop technological capabilities to be able to compete by introducing new products. As the speed of technological development has increased, intense competitive rivalries have led to a proliferation of new products in many markets, many of them "me-too" variants from lead markets (see below). This reinforces competitive rivalry further. Rather than uniqueness and differentiation, which place a premium on superior segmentation and positioning strategies, the key for success is speed and flexibility in new product development—and a well-known and highly regarded global brand.

Successful global marketers are often colorful and idiosyncratic personalities. Akio Morita, Sony's cofounder and former chairman, was famous for going against Japanese traditions, for ignoring his own staff's market research, and for an intuitive understanding of consumers in both East and West. © Reuters/Corbis.

Global and Local Brands

Global brands are brands that are available and well known throughout the world's markets. Examples include Swatch, Mercedes, Nestlé, Coca-Cola, Nike, McDonald's, Sony, and Honda. By contrast, a brand that is well known and strong in some particular market, but unknown in other markets, is a **local brand.** Examples include food retailer Giant in the United States; Luxor electronics in Scandinavia; Morinaga, a food processor, in Japan; and Prosdocimo appliances in Brazil.

Exactly how many countries a brand should cover to be "global" cannot be precisely defined, but the brand should be available in major markets. A 2001 study by ACNielsen, the U.S.-based market research firm, concluded that in the consumer packaged goods category, only 43 brands could be called "global." Even considering that the study excluded certain product and service categories (autos, electronics, credit cards, and liquor, to name four), the number is lower than most observers would have guessed. But the report argues that a global brand should be available with the same name in Bali, Brazil, or Belgium; and its global sales should be above $1 billion annually, with at least 5 percent rung up outside the home region.[17]

In this book the cutoff is more liberal, with "global" and "regional" treated much the same, as long as the brand is identical and the region is large. Some observers even argue that a global brand does not have to be the same everywhere, but this is going too far. For example, the chocolate bar "Marathon" in some European countries was called "Snickers" elsewhere—and the company renamed Marathon to Snickers in order to have exactly that, a "global" brand name. Similarly, when the Nissan company changed its Datsun car marquee in the West to Nissan, it wanted to make its Japanese name the global name. These are major decisions by companies. So, in this text, a global brand may not be found in precisely every corner of the world—but it should have the same name.

In global markets, with standardized global products, a global brand name is necessary for success—which is why many firms consolidate their brand portfolios around a few major brands as globalization proceeds. Nevertheless, because local brands often have their own special market niche and devout adherents, many multinationals maintain a number of acquired local brands as well in their portfolio.

Leading Markets

There are certain country markets where a global firm wants to be present even if competition is fierce and profitability is uncertain. These are so-called **leading or lead markets.**

Lead or leading markets are characterized by strong competitors and demanding customers; they are free from government regulation and protective measures; products and services incorporate the latest technology; and companies are strong at the high end of the product line. They are not necessarily the largest markets, although they often are.

Lead markets are generally found in different countries for different products. Strong domestic competitors emerge because of a country's location-specific advantages, such as natural resource endowments, technological know-how, and labor skills. Over time, these advantages enable domestic firms to accumulate experience. The customers of these firms are sophisticated and demanding, making these markets bellwethers for follower markets. The U.S. PC market, the Japanese camera market, and the German automobile market are examples of such leading markets.

The actual location of a lead market in an industry may also change over time. This is partly a result of the workings of the international product cycle (IPC) discussed in Chapter 2. As follower markets mature and customers become more sophisticated, and as domestic producers develop new competitive skills, the follower markets may become the new leading markets. A good example is Japan in consumer electronics. Conversely, leading markets may lose their status, for as Japan rose, the United States lost its lead in consumer electronics.

An industry can have several leading markets for different segments of the total market, as in the automobile industry. In automobiles, in this sense, Germany, Japan, Italy, and perhaps even the United States can lay claims to preeminence. Different leading markets feature some market segmentation and product differentiation. German buyers place a premium on advanced auto technology, which is why other automakers have located engineering centers there. Italy has a well-developed luxury sports car market, and even German firms such as Porsche hire Italian designers. The Japanese provide mass manufacturing state-of-the-art knowledge, and their domestic customers get perhaps the best value for the money. The United States still provides a sophisticated market for large luxury cars, even if the domestic producers have not performed particularly well.

The existence of lead markets and the need for the firm to be in such markets push the firm toward global strategies in order to take full advantage of the benefits gained from being in lead markets. The firm can draw on lessons from competitors and customers in leading markets to design marketing strategies elsewhere. Product and technology developments in leading markets signal what is likely to happen in other countries. For example, while a semiconductor firm such as Texas Instruments has trouble making money in Japan, the lessons it learns in that difficult market help it to design entry strategies and service support elsewhere in the Asian region.

First-Mover Advantages

An emerging market that has just opened up offers the opportunity to be a first mover and create demand. Since domestic competition is often weak or nonexistent, the marketing tasks are to demonstrate how the product or service fills a need and to educate potential customers in its use. This generic marketing task can be challenging and expensive, with reluctant learners and a need for special promotional material and personal selling. But the brand has a chance to develop brand loyalty before competitors enter.

Being a first mover can create advantages but can also be hazardous. The **first-mover advantages** relative to followers include:[18]

- Higher brand recognition.
- More positive brand image.
- More customer loyalty.
- More distribution.
- Longer market experience.

The drawback for a first mover is that the market is not yet developed, which means that:

- Channel members may need training.
- Customers might have to be educated.
- Advertising has to be more generic.
- Tastes and standards are unknown and perhaps unformed.

Because of the uncertainties involved, some firms decide to become followers, waiting to see how the first entrant does before entering a new market. When they then enter, it is usually with a kind of me-too approach, trying to capture some of the first mover's customers and also help grow the new market. When Saab entered the North American market, it positioned itself as "the other Swedish car," trading on Volvo's image. The leading French beer, Kronenbourg, attacked the U.S. market through a campaign slogan that claimed it was "Europe's largest-selling beer," trying to capitalize on Dutch Heineken's and German Beck's rising popularity.

The Product Life Cycle

One well-known and basic marketing concept must be briefly introduced here because we will make extensive use of it throughout this book. Country markets are often in greatly different stages of the **product life cycle (PLC)**, the S-curve that depicts how the sales of a product category (or a brand, since brands also tend to have a life cycle) progress over time. The stages typically involve Introduction, Growth, Maturity, Saturation, and possibly Decline. For a given product such as mobile phones, some countries (Scandinavia) will be in the saturation stage while others (China) are in the introductory stage. The optimal marketing strategies will vary considerably between these markets.

As Exhibit 1.3 shows, the **diffusion process** that new innovations pass through underlies the shape of the PLC. The first adopters are "pioneers," followed by early adopters (usually the opinion leaders), early majority, late majority, late adopters, and finally, laggards. In the beginning what matters for a company is usually the size and growth rate of the total market. As the market matures market share and profitability become typically more important objectives.

The PLC is also relevant for market segmentation and product positioning, two other prominent marketing concepts. **Market segmentation** involves partitioning a

EXHIBIT 1.3
The Product Life Cycle (PLC)
and the Diffusion Curve

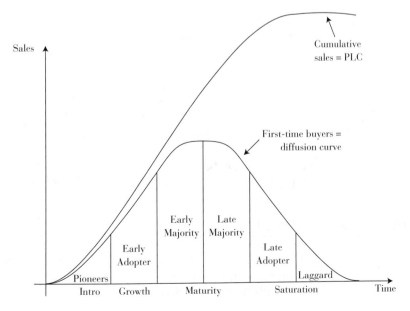

given market into similar customer groupings for which uniform marketing strategies can be used. **Product positioning** refers to the perceptions or image that target customers have of a product or service—or, rather, the image that the firm would like the customers to have. Both market segmentation and product positioning are typically more important in the later stages of the PLC when customers are good at evaluating competing offerings.[19]

In the early stages of the PLC, the pioneer target segment for the product is usually easy to identify. The pioneers are the buyers who have most interest in the product category and who are willing to take a chance on a new product. An example is "computer nerds" in the PC category. Later in the majority stages of the PLC, the buyers are much more heterogeneous. They can come from many different strata of society, and they do not all want exactly the same thing in the product because their needs differ. This means that the marketing mix (the product, the pricing, the promotions and the advertising media, and so on) all have to be tailored to different segments of the total market. The PC for the home user will be configured, priced, and sold quite differently from the PC used by a financial analyst. This is where it becomes important for the marketer to make sure which of the several potential segments to target and how to communicate to the selected segment(s). This is also where product positioning becomes important.

The transition from the growth among the early adopters to the more mature stage of the early majority is not always smooth. For high-tech products, in particular, there is typically a gap or **"chasm"** opening up, creating difficulty for the diffusion of new products.[20] The reason is typically that the motivations behind the purchase have shifted. While early adopters are still enamored by the newness and the technology, and are basically product-oriented, the early majority's basic motivation concerns usage benefits, such as saving time, ease of use, and acceptable prices. To overcome this chasm, it is important for the manufacturers' promotional language to shift from technology specifications (giga bytes, screen pixels, etc.) to customer benefits (number of songs stored, colorful images, etc.). In emerging foreign markets, this kind of chasm can be seen not only for high-tech products. Introducing a new toothbrush brand or a new shampoo can involve a similar kind of newness that can stop a surprised potential adopter from trying the new product. Understanding this is important when entering a new foreign market, something we will return to several times in this book.

Another international application of the product life cycle is to the concept of "the long tail" market. The **long tail theory** is based on the emergence of global online commerce, and the ability of the Internet to provide a sustainable market even for very obscure products and services whose sales are low.[21] There are two parts to the long tail. One is the fact that some products never die—the typical product whose life cycle is shown in Exhibit 1.3 does not disappear from the market but continues to have small but steady sales, shown in an elongated tail to the right. This happens often to products that define generations such as music CDs and films, but also to automobiles, clothes, and accessories and similar products that have nostalgic value. But the long tail also involves new products aiming for very small niches in the marketplace. The low cost of communication via the Internet, the ease of accessing any one online "store," and the low cost of global logistics make it possible to market very special products in small volumes. The "long tail" phenomenon is defined as the ability to sustain a business based on a very small volume of sales to a global niche segment. It means, in fact, that a small business can still be very global. Even though most of this book will reference large multinational and their brands, because they are the ones we are all familiar with, many of the principles apply also to small businesses with a global market.

Why Companies go Global

Today, five classes of variables propel companies toward globalization: Market, competition, cost, technology, and government variables can be referred to as the five major **globalization drivers.**[22]

Market Drivers

Market drivers are the strongest force pushing global marketing. The market drivers include:

1. Common customer needs.
2. Global customers.
3. Global channels.
4. Transferable marketing.

When customers in different countries have the same needs in a product or service category, common customer needs become a compelling factor for companies. With technological progress and global communications, consumers in many countries are exposed to similar messages and products. For many industries, free trade and unrestricted travel have created homogeneous groups of customers around the globe. Preferences tend to become less localized or provincial and approach a global standard.[23] However, some markets—typically culture-bound products and services such as foods, drinks, apparel, and entertainment—stubbornly resist the shift toward globalization and remain multidomestic, with different customer preferences and differentiated products across countries.

Global customers are customers that need the same product or service in several countries. For example, as companies globalize, as global customers they want to buy from suppliers and vendors with global presence. This is why supplier firms in the automobile industry, such as German Bosch, Japanese Nippon Denso, and American Delco, have gone abroad. Global customers have spurred the development of global hotel chains, global ad agencies, and global communications. Hilton Hotels, McCann Erickson Worldwide, and Federal Express are prominent examples of American companies following their customers abroad, in the process putting pressure on competing local services in various countries.

Global channels, distribution and logistics firms that provide seamless transportation and storage around the world, have had a similar positive effect on the emergence of global marketing strategies. Firms can in many cases expand internationally only if the requisite developments in the channel infrastructure keep pace. Thus, new integrated networks make it possible for marketers to sell their products around the world, as a consequence of multinational integration of transportation systems, the spread of large financial institutions, the emergence of worldwide distributors of grain and other commodities, and the globalization of even seemingly localized retailers such as supermarkets (Delhaize of Belgium, for example, is now present not only throughout Europe but also in the United States) and department stores (mainly by acquiring existing stores, but also opening new stores).

Transferable marketing is using the same marketing ideas in different countries. This can mean the same packaging, advertising, brand names, and other marketing mix elements. As campaign ideas in one country prove successful, the global company can use the same or a slightly adapted campaign in other markets. This is how good ideas get leveraged. For example, Nike's successful American ad campaign featuring basketball star Michael Jordan was used in many countries. The multilanguage packaging of many consumer goods has made it possible to offer the same packages with the same colors and the same brand names in many countries.

Competitive Drivers

In many industries the example from competitors who go global provides a strong incentive for firms to follow suit. Such **competitive drivers** energize an organization to match their moves. It is not by coincidence that Swedish Ericsson and Finnish Nokia both attacked the American mobile phone market in the late 1990s. Also, following another company's path means that management can learn from somebody else's mistakes. Toyota's Lexus and Nissan's Infiniti luxury cars were introduced in the North American market following closely the approach used by Honda's Acura, including separate dealer networks. Also, there is legitimacy in trying to match a competitor's move, and it makes the task of convincing doubtful shareholders and reluctant subsidiary management easier. American Whirlpool's coordinated attack on the global market for home appliances (including the acquisition of Dutch Philips' appliance business) thus justified the globalization efforts of Electrolux, the Swedish competitor.

On the home front, the presence of foreign competitors in a firm's domestic market increases the need for the firm to venture abroad, if for no other reason than to counterattack in foreign markets. Benetton's success in the United States has led The Gap and The Limited, two U.S. competitors, to go abroad. The emergence of strong global competitors has served to develop the necessary facilities and infrastructure for domestic companies to go global. Global businesses not only sell their products abroad, but also transfer skills and technology across countries, making it easier for domestic companies to expand globally. The typical head of international operations at a novice entrant abroad has often been hired away from a more successful global company.

Cost Drivers

In industries such as automobiles that require large-scale plants to be efficient, single markets are rarely sufficient to generate **economies of scale.** Scale economies involve the unit cost reductions made possible by long series in a given plant, and to achieve this one plant often needs to supply more than one foreign market. When a new plant is established, it is often designed to assemble one model only, shipping it to neighboring countries in order to gain such scale advantages. Toyota's Kentucky plant, for example, produces the Camry model for the NAFTA market, and the BMW plant in South Carolina focuses on the 325 model, supplying the North American market.

Even where there are no scale economies, **economies of scope** (gains from spreading activities across multiple product lines or businesses) can push businesses to globalize. Thus, in consumer packaged goods, because the dominant global firms have small plants in many countries, they gain scope economies by marketing a wide selection of products. Unilever, Colgate-Palmolive, and Procter & Gamble have mostly uniform product lines and brand names across the EU, but have manufacturing plants in all the major European countries.

Other **cost drivers** include global **sourcing advantages**—cost savings via supply from a low-wage country, improved logistics and distribution systems, and the growth of inexpensive global telecommunications. Also, high product-development costs relative to the size of the national market and fast-developing technology serve to reinforce the need for global strategies to help recoup the investment.

These cost drivers generally induce companies to implement global strategies and some of these strategies further encourage global marketing. Thus, scope economies tend to favor globally uniform brand names and communications, and improved logistics and telecommunications make it possible to manage distribution of products and services centrally. Federal Express is now well known in many places across the globe, and its computerized tracking system makes it possible to monitor the progress of shipments 24 hours a day across the globe.

Technology Drivers

Technological innovations have made global expansion of multinationals both possible and desirable. We have already alluded to how an impetus to global standardization comes from the technological revolution in global media and telecommunications and the resulting homogeneity of preferences. We also saw how technology-based products and services are often natural drivers of global—as opposed to multidomestic—markets. An additional very powerful **technology driver** toward globalization of market strategies is the revolution brought about by the Internet.

The **Internet** is inherently global. The World Wide Web and its home pages can be accessed from anywhere by anyone. Businesses can establish presence in foreign markets without ever setting foot there. The costs of business transactions across borders in industries such as transportation, hotel and travel, and financial services have been substantially reduced. Entrepreneurial start-up firms can create an online presence, receive orders from abroad, get paid via credit card, and ship products instantly and without financial risks. E-commerce allows one-to-one marketing across countries, with customization and personal attention at minimum cost.

Internet technology is now routinely used in international marketing research as well. Survey questionnaires can be administered from Web sites, with appropriate translations for different languages and countries. Respondents can be recruited from e-mail lists or from banner ads on popular Web sites. Software is available that can automatically tabulate responses and provide summary statistics as the survey data comes in. The difficulty of ensuring comparable data across countries, a chronic international research problem, is reduced substantially with the Internet-based surveys. There are still problems with getting representative respondents, but as the Internet access capabilities grow in different countries, this problem will diminish as well.

Government Drivers

Government globalization drivers add favorable trade policies, acceptance of foreign investment, compatible technical standards, and common marketing regulations. All these have a direct and unequivocally positive effect on global marketing efforts. In the past, governmental barriers to foreign market entry kept local markets protected and made global marketing an impossibility. Despite the continued progress toward open markets and free trade, it is important to keep in mind that such barriers can be raised again and that political complications can ruin the best-laid global marketing plans.

A good example of the effect of governments on globalization is the recent introduction of **ISO 9001,** a global standard of quality certification (ISO stands for Industrial Standards of Operation). ISO 9001 encourages global marketing, since it is worldwide. Furthermore, the return on the investment in improved operations to gain certification is higher the more countries the company does business in. At the same time, the higher standards encourage uniformity of operations everywhere.

As one example, faced with myriad conflicting regulations of products and services in the different member countries, the EU Brussels Commission decided to start with a clean slate and adopt the new standards to supersede existing national standards. Of course, each product or service category (telephones, consumer electronics, autos, pharmaceuticals, etc.) has its own category-specific standards. In addition, however, the commission developed an umbrella code in ISO 9001 that serves as a guide for all companies wanting to do business in the EU. A Board of Examiners was created to certify companies under the code, which includes requirements on the safety of facilities, treatment of raw materials, quality inspection procedures, and even customer satisfaction measures. Although approval under the code is not a legal requirement as yet, many companies, European and non-European, have decided to expend resources to improve their operations and gain certification, giving them a competitive edge over competitors not yet certified.[24]

Global Localization

A global marketing strategy that totally globalizes all marketing activities is not always achievable or even desirable. A more common approach is for a company to globalize its product strategy by marketing the same product lines, product designs, and brand names everywhere but to localize distribution and marketing communications. This is the standard approach in consumer durables such as automobiles, cameras, and electronics. By contrast, consumer packaged goods companies have often gone farther in their globalization efforts, with worldwide ad campaigns and frequent in-store promotions in addition to a standardized product line.[25]

Studies of the extent to which successful companies' marketing mix activities are globalized have revealed a fairly consistent pattern. A company's packaging and brand names are most likely to be globalized, followed by its media message and distribution; activities become more localized for in-store promotions; and the pattern ends with very localized personal selling and customer service functions.[26] This pattern holds for American as well as Japanese and European firms. A firm's global marketing strategy has to be flexibly implemented and take account of the different degrees to which the activities need local adaptation and personnel. Canadian and Japanese customers may prefer the same automobile, for example, but they may have different needs when it comes to after-sales support because of the different conditions of use in the two countries.

In general, the closer a marketing mix activity is to the point of purchase or after-sales service, the more need for customization. The coining of the term **global localization,** which has become a new code word in marketing strategy, is a recognition of the fact that the marketing job is surely not finished until products and services are used and consumed!

Developing Knowledge Assets

One unique benefit of global marketing is the opportunity it provides to develop new skills and knowledge. To illustrate how learning through experience happens, it will be useful to relate the experiences of Procter & Gamble in Japan, and how that company had to change its ways of marketing.[27]

A well-known characteristic of the P&G marketing organization had long been its reliance on the brand management concept it helped originate. Briefly, a **brand manager** supports the brand in the marketplace through advertising and in-store promotions and coordinates shipments to warehouses and stocking on store shelves. The job also involves coordinating factory production schedules with special promotional drives, conducting market research, and suggesting improvements to the developmental laboratories. For P&G the system also involved direct competition with other P&G brands in the same product categories. There was a conservative element built into the system in terms of managers' preoccupation with their existing brands.

P&G New Products

For new products, P&G evolved a system in which any proposed introduction needed to be thoroughly tested in laboratory clinics, by home use, and through test marketing. The tests were to be summarized in one-page memos, ideally giving three strong reasons for the advocated action (the famous "keep it simple" memos). Only if definite preferences over existing product formulations were achieved in blind tests would the company give its go-ahead. In the case of Pringle's potato chips, the market tests lasted well over five years. The company wanted to ensure that the product represented a discernible improvement in quality and features over existing offerings.

This system works very well in mature and relatively slow-moving markets where the premium is on incremental improvements to maintain brand loyalty, tracking competitors and customers, and rapid reaction to competitive promotions. It works less well where the competitive edge goes to the firm with the newest product innovation and customer preferences change fast. The latter are characteristics of the Japanese marketplace, where a premium is paid for speed and flexibility, with functional quality taken for granted. Thus, in Japan P&G found it could no longer rely on a great product well supported to be successful. It needed to be able to introduce new products more quickly.

The company tried to revamp its brand management system in Japan and placed brands under group management to avoid the individual responsibility that prohibited brand managers from taking risks. In order to speed up new-product introductions, they also tried to limit "the Pringle syndrome" by making test evaluations quicker and less cumbersome. Because of the new management system, the company now is able to diffuse experiences from various countries throughout the organization faster than before. Reformulated products that succeed in one market are quickly introduced by managers elsewhere. The new compact detergents from P&G were developed in Japan and have now been introduced in most Western markets. The thinner diapers also emerged out of

Japan. In both of these cases, P&G could move faster than its Japanese competitors because of its existing global network—but only after the "not invented here" syndrome typical of the narrowly focused brand management system had been eliminated.

P&G Advertising

Long well known for TV commercials depicting P&G products as problem solvers for the harassed homemaker needing to impress her mother-in-law, the teenager looking for peer approval, or the young man who desperately needs a date, P&G went into Japan displaying Pampers diapers as a solution to a problem. Assuming that a wet baby posed a problem for the young mother, the company positioned Pampers as a new way of dealing with a hassle.

Realizing that grandmothers were important influences in Japan, the P&G commercials made sure the storyboard demonstrated approval from the mother-in-law. Understanding that the homemaker who used the convenient paper diapers could be perceived as lazy, the commercials made sure that the baby's satisfaction showed, as the baby changed from crying to smiling. The commercials also adopted a big sister–little sister format, showing how the young Pampers-using mother followed in the footsteps of the already successful mothers.

Despite such seemingly excellent fundamentals, the advertising failed. The main reason was straightforward: The young Japanese mother simply did not view the baby as a "problem." Sure, there was wetness—but this only meant that diapers had to be changed. To leave the baby unchanged after an "accident" was unacceptable—regardless how "absorbent" the diaper was. Only by adding a color-change wetness indicator did P&G's paper diapers succeed, because then the mother could change the diapers right away after simply checking the color indicator. The indicator was convenient because it helped the mother take better care of the baby. The Japanese mothers responded to the idea of better care, not to more convenience.

Needless to say, this benefit is contingent on the mother's not working outside the home. But it can be transferred to Western markets, by focusing separately on segments of "mother at home" households.

P&G Distribution

Upon entering Japan, P&G learned how strongly the implementation of large-scale in-store promotions depended on sufficient channel capacity. Several distribution layers in Japan are necessary because stores have very limited space, sometimes need replenishment daily, and have little capacity to handle a rush of buyers.

The solution to the distribution problem became the invention of new-product formulations and new packaging techniques. Thus, condensed detergents now allow limited store space to be more efficiently utilized. Similarly, thin diaper designs are preferable since they result in smaller packages. Vacuum-packing techniques are used to compact the fluffy diapers, which then pop up when the smaller packages are opened. All these innovations, born in Japan, are now used by P&G in other country markets.

Global Marketing Objectives

Given the benefits of global marketing, it is logical that the need to market overseas goes beyond pure market considerations. The main objectives the firm going abroad might pursue are as follows:

1. **Exploiting market potential and growth.** This is the typical marketing objective.
2. **Gaining scale and scope returns at home.** Longer production series and capital investment increase productivity.
3. **Learning from a leading market.** Many small market shareholders make no money in very competitive markets, but learn about new technology and about competition.

4. **Pressuring competitors.** Increasing the competitive pressure in the stronghold market might help divert the competitor's attention from other markets.
5. **Diversifying markets.** By adding new countries and markets to the company portfolio, the firm's dependence on any one market will be lessened.
6. **Learning how to do business abroad.** For example, to learn how to deal with former communist countries, entering Poland may be a first step to entering Russia.

The potential diversity of objectives is one reason why global marketing involves more than the traditional one product-one market case typically treated in textbooks.

Three Hats

To get a better grip on the complex job faced by the global marketing manager, it is useful to distinguish between three roles he or she may assume as a company goes global and becomes more extensively involved in international markets.

The Foreign Entry Role

First there is the **export manager** in charge of international sales. In many small and medium-sized companies—but also in some larger domestically oriented companies such as department stores and beer brewers—foreign sales account for perhaps less than 10 percent of the total turnover. As orders from abroad trickle in, someone takes charge of the international sales. As the business grows, this person gradually gains status in the organization, and the foreign business needs to be managed more systematically. The marketing activities initially involve learning about how to export and how to locate reliable middlemen overseas, often carried out with little or no attention to the larger picture. But as sales grow and the potential overseas is recognized by the company, more careful screening of markets overseas becomes desirable, and the possibility of establishing more permanent representation in key markets needs to be considered.

This is the **foreign entry role** or phase of the marketing manager's job. The manager has to learn the intricacies of doing business overseas, of finding the right middlemen, of quantitatively and qualitatively evaluating foreign markets, negotiating for joint marketing ventures, helping to set up a sales subsidiary, and learning to understand foreign customers' product and service requirements. Internally, he or she becomes the company leader in "internationalizing" the company. Externally, the manager becomes the company's spokesperson to the middlemen and customers in the markets entered.

These tasks verge close to a general management position, and the export manager in these companies has to shoulder more tasks than pure marketing. If the overseas entry involves manufacturing, marketing know-how is usually not crucial. But when the company enters a foreign country to gain access to markets, naturally marketers are needed. Nevertheless, many of the basic questions are organizational: setting up a logistics function and a network of middlemen and developing reporting and control mechanisms back to headquarters. It's really basic marketing management—getting products to the customers and getting paid for them.

The Local Marketing Role

In many countries the company can't be satisfied using independent middlemen for the marketing effort. Especially in leading markets, the company needs to be closer to the ultimate consumer. Establishing a sales subsidiary and sending some expatriates to work there is common. In this way the company can ensure that the potential of the market is exploited, that the company capabilities are properly leveraged, that customer trends are monitored, and that moves by the competition are anticipated. In addition, the expatriate marketing manager has to direct the more tactical local marketing effort.

This **local marketing role** involves skills largely the same as those required in the domestic setting. This is the "marketing in Germany" or "marketing in China" hat. The basic marketing skills remain those described in the typical textbooks, although the environment is of course different. This is the quintessential new situation that teaches the manager a thing or two, not only about marketing skills but especially about other cultures and behaviors and, ultimately, about himself or herself.

Because of the different environment, the local marketing effort is usually carried out with the help of several natives. In some countries, the political, economic, social, or cultural environment differs so much that the expatriate becomes ineffective and a drag on the organization. Japan is notorious in this respect, and several foreign companies have decided to rely on Japanese employees altogether. This unfortunately removes many of the learning benefits that come from operating abroad. The typical approach today is to leave day-to-day management to natives, and let Western managers play a more strategic role.

In many companies, the senior managers of foreign subsidiaries are expatriates. The joint ventures and strategic alliances common today feature expatriate managers in senior positions. They have to learn that because of the different environment some of their marketing skills may not be applicable in the local market. Market segmentation is difficult without reliable demographic and economic data. Domestic companies may be protected by tacit agreements between government and industry. In-store promotions run up against uncooperative retailers. The part of this book devoted to local marketing abroad is intended to help the expatriate manager leverage marketing skills learned at home in this new environment.

The Global Management Role

The third hat of the global marketer, and often the next step on the career ladder, is the truly global part of the job. Using the learning and experience gained from foreign entry and local marketing, the marketer is now working on deriving global benefits from the firm's presence in various markets. The idea is to capture the scale advantages and other synergies to be created by more coordinated marketing.

Global management involves questions of global segmentation and positioning, standardization of products and services, uniform pricing around the globe, prototype advertising with a similar theme across countries, global brand names, and international logistics. The basic notion is to rationalize the global marketing operations in order to capture spillovers, scale advantages, and lower costs and to coordinate the marketing campaigns across countries for maximum effect. This is easier said than done. The main body of this book develops the promises and the potential drawbacks of global marketing in much more detail.

Summary

This chapter has emphasized the need for marketers to develop a global mindset, including a sensitivity to local antiglobalization concerns and demands. As markets grow more homogeneous across countries and global competitors win out locally, there is no avoiding globalization. But the global marketer has to be careful in analyzing markets and competitors. If the globalization drivers are weak, with multidomestic markets and mostly local competitors, "going global" may have to be held off for the time being—although "going regional" might still be feasible, the possibility of being a pioneer should always be considered.

Firms pursue several objectives in their global expansion. Although sales and profitability are important, firms will go global in order to track, monitor, and challenge competitors, learn from lead customers and leading markets, and diversify away from reliance on a single market. Thus the marketing manager may find himself or herself in a foreign land, and the stint abroad will often seem unsettling, jarring the manager away from preconceived notions and assumed know-how. In the process, the marketing manager will gain useful experience and learn new skills, which often can be put to good use at home and in other parts of the firm's global network.

The world of the global marketer is complicated, with not only new countries but also new tasks to deal with. It is useful to simplify the situation by separating the job into three parts: foreign entry, local marketing abroad, and global management. The division is not always clear-cut, and the roles of course overlap. But the tasks involved are quite different. Furthermore, the division mirrors the career path of many present and future global marketing managers: first, helping to evaluate and enter new foreign markets, then managing the marketing in one foreign country, and finally coordinating the global effort back at headquarters. These three hats of the global marketer help provide the structure for this book.

The book deals with foreign entry problems in Part Two, local marketing questions in Part Three, and global management issues in Part Four. In Part One of the book, marketing skills and know-how fundamental to all global marketing tasks are introduced.

Key Terms

antiglobalization, *6*	global channels, *21*	lead(ing) markets, *17*
brand manager, *24*	global communications, *5*	local brands, *17*
competitive drivers, *21*	global customers, *21*	local marketing role, *26*
cost drivers, *22*	global localization, *24*	long tail theory, *20*
chasm, the, *20*	global marketing, *14*	market drivers, *21*
diffusion process, *19*	global markets, *14*	market segmentation, *19*
economies of scale, *22*	global products, *16*	multidomestic markets, *14*
economies of scope, *22*	global warming, *9*	product life cycle (PLC), *19*
export manager, *26*	globalization drivers, *20*	product positioning, *20*
fair trade, *8*	government globalization	regionalization, *13*
first-mover advantages, *18*	drivers, *23*	sourcing advantages, *22*
flat world, *10*	green trade, *10*	standardized products, *14*
foreign entry role, *26*	Internet, *22*	technology drivers, *22*
global brands, *17*	ISO 9001, *23*	transferable marketing, *21*

Discussion Questions

1. What are the factors that seem to drive the globalization of the automobile industry? Why is the computer industry not spread more evenly around the globe?

2. Identify three product categories for which you think the markets are global. Can you find three that are multidomestic? What market data would you need to support your assertion?

3. What would a marketing manager learn in the U.S. market that could be useful in Europe?

4. After graduation, many students would like to work in a certain country, and often for a particular multinational. Using one of the Internet search engines (such as **www.yahoo.com** or **www.google.com**), see how much information you can gather about a multinational company's organization and marketing in a country of your choice to help you decide whether it would be a good company to work for in that country.

5. Some observers argue that the coming of electronic commerce on the Internet signals the arrival of a new era of global marketing, as online retailers of everything from books and music to software and outdoor gear make it possible to buy products without visiting stores. Assess how far this development has come by visiting a Web site for a retailer offering online shopping and see what the limits are on which countries they can ship to.

Notes

1. Naisbitt, 1994, painstakingly documents the paradox of global economic integration coupled with political and ethnic fragmentation.

2. Drucker, 1994, is as usual very perceptive in discussing how technology, information, and knowledge affect management.

3. Nonaka, 1992, discusses how the creative inertia in some Japanese organizations has been overcome.

4. The antiglobalization arguments are well presented in books by such noneconomists as Naomi Klein's *No Logo,* William Greider's *One World, Ready or Not,* and Anthony Giddens's *Runaway World.*

5. The economists' counterargumentation to the antiglobalization forces are well represented in Graham, 2000, and Rugman, 2001, although the latter argues that the important international trading areas are regional rather than global in scope. A well-known advocate for globalization is Friedman, 1999.

6. American Brands in the World: Growing Opportunities or Rising Threats? Roper Report, 2004. From Business for Diplomatic Action, Inc.

7. See Fairtrade Labelling Organizations International, 2006, www.fairtradefederation.org.

8. See, for example, Stiglitz, 2008.

9. See Friedman, 2005.

10. This argument has been made most forcefully by Pankaj Ghemawat, a Harvard professor. See Ghemawat, 2007a.

11 See Ghemawat, 2007b.

12. See Rugman, 2005.

13. The term "multidomestic" was first proposed by Hout et al., 1982.

14. This list draws on Yip's original work, 2002.

15. Adapted from Kashani, 1992.

16. See Hamel and Prahalad, 1991.

17. For the ACNielsen study, see the report in Branch, 2001.

18. See Lieberman and Montgomery, 1988.

19. The product life cycle and the related segmentation and positioning concepts are discussed at length in many introductory marketing texts. See, for example, Kotler and Keller, 2005, Chapter 12.

20. The "chasm" notion was originally developed by Geoffrey Moore to explain the marketing failures of high-tech products. See Moore, 2002.

21. The "long tail" phenomenon was first introduced by Anderson, 2006.

22. See Yip, 2002. This section draws directly on Yip's treatment of global strategy. The addition of technology as a driver was suggested by Masoud Kavoossi of Howard University.

23. Levitt, 1983, was the first to recognize this trend.

24. ISO 9001 guidelines are available directly from the EU Commission in Brussels and also from U.S. Department of Commerce offices. Consultants specializing in helping firms get ISO 9001 approval are also available in many countries. For an excellent overview of companies' response to ISO guidelines, see Prasad and Naidu, 1994.

25. This section draws on Quelch and Hoff, 1986, and Yip, 2002.

26. See Johansson and Yip, 1994.

27. The references used here include Yoshino, 1990, and Natsuzaka, 1987. In addition, this section is based on interviews with Mr. Richard Laube, advertising manager for P&G Japan in Osaka, and with Ms. Jennifer Sakaguchi of Grey-Daiko, an advertising agency in Tokyo. A final source is a student report, "Pampers in Japan," by Mike Ando, Yasu Mori, Kazal Roy, and Masa Tanaka, International University of Japan, June 1991.

Selected References

Anderson, Chris. *The Long Tail: Why the Future of Business is Selling Less of More*. New York: Hyperion, 2006.

Branch, Shelly. "ACNielsen Gives 43 Brands Global Status." *The Wall Street Journal,* October 31, 2001, p. 38.

Buzzell, Robert. "Can You Standardize Multinational Marketing?" *Harvard Business Review* (November–December 1968), pp. 98–104.

Drucker, Peter. *Post-Capitalist Society*. New York: Harper and Row, 1994.

Friedman, Thomas L. *The Lexus and the Olive Tree: Understanding Globalization*. New York: Farrar, Straus, Giroux, 1999.

_____. *The World Is Flat*. New York: Farrar, Straus & Giroux, 2005.

Ghemawat, Pankaj. "Why the World Isn't Flat." *Foreign Policy* 159, March–April 2007a.

_____. *Redefining Global Strategy: Crossing Borders in a World Where Differences Still Matter*. Boston, MA: Harvard University Press, 2007b.

Giddens, Anthony. *Runaway World*. New York: Routledge, 2000.

Govindarajan, Vijay, and Anil K. Gupta. *The Quest for Global Dominance.* San Francisco: Jossey-Bass, 2001.

Graham, Edward M. *Fighting the Wrong Enemy: Antiglobal Activists and Multinational Enterprises.* Washington, DC: Institute for International Economics, 2000.

Greider, William. *One World, Ready or Not.* New York: Simon and Schuster, 1997.

Hamel, Gary, and C. K. Prahalad. "Corporate Imagination and Expeditionary Marketing." *Harvard Business Review,* July–August 1991, pp. 81–92.

Hout, Thomas, Michael E. Porter, and Eileen Rudden. "How Global Companies Win Out." *Harvard Business Review,* September–October 1982.

Johansson, Johny K., and Thomas W. Roehl. "How Companies Develop Assets and Capabilities: Japan as a Leading Market." In Beechler, Schon, and Allan Bird, eds. *Emerging Trends in Japanese Management,* vol. 6 of *Research in International Business and International Relations,* ed. Manuel G. Serapio, Jr. Greenwich, CT: JAI Press, 1994, pp. 139–60.

Johansson, Johny K., and George Yip. "Exploiting Globalization Potential: U.S. and Japanese Business Strategies." *Strategic Management Journal,* Winter 1994.

Johnson, Chalmers. *Japan: Who Governs? The Rise of the Developmental State.* New York: Norton, 1995.

Kashani, Kamran. *Managing Global Marketing.* Boston: PWS-Kent, 1992.

Klein, Naomi. *No Logo.* London: Flamingo, 2000.

Kotler, Philip, and Kevin Keller. *Marketing Management.* 12th Edition. Upper Saddle River, NJ: Prentice Hall, 2005.

Levitt, Ted. "The Globalization of Markets." *Harvard Business Review,* May–June 1983, pp. 92–102.

Lieberman, Marvin, and David Montgomery. "First-Mover Advantages." *Strategic Management Journal,* Summer 1988, pp. 41–58.

Micklethwait, John, and Adrian Wooldridge. *A Future Perfect: The Challenge and Hidden Promise of Globalization.* New York: Crown, 2000.

Moore, Geoffrey. *Crossing the Chasm. Marketing and Selling High-Tech Products to Mainstream Customers.* New York: Harper Business, 2002.

Naisbitt, John. *Global Paradox.* New York: Morrow, 1994.

Natsuzaka, Masumi. "Kao and Procter & Gamble in Japan." Class report, University of Washington School of Business, December 1987.

Nonaka, Ikujiro. "The Knowledge-Creating Company." *Harvard Business Review,* November–December 1992.

Porter, Michael E. *The Competitive Advantage of Nations.* New York: Free Press, 1990.

Prasad, V. Kanti, and G. M. Naidu. "Perspectives and Preparedness Regarding ISO 9000 International Quality Standards." *Journal of International Marketing* 2, no. 2 (1994), pp. 81–98.

Quelch, John A., and Edward J. Hoff. "Customizing Global Marketing." *Harvard Business Review,* May–June 1986, pp. 59–68.

Rugman, Alan. *The End of Globalization.* New York: Amacom, 2001.

_____. *The Regional Multinationals. MNEs and "Global" Strategic Management.* Cambridge: Cambridge University Press, 2005.

Stiglitz, Joseph E. "Global Green GDP." www.fora.tv, February 5, 2008.

Vernon, Raymond. "International Investment and International Trade in the Product Cycle." *Quarterly Journal of Economics,* May 1966.

Wind, Jerry, and Vijay Mahajan. *Digital Marketing: Global Strategies from the World's Leading Experts.* New York: Wiley, 2001.

Womack, James P.; Daniel T. Jones; and Daniel Roos. *The Machine That Changed the World.* New York: Rawson Associates, 1990.

Yip, George. *Total Global Strategy II.* Englewood Cliffs, NJ: Prentice Hall, 2002.

Yoshino, Michael. "Procter and Gamble Japan" (A)(B)(C). Harvard Business School case nos. 9-391-003, 004, 005, 1990.

Chapter

Theoretical Foundations

"The method in the madness"

After reading this chapter, you will be able to:

1. Combine a market-oriented analysis perspective with a resource-based analysis when developing a global marketing strategy.
2. Define competitive advantages, by separating country-specific from firm-specific advantages.
3. Assess whether competitive advantages are mobile and transferable abroad, particularly important for country-specific advantages not under the control of the firm.
4. Extend Porter's "five forces" model by analyzing the split between domestic and foreign competitors and the possibility of strategic groups formed by trade barriers or regional treaties.
5. Evaluate the wider repertoire and greater financial clout of global competitors, and their intense competitive rivalry.

The aim of Chapter 2 is to introduce some of the theoretical foundations for global marketing strategy. We define and explain the differences between a market-based and a resource-based strategy and show how the firm that is intent on going abroad needs first to define what it is good at. We introduce the important concepts of country-specific and firm-specific advantages derived from the economic theory of international trade and the theory of the multinational firm, and we explain the role of marketing in leveraging these advantages. Chapter 2 applies and extends these economic principles to actual marketing examples, showing what the theories imply for global marketing strategy. We discuss the role global expansion plays in developing competitive advantages and show how the competitive environment can be analyzed in terms of an extended version of Porter's "five forces" model. The aim is to show how a few simple but powerful theoretical concepts can help guide the international marketer in developing a competitive strategy for the global marketplace. The chapter ends by relating the market-based and resource-based strategies to the three functional tasks of the global marketer: foreign entry, local marketing, and global management.

Competitive Advantage: Here Today, Gone Tomorrow?

For the many people obsessed with sneakers—from teenage sports fans to retired executives, grammar school students to lawyers on the go—the competitive battle in the 1980s was between Nike and Reebok, with Nike pulling ahead. But in the mid-1990s, old favorite Adidas made a comeback, while Reebok fell further behind and Nike suffered several setbacks. In the early years of the new millennium Adidas and Nike were still running even, but Reebok was coming back up. And so on. The industry offers a good illustration of the cutthroat competition between global competitors.

Sneakers (or the "athletic footwear industry" to be politically correct) have never been the same after Philip Knight, Nike founder, began peddling his waffle-soled running shoes out of his car trunk more than 30 years ago. Suddenly the fitness-minded and health-conscious new generation had a product that could take the pounding of feet against hard surfaces and protect weak ankles and tender knees. First jogging, then running, then aerobics became a craze. German Puma and Adidas, long-standing leaders of the sports shoe markets, did not respond, keeping their focus on active sportsmen and women, not wannabes, in the process missing out on a phenomenal growth market. But British Reebok entered the fray, targeting women with an aerobics shoe that took the market and Nike by surprise. In 1987, Reebok passed Nike in annual sales.

But with global competition nothing ever stays the same. In the early 1990s Nike regrouped under Knight, placing its swoosh logo on sports superstars with massive marketing support and speeding up its R&D for new designs. Striking gold, the company came up with the "airpump," a major improvement, and signed basketball legend Michael Jordan. Nike's Air Jordan designs, created around a player who went on to become one of the most celebrated sports stars of all time, helped put Nike back into a solid lead.

Again lightning struck. Competitors soon imitated and improved on the air-pump technology, erasing the temporary competitive advantage. More surprising and important, perhaps, Jordan tired of basketball and decided to get into another sport, baseball. Nike lost one of its major advantages, made worse by the fact that Jordan the baseball player bore no comparison to Jordan the basketball champion. While Michael languished in the minors, Reebok decided to launch a direct attack on Nike's hegemony in sports. Signing the new basketball star Shaquille O'Neal to a multiyear contract, and taking a page from Nike's playbook by designing a product line around him, Reebok went directly against Nike's stronghold.

This time Nike did not sit still. With Knight stepping back in to take the reins he had let go a couple of years earlier, the company launched a massive counter-campaign whose main objective was to create Nike products for all major sports, especially soccer, and to get exposure for the swoosh logo in as many places around the globe as possible. In soccer, an aggressive style pushing the swoosh and the "Just do it" slogan wherever and whenever and, especially, sponsoring the Brazilian national soccer team made Knight unpopular among some soccer purists, but it helped sell shoes. When Jordan returned to basketball and his Chicago Bulls won the championship again, with Shaquille O'Neal's Los Angeles Lakers out in the semifinals, Nike's victory seemed secure.

But Nike's position was challenged again. Family-owned Adidas A.G. put a new professional CEO in place and a renewed sense of mission and global outlook was beginning to bear fruit. While Nike and Reebok were fighting it out for the largest shares of the global market, Adidas had begun a turnaround, which by 1997 showed the company with an annual growth rate of 23 percent in sales and 27 percent in net income. At the same time Nike's marketing war had not been without costs. Nike's sales of footwear in 1997–98 showed only a slight increase, and net income was down 27 percent. Nike still dominated in terms of share and continues to control about 47 percent of U.S. sales compared with 15 percent for Reebok and 6 percent for Adidas. But Adidas was gaining even in the U.S. market where it has been relatively weak, and globally the company captures closer to 15 percent of the market compared with Nike's one-third market share. In July 1998 insult was added to injury. In the World Cup final in Paris, the Adidas-sponsored French team defeated Nike's favored Brazilian team, 3-0. For a while it looked as though Nike and Adidas-Salomon had reached something of a truce, avoiding head-to-head battles. Lately, however, competition has heated up again. As Jordan retired for the second time, Nike signed LeBron James, Jordan's heir apparent. Adidas countered with Kobe Bryant, the Lakers' own superstar. Reebok hired Allen Iverson and Yao Ming, the first Chinese basketball star. Then Nike nabbed Bryant from Adidas, as Adidas bought Reebok in 2005, apparently to consolidate its basketball position in the United States and keep its focus on soccer and David Beckham. And the beat goes on, and on. . . .

Sources: Timothy Egan, "The Swoon of the Swoosh," *New York Times Magazine,* September 13, 1998, pp. 66–70; John Tagliabue, "Once Behind the Pack, Adidas Vies for the Lead," *New York Times,* March 19, 1998, pp. D1, D6; Sharon R. King, "Flying the Swoosh and Stripes," *New York Times,* March 19, 1998, pp. D1, D6; Kenneth Labaich, "Nike vs. Reebok—A Battle for Hearts, Minds and Feet," *Fortune,* September 18, 1996, pp. 58–69; Jodi Heckel, "Nike, Adidas Officials Discuss Sweatshop Issues at University of Illinois," *Champaign-Urbana News-Gazette,* November 29, 2001; Katie Abel, "Reebok, Skechers Aim for Slam Dunks with Endorsement Deals," *FN,* December 10, 2001; *Brandweek,* March 16, 2008.

Introduction

Most students and practitioners of marketing have learned about the advantages of a *market orientation.* "Don't think of the product sold, but the customer need fulfilled." "Deliver customer satisfaction, not just what you think is a quality product." "Your dealer is also your customer." "Understand the consumer better by listening to complaints." "Don't just read research reports but go meet your customers in the store."

For the marketing manager, it is natural to think about overseas opportunities in terms of customer needs and wants. It suggests that the main issue for global marketing is whether there is a demand for the product. But this is only a start. More important, the manager has to identify what the firm has to offer abroad, and whether it can deliver on the promise.

The crucial first factor for the firm is to understand the basis of its own success at home or elsewhere. The firm contemplating going abroad should identify its key strengths and whether its local success is just that, local. Only if there are good reasons to assume that some strengths are applicable in another country should it start examining markets abroad. It is possible to look at foreign entry in terms of learning and increasing competitiveness, but even then existing strengths and weaknesses have to be carefully assessed.

This chapter will discuss the theoretical foundations of such an assessment. It begins by discussing the distinction between country-specific and firm-specific advantages and linking country-specific advantages to the theory of comparative advantage and newer trade theories. Sources of firm-specific advantages are identified and with them the managerial choices to be made between alternative ways of capitalizing on these advantages. The next section expands the analysis to include an assessment of the competitive environment, extending the competitive framework proposed by Porter (1985). We then discuss in depth the firm-specific advantages associated with a global competitor and finish by relating the strategic discussion to the three hats of foreign entry, local marketing, and global management.

Country-Specific Advantages (CSAs)

The fundamental aim of business strategy is to create and sustain **competitive advantage.** This holds true for the global firm. Firms will gain higher profits and superior returns on capital invested to the extent that they can build and exploit advantages over domestic and foreign competitors. Global marketers, although not the only important players, have vital roles in both the creation and the exploitation of competitive advantages. For example, marketers help create global brands, develop global advertising campaigns that communicate with target markets, and design global channels of distribution. In doing so, they must start with an understanding of what the firm's competitive advantages are in the various markets.

For the globalizing company it is useful to distinguish between advantages that are specific to the firm and those a firm possesses because of the country it is from or

Getting the Picture

WHICH COUNTRY HAS WHAT COMPARATIVE ADVANTAGE?

Since the principle of comparative advantage applies at the country level, there have been attempts at identifying exactly what the advantages are in different countries. A now classic example is Dunning's study in 1981, which arrived at the following conclusions:

Japan—textiles, clothing, consumer electronics.
United Kingdom—food and tobacco products.
Sweden—mechanical and electrical engineering.
United States—transportation equipment.
Germany—chemicals.

It should be recognized that although some CSAs persist over time (such as those based on natural resources), there will be changes as new labor skills are developed and technological innovations force new production processes to be employed and new raw materials to become scarce. In today's free and open market system with relatively low transportation costs, international trade should follow the principle of comparative advantage, and thus export and import data can give a rough idea about which country now has what competitive advantage.

For example, after Dunning's study, the advantage in textiles has moved from Japan to other Asian countries, and new technological development has shifted the balance again, toward a greater role for the United States. India has developed a country-specific advantage in computer software development. Cost advantages in southern Europe have been reduced by the opening of eastern European countries as production sites. And while the proximity of the North African countries to the European Union market offered advantages over the rest of Africa, government intervention and a deteriorating political situation have combined to negate this advantage. (See also the discussion of national advantage later in this chapter.)

Sources: Dunning, 1981; "N. Africa Finds Difficulty Sustaining Growth That Made It Continent's Star," *Market Africa Mid-East,* IBC USA, June 2001; International Marketing Data and Statistics, Euromonitor, 2005.

where it produces. To illustrate, producing in a low-cost European country such as Portugal—as Volkswagen does, for example—may give a cost advantage over a competitor producing in Spain—as Nissan does. But this is a **country-specific advantage (CSA)** that can be captured by any producer in Portugal. By contrast, Volkswagen's image and brand name are assets that are unique to the company, **firm-specific advantages (FSAs)** that cannot be duplicated by other firms. When doing competitive analysis in the global context it is important to identify whether a company's strength is firm-specific or not. If it is not firm-specific, the competitive advantage is usually less sustainable since the company cannot prevent imitation.

We will first deal with country-specific advantages (CSAs). Since such advantages have long been analyzed in the economics of international trade, the theory of international trade is a useful starting point.

Comparative and Absolute Advantages

The principle of **comparative advantage** provides the fundamental rationale for the existence of international trade. Free trade between two countries yields economic payoffs to the countries (in terms of higher welfare) provided the countries have different endowments of resources, that is, different advantages. It is not important if one country is better than another in producing all kinds of products, that is, that producers there have an **absolute advantage.** One country might have an absolute advantage (its resource inputs show higher productivity) for all the products involved and trade will still yield positive benefits to both countries. The requirement is simply that in one country production involves less of a sacrifice in the output of alternative products than it does in the other country—which will be the case unless the mix of resources is exactly the same in both countries—so that there is a relative advantage in production.

For comparative advantages to be decisive in international trade patterns they have to be actually fixed to a particular location. Over the years, the increased mobility of labor (the "importation" of south European workers to the northern European countries, the use of Indian laborers in the Saudi oil fields, and the "brain drain" from the United Kingdom to the United States, for example) has made labor less of a country-specific factor. At the same time, the location of plants for textiles, electronic subassemblies, and sporting gear in Southeast Asia is obviously dictated partly by low labor costs. However, on the whole, the theory of comparative or country-specific advantage still explains many of the international trade patterns between countries, especially for raw materials, where location is indeed fixed.

It is also necessary that trade be free. In the absence of free trade, each country has to be more self-sufficient, and less specialization is possible. If the market is large, multinational companies (MNCs) may try to overcome trade barriers by investing in manufacturing within the country. Such import-substituting foreign direct investment (FDI) by the multinational firm is a response to nonfree trade, which is a second-best solution, since now production is not located according to the principle of comparative advantage. Because of the need for several productive inputs in any one manufacturing location, however, the MNC will also usually transfer resources to locations with different advantages. These **technology transfers** serve to give a dynamic character to CSAs. A country with low labor skills, for example, will gradually improve skill levels under such transfers.

The International Product Cycle (IPC)

Potentially, all the factors that create differences in the countries' comparative advantages also create differences in absolute advantages (see the accompanying box on comparative advantages).

When formulating competitive strategy at the firm level, it is the absolute advantages that count. Countries as trade partners are just that, partners, and for the countries the comparative advantage principles apply—an "I win–you win" situation. But at the firm level, the successful company needs to have an edge on competitors, for example, through higher quality or lower cost. This is an "I win–you lose" situation, determined by absolute advantages. And as many countries have found out, a country's absolute advantages can be erased by emerging foreign countries with lower wages or other advantages. This is the working of the **international product cycle (IPC).**

The IPC was initially proposed by Raymond Vernon in 1966, who used it to demonstrate how the manufacturing of new products in the United States shifted over time to new locations overseas and in the process affected trade patterns.[1] The process is depicted in Exhibit 2.1. In the initial stage, the innovator produces and markets the product at home to a growing home market. As production increases above the home market demands, the firm turns to exports and develops markets in other developed countries. Then, as these new markets grow and their domestic production of the product gets under way, trade shifts again to third-world markets. As the production know-how gets more widespread, however, these countries gradually develop their own manufacturing capability, helped by the processes and the technology by now standardized. As low-cost production in these third-world (or newly industrialized) countries gets under way, their imports give way to exports back to the original country's market. The cycle has come full circle, and the original inventor now imports the product.

As many countries other than the United States have become adept at inventing new products and services, the international product cycle as originally developed has become outdated, and Vernon and others have amended it.[2] Today, for example, it is not uncommon to find that a country that started production of a certain innovative product continues as the foremost manufacturing site. The American supremacy in computer design is a good example. This process has been documented in detail by Porter.

National Competitive Advantages

In an important extension of the theory of comparative advantage, Porter has introduced what he calls the **diamond of national advantage.**[3] The diamond comprises four factors that determine the competitive advantage (or disadvantage) of a country:

1. *Factor conditions.* The nation's position in factors of production, such as skilled labor or infrastructure, necessary to compete in a given industry.
2. *Demand conditions.* The nature of the home demand for the industry's product or service.

EXHIBIT 2.1
The International Product Cycle

Source: Reprinted with the permission of the *Journal of Marketing*, "A Product Life Cycle for International Trade?" by Louise T. Wells, July 1968, pp. 1–6. © 1968 by the American Marketing Association.

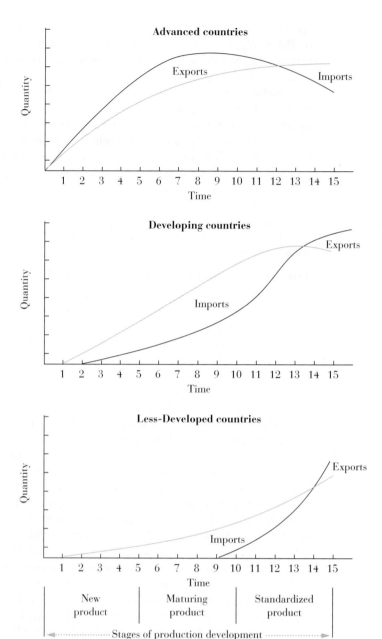

3. *Related and supporting industries.* The presence or absence in the nation of supplier industries and related industries that are internationally competitive.
4. *Firm strategy, structure, and rivalry.* The conditions in the nation governing how companies are created, organized, and managed, and the nature of domestic rivalry.

Exhibit 2.2 shows how these factors interrelate. A nation's competitive advantage—and, consequently, the country-specific advantages for firms from that country—depends on the strength of each of these factors. Favorable factor conditions include the traditional endowment of natural resources that was the basis of the original theory of comparative advantage. Porter argues that, over time, vigorous competition in the industry will help develop stronger firms and support growth and improvement among supplier firms. Furthermore, sophisticated and demanding customers at home help hone the competitive skills of the industry further. If a country offers higher labor skills or lower wages, the multinational firm will locate production there.

EXHIBIT 2.2
Porter's Determinants of National Advantage

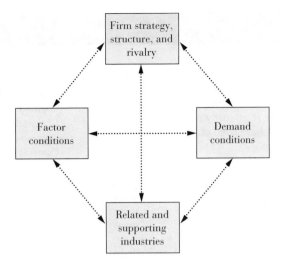

Porter's is a dynamic theory, showing how over time a nation can build up and sustain its competitive advantage in an industry. While firms relying on factor cost advantages (lower-cost labor, for example) can provide the initial stimulus for economic growth, other countries will appear with even lower factor costs. In order to sustain growth, the nation's competitive advantage will have to be extended by capital investments in upgraded machinery and technological development in the industry. But for a nation to sustain its advantage it is also necessary that related and supporting industries follow by upgrading their facilities and expertise (see box, "Porter's Related Industries") and that home market customers become more demanding, expecting the best.

Porter's diamond implies that a country can remain competitive in an industry even as its manufacturing costs rise. Thus, the diamond goes counter to the original IPC theory. While the IPC explains the "hollowing out" of a nation's industrial base, with manufacturing moving to low-wage countries, Porter's diamond suggests that competitive rivalry and capable business management can help nations develop new skills and renew their competitive advantages. While Vernon's IPC concludes that advanced nations will trade for standardized commodities and focus on innovation and new industries ("get out of televisions, and focus on computers"), Porter's diamond shows how the creation of favorable conditions can make a nation stay competitive in a given industry for a long time ("automobiles is what we do best"). Actually, in most economies of the world, both tendencies are at work simultaneously.

The New Trade Theory

In a closely related theoretical development, it has been demonstrated that the trade patterns between countries depend on man-made, Porter-style, locational advantages.[4] For example, as advanced technology centers arise around strong research universities and innovative new firms, the local labor force develops skills unique to specific industries, and companies will find it increasingly attractive to locate in those areas. This **new trade theory** explains the development of high-technology areas such as Silicon Valley south of San Francisco, Bangalore in India, and the Stuttgart-Munich area in Germany. Similarly created CSAs include the skilled labor force in other industries, such as apparel in Italy, optical instruments in Japan, and chocolates in Belgium. These country-specific factors shift the competitive advantages away from what natural resources alone would suggest.

Of particular interest to marketers, Krugman and other "new trade" theorists point out that the products traded are generally differentiated and not homogeneous. Accordingly, international trade patterns will not necessarily follow the original theory's predictions. For example, there is a great amount of intraindustry trade between nations, with a country such as Germany both exporting and importing a

Getting the Picture

PORTER'S RELATED INDUSTRIES

Porter explains how a globally competitive industry spawns the development of globally competitive firms in related industries in the listings given. As can be seen, many of the prominent industries in the world market have been built on more basic innovations in other industries.

Nation	Industry	Related Industry
Denmark	Dairy products, brewing	Industrial enzymes
Germany	Chemicals	Printing ink
Italy	Lighting	Furniture
Japan	Cameras	Copiers
Korea	VCRs	Videotape
Singapore	Port services	Ship repair
Sweden	Automobiles	Trucks
Switzerland	Pharmaceuticals	Flavorings
United Kingdom	Engines	Lubricants, antiknock preparations
United States	Electronic test equipment	Patient monitoring and measuring equipment

Source: Porter, 1990, p. 105.

large quantity of cars, for example. This still begs the question why Germany would not produce all its desired cars and then trade for other products or services. Krugman first demonstrated how the pure theory needs to be augmented to incorporate skills developed. Differentiation leads to specialization and the creation of firm-specific advantages that come from learning by doing. German automakers become good at producing certain types of cars, not others. From a marketing viewpoint this is hardly surprising, since these cars tend to be differentiated and to target alternative market segments.

These ideas suggest that a country can become efficient in the production of goods in which it starts with little or no competitive advantage. As we saw in Chapter 1, at the firm level this process is variously known as organizational learning or knowledge creation.[5] It represents the process by which companies develop new resources. This learning of new skills is of course very much a theme of this text, since the global marketing manager's experiences with foreign countries serve to expand marketing know-how.

CSAs and Country-of-Origin Effects

Country-specific advantages also play another role in global marketing. It is well documented that products or services made in countries with a positive image tend to be favorably evaluated, while products from less positively perceived countries tend to be downgraded. Automobiles are a case in point. German cars have generally a cachet attached to them, just as Korean cars in many markets still have to battle a less favorable image. This effect is called the **country-of-origin effect.**

Made-in Labels

A number of research studies have been conducted on the impact of "made-in" labels.[6] In general, the studies show a pronounced effect on the quality perceptions of products, with country stereotypes coloring consumers' evaluative judgments of brands. It translates into sales as well. In one study it was found that the Japanese automakers' strong penetration in the U.S. market in the 1970s was based more on country advantages than on firm-specific advantages. American auto buyers bought "a Japanese car," not necessarily a Nissan or Toyota specifically.

Country-of-origin effects differ by product category. Not surprisingly, they are less pronounced in products for which technology is widely diffused across the globe (the international product cycle at work), and products from different countries consequently are of similar quality. In apparel, for example, made-in labels ("made in" Malaysia, China, Portugal, Hungary, and so on) tend to have less effect because consumers are becoming accustomed to seeing clothes of similar quality from various places. By contrast, in advanced medical equipment, electronics, cosmetics, and wine, country of origin still counts for a great deal.

Contrary to what one might expect, there is also evidence that these effects do not go away over time as globalization proceeds. Because of increased global communication consumers learn more about foreign countries, and they learn what technologies and products different countries are good at. But even if country-of-origin effects do not seem to go away, country perceptions do change over time. For example, while American products enjoyed a reputation for high quality after World War II, they slipped badly in the 1970s and 1980s as superior foreign products raised customer expectations. British quality perceptions largely followed the same path only earlier and quicker, while Japanese products showed the opposite trend and the German quality image remained strong. Given the intense global competition in many markets, however, there is, not surprisingly, evidence of a convergence of quality ratings in recent years.[7]

Another factor that matters for the country-of-origin effect is whether a country produces at widely different quality levels. If companies in a country tend to adhere to strict quality standards, all in that country stand to gain from country-of-origin effect, just as a global brand name means the company "guarantees" a certain performance level. This is one advantage in Porter's diamond of national advantage. If quality varies greatly, it renders the country name useless—or worse—for quality judgments (just as inconsistent quality would ruin a brand name). The country name has become a brand in its own right, as we will discuss further in Chapter 13.

Brands

With the growth of multinational production, the original emphasis on "made-in" labels has been weakened. However, the country-of-origin effect persists for the brands. The research shows that brands have "home countries" as well, making Sony a Japanese brand anywhere, even though it may have been produced in Taiwan or the United States. The Sony label is taken by the consumer as a sign of insurance that the product will function as a "real" Sony.

Country-of-origin advantages are CSAs, and thus available in principle to all brands from that country. It's the fact of being a German make that matters, whether it is a BMW, a Mercedes, an Audi, a VW, and so on. But there are cases where the brand becomes more or less identified with the country, and thus the CSA becomes an FSA. This has happened with Levi's, for example, which is marketed in Japan as "The Original"—the "real" American jeans. The same effect can be seen in, for example, Coca-Cola and perhaps McDonald's, and Sony and Toyota from Japan. These brands are inextricably linked to their home countries, for better or worse.

Stressing country-of-origin effects in advertising and promotion can be a double-edged sword. A product's country-of-origin might not vary—an American brand is an American brand—but the country image may well vary across markets. This limits the transferability of the advantage. Thus, for example, what may be an advantage to being an American brand in Asia may be a disadvantage in Europe. Marketers recognize this, and many change strategies accordingly. To illustrate, while Levi's may be positioned as the original American jeans in Japan, its American roots are now downplayed in the European Union. Similarly, carmakers Audi's and Mercedes' German roots are emphasized in the United States but not in Europe, since Europeans tend to feel much more ambivalent about the German heritage. Korean brand names are much appreciated in Asia but being from Korea has not yet translated into a strong positive country-of-origin effect for Korean brands elsewhere (although Samsung and Hyundai are making a valiant and seemingly successful effort in consumer electronics and automobiles, respectively).

The Swiss Army home page. Originally made famous by its versatile and high quality pocketknives, the Swiss Army brand has extended into products where its country-of-origin cachet can be fully exploited. Courtesy of Swiss Army Brands.

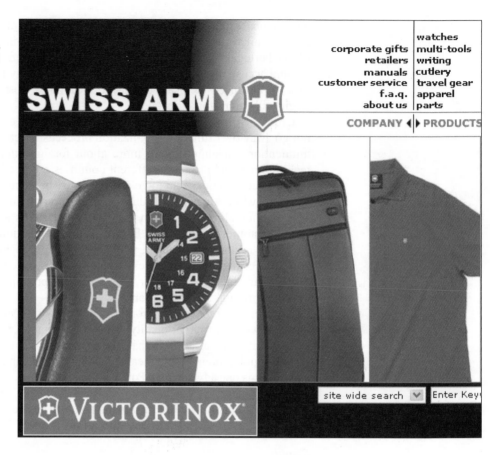

Firm-Specific Advantages (FSAs)

The fundamental premise of any enterprise is that it can transform valuable inputs into even more valuable outputs. The rule for survival of a company is that it provide some desired benefit to the customer better than other enterprises do—it has a sustainable competitive advantage. Similarly, the company entering markets abroad must have advantages that outweigh the increased costs of doing business in another country in competition with domestic firms. These advantages should not be available to competitors and are, therefore, to some degree monopolistic. These are firm-specific advantages (FSAs) to emphasize that they are unique to a particular enterprise. (Since different writers sometimes use different terms, Exhibit 2.3 gives some alternative synonyms for FSAs and CSAs.)

Firm-specific advantages may be of several kinds. They might be a patent, trademark, or brand name or be the control of raw materials required for the manufacturing of the product, access to know-how essential to the development of a service, or simply control of distribution outlets. These advantages could also include process technology, managerial capacity, or marketing skills. They might well have their source in country-specific variables, but the essential point about them is that they can be used by the company alone.

EXHIBIT 2.3
Two Sets of Synonyms for FSAs and CSAs

Level	Synonyms
Country (CSAs)	Comparative advantages; location-specific advantages
Firm (FSAs)	Differential advantages; ownership-specific advantages

Knowledge-Based FSAs

As we saw in Chapter 1, much has been written recently on the topic of the **knowledge-based organization.**[8] Market-based explanations for sustainable competitive advantages have given way to analysis of factors internal to the firm. If competitive advantages traditionally resided in a superior offering in the marketplace, recent rapid changes in products and services have suggested to analysts that competitive sustainability lies more in a company's speed and flexibility in introducing new products and services. These knowledge capabilities are not embedded in the products themselves—their features, quality, image, and so on—but involve know-how, skills, and experiences of the company and its employees. Such know-how can be difficult to articulate and teach, more art than science.

Knowledge is today recognized as one of the (if not *the*) key resources of the firm. **Resource-based strategy** defines the firm not in terms of the products or services it markets, or in terms of the needs it seeks to satisfy, but in terms of what it is capable of. From the resource-based perspective, the first question is what the firm can offer in technology, know-how, products, and services. Only then may the issues of selecting markets and developing a competitive global strategy be successfully tackled.

An internal focus on strengths and weaknesses seems to go counter to the marketing concept but in reality complements it. Whereas a **market orientation** focuses on competitive advantages in the marketplace, the resources perspective fosters a view of the company as a leveraging force for its resources. It generates an appropriate mindset of "getting a return on the assets" philosophy, in which the key management question is how the resources should be deployed to generate the best return.

Marketing-Related FSAs

From a marketing perspective it is important to recognize that the source of a firm-specific advantage can lie in specific market know-how. For example, large consumer goods manufacturers (Nestlé, Unilever, Procter & Gamble) have accumulated experience and skills in many foreign markets that give them an edge over competition. These skills include techniques for analyzing and segmenting markets, developing promotional programs and advertising campaigns, and administering massive introductory campaigns for new products and services. Similar skills in the marketing area might be said to lie behind some of Caterpillar's and IBM's successes in many markets (Caterpillar's policy that a serviceman can reach a site within 48 hours, for example) and also the close relationship with distributors nurtured by many companies in Japan (see box, "Marketing FSAs").

Firm-specific advantages tend to be different in different countries. It is important to identify exactly what the advantages are for the particular country. Marketing research needs to be carried out in order that customer needs and competitive offerings be properly identified and matched against the firm's product or service. Such an analysis will yield guidelines for what features need to be stressed in various countries, so as to place the firm in a position as advantageous as possible vis-à-vis competitors' offerings.

This logic underlies the many multinational firms' practice of providing different products or services from their complete line in different countries. In autos, few of the U.S. makes are sold abroad—they have a differential disadvantage. Many smaller European makes are not introduced in Japan where competition among small cars is intense. Black-and-white television sets are sold in the less-developed countries (LDCs).

Product and service positioning needs to be carried out with a clear understanding of what segments are to be targeted with a differential advantage. Because of weak infrastructure, in developing countries the needs of the customers are often quite different. Large multinational hotel chains such as Holiday Inn entering new markets target either international business customers or tailor their services and price points to the level of economic development in the countries. In countries where voltage surges are common, many home appliances need "shock fuses" to protect against breakdowns. A more rugged and basic version of a product might be designed in order to satisfy customer

Getting the Picture

MARKETING FSAs

Most companies have several marketing strengths, but are sometimes characterized by one or two major FSAs. Among global companies with strong marketing, the following FSAs stand out:

Strong brand names— Nokia, Coca-Cola, Sony
Products with state-of-the-art technology—Intel, BMW, Canon
Advertising leverage—Gillette, Unilever, Nissan
Distribution strength—Starbucks, Microsoft, Kelloggs
Good value for the money—Dell, IKEA, Toyota

Other companies have marketing FSAs not easily exploited overseas: Budweiser's great brand name asset derives from an original Czech beer still brewed and sold, complicating sales in Europe. Also, its light taste relative to most countries' beers slows expansion.

German Henkel's (detergents) strong presence in the European market has been difficult to leverage elsewhere, as it depends on strong distribution and brand loyalty based on special washing traditions with respect to water hardness and temperatures used, less use of tumble dryers, and frequency of washing.

Kao's (detergents) and Shiseido's (cosmetics) strengths in distribution at home in Japan, where they have control at both wholesale and retail levels, cannot easily be duplicated elsewhere.

needs (the "small is beautiful" syndrome). But it's important to gauge the extent to which the FSAs can be kept when redesigning a product, since often if they are lost, the company enjoys no differential advantage and should probably not enter. The big American cars of the 1950s guzzled too much gas and were built too low to be useful on bad roads, so the American automakers exported from their European base rather than from the United States.

Differing levels of market acceptance of the firm-specific advantages limits the degree to which a company can be successful abroad. It also limits the degree to which the marketing effort can be standardized. Volvo, the Swedish car, is positioned as a luxury car in some overseas markets, but at home it is a practical and reliable transportation vehicle. Needless to say, the Swedish advertising is not particularly useful as a starting point for Volvo's marketing overseas. Although more will be said on this topic in later chapters, it needs to be stressed here how the FSAs must be carefully analyzed so that the opportunities (and pitfalls) of a standardized program (with its associated lower costs and improved control possibilities) can be fully realized (or avoided).

Transferability of FSAs

When marketing FSAs are important, the **transferability** of these advantages to other countries becomes particularly important. Not all of them can be transferred.

Various factors might make the employment of marketing FSAs difficult in other countries. Where commercial TV is not available, it is difficult to leverage the skills developed in the area of TV advertising. Procter & Gamble's reluctance to enter the Scandinavian markets is one illustration of this, now partly alleviated as satellite TV and new channels open up the market to TV advertising. When the FSAs are in distribution channels (as in the Electrolux case—see box, "A Marketing Skill Transferred"), going abroad might involve having to create new channels in the local market.

In some of these cases, production in the market country might make the local marketing effort easier. It could, for example, make it easier to recruit capable distributors and dealers, since host country production can be used to assure the channel members that supplies will be forthcoming.

A major difficulty in transferring marketing skills abroad is that these factors often represent **intangibles,** skills that reside in people and are not "embodied" in the product itself (as technology typically is). The principal means of completing the transfer is by employing personnel transfers and education of local people.[9] Because of the new environment in which expatriates have to work, and the uncertain

Getting the Picture

A MARKETING SKILL TRANSFERRED: ELECTROLUX IN JAPAN

The Electrolux Group is today the world's largest producer of powered appliances for kitchen, cleaning, and outdoor use. More than 55 million Electrolux Group products (such as refrigerators, cookers, washing machines, vacuum cleaners, chain saws, and lawn mowers) are sold each year to a value of approximately U.S. $14 billion in more than 150 countries around the world.

Electrolux has long sold its product through door-to-door salesmen demonstrating the virtues of the product in the home of a prospective customer. Over the years considerable refinement in the sales approach was developed and taught to new salesmen. The sales technique became one of the company's distinctive skills.

When entering Japan in the 1970s, Electrolux found initial reactions among the trade people toward this type of selling approach negative. It was said that the Japanese were not used to having unknown people enter their homes and would not allow the salesmen's entrance. Electrolux first decided to follow the standard Japanese approach of selling through department stores and specialty shops. For a period of several years the company attempted several variations on this approach, all with the same result: Sales were too small to cover costs and the higher price of their product (because of transportation costs, tariffs, and distributors' markups) was not considered sufficiently offset by better performance. Competitors among the domestic producers (Toshiba, Hitachi, and others) continued to dominate the market.

Believing that with a proper demonstration of performance the price differential could be justified, management of Electrolux decided against all odds to introduce their particular selling method in Japan. After extensive training of their Japanese salesmen, the door-to-door approach was introduced. The result was an immediate success. Electrolux became a market leader at the upper end of the market.

Electrolux's experience vindicates the idea that we should concentrate on doing what we do best. It also demonstrates the fact that in a new country one does not necessarily have to do things the way they have always been done, not even in a relatively homogeneous or isolated country such as Japan.

Sources: Annual reports; **www.electrolux.com.**

results of the educational effort, marketing skills will often not be transferable at a reasonable cost. Conversely, where marketing skills provide the basic firm-specific advantage, the incentive to go abroad is not as strong as where the advantage rests on factors that can be embodied in the product. An exception to this rule is the growth in franchised services, in which a specific mechanism is created to transfer marketing skills. Successful service companies such as McDonald's, Kentucky Fried Chicken, and Hilton Hotels have standardized their services and relied on training local franchisees in each specific detail of the day-to-day operations, to ensure uniform quality across countries. For manufacturing companies, such an investment in technology transfer is often not necessary, since the final product embodies the advantages already.

The firm establishing manufacturing in a market country can both gain and lose some marketing advantages in the process. Being closer to the customer is always a gain for a firm. For example, distributors can feel more secure about supplies, and customers can rely on after-sales service. The firm becomes more of an insider because it is able to hire a domestic workforce and create goodwill by being a good citizen. Company managers become more attuned to the way of doing business in the country and come to understand the market better.

There is also a possibility that a country-of-origin quality effect comes into play. The exported products embody the production know-how and skills, including the country-specific advantages, of the company at home. Some customers will question whether these can be transferred successfully to the plant in the new country. When Volkswagen started to build its Rabbit model in Pennsylvania in the 1970s, customers rushed to buy the last imports of the model from Germany. The typical strategy to overcome such consumer doubts has been to avoid emphasizing where the product was made. Of course, this approach foregoes some of the positive benefits of manufacturing within a country, and so a more constructive approach is to re-export the product back home. Honda, the Japanese car company, exports its Honda Accord coupe made in Marysville, Ohio, to Japan, thereby assuring the American consumers that the quality of the car is up to Japanese standards.

FSAs and Internalization

There are a number of ways in which a company can enter a given country market. They will be discussed in detail in Chapters 5 and 6 on entry strategies. In principle, four different modes can be identified: straight exporting, licensing, alliances, and direct foreign investment (in production or selling capabilities). In pure exporting the product is simply exported to a distributor appointed in the market country; licensing and alliances "transfer" some ownership advantages via a contractual agreement to an enterprise in the market country; and foreign direct investment (FDI) means the company invests money in subsidiary operations in the country.

The most basic question when going abroad is how the company can get a reasonable payoff or return on its firm-specific advantages. As one alternative, a company could sell its FSAs (be it in patents, brand names, or process technology) to a local buyer for use. This is the licensing or alliance "externalization" option. If the market for such advantages were efficient in the sense that information was perfect, the price the firm could obtain would mirror directly the worth of the advantage in the final market. There are, in fact, a number of such contractual arrangements, some persisting over time (such as Coca-Cola's licensing of bottlers in different countries), others employed primarily in the initial stages of expansion owing to financial and other constraints (such as Mitsubishi's entry into the U.S. auto market using a tie-up with then Chrysler Motor Corporation).

One problem with the licensing and alliance options is that the entering company will not have an opportunity to learn about the new market and to expand its skills repertoire. Furthermore, policing the alliance and overseeing the licensee royalty payments (usually some percentage of sales) can be difficult. As the partner develops the requisite skills of production and marketing, there is a risk that the transferred know-how will be used for its own production, so that over time the firm-specific advantage will be gradually eroded. This **dissipation** problem could be reflected in higher prices for licenses, but with less than perfect foresight it is difficult for the firm to assess the appropriate level of return. Generally, according to the theory, firms turn away from sharing (or "externalizing") because they can get higher returns on their FSAs by "internalizing" them.[10]

In internalizing, the company has a choice between exporting and foreign direct investment. Both avenues imply that the company has decided to retain control over its firm-specific advantages, either by producing at home (the export option) or investment to produce abroad (the FDI option). This is the meaning of **internalization.**

The choice between pure exporting and foreign direct investment (FDI) in manufacturing hinges on, among other things, the number and height of the obstacles to free trade. When trade barriers are low, there is often no particular reason to engage in FDI just to service a market. Because of tariffs and nontariff barriers, however, the case for FDI is often quite strong. An additional factor to consider is the need to assure risk-averse local customers of a steady supply. Furthermore, the case might arise in which the firm-specific advantages are not strong enough to overcome the locational disadvantages of home production, but would be if the manufacturing were done in a third country closer to the market. With the emergence of trade regions, such patterns are common; for example, EU markets are often supplied from Ireland, and the American market from Mexico.

Where production will take place depends on CSAs coupled with the barriers-to-trade encountered from the countries where manufacturing occurs. "Pure" exporting from a home country is simply a special case in which CSAs at home and the firm-specific advantages are great enough to offset the locational disadvantages (including transportation costs and lack of market familiarity—see box, "Country-Specific Advantages and FDI: Rossignol").

FSAs and Transaction Costs

The emphasis on FSAs in the internalization theory can be given an equivalent theoretical interpretation in terms of Williamson's transaction cost framework. Since this framework has proven useful in determining mode of foreign entry, the theory is relevant to the global marketer.[11]

Getting the Picture

COUNTRY-SPECIFIC ADVANTAGES AND FDI: ROSSIGNOL

Foreign Direct Investment can be preferable to exporting even if the formal trade barriers are small. One reason is the country-specific advantage associated with manufacturing in the market country. The French ski manufacturer Rossignol's experience represents one of these cases.

As its share of the French market reached saturation, the management of Ski Rossignol realized that further growth was possible only through expanded international involvement. Initially the company sought to do that by exporting from France, establishing sales offices (commercial subsidiaries) in many of its target country markets, and improving its distributor network.

Because of problems with floating exchange rates and bad experiences with dock strikes and long transportation delays, the company decided to turn to FDI in manufacturing. It established plants in Switzerland, Italy, Canada, Spain, and the United States all within a span of about four years.

These sites, except Spain, were chosen because of their proximity to large ski markets (low labor costs influenced the Spain location). The company management stated: "Skiing trends change quickly, and with differences across countries. Furthermore, skiing conditions vary among countries and even (in the case of Canada and the U.S.) between neighboring countries. With the rapid changes compounded by national and international differences, we needed to stay close to the large individual target markets in order that these trends be anticipated correctly."

From these manufacturing bases, Rossignol has expanded its product line into related sports equipment and clothing, partly by acquiring existing domestic brands and converting them to the global Rossignol name. External production outside France accounted for 40 percent of total revenues in 2000 and increased steadilyover the next few years. In 2005 the company was taken over by American Quiksilver, but retained a French president.

The company has leveraged its acquisitions to establish itself as a leader in a particular niche of the sports and leisure market. Still, warmer winters have taken their toll, and the future of the ski business is uncertain. The company has dubbed itself a "mountain lifestyle brand," and made an effort to smooth out seasonal variations in sales by selling ski and snowboard equipment in the winter and hiking and mountain climbing equipment in the summer. There is some good news. Taking a page from the big advertisers of athletic shoes, the company hired American Lindsey Vonn as their spokesperson, and scored big as she skied to the 2008 World Cup downhill crown on Rossignol skis.

Sources: Thorelli and Becker, 1980, pp. 21–23; "Rossignol Aims for 5% Growth in 2002," *Les Echos,* July 20, 2001; "Adventures on Skis Teams with Club Rossignol, Swissair and Sabena for Unique European Winter Vacations," *PR Newswire,* September 11, 2001; **www.rossignol.com.**

Generally speaking, **transaction costs** are costs incurred when completing a transaction between a buyer and a seller. Apart from obvious costs such as transportation charges, sales taxes, and brokerage fees, there are often other costs incurred as well. Examples include how to establish contact between buyer and seller, translations in order to communicate in different languages, the risk that the product might not follow agreed-upon specifications, misunderstandings in price negotiations, and so on. These obstacles create the costs incurred by the parties in the transaction, and unless sufficient gains from the exchange are obtained, the costs may prohibit trade.

The activities that are required to overcome these barriers can be termed "market-making" functions. Since specialization tends to reduce costs, a sufficient volume of transactions of a certain kind is likely to spawn different agents who specialize in these activities. One example of these kinds of institutions occurs in export marketing, where importers, agents, and distributors serve to link buyers and sellers across borders and rely on their global information network to spot trading opportunities in which they can fetch a profitable commission.

As an alternative to employing external agents or market-makers, a firm might assume such functions itself. The seller of a product might provide the credit, storage, or insurance necessary for the completion of the transaction, while the buyer might take the responsibility for transportation, for example. Establishing a sales subsidiary in the market country, the exporter might even take on the importing, warehousing, and distribution functions without independent agents assisting. These cases of vertical integration represent examples of the principle of internalization. In the framework of transaction cost theory, internalization occurs when the most efficient (least-cost) means of effecting a transaction occurs within the firm itself.

As we have seen, a typical firm-specific advantage is a globally recognized brand name. From a transaction costs viewpoint, an established brand name serves to lower the cost of the exchange since the buyer can trust the quality of the product, and "search" costs are reduced. If this trust is misplaced because company operations abroad are not properly controlled, transaction cost theory predicts that the firm will lose the customer. The brand value will be diluted, and the firm will lose its FSA. This means the transaction costs are very high, and both customers and the firm stand to lose.

Global marketers are fond of saying that "We want to be easy to do business with." What this means is that exchanges are fast and efficient, transaction costs are low, and the value of the brand is sustained. The low transaction costs from a strong brand value benefit both buyer and seller.

FSAs in the Value Chain

The value chain concept suggests that the firm's activities in transforming raw materials and other inputs to final goods can be viewed as a collection of complementary and sequential tasks, each adding value to the product.[12] Some tasks are in operations (purchasing, design, manufacturing, and marketing), others are support activities (finance, personnel). The concept is an elaboration of the value-added notion in economic theory, which does not specify the activities inside the firm but simply views the firm as a transforming black box between inputs and outputs.

The **value chain** is the "internalized" sequence of operations undertaken by the firm. The vertically integrated firm has a long value chain, while a less integrated firm focuses only on some of the operations. "Deconstructing" the value chain is equivalent to externalization. The way McDonald's, the American fast-food restaurant chain, operates in different countries is instructive. In the United States the company has externalized major activities by hiring independent firms to supply the beef, potatoes, bread, and other ingredients and by allowing independent entrepreneurs to open franchised outlets. However, McDonald's inspects operations and keeps tight quality controls on all phases of business. In Europe, suppliers are also independent local producers, but some key franchised locations (including one on Paris's Champs Elysees) are owned by McDonald's itself, mainly for purposes of quality maintenance. In Moscow, McDonald's found it necessary to develop its own suppliers, since the local suppliers could not provide the necessary quality.

Exhibit 2.4 shows how two competing companies, Panasonic and Radio Shack, have configured their value chains in consumer electronics differently. While giant manufacturer Panasonic has no direct involvement at the retail level, Radio Shack, primarily a retailer, does no component manufacturing of its own. This shows how the firms' differing FSAs can be leveraged at different levels in the value chain for electronic consumer goods.

In global marketing, the stage of the value chain that can best be leveraged—and where the FSAs lodge—might not be the same as at home. For example, in markets in which the firm has limited experience or in which products are at a different stage in the life cycle, licensing a technology to a local manufacturer might be preferable to

EXHIBIT 2.4
Value-Added Analysis for Consumer Electronic Products

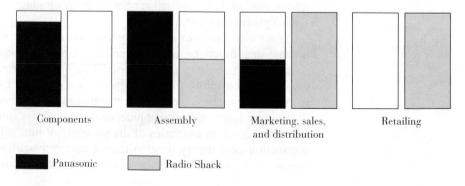

| Components | Assembly | Marketing, sales, and distribution | Retailing |

■ Panasonic   ▨ Radio Shack

IKEA, the Swedish-based furniture and home furnishings specialty retailer, serves a global market. Here, a shopper visits an IKEA store in the United Arab Emirates.
Ed Kashi

making and selling the product. Starting with a market perspective, by contrast, tends to lock management into a narrow focus on selling to foreign markets the same type of product sold at home.

The value chain can change over time, as new ways of combining activities appear and entrepreneurs grasp opportunities to simplify the entire flow, from raw materials to ultimate consumer (a process called industrial rationalization). For example, the Swedish furniture retailer IKEA developed a new formula for selling home furniture. Instead of showcasing finished furniture in downtown stores and later shipping merchandise to buyers' homes as traditional furniture retailers did, IKEA created a self-service store from which purchasers could bring home their furniture the same day.

Designing furniture in easily assembled pieces, and locating in suburban shopping malls where customers come by car, IKEA has been able to offer bookcases, tables, chairs, and even beds in easily transportable cardboard boxes. The assembled showroom furniture is clearly labeled with prices, stocking numbers, and units available, and the customer can walk around and make up a buying list without assistance. Having presented the list to the cashier and made payment, while the order is relayed automatically to the stock room, the customer drives to the back door and picks up the packaged boxes. IKEA has in fact developed a new value chain (or a new "business model"), in which the customer does more work than before. In return, the prices are much lower. IKEA soon ventured abroad, and has become the first successful furniture retailer on a global scale.[13]

FSAs, CSAs, and Regionalization

As we saw in Chapter 1, in many firms' regional strategies dominate total global strategies. Instead of operating throughout the world, the typical multinational focuses on one or two regions, including the home region. Asian firms do business foremost in Asia, and perhaps North America, American firms do business in NorthAmerica and secondarily Europe, and so on.

In such cases, the CSAs and FSAs discussed here need to be defined with respect to the relevant region. In a sense this goes without saying, but the implications need to stressed explicitly. The observed emphasis on regions close to home can be explained by the lesser value of CSAs and FSAs in distant markets.

CSAs are often positive in the home region and the next region, much less so elsewhere. For example, while Japanese cars do well in Asia and the United States, they have a much tougher time of it in Europe. The same is true for Korean cars. Similar patterns can be observed for other product categories. Of course, home-region countries are not always so positive about a brand's country-of-origin. Even though historical ties and similarities in cultures may suggest affinity, the memory of wartime animosities sometimes overrides such sentiment. A typical case is Japan's fragile relationship with China and Korea. By the same token, Korean products do have a special advantage over Japanese competitors in China, for the same historical reasons.

The same advantage applies to the FSAs in the regions closer to home. For example, brand-name familiarity and liking are easier to generate when media spillover is to closer-in nations, where cultural affinity and similarity of language is greater. A truly global brand such as Coca-Cola has more trouble translating its name into Mandarin for the Chinese market than does the Japanese local soft drink Calpis (basically milk with yogurt taste) or its Korean knock-off Coolpis, which can use Chinese kanji characters directly.

Not only is FSA transferability easier to closer countries, but so is the likelihood that the FSAs are positively valued. Traditional product design in Germany emphasizes functionality and durability, qualities desired by its northern European neighbors. By contrast, Italian design is characterized more by style and aesthetics, more appreciated by Mediterranean people. The Japanese early focus on miniaturization has played well in Asian markets where people are smaller, but in Western markets the lightness of touch and feel was not initially accepted. But this changed with the clear superiority of the Japanese technology. Now, of course, even big-boned Western people seem to easily find the small buttons on their cell phones.

The easier transferability and greater acceptance of the CSAs and the FSAs in country markets closer to home help explain why so many multinational firms are actually regional rather than truly global. By the same token, the global marketer will usually find it easier to start expanding abroad by going into countries close to home. We will come back to this again in Chapter 5.

Extending Porter's "Five Forces" Model

Since the competitive advantages lodged in a firm's CSAs and FSAs generally vary across country markets, there is a need to analyze the competitive environment in each country market. This analysis is best based on **Porter's "five forces" model.**[14] The model identifies five sources of competitive pressures on the firm in a given industry: rivalry, new entrants, substitutes, buyer power, and supplier power. The Porter analysis can be extended to deal with global competition across several country markets.

Rivalry

The intensity of competitive rivalry between firms competing directly in a country market is the most obvious competitive force. This is the mode of competition focused on in economic theory. In global marketing it is useful to separate the competitors into domestic and foreign companies. In many industries, such as autos, this division comes close to a division into what Porter calls strategic groups.

Strategic Groups

A strategic group consists of competitors with roughly similar resources and similar target markets. These two factors combine to make rivals follow similar strategies. In autos, the three American automakers (GM, Ford, and Chrysler) tend to form one group, as do the Japanese (Toyota, Nissan, Honda, and Mazda). The two German makers BMW and Mercedes also form a natural group, but Volkswagen is different, perhaps in a group with the Japanese. The groupings themselves are not necessarily important, and they change over time as mergers and acquisitions blur the borders.

But strategic groups are useful for competitive analysis since they suggest the likely strategic direction the companies may take, and which other companies they monitor closely. When Sony introduces a new product, other Japanese electronics makers will usually follow with their own versions. In the ongoing global battle between Coca-Cola and Pepsi-Cola, when Pepsi bought Tropicana, the juice maker, Coke responded by trying to buy France's Orangina, only to be blocked by a French judge alerted by Pepsi lawyers.

Domestic Competitors

In most country markets there will be a group of domestic companies that has traditionally served the home market. In the name of national security, many nations have instituted policies aimed toward self-sufficiency in foodstuffs, transportation, industrial goods, and basic technology. For example, most governments in the past controlled telecommunications and air transportation and subsidized farmers. With similar effect, regulations in support of small businesses and retailers against foreign ownership and customer sentiments in favor of local goods have in the past combined to create entry barriers for foreign firms and advantages for domestic producers.

With deregulation, privatization, and global integration through trading blocs these factors are gradually diminishing in importance. Nevertheless, these changes do not happen overnight, and the global financial turmoil at the end of the 90s led to a backlash in some countries against free markets and economic integration. As a result, in many country markets the domestic competitors still have special advantages. The infamous "Reinheitsgebot" ("Purity law") in Germany, an old, now amended regulation that forbade the use of artificial conservation ingredients in beer, effectively blocked foreign entry and made local production a necessity (which is why many localities in Germany still have their own local beer). Nor do the domestic companies simply stand back and watch as foreign competitors enter. As late as 1998 the three large American auto companies jointly sponsored an advertising campaign encouraging car buyers to show loyalty to their fellow citizens by buying American makes.

Because entry barriers are important in determining the mode of entry into a market, barriers will be discussed in more detail in Chapter 5.

Foreign Competitors

In global markets especially, foreign entrants tend to be the most direct competitors of a globalizing firm. As was mentioned above, the foreign companies can often be analyzed as a separate strategic group, making prediction easier. This does not mean that these companies are colluding or that they imitate each other. Rather, it is the similarity of their strategic situation that tends to suggest similar strategies. The large Korean conglomerates, such as Samsung, LG, and Daewoo, have followed the same initial OEM (original equipment manufacturing) strategy in Western consumer electronics markets to gain access without much knowledge of customer preferences.

Among foreign companies it is useful to single out global companies since, as we saw above, their competitive resources tend to be greater than other firms'. Because this topic is broad, the analysis of global competitors will be dealt with in a separate section below. In general, to understand foreign competitors it is useful to analyze their activities in other markets. For example, to predict the likely strategy of a company such as Mars in the Chinese confectionery market it is useful to observe the company's aggressive attack on eastern European markets.

Regional trade blocs also play a role in determining advantages and disadvantages of the foreign competitors. Foreign companies from inside a trading area have an advantage over other foreign competitors. Although the European Union is not trying to become a fortress Europe with high external tariffs (few tariffs are higher than 10 percent), the advantages of manufacturing inside Europe are such that many North American and Asian companies invest in production inside the EU. The competitiveness of the European companies is high enough that any cost disadvantage matters to non-European entrants.

Getting the Picture

CITIBANK IN EMERGING MARKETS

Banking, both retail and commercial, was one of the slowest areas of the economy to change in eastern Europe. But today, banking in even a country like Russia, although risky, is no longer off limits. As Western banks entered, the target segment they chose was not one might have expected. Rather than aiming for the mainstream market, the early entries were upscale, catering to the elite. The pattern was set by Citibank, the large American multinational bank.

In 1994, when Citibank opened its first branch in Budapest, it decided that the best strategy was to offer up-scale services not matched by any domestic competitors. This made the bank less dependent on building volume, and the bank's research suggested that there would be enough customers for higher-margin service packages. The bank offered cash machines, then still rare in eastern Europe, but to qualify, the customers needed to maintain a minimum balance of $250, a little less than the average salary in the country. In the first year, about 4,000 accounts were opened, 70 percent Hungarians, the rest foreign residents of Budapest.

At the high end, the bank offered special privileges to customers who maintain balances of $100,000. Beyond the rich wood veneer, peach carpet, and potted palms in the main lobby, these customers were given access to a third-floor wet bar with free drinks adjacent to the safe-deposit boxes. Initially the bank found 12 customers who qualified—hardly sufficient for a very profitable operation—but well suiting a prestige-raising business that generated favorable word-of-mouth advertising and intimidated potential competitors.

The same strategy has proved useful in other ex-communist markets as well, and Citibank now has extensive operations in eastern Europe, and even in Russia. And taking the risks has paid off—it does have the strong first-mover advantages with the upper-end account holders.

Sources: Saul Hansell, "Citicorp Announces High-Level Personnel Shifts," *New York Times,* July 1, 1995, p. D5; Jane Perlez, "Citibank in Budapest: ATM's and Potted Palms," *New York Times,* June 22, 1995, p. D7; **www.citigroup.com.**

New Entrants

Another competitive force is the threat of new entrants into a country market. While Porter was mainly concerned with new entrants into an industry—such as Disney buying ABC television, or banks entering the securities business—the threat applies equally, if not more, to potential entrants into a new foreign market. In particular, it is important that the global marketer realizes that other global companies may also enter a country market under consideration, and that the order of entry can directly affect the sales and market shares gained. This is easiest to see in emerging markets that have recently opened. Citibank's early entry into eastern Europe is suggestive (see box, "Citibank in Emerging Markets").

Substitutes

In new markets where conditions are very different from the home market and consumer preferences differ too, the product or service can face new varieties of substitutes. This is particularly true for food products and drinks. Fast food in Asia involves instant noodles, hot dogs are served as full meals with potatoes and vegetables in northern Europe, Belgians love their fritters, and so on. Milk is an unusual drink in many countries, as is coffee in others. Domestic substitutes vary in transportation (rickshas, bicycles), clothing styles, and, of course, sports and entertainment.

In general, where markets are multidomestic, the globalized product or service not only must be adapted to local customs and preferences—it is also likely to encounter different substitutes. When McDonald's opened its first outlets in Russia, the Russians responded with a chain of fast-food stores serving blinis and other Russian specialties. Kellogg's is still trying to convince people around the world to switch from hot to cold breakfast cereals. KFC in Japan successfully fought the habit of mothers of serving hot ramen, a noodle dish, getting many to switch to fried chicken on the premise it helps build strong bodies in young children.

Buyer Power

The last two forces identified by Porter relate to what the economist John Kenneth Galbraith has called countervailing power. Where buyers are strong—either because they are few and large or because they have many alternatives to choose from—they have the power to counter a seller's attempts to raise prices. They simply shift their purchases or put pressure on the seller. These forces carry over directly to the global case. In countries with large government ownership of businesses, the only customer may be a government agency. This can be true of public utilities such as power generation and telecommunications, but other industries are also affected. For example, liquor sales and advertising are highly regulated in many countries, with public monopolies the buying agent, virtually eliminating the ability of companies to create meaningful product or service differentiation and competitive advantages.

Supplier Power

Similar forces can be at work on the side of suppliers to the company. If suppliers are large or there are few supply alternatives, the seller will be forced to pay higher prices for inputs than otherwise, squeezing profit margins. In some countries where there is widespread cooperation between firms, an entrant may find it difficult to establish the required network of distributors and other intermediaries. Domestic competitors with established networks will have a decided advantage.

Rivalry Between Global Competitors

As we saw in Chapter 1, globalizing competitors force many companies to consider "going global." In fact, for any company contemplating a global strategy, the main rivalry will often be with other global companies. Global competitors are always a threat to enter any local market where they presently might not have a presence. In addition, the global competitor usually has available greater resources and a wider repertoire of competitive actions. These assets make for a stronger competitor and also makes prediction of their actions and reactions more difficult.

Competitive Strength

Global competitors tend to possess greater financial resources than other companies, partly because it takes money to go global, but also because their presence in many countries makes it easier to raise funds in the most favorable location, usually where the company has high market share and little competition, using their brands as cash generators ("cash cows" in strategic language). Because of the challenge involved for management in a global company and the possibility of drawing on a larger pool of talent, the global competitor also tends to have access to better managerial capability. If one also remembers that the global network can be a hidden competitive asset, it is not surprising if local firms need protective legislation to be competitive.

The analysis of competitive strength should also deal with the **strategic intent** of the global competitor in any one particular local market.[15] U.S. firms used to considering North America their primary market should remember that so do many multinational companies from other countries, such as Sony and Honda from Japan, Volvo and Saab from Sweden, and Unilever and Shell from Europe. When a global competitor enters a certain market its intent is not necessarily profit making, but (as we saw in Chapter 1) the strategic objective can include a number of other goals. Since what matters to a global competitor is usually the total leveraging of the assets invested in the global network, the global firm can accept losses in one or more markets as long as the spillover to other markets is positive. And since the financial strength of the global competitor makes a long-term view feasible, such a company can wait a long time for the turnaround.

Competitive Repertoire

The broadened **competitive repertoire** of the global competitor includes first of all the capability of attacking a competitor in several markets, and, by the same token, the capability of defending a market by countering elsewhere. The global competitor can also engage in integrated competitive moves.[16] For example, selected price wars can be started in a few markets to occupy competitors, while new products are tested and introduced in other markets. This was the tactic used by the Japanese television manufacturers as they moved into Western markets, using their home market as a testing ground for technical innovation. The global competitor can also sequence new product introductions and the roll-out of a new campaign around the globe, maximizing the effect from word-of-mouth and spillover gains from global mass communication.

It is important to recognize that the skilled global competitor does not have to yield much to domestic companies in local presence. The global competitor employs natives who gain considerably when the global competitor does well. Honda and Toyota dealerships have been tickets to riches for their American dealers, for example. In most countries the locals who have the territorial distribution rights for global companies such as Dunlop, Coca-Cola, and Caterpillar have done very well.

Finally, it is difficult for a domestic manufacturing company to retain the loyalty of the natives when raw materials components are imported from foreign locations. Witness the auto market. Honda is soon likely to employ more Americans than Chrysler, as Honda strives to become an insider in the United States.

Global Rivalry

The increased strength and widened repertoire of the global competitor mean that the scope of marketing competition is enlarged. The Kodak–Fuji story is illustrative. See the box, "The (Continuous) Kodak–Fuji Battle."

The Kodak–Fuji illustration shows how the global competitor can use its global network and its presence in many markets to make surprise competitive moves. Global advertising is also a competitive weapon that can pay off nicely for the global company. The Coca-Cola experience in Russia is an example. Pepsi-Cola, its arch rival, scored a coup in the 1970s when President Nixon helped Pepsi get the lone license to bottle cola in the Soviet Union. When the Russian market opened up after the fall of the Berlin Wall, Coca-Cola had to come from far behind to catch up with ensconced Pepsi. Using globally broadcast commercials on satellite TV emphasizing "The Real Thing" and saturating advertising on CNN's global news channel, Coca-Cola established itself as the cola of the new times and relegated Pepsi to inferior status as an almost domestic Russian brand, reminiscent of the communist past. Within months, Coca-Cola had captured chunks of market share from Pepsi.[17]

Global competitors can elect in which markets to battle a competitor. They can elect how to attack a dominant shareholder in a given market. Global competitors need always to be taken into account even when they are not yet present in a given market or segment. Defending against global competitors can involve some deft maneuvering and some loss-leading efforts when company actions are by themselves unprofitable. The aim is often to neutralize the global threat.

Esco, a small American manufacturer of components and replacement parts for earth-moving machinery, has long had a licensing agreement with Mitsubishi Heavy Industries, a large-company member of the Mitsubishi keiretsu in Japan. Rather than attempting to enter Japan and sell to Komatsu, Kubota, and Caterpillar Japan, Esco has ceded the market to Mitsubishi. Despite the drawbacks, the contract allows Esco to keep a check on Mitsubishi and its possible expansion into Asian markets where Esco is strong. For example, as the contract was renegotiated in the late 1980s, Esco lowered its royalties claim and the control it exercises over actual sales in order to maintain the prohibitions against Mitsubishi sales in Korea and other Asian countries. The alternative was to cancel the licensing agreement, which would have opened the door for Mitsubsihi to go abroad—using technology learned from Esco to start with. Anticipating similar problems in the future, Esco has since engaged in a policy of creating much stronger ties with its Asian distributors, a process that means the company is becoming more and more global.

Getting the Picture

THE (CONTINUOUS) KODAK–FUJI BATTLE

By the early 1980s Fuji film, the Japanese "poor second" competitor to American Kodak, had long tried to make a dent in Kodak's home market. Despite competitive products and successes in Europe and other foreign markets, Fuji had never been able to muster the brand awareness necessary to make it big in America. But in 1984 all that changed. When the Los Angeles Olympic Committee approached Kodak about becoming the "official" film for the 1984 Summer Olympics, Kodak managers vacillated. They thought the potential incremental gains to Kodak consumer-awareness and goodwill hardly justified the steep $20 million price tag suggested by Peter Ueberroth, the business-oriented leader of the Olympic Committee. A small notice reporting the conflict in a British newspaper caught the attention of a Fuji manager in London, who promptly telephoned the Fuji U.S. headquarters in New Jersey. Within hours the Fuji home office in Tokyo agreed to offer Ueberroth what he asked, and Fuji became the official sponsor of the Olympics.

The story does not stop there. The Kodak managers realized that their reluctance had inadvertently opened the door for their main global competitor. Their evaluation of the benefits and costs of the sponsorship had failed to take competitive considerations into account. A counterattack seemed necessary, partly to rejuvenate the flagging spirits within the company. Kodak management decided to launch a marketing offensive in Japan, Fuji's home market stronghold. Developing a revamped but still recognizably "Kodak yellow" package with Japanese print, and capitalizing on a superior new "200" film, Kodak saturated Tokyo with street giveaways and storefront displays. The full-court press worked. Fuji had to refocus its energies from the U.S. market and protect its home turf by matching the new film and its promotions. This was done successfully by working closely with channel members, creating entry barriers by relationship marketing. Claiming unfair discrimination, Kodak challenged these methods in the court of the World Trade Organization in Geneva. In 1998, however, the WTO found no unfair Fuji advantage, admonishing Kodak to "try harder."

The new battlefield is China. Fuji was the first entrant, capturing some first-mover advantages by selecting prime locations. By 1993 Fuji had 70 percent of the market. With Kodak's entry and the presence of an improved and less expensive local competitor, Lucky, Fuji's share had fallen to 30 percent by the beginning of 2001. Launching an all-out counterattack by the Chinese New Year on the famous Bund in Shanghai, Fuji overnight covered all photo stores in Fuji green. No Kodak yellow was to be seen. But the attack backfired when price competition became fierce and no store could make a profit. Striking back, Kodak induced a number of Fuji stores and photo developers to shift to Kodak processing by offering more support and being more selective in its choice of stores, ensuring a more stable profit base.

Of course, with the advent of digital cameras that use no film, this is to some extent a a battle of dinosaurs. But now both companies are duking it out in the digital print market.

Sources: Johansson and Segerfeldt, 1987; *Washington Post,* June 26, 1995, p. A12; "Vivid Picture: Kodak Marketing Prowess Out-Develops Fuji, Lucky," *China Online,* June 15, 2001; "Eastman Kodak, Fujifilm and Konica Minolta Establish EVERPLAY Standard," Kodak press release, February 22, 2006.

Strategy and the Three Hats

The resource-based and the market-based strategy perspectives differ in importance for the three phases of global marketing.

In the foreign entry phase, after a preliminary assessment of the foreign market potential, the resource-based strategic perspective will dominate. The firm must decide what it has to offer, what it can do well, and how it should enter abroad. Foreign entry is frequently initiated by an order from a foreign country for a company's product. Especially in the early stages of global expansion, the assessment of the market, customer segments, and competitive offerings is often done through informal methods and by independent middlemen. The most pressing question is whether middlemen are reliable.

The local marketing phase requires analysis of customers and competitors, the typical market-based approach to strategy. The managerial headaches usually come from unforeseen shifts in customer preferences, potential channel conflict, uncertainty about advertising effectiveness, and competitors' price cuts. The company's resources obviously make a difference for what kind of market strategy can be contemplated and whether an expensive competitive battle can be sustained, but the overriding concern in local marketing is in-depth analysis of customer needs and wants, evaluation of actual and potential competitors' strengths and weaknesses, tactical decisions across the life cycle stages of the product, and issues of quality and customer satisfaction.

With global management, the focus shifts back to headquarters and the resource perspective. The task for the global marketing manager is now to synchronize strategic moves in various countries across the globe, standardizing products and services, coordinating activities, and timing new product entries, all in hope of synergistic efficiency. Will savings from standardization more than offset potential loss of revenues in some countries? How can subsidiary managers be soothed when a new product is rolled out in another country first? How can we get our agent in country X to report quickly any moves by competitor Y? Which are the leading markets for our product? For these kinds of questions, the firm needs to understand its strengths and weaknesses well. Part Four of the book will show how the marketing manager can mold and stretch company resources into a globally effective marketing machine, using global strategies to find the optimal trade-off between local responsiveness and global scale economies.

Summary

When it goes abroad the firm usually can't be certain that the home advantages can be leveraged in foreign markets. Customers will not have the same preferences and competitors will be different. The transfer of advantages into foreign markets is fraught with dangers: Can service be kept at the desired level? To what extent is the marketing infrastructure different? Can the product perform as well in a new environment? When is high quality no longer high quality? These are uncertainties that challenge the marketing strategic plan.

Before the recognition of the learning effects of specialization discussed by Porter and Krugman, the economic theory of international trade and the theory of the multinational firm were basically static, "equilibrium theories" in economic jargon. As we have seen, the global perspective powerfully challenges a static mindset, and suggests that advantages are not a given and fixed fact. "Going global" stretches the firm's capabilities.

The dynamic benefits of foreign entry come from competing against new competitors and supplying new and demanding customers. This is what helps build new FSAs and sustain the competitive edge. Global markets are important not only for their market opportunities, but also for the opportunities they offer to expand the resources of the firm. It is in the constant re-creation of the company's assets and competencies that the dynamic benefits from global marketing come. The global marketer is always learning new concepts and techniques.

This chapter reviewed the main theoretical foundations of global marketing strategy. The discussion first emphasized the need to augment a market orientation with a thorough analysis of company strengths and weaknesses. We then introduced the distinction between country-specific and firm-specific advantages and showed how a firm's country-specific advantages relate to the theory of comparative advantage, Vernon's international product cycle (IPC), Porter's "diamond of national advantage," and newer trade theory. Country-specific advantages also underlie the persistence of the well-established country-of-origin effects.

Firms must also identify their firm-specific advantages, know how these advantages can be transferred abroad, and understand the implications for mode of entry and internalization. In particular, this chapter discussed how global competitors build and use FSAs to help overcome the natural disadvantage of being a foreign marketer abroad. Extending Porter's "five forces" model, the chapter demonstrated the link between competitive strategy and the theory of the multinational firm. We ended with a look at how resource versus market-based strategy impacts the three global marketing tasks—the "three hats."

Key Terms

absolute advantage, *34*
comparative advantage, *34*
competitive advantage, *33*
competitive repertoire, *51*
country-of-origin effect, *38*
country-specific advantage (CSA), *34*
diamond of national advantage, *35*
dissipation, *44*

firm-specific advantage (FSA), *34*
intangibles, *42*
internalization, *44*
international product cycle (IPC), *35*
knowledge-based organization, *41*
market orientation, *41*

new trade theory, *37*
Porter's "five forces" model, *48*
resource-based strategy, *41*
strategic intent, *51*
technology transfer, *35*
transaction costs, *45*
transferability, *42*
value chain, *46*

Discussion Questions

1. Identify the competitive advantages of some market leaders such as McDonald's, Nike, Swatch, and Sony. Are these country-specific or firm-specific advantages?
2. Use Porter's "five forces" model to analyze the competitive environment of a country of your choice (pick a product category that you are familiar with). How does a *market orientation* explain entry into that market? A resource-based view? Why are both perspectives useful?
3. Discuss how the transferability of competitive advantages of a service differs from that of a product.
4. Visit an Internet interactive vehicle-buying service (such as AutoVantage) and compare the various makes offered. Discuss how the close comparisons possible online makes competitive advantages easier to identify. What role is played by a strong brand?
5. On the vehicle Web site, keep track of your own comparisons to create a flow diagram that shows what features were accessed and at what stage (for example, price and engine power). Then compare with others in the class. What does this tell you about how potential buyers arrive at a decision on the Internet?

Notes

1. See Vernon, 1966.
2. See Vernon, 1979, in particular. The later extensions involved introducing dynamic competitive conditions and firm-level rise and decline explicitly. The multinational in the early stage is an innovation-based oligopoly, turning into a mature oligopoly, and then a senescent (aging) oligopoly.
3. See Porter, 1990.
4. See Krugman, 1988.
5. See Nonaka and Takeuchi, 1995, Chapter 7, and Grant, 1998, pp. 435–37.
6. A good early review is that by Bilkey and Nes, 1982. For more recent studies, see Papadopoulos and Heslop, 1993, and Verlegh and Steenkamp, 1999.
7. See, for example, LaBarre, 1994. In this survey covering respondents from North America, Japan, and Europe, Japan was rated overall highest in quality of manufactured products, followed by Germany and the United States. Broken down by respondents from the various regions, however, Germany scored highest among Europeans, the United States among the North Americans, and Japan among the Japanese.
8. See, for example, Nelson and Winter, 1982, and Nonaka and Takeuchi, 1995.
9. Kogut and Zander, 1993, report on these practices.
10. The dissipation problem and the issue of getting a reasonable return on the firm's assets are headaches for managers, since licensing is a very convenient option not requiring much in terms of resources. See Rugman, 1979.
11. Williamson, 1975, is the original statement of the transaction cost framework. The application to foreign entry can be seen, for example, in Anderson and Gatignon, 1986.
12. See Porter, 1985.
13. This extension of the value chain is from Normann and Ramirez, 1993.
14. See Porter, 1985.
15. The emphasis on strategic intent was first suggested by Hamel and Prahalad, 1989.
16. From Yip, 1992.
17. From *The New York Times,* May 11, 1995, pp. D1, D9.

Selected References

Anderson, Erin, and Hubert Gatignon. "Modes of Foreign Entry: A Transaction Cost Analysis and Propositions." *Journal of International Business Studies* 17, no. 3 (1986).

Bilkey, Warren J., and Eric Nes. "Country-of-Origin Effects on Product Evaluations." *Journal of International Business Studies* 8, no. 1 (Spring–Summer 1982), pp. 89–99.

Dunning, John H. *International Production and the Multinational Enterprise.* London: Allen-Unwin, 1981.

———. "The Eclectic Paradigm of International Production." *Journal of International Business Studies,* Spring 1988, pp. 1–31.

Goff, Kristin. "Rental Housing 'doesn't make sense' for builders." *The Ottawa Citizen,* Nov. 27, 1999.

Grant, Robert M. *Contemporary Strategy Analysis,* 3rd ed. Oxford: Blackwell, 1998.

Hamel, Gary, and C. K. Prahalad. "Strategic Intent." *Harvard Business Review,* May–June 1989, pp. 63–76.

Itami, H., with T. W. Roehl. *Mobilizing Invisible Assets.* Cambridge, MA: Harvard University Press, 1987.

Johanson, Jan, and Jan-Erik Vahlne. "The Mechanism of Internationalization." *International Marketing Review* 7, no. 4 (1990), pp. 1–24.

Johansson, Johny K., and Jan U. Segerfeldt. "Keeping in Touch: Information Gathering by Japanese and Swedish Subsidiaries in the U.S." Paper presented at the Academy of International Business Meeting in Chicago, October 1987.

Kogut, Bruce. "Designing Global Strategies: Comparative and Competitive Value Chains." *Sloan Management Review,* Summer 1985, pp. 27–38.

Kogut, Bruce, and Udo Zander. "Knowledge of the Firm and the Evolutionary Theory of the Multinational Corporation." *Journal of International Business Studies* 24, no. 4 (1993), pp. 625–46.

Kotler, Philip; Liam Fahey; and S. Jatusripitak. *The New Competition.* Englewood Cliffs, NJ: Prentice Hall, 1985.

Krugman, Paul R. *Geography and Trade.* Cambridge, MA: MIT Press, 1988.

LaBarre, Polly. "Quality's Silent Partner." *Industry Week* 243, no. 8 (April 18, 1994), pp. 47–48.

Nelson, Richard R., and Sidney G. Winter. *An Evolutionary Theory of Economic Change.* Cambridge, MA: Belknap, 1982.

Nonaka, Ikujiro, and Hirotaka Takeuchi. *The Knowledge-Creating Company.* New York: Oxford University Press, 1995.

Normann, Richard, and Rafael Ramirez. "From Value Chain to Value Constellation: Designing Interactive Strategy." *Harvard Business Review,* July–August 1993, pp. 65–77.

Papadopoulos, Nicolas, and Louise A. Heslop, eds. *Product-Country Images: Impact and Role in International Marketing.* New York: International Business Press, 1993.

Porter, Michael E. *Competitive Advantage.* New York: Free Press, 1985.

———. *The Competitive Advantage of Nations.* New York: Free Press, 1990.

Quinn, James Brian. *Strategies for Change—Logical Incrementalism.* Burr Ridge, IL: Irwin, 1980.

Rugman, Alan M. *International Diversification and the Multinational Enterprise.* Lexington, MA: D. C. Heath, 1979.

Thorelli, Hans B., and Helmut Becker, eds. *International Marketing Strategy,* revised ed. New York: Pergamon, 1980.

Thorelli, Hans B., and S. Tamer Cavusgil, eds. *International Marketing Strategy,* 3d. ed. New York: Pergamon, 1990.

Verlegh, Peeter W.J., and Jan-Benedict E. M. Steenkamp. "A Review and Meta-analysis of Country-of-Origin Research." *Journal of Economic Psychology* 20, no. 5 (October 1999), pp. 521–46.

Vernon, Raymond. "International Investment and International Trade in the Product Cycle." *Quarterly Journal of Economics* 80 (May 1966).

———. "The Product Cycle in a New International Environment." *Oxford Bulletin of Economics and Statistics* 41 (November 1979).

Wells, Louis T. "A Product Life Cycle for International Trade?" *Journal of Marketing,* July 1968, pp. 1–6.

Williamson, O. *Markets and Hierarchies: Analysis and Antitrust Implications.* New York: Free Press, 1975.

Yip, George. *Total Global Strategy.* Englewood Cliffs, NJ: Prentice Hall, 1992.

Chapter

3

Cultural Foundations

"Equal, but not the same."

After reading this chapter, you will be able to:

1. Recognize how culture is not only a fundamental dimension of any society but a very visible force affecting customers as well as managers.
2. See how culture becomes particularly important when it comes to implementing a global marketing strategy.
3. Understand how our own culture has promoted certain behaviors that may well be counterproductive in new cultures.
4. Balance the adaptation to a new culture with an honest articulation of the merits of a proposal so as to build trust.
5. Recognize that cultural differences are examples of market entry barriers and can be overcome with sensitivity, hard work, and a superior product or service.

A global marketer can't avoid the obvious truth that people in Hong Kong, Oslo, or Johannesburg are different, despite the growth of global travel services, global media networks, global hotel chains, and global product offerings. Since marketing is a people-oriented function, this affects the global marketer powerfully.

Culture has two main effects of importance to global marketers. First is the effect on demand. Differences in culture make it difficult to predict customer reactions and understand consumer behavior. Customers around the world have varying needs, face disparate economic constraints, use contrasting choice criteria, and are influenced by different social norms. Although the early discussion about cultures in Chapter 3 will be useful for customer analysis, the demand issues will be dealt with in more detail in Part Three, "Local Marketing," starting with Chapter 7.

The second effect of culture is on the "soft" skills of management. National culture affects organizational culture, how managers deal with subordinates and other employees, how they negotiate contracts, how they control the independent middlemen needed to enter a foreign market, how they establish trust with joint venture partners, and how they manage distribution channels. Simply stated, culture has a direct effect on what people skills the global marketer needs in the foreign environment. This is the main topic of Chapter 3.

Harry Potter and the Global Children

Even though the cultural differences among the world's races remain large, it seems children everywhere have the same yearning for magical storytelling. How else to explain the phenomenal global success of the Harry Potter series of books? It's not just clever global marketing—although global marketing has played a not insignificant role in the achievement.

feels "comfortable"—that is, where culture is similar. Culture affects the way to do business in a country, and therefore influences who should run your subsidiary. In brief, culture does not simply set new limits on the opportunities for buyers and sellers, it also helps determine their goals, preferences, and aspirations.

Chapter 3 begins by discussing the meaning of culture, then stressing the cultural problems with materialism and the fact that the core benefit of a product may well differ between cultures. It then turns to how cultures differ across nations, and the major approaches used to describe cultures. It emphasizes that culture is not simply an underlying driver of behavior but in fact tells us how to behave in many specific ways. The chapter then explains the process by which culture affects what people do well and what they do less well, and how in the process managerial skills are affected. This role of culture becomes particularly important when it comes to negotiations with potential partners overseas, and this chapter discusses how negotiation strategies differ across countries. It explores the cultural effects on industrial buying behavior and relationship marketing. The chapter concludes with culture's effect on the global marketer's main tasks of foreign entry, local marketing, and global management. (The many cultural effects on consumer decision making and choices will be discussed further in Part Three, "Local Marketing," starting with Chapter 7.)

The Meaning of Culture

Culture is usually defined as the underlying value framework that guides an individual's behavior. It is reflected in an individual's perceptions of observed events, in personal interactions, and in the selection of appropriate responses in social situations. The cultural framework encompasses objective reality as manifested in societal institutions and values and subjective reality as expressed in personal but socialized predispositions and beliefs. "Culture" is no abstraction but assumes a quiet physical reality.

Culture manifests itself in **learned behavior,** as individuals grow up and gradually come to understand what their culture demands of them. The functions of a society— "what a society does"—are not very different across countries. Everybody has to get food, lodging, a job, money, clothes, a significant other, success, career, status, social recognition, pride, comfort, peace of mind, a center for his or her existence, power, some influence over others, and all the other things! These are the objectives of people's behavior all over the world. The relative amount of time and resources allocated to these activities may vary, but the tasks remain. The question is how these tasks are accomplished and this varies a great deal across cultures.

When interpreting various cultural manifestations in different countries, the marketer needs to remember that self-referencing can be misleading. Self-referencing is a process by which we form judgments about others. It involves judging others' behavior against our own past experiences and our own conception of self.[1] Other information that may be available when judging people—the particular setting, the other people involved, a project or goal, verbalized motivations, and so on—is often difficult for us to interpret or go by when we face people from a foreign culture. Therefore, self-referencing is all too common when judging people from abroad—we see others through ourselves. We say to ourselves "If I came that late to an appointment, it would mean that I don't respect him. Why is he so late? It must mean that he does not respect me." Not always so.

Self-referencing leads to misperceptions. When people dress casually while you are in a dark suit, when they avoid eye contact while you look steadily at them, when they speak slowly and you speak purposefully, when they smile while you are earnest—such information or behavior may not mean what you think it means. Before reaching any hasty conclusions, you must check with people familiar with the culture, and perhaps bring a knowledgeable companion to any meeting. The bottom line is learn about the culture, don't trust first impressions, and play down self-referencing in favor of more objective information. **Cultural adaptation** as a skill to be honed must be high on the manager's list of priorities, but as with all valuable acquisitions it can't be had on the cheap.

Culture and Buyer Behavior

Understanding people from foreign cultures is often a baffling business. We see that they are born, experience childhood and adolescence, have common human needs, grow up, fall in love, establish families, work hard, and grow old. Everybody has a life. But what kind of life, and what do people choose to make of it, and why? This is where cultural differences come in.

There are striking differences in preferences and tastes between cultures. If a European prefers a car with a stick shift and tight cornering, a Japanese likes a light touch and easy controls. If a Canadian wants a beer with a certain "body," an American may be happy with a light beer. If a Latin American woman wants strong and dark colors, a northern European may dress in lighter colors. These are preferences based on tradition, culture, or simply fashion, malleable within limits, but it is not at all clear whether any one firm can effect many changes alone or how long it will take. These are the cultural differences that have made marketers say that products have to be adapted. The market is multidomestic, not global.

Multidomestic markets typically reflect underlying religious, cultural, and social factors and also climate and the availability (or lack) of various food ingredients and raw materials. Japanese prefer rice and dried fish for breakfast, while Europeans eat ham and cheese or coffee and croissants. Drinking beer with food is strange for the French, while tea is the standard drink at Chinese dinners. The thin-soled shoes favored by stylish Mediterranean men do not fare well in many American settings. And so on. These differences are based on long tradition, education and upbringing, and also agricultural practices and climate. Western people might think that sweets are liked by young and old—but even the children in Asian countries often prefer salty snacks to sweet chocolate cake. One's taste is educated, not something one is born with.

Of course, many groups of people are not in a position to freely choose according to their taste. A great number of people in the world live under such impoverished conditions that showing them vast choices of brands, products, or lifestyles is pointless. They are just as likely to resent the inaccessible materialism they see advertised on the global communication highway.

But even among very poor people there are those who can and do, within limits, choose. The choices made will often surprise an outsider. In a mud hut in central Africa, where clean water is scarce, one will find a Sony TV set. In India a poor farmer is happy to show off his new Philishave electric razor. In the reopened Chinese provinces, one can see Nissans and Toyotas navigating roads intended for oxcarts and pedicabs. And when the consumers in former eastern Europe go shopping, the result can be surprising for other reasons (see box, "Shopping but Not Choosing").

At the outset it will be useful to look at some examples of what culture involves in the business world (see box, "Cultural Idiosyncracies"). As the illustrations in the box suggest, there are hundreds of potential cultural clashes every day in various parts of the world. Some of them are recognized, others are not. Every manager's behavior conveys intended or unintended meanings to his or her counterpart. **Body language,** the often unintended signals that a person projects through dress, body position, hand, and eye movements, fidgeting, and so on, may provoke all sorts of culturally slanted interpretations. In countries with a homogeneous population, such as Italy, a gesture is often sufficient for information to be shared. A "Hai" in Japanese usually means "I see" rather than the more definite "Yes," which is its literal translation. A "Hai" accompanied by a slight bow is a stronger statement (unless, of course, the response is to a speaker of higher status, in which case again it simply means "I see"). And so on and so forth.

Consumption patterns are unpredictable without a feel for local culture. In affluent America, people in expensive Boss suits are happy with junk food but insist on the latest PC upgrade. In Germany, the food seems less important than unsurpassable beds, while in neighboring France, not to mention Belgium, food is a passion. The Japanese, those sticklers for quality details, seem oblivious to leaking roofs patched with plywood and corrugated sheets of plastic.

Getting the Picture

USEFUL ECONOMIC THEORIES

Even though economists have been ignored by most consumer behavior analysts in recent years, understanding consumers was traditionally the job of economists. Some of the old economic theories are useful in countries where the marketer does not have immediate access to market research data on customer attitudes and motivations. James Duesenberry's relative income hypothesis states that consumers' well-being is a function of how much income they have relative to their peer groups—absolute income levels matter less. Another economist, Milton Friedman, proposed that what determines an individual's consumption is his permanent income, defined as the regularly expected income, without "transitory" factors that lead to a temporary increase or decrease in take-home pay.

These behavioral effects are useful to keep in mind when analyzing local consumers as well as local employees. Although from a psychological perspective they are superficial, not spelling out the exact mental processes involved, they offer useful insights when more in-depth psychological data are missing. A similar case can be made for the famous conspicuous consumption concept developed by Thorstein Veblen, about a hundred years ago. Conspicuous consumption refers to the notion that people make purchases of expensive brands and products in order to display their ability to afford them. Again, recent consumer behavior thinking goes further and deals with the underlying psychological processes, but the basic concept is still valid in many cultures.

Sources: Brooks, 1981; Veblen, 1899.

Some examples will clarify this. While the core benefit of an automobile may be transportation in some countries, especially large ones with a well-developed road network such as the United States, the auto is often a status symbol in less-developed countries. While disposable diapers may be bought for convenience in some countries, they are used for health reasons elsewhere. A credit card may offer more security and convenience than cash in some countries, while in others it offers a chance for parents to indulge their teenage offspring.

While these benefits are intermingled in most markets, and some segments of a local market will emphasize some over the others, the identification of a different core benefit is a necessary first step in analyzing local customers. Misunderstanding what the core benefits of a product are in a local market is sometimes a fatal mistake.

Because the product or service has already been marketed at home and perhaps elsewhere, most global marketers—and their headquarters counterparts—assume the core benefits of their offerings are well known, or indeed that they know what they are. But core benefits are not independent of the local environment. In fact, the core benefits of a product are a direct function of the environment. The generic function of a product depends more on the local environment than on innate individual preferences.

The core benefit of a car in the middle of Tokyo, for example, is hardly a matter of transportation. Still, many families do own one to safeguard their social standing and boost their self-perception. Ice cream is bought for its healthy milk in India. Coca-Cola is recommended instead of local water in many countries. Disposable bottles are not convenient when space is limited and garbage difficult to dispose of. Credit cards are convenient only when they are generally accepted and safe only when the charges from a stolen card can be stopped easily. Membership in a low-price club works only when bulk storage at home is possible. Even a simple product such as apples is not the same everywhere (see box, "Fresh Fruit in Japan").

So, the product often takes on a different meaning—or no meaning at all—in a local culture. This means that certain products have no market—yet—in some countries. In others their core benefits have to be reformulated. In fact, the product or service itself may have to be reformulated or "localized." And, to repeat, this reformulation is not adaptation to consumer preferences but to the local conditions of use. The core benefits differ not because people are different but because local culture and infrastructure differ.

Getting the Picture

FRESH FRUIT IN JAPAN

One of the long-enduring trade conflicts between Japan and other countries has been in the fresh fruit industry. Oranges from California, apples from Washington State, grapes from Chile, and bananas from the Philippines are only a few of the cases of entry being denied at the border. Japan's domestic fruit industry is small but strong politically. Gradually, however, the foreign producers have been granted entry and are doing quite well.

The typical justification for keeping products off the Japanese markets is that they do not meet the standards expected by Japanese customers. Although this tends to hide the more important reason of wanting to protect the domestic industry, for fresh fruits there is a grain of truth in this argument. This is not because Japanese consumers want quality per se—it has to do with the core benefit of fruit in Japan. Until recently, fresh fruit in Japan was viewed as a specialty, even luxury product, usually bought during the gift-giving season. It had no particular role to play as a daily food supplement, in salads, for snacks, and so on. Thus, in the beginning, the imported fresh fruit was judged according to standards for apples at $5 apiece, cantaloupe at $40 a melon, and boxed grapes for $70, all turned out in beautifully wrapped gift sets. Not only did the customs officials deem the imported fruit below par, the consumer would not accept it.

It was not until fresh fruit took on the new core benefit of a daily food supplement that the imported fruit was accepted. The industry acceptance was helped by the fact that creating a new core benefit amounted to enlarging the generic market for fresh fruit, also benefiting the domestic growers. It should come as no surprise to the reader that the education of the Japanese consumer as to the new core benefit involved quite an effort in media advertising, in-store and magazine information about diets, and the promotion of fruit in American-produced TV programs broadcast in Japan.

Many of the foreign producers adopted advice by the Japanese officials about packaging, storing and handling the fruit, as well as adhering to demands about pesticide treatments. The imported apples offered for sale in Japan today are not only less expensive than the domestic varieties, but are literally the cream of the crop from the foreign producers. And, in a final twist of what global markets mean, the fresh fruit offered for sale in Western supermarkets today is healthier, packaged better, and more carefully handled than before as a consequence of the Japanese experience.

Sources: Clifford, 1993; "300 Growers Protest U.S. Apple Imports," *Mainichi Daily News,* July 8, 1994, p. 5.

Cultures across Countries

What kinds of cultures are there in the world? There are several useful ways of classifying cultures across countries. First, however, one needs to recognize that cultures and countries do not necessarily go together. Countries with large populations, such as India, China, Russia, and the United States, are really **multicultural,** meaning that they contain a wide variety of cultures within their borders. The same goes for some smaller nations, such as Belgium, Canada, South Africa, and the former Yugoslavia. In other cases, several countries can be seen as one cultural grouping. Examples include the Scandinavian countries (Denmark, Norway, Sweden) and Latin American countries (Venezuela, Colombia, Ecuador, but not necessarily Brazil).

High versus Low Context Cultures

An important distinction between cultures suggested by Hall is that between **high and low context cultures.**[2] In high context cultures the meaning of individual behavior and speech changes depending on the situation or context. Nonverbal messages are full of important—and intended—meanings. Even if no words are spoken, individuals communicate. Things are "understood." And when words are spoken, "reading between the lines" is important. High context cultures have a similarity of backgrounds, a commonness of purpose, a homogeneity in society, careful enculturation and socialization starting at an early age in the family, often one religion, one language, centralized broadcast media, coordinated educational system, and so on.

In low context cultures, by contrast, intentions are expressed verbally. One's meaning should be explicit, not taken for granted. Propositions have to be justified and opinions defended openly. In low context cultures the situation is not allowed to change the meaning of words and behavior—the context conveys little or no extra information. This is quite useful and necessary in a country that is multicultural and where people's value systems and attitudes can be very different.

High context cultures can be found in most of the European countries, some of the Latin American countries (Chile, Mexico, perhaps Venezuela and Argentina), and in Japan and many of the newly industrializing Asian countries (including China and India). In countries with high context cultures—such as Saudi Arabia and Japan—a written contract is not always enforceable if the situation changes or if new people move into executive positions.

Americans, because of their **diversity,** have a low context culture. Low context cultures can also be found in countries such as Australia and New Zealand with large immigrant populations.

"Silent Languages"

In a famous article, Hall also pointed out the important role of nonverbal communication or **"silent languages"** in international business.[3] He identified the use of five different silent languages: space, material possessions, friendship patterns, agreements across cultures, and time. All of the factors have some meaning in interpersonal communication, but are not necessarily mentioned or spoken of. For example, one's conception of *space* relates to matters such as the distance between two people conversing. In the Middle East men will maintain an intimate distance, often too close for comfort for Western people. *Material possessions* of course always speak volumes about one's station in life, particularly where social hierarchies are well developed so that people learn what to look for. The emphasis on well-known brands in Asian markets, for example, reflects a need to clearly identify one's position with signals other people readily understand.

Friendship patterns (whom do you treat as a friend?) are not only reflective of your own cultural upbringing but also involve questions of **trust** and responsibility. In a business deal, it would not be strange for an American to assure a prospective partner that a third person "will agree because he is my friend." By contrast, in a country like Japan, the person might well say, "I cannot speak for him because he is my friend." *Agreements across cultures* are also interpreted differently. While Western business people rely on explicit contracts and keep the letter of the law, Eastern cultures rely more on general agreement and the basic intent of the partners.

Perceptions of *time* vary considerably between even relatively close cultures, and studies have documented the varieties of problems connected with different time perceptions.[4] Latin Americans' perception of their being "on time" even when 30 minutes late for an appointment is counterbalanced by east Asians who think it safest to show up 30 minutes early, just to be on time. While northern people might not like to "waste" time on "small talk" in a business meeting, Latins tend to spend more time on non-business conversation. Differing perceptions of time and its use are responsible for many problems in business negotiations, a topic to be discussed later in this chapter.

Hofstede's Cultural Dimensions

The high versus low context distinction and "silent languages" provide useful concepts by which to think about various cultures. Hofstede's questionnaire study of IBM's employees around the globe in 1980 is a much more systematic assessment of cultures across countries.[5] Although the world has changed considerably since the study was done, cultures have changed less—and judging from recent events in eastern Europe and Russia, ethnicity and cultural roots are stronger than ever.

According to Hofstede's survey findings, countries can be classified along four basic cultural dimensions. The first of **Hofstede's cultural dimensions** is **individualism versus collectivism.** In a collective society, the identity and worth of the individual is rooted in the social system, less in individual achievement. A second dimension is **high versus low power distance.** High power distance societies tend to be less egalitarian, while democratic countries exhibit low power distance (see Exhibit 3.1).

EXHIBIT 3.1   The Positions of the 40 Countries on the Power Distance and Individualism Scales

Source: Geert Hofstede, "The Position of the 40 Countries on the Uncertainty Avoidance and Masculinity Scales," *Culture's Consequences,* published by Sage Publications, Inc., © 1980 by Geert Hofstede. Reprinted by permission of the author.

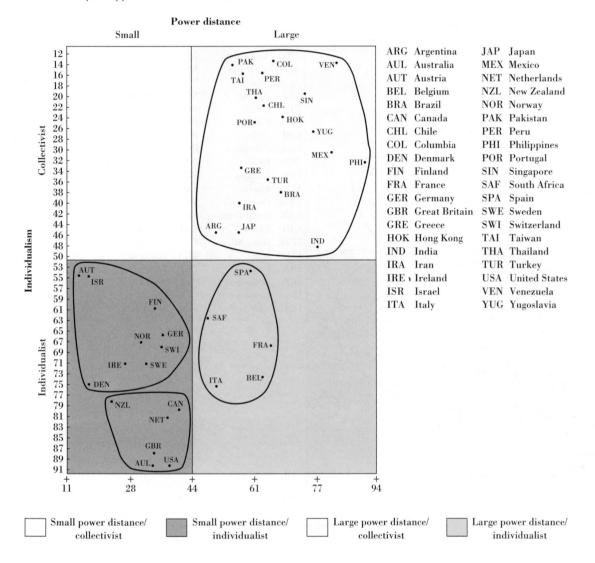

ARG	Argentina	JAP	Japan
AUL	Australia	MEX	Mexico
AUT	Austria	NET	Netherlands
BEL	Belgium	NZL	New Zealand
BRA	Brazil	NOR	Norway
CAN	Canada	PAK	Pakistan
CHL	Chile	PER	Peru
COL	Columbia	PHI	Philippines
DEN	Denmark	POR	Portugal
FIN	Finland	SIN	Singapore
FRA	France	SAF	South Africa
GER	Germany	SPA	Spain
GBR	Great Britain	SWE	Sweden
GRE	Greece	SWI	Switzerland
HOK	Hong Kong	TAI	Taiwan
IND	India	THA	Thailand
IRA	Iran	TUR	Turkey
IRE	Ireland	USA	United States
ISR	Israel	VEN	Venezuela
ITA	Italy	YUG	Yugoslavia

As can be seen from the "map" in Exhibit 3.1, Australians and Venezuelans tend to be diametrically opposite each other on these two measures. While Australians are individualistic and democratic, Venezuelans are much more collectivist and believers in formal authority. (Note that the distances between countries on the map in Exhibit 3.1 represent the degree to which the countries differ culturally.)

Hofstede's third dimension, **masculine versus feminine,** captures the degree to which a culture is dominated by assertive males rather than nurturing females and the corresponding values. Finally, weak versus strong **uncertainty avoidance** rates nations according to the level of risk tolerance or risk aversion among the people (see Exhibit 3.2).

As can be seen from the map in Exhibit 3.2, Australia and Venezuela are not as far away from each other this time. Both cultures tend to be dominated more by males than by females, and although Venezuelans are more eager to avoid risks, the distance—and thus cultural difference—is not that great. Thus, looking at the two maps, the difficulties managers from the two countries might face in dealing with each other might involve individualism and differences in the use of power. While an Australian would act alone and treat others as equals, the Venezuelan might feel better seeking support among peers and then imposing decisions on subordinates.

EXHIBIT 3.2 **The Positions of the 40 Countries on the Uncertainty Avoidance and Masculinity Scales**

Source: Geert Hofstede, "The Position of the 40 Countries on the Power Distance and Individualism," *Culture's Consequences,* published by Sage Publications, Inc., © 1980 by Geert Hofstede. Reprinted by permission of the author.

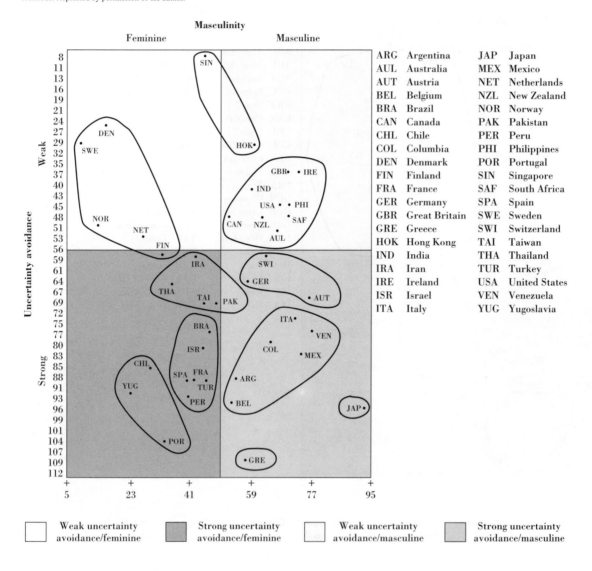

ARG Argentina	JAP Japan
AUL Australia	MEX Mexico
AUT Austria	NET Netherlands
BEL Belgium	NZL New Zealand
BRA Brazil	NOR Norway
CAN Canada	PAK Pakistan
CHL Chile	PER Peru
COL Columbia	PHI Philippines
DEN Denmark	POR Portugal
FIN Finland	SIN Singapore
FRA France	SAF South Africa
GER Germany	SPA Spain
GBR Great Britain	SWE Sweden
GRE Greece	SWI Switzerland
HOK Hong Kong	TAI Taiwan
IND India	THA Thailand
IRA Iran	TUR Turkey
IRE Ireland	USA United States
ISR Israel	VEN Venezuela
ITA Italy	YUG Yugoslavia

In some later applications Hofstede added a fifth dimension, **Confucianist dynamics,** to distinguish the long-term orientation among Asian people, influenced by Confucius, the Chinese philosopher, from the more short-term outlook of Western people.[6]

The Hofstede mapping of countries is useful in that it offers a snapshot of the cultural distances between countries. Marketers can anticipate the degree to which marketing programs, especially communications and advertising or services, might need to be adapted to a new culture. For the multinational company with different product lines in different countries, a close look at these cultural distances can even help with choices about which line should be introduced in a new market.

Thinking along Hofstede's dimensions, managers can evaluate how difficult it may be to do business in a country culturally distant from their own and how severe a cultural shock they and their families are likely to get when moving to the country. The typical American manager going to run a subsidiary in a country whose culture is more risk averse and less individualistic, with more power distance and reverence for authority than her or his own might anticipate some difficulty adjusting.

Getting the Picture

RAPAILLE'S ARCHETYPES: DECODING CULTURES

Dr. G. Clotaire Rapaille is a French-born anthropologist living and working in the United States. He has more than 25 years of experience helping multinational businesses cope with cultural diversity. His experiences have been distilled into seven "secrets" for understanding and, as he calls it, **decoding cultures.**

Secret 1: The structure is the message: People don't buy products and services—they buy relationships.

Secret 2: Cultures also have an unconscious: Cultural archetypes have the power to make or break your marketing, sales, or public relations plan.

Secret 3: If you don't know the code, you can't open the door: Decoding the mindset of the target market opens doors of opportunity.

Secret 4: Time, space, and energy are the building blocks of all cultures: Each culture has a DNA, and you can encode your culture for top marketing and sales performance.

Secret 5: Solve the right problem: You must design and create new products or services to solve the right customer problem.

Secret 6: The more global, the more local: Quality is the passport to global markets, but the code for quality differs from culture to culture, market to market, person to person.

Secret 7: The Third World War is under way—and it is cultural: Cultural awareness is the key to success and to personal and collective freedom.

From one angle, we can see that **Rapaille's archetypes** treat culture as a person. Understanding a culture is similar to understanding a person. A striking illustration of the value of the approach is in his work on quality. Deciphering why the Japanese-inspired "Total Quality Control" programs had failed at AT&T, the giant telecommunications company, Rapaille found that "quality" had a different meaning for people from different cultures.

In Japan, "quality" meant "perfection."

In Germany, "quality" meant "according to standards."

In France, "quality" meant "luxury."

In the United States, "quality" meant simply "it works."

After these findings, it was clear why the Japanese insistence on "zero defects" had little relevance in the AT&T organization.

Source: Rapaille, 2001.

Gannon's Metaphors

There are many useful ways of looking at and analyzing cultures. One way is the Jungian-inspired archetypes proposed by Rapaille (see box, "Rapaille's Archetypes: Decoding Cultures"). Another is through the metaphors proposed by Gannon.[7]

Gannon suggested the use of descriptive metaphors for different cultures, suggestive analogues that characterized cultures in such a way as to help managers anticipate what people's reactions might be in different situations. **Gannon's metaphors** offer a mental anchor for the manager who has to deal with a new culture and cannot foresee all contingencies.

In practice, it is impossible for the global marketer to learn a great deal about all cultures. According to Gannon, learning a smattering of individual "don'ts" ("don't prop your feet on the table, don't blow your nose, don't compliment anybody's wife, don't cross your legs, don't touch your host's son's head," and so on) from the typical "how-to" books is likely to create confusion when more than one culture is covered. Gannon argues that it is more effective to develop a holistic sense of a culture by creating an image (a metaphor) representing how the people think and behave. By planting the image in the back of one's mind, Gannon suggests, one can more comfortably interpret what someone in that culture is trying to say or do. If the metaphor is correct and fairly deeply understood, one's own reactions and responses can become more genuine and instinctive.

Some of Gannon's proposed metaphors are given in Exhibit 3.3. As can be seen, Gannon suggests that the metaphor of American football captures many of the features of American culture, with its emphasis on competition, specialization of individual functions, strong leaders calling the plays, and the desire for individual recognition. By contrast, Italians can be described in operatic terms, where speeches are like tenor and soprano arias, the "bella figura" of Italian dress is represented by the costumes and stage setting, and the major players are all given time to shine in the spotlight.

EXHIBIT 3.3
Gannon's Metaphors

Source: *Understanding Global Cultures: Metaphorical Journeys through 17 Countries,* by Martin Gannon. Copyright 1994 by Sage Publications Inc. Books. Reproduced with permission of Sage Publications Inc. Books in the format Textbook via Copyright Clearance Center.

1. *American football:* Individualism and competitive specialization; huddling; ceremonial celebration of perfection.
2. *The British house:* Laying the foundations; building the brick house; living in the brick house.
3. *The German symphony:* Orchestra; conductors; performance; society, education, and politics.
4. *The French wine:* Purity; classification; composition; compatibility; maturation.
5. *The Italian family opera:* Pageantry and spectacle; voice expression; chorus and soloists.
6. *The Swedish summer home:* Love of nature; individualism through self-development; equality.
7. *The Japanese garden:* Wa and shikata, harmony and form; seishin, spirit of self-discipline; combining droplets.
8. *The Chinese family altar:* Confucianism and Taoism; roundness, harmony, and fluidity.
9. *India: Cyclical Hindu philosophy:* The cycle of life; the family cycle; the social cycle; the work cycle.

The German culture can be characterized by the classical symphony, with its strict discipline under a leader and skilled individuals performing together like a well-oiled machine. And so on. However simplified such metaphors are, Gannon argues, they give the manager the right mindset with which to approach customers, distribution middlemen, potential partners—and bureaucrats!—in the foreign culture.

Culture and "How to Do Business"

The modern conception of culture focuses directly on observable behavior. It recognizes that culture not only predisposes the individual toward certain behavior but eliminates other behavior. Consequently, culture creates a repertoire of behavioral skills. Culture directly influences what people will do and what people can do. This interpretation of culture is very useful for global marketing managers. It suggests that culture is more important for how managers should decide, less to what the decision should be. Culture affects implementation and execution of strategies more than their formulation.

In effect, culture influences what management skills are needed and to what extent experiences from other markets can be applied. Not only are there obvious implications for the way managers treat subordinates and other people; cultural biases influence managers' effectiveness in implementing and managing local marketing.[8]

Managerial Styles

Cultures tend to generate different **managerial styles,** that is, what is considered appropriate managerial behavior in different countries.[9] This can be illustrated with a comparison between companies from the so-called "Triad": Japan, North America, and Europe. First, let's analyze along Hofstede's dimensions the cultures of these three regions.

In terms of the "maps" we saw in Exhibits 3.1 and 3.2, Hofstede's research produces the rough classification for the countries in the Triad seen in Exhibit 3.4. Great Britain is included among the North American countries in Exhibit 3.4 in view of the proximity of scores in Exhibits 3.1 and 3.2. Also, because of their great differences from one another on the Hofstede maps, the European countries are divided into northern Europe (Scandinavia, Finland, and the Netherlands) and continental Europe (the rest, except Great Britain). "Context" has been added as a fifth dimension to account for differences between high and low context cultures.

According to Exhibit 3.4, the Western regions are high on individualism, as one might expect, but differ on the other three dimensions. Power distance is low in democratic North America and northern Europe, higher in continental Europe. The only region low on masculinity is northern Europe, where gender equality is more of an established fact. The tolerance for risk is higher in North America and northern Europe, while Japan and continental Europe tend to avoid uncertainty. Japan's group orientation and hierarchical society are reflected in their low score on individualism

EXHIBIT 3.4
Hofstede's Classification
of Triad Countries

Source: Adapted from Hofstede, 1980.

	Japan	Anglo-Saxon (Canada, United States, Great Britain)	W. Europe Northern	W. Europe Continent
Individualism	Low	High	High	High
Power distance	High	Low	Low	High
Masculinity	High	High	Low	High
Risk tolerance	Low	High	High	Low
Context	High	Low	High	Low
Note: "Context" added.				

and high power distance. Japan and northern Europe are high context societies, while North America and continental Europe are less so, needing more clarification and verbalization.

How do these differences in national cultures affect the behavior of managers whom one meets abroad? Some of the well-known stereotypes of various country managers can easily be derived from these dimensions.[10] One understands why Japanese travel in groups and insist on careful preparation of meeting protocols, why they listen well and slow down their decision making. Western managers can be expected to take responsibility on their own, being individually more confident and trusting their ability to problem solve and improvise. At the same time, continental Europeans want clear agendas and organization of meetings and are more likely to insist on a clear structure of agreements and solutions. The high context cultures of Japan and northern Europe make it less important to justify everything verbally and explicitly, since most managers will be able to "fill in the missing pieces" on their own.

Managing Subordinates

These cultural differences suggest that different types of leadership skills will be needed in managing marketing overseas as opposed to in the home market. Going to a high context culture from another such culture will in general be easier than going to a high from a low context culture or vice versa. Managers from a high context culture will have sensitivities to nonverbal cues that go unnoticed or are ignored by low context cultures. The person from a low context culture is easily seen as a "bull in a china shop" in a high context culture. The American managers are brought up to tolerate and respect others' convictions, but are, because of their low context culture, not sensitive to nuances and not used to placing themselves in somebody else's position. High context individuals, by contrast, may seem to stand out by being reserved and indirect.

It is not surprising if people from high context cultures feel uncomfortable when managers from low context cultures arrive to run a subsidiary. People from high context cultures tend to be fine-tuned—they pay attention to nuances and omissions; they indulge the speaker and fill in the unspoken meaning on their own. On the other hand, while being drunk in the United States is no excuse for badmouthing one's boss to his face—in Japan, that is the manager's unspoken but understood purpose of after-business drinking. The typical manager from a low context culture such as the United States has no ability or will to indulge subordinates to that extent: "If words are spoken, they are meant. There is no excuse."

To help managers cope with—or, even better, avoid—cultural clashes, most companies offer new expatriate managers (and their families) predeparture workshops and briefings about the new culture they are to encounter. As important, most companies make sure that their professional development programs are open to a multinational group of employees. In this way the managers will naturally get "cultural sensitivity training" as a side benefit from internal executive courses. Many of these courses also involve cross-cultural training sessions (see box, "Trompenaars and His Cultural Dilemmas").

Getting the Picture

TROMPENAARS AND HIS CULTURAL DILEMMAS

The spiritual and intellectual heir to Hofstede is another Dutchman, Fons Trompenaars, who, rather than being a pure cultural anthropologist, is a management Ph.D. from The Wharton School. Working out of Europe, where he heads his own multinational consulting group, Trompenaars culls his cultural theories from questionnaires administered in cross-cultural training sessions for various multinationals. By 1998 the data bank contained over 30,000 completed questionnaires.

Trompenaars's basic thrust is that culture is involved in action, and, in the end, is best viewed as "the way in which people solve problems." The "problems" arise primarily in social and interpersonal relationships, when people from different cultures interact. The differences create problems or **cultural dilemmas**. The potential clashes can be grouped into seven categories.

1. *Universalism versus particularism.* Are you always trying to do the "right" thing **(universalist)**, or do you fit your actions to the situation **(particularist)?** This split is especially relevant in ethical dilemmas.

2. *Individualism versus communitarianism.* This is basically the same as Hofstede's distinction between "individualism" and "collectivism."

3. *Neutral versus emotional.* Does a conversation mean an exchange of information ("How long did you stay in Paris?") or emotional as well ("I love Paris").

4. *Specific versus diffuse.* Is the relationship "just business," or is "the whole person" involved? This split becomes especially important in negotiations (discussed later in this chapter).

5. *Achievement versus ascription.* Do you judge an individual on the basis of performance (achievement) or on the basis of pedigree, status, connections, and so forth (ascription)? In class societies, ascription is hard to avoid.

6. *Attitudes toward time.* This is not simply a question of at what point one is "late" for an appointment. It is more profound, whether time moves in a straight line or circular. If the former, the future is focused on. If the latter, the past is as important.

7. *Attitudes toward the environment.* Are you basically responsible for yourself only, or do you attend to others first? Sony's Walkman was conceived to let one person's desire for music not interfere with others. By contrast, in many cultures the Walkman is seen as a way of eliminating interference from others.

It is relatively easy to see that the United States with its low context multiculturalism falls pretty much toward the "left" side of these differences. More traditional cultures such as Japan's tend toward the "right" side. Trompenaars's recipe for solving the cultural dilemmas is to attempt a "reconciliation" of opposing views, allowing both parties to retain their cultural identities by raising the consciousness of the participants and making them see the other side's points. This is accomplished by explicitly discussing the cultural differences, doing role playing, and jointly working out a solution that takes into account the conditions and constraints of the specific task at hand. For Trompenaars, "the one best way of organizing does not exist."

Sources: Trompenaars and Hampden-Turner, 1998 and 2004.

Culture and Negotiations

Establishing a relationship with suppliers, distributors and other middlemen, and potential alliance partners invariably involves some kind of face-to-face negotiations. Foreign entry via licensing or a joint venture necessarily involves finding contract partners. Local marketing puts the marketer in direct contact with channel members who need to be convinced to carry the product. Global management involves trade-offs between local subsidiaries' autonomy and headquarters' need for standardization. Cross-cultural negotiations are a fact of life for the global marketer.

There are several good books on cross-cultural negotiations, and these are recommended for the prospective negotiator.[11] In general, each different culture will require its own particular approach (see box, "It's Never Simple."). The different frameworks discussed above offer some preliminary insights, but in actual negotiations more-detailed advice is necessary. Following are a few basic cross-cultural generalities.

Know Whom You Are Dealing With

In most negotiations, knowing something about the cultural background of the opposite partner is considered a must. It is important to know not only the nationalities involved, but also the particular ethnic background. This holds not only for today's

Getting the Picture

"IT'S NEVER SIMPLE."

The conduct at the negotiating tables varies a great deal across cultures. Where Americans want a prompt answer, Scandinavians can take their time. By contrast, Latin Americans are likely to interrupt when they understand where a speaker is going and are prone to argue a point. Japanese often close their eyes—some even actually go to sleep. Arabs may leave the table because of a telephone call, and simply return later. Mexicans are notorious for arriving late. Italians pay much attention to looks and how an impressive statement can be made. The French often speak among themselves when another speaker is talking. The Germans insist on starting with background information before getting to the point. Chinese are very argumentative among themselves.

These crude generalizations do not always hold up, of course, but it is useful for the negotiator to understand that what seems to be strange behavior is not necessarily so. Leaving the table may seem insulting to some, but is perfectly natural to others. They may not even give it a second thought, since in their own culture it is the way things are done. And in that culture it fills a useful function. Coming late does not mean laziness or carelessness and is usually not even intentional. In a society where clocks are rare, a 10 o'-clock meeting means "sometime in the morning." When the costs of tardiness increase, people will come on time. This is why now in Mexico City, business meetings are much more in sync with the more punctual part of the Western world.

Sources: Graham, 1983; Hall and Hall, 1990; Tan, 2004.

obvious cases in the former Yugoslavia, Russia, Belgium (Flemish versus Valloons), or Nigeria (Ibos versus Hausas), but also in regard to more subtle differences between ethnic backgrounds in the United States, Singapore, or Canada. Further, recognizing you know something about his culture, a clever negotiator may play a game, seeing how far he can push you in that direction.

It is important never to forget that beyond cultural differences, personality can dominate cultural stereotypes. Thus, there are soft-spoken Americans, emotional Japanese, calm Brazilians, and informal Germans. But such persons may also have decided to accommodate a partner's different style, as when a Russian tries to be easy-going in a negotiation with a Brazilian. The experienced negotiator can usually diagnose the case in which the deviant behavior is genuine. And remember, without genuine behavior, trust is difficult to establish.[12]

Know What They Hear

The second caution from experts is the possibility of discrepancies between what the manager thinks he or she is communicating and what is actually received by the other party. Direct and straightforward speech still leaves many things unsaid—and "plain speaking" is in many cultures a typical way to hide something (one might do well recalling Othello's deceitful "honest Iago"). If something needs to be hidden, one ploy is to stress other points strongly, deflecting attention in the same way that most magicians do their tricks. This works against the typically open and direct American negotiators who may not have anything to hide—but who are nonetheless suspect because of the haste and eagerness with which they push negotiations along.

Nonverbal communication is always a mysterious ingredient in negotiations. Research on negotiations has consistently found the other party's attractiveness and grace to be a strong contributor to positive negotiation outcomes.[13] Although in some cases the causal direction seems to be the reverse—we like the person we have just concluded an agreement with—for the most part the effect goes the other way. If we like the manner and appearance of someone, we are more likely to conclude an agreement. Although analysis of proposals and well-timed strategic concessions are the basic components of any successful business negotiation, most managers agree that appreciation of intangibles such as manners, dress, looks, and graceful nonverbal behavior can make for a much more satisfying negotiation experience and may count for more than we think. All the more so in the context of intercultural negotiations.

Know When to Say What

The typical approach by American negotiators is to take a problem-solving view of negotiations, in which the parties are oriented toward information exchange. They try to convey their own preferences and identify those of the other party by focusing on facts, asking questions, probing, and looking for specific data. Members of other cultures are more likely to assume a broader perspective and take a longer-term view of the negotiations, attempting to assess the potential of a general relationship beyond the specific contract agreement.

Graham has analyzed negotiations in many cultures and identified four sequential stages that characterize information exchange in most business negotiations:[14]

1. *Nontask sounding.* This is an initial period when the conversation consists mainly of small talk, designed to get the partners to know each other better.
2. *Task-related exchange of information.* An extended period when the main issues are brought out, facts are presented, and positions clarified.
3. *Persuasion.* This is the stage when the parties attempt to make each other see the issues their way, when there is further explanation and elaboration of positions, and questioning of the other side's evidence.
4. *Concessions and agreements.* Toward the end of most negotiations is a period when mutual concessions might be made, when there is some yielding of fixed positions in order to reach an agreement.

Applying the framework to negotiations between Japanese and Americans, Graham and Sano found the significant cultural differences outlined in Exhibit 3.5.[15] As can be seen, the length and the importance of the stages differ between the two countries. The Americans use less time for nontask soundings than the Japanese, and they are brief with explanations, while the Japanese are more thorough. The Japanese are likely to wait with concessions until the very end, while the Americans move toward an agreement by gradually yielding ground. Against this background it is hardly surprising if trade negotiators from Japan and the United States sometimes seem to be in disagreement about how negotiations are progressing.

Salacuse has classified negotiators from different cultures as proactive "A" types or reactive "B" types.[16] Exhibit 3.6 identifies the major traits of the two types of negotiators. The **type A negotiator** starts with the easily agreed-upon smaller details and works up, while the **type B negotiator** first wants to agree on the overall framework

EXHIBIT 3.5
Four Stages of Business Negotiations

Source: Adapted from John L. Graham, "A Hidden Cause of America's Trade Deficit with Japan," *Columbia Journal of World Business,* Fall 1981, p. 14.

Stage	Japanese	Americans
1. Nontask sounding	Considerable time and expense devoted to such efforts is the practice in Japan.	Relatively shorter periods are typical.
2. Task-related exchange of information	This is the most important step—high first offers with long explanations and in-depth clarifications.	Information is given briefly and directly. "Fair" first offers are more typical.
3. Persuasion	Persuasion is accomplished primarily behind the scenes. Vertical status relations dictate bargaining outcomes.	The most important step: Minds are changed at the negotiation table and aggressive persuasive tactics are used.
4. Concessions and agreement	Concessions are made only toward the end of the negotiations— holistic approach to decision making. Progress is difficult to measure for Americans.	Concessions and commitments are made throughout—a sequential approach to decision making.

EXHIBIT 3.6
Type A and Type B Negotiators

Source: Chart from *Making Global Deals* by
Jeswald W. Salacuse Copyright © 1991 by
Jeswald W. Salacuse. Reprinted by permission
of Houghton Mifflin Harcourt Publishing
Company. All rights reserved.

Trait	Type A Negotiator	Type B Negotiator
Goal	Contract	Relationship
Attitudes	Win/lose	Win/win
Personal styles	Informal	Formal
Communications	Direct	Indirect
Time sensitivity	High	Low
Emotionalism	High	Low
Agreement form	Specific	General
Team organization	One leader	Consensus
Risk taking	High	Low

of the agreement. Most of the traits in the list are self-explanatory. The "agreement building" trait refers to the process through which the agreement is formulated. As the list suggests, the type A negotiator is a more dynamic, energetic, and risk-taking entrepreneur while the B type is a slow, seasoned, mature individual who avoids risk. The A type is closer to the American managers in Exhibit 3.5, the B type closer to the Japanese managers. As Salacuse stresses, both approaches can work—which one is best depends on the cultures involved. It's when they clash that there may be trouble.

Industrial Buyers

Since negotiations are often involved, marketing to local industrial buyers (B2B or business-to-business marketing) is strongly affected by culture. Not only does the purchasing agent's own cultural background play a role, but so does the culture of the organization.[17]

The Business Marketing Task

At the outset it is useful to define the global business marketer's task more precisely. He or she needs to establish the global firm as a dependable supplier to an independent business organization operating in the local market, where the buyer in the customer organization is usually a native of the country. The local business customer uses the product for further processing or resale, in the case of original equipment manufacturing (OEM) under its own brand name. The competition consists of other suppliers, both domestic and foreign, who can also provide the parts and components, the OEM product, or the branded product to be distributed.

In this situation, a global marketer with the appropriate customer orientation has to understand the local buyer's position in the organization, the other people and factors in the organization that influence the buying decision, and the role the product (and the marketer) play in making the buyer successful in his or her organizational role. In short, the local marketer should help the buying organization succeed—and make the buyer look good. A challenging task, especially in a foreign culture.

Cultural Conditioning

Depending on personality and underlying cultural conditioning, buyers tend to develop styles of dealing with vendors. A basic consideration is how the buyer treats the seller—as an equal, or less than an equal. American marketers steeped in a democratic tradition find it hard to accept the inequality and subservience in more hierarchical societies no matter where it's exhibited, but especially when it affects them, as sellers. But it is important to recognize that despite a more advanced product or service offering, the seller is in a sense there to serve, and what is important is to serve the needs of the prospective customer. It is only when competing suppliers are nonexistent that the seller becomes the equal of the buyer. Western companies have long prided themselves on technological uniqueness, but as global competition intensifies, even aristocrats have to adopt a "customer first" attitude.

A culture's openness to change directly influences the buyer's attitude toward risk. For most purchasing agents, changing from an existing domestic supplier to a foreign supplier is perceived as a very risky decision. First, it is not easy to evaluate the new supplier, especially when many of its engineers and managers are foreign. Second, the reliability of supplies is questionable, since many suppliers give priority to buyers in their own country or with whom they have done business for many years. Third, although it is natural to start out with a small order, this is also a means by which the patience and commitment of the foreign firm are tested further. Fourth, terminating an existing domestic supplier sometimes carries with it political negatives (unemployment, plant closings), which make it more than a simple canceling of a business transaction.

Thus, to believe that the global marketer's job is just to present a better problem solution is naive. More has to be done. To signal a strong level of commitment to the new market, the CEO or another top executive might have to visit the prospective customer. Quality questions have to be answered promptly; local language product information has to be offered; and any questions about potential delivery delays on account of time differences, geographical distance, or transportation problems have to be dealt with effectively. As further elaborated below, the risks involved in a buyer's adopting a foreign supplier lead to high up-front costs and require a long-term, relationship-building approach to the transaction.

Organizational Culture

The buyer in an organization is usually only one of the actual decision makers. Buyers are persons with formal authority for selecting the supplier and arranging the terms of purchase. The users of the product or service—engineers, designers, manufacturing managers—often have more influence on the decision as to which supplier to choose. Then there are upper-level executives who have to sign off on a purchase decision. In the line-and-staff linkages between these groups, there are organizational influencers who can wield unseen authority.

These individuals have differential impact at various levels of the buying process depending on the organizational culture. The organizational culture is defined by its routines and procedures for problem solving and decision making. For example, in a purchasing routine users are typically more influential in the early part of the process, up through product specification. The senior executives may have real influence early when resources have to be allocated, but the signing off on the selected supplier may be more a pro forma step, especially in decentralized and bottom-up organizations.

Although ideally a local marketer may wish to establish a strong and trusting relationship with all these parties, such a perfect world rarely exists even at home, but especially not in a foreign setting. For example, in many Asian organizations formal position descriptions tend to be vague or misleading, making it very difficult to identify key people. But it is important anywhere to try to identify the degree to which the buying decision is based on group consensus or whether there is one influential decision maker, which is quite common among Asian companies, even in Japan. In many old-style and hierarchical European companies, it is common for a buyer to affect independence and entrepreneurial initiative, while in fact the decision is made by a group of senior executives. The local marketer needs to remember that it can be slightly embarrassing for a buyer to admit that others in the organization make the decision. Or, as usual, buyers may use others' alleged need for consultation as an avoidance tactic or to postpone a decision.

The group decision making involved in many industrial purchases means that cultural influences will be strong, both from the organizational culture and the culture at large. Most organizations reflect the culture of the country or region where they are located, although there are instances of geocentric organizations that try to remove ethnocentric cultures from the organization (IBM, Philips, and Sony are some examples). In most instances, the local marketer, when approaching the customer, will have to be guided by both local cultural norms and the specific organizational culture involved.

Getting the Picture

BOEING'S SALES PITCH

The Boeing Company, located in Chicago, Illinois, is year in and year out the United States' largest exporter. The company's planes can be found in the fleets of most airlines around the world. What kind of sales pitch sells these planes against the competition of European Airbus and some smaller competitors?

As most newspaper reports suggest, pricing (that is, financing) is perhaps the most potent marketing weapon. The Export-Import Bank of the United States is an important ally of the Boeing Company, helping to offer favorable financing terms. The product is perhaps second in importance, involving attributes such as safety record, advanced technology, fuel efficiency, and customer comfort. And the planes, although they seem to be "off-the-shelf" with standardized designations, same engines, and a few optional "body stretches," actually are somewhat customized in terms of seat sizes, color schemes, and cabin configurations.

In terms of service, the company offers training programs for pilots and mechanics and maintains a regular office with local staff in the cities of major customers (in London for British Airways, in Frankfurt for Lufthansa, in Tokyo for JAL

and ANA, and so on). The company also helps customers in business matters only vaguely related to airplanes, such as helping sons and daughters of high officials find appropriate schooling in foreign countries. While some, if not all, of these efforts can be duplicated quite easily by accomplished competitors, Boeing relies on a trump card that in some cases is hard to match. The company gives the prospective buyer a complete system evaluation of the customer's existing fleet and route structure. Over the years, the Boeing aerospace engineers have developed very sophisticated computer software for forecasting air traffic demand, evaluations of various route structures, and the identification of optimal fleet configurations. In their sales presentations, the Boeing engineers will use the software to analyze the customer's need for new aircraft, given the existing fleet and its age, and suggest additions. As a hypothetical example, if the customer intends to buy two new A320 Airbuses, Boeing might be able to show how a combination of a 747 and two 737s will be more cost effective. The problem solution offered is validated by Boeing's years of experience and high-tech wizardry. This is proactive, relationship-building marketing.

Sources: Personal interviews; www.boeing.com.

Relationship Marketing

For the global marketer contemplating the business-to-business marketing task, it is helpful to anticipate establishing a long-term relationship with the local buyer and the buying organization. Relationship marketing is the term applied to a marketing effort involving various personalized services, creation of new and additional services, and customizing a company's offering to the needs of a special buyer. Although the idea of relationship marketing is adaptable to consumer markets, it is obviously more applicable in business-to-business marketing.[18] The Japanese vertical *keiretsus* provide good examples of what relationship marketing is about. As another example, Citibank has tried to attract and build strong relationships with wealthy customers in many countries by offering extended banking hours, a separate lobby with attractive decor, comfortable seating, and sometimes free drinks. Needless to say, culture influences the creation of a strong relationship in myriad ways.

Relationship marketing takes a long-term view since without it the effort required to build a relationship is hardly worth it. The up-front costs of developing the mutual trust and confidence of a relationship are greater than the revenues from a single sale. A dependable relationship is beneficial to both parties in the long run. The buyer does not have to go through the buying process every time a purchase is required. The seller overcomes the barriers created against competitive entry, thus justifying the investment in learning about the organizational culture, the particular people involved, the product and service requirements, and the local culture. The relationship must create a win–win situation (see box, "Boeing's Sales Pitch").

As in all relationships, power becomes an issue. Bosch, the German supplier of auto components and parts to many European auto companies, strives to maintain a good relationship with its customers. But after the firm opened a modern plant in Japan for the production of ABS braking systems, customers demanded that their new ABS systems should come from the superior Japan plant. Wanting to preserve good relations, Bosch had no choice but to consent, even though it meant curtailing production at its German plant.

The Limits to Cultural Sensitivity

Although the advantages of understanding and adapting to a foreign culture are evident, there can sometimes be "too much of a good thing." There are limits to which the marketing manager should go to try to accommodate the foreign culture if he or she wants to be effective, sometimes depending on the situation.

Nonadaptation

There is a case to be made for **nonadaptation.** First, it is important to recognize that when a country is ready for change, a different culture can be attractive. This is easiest to see in the formerly communist nations. Russians want genuine Americans, not adapted versions. They can do the adaptation on their own and expect the "real thing." The politically mandated changes in these countries have eroded the old norms and paved the way for new approaches. Here, attempting to adapt would be a mistake, since the locals want to learn from a successful foreign culture. It is important for the marketing manager to understand the historical and human context in which the firm's business dealings are taking place.

A second, more obvious caveat should be stated. Adaptation to another culture can easily seem superficial, lacking any deeper meaning or conviction. It can engender the same kind of sympathy as flattery does, but is clearly prone to misinterpretation, and may even create distrust.[19] The businessperson who wants to establish trust needs to present himself or herself sincerely and unequivocally. But when the manager is busy paying attention to his or her behavior in an unfamiliar setting it is very difficult to be clear, honest, and intuitive. It is easy to lose one's bearings; in fact, it is difficult to think. What comes to mind in such situations are often only random bits and pieces, and with bad luck, the manager can come out worse in the process. It takes preparation and a certain nerve to do what one does best.

In the end, adaptation to the customer's culture, while a nice gesture, should not be allowed to interfere with the intrinsic merits of the proposal. The notion that one should let personal likes and dislikes influence a business relationship, so popular in the early discussions of European, Japanese, and even American business, has been torpedoed as too expensive in the open competition in global markets.[20] Even in Japan, loyalties to suppliers and distributors who are not competitive have vanished into thin air as the market has opened up.[21]

Culture and The Three Hats

Culture impacts the three roles of the global marketing manager in different ways. Generally speaking, when foreign entry is contemplated, the skills will involve correct interpretation of some cultural signals and a fair knowledge of local middlemen in the particular country. In the local marketing phase, the specific culture needs to be understood at a much deeper level since customer requirements and consumer preferences have to be deciphered. When it comes to global management, the cultural issues revolve broadly around the question of the extent to which adaptation in the marketplace is always necessary, or whether cultural norms can be challenged.

Foreign Entry

Culture is intimately tied to the "way of doing business" in a country. Whether signed contracts are necessary or a simple handshake is sufficient is largely a matter of custom or business culture. When evaluating potential importers and distributors, not only their financial standing but also their social standing often matters. Establishing trust without personal friendship is impossible in some cultures—but "friendship" may be counterproductive. There are numerous incidents of principals feeling betrayed by their friendly local middlemen in a foreign market.

It is important to bear in mind that culture influences the "how" of business, but not necessarily the "what" of business. The functions of middlemen remain the same everywhere. The product shipped has to be guided through customs at the border; it has to be inspected, stored, and delivered to the appropriate outlets. Installation and after-sale service have to be completed where required, payments have to be made and remitted, and so on. What does differ between cultures is the way these functions are carried out, by whom, how fast, at what price, and so on.

For the marketer planning an entry into a foreign market, therefore, the analysis of its culture should center on what signs indicate a trustworthy and effective middleman or licensee, what are danger signals, and what behaviors suggest strengths and weaknesses. In this analysis there is little use for one's home culture, unless the countries are fairly similar. It is the lack of familiarity with foreign cultures that has made the "psychic" distance between countries a prime determinant of patterns of early expansion abroad. Europeans trade among themselves, Americans go to Canada, and the Japanese focus on Asia. Managers feel more comfortable with people similar to themselves and have more confidence in their evaluation of potential partners. As more experience accumulates, the managers learn to accept and assess very different cultures.

When investment in foreign manufacturing is contemplated, the risk exposure generally increases, and there is a greater need for more expert input. External legal advisers, political risk analysts, and financial intermediaries might all be needed. In addition, it becomes important to predict how cultural factors will affect the management and efficient operation of the plant. This requires specialist advice in local labor relations and a keen appreciation of how culture affects the workers in the country. The expatriate manager needs to have spent some time in the country, to have at least moderate language capability, and be willing to adapt to some of the local customs. One reason foreign direct investment is sometimes forgone in favor of granting a license to a local manufacturer is the cultural complications arising in managing a foreign labor force.

Local Marketing

When we come to local marketing abroad, cultural factors relate directly to the marketplace. In addition to being an influence on managerial behavior, culture is a strong determinant of consumer demand. For the marketer it is no longer sufficient to develop cultural sensitivity and to learn to accept individuals who act in strange ways. Now culture is involved in understanding and predicting local buyer behavior.

For the manager, there is now no escaping the need for first-hand personal experience of the people in the local market. Although market research reports can suggest the needs, wants, and desires of potential and actual customers, it is always necessary to interpret survey findings and related statistics in the context of the actual buying situation. Experience in the domestic setting, where the context is

Monks at a shopping plaza in Bangkok facing modern society. It is not difficult to imagine the curiosity and tension within these young boys sworn to a life of austerity and minimal material possessions when confronted with the new products wrought by capitalism and advanced technology. Dilip Metha/Contact Press Images.

familiar and therefore not so salient, blinds one to this fact. In a foreign market, where the type of outlets, retail assortments, infrastructure, and other contextual factors are different, demand analysis needs to account for underlying cultural drivers and other basic forces.

A few examples will illustrate these points. The first automatic laundromats introduced by Americans in Germany after World War II failed because German housewives, although eager to clean the family clothes, were not about to show their dirty linen in public. Despite a strong demand for Western ice cream, ice cream parlors did not take off in Tokyo until intensive promotion and advertising made it "hip" for young people to stand on the street and eat their ice cream (high rent for space prohibited seating in the parlors). Wearing Western brand-name clothes in the former communist countries was an act of protest and daring as much as a statement of taste and preference.

Western markets tend to be analyzed in terms of individual consumer behavior, treating social and cultural factors as subservient to internal psychological mechanisms for product and brand choice. Although these issues will be covered in more detail later, it should be noted here that this represents a significant bias to be recognized when marketing locally in foreign countries. Of course, in all markets the actors are individuals. But the notion that social and cultural factors in some way are subordinated to the cognitive and affective processes that the individual goes through is sometimes misleading when predicting choices and buying decisions of consumers in foreign cultures. The decisive factors can often be the social and cultural norms.

Examples abound, and not only from group-oriented societies. The desire to belong to a certain social class makes people buy a Mercedes although they would perhaps rather have a BMW. The force of popular pressure makes people order coffee when they want tea. In Germany, and in many other places, the need not to be too different leads consumers to forgo innovative new products in favor of the tried-and-true. More on these factors will be presented in Chapter 7 on buyer behavior.

While such behavior is usually interpreted by Western observers as a simple trade-off between individual preferences and social norms, the process at work is often subtler. The products are not bought to satisfy individuals, but to satisfy others, such as peers and relatives. Of course, one can always argue that "really" the person is satisfying his or her individual desires, but the fundamental lesson is that to predict choices and buying decisions, individual preferences are not so important.

A somewhat extreme example can be used to drive home this point. While in the West most people would marry because they find their partner attractive, in a society where marriages are arranged, as is often the case in India and Japan, the idea that your wife should be attractive is not so important. An attractive partner may attract unwanted attention and even interfere with your life and work—something not completely unknown in the West! When agreeing to an arranged marriage—or buying a car, a house, a suit, a television set—the individual's particular likes or dislikes thus may be much less important to the decision maker than the desire to keep all involved parties at ease. In poorer countries, the focus on the individual can be even more misleading. After all, if you are the decision maker in a large family, your own tastes perhaps should be the last to be satisfied.

Trying to convince a buyer to use disposable, nonrecyclable packaging does not accomplish much when social worth is measured by the sacrifice involved in recycling. In local marketing, it is absolutely necessary to understand the local culture, the moral norms, the social forces that impinge on the individual. Unless this is done, the decision maker cannot interpret market research correctly, since responses and words can mean so many different things in different contexts. Here the manager needs to know when he or she doesn't understand—the first step to "enlightenment."

Global Management

When the task is global integration of the marketing effort across various countries, understanding cultural forces means something quite different again. Here the marketer needs to understand the extent to which cultural forces are malleable and perhaps already changing. The task involves less any particular knowledge about the content of various cultures and more an astute judgment of what the dynamics are and in which direction a country might be heading. Globalization, and any accompanying standardization, often involves going against cultural traditions.

An example will illustrate some of the issues involved. There is less reason to engage in an in-depth assessment of cultural norms in Russia today. The political and economic changes sweeping over the country suggest that a new order is slowly emerging, and the lawlessness and lack of direction reported in the news media are an expression of a culture in which traditional guideposts lack legitimacy and credibility. Russia's mandate is for change—and the promise of American culture and capitalism has opened the door for entrepreneurs who would not have been listened to before. To try to "adapt" to Russia's norms today would be counterproductive and even impossible, since those norms are not yet worked out.

For global management, the issue of standardization of products, services, promotions, communication systems, and control procedures is paramount. To coordinate activities in multiple countries, comparability is necessary, and thus standardization becomes critical. By its very nature, standardization will cut across cultural lines. What the manager has to do is evaluate which lines can (and which cannot) be crossed with impunity and which particular country's standards should be chosen as the general guide. An assessment of the degree of flux in a country needs to be carried out, and a seasoned judgment about the real and imagined obstacles to standardization has to be made. This is transnational management at its most fundamental level, and much more will be said on this topic later.

Summary

This chapter has introduced the central role of culture in global marketing and how to do business. Culture has a direct effect on consumer behavior and on managerial behavior. The modern concept of culture focuses directly on observable behavior. Such behavior is often the result of the enculturation processes of a society. Awareness of culture should affect *how* a manager should decide or negotiate, but not *what* should be decided or negotiated.

After discussing the impact of culture on consumer behavior in some detail, the chapter discussed several frameworks for cultural analysis, identifying some major cultures around the world. We showed how culture helps develop certain managerial skills—and downplays others—which explains why managers from different nations tend to behave differently even though what they want to achieve is the same. This is why culture tends to affect implementation and execution more than strategy formulation, and why a degree of cultural adaptation is so urgent.

The need to develop negotiation skills to establish partnerships was discussed and illustrated with specific examples. From a cultural viewpoint it is important to recognize how one's own words and behavior will be perceived by the potential partner, and vice versa. While some adaption to the behavioral norms of a host country is necessary, facile attempts at complete familiarity may backfire by eroding trust. This is important not only in negotiations but also in industrial marketing, where the organizational culture of the buyer is an important influence on the decision-making process.

Culture plays a different role in each of the three marketing tasks. In foreign entry, culture has a direct impact on negotiations with potential middlemen and alliance partners. In local marketing, the question is how to treat local employees and, in particular, how consumer demand is affected by local tastes and needs. In global management, it's often "forget the cultural differences" time, since it is now a question how far they can be changed, and cultural analysis is useful for assessing the amount of potential damage that can be absorbed in a strategy of standardization.

Key Terms

body language, *61*
Confucianist dynamics, *68*
cultural adaptation, *65*
cultural dilemmas, *72*
culture, *64*
decoding cultures, *69*
diversity, *66*
Gannon's metaphors, *69*
high and low context
cultures, *65*

high versus low power
distance, *66*
Hofstede's cultural
dimensions, *66*
individualism versus
collectivism, *66*
learned behavior, *65*
managerial styles, *70*
masculine versus feminine, *67*
multicultural, *65*

nonadaptation, *78*
nonverbal communication, *73*
particularist, *72*
Rapaille's archetypes, *69*
"silent languages", *66*
trust, *66*
type A negotiator, *74*
type B negotiator, *74*
uncertainty avoidance, *67*
universalist, *72*

Discussion Questions

1. An American manager can often be heard to start out saying, "Well, the way I see it . . . ." while a Norwegian as often will start with, "Well, as we all know . . ." What cultural explanation can you find for this?

2. Look for the Web sites of a few of the companies mentioned in this book. To what extent do they attempt to create a relationship with you? For example, do they offer screensavers with their logo for downloading, offer more information at your request, or allow you to use the site interactively? How many languages are available? Any differences for companies from different countries?

3. Discuss the extent to which electronic commerce (online purchases, Internet shopping, etc.) might be acceptable to a culture. Does this have anything to do with Hall's or Hofstede's dimensions? Give examples of cultures that would be reluctant to accept electronic commerce and others that might accept it more easily.

4. What behavioral differences would you expect to find between the managers in a large German multinational and in an American MNC in the same industry? What factors might make their behavior very similar?

5. In negotiations it is often said that "silence is golden." Give an example of what this might mean. What kind of culture would you expect to favor that rule, high context or low context?

Notes

1. See Sujan et al., 1993.
2. See Hall, 1976.
3. See Hall, 1960.
4. See, for example, Anderson and Venkatesan, 1994; and Levine and Wolf, 1985.
5. See Hofstede, 1980.
6. See Hofstede, 1988.
7. Gannon, 1994.
8. A good introduction to doing business abroad can be found in the books by Brake et al., 1994, and Becker, 2000.
9. Good examples of these cultural effects can be found in Harris and Moran, 1987; Terpstra and David, 1991; and Barsoux and Lawrence, 1991.
10. These characterizations draw on Durlabhji and Marks, 1993; Hall, 1976; and Harris and Moran, 1987.
11. See, for example, Hall and Hall, 1990; Graham and Sano, 1984; and Schuster and Copeland, 1996. All give a good overview of how effective negotiation strategies vary for different cultures and emphasize in particular the techniques for getting into the buyer's network.
12. Fukuyama, 1995, emphasizes strongly the positive role of trust in business transactions and economic success.
13. See, for example, Tung, 1988, and Graham et al., 1994. Tung's treatment illustrates many of the communication problems encountered in international negotiations.
14. See Graham, 1983; Graham and Sano, 1984; and Graham et al., 1994.
15. See Graham and Sano, 1984.
16. See Salacuse, 1991.
17. This section draws on Rangan et al., 1995, and Dwyer and Tanner, 2005.
18. Some European researchers have developed the relationship marketing paradigm into a much broader approach, including applications to consumer goods marketing. See, in particular, Gummesson, 1999.

19. See Francis, 1991.
20. See, for example, D'Aveni, 1994.
21. See, for example, Blustein, 1995.

Selected References

Anderson, Beverlee B., and M. Venkatesan. "Temporal Dimensions of Consuming Behavior across Cultures." Chapter 9 in Hassan, Salah S., and Roger D. Blackwell, eds. *Global Marketing: Perspectives and Cases.* Fort Worth, TX: Dryden, 1994.

Barsoux, Jean-Louis, and Peter Lawrence. "The Making of a French Manager." *Harvard Business Review,* July–August 1991, pp. 58–67.

Becker, Kip. *Culture and International Business.* Oxford: Routledge, 2000.

Bellah, Robert et al. *Habits of the Mind.* Berkeley: University of California Press, 1989.

Benedict, Ruth. *The Chrysanthemum and the Sword.* Tokyo: Charles E. Tuttle, 1954.

Blustein, Paul. "Giant Trading Companies Battle to Preserve Japan Inc.'s Edge." *Washington Post,* April 12, 1995, pp. A18, A19.

Brake, Terence; Danielle Medina Walker; and Walker Thomas. *Doing Business Internationally: The Guide to Cross-Cultural Success.* New York: McGraw-Hill Professional Publishing, 1994.

Brooks, John. *Showing Off in America.* Boston: Little, Brown, 1981.

Clifford, Bill. "Yes, Those U.S. Apple Growers Protest No Access." *The Nikkei Weekly,* April 19, 1993. p. 4.

D'Aveni, Richard. *Hypercompetition.* New York: Free Press, 1994.

Durlabhji, Subhash, and Norton E. Marks, eds. *Japanese Business: Cultural Perspectives.* Albany, NY: SUNY Press, 1993.

Dwyer, F. Robert, and John F. Tanner. *Business Marketing: Connecting Strategy, Relationships, and Learning.* New York: McGraw-Hill/Irwin, 2005.

Fukuyama, Francis. *Trust: The Social Virtues and the Creation of Prosperity.* New York: Free Press, 1995.

Francis, June N. P. "When in Rome? The Effects of Cultural Adaptation on Intercultural Business Negotiations." *Journal of International Business Studies,* Third Quarter 1991, pp. 403–28.

Gannon, Martin, and Associates. *Understanding Global Cultures: Metaphorical Journeys through 17 Countries.* Thousand Oaks, CA: Sage, 1994.

Graham, John L. "Business Negotiations in Japan, Brazil, and the United States." *Journal of International Business Studies* 14 (Spring–Summer 1983), pp. 47–62.

Graham, John L.; Alma T. Mintu; and Waymond Rodgers. "Explorations of Negotiations Behaviors in Ten Foreign Cultures Using a Model Developed in the United States." *Management Science* 40, no. 1 (January 1994), pp. 72–95.

Graham, John L., and Yoshihiro Sano. *Smart Bargaining with the Japanese.* New York: Ballinger, 1984.

Gummesson, Evert. *Total Relationship Marketing.* Oxford: Butterworth-Heinemann, 1999.

Hall, Edward T. *Beyond Culture.* Garden City, NY: Anchor, 1976.

———. "The Silent Language in Overseas Business." *Harvard Business Review,* May–June 1960, pp. 87–96.

Hall, Edward T., and Mildred Reed Hall. *Understanding Cultural Differences.* Yarmouth, ME: Intercultural Press, 1990.

Harris, Philip R., and Robert T. Moran. *Managing Cultural Differences.* Houston, TX: Gulf, 1987.

Hofstede, Geert. *Culture's Consequences.* Beverly Hills, CA: Sage, 1980.

———. "The Confucius Connection: From Cultural Roots to Economic Growth." *Organizational Dynamics* 16, no. 4 (Spring 1988), pp. 5–21.

Huddleston, Jackson N., Jr. *Gaijin Kaisha: Running a Foreign Business in Japan.* Tokyo: Charles Tuttle, 1990.

Levine, R., and E. Wolff. "Social Time: The Heartbeat of Culture." *Psychology Today,* March 1985, p. 35.

March, Robert M. *The Japanese Negotiator.* Tokyo: Kodansha, 1990.

Rangan, V. Kasturi; Benson P. Shapiro; and Rowland T. Moriarty. *Business Marketing Strategy: Concepts and Applications.* Chicago: Irwin, 1995.

Rapaille, G. Clotaire. *7 Secrets of Marketing in a Multi-Cultural World.* Provo, UT: Executive Excellence Publishing, 2001.

Salacuse, Jeswald W. *Making Global Deals.* Boston: Houghton Mifflin, 1991.

Schuster, Camille, and Michael Copeland. *Global Business: Planning for Sales and Negotiations.* Fort Worth, TX: Dryden, 1996.

Sujan, Mita; James R. Bettman; and Hans Baumgartner. "Influencing Consumer Judgments Using Autobiographical Memories: A Self-Referencing Perspective." *Journal of Marketing Research* XXX (November 1993), pp. 422–36.

Tan, Joo Seng. Strategies for Effective Cross-Cultural Negotiation: The F.R.A.M.E. Approach. Singapore: McGraw-Hill (Asia), 2004.

Terpstra, Vern, and Kenneth David. *The Cultural Environment of International Business,* 3rd ed. Cincinnati: South-Western, 1991.

Trompenaars, Fons, and Charles Hampden-Turner. *Riding the Waves of Culture: Understanding Diversity in Global Business,* 2nd ed. New York: McGraw-Hill, 1998.

———. Managing People Across Cultures. London: Capstone, 2004.

Tung, Rosalie. "Toward a Concept of International Business Negotiations." In Farmer, Richard, ed. *Advances in International Comparative Management.* Greenwich, CT: JAI Press, 1988, pp. 203–19.

Usunier, Jean-Claude. *Marketing Across Cultures,* 2nd ed. London: Prentice-Hall, 1996.

Veblen, Thorstein. *The Theory of the Leisure Class.* New York: New American Library, 1899.

Cases

IKEA's Global Strategy: Furnishing the World

IKEA is a furniture manufacturer and retailer, well known throughout the world for its knockdown furniture. Its large retail stores in the blue-and-yellow colors of the Swedish flag are located on the outskirts of major cities, attracting shoppers who are looking for modern designs at good value. The low-cost operation relies on buyers with automobiles to carry the disassembled furniture in packaged kits and assemble the pieces at home.

The IKEA case is interesting because it shows how even retailers can go global once the key competitive advantages of the offering are standardized. The case focuses on the American entry, which posed barriers IKEA had not encountered before and which forced adaptation of some features.

IKEA, the Swedish furniture store chain virtually unknown outside of Scandinavia 25 years ago, has drawn large opening crowds to its stores as it has pushed into Europe, Asia, and North America. Along the way it has built something of a cult following, especially among young and price-conscious consumers. But the expansion was not always smooth and easy, for example, in Germany and Canada, and particularly difficult in the United States.

Company Background

IKEA was founded in 1943 by Ingvar Kamprad to serve price-conscious neighbors in the province of Smaland in southern Sweden. Early on, the young entrepreneur hit upon a winning formula, contracting with independent furniture makers and suppliers to design furniture that could be sold as a kit and assembled in the consumer's home. In return for favorable and guaranteed orders from IKEA, the suppliers were prohibited from selling to other stores. Developing innovative modular designs whose components could be mass-produced and venturing early into eastern Europe to build a dedicated supplier network, IKEA could offer quality furniture in modern Scandinavian designs at very low prices. By investing profits in new stores, the company expanded throughout Scandinavia in the 1950s.

Throughout the following years, the IKEA store design and layout remained the same; IKEA was basically a warehouse store. Because the ready-to-assemble "knockdown" kits could be stacked conveniently on racks, inventory was always large, and instead of waiting for the store to deliver the furniture, IKEA's customers could pick it up themselves. Stores were therefore located outside of the big cities, with ample parking space for automobiles. Inside, an assembled version of the furniture was displayed in settings along with other IKEA furniture. The purchaser could decide on what to buy, obtain the inventory tag number, and then either find the kit on the rack, or, in the case of larger pieces, have the kit delivered through the back door to the waiting car.

This simple formula meant that there were relatively few sales clerks on the floor to help customers sort through the more than 10,000 products stocked. The sales job consisted mainly of making sure that the assembled pieces were attractively displayed, that clear instructions were given as to where the kits could be found, and that customers did not have to wait too long at the checkout lines. IKEA's was a classic "cash-and-carry" approach, except that credit cards were accepted.

EXHIBIT 1 IKEA Sales Data

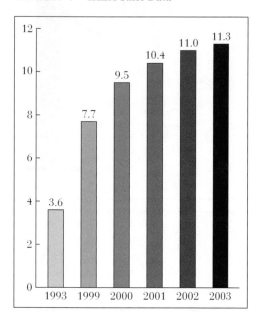

Turnover for the IKEA Group

Sales for the IKEA Group for the financial
year 2003 (1 September 2002 – 31 August 2003)
totalled 11.3 billion euro (US$12.2 billion).

This approach, which trims costs to a minimum, is dependent on IKEA's global sourcing network of more than 2,300 suppliers in 67 countries. Because IKEA's designers work closely with suppliers, savings are built into all its products from the outset. Also, since the same furniture is sold all around the world, IKEA reaps huge economies of scale from the size of its stores and the big production runs necessary to stock them. Therefore, IKEA is able to match rivals on quality while undercutting them up to 30 percent on price.

To draw the customers to the distant stores, the company relies on word-of-mouth, limited advertising, and its catalogues. These catalogues are delivered free of charge in the mailboxes of potential customers living in the towns and cities within reach of a store. The catalogues depict the merchandise not only as independent pieces of furniture but also together in actual settings of a living room, bedroom, children's room, and so on. This enables the company to demonstrate its philosophy of creating a "living space," not just selling furniture. It also helps the potential buyer visualize a complete room and simplifies the planning of furnishing a home. It also shows how IKEA's various components are stylistically integrated into a complete and beautiful whole. Even though furniture is hardly high-tech, the philosophy is reminiscent of the way high-tech producers, such as mobile phone makers, attempt to develop add-on features that fit their particular brand and not others.

As the company has grown, the catalogue has increased in volume and in circulation. By 2003, the worldwide circulation of the 360-page catalogue reached over 130 million, making it the world's largest printed publication distributed for free. In 2003 the catalogue was distributed in 36 countries and 28 languages, showing more than 3,000 items from storage solutions

and kitchen renovation ideas to office furniture and bedroom furnishings.

Sales totaled about 12.2 billion U.S. dollars in 2003, with a net profit margin around 6–7 percent. Of this, Europe accounted for over 80 percent of revenues, with Asia accounting for 3 percent, and North America 15 percent. The huge stores are relatively few in number—only 175 worldwide but growing rapidly—and the company employs about 76,000 people around the world (see Exhibits 1 and 2). Many of the stores have only one expatriate Swedish manager at the top, sufficient to instill the lean Ingvar Kamprad and IKEA ethos in the local organization.

Although the firm remains private, it continues to innovate and reorganize itself. For instance, fast decision making is aided by a management structure that is as flat as the firm's knockdown furniture kits, with only four layers separating IKEA's chief executive from its checkout workers. In 1992 IKEA abolished internal budgets and now each region must merely keep below a fixed ratio of costs to turnover.

European Expansion

In the 1960s and 70s, as modern Scandinavian design became increasingly popular, expansion into Europe became a logical next step. The company first entered the German-speaking regions of Switzerland, thereby testing itself in a small region similar to Scandinavia. Yet expansion so far away from Sweden made it necessary to develop new suppliers, which meant that Kamprad traveled extensively, visiting potential suppliers and convincing them to become exclusive IKEA suppliers. Once the supply chain was established, the formula of consumer-assembled furniture could be used. After some resistance

EXHIBIT 2   **IKEA Retail Operations**

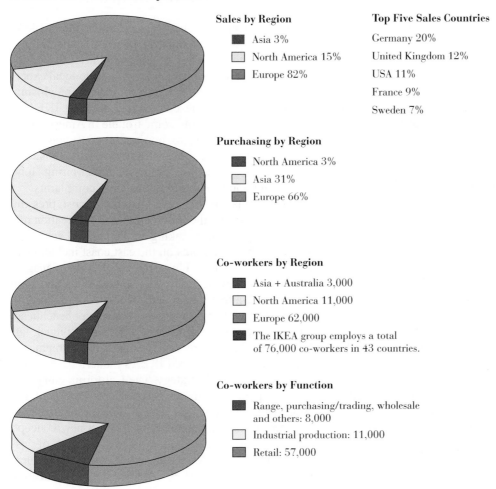

Sales by Region

- ■ Asia 3%
- ☐ North America 15%
- ■ Europe 82%

Top Five Sales Countries

Germany 20%

United Kingdom 12%

USA 11%

France 9%

Sweden 7%

Purchasing by Region

- ■ North America 3%
- ☐ Asia 31%
- ■ Europe 66%

Co-workers by Region

- ■ Asia + Australia 3,000
- ☐ North America 11,000
- ■ Europe 62,000
- ■ The IKEA group employs a total of 76,000 co-workers in 43 countries.

Co-workers by Function

- ■ Range, purchasing/trading, wholesale and others: 8,000
- ☐ Industrial production: 11,000
- ■ Retail: 57,000

Top Five Purchasing Countries

China 18%

Poland 12%

Sweden 9%

Italy 7%

from independent furniture retailers who claimed that the furniture was not really "Swedish," since much of it came from other countries, IKEA's quality/price advantage proved irresistible even to fastidious Swiss consumers.

The next logical target was Germany, much bigger than Switzerland, but also culturally close to IKEA's roots. In Germany, well-established and large furniture chains were formidable foes opposed to the competitive entry and there were several regulatory obstacles. The opening birthday celebration of the first store in 1974 outside Cologne was criticized because in German culture birthdays should be celebrated only every 25 years. The use of the Swedish flag and the blue-yellow colors was challenged because the IKEA subsidiary was an incorporated German company (IKEA GmbH). The celebratory breakfast was mistitled

because no eggs were served. Despite these rearguard actions from the established German retailers, IKEA GmbH became very successful, and was thus accepted, being voted German marketer of the year in 1979. The acceptance of IKEA's way of doing business was helped by the fact that IKEA had enlarged the entire market by its low prices, and some of the established retailers adopted the same formula in their own operations.

To get the stores abroad started, Kamprad usually sent a team of three or four managers who could speak the local language and had experience in an existing IKEA store. This team hired and trained the sales employees, organized the store layout, and established the sales and ordering routines. Although the tasks were relatively simple and straightforward, IKEA's lean organizational strategies meant that individual employees were assigned greater responsibilities and more freedom than usual in more traditional retail stores. Although this was not a problem in Europe and Japan (where its Japanese-sounding name also was an advantage), it was a problem in the United States.

Canadian Entry

To prepare for eventual entry into the United States, IKEA first expanded into Canada. The Canadian market was close to the U.S. market, and creating the supply network for Canada would lay the foundation for what was needed for the much larger U.S. market. Drawing upon a successful advertising campaign and positive word-of-mouth, and by combining newly recruited local suppliers with imports from existing European suppliers, the Canadian entry was soon a success. The advertising campaign was centered around the slogan, "IKEA: The impossible furniture store from Sweden," which was supported by a cartoon drawing of a moose's head, complete with antlers. The moose symbol had played very well in Germany, creating natural associations "with the north," and also creating an image of fun and games that played well in the younger segments the company targeted. The Canadians responded equally well to the slogan and the moose, as well as to IKEA's humorous cartoonlike ads poking fun at its Swedish heritage ("How many Swedes does it take to screw in a lightbulb? Two—one to screw in the lightbulb, and one to park the Volvo"), which became often-heard jokes.

The United States presented a much different challenge, as it offered a much larger market with its population dispersed, great cultural diversity, and strong domestic competition. The initial problems centered around which part of the United States to attack first. While the east coast seemed more natural, with its closer ties to Europe, the California market on the west coast was demographically more attractive. But trafficking supplies to California would be a headache, and competition seemed stronger there, with the presence of established retailers of Scandinavian designs.

Then, there was the issue of managing the stores. In Canada, the European management style had been severely tested. The unusually great independence and authority of each individual employee in the IKEA system had been welcomed, but the individuals often asked for more direction and specific guidance. For example, the Swedish start-up team would say to an employee, "You are in charge of the layout of the office furniture section of the store," and consider this a perfectly actionable and complete job description. This seemed to go against the training and predisposition of some employees, who came back with questions such as, "How should this piece of furniture be displayed?" IKEA's expansion team suspected that the situation would be possibly even more difficult in the United States. The team also wondered if the same slogan and the moose symbol would be as effective in the United States as it had been in Germany and Canada.

Entry Hurdles in the United States

From the outset IKEA had succeeded despite breaking many of the standard rules of international retailing: enter a market only after exhaustive study; cater to local tastes as much as possible; and tap into local expertise through acquisitions, joint ventures, or franchising. Although breaking these rules had not hurt IKEA in Europe, the firm got into some trouble in America with its initial seven stores; six on the east coast and one in California. Many people visited the stores, looked at the furniture, and left empty-handed, citing long queues and nonavailable stock as chief complaints.

IKEA managers believed that their most pressing problem in entering the U.S. market was the creation of a stable supply chain. By taking an incremental approach, starting with a few stores on the east coast including an initial one outside Philadelphia, IKEA managers believed that they had ensured a smooth transition from the eastern United States, with its relative proximity to European suppliers, and its Canadian beachhead. Although the store in southern California was much farther away, its large market and customer demographics—young and active—favored IKEA's modern designs and assemble-it-yourself strategy. The California entry was also precipitated by the emergence of a local imitator, "Stør," which had opened ahead of IKEA, capitalizing on the word-of-mouth generated by IKEA'S new concept.

IKEA's early effort had problems because of less adaptation to the American market than customers desired. For example, IKEA decided not to reconfigure its bedroom furniture to the different dimensions used in the American market. As a result, the European-style beds sold by IKEA were slightly narrower and longer than standard American beds, and customers' existing mattresses and sheets did not fit the beds. Even though IKEA stocked European-sized sheets in the stores, bed sales remained very slow. IKEA ended up redesigning about a fifth of its American product range and sales immediately increased by around 30–40 percent.

The American suppliers, whom IKEA gradually recruited to reduce the dependence on imports, also proved in need of upgrading and instruction in IKEA's way of producing furniture. IKEA sent its people to the suppliers' plants, providing technical tips about more efficient methods and helping the suppliers shop around for better-quality or lower-price materials. IKEA produces about 45 percent of the furniture sold in its American stores locally, up from 15 percent just a few years earlier. Although supplies shifted to Asia for a while once the China market had been entered and new suppliers there had been developed, IKEA has moved back to local suppliers. This has helped against the traditional environmental objection to big-box chain stores, that shipping goods from all over the world is incredibly energy intensive. In turn this has helped the firm cut prices in its

EXHIBIT 3

EXHIBIT 4

It's a big country. Someone's got to furnish it.

American stores. The American difficulties also high-lighted how growth could lead to quality problems in managing its increasingly complex global supply chain, so IKEA began conducting random checks.

Other adaptations to the American market proved just as successful. For instance, new cash registers were installed to speed throughput by 20 percent, with the goal of elimi-nating long checkout lines. Store layout was altered to con-form more to American aesthetics and shopping styles. A more generous return policy than in Europe was instituted and a next-day delivery service was implemented.

Promotion

While some managers helped establish the supply side of the stores, IKEA's marketing staff was busy with the pro-motional side of the business. Store locations had generally disadvantaged IKEA relative to competitors. Because of the huge size of the stores (typically around 200,000 square feet), the need to keep a large inventory so that cus-tomers could get the purchased furniture immediately, and the amount of land needed for parking around each store, most stores were located in out-of-the-way places—next to the airport in New Jersey in one case and in a shopping mall 20 miles south of Washington, DC, in another. Thus, advertising was needed to make potential customers aware of store locations. It was thought that lower prices and

selection would do the rest—positive word-of-mouth had proven the best advertising in most other markets.

But in the United States' competitive retail climate IKEA found that more-focused media advertising was needed. As one manager stated: "In Europe you advertise to gain business; in the United States you advertise to stay in business." The diversity of the consumers made word-of-mouth less powerful than in ethnically more homogeneous countries. Management decided that a strong slogan and unique advertising message were going to be necessary to really bring awareness close to the levels in other countries.

The Moose symbol of IKEA (see Exhibit 3), although successful in Germany and Canada, was considered strange and too provincial for the U.S. market and would project the wrong image especially in California. Instead IKEA, in collaboration with its New York–based adver-tising agency Deutsch, developed a striking slogan that combined the down-home touch of the company philos-ophy with the humorous touch of the Moose: "It's a big country. Someone's got to furnish it" (see Exhibit 4).

Following the success of this advertising strategy, the company ventured further to establish itself as a pioneer-ing store and to attract new kinds of customers. IKEA and Deutsch developed a series of eight TV advertising spots that featured people at different transitional stages in their lives, when they were most likely to be in the market for furniture. One spot featured a young family who had just bought a new house, another a couple whose children had just left home, and so on. IKEA even developed one spot that featured a homosexual couple, two men talking about furnishing their home. It was a daring step, applauded by most advertising experts and impartial observers. The campaign had a positive impact on IKEA's image—and on IKEA's sales. The company has continued the trend. One 30-second TV spot showed a divorced woman buying fur-niture for the first time on her own.

The privately held company won't reveal income figures, but it is successful in each of the market areas where it has located its U.S. stores. It is credited with being partly respon-sible for a shift in furniture buying behavior in the United States. Choosing furniture has become a matter of persona-lity, lifestyle, and emotions in addition to functionality. IKEA's managers like that—they want IKEA to be associated with the "warmest, most emotional furniture in the world."

Discussion Questions

1. What are IKEA's firm-specific advantages? Country-specific advantages?

2. What are the cultural factors that make expansion abroad in retailing difficult? What has made it possible in IKEA's case?

3. Describe how IKEA's expansion has reenergized mature markets around the world and changed the competitive situation.

4. How does the TV advertising campaign initiated by IKEA overcome the entry barrier of high advertising expenditures?

5. Should IKEA expand further in the United States or focus on other countries?

Sources: Case compiled by Paul Kolesa from Rita Martenson, "Innovations in International Retailing," University of Gothenburg, Sweden: Liber, 1981; "Furnishing the world," *The Economist,* November 19, 1994, pp. 79–80; Richard Stevenson, "IKEA's New Realities: Recession and Aging Consumers," *New York Times,* April 25, 1993, p. F4; Kate Fitzgerald, "IKEA Dares to Reveal Gays Buy Tables Too," *Advertising Age,* March 12, 1994, pp. 3, 41; Vito Pilieci. "The IKEA catalogue: Swedish for massive circulation," *Calgary Herald,* August 27, 2003, p. C1; David Roberts, "Swedening the Pot," www.grist.org, February 27, 2007.

Case 1-2

Globalization Headaches at Whirlpool

Whirlpool is a leading American home appliance manufacturer. Predicting that the appliance market would gradually be globalized, the company bought the appliance business of Dutch Philips in 1989 and embarked on a global strategy.

The case details what happened in the globalization process. It is an interesting story because the process has not been smooth, and the case shows the potential problems involved in shifting to a global strategy. The Whirlpool experience provides an illuminating counterpoint to the relative success of IKEA.

For Whirlpool, the Benton Harbor, Michigan, company going global was initially "less than rewarding," according to Russell Leavitt, an analyst with Salomon Smith Barney. Since 1994, Whirlpool, which dominated the U.S. appliance market with sales of $12.2 billion in 2003, and a 35 percent share of the U.S. market, had tried to enter the European and Asian markets. Unfortunately, this resulted in $60 million in operating losses in Asia in 1997, $16 million in 1998, unprofitable quarters in Europe, and the redesign of half its products.

Background

Whirlpool was the leader in the U.S. appliance market ($22.5 billion) with brands such as Whirlpool, KitchenAid, and Roper. In the United States, General Electric (GE) was second, with a 32 percent market share, followed by Maytag, with 15 percent, Electrolux's Frigidaire, with 10 percent, and Raytheon Corp.'s Amana division, with 7 percent. Whirlpool made washers and dryers for Sears Roebuck and Co.'s Kenmore brand. Whirlpool was also the number one appliance maker in Latin America in a partnership with the Brazilian manufacturer Brasmotor SA, which made most of its appliances. Exhibit 1 provides the overall financial summary for 2002 and 2003, the development of key financial

ratios over a 10-year period is shown in Exhibit 2, and regional sales and profits are given in Exhibit 3.

EXHIBIT 1   Financial Summary

(Millions of U.S. $, except per share data)	2003	2002	% Change
Net sales	$12,176	$11,016	10.5%
Earnings from continuing operations	$ 414	$ 262	58.0%
Per share on a diluted basis	$ 5.91	$ 3.78	56.3%
Net earnings (loss)	$ 414	$ (394)	NM
Per share on a diluted basis	$ 5.91	$ (5.68)	NM
Stockholders' equity	$ 1,301	$ 739	76.0%
Total assets	$ 7,361	$ 6,631	11.0%
Return on equity	42.9%	14.8%	
Return on assets	6.1%	3.4%	
Book value per share	$ 18.56	$ 10.67	73.9%
Dividends per share	$ 1.36	$ 1.36	–
Average dividend yield	2.2%	2.2%	
Total return to stockholders	41.7%	(26.9)%	
Share price			
High	$ 73.35	$ 79.80	
Low	$ 42.80	$ 39.23	
Close	$ 72.65	$ 52.22	39.1%
Total return to stockholders (five-year annualized)	8.1%	1.4%	
Shares outstanding (in 000's)	68,931	68,226	1.0%
Number of registered stockholders	8,178	8,556	(4.4)%
Number of employees	68,407	68,272	0.2%

EXHIBIT 2 Key Financial Ratios

(millions of U.S. $, except share and employee data)	2003	2002	2001	2000	1999	1998	1997	1996	1995	1994	1993
Key Ratios											
Operating profit margin	6.8%	6.3%	3.0%	7.8%	8.3%	6.7%	0.1%	3.3%	4.5%	4.7%	6.8%
Pre-tax margin	5.4%	4.5%	0.9%	5.6%	4.9%	5.5%	(2.0)%	1.2%	2.6%	3.4%	5.7%
Net margin	3.4%	2.4%	0.3%	3.6%	3.3%	3.0%	(0.5)%	1.7%	2.4%	1.8%	3.5%
Return on average stockholders' equity	42.9%	14.8%	1.3%	20.7%	17.9%	17.2%	(0.8)%	8.2%	11.6%	9.4%	14.2%
Return on average total assets	6.1%	3.4%	0.4%	5.5%	4.2%	4.6%	(0.7)%	1.8%	3.0%	2.8%	4.0%
Current assets to current liabilities	1.1x	0.9x	1.1x	1.0x	1.1x	1.2x	1.2x	0.9x	0.9x	1.0x	1.0x
Total debt-appliance business as a percent of invested capital	50.9%	65.1%	48.0%	49.4%	37.7%	43.5%	46.1%	44.2%	45.2%	35.6%	33.8%
Price-earnings ratio	12.3x	(9.2)x	236.5x	9.2x	14.3x	13.0x	–	22.4x	19.2x	23.9x	21.2x
Interest coverage	5.8x	4.5x	1.6x	4.2x	4.1x	3.2x	–	1.6x	2.7x	3.6x	5.0x
Other Data											
Number of common shares outstanding (in thousands):											
Average—on a diluted basis	70,082	69,267	68,036	70,637	76,044	76,507	74,697	77,178	76,812	77,588	76,013
Year-end	68,931	68,226	67,215	66,265	74,463	76,089	75,262	74,415	74,081	73,845	73,068
Number of stockholders (year-end)	8,178	8,556	8,840	11,780	12,531	13,584	10,171	11,033	11,686	11,821	11,438
Number of employees (year-end)	68,407	68,272	61,923	62,527	62,706	59,885	62,419	49,254	46,546	39,671	40,071
Total return to stockholders (five-year annualized)	8.1%	1.4%	12.2%	0.3%	7.9%	(1.2)%	6.8%	6.3%	20.8%	12.0%	25.8%

Global Expansion

In the 1990s, Whirlpool invested heavily in its overseas operations. To convince shareholders and reflect its new "cosmopolitan" face, Whirlpool's 1990 Annual Report featured postage stamps from all around the world. In 1993, the annual report had a tiny compass attached to the front cover and, in 1994, Chairman David R. Whitwam

EXHIBIT 3 Business Units Sales and Operating Profit

Source: Whirlpool Annual Reports (2003, 2002)

	2003	2002	Percent Change
Net Sales (U.S.$ in millions)			
North America	$ 7,900	$ 7,300	8%
Europe	2,700	2,200	23
Asia	416	391	6
Latin America	1,400	1,270	10
Operating Profit (U.S.$ in millions)			
North America	$ 810	$ 830	−2%
Europe	124	n/a	n/a
Asia	7	n/a	n/a
Latin America	89	107	−17

gave an interview to the *Harvard Business Review* entitled "The Right Way to Go Global." In 1992, Mark Gray, vice president of technology services, was seeing the move toward globalization as a move toward standardization and product homogeneity with simplified manufacturing processes and economies of scale. Whirlpool seemed to be in a good position. It was building plants with local partners in Mexico, Brazil, and India, while its strategy overseas was vertically integrated manufacturing.

In 1995, Whirlpool was controlling joint ventures in India and China (to make refrigerators and air conditioners) and hoping to break even in Asia by 1997. In Europe, Whirlpool had purchased Philips Electronics NV for $2 billion in 1989 as rivals such as Maytag were pulling out. Until 1989, only 10 percent of Whirlpool's business was truly global; after the purchase, international operations increased to 40 percent. To perform better in a global environment, Whirlpool tried to integrate international and domestic managers into a cohesive global team by holding worldwide leadership conferences. In 1991, 140 senior leaders participated in workshops and networked for seven days!

Whirlpool's profits hit a record $205 million in 1992 but, in April 1993, its finance company, Whirlpool Finance Corporation, took a $40 million after-tax write-down. This charge wiped out almost 50 percent of the unit's earnings over the past three years. A litany of internal issues such as manufacturing inefficiencies, start-up costs associated with production of a redesigned midsize refrigerator, and restructuring of the pan-European sales force resulted in 1995 being just as disappointing. External pressures were also applied to the industry worldwide: unprecedented raw materials cost increases, inability to get immediate price relief, product mix erosion, and intensifying competition in Europe as customers sought greater value. Additionally, Mexico's peso devaluation crisis resulted in a market decline of 40 percent in Mexico.

Going global was risky. In developed markets such as Europe, newcomers faced many entrenched players. Overcapacity was particularly endemic in Europe, where the top four appliance manufacturers had 55 percent of the market and new entrants faced 300 local manufacturers (ready to use price wars and other tactics). Higher material costs, pinching margins, poor economic conditions as well as its own miscalculations cut Whirlpool's profit margins. Whirlpool's name was not well known in Europe where Sweden's Electrolux dominated the market. Whirlpool did not realize the appliance business was considerably tougher in Europe than in the United States because of the countless variations in what consumers from different countries need and want. For example, due to very different climates, Danes needed to spin-dry clothes, whereas Italians often line-dried their clothes. The British wanted refrigerators well constructed, the French were more concerned about the refrigerator's capacity to keep fruit and vegetables fresh, and the Spanish cared about its capacity to keep meats. Furthermore, Italians regarded childproof safety features as vital, and Germans looked for environmental features.

In Asia, Whirlpool's strategy was anchored on "five Ps": partnerships (majority-owned joint ventures, four in China, one in India), products (development of a new frost-free refrigerator platform and of a global washer), processes (all aspects of quality are included), people (foreign assignments for top members of Whirlpool's management), and a pan-Asian approach (build on commonalities between the many national markets). Whirlpool faced the same problem in China it encountered in Europe: market saturation. In developing countries such as China, the risk was increased by vague laws governing taxation and commerce.

Competition

Whirlpool's rivals were also bruised by going global. Its U.S. rival Maytag ($3 billion in sales) pulled out of Europe in 1995, giving up its six-year effort to penetrate the region. "Europe is not an attractive place to try to go in and dislodge the established players," said Leonard Hadley, Maytag's chairman. "I am nothing but satisfied with our exit. The U.S. is still the best place in the world to make money." Hadley was instrumental in Maytag's divestment in Europe. Maytag's financial returns in Europe were only half of those they could earn in North America. Maytag was now pouring money into new

products, advertising, and share buybacks in its North American business. In 1993 Hadley created a "Galaxy initiative," a lineup of nine top-secret new products, each code-named after a different planet. In 1997, Maytag launched Neptune, a front-loading washer and the talk of the industry. In March 1998, it reached an agreement to sell its product through Sears, the outlet for a third of the appliances sold in the United States. In September 1998, Maytag was estimating its third quarter earnings would exceed 70 cents a share with sales rising as much as 20 percent. Since Maytag was oriented to the higher end of the appliance and floor-care markets, the domestic economy's stable growth was helpful in making consumers less price conscious. In general, Neptune earned about $4 for every $1 Whirlpool made on its high-end washer.

Maytag was also revising its relationship with its suppliers. During the 1998 AHAM Supplier Division Forum, Maytag's director of procurement, Mike Rosberg, described his company's 3-3-4 Initiative as a "journey" with impressive goals: 300 suppliers; 3 parts per million defect rates; and 4 years to accomplish the goals. The effort began in 1996 when Maytag's supplier base was 936. In 1998, Maytag's supplier base was approximately 870. Parts per million rates in 1996 were 10,000. By 1998, the rate was 2,800. For suppliers wanting to be among Maytag's chosen 300, Rosberg stressed the importance of partnerships. "There's been a shift away from procurement thinking and commodity sourcing in our company, to relationship sourcing." Maytag expected margins of about 135 in 1999.

GE, with 32 percent of the U.S. market and $6.38 billion in sales in 1996, had tried for years to dislodge Whirlpool. Its profits were bigger, with $750 million compared to Whirlpool's $300 million. GE gained two percentage points of market share in 1996. (Each percent roughly translates to about $200 million in sales.) In the United States, GE was in a nationwide price-cutting contest with Whirlpool.

In its effort toward globalization, GE took a different approach from Whirlpool's. GE Appliances strived to be a leader in cost, speed, and international expansion, while Whirlpool decided to build a dominant consumer franchise on cost and quality and would deal with speed later. Despite all its setbacks, Whirlpool turned out to be more successful. By 1994, GE and Whirlpool were either number one or two in the United States, Canada, and Mexico. In 1988, both companies were leaders in the United States and Canada, with Whirlpool among the leaders in Brazil. In addition, GE Appliances became a leader in Colombia and Venezuela. But Whirlpool was either number one or two in the rest of Latin America, Europe, and India, as well as a leader among Western firms in China. Whirlpool preempted GE in many of the emerging markets of the world.

Abroad, GE launched a strategy it called "smart bombing." This involved GE executives examining each country microscopically and tailoring a mix of products to market in each. GE Appliances CEO David Cote stressed that "this industry doesn't reward investment, so we have to spend money sparingly and carefully." Since refrigerators that once cost $800 now sold for about $750, there was little room for further price cuts. GE bought 80 percent of a Chinese distribution company, Shanghai Communications & Electrical Appliances Commercial Group. Its job was to find Chinese companies capable of making GE-designed products under contract. To make sure its standards were met at each factory, GE flew a team of experts on "bubble assignments" for a week to six months to assist in quality control, technology, service, manufacturing, billing, collecting, and other skills. Total sales amounted to $20 million in 1997. With little money invested, it was a positive return on assets.

In Japan, GE collaborated with the big discount retailer Kojima in order to eliminate several layers of distribution and turn American-made appliances into irresistible bargains. In India and the Philippines, GE established partnerships with Godrej, the Bombay-based top Indian manufacturer of refrigerators and laundry products, and with Philacor in Manila, the number two appliance manufacturer in the Philippines. Both companies were healthy and sophisticated partners and surpassed GE's criteria for quality and costs. In 1996, GE operating earnings rose to 11.8 percent of its $6.4 billion sales. Overseas GE was estimated to have made up to $320 million in profits between 1994 and 1997. GE also had a joint venture in Britain with Hotpoint (Britain's General Electric Company) and was trying to enter the luxury end of the European market. It bought licenses from European manufacturers to sell their products under the GE name. In 1996, GE bought a Brazilian stove maker in order to return to Latin America and compete with BoschSiemens, a joint venture between two of Germany's biggest companies, Robert A. Bosch GmbH and Siemens A.G. This German joint venture acquired Brazil's largest maker of cooking appliances in 1994. It has since built factories to make refrigerators and drying machines in Brazil and started construction of a refrigerator factory in Peru.

Sweden's Electrolux, with a 25 percent market share in Europe, was part of a constellation of public companies controlled by the Wallenberg family. The global strategy Electrolux announced in 1995 was to segment geographical markets with one global Electrolux brand and three pan-European brands (Electrolux, Zanussi, and AEG), as well as with local brands (Faure in France, Tricity Bendix in the United Kingdom, and Zanker in Germany). Chairman Michael Treschow aimed to develop new products, such as the Euro oven (with 46 variations on a single platform), to address the fragmented European market. The company expected to double sales in its new markets (central and eastern Europe, China, India, Southeast Asia, Latin America, and Africa) within three to five years.

In China, a $100 million investment program included a joint venture to manufacture water purifiers at a plant outside Beijing and a joint venture to manufacture compressors and a vacuum-cleaner manufacturing plant. Only 2 to 3 percent of Chinese homes had vacuum cleaners and it was a huge market to seize. In India, Electrolux had acquired majority shareholdings in production facilities for refrigerators and washing machines, and in Latin America, Electrolux had a minority interest in Brazil's second-largest white-goods manufacturer, Refripar. But despite these successes, Electrolux announced a $320 million write-off to pay for shedding 12,000 workers and planned to close 25 plants in several countries.

New Energy Standards

It was not only abroad, but also in the U.S. market that Whirlpool and its rivals had to face new challenges. One such challenge was the Department of Energy's (DOE) more stringent energy standards. The DOE had been prodding manufacturers to produce front-loading washing machines, which consumed less water and energy than top-loaders. They were standard in Europe, and were considered to be better cleaners. However, they were also much more expensive and American consumers might not be ready to pay for them. The new energy standards for refrigerators mandated a 30 percent reduction in energy usage for refrigerators manufactured after July 2001. The original goal was to enforce the regulation in 1998, but the Association of Home Appliance Manufacturers (AHAM) lobbied for a delay. This riled Whirlpool, which had already redesigned its line for 1998 sales, and caused the company to cancel its membership in AHAM.

During the 1998 meeting of the Association of Home Appliance Manufacturers, Whirlpool's corporate vice president of global procurement Roy Armes said the company's OEM division had cut its supplier base worldwide by half over the past three years. Armes stressed the importance of early design efforts involving suppliers. "Today, 80 percent of the product cost occurs well before the product is produced and even before the first components are bought." Larry Spang, vice president and general manager of the laundry and specialty division at Siebe Appliance Controls, opined that there was a "segment of the buying population that is paying close attention to higher-end products." Emerson's Jehling challenged the appliance industry and its supply base to do "a better job of consumer analysis." And Dow's Moran said his company "is aware and sensitive to the market demand for low-noise appliances."

A summary of the Appliance Manufacturer's Major Appliance Dealers 1998 Study revealed that (1) capacity and low-noise were features for which consumers were willing to pay more; (2) price continued to drive the majority of appliance purchases; and (3) dealers and consumers alike were very conscious of service-oriented brands. Dealers and consumers were not yet starting to care about

Design for Recyclability. The 1998 survey showed that even fewer respondents (10 percent versus 13 percent five years earlier) said that Design for Recyclability was a selling point. Even more telling was that when asked if Design for Recyclability would be a selling point five years from now, only 54 percent said yes. When that same question was asked in 1995, 74 percent answered yes.

Appliance manufacturers were also learning to probe consumers' psyches early in the cycle to design features and elements meeting the escalating needs of women (key decision makers on appliance purchases). Consumers were more and more concerned about clean water, energy savings, softening products, and water filtration in washing machines and dishwashers. Whirlpool enlisted French anthropologist G. Clotaire Rapaille (see Chapter 3) in 1995 to tap into consumers' feelings about and interactions with their appliances.

Whirlpool's Global Strategy

In spite of its own losses and lessons from its rivals, Whirlpool remained committed to its foreign operations. The Asian economic crisis did not threaten Whirlpool's sales since Asia accounts for only 5 percent of its sales. Moreover, developing countries remained a place where appliance sales were growing at double-digit percentage rates (in Brazil, the growth was 25–30 percent per year).

However, the financial crisis spread in South America. Brazil doubled interest rates in October 1997 and again during the fall of 1998. As of December 1998, Whirlpool appliance sales plummeted by about 25 percent in Brazil, to $1 billion or about 10 percent of the company's 1998 revenues. Brazil was still by far the jewel of Whirlpool's global expansion strategy. Through much of the 90s it was the company's most profitable foreign operation. Brazilian affiliates contributed 1997 earnings of $78 million compared with $11 million operating profit from the parent, but the company announced in 1998 that it would reduce its Brazilian workforce by 25 percent, resulting in the loss of 3,200 jobs. However, growth in home appliances was most likely to come in emerging markets thanks to the low penetration rate of appliances. As of December 1998, only 15 percent of Brazil's households owned microwave ovens. Once Brazil recovered, the company projected a 5–6 percent growth compared to 1–2 percent in the United States and Europe. The market was not following Whirlpool's optimism but recognized that Whirlpool remained the only major white-goods maker still making money in Brazil. Paulo Periquito, Whirlpool's executive vice president for Latin America, was trying to cut costs and improve efficiency, flexibility, and agility necessary in the unsteady Brazilian environment. He was pinning his hopes on interest rates falling gradually in 1999 and confident as to the fact Whirlpool had already survived Brazil's many debt crises, hyperinflation, and military governments.

Whirlpool also intended to experiment with licensing as opposed to participating in manufacturing. It restructured its international operations, spent $350 million to exit from two of its four joint ventures in China, and reorganized its European business. Even if it was laying off 10 percent (4,700 employees) of its corporate force hoping to save $180 million a year by the year 2000, its choice was to remain global.

Being global offered the possibility of being the first to transfer new technologies between continents and to recruit management from a more diverse pool. Whirlpool management learned from globalization to embrace dual executive roles. The company's chief technology officer was also responsible for worldwide purchasing. Whirlpool's relationship with its suppliers became more important as it had to coordinate multiple product lines along geographic regions and as components makers have driven technology. Whirlpool wanted to avoid organizing the two tasks, technology and supply management, as separate functions in order to accelerate processes. People in purchasing tended to favor current suppliers while people in technical departments tended to experiment. Whirlpool concluded that an executive wearing two hats could develop and test new ideas more quickly.

Like Whirlpool, most of the appliance makers remained engaged in globalization, and they were committed to dodge setbacks and try again. Despite its lack of success in Europe, Maytag decided in 1996 to reinvest abroad and put $35 million in a joint venture with China's leading washing-machine company. Another $35 million was used to expand the joint venture operations into refrigerators.

End-of-the-Decade Expectations

Whirlpool Europe completed 1998 with a 125 percent gain in operating profit along with substantial gains in unit shipments and sales. Full-year 1998 earnings from continuing operations were up 37 percent from $226 million for the 1997 period to $310 million. Full-year 1998 net earnings were $325 million, versus a reported net loss of $15 million in 1997. Full-year 1998 sales were $10.3 billion, up 20 percent from full-year 1997 due to the consolidation of the company's Brazilian subsidiaries. In 1998 the company aggressively lowered costs and improved efficiency and productivity. Several new product introductions in clothes washing, refrigeration, air conditioning, and cooking under the company's leading Brastemp and Consul brand names were made. Whirlpool Asia reported a 73 percent improvement in operating performance for 1998. The company grew its unit shipments in India as consumers continued to make Whirlpool brand refrigerators and washing machines the top choice. Exports of Whirlpool brand microwave ovens built in China rose sharply.

For 1999, the company planned further performance improvements from growing contract sales, ongoing efficiency gains, and additional new product introductions including exciting new clothes washers and dishwashers. The company estimated that U.S. appliance industry shipments in 1999 would approximate 1998 levels.

In 1999, the company expected to continue this momentum through a combination of sales growth initiatives and additional new product introductions in the clothes washing and cooking products categories. Whirlpool anticipated appliance industry shipments in western Europe to grow about 2 percent in 1999. For 1999 the company forecasted that the Latin-American economy, as well as the appliance industry, would remain under stress, as the timing of economic recovery is uncertain.

The company anticipated that full-year 1999 appliance industry volumes in Brazil would decline between 5 and 10 percent from 1998 levels. Whirlpool's strategy was a combination of new product introductions, consumer-focused service offerings, and additional cost reductions. Whirlpool expected that its Asian business would perform soon at a breakeven level or better as unit volumes and the Whirlpool brand name continued to grow across the region.

Whirlpool's chairman estimated that "despite continued uncertainty in Brazil, we expect operating profit to show improvement in the first quarter of 1999 and to grow between 10 and 15 percent for the full year, driven by strong performances in North America and Europe as well as a continued turnaround in Asia. In spite of difficult economic and business conditions in Brazil and elsewhere, we currently expect to deliver year-over-year net earnings growth of between 5 and 10 percent."

Success at Last

By the time he retired in mid-2004, CEO David Whitwam was considered a global visionary and global success. Whirlpool's status as a leading global company was well established, and its worldwide reach had become the industry success model, forcing competitors such as Electrolux to follow its lead. As he described his ultimate success over two turbulent decades at Whirlpool, Whitwam explained that he had finally found the right formula—and that only about a third of the total potential benefits from globalization of the corporation had yet been harvested.

The key innovation, according to Whitwam, was the way Whirlpool resolved the paradox of being global and local at the same time. While initially centralization of the organizational structure and the decision-making process seemed absolutely necessary, the problem was how to motivate local subsidiaries with such a top-down approach. This classic dilemma (global integration balanced by local sensitivity) required more than simple order-giving exchange and person-to-person interactions. It required a systematic process understood and accepted by everybody in the global organization.

To establish such a process, Whitwam used a team approach. He created a large set of worldwide teams comprising representatives of various regions as well as upper and lower management levels. Each of the teams was assigned the task to evaluate some particular international project, such as a coordinated new product introduction, globally uniform advertising, location of R&D activities, and so on. Many teams had overlapping responsibilities, requiring team-to-team interactions. Team activities were staggered so that starting and ending points differed, making it possible for a team to learn from another team's experience and, if necessary, adapt its own work. In addition, each team was taught to perform small real-world experiments to test assumptions and new ideas. These small experiments helped quick learning from trial and error, without exposing the larger organization in case the assumptions and ideas proved mistaken. For example, the easy assumption that office workers would prefer gourmet food to "junk food" in vending machines quickly proved faulty in a small European test.

The team approach helped Whirlpool create an innovative and flexible global organization that could be locally sensitive and still gain the benefits of global sharing of best practices and shared learning. Using its intranet IT network for communications and significantly improving responsiveness to its customers, the organization was held together as much by a common culture and understanding of "how things got done" as by person-to-person relations. Not easy for any company, especially one that has had so many headaches.

Discussion Questions

1. To what extent is the appliance market regional rather than global?
2. What seem to be the key success factors in the appliance business?
3. Are Whirlpool's difficulties with its global strategy due to internal factors or to external factors beyond its control?
4. To what extent does Whirlpool's experience suggest that globalization is not a good idea in the appliance business? Explain fully.
5. To what extent should Whirlpool adapt its global strategy? (You may want to access Whirlpool's Web site and annual reports to see how the company has fared recently and whether its international commitment remains strong.)

Source: This case was prepared by Michèle van de Walle and Professor S. Tamer Cavusgil, Michigan State University, for class use only. See also Pierre Loewe and Jorge Rufat-Latre, "The Changing Face of Global Business—Five Guidelines Can Ease the Pain of Change Management," *Optimize*, June 1, 2004, p. 32.

Part 2

Foreign Entry

Global marketing can be implemented only after the firm has entered foreign markets. In Part Two, we turn to the process of market entry and global expansion. Although conceptually there are many similarities between a national roll-out of a new product and international expansion to new countries, going across borders poses new difficulties.

When a business enters a foreign country, exposure to political risks now must be managed. When products are to be shipped across borders and into another country's distribution channels, foreign importers have to be identified and put under contract. When transactions are across borders, exchange rate fluctuations and customs duties affect revenues. When sales have to be promoted overseas, advertising agencies with a local presence must be used. These are only some of the complicated issues in choosing which country to enter, what mode of entry to use, and what global expansion path to follow.

Although much of the material in Part Two deals with the novice exporter, large multinationals that operate in many markets must follow the same principles. Exporting mechanics and customs barriers directly affect where a multinational will locate new facilities. A multinational corporation (MNC) will often have to change the chosen entry mode when its strategic objectives change. If political or economic conditions in a country change, an MNC will sometimes exit and then reenter as conditions improve. And even for the largest multinationals, there are usually still markets left to conquer.

Chapter

Country Attractiveness

"But this is not Kansas!"

After reading this chapter, you will be able to:

1. Evaluate country attractiveness by considering environmental factors such as political developments, trading bloc membership, and entry barriers, in addition to market potential.
2. Test the sensitivity of a country's ratings against alternative scenarios of political developments and competitive reactions.
3. Find the relevant data needed for country evaluations, including the available data on the Internet as well as data from independent research agencies that provide customized analysis on specific products and markets.
4. Do sales forecasting for a given country, using techniques appropriate for the stage of the product life cycle (PLC) that the country market is in.
5. Combine the quantitative forecasts with subjective estimates from personal visits and channel interviews.

In theory there are several reasons for the firm to enter a foreign market. From a pure marketing perspective, it is most natural to view expansion abroad in terms of entering new countries because of their market potential. But as we saw in Chapter 1, the firm may also enter in order to get access to a larger regional trade bloc, to learn from customers and competitors in a leading market, or to attack a competitor's major market. A country can look attractive not only because the firm can sell a lot of product but also because the firm can derive other benefits from a presence there.

Chapter 4 will outline the principles and techniques involved in systematically researching country markets for entry. Early considerations include broad political, economic, and social indicators, a matter of making sure that the "basic fundamentals" are in place. The chapter will discuss research on these environmental forces first and then proceed to the research needed to scope out the competition, domestic as well as foreign. We then present a stepwise procedure that companies use to gradually narrow down the set of candidate countries, and we give a real-life running illustration of how the procedure is applied. The chapter describes various data sources, but also emphasizes the importance of first-hand experience before making a final choice. A more technical section on how companies forecast sales in a country ends the chapter.

The Internet Aggregators: Cheaper and Better Country Data

The globalization of business has been good for many market research firms. The need to find out more about a potential market opportunity abroad has forced many companies to turn to outside research vendors with international expertise.

99

These research firms in turn have found it profitable to strike up alliances with local market researchers abroad, creating regional and global networks of affiliated firms. As multinationals have expanded abroad, the research firms have established branches in prime foreign locations, even acquired or merged with some of their previous partners. Large marketing research firms such as ACNielsen in the United States, London-based Taylor Nelson Sofres, and GfK out of Germany are truly multinationals in their own right.

Globalization has also had the effect of broadening the scope of market research. Entering new markets abroad requires assessment of their political and economic stability, infrastructure development, and local climate, factors that in the home country are well known and taken for granted. These needs have meant that assessing country attractiveness involves not just marketing researchers but also experts on political risk, currency volatility, and ethnic violence. One is not surprised to learn that Henry Kissinger, the former U.S. secretary of state, runs a very successful global consulting firm out of New York.

The cost for the country reports generated by these firms can run into the tens of thousands of U.S. dollars. Because conditions can change quickly, the firms typically produce monthly or quarterly updates, in addition to annual summaries. Subscription fees for these syndicated reports can run $10,000 to $20,000 per year. Customized assessments of a specific country's situation can run much higher than that. These are steep figures for many firms considering foreign entry.

With the advent of the Internet, however, things are changing. A new industry of "market research aggregators" has emerged. These aggregators make their living from the business of acquiring, cataloging, reformatting, segmenting, and reselling reports already published by large and small research firms. These reports are made available to customers on the Internet at prices typically in the hundreds to a few thousand U.S. dollars per report, much less than the original data. In addition, the Internet allows easy customization of the reports to the needs of each buyer.

The market research aggregator is typically a small Internet start-up with ties to one or two large researchers and several smaller, specialized research firms. They are not fly-by-night hackers breaking into the data banks of the original suppliers. Rather, the aggregator firm contracts with these firms for access to their data banks and reports. The revenues and profits are divided between the aggregators and the original researchers according to contract provisions.

The size and growth numbers for the new industry are impressive. At the end of 2001, an aggregator such as Profound.com offered about 150,000 research reports for sale. This represented a 34 percent increase over the 112,000 in 2000 and up 75 percent from 86,000 in 1999. Another aggregator, AllNetResearch.com, had a database with about 3,000 reports from 95 firms in December 2001, up from 400 reports and 30 firms in 2000. Of course, such success does not go unnoticed. With customary speed, the smaller startups were soon swallowed up by larger players. Accessing AllNetResearch on your search engine is likely to bring up Jupitermedia Corp. or Internetnews.com. But the aggregators' role has stayed the same and keeps growing.

Why do the original researchers allow these intermediates access to their data? In the beginning the firms were wary of these "interlopers," fearing that they would take away loyal customers paying high prices. But the experience for the large research firms has been that they now get access to a lower-priced market segment they would otherwise not be able to tap into. And for the smaller researchers, the aggregators serve as the main sales channel, allowing the firms to concentrate on data gathering and analysis. Think about it: You might know something important about a country that really very few people know. Now you could verify your sources, write it up, and get the valuable information sold via an aggregator to someone who is in desperate need to know.

The Internet sometimes lives up to its hype.

Sources: "Total Research Announces Sales of Its 51% Stake in Romtec-GfK Joint Venture," *Business Wire,* July 2, 2001; Steve Jarvis, "Sum of the Parts: Fast-Growing Industry Delivers Data to New Markets, Piece by Piece," *Marketing News,* January 21, 2002.

Introduction

In the global turmoil of the new millennium, researching country markets' potential and especially the risks involved in entry is more critical than ever. At the same time, the possibility of relying on hard data to make serious commitments to market in countries has become more elusive. This is not because the data are worse than before; with the advent of the Internet it is quite the contrary. The problem is that one can no longer be sure that the data reflect what is in store in the future. The convulsions in the economic networks engendered by terrorists and antiglobalization activists not only are inducing volatility in international financial flows but also threaten the freedom of international trade and the openness of markets, two factors much more crucial to the global marketer than free capital movement.

Even without these complications from the environment, it is hardly surprising to note that choosing countries to enter in a systematic way is always fraught with problems. Even though vast improvements have come with the emergence of global databases, international online data services, and global research agencies, market-level data quality is still usually uneven and comparable data across countries are often nonexistent. Lack of familiarity with conditions abroad means that predictions of market potential and long-term prospects are even more hazardous. The notion of matching the company know-how against foreign opportunities might be good in principle, but in reality it is very hard to do.

So what is a rigorous and systematic approach to country selection that is also realistic? The answer comes in two parts. First, the initial screening should be based on a well-articulated vision of why the company wants to go abroad and what kinds of resources it can marshal. For example, the aim of the foreign entry might be to attack a competitor's cash-generating home base or enter a leading market. Or, the aim might be to preempt a competitor's entry into a new market by entering first and gaining first-mover advantages. In either case, the choice of country is often a given. Also, any limiting constraints should be clarified and be used to screen countries out of contention as early as possible. Second, when more than one country remains in the choice set, the final choice should be made only after in-country visits have confirmed what the available published data reveal about market size, growth, entry barriers, and the competitive market shares. The iron rule is never to commit resources without first-hand information.

Chapter 4 delineates this process in more detail. We describe what market research across the world's regions and countries involves and how to evaluate country markets in terms of market potential and resource demands. We introduce a systematic screening procedure and discuss how to handle various obstacles and special factors complicating the systematic process. We describe the various data sources available, stressing the emergence of online databases, and end with a description of several different approaches to forecasting sales in a foreign country.

Regional and Country Indicators

The initial research across various regions and countries tends to be quite informal and wide-ranging. Here, one might use quite broad country indicators—an example is Anholt's development of country branding indices (see box, "Attractive Countries?"). The later research should be more formal and systematic.

In this section we will discuss the broader analysis of the potential of regional and country markets. The first area of concern is typically the political risks associated with the various regions and countries.

Getting the Picture

ATTRACTIVE COUNTRIES?

A British policy advisor and researcher, Simon Anholt, has produced a general measure of country attractiveness. Anholt proposed that there are six basic components of a country's attractiveness:

1. Exports
2. Governance
3. Culture
4. People
5. Tourism
6. Immigration

Basically, as a country scores higher on these six factors, it is becoming a more attractive country. The reasoning is as follows.

If a country is perceived to produce desirable products, then consumers are more likely to favor—and pay a premium for—products produced in that country. If its government is perceived to be benign and stable, it will find it easier to win support from the "international community." If its people and culture are admired, they will have less trouble living and working abroad and immigrants will be attracted. If the country is attractive as a tourist destination, it will attract more tourists. Combined, these six factors help identify whether a country is attractive to the various customer groups—potential tourists, investors, expatriates, former emigrants returning home, and global marketers who are looking for new growth markets.

Anholt has combined with GMI (Global Market Insite), a U.S. research firm, to collect data on the six factors for a number of countries. Instead of using published data, the data collection involves customer surveys with representative samples in 35 countries. Respondents rate not only their own country but other countries as well. Pooling the data across countries, a composite ranking of countries on the six dimensions can be calculated. This ranking provides useful insights into how a country is perceived by people from

other countries. The overall score summed across the six factors gives a thumbnail picture of how attractive a country seems to people around the world. The following list gives the rankings for the top 15 countries in 2007.

1.	United Kingdom	128.41
2.	Germany	127.59
3.	France	126.41
4.	Canada	126.30
5.	Switzerland	125.21
6.	Sweden	124.41
7.	Italy	123.92
8.	Australia	123.56
9.	Japan	123.46
10.	United States	122.65
11.	Netherlands	121.54
12.	Spain	120.53
13.	Denmark	119.92
14.	Norway	119.89
15.	New Zealand	117.84

It deserves to be emphasized that most of a country's residents tend to rate themselves highly and also that various stereotypes play a definite role in the ratings. For example, among American respondents, the United States is rated number one and France is in 14th place. Conversely, among French respondents, France is number one and the United States is in 16th place. Even with such differences in perceptions, these country assessments are still very useful when they are tracked over time, and changes can be observed. They are, of course, also useful as starting points for a more in-depth analysis.

Anholt has also developed a concept of "place branding" and "nation branding," which we will return to in Chapter 13 on "Global Branding."

Sources: Anholt, 2003; **www.gmi-mr.com.**

Political Risk Research

Today for many firms the standard first question asked about a country concerns **political risks,** the danger that political and military upheaval will change the nation's economic rules and regulations overnight. There are many ways of analyzing the risk and of assessing the level of exposure, and the sources of information vary from very detailed statistical reports on the history of the country's political development to impressionistic tales by recent visitors to the country. The factors that need to be considered can be arranged in a descending order of importance for the investor, as in Exhibit 4.1.[1]

Political risk analysis proceeds from the first to the fourth level in the table. The data used will usually come from any one of the several firms offering political risk analysis.[2] If at any of the levels the risk is deemed unacceptable, the investment project receives a "no-go" stamp and is discontinued in favor of foreign direct investment

EXHIBIT 4.1
Political Risk Factors

Source: Reprinted by permission of Macmillan Publishers Ltd: *Journal of International Business Studies,* Steven J. Korbin, "Political Risk: A Review and Reconsideration," 10, no. 1, pp. 67–80, copyright 1979 by Palgrave Macmillan.

Factors	Examples
Level 1: General Instability	Revolution, external aggression
Level 2: Expropriation	Nationalization, contract revocation
Level 3: Operations	Import restrictions, local content rules, taxes, export requirements
Level 4: Finance	Repatriation restrictions, exchange rates

(FDI) elsewhere or simply export or licensing negotiations. Even though the economics of an FDI project are quite acceptable—in the sense that projected discounted returns sufficiently clear the hurdle return on investment (ROI) rate—the political risks may be great enough to stop the project. This is more likely to happen when the investment is aimed at the acquisition of raw material or low-wage costs than when the penetration of markets is at stake.

The rise of international **terrorism** is a new type of political risk. Even before the September 11, 2001, attacks on the twin towers of the World Trade Center in New York, terrorism was listed as a top concern among multinationals. The Iran revolution, politically motivated murders in South America, and the crime wave in newly capitalist Russia have made multinational companies and their expatriate managers very uneasy and eager to purchase insurance. Although terrorism's international reach can make almost any country unsafe, as the attacks on the World Trade Center in New York showed, terrorism and escalating crime have put an especially dark shadow on certain countries' and regions' attractiveness. For example, in a Gallup survey of British executives' evaluation of political risk in various countries, Russia was rated as "difficult"

French farming union leader Jose Bove inside a makeshift cell at the courthouse in Millau in southern France, on February 6, 2002. The charismatic M. Bove became a globally famous antiglobal hero after he led the ransacking of a new McDonald's restaurant in Millau, claiming that globalization destroyed the livelihood of French farmers. He served three weeks of his three-month prison term and was then released for good behavior. Wide World Photos.

Getting the Picture

POLITICAL RISK: THE CASE OF IRAQ

The dust has not quite settled in war-torn Iraq, but sovereignty has been passed from the U.S.-led coalition to the country's own leaders. Now Iraq must ready itself for another invader: big business.

How should a company, looking to expand its business into Iraq, assess political risk? How does it protect itself? The answer is simple: Pay somebody else to figure it out.

Enter Aon corporation. Aon is a holding company for an international family of insurance brokerage, consulting, and insurance underwriting subsidiaries. According to Aon Trade Credit's chief economist, Dr. Michel Leonard, the global cost of political risk could reach $1 trillion in 2004. In January 2004, Aon released its 2004 Political and Economic Risk Map rating the economic, currency, and political risks for doing business in more than 200 territories worldwide.

Brokers and underwriters such as Aon are helping many organizations to protect employees, equipment, and other assets in Iraq. Companies can get personal accident insurance for Iraq, if they are prepared to pay for it. Personal accident insurance rates for Iraq are the highest in the world, but rates for southern Iraq were 33 to 50 percent lower than in northern Iraq and Baghdad. Political risk insurance for equipment, machinery, and other mobile assets taken to Iraq typically covers physical loss or damage due to political violence, abandonment, confiscation, expropriation, and inability to re-export the equipment on completion of the contract. Coverage can be adjusted and rates can be reduced by hiring Aon as a consultant to help arrange for local security, brief and train staff on security issues, develop an information network to monitor security in all parts of the country, and plan responses for likely incidents and be aware of nearest medical facilities.

The U.S. Department of Commerce now has an Iraq Investment and Reconstruction Task Force that provides information and counseling to companies pursuing business opportunities in Iraq. A 2007 Task Force survey shows that a majority of Iraqi businesses are optimistic for further economic growth and improvements in security for 2008. The survey found that 78 percent of business owners expect the economy to significantly grow over the next two years and the majority of business leaders (84 percent) believe security is better now than the previous year.

Corporations are faced with a dilemma. Are the potential revenues in a country such as Iraq sufficient to cover the research costs before entry, justify the risks of operating there, and pay for the high insurance costs necessary to do business there? Even though the Iraqi businesses are welcoming, in the short term, many foreign companies are likely to pass up the opportunity.

Sources: Carolyn Aldred and Michael Bradford, "More Buyers Seeking Policies for Iraq Risks," *Business Insurance,* February 2, 2004; "Aon Unveils 2004 Political and Economic Risk Map," *Business Wire,* January 28, 2004; **http://trade.gov/Iraq/.**

---

by 57 percent followed by Africa (47 percent), and South America (46 percent).[3] High-risk countries included Angola, South Africa, Zaire, Colombia, Haiti, Papua New Guinea, and Turkey. With the spread of terrorism, these risk indicators can change quickly, and once complacent countries and firms need to keep updated on any changes. The political risk assessment industry is also responding well to the increased demand created by the Iraq War (see box, "Political Risk: The Case of Iraq").

As governments change and new regimes come to power, political risk can be temporary, but it is important that the company makes sure to follow risk indicators closely and keep them updated. Where the risk index is high, scenario planning becomes necessary, with any proposed strategy tested against alternative political developments. Predicting political change in Russia may be difficult, but alternatives can be sketched out (from "worst" to "best" scenarios) and the most robust strategy identified. Of course, "most robust" does not necessarily mean "very robust." Given the Russian scene under Putin, it is not surprising if many firms have been pulling out—even the most robust strategy is not attractive enough, given the risks involved.

Environmental Research

Once political risk has been analyzed, environmental factors affecting marketing should be researched. This is partly a matter of getting "back to basics." For example, environmental variables affect how products are used and analyzing them can be useful in different countries as they affect customer choices directly. It is not a matter of attitudes and preferences, but simply "reality." Home furniture does not sell well where homes are small. Electric toothbrushes are less than useful when electricity is expensive. Small cars and thin-soled shoes make big people uncomfortable, with good reason. Placing a PC on the desk of an executive in many countries insults a hard-won status. And so on.

It is not useful to research customer evaluation of a product if its basic functionality is not understood. One study tried to identify the demand for and desired course content of an international executive program by asking managers in Asia, Europe, and North America for rankings of various topics. The study sponsor did not realize that for many managers one major motivation to participate lay simply in the status it conferred upon the manager, independent of the content of the course, something uncovered when telephone callbacks were made.

Thus, in new local markets, the most valuable market research centers on very basic environmental determinants of consumption and buying behaviors. The local marketing campaign that goes wrong abroad often does so because of unexpected differences in environmental factors (different from the home market) that are missed or ignored.

For country evaluation purposes it is common to distinguish among four **environmental dimensions:** (1) physical; (2) sociocultural; (3) economic; and (4) trade blocs and regulatory environment.[4]

Physical Environment

The most obvious environmental factor affecting people's behavior is the climate. The humidity and heat of the eastern seaboard of the United States in the summer (and of many other countries as well) dooms polyester fabrics, encourages air-conditioning installations, and raises property values for summer houses in cooler places like Vermont or Maine. The heat and humidity should raise air-conditioning sales also in Southeast Asia, but the soft housing construction, necessary because of the region's propensity for natural disasters, prohibits effective insulation. The cold of Russia has made furs a particularly common Russian export product, although the lack of adaptation to Western styles and to countries with less chill (thus needing lighter furs) has prevented further penetration of the best markets.

One particular aspect of the physical environment is the risk of epidemics. After the outbreak of SARS in South China in 2002, tourism and travel to the area virtually stopped, affecting businesses severely. Once the potential pandemic had been averted, travel and the economies quickly recuperated, helped by the continued growth of China's economy. Nevertheless, with the repeated occurrence of avian flu among chicken farmers in Southeast Asia and the increasing problem of air pollution in China, it is clear that in some ways the physical environment in Southeast Asia cannot be rated as very good for many businesses. The point here is simple: These risks have to be assessed, and in addition to government warnings, the World Health Organization should be relied on for up-to-date information.

Sociocultural Environment

As we saw in Chapter 3, cultural influences are pervasive in most country markets and are reflected in the social class groupings and the social stratification of a society. It is not important at this stage to decide whether culture or social factors are the primary drivers. What is important is that both tend to be important when analyzing the receptiveness of a country market to a new entrant.

Social and cultural influences are of course less obvious than physical factors. The researcher needs to start by collecting quantitative data and reading newspapers, and later, if needed, make a personal visit to observe and talk to people directly. The initial research can rely on secondary sources such as the United Nations, the World Bank, or general information about culture and language. The aim is to uncover those countries or regions with more or less cultural affinity with the home country. Since distance often does matter for the successful transfer of core FSAs, another aim is to develop a general understanding of the possible sociocultural obstacles the firm faces in the new environment. More in-depth analysis will have to wait for personal visits and more direct dealings with people in the country, something that takes time and is best done once the country is on the short list of candidates for in-depth screening.

Getting the Picture

THE EASTERN EUROPEAN CUSTOMER

When the east European countries opened up after the fall of the Berlin Wall, most Western manufacturers assumed that customers there would be eager to buy their products. In many cases they were disappointed by customers who seemed reluctant to switch to the new and better brands. Price and purchasing power were a problem, but interviews with shoppers who stayed with their old brands showed that many of them had enough money to buy the new products. According to the interviews, the problem was that the consumers could not choose between the new variants on the market, since they simply did not have enough understanding of the different features. The Western brands in shampoos, for example, offered "conditioning" and "rinse" and other features such as "two-in-one" and "hair repair," confusing attributes that the eastern European customers could not translate into benefits. The solution was to change the advertising copy and to offer in-store descriptions on the shelves.

Source: M. Wolongiewicz, personal interview.

Economic Environment

The level of economic development is naturally a major determinant of local buyer behavior. Disposable income data are easily available from secondary sources and are, by and large, reliable. But without more information on the income distribution and the social impact of economic well-being, income-per-household data can be interpreted incorrectly. For example, in some countries there can be a dramatic difference in spending power between the rich few and the many poor. Some basic understanding of the stage of the product life cycle is useful and possible to get as well from secondary data. Consumption figures and product penetration for the category can be used to assess market maturity. One approach is to simply identify the date of the first sales of the product (as in "When did mobile phones first become available?") and then use income data to compare the country to other known markets. The aim is to gain information about level of product awareness and interest (see box, "The Eastern European Customer").

Trade Blocks and Regulatory Environment

The initial assessment should always include information about membership in regional trade blocs. In fact, for many situations the first question to answer is whether a country is a member of a desirable trade bloc, such the European Union or Mercosur. Nonmembers might be screened out at that early point. In most cases the trade bloc information will also clarify the specific regulations and institutional framework under which the business will have to operate in the foreign country.

The institutional framework within which markets function is designed to enable or prohibit certain business practices. Although detailed information on internal regulations is time-consuming and best postponed until the in-depth stage, it is necessary to gain some understanding of trade barriers and major regulations as early as possible. A country's membership in the World Trade Organization (WTO) and basic openness to external trade is easily assessed using Internet sources.

Systematic Entry Screening

After the initial wide-ranging and informal analysis, the more systematic and in-depth analysis of country choice can be divided into four stages: country identification; preliminary screening; in-depth screening; and final selection.[5] The discussion of each stage will be illustrated by an actual application at a company called Microlog. See box, "Microlog Goes to Europe (A)."

Stage 1—Country Identification

In the **country identification** stage, various statistical data are used to identify candidate regions and countries. Typically, the company decides to enter a particular trade area. For example, companies opt to focus on Europe or Latin America or East Asia,

Getting the Picture

MICROLOG GOES TO EUROPE (A)

Microlog Inc. is a small company located in Germantown, Maryland, just outside the Washington, DC, beltway. Its business is in telecommunications and it has managed to survive over a decade in a very competitive industry. The company markets and services voice processing systems; that is, computerized electronic telephone systems that help direct incoming calls, record messages, and generally serve as an online mail and audio information service. Such integrated hardware–software systems saw tremendous growth in the United States in the early 1990s. Microlog is one of the many small companies that helped develop the systems. Its domestic market includes local businesses as well as the U.S. government.

Early on the company wanted to expand overseas. Domestic markets were growing, but competition was intense. Microlog management decided that the best strategy would be to capture first-mover advantages in new and growing foreign markets such as the EU. Once a system is installed, a company will not easily change vendor, and the servicing brings in business. Furthermore, word-of-mouth from a successful entry would travel fast to geographically close companies. The story of its first entry offers a good illustration of what systematic entry research entails.

Source: Adams et al., 1993, **www.mlog.com.**

and then do a more in-depth analysis within each of the regions to identify where to place their sales headquarters and which countries to enter first.

The statistical variables typically define level of development (including per capita income) and cultural similarity of the countries. To get a sense of the total potential, population comparisons are necessary as well. Indonesia has 178 million people, while Malaysia has 17 million, a big difference. The unified Germany has about 80 million people, biggest in Europe (not counting Russia), much bigger than another country with German culture, Austria, at 8 million. France and the United Kingdom have about 55 million each, while Sweden has 8 and Denmark 5 million people, much smaller markets. Hungary at 11 million is small compared to Poland's 40 million, and in Latin America, Chile at 13 million is small compared to Brazil at 150 million. Japan is 2.5 times as large as South Korea's 44 million, while another "tiger," Hong Kong, has a limited home market of 5 million people.

The country identification process at Microlog is described in the Microlog (B) box.

Stage 2—Preliminary Screening

After the candidate countries have been identified, the **preliminary screening** stage begins. This involves rating the identified countries on macrolevel indicators such as political stability, geographic distance, and economic development. The idea is to weed out countries from consideration. For example, if profit repatriation or currency convertibility is questionable, the country may be eliminated. Also, countries with signs of political instability may be ruled out at this stage. Generally, exchange rate volatility is an important indication of underlying economic or political problems.

At this stage, the anticipated costs of entering a market should be broadly assessed to match financial and other resource constraints. In addition to data on transportation costs and customs duty, which are comparatively easy to assemble, costs involve storage

Getting the Picture

MICROLOG GOES TO EUROPE (B)

To screen candidate countries, the marketing director and his assistant first decided among three regions: Southeast Asia, Latin America, and Europe. All three regions showed promise, with increasing penetration of telephones and promising economic prospects. Southeast Asia showed the fastest growth, while Latin America was bound to get a boost from the NAFTA accord. Europe was very attractive because of the 1992 homogenization of regulations. Given

their limited resources, the two managers decided to first focus on Europe, partly because of their own ease and comfort there (the manager had extensive experience in Europe, and the assistant was British). They also sensed that Europeans might be more culturally prepared for a computerized response to a telephone call than the other regions (although partially correct, later acceptance in the Southeast Asian countries proved to be even quicker).

Source: Adams et al., 1993, **www.mlog.com.**

Getting the Picture

MICROLOG GOES TO EUROPE (C)

To collect preliminary screening data on the European countries, the marketing manager asked for help from a team of MBA students at a nearby university. The five-member team collected U.N. data on the size and growth of the GNP, population size, infrastructure, and level of industrial activity from the university library. Visits to the World Bank yielded information on political risk factors, ethnic diversity, and potential language and cultural problems. Informal interviews with fellow European MBA students and faculty members with European experience were used to verify information and check indicated ratings.

The preliminary screening led to a selection of 11 countries for in-depth evaluation. The set of countries included Belgium, Denmark, France, Germany, the Netherlands, Ireland, Italy, Norway, Spain, Sweden, and Switzerland.

Source: Adams et al., 1993, **www.mlog.com**.

and warehousing, distribution in the country, and supporting the product in the market. These usually have to be rough estimates, drawing on industry experts and personal experience in the country.

Preliminary screening by Microlog is described in the Microlog (C) box.

Stage 3—In-Depth Screening

The **in-depth screening** stage is the core of the attractiveness evaluation. Data here are specific to the industry and product markets, if possible even down to specific market segments. This stage involves assessing **market potential** and actual market size, market growth rate, strengths and weaknesses of existing and potential competition, and height of regulation and entry barriers, including tariffs and quotas. Where possible, in-country segmentation should also be explored, with an eye to capturing more precise target segment forecasts. Furthermore, at this stage the company resource constraints—money, managers, supply capacity, and so on—should be revisited to make sure that contemplated entries are feasible.

Several screening criteria for the in-depth stage can be useful to the prospective entrant. Generally, studies have shown that almost all entrants use information relating to market size and growth rate, level of competition, and trade barriers and regulations.[6]

Market Size

For market size, it is useful to distinguish between the current market and the potential future market. To assess the size of the current market and the target segment size, three sets of data are useful:

- Population, age-groups, number of households (in B2B, number of businesses).
- Disposable income per capita.
- Per capita spending on product category.

The future potential requires an analysis of the product life cycle:

- Current stage of the PLC.
- Potential saturation level.
- Percent of saturation potential sold (penetration).

A crude measure of market size can be computed from local production, minus exports, plus imports. An indirect measure can be derived from the widely available GNP measure, population size, growth in GNP, and imports of relevant goods. Data for the product life cycle involves penetration data such as percentage of households in possession of the product or in the market versus the likely total saturation level. Data availability is discussed later in this chapter.

Market Growth

For market growth, it is useful to distinguish between three growth components:

- *Growth among existing buyers.* This could be growth in buying frequency and also growth in amounts bought.

- *Growth in penetration.* These are new buyers coming into the market as awareness grows and product diffusion occurs.
- *Growth rate of new buyers.* With population growth and growth in disposable income, these are new incoming buyers who are old enough and have enough buying power to purchase.

Growth estimates can be obtained by getting the market size measures for different years and computing the growth rates. When deriving the growth rate in this manner, it is important that cyclical changes in the economy are accounted for. When the business cycles turn up, even slow-growing mature markets will show strong growth.

Competitive Intensity

The level of competitive rivalry in the market can be measured by the number of competitors in the market and the relative size distribution of market shares. Distinguish the following:

- Total number of competitors.
- Number of domestic and foreign competitors.
- Domestic companies' market shares.
- Multinational competitors' market shares.

Then assess your own company's strength in terms of competitive advantages and disadvantages, to reach a range of potential levels of market share.

Many governments' departments of commerce track market shares for many industries in different countries in their market shares reports.[7] Competition is generally toughest where a few large domestic companies dominate the market. When existing companies all have small shares, or when foreign companies have already made successful entry, the competitors will generally be less concerned about a new entrant.

Trade Barriers and Regulations

Tariffs, taxes, duties, and transportation costs can be ascertained from official government publications. One problem in analyzing tariff data is that the level of the barriers depends on the exact specification of the entering goods. The company can often decide to do some assembly in the foreign country to avoid high tariffs on finished products, for example, or it can decide to purchase a component from a local manufacturer in another country to get a better rate because of increased local content. Accordingly, the country rating on tariff barriers can only be assessed accurately after preliminary decisions have been made as to whether a final or some intermediate product will be shipped to that country. Since tariffs also vary by country-of-origin, it is important to research which sourcing country would be best to utilize. When a multinational has several alternative plant locations around the world, it is necessary to research all feasible locations.

Internal business regulations pose special problems. Here it is very desirable to have a command of the native language, and also the help of a lawyer. This is doubly true when it comes to nontariff barriers such as customs procedures and preferential treatment. It is also necessary to assess the role of corruption, often using unorthodox methods (see box, "The World Bank Does Corruption Research").

It is very important that on-the-spot research uncover exactly what is and is not possible under local laws and ordinances. In-store promotions, for example, are usually subject to various limitations the new local marketer must identify. Such research is best done through a research assistant who can contact government agencies, trade associations, and various libraries. Research also should be used to uncover the extent to which trade associations and similar networks of actual and potential competitors are present. This research usually involves the local marketer directly. For example, researching distribution in a local market is best done through lots of personal visits and face-to-face interviews.

Getting the Picture

THE WORLD BANK DOES CORRUPTION RESEARCH

Under its previous president, James Wolfensohn, the World Bank took on corruption as one of the major barriers to doing business in developing countries. But fighting corruption is akin to fighting a phantom. It is hard to find and prove. Since the parties involved are unwilling to talk, simply assessing levels of corruption in a country is hard. Traditional research approaches such as survey questionnaires or focus groups will not work. Imaginative methods are required. One such study, aiming to document and demonstrate the social cost of corruption, is a great example of how country research can be carried out.

Through its affiliated International Finance Corporation, the World Bank devised a small case study of how people in India use bribes to obtain a driver's license. Between October 2004 and April 2005, researchers followed 822 applicants through the process of obtaining a driver's license in New Delhi, India. Participants were recruited from actual applicants, and randomly assigned to three groups: "bonus," "lesson," and comparison groups. In the bonus group, participants were offered a financial reward if they could obtain their license fast; in the lesson group, participants were offered free driving lessons. The comparison group was given no incentives. To gauge driving skills, a surprise driving test was administered after participants had obtained their licenses.

Several results stood out. First, the bureaucracy was responsive to individual needs in that those who were in the bonus group got the license 40 percent faster and at a 20 percent higher rate. This was because most of them hired an agent with special access and expertise to get their licenses. Second, those in the lesson group, despite superior driving skills, were only slightly more likely (by 8 percentage points) to actually get a license than the comparison group and far less likely (by 29 percentage points) than the bonus group. The fact that they had trained more was not very decisive. In fact, the bureaucrats created red tape by arbitrarily failing drivers, independent of their actual driving skills. This ensured that the hired agents would be able to sustain their marketability and get customers. Driving safely was not how those in the bonus group obtained their license: in fact, 69 percent of them were rated as "failures" on the dependent driving test.

To get a license—and to get it faster—the "bribes" to the agents were necessary. Corruption did "grease the wheel." As for the social costs of corruption, the research documented that requiring a driver's license did not mean that unsafe drivers were kept off the roads.

Sources: Marianne Bertrand, Simeon Djankov, Rema Hanna, and Sendhil Mullainathan, "Obtaining a Driver's License in India: An Experimental Approach in Studying Corruption." *Quarterly Journal of Economics* 122, November 2007; "Doing Business," World Bank, 2008.

The in-depth screening stage at Microlog is described in the Microlog (D) box.

Stage 4—Final Selection

In the **final selection** stage, company objectives are brought to bear for a match, and forecasted revenues and costs are compared to find the country market that best leverages the resources available. Typically, countries similar to those the company has already entered show lower entry costs, less risk, and quicker returns on the investments required to build up the market franchise. With a longer time horizon, less risk-averse management, and lower target rates of return, the firm can select countries that show greater long-term prospects and that promise to expand the firm's capabilities.

Getting the Picture

MICROLOG GOES TO EUROPE (D)

After the choice of the 11 countries had been accepted by Microlog's manager, the team and the manager discussed the selection of in-depth screening criteria. The selected criteria involved market size, growth potential, a "loose brick" factor indicating ease of entry, competitive factors, distribution possibilities, cultural distance to the United States, technological development, likely receptivity to voice processing, and importance of the market in the EU.

Once the criteria were agreed upon, the team set about collecting data, scoring each of the 11 countries on the selected criteria. This entailed some hard legwork. For example, regulatory data of the telecommunications industry were collected from the countries' consulates in Washington, DC, a laborious job divided up among the team members. Competitive data came from Microlog's management, trade association figures, U.S. Department of Commerce publications, and computer searches across various publications. In the end, many of the ratings came from the team's (and the manager's) subjective judgments.

Source: Adams et al., 1993, **www.mlog.com.**

Getting the Picture

MICROLOG GOES TO EUROPE (E)

Before calculating the attractiveness scores for the various countries, the team met with the manager and his assistant in order to come up with weights reflecting the importance of the various criteria for the voice processing system's market success. The cultural and linguistic similarity with the United States and the compatibility of the phone system and its regulation were judged to be particularly important. The manager had visited Europe and decided that even though the voice recordings on the system would have to be in the native tongue, for Microlog to transact business in any other language than English would be difficult. At the same time, size of the market was seen as unimportant or even slightly negative, since it was deemed that entry into a smaller market to start with might be a more manageable task for the firm. Also, in one of these meetings the ease of expansion from the entry base into other countries emerged as an important criterion.

The weights and attractiveness scores of the countries showed that the Netherlands and Ireland were rated highest. In both cases the telecommunications market was well developed, the industry regulations were not as severe as elsewhere, and the countries seemed to be natural entry gates for the northern European market. The Scandinavian countries, although attractive in many ways, were not sufficiently close to continental Europe to be good gateways. In addition, Sweden's Ericsson was a feared potential competitor. Germany was ruled out mainly because of its byzantine regulatory system that raised barriers and made entry costly. France's regulations were also a barrier—raised further by the dominance of Alcatel, the French telecommunications giant and a potential competitor. Because the team considered the Netherlands' location more favorable than Ireland's, it recommended the Netherlands for initial entry. As a second alternative for an entry into southern Europe, the team recommended Italy.

Source: Adams et al., 1993, **www.mlog.com.**

The firm's objectives in contemplating foreign entry can be used to assign "importance" weights to the various criteria, such as costs, to get a weighted sum across the criteria. There are several ways to assign scale numbers to the ratings and the importance weights. The process leads to a ranking of the countries from highest to lowest attractiveness for the firm.

The final selection stage of the team's assessments in the Microlog case is described in the Microlog (E) box.

Personal Experience

The final selection of the country to enter cannot and should not be made until personal visits have been made to the country and **direct experience** acquired by the managers. There is no substitute for on-the-spot information and the hands-on feeling of a new market. There are lessons to be learned from the flexibility with which the hotel staff responds to unusual requests; the language capabilities of the average person in the street; the courtesy, or lack of it, in stores; the degree to which a doctor responds to a client's questions; the ease with which a phone call home can be made; and the speed with which currencies may be exchanged. Countless such observations may be made on the local scene. And the visits will often have serendipitous effects, creating marketing opportunities not recognized before, as happens to Microlog in box (F).

Getting the Picture

MICROLOG GOES TO EUROPE (F)

The final choice? The Netherlands. A first trip to the European CeBIT fair in Hanover yielded several contacts, including a couple of leads to distributors in the Netherlands. Rerouting his return trip through Hilversum, the manager met with executives at Philips, the big electronics manufacturer. Philips was interesting not simply as a prospective customer, but as a partner in the European market. With the kind of strong European connection provided by Philips, Microlog would be able to quickly establish credibility and create a base for future European expansion. As the manager put it: "We wanted Philips to be the long pole in our European tent." For its part, Philips's manage-

ment recognized the potential value of Microlog's voice processing system and was interested in having Microlog provide an OEM system to be marketed under the Philips name in their telecommunications division. Signing a nonexclusive "best efforts" contract with Philips enabled Microlog to gain immediate credibility in Europe and gain a strong base for further expansion via independent value-added resellers (VAR). In this way, Microlog could gain entry into several European markets by piggybacking on Philips's sales force and also selling via the VARs under its own brand name.

Source: Adams et al., 1993, **www.mlog.com.**

An advertisement for Dutch Philips's new color monitor. Despite the loss of its brand name in the United States, where Philips is an oil company, Dutch Philips is a global giant in consumer electronics. Its technological prowess makes it a worthy competitor of the world's best, and its European styling flair emphasizing ergonomic features makes for people-friendly products. Courtesy Philips Taiwan Ltd.

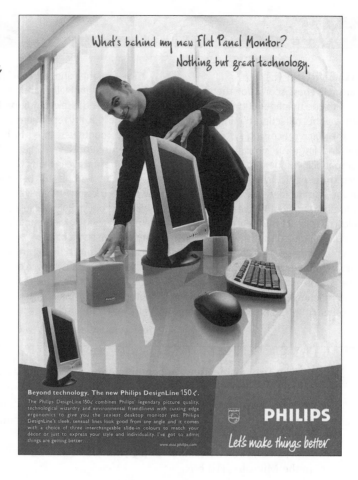

Country Data Sources

Despite the important role of personal visits to the top candidate countries, most of the data used in the screening of countries come from secondary, not primary, sources.

A useful start when doing research is to look at the easily available secondary data sources, such as the U.N. publications, the OECD and GATT/WTO reports, and the Department of Commerce reports in the United States. A large number of organizations—consulates, commerce departments, newspaper and magazine affiliates, information agencies—can be helpful. The data are today often accessible through their Web sites, and can easily be found with the help of an Internet search engine such as Google or Yahoo. Some of the more prominent organizations and sources are listed in Exhibit 4.2.

Actually, with the globalization of markets and Internet growth, the availability of **secondary data** (data already collected for some other purpose and readily available) has grown exponentially. Internet and online services such as Lexis–Nexis and Google have made it easy to access basic economic and demographic data as well as newsworthy developments. Basic data availability online continues to improve for companies (annual reports, for example) and for people in various regions or trade blocs (the Eurostat, for instance).

For more in-depth analyses, various independent firms, from advertising agencies to international research firms to electronic news media, have emerged to gather and sell information on specific industries across the globe. Leading research firms are increasingly building representation and capability to do market surveys in different countries, including the emerging economies. Some of the sources are listed in Exhibit 4.3.

EXHIBIT 4.2
Country Data Sources

Africa Briefings
Macroeconomic and economic sector data for African countries.

Business Environment Risk Intelligence (BERI)
Provides political risk ratings for 130 countries on a scale from 0 (greatest risk) to 100 (least risk).

CIA World Factbook 2008
Economic and political profiles of countries worldwide.

Council of European Social Science Data Archives (CESSDA)
Listing of European macroeconomics data archives.

Economist Intelligence Unit (EIU)
Analysis and forecast of economic, political, and business environment for over 180 countries.

EIU Country Commerce
Provides operating conditions, commercial laws, and business regulations of approximately 60 countries worldwide.

EIU Country Data
Economic indicators and forecasts providing data series on economic structure, foreign payments, external debt stock, external debt service, external trade, trends in foreign trade, and quarterly indicators.

EIU Country Reports
Provides quarterly analyses and forecasts of the political, economic and business environment in more than 180 countries.

Eurostat
Economic data for the European Union (EU).

Global Risk Assessment, Inc.
Analysis and research for political, investment, and trade risk.

Global Prospectus LLC
Global market and industry data.

Internet Center for Corruption Research
Country ranking according to level of corruption.

PRS Group
Data on country and political risk analysis.

Transparency International
Annual ranking of perceived corruption in 90 countries.

World Bank Country Data
Contains profiles on 206 countries.

Doing Business 2008
Regulatory obstacles in 178 countries.

In the country identification stage, the analysis usually has to make do with general information. A good place to start is with the United Nations annual compilation of world economic and social data, which will give a broad picture of the various countries. This can be followed by data from the U.S. Department of Commerce and other government offices and data from international organizations such as the EU Commission, World Bank, and the International Monetary Fund (IMF).

In the preliminary screening phase, more in-depth data become desirable. Syndicated reports from Business International, Dun & Bradstreet, or The Conference Board

EXHIBIT 4.3
Selected International Data Sources

The Economist Intelligence Unit (EIU): Marketing in Europe (product markets in Europe—food, clothing, furniture, household goods, appliances). EIU now also owns BI (see below).
Business International: BI database (consumption patterns in different countries).
Frost & Sullivan: Syndicated market research for various industries in different countries.
Euromonitor: European marketing data and statistics (population, standard of living index, consumption).
Bates Worldwide: Global scan (spending patterns, media habits, and attitudes in different countries).
U.S. Department of Commerce: Global market surveys (research on targeted industries); country market surveys (more detailed reports on promising countries for exports); overseas marketing report (market profiles for all countries except the United States).
World Bank: World Development Report.

should be considered. Bates Worldwide, the global ad agency headquartered in New York, publishes its "Global Scan" database. The database covers 20 countries and offers demographics and socioeconomic data for subgroups of the population of the various countries. Euromonitor International is another source that offers data on attitudes and opinions in addition to socioeconomic data on the European countries. The so-called VALS (Values and Lifestyles) program initiated by Stanford Research Institute has been expanded internationally, identifying lifestyle segments of many developed markets. The data cost money, but usually syndication keeps report costs down to reasonable levels for most firms (under $1,000).

A good data source for the preliminary screening phase is the *Business International Market Report,* published annually for the last 30 years. The report gives weighted indicators of market size, growth, and market intensity for the world's markets. The market size data are based on a combination of measures including population size; urban percentage; private consumption expenditures (disposable GNP minus private savings); ownership figures for telephones, cars, and televisions; and electricity production. The market growth indicator is basically the average shift in market size over five years. The market intensity measure is intended to capture the dynamics of the marketplace by double-weighting the private consumption expenditures, the car ownership figures, and the proportion of urban population.

The BI indices, now published by the Economist Intelligence Unit, are particularly useful for spotting promising growth countries and thus suggesting newly emerging markets where a global marketer may want to have a presence. The indices need to be buttressed by political risk indicators and some data on the degree to which the market is open and free of government interference. Such data can be obtained from the *Political Risk Yearbook,* published annually by Political Risk Services in Syracuse, New York. These data provide expert assessments of political instability in a country, including the chances of a violent change in government and the degree of social unrest. They also contain summaries of restrictions on business, such as limitations on foreign ownership and constraints on the repatriation of funds. Countries that score high on political instability and restrictions on business can usually be eliminated from consideration early.

The best guide for entry barriers and regulatory obstacles is probably the annual "Doing Business" reports from the World Bank. They offer data on regulatory barriers to doing business in a wide variety of countries. The 2008 publication covers 178 countries (see box, "Business Barriers Across Countries").

In the in-depth screening stage, when data on specific markets are needed, the data availability varies by industry. Trade associations are usually the place to start, followed by government agencies. The U.S. Department of Commerce, and its counterparts in other countries, publishes some data at the industry level, even some market share data for various countries and products. Where trade conflicts have occurred, more data tend to be available. In highly visible industries such as automobiles, computers, and consumer electronics, reasonably good data are usually available from the trade press. There are also syndicated data. Frost and Sullivan in New York, for example, provide worldwide studies of market growth and potential for specific industries. The problem in the in-depth screening stage is the lack of comparability between countries and the incompleteness of some countries' data. The dynamic potential of a country such as Italy, for example, with its large underground economy, is difficult to capture in published statistics. The lack of information serves, in fact, as a barrier to entry.

Data on product-specific criteria can be used to cluster candidate countries into groups of high and low potential. In the Microlog case the team clustered the countries on two criteria at a time. Exhibit 4.4 shows the resulting clusters for the mapping of "competition" against "growth potential." In the upper northeast corner is a cluster of countries with high growth potential and relatively weak competitive intensity, obviously presenting more opportunity than France, with so-so growth and a high degree of competition (1 = strong competition). This graph alone quickly suggests why France may be a bad choice for Microlog's entry into the EU.

Getting the Picture

BUSINESS BARRIERS ACROSS COUNTRIES

When assessing country attractiveness for trade and investment, entry barriers and business regulations can reduce a high-scoring country to an also-ran. Japan's prohibition against large-scale stores and Germany's restrictions on store opening hours (now both history) are perhaps the most obvious examples, but many other countries with low tariff barriers turn out to be less than attractive because of inhibiting business regulations. For example, India has enforced mandatory certification for 109 products, covering a wide range of products (e.g. various food items, food colors, cements). For certification of these 109 items, detailed requirements have been issued under seven different acts. Even with no external tariffs, imports would not have an easy entry.

In recent years a World Bank team under the leadership of Dr. Simeon Djankov has produced an assessment of business regulations in a growing list of countries. The 2008 report covers no less than 178 countries, each country showing updated regulatory requirements for ten categories of business activities. The categories are:

Starting a business

Getting licenses

Hiring and firing workers

Registering property

Getting credit

Protecting investors

Paying taxes

Trading across borders

Enforcing contracts

Closing a business

Available in one volume or by country, the "Doing Business" annual reports update all 10 sets of indicators and rank countries on their overall ease of doing business. The reports identify which countries are improving their business environment the most and which ones have slipped. Economies are ranked on their ease of doing business, from 1–178, with first place being the best. A high ranking on the ease of doing business index means the regulatory environment is conducive to the operation of business. The list of the top 10 countries from the 2008 report, covering the period April 2006 to June 2007, follows:

1. Singapore
2. New Zealand
3. United States
4. Hong Kong, China
5. Denmark
6. United Kingdom
7. Canada
8. Ireland
9. Australia
10. Iceland

The bottom 10 were, predictably but sadly, mainly developing countries, especially African countries, with the Democratic Republic of Congo in last place.

Sources: www.doingbusiness.org; Parvaiz Ishfaq Rana, "Softening of Indian Trade Barriers," *Dawn,* Internet edition, April 30, 2007.

The final selection stage requires no new secondary information in principle, but it is here that the subjective judgments and experiences during the visits to the prospective country play a bigger role. Now managers can substitute subjective "guesstimates" for missing data and correct other data that seem out of line. Although this

EXHIBIT 4.4

Microlog's Country Clusters

Source: Adams et al., 1993.

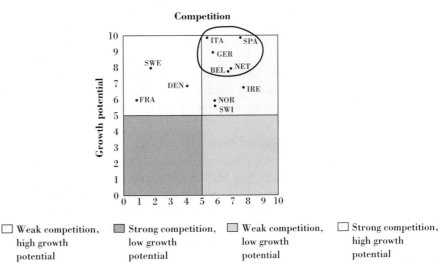

☐ Weak competition, high growth potential   ■ Strong competition, low growth potential   ▨ Weak competition, low growth potential   ☐ Strong competition, high growth potential

may introduce bias into the final assessment, it is at least clear where it comes from. Thus, it is possible to do a sensitivity analysis and evaluate the extent to which the overall ratings vary for potential biases in either direction. This is also where the competitive research should have yielded possible scenarios for competitive reaction that can be played out against the option chosen. When door-to-door cosmetics seller Mary Kay decided to enter China, the company judged that first-mover Avon would not react defensively, since the two could grow the huge market together. The prediction proved correct—but both companies were stunned by the later political crackdown on pyramid sales, which forced the companies to stop door-to-door selling in China and instead open stores.

Researching Competitors

As we saw in Chapter 2, in most markets the local marketer is faced with competition from both domestic competitors and other foreign competitors, and research is important to identify who they are, what their strengths and weaknesses are, and how they are likely to react to a new competitor. This research is particularly useful when developing alternative scenarios of competitive reactions, for sensitivity testing of the final choice.

Strengths and Weaknesses

From company annual reports, if available, 10K or corresponding stock exchange filings, and similar sources, it is possible to get a sense of the financial capability of the competition. Recognize, however, that a company with a large consolidated financial base is not necessarily active in any one country market. It's important to judge the strategic importance of the market for the competition and the strategic intent of the competitors operating there.

The overall importance of the market for the competitors is usually higher for domestic companies than for foreign entrants. However, FDI in manufacturing tends to make a foreign company an "insider" in the country and thus likely to behave similarly to a domestic company. IBM Japan is in many respects a truly Japanese company, with only a handful of Western employees and not at the top level.

Understanding the organizational structure of the competitors helps gauge their local strengths. A multinational such as Philips, the Dutch electronics company, with strongly independent country operations, is not likely to engage in massive support for a particular country's operations. By contrast, a company with a globally integrated strategy such as Caterpillar will be able to take a loss in one market and make it up elsewhere. Its country operations can draw on the global resources to a greater extent than can the Philips subsidiary.[8]

As for the local marketing efforts of competitors, research will identify whether strategies involve low prices rather than unique differentiation, will reveal the strengths and weaknesses of their distribution and after-sales service systems, and so on. This type of information is usually available from middlemen, trade magazines, and even newspaper articles. More often it's easier to "scope out" the strengths and weaknesses of competitors than to get a handle on what motivates customers.

Competitive Signaling

The local marketer must read competitive signals to judge what competitors' future actions may be. In most markets, not only emerging ones, deregulation and the privatization of industry have led to chaotic conditions, and forecasting competitive behavior is not easy. This is especially true in high-technology areas such as telecommunications and computers where premature announcements are sometimes used to mislead competitors or foil a takeover bid.

Competitive posturing can be difficult to interpret for a new entrant, and it may be necessary to hire experienced local talent precisely to deal with relationships with competitors, as well as with the public and with the authorities. In most countries the type of "hands-off" bureaucratic stance assumed in the United States is unusual, and it becomes important for the new manager to develop a network of contacts so that communication in the trade can be facilitated. Although from one angle such networks may be seen as collusive and anticompetitive, from another viewpoint they simply represent the way business is done in the foreign industry. With the advent of strategic alliances and related cooperative alignments between companies and competitors, the local marketer needs to study and learn how the network can be used to the firm's benefit.

Forecasting Country Sales

This chapter has so far dealt with research to evaluate the market potential in a foreign country. Such research identifies what could potentially be achieved under "ideal" conditions, while a **sales forecast** assesses what is likely to be obtained given the probable situation and contemplated strategies. Here the focus is on the derivation of sales forecasts at two levels: industry sales and market share.

The forecasting of total market sales and market share involves technical skills, many of which are valid in any market. But there are additional factors that need to be considered in foreign markets. Economic and demographic data might not be available or not be comparable because of different classifications. The marketer often has to leverage past data from other markets, including the home market, into a kind of "bootstrap" forecast of what is likely to happen in a new market. Forecasting sales in a foreign market is a matter of combining technical skills and country knowledge imaginatively.

A Basic Equation

Few companies are as fortunate as Mazda when it comes to forecasting sales in foreign markets (see box, "Mazda's Shorthand Forecast").

The Mazda approach provides the basic components that companies have to estimate in order to generate a forecast:

$$\text{Sales} = \text{Industry sales} \times \text{Market share}$$

The division between industry sales and market share serves to isolate what factors need to be considered. To develop an estimate of industry sales, the well-known determinants such as economic growth, disposable incomes, social and political developments, as well as dynamics of the product life cycle need to be incorporated. The market share prediction, on the other hand, relates directly to factors such as competitive situation and marketing effort. The basic idea tends to be that what affects the market size is one thing, what affects the share we get in the market is another. Although in international marketing this represents an oversimplification because of various trade obstacles (tariff and nontariff barriers), such factors can be incorporated and accounted for as we will show.

Stage of the Product Life Cycle

In the early stages of the product life cycle relatively little data are usually available for statistically based forecasting, and more inventive methods have to be relied on. In later stages, past sales and market share data are available, and more sophisticated methods can be employed. Three types of forecasting techniques can be used in the early stages. One is the evaluation via a "build-up" method from industry experts and distribution channel units; another is forecasting by analogy, doing a comparison with a lead country. When all else fails, judgmental methods have to be used.

MAZDA'S SHORTHAND FORECAST

Even before 1981, when their agreement to voluntarily restrict exports to the United States took effect, the Japanese auto companies had an easy time forecasting their American sales (after 1981 the Japanese simply divided up their market share among themselves). Mazda, for example, was able to employ a "shorthand" type of quick forecasting method. First, projected industry sales, in units, were polled from various sources, including economists in Washington, DC. Second, the market share going to imports as a class was identified, also provided by these same sources. Next, the Japanese share among these imports was estimated on the evidence of past

performance and projected competitive developments worldwide—the Japanese Automobile Manufacturers' Association (JAMA) was instrumental here. Finally, the share falling to Mazda from the Japanese piece of the pie was estimated on the basis of in-house data and probable developments in styles and specifications and against previous performances abroad. Computing the forecasted sales then was simple. They equaled Industry sales × Import share × Share for the Japanese × Share for Mazda among the Japanese. Time and cost to develop the forecast? Negligible. Accuracy? Almost perfect.

Sources: Personal interviews with company spokesmen, Mazda North America.

Industry Sales

The Build-Up Method

For the early stages of introduction the best estimates of future sales usually come from industry experts and knowledgeable channel members. If the company can contact some of these individuals—travel is usually necessary—an estimate of the market size can be based on their information. The "build-up" connotation of the **build-up method** comes from the fact that the market sales are estimated on the basis of separate estimates from individuals knowledgeable about certain segments of the market. These single estimates of various parts of the market are aggregated ("built up") into an evaluation of total market size.

For example, when one company attempted to forecast sales in Europe of a new consumer audio product, it divided each country market into three segments each served by different channels. The teenage segment purchased mostly through convenience outlets. The high-performance segment purchased through specialty stores. The family user purchased through general merchandise and department stores. The company then collected estimates from each of these channels in the main European countries to build up a forecast.

Given that these estimates are subjective, it is important that the marketer gather additional information from whatever other sources are available so as to develop a sense of the reliability of the subjective estimates.

The information from the build-up method should always be compared to managerial experiences of the product in other countries—provided of course there are other countries further along the product life cycle process. In these cases forecasting by analogy has become quite popular.

Forecasting by Analogy

The basic premise underlying **forecasting by analogy** is that the sales in one "lagging" country will show similarities to sales in another "leading" country where the product is already marketed. Since the 1960s, when the theme of global interdependence and convergence first emerged strongly, such similarities have been used to forecast a similar rate of acceptance of a new product in many different countries, especially those belonging to a common regional grouping. A standard example was television. Its introduction in the United States had been shown to exhibit a growth curve replicated with minor modifications in a number of other countries (the so-called demonstration effect). Most examples fall within the durable category of products, where market penetration in terms of first-purchase rates is used as a standard indication of stage of market development.

According to this technique, a reasonably quick and cheap way of assessing the sales potential at a given point (and for the future) in a country where a product introduction is contemplated would be to ascertain at what stage of the growth curve (the product life cycle) the product will be when entering the new market. If the product is new, the assumption is made that the growth curve will have approximately the same slope as in a "lead" country where the product is already introduced. Empirical analyses have demonstrated that the speed of adoption tends to be quite similar in new countries—but also that (because of differences in economic rates of growth), the saturation level will be lower (or higher). These differences are usually adjusted for judgmentally when the final forecast is developed.

An Illustration: TV Penetration

An example of the possible use of forecasting by analogy is provided by the introduction and market penetration of TV sets in various countries at different points in time.[9] Exhibit 4.5 shows the percent of ownership and annual increases in sales for three countries.

According to the exhibit, the penetration rate was slightly faster in the United States compared to Germany and the United Kingdom, and large annual increases occurred correspondingly earlier in the life cycle. Other countries showed different patterns. Sweden, for example, exhibited a penetration rate steeper than that of the United States, often ascribed to the "demonstration effect" of the United States and other countries in which TV stations came on the air earlier.

Exhibit 4.5 illustrates the opportunities and problems in forecasting by analogy. Yes, the patterns are the same, generally speaking. But the timing of the takeoff and rapid growth stages are different, and the lags involved are not identical. By introducing variables to explain the variations in the penetration curves it is possible to adjust the forecast by analogy to more properly reflect the likely time path.

To account for the difference in size between countries, the sales figures are usually weighted by a measure such as GNP or population size. For example, forecasted sales might be computed from an expression such as the following:

$$S_b(1995) = [S_a(1991)/\text{GNP}_a(1991)] \times \text{GNP}_b(1995)$$

where S stands for unit sales, the subscript a stands for the leading country, b stands for the lagging country, and there is a lag of four years (1995–1991). In words, the ratio of sales to GNP in the lead country in 1991 gives the unit sales per dollar GNP. By multiplying this factor into the lagging country's GNP in 1995, a sales forecast is arrived at.

It goes without saying that such a simple formula requires a careful assessment of the comparability between the two countries. What is relevant is whether there is any reason to expect the ratio between sales and GNP to differ between countries. The United States and Canada are two quite different countries in some respects—but there might be little reason to expect these differences to be very important once the discrepancy in the size of population has been taken into account. On the other hand,

EXHIBIT 4.5

Yearly Increase in Household Ownership of TV Sets, 1946–70

Source: Lindberg, 1982. Adapted with permission. © 1982 by the American Marketing Association.

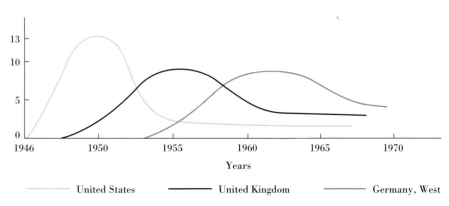

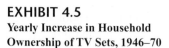

comparing Japan and West Germany, countries with quite comparable economic output records, might be more difficult: The TV might play a very different role in the Japanese household with the absent husband working until 11 PM as compared to the German household in which the larger homes and less time on the job allow the family to spend more time together. These differences might induce the suspicion that GNP will not account for differences in sales (as it turns out the penetration ratio is higher for Japan where color TV has become more of a status symbol than in Germany).

Judgmental Forecasts

If the product has no history in any comparable country (as might be the case when entering the former communist countries), analogies can be misleading. Furthermore, channel members may know too little for a build-up method to have any validity or reliability. Purely judgmental methods may have to be used.

Judgmental forecasting techniques generally attempt to introduce a certain amount of rigor and reliability into otherwise quite arbitrary guesses.[10]

The Jury Technique

The use of executive judgment based on first-hand experience and observation in estimating foreign sales is indispensable. The **jury technique** is basically a structuring of the standard executive committee meetings, in which the members are asked to submit their separate forecasts, either before or after intensive discussion. The individual forecasts are then pooled and the results again evaluated before a final figure or range is arrived at. The concept is that a group of experienced executives would have more insights when combined than any single one. When coupled with the Delphi method (see below), the method gains additional power.

It is important that whatever data exist are made available to the jury and also that staff members from overseas are included in the process. It should be emphasized that this type of managerial judgment becomes especially important in decisions involving major commitments and high risk, since then the consensus arrived at by the jury automatically assigns responsibility to the whole group, not an individual manager. In this respect, foreign entry is more naturally the domain of several executives rather than a small number or one person with good knowledge of operations in one country but not in others.

Expert Pooling

There is no doubt that consultation with experts **(expert pooling)** on the country contemplated will always be a cornerstone in sales forecasting where new entry is concerned. Without a firm's having previous experience in a new country's markets, the reliance on independent experts (academicians, consulting firms, or host country nationals) is almost unavoidable. Judging from the literature on export initiation, it is precisely this type of information source about market potential that best serves the process of exploring entry into a new country.

Panel Consensus

The **panel consensus,** much like the jury of executive opinion, tries to pool the available information from more than one source. The Microlog team used this type of pooling to arrive at country ratings on the selected criteria, essentially taking averages across each team member's subjective rating. The Delphi method is a more systematic approach.

Delphi Method

The **Delphi method** consists of a series of "rounds" of numerical forecasts from a preselected number of experts. These experts may or may not know the identity of the other members of the panel. They are asked to provide individual estimates, independently of their colleagues. The estimates are tallied, the average forecast is computed, and summary statistics (but not individual estimates) are returned to the experts. Another round of estimates is collected, tallied up, and the summary is again distributed. As these rounds continue, the feedback provided will tend to bring the estimates into line. The expert whose initial estimate is far off the average forecast will tend to converge toward the mean—unless, of course, he or she has strong prior belief that the estimate is more correct. In either case, the process gradually converges, as those with weaker opinions yield to those with strong opinions under the influence of the pressure to adjust toward the average forecast received.

The Delphi method has been discussed widely and has come in for its share of criticism. The basic problem is that "bad estimates might drive out good estimates" when the panel members show unequal degrees of stubbornness. In general, however, the type of pooling of various opinions offered by this technique has been its greatest advantage. When judgmental analysis is carried out by using several individuals with some experience or direct knowledge of a country's market, it serves to prohibit one particularly strong personality (a headquarters executive, for example, or the general manager of a subsidiary) from dominating the proceedings. The anonymity provided serves to ensure that everybody "has a voice."

Time Series Extrapolation

When the product in the market country has reached a more mature stage in the product life cycle, forecasting using past data becomes possible. There are essentially two approaches available for carrying out these forecasts. One is based on historical data of industry sales alone, simply extrapolating past trends into the future. The second allows for more in-depth analysis, incorporating the variables that underlie sales developments in the country. This method is based on regression analysis.

Time series data represent a form of "history in numbers." In other words, statistics are based on past performance, behavior, and developments, and the statistical analysis of the data generated by these histories will simply ferret out what happened in a more comprehensive and objective manner than subjective evaluations. Thus, the primary requirements for statistical forecasting of foreign sales are (1) that data are available, (2) that past events are relevant for the future, and (3) that statistics will be a better judge of what happened than more informal or anecdotal accounts. Although in domestic forecasting the reliance on statistical analysis often seems great (because the requisite data are indeed available), in international marketing all three requirements typically pose problems. For example, recent dramatic political and economic changes in Asia, Eastern Europe, and Latin America suggest that historical time series may be a poor guide for the future.

Extrapolation refers to the method by which a time series of (sales) data observed over some periods in the past is extended into the future. It represents, in a sense, the purest form of forecasting, in that the concern is entirely with the future: The current level of sales provides but one data point among many. At the same time it represents a very naive form of forecasting in that the only information employed is the numbers of the sales series in past periods. The focus of the forecaster's job is on detecting patterns in these numbers to be projected into the future. There are many excellent texts on this topic, and since the international context adds little to these treatments, they will not be covered here.[11]

Regression-Based Forecasts

The first considerations in developing a regression forecast involve the use of some prior knowledge to develop a forecasting equation. First, the relevant dependent variable of interest needs to be determined. Is it a matter of annual industry sales, in units (the most common choice)? In dollars? The growth rate of sales per annum? The import sales alone?

Second, the forecaster must try to identify what factors will affect the dependent variable selected. For most country analyses, GNP and population figures become relevant since they tend to measure the "size" of the market. But more specific measures are often needed. How many people or firms could one consider to be potential customers, or, stated differently, what is the "in-the-market" proportion? If a country has a large population but few single-person households, the market for labor-saving prepared foods might be correspondingly smaller. Where a large number of small manufacturers exist, but only few large-scale corporations, the market for mainframe computers and associated software might be minimal, despite a high GNP per capita.

The Size Component

It is useful at this stage to break up the independent variables into different categories. One set deals with "size": how many firms, or people, are potential customers, for example. A useful approach is sometimes to segment the total number into homogeneous subsets: how many heavy industry firms, how many in services, or, for consumer goods, how many households with children, how many with incomes over a certain level, how many in the big cities versus the rural areas, and so on depending upon the product. This type of evaluation can usually be done using the "chain ratio rule," in which the initial figure of size is broken down by the percentages falling into the separate segments: For example, the size M of one segment may be calculated as

$$M = \text{Number of households} \times \text{Proportion with children} \times \text{Proportion with incomes over \$10,000 a year}$$

Willingness to Buy

A second group of independent variables influences the willingness to buy the product. In consumer goods, need for the product among types of consumers, existing attitudes toward foreign products, and fit between product use and buyer lifestyles are all important considerations. In industrial markets, sophistication of the process technology employed in manufacturing, attitude toward foreign products, special features the product offers, and other similar considerations are relevant. Needless to say, this portion of the analysis must be based on intimate knowledge of the country's people, be it through formal market research or personal experience.

Ability to Buy

The last category relates to consumers' ability to pay for the product. Variables here are income, per capita expenditures on related products, profit performance of company customers, and other similar economic factors. It's important to identify trends in these figures so that precautions can be taken and future opportunities are not missed.

Sales per Customer

Combining the willingness and ability to buy, one can develop an estimate of the amount of probable sales (units or money) per customer in the target segment. A typical method to use is regression, in which the various factors that determine willingness and ability are regressed against sales, the data coming from other countries where the product has already been introduced. A typical example is given by Armstrong for a forecast of camera sales (see box, "Armstrong's Regression Model").

Market Sales

Customers' willingness and ability to buy can now be combined into a total sales estimate. Using the market size multiplied by the average sales per customer, a simple version of the model is:

$$S = M \times r$$

where r is the average sales per customer (in units or money).

Getting the Picture

ARMSTRONG'S REGRESSION MODEL

Armstrong forecasted camera sales in a given country in three steps. First, a regression was specified to predict camera sales per potential buyer:

$$R = f(E,P,B,T,W,C,G)$$

with E = Beckerman's standard of living index

P = Price of camera goods

B = Buying units index (households per adult)

T = Temperature

W = Rainfall

C = Proportion of children in the population

G = Growth of per capita income per year

This regression equation combines the willingness and ability to buy into a forecast of average of sales per potential buyer (R). It was estimated using data on camera sales for existing country markets.

The second step specified the size of the potential market using a multiplicative chain:

$$M = (T) \times (L) \times (A) \times (N)$$

with M = Number of potential buyers

T = Total population

L = Literacy rate (proportion)

A = Proportion of population aged 15–64

N = Proportion of nonagricultural employment

This equation was not estimated since the variables were straight proportions. These are segmentation variables, eliminating people outside Kodak's target segments. For example, Kodak's experience showed that most sales occurred outside the nonagricultural segment.

The third step combined sales per potential buyer and the size of the market to derive the forecasted sales:

$$S = (R) \times (M)$$

where S = Forecasted camera sales in units per year for the given country.

Regression is widely used for forecasting and market planning as we will see in Chapter 11.

Sources: Armstrong, 1970; Corstjens and Merrihue, 2003.

Forecasting Market Share

After forecasting industry sales it becomes necessary to predict what portion of total industry sales the particular company can obtain. This entails a forecast of market share.

Predicting Competition

Market share forecasts involve prediction of competitive moves. This requires not only knowing who actual and potential competitors might be in a given country but also assessing competitors' strengths and weaknesses. Hard enough when it comes to understanding what is currently going on, when attention is directed toward the future, the forecasting problem becomes very thorny. Small wonder that subjective managerial judgment plays a relatively great role.

Market share forecasts are usually done best by breaking up the problem into its separate components. First, the likely competitors must be identified, including domestic firms and multinational companies operating in the country. Second, country-specific advantages of the domestic companies over foreign competition should be well understood. Third, the company's strengths against the other firms have to be objectively assessed, particularly against other foreign firms operating in the country.

Identifying Competitors

Drawing on informal in-house knowledge and on selected contacts in the market country, a list of competitors is compiled. One difficulty is identifying what future entries may be made—here also, less formal research methods will be reliable indicators. It is important that potential entrants be included, particularly when the product in the new country is at an early stage in the life cycle while in other countries its development has progressed further. When a competitor is already well established in other markets, entry into a new market can be undertaken quite quickly. A good example is the burgeoning auto market in Saudi Arabia that was rapidly covered by major automakers from Europe and Japan once the oil revenues had radically increased the spending power of the population.

Domestic Competitors

The fact that tariff and nontariff barriers make entry difficult by raising foreign firms' prices and giving advantages to domestic producers must be considered very carefully. Not-so-prohibitive existing barriers could be changed all too quickly after an entry has been successfully made, and the possibility of direct foreign investment must be considered at this stage. For forecasting purposes, the critical figure is the proportion of the market available to foreign competitors ("country share"). In most countries there are (possibly unstated) limits on market capture that the entering firms can reach without inducing protectionist measures. Managerial judgment and informal inquiries might disclose what those limits are. The forecasted share might well need be to constrained a priori using this information, with the understanding that the company will have an upper limit on the share it can obtain in the market.

Apart from such political considerations, the forecaster needs to evaluate the strength of a possible "pro-domestic" attitude on the part of buyers. There is sometimes covert or overt pressure on buyers to stay loyal to their domestic companies, the "Buy American" movement being one example. In addition, there are attitude differences toward products from different countries, as well as formal requests to companies that entry into certain other countries be restricted (at the time of this writing, certain Arab states demanding that suppliers not do business with Israel, for example).

In addition to these extra-economic considerations, the forecaster needs to be aware that many domestic producers provide a product or service that is particularly well suited to the special needs and wants of the country, even though it might make little headway in the international marketplace. America's big cars, the dark beer of England, and "small-is-beautiful" farm equipment in India may be hard to compete with in local markets. In these cases the evaluation of the competitive strengths of the domestic producers needs to be adjusted beyond a straightforward application of strengths and weaknesses of products. Needless to say, such adjustments become subjective and judgmental.

In the end, the forecaster should be able to come up with a reasonable estimate of the market share "available" to imports (import share versus domestic share). This step serves well in accounting for factors affecting market performance that are not encountered in the home market.

Foreign Competitors

How well will the company fare against other foreign competitors in the local market? Here more objective data are sometimes available, since these firms might have been encountered in other world markets. Motorola can assess fairly directly how well its products may perform relative to Samsung, Sony-Ericsson, or Nokia using its experience with these companies in other parts of the globe. Market share estimates can't be assumed equal to those in other markets, but a fair evaluation can be made.

If appropriate, this last step can be broken down into evaluating foreign competitors first and then firms from the company's home country. Westinghouse might first assess a probable U.S. share, and then go on to comparing itself to General Electric. We saw Mazda's approach, first identifying the probable Japanese share and then comparing its strength against Japanese competitors. This breakdown becomes particularly necessary when the tariff, quotas, and other nontariff barriers (including country-of-origin stereotyping and attitudes) differ for different home countries. A typical example would be automobiles in the EU. Semiofficial quotas help Italian and French authorities keep domestic auto firms' market shares up to protect employment. Once the "desired" domestic share has been ascertained from industry experts, the foreign automakers can focus on the remaining available market share.

Summary

Chapter 4 examined how companies do global market research to evaluate countries' attractiveness for foreign market entry. The basic research on each country involves political risk analysis and environmental data on trade barriers, economic regulation, and social and physical conditions. An assessment of domestic and foreign companies' competitive strength in each specific market being considered is also warranted.

The evaluation process typically proceeds in stages, with an initial identification of a set of countries based on matching the macrosegments and the company's strategic intentions, such as a desired presence in a particular free trade region or clusters of similar countries. A preliminary screening using situational indicators such as geographic distance, political uncertainty, and exchange rate volatility reduces the set, after which an in-depth screening of the most promising candidates reduces it further. The chapter described the various data sources that exist for the different stages of the evaluation process. However, even though data sources have grown substantially in the last few years, the screening requires a personal visit to the top candidate countries to get a direct feel for the market and marketing infrastructure. Such "hands-on" contact by managers with the new market should never be missed, especially now with financial and political turmoil intense.

Secondary data on buyer behavior in different countries have become more available with the advent of the Internet, online public data from trade regions, and syndicated data from private research firms.

The chapter also showed how to adapt sales forecasting techniques applicable in domestic markets to foreign country markets. Despite data differences and differences in product life cycle stages, among many other factors, the standard breakdown of the forecasting problem into industry sales and market share forecasts as separate issues can be used. It should be modified by introducing "import share" to deal with tariff and nontariff barriers and "country share" to deal with country-of-origin attitudes.

As always, it is useful if several independent forecasts are carried out, if feasible, and the results "pooled" to arrive at the best forecast possible. This pooling effort draws on many individual judgments, based on managers' valuable direct personal experience with the country in question. The low likelihood of intimate knowledge of every country on the list makes group consensus forecasts generally superior to an individual's projections.

Key Terms

build-up method, *118*
country identification, *106*
Delphi method, *120*
direct experience, *111*
environmental dimensions, *105*
expert pooling, *120*
extrapolation, *121*
final selection, *110*
forecasting by analogy, *118*
in-depth screening, *108*
jury technique, *120*
market potential, *108*
market share forecasts, *123*
panel consensus, *120*
political risk, *102*
preliminary screening, *107*
sales forecast, *117*
secondary data, *112*
terrorism, *103*

Discussion Questions

1. Company spokespeople are often heard to say, "We have to be in that market." What is a likely explanation for this statement if the market is (a) China; (b) Germany; (c) Brazil; (d) Japan; (e) the United States? Give examples of products or services.
2. What factors would you consider when helping an already global manufacturer of household vacuum cleaners choose between Mexico, India, and China as the next country to enter?
3. Access the available online services to create a database that would help a company decide how attractive a country market is. Product category and country are your choices.
4. Use the Web sites of companies in a given product category—such as pharmaceuticals, autos, or consumer electronics—to develop a short report on how their respective product lines overlap and therefore compete in a country market of your choice.
5. New high-tech products—such as the Apple iPod—are often said to generate their own demand. What does this imply about the possibility of forecasting sales when such a product is first introduced? How could one forecast sales for it when later entering a market such as Russia?

Notes

1. Adapted from Kobrin, 1979, and De la Torre and Neckar, 1990.

2. These firms include, for example, Business International and Frost and Sullivan—see the discussion on country data sources, and Exhibit 4.2.

3. See "War Cited as Top Risk to Business," *Chicago Tribune,* January 17, 1994, p. 1.

4. Note that the breakdown here relates directly—although in slightly different order—to the Ghemawat CAGE framework (cultural, administrative, geographical, and economic distance) discussed in Chapter 1. The regionalization strategy observed for many multinationals derives precisely from the fact that the environmental variables in similar regions are more conducive to successful transfer of the firm's FSAs and CSAs.

5. This section draws on Douglas and Craig, 2000, and Kumar et al., 1994.

6. See, for example, Douglas and Craig, 2000.

7. See Exhibit 4.3 for where to get these reports.

8. See Hamel and Prahalad, 1989.

9. This example is adapted from Lindberg, 1982.

10. This section draws on Armstrong, 1985, Makridakis, 1990, and Corstjens and Merrihue, 2003.

11. Armstrong, 1985, is useful and relatively accessible for the nontechnical reader. Lindberg, 1982, and Makridakis, 1990, offer interesting applications.

Selected References

Adams, Jonathan; Shubber Ali; Leila Byczkowski; Kathryn Cancro; and Susan Nolen. "Microlog Corporation: European Market Evaluation." Class project, School of Business, Georgetown University, May 12, 1993.

Alden, Vernon R. "Who Says You Can't Crack the Japanese Market?" *Harvard Business Review,* January–February 1987, pp. 52–56.

Amine, Lyn S., and S. Tamer Cavusgil. "Demand Estimation in a Developing Country Environment: Difficulties, Techniques, and Examples." *Journal of the Market Research Society* 28, no. 1 (1986), pp. 43–65.

Anholt, Simon. *Brand New Justice: The Upside of Global Branding.* Oxford, UK: Butterworth and Heinemann, 2003

Armstrong, J. Scott. "An Application of Econometric Models to International Marketing." *Journal of Marketing Research* VII (May 1970), pp. 190–98.

———. *Long-Range Forecasting,* 2nd ed. New York: Wiley, 1985.

Bartlett, Christopher A., and Ashish Nanda. "Ingvar Kamprad and IKEA." Harvard Business School case no. 9-390-132, 1990.

Corstjens, Marcel, and Jeffrey Merrihue. "Optimal Marketing." *Harvard Business Review* 114, October 2003, pp. 1–7.

De la Torre, Jose, and David H. Neckar. "Forecasting Political Risks for International Operations." In Vernon-Wortzel, H., and L. Wortzel, eds. *Global Strategic Management,* 2nd ed. New York: Wiley, 1990.

Douglas, Susan, and Samuel R. Craig. *International Marketing Research,* 2nd ed. Upper Saddle River, NJ: Prentice-Hall, 2000.

Dubey, Suman. "After 16 Years Away, Coca-Cola to Return 'The Real Thing' to India." *The Wall Street Journal,* October 22, 1993, sec. A, p. 9E.

Hamel, Gary, and C. K. Prahalad. "Strategic Intent." *Harvard Business Review,* May–June 1989, pp. 63–76.

Kobrin, Stephen J. "Political Risk: A Review and Reconsideration." *Journal of International Business Studies* 10, no. 1 (1979), pp. 67–80.

Kotler, Philip. *Marketing Management: Analysis, Planning, Implementation, and Control,* 9th ed. Upper Saddle River, NJ: Prentice Hall, 1997.

Kumar, V.; Antonie Stam; and Erich A. Joachimsthaler. "An Interactive Multicriteria Approach to Identifying Potential Foreign Markets." *Journal of International Marketing* 2, no. 1 (1994), pp. 29–52.

Lindberg, Bertil. "International Comparison of Growth in Demand for a New Durable Consumer Product." *Journal of Marketing Research,* August 1982, pp. 364–71.

Makridakis, Spyros G. *Forecasting, Planning and Strategy for the 21st Century.* New York: Free Press, 1990.

Mitchell, Arnold. *The Nine American Lifestyles.* New York: Macmillan, 1983.

Naisbitt, John. *Global Paradox.* New York: Harper and Row, 1994.

Porter, Michael E. *Competitive Strategy.* New York: Free Press, 1980.

Rugman, Alan. *The End of Globalization.* New York: Amacom, 2001.

Smart, Tim; Pete Engardio; and Geri Smith. "GE's Brave New World." *BusinessWeek,* November 8, 1993, pp. 64–70.

Thorelli, Hans B., and S. Tamer Cavusgil, eds. *International Marketing Strategy,* 3rd ed. New York: Pergamon, 1990.

Yoshino, Michael. "Procter and Gamble Japan" (A)(B)(C). Harvard Business School case nos. 9-391-003, -004, -005, 1990.

5

Export Expansion

"Over the river and into the trees"

After reading this chapter, you will be able to:

1. Analyze barriers to entry, including tariffs, quotas, and discriminatory customs procedures, to decide between exporting and alternative entry modes.
2. Handle a number of activities that are new to a marketer, including export pricing and how to find a local agent.
3. Decide between having an agent and a distributor handle the local marketing or establishing your own foreign sales subsidiary.
4. Select a local distributor who can help overcome restrictive government regulations, limited access to distribution channels, and pro-domestic consumer biases.
5. Understand the important role of importers as partners who have more intimate knowledge of the market demand in their country.

After identifying various opportunities in foreign countries, the question becomes how the chosen country or countries should be entered and what strategy the global expansion should follow.

For marketing, it helps to distinguish between modes of entry that ship the product to the selected market and those that transfer know-how to the host country. Exporting is the standard exchange of product for money, while licensing, franchising, strategic alliances, and investment in manufacturing are entry modes that share technology and know-how with host country partners. Exporting is more straightforward and less risky, since it is expansion into new markets with an existing line of final products, while transfer of know-how involves trade in markets for company knowledge, an intermediate good. Selling Coke cans is simpler and safer than selling the formula. This is why many firms expanding abroad start with exporting.

Chapter 5 will concentrate on the export mode of entry and expansion. Exporting is the international equivalent of trade across geographical regions, often the preferred mode when trade barriers (including tariffs and transportation costs) are low. The local marketing effort can be directed through independent middlemen, but it is usually preferable to establish a foreign sales subsidiary.

"Made in Brazil" Becomes Badge of Pride

When it first started exporting products, the Brazilian subsidiary of Stanley Tools had to omit the "Made in Brazil" labels from at least half its products because customers had a negative impression of Brazilian quality. Five years later, only one Chilean customer wanted tools without the label.

If "Made in Brazil" was once synonymous with shoddy work, that is no longer the case. Brazil far surpasses its Latin American neighbors in receiving certificates of quality from the International Organization of Standardization (known as ISO).

Over 1,000 Brazilian companies have received ISO certification, which means that their products meet international standards of quality. An example of an ISO-certified company is Grupo Siemens, the Brazilian subsidiary of German-based Siemens AG. In a recent four-year period, exports from Grupo Siemens quadrupled, reaching an impressive $80 million.

Besides showing they can deliver world-class quality, Brazilian companies keep their prices competitive by improving productivity. At BASF da Amazonia S.A., productivity improvements saved the subsidiary of the German conglomerate from shutdown. The Brazilian factory now exports tapes to Europe, Latin America, and the United States. Brazil's steel industry has doubled its productivity to a level rivaling Japanese firms.

Despite being hurt by the global financial turmoil at the end of the 1990s, in the 2000s Brazilian companies are becoming a formidable presence in the world economy. For example, exports to the United States totaled $8.3 billion in the first seven months of 2001 compared with $7.5 billion for the same period in the year 2000. The trend has continued—exports from Brazil to the United States in 2006 stood at $26.4 billion. As the export-oriented high-technology sector in Brazil grows, the country also faces problems once reserved for economically advanced countries. For example, in 2001 Brazil was in a protracted trade dispute with Canada about export subsidies—in airplanes! The Canadian firm Bombardier manufactures a 44-passenger jet airplane, a relatively small airplane that occupies a niche as a regional jet below Boeing and Airbus and above the corporate jet market. A major competitor to Bombardier turns out to be a Brazilian aircraft manufacturer, Embraer.

Aircraft being very expensive, it is quite common for governments to provide inancing for potential foreign buyers contemplating the purchase of a plane from the country's manufacturer. To support Embraer's push into foreign markets, the Brazilian government offered loans to potential customers in the United States and elsewhere. The problem was, according to the Canadians representing Bombardier, the loans were interest-free, a clear violation of World Trade Organization (WTO) rules about fair competition. Canada has repeatedly complained to the WTO about this practice, but the dispute has yet to be finally settled. In desperation, Bombardier has adopted the practice as well, winning two large contracts in the United States by matching the Brazilian offers.

With the rise in the global economy and the strength of multinational corporations, Embraer has grown its commercial sales and targeted the executive jet market worldwide. Its product line has been extended to satisfy the need of moguls for larger jets, and with rise in executive compensation around the world, the strategy has so far been very successful. Embraer has even developed a special trademark, turned-up wingtips. Despite a slight dip after September 2001, total sales have gone from US$2.7 billion in 2000 to $5.2 billion in 2007.

Brazil's two-term president, Luiz Inacio ("Lula") da Silva, is a socialist originally elected in October 2002. Despite his left-wing credentials, Lula has applied conservative economic policies in pursuit of growth. Although this conservative stance angers many, observers claim these economic decisions have made Brazil's economy more stable. *The Economist* agrees, and predicted in 2008 that Brazil will be able to keep on its path of around 6 percent annual growth for the foreseeable future.

Sources: James Brooke, "A New Quality in Brazil's Exports," *New York Times,* October 21, 1994, pp. D1, D6; "Brazilian Exports to the U.S. Rise," *O Globo,* October 4, 2001; John Ward, "Brazil Broke Rules: WTO," *The Gazette* (Montreal), July 27, 2001; "The Tortoise and the Hare," *The Economist,* March 22–28, 2008, pp. 39–40.

Introduction

Several strategic questions arise about how to reach foreign markets and conduct an orderly global expansion. What should the mode of entry be? How fast should new country markets and new products be added to existing ones? What is the best expansion path, considering the learning and experience already accumulated? Will similar countries be preferable or should one strike out into new ground completely? What added advantages would a product and country diversification strategy entail? How should new entries be chosen so as to maximize total benefits?

Immediate global expansion into all markets is usually not feasible. Financial, managerial, and other resource constraints often dictate a more sequential approach. Even if the company is resource-rich, prudence suggests a more deliberate approach. The company must establish defensible market positions in each country before moving on to other countries. Foreign direct investment might be avoided at the early stages because of the risk exposure. The learning associated with exporting and doing business abroad needs to be assimilated and diffused to benefit company managers.

Chapter 5 first introduces the major modes of entry and discusses each briefly, then relates the mode of entry decision to the question of entry barriers in the local markets abroad. The chapter then discusses the many new exporting tasks involved in entering a single country, including the transportation documentation, export pricing problems, and the important payment alternatives. The functions of the independent middlemen and the key issues in their selection are then discussed, and the need for a wholly owned sales subsidiary assessed. Criteria for the selection of the independent agents and distributors are shown, and the need for legal advice is stressed. The chapter ends with a discussion of the way potential importers often take the initiative in stimulating exports and become important partners in the exporting process.

Modes of entry that transfer know-how are discussed in more depth in Chapter 6.

Four Modes of Entry

It is useful to distinguish between four principal **modes of entry** into a foreign market: exporting, licensing, strategic alliance, and wholly owned manufacturing subsidiary. These four modes break down into several different activities. A typical breakdown is given in Exhibit 5.1.[1] These alternatives will be discussed in detail in this and the next chapter. At the outset, we take a quick look at the options available.

Exporting

Indirect exporting refers to the use of home country agencies (**trading companies,** export management firms) to get the product to the foreign market. "Piggybacking" is the use of already exported products' transportation and distribution facilities. Consortia are used by some smaller exporters banding together to sell related or unrelated products abroad. **Direct exporting,** by contrast, means the firm itself contacts the buyers abroad, be they independent agents and distributors or the firm's own subsidiaries. There is also direct sales, including mail order and

EXHIBIT 5.1
Entry Modes for Foreign Markets

Source: Adapted from F. R. Root, *Entry Strategies for International Markets,* Revised and Expanded. Copyright © 1994 Jossey-Bass Inc., Publishers. First published by Lexington Books. Reprinted with permission from John Wiley & Sons, Inc. All rights reserved.

Exporting	*Strategic alliance*
Indirect exporting via piggybacking, consortia, export management companies, trading companies	Distribution alliance
Direct exporting, using market country agent or distributor	Manufacturing alliance
Direct exporting, using own sales subsidiary	R&D alliance
Direct sales, including mail order and e-commerce	Joint venture
Licensing	*Wholly owned manufacturing subsidiary*
Technical licensing	Assembly
Contract manufacture	Full-fledged manufacturing
Original equipment manufacturing (OEM)	Research and development
Management contracts	Acquisition
Turnkey contracts	
Franchising	

e-commerce, a new but rapidly expanding mode of foreign entry particularly useful for small businesses and for initial entry. Direct sales can involve products as well as services. Dell computers can be bought online, paid for with a credit card, and shipped via an express carrier such as UPS, which can also handle the customs clearance and delivery inside the country. Cross-border catalog sales have a long history, expanding with the arrival of telephones and the credit card. The typical Web site used in electronic commerce is similar to a catalog with no need for a telephone call (although phone orders are a common alternative to online ordering) and with the payment transacted online as well. More e-commerce issues will be discussed in Chapter 17 on global promotion.

Licensing

Licensing involves offering a foreign company the rights to use the firm's proprietary technology and other know-how, usually in return for a fee plus a royalty on revenues. Among licensing modes, franchising has become a well-known alternative with the expansion of global hotel and fast-food chains. In **franchising,** the firm provides technical expertise to the reseller abroad, shows how to manage the franchise, and provides advertising support behind the brand. The other licensing options are all similar, differing mainly in the type of know-how transmitted. **Turnkey contracts** provide for the construction of whole plants and often the training of personnel capable of running the operations; **contract manufacturing** involves hiring a firm to produce a prespecified product (jeans produced by Filipino and Chinese textile mills for overseas manufacturers).

Strategic Alliances (SAs)

Strategic alliances (SAs) are collaborations between companies, sometimes competitors, to exchange or share some value activities. Examples include joint R&D, shared manufacturing, and distribution alliances. Strategic alliances in the form of **joint ventures** also involve capital investments and the creation of a new corporate unit jointly with a foreign partner. Such joint ventures have long been common, especially in countries such as India where government mandates participation by locals and in countries such as Japan where market access is difficult for outsiders.

Joint ventures are a type of strategic alliance in which partners create an equity-based new unit. In recent years, nonequity-based strategic alliances have become very common. An international strategic alliance is typically a cooperative collaboration between companies, even between potential competitors, across borders. The alliance could encompass any part of the value chain—although the focus is often limited to manufacturing, R&D, or distribution. In distribution alliances, the partners agree contractually to use an existing distribution network jointly. A typical example is the linkup between Lufthansa and United Airlines to pool route information and passengers.

Wholly Owned Manufacturing Subsidiary

When production takes place in the host country through a wholly owned manufacturing subsidiary, the company commits investment capital in plant and machinery that will be at risk in the country. This is traditional **foreign direct investment (FDI).** A wholly owned subsidiary in manufacturing can involve investment in a new manufacturing or assembly plant (such as Sony's TV plant in San Diego) or the acquisition of an existing plant (such as Matsushita's purchase of Motorola's TV plant outside Chicago). The presence of actual manufacturing operations helps support marketing activities. For example, a local plant is more likely to provide a stable flow of products, and it will be easier to adapt the products to the preferences of local customers than with a plant located outside the country's borders.

It is important to recognize that FDI usually leads to exporting. As manufacturing is established abroad through direct investment, parts and components are often shipped (exported) from the home country. About a third of U.S. international trade involves such shipments between units of the same company.[2] Although such intra-organizational transfers are quite different from market exchanges, more and more companies set transfer prices at market levels and allow subsidiaries to buy from local suppliers if quality and price are more favorable. This means the supplier plant has to engage in "internal" marketing, satisfying internal customers in the subsidiaries abroad.

A sales subsidiary is fundamentally different from a wholly owned manufacturing subsidiary. A sales subsidiary manages distribution and marketing of the product in the local market. Usually the product is exported from the home country or from another foreign plant. Volvo North America, located in Northridge, New Jersey, imports and distributes Volvos shipped from Europe.

Establishing a sales subsidiary requires relatively low levels of capital investment. Although operating costs for even a small sales office can be high in a country like Japan, with major expenditures for "general administrative and sales," the investment exposed to risk is often low. At the same time, establishing a sales subsidiary involves taking control of the marketing in the country and is thus strategically important. For marketing effectiveness, the control of the sales effort should generally be in the hands of the company itself.

The Impact of Entry Barriers

Before examining entry options in more detail, we look at the import barriers or **entry barriers** that always exist to entering a foreign market. The height and nature of the market entry barriers directly influence the entry mode chosen by a company. Entry barriers increase the cost of entry and constrain the options available, and where they are high, the company might have only one choice of entry mode or else have to stay out.

Entry Barriers Defined

The concept of entry barriers comes from the economics of industrial organization. It generally connotes any obstacle making it more difficult for a firm to enter a product market. Thus, entry barriers exist at home, as when limited shelf space prohibits a company from acquiring sufficient retail coverage to enter a market. Overseas it can mean that customs procedures are so lengthy that they prohibit an importer's fresh produce from getting to the stores before spoiling.

In global marketing it is convenient to classify the entry barriers according to their origin. Although gradually less important because of dramatic improvements in technology, transportation costs sometimes force new investment in manufacturing to be close to the market. Proximity of supplies and service still matters when transportation costs are high. **Tariff barriers** are obvious obstacles to entry into the country. Less visible **nontariff barriers,** for example, slow customs procedures, special product tests for imports, and bureaucratic inertia in processing import licenses, can also make entry difficult. Government regulations of business, domestic as well as foreign, constitute another set of market barriers, sometimes creating local monopolies. A special subset of these barriers is regulations directly intended to protect domestic business against foreign competitors.

Other barriers are more subtle. Access to manufacturing technology and processes, component suppliers, and distribution channels can be restricted by regulation, territorial restrictions, competitive collusion, or close ties between transacting partners (see box, "Sky-High Entry Barriers"). These barriers constitute artificial value chain imperfections and become important for the marketer to consider when deciding the configuration of the overseas operation.

There are also "natural" entry barriers that arise because of competitive actions. Many of the typical marketing efforts—creation of brand loyalty, differentiation

Getting the Picture

SKY-HIGH ENTRY BARRIERS

Barriers to entry vary from the most obvious ones—like a refusal to allow foreign lawyers to practice in a country, a rule most countries adhere to—to the most subtle and devious ones, such as officials always keeping foreign applications for custom clearance at the bottom of the pile of applications. International airports tend to exhibit both kinds of barriers to foreign competitors. So-called "open skies" bilateral agreements between countries, intended to provide easy access for all comers to an international airport, have proven almost impossible to negotiate because of conflicting national interests.

One typical airport barrier is the government's refusal to assign parking slots at an international airport to a foreign airline—or having their flights dock farthest away from check-in and baggage facilities. Furthermore, each country's national airline usually has first pick of the slots available and a strong voice in the approval (or rather disapproval) of new competitors entering. The national airline also has first pick

of routes and times of flight, optimizing profitability and passenger convenience. And when airport facilities are upgraded, the main beneficiaries tend to be national airlines. For example, if more passport controllers and baggage handlers are added, they are likely to show up at the times when the national airline's flights arrive. As a result, seasoned travelers interested in convenience and service—and for whom price is no object—choose airlines based on destination. Into Paris, fly Air France, with the best facilities at De Gaulle Airport. Heading for London? Fly British Airways, "the world's favorite airline," which controls most slots at Heathrow. Frankfurt is virtually synonymous with Lufthansa, Hong Kong is Cathay, and Singapore is, yes, Singapore Air. Flying out of Tokyo, you can use All Nippon Air, but you can't use the air terminal check-in service, which is reserved for Japan Air Line's travelers.

Sources: "Former U.S. Transportation Officials Say American Airlines/British Airways Pact Would Harm Competition, Lead to Higher Fares," *PR Newswire*, December 19, 2001; Rugman, 2001, p. 169.

between products, high levels of promotional spending—are factors that, when successful, lead to barriers or defenses against competitive attack.

The Cost of Barriers

The economic costs of entry barriers are well known. The inefficiency created by barriers translates into higher prices for consumers. What this means to the marketer is that the barriers create additional costs for the foreign entrant.[3]

Regardless of the source of the barriers, their existence means that some firm or individual will have a chance to profit from a monopolistic position. This individual is sometimes referred to as a **gatekeeper,** since he or she holds the keys to the market. For example, where regulations prohibit foreign ownership of broadcast media, domestic cable companies can keep prices high and service levels low. Where a domestic company has built a viable defense for its products with a strong brand image, it can collect "rent" by charging premium prices. Where close ties in distribution channels are necessary, natives with good contacts garner considerable fees by simply arranging a meeting between two prospective partners. The cost of doing business is very high in some countries because of such barriers.

The Importer's View

Entry barriers can give some importers a protected market position, especially when combined with exclusive distribution contracts. This has in fact happened in some countries with high trade barriers. In many Asian and European countries, for example, the possession of the exclusive rights to represent a particular global brand—such as Dunlop in golf clubs, Blaupunkt in car radios, and Canon in cameras—when coupled with restricted entry has been a virtual license to raise prices high. As countries lower their tariff and nontariff import barriers, exclusivity means less since unauthorized gray trade distributors can import the products as well. Prices come down.

But import barriers are not simply a boon for authorized importers. When trade barriers are high, the supplier company may opt to invest in production within the country, eliminating the need for an importer. Also, high barriers have to be paid for by all importers, and the importer may not always be able to pass the extra costs on to the consumer. The large American sport utility vehicles are not only expensive to drive in

Europe where gasoline is priced even higher than in the United States, but also because the tax on vehicles in Europe is sharply progressive with the weight of the vehicle. The tax serves in fact as a nontariff trade barrier. Finally, even if the native importer may have an advantage with personal contacts among the country's customs administration, the need to cultivate such contacts can also be a drag on the importer's bottom line. In the end, according to their own testimony, a lot of importers would be happy to compete without the help of the government.

Tariff and Nontariff Barriers

The firm on its own or through its trade association or local chamber of commerce can attempt to lobby its own or the host government for a reduction in tariff and nontariff barriers. Examples abound. American companies demand that the U.S. trade representative pressure Japan to open its markets. European companies appeal to the WTO for the reduction of tariffs on steel exported from the EU into the United States. Automobile quotas on foreign cars in Italy are under pressure from the EU Commission. These negotiations are sometimes emotional and clouded by national pride and are always difficult.

The firm should analyze the tariff base carefully to identify how the tariff rate is calculated.[4] Most often the tariffs are higher for a complete assembly, lower for parts and components. In the early 1980s when the United States raised the tariff rate for imported trucks to 25 percent, Nissan shipped every truck in two parts, the body and the flatbed, which could be assembled in a one-step operation. In this way the trucks entered as unfinished goods, with a lower tariff rate of 2.5 percent. Such "screwdriver assembly plants" exist in various parts of the world precisely as a way of avoiding high tariffs, but governments are also learning to write more stringent classification codes for the imported parts to capture more of the rent or profit generated.

It is common to lower or even waive a tariff when the imported product or component has a certain level of "local content" or when imports involve production for reexport. The foreign entrant has an incentive, therefore, to add parts and labor from the foreign market. When such parts are not available, it is not uncommon for the entrant to help establish a supplier of the parts in the country so as to obtain the lower tariff rate. This is an example of how tariff barriers can lead to foreign investment in plants.

In general, trade barriers will lead the foreign entrant to reexamine the firm's existing integration of activities in its value chain, from supplies to final sale. It becomes

One of Europe's traffic bottlenecks, the border crossing between France and Spain. As the EU integration continues and the customs checkpoints are eliminated, market entry barriers have quite literally been dismantled. Raphael Galliarde/Gamma-Liaison.

important to identify if some activities in the chain need to be broken out and to internalize only those activities that cannot be done better elsewhere. For example, when Volkswagen entered Japan, the difficulty and expense of establishing its own dealer network made the company decide to contract with a competitor, Nissan, to distribute Volkswagens in Japan. Thus, even though the barriers represent imperfections in the market, skillful management can help reduce the negative economic effects from these imperfections. As economists have shown, where trade is prohibited by tariffs, multinational production is often an efficient response, with gains for the firm and the country as well.[5]

A final tactic, increasingly employed as regional trade agreements proliferate, is to establish manufacturing in a member country in the regional trade group. Then the firm can export to the market country in the region at lower tariff rates from the transplant operation inside the region.

Government Regulations

When it comes to **government regulations** of business—involving questions ranging from "Who can start a business?" to "Can free product samples be sent in the mail?"—the foreign firm can do little but to adapt to them. Some assistance from the home government might be available. The U.S. government's negotiation in the late 1980s of the so-called Structural Impediments Initiative (in which Japan was asked to change things like its retail store regulations) is an interesting example of intrusion into a country's domestic policies by a foreign nation.[6] The EU homogenization of myriad regulations is another example of how government rules are changing in the globalizing economy. In this process, a global entrant can be a catalyst (see box, "Going against the Rules—In Germany").

The foreign entrant will need to study in detail the specific regulations affecting its industry and the sales of its products and services. In this process the foreign services of government offices (including the consulate abroad) and the local chambers of commerce can be of help. In other instances, the company needs to hire professional specialists who can decipher the foreign regulations. International law firms are often a good place to start.

Government regulations may be so severe and limiting that the company can do little without a native partner. As a member of a joint venture or some other collaborative alliance, the native partner can be assigned the task of carrying out negotiations with government authorities and local regulators. When Toys "R" Us established its operations in Japan, it selected Mr. Den Fujita, the general manager of McDonald's Japan, as its representative. The most pressing problem, getting building codes and retail regulations changed, required a strong local presence. Once in, the firm became an insider with claims on the same local protection as domestic firms.[7]

Distribution Access

In many countries it is very difficult to get members of the distribution channels to carry the firm's product. Retailers have no shelf space, they carry competing brands, and they don't trust that the new brand will sell. Wholesalers can't depend on supplies from overseas, they are not familiar with the distributor, and they need extra rebates if they are to take a new brand on. Again, tracking the new brand requires that price and packaging information be entered into the computer so the scanners will work, and so on. In many countries, including the United States, new brands need to pay a "slotting" fee—a "tip" or bribe—to get the trade interested. Thus, the difficulty of gaining **distribution access** means that the firm, even after successful entry, might compete with a handicap. As seen in Chapter 2, this is not an unusual situation in foreign markets (since such network ties lower transaction costs and are thus economically justified).

There is a downside to close distribution or supply ties. When the channel members or suppliers are not efficient, the ties may be more a burden than a benefit. Thus, some smaller parts manufacturers in Japan who are suppliers for Nissan, say, lack scale

Getting the Picture

GOING AGAINST THE RULES—IN GERMANY

After successful entry into Switzerland against entrenched domestic retailers, IKEA, the Swedish furniture retailer, decided in the late 1970s to go for the big prize and enter (then) West Germany, Europe's largest market. The low-price store chain, with a business concept of fiberboard furniture sold in kits for home assembly, was not welcomed by the German retailers. But they were not worried—they "knew" that the German consumers would not take easily to lower prices for unfinished furniture. The German consumers knew quality and would not be taken in by any promotional stunts.

It turned out quite differently. The Swedish company defied tradition and entered with a high promotional profile. It positioned itself as "the impossible store" from Sweden, sporting a Moose as a spokesperson. At the first store opening it offered all comers an early morning breakfast, contests, and free samples. It emphasized its Swedish origin by flying the Swedish flag and stressed the easy-to-assemble furniture by simplifying instructions and relying entirely on pictures drawn partly from European traffic symbols. Its opening in Munich drew more people than the local football champions, the Bayern Münich with national hero Franz Beckenbauer.

The German retailers were not slow to retaliate. They sued the Swedish company for upsetting an orderly market and for false advertising. One claim was that most of IKEA's products were not made of solid wood and could therefore not be sold as wood furniture. Another argument was that the Swedish origin was misleading because most of the products came from east European suppliers. It was also argued that since the free breakfast did not include eggs, it was misleading to serve it as a breakfast.

The arguments were of course formally correct and were all accepted by the court. But IKEA won the market battle; its success led to a revision of industry regulations. The final blow came when one of the largest German chains established its own chain of low-priced unassembled furniture, reasoning that "if you can't fight them, join them." Today, the German market is a much more competitive market than previously. It is also IKEA's biggest market, with 43 successful stores.

Sources: Mårtensson, 1983; Christopher A. Bartlett and Ashish Nanda, "Ingvar Kamprad and IKEA," Harvard Business School case 390–132; **www.ikea.com.**

economies and may not be as efficient as suppliers in South Korea, Taiwan, or even Europe and the United States, especially when the yen is very strong. In a similar vein, the vertical integration by Mercedes through its purchase of the electronic component business of AEG, one of its German suppliers, might not be very profitable if AEG quality is weak.[8] Where free market supplies are available, free competition typically ensures competitive prices and consequently lower costs.

Lack of access to distribution channels usually means that the firm has to consider a strategic alliance or even sell the product unbranded in an OEM (original equipment manufacturing) arrangement with a firm already established. Volkswagen distributes Toyota trucks in the EU countries. Mitsubishi cars were once sold in the United States through Chrysler dealers. Taking the OEM route, Japanese Ricoh makes copiers that are then marketed under the American firm Savin's brand name in the West, although the Ricoh company has recently begun to market copiers overseas under its own name. There is also the (usually expensive) alternative of establishing a new channel. When Honda motorcycles entered the United States, the company saw fit to help train and finance new dealerships across the country.

Another access barrier is the possibility that the firm cannot hire capable local talent. Where people find working for a domestic firm preferable, either because of pay or some status-related reason, the firm may have trouble entering the market alone. This is especially striking when the market is very new to the firm, so that access to local workers is important. On the other hand, in some countries, especially developing countries, working for a foreign firm may be seen as desirable, and to that extent foreign entry is facilitated.

Natural Barriers

Competition among several differentiated brands tends to create so-called **natural barriers,** allowing strong brand names to charge a premium price over more generic or no-name competitors. This is the case in "pure domestic" markets, in which all companies compete on an equal footing (hence "natural").

Market success and customer allegiance are the factors behind natural barriers. When customer satisfaction and brand loyalty are high, or country-of-origin biases favor a domestic brand, it may be difficult to break in. Further, if advertising expenditures are large and price promotion common—typical of North American markets—the prospective entrant has to offer something special and match promotional spending. This is where firm-specific advantages are important. Natural barriers depend as much on subjective consumer perceptions as on real differences between products. Thus, it may not be sufficient to have a "superior product" in terms of objective tests. The marketing effort in the new country has to convey the superiority effectively.

Advanced versus Developing Nations

In developing countries, the important barriers are usually tariffs and other government interventions into the free market system. If the firm is able to invest in product assembly in order to get under the tariff barrier, the markets are generally less competitive and a strong position can often be gained at relatively low cost. Pepsi gained entrance to the former Soviet Union with the help of President Nixon and dominated the Russian market for colas until the fall of the Berlin Wall (of course, it failed to hold on to its first-mover advantage as Coca-Cola deftly played up its "new dawn" aura).[9]

By contrast, in advanced countries it is usually natural barriers that are high. Here entry may be easier, but it is difficult to establish a strong and defensible position. This is important to remember when evaluating the firm's strategy for learning and gaining expertise in global markets. Advanced countries with open markets are a learning ground for marketing strategy and tactics. Developing countries with their tariff and nontariff barriers and myriad government regulations produce subsidiary managers with savvy about negotiations with foreign governments.

Exit Barriers

The firm usually faces exit barriers after entry—nonrecoverable investments have been made, people hired, contracts signed—and if there is likelihood of a forced exit, a firm will be reluctant to commit. Another consideration for the marketer is the potential loss of goodwill accompanying withdrawal from an important and visible market. The French automaker Peugeot probably lost a great deal of brand equity (and money) in the U.S. market before finally exiting in 1992. When future exit is a distinct possibility because of uncertainties, an otherwise attractive foreign market can be entered by choosing a less visible and less committed mode of entry, such as OEM manufacturing or licensing. If a global brand name might be hurt by withdrawal, the company could conceivably market the product under another name. With the advent of global markets, however, companies are less willing to forgo the advantages of leveraging a global brand name. In the era of global marketing, the company needs sufficient resources and capability to nurture and sustain its products and brands, thus surmounting exit barriers by never having to face them.

Effect on Entry Mode

In sum, barriers to entering a foreign market make entry mode decisions more complex than just the arithmetic of a simple geographical expansion.

The company can expand into some markets only by unbundling its know-how. That is, even though the company may want to be a player in final product markets everywhere, in country markets where government regulations or the company's lack of market knowledge would force the use of joint ventures, the company might opt only to sell components, so as not to give up crucial know-how. An obvious instance is China's insistence that foreign auto manufacturers entering the Chinese market team up with a Chinese joint venture partner. "Unbundling" is one of the possible outcomes of negotiations by potential foreign entrants into China's auto industry. This can also happen in other countries when protectionist sentiment heats up (see box "Taking the Plunge").

Where local-content requirements are high, the company may contract with a local producer to contract manufacture of simpler versions of the products. Toshiba television

Getting the Picture

TAKING THE PLUNGE

"With our fleet of specially built ships, we would rather build the cars here in Japan and export them to the United States and Europe. There is no economic reason for us to invest in an assembly plant in those countries. Now, of course, with the European trade barriers and the U.S. protectionist voices becoming louder, we may have to make some local investment and meet the local content requirements. But how will our customers react if we cannot maintain our quality level? So, we decided to start with the joint venture with GM in Fremont to see whether we could manage the workforce in the United States and satisfy our quality conscious customers. Finally, I think we have succeeded."

Source: Toyota spokesperson in 1986 before the company started assembly plants in Derbyshire, England, and in Kentucky.

sets are assembled in the Czech Republic in a plant built by Toshiba but operated by local Czechs, with Toshiba's reward being a royalty on the sales.

In other markets where distribution is complex or customer requirements idiosyncratic, the company might opt to engage in a **distribution alliance** with a competitor. As noted earlier, Japan's Ricoh produced OEM and let the Savin company sell their copiers in the United States in order to gain quick market penetration. The global expansion path is often more complex than simply a question of where the firm's final products will be sold.

Many companies develop managerial expertise with a particular mode of entry, and this entry mode becomes the preferred mode of expansion. Some Western multinationals have long preferred wholly owned subsidiaries, run by an American expatriate. This mode has been sustained even when the cost of financial exposure and the growth of local management expertise weakened the rationale for them. Companies such as Union Carbide, IBM, Honeywell, Philips, and the American auto companies fall into this category. Other companies, such as small technology-based entrepreneurs, will often expand through licensing or joint ventures. The reason for one sustained company policy or another is usually that management feels more comfortable with it, having developed skills dealing with that form of overseas involvement.

Each mode of foreign entry involves quite different managerial skills. Overseeing a number of licensees in various countries is one thing, running a network of wholly owned subsidiaries quite another. Direct exporting involves learning about overseas transportation, international trade credit, tariff barriers, and so on; quite an investment for the beginner. The growth of various forms of cross-border strategic alliances in the recent past has been accompanied by the emergence of a cadre of international contract lawyers and managers skilled in international negotiations. The start-up costs of learning to manage any one of these modes of entry are considerable, and it is not surprising that companies tend to leverage their particular skills by staying with the same approach.

Consequently, even though the firm's value chain may be broken up to get under a certain country's barriers or in accordance with government regulations, its expansion path will be likely to follow the same mode of entry everywhere. Xerox and 3M are good at running international joint ventures; IBM and Ford like wholly owned subsidiaries; the Body Shop and McDonald's prefer franchising. Staying with the "tried-and-true" leverages the company's expertise properly, minimizes the obstacles to entering, and maximizes the chances of success. When these companies have used another mode of entry, chances are they were forced to do so by government regulation or some other market access barrier.

The Exporting Option

For the newcomer to the international scene, the exporting option is often the most attractive mode of foreign entry. Then, sometimes it is just through the experience of exporting that the idea of a full-fledged market entry is developed. At any rate,

Getting the Picture

JAPAN'S GIANT TRADERS

Although Toyota may employ more people, the biggest companies in Japan in terms of total turnover are traditionally the giant trading companies. The big traders do business in all kinds of products all over the world. They finance salmon fishing in Alaska and sell the fish in Hong Kong; they ship iron ore from Australia to Japan and steel from Korea to Indonesia; they ship cars to Europe and bring beer back to Japan. They are active in oil exploration, build paper mills in Peru and chemical plants in China, and organize international consortia for the exploration of minerals in New Guinea. Their take is usually a small commission or fee on the transaction created, but they also speculate in the spot market for various commodities, sometimes winning, sometimes losing. Their global information network is the envy of any spy ring, and they announced the Iranian revolution before the CIA learned about it. The largest trading companies and their sales in 2003 are shown in the table.

Each of these traders belongs to *keiretsu* groupings in Japan, which bring together a number of companies in different industries. Thus, Mitsubishi Corporation is part of the Mitsubishi group, which also includes Mitsubishi cars, Mitsubishi Bank, Mitsubishi Electric, and about 50 other companies.

These traders are able to help many companies enter foreign markets. Thus, Marubeni was active in assisting Nissan in its initial stage in the United States, and in Algeria, Toyota trucks are still sold by a trading company. Non-Japanese can also employ these traders, provided they are not competitors of keiretsu members. It is important to keep in mind, however, that these companies are always on the lookout for new deals and will sometimes develop a competing business. For example, the Swedish Nobel company, maker of dynamite, found that its trading partner in Japan had initiated domestic production in direct competition with Swedish imports.

Sources: Eli, 1991; Rugman, 2001.

Name	Sales Revenue (U.S. $ in millions)	Operating Earnings (U.S. $ in millions)	Number of Employees	Strengths
Mitsubishi Corp	$ 81,733.3	$ 561.7	n/a	Government business
Mitsui & Co	90,335.4	547.0	5,831	Telecommunications
Sumitomo Corp	56,966.8	249.1	4,072	CATV business
Itochu Corp	55,790.7	62.6	3,070	Textiles
Marubeni Corp	53,429.8	214.7	2,351	Pulp/paper

Source: yahoo.co.jp finance (2003 data).

when unsolicited orders have started flowing in from abroad, the firm begins to pay more attention to the potential in foreign markets, and exporting becomes the natural first step.

Indirect Exporting

The simplest way to manage the firm's export business is to employ outside specialists. The firm may hire a trading company, which becomes the "export department" for the producer (see box, "Japan's Giant Traders").

In the United States the arrangement whereby an **export management company (EMC)** performs all the transactions relating to foreign trade for the firm has a similar character. EMCs are independent agents working for the firm in overseas markets, going to fairs, contacting distributors, organizing service, and so on. They serve basically as an external "export department" for the firm, an example of value chain deconstruction. This type of "indirect" exporting has its great advantage in that the firm avoids the overhead costs and administrative burden involved in managing their own export affairs. On the other hand, there is the disadvantage that the skills and know-how developed through experiences abroad are accumulated outside the firm, not in it.

In most cases, the domestic firm wants to make only a limited commitment to its facilitating agencies, keeping open the option of taking full responsibility for its exporting at a later date. This is one reason why EMCs lead rather precarious lives. If they are too successful, the producer may decide to break the contract and internalize the exporting function.

Direct Exporting

Direct exporting has the advantage over indirect exporting in the control of operations it affords the producer. Going through an intermediary trading company, the firm may not even know in which country the product is sold. With direct exporting the firm is able to more directly influence the marketing effort in the foreign market. The firm also learns how to operate abroad. Without involvement in the day-to-day operations of overseas affairs, the firm will not generate much in-house knowledge. It is not until the firm decides to hire its own staff that a more strategic involvement in foreign markets becomes feasible.

For the direct exporter, the principal choice is between establishing a sales subsidiary or employing independent middlemen. The latter option means an agent to manage sales and administration paid through fees and commissions and a local distributor who supplies the product to the trade and adds a markup to the cost. The choice between a sales subsidiary and independent middlemen depends on the degree to which control of the marketing effort in the country is desired and on the resources the firm can muster. To strike the optimal balance, the volume of operations (current and anticipated), the firm's willingness to take risks, and the availability of suitable local distributors are critical determinants. Investing in a wholly owned sales subsidiary is a bigger commitment and requires more resources than the use of independent people. But where the market is potentially large, the firm would generally be better off with more central control of operations and, in particular, the marketing effort.

The Exporting Tasks

There are many separate functions to be managed in direct exporting. The major tasks are listed in Exhibit 5.2. The exhibit and the discussion to follow cover only the major tasks. Some of them, such as those relating to legal issues, are only marginally related to marketing, while others, such as after-sales support, directly relate to customer acceptance. Many of the functions can be handled by independent specialists who can be found through department of commerce contacts, at industry fairs and conventions, through the local telephone directories, or by contacting the consulate. Associated with these tasks are many different documents needed for exporting. Exhibit 5.3 gives a list of the principal documents. They will also be discussed below.

Product Shipment

Transportation

The shipment of the product to the border of the country is usually handled by an independent freight forwarder in combination with a shipping agency. In the typical case, freight forwarders who might specialize in certain types of products or countries pick

EXHIBIT 5.2
Direct Exporting Functions

Source: Adapted from Franklin R. Root, "Direct Exporting Functions," *Entry Strategies for International Markets,* revised and expanded, p. 6. Copyright © 1994 by Jossey-Bass Inc., Publishers. First published by Lexington Books. Reprinted with permission from John Wiley & Sons, Inc. All rights reserved.

Product shipment
1. Transportation to the border
2. Clearing through customs
3. Warehousing

Export pricing
1. Price quotes
2. Trade credit
3. Price escalation
4. Dumping

Local distribution
1. Finding a distributor
2. Screening distributors
3. Personal visit
4. Negotiating a contract

Getting paid
1. Checking creditworthiness
2. Getting paid in local currency
3. Hedging against currency losses
4. Converting funds to home currency
5. Repatriating the funds

Legal issues
1. Export license
2. Hiring an agent
3. Transfer of title/ownership
4. Insurance

After-sales support
1. Service
2. Parts and supplies
3. Training of locals
4. Creating a sales subsidiary

EXHIBIT 5.3
Principal Documents Used in Exporting

Source: Adapted with permission from Franklin R. Root, "Principal Documents Used in Exporting," *Entry Strategies for International Markets,* revised and expanded, p. 71. Copyright © 1994 by Jossey-Bass Inc., Publishers. First published by Lexington Books. Reprinted with permission from John Wiley & Sons, Inc. All rights reserved.

Foreign customer
1. Pro forma invoice
2. Acceptance of purchase order
3. Ocean (airway) bill of lading
4. Certificate (or policy) of insurance
5. Packing list

Exporting manufacturer
1. Purchase order
2. Letter of credit or draft (trade) acceptance

Freight forwarder
1. Shipper's letter of instructions
2. Domestic (inland) bill of lading
3. Packing list
4. Commercial invoice
5. Letter of credit (original copy)

U.S. government
1. Export declaration
2. Export license (strategic goods and shipments to designated unfriendly nations)

Foreign governments
1. Certificate of origin
2. Customs invoice
3. Consular invoice

Exporter's bank
1. Exporter's draft
2. Commercial invoice
3. Consular invoice
4. Insurance certificate
5. Ocean (airway) bill of lading

up the product at the factory, transport it to the embarkation point, and load it onto the transnational carrier. Federal Express and DHL serve as freight forwarders in the case of express mail, and they usually own their own transportation fleets (although some shipments, such as air transport to Africa, might go by a regular airline).

Clearing through Customs

Unloaded at the national border, the product will go from the ship or airline to a customs-free depot before being processed through customs. This depot can be a large free-trade zone, such as the one outside of Canton in China or in Gibraltar at the bottom of the European continent. From this free-trade area the product can be shipped to another country, never having crossed the border. In the typical case, the free-trade zones allow workers to further add value to the product. For example, along the Mexican border with the United States, the so-called maquiladoras are small factories located in the free-trade zones, and Mexican workers can be used to work on the products with no cross-border shipment of products. Thus, they can be shipped anywhere in the United States after the Mexican labor value added, without having to cross custom lines.

Transportation companies serving multinational firms stress their global capability, as in this ad for DHL Worldwide Express.
Courtesy DHL Worldwide.

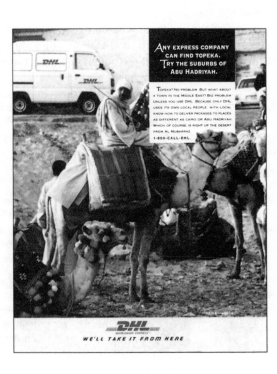

The customs officials will process the goods for entry once a claimant appears. This is usually the buyer, but can also be an independent importer or customs facilitator who specializes in getting the customs procedures done quickly. By presenting shipping documents—the **bill of lading**—the buyer or his agent can get access to the goods after paying the assessed duty. The tariff rate is decided on by the local customs official on the spot. In some countries, this is where there is often a temptation for bribes, the buyer "inducing" the customs official to assign a lower tariff classification.

Warehousing

After entering the country, the goods will often require storage, and there are usually facilities in the destination port to be rented. The price is often quite high—as is the daily storage rental for goods waiting to be processed in the free-trade zone. Companies try to save money by getting the goods through customs quickly and warehoused at a less expensive location.

Export Pricing

Price Quotes

Export pricing quotes are considerably more complex than domestic quotes. The more common pricing terms of shipment have been standardized by the International Chamber of Commerce and codified as Incoterms (see Exhibit 5.4). The firm selling abroad would generally be in a stronger competitive position by quoting prices **CIF** (cost-insurance-freight, that is, by accepting the responsibility for product cost, insurance, and freight, and factoring these items into the quote) rather than **FOB** (free on board), which means that the buyer has to arrange shipping to his country. Quoting CIF still leaves the buyer with the responsibility for checking and adding tariff charges and other duties, and if, in addition, the buyer has to arrange transportation from the seller's country, the transactions costs can be very high.

For products whose value is high relative to weight and size, air transportation is often used. Computer software, for example, is sometimes shipped overseas by air, cash on delivery. In many cases the seller will force these shipments to be prepaid, however, especially after a few mishaps and, in particular, when the buyer is from a less-developed country. In this way price quotes for overseas markets are very much tied into the question of trade credit.

Trade Credit

The importance of the level of price quoted depends very much on what credit arrangements can be made. A high price can often be counterbalanced by advantageous trade credit terms, especially where the seller takes the responsibility for arranging the

EXHIBIT 5.4
Terms of Shipment

Source: Incoterms 2000, **www.iccwbo.org**.

Ex-works (EXW) at the point of origin	The seller agrees to deliver the goods at the point of origin or some specified place. All other charges are borne by the buyer.
Free Alongside Ship (FAS) at a named port of export	The price for the goods includes charges for delivery of the goods alongside a vessel at a port.
Free on Board (FOB) at a named port of export	In addition to FAS, the seller loads the goods on the vessel to be used for ocean transportation.
Cost and Freight (CFR) to a named overseas port	The price for the goods includes the cost of transportation to a named overseas port of disembarkation.
Cost, Insurance and Freight (CIF) to a named overseas port	The price includes insurance and all transportation and miscellaneous charges to the port of disembarkation from the ship or aircraft.
Delivery Duty Paid (DDP) to an overseas buyer's premises	The exporter delivers the goods with import duties paid, including inland transportation to the importer's premises.

trade credit. For many foreign buyers, governments as well as companies, the actual price is of less concern than what the periodical payments will be. This is nothing very peculiar to specific countries, but rather hinges on the magnitude of the money involved. Credit is of particular importance in exchanges that involve large items such as turbines, industrial plants, aircraft, and so on, in which no buyer can realistically be expected to pay the total bill in cash.

What makes the credit question particularly interesting from a global marketing perspective is that in many cases the competitive advantages depend critically on this question. For the seller to have strong support from a dominant international bank is of unquestionable advantage in many of these cases. The Japanese trading companies are provided such support through their affiliated keiretsu banks, which can also help organize financial support from related companies. If, in addition, the government in the home country can be persuaded to use its financial leverage to provide further credit the competitiveness of the seller can be increased dramatically. For example, the Airbus sales are generally made at relatively high prices per plane but are accompanied by advantageous loans extended by the governments involved in the consortium (France, United Kingdom). To compete against the Airbus, it might not be sufficient to offer lower prices but more important to offer good terms for credit payments. The Boeing aircraft company undertakes a heavy lobbying and advertising effort supporting the Export-Import Bank in Washington, DC, partly because the Ex-Im Bank helps the company offer competitive credit terms.[10]

Price Escalation

In general, prices abroad can be expected to be higher than prices at home for the simple reason that there are several cost items faced by the exporter not encountered in domestic sales. The factors relate to transportation costs, tariffs and other duties, special taxes, and exchange rate fluctuations. The resulting increase in price overseas is commonly denoted **price escalation.** An example of how price escalation works is presented in Exhibit 5.5. As can be seen, there are several added cost items incurred when selling overseas. Shipping costs are only part of the problem—added are applicable tariffs and customs duty, insurance, and value-added taxes. Also, the fact that several middlemen (importer to take the goods through customs, freight forwarder to handle the shipping documents, dock workers) are involved in the channel adds to the costs and cuts into the profit margin unless prices are raised.

The escalation of price means not only that prices become higher than intended, it also makes it more difficult to anticipate what the final price in the market will be. The methods used to cope with the problems are several. Companies attempt to redesign the product so as to fit it into a lower tariff category, sometimes by shifting the final stages in the assembly process abroad. For example, truck tariffs for completed assemblies are usually much higher than for semifinished trucks, and the industry has responded by creating a "knockdown" (KD) assembly stage consisting essentially of putting the flatbed on the chassis, "knocking it down" into place. The same formula has been applied with success to passenger autos, so that FDI in auto production now might simply mean a "KD plant" with perhaps 20 employees.[11]

Another solution to the escalation problem has been to lower prices and thus absorb some of the trade barrier cost on the part of the company. It also means that duties that are paid on value (ad valorem) will be lower. The problem is then that the host country subsidiary will show large profits and repatriating these funds might be a problem (see "Transfer Pricing" in Chapter 14). When entering the newly opened Russian market, many companies are tempted to quote low prices for goods sent to their Russian operation in order to avoid taxes. The problem is that this tends to inflate profits unrealistically, since costs will be low and consequently profit margins will be high for the Russian sales. This makes for a very profitable operation in rubles, but rubles can be devalued and are not so easily turned into Western currency.

EXHIBIT 5.5
International Price Escalation Effects (in U.S. $)

Source: Becker, 1990. Reprinted by permission of Butterworth-Heinemann, Ltd., and the editors.

International Marketing Channel Elements and Cost Factors	Domestic Wholesale-Retail Channel	Case 1 (same as domestic with direct wholesale import c.i.f./tariff)	Case 2 (same as case 1 with foreign importer added to channel)	Case 3 (same as case 2 with V.A.T. added)	Case 4 (same as case 3 with local foreign jobber added to channel)
Manufacturer's net price	$6.00	$6.00	$6.00	$6.00	$6.00
+ insurance and shipping cost (CIF)	*	2.50	2.50	2.50	2.50
= *Landed cost* (CIF value)	*	8.50	8.50	8.50	8.50
+ tariff (20% on CIF value)	*	1.70	1.70	1.70	1.70
= *Importer's cost* (CIF value + tariff)	*	10.20	10.20	10.20	10.20
+ importer's margin (25% on cost)	*	*	2.55	2.55	2.55
+ V.A.T. (16% on full cost plus margin)	*	*	*	2.04	2.04
= *Wholesaler's cost* (= importer's price)	6.00	10.20	12.75	14.79	14.79
+ wholesaler's margin (33 1/3% on cost)	2.00	3.40	4.25	4.93	4.93
+ V.A.T. (16% on margin)	*	*	*	.79	.79
= *Local foreign jobber's cost* (= wholesale price)	*	*	*	*	20.51
+ jobber's margin (33 1/3% on cost)	*	*	*	*	6.84
+ V.A.T. (16% on margin)	*	*	*	*	1.09
= *Retailer's cost* (= wholesale or jobber price)	8.00	13.60	17.00	20.51	28.44
+ retailer's margin (50% on cost)	4.00	6.80	8.50	10.26	14.22
+ V.A.T. (16% on margin)	*	*	*	1.64	2.28
= *Retail price* (= what consumer pays)	$12.00	$20.40	$25.50	$32.42	$44.94
Percent price escalation over: Domestic		70%	113%	170%	275%
Case 1			25%	59	120
Case 2				27%	76
Case 3					39%

*Indicates "not applicable."

It is also important to consider the possibility of FDI to assemble or manufacture in the market country, thus avoiding the escalation problems entirely. This is exactly what many trade barriers are intended to make firms do. Such FDI could also be made in a third country with more favorable tariffs compared to the market country. The problem with relying too heavily on the tariffs as the only justification for FDI is that such barriers can be removed or changed on a moment's notice and it becomes important to recognize that escalation as a reason for FDI is simply too shortsighted.

In the end, exporters learn to live with the escalated costs and to avoid more outrageous customs duties by modifying the escalated products, shipping semifinished goods, and, in general, making such moves as will allow the product to fall into a relatively moderate transport and tariff classification. Having done that, they are generally on par with other importers, if not the domestic producers, and given the existence of at least some unique FSAs they are able to avoid further costly redesigns or shifting production location.

Getting the Picture

LAWYERS TAKE TIME—AND MONEY

Dumping cases are initiated by the presumed victims of the dumping actions. The injured party files a complaint with the appropriate government agency, in the United States the Department of Commerce. The defending firms are then asked to appear and present their side of the case. After deliberations are finished, the government agency issues a verdict, finding the defendants guilty or not guilty as the case may be. Appeals can typically be made to a higher court, in the United States to the U.S. International Trade Commission. Once a verdict is upheld, the appropriate remedy is decided upon, countervailing duties and/or antidumping fines. These proceedings all take place in the country of the complainants, consistent with the WTO rules and directives.

Protracted dumping proceedings lessen the competitive effectiveness of the laws. Consequently, in recent years the governments and the courts have made an effort to shorten the time involved and make the laws more effective. When it comes to a speedy trial, India is ahead of other countries. Data show that antidumping proceedings may be finished in

as little as 3 months, against 4–5 months in the United States, about 5 months in Australia, 5–6 months in New Zealand, and roughly 7–8 months in the European Union.

When it comes to legal expenses and court costs, the United States wins hands down. In the typical case of steel producers, just to hire a legal defense team a firm might have to shell out a retainer of US$1.5–2 million. Add to that the requirement in U.S. law that all defendants have to make their case (that is, hire a lawyer) or else forfeit the case, and one can see that a dumping case involves a lot of money for at least some people. Lawyers have a strong interest in keeping dumping cases coming, perhaps one explanation for why the United States dominates the number of cases.

Many people outside the United States claim not to understand why America has so many lawyers. One simple answer is that there is money in it.

Sources: "India Takes Only Three Months to Probe Dumping Cases," *Financial Express,* December 31, 2001; "Heavy Legal Costs Weigh Down Steel Exporters to U.S.," *India Business Insight,* December 25, 2001.

Dumping

Even though pricing on the basis of costs alone is not recommended in theory (demand must be taken into account, for example), cost-based pricing has one strong justification: It is the pricing procedure easiest to defend against dumping charges.

Dumping is commonly defined as selling goods in some markets below cost. There are sometimes good management reasons for doing that. A typical case is an entry into a large competitive market by selling at very low prices; another case is when a company has overproduced and wants to sell the product in a market where it has no brand franchise to protect. *Reverse dumping* refers to the less-common practice of selling products at home at prices below cost. This would be done in extreme cases where the share at home needs to be protected while monopolistic market positions abroad can be used to generate surplus funds ("cash cows" in foreign markets). Regardless, dumping as defined is often illegal since it is destructive of trade, and competitors can take an offender to court to settle a dumping case. The usual penalty for manufacturers whose products are found to violate the antidumping laws is a **countervailing duty,** an assessment levied on the foreign producer that brings the prices back up over production costs and also imposes a fine.

Dumping cases are notorious for their protracted duration. The 1968 case against Japanese TV producers in the U.S. market, for example, took three years to decide, and by 1977 the assessed extra dumping duties were not yet fully collected. At this later date the U.S. low-price importers had already shifted their sources of supplies from Japan to Taiwan and South Korea. Things have gotten better, even if time and costs are still high (see box, "Lawyers Take Time—and Money").

The manner in which the relevant costs are used to define dumping varies between countries, reflecting the fact that economists have difficulty agreeing on a common definition. China is an interesting special case. The country ranks first in the world for the number of antidumping suits lodged against it. By the end of 2000, there were 450 antidumping cases involving tens of billions of U.S. dollars against Chinese producers, and the number was expected to increase with China's WTO entry. One problem has been that without a true market economy, the cost basis for determining potential dumping practices does not exist. Foreign governments have used third-country prices to arrive at a proper cost figure. The argument is that in China, where state-owned exporters receive subsidies and bank loans they never have to repay, under a system that is largely secret, there is no basis to assess costs. Although China's WTO entry will force a change, experts suggest that it will be at least a decade before these practices are eliminated.[12]

The United States is the leader in dumping complaints brought, responsible for about 56 percent of all countervailing duty actions and 28 percent of antidumping fines since 1980. Other active countries include Australia, Chile, and Canada. With greater European unity, the EU is expected to take a more active stance in the future. Most countries and regional groupings have established their own particular version of antidumping regulations. Under the new WTO trade laws, the antidumping rules that are to apply to all members are more liberal than usual, making penalties more difficult to assign. The new rules, developed with the intent to support emerging countries' exports, feature (1) stricter definitions of injury, (2) higher minimum dumping levels needed to trigger imposition of duties, (3) more rigorous petition requirements, and (4) dumping duty exemptions for new shippers.[13]

Local Distribution

Finding a Distributor

The next step is to get the product into the distribution channels. The most common approach is not to try to create new channels, but to use existing ones. Although there are some instances in which the creation of new channels has been instrumental in a company's success (the Italian apparel maker Benetton's franchised stores in the United States, for example, and the U.S. cosmetics firm Avon's door-to-door system in Asia), in most cases existing channels will have to do. This means identifying one or more independent distributors who can take on storage and transportation to wholesalers and retailers. These **distributors** usually take ownership of the goods, paying the producing firm, and often will handle the importing and customs process, in addition to storage and distribution in the country. Generally, the firm appoints one distributor for the whole country, with an exclusive territory. However, in large nations such as the United States overseas-based companies often have two or three distributors in various parts of the country (East Coast, Midwest, and West Coast, for example).

It is crucially important for the firm to find the best distributor available. According to one report, exporters find that the range of distributor performance can vary from zero to 200 percent of what is expected.[14] There are only a few excellent distributors in any one country, and the best ones are often not interested in taking on another supplier unless offered a well-known global brand.

Identifying potential distributors can be done with the assistance of governmental agencies. Many countries maintain trade facilitation agencies to assist in the search for local distributors. The U.S. Department of Commerce, for example, will assist in identifying the names and addresses of many potential distributors in various countries and industries. But more commonly, potential distributors will be found at **trade fairs** and international conventions. At these fairs, held in places such as Frankfurt, Cologne, Hong Kong, and Las Vegas, distributors will come to spot new products that might have a market in their country and try to establish a relationship with a vendor. The export manager participating in a fair should try to identify beforehand potential distributors who might come to the fair and arrange meetings ahead of time, but this is of course not always possible.

Screening Distributors

Once a few select candidates have been identified, they must be screened on key performance criteria. In many cases a late entrant to the country market might have trouble finding a good distributor, making it particularly important that the screening process does not miss some key characteristic. The criteria include the ones given in Exhibit 5.6.

EXHIBIT 5.6
Criteria for Choosing
Distributors

Source: Adapted from Franklin R. Root,
"Criteria for Choosing Distributors," *Entry
Strategies for International Markets,* revised
and expanded, pp. 63–65. Copyright © 1994
by Jossey-Bass Inc., Publishers. First
published by Lexington Books. Reprinted
with permission from John Wiley & Sons,
Inc. All rights reserved.

Previous experience (products handled, area covered, size)
Services offered (inventory, repairs, after-sales service)
Marketing support (advertising and promotional support)
Financial strength
Relations with government
Cooperativeness
Whether or not handling competing products

Which of these criteria are judged important and which not depends on the situation and the significance the company attaches to the criteria. For example, consumer non-durables typically require little after-sales service. The financial strength of the distributor is less important if the firm can support the company in the start-up period. Distributor strength can even be a drawback when the initial arrangements are seen as temporary, to be superseded by a more permanent, FDI position if the market is as large as expected.

Personal Visits

Once some promising leads have been developed, a personal visit to the country is necessary. On the trip managers should do three things:

- Talk to the ultimate users of the equipment to find out from which distributors they prefer to buy and why. Two or three names will be likely to keep popping up.

- Visit these two or three distributors and see which ones you would be able to sign up.

- Before making the final choice, look for the distributor who has the key person for your line. This is a person who is willing to become the champion for the new product line. Experience has shown that the successful distributor is the one who has one person in the organization willing to take the new line to heart and treat it as his or her own baby.[15]

Negotiating a Contract

The contract has to be very specific as regards the rights and obligations of the manufacturer and the distributor, the length of the contract, and conditions for its renegotiation. A checklist is given in Exhibit 5.7. The conditions under which competitive product lines might be added and the degree of exclusivity that the distributor is granted figure prominently among the rights and obligations. Although local regulations and the letter of the law naturally must be followed, the usual situation is one in which the actual formulation of these contracts hinges directly on the size and strength of the two parties.

In Western countries these negotiations tend to be rather open and confrontational so that all key points get hammered out fast, while in Far Eastern and other nations negotiations may be protracted, indirect, and often quite trying on Westerners' patience. Regardless, the spirit of the contract should be reflected in the subsequent actions of both the manufacturer and the distributor. Where it is not, neither of the parties will be happy. The relationship between the two should not be a zero-sum game, but a win–win proposition. (See the discussion of negotiations in Chapter 3.)

Payment

Local Currency

Getting paid can be a headache, especially if the country imposes convertibility restrictions. Today in China, India, Russia, Mexico, and other countries, it is very difficult to get access to hard currencies such as dollars, yen, or euros. The local currency is either very weak (Mexico) or not easily convertible (China, India). And despite

EXHIBIT 5.7
Master Foreign Distributorship Agreement Checklist

Source: Adapted from Hall, 1983, pp. 65–66. Courtesy of Unz & Co.

Appointment	*Confidential information*
Appointment	*Sales literature*
Acceptance	Advertising literature
Territory–products	Quantities
Sales activities	Mailing lists
Advertising (optional)	*Trademarks and copyrights*
Initial purchases (optional)	*Subdistributors*
Minimum purchases (optional)	*No warranty against infringement*
Sales increases (optional)	*No consequential damages–indemnity*
Orders	*Product warranty*
Distributor resale prices	*Relationship between parties*
Direct shipment to customers	*Effective date and duration*
Product specialists (optional)	Effective date and term
Installation and service	Early termination
Distributor facilities (optional)	Breach
Visits to distributor premises	Insolvency
Reports	Prospective breach
Financial condition	Change in ownership or management
Business structure	Foreign protective act
Competing products	*Rights and obligations upon termination*
List prices	No liability for principal
Prices	Return of promotional materials
Taxes	Repurchase of stock
Acceptance of orders and shipment	Accrued rights and obligations
Acceptance	*Noncompetitive*
Inconsistent terms in distributor's order	*No assignment*
Shipments	*Government regulation*
No violation of U.S. laws	Foreign law
Passage of title	U.S. law
Defects, claims	Foreign Corrupt Practices Act
Returns	*Force majeure*
Payments	*Separability*
Terms	*Waiver*
Letter of credit	*Notices*
Deposits	Written notice
Payments in dollars	Oral notice
No deduction by distributor	*Arbitration*
Set-off by principal	ICC rules
Security interest	Jurisdiction
	Article titles
	Entire agreement and modifications
	Entire agreement
	Modifications

heroic efforts to participate in global capital markets, many former communist countries (Russia, Bulgaria) still have trouble paying for their imports in hard currency.

Creditworthiness

In most countries, checking on the creditworthiness of the buyer can usually be done through banking connections. Regardless, many exporters avoid relying on credit, not shipping goods until an intermediate bank, preferably in the seller's country, guarantees payment.

Letter of Credit

Payment in advance is traditionally done via some form of **letter of credit.** This is arranged for by the buyer. Exhibit 5.8 shows the linkages involved. As can be seen, once the buyer approaches the local bank, opening a credit line, this bank will contact its corresponding bank in the selling firm's country. This latter bank will inform the

EXHIBIT 5.8
Letter of Credit Model

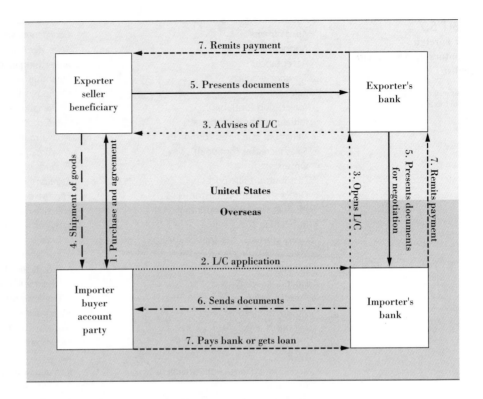

seller that a letter of credit has been issued, assuring the seller that payment will be made. Once the seller ships the goods, the bill of lading can be presented to the bank, which will contact the overseas bank in the buyer's country and will pay the seller. This transaction usually takes place before the goods have reached the buyer's country. Once they arrive, the buyer can claim the goods at customs against the bill of lading sent by the bank.

Converting Funds

Because letters of credit involve several intermediaries and a fair amount of administrative work, the fees tend to be high. Importing companies try to reduce costs by negotiating standing letters of credit, amounting to an international credit line. In other cases, the buyer will try to induce the seller to simply accept payment within 30 or 90 days of delivery, similar to typical domestic arrangements. As international financial markets and banking institutions become further integrated, conversion to home currency and payment is likely to become less of a problem. The diffusion of internationally accepted credit cards has greatly reduced payment risks, since funds can be obtained before shipping an order.

Repatriation, Hedging

The problem of repatriating funds from a weak currency country has made financial intermediaries develop so-called swaps, through which the funds will be exchanged (at a discount) against funds elsewhere. There are also, of course, various ways of hedging against shifts in exchange rates, and many importing firms use futures options to purchase funds in a currency they know will have to be used in the future.

For the marketer, it becomes important to stay close to the financial managers in the company and make sure they are consulted before an order from a new country is accepted. Standard sales techniques, such as offering delayed payments, installment pay schedules, or no-money-down credit sales might have to be forgone in favor of more prudent pricing schemes. Again, however, credit cards have come to the rescue, since by using Visa or MasterCard or several other cards, funds are automatically converted.

Legal Issues

Export License

Many products require an **export license**—in the United States usually issued by the Department of Commerce—in order to be shipped out of the country. In the Cold War era, many computers and other electronics products could not be exported from the United States—exporters could not get an export license. The issue of national security concerns was used to block many exports on the grounds that the Soviets might get hold of technology with military value. Even today, when many license requirements have been voided or are approved liberally, there is often a need to get a pro forma license. In the importing country, especially where currency restrictions are in place, import licenses are needed for many foreign products. The local department of commerce office will offer help on the license matter.

Transferring Title

The **title** of ownership of the exported goods generally follows the bill of lading. Whoever holds the bill of lading has access to the goods. The business risk—and thus exposure to normal loss, such as lack of sales in the marketplace—shifts with the title. The local distributor who borrows money to pay for the goods will be exposed to risk at the point when the bill of lading is accepted by the seller's bank—or, sometimes, as the seller's bank delivers the bill of lading to the buyer's bank.

Insurance

If damage to the goods occurs during transit, **insurance** questions arise. As we have seen, the recommended procedure is for the seller to quote a price CIF (cost-insurance-freight), in which case the seller will arrange for insurance and shipment to the border. This simplifies the whole exporting process but also makes the seller responsible for following up with insurance claims. Alternatively, the seller can quote FOB (free on board), in which case the buyer is saddled with the need to arrange for shipment and insurance. Good marketing thinking suggests that the company should quote its prices at the higher CIF rate and not bother the buyer with extra work.

Hiring an Agent

The seller must pay attention to legal matters in the market country. Product liability and warranty issues can become a problem, after-sales service responsibility questions may come up, conflicts with distributors about contracted quotas and sales efforts may arise, and so on. Since most countries do not allow foreigners to work on legal questions, a company representative, an agent, is needed.

The **agent** will be the legal representative of the firm (the principal) in the local market, usually working for a retainer fee and a contract that provides hourly compensation on special cases. Exhibit 5.9 offers a checklist of things to consider when hiring an agent. Where their responsibilities involve some sales activities—such as, for example, visiting distribution outlets to monitor in-store support—agents can also be remunerated via a commission percentage of revenues. Many agents work for more than one principal, but not for competing firms. Agents can be found through the same sources as distributors.

After-Sales Support

Service, Parts Supply, Training

In order to support the local marketing effort, the firm needs to establish after-sales service, stock spare parts and supplies, and train local staff. These tasks are often managed by the distributor, aided by the agent. The contract specifying the responsibilities of the distributor (see Exhibit 5.7) should make clear what marketing role he or she should play, and the agent is expected to enforce the contract.

EXHIBIT 5.9
**Master Foreign Agency
Appointment Checklist**

Source: Adapted from Hall, 1983, pp. 67–68.
Courtesy of Unz & Co.

Appointment	*Product warranty*
Territory–products	*Effective date and duration*
Sales activities	*Effective date and term*
Promotional efforts	Breach
Introductions (optional)	Insolvency
Prices	Prospective breach
Acceptance	Change in ownership or management
Agent representations	Foreign Protective Act
Minimum orders (optional)	*Rights and obligations upon termination*
Increase in orders (optional)	No liability of principal
Agent facilities	Return of promotional materials
Competitive products	Repurchase of stock
Confidential information	Accrued rights and obligations
Reports	*Indemnity*
Operations report	*No assignment*
Credit information	*Government regulation*
Visits to agent premises by representatives	Foreign law
of principal	U.S. law
Sales literature	Foreign Corrupt Practices Act
Trademarks and copyright	*Force majeure*
Acceptances of orders and shipments	*Separability*
Acceptance	*Waiver*
No violation of U.S. laws	*Notices*
Commissions	Written notice
Commission percentage	Oral notices
Accrual	*Governing law*
Refund	*Arbitration*
Discontinuation of products	*Article titles*
Repair and rework	*Entire agreement and modifications*
Relationship between parties	Entire agreement
Subagent	Modifications
No warranty against infringement	

As the firm's sales in a country grow larger, control of the local marketing effort becomes a very important issue. Not only does after-sales support need to be monitored more closely, but the whole marketing program (pricing, product line offered, promotion, and channel management) might need more effective management. A single agent and one or two independent distributors can't usually be counted on for that kind of marketing support.

Sales Subsidiary

At that point the company often decides to establish a **sales subsidiary,** staffed with locals and a few top managers from headquarters.

Such a sales subsidiary will run the local marketing effort, conducting market research; dealing with local advertising agencies; monitoring distributors' performance; providing information on competitors, market demand, and growth; and generally managing the local marketing mix—sometimes going against top management's recommendations and shared wisdom. More on this will be discussed in Part Three, "Local Marketing."

Importers as Trade Partners

Throughout the discussion in this chapter we have looked at the exporter or market entrant as the initiator of a trading relationship. Although this is natural in a marketing text, it is important to recognize that importers can also initiate trade. The most obvious example is when a company establishes sourcing abroad. For example, when Nike locates its sneaker production in Asia, the company acts as the future importer of the planned production. When Volkswagen subcontracts with a Portugese plant for the assembly of a new van, it is the importer that creates trade, just as when H&M from Sweden sources its teenage fashion wear from eastern Europe.

But there are less obvious cases in which importers take the initiative to create exchange. Where new markets emerge and grow at a fast rate (several examples are given in Chapters 8–10 on local marketing abroad), local businessmen are often quicker to see the potential of attracting well-known foreign brand names into their countries. As we have seen above, global companies (such as McDonald's, Levi Strauss, Toyota, Sony, Mercedes, and Dunlop) may owe their initial presence in many smaller countries not to a grand global strategy, but to the daring initiative shown by local entrepreneurs who convince the company to let them represent the brand in the country. The fact that one can find Heineken beer in most countries is mostly a testament to local entrepreneurs with import licenses who have approached Heineken and acquired local distribution rights. Typically, success leads to greater involvement by the parent company, sometimes leading to the contract disputes discussed earlier. As was stressed then, it is important to view these entrepreneurial importers as key local partners from the outset, and treat them accordingly.

The buyers of components and supplies in large companies can of course also be the ones initiating trade from abroad. But here studies of importers' initiatives have revealed that most buyers prefer to deal with domestic suppliers. Furthermore, these studies show that a shift from domestic to foreign suppliers is often motivated by dissatisfaction with existing suppliers. In other words, industrial buyers tend to be reluctant to change to imports from a foreign supplier unless they are unhappy with their domestic sourcing.[16]

This research also shows that a major reason for the reluctance of buyers to become importers is the perceived risk associated with imports from abroad. This perception of risk also leads importers to use different criteria when evaluating potential suppliers from abroad. While domestic suppliers are assessed in terms of quality and price of their product, foreign suppliers are also judged in terms of location and size. This underscores what has been stressed already, namely, that it is very important for the supplier to demonstrate not only product quality and reliability, but also logistical capability, ensuring timely supplies. Again, follow the golden rule, and treat these partners as you would like to be treated.

Summary

In this chapter the discussion has centered on the exporting mode of entering foreign markets and the ways companies tend to expand their global market reach. Four major entry modes were identified: exporting, licensing, strategic alliances, and wholly owned subsidiary in manufacturing. Each mode has advantages and disadvantages for the entrant depending on the barriers to entry. It was shown how high trade barriers almost always lead the firm to avoid exporting, and instead leads to licensing, alliances, or FDI.

The chapter then discussed the exporting option in detail. It showed how price is affected by the transaction costs in international trade, including tariffs. The various functional tasks involved in exporting were discussed in detail. Since many of them will be new to the typical marketing manager, the discussion went into detail to show what is involved and how the export manager, in many ways, needs skills quite different from the typical marketing manager. Nevertheless, these skills are essential for the global marketer, since it is important to understand the difficulty one might face in implementing international strategies. In today's multinational firm, all senior managers need some international experience and know-how, and exporting procedures are as basic to global marketing as accounting is to the financial manager.

The chapter ended with a discussion of importers as trade initiators and important partners in the local market.

Key Terms

agent, *151*
bill of lading, *143*
CIF, *143*
contract manufacturing, *132*
countervailing duty, *146*
direct exporting, *131*
distribution access, *136*
distribution alliance, *139*
distributors, *147*
dumping, *146*
entry barriers, *133*
export license, *151*
export management company (EMC), *140*

FOB, *143*
foreign direct investment (FDI), *132*
franchising, *132*
gatekeeper, *134*
government regulations, *136*
indirect exporting, *131*
insurance, *151*
joint ventures, *132*
letter of credit, *149*
licensing, *132*
modes of entry, *131*

natural barriers, *137*
nontariff barriers, *133*
price escalation, *144*
sales subsidiary, *152*
strategic alliances (SAs), *132*
tariff barriers, *133*
title, *151*
trade credit, *144*
trade fairs, *147*
trading companies, *131*
turnkey contracts, *132*

Discussion Questions

1. What kind of entry barriers might be faced by Amazon.com in expanding its online bookselling business into European, Asian, and Latin American markets? How would entry mode be affected?

2. Because it is located in the southern hemisphere, Chile's strong fruit-growing industry has the advantage (an example of a CSA) in many northern markets of counterseasonal harvesting. What is involved in arranging for the exporting of the fruit crops to a market such as the European Union? What trade barriers might Chilean fruit-growers face with this entry mode? How would you try to control the marketing effort in Europe?

3. For an industry or product of your choice, use Internet Web sites, library sources, U.S. Department of Commerce publications, and trade publications to find out when and where the major international trade fairs and conventions are held. Estimate how much participation would cost for a company (registration fees, booth charges, travel, food and lodging, preparation of pamphlets, etc.).

4. What might be the natural entry barriers against foreign cars, if any, in the United States? In Germany? In Japan? Any natural barriers against foreign foods for the same countries?

5. What are the advantages of the Internet in distributing your final product? What mode of entry would you propose?

Notes

1. Adapted from Root, 1994.

2. From U.S. Department of Commerce statistics.

3. The cost of entry barriers is not an issue of free versus managed trade. All agree that barriers cost money and that consumers have to pay more for products and services. The policy difference is rather in terms of whether managed trade is worth it for the nation, since tariffs protect firms and jobs, however inefficient, at least in the short run. In the longer run, the added economic benefits from lower barriers are supposed to result in new investment and new job opportunities in competitive industries. At least that is the theory. Since the foreign marketer will be confronted with sometimes hostile reactions from workers who have lost their jobs because of trade (as has happened in central Europe, Russia, and elsewhere), this theory should be kept in mind. It provides some modicum of defense for global competition.

4. The departments of commerce in different countries will have the tariff schedules for many countries and be able to give advice on how to analyze them. Also, some direct experience is, as always, useful. Watching a customs official decipher the schedules to assign the correct tariff instills some sense of humility and respect for government officials.

5. Recognizing FDI and the multinational firm as an efficient response to barriers is one of the core propositions of the modern theory of the multinational—see Buckley, 1987.

6. See Czinkota and Kotabe, 1993.

7. Personal interview with Mr. Isoda of Daiwa Securities, June 5, 1993.

8. Although the close company groupings in Japan called *keiretsus* have been acclaimed as a source of overseas success and a barrier to foreign entry at home, they are now also a burden as Japan's financial crisis and recession mean that inefficient partners can no longer be supported by other members.

9. See Elliott, 1995.

10. See, for example, "U.S. Says Talks," 1987.

11. The host country governments have gradually grown in sophistication and try to stem this loophole in the trade barriers by requiring a certain percentage of local content in the value of the imported product. In autos, figures around 60–80 percent are typical.

12. From O'Neill, 2001.

13. These are only the main changes. For further information, see Horlick and Shea, 1995, and Suchman and Mathews, 1995. Effective enforcement of the new rules is still in question, especially since individual countries may not agree to the binding arbitration stipulated through the new DSM (dispute resolution mechanism). See Horlick and Shea, 1995. See also Rugman, 2001.

14. See Beeth, 1990.

15. Ibid. offers a brief but enlightening discussion of what makes for a great distributor.

16. See, for example, Alden, 1987, and Rangan et al., 1995.

Selected References

Alden, Vernon R. "Who Says You Can't Crack the Japanese Market?" *Harvard Business Review,* January–February 1987, pp. 52–56.

Becker, H. "Price Escalation in International Marketing." Reading no. 43 in Thorelli, Hans B., and S. Tamer Cavusgil, eds. *International Marketing Strategy,* 3rd ed. New York: Pergamon Press, 1990, pp. 523–26.

Beeth, Gunnar. "Distributors—Finding and Keeping the Good Ones." In Thorelli and Cavusgil, *International Marketing Strategy,* pp. 487–94.

Buckley, Peter J. *The Theory of the Multinational Enterprise.* Studia Oeconomiae Negotiorum 26. Uppsala, Sweden: Acta Universitatis Upsaliensis, 1987.

Contractor, Farouk, and Peter Lorange, eds. *Cooperative Strategies in International Business.* Lexington, MA: Lexington Books, 1988.

Czinkota, Michael R., and Masaaki Kotabe. *The Japanese Distribution System.* Chicago: Probus, 1993.

Czinkota, Michael R., and Jon Woronoff. *Unlocking Japan's Markets.* Chicago: Probus, 1991.

Eli, Max. *Japan, Inc: Global Strategies of Japanese Trading Corporations.* Chicago: Probus, 1991.

Elliott, Stuart. "At Coke, a Shift to Many Voices." *New York Times,* January 20, 1995, pp. D1, D6.

Emmott, Bill. *Japan's Global Reach.* London: Century, 1992.

Hall, R. Duane. *International Trade Operations.* Jersey City, NJ: Unz, 1983.

Hanssens, D. M., and J. K. Johansson. "Synergy or Rivalry? The Japanese Automobile Companies' Export Expansion." *Journal of International Business Studies,* Spring 1990, pp. 34–45.

Horlick, Gary N., and Eleanor C. Shea. "The World Trade Organization Antidumping Agreement." *Journal of World Trade* 29, no. 1 (February 1995), pp. 5–31.

Lee, Chong Suk. *Export Market Expansion Strategies and Export Performance: A Study of High Technology Manufacturing Firms.* Doctoral dissertation, University of Washington, 1987.

Mårtensson, Rita. *Innovations in Retailing.* Lund, Sweden: Liber, 1983.

O'Neill, Mark. "Anti-dumping lawsuits rankle." *South China Morning Post,* October 28, 2001.

Piercy, Nigel. "Export Strategy: Concentration on Key Markets vs. Market Spreading." *Journal of International Marketing* 1, no.1 (1982), pp. 56–67.

Porter, Michael. *The Competitive Advantage of Nations.* New York: Free Press, 1990.

Rangan, V. Kasturi; Benson P. Shapiro; and Rowland T. Moriarty. *Business Marketing Strategy: Concepts and Applications.* Chicago: Irwin, 1995.

Root, Franklin R. *Entry Strategies for International Markets,* Revised and Expanded. San Francisco: Jossey-Bass Inc. Publishers, 1994.

Rugman, Alan. *The End of Globalization.* New York: Amacom, 2001.

Suchman, Peter O., and Susan Mathews. "Mixed News for Importers." *China Business Review* 22, no. 2 (March–April 1995), pp. 31–34.

Thorelli, H. B., and S. Tamer Cavusgil, eds. *International Marketing Strategy,* 3rd ed. New York: Pergamon, 1990.

"U.S. Says Talks with Common Market over Airbus Subsidies Are Deadlocked." *The Wall Street Journal,* December 18, 1987.

Vernon, Raymond. "International Investment and International Trade in the Product Cycle." *Quarterly Journal of Economics,* May 1966.

Chapter

6

Licensing, Strategic Alliances, FDI

"Can't we be friends?"

After reading this chapter, you will be able to:

1. Avoid entry barriers by unbundling the value chain and engage in nonexporting modes of entry.
2. Spot when licensing and strategic alliances involve transfer of know-how and, therefore, possible dilution of firm-specific advantages.
3. Work effectively with licensing and alliance partners who may be competitors in some product markets.
4. Find the optimal mode of entry by first finding a way over entry barriers and then making the necessary trade-offs between strategic posture and the market stage of the life cycle.
5. Decide between a waterfall-expansion strategy with gradual entry versus a sprinkler strategy that attempts to cover all markets at once.

Exporting might be the mode of entry into foreign markets that most closely resembles market expansion at home. But it is only one mode of entry, and because of transportation costs, tariffs, and other entry barriers—and because they want to be closer to the customers—companies find it necessary to contemplate using other modes of entry. These alternative modes generally involve some amount of technology transfer and know-how sharing. The three principal modes are licensing, strategic alliances, and FDI (foreign direct investment) in wholly owned manufacturing subsidiaries. The global marketer must understand how these modes operate and how the deconstruction of the value chain affects the marketing effort. In licensing and strategic alliances there may be no need—or no role—for local presence of marketers from the company, as the partner becomes responsible for the local effort. By contrast, FDI in a manufacturing plant might lead to a marketing effort not only in the country itself but throughout a whole trade region.

The Ubiquitous Global Marketing Alliance

In the 2000s, global marketing alliances have become as common as failures among the dot-com start-ups. Actually, marketing alliances, even across borders, have been common in some industries for a long time. Marketing alliances can involve a simple arrangement for one company to distribute another company's products through its sales force. Such an arrangement might allow the seller to offer a complete product line in one sales call, as pharmaceutical companies frequently do. Or it might be limited in scope and time, such as cross-promoting Coca-Cola and a Disney film. Calling the alliance "global" seems sometimes a matter of definition. Today the term seems to be used when the partners are simply from different countries, so that "global" really stands for "international." "Global" has the cachet—although attaching "global" to such an alliance is perhaps an exaggeration.

Nevertheless, the global alliance formula has become ubiquitous for a sound business reason: It allows access to foreign markets with a minimum of up-front investment. Intense competition among large global firms stretches their resources thin, and cooperation allows firms to focus on what they do best but still compete across the whole global market. Smaller local companies can use global marketing alliances to beef up their marketing muscle and put up a good defense against the large globals. The leverage that can come from a global marketing alliance is in a way like putting a company on steroids.

Some examples will show how these alliances can crop up anywhere. Warsteiner Brauerei is Germany's largest private beer brewer. In September 2001, Warsteiner announced its intention to set up marketing alliances with foreign private breweries to increase beer exports quickly without having to spend large sums of money. Head of distribution and marketing Frank Spitzhuettl explains: "Heineken and Interbrew are buying up wholesalers [for beer sales in the catering trade] one after the other. We must find a way of working together with foreign breweries which want to remain private and independent."

In March 2000, the Whirlpool Corporation and the Tupperware Corporation formed a global marketing alliance. The idea is that Whirlpool's kitchen appliances and Tupperware's food containers present synergies in R&D and promotion. The alliance, started in Europe and then expanded to the rest of the world, works on collaborative cooking and refrigeration methods, including joint promotions. According to Jeff Fettig, Whirlpool's president and chief operating officer, "This will include gathering and sharing of consumer research, development of new high value products and co-promoting new and current products."

The airlines industry offers numerous examples from the past and present since code-sharing is a marketing alliance. The 1999 proposed alliance between global giants British Airways and American Airlines was denied by antitrust regulators, but in the same year Delta, Air France, and AeroMexico were allowed to code-share. Then there is the big Star Alliance, including United Airlines, Lufthansa, Varig Brazilian, Thai Airways, SAS, and others (the number of members is now up to 19). The code-sharing means that the members' flights are listed jointly, so that UA 4177 and LH 1342 might be the same flight from London to Frankfurt. Only one aircraft is necessary, but each alliance member can feature the flight in its "product line" (the destinations it flies to).

Other alliances are less well known. The Leading Hotels of the World is a global marketing alliance that markets luxury hotels around the world. A potential member hotel applies for membership and, after inspection and approval, pays a membership fee that is used to advertise and promote the destination jointly with other upscale luxury hotels around the world. One recent member is Datai Langkawi on Pulau in Malaysia, an idyllic retreat in the depths of a centuries-old virgin rain forest with an 18-hole golf course and a private beach.

More mundane, B2B (business-to-business) alliances are also in vogue. In 2002 Parker-Hannifin of the United States, the world's leading manufacturer of motion and control technologies and systems for industrial use, and Myotoku Ltd. of Japan, a specialist in vacuum technologies, announced a global marketing alliance. Says Parker-Hannifin group President Bob Bond: "The alliance with Myotoku fills a major gap in our vacuum offering and allows us to pull through additional product opportunities." As for Myotoku, its President Toshio Nakamori is also pleased, saying: "Parker's global reach and Myotoku's design and manufacturing capabilities in vacuum products should bring important growth to our companies."

There seems to be no limit to what a cross-marketing global alliance can accomplish.

Sources: "Warsteiner Plans Marketing Alliance with Foreign Private Breweries," *AFX.com,* September 16, 2001; "Whirlpool Corp. and Tupperware Corp. Said They Formed a Global Alliance to Share Research and to Jointly Promote New Products," *AFX European Focus,* March 28, 2000; "Parker Establishes Global Marketing Alliance with Tokyo-based Vacuum Technology Firm," *PR Newswire,* January 11, 2002; "Datai Langkawi in Global Marketing Alliance," *Business Times* (Malaysia), March 20, 2000; www.staraliiance.com.

Introduction

Exporting no doubt introduces a new and unfamiliar set of activities for the global marketer. But complicated as exporting is to manage in a practical sense because of the number of tasks and the various middlemen involved, conceptually it is a natural extension of traditional market expansion. This is not the case for the alternative modes of entry. Licensing, alliances, and FDI all involve management skills and concepts different from the standard marketing repertoire. This chapter will cover the basic new points.

Licensing used to have a bad name as an entry mode. As we saw in Chapter 2, licensing runs the risk of **dissipation,** that is, a firm's know-how and FSAs will easily leak to its competitors. The oft-told stories about American companies such as RCA, Honeywell, and General Electric selling technology licenses inexpensively to the Japanese after World War II only to witness the later incursions of Japanese companies into Western markets have helped put licensing in a bad light. In recent years, however, as technology sharing between competitors has become commonplace, licensing is no longer the black sheep. Although the 2001 WTO meeting in Doha, Qatar, produced a weakening of the patent protection in pharmaceuticals, the general thrust of recent negotiations has been to encourage recognition of intellectual property rights across countries. Technological leaks can be pursued more legitimately now, and anyway technological change is often so fast that some licenses lose their value even before the clones and "me-too" copies appear.

Still, many firms prefer to invest in wholly owned manufacturing subsidiaries abroad rather than run the risk of dissipating their firm-specific advantages and not getting sufficient up-front compensation for the use of their patented know-how. In fact, the standard definition of a multinational corporation is not simply a company that sells its products in many markets but one that also has several manufacturing and assembly plants operating abroad, thus controlling the use of its FSAs.

The chapter presents in-depth descriptions of the three main nonexporting modes of entry, licensing (including franchising), strategic alliances, and wholly owned manufacturing subsidiaries, in more detail. The licensing part features separate sections on franchising and original equipment manufacturing (OEM). The alliances part discusses both distribution and manufacturing alliances, and also R&D alliances and joint ventures. Then the chapter shows how marketing can be controlled under the different modes of entry and a sketch of the **optimal entry mode** under different assumptions of company strategic objectives and market maturity. We then discuss global expansion paths, the effect of "cultural distance" on the internationalization path of firms' expansion, and the important benefit of learning how to do business abroad. Then we show how the gradual "internationalization" of the company is reflected in changes in the modes of entry and also how "born globals" leapfrog these stages. A section presents the benefits and costs of "sprinkler" and "waterfall" expansion strategies.

Licensing

Licensing refers to offering a firm's know-how or other intangible asset to a foreign company for a fee, royalty, and/or other type of payment. Its advantage over exporting is its avoidance of tariffs and other levies that might be assessed against an imported product. For the new exporter, it also has the advantages that the need for market research and knowledge is reduced and that, as opposed to the use of a distributor, it is often possible to induce the licensee to support the product strongly in the market. This is because in licensing, the firm in the host country gets specific know-how from the licensing firm and thus is able to develop some skills on its own; it does not just resell the product as the distributor does. Licensing is therefore a form of technology transfer—but this is also its greatest weakness for the licensor. Because the licensee gets access to certain firm-specific knowledge, it will share in the competitive advantage of the licensor—and can then potentially use this knowledge in further applications other than the ones specifically stated in the licensing contract.

To avoid this dissipation of firm-specific advantages, the licensing firm needs to handle contract negotiations with considerable skill. Exhibit 6.1 shows some of the elements of the typical licensing contract. It is important, for example, to limit the geographical area within which the licensee might sell the product so as not to engender competition with the firm's own sales in other countries (see box, "How Not to Do It").

It is also important to make sure what the conditions for terminating the contract are, what the time limit is, and how the specific know-how is to be used. Contracts identify the level and kind of marketing support the licensee is supposed to generate and the appropriate steps to be taken should this support not be forthcoming. The licensor, for its part, pledges its supply of the requisite transfer of knowledge, including managerial and technical support, patents with or without trademark, or brand name transfer.

The royalty level and payment structure vary with different forms of licensing. **Straight licensing** of a certain technology in processing, for example, tends to bring **royalties** of 5 percent of gross revenues, sometimes more (the Disney World Corporation receives 7 percent from its Japanese licensee), sometimes less. Occasionally there are also payments in the form of technical assistance fees and the possibility of lump-sum royalties, paid out only intermittently. Another attractive alternative is to negotiate for an equity option in the licensee's firm that can be exercised when further in-depth penetration into the country market is desirable.

Alliances have become common in the international airline industry. They allow different national airlines to combine routes and share seating codes for seamless travel around the world—and for valuable frequent flier miles for the fatigued business executive.
Courtesy of Young & Rubicam New York.

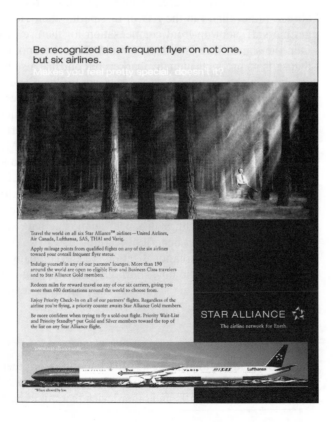

EXHIBIT 6.1
Elements of a Licensing Contract

Source: R. Duane Hall, *International Trade Operations*. Jersey City, NJ: Unz & Co., 1983, pp. 67–68.

Technology package	*Compensation*
Definition/description of the licensed industrial property (patents, trademarks, know-how)	Currency of payment
	Responsibilities for payment of local taxes
	Disclosure fee
Know-how to be supplied and its methods of transfer	Running royalties
	Minimum royalties
Supply of raw materials, equipment, and intermediate goods	Lump-sum royalties
	Technical assistance fees
Use conditions	Sales to and/or purchases from licensee
Field of use of licensed technology	Fees for additional new products
Territorial rights for manufacture and sale	Grantback of product improvements by licensee
Sublicensing rights	Other compensation
Safeguarding trade secrets	
Responsibility for defense/infringement action on patents and trademarks	*Other provisions*
	Contract law to be followed
Exclusion of competitive products	Duration and renewal of contract
Exclusion of competitive technology	Cancellation/termination provisions
Maintenance of product standards	Procedures for the settlement of disputes
Performance requirements	Responsibility for government approval of the license agreement
Rights of licensee to new products and technology	
Reporting requirements	
Auditing/inspection rights of licenser	
Reporting requirements of licensee	

Franchising

Many multinational firms, especially in the service sector, are turning to franchising as a way to enter foreign markets and still retain some control over their marketing and brand image. In **franchising,** the entering firm (the franchisor) offers to help a local entrepreneur (the franchisee) to establish a local business that is allowed to sell the franchisor's well-known branded product in the new market. In return, the franchisee will raise the necessary capital and agree to pay the franchisor a royalty on sales and usually an up-front fee. For its part, the franchisor promises to maintain the brand through advertising and promotion, including sponsorship of various events. The franchisor also provides a wide range of market support services to the franchisee, in particular local advertising to sustain the brand name, of which the franchisee usually will pay a portion. Training manuals for employees, help with product lines and production scheduling, accounting manuals, and occasional assistance with financing are some of the services provided to the franchisee.

In order for franchised brands to be effectively promoted by global advertising, product lines and customer service need to be standardized, two important features from a marketing perspective. Although cultural differences might require some adaptation—in Europe, McDonald's serves beer, and in Asia, rice is added to the menu—the franchising concept works precisely because of standardization of product and service. Products should be predictably the same ("too good" can be as dangerous as "not good enough" since customers rely on "what to expect"). The same for service—although "personal service" in franchising should perhaps be called "impersonal service," since even the smiles are obligatory.

A number of fast-food firms have utilized franchising to penetrate new markets by leveraging on their brand name and the local market knowledge of their franchise owners. U.S. fast-food firms have fueled the growth of franchising over the last decade, driven by such brand names as McDonald's, KFC, Taco Bell, Pizza Hut, Burger King, and Wendy's. All of these firms were able to successfully identify the core features of their service systems and their product-specific advantages in order to determine how to export their winning concepts. For instance, McDonald's successful system consists of not only the cooking method and serving procedure but also the training of the

Getting the Picture

HOW NOT TO DO IT

A neophyte American firm decided to avoid managerial and research expense to explore foreign markets and to simply license the manufacturing and sales of their product to a U.K. firm. The English firm was granted the right to sublicense the process know-how to other parts of the world. After a few years the foreign markets for the company's product increased greatly in potential, but the U.S. company gained only a small share of the increase in revenues. It had already "sold" those markets to the English company and could only watch as that company's sales took off.

Actually, even more savvy multinationals make these kinds of mistakes. Early in its global expansion, American Gillette licensed its razor blade manufacturing technology to British Wilkinson—forgetting to exclude continental Europe from Wilkinson's sales territory. The result: Gillette has had a long uphill fight against Wilkinson to gain dominance in European markets.

Source: Adapted from M. L. Mace, "The President and International Operations," *Harvard Business Review,* November–December 1966, p. 76.

workers, their attire and attitude, and the management and bookkeeping system. Franchisees are required to attend "Hamburger University" in order to learn how to manage the business and train their staff. These franchisees must also adhere to established McDonald's standards in terms of the quality of the ingredients and the preparation and sale of the product (see box, "The McDonald's Way").

One drawback of franchising is the need for careful and continuous quality control. If the franchisor does not perform, the company might have to terminate the contract. When the McDonald's restaurant on Champs Elysees in Paris gave mediocre service in unclean premises, the McDonald's corporation stepped in and took over. Such close supervision of the various aspects of far-flung operations requires well-developed global management systems and labor-intensive monitoring. Because of the managerial skills required, international franchising has become successful largely among those businesses having long experience with franchising at home before venturing out globally. Examples include the successful American fast-food purveyors McDonald's and Kentucky Fried Chicken, Hilton hotels, and the British-based Body Shop (but not Starbucks, which owns its stores, and Italy's Benetton, which has developed a unique system of independent retailers supported by entrepreneurial sales agents appointed by the company).

Original Equipment Manufacturing (OEM)

In terms of the theory of the multinational, OEM usually falls in the "exporting" subcategory, involving shipments of components from home to overseas. From a marketing viewpoint, however, it fits better with licensing and strategic alliances since the company brand name is suppressed, usually not the case in exporting. OEM is like selling a generic brand, letting another firm put its name on the product.

In **original equipment manufacturing (OEM),** a company enters a foreign market by selling its unbranded product or component to another company in the market country. The buyer then sells the final product under its own brand name. For the supplier firm, there is little or no expense in marketing its product overseas, and the buyer gets a product ready to use and to market. The supplier has to give up its own effort to market the product overseas, but often tries to change its strategy later if the overseas market for its product is strong.

Some examples will illustrate the principles. Canon provides the cartridges for Hewlett-Packard's very successful laser printers and also for Kodak's copiers, both OEM arrangements. After several years of successful market development, Canon now also markets its own copiers with success. Esco, an Oregon-based heavy machinery firm, supplies parts OEM to Mitsubishi Heavy Industries, to be distributed under Mitsubishi's name as spare parts in Komatsu and Caterpillar earthmovers.

The large Korean consumer goods manufacturers such as Samsung and Lucky-Goldstar initially opted for the OEM entry mode in the U.S. market. By selling unbranded color television sets, microwaves, and VCRs to resellers such as Sears, Amana, and Emerson, they avoided the need to spend money on establishing a brand

Getting the Picture

THE MCDONALD'S WAY

With more than 30,000 restaurants in over 120 countries, McDonald's is in all likelihood the world's largest and best-known food service retailer. Despite already possessing possibly the most developed global franchise system anywhere, McDonald's is still driven to expand. It aims to serve 1 percent of the world's population. This vision is focused on three worldwide strategies: be the best employer for its people in each community around the world; deliver operational excellence to its customers in each of its restaurants; and achieve enduring profitable growth by expanding the brand through innovation and technology.

Currently, about 70 percent of McDonald's worldwide restaurant businesses are owned and operated by independent businessmen and women. A new franchise costs around $500,000 depending on the size of the facility, inventory, decor, landscaping, and other factors, and an initial fee of $45,000 must be paid to McDonald's. McDonald's charges a 3.5 percent service fee and a rental charge of 8.5 percent of the franchisee's volume. Additional support is available for prospective franchisees throughout the countries in which McDonald's operates.

In certain countries, such as Russia, McDonald's has ownership interests in restaurants. When McDonald's opened its first Moscow outlet in 1990, its 700-seat restaurant served 30,000 meals in one day. McDonald's now serves more than 200,000 Russians every day, which is particularly notable considering that its food prices are comparable worldwide while Russian incomes are only a fraction of those in developed countries. From the initial Pushkin Square restaurant, which received its ingredients almost totally from abroad, McDonald's now purchases over 75 percent of its ingredients from more than 100 independent Russian suppliers. The Moscow McDonald's has invested in a $45 million warehouse ("McComplex") in order to supply its restaurants with the quality ingredients necessary to meet their global standards. Today this centralized distribution facility supplies all of McDonald's 74 restaurants throughout Russia as well as those in 17 other countries, including Austria, Belorussia, Czech Republic, Germany, Hungary, Moldova, and Ukraine.

Even with McDonald's new flexibility toward local preferences, to reduce antiglobalization and anti-American reactions, it is hardly surprising that some non-Americans—as well as some Americans—consider McDonald's a threat to a country's traditions.

Sources: **www.mcdonalds.com;** "Moscow-McDonald's Backgrounder," October 1994; Barbara Marsh, "Franchise Realities: Sandwich-Shop Chain Surges, but to Run One Can Take Heroic Efforts," *The Wall Street Journal,* September 16, 1992, pp. A1, A5; Michael Specter, "Borscht and Blini to Go: From Russian Capitalists, an Answer to McDonald's," *New York Times,* August 9, 1995, pp. D1, D3.

image in the market. At the same time, however, they gave up the chance to establish their own recognizable identity in the way the Japanese did. Opting for a Canon-like approach, the Korean automaker Hyundai decided to establish its own dealer and service network in the United States. Now the other Korean companies, with Samsung and LG (formerly, Lucky-Goldstar) in front, are doing the same. Today, having a globally recognized brand is key to global success.

Strategic Alliances

An international **strategic alliance (SA)** is typically a collaborative arrangement between firms, sometimes competitors, across borders. The joint venture is today often viewed as an equity-based SA, while new forms of alliances involve nonequity-based collaboration (partnerships, agreements to share, contractual participation in projects).[1]

SAs are a new type of entry mode increasingly prevalent in the last decade. Because they often represent collaboration between potential competitors, one effect has been to weaken the tie between ownership advantages and company control. Strategic alliances are based on the sharing of vital information, assets, and technology between the partners, even though they might in the process lose their proprietary know-how. Thus, alliances tend to be akin to licensing agreements, with the exception that the royalty and fee payments to one partner are replaced by active participation in the alliance by both partners.

The Rationale for Nonequity SAs

Since nonequity strategic alliances, especially between competitors, are a relatively new form of entry mode, it is useful to explain why they have emerged now.

The economic gains from strategic alliances are usually quite tangible. A company accesses technology it otherwise would not get. Markets are reached without a long buildup of relationships in channels. Efficient manufacturing is made possible without investment in a new plant, and so on.

However, given the risks of losing control of the firm's know-how, one wonders why alternative organizational forms—joint ventures, wholly owned subsidiaries, licensing, or mergers, for example—have proven insufficient. The reasons quoted by companies include the sheer size of the financial investments required, the speed with which market presence can be established in SAs, and the lessened risk exposure.[2]

Two other factors play a role as well. One is the crumbling of the value of control itself. As we saw above, leading know-how is being diffused faster than ever, and products and manufacturing processes embodying new technology are now readily copied through widespread reverse engineering and competitive benchmarking. Companies that have presence in most leading markets will have quick access to most new technologies. Even though patents can be policed across borders, the speed with which technology ages makes leakage less of a problem.[3]

A second factor is the new urgency about competing in several country markets at once. Having a presence in leading markets is often necessary to observe customers, monitor competitors, and to disturb competitors' sources of cash. Alliances allow firms to expand the use of existing managerial resources.[4]

Hence, nonequity SAs represent more of an expansion of a company's repertoire than the replacement of existing forms of business venture. The company can now do things it could not do before. SAs allow two companies to undertake missions impossible for the individual firm to undertake. Strategic alliances constitute an efficient economic response to changed conditions.

Distribution Alliances

Since their marketing implications differ considerably, we will distinguish between three types of nonequity alliances: distribution, manufacturing, and research and development (R&D).

An early and still common form of SA is the shared distribution network. The tie-up between Chrysler and Mitsubishi Motors to distribute cars in the United States is one example. So are Nissan's agreement to sell Volkswagens in Japan, the licensing of Molson's of Canada to brew and sell Kirin beer in North America, and the tie-up between SAS, KLM, Austrian Air, and Swiss Air to share routes in European air corridors. More recently, the STAR alliance involving United Airlines, Lufthansa, Air Canada, SAS, and Thai Airways (and now Varig Brazilian Airlines) has been created to provide global route access and seamless booking through code-sharing agreements.

Even if the scale of these alliances is "larger than ever," these types of arrangements are not new. In the traditional textbooks they fall under "piggybacking," "consortium marketing," and licensing. Their strategic rationale usually lies in improved capacity load and wider product line for one partner and in inexpensive and quick access to a market for the other. Assets are complementary, and the partners can focus on what they do best.

One drawback of these SAs is that over time the arrangement can limit growth - for the partners. The partner with the established distribution network may want to expand its product line, competing with the other partner's products. It may want to expand into other markets, shift resources from the existing markets, and thus give less support to distribution than the other partner would find acceptable. Growth will be constrained.

As for the other partner, the arrangement hinders its learning more about the market and how to market the product in the foreign country and thus creates an obstacle for further inroads. If this partner decides to develop greater penetration in the market, adding products to the line and increasing marketing support, it might be competing with the first partner's products, and also tax the capacity limitations of the existing channel network. Mitsubishi's lackluster performance in the U.S. auto market is partly due to the difficulty of working through Chrysler's dealer network and the late creation of an independent dealer network. Its growth has been stymied.

Because of such limits to growth, this type of SA does not last long when market expansion is an important goal of a partner.[5] The association can be convenient and economical, however, and when there is less pressure to grow, the alliance is justified.

Manufacturing Alliances

Another early form of strategic alliance is **shared manufacturing.** In Japan, Matsushita agreed to manufacture IBM PCs, using up excess capacity. Volvo and Renault shared certain body parts and components, even after their full-fledged merger was scrapped. Saab engines are now made by GM Europe in its Opel factories (an alliance emerging from GM's purchase of 50 percent of Saab stock).

It is not always easy to distinguish these arrangements from OEM and similar agreements. The difference is that OEM arrangements are simple contracts for selling unbranded components to another manufacturer. Potentially they sell the components to many customers. By contrast, **manufacturing alliances** involve the brands of both manufacturers with existing capabilities in the manufacturing of the parts; the subcontracting is a special arrangement for both partners.

These alliances are complementary more in economics than in technology. The arrangement is convenient, saves money, and is similar to a distribution agreement. The partners fill unused capacity and save money and time by not having to invest in new plant and equipment. From a marketing viewpoint, the alliance is sometimes a drawback since the sales organization has to deal with two principals in charge of production. It is harder to get the alliance to listen to customer feedback.

As in the case of distribution tie-ups, these SAs are likely to put a constraint on further growth. Limits to further expansion come from limited capacity, less learning from the partner, and difficulty in changing the product mix for further expansion. A change in growth objectives may spell the end of the arrangement.

R&D Alliances

SAs in R&D are different from those in distribution and manufacturing. In addition to providing favorable economics, speed of access, and managerial resources, **R&D alliances** are intended to solve critical survival questions for the firm.[6] R&D tie-ups with competitors are a means of keeping pace while making sure that competitors work toward the same technological standards. In essence, the amount of funding involved in R&D leads the company to hedge its bets and try to make sure the direction of research is the same throughout the industry. The firms have confidence in their own implementation of the new technological ideas, and marketing can be the competitive edge when technology can no longer be.

This is a striking departure from past practices, at least in the West. The R&D labs of the major companies provided the basis for their competitive edge, with super-secret research patented and policed for infringements and with full-fledged new discoveries emerging unannounced. Today, the companies are eager to announce the start of their research rather than its completion; they want competitors and customers to know what they are working on; and they listen attentively for news from competing firms. When differences in standards threaten to emerge, the firms gather eagerly under the auspices of the industry association to iron out differences. As one company introduces a new product based on a new technology, customers know that competitors will announce similar products within a few months. If a competitor misses a beat, it can spell disaster.[7]

Microsoft, the PC software giant, has always made a special effort to protect the integrity of its unique software. Recently, however, it has decided to share some technological developments with actual and potential competitors in order to induce other software writers to use the Microsoft standard. Furthermore, it is under pressure from several industry SAs, and Microsoft has also found it necessary to license (and "improve") the new Java network software from Sun Microsystems. However, the 1998 court case pitting Microsoft against Netscape, leader in Internet access software, and other software producers shows how fragile alliances and partnerships can be when technology evolves as rapidly as in computer software.

Increasing R&D activity has been accompanied by a proliferation of new products in the markets, which in turn has increased competitive rivalry. To compete effectively, companies have been forced to increase and speed up their R&D efforts even more or risk losing their technological competencies. Strategic alliances provide one way of doing this and alleviating the accompanying financial strain on the organizations.

In many markets the products have to embody the new technology even to be considered by buyers. While once a Saab car could tout the special advantages of an aerodynamic shape and front-wheel drive, now even antilock brakes, air bags, and 16-valve turbo engines are standard. It is this relentless emphasis on the most recent technology in new products that has raised the ante of global participation in so many industries and has led to the need for SAs in R&D. As we will see in Part Four, "Global Management," technology has changed the nature of marketing in many global markets.

Joint Ventures

Even though **joint ventures (JVs)** have undeniable strengths from a marketing viewpoint, many corporations have been reluctant to enter into JV agreements unless forced to by government regulations or pressure. The JV involves the transfer of capital, manpower, and usually some technology from the foreign partner to an existing local firm, whose main contribution tends to be expertise and understanding of the local market. The contract guiding the formation of a JV has often been likened to a marriage contract, and for good reason.[8]

The transfer of technology is the main problem. Since the JV implies that equity is shared among the partners, there is a decided risk that the know-how (and thus the firm's specific advantage) will become diluted by the necessary sharing of information. The point is well illustrated by the protracted negotiations that preceded the GM–Toyota JV agreement in 1982 to produce a small car for the U.S. market. The U.S. Justice Department was reluctant to approve the agreement between two of the world's largest automakers on antitrust grounds. From Toyota's perspective there was little about car manufacturing or marketing to be gained from the venture, as compared to GM's potential gains, and the company was reluctant to share its manufacturing know-how with a competitor. Toyota, however, saw the agreement as defusing the concern about Japanese imports that threatened (and still does) to force U.S. lawmakers into a protectionist stand. Consequently, Toyota could be indifferent to the delays caused by the U.S. government. At least for some time, the political risks could be "managed" by Toyota in this manner.[9]

Manufacturing Subsidiaries

Foreign direct investment **(FDI) in wholly owned manufacturing** subsidiaries is undertaken by the international firm for several reasons. The aims could be to acquire raw materials, to operate at lower manufacturing costs, to avoid tariff barriers and satisfy local content requirements, and/or to penetrate local markets.[10] The last rationale is of prime interest in the marketing context.

Manufacturing FDI has several advantages in market penetration. First, local production means price escalation caused by transport costs, customs duties fees, local turnover taxes, and so on can be nullified or drastically reduced. Availability of goods can usually be guaranteed to resellers, minimizing potential channel conflicts over allocation decisions and eliminating delays for ultimate buyers. Location of production in the market country may lead to more uniform quality, although in some cases the basis of initial reluctance to go to manufacturing abroad may well have been the risk of lowered quality.

Today, however, with the global spread of manufacturing skills, the risk of lower quality is reduced, and companies can count on local suppliers to provide quality and service (see box, "A BMW Made in America? Yes!")

Getting the Picture

A BMW MADE IN AMERICA? YES!

The BMW Z3 roadster is a slick, sporty automobile, a product of German precision engineering and craftsmanship. It's the "ultimate driving machine," James Bond's vehicle of choice in the movie *GoldenEye.* Where is the BMW Z3 made? The last place you'd think of would probably be Spartanburg, South Carolina. A German icon mass-produced in the heart of the United States? Yes. The Spartanburg facility is the first full BMW manufacturing plant to be located outside Germany.

The BMW Spartanburg plant was launched in March 1994. The company invested roughly $1.4 billion in the facility, employing more than 3,500 workers ("associates"). In addition to the Z3 and the Z3 coupe, the plant produces the M coupe and the sport utility vehicle X5 (BMW's new SUV offering) for both the domestic and the international markets. The Spartanburg plant is in fact the only BMW plant that makes the X5. Although the BMW brand is uniquely German, the SUV concept is purely of American origin.

Why would BMW consider the United States as a manufacturing facility location? You would think the main reason is ready access to the large market. But with tariff barriers low or nonexistent, and with transportation and logistics increasingly efficient, market access is not the major factor. Instead, the main reason for the move to North America was for better supplier relations.

BMW found that U.S.-based suppliers were nimbler and more flexible than their European counterparts. European suppliers, used to comfortable relationships with the abundant European automakers, were less open to new part requirements, just-in-time systems, and supply-chain improvements. The company was able improve its supply chain by using American suppliers.

The number of BMW customers in the United States has tripled over the last ten years. And BMW reached a new global sales record in 2001, delivering 905,653 models to customers around the world.

Sources: "BMW: Spartanburg Plant Key Facts," *Auto Intelligence,* Internet Online, available from **www.autointell-news.com/-european companies/BMW/bmw3.htm;** *The Economic Impact of BMW on South Carolina.* The Division of Research, Moore School of Business, University of South Carolina, May 2002, available at **www.bmwusfactory.com**

The most striking marketing advantage of local production is usually the projection of an ability and willingness of the company to adapt products and services to the local customer requirements. Examples include U.S. automakers' production of cars for European markets and French ski manufacturer Rossignol's location of plants in the United States and Canada (as we saw in Chapter 2). In both cases there was a desire to be closer to major markets and to be able to anticipate and quickly adapt to major changes.

There is a potential problem in overseas manufacturing when country-of-origin effects are strong, that is, for products whose quality consumers tend to judge by the "made in" label. Research shows there can be a significant effect on product and brand evaluation from a shift in manufacturing location.[11] This can work to the disadvantage of the firm establishing production in a low-wage country where workers have lower skills. In some cases, as customers realize that what they intended to buy is actually manufactured in a developing country, they reject the product.[12]

The solution adopted by companies is to shift lower-skill operations overseas, keeping more advanced operations at home. Although companies are criticized for this strategy (see below), it is often justified not only because it protects product quality and established brand equity, but also because it is a natural step in the gradual upgrading of labor skills in the low-wage countries. Finally, companies with global brands strive very hard to ensure that quality standards are met, and research suggests that a strong brand image can override any negative country-of-origin effects.[13]

Outsourcing

One risk factor that today needs to be incorporated in the overall evaluation of FDI is the potentially negative fallout at home when a company moves production overseas. The so-called **off-shoring** or **outsourcing** practice where a company shuts down production in one country, fires the workers, and starts production in a lower-wage country, has come under strong criticism in many developed countries. Manufacturing costs tend to be higher in advanced economies because workers' wages are higher. To be more cost efficient, companies look for lower-wage locations, especially in industries that are labor intensive (so that labor costs are a significant part of total cost). Textiles, shoes,

Getting the Picture

NOKIA'S ASIAN CONNECTION

Finland-based Nokia is the world's largest mobile phone manufacturer, with a 35.9 percent share in the global handset market in 2002. It attributes its success to some tangible—and some intangible—associations with Asia.

First, your Finnish mobile phone is most likely made in Korea or China. As early as 1984 Nokia established a factory capable of churning out 10 million mobile phone handsets in Masan, South Korea. Nokia has other production locations in Brazil, Germany, Great Britain, Hungary, Mexico, the United States, and, most recently, China—and also at home in Finland. But Nokia's Masan facility is one of its largest plants. Most of the mobile phones from Masan are being exported out of Korea for sale into the Americas, Europe, and Asia.

Then there is a more intangible association. With a world electronics market dominated by Asian companies with exotic-sounding names—Fujitsu, Sony, Ricoh, Samsung, Epson, and their likes—Nokia seemed just another Asian brand. Consumers embraced the newcomer because of its quality technology and user-friendly products—and its Japanese-sounding name.

Asia is a leading market for cell phones, and Nokia also wants to monitor innovations there. It is not uncommon for new products in Asia to be just half the size of cell phones sold at the same time in the United States, a follower market

in cell phones. The phones may have up to three times as many design features as those in the United States. It is common for a Japanese student or Taiwanese executive or Singaporean housewife to purchase a new cell phone every six months. This is about how fast new mobile phones come into the market, rendering the previous model obsolete (or at least not as fashionable).

Some of Nokia's investments also involve outsourcing strategies. In 2001 Nokia shifted a large proportion of mobile phone manufacturing from the United States to factories in Korea, Mexico, and Brazil. During a five-month period some 800 factory workers in Nokia's northern Texas facilities were laid off. The Texans were too expensive compared with workers in Korea. Factoring in overhead, rapidly changing technology, and market access, a new Korean plant was a better choice than the Texan facility. Avoiding layoffs in Finland protected Nokia from the home country criticism that its American competitor Motorola faced that year after shutting down its Harvard, Illinois, plant and also moving to Asia.

Sources: Jay Wrolstad, "Nokia Overhauls Phone Manufacturing Strategy," *Newsfactor Top Tech News,* Wireless Newsfactor, February 5, 2001; "Nokia Quits CDMA Business in Korea," *The Korea Herald,* January 13, 2003; "More Foreign Branches in Korea Hit over Trillion Won in Sales," *Financial Times,* December 10, 2002; **www.nokia.com;** "Korea's Manufacturing Technology 5 Years Ahead of China," *Asia Pulse,* October 30, 2002.

apparel, and consumer electronics are examples of such industries, but now even services such as telemarketing, customer service, hotel bookings, travel reservations, and computer programming are being outsourced to lower-wage countries.

Companies that outsource are criticized for firing workers at home and not offering alternative work. According to economic theory, outsourcing is good because resources are allocated according to the principle of comparative advantage, allowing more goods to be produced at a lower price and thus benefiting consumers. The laid-off workers, perhaps after retraining, supposedly will find new jobs in industries where the country is competitive. The problem is, of course, that these companies may not be hiring, and that at least for a time the workers will stay unemployed. While traditional economic theory argues that sooner or later the rise in productivity will generate more jobs, in recent years reality has not followed economic theory. Unemployment rates are up in many advanced countries. The result is that there is increasing political pressure to back off from outsourcing, and a company that stays home can perhaps count on potential tax breaks and improved consumer goodwill.

The revised economic theory now acknowledges that in a global economy the new jobs created may simply be somewhere else, not in the country with the laid-off workers. The globalization process continues, but the number of manufacturing subsidiaries for outsourcing purposes might be reduced (see box, "Nokia's Asian Connection").

Acquisitions

Rather than establish the wholly owned subsidiary from scratch (a **greenfield investment**), the multinational company can consider the **acquisition** of an existing company. The advantage lies in the speed of penetration: An existing company will already have a product line to be exploited, the distribution network and dealers need not

Getting the Picture

TALKING GLOBALLY

T-Mobile is the only wireless operator to offer services on both sides of the Atlantic under a single, global brand name—underscoring the choice it brings to consumers to use "one number, one phone" when traveling worldwide.

T-Mobile is a member of T-Mobile International group, the mobile telecommunications subsidiary of Deutsche Telekom (NYSE: DT). The company acquired U.S. mobile phone operator VoiceStream Wireless Corp. for $46.04 billion in cash and stock, acting on a long-stated goal to extend its reach onto American soil. The deal created a powerful international wireless concern with roughly 19.8 million wireless subscribers worldwide, including 1.8 million in the United States, and licenses to provide services to roughly 375 million people around the globe.

"Deutsche Telekom is now on par with the other two big wireless players in the world, those being Vodafone Airtouch and France Telecom's Orange Group," said Jeffrey Hines, an industry analyst. "And unlike France Telecom and Vodafone, they would be the only ones with a significant presence in the United States."

From a global brand viewpoint, DT still lacked a global brand. It was known as Deutsche Telekom in Europe but was known only as VoiceStream in North America. The company remedied this by relaunching themselves as T-Mobile, the global brand, in 2002.

The rebranding scheme marked the beginning of internationally acclaimed actress Catherine Zeta-Jones's reign as T-Mobile's global spokesperson, appearing in several television, print, and radio advertisements showing consumers how they can use T-Mobile to "get more from life!"

Sources: www.t-mobile.com; "Deutsche Telekom to Acquire VoiceStream for $50.7 Billion," *FKLaw News,* Internet Online, available from **www.fklaw.com/news-37.html.**

be developed from scratch, and the company can simply get on with marketing its new product(s) in conjunction with the existing line. German Siemen's purchase of compatriot Nixdorf to improve penetration in the European minicomputer market is a case in point. Another example is the purchase of American Borden by Swiss Nestlé in order to expand in the U.S. dairy food market. A recent example is Deutsche Telekom's expansion into the United States (see box, "Talking Globally").

The disadvantages of acquisition are many, however. In a narrow sense, the existing product line and the new products to be introduced might not be compatible, and prunings and adjustments that have to be made require reeducating the sales force and distribution channels. In general, it is not so easy to find a company to acquire that fits the purposes of entry very well. In many countries the acquisition of a domestic company by a foreign firm is not looked upon favorably by the government, employees, and other groups. From a marketing viewpoint the particular advantage of acquisition lies in the market acceptance of the company's products, gaining sales as a spillover from goodwill toward the acquired company's lines. But this benefit can be gained from a joint venture, and many of the political drawbacks of acquisitions are eliminated with a joint venture.

Entry Modes and Marketing Control

The effect of entry mode on the degree to which the firm can exercise control over its local marketing effort is not simple and direct. It is important to distinguish between the question of where and by whom the product or service is produced (which is the main concern of the discussion in Chapter 5 on mode of entry) and the way the marketing is managed.

It is useful to separate three alternative ways of organizing the local marketing effort. They are, in increasing order of control: (1) independent agents and distributors; (2) alliance with a local marketing partner; and (3) a wholly owned sales subsidiary.

There is a rough correspondence between the modes of entry and the means of organizing the marketing. Exporting typically involves independent agents and distributors. As we saw earlier, the local partner in a strategic alliance is often also in charge of local marketing. FDI in manufacturing often means the creation of a wholly owned subsidiary that may also handle the local marketing.

But in practice, the picture is not so simple. For example, exporting is often undertaken from a home country plant to a wholly owned sales subsidiary abroad. This is a common organization when the local market is large and the company has had some success in the market, as in the automobile industry. European and Japanese cars are generally shipped to the U.S. sales subsidiary of the automaker. When FDI in assembly and manufacturing is undertaken, such as Nissan in Tennessee, the companies create a free-standing manufacturing subsidiary, which sells and ships its cars to the sales subsidiary.

In the case of sales subsidiaries handling the marketing, the logistics and the distribution may still be handled by independent carriers and distributors. The sales subsidiary is in charge of promotion, including advertising, pricing, market research, and the management of the channels of distribution.

It is actually quite common to find real-world cases in which the preferred marketing control mode is different from the product entry mode. Exhibit 6.2 shows some of these cases.

The example of Absolut vodka (from Sweden) sold in the United States represents an instance of pure exporting, with Seagrams functioning as the independent agent with territorial marketing control in the United States. A Toshiba-EMI joint venture in Japan markets EMI's music recordings in Japan, many localized by translations of covers into the Japanese language. Volvo cars exported to the United States are marketed by the company's U.S. subsidiary located outside Chicago.

Licensing usually means less control over the marketing effort, as in the case of Disneyland in Chiba outside Tokyo. The Japanese marketing effort is controlled by the independent Japanese licensee. In the case of EuroDisney, in which Disney took a joint venture stake in the operation, the marketing effort is basically under the control of the local European partners. Microsoft's early entry into Japan was via ASCII, an independent licensee (although disagreements over the local marketing strategy later forced Microsoft to establish its own Japanese subsidiary, which markets the software in Japan). And Nike, the athletic shoemaker, has licensed manufacturing in Asia, but controls the marketing.

To enter via a strategic alliance and then allow the marketing to be done independently is unusual, since the partner is a natural marketing agent. However, some new joint ventures in China seem to be planned according to this model. For example, in autos the marketing may have to be controlled by the Chinese government. On the other hand, for other products, with Western manufacturers establishing plants in joint ventures with Chinese government affiliated manufacturers, the marketing is managed separately by Western sales subsidiaries. An example is American Black and Decker, maker of power tools, which has its own marketing subsidiary in China.

Entering via FDI in manufacturing and then allowing independent agents to do the marketing can be illustrated through an OEM agreement. Lucky-Goldstar, now LG, a Korean company, has invested in a television plant in Arkansas, which builds television sets for the Sears private label. The lack of control over marketing is a drawback, and in the long run most companies would like to take over the marketing and establish their own brand name as Goldstar is now doing.

Mitsubishi Motors now manufactures cars in Illinois that are marketed through its joint venture with Chrysler (although the arrangement is being gradually phased out as Mitsubishi establishes a parallel dealer network to gain more control over the marketing).

EXHIBIT 6.2
Product Entry and Marketing Control Can Be Different

	Marketing Control		
Mode of Entry	**Independent Agent**	**Joint with Alliance Partner**	**Own Sales Subsidiary**
Exporting	Absolut vodka in the U.S.	Toshiba EMI in Japan	Volvo in the U.S.
Licensing	Disney in Japan	Microsoft in Japan (initially)	Nike in Asia
Strategic alliance	Autos in China	EuroDisney	Black & Decker in China
FDI	Goldstar in the U.S.	Mitsubishi Motors in the U.S.	P&G in the EU

Delivering Coca-Cola in Guang-dong, China. Coca-Cola's typical entry mode into foreign markets is to license independent bottlers in a franchising arrangement. But in some emerging countries Coca-Cola invests directly in the bottling plants to control quality. RonMcMillan.com.

The combination of wholly owned manufacturing plants and sales subsidiaries is common. Procter & Gamble operates several plants in Europe, with products marketed through its European sales subsidiaries.

Two major lessons from these various cases should be emphasized.

1. Local marketing control often can be effectively exercised via a sales subsidiary, regardless of the entry mode of the product.
2. Even with a sales subsidiary, however, product entry mode is not irrelevant. For example, reliable and timely supplies to the local market cannot be ensured through exporting when protectionist pressures mount or when transportation is long and hazardous. Licensees may not perform as agreed, and partners in alliances may or may not prove to be good partners when conditions change.

In the end, choosing the best entry mode depends not only on marketing factors, but also on the business strategy as a whole, including the strategic objectives of the involvement in the foreign market.

Optimal Entry Strategy

Which mode of entry into the foreign market should be chosen? Can an optimal entry strategy be found?

With all the factors internal and external to the firm to be taken into account, it's impossible to give a single answer to this question. A mode that offers protection from political risk (such as licensing) may offer little help with control of product quality. A mode that maximizes control over company-specific advantages (such as FDI in manufacturing) involves the maximum political risk, and so on. Entry barriers sometimes force a mode, such as joint ventures in China. But it is possible to identify conditions under which a particular mode would be preferable.

The Entry Mode Matrix

One can distinguish several strategic situations and the preferred mode of entry in each. The entry strategy is affected both by company factors (the FSAs in particular) and by market factors (opportunities and threats). The company factors can be grouped into an entry mode matrix with three strategic postures. The market factors are different in emerging economies as compared to high-growth and mature markets. Services need to be treated separately (see Exhibit 6.3).

Strategic Posture

One company posture is when few resources can be dedicated to entry, and this is the usual case when entry is the first step in the internationalization process. The major

EXHIBIT 6.3
An Optimal Entry Mode Matrix

Company Strategic Posture	Product/Market Situation			
	Emerging	High-Growth	Mature	Services
Incremental	Indirect exports	Indirect exports	Direct exports	Licensing/alliance
Protected	Joint venture	Indirect exports	Alliance/licensing	Licensing
Control	Wholly owned subsidiary	Acquisition/alliance	Wholly owned subsidiary	Franchising/alliance/exporting

characteristic of the entry strategy then tends to be its tentativeness and the desire to keep future options open. This strategic posture will be called *incremental.*

A second strategic posture is when the firm possesses a well-protected trade secret or patentable know-how whose potential abroad is clear, but needs to learn about the market and develop more local familiarity. This situation will be denoted *protected.* Typical examples would include patented innovations, the computer-on-a-chip, and electronic banking technology. In such cases there are usually real or self-imposed limits to the resources (manpower, operating capital) allocated to the entry.

In a third strategic situation the company has well-established firm-specific advantages, is large enough to encounter relatively few resource obstacles to expansion, and offers a product with definite potential abroad. This is the typical "global" situation, with the company committed to expanding abroad without jeopardizing any of its firm-specific advantages. This will be called the **control posture.**

Product/Market Situation

A first distinction among various product/market conditions that might prevail in the market country is between products and services. The characteristics of service markets are different from those of markets for physical products when it comes to entry mode considerations. Whereas the product embodies many of the firm-specific advantages in its physical attributes and can thus be viewed separately from the actual transaction through which ownership is exchanged, the quality and benefits of services reside in the transaction itself. This is why export of services often takes the form of people's travel (professionals in various fields, doctors, engineers, consultants, and so on) to perform the service. Services will be dealt with in more detail in Chapter 12.

Among product markets it is useful to distinguish between three situations. Emerging markets are those recently opened up because of political changes and that show generally weak infrastructure, difficulty in accomplishing market-based exchanges, lack of distribution alternatives, and risk of default on payments. Some less-developed countries also fall into the emerging category.

A second situation is high-growth markets, such as some high-technology markets in advanced economies and markets in many fast-growing countries, including the newly industrialized countries. The main marketing issues tend to be to quickly establish presence in the country and to support the product sufficiently in the marketplace so as not to lose out against competitors. The sales growth will go to the entrant who quickly establishes leadership and captures first-mover advantages in the high-growth market.

A third situation is the market in the mature stage, when the name of the marketing game is market share, including dominance in at least a niche in a well-differentiated marketplace. Many markets in advanced economies are mature. The emphasis in entry in mature markets is not so much on speed of penetration as on the total amount of marketing expenditure needed to establish presence and maintain loyalty.

Optimal Modes

For preferred choices among the alternative modes, see again Exhibit 6.3.

Incremental

The resource-poor entrant that wants to stay flexible for the future will most likely be best off with exporting using a gradual "waterfall" strategy (described later in this chapter). For emerging markets, indirect exporting may be the only feasible option. If the market in the country is growing quickly, indirect exporting might be preferable since the start-up costs are lower and market presence can be established more rapidly. In supplying services, the actual start-up usually requires people to be sent abroad (a form of "direct exports") but also requires some continued presence from local people, making licensing the preferred option.

Protected

The firm with strong and protected know-how but without very keen interest or skills in foreign markets might also be best off with indirect exporting in high-growth markets (if speed is of the essence). An alliance with a local competitor with distribution capability might be a viable alternative. Where slower penetration is acceptable, the alliance alternative should be expanded to include the possibility of a joint venture or possibly licensing, should a suitable partner be found. In an emerging market, against its better judgment as it were, the firm may have to accept a joint venture, keeping its partner in check to the extent possible. If the offering is a service, licensing should be the first alternative. It would run relatively low risks of dissipation because of patents or other protection and would allow the proper adaptation to local market conditions.

Control

The larger firm interested in global expansion and control over production and marketing in various countries would usually do best with some type of FDI in manufacturing and local sales subsidiaries. In emerging markets, a wholly owned subsidiary may be the only viable option. If the market is growing rapidly, acquisition of (or an alliance with) a local firm may be the most advantageous alternative. Where the market is large, establishing a manufacturing subsidiary with 100 percent ownership is more easily justified. However, if there are large economies of scale in manufacturing (the case in autos, but not in electronics, for example), the company would do better focusing all manufacturing in one or two plants and sourcing worldwide from there through exporting. Tariff barriers against imports might preclude such an option, of course. If the company's business is in services, the use of franchising is probably the best bet. It offers good control possibilities coupled with local adaptation (of great importance in most services) and also allows local capital to be used, an advantage from a political risk point of view.

Real-World Cases

The suggested entry modes can be illustrated with reference to some real-world examples (see Exhibit 6.4).

Incremental Strategy

Supervalu, a wholesaler of food products from Washington state, has entered the Russian food market on a small scale. An intermediary trading company located in Boston specializing in Russian trade approached the wholesaler about exporting packaged food products to Russia. The products were to be sold in a Moscow supermarket the intermediary had established. Reluctant at first, Supervalu finally agreed when the financial risk

EXHIBIT 6.4
Entries under Different Conditions

Company Strategic Posture	Product/Market Situation			
	Emerging	High-Growth	Mature	Services
Incremental	Supervalu to Russia	North American fish to Japan	Rossignol skis to U.S.	Dialogue to Europe
Protected	Pharmaceuticals in China	Sun Energy technology to Europe	Coca-Cola bottling; Toyota-GM tie-up	Disneyland in Japan
Control	New FDI in India	Matsushita in U.S. TV market	IBM Worldwide, autos into U.S.	Hilton, Sheraton; McDonald's

was assumed by the trading company and its Russian partner. The wholesaler is now attempting to increase its presence in the Russian market, with or without the help of the intermediary.[14]

The U.S. fishing industry, characterized by numerous small establishments, has found a large and rapidly growing market in Japan, whose supplies from northern waters have been effectively cut off by Russian ships. But, by necessity, sales to Japan are characterized by indirect exports via the large Japanese trading companies. Despite some attempts by the Americans to join together and establish some profitable processing followed by direct exports, the market knowledge and financial power of the trading companies has made the fishing industry on the American west coast simply raw materials suppliers to Japanese processors.

A more positive experience of an incremental exporter maintaining flexibility is the case of Rossignol, the French ski maker. As we saw in Chapter 2, the initial entry into the North American market was via direct exports to American distributors. This choice was predicated on the lack of financial clout and market knowledge possessed by the company. As its experience and success in the European (primarily French) market grew, so did the recognition that the U.S. and Canadian markets were not only important but also quite different from the European market in terms of skiing conditions, customer preferences, and so on. The decision was then made to establish wholly owned manufacturing in both countries to enable the company to adapt its products and stay in close touch with market developments. The initial choice of direct exports allowed the company the requisite time for learning and for accumulating resources before a more committed move was undertaken.

A small consulting firm in the computer software business, Dialogue, Inc., operates out of New York City. The demand for its services abroad is growing rapidly, and the company has had problems identifying the right mode for serving this market. The strategy the company has evolved consists of service and distribution alliance tie-ups with different consulting firms in various European countries, sharing the software know-how with them through seminars and training sessions both in Europe and in New York and then using the company's established sales force and local market presence to help sell the software with the requisite quality control and backup services.

Protected Know-How

Western pharmaceutical companies eyeing the vast Chinese market see tremendous opportunity. There is some need for the companies to worry about leakage of formulas, but China has a very different tradition in medicine, and there are few pharmacologists educated in the West. But the unfamiliar market, the need to establish good relationships with government agencies, and, not the least, the Chinese government's rules meant that joint ventures for some time was the only entry mode for Schering-Plough, Merck, Pfizer, and the rest.[15] China's WTO entry in 2001 has made it possible to establish wholly owned subsidiaries, but pharmaceuticals are still a highly regulated business, and not just in China.

The Atlas International Company of Seattle, Washington, is an export management company (EMC) specializing in sales of U.S.-developed sun energy technology. The innovating companies are too small and too unskilled at marketing abroad to be able to take advantage of the opportunities that present themselves and have turned to indirect exporting using Atlas. Many of the rapid growth markets are a consequence of government resource allocations to the sun energy field, and Atlas provides a service by keeping abreast of the rapidly developing opportunities in different countries. Nevertheless, Atlas recognizes that if any one company's exports start taking a large share of total sales, that firm will look for ways of managing "its" part of the business.

Coca-Cola's licensing of local bottlers is its standard approach in overseas markets, sometimes aided by a joint-venture ownership structure. The protection of the formula is the keystone of this policy—the bottlers are given a concentrate and instructions for adding carbonated water to produce the drink but do not get access to the formula itself.

Another case of a joint venture in a mature market is Toyota's tie-up with General Motors in Fremont, California, where small cars under the Corolla name are assembled. To questions about the possible dissipation of Toyota's firm-specific know-how, the company has said little, but observers tend to agree that the effects are small. Not much of the actual know-how has been transferred, since many of the assembly tasks have been adapted for American workers. In addition, by now the technology from Japan represents quite standard process knowledge, available to most if not all carmakers in one form or other already. The basic strength of the agreement seems to be that GM gets Toyota's people to implement the new procedures and assembly technology.

In a reverse situation, Disney World agreed to license its name for use at the entertainment park in Chiba outside Tokyo. Satisfied with a substantial 10 percent of gross sales in royalties and the provision that quality controls would be stringent, the Disney company apparently judged its expertise in the Japanese market insufficient for a wholly owned subsidiary operation. The company was a bit more secure in its knowledge of the European market and opted for an equity investment in a joint venture with French partners, but it is encountering a fair number of problems. Hong Kong Disneyland, opened in 2005, is a joint venture with the Hong Kong government.

Control Posture

Now that India has relented on its ban on foreign ownership, many companies are coming back. Whether through greenfield investments, acquisitions, or reacquisitions of abandoned facilities, companies are establishing wholly owned subsidiaries in which they can control operations and use of their know-how. These companies include American and Japanese car companies, Korean conglomerates, and European electronics manufacturers, eager to cash in on the future growth of the Indian market.

When the American color TV market took off toward the end of the 60s, the Japanese electronics giant Matsushita (brand name Panasonic) faced the choice of establishing production in the United States or being left behind. Trade barriers were high and Sony was already present at its San Diego plant. By acquiring the troubled Motorola TV plant outside Chicago, Matsushita at great cost managed to kill two birds with one stone. One, it acquired the desired manufacturing base in the market and could enter quickly (especially since they kept the Motorola brand name Quasar), and two, political pressures were assuaged, especially since the plant was scheduled to close. The cost was the problem inherited at the plant of low productivity and fractious labor-management relations. After considerable effort (including the introduction of some of the vaunted Japanese management techniques such as quality control circles), productivity has still not picked up. Quasar as a brand name has now been largely replaced by Panasonic.

The control strategy of IBM in the mature markets of Europe and Asia has been based specifically on 100 percent ownership of sales subsidiaries for its IT services. The objectives of protecting its hard-won technical know-how and maintaining its corporate philosophy of providing outstanding service to back up its systems were factors in determining the FDI strategy. In personal computers, by contrast, the company has been more willing to engage in alliances, including joint ventures. IBM's know-how in the PC field is much less on the cutting edge than in mainframes.

Scale returns in manufacturing have made automakers in Europe and Japan hesitant about setting up plants abroad. Although transportation costs to the large North American market are relatively high, all the Japanese and European automakers have followed basically the same path of direct exports marketed through wholly owned sales subsidiaries. Establishing a dedicated distribution network, an expensive and resource-consuming undertaking, the marketing effort can be controlled without investing in manufacturing or assembly. In 1976, Volkswagen established production in Harrisburg, Pennsylvania, in order to be closer to its main overseas market, but quality problems forced the company to close the plant after five years. It was not until the voluntary quotas with Japan were enacted in 1981 that Japanese automakers started manufacturing in the United States. In 1994, both Mercedes and BMW announced plans to start manufacturing in the United

States, reducing transportation costs of sports models specially designed for the North-American markets. When economies of scale in manufacturing are great, exporting world-wide from one or two plants is preferable, unless entry barriers to major markets are high.

The franchising of fast-food companies such as McDonald's is well known in many parts of the world. The main ingredient in this successful global expansion is the emphasis on (control of) standardized service more than the product itself (the food). This is generally true also in the companies' domestic markets. The hotel chains that have sprung up in many metropolitan centers of the world, the Hiltons and the Sheratons well known to many travelers, are not wholly owned subsidiaries as one might have thought but franchise operations typically capitalized by local interests and supported by worldwide promotion and advertising.

These services aim less at a local market and more toward a global market of international business people and tourists. The standardization of the service has a distinct "consumer confidence" or "trust" aspect to it—the customer using these services avoids taking chances with unknown offerings. This is why franchising, with its greater possibilities of controlling quality, is preferable to alliances or simple licensing of a trademark or brand name.

Global Expansion Paths

The "Cultural Distance" Effect

As we saw already in Chapter 1, most companies find it natural to expand first into neighboring countries and regions. This is where their experiences in the home market would be most useful, and where their FSAs and CSAs are usually best leveraged. This has been called the "cultural distance" effect.[16] Geographical proximity plays a role but is only one part of the broader notion of **cultural distance** at the heart of regional expansion (remember the Ghemawat CAGE framework in Chapter 1).

There are numerous examples of the cultural distance effect at work. The United States and Canada are each other's most important trading partners, and many small businesses in Wisconsin, for example, trade more with Canadian businesses than they trade with California or the East Coast. Japan's exporting companies generally started trade with the Southeast Asian countries before moving on to Latin America and Australia. Most European companies export first to their immediate neighbors, an old habit much encouraged by the establishment of EU ties. And the strength of old ties is not to be forgotten (see box, "Cultural Distance and Colonialism").

The International Learning Curve

The cultural distance path can be justified not only on the basis that it seems to achieve a maximal capitalization of FSAs, CSAs, and previous experience. It also allows the gradual accumulation of know-how about how to do business abroad, like following a **learning curve** that gradually increases the skills and productivity of the managers involved. At least in the initial stages of expansion, this learning effect is a common rationale for choosing which countries to enter (although not always—see box, "Seizing the Moment").

Gradually entering more countries in an expanding circle away from the home market, the company learns to do business globally, understands how to analyze foreign environments, and gains capability and a widened repertoire. In short, the firm develops new resources. Naturally, foreign market potential also matters—but in the beginning even a great potential in a psychically distant market may not be exploited because of the additional transaction costs.[17] As experience is gained, the possibilities open up, and the firm goes global. For example, the Swedish furniture retailer IKEA entered the European markets, established a strong market position there, and waited until its Canadian operations were fully mature before entering the United States.[18]

Learning periods are routinely incorporated into the expansion paths of Japanese firms, which tend to enter Southeast Asian markets following the minimum cultural

Getting the Picture

CULTURAL DISTANCE AND COLONIALISM

An interesting example of the principle of "cultural distance" is the relationship between old colonial powers and their ex-dominions. One would have expected that because of the historical events preceding independence many formerly colonized countries would spurn companies from the colonial powers. In many cases, however, the opposite has happened. British companies are still very active in India, Australia, and countries in Southeast Asia; and French firms do a majority of the international business in their old colonies in West Africa. The reasons are basically to be found in the cultural ties and traditions established during colonial rule. The colonial language used for business, the educational system of the country, the financial connections with the outside world, the newspapers read, and expatriates staying in the country after independence are all factors that contribute to a paradoxical degree of dependence upon the previous colonizers on the part of many newly independent countries.

distance path first and then, looking for diversification, enter Latin American markets (focusing on the Japanese expatriate markets). As skills and confidence grow, the companies eye the U.S. market with its great potential. Before entering it (or the European market), however, many Japanese companies will enter the Australian market to make sure they will be able to sustain penetration in a country with similar characteristics. Only with sufficient success and learning in the Australian market will they attempt to enter the U.S. market.[19]

The Internationalization Stages

As several researchers have found, the gradual expansion sequence suggested by the cultural distance effect is reflected in the mode of entry chosen. Although companies differ, the general pattern is for gradually increased commitment to foreign markets. Five stages can be identified:[20]

Stage 1: Indirect exporting, licensing.

Stage 2: Direct exporter, via independent distributor.

Stage 3: Establishing foreign sales subsidiary.

Stage 4: Local assembly.

Stage 5: Foreign production.

Several deviations from these **internationalization stages** are uncovered as globalization has proceeded further. For example, the early use of licensing has been questioned by proponents of the "internalization" school, which places more importance on preservation of the FSAs and worries about the dissipation threat in licensing (see Chapter 2). Also, in recent years, as strategic alliances have become common, companies utilize joint ventures and alliances at almost any stage in the process. In

Getting the Picture

SEIZING THE MOMENT

Toyota, the Japanese automaker, exported overseas first to its Southeast Asian neighbors, then to Australia. As a former export manager remembers: "The Asian markets we were familiar with, and the expansion was natural. Australia we didn't know very well, but it was sort of a rehearsal for entering the United States. We had decided that Toyota needed to be in the United States because of its market potential and for the status it carried here at home. Europe? Well, that's different." He smiles sheepishly. "This Danish businessman came to Tokyo in 1958, I think, and wanted to be our representative in Denmark. We didn't know what to do, but he simply ordered a few cars from us, prepaid, and we had to ship them. That's how Europe got started. No systematic planning—but the Danish businessman made good, and Denmark is still one of our strongest European markets."

Source: Personal interview, Toyota sales headquarters, Tokyo.

fact, the traditional notion that firms will go global gradually and in stages has been challenged. Some firms go global from the beginning. They are "born globals."

Born Globals

Based on research among newly formed high-technology start-ups, the term *born global* was apparently first coined by a McKinsey report in 1993.[21] **Born global** firms are firms that from the outset view the world as one market. They are typically small technology-based businesses, and their FSAs lie in new innovations and technological breakthroughs. The entrepreneurial spirit of the founder coupled with the threat of competitive imitation and alternative technologies mean that rapid internationalization is necessary to capture the first-mover advantages in world markets.

Born global firms rely on networking for most of their expansion abroad. They may start as exporters, selling to customers identified and reached through alliances and network relationships. Their FSAs involve technical eminence, with substantial added value and differentiated designs. Because of limited organizational and managerial resources, the born globals tend to rely on advanced communications technologies to reach their customers in different countries—facsimile, electronic mail, the Internet, and electronic data interchange (EDI). The advanced communications allow the company low-cost exchange with partners and customers. In addition, substantial market data availability on the Internet, previously unavailable to smaller firms, facilitates their overseas penetration. In a pioneering Swedish study of smaller firms' internationalization paths, the importance of creating a strong network of communications and logistics is similarly stressed.[22]

Born globals are typically found in business-to-business markets, where targeted sales and network relationships matter a great deal (see box, "What Do Born Globals Do?"). Few of the company names are household words. Biogen, a gene splicing technology company based in Massachusetts, is a reasonably well-known born global company partly because of its controversial business. And even though companies such as Computer Network Technology, Progress Software, and Auspex Systems may not register on many marketers' radar screens, there are actually numerous born globals. Defining born globals as companies that went overseas within one year of their founding, one U.S. study found that 13 percent of a national sample were born globals.[23] Because of less reliance on a large home market, some foreign companies show even more impressive figures for born global firms. A pioneering Australian study found that among the sample of born global Australian firms, exports accounted for 76 percent of turnover within two years of founding.[24]

In the end, it looks as though the advances in global communication have made traditional internationalization patterns simply history. Although high-technology markets differ from mainstream markets, there are reasons to suspect that in the future many small companies will see the world as their market from the beginning, using the Internet to research foreign markets, identifying distributors and potential partners on the World Wide Web, and creating alliances and relationships through e-mail and voice-mail.

Waterfall versus Sprinkler Strategies

After building up experience and confidence, internationalizing companies usually start considering a more orderly and strategic international expansion. For one thing, when companies find that over 10 percent of their revenues comes from overseas markets, management starts paying more attention to overseas potential.[25] But there are other instances when coordinated expansion strategy is needed. When the firm has a new successful product at home, it is faced with the question of how fast to introduce it elsewhere. There is also the question of how fast to enter markets that suddenly open up, as was the case with Russia, China, and even India. Should all three be entered at the same time or not?

There are usually two alternative strategies to consider. Under a "waterfall" scenario, the firm moves gradually into overseas markets, while in the "sprinkler" mode the company tries to enter several country markets simultaneously or within a limited period of time.[26]

Getting the Picture

WHAT DO BORN GLOBALS DO?

Although "born global" firms can nowadays be found in most industries, by far the greatest percentage appear in Internet-related technology businesses. All new Internet businesses are in a sense automatically "global" in that their customers can be found anywhere on the planet. But this is especially true of start-ups that offer value-added products to Internet users—value-added products that uninitiated outsiders often have trouble even understanding.

One such company is Digital Paper Corporation, based in Alexandria, Virginia. A privately held company, Digital Paper is a "developer of post-design collaboration software and solutions that improve customers' business performance by enabling fast, secure collaboration and exchange of intellectual capital over the Internet." Many of us might be excused for saying "Huh, what?" to that. In plain language the company has a software package, Intranet Docs, which enables the transfer of engineering drawings between subsidiaries of a multinational, using the Internet. Digital's key competitive advantages are two: One, the transfer is guaranteed safe

from potential commercial spies, and two, the software can be easily retrofitted onto a company's existing intranet. The company has customers across the globe in a variety of industries, including aerospace, automotive, and governments, and works with companies such as General Electric, Volvo cars, and Marconi Corporation in mobile communications.

Another born global is Vignette Corporation in Austin, Texas, whose Internet products "allow businesses to create and extend relationships with prospects and customers, and to facilitate high-volume transaction exchanges with suppliers and partners." In plain Texan language this means that Vignette takes charge of updating a company's Web site and expanding its customization capability. Can they handle different languages? You bet. There is now software that will not only translate between languages but also adapt Web design to various countries.

Sources: "Digital Paper Expands Customer Base with Four New Wins," *Business Wire,* August 8, 2001; "Cool Company on the Net: Carrier Selects Vignette to Power Its Corporate and Consumer Sites," *Business Wire,* July 11, 2001.

Waterfall

Traditionally, the **waterfall strategy** was the preferred choice. It goes well with the cultural distance and learning patterns discussed already, and also helps explain the international product cycle (IPC) process discussed in Chapter 2. After success in the home market, the company gradually moves out to culturally close country markets, then to other mature and high-growth markets, and finally to less-developed country markets. This is the pattern followed by many well-known companies including Matsushita, BMW, and General Electric.

The advantage of the waterfall strategy is that the expansion can take place in an orderly manner, and the same managers can be used for different countries, which helps to capitalize on skills developed. For the same reasons it is also a relatively less-demanding strategy in terms of resource requirements. Launching a new product requires investments in manufacturing, inventory, advertising, distribution, sales force, and staff. A waterfall strategy requires a relatively low investment because the new product is introduced in only a subset of countries. If the product fails in those countries, a manager need not launch in the remaining countries, thus saving the investment in the latter countries. This is why it is still the most common approach also for newer companies such as Dell, Benetton, and the Body Shop—and, as we saw in Chapter 4, also for Microlog, the fledgling voice communications company. But in fast-moving markets the waterfall strategy may be too slow.

Sprinkler

Compared with the waterfall, the **sprinkler strategy** has the opposite strengths and disadvantages. A sprinkler strategy can fully exploit economies of scale and experience in R&D and manufacturing by exposing the new product to a maximum number of markets as rapidly as possible. It is a much faster way to market penetration across the globe, it generates first-mover advantages, and it preempts competitive countermoves by sheer speed. The drawback is the amount of managerial, financial, and other resources required and the risk potential of major commitments without proper country knowledge or research.

Examples of the sprinkler approach are becoming more frequent as the competitive climate heats up and as global communications such as the Internet make access to country markets easier. The typical cases involve new product launches by companies with established global presence such as Sony (the handheld camcorder, for example, and the Walkman), Microsoft (Windows XP and Vista), and Gillette (the Sensor, for example).

But the sprinkler strategy is also used by expanding companies to establish a global presence. For example, America Online, the Internet access provider, launched its service simultaneously in countries in Europe, Asia, and Latin America. Catalog-based retailers such as Lands' End, Eddie Bauer, and L. L. Bean have also entered a large number of foreign countries within a limited time period. Telecommunications companies have also followed the sprinkler strategy, although partly by necessity: Not many country markets were open to foreign competitors before deregulation and privatization. The fact is that with the great advances in global communications in the last decade, the sprinkler approach has become much less resource demanding, and companies can reach almost anywhere on the globe to sell their wares.

In research focusing on the European market, researchers found that there are distinct advantages to a waterfall strategy over a sprinkler strategy.[27] The waterfall strategy was supported for three reasons. First, introducing in a few countries that are likely to show early takeoff can win internal support for continued marketing of the new product. This means the first entries should be not necessarily in the largest markets or the most similar markets, but in markets where the acceptance of innovations is greater.

Second, takeoff in one country increases the likelihood the company can convince distribution channels in other countries with slower takeoffs to carry the new product and support it adequately. Third, an early takeoff generates revenues and profits for the company, which it can use to improve the product, market it more aggressively, and introduce it in other international markets.

Basically, the tradeoff between a waterfall and sprinkler strategy reduces to a tradeoff between sales maximization (sprinkler) and risk minimization (waterfall). In consultations with analysts and managers, the researchers found that analysts tend to favor a rapid deployment across all countries to maximize sales and market share. However, managers are deeply concerned about the risk of failure. They have no certainty of the success of their new products, especially early on. Even if they are convinced that the new product will succeed, they remain uncertain of the dates of product takeoff and the rate of growth.

Summary

This chapter first discussed the three main nonexporting modes of entry: licensing, strategic alliances, and FDI in wholly owned manufacturing subsidiaries. The marketer's role differs in these entry modes from that of simple exporter, since the company is marketing its FSAs directly rather than having them embodied in the final product. The relative advantages and disadvantages of the modes were shown to depend on industry and firm characteristics, but also on the existing trade barriers.

We then discussed the questions of how marketing control could be exercised under the different modes and what the optimal mode of entry should be. The answers depend on a number of strategic and situational considerations that favor one mode over another. We summarized these considerations in a matrix of strategic market and resource situations facing the entrant into a country. Matching typical strategic postures (incremental, protected, or control) and typical market situations (emerging, high-growth, mature, and service versus product), the global marketer can get a feel for which mode may be the preferable choice. Several real-world examples demonstrated the application of the choice-of-mode matrix and showed how companies have actually attempted to make entry decisions recently that are good for today and also leave room for future change and growth.

The traditional pattern followed by exporters into foreign markets shows the cultural distance effect and the learning curve at work leading to the kind of regional concentration already discussed in Chapter 1. The traditional pattern is reflected in the internationalization stages through which a firm gradually becomes a savvy global competitor. Today's faster global expansion by the so-called born globals, smaller start-ups in high technology that begin exporting within a year of their founding, deviates from the standard pattern.

The company needs to decide whether expansion into new countries should follow a waterfall or a sprinkler strategy. For rapidly moving markets, the firm may have to go with the quicker but also riskier sprinkler approach, entering several countries simultaneously. Research findings have shown that the main point is to develop a clear and coherent strategy for expansion, whether a waterfall or a sprinkler strategy.

Key Terms

acquisition, *168*
born global, *178*
control posture, *172*
cultural distance, *176*
dissipation (of FSAs), *159*
FDI in wholly owned manufacturing, *166*
franchising, *161*
greenfield investment, *168*

internationalization stages, *177*
joint ventures (JVs), *166*
learning curve, *176*
licensing, *159*
manufacturing alliance, *165*
off-shoring, *167*
optimal entry mode, *159*

original equipment manufacturing (OEM), *162*
outsourcing, *167*
R&D alliance, *165*
royalties, *160*
shared manufacturing, *165*
sprinkler strategy, *179*
straight licensing, *160*
strategic alliances (SAs), *163*
waterfall strategy, *179*

Discussion Questions

1. While Disney World entered the Japanese market by licensing its name to a Japanese company, EuroDisney (now Disneyland Paris) outside Paris was established as a joint venture with European backing but with Disney holding majority control. To what would you attribute the difference in entry mode? Given the lack of early success in Europe, do you think another entry mode would have been better? Why, or why not?

2. In fast-food businesses (McDonald's, KFC, Pizza Hut) franchising has become a popular mode of entry into foreign markets. Discuss the reasons for that. What alternatives could be used? Can you find any real-world illustrations of such alternatives?

3. How can control over local marketing be managed in exporting? In franchising? How can Starbucks, the specialty coffee retailer, maintain marketing control over its franchise operations in Japan?

4. The regional trade blocs represent "ready-made" target segments where trade barriers are low and therefore exporting is typically a strong option. Discuss the pros and cons of FDI versus an alliance when entering such a trade bloc for the first time.

5. Use the Internet to locate the Web site of a global company that has recently introduced a new product, brand, or model. Then assess from the information provided whether the introduction followed a sprinkler or a waterfall strategy.

Notes

1. The terminology varies between writers. Some keep joint ventures separate from strategic alliances, arguing that the latter do not involve equity investments but are simple collaborations. From a marketing perspective, however, joint ventures and strategic alliances pose similar problems. See Contractor and Lorange, 1988; and Varadarajan and Cunningham, 1995.

2. See, for instance, Hamel, Doz, and Prahalad, 1989; and Bleeke and Ernst, 1991.

3. See Johansson, 1995.

4. See Terpstra and Simonin, 1993.

5. Bleeke and Ernst, 1991; and Parkhe, 1991, show the lack of durability of many strategic alliances.

6. Bleeke and Ernst, 1991.

7. Hamel et al., 1989, give an upbeat view of competitive collaborations.

8. See Contractor and Lorange, 1988; and Geringer and Hebert, 1991. There are many other forms of international ventures that are quite different organizationally—for example, the American

Bethlehem Steel and Swedish Granges JV for the mining of iron ore in Liberia—but such alliances are of less interest here.

9. See Hamel, 1991.

10. This discussion of FDI in overseas manufacturing is necessarily brief. A lot has been written on the topic, and the interested reader can find a good comprehensive statement of the modern FDI theory in most multinational texts, including Rutenberg, 1982.

11. See Johansson and Nebenzahl, 1986.

12. See, for example, the reaction of Chrysler buyers to learning that the cars were built in Mexico (Nag, 1984).

13. See Tse and Gorn, 1993.

14. This example is from "Food Distribution in Russia: The Harris Group and the LUX Store," Harvard Business School case no. 9-594-059.

15. See Beamish, 1993.

16. The cultural distance and internationalization effects were first brought out by researchers at Uppsala in Sweden—see Johansson and Vahlne, 1977, 1992.

17. An empirical evaluation of how transaction costs influence mode of entry is presented in Anderson and Gatignon, 1986. See also the discussion of transaction costs in Chapter 2.

18. See "Ingvar Kamprad and IKEA," Harvard Business School case no. 390-132.

19. As their annual reports show, these are the typical steps taken by Japanese firms in autos, electronics, and heavy equipment.

20. See, for example, Cavusgil, 1980; Czinkota, 1982; Nordstrom, 1991.

21. See McKinsey and Co., 1993. The discussion of born globals here draws on the excellent overview of the research by Knight and Cavusgil, 1997.

22. From Hertz and Mattsson, 1998.

23. See Brush, 1992.

24. See McKinsey and Co., 1993.

25. The figure of 10 percent keeps coming up in many informal conversations with executives. It is of course not a hard-and-fast figure—overseas potential should always be considered—but it seems that at about 10 percent of revenues, overseas markets develop enough "critical mass" to demand more attention. The actual figures for most multinationals lie closer to 50 percent, even though American MNCs tend to be somewhat lower because of the large home market.

26. This terminology is suggested in Riesenbeck and Freeling, 1991.

27. See Tellis et al, 2003.

Selected References

Anderson, Erin, and Hubert Gatignon. "Modes of Foreign Entry: A Transaction Cost Analysis and Propositions." *Journal of International Business Studies,* no. 3 (1986), pp. 1–26.

Beamish, Paul W. "The Characteristics of Joint Ventures in the People's Republic of China." *Journal of International Marketing* 1, no. 2 (1993), pp. 29–48.

Bleeke, J., and David Ernst. "The Way to Win in Cross-Border Alliances." *Harvard Business Review* 69, no. 6 (November–December 1991), pp. 127–35.

Blustein, Paul. "Giant Trading Companies Battle to Preserve Japan Inc.'s Edge." *Washington Post,* April 12, 1995, pp. A18, A19.

Brush, Candida. *Factors Motivating Small Firms to Internationalize: The Effect of Firm Age.* Doctoral dissertation, Boston University, 1992.

Cavusgil, S. Tamer. "On the Internationalization Process of Firms." *European Research* 8, no. 6 (1980), pp. 273–81.

Contractor, Farouk, and Peter Lorange, eds. *Cooperative Strategies in International Business.* Lexington, MA: Lexington Books, 1988.

Czinkota, Michael R. *Export Development Strategies: U.S. Promotion Policy.* New York: Praeger, 1982.

Geringer, J. Michael, and L. Hebert. "Measuring Performance of International Joint Ventures." *Journal of International Business Studies* 22, no. 2 (1991), pp. 249–63.

Hamel, Gary. "Competition for Competence and Inter-Partner Learning within International Strategic Alliances." *Strategic Management Journal* 12, Summer 1991, pp. 83–103.

Hamel, Gary, and C. K. Prahalad. "Creating Global Strategic Capability." In Hood, Neil, and Jan-Erik Vahlne, eds. *Strategies in Global Competition.* London: Croom Helm, 1988.

Hamel, Gary; Yves Doz; and C. K. Prahalad. "Collaborate with Your Competitors—and Win." *Harvard Business Review,* January–February 1989, pp. 133–39.

Hertz, Susanne, and Lars-Gunnar Mattsson. *Mindre Foretag Blir Internationella* (Smaller Firms Go International) Malmo: Liber, 1998. (In Swedish.)

Johansson, J., and J. E. Vahlne. "The Internationalization Process of the Firm—A Model of Knowledge Development and Increasing Foreign Market Commitments." *Journal of International Business Studies,* Spring–Summer 1977, pp. 23–32.

_____. "The Internationalization Paradigm: A Review and Assessment." International Marketing Review, 1992.

Johansson, Johny K. "International Alliances: Why Now?" *Journal of the Academy of Marketing Science,* Fall 1995.

———, and Izrael D. Nebenzahl. "Multinational Expansion: Effect on Brand Evaluations." *Journal of International Business Studies* 17, no. 3 (Fall 1986), pp. 101–26.

Knight, Gary A., and S. Tamer Cavusgil. "Early Internationalization and the Born-Global Firm: An Emergent Paradigm for International Marketing." Working paper, 1997.

McKinsey and Co. *Emerging Exporters: Australia's High Value-Added Manufacturing Exporters.* Melbourne: Australian Manufacturing Council, 1993.

Nag, Amal. "Chrysler Tests Consumer Reaction to Mexican-Made Cars Sold in the U.S." *The Wall Street Journal,* July 23, 1984, sec. 2.

Nordstrom, Kjell A. *The Internationalization Process of the Firm: Searching for New Patterns and Explanations.* Stockholm: Institute of International Business, 1991.

Otterbeck, L., ed. *The Management of Headquarters-Subsidiary Relationships in Multinational Corporations.* Aldershot, U.K.: Gower, 1981.

Parkhe, Arvind. "Interfirm Diversity, Organizational Learning, and Longevity in Strategic Alliances." *Journal of International Business Studies* 22, no. 4 (1991), pp. 579–601.

Pucik, Vladimir. "Strategic Alliances, Organizational Learning, and Competitive Advantage—The HRM Agenda." *Human Resource Management* 27, no. 1 (Spring 1988), pp. 77–83.

Riesenbeck, Hajo, and Anthony Freeling. "How Global Are Global Brands?" *McKinsey Quarterly,* no. 4 (1991), pp. 3–18.

Root, F. R. *Foreign Market Entry Strategies,* 2nd ed. New York: Amacom, 1989.

Rugman, Alan. *The End of Globalization.* New York: Amacom, 2001.

Rutenberg, David P. *Multinational Management.* Boston: Little, Brown, 1982.

Tellis, Gerard J.; Stefan Stremersch; and Eden Yin. "The International Takeoff of New Products: The Role of Economics, Culture, and Country Innovativeness," *Marketing Science* 22, no. 2 (Spring 2003), pp. 188–208.

Terpstra, Vern, and Bernard L. Simonin. "Strategic Alliances in the Triad: An Exploratory Study." *Journal of International Marketing* 1, no. 1 (1993), pp. 4–25.

Thorelli, Hans B., and S. Tamer Cavusgil, eds. *International Marketing Strategy,* 3rd ed. New York: Pergamon, 1990.

Tse, David K., and Gerald J. Gorn. "An Experiment on the Salience of Country-of-Origin in the Era of Global Brands." *Journal of International Marketing* 1, no. 1 (1993), pp. 57–76.

Varadarajan, P. Rajan, and Margaret H. Cunningham. "Strategic Alliances: A Synthesis of Conceptual Foundations." *Journal of the Academy of Marketing Science,* Fall 1995.

Toys "R" Us Goes to Japan

Toys "R" Us, the giant "category killer" in toys, represents a very special kind of firm. The category killers are specialty retailers that operate on a much larger scale than the typical boutique specialty retailer. Examples include Home Depot in hardware and Best Buy in home appliances and consumer electronics. Wal-Mart, other superstores, and discount outlets threaten these specialty retailers. Toys "R" Us was bought out by an American consortium in 2005, but has continued to operate with fewer stores. The Japan operation has continued, managed as a separately incorporated subsidiary in Tokyo. At the time of its Japanese entry, the question was mainly whether its retailing formula could succeed in such a different market environment.

The Toys "R" Us case shows how high barriers to entry can be overcome, at a cost, and how protected businesses easily become uncompetitive. The case also demonstrates how a new service format requires promotion that educates customers about its advantages.

Toys "R" Us, Inc., a children's specialty retailer concentrating on toys and children's clothing was headquartered in Paramus, New Jersey. In the early 1990s, after successful penetration of the North American market and selected European markets, company executives were formulating their expansion plans for the Japanese market.

Company Background

Toys "R" Us was, by early 1990, the largest toy retailer in the world, with about 20–25 percent of the U.S. market, and 2 percent of total international sales. It was founded in the late 1940s by an American, Charles Lazarus, as the first "toy supermarket," and was acquired in 1966 by department store chain operator Interstate, Inc. Interstate went bankrupt in 1974 after becoming overextended through buying a number of discount chains, but continued to build more Toys "R" Us stores through a court-ordered reorganization. After the reorganization was finished in 1977, Interstate divested all its other assets and became Toys "R" Us, Inc.; Lazarus became chairman and CEO. Toys "R" Us grew fast through the late-1970s and 1980s via an aggressive expansion campaign that undercut existing retailers. The first Kids "R" Us stores, a clothing extension, were opened in 1982; and the first international stores were opened in 1984. Since going public in 1978, sales rose every year, although earnings showed only nominal gains between 1989 and 1991.

At the beginning of the 2000s, encountering increased competition from Wal-Mart, sales and profits of Toy's "R" Us had stagnated in the United States. Still, the company operated about 700 stores in the United States, and was growing steadily overseas (see Exhibit 1). Sales for 2003 were $11.6 billion. The company was not quite this big in the beginning of the 1990s when the Japanese entry took place. In 1993 the company operated 1,032 stores, with 581 Toys "R" Us stores and 217 Kids "R" Us stores in the United States, and with 234 Toys "R" Us stores managed through international subsidiaries in 18 countries. Sales in 1993 were $7.9 billion, making Toys "R" Us the 50th-largest retailer in the world and the 22nd-largest in the United States. By comparison, Japan's largest retailer, Daiei,

EXHIBIT 1   Financial Highlights Toys "R" Us, Inc. and Subsidiaries, 1999–2004

(Dollars in millions, except per share data)

	Jan. 31, 2004	Feb. 1, 2003	Feb. 2, 2002	Feb. 3, 2001	Jan. 29, 2000	Jan. 30, 1999
Operations:						
Net sales	$11,566	$11,305	$11,019	$11,332	$11,862	$11,170
Net earnings (loss)	88	229	67	404	279	(132)
Basic earnings (loss) per share	0.41	1.10	0.34	1.92	1.14	(0.50)
Diluted earnings/(loss) per share	0.41	1.09	0.33	1.88	1.14	(0.50)
Financial Position at Year End:						
Working capital	$ 1,912	$ 1,208	$ 657	$ 575	$ 35	$ 106
Real estate—net	2,461	2,398	2,313	2,348	2,342	2,354
Total assets	10,218	9,397	8,076	8,003	8,353	7,899
Long-term debt	2,349	2,139	1,816	1,567	1,230	1,222
Stockholders' equity	4,222	4,030	3,414	3,418	3,680	3,624
Common Shares Outstanding	213.6	212.5	196.7	197.5	239.3	250.6
Number of Stores at Year End:						
Toys"R"Us—U.S.	685	685	701	710	710	704
Toys"R"Us—International	574	544	507	491	462	452
Babies"R"Us—U.S.	198	183	165	145	131	113
Kids"R"Us—U.S.	44	146	184	198	205	212
Imaginarium—U.S.	—	37	42	37	40	—
Total Stores	1,501	1,595	1,599	1,581	1,548	1,481

had about $14 billion annually in sales. After-tax profits of $483 million were realized in 1993, and 18 percent of total sales and 14 percent of profits were from the international operations. Financial highlights from 1989 through 1994 are given in Exhibit 2.

Company Strategy

Toys "R" Us succeeded by using a "category killer" strategy, which combined strong advertising to promote name recognition and discounts on the most popular

EXHIBIT 2   Financial Highlights Toys "R" Us, Inc. and Subsidiaries, 1989–1994

(Dollars in millions, except per share data)

	Jan. 29, 1994	Jan. 30, 1993	Feb. 1, 1992	Feb. 2, 1991	Jan. 28, 1990	Jan. 29, 1989
Operations:						
Net sales	$7,946	$7,169	$6,124	$5,510	$4,788	$4,000
Net earnings	483	438	340	326	321	268
Basic earnings per share	1.66	1.51	1.18	1.12	1.11	0.92
Diluted earnings per share	1.63	1.47	1.15	1.11	1.09	0.91
Financial Position at Year End:						
Working capital	$ 633	$ 797	$ 328	$ 177	$ 238	$ 255
Real estate—net	2,036	1,877	1,751	1,433	1,142	952
Total assets	6,150	5,323	4,583	3,582	3,075	2,555
Long-term debt	724	671	391	195	173	174
Stockholders' equity	3,148	2,889	2,426	2,046	1,705	1,424
Number of Stores at Year End:						
Toys "R" Us—United States	581	540	497	451	404	358
Toys "R" Us—International	234	167	126	97	74	52
Kids "R" Us—United States	217	211	189	164	137	112
Babies "R" Us—United States	—	—	—	—	—	—
Kids World—United States	—	—	—	—	—	—
Total stores	1,032	918	812	712	615	522

items (loss leaders such as diapers) to create a perception that everything was discounted. The stores were large and offered a wide selection of brand name merchandise. Such stores were the progenitors of the low-cost, low-service, warehouse-style discount store concept that was later to take a large share of the U.S. market. In the United States, a computerized inventory system was used to track demand on a regional and store-by-store basis to maintain low standing inventories and capitalize quickly on trends. This system was continually upgraded with even better communications technology and improved regional warehouse facilities. Toys "R" Us also owned and operated its own fleet of trucks to save on shipping. Bargaining power from the high market share was occasionally wielded by Toys "R" Us to keep its suppliers in line. Prices on most goods were competitive with other retailers, but in general they were not deeply discounted. Some years, Toys "R" Us used coupon promotions aggressively in the period before Christmas to increase market share during their major sales period.

The long-term strategy for Toys "R" Us was to expand in international markets. Toys "R" Us International operations followed the home country strategy, but as competition from other large-volume discount-type stores was less in most of the international markets, prices were correspondingly higher. Inventory was chosen with more than half from the Toys "R" Us U.S. inventory, and the rest to reflect local tastes. As of 1993, Toys "R" Us started making franchising deals to enter foreign markets with local partners; deals to enter six such markets had been made, primarily in oil-rich developing countries in the Middle East. Of the 115 stores Toys "R" Us opened in 1993, 70 were in foreign countries.

The Japanese Toy Market

As in many product categories, the toy retail market in Japan was dominated by small specialty stores and general retailers. Of the 29,413 stores that had toy sales as a significant percentage of overall sales in 1991, 11,628 were toy and hobby specialty retailers (including computer game shops), and 12,582 were small general retail shops; an additional 2,772 were convenience stores, and 1,227 were large toy specialty retailers; less than 500 larger general retailers made a significant portion of their income from toy sales. By comparison, in 1987 the United States had only 9,629 stores that fell into the specialty retailer category, and a significant percentage of total sales were made by large general retail chains such as Kmart, Sears, and Wal-Mart.

Japanese statistical reporting did not separate toys from other leisure goods, but statistics indicated that yearly sales for toys, sporting goods, and musical instruments were approximately ¥3.3 trillion ($25 billion at a 1991 exchange rate of ¥130/$) in 1991. The largest exclusive toy retailer in Japan, Kiddyland, had 1992 per store sales of ¥230 million ($1.8 million) from 52 stores for a total of ¥11.96 billion ($92 million), as compared to Toys "R" Us's $7.9 billion from 1,032 stores ($7.6 million per store). All in all, there were 21 toy/hobby store chains (defined as having more than one store) in Japan, with the largest, Pelican, having 71 stores.

The 29,000 toy and sporting goods retailers were serviced by a network of 5,692 wholesalers and dealt almost exclusively in Japanese-made products. There were upwards of 15,000 toy manufacturers in Japan, but only six of all of these (including game giants Nintendo and Koei) employed more than 50 people; the vast majority was one- to two-person operations. The most popular products were computer games and dolls or toys with linkages to animated television characters.

The average Japanese household spent ¥83,724 per year in 1992 ($650) on health and leisure products (again, the two are not differentiated in statistical analyses). There were approximately 39 million households in Japan, which ranked Japan with the United States and Europe as one of the three largest and wealthiest markets in the world for leisure products. In general, they were motivated as much by quality as by price, and showed a preference for established brand name merchandise over lesser-known goods.

Overcoming Barriers to Entry

Toys "R" Us first made public its plans to enter the Japanese market in 1989, signing a high-profile alliance contract with McDonald's Japan. A new subsidiary, Toys "R" Us Japan, was established with Toys "R" Us owning 80 percent and McDonald's Japan holding the remaining 20 percent. The long-time president of McDonald's Japan, T. Fujita, came on board as vice chairman of the new joint venture, and almost the entire staff was locally hired. There were no foreign permanent employees at Toys "R" Us Japan's headquarters in Kawasaki City, 20 minutes outside central Tokyo. The two companies presented a formidable team to local competitors; Toys "R" Us, with its commanding share of the U.S. market and excellent marketing strategy, had the industry power and experience in cracking foreign markets, while McDonald's, so firmly established in Japan that it was almost considered a Japanese company by many, had the depth of market knowledge and research skills as well as the communications lines to the target groups of children and young families. As part of the deal, McDonald's had the right to establish a restaurant in any location Toys "R" Us picked for a store.

After the plans to enter Japan were made public, a number of issues were pointed to and voices were raised to suggest that Japan was not ready for the retailing revolution Toys "R" Us represented. The issues took a number of forms: suggestions that Toys "R" Us would not be able to get the necessary permissions and empty space it needed to open huge stores; statements that major Japanese manufacturers would not be willing to enter into direct deals with Toys "R" Us, instead preferring to work through middle wholesalers and preserve their traditional trade links; analyses that claimed that Toys "R" Us, like many other multinationals, would find that the tools that worked so well in the rest of the world would come up short when confronted with the sensitive Japanese consumer; and contentions that discount retailing was antithetical to the Japanese psyche, which linked quality with price, and so Toys "R" Us, by competing on price, would class themselves out of the market.

However, Toys "R" Us was able to draw on the successful experience of McDonald's, which had been able to adjust to Japanese rules while still maintaining its innovative nature (as the first Western-style fast-food chain) to become a market leader. When McDonald's came to Japan, it had faced and beat the same issues of establishing distribution and supply channels, and its experience was valuable for Toys "R" Us to draw on.

Market Penetration

The timing of the Toys "R" Us market entry was fortunate. In 1989, the bubble economy was in full swing, but by December 1991, when the first store opened in Japan, the economy had lapsed into recession. The slogan "Everyday Low Prices" was therefore appealing to many who were looking for value as well as quality, and the minimal level of service (no gift-wrapping) was more acceptable as fewer gifts were being given.

The entry was also well timed in coinciding with an antistructural impediments initiative by the Bush administration. The Japanese government, looking for positive PR, pushed a regional government to waive the "Big Store" laws under which existing retailers could veto the entry of a large retailer into the area. The first store, at 3,000 square meters and offering 18,000 items in inventory, was the perfect example of what has come to be called in America a "category killer": By creating an overwhelming advantage, it was intended to stop competitors from opening opposing stores before they started.

The first store was opened outside of Niigata in Ibaraki Prefecture in December 1991. By 1993 the company had opened 15 more stores. It relied on McDonald's market research to target suburban areas with young families as a primary growth base. City stores were initially limited to Osaka and Nagasaki, but most stores were near enough to major cities that they could be reached within a one-hour drive. Despite the high cost of land, the stores provided ample parking.

Toys "R" Us's primary advertising media strategy was the use of colorful inserts in newspapers, rather than television or radio, which were far more expensive and scattershot, not necessarily reaching the targeted audience. Newspaper inserts for home deliveries ensured that advertising reached the home, where mothers and children, the primary targets, were more likely to see them. It was also possible in this way to localize advertising to areas near stores; there were as yet too few stores in operation to make television a valuable alternative.

Localization

As Toys "R" Us Japan imported more than half of its supply from the United States, finding capable suppliers was not the pressing issue it was first thought to be. Toys "R" Us adopted a flexible strategy, working through existing channels in Japan where available, but utilizing the central Kobe warehouse as a way station to control in-store inventory more precisely. Only one major Japanese manufacturer signed on to ship directly to Toys "R" Us stores, but that one was Nintendo, which extended its American direct-shipping agreement to cover Japan as well in June 1991, before the first store in Japan was opened. On the other hand, neither was it true that, with this deal, "the Japanese toy distribution system, hit by a wave of internationalization, had taken a first step toward significant reform," as some newspapers suggested. No other manufacturers had made a similar deal, and no other toy retailer had been able to crack the distribution network and deal direct.

Before entering the Japanese market, Toys "R" Us had operations in eight other countries. It drew on these experiences, especially those of its successful stores in two other Asian cultures, Hong Kong and Singapore. There was thus a willingness to adapt to local conditions. For example, although corporate policy dictated that no store could be less than 3,000 square meters, the Japan group decided that a new store in Himeji, Hyogo Prefecture, could be viable at 2,800 square meters, and succeeding stores were sometimes even smaller than that.

Toys "R" Us positioned its fundamental system as a positive innovation that provided value to Japanese consumers, and marketed it as such. Toys "R" Us stores, rather than focusing on "Everyday Low Prices," promised unparalleled inventory, essentially guaranteeing that even the most popular items would be in stock at all times, which small local retailers were unable to do. Rather than being forced to get up at 4 a.m. and get in line to get the new Mortal Combat 4 the day it came out, all a consumer had to do was come to Toys "R" Us any time to be sure they could get the game.

The relative lack of service, while off-putting to some Japanese consumers, was not unique to Toys "R" Us. At the same time, other discount stores such as Topos had made inroads, offering a wide selection, low prices, and economy packaging. Only Toys "R" Us, however, had combined the by now accepted discount store with the specialty retail niche; but given its success at home, it seemed likely that Home Depot, Comp USA, and other large-scale niche retailers were monitoring the progress of Toys "R" Us very carefully.

Toys "R" Us Japan was willing to carry a lot more debt than its low-leverage parent firm, in line with the practices of Japanese competitors. The company also leased their land short-term, a concession made as part of the price of goodwill, but not a serious drawback in the depressed land market. Despite the low rents and interest rates, in general, operating costs were three times as high as in the United States. Toys "R" Us also imported large quantities of goods, profiting from the cheap dollar. However, this triple positive of cheap land, cheap money, and cheap imports would have to end sooner or later, and sharp swings upward in any or all of them would certainly have a negative effect on the bottom line.

Threats and Opportunities

Interestingly, in Japan it was two footwear dealers that took the lead in opening shops modeled on Toys "R" Us. Chiyoda's "Harrowmark" chain and Marutomi's "BanBan" were both expanding nationwide, offering low prices compared to Toys "R" Us, but unable to finance the same size stores or inventories. The price wars spawned cut into Toys "R" Us Japan's bottom line for some time. Other stores adopted nonprice techniques to compete, such as "do-it-yourself" toy days, where children were helped to build models or stitch together dolls, or the hiring of "toy consultants" to get into kids' heads and guess the next big hit so stores could stock up.

Just as threatening was a move by smaller retailers to unite in opposition to Toys "R" Us. The ostensible goals of the 600 company-members Toy Shop Specialist Council (Gangu Senmontei Kai) were to research new management techniques, examine the possibility of making direct deals with producers, and cooperate to establish a new joint distribution system, all laudable goals. However, they had also taken less benign steps: They approached distributors and asked that they boycott Toys "R" Us for its policy of dealing direct. While they had had some successes, few distributors wanted to cut off hope of dealing with the toy giant, and so were taking a wait-and-see approach. "Distribution retribution" had not yet come to hurt Toys "R" Us.

While value was important to the Japanese consumer, quality was traditionally more of a watchword than price. Given two equivalent products, the consumer would choose the cheaper one; differentiate them and quality would win

over price in most product areas in Japan. It was important for Toys "R" Us not to veer into the part of the low-price zone that was seen as equivalent to low quality. To that end, their policy of carrying only established brand name items was good, as was the marketing emphasis on inventory rather than price, but in the future, as price competitors arose, it would be important for Toys "R" Us to walk a fine line between becoming too expensive for the young target market it aimed for and so cheap that consumers decided the store had nothing else going for it.

Toys "R" Us Japan executives indicated that they felt that Japan was an almost untapped market, easily capable of supporting five times as many stores as were now in operation. At the same time, they discounted the idea of competition rising to fill that niche before Toys "R" Us could preempt it. However, examples of other American companies that took a lead in market share, then became sanguine and saw that lead slip away, were legion. While Toys "R" Us to date had shown no tendency to give in to wishful thinking, it was still necessary to look at the challenges to be faced in the future. These included not only increasing competition, but also increasing costs, possible positioning problems, and the steady deterioration of the Japanese economy and consumer spending.

Source: Case compiled from a report developed by Michael Chadwick and Jeong-Soe Won, Waseda–Georgetown Graduate Business Program, Tokyo, 1994, revised by Paul Kolesa.

Discussion Questions

1. Was Japan an attractive market for Toys "R" Us? Do you think there were any cultural obstacles to product acceptance? Strong competitors?

2. What were the entry barriers into Japan? Any culturally based barriers, in terms of how to do business?

3. How did Toys "R" Us manage to cross the entry barriers into Japan? What alternative modes of entry could have been tried?

4. What were the problems in transferring the Toys "R" Us competitive advantages to a foreign market? Why did Toys "R" Us internalize the firm-specific advantages rather than license another retailer abroad?

5. Given Wal-Mart's threat in the U.S. market, what should Toys "R" Us future strategy in Japan be?

Case 2-2

Illycaffe (A): Internationalization

Illycaffe is a medium-sized Italian company which produces and sells premium coffee to restaurants and coffee-bars. Its success in Italy provided the impetus for international expansion, and also the inspiration for Starbucks, the American-based coffee-bar chain that is expanding internationally.

The Illycaffe case deals with the problems involved in going abroad and maintaining quality and other firm-specific advantages while relying on independent distributors to deliver the product.

Illycaffe was founded in Trieste, a large city in the northeast of Italy, by Francesco Illy in 1933. Francesco

Illy was a true gourmet, who sought to provide his customers with the highest-quality espresso coffee. By 1990 Illycaffe had a total of 150 employees and its sales had grown from 21 billion lire in 1983 to 67 billion lire in 1990. It was a family-owned company whose shares were divided between Ernesto Illy (the founder's son), his wife, and their four children, all of whom occupied various management positions within the company. Riccardo Illy was marketing manager.

What's Espresso?

Italy is well known for its history, culture, art, and beauty. Italian wine and cuisine are also part of the mystique that attracts people from around the world. Espresso coffee is an element of the cuisine and therefore of this mystique. Espresso is a symbol of the Italian culture.

What makes espresso so different from other types of coffee? There are several methods to percolate coffee: the "filter" or "napoletana" method of letting the weight of the water itself (gravity) pull it through the coffee powder; the "moka" method of creating steam pressure to push water through the coffee; the "espresso" method, which uses water at 194 degrees fahrenheit and 9–10 atmospheres of pressure. The higher the pressure, the less time it takes for the coffee to percolate; the filter method requires several minutes, while the moka method requires one minute, and the espresso method only 30 seconds. The different methods also result in different levels of caffeine in the coffee cup; the filter method (common in North American and in northern Europe) results in 90–125 mg. of caffeine per cup, while the espresso method produces a cup with only 60–120 mg. of caffeine.

Marketing Strategy

Being a single-product company, Illycaffe differentiated its packaging of espresso coffee based only on format (from 3 kg. for professional consumption; from 125 gr. to 250 gr. for domestic consumption), on the form (ground coffee, beans, or E.S.E. servings), and on the type (regular or decaffeinated).

The unique preservation of the product, by the use pressurization, allowed the expansion of Illycaffe in strategic areas such as the United States, Europe, and even Japan.

The company's mission, which was "to delight customers around the world with an excellent cup of espresso and to do everything to improve its quality," reflected the high level of specialized experience capable of meticulously evaluating both the product level and the process level. The direction of excellence always made reference not only to the product that left the establishment but also to "the cup of espresso perfectly served, in every moment and in every place in the world."

Illycaffe's positioning strategy in the crowded coffee market was based on the quality concept. In order to

© Anna Kubato

maintain high standards, the management had patented a packaging system that was able to guarantee high levels of flavor and aroma. But the quality system was also based on the careful selection and control of the coffee beans used in production. Illycaffe used only 100 percent Arabica beans in production and had contributed to the invention of sophisticated machinery that was able to eliminate any defective beans from each batch used in production. The company also dedicated 3 percent of annual sales to research and quality control.

The advertising and promotion policies also focused on the quality of the product, linking it to the brand name in order to increase brand loyalty. It was difficult for producers to ensure that coffee served in cafes was identified by brand. But because most consumers believed coffee made in bars and restaurants was better than that made at home, a strong presence in this segment was necessary to build the brand's image in the home segment (food retailing). Illy reinforced its brand name in cafes and restaurants by asking the owners to display Illy signs and logos both outside the premises to attract customers and inside to recall the brand name. The marketing policies and brand image established by the management helped Illy to get a premium price for its coffee, often even doubling the price of the next highest competitor in this market.

The Quality Problem

One of the company's major problems in maintaining its quality image was the high rate of personnel turnover in the bar and restaurant business. Many employees took on temporary positions as they were looking for other lines of work. This was true in most advanced economies, but it meant that bar operators constantly had to train new personnel in the art of producing a quality cup of espresso.

The quality depended as much on the human input and machinery as on the quality of the coffee used. According to Illy, in fact, a good cup of espresso depended on several elements including the quality of the beans, the roasting of the beans, the correct mix of roasted beans, the quantity of coffee powder used to prepare each cup of coffee, the degree to which the coffee was pressed into the filter of the espresso machine, the water temperature, the pressure at which the water was expelled during the preparation, the cleanliness of the filter, the size of the filter holes, and the quality of the water used in preparation.

The company decided that this was a strategic area for innovation and began to offer technical assistance and training/consultancy to its clients. As Riccardo Illy noted, "A good product is not enough in this market. . . . You also have to teach the operators of the espresso machines how to use them in the best way if you want to guarantee an increase in sales."

Global Strategy

As the company grew to serving about 3 million servings every day worldwide, more emphasis was placed on retail sales. Outside Italy most sales had focused on the professional sector as Illycaffe had looked to restaurant chefs and cafes for the majority of its business. However, the company's marketing director, Franco DiLauro, indicated that while 63 percent of company sales were still in Italy this was expected to soon change. He stated that sales growing in other countries at 25 percent or more should soon eclipse the current 8–10 percent domestic growth expected in Italy's saturated, caffeine-driven marketplace.

As the firm had grown, its dilemma had become its image as a premium product that people should save for special occasions. This notion was reinforced by an advertising campaign that featured Spanish actress–model Ines Sastra choosing Illycaffe as the perfect perfume. In order to encourage consumption and convey that the extraordinary can be found in ordinary, everyday life, Francis Ford Coppola, the director of the *Godfather* movies, was enlisted to film his first-ever commercial. Coppola also owned a California vineyard and had a store in San Francisco that sold Illycaffe. With a $2 million budget and $4 million cost to run the commercial in Italy, Illycaffe was counting on Coppola to craft a coffee story juxtaposing illusion and reality. The result was a homage to the Italian barista, or coffee bar operator, that had distributors in the United States and other markets clamoring to air.

The U.S. Entry

Illycaffe first entered the U.S. market in 1981 after a long history and success in many high-end shops and restaurants throughout the world. At that time, espresso could be found in few places other than Italian stores and restaurants, and the initial American reaction was not very enthusiastic toward the bitter beverage served in a tiny cup. The company began focusing on the foodservice industry, courting top chefs and owners of fine restaurants throughout the country. Statistics clearly showed that Illycaffe was in the right market at the right time. According to the National Coffee Association, Americans drank just 1.87 cups of regular coffee a day in 1993, down from 2.22 cups in 1975. But the Specialty Coffee Association said its industry was booming, doing more than $3 billion in retail business in 1993, with that figure expected to reach $5 billion by 2000. Thus, Illycaffe saw its sales increase by 53 percent in 1992 and another 45 percent in 1993. In 1994, the company expected sales to perk up another 38 percent and increase three-fold from the current level in just four more years.

Initially, Illycaffe faced sizable entry barriers into the U.S. market. For instance, since the 1950s U.S. coffee consumption halved as a result of competition from soft drinks. So Illycaffee not only had difficulty adapting American lifestyle and taste to espresso but also educating and training barmen how to serve a good espresso by handling the machine properly and using consistently the right dose of coffee. But Illycaffe saw further growth in the American market based on sheer numbers alone. In Italy there is one espresso bar for every 400 inhabitants, but in the United States the ratio is about one for every 30,000, according to Andrea Illy. Japan was also viewed as a market where espresso could similarly become a fashionable drink.

The German Entry Problem

Even though successful elsewhere, by the early 1990s Illy faced some difficulties in its German entry. The position of Illy in Germany was somewhat different from its position in other European countries where sales were made through agents and sales subsidiaries. Originally (1974), an exclusive agreement had been signed with a German distributor. Despite the limits of this strategy, the company's sales grew from 10 tons in 1974 to 30 tons in 1978. In 1978, however, one of the major German coffee producers, Hag, approached the management of Illycaffe with a proposal to form a distribution alliance. Hag was a family-owned and family-run business with a long tradition in the coffee industry. The company produced both caffeinated and decaffeinated filter coffee, as well as a line of supplementary products such as sugar and cream. Hag had an extensive distribution network throughout Germany and had noted a growing interest in espresso coffee among its clients. The company had tried to produce its own brand of quality espresso, but had failed and was now looking for an Italian producer who would be interested in an alliance for the German market.

Ernesto Illy realized that any significant increase in sales in Germany would require much greater investments in both sales force and promotion. But 1977 had not been a profitable year in the domestic market, and the company's financial situation would not permit such investments. Nor was the existing German distributor willing to take on further commitments. Ernesto therefore decided to accept Hag's proposal. As he concluded: "This was a great offer from a significant player in the German coffee industry who believed in our product. This was all the assurance that I needed."

The Hag-Goldene Tasse Era

The contract that was signed by the two companies in 1978 gave Hag exclusive rights to the sale of Illy coffee in Germany. Illy's German distributor, in fact, was required to turn over its client lists to Hag. The job of Illy's distribution was reduced to acting as an interface between the two headquarters and to supplying smaller customers.

Illy maintained control over the brand name and the product, while Hag was given responsibility for promotion and distribution decisions in Germany. Rough sales targets were indicated in the contract (80 tons by 1980, 150 tons by 1981, and 250 tons by 1982), although Hag was under no obligation to reach these targets. No provisions were made for Illy to receive any information about the clients.

Three years later, Hag was acquired by another company in the German coffee business, Goldene Tasse. No significant changes were made in the Illycaffe agreement as a result of this acquisition. In fact, the meetings between the two companies during these years were rare and the contract was typically renewed at the end of each period without any direct contact between the two partners.

According to the original contract, Hag had agreed to pay Illy 13.70 DM for each kilo of coffee received. The price was broken down into two parts: one half was pegged to the price of green coffee on the international market, while the other half was pegged to Illy's production costs.

Price changes were provided for only the half related to the raw coffee: These changes could be effected only every three months according to the fluctuations in the trading price established on the international market. Requests for price increases due to rising production costs, on the other hand, could be made by Illy only once at the beginning of each contract year and had to be supported by documentation explaining the actual cost increases.

Following the signing of this agreement in 1978, Illy witnessed a steady increase in sales. But as Riccardo complained as he looked over the records in 1990, "The sales may have been increasing, but we weren't making any money. Our selling price was too low to earn any margins and we had to absorb the high rates of inflation in Italy. Moreover, as the price of green coffee continued to fall on international markets due to the excess in supply throughout the 1980s, we had no way to raise the price of our product to Hag in any substantial way."

Globalizing the Strategy

As Riccardo Illy took over responsibility for the company's international activities in 1990, he quickly decided to change Illy's strategy in the European market. He was convinced that the move toward a more unified European market provided an excellent opportunity for Illy to appeal to a pan-European consumer through a standardized marketing program in line with the strategy followed in the Italian market. In order to carry out this plan, however, he understood that he needed to create a cohesive team and to bring the various subsidiaries under his direct control. The most effective way he saw to begin this process was to acquire distributors in each major market.

Once the buyout process was completed, Mr. Illy gave one of his export managers, Mr. Giacomo Biviano, responsibility for the company's activities in Europe. Mr. Biviano, a young and decisive manager with a strong background in both international marketing and administration and control, was named CEO for France and Germany, and also appointed to the supervisory board of the new company in Holland. As Biviano described it, "We needed managers who would be loyal to our ideas and would implement a standardized set of policies that were to be decided at the central level."

Ownership Complications

Just about this time, however, Riccardo Illy also learned that Hag-Goldene Tasse had been acquired by General Foods, a diversified multinational in the food industry, which was itself later acquired by Philip Morris International. By 1990, both Kraft, another American-based multinational in the food business, and Jacobs Suchard, a Swiss producer of coffee and chocolate with its own line of espresso, had also come under the wing of the Philip Morris group. As a result, a merger was made between Hag's coffee division, Goldene Tasse, and Jacob Suchard's coffee business in Germany. The new company, called Jacobs-Goldene Tasse, took over Hag's position as Illy's partner in the German market. Riccardo Illy immediately called for a meeting with the new partners to discuss the potential effects of the changes on the distribution agreement between the companies.

Although Hag-Goldene Tasse had its own line of espresso coffee, and Jacobs Suchard had a line of both espresso coffee and espresso beans, all of which were sold to the bar segment in Germany, Riccardo Illy underlined the fact that none of these products were of the same quality as Illy's brand of espresso coffee. At the meeting the parties agreed to continue the existing arrangement until Jacobs had time to do more research, with one significant change. To protect its quality image, Illy was allowed to have a technical assistant accompany Hag's salesmen during client visits, providing consultancy on the use and maintenance of espresso machines. Although the arrangement lasted only a few months, Illy gained some important insights from these visits. As Biviano noted, "One significant lesson we learned from these direct contacts with the clients was that it was unusual for bar and restaurant operators in Germany to demand trade credit from small suppliers. Such financing was required only from suppliers whose products represented a large share of the business, such as filter coffee and beer."

The Second Meeting

Riccardo Illy and Giacomo Biviano prepared a list of changes that they wanted made in the contract for the subsequent meeting:

1. The selling price of Illy coffee to Hag-Goldene Tasse would be the same as in other European markets, and with the same payment conditions.

2. All marketing activities (especially advertising to the trade, to the consumer, and at the point-of-sales) would be managed and controlled by Illy's new German subsidiary.

3. Hag-Goldene Tasse would be granted exclusive rights to the distribution of Illy coffee in Germany, contingent on the requirement that Hag-Goldene Tasse distribute only Illy's brand of espresso coffee.

4. Clear growth objectives would be stipulated in the contract. These objectives should be in line with Illy's overall objectives for growth, and Hag should be obliged to achieve the stated objectives.

5. A unit to supervise technical consulting/quality control at the point-of-sales would be created and managed by Illy-Germany.

6. A new policy of communication at point-of-sales would be implemented through the use of Illy cups and billboards. Illy should have the authority to control the implementation of this activity through contracts and regular visits to clients.

By the end of the meeting, Jacobs Suchard and Hag-Goldene Tasse had agreed to points (1) and (4), but had refused to accept point (3). The companies did not adopt a position concerning points (2), (5), and (6). No new meeting was scheduled between the parties.

Uncertain Future

At the end of the current contract period in June 1991, the manager of Illy-Germany terminated the contract between Illy and Hag-Goldene Tasse, offering an interim option to renegotiate a new contract. The option was left open until the end of August.

In the meantime, Riccardo Illy and Giacomo Biviano began to study the three major alternatives:

1. Give full responsibility for rules and distribution back to Illy-Germany and work together with the German team to establish an effective sales force.

2. Look for a new partner in Germany who could offer a solid sales network and would agree to the terms outlined in the proposal prepared for Hag-Goldene Tasse.

3. Work toward a new contract with Hag-Goldene Tasse/Jacobs Suchard.

In the latter two cases, given that it was unlikely that all of Illy's requests would be accepted by any partner, it would be necessary to rank the requests in order of importance and to establish the minimum requirements for any agreement.

As the next step, therefore, the two managers had to decide whether or not to attempt to revive the piggyback agreement with Hag, to look for a new distributor, or to create their own network in accordance with their new Euro strategy.

Source: This case was prepared by Pamela Adams, SDA Bocconi, Milano, and revised by Paul Kolesa. Used with permission.

Discussion Questions

1. To what extent do you think a global strategy in coffee is well-founded? For example, is the espresso market global or multidomestic?

2. How would you define Illycaffe's FSAs? CSAs? Can they be transferred abroad?

3. What were the difficulties Illycaffe faced when expanding abroad? How did these impact its choice of entry mode?

4. What created the problems with the existing distribution strategy in the German market? Was the distribution alliance with Hag ill-advised?

5. What negotiation strategy would you have recommended for Mr. Illy?

Case 2-3

Illycaffe (B): The Starbucks Threat

Throughout the 1990s and into the new millennium, Illy continued to expand its relationships with restaurants and hotels around the world. As of 2004, Illycaffe was sold in over 70 countries. Europe and the United States were the primary strategic markets, where the group held close to 30 percent of the market for quality coffee. Approximately two-thirds of its business came from the hotel, restaurant, and cafe sectors. The proportion of sales earned outside of Italy was constantly growing and had reached over 40 per-

cent. The company's global presence was strengthened after it became the only global agro-industrial company to have double quality certification. In 1996, the company was granted ISO 9001 certification for its production process, after having received the Qualite France certification for its product quality in 1992.

In Italy, Illy was still number one in Italy's highly fragmented hotel, restaurant, and bar segment, but held only a 6 percent market share. The company had 27 percent of the home espresso market, however. Among Italian connoisseurs, Illy was deemed the elite brand. Illy went to much greater lengths than most firms to promote quality and consistency. "It was 'La Dolce Vita' in a cup," according to its loyal customers.

By the beginning of the new millennium, however, Illy faced a new and surprising global threat: An American chain of coffeehouses. American coffee had always been disparaged as weak and watery, just like American beer. But now Starbucks, a small company from Seattle, had revolutionized the coffee market in the United States, with high-quality lattes, mochas, and espressos. There were also typical American "innovations" like "frappuccino," an ice and coffee concoction, and paper cups of different sizes (all big compared to Illy's standard cups). Espresso in a paper cup? To CEO Andrea Illy, son of Ernesto Illy, it seemed heretical and an insult to the coffee. But Starbucks was very successful, not only in the United States, and the chain was expanding globally at a fast clip. Should Illy worry about Starbucks? How big was the threat? Were Illy and Starbucks competing for the same segments of coffee drinkers? Perhaps Starbucks was simply creating new coffee drinkers, enlarging the total market? Andrea Illy decided he must take a closer look at the company, its history, and its financials.

The Starbucks Threat

At the beginning of the new millennium, Starbucks seemed to be everywhere. The world's number one specialty coffee retailer, Starbucks operated and licensed more than 7,500 coffee shops (yes, they were referred to as shops rather than coffee bars or coffeehouses) in more than 30 countries. Starbucks owned more than 4,700 of its shops (mostly in the United States), while licensees operated more than 2,800 units (primarily in shopping centers and airports). The company also owned and franchised the Seattle's Best Coffee and the Torrefazione Italia chains in the United States (with more than 100 shops). During 2004, the company planned to open more than 550 company-owned units and an additional 375 licensed locations, primarily abroad.

The shops offered a variety of coffee drinks and food items as well as coffee and coffee accessories. The strategic notion was that the coffeehouses would be destination points, where people could meet friends, drink coffee, chat, and spend time reading, doing homework, or surfing the Internet. Starbucks was one of the first businesses to jump on the Wi-Fi bandwagon, teaming with Hewlett-Packard and Deutsche Telekom's T-Mobile unit to offer high-speed wireless Internet access at 1,200 of its locations in the United States, London, and Berlin. In March 2004, Starbucks and Hewlett-Packard unveiled their Hear Music service that allowed Starbucks's customers to download songs and create custom music CDs

in shops. The company intended to offer Hear Music in 2,500 Starbucks stores by 2006. The company offered loyal patrons its Starbucks Card, which allowed customers to prepay up to $500 on a store card, which doubles as a gift certificate. The program's success enticed Visa to team up with Starbucks to offer Visa cards for the same purpose.

The company also leveraged its popularity to extend its brand beyond coffee to a host of home goods and lifestyle products. It partnered with Amazon.com to sell branded kitchenware and coffee supplies. Starbucks also marketed its coffee through grocery stores and licensed its brand for other food and beverage products.

History of Starbucks

Starbucks opened its first location in Seattle's Pike Place Market in 1971, selling quality ground beans over a small counter in an open-air market. It was started more or less as a hobby for three good friends, strong on ideas but not very profit-oriented entrepreneurs. Eleven years later, Howard Schultz joined Starbucks as director of retail operations and marketing. Starbucks began providing coffee to fine restaurants and espresso bars in Seattle.

In 1983 Schultz traveled to Italy, where he became impressed with the popularity of espresso bars in Milan. Seeing the potential to develop a similar coffee bar culture in Seattle (where a young Bill Gates had just started a promising software company named Microsoft), he convinced the founders of Starbucks to test the coffee bar concept in a new location in downtown Seattle. This successful experiment was the genesis for a company that Schultz founded in 1985 called Il Giornale, offering brewed coffee and espresso beverages made from Starbucks's coffee beans. With the backing of local investors, Il Giornale acquired Starbucks's assets and changed its name to Starbucks Corporation in 1987. The company opened coffeehouses in Chicago and Vancouver, B.C.

In the early 1990s, Starbucks expanded headquarters in Seattle and built a new roasting plant. The company also became the first privately owned U.S. company to offer a stock option program that included part-time employees. The company expanded into California, Washington, DC, Minneapolis, Boston, New York, Atlanta, Dallas, Houston, and negotiated contracts to serve Starbucks coffee with Horizon Air, United Airlines, Nordstrom, Barnes & Noble, and ITT/Sheraton/Westin (now Starwood Hotels). By then the company had 676 Starbucks locations.

International Expansion

In the late 1990s, Starbucks expanded internationally, opening locations in Japan, Hawaii, Singapore, the Philippines, Taiwan, Thailand, New Zealand, Malaysia,

China, Kuwait, Korea, Lebanon, and the United Kingdom. They were as aggressive in the domestic retail market, opening more locations in the United States. This was when the strategy known as "a Starbucks on every corner" was developed, saturating downtowns with shops sometimes only one block away from each other.

By the year 2000, Howard Schultz transitioned from chairman and CEO to chairman and chief global strategist. Orin Smith was promoted to president and CEO. Within the three years that followed, the company continued to push for more retail locations abroad, launching shops in Dubai, Hong Kong, Shanghai, Qatar, Bahrain, Saudi Arabia, Australia, Switzerland, Israel, Austria, Oman, Indonesia, Germany, Spain, Puerto Rico, Mexico, Greece, southern China, Turkey, Chile, and Perú. In 2004, Starbucks Coffee International opened in Paris, its first shop in the bastion of lovers of strong coffee.

As of mid-2004, the count of Starbucks locations around the world was at 7,569. Each of these locations was focused on providing the Starbucks experience: making various incarnations of coffee drinks available to people for enjoyment in the coffeehouses and for "to-go" consumption or takeout trade.

Starbucks' international expansion had not gone completely smooth. High startup costs and cultural resistance to the Starbucks brand were obstacles in some countries. Tensions in the Middle East forced the company to pull out of Israel in 2003. Some of the licensees did not perform as well as expected or encountered unforeseen difficulties. In June 2004 Starbucks decided to buy 35 stores from its Singapore licensing partner, Bonvests Holdings Limited, and in July 2004 the company agreed to acquire a 49.9 percent equity stake in its Malaysian licensee. Adding to the pressure was the fact that back home fast-food restaurants like McDonald's and Dunkin' Donuts had started offering a selection of higher-quality coffees at much lower price points than Starbucks. And loyal but finicky customers were complaining about deteriorating quality and service, also threatening Starbucks's customer franchise. In February 2008 Chairman Schulz proclaimed a three-hour "sabbatical closure" of all U.S. stores so that "Starbucks's partners will have an opportunity to connect and deepen their passion for coffee with the ultimate goal of transforming the customer experience."

Financial Performance

Starbucks Coffee Company was the leading retailer, roaster, and brand of specialty coffee in the world. According to its mission statement, the company was committed to offering the highest-quality coffee and the Starbucks experience while conducting its business in ways that produce social, environmental, and economic benefits for communities in which it did business. Its coffee was advertised as "fair trade." Its sales and profits

EXHIBIT 1 **Starbucks Sales and Income**

	2003	2002	2001	2000
Annual Sales ($ mil.)	4,075.5	3,288.9	2,649.0	2,169.2
Annual Net Income ($ mil.)	268.3	215.1	181.2	94.6

had been growing steadily as the international expansion has occurred (see Exhibits 1 and 2).

Illy versus Starbucks?

Summarizing the Starbucks information after making several personal visits to the shops, CEO Andrea Illy had come to some conclusions. He thought the U.S. chain, which measured its sales in billions of dollars, not millions, over-roasted its coffee and concentrated too heavily on takeout trade. But he also voiced admiration for what Starbucks had achieved. "Starbucks piggybacked on the Italian concept of the coffee bar," he said. "They were able to internationalize espresso as no one else had done. We see them as an opportunity for us, not a threat. After they're educated about coffee by Starbucks and others, we think they'll want the real thing. Us."

As opposed to the Starbucks shops, Illy had successfully pursued cobranding relationships with restaurants, cafés, hotels, and coffeehouses, where Illy provided equipment and coffee to augment the establishments' existing menu. It was very common to see the trademark red Illy logo, usually outside these cafés and restaurants underneath the café's or restaurant's own sign. These cobranding arrangements were similar to the "Intel Inside" strategy adopted by Intel in the personal computer field. It was also common to see Illy signage inside the establishments.

Also, Illy's product line was more limited than Starbucks's. Illy tended to stress its espresso roots, playing down the mochas and cappuccinos that masked the true quality of the coffee. Furthermore, Illy espressos were always served in specially designed small porcelain cups and saucers.

EXHIBIT 2 **Financial Overview**

Share price: Close 23-Jul-2004	$47.06
52-Week High	$47.87
52-Week Low	$26.00
Basic Earnings per share	$0.87
Price/Earnings Ratio	54.09
Current Ratio	1.76
R&D Expenses (mil.)	$5.40
Advertising Expense (mil.)	$49.50
% Owned by Institutions	72.90%

Andrea Illy shuddered at the thought of having Illy-caffe served in a paper cup. Still, he could not deny the strength in Starbucks's numbers, both in terms of sales figures and store locations. To what extent should Illy concern itself with the Seattle giant? Was there a need for a defense strategy? Was Starbucks's expansion really an opportunity for Illy, or was that just wishful thinking?

Sources: This case was developed by Cipriano De Leon from the following sources: R. W. Apple, "Discovering La Dolce Vita in a Cup," *New York Times*, October 24, 2001; "Starbucks Timeline and History," Starbucks The Company, Internet Online, available from **www.starbucks.com/aboutus/timeline.asp** [2004]; "Starbucks Celebrates Five Years in South Korea With the Opening of its 100th Store," *Business Wire*, July 26, 2004; "Starbucks Corporation," Hoovers Online, Internet Online, available from **http://premium.hoovers.com/subscribe/co/fin/factsheet.xhtml?COID=15745**.

Discussion Questions

1. What are Starbucks CSAs and FSAs? How do these advantages explain the chain's success in the United States?
2. How internationally mobile is the Starbucks concept? Any barriers to entry?
3. Franchising would seem a natural entry mode for Starbucks, but the chain sometimes owns the shops even abroad. What could be the explanation?
4. Do Illy and Starbucks compete or not? How likely are they to compete in the future?
5. If you were Andrea Illy, what strategic plan would you develop?

Case 2-4

AOL: International Expansion

America Online (AOL) is one of the largest providers of online services. With a large membership base in the United States and increasingly overseas, the AOL portal offers e-mail, Internet access, and instant messenger (IM) services to its members. AOL's network of Web properties is one of the top three in the United States, attracting an average of 110 million unique visitors each month during the quarter ending March 31, 2008, according to comScore Media Metrix, and many are leaders in their categories. As part of its international growth plans, AOL has launched 19 international Web sites and has plans to expand to 30 countries outside the United States by the end of 2008. In addition, AOL has teamed up with HP—a leading PC maker in the United States—to include localized versions of the AOL.com portal and other AOL services as the default setting on HP computers shipped in the United States and more than two-dozen countries worldwide. This case focuses on how the company expanded internationally and the problems involved in entering and managing virtual services in foreign countries.

07:28 a.m. EDT 5 August 1998—AOL announced that its combined CompuServe and international subscribers surpassed 2.5 million members. AOL total subscriber base is now over 15 million, up almost 70% over last year. We do not believe there is another company that strategically or financially is better positioned than AOL in the online/Internet marketplace. AOL's ability to leverage its massive infrastructure to deploy multiple brands (AOL, AOL.com, Digital Cities, Mirabilis, and CompuServe) on a worldwide basis is unmatched. Conference call comments indicate the potential for international profit recognition as early as fiscal 1999, ahead of our 2000 expectations.

Scott Geltz, manager of New Market Operations for AOL's international organization, was reading his e-mail on the plane back from Hong Kong to Washington, DC. The e-mail contained a collection of reports from Wall Street's stock analysts on AOL like the one above. There were no surprises but Scott could see a discernible trend in these reports over the last few months: Everyone seemed to be counting on an aggressive strategy by AOL to expand its operations internationally.

Scott had just spent two weeks in Hong Kong working on the first steps toward launching the AOL service there. In May 1998, AOL had signed a licensing agreement with China Internet Corporation (CIC), giving it a license to market, promote, and distribute AOL services to Hong Kong, as well as to use AOL's proprietary publishing tool (i.e., Rainman) to develop local contents. Like AOL's other international ventures, once the deal was signed, the responsibility for the "program" would gradually shift from "market development" to "operations" within the international organization. Scott Geltz, Lisa Zimmermann (an operations coordinator), and an intern made up the New Market Operations unit in AOL International. Greg Consiglio, who had accompanied Scott on this trip, and an intern composed the Business Development unit. Mark Minkin, the group's vice president, presided over both the operational and

Source: Professor Kasra Ferdows, from Georgetown University, prepared this case as the basis for class discussion rather than to illustrate either effective or ineffective handling of an administrative situation. Certain facts and figures have been disguised. Materials presented in this case do not necessarily represent the views of AOL or its officers. Copyright © Kasra Ferdows, Georgetown University, Washington DC, 20057, USA.

EXHIBIT 1   **AOL International Organization Chart**

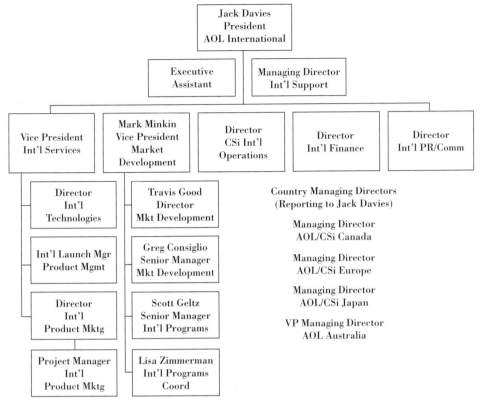

business development functions. (See Exhibit 1 for organization chart of AOL International.)

Scott's workload had been increasing rapidly in the last year. Until November 1995, AOL did not have any subscribers outside the United States. But since then, in one form or another, it had started to offer its service in eight countries. Every country was different, with Hong Kong, the ninth one, being even more unique. Hong Kong was a potential gateway to mainland China and possibly Taiwan. It was important that AOL start on the right foot in this market.

Moreover, unlike all the previous international deals, Hong Kong was not a joint venture. AOL had chosen to set up a franchise rather than hold any equity. What did that mean in terms of day-to-day running of the Hong Kong operations? How would CIC work with AOL? What would AOL provide, and how would it protect the reputation of the AOL brand name?

There were even broader issues. As the Wall Street analysts were saying, there was no question that international expansion was an important, if not the most important, source of future growth and profitability for AOL. In fact, given the rush of potential competitors, like Yahoo!, into the global markets, AOL had no choice but to expand its international operations quickly. The international business development team was currently involved in assessing or signing deals in a half-dozen new countries. But in all this rush, was it clear why one country was chosen over another? What about a regional approach—for example a

Spanish language service for several South American countries? It seemed that so far, AOL had responded to opportunities in countries that could apply the "AOL System" smoothly. Had AOL reached a point that it needed to change its approach to international expansion? Should it now ask what it had to do to enter critical markets like China, Latin America, or India, even if it meant changing some of the key features of the "AOL System"?

Given the fast pace of life at AOL, Scott knew that he didn't have much time to delve into these questions. He and Greg had another 15 hours on the plane and the weekend to prepare for a debriefing session with Mark. Although the target date for starting full-fledged AOL service in Hong Kong was some months away, there were already urgent decisions to be made. He wondered how many more trips to Hong Kong he would be taking in the next few months. A franchise operation was supposed to require minimal investment by AOL, but it sure did not seem so. Could he really manage a smooth start-up in Hong Kong from northern Virginia—12 time zones and 11,000 miles away? Should he ask Mark to send him and a small team to Hong Kong for at least six months to ensure that AOL started well in East Asia?

Company Background

America Online was founded in 1985 as Quantum Computer Services. It started by providing interactive services for personal computers, first for Commodore 64 and 128,

EXHIBIT 2   **Partial Organization Chart of AOL**

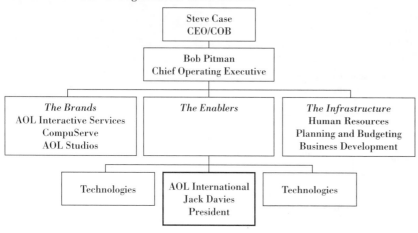

then for Tandy (1986), then for Macintosh (1989), and finally for IBM PCs (1990). By then it had 100,000 members and 150 employees. In 1991 it changed its name to America Online and by 1994, reached the million-member mark. In 1995 AOL, by then the largest provider of online services in the United States, started to enter international markets. The first move was through a joint venture with Bertelsmann AG, one of the world's largest media companies, to provide AOL service to selected European countries. By 1998 and after two additional international ventures, AOL was serving subscribers in six European countries, Canada, and Japan.

AOL also started to acquire other companies in 1994. By mid-1998, it had acquired 12 companies, including CompuServe (in 1997). CompuServe had been founded in 1969 in Columbus, Ohio, and by 1980 had started to provide interactive service targeting computer enthusiasts, researchers, and business professionals. By mid-1998, CompuServe had over 2 million subscribers.

Meanwhile, AOL had also entered into a number of important alliances with major companies in the industry, including IBM (in 1990), Netscape, and Microsoft (in 1996). By mid-1998, AOL had organized itself into three business units: AOL Interactive Services, CompuServe Interactive Services, and AOL Studios. (See Exhibit 2 for a partial organization chart.) AOL Interactive Services was responsible for AOL's core online service (offering a variety of popular features like e-mail, chat, Instant Messenger, AOL Channels, etc.). CompuServe, also an online service, focused on the professional and business markets and was managed separately from the rest of AOL. The AOL Studios developed original content programming for AOL and other online services. AOL had also owned ANS Communications, a provider of global networks of communication systems to businesses, but sold this division to WorldCom Inc. for $175 million in early 1998 (while continuing to use it as a customer).

Worldwide, AOL employed approximately 10,000 persons. Over 3,000 employees worked in the headquarters

offices located in suburbs of Washington, DC, in northern Virginia. AOL Networks operated eight call centers; five in the United States, one in Germany, one in Ireland, and one in Japan. It also had sales offices in five other U.S. cities. AOL had no sales offices located outside the United States.

AOL employed a diversified portfolio approach in designing, structuring, and operating its network services. It managed the AOLnet, a TCP/IP network of third-party network service providers, including Sprint, BBN (a part of GTE Internetworking), WorldCom's wholly owned subsidiaries ANS Communications (recently acquired from AOL), and UUNET Technologies. Buildup of network capacity required substantial investment in telecommunications equipment, and demanded a careful matching of anticipated demand with supply in a highly volatile market. The risks were significant.

While revenues had been increasing substantially from year to year, expenses had grown even faster. In 1997, AOL posted almost $500 million in losses from operations, $385 million of which was a write-off of "deferred subscriber acquisition costs."[1] (See Exhibit 3 for Consolidated Statements of Operations and Exhibit 4 for Consolidated Balance Sheet.)

Competition

AOL competed in a rapidly changing marketplace with a wide range of other companies in the communications, advertising, entertainment and information, media, direct mail, and commerce fields. There was no other company similar to AOL, but the company had many competitors in each of these fields. Competitors for usage, subscribers, advertising, and electronic commerce included Internet service providers (ISPs) like the

---

[1] Until 1997, AOL had regarded part of the marketing and promotion costs as investment for acquiring subscribers. However, in 1997 it decided to regard all these costs (including what had been accumulated from previous years) as expense.

EXHIBIT 3   Consolidated Statements of Operation *(amount in thousands, except per share data)*

	Year Ended June 30,		
	1992	1996	1999
Revenues:			
Online service revenues	$1,429,445	$991,656	$344,309
Other revenues	255,783	102,198	49,981
Total revenues	1,685,228	1,093,854	394,290
Costs and expenses:			
Cost of revenues	1,040,762	638,025	232,318
Marketing			
Marketing	409,260	638,025	77,064
Write-off of deferred subscriber acquisition costs	385,221	—	—
Product development	58,208	43,164	11,669
General and administrative	193,537	110,653	42,700
Acquired research and development	—	16,981	50,335
Amortization of goodwill	6,549	7,078	1,653
Restructuring charge	48,627	—	—
Contract termination charge	24,506	—	—
Settlement charge	24,204	—	—
Total costs and expenses	2,190,874	1,028,611	415,739
Income (loss) from operations	(505,646)	65,243	(21,449)
Other income (expense), net	6,299	(2,056)	3,074
Merger expenses	—	(848)	(2,207)
Income (loss) before provision for income taxes	(499,347)	62,339	(20,582)
Provision for income taxes	—	(32,523)	(15,169)
Net income (loss)	$(499,347)	$29,816	$(35,751)
Earnings (loss) per share:			
Net income (loss)	$(5.22)	$0.28	$(0.51)
Weighted average shares outstanding	95,607	108,097	69,550

Microsoft Network, Prodigy Services company, and various national and local Internet service providers. Long distance and regional telephone and cable companies also competed with AOL, including among others, AT&T Corp., MCI Communications, and various regional Bell operating companies. Also competing in these fields were the so-called "portal" sites—Web-based services like Yahoo!, Netscape, Infoseek, CNET, Excite, and Lycos—each providing interactive services that were becoming increasingly functional equivalents of AOL's online services. Another group of competitors were global media companies such as newspapers, radio and television stations, and content providers like Disney, Time-Warner, CBS, and Sony.

There were more. New technologies were bringing in new competitors constantly. The development of midband and broadband distribution technologies for offering cable Internet services had brought in new competitors like @Home Networks, Road Runner Group (owned by Time Warner), and MediaOne (a subsidiary of US West Media Group). Advanced telephone-based access services offered through digital subscriber line (DSL) technologies and other advanced digital services offered by broadcast and satellite companies were intensifying the competition even further. Emerging convergent technologies offering combinations of television and interactive computer services, such as those offered by Web TV and NetChannel, posed yet additional competitive challenges for AOL.

International Expansion

The joint venture with Bertelsmann in 1995 to expand AOL services into Europe was a major move for the company. The joint venture itself was a 50–50 split, with Bertelsmann contributing DM 150 million (about $100 million), and AOL providing its technology, know-how, network, program contents, and the AOL brand name. In addition, Bertelsmann purchased approximately a 5 percent stake in AOL for about $50 million and put a director on the AOL Board.

From its 19th-century German roots as a small printing firm and religious book publisher that began the world's first book club, Bertelsmann had grown into a global group of companies involved in book, magazine, and newspaper publishing and distribution, music and entertainment, radio, television, video, printing, and manufacturing. Among its best-known North American enterprises

EXHIBIT 4 Consolidated Balance Sheets *(amount in thousands, except per share data)*

	1997	1996
Current assets:		
Cash and cash equivalents	$124,340	$188,421
Short-term investments	268	10,712
Trade accounts receivable	65,306	49,342
Other receivables	26,093	23,271
Prepaid expenses and other current assets	107,466	65,290
Total current assets	323,473	267,036
Property and equipment at cost, net	**233,129**	**111,090**
Other assets:		
Restricted cash	50,000	—
Product development costs, net	72,498	44,330
Deferred subscriber acquisition costs, net	—	314,181
License rights, net	16,777	4,947
Other assets:	84,618	29,067
Deferred income taxes	24,410	135,872
Goodwill, net	41,783	51,691
Total assets	**$846,688**	**$958,754**
Current liabilities:		
Trade accounts payable	$ 69,703	$105,904
Other accrued expenses and liabilities	297,298	127,876
Deferred revenue	166,007	37,950
Accrued personnel costs	20,008	15,719
Current portion of long-term debt	1,454	2,435
Total current liabilities	554,470	289,884
Long-term liabilities:		
Notes payable	50,000	19,306
Deferred income taxes	24,410	135,872
Deferred revenue	86,040	—
Minority interests	2,674	22
Other liabilities	1,060	1,168
Total liabilities	718,654	446,252
Stockholders' equity:		
Preferred stock, $.01 par value; 5,000,000 shares authorized, 1,000 shares issued and outstanding at June 30, 1997 and 1996	1	1
Common stock, $.01 par value; 300,000,000 shares authorized, 100,188,971 and 92,626,000 shares issued and outstanding at June 30, 1997 and 1996, respectively	1,002	926
Unrealized gain on available-for-sale securities	16,924	—
Additional paid-in capital	617,221	519,342
Accumulated deficit	(507,114)	(7,767)
Total stockholders' equity	128,034	512,502
Total liabilities	**$846,688**	**$958,754**

were RCA Records and the Bantam Doubleday Dell Publishing Group. Bertelsmann employed 52,000 people in more than 300 companies in 40 countries. In 1995, when the joint venture with AOL was signed, Bertelsmann's sales were $11 billion; AOL's were $ 0.4 billion.

The first service was launched in November 1995 in Germany, and was followed by the United Kingdom in January 1996 and France in March 1996. Since Bertelsmann also had experience in Australia, AOL formed another joint venture with Bertelsmann to offer AOL service in Australia in late 1998. Meanwhile, AOL also introduced service in Canada (January 1996), and with the help of the joint venture with Bertelsmann, in Switzerland (November 1996), Austria (1996), and Sweden (January 1997).

In April 1997, AOL formed another joint venture, this time with Mitsui, one of the world's largest trading companies, and Nihon Keizai Shimbun, Inc. (Nikkei), publisher of Japan's leading business newspaper and a leader in the publications of online services. Mitsui owned 40 percent, Nikkei 10 percent, and AOL 50 percent. Mitsui and Nikkei contributed 6 billion yen ($56 million) with AOL bringing its technology, know-how, network, access to its online services in the United States and Europe, and its brand name. In addition, Mitsui purchased approximately $28 million of convertible preferred stock in AOL. In 1997, Mitsui employed 11,600 people in 226 cities in 90 countries and conducted transactions in excess of $195 billion per year. Nikkei, founded in 1876, was a large media company with book publication, broadcasting, exhibitions, and seminars as well as being publisher of *Nihon Keizai Shimbun,* a daily newspaper with a circulation of approximately 3 million and a primary source of business information in Japan.

Many experts believed that the international market was the next major battlefield in the Internet online industry. In August 1998, AOL reported 135,000 net new international members, bringing the total number of international members to 1.4 million (not including 1.2 million CompuServe members). There was no question that the potential markets, especially in Asia, were huge. There was also no question that competition for these markets was becoming fierce, rapidly. In spite of the financial and economic troubles in east Asia in 1998, many of the global Internet service providers were seeking entry into the large economies in this region. For example, Yahoo! had recently opened a sales office in Singapore.

Up to 1998, AOL had entered international markets essentially through joint ventures. Hong Kong, being the first venture in which AOL did not hold equity, was essentially a franchise and could prove the new model in which AOL would enter other international markets. Franchising promised several advantages over joint ventures. It would require not only a limited initial investment, but if there were any up-front payment by the franchisee, it could result in a net positive cash flow. It would generate net revenues quickly, require fewer AOL employees during start-up, and often none thereafter. In short, franchising promised the possibility of building brand awareness and a customer base quickly without taxing the company's financial and managerial resources too much. The disadvantages were partial loss of control over brand name and potential future revenues.

AOL had devised yet another model for introducing its brand name in new international markets. The AOL Instant Messenger (AIM) was a message exchange service that AOL offered free of charge to anyone (including non-AOL subscribers) who asked for it. Once connected to the Internet, the users, in any country, could exchange messages with other users. For AOL, the great advantage of AIM was that the users had to first register with AOL.

This gave AOL not only valuable information about potential customers, but because registration involved choosing a screen name, it was almost like the first step in joining AOL as a subscriber. Moreover, AIM kept the AOL brand name in front of potential customers and allowed assessment of potential partners for franchising or joint ventures in promising markets. In 1998, AOL planned to distribute AIM worldwide to speakers of English, German, French, Spanish, Japanese, and Portuguese. The annual cost of offering this service (for AOL) was small, less than $100,000 per country.

Yet another model for spreading the AOL name internationally was the AOL.com Web site. The intent here was to create an Internet search service like Yahoo!, Excite, or Lycos, with the goal to make it the most visited Web page on the Internet. It would put AOL's brand name in front of the worldwide audience and could enhance advertising revenues. The costs for this project were minimal.

In summary, AOL could enter a new country with as little investment as just creating a customized Web site. As it increased its financial and managerial investments, AOL could offer free AIM service, offer basic AOL (not customized for the country) through a local Internet service provider (almost like a franchise), create a full franchise with local contents (like the one in Hong Kong), or establish a joint venture (like the ones with Mitsui and Bertelsmann). So far, AOL had not considered a wholly owned greenfield subsidiary as a way to enter a new country.

Serving International Subscribers—Operational Issues

To provide AOL.com or AIM internationally, AOL did not have to set up an establishment in a country to allow individuals in that country to use those services. However, once there were paying subscribers, AOL had to establish call centers and provide member services. From an operational viewpoint, it did not make much difference whether the unit in the country was a joint venture or a franchise. Besides operating the call centers, there were a number of tasks that had to be done by the unit. These tasks could be grouped into the following categories:

1. Marketing
2. Public relations and communications
3. Legal and local regulations
4. Fraud prevention and security
5. Management of local network
6. Billing and collection
7. Design and layout of service
8. Design of local content
9. Production of local content
10. Finance
11. Human resources and administration

EXHIBIT 5   **Typical Network Structure**

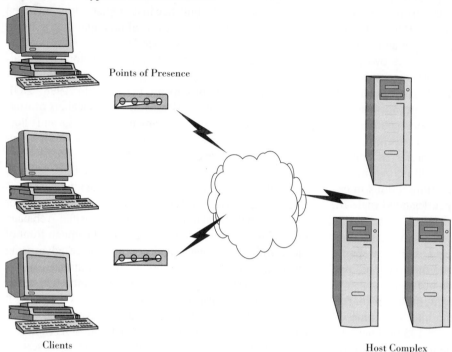

Points of Presence

Clients   Host Complex

AOL's headquarters staff would provide the technical help with software and host infrastructure to allow subscribers the ability to connect with the AOL network. They would provide a range of services: from providing the "Golden Master" for production of AOL CDs to be sent to subscribers to programming assistance for all the steps in getting a signal from a subscriber's computer to the AOL central computers in northern Virginia and back. (See Exhibit 5 for a schematic diagram of the typical network.)

The difference between a joint venture and a franchise operation was in who performed the tasks. "We have to provide everything that we usually provide in these markets. We have to provide 'the AOL experience' for the subscribers whether we have a joint venture or a franchise. In our joint ventures so far, we have used a few experienced AOL employees who understand the AOL system almost instinctively. They have stayed around during the start-up phase and answered the myriad of inevitable questions. Even after the start-up phase is over, we have AOL employees in the organization of the country who not only monitor what is going on, but more importantly, help in solving the local operating problems as they arise. In a franchise, we must do all that remotely and rely on people who are not employed by AOL," said Scott Geltz.

Launch of Service at Hong Kong

In 1998, in spite of the economic problems in east Asia, Hong Kong was an attractive market for Internet services. According to American International Data Corporation, Hong Kong was experiencing the fastest Internet user growth rate in Asia. There was an estimated 300–600,000 Internet users, projected to hit 1 million by 2000. There were already a large number of local ISPs in Hong Kong, but AOL counted on its brand name and the features of the AOL experience to compete. These features included AIM, access to unique AOL content from AOL's other international services, and local content from CIC geared to Hong Kong consumers, in both English and Chinese.

The Web page was to be introduced first. AOL.com had its own NetFind search engine, but a new search engine in Chinese was also under development. AIM would be provided soon after. These introductions were straightforward. The real challenge was in the launch of the full AOL service, scheduled in the second quarter of 1999. With all that having to be decided first, it was difficult to tell if everything was on schedule.

There were big decisions like pricing of the subscription (including whether it would be a flat rate or not) and on the marketing plan for Hong Kong (including the logistics of production and distribution of the AOL discs). Smaller decisions like whether the "Terms of Service" shown during signup to new subscribers would be in English, Chinese, or both languages also had to be ironed out. Were there any local laws, procedures, or customs that had to be taken into account? Who would prepare the Chinese text of this agreement, and what were the steps to clear it through the AOL lawyers?

There were a host of decisions about the layout and the artwork. On one hand, it was essential to preserve the AOL "feel"—the familiar layout, colors, channels, sequence of pages, and so forth. On the other hand, it was important to customize the context to fit the Chinese language and thinking. Even if guidelines that codified the "AOL feel" could be written, would they be sufficient? There were many detailed decisions often involving trade-offs. Especially during the start-up phase when many of these decisions were made for the first time, someone from AOL had to sit across the table from CIC and help reach a good compromise. For example, the side screen in the sports channel should be the usual size, but it could show horse-racing news in Hong Kong instead of baseball often shown in the United States and Japan.

Undoubtedly, the fact that Hong Kong was AOL's first experience with franchising made this venture even more challenging. Unlike McDonald's or Coca-Cola, AOL had neither the experience nor established guidelines for how a franchise should operate. In a sense, Hong Kong was a pilot for testing the proposition that it was possible to codify what was AOL. As Scott Geltz saw it, "To operate a franchise successfully, we must first be able to gather the collective knowledge at AOL, and translate it into specific guidelines, procedures, and methods of doing things. These are not easy tasks, and for the moment, they fall on us in the AOL International group because we need this form of knowledge more than the rest."

Scott had already started to write an inch-thick manual going over some of the common questions, ranging from what should be put behind "firewalls," to how long it took to obtain a new layout design from AOL's central staff. There was no question that such a document would be helpful for Hong Kong and future franchise operations. Anyway, one could argue that it was crucial for AOL to capture and document its tacit knowledge and this was an important step in that process. However, no one (including Scott himself) believed that a manual, even a very good one, would ensure that all would go well in Hong Kong. It was important both to suggest what to do and to make sure that it would be done.

CIC was a large organization. The Chinese news service, Xinhua, had a 60 percent stake in CIC and already had strategic partnerships with other large international information services such as Reuters and Bloomberg. The deal with AOL was another strategic partnership for CIC and it was reasonable to assume that some of CIC's senior managers would have more than AOL to worry about. In the last two weeks, Scott had tried to pinpoint exactly who in the CIC organization would be in charge of the various functions related to the AOL franchise. However, the answers had not been very clear. It seemed that CIC was falling behind schedule in recruiting some of the key managers for this venture. Consequently, some of the tasks were starting to fall behind schedule and Scott was wondering if or when he should intervene. An example was a piece of artwork that was supposed to be done by mid-September. So far, CIC had not hired anyone to do that and it seemed likely that the deadline would be missed. Scott knew of someone in Australia who had recently done similar work for AOL and wondered if he should ask the Australian to step in. He also wondered about the portal, HongKong.com. He had been told that this portal was primarily for tourists. It could nicely complement the travel section of AOL, but could it also compete with AOL?

Getting the needed attention was also a problem at the AOL headquarters. AOL U.S. had been expanding rapidly, and demanded the full attention, time, and energy of key managers in the AOL organization. Many of these managers regarded the international operations to be of a lower priority than the fast-growing U.S. operations. Changing this "culture" was not going to be easy or fast.

Discussion Questions

1. How would you define the business that AOL is in? What are the key success factors (KSFs) in that business?

2. What are the main obstacles to international expansion in this business? Is the service mobile, with competitive advantages (FSAs and CSAs) intact?

3. How would you evaluate the market opportunity for AOL abroad? Where is demand strong? Local competition? Any first-mover advantages (FMAs)? Any positive or negative country-of-origin effects? Any lead country benefits?

4. What are the different foreign entry modes for the service? Their pros and cons?

5. What should AOL do in Hong Kong?

Part 3

Local Marketing

In Part Two, Foreign Entry, we focused on how the firm establishes its presence in foreign countries. Part Three now looks at the local marketing activities in the new countries.

The marketer is no longer at headquarters but located abroad. This shift has several important consequences. First, the marketer must analyze and segment markets, manage distribution channels, position products and services, develop effective promotions, capture market share, and increase sales. Even though the main strategic objective of the firm's presence in the country might be to check competition, monitor leading customers, or cross-subsidize a business elsewhere, the marketing job is still to be as successful as possible within the corporate constraints.

Second, the marketer must learn more about the environmental factors, as the political, financial, and legal restrictions on business can create unforeseen headaches. Also, the social and cultural networks among customers and competitors work in new and mysterious ways. The marketing infrastructure has developed under different conditions, so that the functions performed by wholesalers, retailers, advertising agencies, and other middlemen may deviate from expectations. Co-workers speak a different language, pledge allegiance to their own nation, believe in a different religion, and behave in unfamiliar ways toward each other.

Third, the focus is no longer on national boundaries. The local marketer is now concerned with the market—and the market may or may not be the same as the nation. The market could be larger, a free trade region or geographically close countries, or it could be smaller, ethnic or urban subgroups within a country.

In our discussion of local marketing in Part Three, the manager will be seen as a marketer who is working within the special constraints created by a new and unfamiliar environment, with an arm's-length relationship to the home office. Chapter 7 presents the conceptual models underlying the marketer's understanding of customers, how local buyer behavior research can be done, and how segmentation and positioning are affected when new foreign brands enter a local market. Chapters 8, 9, and 10 show how the different market environments in maturing, new growth, and emerging economies affect the local marketing effort. These chapters deal with strategy formulation, implementation, and execution under quite different conditions.

Chapter

Understanding Local Customers

"Buyers everywhere are the same—only different"

After reading this chapter, you will be able to:

1. Handle the conceptual rethinking that becomes necessary when trying to understand buyer behavior in a new local market.

2. Adapt existing concepts and models of consumer behavior by incorporating new data about the local environment uncovered by marketing research.

3. Do local market research with translated questionnaires, controlling for measurement problems, differences in how people respond to surveys, and problems of sample equivalence.

4. Tailor the segmentation scheme to the stage of the life cycle and to local attitudes, social norms, and existing loyalties.

5. Configure product positioning to account for the possible shifts in the market as the new brand enters.

Ultimately, customers in different places may want the same basic things, but specifically, their product and service needs and preferences vary considerably. The reasons for the variations lie in cultures and socioeconomic and geographic environments, that is, the conditions under which products and services are used and consumed. These locational and cultural factors affect buyer behavior directly and they demand a corresponding variety in local marketing activities. A good deal of the local marketer's hard work abroad involves adjusting his or her understanding of what customers specifically want as well as of how and why customers and competitors behave as they do.

This adjustment of one's understanding is not a matter of acquiring advanced marketing skills but of stretching basic conceptual skills. To the extent they are relevant and applicable, most of the technical marketing skills required in a local market are very similar to those at home. This chapter will not deal extensively with those. On the other hand, there are sophisticated conceptual skills needed, especially when the local market is a leading market. To understand customers and competitors, the local marketing manager needs to develop a "theory" of what motivates the people. As a start, it is useful to look back at relatively simple models of buyer behavior—stages of consumer decision making, how information is processed by consumers, what external influences play a role in buying decisions, and how the individual buyer handles risk-taking—and reevaluate the assumptions underlying these models. Such conceptual rethinking requires a stretch of the imagination and constitutes part of the learning that goes into marketing abroad. The local marketer abroad will develop larger conceptual skills, fresh ways of thinking about marketing, which in the future can be usefully applied in other parts of the world. Again, significant features of buyer behavior in the home market will also be better understood when contrasted against buyer behavior in other countries.

Disneyland Paris Tries to Rekindle Marketing Magic

Just a year and a half after opening its gates in 1992, the EuroDisney theme park situated at Marne-La-Vallee just outside Paris was teetering on the brink of bankruptcy. The company reported disappointing revenues and an unexpected $900 million loss for its first full year of operation. Unless it could negotiate financial help from its creditor banks and parent Walt Disney Company, EuroDisney would have to shut down. What went wrong?

At one point, EuroDisney seemed to be a promising concept: Based on Disney's success in Japan and North America, the company's theme park concept seemed to have worldwide appeal. However, park attendance at EuroDisney was less than expected, and the visitors who came did not spend much money. Perhaps most devastating to EuroDisney's bottom line was that the resort had constructed too many hotel rooms. Tourists did not book rooms for visits to the park as expected.

Disney responded by gradually modifying its marketing approach, renegotiating the financial package, and changing the way it treated its employees. For example, the familiar "Disney culture" was relaxed to fit the local culture and the expectations of the European managers and workers. The French "cast" (Disney employees) did not take lightly to the idea of being lectured about personal grooming, what makeup to use, and what clothes to wear even coming and going to work, as they felt such demands were tantamount to invasion of privacy. And European middle managers cared more about prestige and status than the democratic ideals of American management. For these reasons, Disney eased up on its strict behavioral code.

Other changes involved adaptation of the "product." For instance, the French—over one-third of EuroDisney's visitors—expect wine with their lunch, so the park loosened Disney's no-alcohol policy. And contrary to the relaxed eating habits of snacking Americans, the French visitors expected their lunch promptly at 1 p.m., causing long lines and some frustration. So, the park opened additional restaurants to accommodate local tastes and habits. In addition, EuroDisney invested in a spectacular new ride, the Space Mountain roller coaster, reportedly the fastest Disney attraction in the world, to generate excitement and lure new visitors. EuroDisney also set more affordable prices—up to 20 percent less for tickets, food, and hotel rooms.

A major change was a 1996 decision to disassociate the park from the "Euro" name. The Euro connotation had grown stale from overuse in various media and even turned negative as nationalist sentiments surfaced. Instead, Disney opted for a Frenchified institution. One move was to rename the park Disneyland Paris, drawing on the success with Tokyo Disneyland in Japan and doing away with all references to Euro. Another significant move was the release of a successful film adaptation of the Victor Hugo classic, *The Hunchback of Notre Dame.* Produced as the typical Disney cartoon, the feature-long film became a worldwide hit, and the French theme was emphasized in cross-marketed merchandise from the film. In addition, the traditional daily parade down "Main Street" in the Disneyland Paris park was changed to feature characters, music, and songs from the movie.

Naturally, the Frenchification also included considerable upgrades in the park's restaurants and menus and the Parisian (and Parisienne) visitor can now enjoy a truly French meal in the park, with accompanying fine wines and high prices.

Disneyland Paris has kept improving, adapting, and expanding its product line. One recent effort involves building a small town at the Val d'Europe location, to accommodate employees and visitors, but primarily to attract French families with attractive and affordable housing. The town square is a replica of the famous square in Lucca, Tuscany, and the houses are modeled on Regents Park houses in London. Streets are lined with well-groomed trees and flowers. The town and the homes are Disney's version of a traditional European town, complete with modern facilities and conveniences.

Despite the efforts, success continues to be elusive. And even though the experiences in France were helpful in creating Disneyland Hong Kong, opened in 2005, the differences between France and China were great enough to raise a host of new problems. Everybody loves Mickey, sure, but maybe not everybody wants to pay the price.

Sources: Roger Cohen, "Euro Disney '93: $90 Million Loss," *New York Times,* November 11, 1993, p. D4; Nathaniel C. Nash, "Euro Disney Reports Its First Profits," *New York Times,* July 26, 1995, p. D3; David Churchill, "Disney Shows How It Is Done," *The Sunday Times,* January 13, 2002. Damian Barr, "Buyers Flock to Disney's 'Copycat' New Town at Val d'Europe, Paris," *The Times,* March 28, 2008.

Introduction

Good marketing basics are good marketing basics everywhere. Really, local marketing is no different. Understand buyer behavior, treat the customer right, and offer quality that justifies consumer loyalty. At the same time, in the local marketing context, offer products and services appropriate to the local usage conditions and that have some local competitive advantage. Empathize with the customer's situation, don't fight it. Fight the headquarters instinct that says, "What we do is what they get." As we have said above, fight the kind of ethnocentric rigid mindset that translates to "since it's good enough at home, it's good enough here."

After that, though, it is good to remember that, as we saw in Chapter 3, it is not always true that one has to bend over backward to adapt to local cultural norms, do it exactly the way the locals want it, or forget about one's own heritage or pride in what one's company produces. There are times when breaking such rules is good. Foreign companies successful even in idiosyncratic markets warn against overplaying the "cultural sensitivity" theme. Offering superior value to customers is as good a plain recipe for success in Asian, Latin American, and European markets as in the United States.

It is just that what ultimately constitutes "value" may differ depending on actual usage conditions, what functions are really needed, and culturally contingent expectations about performance.

The diagram in Exhibit 7.1 demonstrates the various forces that need to be assessed when predicting buyer behavior in local markets. Apart from culture, other external factors (in the box on the left in the exhibit) are important as well, including economics, technology, and politics. These and related external influences determine the overall context in which the buyer makes purchasing decisions. This is one's general knowledge of the country environment.

The buyer box on the right in Exhibit 7.1 involves the psychological, demographic, and sociological models of man, which underlie marketer analysis of how customers should actually be approached. Buyer characteristics, such as personality, age, marital status, and life-cycle stage are internal determinants of behavior and will be useful when segmenting the local market. The buyer decision process relates to the way the buyer processes information and makes purchasing decisions, which is a major issue for the local marketer since people's decision processes vary across markets and cultures. This is the stage at which the marketing effort comes into play and can make a difference (see the local marketing effort box and arrow in the exhibit). Finally, as the purchasing decision is made, the firm's controllable marketing factors (including

EXHIBIT 7.1
Diagram of Major Factors Influencing Local Buyer Behavior

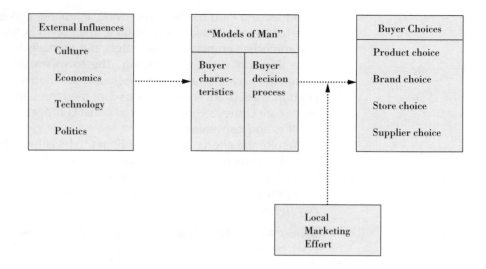

product design, price, promotion, and distribution) have become important influences on the choices that consumers make.

This chapter focuses on the middle box in the exhibit, the "models of man" that immediately underlie local buyer decision making and therefore should inform market segmentation and positioning decisions for the local marketer. The chapter starts by discussing the typical stages of a buyer decision-making process, and how the local economic and cultural environment changes the way people behave in each stage. We then discuss local market research, and review the problems and pitfalls of local buyer behavior research and the changes in approach necessary. Then the chapter explains how the entry of a new foreign brand into a local market can affect existing segments and brands' positioning. It demonstrates how the selection of local target segments and product positioning can be adapted to account for the likely shifts in perceptions and **preferences** when a new brand enters.

The chapter ends with a section identifying three significantly different market environments (mature, new growth, and emerging markets) and how the local buyer situation and the marketing tasks differ across these markets.

Buyer Decision Making

When analyzing local buyer behavior, the good news is that there is one simple truth about buyer behavior in all markets. It is that most people are doing what they do for a reason. Consumers perceive a link between behavior and desired results. Buyers do not choose products or services for no reason, even in the most fatalistic of cultures. In other words, buyers are **goal oriented.**[1]

Thus, if one can find out what people in a local market are trying to achieve, one can start to understand their behavior. The local marketer should start by attempting to find out what motivates buyers by asking them what and why they buy, or by observing them buying certain products or choosing certain brands. The results of such an investigation are sometimes startling, because of **hidden motivators** (see box, "Finding the Hidden Motivators").

Given the goal orientation, it is useful to see consumers as conscious decision makers. To analyze their decision-making process, an adapted version of the flowchart model of individual consumer decision making first introduced by Engel, Kollat, and

Getting the Picture

FINDING THE HIDDEN MOTIVATORS

When Marriott, the American-based hotel chain, opened up a new luxury hotel in Jeddah, Saudi Arabia, it became an instant attraction for local luminaries and international travelers. The grandly decorated lobby with its large windows and magnificent entrance drew not only travelers and hotel guests but also local visitors. The large number of people crowded in the lobby delayed check-in and check-out operations, and long lines formed in front of the service counter. Managers at the Marriott headquarters in the United States soon determined that it was necessary to install the quick check-out system already in place in many of its hotels worldwide, which would allow the guests to leave quickly without waiting in line.

But when the system was proposed to local management, objections were immediately raised. The managers explained that the customers of the new Marriott wanted to spend time in the lobby, to see and be seen, and to enjoy the status it conveyed; the long lines supplied a simple but legitimate reason for doing this. It was decided that a more rapid check-out process would be a negative benefit and the proposal was scuttled.

Source: Bruce Wolff, Vice President of Distribution Sales, Marriott Hotels.

Blackwell is helpful.[2] The authors distinguish between five sequential stages of a consumer decision process (see Exhibit 7.2).

This flowchart can be useful to understanding consumers anywhere. Buyers uncover needs or problems, look for alternative ways of satisfying their needs (where alternatives are available), evaluate the alternatives against each other, make a choice, and get satisfied or not. But local market environments differ, affecting both how these steps are taken and what starts and ends the process. The flowchart can't be applied the same way everywhere. Understanding the American consumer of detergents does not mean understanding the German consumer of detergents. To paraphrase the Romanian playwright Ionesco, consumers are not always consumers.

Problem Recognition

Problem recognition is what happens when an individual perceives a difference between an ideal and an actual state of affairs. The resulting tension generates a motive for the individual to start the buying decision process in order to satisfy the perceived need. New products often lead to tension and a recognized "problem," the way underarm deodorants suggest that "humans smell."

Because the core benefits may differ between local markets, the ability of a product or service to create a problem and satisfy the ensuing need will differ as well. The buyer may not perceive the offering as relevant or suitable, and the product will not be considered—the brand will not be included in the **evoked set.** Large, Western-style furniture, for example, is simply not considered in some Asian markets—it is more or less useless for the Asian consumers' needs in their smaller homes.

In other cases, the introduction of a new foreign product or service leads to an increased awareness of new possibilities. The "ideal state" is changed; the consumer is made aware of the deficiencies of what was available before; the buyer's aspiration level is raised; and the offering "educates" the consumer. The new entry has "created a need," although one can argue that at some deeper level there was a latent need for this offering.

EXHIBIT 7.2
Consumer Decision Process

Source: *Consumer Behavior,* Third Edition by James F. Engel, David Kollat, and Roger D. Blackwell, copyright © 1978 by The Dryden Press, reproduced by permission of the publisher.

Problem recognition → Search → Evaluation of alternatives → Choice → Outcomes

For the local marketer it is important to recognize that education about the core benefits might be necessary in order to create a demand for the product. But such promotion must first ensure that the core benefits are deliverable in the local market. To advertise "smooth ride" in a country with no paved roads will backfire.

This type of consumer education is not only about raising functional performance standards with new products or services. It is also about teaching the consumer to make finer distinctions between alternatives. These issues become important not only in the "evaluation of alternatives" stage of the decision process but also serve to create the stimulus for problem recognition. Increased awareness of what a product or service can deliver—a new shampoo with rinse and conditioning in one, for example—will create new criteria for choice. When entering a local market, such "firm-specific advantages" may have to be taught before the consumers recognize that they have a "problem" with their less-advanced existing products. This "need-stimulating" aspect of opened-up trade is one reason why foreign products are sometimes viewed by public policy makers as problem creators rather than problem solvers.

Search

The next step in the process, a consumer's search for alternative ways to solve the problem, is closely related to his or her level of involvement with the product category. For products with which involvement is high—because of a large money outlay, interesting products, or high **perceived risk**—search tends to be more comprehensive and time consuming, although previous experience and brand loyalty can reduce the effort. For convenience and habit purchases, the decision process is shorter, with little need for extensive searches or alternative evaluations.

However, the search intensity is also dependent on the perceived availability of alternatives. In markets that have been closed to trade, consumers have had less exposure to alternatives, and then searching for alternative choices has not been worthwhile. The motivation to search is low, and the consumers' incentive to make an effort needs to be stimulated by the new entrant. There is often an aversion to innovations in such markets, the old product having a monopolistic advantage the consumer initially assumes is based on true superiority. No one really wants to find out that the tea they like so much is really not as good as the new varieties on the market, or that the old beloved manual SLR camera is inferior to a new automatic. The introduction of these new versions often needs to be done with a fair amount of persuasion by a credible spokesperson.

One advantage for products with high global brand awareness is that this initial distrust is easier to overcome. In fact research shows that in Internet searches, brands with large market shares and well-known names receive a majority of the hits. In many emerging markets the consumers have long waited for the arrival of these brands. There is a pent-up demand that the newly arrived local marketer can capitalize on. It is important to realize, however, that such a release will not automatically translate into future success. Once the mystique of a long-desired goal is dissolved, the consumer is likely to engage in more sober evaluation of the product's benefits.

Evaluation of Alternatives

Once a new product or service is available to the consumer and is in the "consideration set" of alternatives, a highly involved individual will process the available information, matching the pros and cons of the alternatives against preferences. How this is done by people in different cultures is important to know, especially for positioning purposes.

There are several ways that consumers deal with these kinds of **multiattributed evaluations.** Consumers can, for example, use gradually less-important features to successively screen out alternatives (a "hierarchical" decision rule) or consider all features simultaneously (a "compensatory" rule). The choices depend on factors such as involvement, product experience, and time pressure. For example, in Internet searches savvy consumers can spend a long time comparing different brands on a number of features as well as price. Where customers are sophisticated, as in leading markets, compensatory evaluations are likely. By contrast, in follower markets, especially in the early stages of the product life cycle, consumer evaluations tend to be more hierarchical. A desirable country of origin or the cachet of a Prada or Nike can be sufficient for purchase.

Even when more attributes are evaluated, which features are important can vary considerably between markets. Part of the reason is that the core benefits can vary. While a Mercedes may be bought for its luxury status in the United States, a used Mercedes may be bought for its dependability in eastern Europe. While Levi's are practical and functional in the United States, they may convey status in Germany.

In markets such as North America, where many similar products vie for attention, simple functional superiority is not easy to gain or sustain. At this point, the consumer is likely to focus on less-tangible benefits, such as brand image, up-to-date features, and aesthetics. The success of the Jeep in Europe and Japan is not based on the functional aspects that might dominate in Australia but on its status. The local marketer should not forget the functional aspects, however, since quality performance is a necessary condition for purchase. Inferior performance on essential features will not go unpunished.

For low-involvement purchases, it is well known from market research that the time and effort required for a thorough evaluation of the available information are often too demanding on the average consumer,[3] who resorts to simplified rules of thumb, such as "choose the brand with the second-lowest price." Such rules are difficult to discern without keen observation on the part of the marketer and an understanding of the foreign culture (as well as his or her own culture).

Choice

The final choice of which alternative to select or try is typically influenced by social norms and by situational factors, including in-store promotions.

Social Norms

Where group pressures to comply are strong, as in many non-Western cultures, one can expect the influence of **social norms** to override any multiattributed evaluation. The social norms can be usefully analyzed by the so-called extended Fishbein model.[4] A flow diagram of the Fishbein model, as simplified and adapted to marketing, is given in Exhibit 7.3. Fishbein hypothesizes that a person's behavioral intention derives from the multiattribute evaluation of the alternatives but is modified by the social norms (Fishbein originally used the term behavioral norms) affecting the choice. The multiattribute evaluation results in an overall ranking of the alternatives in order of preference. As Exhibit 7.3 shows, the social norms involve two aspects: the social forces themselves and the individual's motivation to comply.

EXHIBIT 7.3
The Extended Fishbein Model

Source: Adapted from M. Fishbein and I. Azjen, *Belief, Attitude, Intention, and Behavior*, p. 334.

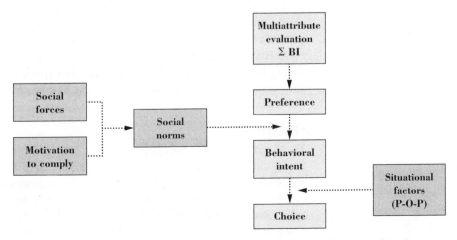

B = beliefs about product attributes; I = importance of the beliefs; P-O-P = point of purchase.

A family in Xinjiang, China, watching TV in their courtyard. In less-developed areas of the world, the electric power supply can be unreliable and the cable hookups are often makeshift. Nevertheless, many poor now consider TV a "necessity." Robert Van Der Hilst/Stone/Getty Images.

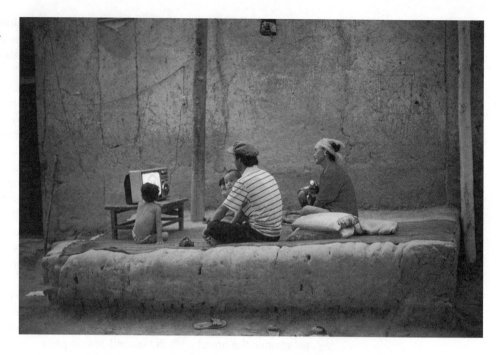

Social forces represent the pressures and normative suggestions that come from an individual's family, peer groups, social class, and other external forces. For example, an autoworker in Germany will face some pressure to buy a German car, regardless of individual preference. A successful pension fund manager in the City of London is more likely to wear an expensive analog Rolex than a cheap digital watch however versatile and reliable.

Motivation to comply relates to the willingness of the individual to listen to what others say and think. This is very much a matter of culture. In high context and homogeneous cultures where norms are both enforceable and enforced, the motivation to comply will usually be great. Most people will know what products, features, brands, and stores are "acceptable," and adhering to the norm will have tangible benefits. Buying the right brand brings memberships, invitations, and opportunity. You "belong." Individualism, on the other hand, which represents low motivation to comply with others' demands, will be costly, since sanctions can be enforced. You are an "outsider," not always unattractive, however, in low-context cultures where sanctions can't be effectively imposed. James Dean, the late actor and quintessential American outsider, is used by Levi's to advertise its jeans in Japan. Paradoxically, but not surprisingly, for the "young rebels" in Japan, wearing Levi's means that they "belong."

The high value placed by Confucian cultures on the importance of social norms suggests that, in general, Eastern cultures show much more of an impact from social norms than do Western cultures. This was borne out in one study of athletic shoes comparing behavioral intentions of Koreans and Americans. As hypothesized, Koreans showed a significantly greater willingness to consider peer group influence than did Americans.[5]

Outcomes

The degree to which consumers achieve satisfaction with their purchases also varies across cultures, as recent customer satisfaction surveys amply demonstrate. This is not surprising, considering what factors make for high satisfaction.

The most obvious determinant of satisfaction is the actual performance of the product or service when used or consumed. But basic functionality does not necessarily mean that satisfaction is high. As we saw in the evaluation section, where product and service quality are high, basic performance is not necessarily a big factor in consumer evaluations. That the car starts in the morning is usually no cause for rejoicing—unless, of course, one's expectations are very low, as must have been the case with buyers of the notorious Trabant in former East Germany. Satisfaction is very much influenced by the **expectations** of the buyer.

Customer satisfaction tends to be high when expectations are exceeded and the consumer is pleasantly surprised. It is important to recognize that the competition existing in the local market helps set the hurdle for the new arrival's acceptance. The new entrant has to offer something new or special. This is why entries from a leading market have a better chance of success than others.

Another determinant of satisfaction is previous experience—or lack of it—with the product category. To some extent, this experience helps form the expectations about acceptable performance. In markets where products have only recently become available, expectations are based on reputation, not previous experience. This, however, does not mean that expectations are low. Unverified stories and word-of-mouth information in emerging markets have made many consumers hold unrealistic expectations about the general happiness they will experience when markets are flooded with products. Any one product's performance can generate dissatisfaction when expectations are unrealistically high.

The lack of supporting infrastructure can also be a problem in emerging and developing markets. The promise of a new shampoo might only be realized where showers are available and the water is clean. Expecting personal computers to significantly raise white-collar productivity might be unrealistic in societies where computer literacy in the educational system is low and company managers lack skills.

In the end, the consumer is back to the core benefits and the degree to which the use and consumption experience manage to validate those essential benefits, and possibly satisfy other, more esoteric desires. Consumer well-being is the aim of all marketing, and it is important that the new local marketer realize the challenge that the local consumer is confronted with. In many cases the need is not yet recognized by the prospective buyer, in others the new product may not be able to deliver because of lack of infrastructure support, and in yet others the new product may be out of reach of the customer's budget. New products and brands not only bring improvement and a better quality of life; they also create problems that need to be solved and wants that need to be satisfied. The local marketer must make sure the firm's offering can solve the problems and satisfy the needs.

Local Buyer Research

As in purely domestic marketing, to better understand the local customer requires marketing research. The marketing research expenditures in the top three countries from different regions are shown in Exhibit 7.4. With the exception of China, where marketing research is still in an embryonic stage, the expenditure rankings correspond closely to the size of the population in the countries. There are some differences between regions, however, with Latin America showing lower expenditures relative to population size, reflecting their lower GDP.

The typical marketing research process is shown in Exhibit 7.5. Except for the last stage, data analysis, all the stages can be affected by a foreign environment. The stages will be discussed in order (secondary data was covered in Chapter 4).

Problem Definition

It is common to distinguish between the marketing decision problem and the marketing research problem. The decision problem in a market might revolve around the question of what to do about declining sales, and the research problem might be to assess customer attitudes and satisfaction levels. The same research might not be applicable in another market, even though the decision problem is the same.

EXHIBIT 7.4
**Marketing Research
Expenditures in Top Three
Markets, by Region (2002,
US$ in millions)**

Source: *Marketing News,* July 15, 2004,
pp. 12–13.

Europe	
United Kingdom	1,755
Germany	1,490
France	1,260
Asia–Pacific	
Japan	1,037
China	302
Australia	272
Latin America	
Mexico	243
Brazil	188
Colombia	47
North America	
United States	6,307
Canada	449
World total	**16,610**

For example, over several years the California Almond Growers Exchange was unable to penetrate the Japanese market even though there were no real trade barriers and domestic competition was weak or nonexistent. Planning to do a study of consumer attitudes toward almond nuts, the association first decided to do a marketing audit, tracing the sales through the distribution channels. The real cause of low sales was found

EXHIBIT 7.5
**The Stages of Consumer
Research**

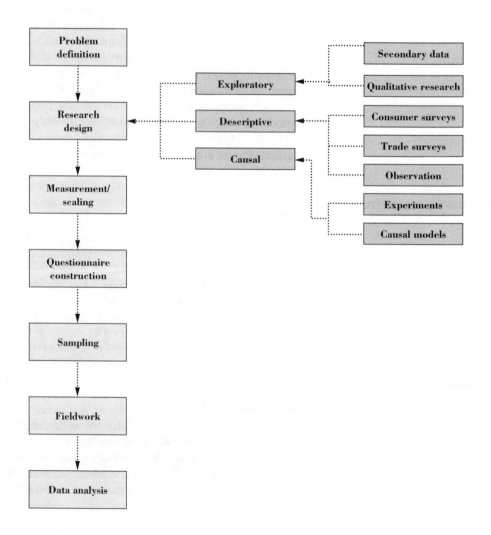

to be the lack of distribution coverage. A deal was struck with Coca-Cola Japan, which had in place 15,000 salespeople and over 1 million sales locations throughout Japan. The association has now captured over 70 percent of a growing market.[6]

Qualitative Research

Although there are many forms of qualitative research, the well-known **focus groups** have become standard for initial **exploratory research** in many markets.[7] Recruiting carefully screened users and potential buyers of a product, research companies gather 8 to 10 individuals around a table to share opinions about a product or service. Guided by a moderator's questions, the participants are encouraged to voice any misgivings about a design or dislikes about a color pattern, to point to ambiguities in translated advertising copy, and so on. The responses are taped, usually on video, and the sponsoring marketer can observe the proceedings from behind a one-way mirror.

In foreign markets, focus groups have the advantage of being relatively inexpensive, can be completed quickly, and can reach local pockets of the total market. Unfortunately, they can also constitute an **unrepresentative sample** because typical screening criteria are incorrect in the new environment or are not implemented correctly. For example, when the Italian maker of Campari, the aperitif, asked for a series of focus groups of "buyers" in the United States, the local research firm could not find any buyers to recruit. Agreeing to lower the screen to "those aware of the name," the Campari maker was dismayed to find that the users recruited knew too little about the beverage to give any useful information. The Italian company refused to pay for the research.

In general, the small nonrandom sample sizes of focus groups make assumptions about representativeness tenuous at best. It is also important to remember that respondents get paid, and even if it is usually a small amount (typically $25 in the United States, about the same in Europe—the amount varies by city and by respondents' occupation, more than by country), this will tend to inhibit the expression of negative feelings. Another problem is that the moderators—and the research firms—are usually specialized in certain products and customers, and may be less than ideal for other consumer groups. A German company sent the videotapes of five focus groups to a Japanese client, who was surprised to observe the dominating attitude of the moderator toward his respondents. The moderator, not without pride, explained to the perplexed sponsor that he usually dealt with corporate customers for industrial products, not teenagers discussing audiotape design.

These and related problems can be overcome with careful planning of the focus groups. Representativeness in terms of geographical areas is usually dealt with by selecting certain cities that are leading markets for the products. In the United States, New York and Los Angeles are often viewed as trendsetters—in Germany, it is Berlin and Munich. Few U.K. studies can avoid London, and the same is true for studies in France (Paris), Italy (Milano), Spain (Madrid), and Scandinavia (Stockholm).[8] The moderators chosen should be professionals who can identify in some way with the subjects and make them feel at ease. The amount paid should be sufficient to make a difference and thus be an incentive, but not so large as to invite praise. The screening criteria should be related to the level of market sophistication. To get consumers in emerging markets to help adapt the product is often pointless, since they usually have little experience and no confidence in their own judgment. By contrast, local users in leading markets are often ideal key informers for the adaptation of a global product.

Consumer Surveys

Surveys of relatively large ($n = 5,000$ and above) random samples drawn from a **sampling frame** of representative product users constitute the core component of **descriptive market research.**

Whether administered by mail, phone, or in person, such surveys are used for a variety of marketing purposes, including segmentation and positioning, concept testing, and customer satisfaction and competitive product evaluation. But the problems with survey research methods in certain markets have been well documented.[9]

Getting the Picture

TELLING IT LIKE IT IS

The researcher followed the family on the weekly Saturday shopping trip to the local open-air market. The goal was to document spending patterns for various household products by urban families in a large Mediterranean country. Walking by the various stalls offering all kinds of produce, clothing, and electronic products, the observer dutifully recorded the family's bargaining for a better deal and the actual prices paid. Returning home, he discussed the trip with the husband and double-checked the figures. The husband corrected him, doubling the price for the shirt bought, and lowering the price for the red wine. "But I saw how much you paid," protested the researcher. "You don't understand," responded the husband. "I can't wear such a cheap shirt, and I can't spend that much on wine." Survey responses sometimes do not match reality.

Source: Doctoral researcher in anthropology at the University of California at Berkeley.

There are many cultural aspects affecting the application of the kind of direct questioning involved in the typical consumer survey. In high context cultures the idea that one can understand consumers from their responses to a formal survey is naive. Open-ended questions are often left blank by respondents in hierarchical cultures who are not used to explaining their reasoning or are afraid of being too transparent. Answering truthfully to a stranger is not necessarily proper in some nations, especially those in which an authoritarian regime has made people wary of questions. Americans have no hesitation about fabricating an opinion on the spur of the moment—Europeans will leave questions unanswered "since they have no direct experience using that product." Asked for their "perceptions" of the gas mileage of a certain car model, Japanese respondents may ask for time to check automobile specifications in a car magazine.

Face-to-face interviews are prone to bias because of **demand characteristics**, that is, respondents who try to answer in a way that satisfies the interviewer (or the respondent's own ego). Such demand pressure is handled differently in different cultures. Western people are known either to try to please ("yea-sayers") or go against ("nay-sayers") according to their attitude toward the assumed sponsor. Respondents everywhere may try to answer more or less conscientiously, often opting for the least inconvenient multiple-choice alternative. Or they may lie. For example, respondents may be eager to show off a socially desirable image (see box, "Telling It Like It Is").

One drawback of surveys can be the attitude of the respondents toward the study itself. In Western as well as Eastern societies, there will be prospective respondents who refuse to divulge any opinions simply because they "do not want to be taken advantage of," distrusting the function of market research. In more insidious cases people will consent to participate only to fake their responses so as to distort findings. To handle these problems of respondent noncooperation, the firm does well to interview the research firm carefully so as to thoroughly understand the general sentiment in the local market vis-à-vis formal **questionnaires.** It is also a good idea to monitor the process by observing some pilot interviews if at all possible.

Trade Surveys

The quickest, least expensive, and most commonly used method for learning about customers in a market is to do a **trade survey,** interviewing people in the distribution channels and trade associations. These people can often explain the basic segments in the market, who the buyers are, the type of buying processes used, and the sources of buyer information. They can answer the who, when, what, and how-much questions but will usually not be able to more than speculate about the why. These people provide a good starting point for further data gathering and analysis.

In the United States, the use of middlemen for information about consumers is usually limited to the sales and scanner records of retailers and wholesalers. More attention is usually given to middlemen in the business-to-business sectors, if only because there are a limited number of ways to use formal research methods on business customers. In many other countries, the middlemen are a much more important—and perhaps the only—source of information.

In countries with less social mobility and less diversity than the United States—and that includes a majority of the world's nations—key informants in the trade are good sources of information about buyers. Cultural homogeneity makes it possible to get a sense of people through a few personal interviews, since the informants usually can speak for a large share of the population. Furthermore, social stability means that many middlemen have been in the same position for many years, and they can speak from experience. In the United States, by contrast, people are diverse and no one person can speak for the many subcultures. And people are likely to change jobs frequently, not building up much experience in the trade.

Interviewing middlemen is, it should be remembered, only one aspect of getting data on the trade. Store visits to observe customers and talk to them directly, inspecting store layouts and atmospherics, and collecting sales and turnover data are other activities that yield market information.[10]

Observational Studies

Research involving **direct observation** of customers buying and using existing products can be very beneficial. Existing products give important clues to customer preferences, especially in mature markets. In markets where access is free and the customers have well-developed preferences, the sales records of the various products constitute, in fact, a shortcut to understanding customer preferences. The products "reveal" consumer preferences.[11]

By analyzing best-selling products—and those that don't do so well—the local marketer can start to identify which features of a product are valued by the market and which are not. Although these points are in a sense obvious, Western marketers have been slow in exploiting this potential. The Japanese have been much faster. The Japanese successes in Western markets have not been based on thorough market research in the traditional sense.[12] Instead, they have learned about customers by analyzing the products that are successful in Western markets.

For example, the way drivers enter their cars has a direct bearing on design. The Japanese small cars were built originally for men, who can easily put one leg in and then sit down in the driver's seat pulling the other leg after. But in the West, the small Japanese cars became popular with women, whose skirts prohibited such an entry. Thus, the Japanese had to make the door larger, to allow the woman driver to first sit down, and then pull both legs in. This redesign came about when Toyota engineers traveled to Los Angeles and watched people get in and out of their cars. Similar research lies behind the lowered threshold of the trunk (to make it easier to slide baggage in and out), the coffee cup holders in cars, and the height of the fastback door.

This approach has been very successful. As a leading American businessman once said, "The Japanese have gotten the American consumers' number." But for the practice to work well in general, it is necessary to assume that current products reflect customer preferences. This assumption is likely to hold only in mature markets with no entry barriers. Where customers have been deprived of products because of trade barriers, consumer preferences might well display a yearning for something different. The same holds where economic development is too low for some products to be affordable. Such latent preferences can't be uncovered through observation. A better way would be informal interviews with experts in the trade.

Explanatory (Causal) Research

Explanatory marketing research attempts not only to describe attitudes and preferences but also to explain why buyers have certain attitudes toward a product or why they prefer certain brands. The aim is to determine whether—and the extent to which—a marketing variable such as price or advertising has an effect on variables such as, attitudes, brand preference, or purchase. Typical research designs involve experimental methods and the estimation of links in causal models. The problems attacked tend to be the fine-tuning of price levels, testing of alternative advertising copy and visuals, and the connection between after-sales service and customer satisfaction. The basic notion underlying the research is that the local marketer needs to understand exactly what impact the contemplated marketing activities will have on the results.

In new foreign markets this kind of research is rarely worth the cost. The decisions to be made are much too basic to need that much fine-tuning, and the action alternatives facing the local marketer are often rather crude. The exception is advertising if there is good reason to try out some alternatives because the local consumers might not be receptive to the kind of advertising coming from headquarters. Storyboard tests with alternative copy, for example, are not expensive and can be done quite quickly.

For the firm with long-established presence in the country, on the other hand, the fine-tuning involved in causal research can very much be worthwhile. Then the standard marketing research approaches can be applicable. The use of scanner data and associated buyer panels, through which household spending patterns and demographic profile can be matched against sales promotion activities in stores, is becoming possible in most mature economies. The emergence of global markets has in this respect been accompanied by a globalization of market tracking measures, and the local marketer will do well to check out the available services in the new market.

Measurement and Scaling

Measurement errors are likely to occur in any research, and the problems are magnified when dealing with a foreign culture. Here we can only suggest the flavor of the problems involved—expert publications in international marketing research should be consulted for further reading.[13]

Equivalence Issues

There are four **measurement equivalence** issues in cross-national marketing research:[14]

1. **Construct equivalence.** Construct equivalence refers to the question of whether the variables used for measurement have the same meaning across countries. For example, an American might "love" his car—not what a Japanese would say. Solution: Use synonyms that have direct translations.
2. **Translation equivalence.** Translation equivalence refers to the problem that there may not be an equivalent word in another language. For example, few languages make a distinction between "assertive" and "aggressive." Solution: Use simple words.
3. **Calibration equivalence.** Calibration equivalence refers to the comparability of category cutoffs. The use of official exchange rates can mean that a high income in one country might be barely above the poverty level elsewhere. Solution: Most market researchers go for adapted ranges, but then the comparability can be lost.
4. **Score equivalence.** When is a score of "5" in one country equal to a score of "5" in another country? Solution: Use deviations from the average score in the country, although this also makes it difficult to compare levels between countries.

Attitude Research

These problems of equivalence become particularly important in attitude research. Attitude research involves finding out what people in a country think and feel and how they perceive competing products and services. The research typically involves a representative sample of the population and survey questionnaires with one or more batteries of attitude scales.

In **attitude scaling,** the way of measuring an individual's intensity of feeling vis-à-vis some product or company, very basic factors can create headaches. Using numbers for scale points raises questions of cultural significance of different numbers (the number "4" carries negative connotations for some Chinese, for example, as "13" does for Western people). It also raises questions about the validity of numbers as indicators of emotions or value ("he's a 10" may be easy to grasp for Westerners used to quantification, confusing to others). There is always the question about how many scale points should be used. Since scaling numbers are designed to reflect underlying emotions, one would like to have an approximate verbal equivalent of any number (or—complicating matters much further—does the culture have "emotions without words"?). There is also the problem of equal-appearing intervals. Even in Western applications, it is not always clear that the difference between a "1" and a "2" is equal to that between a "6" and a "7."

These are only a few of the problems associated with one technical question about scaling. On a more basic level, the cognitive and emotional concepts measured—such as attitudes and preferences—might not be equivalent across cultures. In some cases the corresponding mental state does not exist. For example, "assertive" is a notorious English language concept for which there are few counterparts in any language. In other cases, the same word has a different meaning—"love" has a much stronger sense of "obligation" in Asia than in the self-centered West. In yet other instances the foreign language has a much more nuanced set of emotions—the word "disagree," which is commonly used in attitude scales, can be expressed in at least five different ways in Japanese.

Questionnaire Construction

The questionnaire employed in the typical consumer survey needs to be carefully pretested, especially if it is simply a translation from a standardized version in another country. Translated questions are often very prone to misunderstandings, even when literally correct, because of differences in context.

The local market researcher should first translate the original questionnaire into the foreign language and then have someone else "back translate" the questionnaire into the original language. Differences will appear, and they have to be resolved through discussions, pretests with target respondents, and repeated **back translations.** It is common for this process to yield a questionnaire of different length than the original, since different languages require different levels of polite indirectness. Even in the new European Union, language differences continue to create problems (see box, "Getting to Know the European Consumer").

Typical screening questions such as, "Do you do most of the shopping in this household?" can be ambiguous because the meanings of the words "most," "shopping," and "household" depend on cultural norms and the family's economic situation. These difficulties can be overcome by careful design of the questionnaire and painstaking pretesting.

"What do you like about it? How can it be improved?" A new Colgate package is tested in Brazil. As markets globalize and consumers face more choices, the importance of research increases. Courtesy of the Colgate-Palmolive Company.

Getting the Picture

GETTING TO KNOW THE EUROPEAN CONSUMER

Despite all the talk about an integrated European Union, the European consumers are hardly homogeneous. According to Tom Broeders, an independent marketing consultant in Belgium, "Europe is a collection of different cultures related to language and habits."

Marketing research in Europe must blend flexibility, intuition, and knowledge of what information resources exist in each country. The researcher's first lesson is that multiple sources are usually necessary. For demographic data about European consumers, researchers must rely mainly on national and regional government agencies, such as each country's national statistical institute. However, privacy concerns in some countries limit data availability. In Germany, for example, the notion of a census was rejected for many years—Germans feared government interference in their private lives.

Language differences make the creation of pan-European survey questionnaires difficult and expensive. These problems will diminish as the European nations begin providing more data for cross-national comparison and market researchers test pan-European strategies. One example is the joint European development of a standardized questionnaire that is administered annually and collects comparable data on a number of sociodemographic, political, and economic indicators. Called the Eurobarometer, it was originally written in French and English, translated by native speakers into 12 other languages, then back translated into French and English to check for subtle variations in meaning.

Sources: Blayne Cutler, "Reaching the Real Europe," *American Demographics,* October 1990, pp. 38–43; Thomas T. Semon, "Red Tape Is Chief Problem in Multinational Research," *Marketing News,* February 14, 1994, p. 7; and Lisa Bertagnoli, "Continental Spendthrifts," *Marketing News,* October 22, 2001, pp. 1,15.

Sampling

The lack of comprehensive and reliable sampling frames from which to sample respondents has long been holding back market research in many countries. Telephone directories are not very useful when few households have telephones. Postal addresses won't work well when people are mobile, when one address covers many individuals in extended families, and when postal service is unreliable.

However, the problems involved in getting acceptable sampling frames are being gradually solved with the emergence of service firms that specialize in developing lists for direct marketing and survey research purposes. The increasing importance of global direct marketing has encouraged American research firms to invest in the development of lists in many foreign countries, using alliances and joint ventures with local entrepreneurs. The researcher who pays for the use of such lists can ask that customized lists be developed, using standard target **segmentation criteria** about geographic location, income, family size, and so on. Although an emerging country such as China might still be relatively uncharted, consumers in many other countries in Asia and Latin America are becoming accessible to global market researchers.

One particularly elusive issue in international sampling is the question of sampling equivalence. **Sampling equivalence** refers to the question of whether the samples in different countries are comparable. This is different from the question of whether the samples are each representative of the different countries, or whether they have the same socioeconomic characteristics. For example, one might want to get responses from a sample of the primary decision maker for a product in each country. But if the primary decision maker is different in the different countries, one should not aim for the same subset in each country. Thus, research first needs to be done to identify the correct sample member and then let the sample be drawn from different subgroups in different countries. Even though this makes it difficult to compare results across countries, at least the appropriate target segments are reached.

Fieldwork

Throughout the research process, and in particular when it comes to the fieldwork, usually the firm will work with a market research firm, sometimes a full-service advertising agency. The choice is usually between a branch of a multinational firm and an independent local firm. The multinational firm has the advantage when cross-national comparability is desired. Nevertheless, the local firm will often be more cost-efficient and will sometimes have better knowledge of local situations (even if, in general, the multinational firm will be able to attract very good local talent because they can offer career opportunities abroad). Independent local firms will in many cases be part of a wider international network of local research firms, and working with local firms in many different countries can still provide cross-country comparability without too severe coordination problems.

As always, it is important that the administration of the survey be carefully monitored, since it is tempting for interviewers to cheat by returning bogus questionnaires, especially when they get paid by the number of completed interviews. But in many countries it is difficult to completely control the process. In the United States, for example, it is not always legal for a representative of the sponsor to listen in on a phone interview, or even tape it, without the respondent's explicit permission. Callbacks making sure that a respondent was interviewed can be made, provided the respondent agrees.

In most developed markets, many of the large research firms, such as ACNielsen (part of VNU NV), have branches that can carry out local research as advanced as that at home. Some of the largest firms are given in Exhibit 7.6.

Accounting firms are also potential sources for data—Ernst & Young, for example, does a considerable amount of international market research in services—as are legal professionals, or industry-specific research firms (wood products, automobiles, airlines, and computer software, for example). The reason specialization occurs is simply that the research firms have to invest a great deal of time to be sufficiently well informed about the global situation for an industry, and the payoff comes when more than one client can be served on the basis of the same material. This does not mean that the firms send the same customized report to all clients—rather that the customization is done on top of a common data set for the industry.

EXHIBIT 7.6 **Selected Top Global Research Organizations in 2002 (rank is the rank by revenues among all global research organizations)**

Source: Jack Honomichl, "Top 25 Global Research Organizations—2002," *Marketing News,* Aug. 18, 2003.

Rank 2002	Rank 2001	Organization	Headquarters	Parent Company	No. of Countries with Subsidiaries or Branch Offices[1]	Full-Time Employees (research only)[2]	Global Research Revenues[3] (US$ in millions)	Percent Change from 2001[4]	Percent of Global Revenues from Outside Home Country
1	1	VNU NV	Haarlem	Netherlands	81	32,625	$2,814.0	1.2%	99.0%*
2	2	IMS Health Inc.	Fairfield, Conn.	U.S.	75	5,900	1,219.4	3.9	60.0
3	3	The Kantar Group	Fairfield, Conn.	U.K.	62	6,000	1,033.2	20.7	69.7*
4	4	TNS (Formerly Taylor Nelson Sofres plc)	London	U.K.	54	9,063	908.3	0.2	80.6
5	5	Information Resources Inc.	Chicago	U.S.	20	3,600	554.8	20.2	25.8
6	6	GfK Group	Nuremberg	Germany	51	4,879	528.9	4.2	63.5
7	8	Ipsos Group SA	Paris	France	35	3,828	509.0	14.0	83.1
8	7	NFOWorldGroup Inc.	Greenwich, Conn.	U.S.	40	3,900	466.1	3.0	63.9
9	10	Westat Inc.	Rockville, Md.	U.S.	1	1,600	341.9	17.9	
10	9	Nop World	London	U.K.	6	1,648	320.0	211.3	70.3

[1]Includes countries that have subsidiaries with an equity interest or branch offices, or both.
[2]Includes some nonresearch employees.
[3]Total revenues that include non-research activities for some companies are significantly higher. This information is given in the individual company profiles.
[4]Rate of growth from year to year has been adjusted so as not to include revenue gains or losses from acquisitions or divestitures. Rate of growth is based on home country currency and includes currency exchange effects.
*Estimated by Top 25.

Finally, it is important to emphasize that as economic growth occurs, mature markets with differentiated demand requiring formal and scientific market research applications will emerge in many countries. As consumers grow more sophisticated, so necessarily must the techniques used to track their preferences.

Local Market Segmentation

The basic management question in market segmentation is to find homogeneous groups of customers with high demand potential for the firm's products or services. Differing segments exist, of course, in all country markets. People's lifestyles, usage levels, demographics, and attitudes vary among any population. But to be useful for marketing purposes, targeted segments have to possess the following characteristics. They have to be:

1. Identifiable (What distinguishes them?).
2. Measurable (How many belong to each segment?).
3. Reachable (How to distribute to, communicate to, each segment?).
4. Able to buy (Can they afford it?).
5. Willing to buy (Do they want it?).

It goes without saying that each of these requirements, except possibly the last one, can be difficult to satisfy in emerging and less-developed markets. If, in addition, the potential customers in these markets have only weakly developed preferences—because of a lack of exposure to products and services—research to identify market segments will be akin to searching for Atlantis, the mythical sunken city.

Segmentation Criteria

The construction of market segments can be based on many different criteria. Whether global or domestic, the most useful segmentation criteria are those that accomplish three things:

1. The criteria help to recognize the factors influencing the segment's buying behavior, both consumption level and choice between competing brands. "Political party affiliation" may be a less useful criterion than "Number of children" from this perspective.
2. The criteria should be reflected in published data so that the size of the segment can be calculated. "Lifestyle" may be less useful than "Level of education" in this regard.
3. The criteria should facilitate the selection of adequate media through which marketers can communicate with the segment. This requirement suggests that "Teenagers" is a more useful criterion than "Social class."

In reality, firms tend to use several criteria in combination. The most common bases for segmentation are the following (in order from the most basic country factor to more specific market factors).

Economics

The most basic local segmentation criterion is still economic development. Even for low-priced consumer necessities such as detergents, soap, and toothpaste, level of GDP per capita matter. The reason is that it is difficult to globalize marketing mixes where package sizes have to be downsized, distribution channels are different, and some communications media are unavailable.

Demographics

The age and family structure in different countries also play an important role in determining local segments, especially in terms of size. The fact is that for many consumer products, age and family size are strong determinants of consumption levels. As in the case of economics, published data are usually available and quite reliable. But they rarely determine the choice between competing brands. Demographics, like economics, help determine consumption levels, but they do not always satisfy the first requirement of a good segmentation criterion, that is, influencing choice between competing brands.

Values

One general culture-related criterion popular in local segmentation is value-based segmentation. Because individual values are so basic, the derived segments are often found to be similar across countries. What differs is the percentage of a population that falls into each of the segments. A typical list of value-based segments is the following from Roper's Worldwide Global Consumer Surveys (with percentages of the global population in parenthesis):

Strivers (12 percent)—Emphasis on material and professional goals. Most common in developing Asia.

Devouts (22 percent)—Emphasis on religion and tradition. Least common in developed Asia and Western Europe.

Altruists (18 percent)—Emphasis on social and welfare issues. More common in Latin America and Russia.

Intimates (15 percent)—Emphasis on family and personal relationships. More common in America.

Fun seekers (12 percent)—Emphasis on hedonistic pleasure and fun. Most common in developed Asia.

Creatives (10 percent)—Emphasis on knowledge and technology. More common in Western Europe.

Value-based segments have the advantage of being stable over time. They are also applicable for a wide variety of products, but because they represent very fundamental characteristics of individuals they need to be coupled with more product-specific criteria in order to be effective.

Ethnicity

One cultural factor that has become increasingly important as globalization progresses is ethnicity. As people move away from their home country in search of better work and living conditions elsewhere, they start forming enclaves of their home culture in the new country. Gradually, as more immigrants arrive and as economic progress continues, these ethnic groups become large and prosperous enough to justify targeting as separate segments. In the United States, for example, a number of firms target the Hispanic population. The same opportunity is of course open also for companies from the old home country, which is why you can find food products from many countries in any large urban supermarket in the developed world. As the ethnic groups grow, their influence spreads to the rest of society, and we all learn to like Mexican flautas, Korean kimshi, Moroccan couscous, and Indian pan. Gradually, the influence diffuses further and affects not only what we eat but what we see and hear (see box, "Global Entertainment: Bollywood and Telenovelas").

Peer Groups

Even though a lot has been said in the media about the emergence of global segments of people with no regard for nationality and culture, the reality is that people still care about their peer groups. Famous companies such as Benetton, Nike, Levi's, and British Airways have promoted their universality only to find that customers still want to be recognized for what kind of groups they belong to, and want their brands to reflect that. Thus, global segments are still often defined in terms of group belonging: Benetton's target is generation X, Nike's runners are "rebels," Levi's target

Getting the Picture

GLOBAL ENTERTAINMENT: BOLLYWOOD AND TELENOVELAS

It was once safe to assume that every moviegoer and TV watcher around the world sought entertainment from Hollywood films and American must-see TV. Emerging markets and Third World markets caught a glimpse of a "better life" via the window of multimillion-dollar Hollywood movies and American prime-time TV. This is changing. America is taking a backseat when it comes to the film and TV industry.

Enter Bollywood. Every year, the Indian film industry turns out 800 to 1,000 films. These films reach an audience of such staggering size no one seems to be sure how big it is, with estimates ranging from 12 million per day to the 23 million per day suggested by the *Encyclopedia of Indian Cinema*. And that doesn't count the global communities of nonresident Indians, estimated at upwards of 3.6 billion souls.

Bollywood outside of India first manifested itself in the United Kingdom, where the largest ethnic minority is Indian. Films such as *Bend it Like Beckham, Monsoon Wedding,* and *Moulin Rouge* embrace Bollywood influences. Indian music is becoming more mainstream through hip-hop samples and pop song remixes. *Bombay Dreams,* a musical about the Indian movie industry imported from London and revised for American audiences, has brought Bollywood to Broadway. The millions of South Asians who live in America retain a very vibrant link with their motherland through Bollywood. They keep their culture alive watching Bollywood movies.

Bollywood is giving viewers an alternative to the typical Hollywood movie laden with computer-generated explosions and car chases. You know you're watching a Bollywood film when you're hearing people bursting into song in all kinds of unlikely places and seeing a successful mixture of genres (comedy followed by music followed by dance followed by romance followed by drama) that's called the masala style and would cause less sure films to collapse into chaos.

Jumping from Indian movies to Mexican television, there is a surging popularity in the "telenovela" all over the world, targeting Spanish-speaking ethnic populations.

The telenovela or television novel (the usual but inapt translation is soap opera) offers audiences love, drama, and hope, through plots that unite the right couples, where good triumphs over evil, people can be redeemed, and impossible love is given fruition. The programs are exported via Miami or Mexico to the various Spanish-language markets in various countries. In heavily Hispanic cities such as Los Angeles, the telenovela sometimes gets higher prime-time ratings than any English-language network. They are also dubbed into other languages and sent to networks in Singapore, Thailand, Canada, the Philippines, Brazil, and the Czech Republic. Just as the Bollywood movies, the telenovelas threaten the assumed global dominance of American entertainment. In the Czech Republic, for example, English-language soap operas have only achieved market shares of a few percent while telenovelas may garner 50 percent of viewers.

During the 1990s, the global audience was watching U.S.-produced *Friends* and *Baywatch* on TV, and Julia Roberts and Tom Cruise in the movies. Now we are watching *Betty la Feya* (Ugly Betty) and *Un Amor Real* (A True Love) on TV, and Indian stars Aishwarya Rai and Sanjay Dutt in the theaters.

Sources: Kenneth Turan, "By Way of Bombay; a UCLA film series is proof: Bollywood has arrived with a flourish," *Los Angeles Times,* April 15, 2004, p. 36; Susan Carpenter, "Hollywood, Meet Bollywood," *Los Angeles Times,* April 15, 2003, p. 37; Vivek Wadhwa, "My Entertaining Education in Movieland," *BusinessWeek Online,* August 11, 2004; Jonathan Schlefer, "Global Must-See TV: Telenovelas," *The Boston Globe,* January 4, 2004, p. 12.

are the American wannabes in foreign countries, and British Airways targets Anglo-Saxon businesspeople around the world. These segments are no longer bound by country borders, but they have a strong group identity nevertheless. Furthermore, global peer groups influence choice between competing substitutes more than actual consumption levels.

Lifestyle

As economic development takes place, and buying behavior involves more than simple necessities, consumers start developing their own lifestyle. They choose products and brands on the basis of what they want, not simply on what they need. Consumers become more sophisticated and fickle, and markets move toward the maturity stage. Their AIOs (attitudes, interests, and opinions), not economics or demographics, determine what they choose.

Lifestyle segments tend to be similar to value-based segmentation, although more geared to consumption patterns. For the 1994 European market, the research agency

RISC developed the following six pan-European lifestyle segments (the relative size of the segments in percent):

Traditionalist	18 percent
Homebody	14 percent
Rationalist	23 percent
Pleasurist	17 percent
Striver	15 percent
Trendsetter	13 percent

Because it is not tied to a specific product category, this type of general lifestyle segmentation, although suggestive for creative advertisers and copywriters, does not always link directly to particular consumption choices. It is typically employed in combination with other segmentation criteria.

Benefits

A more product-specific criterion useful in local segmentation is one that focuses on the benefits sought. In general, different people may look for different benefits, but local segments can be identified that are looking for roughly the same benefits. Anita Roddick's Body Shop seems to have identified a global segment that looks for "green" products in personal care, with benefits both in terms of functional quality and environmental care. One problem in using benefits sought for segmentation is that it requires good understanding of the local markets, solid marketing research, and a product that scores high on the specific benefits sought. It also works less well in technology products, where consumers do not have enough product understanding to give useful information about benefits. Often, as in the Body Shop case—and in other cases such as Swatch watches, PC software, and mobile phones—consumers do not comprehend the benefits until the products have been introduced on the market.

Local Product Positioning

Product positioning refers to the activities undertaken by the marketer to communicate the features and the benefits of the product and the image of the brand to the actual and potential customer. A product's or brand's "position" refers to the place in a customer's mind that the brand occupies, that is, the customer's perception of the brand. For example, does the customer think the brand is of high quality, expensive, good value, durable? To what extent is the brand fun, prestigious, global? And so on. The marketer will of course have a planned position in mind, but it is not always easy to make sure it is the one the customer ends up with. Ford Explorer's marketers might intend for people to see a powerful, sporty, and safe design but some customers might find the SUV boring, truck-like, and unsafe.

In some ways, local product positioning is no different from positioning in any market. The firm has to identify what attributes and benefits the customers look for, and how the product or service measures up on these features against competition. But there is one principal difference with globalization. The local marketer is looking for cost savings and demand spillovers from coordination of global products and brands. This means there are limits to how much features and communications can be adapted to consumer preferences. What the local marketer needs to find out is how far he or she can stray away from buyer preferences before sales and market shares get punished. For this assessment it is necessary to understand how local product positioning relates to local customer choice.[15]

The Product Space

To describe a brand's position marketers typically use so-called **perceptual maps,** also known as product space maps.[16] We will show some of these maps below. These

EXHIBIT 7.7
Market Positioning Map of Selected Automobile Brands (1970s)

Source: John Koten, "Car Makers Use 'Image' Map as Tools to Position Products," *The Wall Street Journal,* March 22, 1984, p. 31. Copyright © Dow Jones & Company, Inc. Reproduced with permission of Dow Jones & Co. Inc. in the format Texbook via Copyright Clearance Center.

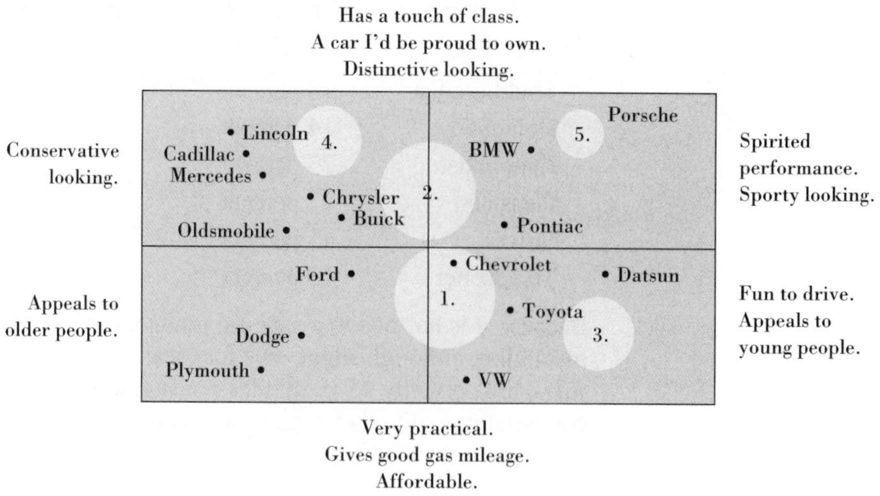

two-dimensional maps are based on customers' ratings of competing brands on the various attributes that are important, and show the position of each brand on the map. The **product space** also indicates the preferences of the customers, as well as what kind of combination or "bundle" of attributes they prefer (more power, better mileage, etc.).

An example of a product space for automobiles is given in Exhibit 7.7.[17] The axes of the diagram are described in terms of the various attributes that people consider important. The location of the various automobile marques on the axes—their "position" in product space—is derived from people's ratings of the makes on the various attributes. For example, a Lincoln scores high on "Has a touch of class" and is also high on "Appeals to older people." The map also shows the preferences of different market segments through ideal points circles. The size of the circles reflects the size of the market segment. The location of the circles—which is drawn from people's expressed preferences—shows what kind of attributes would appeal to the segments. For example, the relatively small segment 5 would like a "Sporty looking" car which still "Has a touch of class."

Strategic Implications

The distances in the diagram between makes reflect the degree to which they compete. For example, the Lincoln seems to compete more with Cadillac than with Mercedes, but not at all with VW. Similarly, the cars that are located closer to a segment are better positioned to capture that segment. Lincoln most likely would sell better in the relatively small segment 4, really a niche segment, than in the largest segment, number 1.

These implications need to have some credibility or "face validity," helping managers to trust the results. As always with market research, managers need to exercise judgment in relying on the kind of advanced data analysis represented by the product positioning technique. Some portion of the results should match what managers already know.

The traditional idea of product positioning was that new entries simply were added somewhere in the consumer's existing perceptual maps. This is still the basic rationale behind the use of these maps. Identify the existing competitive positions and consumers' ideal points, and then target a "hole" in the market where no competitor is positioned but where a potential target segment of customers is located.

Exhibit 7.7 shows the American automobile market in the middle of the 1970s. The Japanese makes Toyota and Datsun (now Nissan) are positioned close to the third-largest segment in the market. This segment desires good gas mileage and a car that is both sporty and fun to drive—preferences that the Japanese-made cars had already targeted in their home market. But even though these two makes were well positioned relative to American makes, there is also a "gap" open in the back of the Japanese makes (segment 3); a gap that Honda was to fill.

Overcoming Mispositioning

A drawback of a standardized global product or brand is typically that it is not adapted to the actual preferences in a particular foreign market—it is not adapted to the local market preferences. In marketing language this means that it is **mispositioned** relative to the preferences or **ideal points** of the consumers in their **perceptual space**.[18] This is why local managers often claim that adaptation is necessary because "in our market, customers are different."

Why would customers buy a mispositioned offering if they have alternatives closer to their ideal? The usual answer is a lower price. This is one reason why one can see so many "special discounts" in various markets around the world, as firms try to sell products that customers don't really want. But as many marketers have learned, inducing the customer to purchase a less-desirable product by offering a discounted price often leads to customer dissatisfaction, as the favorable discount is soon forgotten but the less-desirable product remains.[19]

Another and more common reason why mispositioned global products are attractive to potential consumers is brand image and status. While local products and services may be better adapted to the market, the global competitor with a strong brand name offers "value-added" status that the locals can't easily match. To lower perceived risk and cognitive dissonance, the doubts that you might have bought the wrong thing, a well-known global brand name will often do much better than a local brand. The same is often true for conspicuous consumption, showing off—and to impress someone special.

Changing the Product Space

The product space graph is a picture of the local marketplace at one point in time. It is a static representation of the market. In practice it is unlikely that customers' perceptual maps stay unchanged when a new product or brand enters the market, especially if it is a global brand. More often than not, the introduction of new "stimuli" (again using the standard consumer psychology terms) will change the perceived product space. The space gets elongated or compressed, and new dimensions might be added. Think of cell phones, for example. What features (**salient attributes**) you look for today are quite different from what they were just a few years back; back then it might have been size and battery length, now it might be screen resolution and Internet access.

The elongation of the dimensions defining the product space occurs when the new entrant offers more of the salient features. This happens frequently, since the global products often incorporate the newest technology.

A good illustration of extending the product space is the introduction of the Honda Accord in the U.S. auto market in 1976. Exhibit 7.8 shows a positioning map with the Accord and several competing models included.[20] As can be seen, the Accord offered a unique mix of characteristics, being much more economical than even the Japanese

EXHIBIT 7.8
How the Honda Accord Extended the Product Space

Source: Johny K. Johansson and Hans B. Thorelli, "International Product Positioning," *Journal of International Business Studies* 16, no. 3 (Fall 1985), pp. 57–75. Reprinted by permission of the *Journal of International Business Studies.*

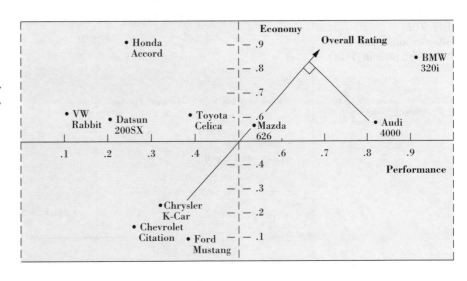

competitors. As the overall rating vector shows, the BMW was the preferred choice—but the price was much higher for that car. The American makes were not competitive in this market segment without large rebates.

The new entrant is likely to offer novel features as well. This means that new salient dimensions are added. Products that do not offer the new features (digital audio, antilock brakes, and low cholesterol) will be left out of the consumers' evoked sets. Older brands, often local-only, are now mispositioned. They might not even register in the appropriate evoked set any longer. The main players are global. See, for example, what is happening when Starbucks moves into a new neighborhood or a new market and the local cafes that don't offer the same selection or quality close shop.

The advances in technology restructure the space in other ways. Features that in the past could be had only by giving up other features can now be accommodated without sacrifice. In automobiles, comfort can now be had without compromising fuel economy. Safety does not require heavy car bodies. Noiseless air-conditioning is available. These innovations are not necessarily limited to global products—but the advantage of the global product is that it can incorporate these advanced features at a reasonable cost to the consumer, because of scale economies.

Again, the American automobile market offers an instructive illustration. Exhibit 7.9 shows the market in 1968, before the two oil crises in the 1970s. As can be seen, there is little evidence of miles-per-gallon or economy as a buying criterion. This can be contrasted with the earlier map in Exhibit 7.7. In Exhibit 7.7 "economy" was emerging strongly, opening up a window for the Japanese entrants. At the same time, there was no need to give up on sporty performance, as would have been the case in 1968.

Changing Customer Preferences

Finally, the entry of a new global brand might well change customer preferences in addition to perceptions. Traditionally, consumers' tastes and preferences were formed by brands and products they could see, touch, and buy. With global communications, things have changed. Global media and sponsorships of events ensure that many people will be exposed to a brand name even before they have seen the real product. For example, TV advertising during the Superbowl in 1998 reached an estimated 150 million people. Although some countries blacked out the commercials shown, there were considerable spillovers from satellites and Direct TV. The 1998 World Cup drew an audience of over 250 million viewers for a month, not all in the target market for Mars's candy bar Snickers but many of those viewers are now aware of the Snickers name. The fact is that a brand name can cross trade barriers much more easily than a product or service can. This means that a pent-up demand for a branded product in a protected market can easily be created by global communication of the brand name.

EXHIBIT 7.9
Illustration of Joint Space of Ideal Points and Stimuli (1968)

Source: Paul E. Green and Donald S. Tull, *Research for Marketing Decisions,* 3rd ed. (Englewood Cliffs, NJ: Prentice Hall, 1975), p. 611. © 1975. Adapted by permission of Prentice Hall, Inc., Upper Saddle River, NJ.

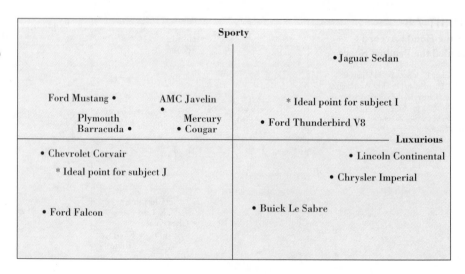

For younger people, global brands such as Coca-Cola and McDonald's have become as familiar as the local brands. The advantage of a local-only brand is that the immediate recognition and subliminal identification that comes with familiarity and tradition is then achieved also by the global brand. As one little boy from Hong Kong happily exclaimed upon arriving in Los Angeles: "They've got McDonald's here, too!" It is not surprising that many of the global segments in consumer goods refer to markets for children and teenagers—toys, clothes, shoes, and music. For them, "tradition" means last-year's styles.

The final choice usually involves social norms. These norms can favor the domestic or the foreign brand. Where patriotic feelings run strong, domestic brands are usually favored. Where peer group pressure is for status brands, global brands are usually winners. In either case, if the buyer is highly motivated to comply with social norms the brand suggested by the norms will be preferred. In Exhibit 7.7, Mercedes, whose positioning relative to segment 4 is weaker than Lincoln's, is a good example. The mispositioning is not compensated for by price—the Mercedes being more expensive than the Lincoln—but by brand image and the status conferred upon the owner.[21]

Three Local Market Environments

The "External Influences" in Exhibit 7.1 combine to create the local buyer environment which makes for different buyer behavior and different marketing effectiveness. It is useful to distinguish between three significantly different market environments. They are *emerging* markets, *new growth* markets, and *mature* markets (see Exhibit 7.10).

Marketing Environment

As can be seen from the exhibit, the *emerging markets* are characterized by low levels of product penetration, weakly established marketing infrastructure (especially in terms of advertising media and distribution outlets), relatively unsophisticated consumers with weak purchasing power, and weak domestic competitors. Even with high tariffs, foreign products are potentially making inroads.

New growth markets in NIEs, by contrast, show greater purchasing power and more demanding customers. Consumers can buy more than just basic products, and brand names are important. Because of a high growth rate, there are some strong domestic companies, and foreign competitors face entry barriers. These markets possess a rapidly developing marketing infrastructure.

Most *mature markets* show slow growth apart from some high-technology markets. The customers in these mature markets are pampered by strong domestic and global companies who compete intensely for customer satisfaction. Although some of these markets are still protected by trade barriers, customers are able to choose from among the best products in the world and tend to be confident about their

EXHIBIT 7.10
Three Market Environments

Feature	Emerging	New Growth	Mature
	Market Environment		
Life cycle stage	Intro	Growth	Mature
Tariff barriers	High	Medium	Low
Nontariff barriers	High	High	Medium
Domestic competition	Weak	Getting stronger	Strong
Foreign competitors	Weak	Strong	Strong
Financial institutions	Weak	Protected	Strong
Consumer markets	Embryonic	Strong	Saturated
Industrial markets	Getting stronger	Strong	Strong
Political risk	High	Medium	Low
Distribution	Weak	Complex	Streamlined
Media advertising	Weak	Strong	In-store promotion

ability to make informed purchase decisions, such as, for example, separating high value from high price.

Even though there are many similarities, new growth markets in the NIE countries differ from the typical growth markets in mature economies. The latter are usually driven by product innovation and high technology, while NIE growth markets result from a general economic expansion and require much less product innovation.

Marketing Tasks

Execution of the key tasks for the various marketing functions differs in these three environments. Exhibit 7.11 shows some of the main dimensions. The marketing effort by the local marketer in emerging markets tends to focus on the development of a **marketing infrastructure,** which involves enlarging market reach through improved logistics and establishing functioning distribution points. Analyzing customer needs involves primarily on-location visits to assess feasibility of entry, and a major question is whether the company should be the first to enter or wait and let others go ahead building up the infrastructure. A question mark is the degree to which disposable per capita incomes are sufficient for the market to take off, and the product offered is often a simplified and less-expensive version. Often the primary aim is to make the product available in selected locations, typically urban, and then build up from there by creating awareness and positive word of mouth.

In new growth markets, the typical strategic aim of the local marketer is generic **market development** efforts involving promotional efforts to get more customers into the market and generate economies of scale for an existing product line. The aim of market research is to identify the dominant design requirements of demographic subgroups, and the local visits are meant to gain distribution in the leading channels. The product line now includes the top of the line, even though entirely new products are not yet common. Image, high price, and special service are all aspects that can be used to distinguish the offering at the high end, while the lower-end products tend to be less attractive because of the competition from domestic or other foreign brands.

In mature markets, the strategic focus for the local marketer is typically on gaining **market share.** This is when fine-tuning of the marketing effort is necessary; and sophisticated market research, new product introductions to develop new niches, and value-based pricing are used to appeal to a fickle and difficult-to-satisfy customer.

EXHIBIT 7.11
Dominant Marketing Dimensions

| Task | Market Environment | | |
	Emerging	New Growth	Mature
Marketing analysis:			
Research focus	Feasibility	Economics	Segmentation
Primary data sources	Visits	Middlemen	Respondents
Customer analysis	Needs	Aspirations	Satisfaction
Segmentation base	Income	Demographics	Life style
Marketing strategy:			
Strategic focus	Marketing infrastructure	Market development	Market share
Competitive focus	Lead/follow	Domestic/foreign	Strengths/ weaknesses
Product line	Low end	Limited	Wide
Product design	Basic	Advanced	Adapted
New product intro	Rare	Selective	Fast
Pricing	Affordable	Status	Value
Advertising	Awareness	Image	Value-added
Distribution	Build-up	Penetrate	Convenience
Promotion	Awareness	Trial	Value
Service	Extra	Desired	Required

Country Markets

Mature markets include the so-called triad countries in Western Europe, North America, and Japan, and also Australia and New Zealand. The NIE growth markets comprise what used to be called the "four Asian tigers" (Hong Kong, South Korea, Singapore, and Taiwan, the original newly industrialized countries or "NICs") and also other fast-growing markets such as Chile and other Latin American countries, several ASEAN countries, some Middle Eastern countries, Israel, and South Africa. Growth markets also include poorer western European countries such as Greece and Portugal for which the EU membership has been very beneficial.

Emerging markets include the newly democratized postcommunist nations, including Russia and China (still communist but with a more open economy), and other developing countries (for example, Vietnam). Many emerging markets have a history of central control that still colors their approach to free markets.

This classification is not necessarily the one used by public agencies or global companies. For example, "emerging" sometimes refers to all markets outside the triad, and an emerging country such as China can also show high growth. Furthermore, there are product markets with high growth in mature economies, especially in high-technology industries. Nevertheless, the split serves to highlight the main distinctions with marketing relevance. The correspondence to the product life cycle (PLC) is useful for marketing purposes, since the marketing problems encountered reflect the PLC stage the markets are in.

Summary

As a new local entrant, the global marketer's assumptions about reasonable buyer behavior have to be put on hold. It is important to "zero-base" one's mind to the extent possible and approach buyers with an open mind. It helps to remember that most people make purchase decisions for a reason, however vague or hidden. Understanding new customers abroad often involves getting to know complete strangers.

It is important for the marketer to look at how the consumer goes through the usual steps of decision making, from product evaluation to final choice. At each stage of this decision process the environmental differences between different local markets will affect how the consumer acts and what happens next. Understanding the consumer abroad involves not only rethinking how people make decisions but also how local peer groups and other social influences affect the decision-making process.

Market research in local markets often needs to be adapted to the local conditions even more than the products or services offered. This is because the typical research methods—focus groups, surveys, interviews—involve people-to-people interactions and thus culture and language come into play. Back translating questionnaires is a necessary but not sufficient requirement. Efforts also have to be made to ensure equivalence in measurement, scaling, and sampling. As economies develop and grow more advanced, market research can also become more sophisticated and in-depth. This is possible because respondents become more familiar with products and services, but is also necessary as consumers grow more sophisticated and demanding of variety in their choices.

To identify local segments for targeting, various criteria can be applied. Some general data are usually available about the basic consumer groups in the local market, but the analysis also has to consider competition and the firm's strength in a segment. The aim is to predict the market share that the company can be expected to capture, given the planned positioning.

Local product positioning involves predicting how segments abroad might react to the arrival of a foreign, perhaps global, brand. Several scenarios are possible, including a shift in the product space as new features are introduced. The global marketer has to evaluate the risk that a standardized product might lead the brand to be mispositioned, and to assess the degree to which its brand can counter the lack of ideal fit. If not, price may have to be reduced—or, of course, the product could be adapted to local preferences. Some local adaptation is often necessary in today's markets, as localization is becoming the new imperative.

For local marketing purposes it is useful to divide countries into three categories: advanced economies with basically *mature* markets, newly industrialized economies (NIEs) with strong *growth* markets, and developing economies with gradually *emerging* markets.

Key Terms

attitude scaling, *220*	goal oriented, *210*	preferences, *210*
back translation, *221*	hidden motivators, *210*	product positioning, *227*
calibration equivalence, *220*	ideal points, *229*	product space, *228*
construct equivalence, *220*	market development, *232*	questionnaires, *218*
customer satisfaction, *215*	marketing infrastructure, *232*	salient attributes, *229*
demand characteristics, *218*	market share, *232*	sampling equivalence, *222*
descriptive market research, *217*	measurement equivalance, *220*	sampling frame, *217*
direct observation, *219*	measurement error, *220*	score equivalence, *220*
evoked set, *211*	mispositioned, *229*	segmentation criteria, *222*
expectations, *215*	motivation to comply, *214*	social norms, *213*
explanatory marketing research, *219*	multiattributed evaluations, *212*	surveys, *217*
exploratory research, *217*	perceived risk, *212*	trade surveys, *218*
focus groups, *217*	perceptual maps, *227*	translation equivalence, *220*
	perceptual space, *229*	unrepresentative sample, *217*

Discussion Questions

1. The text suggests that people buy what they buy for a reason. Why do college professors in the United States favor bag lunches while college professors elsewhere have lunch in a restaurant? Why do Americans of both sexes favor (light) trucks, while Europeans like sporty sedans with stickshifts, and Asians prefer light and smooth cars?

2. To what extent do you think consumers in different countries will take to shopping on the Internet? For which part of the consumer decision process would the Internet be especially relevant?

3. How would you go about doing consumer research to find if a product has different core benefits for different local markets abroad? Motivate and explain your research design.

4. How would you go about finding out whether consumers in a country are against global brands or not? Whether they are anti-American brands only? Whether they are more in favor of domestic brands than before?

5. When discussing product positioning, the chapter used examples of Japanese cars entering Western markets. Using this framework, how would you analyze the reception given to the Japanese luxury marques (Acura, Infiniti, Lexus)? What did change in people's perceptions—and what did not?

Notes

1. The idea of goal-oriented consumer behavior is by no means new—see, for example, Hall, 1976, or Solomon, 2008. But it is important to keep it in mind, since some non-Western religions have a fatalistic bent, which tends to make human action pointless. Usunier, 1996, provides an excellent treatment of the way different cultures view human behavior and the implications for marketing.

2. See Blackwell et al., 1995.

3. There are many studies of "information overload," including Jacoby et al., 1974, and Keller and Staelin, 1987.

4. See Fishbein and Ajzen, 1975. An early application in marketing is presented in Ryan and Bonfield, 1975.

5. See Lee and Green, 1991.

6. See Alden, 1987.

7. Malhotra, 1993, Chapter 6, offers a thorough discussion of qualitative research with an international flavor.

8. The actual cities chosen depend of course on the type of product involved, where the target segment is located, and what the available resources are. In general, however, foreign entrants tend to have a predilection for choosing the capital or big cities, because that is where media headquarters and opinion leaders are located.

9. See Craig and Douglas, 2005. This book and the one by Churchill and Iacobucci, 2004, are drawn on for much of the material in this section.

10. Johansson and Nonaka, 1987, give examples of how the Japanese companies do this.

11. The "revealed preference" theory in microeconomics is based on the same notion.

12. The examples of the Japanese approach to marketing research here and in several other places in this chapter are mainly drawn from Johansson and Nonaka, 1996.

13. See, for example, Craig and Douglas, 2005.

14. This section draws from Steenkamp and Ter Hofstede, 2002.

15. The standard terminology is used here with "product" positioning also covering services. Ries and Trout, 1982, give the classic account of the psychology of positioning. A good treatment of the basics of positioning techniques can be found in Urban and Hauser, 1993. The Reatta case in Urban and Star, 1991, is an excellent example of the empirical application of positioning.

16. Most marketing texts will have a discussion of the basics of product space maps. See, for example, Kotler and Keller, 2006.

17. This illustration is adapted from Koten, 1984.

18. In an interesting study of consumers in France, Korea, and Spain, Du Preez et al., 1994, showed how ideal points and attribute importance in automobiles differed between the countries. A standardized car model offering similar features in all three countries would have been mispositioned in at least two of them.

19. This is the problem of extrinsic (discounted price) versus intrinsic (less than ideal features) motivations, a topic researched in consumer behavior. See, for example, Szybillo and Jacoby, 1974.

20. Adapted from Johansson and Thorelli, 1985.

21. Global brand names also give the manufacturers more clout in international distribution channels, a topic we will return to in Chapter 15.

Selected References

Alden, Vernon R. "Who Says You Can't Crack the Japanese Market?" *Harvard Business Review,* January–February 1987, pp. 52–56.

Blackwell, Roger D.; Paul W. Miniard; and James F. Engel. *Consumer Behavior,* 9th ed. Fort Worth, TX: Harcourt College Publishers, 2001.

Brooks, John. *Showing Off in America.* Boston: Little, Brown, 1981.

Churchill, Gilbert A., Jr., and Dawn Iacobucci. *Marketing Research: Methodological Foundations,* 9th ed. Mason, OH: South-Western, 2004.

Craig, Samuel C., and Susan Douglas. *International Marketing Research,* 3rd ed. New York: Wiley, 2005.

Dichter, Ernest. *Handbook of Consumer Motivations.* New York: McGraw-Hill, 1964.

Du Preez, Johann P.; Adamantios Diamantopoulus; and Bodo B. Schlegelmilch. "Product Standardization and Attribute Saliency: A Three-Country Empirical Comparison." *Journal of International Marketing* 2, no. 1 (1994), pp. 7–28.

Fishbein, Martin, and Icek Ajzen. *Belief, Attitude, Intention, and Behavior.* Reading, MA: Addison-Wesley, 1975.

Fornell, Claes. "A National Customer Satisfaction Barometer: The Swedish Experience." *Journal of Marketing* 56, no. 1 (January 1992), pp. 6–21.

Hall, Edward T. *Beyond Culture.* Garden City, NY: Anchor, 1976.

Hanssens, D. M., and J. K. Johansson. "Rivalry as Synergy? The Japanese Automobile Companies' Export Expansion." *Journal of International Business Studies,* Third Quarter 1991, pp. 503–26.

Hochschild, Arlie Russell. *The Managed Heart: Commercialization of Human Feeling.* Berkeley: University of California Press, 1983.

Hofmeister, Sallie. "Used American Jeans Power a Thriving Industry Abroad." *New York Times,* August 22, 1994, p. A1.

Jacoby, J.; D. E. Speller; and C. Kohn. "Brand Choice Behavior as a Function of Information Load." *Journal of Marketing Research* 11 (1974), pp. 63–69.

Johansson, Johny K., and Ikujiro Nonaka. "Marketing Research the Japanese Way." *Harvard Business Review,* May–June 1987, pp. 16–22.

————. *Relentless: The Japanese Way of Marketing.* New York: HarperBusiness, 1996.

Johansson, Johny K., and Hans B. Thorelli. "International Product Positioning." *Journal of International Business Studies* XVI, no. 3 (Fall 1985), pp. 57–76.

Keller, K. L., and R. Staelin. "Effects of Quality and Quantity of Information on Decision Effectiveness." *Journal of Consumer Research* 14 (1987), pp. 200–13.

Koten, John. "Car Makers Use 'Image' Map as Tool to Position Products." *The Wall Street Journal,* March 22, 1984, p. 31.

Kotler, Philip, and Kevin Keller. *Marketing Management,* 12th ed. Upper Saddle River, NJ: Prentice-Hall, 2006.

Lee, Chol, and Robert T. Green. "Cross-Cultural Examination of the Fishbein Behavioral Intentions Model." *Journal of International Business Studies* 22, no. 2 (1991), pp. 289–305.

Malhotra, Naresh K. *Marketing Research: An Applied Orientation.* Englewood Cliffs, NJ: Prentice Hall, 1993.

Mitchell, Arnold. *The Nine American Lifestyles.* New York: Macmillan, 1983.

Nash, Nathaniel C. "Bunge & Born: More Mindful of Latin America." *New York Times,* Jan. 3, 1994, p. C5.

Ries, Al, and Jack Trout. *Positioning: The Battle for Your Mind.* New York: Warner Books, 1982.

Robinson, Eugene. "In Argentina, Private Firm a Power Player; Bunge & Born, a Multinational Wields Clout in Nation's Economy." *Washington Post,* December 6, 1989, p. G1.

Ryan, Michael J., and E. H. Bonfield. "The Fishbein Extended Model and Consumer Behavior." *Journal of Consumer Research* 2, no. 2 (1975), pp. 118–36.

Solomon, Michael R. *Consumer Behavior,* 8th ed. Upper Saddle River, NJ: Prentice-Hall, 2008.

Steenkamp, Jan-Benedict E.M., and Frankel Ter Hofstede. "International Market Segmentation: Issues and Perspectives." *International Journal of Research in Marketing* 19 (September 2002), pp. 185–213.

Szybillo, George J., and Jack Jacoby. "Intrinsic versus Extrinsic Cues as Determinants of Perceived Product Quality." *Journal of Applied Psychology* (February 1974), pp. 74–78.

Urban, Glen L., and John R. Hauser. *Design and Marketing of New Products.* 2nd ed. Englewood Cliffs, NJ: Prentice Hall, 1993.

Urban, Glen L., and Steven H. Star. *Advanced Marketing Strategy.* Englewood Cliffs, NJ: Prentice Hall, 1991.

Usunier, Jean-Claude. *Marketing Across Cultures,* 2nd ed. London: Prentice Hall, 1996.

Womack, James P.; Daniel T. Jones; and Daniel Roos. *The Machine That Changed the World.* New York: Rawson Associates, 1990.

Chapter

8

Local Marketing in Mature Markets

"The customer is king"

After reading this chapter, you will be able to:

1. Analyze the increasingly fickle consumer in mature markets where "*The customer is king*" and the most advanced marketing tools and techniques apply.
2. Understand how mature markets are often different because the consumers want to—and can afford to—get back to their cultural roots.
3. Recognize that despite surface similarities between mature markets, fine-tuned segmentation and positioning strategies are necessarily localized.
4. Use trade blocs as important determinants of regional market segments, encouraging the development of pan-regional products and programs.
5. Develop regional strategies by identifying specific segments that are similar across markets.

As we saw in the previous chapter, good marketing at home or in one country is not necessarily good marketing elsewhere. Since each country has its own special character, the local marketing job is never exactly the same anywhere. But for some countries in a few broad categories, the job is in fact more approximately the same. This chapter deals with the similarities and differences across mature markets.

Barilla: The Global Pasta Powerhouse

Barilla Holding Societa per Azioni, the planet's Italian pasta producer and purveyor, keeps its plate (and its customers' plates) full. It dominates the pasta market in Italy, the leading market for pasta. It also dominates the rest of Europe and is the number one pasta seller in North America.

It is striking to see a family-owned Italian company succeed in a mature market like the United States, where food company Kraft spends $850 million a year on advertising—nearly five times Barilla's U.S. sales in 2001. But its success in the saturated and competitive American market has been achieved through excellent but traditional marketing efforts: supporting a high-quality product with strong advertising and extensive distribution coverage.

Parma-based Barilla started out as a small regional pasta-maker in 1877. Over the years its fortunes waxed and waned. In the 1970s the company was sold and then bought back by the family. By adopting novel packaging techniques and using celebrities in its advertising (filmmaker Federico Fellini, opera star Placido Domingo, tennis champion Steffi Graf, and others), by the mid-1990s Barilla had become the market leader of Italy, with a 41 percent market share. But for Guido Barilla, chairman of the Barilla Group, the real future of their company was in conquering the U.S. market. He had attended Boston College and spent a year in the United States selling pasta to specialty stores and Italian restaurants in the 1980s.

Encouraged by a former Procter & Gamble executive who had married into the family, Guido began exporting Barilla spaghetti and fettuccine to America in 1996. Within three years Barilla had become the dominant pasta seller in America. By 2002 it claimed a 15 percent share of the $1 billion market in the United States, twice that of its closest competitor, Ronzoni.

The recipe behind this success was innovative in one respect. According to traditional thinking, American customers tend to be price conscious about food, and it's hard to persuade them to pay more even if the quality is better. But Barilla studied the experience of Kikkoman, the leading Japanese soy-maker, which had been successful in the United States maintaining quality and prices. Following this lead, Guido decided not to compromise on quality and price, but instead try to educate the American consumers about quality pasta. Barilla spent heavily on advertising, especially in daytime television to target its biggest customers: housewives. "Too many people think that a 'poor' product like pasta is a commodity—they don't know how a good pasta should taste. And we can handle big spending on advertising," says Guido.

Barilla's initial sales in America got started via high-end Italian restaurants where the demand was for a high-quality pasta that holds up well between the kitchen and the table. Most restaurants bought their ingredients through the fiercely competitive food-service industry. By getting chefs to demand its pasta, Barilla's "pull" strategy put food-service middlemen in a position where they had no choice but to offer it.

Barilla also spent a lot on purchasing shelf space in supermarkets, a common U.S. practice where slotting fees can be over $1 million per stock item. Barilla is known for its eye-level "facing" row of blue boxes and the variety of pasta it sells. It didn't limit itself to just the spaghetti and elbow macaroni that most Americans were used to, but offered linguine, spaghettini, tortellini, penne, and other varieties. Also, Barilla was the first pasta-maker to take advantage of nationwide suppliers such as Wal-Mart and Costco to market its products across the entire country.

A problem in early 2004 threatened Barilla's sales in the United States. American consumers began embracing the Atkins diet, where carbohydrates such as bread, pasta, and rice were shunned. Barilla counterattacked the trend by hiring Young & Rubicam to launch advertisements that would play on Barilla's Italian heritage. The $8 million ad campaign focused on Barilla's sauces, fresh ingredients, and premium-quality pasta. The ads did not mention the Atkins diet nor offer any defense. It has so far been a successful attempt, positioning the proud Italian company above fad diets and fleeting food trends.

Barilla leveraged its firm-specific advantages while adapting to the local American market. The company had to adapt the American style of supply chain management and distribution in order to cater to the huge American market. Through consistent product quality, advertising to create more demand, a thorough understanding of local retailing, and its national heritage, Barilla rose to dominance in a saturated and mature market.

Until 1992, Barilla did only 10 percent of its business overseas. By 2004, well over half of Barilla's sales came from outside Italy. The company is now looking to feed China's hungry billion.

Sources: "Barilla Holding Societa per Azioni," *Hoovers Online,* Internet Online, Available from **http://premium.hoovers.com/subscribe/co/factsheet.xhtml?COID=91684;** Deborah Orr, "A Passion for Pasta," *Forbes,* November 25, 2002; Sonia Reyes, "Atkins-Defying Barilla Touts Sauces Via TV Push," *Brand Week,* April 12, 2004; "Academia Barilla Opens As World's Foremost Center of Excellence for All Things Concerning Italian Gastronomy; State-of-the Art International Center to Celebrate, Promote and Safeguard Italian Food and Culture," *PR Newswire,* May 4, 2004; "Italian Barilla Posts 4.4 Billion Euro Turnover 2003," *ANSA English Corporate Service,* March 18, 2004; **www.barillagroup.com.**

Introduction

In this first of three chapters that deal with local marketing in differing environments, the focus will be on *mature* markets. Since many of the standard marketing techniques are applicable in these markets, the emphasis will be on the adaptation of this know-how to local conditions and the differences between various types of markets. *New growth* markets and *emerging* markets, especially newly democratized countries, are quite different, and Chapters 9 and 10, respectively, are devoted to them.

This chapter starts with a general discussion of local marketing in mature markets. This is followed by four special cases: pan-European marketing, marketing in Japan, in Australia and New Zealand, and in the North American market, in that order.

Local Marketing in Mature Markets

We focus first on the main issues that make a difference in the implementation and execution of traditional marketing know-how in mature foreign markets.

Market Segmentation

An important feature in mature markets is the need for *market segmentation.* In mature markets customers are increasingly particular, with well-developed preferences; they are eager to satisfy varied and idiosyncratic tastes. Small differences in products and services make a big difference to the customer. The ability of firms to target increasingly narrow niches of the market increases accordingly. New media—such as satellite TV and the Internet—as well as direct marketing techniques—such as e-commerce and catalog sales—help manufacturers target narrow consumer segments.

The fragmentation of mature markets presents an opportunity, but also a headache, for the foreign entrant. The opportunity lies in the fact that there will often be a part of the market that has yet to find the kind of product desired. With the large populations of Europe, North America, and Japan, even small such niches may represent a large enough market. The problem is that the foreign entrant has to spot these niches. The stereotypical descriptions of the consumers in these markets will be misleading, and conventional wisdom has to be shunned.

There are many examples of this. Baskin-Robbins has done very well in Japan, even though "Japanese do not eat ice cream standing up." Now teenagers do, even if other people don't. Armani, the Italian designer, has been very successful in the United States, even though "American men don't want to look too stylish." Businessmen wear Armani suits after hours, if not on the job. Japanese autos are a big threat in Europe, despite the notion that "Europeans drive their cars too hard for the light Japanese autos." Not all Europeans drive like Arnold Schwarzenegger. And even in a staid and mature industry such as banking, segmentation is needed.

Product Positioning

Product positioning, the creation of a particular place in the prospect's mind for the product or service, goes hand in glove with market segmentation. In mature markets, successful products have to provide "something special."

Traditionally, this "something special" involved offering a function or feature that no competing product had—"product differentiation" in economic theory. These features were often protected by differing or superior technical standards or even patents. For example, Mercedes offered a soft ride because of its special split rear axle design, the Saab was one of the few cars with front-wheel drive, and some sports cars featured a unique and responsive rack-and-pinion steering column. Over time, as technology diffused, such differences were eliminated as most car makers adopted the best technology. The diffusion rate has speeded up over time—side air bags, antilock brake systems, and all-wheel drive were soon imitated by other makes and models. Today the differences that companies have to use for positioning are more superficial, not only for cars but for many other products. Different brands of toothpaste offered special whitening formulas, cavity fighting ingredients, or transparent gel—but all the major brands can be had with a variety of combinations of these features. Positioning in mature markets often becomes a matter of customer perceptions and competitive imitation. This is where factors such as image, brand name, and country of origin come into the picture.

A strong *brand image* conveys not only the benefits of status and recognition for the customer. It also guarantees that the product will function well: Otherwise, the image would have lost its luster. The global brand names that have emerged over the years represent considerable assets, or "brand equity" (much more will be said about brands in Chapter 13, which covers global branding).

The "made in" labels of foreign-made products can in the same way generate a **country-of-origin effect.** As we saw in Chapter 2, a country well known for high-quality manufacturing, such as Germany, offers an advantage to firms with products made in Germany, a country-specific advantage (CSA) in fact. When Volkswagen started the production of the Rabbit model in the United States in the late 1970s, some American customers rushed to buy the last German-made ones (for good reason, as it turned out, as the Pennsylvania plant had quality problems from the start). French fragrance products are rated highly, so in the early 1980s Shiseido, the Japanese cosmetics firm, hired Serge Lutens in Paris to do its new line of fragrances. Swatch, the very successful Swiss watchmaker, hired Italian designers for its initial line, knowing that "Swiss design" was not particularly good for styling. Companies recognize that country-of-origin effects can be useful marketing tools.[1]

As more countries develop the skills and know-how to produce quality products, one can expect such country-of-origin effects to change. The process is a matter of market success. For example, as Honda, the Japanese carmaker, successfully marketed its Ohio-assembled Accords back in Japan, the company made sure the news media knew about it. This had two results. One, it assured the American buyers that the Hondas built in Ohio were every bit as good as those built in Japan. Second, it made consumers reevaluate their perception of the ability of Americans to build reliable cars.[2]

For many foreign entrants from Third World countries, it is tempting to enter mature markets with low-end and inexpensive products. This may be unavoidable for them, but over the longer run such a strategy tends to be untenable. As industrial development progresses across the globe, other countries develop the requisite know-how and labor skill to become the new low-wage producer. In apparel, Hong Kong first gave way to the Philippines, and now Pakistan, Turkey, and China has taken over. The solution is to upgrade, positioning the products at a higher end in the marketplace. Hong Kong is now a quality manufacturer of apparel.[3]

Marketing Tactics

Product Policies

In mature markets a company's product lines typically follow one of two strategies. A dominant shareholder will usually have a full product line, with a range of models or versions for the different segments and preferences in the market. The alternative is for the company to focus on a specific niche, usually a high-end niche, where a shorter line can be focused on models with high profit margins. In either case, since the customers at the mature stage tend to be fickle, advanced design, fancy packaging, customer service, and other value-adding features play a major role in consumer choice.

In these markets new product innovation tends to play a major competitive role. Whether it is a new or modified product, or simply a new package size or color, companies tend to look for surface differentiation that appeals to specific subsets of the market. The lower end of the market is typically attractive only to large-scale, low-cost producers with standardized products who compete on price.

Many Third World countries tend toward selling a low-cost **"me-too" product** in a mature market. A "me-too" product is basically a copy of another product, often with simpler features and at a lower price. The key to success of a "me too" is the price sensitivity of the marketplace. A tractor from the former Soviet Union, such as the Belarus, can be sold at a discount; the main uncertainty is the necessary amount of the discount. This can usually be researched. By contrast, a completely new product offers a more high-margin opportunity but also poses a greater challenge.

The global marketer introducing a *new* kind of product to a local market has the advantage of little or no competition. Being the first into a previously untapped segment generates the kind of first-mover advantage discussed in Chapter 1. Brand name recognition is often greater for the first entry. Customer loyalty and distribution networks are easier to develop. Distribution accessibility tends to be more limited for latecomers. Necessary product modifications can be spotted faster. Reputation as an innovator and pioneer can be capitalized on in advertising. These are firm-specific advantages (FSAs) that translate into a strong market position.[4]

Real-world examples are plentiful. The Walkman has become synonymous with Sony all over the globe, despite determined copying of the designs by other Japanese electronics firms. Swatch is still the leader in fashion watches despite attempts by Fossil, Seiko, Timex, and lesser competitors to challenge Swatch's leadership. Schick is still the leader in razor blades in Japan, where it entered before the world leader Gillette.

Pricing

In mature markets it is common to think of pricing in terms of selecting a target position—high-end or low-end, depending on the positioning desired—and then using temporary deals and offers to attract customers—and to fight competitors—in the short term. By making the price cuts temporary, the brand can be maintained at the higher position, while still competing with lower-priced entries. Low-priced entries from the Third World countries can expect such competitive defenses from established brands.

One might think that in mature markets price would not be an important factor for consumers. However, competition in mature markets is often so fierce that pricing and discounts become very important competitive tools. Discounted prices are also used to smooth reasonable variations in demand, as in the case of airline tickets.

In many mature markets it is common to encounter regulations against price discrimination, the practice of charging different prices to different customers. The thrust is toward not allowing any discrimination that is not justified by differences in costs in serving the customer, but the global marketer is not always in control of the local prices. In many countries manufacturers can only suggest prices at the retail level, but the retailers have the right to offer discounts and cents-off without necessarily asking the firm. Many global firms would like to maintain similar prices across markets for positioning purposes, but in a country such as the United States it is not always clear what the actual prices charged are. The so-called intrabrand competition common in the United States means that the identical model of a Sony digital camera can be sold at widely different prices in two states, even two different sales outlets. This kind of competition also takes place across national borders—we will discuss "gray trade" in more detail in Chapters 14 and 15.

Another reason manufacturers are not always in control of local prices is that governments sometimes interfere, be it through regulations, value-added taxes, luxury taxes, and so on. This is a particularly salient problem for pharmaceuticals, since many governments keep strong controls on ethical and over-the-counter drugs, and insurance reimbursement policies can vary considerably across countries.

Distribution

In mature markets the distribution system is usually well developed, and there are few or none of the infrastructure problems so common in emerging countries. But there is another problem: Getting into the appropriate channel is often very expensive and sometimes impossible.

For example, to get a supermarket chain in a mature market to add a new foreign product on the shelf takes more than dealer margins, promise of secure and timely delivery, and extensive promotional support. There are also direct payments to be made—"slotting fees"—and a very short probation period. If the brand proves itself (a matter of quick turnover) the future might be bright. But a small mistake in execution (a slipped delivery date, a faulty package, inappropriate promotional language) can easily waylay the best promise.

Entry through department stores is hardly easier. Kao, the Japanese company, spent several unsuccessful years attempting to get its cosmetics line on the floor of the large German stores. And the perfumeries that offered an alternative distribution channel proved equally resistant. In autos, where the necessity of dealer service and trained repair personnel makes entry very expensive, many companies spend years developing a network. BMW, the German carmaker, found it necessary to create its own subsidiary in Japan to help support the independent dealers that dared stock its cars. Before that, a typical dealer showroom in central Tokyo might feature one car in a small one-room window. As the Japanese began to shop for cars outside the inner city, new dealers with larger showrooms on the outskirts of Tokyo could be established.

One distribution strategy is "piggybacking." In piggybacking, an existing network controlled by another company, often a potential competitor, is used to distribute the product through contracting with the competitor to move products on a fee or commission basis. Toyota trucks are sold through Volkswagen dealers in Germany. Nissan sells some Volkswagen cars in Japan. The now common international alliances between airlines often involve the sharing of reservation systems for complementary routing. Pharmaceutical companies sometimes market their drugs in co-marketing arrangements with manufacturers of medical instruments and devices relating to the same injury or illness. The large-scale dealers selling a large number of competing auto makes, the multiple-brand electronics stores, the personal computer stores, and other similar retail innovations initiated in the United States are spreading to other mature markets. As this transformation unfolds, one can expect better access for foreign marketers.

Promotion

In many mature markets where market share is the criterion of success, sales promotions such as free samples, coupons, and point-of-purchase displays are used to break the habitual choice of the loyal customer. The supporting marketing communication attempts to increase the saliency of features on which the brand is superior to competitors. This leads to the kind of hard-hitting ad campaigns so often derided by foreign visitors to the United States. Because of the immense media clutter in the United States, and the proliferation of product variety, marketing communications need to have an impact during the short interval the customer is exposed.

Advertising also helps add value to the brand by creating a positive image, high recognition, strong status appeal, and so on. Advertising intended for this purpose uses more of a soft sell; such market communications tend to be favored in Europe and, perhaps especially, in Japan. When members of the distribution channels are able to furnish necessary product information (as in traditional European stores) or the consumers have time to examine products in the store (as in Japan), such softer advertising is often more effective.[5]

The variety of media available in mature markets also makes it necessary to clearly develop a target segmentation strategy in order to identify the best media vehicles to reach the potential buyers. This holds for print vehicles (which magazines and newspapers are appropriate?) as well as broadcast media (which radio and television programs should be selected?). In addition, because of the wealth of traditional media, direct mail, telemarketing, and online marketing need to be considered.

Customer Satisfaction

In many mature markets intense competition has produced a management focus on **customer satisfaction** (CS), and making sure that existing customers will stay loyal.

Typically, two things make for a satisfied customer in these markets. First there is product *quality,* in a broad sense, including functional performance factors (reliability, flexibility, and so on). Second are emotional factors, a matter of pleasing the customer. Here personal attention and after-sales service factors (delivery, warranty, and

EXHIBIT 8.1
Customer Satisfaction and Two
Kinds of Quality

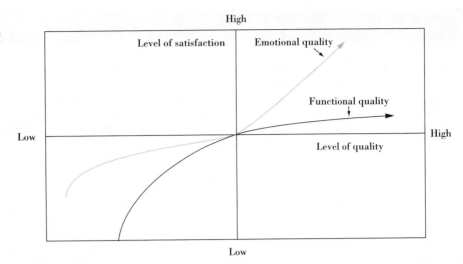

so on) become important. The idea of customer satisfaction also includes what is usually called "the surprise quotient," the degree to which the company can offer an unexpected technical feature or personal service.

While a lack of functional quality is certain to negatively affect satisfaction, managers can't assume that perfect functioning alone will produce any customer euphoria: In mature markets it may simply be taken for granted. The real satisfaction—which creates repeat business, customer loyalty, and positive word of mouth—comes from emotional factors, which are seen to yield "extra" or value-added quality. These relationships are depicted in Exhibit 8.1. A customer's typical experience with an automobile can be used to illustrate the way quality affects satisfaction in the exhibit. When the car does not start in the morning, or when the steering wheel rattles, functional quality is low. This kind of trouble leads to dissatisfaction (lower left-hand corner of the graph). Even a kind service repairer will have trouble raising satisfaction levels. On the other hand, the fact that the car starts and the wheel does not rattle does not generally lead to satisfaction: It is taken for granted.

In order to produce high levels of satisfaction, the customer needs to be given something not so obviously expected—something for which the "surprise" quotient is high. This can involve simple things such as a pickup when service is due or a cleaned-out ashtray after service is done. It can also involve semifunctional things such as more elbow room for the driver, clear instrument panels, and an easy-to-program radio. Although not necessary in a functional sense, these things often make the driver happier: They raise the emotional quality and therefore satisfaction (upper right-hand corner of the graph).[6]

In advanced countries with mature markets and intense global competition, customers' expectations continue to rise, and they demand ever higher quality products and improved service—at competitive prices. This is a stiff management challenge, which must be met for the local marketer to be successful in today's mature markets.

So far we have dealt with the basic strategies for mature local markets. The local marketer has, of course, to add specifics pertinent to his or her special market environment. Four special cases follow: pan-European marketing, marketing in Japan, in Australia and New Zealand, and in North America. The discussion follows whenever possible the same basic outline: market environment, including foreign trade agreements; competitive situation; market segmentation; product positioning; and marketing tactics (product, pricing, distribution, and promotion).

Close-up: Pan-European Marketing[7]

The 1992 European integration has stimulated many companies to analyze the potential of **pan-European marketing** strategies. Although pan-European marketing is not truly "local," the creation of the EU (European Union) is intended to lead to a "single market."

Getting the Picture

CENTRAL EUROPE: FROM USSR TO EU

The promise of being able to live, work, and do business throughout the European Union resulted in a host of applicants for membership from the former Soviet bloc. Since any enlargement of the EU would necessitate that a country demonstrate compliance with various political, legal, and economic criteria, some nations have been admitted in advance of others.

Near the top of the list (and admitted in 2004) were the central European countries Poland, the Czech Republic, Slovakia, and the three Baltic States: Estonia, Latvia, and Lithuania. Further down were Romania and Bulgaria, which still must make significant progress to meet EU membership requirements. This was also the case for the war-torn former Yugoslavian countries and Albania. These former Soviet satellite countries have shed the communist yoke and the countries at the top of the list have made substantive progress toward ensuring personal freedoms and developing free market systems. Since these states were brought into the communist camp only at the end of World War II, all have a strong capitalistic and democratic heritage. In fact, Poland's strong trade unions contributed to the region's first freely elected democratic leader without any ties to communism.

Along with its strong democratic movement, Poland has made significant progress in restructuring its economy away from heavy industry and toward an expanding service sector, particularly business services and real estate. Nonagricultural employment reached 61 percent by 1999 in Poland, and privatization in the manufacturing sector continues to raise the private sector's contribution to GDP.

Similar transformations are occurring throughout central Europe as the rise of the iron curtain has contributed to rapid productivity growth and a resulting increase in foreign direct investment. In Hungary FDI reached just under US$2 billion by the end of 2000, or about 46 percent of the country's GDP. Much of this production capacity has been steered toward trade with EU member nations. For instance, the EU is the Czech Republic's largest trading partner with 69 percent of exports and 62 percent of imports in 2000. Most encouraging of all has been the growth of small enterprises (those with up to 49 staff). Such enterprises grew in Slovakia to 59,408 in 1999, with individual entrepreneurs accounting for another 75,054 members of the labor force.

Change has come a bit more slowly and erratically in Bulgaria and Romania. However, both nations have instituted a host of structural reforms that have resulted in growing service sectors and increasing trade with the West. The key for both nations is to continue the privatization of inefficient enterprises and to stimulate new investment. But if they both were able to survive the Soviet era, EU membership hardly sounds unrealistic. Both countries were conditionally admitted in January 2007.

Applicants hope to revel in the benefits of the EU's enlargement—reunification, stability, and prosperity. Clearly enlargement will unify some parts of Europe and create stability by expanding the number of countries committed to democracy and cooperation. Further, enlargement will contribute to overall prosperity by further encouraging trade and investment. The challenge now is to resolve some remaining issues prior to deciding which countries will occupy the slots on a time line for membership.

Sources: Allan Hall, "Some Europeans Migrate to New Places to Seek Employment," Evening Standard, September 12, 2001; Gideon Rachman, "Europe's Magnetic Attraction," The Economist, May 17, 2001.

Market Environment

The decision in 1986 to establish a single European market within the EU by 1992 led to a completely changed strategic environment for most businesses, European and others. Tariff barriers and customs duties were scrapped, and goods and labor were to move freely between countries. Product standards were harmonized. Cumbersome border controls were abolished, and a common European passport was created. Commercial vehicles needed a single loading document for shipments across Europe, where before each country had its own set of documents and standards. The resulting savings were estimated at $5.8 billion. National price controls were eliminated, helping to create a large and unified market with competitive prices. A single currency, the euro, was introduced in 1999, simplifying payments and equalizing prices (although not all countries joined the euro, with the United Kingdom holding on to its pound £, for example).

The EU moves steadily closer to a fully integrated marketplace, while at the same time preparing to include new countries, especially those formerly under Soviet control (see box, "Central Europe: From USSR to EU"). The original six countries (France, Germany, Italy, and the Benelux countries) became nine in 1973 with the addition of Ireland, Denmark, and the United Kingdom. Greece followed in 1981; Portugal and Spain in 1986. Austria, Sweden, and Finland made it 15 members in 1995. And on May 1, 2004, ten new members were added: three Baltic countries (Estonia, Latvia, and Lithuania), five Central European countries (Hungary, Poland,

EXHIBIT 8.2
GDP Per Capita in the EU (2007, in U.S.$), Rank in World, and Population

Sources: Data from www.worldbank.org; www.imf.org.

Nation	GDP Per Capita (PPP)	GDP Rank in world	Population
Original six members			
Luxembourg	80,457	1	480,222
The Netherlands	38,486	13	16,570,613
Belgium	35,273	21	10,392,226
Germany	34,181	23	82,400,996
France	33,188	25	63,718,187
Italy	30,448	27	58,147,733
New members added 1973–1995			
Denmark	37,392	16	5,468,120
Sweden	36,494	18	9,031,088
United Kingdom	35,134	22	60,776,238
Finland	35,280	20	5,238,460
Ireland	43,144	9	4,109,086
Austria	38,399	15	8,199,783
Spain	30,120	29	40,448,191
Greece	29,172	30	10,706,290
Portugal	21,701	39	10,642,836
New members added 2004			
Cyprus	46,865	7	788,457
Slovenia	27,205	31	2,009,245
Malta	53,359	3	401,880
Czech Republic	24,236	36	10,228,744
Hungary	19,027	43	9,956,108
Poland	16,311	50	38,518,241
Estonia	21,094	40	1,315,912
Slovakia	20,251	41	5,447,502
Lithuania	17,661	46	3,575,439

Czech Republic, Slovakia, and Slovenia), and two small Mediterranean islands (Cyprus and Malta).

The EU is now a single market with upward of 450 million consumers, the biggest mature market in the world. Of course, not all of these countries are really in the mature stage. As can be seen in Exhibit 8.2, the 2003 per capita incomes varied widely. At the upper end is tiny Luxembourg, followed by the Scandinavian countries and the larger and older European members. Ireland has risen strongly recently on the basis of FDI from many multinationals moving into the EU market. At the lower end are several of the newly admitted central European countries.

Needless to say, for many of the large multinational companies with a long-established presence in a fragmented Europe, the changes have presented an exciting challenge. In addition to the need to coordinate marketing strategy (segmentation and positioning) and tactics (the marketing mix) across the EU, there have been questions about the appropriate organizational structure to implement the changes. Paradoxically, the challenge has been greatest for the European companies themselves.

Foreign Trade Agreements

The EU has now taken over the role as the primary trade negotiating entity for its member countries. Still, the traditional bilateral and multilateral relationships at the national level are only gradually being replaced, and in some cases sustained indefinitely. Thus, for example, the 54 member nations belonging to the Commonwealth—a regional grouping dating back to the British colonial domination in the 1900s—still pursue preferential trade among its members. But the main trade negotiating power rests with the EU.

The EU generally undertakes trade negotiations and dispute resolution with other regional groupings, often under the World Trade Organization (WTO) umbrella. For example, the EU deals directly with the NAFTA and the ASEAN groupings. At the same time, special task forces are created to work on specific issues. The Asia-Europe Meeting (ASEM) is a group of Asian and European countries (EU members) that meet regularly to discuss issues of trade and investment. There are similar groups dealing with Latin America (the EU-Andean Community, the EU-Mercosur, for example), with Africa (the Euro Mediterranean Partnership, focusing on North Africa, for example), and a cooperation agreement with the Gulf Cooperation Council focused on the Arab states in the Persian Gulf.

The EU also takes the lead in conflict resolutions with other trade regions. For example, when the United States imposed higher tariffs on imported steel, the EU raised the issue in the WTO, where the tariffs were judged illegal. This set the stage for possible retaliation by the EU, forcing the Americans to back down. On the other hand, the EU has to cope with sometimes conflicting trade demands and practices from its own members. For example, the high French agricultural subsidies that help create trade conflicts in the WTO have threatened EU cohesiveness. Although it looks as if France is gradually yielding ground, it is probably safe to assume that the EU will continue to face internal problems, especially now that the central European countries have been admitted. Nevertheless, in the big picture, the EU will continue to be an important player in the world's trade negotiations.

Competition

The integration forced large European corporations to start coordinating previously independent national operations. The new rules meant that national subsidiaries had to be given stronger central direction to gain the projected savings from eliminating unnecessarily costly national differences in product designs, brand names, and promotions. It also meant that smaller plants in local countries would be closed and more efficient larger-scale units created. With decades, even centuries of hostility between countries, all this was no easy task.

By contrast, many large non-European companies were unburdened by old and outdated affiliations and practices. With an existing manufacturing foothold in the EU market and global brand name recognition, many were well placed to take advantage of the integrative opportunities, be they low-cost labor in Italy, financial problems for middle-sized business as in Austria, or no-longer-protected electronics businesses in France.

For smaller European companies—and even the many large firms—the threat from these foreign entrants has been met by the creation of larger and stronger companies. The result has been a spate of mergers and acquisitions. Stella Artois and Jupiler, the two dominant Belgian beer brewers, merged. Heineken in Holland bought Amstel. German Siemens, the large maker of electronic machinery, bought Nixdorff, a computer maker. Asea, in the large-scale power transmission business, bought Brown-Boveri, a Swiss competitor. Virgin Records in London bought FNAC, a French retail firm. Where acquisitions failed or were disallowed, alliances were formed. German Lufthansa agreed with United Airlines to share routes and frequent fliers. Similarly, Swiss Air, Caledonia, and SAS agreed to cooperate.

In fact, at the corporate level, there seems to be only one strategic response possible for European firms: Get bigger and go pan-European. The new mergers tend to be initiated by organizations based in the larger markets, such as Germany and France.[8] They are more likely to have the financial and managerial resources required to go pan-European. The "merger mania" has been further stimulated by the 1999 introduction of the common currency, the euro (see box, "Bigger is Better?").

Japanese companies have tried to decide whether a full-fledged European subsidiary is necessary and where to locate it. While Toyota made do with an enlarged presence in Brussels, Nissan established European headquarters in Amsterdam to be close to port and warehousing facilities and thus be able to better coordinate a pan-European approach. But

Getting the Picture

BIGGER IS BETTER?

The arrival of the euro for electronic transactions on January 1, 1999, set the stage for intensified pan-European tie-ups among companies. From hotel chains and automobiles to book publishers and stock markets, the name of the game is that "bigger is better." Nation-based players are now going pan-European through alliances and outright mergers with former competitors of equal size. In the first three quarters of 1998 alone, European mergers and acquisitions totaled $643 billion, about a third of that between companies of approximately equal size, an unusually high percentage. Even though some member countries are still outside of the Euro zone—Britain and Sweden among them—cross-border alliances included those countries as well.

Pharmaceutical companies were particularly active, partly in response to increasing homogeneity in national reimbursement policies for prescription drugs and also under competitive pressure from American companies. Chemical giant Hoechst of Germany merged its drug and agricultural products operation with that of French Rhone-Poulenc, and drugmaker Zeneca of Britain bought Astra of Sweden in one of the biggest mergers valued at $35 billion. In 2004 two large French drug makers, Aventis and Sanofi-Synthelabos, joined forces, encouraged by their government, which feared a takeover by Swiss Novartis, another pharmaceutical giant. But is bigger necessarily better? One problem that plagues these combinations is the difficulty of integrating different corporate cultures. Then there is always a question about who is to run the combined operations. A planned merger between two of Britain's largest pharmaceuticals, Glaxo Wellcome and Smith-Kline Beecham, almost fell apart when the two CEOs could not agree on who would run the merged businesses. But since 2000 the company is known as GlaxoSmithKline—no hyphens.

Sources: Anne Swardson, "Discord in Europe's Unity," *Washington Post,* October 13, 1998, p. C1; Alan Cowell, "Zeneca Buying Astra as Europe Consolidates," *New York Times,* December 10, 1998, pp. C1, C2; Robert Stevens, "Glaxo Wellcome-SmithKline Beecham Merger Creates World's Largest Drug Company," **www.wsws.org,** January 22, 2000.

most Japanese companies established European headquarters in the English countryside, where language and simple village customs made the transition from Japan easier.

Within Europe, the Americans shifted and centralized responsibilities. Ford pulled some of the decision-making power from country heads to its European headquarters in Dagenham outside London. Product design responsibilities were centralized, and pan-European design teams were assembled in Dagenham. Financial controls and reporting back to headquarters in Dearborn, Michigan, were tightened up by a new European head, sent in from the United States. The head of Ford Werke AG in Cologne quit rather than lose power.

Rather than centralizing decision-making power within Europe, Honeywell, manufacturer of electronic measurement devices and computer controls, decided to adopt a **distributed headquarters** model with each country organization taking the European lead in certain functions. The French unit would focus on R&D, the British would handle the marketing, and the Germans would handle the existing customer support and service functions. This reorganization met with some resistance. Xerox was able to attract some of the top German development engineers from Honeywell to its German subsidiary in Düsseldorf. The Germans did not want to relocate to France and play second fiddle to the French.

Market Segmentation

As most companies developed organizational capability for a pan-European strategy, the businesses' segmentation and positioning plans followed predictably. Europeanwide segments were identified and targeted. Pan-European product designs and marketing communications were created to achieve the same synergistic positioning in all countries.

The experience of Volvo Trucks, one of the largest truck manufacturers in the world, is instructive.[9] Before the integration, segmentation of the European market had been localized and specific to each country. It had been up to the marketing manager of each country subsidiary to develop a segmentation scheme for the customers in that country. Because each country had special traffic regulations and transportation laws, there had been no effort to use the same segmentation scheme elsewhere. The only criterion common across countries was the carrying capacity—large trucks above 16 tons,

EXHIBIT 8.3

**Six Basic Plus Four Potential
European Segments**

Source: Tevfik Dalgic, "Euromarketing:
Charting the Map for Globalization," *International Marketing Review* 9, no. 5 (1992),
p. 37. Reprinted with permission from *International Marketing Review*.

Cluster 1. United Kingdom and Irish Republic (total population 60.350 million)
Cluster 2. France, French-speaking Belgium, and Switzerland (total population 54.518 million)
Cluster 3. Iberian Peninsula (total population 56.363 million)
Cluster 4. Italy and Italian-speaking Switzerland (total population 71.498 million)
Cluster 5. South Mediterranean, including Greece, southern Italy, and Island of Sardinia (total population 31.252 million)
Cluster 6. Northern Europe and the Scandinavian Peninsula including the northern part of Germany, Flemish-speaking Belgium, the Netherlands, Denmark, Sweden, Norway, and Finland (total population 57.618 million; if former East Germany is added to this cluster, the total population will be 74.242 million)
Cluster 7. East European countries: present Czechoslovakia, Hungary, and Poland (total population 63.771 million)
Cluster 8. Balkan states: Turkey, Albania, Bulgaria, old Yugoslav Republics, Romania, Moldova, Cyprus, and Malta (total population 113.142 million)
Cluster 9. Black Sea region: Russian Federation, Ukraine and Caucasian states (Armenia, Azerbaijan, Georgia) (total population 205.729 million)
Cluster 10. Baltic region: Lithuania, Estonia, Bylerus, and Latvia (total population 17.767 million)

medium-sized trucks between 10 and 16 tons, and small trucks under 10 tons. This division was dictated by Volvo's manufacturing plants but served no particular marketing purpose.

As the single market demanded greater market orientation, Volvo commissioned research that would lead to a more in-depth segmentation scheme to be used across countries. The research helped to identify different customer segments based not only on tonnage transported but also on usage situation, type of shipment, and differences in performance criteria. The usage situation distinguished between urban and long-haul transportation, allowing the company to develop special features (such as small turning radius) useful in Europe's narrow streets. Identifying common types of shipment (heavy machinery versus electronic components, for example) allowed the company to add certain loading features. Differences in performance criteria, such as speed versus fuel efficiency, helped salespeople advise the customer about which engine options to choose. These segmentation criteria were "portable" between countries, allowing the company to run a series of training and support sessions where the local managers and sales staff were shown how the segmentation scheme could be adapted to help their operation.

One researcher has identified six basic segments, with another four groupings added as the EU expands.[10] As can be seen from Exhibit 8.3, these clusters of countries form large markets by themselves, making it possible to gain many scale advantages without necessarily operating across the whole EU region. Going beyond geography and cultural-linguistic affinity, other researchers have identified further segmentation possibilities in the EU. For example, one study of the yogurt market in Europe identified four separate segments, the largest of which was clearly pan-European. This segment consisted of younger and higher-income consumers, who spend the most on yogurt, and buy in larger stores. The study also found that the benefits of "low-fat" yogurt—good for health, but also seen as a "fun-and-enjoyment" product—stretched across all four segments, suggesting the possibility of less-differentiated mass-marketing.[11]

Product Positioning

The shift to a pan-European market segmentation focused around the customer has taken place in many other European markets as companies find it worthwhile to analyze and target the enlarged customer base in the single market. Positioning has followed suit, partly by sheer force of the drive to a single market. There are very few products today that can maintain different images in different countries of Europe. Whereas before French wine might have been expensive, associated with a high-status image in some high-tax European countries, today most Europeans judge French wine as the French

EXHIBIT 8.4
Three Strategic Options

Source: Chris Halliburton and Reinhard Hünerberg, "Executive Insights: Pan-European Marketing—Myth or Reality?" *Journal of International Marketing* 1, no. 3 (1993), p. 85. Reprinted by permission of Michigan State University Press.

Options	Strategies	Remarks
1. Market retreat	• Sell out to pan-European player (example, Nabisco) • Seek a different, less competitive market (example, Nokia Data)	• May be preferable to a stuck-in-the-middle position
2. Pan-European competition	• Identify true pan-European market segments (example, Perrier) • Organic penetration from existing national markets (example, Pilkington) • Aggressive policy of acquisitions to complete European portfolio (example, BSN) • Cooperation with other national players to form pan-European organizations (example, Carnaud-Metal box) or alliances (example, European Retailers Association)	• May be few true segments • Excessive time required • Few winners • Complex and risky but increasingly important in "post-1992" Europe
3. Niche position	• Consolidate national position through realignment, merger, or acquisition (example, Mannesmann-VDO) • Identify new Euro-regions • Identify segments across limited number of countries (example, Campbells Biscuits) • Seek economies at component level while retaining niche brands (example, Electrolux) • Become an OEM supplier to pan-European companies	• Vulnerable to standardized Euro-products if national differences are marginal • Information access • Need to accumulate scale benefits • Organizational complexity • Vulnerable to pan-European OEM suppliers

themselves do—by drinking it. Germany has had to relax its ban on artificial ingredients in beer, leaving its market open for Carlsberg, Budweiser, Molson, and other foreign beers and allowing its outstanding German beers to stand out—and the other German beers to falter.

Before integration, a product such as Swatch might have had different images in different European countries; now, gradually, the differences are between cross-border segments, not nations. In pan-European marketing, product positioning is the same across countries, but different product lines or models target different customer segments. There are Swatches for upscale consumers and for teenagers, for business and for play. Similarly, there are different clothes, foods, and drinks for these segments. These target segments are not limited by nationality.

But a pan-European strategic response is not necessarily the correct approach for all companies in all industries. Given the right industry and company conditions, there is also opportunity in niche strategies. Research has shown three viable strategic alternatives,[12] given in Exhibit 8.4. Some companies have actually benefited by simply retreating from the market, cashing in on the existing brand and company equity, and allocating funds elsewhere. More commonly, the alternative to a pan-European approach is to seek out a niche or create one. Since the unification of Europe in economic terms has not been accompanied by a similar unification in terms of politics and national borders, there will undoubtedly be good opportunities for smaller firms that wish to cater to ethnic tastes and traditional preferences (see box, "The Teeming Euro-Teens").

Getting the Picture

THE TEEMING EURO-TEENS

American and, perhaps especially, Japanese teenagers have long been considered a lucrative market segment, spending their parents' money seemingly at whim and will. Now come the Euro-teens—and the Euro-'tweens.

The teenage market includes boys and girls from 13–19, and the 'tween market is the name for the younger slice of 8–14-year-olds. With the children of older "baby-boomers" now in their teenage years, this Euro-segment is coming on strong. Yes, they do sport the fashions, the mobile phones, the music, the films—and the attitudes—of their peers on the other side of the globe, but they also have their own identities.

Compared to teens elsewhere, the Euro-teens tend to be further into the job market than others. A survey in Germany showed that among the 16–18-year-olds, a healthy 60 percent had a job—and 92 percent were still receiving an allowance from home. They seem to be more aware of, and sympathetic to, the antiglobalization sentiments. Even though they do watch television and use the Internet, another survey showed that 67.5 percent of boys and 47.1 percent of girls found the Internet "too American," and just over 35 percent said they would prefer to buy a local rather than an American product online. Similar to the Japanese teens, the Euro-teens are also likely to use their mobile phones for games and text services, and wireless marketing is much more advanced in western Europe than in the United States.

As always, the teens in different nations in Europe take pride in being just that, different. This is why marketing even to this Euro-segment has to be localized. Maurice van Sabben is the head of online and interactive business development for Fox Kids Europe, a joint venture partly owned by Fox Broadcasting. Fox broadcasts to 54 countries in 17 languages and operates 14 localized websites. "Keep it local," he says. "Make it relevant to the kids and 'tweens in their respective countries."

Parents? Proud but poor.

Sources: Lisa Bertagnoli, "Continental Spendthrifts," *Marketing News,* October 22, 2001, pp. 1, 15; Daniel Rogers, "An End to Fair Play," *Financial Times,* July 31, 2001, p. 7.

Marketing Tactics

Product Policies

The marketing mixes of the European marketers have moved toward uniformity as the pan-European strategies are implemented. Many companies have attempted to develop pan-European products and brands. One of the earliest examples was Procter & Gamble's "Vizir" brand name for a new liquid detergent, whose development process and success record have been used as a model for other similar efforts.[13] The lead country for Vizir was Germany, with the biggest market and the most promising test results. A global product team was organized with representatives from several European countries. Despite difficulties with cross-country coordination of introductions, delays by headquarters back in Cincinnati, and uneven support from the various country heads, the launch was a success in most countries (even though the delays allowed Henkel, the main German competitor, to catch up quickly with a "me-too" product).

Today such **Euro-brands** are common and are becoming global. And even though brand names may vary because of language differences (the Snuggle fabric softener comes with at least 15 different brand names), the product itself may be identical across countries. Most packaged goods in Europe feature packaging in at least four languages: English, French, German, and Spanish. Euro-designs of durable products are also common. France's Thomson, Italy's Olivetti, and Swedish Electrolux have long designed household appliances and office products aimed primarily at the European market. But now other companies follow suit. In its Bordeaux plant Pioneer makes loudspeakers with a European design (thinner, sharper lines); Sony makes some design alterations for the European market with slimmer and elongated shapes and less flashy colors; the Mercedes product line in Europe has more models than in the United States, making finer discriminations in the intermediate range; Japanese camera companies make their European product lines unique by adding a few features demanded by customers and deleting other features (partly to enable the companies to control the gray European trade in cameras from Hong Kong and the United States).

Pricing

Other tactical marketing mix decisions are also being adapted to the new reality. Pan-European pricing is a particularly complicated issue as the single **euro currency** is

Getting the Picture

WAL-MART GOES TO EUROPE

Wal-Mart, the American suburban phenomenon, has now been at the top of the Fortune Global 500 list for several consecutive years. The Arkansas-based retailer is the largest company in the world in terms of sales revenues ($256 billion in 2003). After much success in the United States, it has begun the inevitable expansion overseas. Although doing well in both Canada and Mexico (where it is the biggest private employer), when Wal-Mart tried to go into Germany the company stumbled for the first time since it achieved domination.

To enter the German market (third largest after the United States and Japan), Wal-Mart bought two smaller local chains, Wertkauf and Interspar. Although Wertkauf proved a success, Interspar did not. Its run-down stores have stopped Wal-Mart from turning a profit since the 1997 purchase. German laws have also presented Wal-Mart with three major problems: price controls that prevent below-cost selling, strict zoning laws that make it difficult to get permission to construct big stores, and rigid labor laws that prohibit some of the low-wage and overtime work practices of Wal-Mart at home. In addition, Germany also has well-established Wal-Mart rivals like Metro, Aldi, and Lidl, that are comfortable with slim profit margins. Strong price competition, especially from Aldi, a limited-range discount chain that cut prices on the most basic lead items featured in Wal-Mart, eliminated any profit margins. Coupled with several missteps—including a lack of language competency on the part of top management—forced Wal-Mart to withdraw from the German market in 2006.

Wal-Mart has found no more luck in Britain where it also bought one of the local chains, Asda, in 1999. Asda is the second biggest supermarket retailer after Tesco, one of Europe's largest retailers, and a global competitor for Wal-Mart. A concerted counterattack in England by Tesco, with superior service, and more convenient locations with new and smaller store units, has proved quite a match for Wal-Mart. As of 2008 Wal-Mart is still in England, but making little or no money.

In 2004, Wal-Mart made public the possibility that it will expand into other European countries. While on a business trip to Brussels, H. Lee Scott, CEO of Wal-Mart, said that he would want stores in every European country if he could have it. The threat is still there, but the Europeans are slightly more sanguine than they were before.

Sources: Daniel Dombey and Susanna Voyle, "Wal-Mart Eyes Basket of European Stores," *Financial Times*, May 25, 2004, p.1; "How Big Can It Grow? Wal-Mart," *The Economist*, April 17, 2004, Special Report; Mike Lydon, "Wal-Mart Struggles, Pulls Out Of Europe," **www.planetizen.com**, August 6, 2006.

introduced and companies have to set a common euro price throughout the region. Companies in some industries (such as autos) needed to price in euros by 1999 and began before that to phase in a common price level across Europe. Price differentials on the same product and brand in different countries are being minimized to avoid inducing customers to buy in a neighboring country (this so-called gray trade problem will be discussed in more detail in Chapters 14 and 15). But long-standing practices are not easily changed, especially since in many protected local markets the high prices have made some products cash cows for the distributor. Pharmaceutical companies, for example, are faced with controlled prices in many markets, with governments reimbursing patients' medical expenses. But if, because of these controls, its drugs can be bought less expensively in some countries, there is nothing to prohibit massive purchase by a foreign pharmacy for resale at higher prices. Telecommunication equipment manufacturers face similar complications, as in the case of Finnish Nokia and Swedish Ericsson. More will be said about the pricing problems in Chapter 14, "Global Pricing."

Distribution

In addition to the rationalization of the manufacturers' sales network, retail and wholesale distribution is gradually being transformed, from locally based smaller units to large integrated organizations resembling those common in North America. The French hypermarket chain, Carrefour, has expanded throughout the EU, as have Standa's Italian-based Euromercatos. Marks & Spencer, Britain's clothing chain, is developing a pan-European presence. Belgium's Delhaize supermarket chain is attempting to expand using mergers and acquisitions in addition to new store investments. Germany's Kaufhof department store chain is also developing a pan-European strategy.

Some of this development has been spurred also by entry from non-European retailers. In particular, Wal-Mart has been active in trying to enter the EU (see box, "Wal-Mart Goes to Europe").

A French and German ad for Mach III, Gillette's new razor cartridge. Through standardized visual elements and use of the same selling proposition about a better shave with less skin irritation, the ad needs only language translation for pan-European use.
Courtesy of The Gillette Company.

These new large units help facilitate the introduction of pan-European strategies among manufacturers. The savings created through large centralized negotiations between the manufacturer and a large distribution chain are well known in the American marketplace but are relatively new in Europe. From a marketing viewpoint, this development is likely to generate the same kind of interest in, and need for, more relationship marketing as it has in the United States.

Promotion

Even though there are no pan-European networks comparable to CBS, NBC, ABC, or Fox in the United States, another striking development is the increasing use of pan-European TV advertising, taking advantage of the satellites beamed across previously closed borders. As public ownership of TV broadcasting lessens and commercial airtime is made available, even previously "protected" countries such as Norway and Sweden are exposed to the same mass media messages as the British, the French, and the Italians, who have long had commercial TV. Language differences are overcome by limiting copy to voiceovers, making it possible to quickly adapt a given commercial to broadcasting in a different language. This allows the local branches of the agency handling the Honda account to use the same commercial everywhere. Coca-Cola does not need many words to put across its message, and in some cases even the American English stays intact. The satellite channels feature commercials with a limited number of words, usually English. To appeal to the many different nationalities with a common theme, American Clairol uses rapid scans over pictures of women from easily recognized places in Europe, all using the same Clairol shampoo. And, as always in Europe, sex and humor play important parts (see box, "European Advertising—Same Old, Same Old?").

Getting the Picture

EUROPEAN ADVERTISING—SAME OLD, SAME OLD?

Combining the tradition of sex in French advertising with the humor in British ads should work well in pan-European advertising, no? In one commercial for the female body spray Impulse from Lever Fabergé, the firm's agency, Ogilvy and Mather Worldwide in London, had a naked male model posing for a painting class. With the slogan "men can't help acting on Impulse," the man is unable to hide his reaction when a girl wearing Impulse runs in late for class and a waft of her fragrance reaches him. A follow-up commercial features what seems to be a similar frisson between the male model and the girl, only to have the man turn out to be gay. The commercial ends with him leaving hand-in-hand with his partner.

One wonders how this commercial would play in Peoria, Illinois. Probably not too well. Fact is, Ogilvy and Mather lost the account when sales of Impulse in Europe did not respond as quickly as the male model in the first commercial.

Sources: "BBH Wins Unilever's Pan-Euro Impulse from O&M," *Euromarketing via E-mail,* February 16, 2001; Matthew Valencia, "Lean, Mean, European," *The Economist,* April 27, 2000.

Close up: Marketing in Japan[14]

Japan's situation is sufficiently unusual that it deserves separate treatment. Despite its continued economic downturn in the 2000s, Japan remains one of the prime markets in the world. In addition, the competitiveness of its companies and products abroad makes an understanding of the home market situation useful. This is where the Japanese multinational companies hone their skills.

Market Environment

Japan is a country the size of California with over 120 million people concentrated in small pockets of inhabitable land. Its economic performance in the 40 years up to the 1990s was phenomenal, per capita incomes growing from poverty level to among the highest in the world, reaching $34,500 (PPP) in 2003 at official exchange rates, where it has leveled off (the figure in 2007 was $33,800). The Japanese market still has great potential for foreign firms in a wide variety of products and services: It is just very hard to succeed there.

The Japanese economy took off in the early 1950s during the Korean War as the United States pumped millions of dollars into its industry. After the war, consumers in Japan and elsewhere (from the beginning, Japan's expansion was export-led) were the beneficiaries of intense competition among Japanese domestic suppliers in many product categories. Since foreign suppliers started with the handicap of not understanding how to do business in Japan very well, especially given a difficult language, most customers in Japan, both industrial and ultimate consumers, preferred to deal with domestic suppliers. The domestic suppliers could be pitted against each other, following the old samurai tradition of feuding daimyos during medieval times.

The recurring recessions in the decade of the 1990s and into the new millennium have been very hard on the Japanese psyche, producers as well as consumers. Hailed as the new "Number One" in the 1980s, Japan's domestic economy has performed miserably, with growth rates of 1 to 2 percent annually. The problems stem largely from inflated valuations in real estate and speculative investment in plant and equipment, based on inflated expectations about future earnings. Once the downturn began in the early 1990s after a minor hike in interest rates, business failures in the domestic economy shook consumer confidence. Without a strong social welfare system and with an aging population, individuals and households soon decided to start saving instead of spending. But as predicted by the "majority fallacy" in economics, what was proper for one family led to problems when everybody followed the same pattern. First retail sales slumped, then orders were cancelled, suppliers were put on hold, and producers found themselves with mounting inventories. There is still, as of early 2008, no evidence that government's desperate attempts to prime the economy are having an effect, since consumers are still holding back.

It is not clear what will turn the situation around. Various retailers' marketing efforts—lower prices, special deals, promotional campaigns—seem to have had little or no effect on demand. There was some hope that the arrival in late 2001 of a first baby child, a daughter, to the crown prince and princess Masako would stir optimism, but the effect seems to be limited to the toys and memorabilia trade. Credit cards, which had slowly been gaining acceptance, are giving way to debit cards with conservative limits on spending and, recently, smart cards with built-in chips. Text-messaging mobile phones are popular among the younger set, both female and male, and new electronic gadgets such as the minidisc are always a draw. There is also some consolation in the fact that since there is little or no population growth in Japan, per capita incomes have stayed relatively high. This means that Japan is still a prime market for new high-end products and for luxury products from abroad. Overall, however, the Japanese marketplace at the start of the new millennium is in a holding pattern. Once the economy picks up, it is likely to show more of its true colors as the second-largest market in the world.

Foreign Trade Agreements

Japan has a long history of deliberate isolation from the rest of the world, which has made it reluctant to engage in trade agreements. One reason is the country's relative isolation, geographically and culturally. Except for Australia and New Zealand, Japan is very far away from other developed countries. Its language and customs are different from others and difficult to learn or understand, even for other Asians.

This has meant that Japan is an outsider in the sense that the country is not a member of any trading bloc of significance. In addition, from the beginning the industrial policies developed by Japan's Ministry of International Trade and Industry (MITI) involved tariff protection from foreign competitors.

Today much of the tariff if not the nontariff trade protection is dismantled. Japan has eased control over foreign capital investments, and consumers are more than willing to purchase foreign products. The combination of high incomes, high-productivity workers, state-of-the-art technology, and success in exporting has diminished the need for protection. Pressure from American and European trading partners and the threat of protectionist countermeasures have made the Japanese eager to attract foreign products to Japan. But marketing in Japan is not all that easy. The distribution system is complex and costly, and the consumer is very demanding.

Competition

One would have thought that with the home market protected, the competition in Japan's markets would be limited. And in one sense it has been. Prices have long been "coordinated" by directives from government bureaucrats, who fear the ill effects on small- and medium-sized businesses from cutthroat competition. In particular, so-called intrabrand price competition has been suppressed, meaning that a particular brand and model—Sony Walkman, say—will cost the same in all stores in Japan.

But from the beginning, competition between brands from different manufacturers ("interbrand" competition) has been absolutely fierce. Inspired by the bushido or "warrior" tradition in medieval Japan and its samurais, companies from different groups have competed fiercely for customers in terms of product innovation, quality, and service. This intense competition between domestic competitors spawned the development of quality circles and "total quality management" (TQM) techniques by leading Japanese companies. Gradually, the Japanese consumers learned that functionality, reliability, and features could be taken for granted. Their choices between close competitors were based on design, brand image, and other "intangibles." Price was no object, as most stores offered the same brands at the same price.

With the economic slowdown, this has changed. Deregulation has allowed discount stores and "category killers" to enter in suburban locations. Tariff reductions and elimination of certain trade barriers have allowed foreign firms to enter more easily. Among

Getting the Picture

TOYS "R" US JAPAN—BACK TO SERVICE

Toys "R" Us, the American "category killer" in children's goods, opened its first discount warehouse-style toy store in Japan in December 1991. Their low-price, wide and deep assortment, and "help yourself" style of merchandising became increasingly popular as the Japanese economic slump continued (see Case 2-1 in this text), But the no-frills policy has lately come under reevaluation.

As the market has become saturated, limiting the growth through new customers, the company has found that in order to grow revenues, increased sales levels could be reached only by increased service. In April 2001 the company introduced a system of "sales associates" in 13 Japanese outlets. The associates help explain how to operate the toys, ask customers if they need help, and even suggest new items for the shelves. These "innovations" would hardly seem noteworthy for most customers, except for those who have had some experience with Toys "R" Us stores, where in

the past salespeople had been eliminated in the name of efficiency. The Japanese customers even had to scan the barcode on an item themselves to find out the price. But as frustrated shoppers led to a sales slump in 1998, the subsidiary of the company requested the freedom to introduce changes. Reluctantly, headquarters gave the permission, and now sales and profits—and service—are up again in the Japanese unit.

Intense competition from Japanese firms has continued to make life difficult for the subsidiary. But McDonald's Japan, its partner with shares in the company, has provided support—combining the locations of Toys "R" Us and McDonald's still seems to draw in the little ones.

Sources: Michael Chadwick and Jeong-Soe Wong, "Toys 'R' Us Japan," Case report, Georgetown University, 1994; Fumiko Murakami and Wataru Yoshida, "Toys 'R' Us Recasts Sales Approach," *The Nikkei Weekly*, November 26, 2001; William Spain, "Expect More Good News from McDonald's," **www.MarketWatch.com**, April 18, 2008.

consumers there is a new emphasis on price and value, more in line with the typical Western markets. With this new emphasis, the Japanese consumer markets have become more similar to other mature markets, and therefore more differentiated than previously. And just relying on lower prices is sometimes not enough (see box, "Toys 'R' Us Japan—Back to Service").

Market Segmentation

The demanding Japanese customer is a hard nut to crack for the newly arrived local marketer. For example, Japanese consumers have long been accustomed to thinking that the only reason an imported product should be bought is that it provides something special. Of course, if Japanese producers were able to manufacture products that are as good or better by taking apart the foreign product ("reverse engineering") and making a similar version, Japanese consumers would often opt for the Japanese version.

Japanese consumers are, in some ways, the most spoiled buyers in the world.[15] But with the economic slowdown, this has changed to some degree. Although the Japanese are still demanding quality products, they are finally finding it worthwhile to get into the family car, drive to the large supermarket or out to the suburbs, and do their shopping once a week. Improved storage conditions in the home, with efficient refrigerators and freezers, make it possible to buy in larger quantities. Packaging innovations, such as condensed detergents and vacuum packs, alleviate the still severe space problems. As Jeeps and four-wheel-drive off-the-road vehicles become ever more popular, the family today has a car that can carry the purchases comfortably. The Japanese are becoming more similar to Westerners in their leisure and shopping behavior, if not in their work habits.

For each product category, there are now (1) upscale segments; (2) middle-of-the-roaders who buy the tried and true; and (3) those buying on price, looking for cheaper imports and private labels. In short, the Japanese market segments have become more similar to other mature markets. While Japanese customers were always demanding in terms of quality, service, and up-to-date technology and design, they are now also open to discounted prices. *Bargain* is no longer a dirty word.

Product Positioning

When the Japanese consumers' disposable incomes were growing, there was a considerable amount of status-oriented consumption. Well-known global brand names fetched high price premiums, especially in the luxury product categories.

Although there are still signs of this behavior, things have now changed. Less secure financially, consumers take time to evaluate products and compare prices. They have become what one informant calls "value conscious" and don't necessarily demand the very latest (although for some product categories and for some consumers this is of course not uniformly true). Rather than focusing on brand and all the latest features, many consumers are learning to make trade-offs between what they really need to have and what the price is.

This does not mean lesser quality is accepted. Quality does not reside in the features of a product. For the Japanese it is not an attribute defining the product. Quality for the Japanese simply means that the product performs the promised function without fault. The many new features desired before the present slowdown were all to come with zero-defect quality, which they largely did, thanks to the vaunted Japanese manufacturing skills. When the Japanese consumer trades off features and prices today, there is no compromise with quality.

Marketing Tactics

Product Policies

Adapting products and services to the Japanese customers' requirements has been, and continues to be, a problem. The basic demand in Japan has long been for quality products and luxury products. Western luxury brands and special cultural items with strong country-of-origin affiliation—such as Italian designs, French specialty foods, and American sports apparel—have been staple items in Japanese consumption. This is no longer so common, as incomes decline and as foreign products are entering often at lower price points. But Western quality levels are still a concern to the Japanese consumer.

Packaging is also of continued importance. Reflecting the emphasis the culture puts on attention to detail, the Japanese demand zero defects in packaging. Even mundane products such as toilet soap, audiotapes, and compact discs are examined for imperfections in packaging. Variations in label position, blemishes in the wrapping material, and unappealing color combinations are taken as signs of a poor-quality product. Apparel in stores is painstakingly examined by fastidious shoppers who look for double stitching, depth and variability of colors, and evenness of cut. Cost-saving shortcuts, such as replacing metal with plastics or noncentered labels are going to backfire in the Japanese market.

Pricing

As the distribution system opens up, imports pose a stronger competitive threat to domestic companies in Japan. Not surprisingly, price sensitivity on the part of the Japanese consumer has increased considerably in the last few years. Lower-priced imports are now more generally available in the new distribution channels, and they have put pressure on domestic retail prices. Some of these imports are private label brands of retailers. Accordingly, the consumer is faced with lower-priced alternatives not only in new discount outlets but also in established retail stores. The Japanese consumer today benefits from strong interbrand price competition and has learned from exposure to overseas markets that lower prices do not always mean lower quality.

While traditional retail outlets try to sustain premium brand prices, discount outlets have begun to sell brand name products at reduced prices, and a good deal of the brand name products are direct imports from overseas. Accordingly, while uniform prices made comparison shopping useless in the past, because of parallel imports there is now price competition within brands. Even not-so-poor consumers get price-sensitive when there are large savings to be gained.

Getting the Picture

ILLEGAL BARRIERS—OR RELATIONSHIP MARKETING?

Even though the warfront in the competitive battle between Kodak and Fuji has shifted to China—see box "The (Continuous) Kodak—Fuji Battle" in Chapter 2—their past conflicts inside Japan's market offer good examples of how distribution channels can be formidable barriers to entry. According to the Eastman Kodak Company, makers of world-leading Kodak films, its Japanese competitor Fuji film has illegally blocked access to distribution in Japan. In a complaint lodged with the U.S. Trade Representative, Kodak charges Fuji with illegal rebates and strong-arm tactics to control the four largest film wholesalers in Japan and keep Kodak out of retail stores. Only about 15 percent of Japan's film retailers stock Kodak film, and Kodak has only 10 percent of the market compared with Fuji's 70 percent.

Fuji's view is, not surprisingly, different. It claims its rebates are legal and amount to cooperative sharing of channel members' promotional budgets. As for distribution access, Fuji film is sold everywhere, but so is Kodak film in the United States. The little green boxes are seen by Japanese everywhere from an early age. Schools receive complimentary supplies of the little green boxes for class photos, and high school students on class trips carry Fuji disposable cameras. Past tariff protection is gone, and Japanese tariffs are at zero, although American duty on imported film is at 3.7 percent. And while Fuji has 70 percent of the market in Japan, it proves nothing: Kodak has nearly 70 percent of the market in the United States. Not surprisingly, the World Trade Organization in its 1997 review of the case found no reason to intervene against Fuji.

That slowed down the conflict between the two companies, at least for a while. But in 2004 when Kodak decided to make its single-use cameras in Mexico and China instead of Rochester, observers noted that Fuji still produced such cameras in Greenwood, South Carolina. The goodwill accruing to Fuji was noted by the press, as was the loss in pro-Kodak feelings among U.S. workers. The company made no comment. Good relationship marketing does not depend on borders.

Sources: Washington Post, June 26, 1995, p. A12; *New York Times,* July 5, 1995, p. D4; Jay Gallagher, "Kodak, Fuji put focus on loss of factory jobs," Albany Bureau, *Rochester (NY) Democrat and Chronicle,* January 25, 2004.

Distribution

The SII (Structural Impediments Initiative) and related efforts by Western powers to pry open the Japanese distribution system have won some victories, including the easing of the limiting large-store law, putting pressure on entrenched domestic marketers.[16]

The traditionally fragmented nature of the **Japanese distribution** system has frequently been noted by foreign companies. Western wholesale and retail middlemen are rationalized into large-scale units performing integrated functions; the Japanese system features several layers of small, specialized units, each handling small quantities of products. For each sale at the retail level, the product in Japan will go through many more hands, each siphoning off its fees and commissions. At one point the typical wholesale-to-retail ratio was 4 to 1 in Japan, while in the United States the corresponding figure was 2 to 1.[17]

For the local marketer in Japan, the cost of the system is only part of the problem. The need for frequent and close contacts between middlemen creates a preference for dealing with the same people and an aversion to change. Each middleman is treated as a customer. For a newcomer to break into an established relationship is not easy, especially if the product or service offered competes with a domestic alternative. There are still cases in Japan where a retailer is threatened with a cutoff of supplies from a domestic manufacturer or wholesaler if a competing product is added to the shelf. Although illegal and thus kept as "an understanding," the pressure can be very real. These pressures are now relenting, but they kept American cigarettes, European beer, and Western PCs off the retail shelves for a long time. The Kodak example is illuminating (see box, "Illegal Barriers").

Creating a new distribution channel is possible, but very expensive. Not only is it difficult to entice middlemen to give up their existing business, but the new people that may be attracted are often not the best. Add the cost of training and stocking and the cost of space and display locations, and the investment can be very large. It has been done successfully, as in the Toys "R" Us case, but one can understand why many Western firms find it too expensive a proposition.

Promotion

The Japanese penchant for polite indirectness has made their advertising singularly unfocused and "nonsensical." Sometimes brand names are not even mentioned, although alluded to or shown obliquely. Advertising is seen as a kind of art form, rather than a functional sales tool. Part of the reason is that the typical Japanese buyer spends more time contemplating purchases than most people in the West. Fewer housewives are working outside the home. The husband's workmates and the children's schoolmates are peer groups with which the interactions are frequent and long-standing. Add to that a distribution structure with clerks knowledgeable about their products, and there is little real need for advertising to provide information. The focus can be on entertainment and the creation of an attractive image.

But for mundane packaged goods, the advertising has shifted to more of an American style "unique selling proposition" approach. The reason is that as people encounter economic difficulties, the buyer needs specific reasons for purchasing the more expensive branded product. Image, status, and "fun" are not sufficient anymore. Thus, one can discern a clear shift toward functional advertising in Japan, also underscored by a greater willingness to speak about low prices. Economic necessity imposes itself on the advertising artistry.

The lack of store space affects promotional efforts directly. There is a need to offer smaller packages, fewer units, and faster restocking of supplies. When Procter & Gamble introduced its Cheer detergent brand into Japan using point-of-purchase promotions and dealer rebates, the consumers often found the stores sold out; there was simply not enough shelf space available to do the necessary stocking. Although Japanese consumers are now able to shoulder some of the storage functions as their cars, houses, and refrigerators become larger, there is still a premium price paid for space.

Close-up: Marketing in Australia and New Zealand[18]

Australia and New Zealand are mature economies with a British heritage. Their economies have grown at a slower pace than those of the Asian countries, with growth rates at about 2 to 4 percent, typical of other developed nations. Both Australia and New Zealand have targeted Asia and in particular the ASEAN region as the future source of growth and are in the process of shifting away from their European past. In 1994, trade between Australia and ASEAN countries reached $8 billion, growing at 20 percent annually. Following in Australia's footsteps after its emergence in the 1980s from a socialist government with high tariffs and import controls, New Zealand is also targeting Asian countries. Its largest trading partner is Japan.

Market Environment

Australia, a vast country more than twice the size of India, has only 21.2 million inhabitants. The per capita income was $34,359 in 2007. The country was ranked third in the United Nations' 2007 Human Development Index and sixth in *The Economist's* worldwide quality-of-life index 2005. Its economic base is in raw materials, in particular minerals, and in agriculture. A free-floating exchange rate was introduced in the early 1980s as the financial sector was deregulated and foreign direct investment increased. The change moved Australia away from the concept of a self-sufficient economy and toward a more open marketplace, which in turn has allowed Australia's raw materials better access to foreign markets. The absence of an export-oriented manufacturing industry has been a weakness of the Australian economy, but rising prices for its mineral exports and increasing tourism has helped economic growth. In addition, both Australia and New Zealand in recent years have developed a large and expanding wine industry with a strong export performance. Given the soil and climate conditions, the best wines are the whites, and Australian wineries have garnered accolades around the world for high-quality white wines at good prices.

New Zealand with its 4.2 million people is basically agrarian. The per capita income was $27,300 (PPP) in 2007. The domestic economy can be subdivided into five industries, all with substantial international involvement: forest products including paper, dairy products, meat products, fruits, and wool. Traditionally the country has exported agricultural and forest products and imported manufactured goods, still the dominant pattern. Since 2000 New Zealand has made substantial gains in median household income. New Zealand, along with Australia, largely escaped the early 2000s recession that impacted upon most other advanced countries. New Zealanders have a high level of life satisfaction as measured by international surveys, and ranked first in life satisfaction and fifth in overall prosperity in a 2007 prosperity index.[19] Economic growth and foreign direct investment by global firms have combined to make New Zealand a player in the telecommunications, information technology, and office equipment industries. Because of its small size and relative isolation from world markets, multinational companies such as IBM, Microsoft, Ericsson, Honeywell, Canon, and Philips approach New Zealand as a low-cost and low-risk test market for new products.

As a result of the growing trade exchanges, the centuries-old fear of large-scale immigration from the Asian countries seems to have waned; and in New Zealand in particular, with its Maori native culture, there is growing public acceptance of the contributions made to the economy by professionals and other immigrants from Asian cultures.

Foreign Trade Agreements

Like Canada, Australia and New Zealand have traditional ties to the British Commonwealth, which gave the countries preferred trading status with the United Kingdom. When the United Kingdom joined the European Common Market in 1973, however, the favored trading status was lost, which led to severe economic strains and ultimately new open-market policies in both countries. They have since reoriented their economies, and have long sought a free trade agreement with ASEAN.

The countries are both members of the APEC (Asia-Pacific Economic Cooperation) grouping and also participate in the ARF (ASEAN Regional Forum). These are still very heterogeneous associations, far from the integrated trade area concept of ASEAN proper, but nevertheless instrumental in the trade growth with Asia (see box, "Foster's: Australian for Beer").

The two countries have close trade ties with each other, manifested in the ANZCERTA pact (Australia New Zealand Closer Economic Relations Trade Agreement). For most global marketers, the two countries can be approached as one regional market.

Competition

The relatively limited size and the geographical distance to this region make some companies reluctant to enter the market, and thus competition is not as intense as in other mature markets. Those that do enter often produce on location to offset costs and to get under tariff and other trade barriers. But wages are high relative to many countries, and not only when compared with Asia (for example, two electronics companies, Panasonic from Japan and Motorola from the United States, found manufacturing to be between 25 and 50 percent more expensive in Australia than even in Europe and the United States). These high costs suggest that in the future, as trade barriers come down, import competition will increase dramatically.

Market Segmentation

As developed and mature markets, the Australia–New Zealand region offers typical consumer markets where careful targeting and segmentation become important. Natural segmentation criteria involve cultural roots, urban versus rural, and demographics, including age. Cultural roots do not simply involve the old-world heritage from Britain, although the college sports of the British Isles (rugby, cricket) are still very much in view. It is noteworthy how soccer—a sport where England, Scotland, Wales, and Northern Ireland also excel—seems not to have caught on in Australia and New Zealand, possibly because it is less uniquely identified with the United Kingdom.

Getting the Picture

FOSTER'S: AUSTRALIAN FOR BEER

One of the largest Australian companies is Foster's Brewing, the leading beer producer with revenues close to US$4 billion in 1996. Foster's operates in more than 120 countries and in 1997 was the third-largest selling beer globally. It expanded vigorously into Asia in the mid-1990s and found itself with overcapacity in China as the Asian crisis hit in 1998. The company is refocusing its China strategy around its Shanghai brewery, selling off operations in Guangdong and Tianjin. It plans to use its two Vietnamese breweries as the central supply location for the ASEAN markets and its expanded facilities in India to gain first-mover advantages over other foreign brewers in that market, subsequently moving further into the Middle Eastern markets.

In its marketing communications, Foster's relies on a country-of-origin cachet, Australia being a leading market for beer consumption. For the Sydney Olympics in 2000 one of its billboard slogans was "I live in Australia, the best address on Earth." In the United States its advertising focuses on the theme of "Foster's: Australian for Beer," showing stereotypical Australian characters (rugby players, hat-wearing outback men) in slightly absurd and comical vignettes, and with strongly accented Australian voiceovers. It is a strategy clearly targeting the heavy user segment among young males with the "work hard–play hard" lifestyle that seems to come naturally to the pioneering spirit of the Australians. It has also translated this spirit to some of the commercials in foreign markets, improbably showing suave and well-dressed Southern Europeans behave like real Australian mates.

While this strategy has continued for its main lager brand, Foster's has extended its product line with the introduction of other beers. One was the 2008 launch of a "green" beer. The eco-friendly brand is named Cascade Green and is described as a "100 per cent carbon-offset beer." The green color of the bottle is replicated by point-of-sale items, including bottles and cans as well as packaging. To minimize the product's carbon footprint, Cascade Green uses two-color biodegradable vegetable inks and materials that are 100 per cent recyclable for the cartons.

So as not to diffuse its alpha-male image for the main brand, Foster's name is not displayed on the Cascade Green bottle. There are limits!

Sources: Russell Baker, "Foster's to Sell Two of Its Three China Breweries," *Business Times* (Singapore), August 25, 1998, p. 17; "Foster's Entry May Change Indian Beer Market's Complexion," *The Hindu*, September 14, 1998; Emma Germain, "Foster's Launches Green Beer Down Under," *Design Week*, **www.designweek.co.uk**, April 15, 2008.

There is also a certain pioneer spirit in these countries that to some extent resembles that found in North America. For example, Australian Queenslanders are compared to Texans in the United States. This is not surprising considering the relatively late formation of these countries. Permanent European settlement of Australia began in 1788, and New Zealand's Waitangi Treaty between the Maori and the British settling their feuds dates from 1840.

The end result is that, as is typical in many mature markets, there are young people ready for the new global markets and there is an older generation nostalgic for what was. An American style might be more appealing to the younger age groups, whereas the older generation tends to be much more tradition-bound and in this case feels more empathy with British ways.

Product Positioning

Despite the relatively recent protectionist history in the region, global products and brands are appreciated in these markets. Part of the reason is a certain sense of deprivation because of past policies, made salient by global communications and frequent visits by people to other developed countries, in particular to Britain and the old home country.

There is still a fairly strong pro-home-country bias in several product categories, but presumably mostly because of social and cultural habits formed during the protectionist years. As always with globalizing markets, one would expect some—but not all!—of the pro-home allegiances to vanish as lower trade barriers induce competitive foreign producers to enter. The local survivors will be those who upgrade their products and stay competitive. On this count it is interesting to note that exported products from the region—kiwifruit from New Zealand and Foster's beer from Australia, for example—tend to use their country of origin in promotions abroad to create a unique positioning, drawing on the pioneering spirit of the country to position the products as fresh and irreverent newcomers.

Marketing Tactics

Product Policies

Most global products and services need only slight adaptation to appeal to customers in these markets. For example, the Toyota Camry, a best-seller in the U.S. market, is sold as a globally standardized vehicle, although the color preference in Australia is for dark and glossy, not necessarily the same as elsewhere. In the same way, companies in packaged goods such as P&G and Nestlé make little or no modifications of their products and may forget about those items that might need major localization changes. As for new technology, the markets are very up-to-date. A product such as mobile phones has penetrated the market particularly quickly because of difficult terrain and vast distances. Australian growth in mobile phones approached 70 percent in 1994, and by 2003 about 15 million, or three-quarters of the country's population, were mobile phone users. The country may have the highest penetration rate in the world.

Because of its terrain, the region offers conditions for product testing that some companies take advantage of. For example, the tough road conditions in Australia's Northern Territory make it particularly useful for testing automobile suspension and new truck designs. The steep coastline on New Zealand's Southern Island spawned the bungee jumping craze.

Pricing

Because of the distance from other markets and production locations, the small market size and high labor costs that make local production inefficient, and the historically high tariff rates, prices in the Australian and New Zealand markets are relatively high. Even though tariff rates have come down from an average of about 15 percent in 1988 to 6 to 7 percent in 1996, local regulation of business is still keeping some prices up. For example, just as is traditional in many European countries, book prices are controlled to allow small stores to maintain their profit margins, a system likely to be challenged by globalizing online booksellers such as Amazon.com.

The upshot is that although many global products and brands are available in the region, prices tend to be higher than elsewhere.

Distribution

Despite Australia's vast geographical expanse, its distribution is fairly efficient because its prime markets are clustered around the coastline and a few metropolitan areas, including Sydney, Melbourne, and Perth. The same holds true of New Zealand, with its mountainous interior. Where in the past the seafaring routes were key to transportation, today air travel is instrumental in connecting the local markets.

In the metropolitan areas of the two countries, the distribution system is modern and up-to-date. The shopping malls and busy streets offer the same amenities as elsewhere in developed countries. In fact, many large corporations use Australia for their regional Asian headquarters not because of its location but because of access to a well-developed infrastructure and telecommunications. For example, Dun & Bradstreet, the American financial data services company, uses its Australian location as headquarters for its Asian data distribution.

Promotion

When it comes to global communications media, there is very little that separates Australia and New Zealand from the rest of the developed world. In fact the relative isolation of these countries in the past because of government policies and distance from the northern hemisphere has made global communications particularly welcome. It's a two-way street. As global communications help open up these markets, Australia's and New Zealand's companies are fast becoming players abroad.

Global communications make it feasible to reach these markets with globally integrated promotional messages. At the same time, the countries' cultural ambivalence between the old world and the new makes for a need to segment targets. The young age segments are perhaps ready for the American-style media and global program vehicles, including CNN, *The Simpsons,* and the *Late Show with David Letterman;* while older segments are likely to favor the familiar humor and verbally adept British commercials and sitcoms.

In the end, it is clear that Australia and New Zealand have linked their future much closer to that of Asia. They will suffer as the Asian crisis unfolds, but also prosper as the Asian countries get back on the growth track.

Close-up: Marketing in North America

Viewed from any perspective, the North American market (the United States and Canada—Mexico is treated as part of the Latin American region in the next chapter) offers huge potential. It has a large population, with about 298.4 million people in the United States and 33.1 million in Canada in 2007. Depending on the current exchange rate, the region has the highest or one of the highest incomes per capita in the world. The per capita income in 2007 was $46,000 (PPP) in the United States and $38,200 (PPP) in Canada. It harbors a heterogeneous population with a variety of ethnic segments large enough to offer a target for many diverse products. Apart from some aberrations—steel, some agriculture, and apparel—it may be the most open market in the world. It certainly ranks as one of the most competitive markets in the world for most products. It may not be entirely correct to say so, but Frank Sinatra's words from the song "New York, New York" are perhaps applicable: "If you can make it there, you can make it anywhere."

Market Environment

As of 2008, perhaps the most dominant aspect of the market environment in the United States was the aftermath of the 9/11 terrorist attacks, the Iraq War, a weakening dollar, and threatened recession. The enhanced security concerns, the broadened surveillance effort, and inspection procedures at the nation's borders served to slow down tourism, trade, and travel, and increased the costs of transactions and exchanges across borders. One would hope that these obstacles to global marketing would gradually be reduced and eliminated in the near future.

Marketing in the North American context is what many if not most basic marketing textbooks cover. There is no need—and no room!—to discuss here all the aspects of marketing in this region. Instead, this section will focus on four aspects of the market that help make marketing there different and are not necessarily discussed in the typical marketing text. The four aspects relate to:

- Ethnic diversity.
- Religion, and the separation of state and church.
- Diffused economic activity.
- Local marketing regulations.

Although not necessarily unique to North America, these four aspects combine to create a marketing environment quite unlike that found in many other countries. They will be discussed in order.

Ethnic Diversity

A fundamental cultural factor is the region's ethnic diversity. But there is a difference between the "melting pot" of the United States and Canada's more segmented approach to diversity.

In the United States the tradition of the "cradle of freedom" symbolized by the Statue of Liberty is still strong. New immigrants from foreign countries arrive every year: In 2002 alone the number of legal immigrants was 1,063,732 (to which should be added an untold number of illegal immigrants). Since many of the new arrivals are poor, the cultural norm for Americans is to be helpful and to also be tolerant of seemingly strange behaviors. However, the driving concept is still the melting pot. Immigrants should be assimilated and become "real Americans." Even though this idea has come under attack

The iPod advertising establishes a fun, easy-to-use, young, and exciting image of the iconic white Apple MP3-player. It also uses cartoon-style figures, easily blending into any multicultural and ethnic setting. From the iPod Web site.

in the last few years as various minorities have attempted to assert their own cultural heritage, many Americans naturally assume a "teaching" role rather than a "learning" role toward other cultures. This attitude partly explains why they sometimes appear insensitive to local cultures abroad.

Although Canadians share some of these pioneer traits, their British roots have led to a more European approach, with cultural identity, old-world customs, and different languages nursed with pride. In Canada, ethnic subgroups are still strong and supportive of their cultural traditions. The Quebecois are only the most visible example of this. Boys' soccer leagues in Vancouver can still feature matches between Italian and British teams. In the language of Chapter 3, Canada's approach to ethnic and cultural diversity is more "high context" than the United States'.

Religion

In North America, church and state are separated by law. The government—federal, state, township, county—can impose no restrictions on individual freedom or freedom of enterprise using religion as a rationale. Various religious sects have their particular customs and holidays, but it is impossible and in fact illegal to impose any constraints on commerce because it is a "religious holiday." In the United States many stores (except in some places liquor stores) can stay open 24 hours a day and 365 days of the year.

For most foreigners, such open flaunting of commerce suggests extreme materialism. Expatriates from foreign countries sometimes succumb to the "convenience" of the American markets, making it difficult for them to return home to where strict store regulations make sure that some decorum is maintained and commerce is kept in check. In many religions trade or marketing is often viewed as slightly immoral. When religion is not separated from the state, this sentiment directly affects regulations of trade. The fact is that in most countries, retail distribution is much more regulated in terms of opening hours, zoning requirements, competition, and new store locations than in the United States. In American marketing, nothing is sacred. Literally.

Decentralization

Most countries tend to have a central government and business headquartered in close proximity. In Europe, London is the key to Britain, Paris to France, and now Berlin to a unified Germany. In Japan the headquarters of most large companies can be found in Tokyo, the capital, or Osaka. By contrast, in North America firms are spread all over the map, even into small towns. Caterpillar, a leading earthmoving machinery company, is headquartered in Peoria, a small town in Illinois. Washington, DC, the U.S. capital, has very little big business presence (except for the lobbyists and trade associations). The 50 states in the United States and 9 provinces in Canada all claim a degree of independence from the federal center. In the United States, major economic activity and viable customer agglomerations exist in 15 to 20 large metropolitan "spot markets," including New York, Los Angeles, Chicago, and Atlanta.

While the customers in most foreign markets take their cues from the center, many American consumers are blissfully ignorant about what New Yorkers or Los Angelenos like to do or wear. One can still use these latter two areas as bellwether test markets, as foreign companies often do, but such simplifications are usually more misleading than they would be in Tokyo. Mexico City may be the key to the Mexican market, but for many packaged goods Des Moines, Iowa, is a better test market than New York or LA.

Regulations

A particular headache for foreign companies entering the North American market is the prevalence of many regulatory differences between central and regional governments. As most readers will know, the French-language province of Quebec offers many challenges to standardized marketing programs in Canada, and packaging and labeling have to be dual English and French. Even brand names are affected. Procter & Gamble's Pert shampoo is Pret in Quebec. In the United States, the 50 states have independent jurisdiction over several important areas affecting business, including franchising contracts, resale price maintenance, pollution control, energy, transportation, banking, and industrial safety. Thus questions of product adaptation, after-sales service, packaging, and warehousing often become quite complicated.

As in other mature markets, there are also stiff regulations protecting the consumer. Promises in advertising must be kept (unless they are "puffery," that is, extravagant and thus "obviously untrue" in legal jargon). Test data on products must be made available for objective examination. Audience figures quoted for various media need to be validated by an independent agency. Stiffer laws regarding privacy from Europe are also under consideration. And as most foreigners know, the number of lawyers in the United States is sufficient to ensure that these and other regulations are enforced.

These basic differences help explain a few of the unique features of how marketing is done in North America. Some of the differences will be highlighted.

Foreign Trade Agreements

The 1994 NAFTA (North America Free Trade Area) agreement has created increased exchange between Canada, the United States, and Mexico. But the Canadian and U.S. markets were already very closely aligned through earlier free trade agreements, sometimes hotly contested. For example, the Pacific Northwest salmon fishing industry and forest industry have a long tradition of conflicts and infringement allegations between American and Canadian firms.

The ties are close also because the large Canadian multinationals, such as Seagrams in distilled liquor and Nortel in telecommunications, saw the United States as their largest market. And American multinationals, such as the automobile companies, had long been locating assembly and production in the Canadian market. Honda's 1998 Odyssey minivan was produced in Ontario, Canada, for export to the United States and Europe. European automobiles and Japanese television sets destined for the U.S. markets are often arriving across the Canadian border, drawing on preferential tariff rates. In fact, foreign firms entering the U.S. market often come across from Canada, using excellent port facilities in Halifax and on the St. Lawrence Seaway on the East Coast and in Vancouver on the West Coast. Canada is closer than the United States to both northern Europe and northern Asia.

Competition

The United States is by most measures one of the most competitive markets in the world. Its huge potential has attracted many of the strongest multinationals, helped by relatively low trade barriers in many industries. But because of competition, success does not come easily. For the many successful foreign entrants, there are many that have found success elusive. Mercedes and BMW have succeeded where Peugeot and Rover have not. Adidas and Puma have found the going tough, while Reebok's early success has been difficult to sustain. The Body Shop and Benetton have had trouble keeping their U.S. operations in the black. While Sony, Honda, and Toyota have been consistently strong in North America, the same cannot be said for Mitsubishi, Nissan, and Mazda. And so on.

Although there are many reasons for such failures, one underlying factor is often the marketing complexity fostered by the cultural diversity in North America. The diversity in both the United States and Canada is not simply reflected in varying customer preferences but also makes for complexity in marketing communications. Simple messages can be misinterpreted and misunderstood, and there is less agreement on fundamental values than elsewhere. Add the fact that so many competitors vie for attention, and the end result is that marketing budgets need to be much larger than elsewhere. Novice foreign marketers are often baffled and have a hard time understanding the huge amount of advertising required for successful entry into the North American market.

Market Segmentation

Because of the maturity of the North American market and the large geographical area covered, *market segmentation* is a "natural." For segmentation purposes cultural identity can serve as a useful criterion even in the United States. Marketers target the Hispanics in larger cities with advertising on Spanish-language cable TV stations such as Univision, and African American audiences are targeted through advertising on prime-time shows featuring African American actors.

Product Positioning

Diversity has helped keep the American culture "low context" and "young." In positioning, a premium is placed on direct and straightforward explanations. If nothing is said, nothing is meant. If you can't hear or understand what was stated, you had better ask for a repeat. For products with a mass audience it also makes it reasonable to communicate the positioning in concrete terms so as to be sure that "they get the message," since shared cultural norms may not exist. Subtle sales pitches get nowhere fast; hard sell becomes the norm. By contrast, the Canadian approach treats differences in cultural norms with much more sensitivity—and more soft sell. Still, individual consumers are assumed to make rational purchase decisions based on the trade-offs between various attributes or benefits, just as they or their forefathers might have done when they weighed the pros and cons of moving to these countries.

Marketing Tactics

Product Policies

Market size, affluence, and diversity have meant that the North American market offers a dizzying array of choices of products and services. Affluence and diversity not only help explain the wide assortments of products offered in stores or the ethnic variety of restaurants. They also help explain the emergence of the United States as a champion of fast foods. Pioneers, as contrasted to more established citizens, have many things to do and cannot spend too much time on unproductive activity. Also important is the fact that fast food represents a "least common denominator" offering for a diverse society, the kind of energy replenishment that everybody can partake in. McDonald's is the United States' answer to the communal sharing of food in more traditional societies.

Pricing

The attractiveness of the North American market has made it a very competitive arena for many domestic and foreign producers, with consumers reaping the benefits in terms of favorable price-to-quality ratios. For example, many foreign tourists, including Canadians, find prices in the United States lower than at home, even for their own countries' products. Free trade works.

The freedom from restraints on trade affects prices in many ways. Resale price maintenance ("fair trade") is usually illegal under the Robinson–Patman Act. To deny off-price outlets product shipments because they undercut prices is an offense. Competition is encouraged between brands but also intrabrand, between retail outlets. In the United States the same pair of Ralph Lauren eyeglass frames can be sold in two different stores with a 50 percent difference in price (see box, "Why Americans Are Price Sensitive").

Getting the Picture

WHY AMERICANS ARE PRICE SENSITIVE

When John Kenneth Galbraith published *The Affluent Society* in the 1960s, his assertion was that prices do not matter much in a society where people are affluent. This led many foreign observers to assume that in America, the land of milk and honey, prices do not matter. Many of them were surprised to find that, in fact, the United States may have the world's most price-conscious consumers. The Japanese, for example, have long been wondering why Americans are so focused on price.

The explanation is simple. It has to do with something called *intrabrand competition*. Intrabrand competition means competition between two offerings of the same brand.

In the U.S. marketplace, suggested retail prices can usually not be enforced. Attempting to not ship to stores that undercut suggested prices is illegal, and this is enforced through the justice system with its many lawyers. The principle is that any store legitimately selling, say, coffeemakers should be able to feature Braun models. The price they charge is theirs to decide, not Braun's. Nor can Braun charge the store a higher price than it charges other similar stores—again, a law that is actively enforced. When a big cost-cutting retailer begins to offer Braun's products, the company can try to avoid shipping, claiming lack of supplies or some other problem, but such defenses have been challenged successfully in courts and do not usually hold up.

The result is that a Braun automatic coffeemaker that in a department store retails for, say, $95 can be had at a cost-cutting suburban warehouse for $49.95. A Ralph Lauren eyeglass frame at $250 in the city can be had for $129 across a state line. London Fog coats are sold at a 40 percent discount in off-price outlets. And these are not copies but the real thing (although knockoffs are also a big market). American consumers are price sensitive for good reason: Price differentials can be huge. American stores have also wised up, many promising to pay the difference if the customer can find the same product at a lower price elsewhere.

In most other countries such discrepancies would perhaps suggest to the buyer that the cheaper version is counterfeit. It might be in the United States as well—but so, alas, may be the more expensive version in the other store (the problems of counterfeits will be dealt with in Chapter 12, "Global Products and Services").

Distribution

The great size of the North American continent and the wide spread of its people would seem to be the main cause for the large-scale stores and the nationwide chains that have made distribution in the United States very efficient. The creation of efficient transportation highways, the ownership of automobiles, national broadcast networks, and the technological developments in packaging and storage techniques, including plastic wrapping and the refrigerator, made the large-scale supermarkets and nationwide distribution possible.

But this has also meant that distribution channels carry more clout in the United States than in many other markets. For a foreign entrant used to a more fragmented system, it is surprisingly easy to gain coverage of the North American market quickly, provided an agreement can be reached with one of the large nationwide distributors or chain stores. The problem is that such an agreement can be very expensive to reach. Conversely, in many other markets national distribution may be difficult to attain without negotiations with many local small and independent channel members. For the North American marketer used to the simpler system at home there is little preparation for such distribution headaches.

Promotion

North American communications media are in principle not that much different from media elsewhere, but the use of advertising and commercials is greater. The United States shows larger advertising expenditures per capita than any other nation, including Canada (Japan is a distant second). Clutter is a real problem for advertisers since it is hard for one ad to get noticed. Nevertheless, advertising is absolutely necessary for consumer goods to reach any penetration in American markets; TV advertising, in particular, serves as the "great equalizer" carrying the message to the many different segments in the market. Foreign brands frequently have to spend 5 to 10 times more advertising per dollar sales in the United States than at home. The big market is there for the taking—but at a steep price.

The wide media choices available to North Americans are partly another result of the diversity. Cable TV offers 75 or more channels in most areas. TV programming is accordingly varied, and many programs cater to special subgroups in the population. In contrast to most other countries, there are no government-owned noncommercial broadcasting stations, an expression of the desire to keep the government from unduly influencing the population. This also means, of course, that there is no commonly accepted view of events or issues but that each citizen is forced to take responsibility for whatever opinions he or she may have. In the United States, it is rare to hear someone refer to the kind of "As we all know" evidence that forms such an important part of arguments in more collectivist cultures.

Summary

In the mature markets of the advanced countries, local marketing should become "just marketing." It can, but with a twist. Even among the triad nations of Western Europe, North America, Japan, Australia, and New Zealand, there are plenty of differences the marketer must take into account. This chapter has spelled out some of the more obvious differences but has really only scratched the surface. The local marketer has to develop a more in-depth sense of the local marketing scene in order to be effective.

Market segmentation is usually a "must" in mature markets, and in these open markets competition is intense. New entrants will often have to use niche strategies, positioning their products not in the core of the market but in a specialty area. Even when the entrant is a strong core brand in a leading market, the differences between mature markets can be great enough that the niche approach is preferable. On the other hand, when the product is new, the entrant has a chance to develop a new market and gain favorable first-mover advantages, something that takes resources, focus, and continuous monitoring of penetration.

Key Terms

country-of-origin effects, *240*
customer satisfaction, *242*
distributed headquarters, *247*

Euro-brands, *250*
euro currency, *250*
Japanese distribution, *257*

"me-too" product, *240*
pan-European marketing, *243*

Discussion Questions

1. From library research (including the Internet), identify how a product and brand of your choice is advertised differently—or similarly—in a European country and North America. How are the differences (similarities) related to differences (similarities) in positioning?
2. Use the Internet and company Web sites to find out the competitors in the Australian/New Zealand market for beer. Which global brands are present, and which are not?
3. Other than offering low prices, what can a Third World country do to get its products accepted by consumers in a mature economy? Can you find an example of a successful entry from such a country?
4. What are the reasons why entry into the Japanese market is so expensive?
5. Use news media and online access to track the impact of the single European currency introduction in January 1999. What seem to be the main marketing implications from the euro's arrival? How has the forced pricing in both national currency and the euro been handled by the various companies?

Notes

1. Country of origin effects have been the focus for a number of research studies for three decades or so. The sustained findings are that made-in labels matter for customers' quality perceptions. While consumers often protest that where a product is from does not matter, they still use country of origin as a clue to quality. It is less common, apparently, that consumers buy things because of some patriotic feeling. See Papadopoulos and Heslop, 1993.

2. As the multinational companies expand their manufacturing operations across the globe, the same process can be expected to make customers reevaluate their stereotypes of the countries. So, Indonesian-made calculators won't raise any eyebrows. What seems to be happening, according to research by David Tse and others, is that a strong brand name serves to reassure the buyer. A Hewlett-Packard printer made in Malaysia is still an H-P product. A BMW Z3 roadster built in South Carolina is still of German quality. A Sony TV made in San Diego is still a Sony, and to many consumers, its positioning is still that of a "Japanese product." See, for example, Tse and Lee, 1989.

3. The diffusion of manufacturing technology that drives this development exemplifies the Vernon international product cycle (IPC; see Chapter 2).

4. See Kerin et al., 1992.

5. See Johansson, 1994.

6. See Albrecht, 1992, and Fornell, 1992, for a fuller presentation of what customer satisfaction involves in different markets.

7. This section is based on Cecchini, 1988, on Quelch et al., 1991, on Johansson, 1989, and current newspaper sources accessed on the Internet. Here, as elsewhere, Raul Alvarez of Comcast provided invaluable insights.

8. See Halliburton and Hünerberg, 1993.

9. From "Volvo Trucks Europe," case no. 17 in Kashani, 1992.

10. See Dalgic, 1992.

11. See Hofstede et al., 1999.

12. From Halliburton and Hünerberg, 1993.

13. See Bartlett, 1983.

14. This section draws on Johansson and Nonaka, 1996, and Internet sources. Thanks are due to Kennedy Gitchel for reviewing and updating the material.

15. Fields, 1989, paints a vivid picture of Japanese consumers.

16. This section draws on Johansson and Hirano, 1995. The Structural Impediments Initiative (SII) was an agreement in the early 1990s between the United States and Japan to dismantle distribution and other barriers that prohibited entry into each other's markets.

17. See Czinkota and Woronoff, 1991, p. 91.

18. This section draws on FitzRoy, Freeman, and Yip, 2000, and on Cartwright and Yip, 2000.

19. See "Kiwis world's most satisfied," *National Business Review*, July 5, 2007.

Selected References

Albrecht, Karl. *The Only Thing That Matters.* New York: Harper Business, 1992.

Bartlett, Christopher A. "Procter & Gamble Europe: Vizir Launch." Harvard Business School, case no. 384–139, 1983.

Cartwright, Wayne, and George S. Yip. "New Zealand—Resource Play." Chapter 15 in Yip, 2000.

Cecchini, Paolo. *The European Challenge 1992.* Aldershot, UK: Woldwood House, 1988.

Chadwick, Michael, and Sue Won. "Toys-R-Us in Japan." Project report, Waseda-Georgetown program, Summer 1994.

Czinkota, Michael R., and Jon Woronoff. *Unlocking Japan's Markets.* Chicago: Probus, 1991.

Dalgic, Tevfik. "Euromarketing: Charting the Map for Globalization." *International Marketing Review* 9, no. 5 (1992), pp. 31–42.

Dreifus, Shirley B., ed. *Business International's Global Management Desk Reference.* New York: McGraw-Hill, 1992.

Fields, George. *The Japanese Market Culture.* Tokyo: The Japan Times, 1989.

FitzRoy, Peter; Susan Freeman; and George S. Yip. "Australia—Asian Future." Chapter 14 in Yip, 2000.

Fornell, Claes. "A National Customer Satisfaction Barometer: The Swedish Experience." *Journal of Marketing* 56, no. 1 (January 1992), pp. 6–21.

Halliburton, Chris, and Reinhard Hünerberg. "Executive Insights: Pan-European Marketing—Myth or Reality?" *Journal of International Marketing* 1, no. 3 (1993), pp. 77–92.

Halliburton, Chris, and Ian Jones. "Global Individualism—Reconciling Global Marketing and Global Manufacturing." *Journal of International Marketing* 2, no. 4 (1994), pp. 79–88.

Hofstede, Frenkel ter; Jan-Benedict E.M. Steenkamp; and Michel Wedel. "International Market Segmentation Based on Consumer-Product Relations." *Journal of Marketing Research* XXXVI (February 1999), pp.1–17.

Johansson, Johny K. "Japanese Marketing Strategies for Europe 1992." Paper presented at the conference on "The New Japan–U.S. Relationship," New York University, New York, April 4–5, 1989.

———. "The Sense of 'Nonsense': Japanese TV Advertising." *Journal of Advertising* 23, no. 1 (March 1994), pp. 17–26.

Johansson, Johny K., and Ikujiro Nonaka. *Relentless: The Japanese Way of Marketing.* New York: HarperBusiness, 1996.

Johansson, Johny K., and Masaaki Hirano. "Japanese Marketing in the Post-Bubble Era." *International Executive* 38, no.1 (January–February 1995), pp. 33–51.

Kashani, Kamran. *Managing Global Marketing.* Boston: PWS-Kent, 1992.

Kerin, Roger A.; P. Rajan Varadarajan; and Robert A. Peterson. "First-Mover Advantage: A Synthesis, Conceptual Framework, and Research Propositions." *Journal of Marketing* 56, no. 4 (October 1992), pp. 33–52.

Kotler, P.; L. Fahey; and S. Jatusripitak. *The New Competition.* Englewood Cliffs, NJ: Prentice Hall, 1985.

Papadopoulos, Nicolas, and Louise A. Heslop, eds. *Product–Country Images: Impact and Role in International Marketing.* New York: International Business Press, 1993.

Quelch, John A.; Robert D. Buzzell; and Eric R. Salama. *The Marketing Challenge of Europe 1992.* Reading, MA: Addison-Wesley, 1991.

TeleVeronique and TV 10. "Launch of Dutch Commercial TV Good News for U.S. Distributors." *Television/Radio Age* 36 (July 24, 1989), p. 19.

Tse, David, and W. Lee. "Evaluating Products of Multiple Countries-of-Origin Effect: Effects of Component Origin, Assembly Origin, and Brand." Working paper, Faculty of Commerce, University of British Columbia, Vancouver, Canada, 1989.

Updike, Edith Hill, and Mary Kuntz. "Japan Is Dialing 1-800 BuyAmerica." *BusinessWeek,* June 12, 1995, pp. 61, 64.

Womack, James P.; Daniel T. Jones; and Daniel Roos. *The Machine That Changed the World.* New York: Rawson Associates, 1990.

WuDunn, Sheryl. "Japanese Do Buy American: By Mail and a Lot Cheaper." *New York Times,* July 3, 1995, pp. 1, 43.

Yip, George S. *Asian Advantage: Key Strategies for Winning in the Asia-Pacific Region.* Reading, MA: Addison-Wesley, 2000.

Chapter

Local Marketing in New Growth Markets

"The future is now"

After reading this chapter, you will be able to:

1. See how new growth markets in Asia, Latin America, and elsewhere have become the new sources of growth for global companies.

2. Understand how many of these countries are directly affected by global turmoil but still have strengths both as markets and as producers with sustained potential for the longer run.

3. Use trade blocs as markets for these economies because the blocs are large enough compared to the stand-alone markets, which tend to be too small for targeting.

4. Develop marketing programs for new-growth market in a newly industrialized economy where there is less stress on new-product development and more on generic market development for existing products.

5. Tap into the pent-up demand in these markets where standardized global products and brands can be successful at an early stage, but where customers very quickly become more similar to the fickle consumers in mature markets, demanding adaptation and customization.

   Chapter 9 deals with local marketing in the context of fast-growing markets in countries that have appeared as players in the global marketplace. The chapter discusses these new markets in terms of opportunities for global marketers, but it is useful to remember that they also serve as sourcing locations for multinational firms (as we saw in Chapter 5's opening vignette about Brazil's exports, for example). This means that many companies are relatively familiar with the cultures involved and how to do business in the countries. It also means that manufacturing technology has been transferred, and many of these countries have viable domestic firms that can be strong competitors in their home markets as well as export markets.

   The chapter stays close to the traditional marketing model involving market segmentation, product positioning, and the marketing mix. It first deals with these markets at a general level and then goes into more detail for three special cases: Latin America, the new Asian growth countries, and India.

Samsung Overtakes Sony

In the last couple of decades, the Japanese companies have been the undisputed kings of the consumer electronics products world. Subduing first the German (Grundig, Telefunken) and British (Garrard, Burroughs) firms, and then the Americans (Fisher, RCA), the Japanese brands with Sony in the lead used the invention of the transistor (by American scientists at Bell labs) to take over the world's market for radios, televisions, and stereos. Product inventions such as the Trinitron color tube, the Walkman, the Discman, and Playstation 2 helped solidify the dominance. Helped by a large, demanding, and discerning consumer market at home, by the end of the century Japanese consumer electronics had virtually no competition in the global consumer electronics market.

Neighboring Korea, however, had a burgeoning electronics industry of its own. Spurred chiefly by Japanese foreign direct investment for low-cost manufacturing, the Koreans had become the primary OEM suppliers for store and generic brands around the world. In 1993, the new chairman of Samsung, Mr. Kun Hee Lee, decided that it was time to emulate the Japanese and create Korean brand names that the consumer could recognize. A beginning had already been made by Korean competitor Lucky Goldstar (LG) whose Goldstar television sets had already shown some promise in the U.S. market. Mr. Lee invoked a seemingly impossible aspiration, that Samsung one day would overtake Sony, a key competitor and one of the world's most valuable brands.

Turning a manufacturing company with B2B (business-to-business) sales to other vendors into a B2C (business-to-consumers) branded consumer goods company is not an easy task. IBM never did manage to get hold of its PC business and sold it to Chinese Lenovo at the end of 2004. After several difficult years, Hewlett-Packard seems to have finally succeeded in developing products attractive to consumers, while Ericsson, one of the original mobile phone developers, never did really understand consumers, and turned to Sony for a joint venture, Sony-Ericsson. But Samsung seems to have found the key. In Interbrand's annual ranking of the Top Global Brands, Samsung came from nowhere, then ranked number 42 to Sony's 20 by 2001, and in 2005 Samsung finally surpassed Sony, ranked at 20 to Sony's 28.

Several factors came together to produce this success. First, Samsung never veered away from its core business and manufacturing prowess, but instead invested heavily in R&D and state-of-the-art semiconductor plants. Sony, in contrast, moved further into what the industry calls "content," including movies, music, and entertainment. Samsung focused heavily on cell phones, a global growth market and one in which Samsung's technical expertise proved critical to solve the problem of sending radio signals over the jagged mountains of Korea. The Japanese cell phone producers, by contrast, were hampered by restrictive regulation and three different standards for transmission.

On the marketing side, the Samsung shift to become more consumer oriented was spearheaded by a new head of marketing. Eric Kim, a Korean-American with a background in technology marketing in the United States, was hired in 2000. Drawing on his branding experience, Kim clearly realized the need for Samsung to establish brand awareness and affinity among consumers, but also that he would have to find a way to sell any increased branding effort internally in Samsung. Understanding the strong engineering culture in Samsung, Kim realized that he needed quantitative data to show the benefits of any required marketing spending. Creating an in-house decision support data bank allowed Kim to show the results of past spending, and predict the likely results of alternative spending patterns. The M-net program, as the data bank was called, helped Kim convince hard-core engineers about the value of an advertising campaign stressing digital convergence (the "DigitAll" campaign), sponsoring the Olympics, and developing a special cell phone designed by the Wachowski Brothers for product placement in *The Matrix Reloaded*.

Now Hyundai is waiting in the wings.

Sources: www.Interbrand.com/best_brands; John Quelch and Anna Harrington, "Samsung Electronics Company: Global Marketing Operations," Harvard Business School, case 9-504-051, April 3, 2007; Marcel Corstjens and Jeffrey Merrihue, "Optimal Marketing," *Harvard Business Review,* October 2003, pp. 2–9.

Introduction

The new growth markets comprise a varied set of countries. In addition to Southeast Asian and Latin American countries, one can also include several Mediterranean countries, South Africa, and now also several of the central European countries. The main focus here will be on the Asian countries (except China and Vietnam, which will be dealt with in Chapter 10), Latin America, and India.

The local marketer in a **newly industrialized economy (NIE)** with fast economic growth faces a situation not unlike that of early marketers in mature markets. Although some of the markets are small in terms of population—Hong Kong and Israel at about 7 million, Singapore at 4.6 million—others are in the range of the European mix of populations, or between Chile's 16.6 million and Korea's 48.2 million.

India's 1.1 billion places it in a league of its own. India is usually seen as an emerging country, but its impressive recent growth justifies its inclusion here. Also, in contrast to communist China, it has a democratic tradition that makes its marketing environment more similar to the new growth countries.

Two Kinds of Markets

For global marketing purposes, it is useful to distinguish two kinds of new growth countries. There are those that are relatively rich in natural **raw materials,** but where the majority of the people have suffered pain inflicted to equal degrees by **authoritarian political regimes** and **colonial domination.** Broadly speaking, this is the history of many Latin American countries and also South Africa. The growth of consumer demand in these countries is fueled by a more even distribution of the wealth created by their natural resources. Many of these peoples have witnessed at close range the affluence made possible by capitalism, but have not been able to share in it before. Their outlook as consumers is cautiously optimistic, with the fear of renewed autocratic rule still very real.

Another kind of new growth market involves countries that have turned toward Western-style capitalism more recently, with the help of foreign direct investment. Not so well endowed with natural resources, their wealth creation has been spurred by multinationals locating export-oriented plants to take advantage of low **labor costs.** Included are several of the Asian countries and to a lesser extent Israel. These countries are newcomers to economic affluence and tend to be basically optimistic about the future.

Although the global financial turmoil, the antiglobalization trend, and the terrorist acts in the new millennium have shifted these general sentiments downward, the basic distinction remains. The Latin American growth markets tend to be strong for consumer durables and related products as households attempt to create a better quality of life for children and extended families. Meanwhile Southeast Asia has been the source of phenomenal growth for Western luxury products and global brands, as the newly acquired wealth is channeled into hedonic consumption and individual gratification.

The difference in economic and political history between these countries is generally related to differences in religion and culture. While the Catholicism of Latin America has emphasized submission to authority and acceptance of the essential pain of ordinary life, the Buddhism of Asia offers fatalism and an emphasis on the basic insignificance of individual life. While Christianity preaches original sin and guilt, Buddhism offers meditation and transcendence of worldly constraints. Although these distinctions are oversimplified, they suggest clues as to why consumer demand in some new growth markets seems more frivolous than in others.

Despite these fundamental differences, there are several marketing similarities among these new growth markets. As we saw in Exhibit 7.10 of Chapter 7, markets in these countries are typically in the growth phase of the product life cycle, which makes them attractive for entry. Certain markets might seem mature—food, basic household products, apparel—but there is generally potential for new variants and more international offerings. Other markets might be embryonic and in the introductory stage, including leisure products and services, Western furniture, and frozen food. But as incomes are rising, people in these countries are demanding the variety and experiences offered by the markets in more mature economies.

The Role of Trade Blocs

For many new growth markets, membership in **trade blocs** plays a very important role. There are two basic reasons for this. One, it makes the country more attractive to foreign investors, since manufacturing plants can be located there and receive preferential treatment for exports to other member countries. This is a key factor behind Malaysia's and Thailand's economic growth, fueled by membership in the ASEAN grouping. It helps in particular where components and parts need to be shipped between different assembly plants of a multinational. The large Toyota automobile plant in Indonesia exports to other ASEAN markets but also receives parts and supplies from its subsidiary operations in other ASEAN countries. Separating its manufacturing of engines, transmissions, and components between the different ASEAN countries to gain scale advantages, Toyota manages to obtain a preferential treatment for cross-shipments at half the regular tariff rates.

A second factor increasing the importance of trade blocs for the new growth countries is the enlarged market potential. Mercosur membership allows Argentina, a country with a population of about 41 million, to boost its market size to more than 200 million, adding Brazil, Paraguay, and Uruguay. Market entries and foreign investment that could not be justified with a smaller population can be attracted much more easily. Conversely, the lack of a trade bloc among geographically close neighbors will be a drawback for a region. In the Middle East, for example, the Arab request that entering multinationals not deal with Israel has made it difficult to realize the full growth potential for the small Israeli economy. Trade blocs do tend to reduce political risk.

The relationship between trade bloc membership and growth is of course reciprocal. New growth usually occurs when the trading blocs are created. At the same time, growth is necessary for the country to show sufficient promise—passing the critical takeoff point for sustained growth—in order for other countries to see the benefits of a trade bloc. If the country's economy is weak, its domestic businesses will fear and fight new entrants, and prospective bloc members will hesitate to partner with an inferior candidate. Africa is a good example of this vicious circle. Apart from their seemingly intractable tribal conflicts, the weakness of their domestic economies and market demand has prohibited many African countries from pursuing effective trade coordination. Fortunately, with the end of apartheid, South Africa might be able to lead the continent's revival (see box, "South Africa Moves Up").

Market Segmentation

Market segmentation in these countries differs from that in the developing countries primarily in the higher degree to which a **core middle class** has developed. The emergence of such a core group of consumers with some spending power in the NIEs means that segmentation techniques are directly applicable. In other words, these consumers demand variety and are willing—and able—to pay for it. In some cases, the requisite basic information—demographics, incomes, location—is unreliable because of large but hidden extended families, a desire to avoid taxes, and increased mobility of the populace. But as economic growth continues, consumer segments can be defined based on spending according to preferences and not only in terms of necessity; that is, not just according to "needs" but to "wants." It becomes important to recognize this and augment the official data available with primary data collection and personal observation and interviews.

Product Positioning

In new growth markets it is easy to observe the attention given to well-known **brand names.** Many people from these countries are aware of foreign products, either through travel or through the global communication network. Global brands carry a cachet, and companies capitalize on this by high-profile promotions, including very visible outdoor

Getting the Picture

SOUTH AFRICA MOVES UP

It was not that long ago—1994 to be exact—when South Africa threw off its apartheid policies and stopped being a pariah state shunned by many multinationals. Despite some setbacks—high unemployment among the black population, and an AIDS epidemic that is still out of control—the transformation to a free market and expansive economy has been proceeding apace. Today, South Africa has a well-developed stock exchange, banks, telephones and other infrastructures that work, a vital automobile industry, and a high-technology industry in telecommunications and computers. It's 2007 GDP per capita stood at US$9,761, far above other African nations. Not only has the country become one of the new growth markets of the world, it has also spearheaded an ambitious plan for the economic and political development of sub-Saharan Africa.

In fact, there is a decidedly pan-African focus by South African leadership in business and government. Other markets around the globe have not been neglected. South African wines, for example, have made inroads in most major markets, helped not only by unbeatable prices but also assertive promotional campaigns. But the country leadership has decided that without a stronger African economy—and less political and ethnic turmoil—its own future is limited. So, with the prompting of the government, South African businesses can today be found active in many of the sub-Saharan economies. Building on a skilled and experienced class of entrepreneurs, educated during white rule, South African businesses have entered markets from Nigeria and Mali to Ethiopia, Kenya, and Mozambique.

Since the native business entrepreneurs tend to lack skills and financial strength, the entry mode typically involves some direct investment as well as expatriates from South Africa to manage operations locally. South Africans can be found managing the railroads in Cameroon and power plants in Mali and Zambia. They are the brewers of local beers in Ghana, and the leading providers of cell phone service in Nigeria and Uganda. They control banks and supermarkets in Kenya and Tanzania.

Since many of these expatriates are whites, the foreign entrants have sometimes been received less than enthusiastically by a population that has only recently thrown off the colonial yoke. But in the end what matters more seems to be the quality-of-life benefits for people in the various countries who are finally getting reliable suppliers of products, services, and public utilities. So, South African exports to other African countries have risen steadily, from less than 10 billion rand in 1994 to close to 30 billion rand in 2000. While the share of South African exports that went to African countries was a pitiful 1.7 percent in 1991, the share rose to 12.8 percent in 2000. By early 2002, South Africa accounted for approximately 40 percent of the entire continent's economy. South Africa is poised to be the one country that just might have enough economic strength and vitality to lead Africa out of the economic wilderness. In 2002, the South Africa Brewers (SAB) company merged with U.S. beer giant Miller Brewing Company to create SABMiller. The combined company is the world's second largest beer brewer (after Anheuser-Busch). SABMiller occupies a top three position in more than 30 countries across four continents. It is the world's leading brewer in developing markets, with major brewing and distribution operations in Africa, Central Europe, Central America, and Asia.

Now if only the political leaders in other African countries like Kenya and Zimbabwe take heed, Africa may be on the right path.

Sources: Andrew High, "Envoy Cracks It with Boost for SA Wines," *Business Times (South Africa),* August 6, 2000; Rachel L. Swarns. "Awe and Unease as South Africa Stretches Out," *New York Times,* February 17, 2002, C1, 10; "Human Wave Flees Violence in Zimbabwe," *New York Times,* April 21, 2008.

and transit advertising. However, this does not mean that these customers are necessarily gullible; rather, they are open to indulging themselves occasionally. For more basic and essential products and services—foods, household appliances, autos—the demand for quality and performance can be as high as in an advanced market.

These countries often use foreign technology and capital to fuel their growth, which tends to create a certain advantage for foreign entrants since they represent the "real thing." Unlike more mature markets, domestic products tend to be seen as less desirable, even though their functional performance may be superior. This **neocolonial** attitude on the part of the customers does not mean that one particular foreign country is necessarily favored, although one is struck by the apparent preference for European styles in Argentina, Japanese products in Korea, and for anything British in Hong Kong and Singapore. The country-of-origin effect generally reflects how the economic development of these countries has depended on these supplier countries to a great extent; and, consequently, the products on the market tend to come from these countries.[1]

Marketing Tactics

The marketing mix in new growth markets can often be handled with a minimum of adaptation from more mature markets.

Product

Basic localization to make sure the product functions well (adapted electric currency, smaller package sizes, translation of directions, etc.) is necessary in these markets, and customers can be as demanding as elsewhere. But since there is often a cachet to being "foreign" for certain segments and occasions, the "no adaptation" option should be given serious consideration. It is important that the brand name be strongly supported; generic products in these markets rarely stand a chance against the domestic variants.

Pricing

Pricing is important but can largely reflect the same considerations as in the advanced markets—demand, costs, and competitive conditions. If the unique selling proposition involves status positioning, a high price is warranted. These markets are growing, and people are ready to spend money. At the same time, it is important that price not be too limiting: Building a brand franchise with a large and loyal following is very much the name of the game.

Distribution

Distribution and service activities should also be viewed for the potential long-range benefits. Distribution is very important and warrants larger margins and more support services than elsewhere. Participating in a growth market usually involves spending money to increase the number of outlets, the coverage of segments, and the response to competitive threats. These markets are not cash cows yet. Except for the upper niche of luxury consumption, they will not really produce a large net cash flow until later.

Promotion

Products and services should be supported for the future potential benefits they offer. Creating a strong image for a brand is important. Sharing information and building trust among customers for industrial products is similarly important. The sales personnel need to be careful not to divulge trade secrets that can be used by domestic producers against the innovating firm. The NIEs have often shown themselves impervious to international copyright laws and patent enforcement, although under the influence of the WTO this is now changing. Microsoft, the large U.S. software producer for personal computers, has had a policy of avoiding entry into Korea, Hong Kong, and Singapore because of these countries' copyright infringement practices (pirated Microsoft software still finds its way into these markets).

Nevertheless, with free trade issues still politically salient in attractive markets such as the United States and Canada, the NIEs will find it necessary to curb such activities in order to be part of the global trade system. Thus, promotional support, tie-ins with local representatives, and an open mind in regard to sharing with and trusting locals will be more justified in the future than in the past.

Close-Up: Marketing in Latin America[2]

These general considerations provide a starting point for the local marketer in an NIE. But more details on local conditions are needed to formulate, implement, and execute marketing strategy. Three major growth regions will be discussed in more detail: first, the Latin American market; then, the new Asian growth markets; and, finally, the Indian market.

Latin America is coming back as one of the growth markets of the world. This has also meant that the multinational companies have entered and that local companies have to face global competition, sometimes less than successfully (see box, "Bunge & Born").

The economic growth is fueled by regional trading blocs, a political shift toward increased democracy, and a gradual emergence from a large debt burden in several of the countries. For the local marketer, of special importance is the culture (religious and ethnic heritage), which affects communication strategy in particular; an uneven income distribution, which strongly affects segmentation; and a drive toward pan-regional marketing. More on this below; first, some background information.

Getting the Picture

BUNGE & BORN: WINNING AND LOSING THE BRAND WAR

Bunge & Born S.A. was long South America's largest consumer goods company, a multinational especially strong in food products. In the 1990s as the Latin American market improved, the company faced increased competition from domestic producers and imports in the various country markets. According to Ricardo Esteves, a director of the company: "During high inflation the fear was simply to be able to get the products, and you did not worry about quality or price. Now the shopper is comparing local goods with imported goods and other brands. So we had to produce better products at more competitive prices."

The solution? Uniform standards of products from the various country subsidiaries. And establishing strong regional brand awareness. "Before people would buy whatever pasta was on the shelves, even though they did not know what little company made it," says Mr. Esteves. "But people wanted to feed themselves better; they were looking for better taste, more purity, as well as a company that would stand behind the product. We want them to look for our brand."

Unfortunately for Bunge & Born, the consumers looked beyond its brands. The market positions seemed strong. Santistas Alimentos, its Brazilian arm, had sales of $2 billion in 1997 and was that country's market leader in flour, bread, and margarine.

In Argentina, its Molinos Rio de la Plata unit with 1997 sales of $1.4 billion led the market in cooking oil, margarine, processed meat, and pasta. However, as markets opened up, the multinational firms with global brands moved in. Also, retailers became more powerful. The supermarket industry began consolidating, led by multinationals such as Carrefour, Wal-Mart, and Ahold of the Netherlands. Bunge & Born suffered because of its past history as well. Bread and margarine may go together in a sandwich, but require very different operations, creating inefficiencies. Few international food companies mix fats and oils with wheat products because of this.

By the year 2000 Bunge & Born had divested itself of both the Santistas and the Molinos businesses, changing its name to Bunge International and shifting its business focus to agribusiness. Luckily for sentimental consumers, the new owners have pledged to keep at least some of the well-known brand names. Today, Bunge is a leading agribusiness and food company with integrated operations that circle the globe. Bunge's 22,000 employees work at over 450 facilities in 32 countries. It has moved away from South America, is registered as a Bermuda company for tax reasons, but has headquarters in White Plains, New York.

Sources: Nash, 1994; Robinson, 1989; "Bunge International: Sunset over the River Plate," The Economist, June 6, 1998, U.S. edition; **www.bunge.com.**

Market Environment

Latin America is a geographical area that stretches from Mexico down through Central and South America to Cape Horn. It is tied together by a common cultural heritage of native Indians, colonial dominance by Spain and Portugal, and the Roman Catholic Church. The language is Spanish except in the largest country, Brazil, whose 187 million inhabitants speak Portuguese. The total population is over 560 million, of which Mexico accounts for 107 million. The income per capita is still relatively low (see Exhibit 9.1).

Latin America exhibits a varied ethnic mix of descendants of the ancient, highly developed civilizations of Incas and Aztecs and the conquering Europeans—largely Spanish and Portuguese, but also German, Italian, and British. There are also African, Asian, and Polynesian influences and a significant Japanese presence in Peru and

EXHIBIT 9.1
GDP Per Capita in Latin America (2007, in U.S.$, PPP), GDP Rank in World, and Population

Source: Data from **www.worldbank.org**; **www.imf.org**.

	GDP Per Capita	GDP Rank in World	Population
Mexico	12,775	60	106,535,000
Chile	13,936	54	16,598,074
Argentina	13,308	57	41,000,000
Venezuela	12,166	62	28,272,666
Brazil	9,695	78	186,576,380
El Salvador	5,842	95	6,857,000
Peru	7,803	83	27,903,000
Guatemala	4,699	107	13,354,000
Colombia	6,724	92	44,082,284
Ecuador	7,195	88	13,341,000
Honduras	4,082	113	7,106,000
Bolivia	4,013	116	9,525,000
Nicaragua	2,617	127	5,603,000

An Argentine advertisement for Tropicana orange juice, emphasizing its purity. The Spanish language ad is a logical pan-regional advertisement as Tropicana expands from its Argentine entry point to the rest of Latin America. Courtesy of Tropicana.

Brazil. These varied influences combine uneasily, with ethnic heritage strongly linked to social class. There is great disparity between the political, social, economic elite and the often illiterate, poor peasants of Indian heritage. Society is stratified with two classes: very rich and very poor. This has given rise to political/military instability, a history of revolutions and coups, and terrorism as a means of changing the status quo. Economic progress should serve to lower this propensity for violence, and there is some indication of a growing middle class.

The Roman Catholic Church is still the most important **religious influence;** it has been shifting from its traditional role of supporting the oligarchy to supporting movements for social justice. There has been some growth in Protestantism and an evangelical movement (principally Pentecostal), heavily influenced by TV evangelism from the United States. The shift toward Protestantism goes hand in hand with the industrialization and urbanization of Latin America and the cultural shift toward democratization and self-reform.

Overall the region is poor, with at least 50 percent of wealth controlled by 20 percent of the people in almost all the countries in Latin America. Affluent consumers with buying power equivalent to that in developed countries are only about 10 to 20 percent of the population in most countries. Broadly speaking, these are countries in the process of moving from an agricultural to an industrial society. Venezuela is a special case, with a populist president in Hugo Chavez and increased wealth because of its oil and the rising oil prices.

Foreign Trade Agreements

Several regional trade agreements affect marketing in Latin America directly by enhancing the opportunities for regionwide marketing strategies. The major agreements are as follows:

LAIA—Latin American Integration Association

This agreement between all South American countries and Mexico expands a previous free trade agreement (LAFTA) into a customs union with free flow of goods and a common tariff rate toward nonmembers.

ANCOM—Andean Common Market

In February 1993, Bolivia, Colombia, Ecuador, and Venezuela began operating a common market. ANCOM means reduced tariffs, increased intraregional trade, free factor mobility, and a political climate more favorable to foreigners. Peru has now also been added to the group.

Mercosur—Southern Cone Common Market

A common market consisting of Argentina, Brazil, Paraguay, and Uruguay, with the economies of Brazil and Argentina performing well, this has become perhaps the strongest grouping in Latin America. The member countries have agreed to establish a common external tariff (in 1998 still at a relatively high average level of about 20 percent) and lower tariffs for intraregional trade. There have been problems in adjusting internal tariffs on a smooth schedule (in 1995, for example, Uruguay had 950 products listed as "exceptions" to the common agreement), but the sheer growth of the countries has generated a strong momentum in internal trade. For example, the Brazilian shoe industry benefits from a supply of less-expensive Argentine leather, while competition from Argentine wheat has reduced Brazilian wheat production by a third compared with levels before the agreement.

NAFTA—North American Free Trade Area

The 1994 ratification of NAFTA has meant that Mexico has moved closer to its northern neighbors. But rather than seeing this as a step away from the Latin American region, from a marketing viewpoint Mexico has become a natural entry gate to the larger Latin American market for North American businesses. This would be reinforced with the proposed admission of Chile to the trade agreement.

FTAA—Free Trade Area of the Americas

At the Summit of the Americas in 1994, the participating 34 countries agreed to construct a free trade area of the Americas. The negotiations about reducing tariffs and other obstacles to trade were scheduled to be finished by 2005, although the delays in WTO with the Doha round of global trade facilitation have slowed the progress.

Market Segmentation

Market segmentation in Latin America is often based on the simple distinction between **urban versus rural population,** combined with age and income level. A typical rule of thumb says that 80 percent of the purchasing power is in urban areas, with 20 percent in rural areas.

Urban Latin America also has a young, style-conscious segment. Approximately 56 percent of Latin America's population is under the age of 24. Many young adults live with their parents and spend disposable income on luxury and semiluxury items. The youth market can have a large influence on the buying patterns of their parents and other consumer groups.[3]

In rural Latin American markets, the cultural heritage of poverty and sometimes fatalistic religion creates a large tradition-bound family-oriented core customer segment. Authority is centered in the father, with a culture of "machismo" and the strong male figure. There is still a willingness to leave things to destiny and chance, to view the future as inevitable, and to put off till tomorrow (the well-known "mañana") anything that can wait and hope that it will take care of itself. But change is under way, and the global marketer should certainly not suppose that this tendency makes it unnecessary to answer requests and fill orders on time.

Product Positioning

Companies targeting affluent urban buyers can generally apply the strategies used in more mature markets. The urban segment is a status-conscious and aspiring market with working- and middle-class households spending a large portion of their income to upgrade the quality of life for their families through appliances, TVs, VCRs, and so forth.

Getting the Picture

VOLKSWAGEN MADE IN BRAZIL? YOU BET

Even though income per capita might be low given Latin America's traditional income inequalities, you can find high-priced import cars on the streets of every major Latin American city. In fact, as Argentina's currency became shaky toward the end of 2001, sales of new Mercedes and other luxury cars skyrocketed, as rich customers tried to buy before the peso was devalued. However, the general picture is different. Because of high tariffs and high transportation costs, automobiles in Latin America are rarely large luxury imports. Rather, they are small cars built by multinational carmakers in local assembly plants. The core of the industry is in Brazil with the largest car market in all of Latin America. Centered around Sao Paulo and Belo Horizonte in the south, the plants of the multinational manufacturers assemble cars destined for the Brazilian home market, for the other Latin American countries, and also for exports overseas.

Thus, even if the market shares of cars in Latin America feature well-known names, they are made locally. The 1999 Latin American market was divided as follows:

Volkswagen	23%
Fiat	22
GM	21
Ford	11
Renault	7
Other	16

Where are the Japanese, you may ask. The answer is that they are latecomers, and their initial investment was in Mexico where they could produce for the North American as well as the South American markets. But as the markets open up, they and the Koreans are eyeing the opportunity.

As Latin America's growth continues, customers for new cars are getting increasingly sophisticated, and the competitive rivalry is heating up. In March 2000, GM and Fiat agreed to a financial tie-up (GM bought 20 percent of Fiat for $2.4 billion, while Fiat agreed to take a 5.1 percent stake in GM) and have agreed to pool purchasing and combine engines and transmissions. The two carmakers have just finished building new plants in Latin America. While at present their small affordable cars—Chevrolet's Corsa and Fiat's Palio and Uno—are sales leaders, the plan is for more upscale cars and light trucks. Says David Rand, general director of design for GM Brazil: "Brazilian consumers now want the latest products. They watch America; they watch German television."

The Brazilian auto market is different from the rest of the Latin American market. In 2007 the Brazilian government instituted a compulsory 2 percent biodiesel blend in all diesel fuel beginning January 1, 2008. Brazil is a big soybean producer, and soybeans are used to produce biofuels in over 50 plants nationwide. The compulsory rule means that cars destined for the Brazilian market need to offer more hybrid engines—and places Brazil at the forefront of the green car movement.

The girl from Ipanema in a hybrid SUV?

Sources: David Phillips, "GM, Fiat Marriage Spells Profits," *Detroit News,* November 22, 2000; Christine Tierney, "Volkswagen," *BusinessWeek,* July 23, 2001; "Brazil Requiring 2% Biodiesel Blend Starting 1 Jan 08." Green Car Congress, December 28, 2007.

Global brands and products carry the usual cachet. One company, Prosdocimo in Brazil, was a leading competitor in the home appliance business for many years. Now bought up by European Electrolux, its products have been upgraded in line with the rising affluence of the Brazilian market, and the brand name has been changed to the higher-status name of Electrolux (see also box, "Volkswagen Made in Brazil? You Bet").

Marketers targeting the huge pool of low-income consumers have a tough challenge. Successful mass marketing can possibly be achieved through creative packaging (small-volume, low-price units), taking new product rollouts one step at a time, establishing one product firmly before launching another, and spending heavily on advertising.

Companies also have to rethink their strategies for reaching outlying markets/rural populations in Latin America. Face-to-face interviewing and observation are generally necessary to gauge reaction to promotions and products. It is very important to be sensitive to religious, political, ethnic, and cultural issues. Cultural idiosyncrasies—such as symbolism of certain colors, flowers, and animals—have to be reckoned with in advertising and promotions. In some rural areas consumers have not had extensive contact with the developed world.

Marketing Tactics

Product Policies

During the growth of the 1990s the Latin American marketers, whether domestic or foreign, have continually upgraded their products and services. The process has been driven by two factors. One is the increased competition from foreign producers as domestic markets have been opened. A second driver is the implementation of trade agreements between Latin American countries, opening neighboring countries to within-region exports.

A typical example is the beer industry. Major international beer companies, including SABMiller, headquartered in London, and Labatt's from Canada (now owned by Interbrew), have focused on Latin America as a new growth region. Investing in brewing capacity in these countries not only increased supply but also introduced modern brewing techniques and global brands, putting pressure on the local brewers. As a result, the locals consolidated and upgraded their brewing facilities, and many started exporting to other countries. Not surprisingly, and typical of this type of new growth markets, generic demand increased sharply as beer consumption soared. While in 1990 annual beer consumption in South America was 37 liters per capita, the 2006 figure was close to 50 liters. This left room for both global and local brands, such as Brazil's favorite, Brahma, with almost 50 percent of the Mercosur beer market.[4]

Apart from obvious localization changes such as using Spanish (and Portuguese for Brazil) on packages and instruction booklets, these markets so far require fairly limited product adaptations. But it is important that the right choices among a company's assortment be chosen. Latin American people can be much more serious and formal than European or American managers might expect. For example, when J. C. Penney, the American lower-end department store, entered Chile in 1996, it offered expensive lines in the flashy colors popular in more tropical markets such as Miami and Mexico. After a disappointing performance, the store replaced American managers with local talent, put greater emphasis on less-expensive and more-functional items, and went after Chile's growing maternity market. Sales picked up, and soon Penney opened a second store.[5]

Overall, however, the pent-up demand is for global brands and products that have been seen on television broadcasts of sports and entertainment events. In time, as the markets move closer to maturity and pan-regionalism, one can expect to see a need for more specific targeting of Latin American consumers and their specific tastes. To some extent, that demand will be satisfied by advanced local companies, but one would also assume that global marketers will find the market sufficiently attractive to want to develop pan-regional products for Latin America as well.

Pricing

As long as the historical inequality in incomes holds in Latin America, global entrants will have to focus on the urban markets, leaving the lower-price end of the range to local companies. This means that the standard advice for foreign companies is to price products slightly higher to create a semi-upper-middle-class image attractive to upwardly mobile families. As the middle class is developing rapidly, however, the foreign companies have found it useful to avoid too high a skimming price, instead extending the price range from the high-end (for the top-of-the-line products) to include also the mid-range prices.

The real potential in Latin America being the huge middle market, it is not surprising to see that many mid-range producers are doing increasingly well. Wal-Mart discount drugstores and Home Depot's hardware "category killer," both American retail chains with middle-of-the-road products at affordable prices, have done well in targeting the new middle class. But here the local producers and retailers are also active, and the competition can be fierce. Sears, Roebuck and Co., with long-standing presence throughout Latin America, was forced to withdraw from Chile in the early 1980s. Local chains such as Sodimac Homecenter offer comparable products and matching prices—and are more attuned to the local market.[6]

There are also plans for a common Mercosur currency. If implemented, this will directly affect prices because of the need to have transparent uniformity in different country markets.[7] If the brief experience in Europe is any guide, the effect will be to force companies to price at relatively lower levels than previously in most countries, a sort of "lowest common price" level based on prices in the most competitive market.

Getting the Picture

GETTING STARTED IN MEXICO: AMWAY FINDS LOCALIZATION LEADS TO RAPID GROWTH

When entering Mexico, Amway, the American direct home sales company, had to modify its system to conform to local laws and adjust for the lack of service infrastructure.

First was a change in the organizational system to avoid responsibility for social security payments and income tax withholdings for its individual distributors. Each Amway distributor must therefore register as an individual business so that there is absolutely no labor connection with the company.

Instead of the home delivery from a central warehouse used in the United States and Europe, the lack of adequate service by shippers in Mexico forced Amway to use eight distribution centers in six cities. It also works with a Mexican express delivery company for service to areas not covered by its own depots.

One challenge was the inadequate telecommunications system. The Mexican telephone company's (Telmex) rapidly expanding toll-free 800 service couldn't keep up with Amway's needs for quick order taking from its distributors. Service is still relatively inefficient and expensive. Also, Amway has had trouble securing a dedicated line for computer communication between HQ in Monterrey and outlying distribution centers.

Trademark registration and health authorization processes for imported products cause significant delays: Average wait is up to three months versus one month in Europe.

After these start-up pains were overcome, Amway Mexico became very successful, benefiting from a surge of enthusiasm for entrepreneurial self-sufficiency among Mexicans without steady employment in their home country. The initial suspicions about pyramid selling have been alleviated by strong advertising campaigns by the American firm. Amway goes to some length to explain itself on its corporate site, Amway.com. "Some people confuse the Amway business opportunity with disreputable pyramid schemes. However, there are major differences, which have been officially recognized by the U.S. Federal Trade Commission," the company says. It explains that Amway's multilevel "network" marketing is driven by one-to-one sales of quality products, and that entry requires a small refundable entry fee and no minimum order, and that it doesn't pay bonuses for sponsoring another person.

Sources: Dreifus, 1992; American Chamber of Commerce in Mexico, 1992; Karl Greenberg, "Amway Taking Back Its Name In Multimillion-Dollar Campaign," *MediaPost's Marketing Daily,* Friday, March 28, 2008.

Distribution

Distribution in Latin America is moving toward the larger integrated units and the chain concept common in European and North American markets. For example, large supermarkets with expanded assortments of leisure products and home appliances—so-called hypermarkets—are growing in importance. Carrefour, the French chain of hypermarkets, has a large presence there.

In terms of establishing distribution at the time of initial entry, barriers exist. Even though things are gradually improving, some find that a weak infrastructure and lack of legal protection create problems. Amway's experience in the early 1990s still provides some valid illustrations (see box, "Getting Started in Mexico").

Foreign companies have found that it is a mistake to rely on selling products through large and established Latin American distributors, who may only take on products that are easy to sell and who do not have a commitment to specializing in their products. For North American firms, joint ventures with strong local partners are advisable at entry to help open up the doors to Latin America's clubby business world. Some companies, such as the Philadelphia hospital company AMSCO, avoid allowing middlemen to define their markets and concentrate on learning the market and getting to know the end customers firsthand.[8]

Tropicana Dole Beverages International, now a unit of Pepsico, entered the South American market by launching its Pure Premium Orange and Grapefruit juices and Pure Tropics line of fruit juice blends in Argentina. Tropicana has a joint venture with La Serenisima, Argentina's largest dairy and a partner with similar high-quality products and brand-loyal customers. Tropicana entered into Argentina because of its strong economy, concentration of affluent consumers, and lack of premium chilled juice competitors. Argentina is also to be used as a springboard for entry into other Mercosur markets.[9]

Promotion

In general, Latin America is no longer in its infancy in terms of knowledge and awareness of world-class brands and products. Globally established brands have invested considerably in raising brand awareness and creating a market presence, and smaller local brands have had to fight for their existence.

Among urban consumers, research has shown that adult Latin Americans want detailed product information in advertising and tend to reject image-oriented ads. They want to understand immediately what the commercial is for and what it claims to deliver. Product demonstrations and testimonials are effective.[10]

Television commercials often revolve around family life, as households frequently have three generations under one roof. Women have been shown to respond well to commercials that convey a sense of pleasing the family through traditional roles of caring for the home and making meals. The Hispanic culture is upbeat and happy, and Hispanics react most favorably to ads that portray them as colorful and lively.

Sponsoring the popular daytime soap operas on television allows the advertiser to reach a huge audience of women of all ages. For the male audience, sponsorship of movies or sporting events is also fruitful. Endorsements by well-known entertainers or athletes can be powerful. Cafe Pele, named after the soccer star, has been very successful for Brazilian coffeemaker Cacique de Alimentos. When Gatorade featured soccer star Pele in a TV commercial in which he was seen drinking Gatorade after a game, no words were necessary. Sales took off, and success was ensured throughout the region.

In rural areas marketing communications are dominated by the need to overcome illiteracy. High illiteracy rates mean that there is a need for product identification through nonverbal/pictorial means. The accompanying music becomes very important: Brazilian commercials typically rely heavily on the popular dance music of the region. Package shape and design become very important. Repetition of identical posters and reinforcing the product and its name are useful, accompanied by easily memorized music.

As for sales promotion, because many retailers do not accept cents-off coupons, inducing new product trial is a challenge. Companies have used inventive promotional tools such as vans and sound trucks stationed at markets to play music and offer free samples to passersby.

Major Country Markets

Latin America has four major markets. Argentina, Brazil, and Mexico have large populations, while Chile has the highest per capita GDP. Some marketing highlights are discussed below.

Argentina

The currency crisis of Argentina at the beginning of 2002 initially threw the country with its 41 million people and the highest standard of living in Latin America into turmoil. Ten years of growth and prosperity was based on a peso pegged to parity with the dollar, and as the dollar rose against all major currencies at the end of the 1990s, Argentina's export products became overvalued. While imports soared, exports declined, creating an untenable trade imbalance funded by dollar-denominated loans from abroad. The cancellation of the peg to the dollar and the ensuing devaluation led to a crisis situation. To the surprise of many, especially the IMF economists, the crisis turned out to be brief, although painful. Defaulting on its $38 billion foreign debt, the country saw foreign investors flee, but prepared the ground for a domestic recovery. Once the economy stabilized at a lower peso rate, the country got back to its growth path—and its soaring exports became one of the new success stories in Latin America.

In the early years after World War II Argentina was one of the 10 richest countries in the world, on a per capita income basis. Politics changed that, but now the country is coming back again. The country has a highly sophisticated industrial and agricultural sector, making it able to withstand the Latin American turmoil and maintain free markets.

Increased purchasing power has contributed to increasing sales in consumer markets. With their European heritage and past affluence, the Argentine consumers are

Getting the Picture

TANGO AT HARROD'S

In 1913, as Europe lurched toward the Great War and faraway Argentina with its agricultural resources and prime beef was one of the high-potential countries in the world, Harrod's, the great London-based department store, built a branch in downtown Buenos Aires. Its glory faded after the Peronistas had reduced the potential for luxury consumption in Argentina, and in 1960 the owners sold the store to an Argentine company. But the Londoners apparently forgot to check the fine print carefully. The 1913 holding company contract gave the store the right to "carry on in the Argentine Republic and elsewhere in South America." By selling the store, Harrod's had also sold the South American rights to its name.

Throughout the 1990s, as economic growth made the Latin American market increasingly attractive, Harrod's owner Mohammed Al Fayed (whose son Dodi was killed with Princess Diana) made furious attempts in court to get its name back. But the courts held fast, and in 1998 Harrod's name in South America was the confirmed property of the Argentine company Harrod's BA, Ltd. Now, the old store in Buenos Aires is under Argentine ownership and has a special department for tango outfits. Perhaps as an act of revenge of sorts, when Harrod's in London organized an "Argentina at Harrod's" event in May 2006, one of the main features was a tango exhibition, with dancers from Argentina demonstrating the moves and the London audience invited to join.

If you can't beat them, join them!

Sources: Faiola, 1998; Schemo, 1998; **www.viewlondon.co.uk**, 2006.

---

highly sophisticated and oriented toward Western products and global brands (see box, "Tango at Harrod's").

The 12 million people in the greater Buenos Aires metropolitan area serve as a lead market not only for the rest of the country but also for the larger Mercosur region. It can be very competitive. One example is the soft drink market. Fierce competition exists between Pepsi and Coke for brand penetration and customer loyalty. Both companies are targeting young consumers and installing large numbers of vending machines as well as sponsoring rock concerts and special promotions. After nearly falling into bankruptcy during the years of hyperinflation and price controls, Pepsi has recently been relaunched in Argentina, achieving a 39 percent market share. Coke has responded by restructuring its distribution channels to work more closely with supermarket chains, bars, restaurants, and other retailers.

Brazil

Brazil is the largest of the Latin American countries with 187 million people. Under President Lula's regime, past restrictions on inward investment and capital movements have been lifted, runaway inflation has been stopped, and the country has become a Latin American engine of growth again. Brazil generates a third of South America's economic output and is a major consumer of its exports.

The currency devaluation in Argentina in 2002 also threatened Brazil's real and the country's attraction for foreign investors. However, Brazil held fast to the IMF recipe of maintaining a stable currency and honoring commitments to foreign investors. This has meant that the real is rising in value, making Brazil's exports relatively expensive. Still, because it possesses great wealth in raw materials, especially in minerals but also in oil and agriculture, rising raw material prices have helped fuel strong economic growth. With strong trade ties to China and the United States, the longer-term future looks bright. In 1998 there were over 300 joint business projects under way with Argentine companies alone, and more than 70 percent of Brazilian exports were of manufactured goods, including automobiles from Brazilian plants of Volkswagen, Fiat, General Motors, Honda, and Toyota.[11]

Chile

Chile, with its 16.5 million people, has been perhaps the most consistent example of recent Latin American growth, and its consumer markets are booming. A raft of new shopping malls have risen around metropolitan areas, and are emerging as the kind of consumer destination they are elsewhere. The new shopping malls range from a $59 million luxury mall

Getting the Picture

COLAS IN MEXICO: BRANDING GLOBALLY, MARKETING LOCALLY

Not surprisingly, global companies are finding that marketing and brand promotion strategies that work in developed mature markets do not always work in developing regions. Traditional rivals Coke and Pepsi provide a Mexican illustration.

Mexicans eat and drink on the go. They are also used to trekking to the corner store more than once a day, for small shopping errands. Slick TV spots featuring wannabe athletes carrying a six-pack of Cola do nothing for them. To overcome its weak number two position, Pepsi evolved a "Power of One" strategy that focused on selling one can of Pepsi each time. Furthermore, the can is downsized and costs less than the usual 12-ounce container. The can is cross-marketed with Pepsi-owned Frito-Lay's leading snack brand "Sabritas," which has 81 percent of the Mexican salty snack market, and downsized Sabritas packages are also available. As the thirsty consumer enters a store he or she is greeted with large displays of Pepsi and Sabritas, the least expensive combination selling for a few pesos.

As the Power of One promotion succeeded in raising Pepsi's sales by 26 percent, longtime leader Coke did not sit still. In February 2000, its local franchisee Panamco was given authority to localize its marketing and distribution of Coke further. The bottler has been experimenting with various niche programs, including a "Condominium Plan," a "School Plan," and a "Liquor Store Plan." The core counter-strategy, however, involves a plan called the "100 meters program." The idea is that in any urban center, no one should have to walk more than 100 meters to buy a Coke.

The results? By end of 2006 Coke controlled 60 percent of the Mexican soda market, while Pepsi had 30 percent. Coke's hold on Mexico extends far. Vicente Fox was serving as president of the Coca-Cola Corporation of Mexico and Latin America before becoming Mexico's president in 2000.

Sources: "Stomach Share," *Brandmarketing,* May 2000; Alan Waldman, "Branding Globally, Marketing Locally," *Multichannel News International,* June 1, 2001; Beverly Bell, "Cola Wars in Mexico," **www.inthesetimes.com,** October 6, 2006.

to Chile's very first outlet mall, where one-third of the new stores will be foreign chains. An increasing number of Chileans frequent shopping malls, but the basic attraction is slightly different from the United States. One study showed that while as many as 45 percent of Americans are attracted to malls because of the atmosphere, the majority of the Chilean shoppers come to purchase a specific item.[12]

As elsewhere in Latin America, credit card issuers are helping to fuel growth in spending by lowering the minimum household income required to obtain a card (for instance, Banco Santander requires only $500 to $600 monthly income, versus $1,000 previously).

Mexico

The 107 million people of Mexico make the country the second-largest market (after Brazil) in Latin America. Its membership in NAFTA has reinforced foreign investors' confidence in the country despite various political problems and ethnic disturbances. In the past many foreign companies (Japanese and European in addition to American) located plants in Mexico to serve the Latin American market. With the advent of NAFTA, capacity at these plants has now increased to serve the North American market as well. The economy is also given a boost from Mexican workers in the United States who send money back home to their families and relatives.

The Mexico City metropolitan area, home to almost 20 million people, provides a major market for global brands and upscale consumer goods. As in so many other countries where business and government are concentrated in the capital city, Ciudad de Mexico is a trendsetter for the rest of the country but also atypical in its cosmopolitanism. For example, a 24-hour home shopping network was introduced in Mexico City as early as 1993, and many of the world's major retailers can be found there (although Home Depot, the American hardware superstore, scrapped plans for Mexico in the 1995 crisis and instead went into Chile in 1998).[13] Some marketers are successful with the integrated marketing approaches common in mature markets to reach consumers. For example, the Kellogg's cereal company sponsored a conference on nutrition and fiber that generated a large amount of publicity. This was followed by an equally successful introduction of recipes and nutrition messages on cereal boxes. However, localization is often desirable (see box, "Colas in Mexico").

Getting the Picture

PAN–LATIN AMERICAN STRATEGY? YES AND NO

As the Latin American TV market is poised for strong growth and regionwide networks are created, advertisers are starting to think pan-Latin. So do firms selling everything from pizza to natural gas.

In August 2000, Venezuelan media giant Cisneros Group launched a pan–Latin American entertainment and news television network that ultimately aims to reach 40 million viewers in Latin America, Spain, and Portugal. The Spanish-language channel is delivered by satellite and cable and will aim at a mix of soap operas, magazine-type shows, humor, and news for Latin American viewers of all ages. As advertisers join up, TV revenues from Latin American advertising are expected to triple to a total of $41 billion by the year 2010.

Many of the products and services advertised are the "usual suspects" of global brands, including Coke, Sony, Volkswagen, and Goodyear. But the advertisers also include more exotic brands such as TelePizza, the Spanish fast-food company that entered the Central American market in 2000. TelePizza has had great success with its dial-a-pizza business model in Europe and plans to expand into at least three new countries a year. In Latin America the plan is to expand southward from a base in Guatemala via the Gutierrez group, which is a partner of the Spanish telecom group Telefonica SA.

But pan-regional strategies are not always preferable to more localization. The famed TV station Music Television, a.k.a. MTV, has long treated the Latin American market as one, with a single station serving the entire region from Mexico to Tierra del Fuego. But in 1996 the company made a decision to split the region into a northern and a southern part, and in 2001 it took the next step of localizing programming by country. The new format will allow stations to focus less on multinational megastars and more on local talent. This could be a mixed blessing for local artists who had been critical of the pan-regional strategy. It is nice for, say, Chilean artists who previously had been denied access to airtime. On the other hand, with the new structure they will not get exposed to the greater audience outside Chile.

Does this mean we up North will not get to hear the next Ricky Martin, Marc Anthony, or Jennifer Lopez? Don't count on it. As long as the Spanish-speaking half of the globe keeps growing they are likely to give us more, not less, of their culture—performers like Daddy Yankee, Camila, and Juanes.

Sources: "Pan–Latin American TV Channel Launched," *National Post*, August 29, 2000; "Latin American TV Market Poised for Tremendous Growth," *Multichannel News International*, July 2000; "TelePizza to Enter Central America," *Expansion*, October 25, 2000; "Regional MTV Station Is a Mixed Blessing for Chile," *Santiago Times*, April 4, 2001; **www.billboard.com.**

Pan-Regional Marketing

Some observers argue that the Latin American market is **pan-regional**, and that a marketing strategy aimed at the Latin American region overall will be effective.[14]

Advertising agencies such as McCann-Erickson and DDB Needham believe that there is a strong trend toward increased regionalization and integration in Latin America.[15] They anticipate that this will lead to more pan-regional advertising and media buying. However, cross-border advertising is currently hampered by the media infrastructure, which is still very localized and not very extensive in some countries.

One American companies' Latin American strategies can be used to demonstrate how global marketers are approaching the region (see also the globalization of Goodyear's Latin American advertising discussed at the end of Chapter 16).

Burger King in Latin America

Burger King, the fast-food restaurant chain, has expanded into Mexico, Brazil, Chile, Peru, Argentina, Colombia, and Puerto Rico during the last few years. This expansion has taken the form of joint ventures, franchise agreements, and alliances with U.S. consumer products companies such as Coca-Cola. Burger King spent about $5 million in advertising annually to introduce its name into the region.

The company's objective in expanding in Latin America is to "think globally and act locally." It has established headquarters for the Latin American division in Miami but is also setting up corporate offices in the local markets including Rio de Janeiro, Mexico City, and São Paulo.[16]

In the end, however, it is misleading to believe that Latin America is a single, borderless market like the European Union. Manuel Mencia of the Beacon Council, a Florida economic development group, says that non–Latin Americans tend to ignore that "what divides Latin Americans is much more important than what binds them."[17] Marketers may do better understanding one country's culture at a time and, for the time being at least, emphasizing localization (see box, "Pan–Latin American Strategy? Yes and No").

Close-Up: Marketing in the New Asian Growth Markets[18]

Up until July 1997 when the Thailand currency (the baht) was devalued, setting off a worldwide financial crisis, the Southeast Asian countries had been the fastest growing economies in the world. Annual growth rates for the region typically ranged between 5 and 10 percent, significantly above the 2 to 4 percent growth rates of the mature economies (see Exhibit 9.2). With the precipitous fall in the exchange rates as investment capital fled the countries, growth rates were sharply down and even negative in 1998. With China's awakening, however, one can expect the region to bounce back and resume its economic progress (see box, "Asian Comeback?").

The countries of primary interest here are South Korea, Taiwan, Hong Kong, and the original ASEAN members (Indonesia, Malaysia, the Philippines, Singapore, and Thailand). India will be treated separately, and China and Vietnam are covered in Chapter 10, which deals more directly with newly opened markets.

Even though all of these countries suffered significant economic damage at the end of the 1990s, caught in the grip of financial crises and currency devaluations, they have recently returned as high-growth markets.

Market Environment

As can be seen in Exhibit 9.2, these countries vary in size from Indonesia's almost 232 million people to Singapore's 4.7 million. Several are ethnically homogeneous (Taiwan, Korea), while others (Malaysia, Singapore) are populated by several racial groups (Chinese, Indian, Malay). They also vary in geographic scope, from the city-states Hong Kong and Singapore to Indonesia's and the Philippines' archipelagoes with a vast number of islands. Indonesia alone possesses an estimated number of 13,700 islands, it has the world's largest Muslim population (over 200 million), and its people speak some 250 regional dialects. Their economic performance also differs, the longer-established "four dragons" (Korea, Taiwan, Hong Kong, and Singapore) clearly outperforming relative newcomers such as Thailand, Indonesia, and the Philippines. In 2007 Hong Kong and Singapore had per capita incomes in the top 10 of the world, a remarkable feat.

One common characteristic of several of these countries is a sort of love–hate relationship with Japan. Most were occupied by Japanese forces in World War II, and some, such as Korea, had been under Japanese domination before. At the same time, the recent economic resurgence of these countries has been modeled on the Japanese pattern, basically an export-led expansion. In addition, the Japanese multinationals have invested heavily in the Asian countries, with operations ranging from sourcing of raw materials (Indonesian lumber, oil) to technology products such as automobile components and computer chips (Malaysia, Thailand). Despite the occasional animosity against Japan because of atrocities committed during the war, the Japanese businesses are basically well positioned and welcomed in these countries.

EXHIBIT 9.2

GDP Per Capita in Asia (2007, in U.S.$, PPP), GDP Rank in World, and Population

Source: Data from www.worldbank.org; www.imf.org.

Nation	GDP Per Capita	GDP Rank in World	Population
Hong Kong	41,994	10	6,963,100
Singapore	49,714	6	4,681,000
Taiwan	30,126	28	22,975,000
South Korea	24,783	35	48,224,000
Malaysia	13,315	56	27,452,527
Thailand	7,900	81	63,038,247
Philippines	3,378	122	88,574,614
Indonesia	3,725	120	231,627,000
Vietnam	2,587	129	87,375,000
China	5,292	99	1,323,361,000
India	2,659	126	1,131,813,000

Getting the Picture

ASIAN COMEBACK? YES—THANKS TO CHINA

Most analysts of Asia's prospects in the wake of the financial crisis at the end of the 1990s pointed to the need for Japan to serve as the engine of recovery. As long as Japan was in the doldrums, the argument went, there is not much hope for much growth. Asia—in fact, the world—needed a strong Japan.

This argument was perhaps accurate at one point. But it is not the whole story, and as the Japanese malaise lingers, the other economies are finding ways to cope. Excepting Indonesia and Thailand, most of the countries have grown at a pace of about 5 percent a year since the start of the new millennium, slower than the 7 percent or so in the mid-1990s but still better than most other countries.

One saving grace has been the strong performance of the Chinese economy. With China growing at almost a 10 percent annual rate, its size has helped the other countries to substitute trade with China and investment there for the slack on the Japanese side. Hong Kong has clearly gained considerably because of its function as a gateway into China, and although this role has diminished as Shanghai and other cities take on a greater role, Hong Kong is still strong.

Singapore's Chinese ties are also healthy, but the strength of Singapore has always been closely tied to the West and if the United States falters, Singapore is not doing as well.

Korea and Taiwan, once "tigers," are also helped by a strong China. Korea still has considerable investments in China, and with China and Taiwan entering the WTO together in 2001, the latter country seems to have buried long-standing conflicts with the mainland. And even the Japanese companies have found China to be one of the few bright spots in their forecasts. The Japanese and the Americans are in fact the largest foreign investors in China. As the Chinese economy has opened up further in the wake of the WTO entry, one can expect its importance as a growth engine to increase further.

As China seems to be putting everyone back on track, the economies of Asia are, on the whole, ready to move on to the next level of development and growth.

Sources: Brian Barry, "The Faltering Firefighter," *The Economist,* July 6, 2000; "Ad Agencies' Hopes Still Buoyant across Asia Despite Slower Growth," *Asian Wall Street Journal Weekly,* January 8, 2001; Philip Kotler and Hermawan Kartajaya, *Repositioning Asia: From Bubble to Sustainable Economy* (Singapore: Wiley and Sons, Asia, 2000); "Global slowdown tests China's goals," **www.atimes.com,** April 4, 2008.

Foreign Trade Agreements

There are several regional trade agreements among these countries that offer good starting points for pan-regional strategies.

ASEAN—Association of South East Asian Nations

ASEAN was created in 1967. It includes Indonesia, Malaysia, the Philippines, Singapore, and Thailand, with Brunei added in 1967, Vietnam in 1995, Myanmar and Laos in 1997, and Cambodia in 1999. Originally a political union, it has evolved into a free trade area.

Shopping in warehouse stores at discounted prices is becoming a global phenomenon as chains go into new growth markets. Here shoppers in Malaysia push the limits of their carrying capacity at Makro, a Dutch-owned retail chain. Munshi Ahmed.

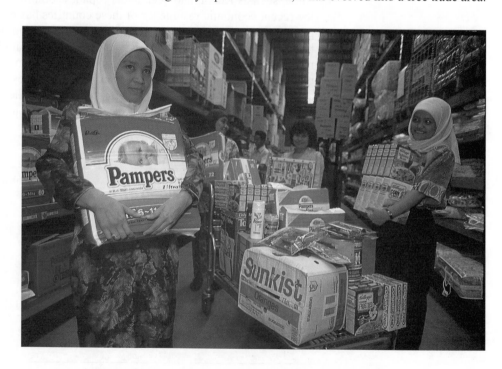

AFTA—ASEAN Free Trade Area

In 1992, ASEAN countries met to formalize a far-reaching trade agreement, forming AFTA. Created to match the emergence of the European Union, the principal result was a preferential tariff rate no higher than 5 percent between member nations (with the ultimate aim of reducing tariffs to 0 percent), reduction of nontariff barriers, and a common external tariff rate. The AFTA development is a significant step toward creating the kind of common market one finds in Europe's EU and Latin America's Mercosur, and it is likely that "pan-AFTA" products and marketing campaigns will gradually emerge.

APEC—Asia-Pacific Economic Cooperation

APEC is a large association that spans both sides of the Pacific from Canada and Chile to Australia.

ARF—ASEAN Regional Forum

ARF is an extension of the ASEAN bloc to include Russia and Cambodia.
These broader groupings represent tentative efforts to extend the region politically and economically, and have been slowed by the turmoil at the end of the 1990s.

New trade agreements are being negotiated, especially with the pivotal ASEAN grouping. With China's size and rapid growth, experts predict the next agreement is likely to be an ASEAN-China Free Trade Area. Closely behind is a Japan tie-up, the ASEAN-Japan Comprehensive Economic Partnership. A Korean agreement is also on the horizon, creating an "ASEAN-plus-3" trade area. India is also interested in an agreement with ASEAN but this is being pushed further into the future.

Market Segmentation

The economic upswing in the Asian high-growth markets has led to the emergence of a significant middle class, in Thailand known as the "have somes." Its size varies with the population and the level of growth. In Korea, with a GDP ranked 35th in the world, the majority of the 48 million inhabitants can be classified as middle class, while less than 15 percent of Indonesia's 232 million people are middle class. Most of these people live in the urban areas. In fact, the core of the market for global companies is in the large metropolitan areas, from Bangkok and Jakarta to Manila and Seoul.

However justified from an economic perspective, avoiding the rural areas where people tend to be less well-off can create some political problems. Multinational entrants cannot always count on a welcome with open arms, especially from governments with socialist leanings. So far the Asian growth markets have been led by pro-Western capitalist governments, but the financial crises at the end of the 1990s threatened to change this. In 1998, for example, Malaysia closed its door to free capital flows, essentially cutting itself off from the foreign money that had so far fueled much of its growth. One would expect that once the capital flows are again freed up, the multinational entrants would have to pay attention not only to economic fundamentals but also to the social problems in these countries, just as the World Bank has urged them to do.[19]

Segmentation in most of these markets does in fact have to start with the underlying cultural, ethnic, and religious roots. The cultures in these countries vary a great deal. People in Hong Kong and Singapore are basically Chinese but also cosmopolitan. Taiwan and Korea each have quite unified national cultures, while the Philippines' long relationship with Western Catholicism and more recent American ties have made for a very special culture. South Asia generally exhibits a mix of Chinese, Indian, and native cultures.

Product Positioning

The most visible products for these markets are perhaps the global luxury brands (Gucci, Chanel, Dunhill, and others) positioned at the upper end of the market, skimming the demand from the very affluent and the occasional buyers who want to indulge themselves. Before the financial turmoil, there was no doubt about the continuing fascination with status and premium prices. These countries are relative newcomers to economic prosperity, and with little stigma attached to hedonic pleasures in their

Buddhist credos, it was natural to follow the "If you've got it, flaunt it" maxim. It is not surprising to learn that in 2008, as much as 37 percent of the sales of European luxury goods makers came from Asia.[20]

The Asian markets' desire for **global identification** has made many multinationals with more mundane products use global standardization in their positioning strategies as well. In addition to Lux soap, Unilever has introduced well-known brands such as Lipton tea, Persil detergent, and Pepsodent toothpaste using essentially global campaigns. Procter & Gamble's Pampers diapers, Pantene shampoo, and Whisper sanitary napkins are also positioned with limited adaptation.

But as in the case of Toyota, Unilever, and P&G, to appeal to the less-affluent core segments, multinational companies are forced to offer less-advanced, localized products. The companies also use acquired local brand names to help establish local identity and supply the lower end of the market. Then there is the need for more specific adaptations because of country-specific factors. For example, American Motorola used a global campaign in Korea to position its cellular phone as leading in technology. But the appeal of "a world everybody dreamed of" made little sense in mountainous Korea where Motorola's older technology was inferior to that of Samsung's newer technology. In 1995 Samsung's domestic Anycall brand decisively took over market leadership from Motorola's global Microtech series. Samsung has kept it ever since.[21]

Marketing Tactics
Product Policies

The emphasis on these markets as followers of global mature markets makes standardized product policies natural. Nevertheless, there are some idiosyncratic factors that product policies need to pay attention to.

Product Design   Because of limited storage space in the homes, many of the products for these markets need to be localized by offering smaller package sizes. Furthermore, as in Japan, buyers prefer slimmer designs, and robustness is not as important an attribute as elsewhere. Basically, Asian people tend to be less dominating toward their possessions, taking a caring approach as opposed to the cruder "use and discard" attitude common in the West. This also means that style and finish are more important than elsewhere. Again, the Japanese market and its products provide good illustrations. One reason the Japanese companies have a country-specific advantage in the Asian markets is simply that their home market is similar to that of their neighbors.

Product Line   The Asian consumer is generally more eager to achieve a **"harmonious whole"** than Western individuals. In clothing, for example, Asian customers aim for "the complete look," wanting all parts of their outfit coordinated. While this desire has some vague cultural background in collectivist "groupthink" and traditional aesthetic norms from the Orient's imperial past, it also reflects an underlying uncertainty among consumers about Western-style dress codes, as in "Exactly what goes with what?" Retail stores and apparel makers have turned this problem into an opportunity by providing head-to-toe outfits, from hats and scarves to dresses, skirts, stockings, and shoes, creating within a single store and brand environment a complete line of interrelated products. A New York designer like Anna Sui develops whole ensembles specifically tailored to the Asian woman.[22]

The same desire for **full-line policies** has long inspired the Japanese manufacturers in consumer electronics, cameras, and autos. In Western markets, such a policy goes well with brand loyalty and the notion that once you have bought a brand, you should be able to stay with it as your needs change or your income goes up. In Asia, the notion is broadened to the idea that the brand defines who you are. This is not so far-fetched even in the West, especially for some market segments such as teenagers. But in Asia, where individualism and egos are not so highly developed, one's material possessions clearly signify one's worth. Firms that make sure that their product line offers complementary products and upgrades will do better and can price accordingly.

Getting the Picture

ASIA AS A TRENDSETTER?

According to a leading international marketing research firm, Taylor Nelson Sofres in London, young people of Asia are poised to become the new trendsetters for the young generation.

The evidence, according to the firm's executive director for Asia Pacific, John Smurthwaite, is in the aging of the West's population. For example, in Europe, 20 percent of the population is aged 60 years and older and that will grow to 35 percent by the year 2050. "As there will be more young people in Asia, marketing ideas for the young will probably shift to Asia, while advertising and marketing in Europe will focus on the older consumers," says Smurthwaite. In 2000, just emerging from a regionwide financial crisis, Asia made up 30 percent of the world's GDP. This "will rise to 42 percent over the next 15 years because of population growth as well as GDP per head growing," he asserts. His concept is that as marketers in Europe and the United States spend more time developing products and services for the elderly, the lead markets for the young will be in Asia.

Taylor Nelson Sofres has established a nationwide consumer panel in Malaysia recruiting young participants to help forecast future tastes. Another expression of the belief in Asian trendsetters comes from the Consumer Electronics

group of Philips. The large Dutch multinational decided in 2001 to spend about 80 million euros on marketing to tech-savvy youths in Asia. For example, the company launched the Rush X extreme sports competition for skateboarding, BMX bicycles, and inline skating. The event received an overwhelming response. Further, Absolut Vodka's Asia Pacific unit decided to launch its latest variant, Absolut Mandrin, in the Philippines. And Japan's Toshiba Corporation, the large electric appliance manufacturer, announced in August 2001 that it would shift responsibility for Asian marketing from Tokyo to its subsidiary in Thailand.

There is even a spillover in other ways from Asia. A 2006 study on the cultural influence of Asian American youth reveals that Asian American youth are increasingly generating some of the key trends in U.S. pop culture. In three areas in particular (technology/gadgetry, anime/manga, and video-gaming), young Asian Americans are said to drive overall trends in the U.S. marketplace.

Sources: "Asia Poised to Be Center of Marketing Ideas for the Young," *The Star* (Malaysia), September 23, 2000; Nicole Yeong, "Philips Targets Hi-Tech Products at Youths," *New Straits Times,* April 2, 2001; Amelita R. Remo, "Absolut Splashes Flavored Vodka on Pinoy," *Philippine Daily Inquirer,* July 6, 2001; "Asian American Youth: America's New Trendsetters," **www.hiphoppress.com,** July 27, 2006.

In Korea, the Philips company from Holland offers a product line from small electronic tools to home appliances and advanced state-of-the-art TVs and VCRs, to more sophisticated microchip products, all with distinctive European designs and a well-recognized brand name. Despite the presence of domestic giants Samsung and LG, Philips can charge premium prices about 10 to 15 percent higher than the competition.[23]

New Products   At first glance, there are few compelling reasons for the introduction of new products specially designed for the Asian markets. The buyers are basically eager to get access to the products they see available in mature foreign markets. These are not lead markets but followers. Their insistence on the "whole harmonious picture" also makes an attempt to introduce a single new product less likely to succeed. Furthermore, because of the newness of the market, there is a lack of independent judgment on the part of buyers, and without the endorsement of success elsewhere, a new product will not be easily accepted.

But the Asian countries can serve as **leading markets** for the emerging markets dealt with in the next chapter. That is, the global marketer can use the lower-end product line extensions carried out for the Asian market to get a foothold in China, Russia, and other emerging markets. In addition, the experience with the upper end and the middle classes in the new growth Asian markets may well be transferable to emerging markets, especially China, where underlying cultural and ethnic segmentation criteria suggest similarities. And, to be sure, in some products such as watches and cameras, Hong Kong, Singapore, and Seoul are joining Japan as lead markets for the West (see box, "Asia as a Trendsetter?").

Pricing

In Asia as elsewhere, the global marketer faces a choice between a high **skimming price** strategy and a lower **penetration price** strategy. As we have seen, the natural positioning of a global brand entering the market is at the upper end of the price range, a skimming strategy. To penetrate the core of the market, a lower price is necessary. To justify this price without losing the strength of the high-end brand name, companies develop the lower-end product alternatives discussed above. In addition, some companies acquire a local manufacturer with a local brand.

These are not particularly unique pricing policies for Asia, but changing price position there without losing loyalty is not easy. The entry price will lock in the brand's positioning. In the West one can shift the price level for the brand downward, but in Asia the repercussions would likely be more severe, because it would ruin the brand loyals' sense of what the brand stands for and would hurt the "whole harmonious picture."

Pricing in the Asian region also needs to take into account the risks of gray trade. Many of these markets have a long-standing inclination to engage in pirating and cross-shipment of products, especially top global brands. Although this danger is lessened as the countries achieve economic growth, the lack of effective copyright protection and the Japan-induced predilection for technology diffusion rather than technology protection have made it difficult to erase these practices completely. The upshot is that multinationals need to make sure that prices in the Asian region are not entirely out of line with those in other parts of the world, especially if the brands and products sold are pretty much the globally standardized versions.

Distribution

Many observers agree that the most visible sign of economic growth in the Asian markets is the dynamism of the urban retail sector. Modern department stores dominate the vibrant shopping areas not only of Hong Kong and Singapore but also of Bangkok and Kuala Lumpur. Hypermarkets attract large crowds in Taipei, and just as in the Mall of America in Minnesota, shopping malls in Manila have become entertainment centers with ice rinks, cinemas, and children's playgrounds. Personal computers can now be bought through superstores as shopping has become a social activity and old mom-and-pop small stores rapidly disappear.

Outside of the big cities, however, several of these countries still suffer from a weakly developed infrastructure, including underdeveloped transportation networks and weak retail structures. Transportation gets especially difficult in countries like Malaysia, the Philippines, and Indonesia where large and disconnected archipelagoes make distribution costly, time-consuming, and risky, what with the uncertainties of a tropical climate and accompanying weather patterns. Even in the immediate surroundings of the big cities, crowding and overstretched city budgets make for less than optimal distribution conditions, especially in the south, where one can still see very picturesque and quaint rickshaws in the street. But as in Hong Kong and Singapore, the capitals of the Asian countries are modernizing rapidly with high-rise buildings downtown, broad avenues, clean streets, and global symbols of achievement. The once tallest buildings in the world, the Petrona Twin Towers in Kuala Lumpur (450 meters, or 1,483 feet), were demoted by Taipei's 101 Tower (508 meters, or 1,667 feet), although purists claim that the tall spire on top of 101 Tower unfairly raises the height. Due to open in 2008 is Shanghai Financial Center, which reaches 492 meters (1,614 feet) without a spire and with a strikingly modern design (for a look, go to www.kpf.com/ projects/mori.htm). Of course, the Burj Dubai, nearing completion in 2008, is planned to rise an astounding 800-plus meters above ground.

Promotion

By and large, the promotional strategies employed by multinationals in Asian markets have been only minimally adapted from elsewhere. As with their product policies, the rationale is the pent-up demand for Western products. But even though positioning messages, unique selling points, brand names, and slogans may stay the same, companies have had to adapt to the local language, and in many cases used native endorsers, including local sports heroes and television stars.

In the Philippines where many natives speak English, global campaigns often use "Taglish," a mix of English and the local Filipino language (Tagalog). Global advertising

Getting the Picture

MARKETING IN KOREA

Not all NIEs are the same when it comes to marketing. While a country such as Taiwan has high trade tariffs and little regulation of how to do business, South Korea has lower tariffs; but when it comes to marketing regulations, it is considered by some observers to be one of the most restrictive countries in Asia. For example, most aspects of promotion are heavily regulated: how, what, when, and where. Price cuts should not exceed 60 days per year, any one individual period being limited to 15 days for a manufacturer, 7 days for a retailer. Any one business can have only four promotions per year. The price cuts have to be related to the product value according to a complicated formula. Commercial TV is available, but until 1995 the advertising industry was strictly local. Liberalization of TV time buying and the advent of cable and satellite TV promise to increase competition for local agencies, which lag behind their foreign counterparts.

Distribution, a key element of the marketing mix since promotional tools are limited, has its own share of regulations. For example, store limits have been at 300 square feet for foreigners, roughly the size of an average 7-Eleven store. A liberalization package, passed on July 1, 1993, as a first step in a campaign to gain World Trade Organization membership for Korea, has led to increased store construction in the big cities by Korean entrepreneurs eager to position themselves ahead of an expected foreign influx. Most foreign firms enter via joint ventures, needing a local partner to handle the regulatory obstacles if not the business itself. Price Club/Cosco, the American warehouse retailer, established links with Shinsegae, and its low prices are revolutionizing the market—30 percent below Korean competitors.

Korea was admitted to the WTO in 1995, before Taiwan, which helps explain the higher tariffs in Taiwan. In 2002, Taiwan (or "Chinese Taipei" as it is diplomatically called to avoid ruffling Chinese feathers) was finally admitted, and the tariff barriers are coming down. But judging from the difficulties in Korea, nontariff barriers in the form of business regulations may still cause problems, even though the WTO promises to change those as well. The hope is also pinned to the bilateral talks initiated separately by the United States with both Korea and Taiwan in the new millennium to overcome the impasse in the Doha multilateral round.

Sources: Boddy, 1994; Taylor, 1994; Balbina Y. Hwang, PhD, "Round One of the U.S.-ROK FTA Talks Sails Through," The Heritage Foundation, WebMemo #1129, June 15, 2006.

campaigns by Unilever and Procter & Gamble use Tagalog and local movie and native personalities to reach housewives and their maids, many of whom may be illiterate.

Not all promotional tools can be directly extended. For example, sales calls to the home, a standard approach employed by Japanese auto companies in Japan, cannot be used in Taiwan where the intrusion is considered too great. At the same time the family is the decision-making unit for cars, creating a dilemma. The solution has been to attract the whole family to the showroom, with the help of inducements such as toys for the children as well as flowers for the wife; a generally pleasant atmosphere with soft music, clean windows, and carpets; and a seating area for relaxed contemplation of the new cars.

Major Country Markets

South Korea

One of the original Asian NIEs or "four dragons" (together with Taiwan, Hong Kong, and Singapore), Korea has 48 million people and a per capita income on par with many European countries. This makes Korea a worthwhile stand-alone market for many products (although market entry barriers can be high—see box, "Marketing in Korea").

The Korean economy is dominated by the giant conglomerates called *chaebols*, family-owned groupings of companies that hold considerable power over the economy, from manufacturing to distribution channels. There are about 30 such chaebols, led by world-class manufacturers such as Samsung and LG in electronics and Hyundai in automobiles. Together they control about 40 percent of the Korean economy, and a new entrant will often have to deal with them as partners or else encounter various kinds of obstacles. The family structure invites favoritism and corruption. In 2008, the chairman of Samsung, Kun-Hee Lee, whom we met in the opening vignette, was indicted for tax evasion and breach of trust, and abruptly resigned.[24]

There is still a cachet to Western goods in Korea, especially in luxury products but also in other categories. For example, foreign fast-food restaurants, including KFC and Pizza Hut, are very successful. Small home appliance sales still show advantages to foreign makers like Philips and French Moulinex in competition with Korean giants Daewoo, Samsung, and LG.

Western companies such as France's Carrefour and American Wal-Mart in retailing, German Siemens in heavy electric equipment, and a number of Japanese companies are active in Korea as business and distribution regulations are gradually eased. Korea is not an easy market, with very strong domestic competitors, but its openness to foreign direct investment—Nokia, Nike and other companies produce there—has helped the country become a more promising market than neighboring Japan. Despite the political problems with North Korea, and internal questions about business ethics, Korea seems to be on a strong growth path in the long run.

Taiwan

The overriding question for Taiwan's 23 million people is the relationship with mainland China, which wants to incorporate Taiwan under a "one China" rule. Depending on the outcome of that political struggle, the Taiwanese market may or may not be viable for foreign entry, especially with a relatively small population.

Because of its relatively late WTO entry in 2002, Taiwan has had relatively high tariff barriers behind which its small- and medium-sized companies have used a low-cost and highly efficient workforce to create a vigorous export industry. As affluence has increased, the low-wage emphasis has given way to a stress on skilled labor and high-technology products—personal computer maker Acer is a prominent success story in Taiwan—again supported by government. This development has allowed entry barriers for many consumer products and services to come down. Many of the large MNCs are active in Taiwan (P&G, Unilever, the Japanese automakers, etc.). Just as in Korea, loosening regulations in distribution have allowed foreign retailers to enter, and in Taipei one can now see many Japanese-owned 7-Eleven convenience stores, volume discount stores such as Makro from the Netherlands, the Wellcome supermarket chain from Hong Kong, and other foreign chains.

Taiwan is considered to have particularly exacting customers, which makes the country useful as a test market for new products targeting Asia. For example, P&G designated Taiwan the lead country for the introduction of its new Pantene Pro-V shampoo-and-conditioner product. After success in Taiwan, the product was successfully rolled out in other Asia-Pacific countries.

Hong Kong

The 7 million inhabitants of Hong Kong have long been one of the most affluent of the East Asian people, and its central hub location has made it a natural entry point for many companies venturing into Asia, especially mainland China. Because of its international flavor it is not a typical Asian market, but like New York in the United States, Hong Kong still serves as a lead market and trendsetter for the rest of Asia.

The 1997 changeover of Hong Kong from a British Crown Colony to a Special Administrative Region of China has so far not forced any changes in this role. Even though there has been a shift of some company headquarters from Hong Kong to Singapore, and some people left Hong Kong or shifted resources to other locations before 1997, the city is still strong and vibrant (see box, "Hong Kong: Love It—or Leave It?"). The relatively small population makes it a less attractive stand-alone market, but high-end luxury goods makers such as Vuitton, Hermes, Armani, and Cartier do very good business in Hong Kong, especially since the financial turmoil at the end of the 1990s was contained quite successfully by the city's financial rulers.

Pan-Regional Marketing

The Asian markets naturally lend themselves to **pan-regional** strategies because of their cultural similarity and parallel development paths, now with China rather than Japan as the lodestar. However, the differences in economic development are still large enough to make implementation of standardized products and communications strategies often premature. What sells well in Seoul and Hong Kong and

Getting the Picture

HONG KONG: LOVE IT—OR LEAVE IT?

In 1997, as Hong Kong came under Chinese rule, many residents vacillated between staying or leaving. But the mainland government treaded softly, leaving much of the entrepreneurial Hong Kong economy in peace. Under Deng Xiaoping's "one country, two systems" concept, Hong Kong not only survived but thrived. The Asian financial crisis at the end of the 1990s was quickly overcome, and despite the SARS scare in 2003 and the uncertainties created by the wars in Afghanistan and Iraq, Hong Kong has continued strong. A new airport was constructed (Chek Lap Kok), the opening of a Hong Kong Disney theme park in 2005 was announced, its universities expanded and attracted world-class talent—and banks such as the Hong Kong and Shanghai Banking Corporation (HSBC) went global (HSBC, "The world's local bank," is actually headquartered in London).

With China's entry into the WTO and Beijing hosting the 2008 Olympics, the future looks bright for Hong Kong—provided, of course, it is allowed to continue playing by different rules than the mainland. In 2004, there were signs that pro-democratic demonstrations in Hong Kong would not be tolerated by Beijing. An editorial in the official Chinese news agency's *Outlook Weekly* rebuked some demonstrators for lack of patriotism. One hopes this is simply a warning about a particular event, not a shift in policy.

Hong Kong residents enjoy many freedoms, the prosperity of a first-world city, and the protection of a legal system—all of which are not as evident in mainland China. However, even though Hong Kong has often been categorized with Singapore in the top slots on rankings of fast growth and economic freedom, one relic from the past is a weak competition law. The economy is hobbled by cartels in banking, utilities, telecommunications, real estate, and transportation, considerably raising the cost of working and living in Hong Kong. The fact is that doing business in Hong Kong is expensive enough that some firms are already considering moving inland to Shanghai and other places—ironic, since only a few years ago the high cost of doing business drove some multinationals' Asian headquarters from Tokyo to Hong Kong.

As part of the deal made for the former British colony's return, China's communist leadership promised Hong Kong autonomy until 2047. This helped the Walt Disney Company decide to open its new theme park in Hong Kong in September 2005. Despite some early troubles, including travel restrictions from the mainland and a lack of adaptation to the Chinese holiday schedule, the Hong Kong Disneyland manages to attract visitors to the old city-state and helps make it one of the world's most exciting—and expensive—cities.

Sources: "Meddling in Hong Kong," *The Economist,* September 30, 2000; Normandy Madden, "View from Hong Kong," *Ad Age Global,* January 1, 2002; Michael Schuman, "Disney's Hong Kong Headache," **www.time.com,** May 8, 2006.

Shanghai might still be out of reach for people in Malaysia and Thailand and rural China. In addition, as we have seen, the religious factor plays a role, limiting the applicability of uniform advertising and other communications.

The trading blocs, however, offer a good starting point for pan-regional strategies. Although the APEC grouping is too loose and heterogeneous to be an effective market area, ASEAN, in particular after the expanded 1992 AFTA Trade Agreement, constitutes a natural regional market, with low internal tariffs and acceptance of foreign capital and goods. One would expect pan-AFTA strategies to be very viable in the future.

Because of the vast distances in Asia (Tokyo is as far from Singapore as London is from New York), industrial activities—and thus markets—tend to concentrate around regional transportation hubs, where raw materials, plants, and skilled labor come together. These "growth triangles" (or "growth polygons," to be more correct) can be found around Hong Kong and southern China; around Singapore (called SIJORI for Singapore, Johore in Malaysia, and Riau in Indonesia); between Korea, Japan's Kyushu island, and China's North East coast (the "Yellow Sea" triangle); and in several other places. Actively supported by local and national government planners, these growth polygons have become the preferred development path of Asia and naturally serve as leading markets within the larger trading areas.

Close-Up: Marketing in India[25]

Since 1947, when British colonial rule ended, India has been the world's largest democracy. Despite religious and ethnic violence, the country's leaders have continued to be elected through a democratic process, without the military coups that have plagued less fortunate Third World countries.

Market Environment

India has now over 1.1 billion people. It has long been one of the poorest countries in the world, but in recent years political strife and socialism have taken a backseat to a more open and free-market economy, and the educational elite has helped put the country back on the economic progress track. Taking advantage of the upsurge in outsourcing by large multinationals and its own entrepreneurial talent in electronics, telecommunications, and especially computer software, India has been able to rack up strong growth figures for several years.

The Indian economy showed a GDP growth of 9.0 percent during 2005–2006, rising to 9.4 percent during 2006–2007. Projections are for a sustained growth momentum and achieving an annual average growth of 7 to 8 percent in the next five years. However, because of rapidly increasing population, the per capita figures are still low. By 2003, its per capita gross national income stood at US$2,880 at PPP and in 2007 they were at US$2,659, an actual decrease. Compared to China, with its one-child per family policy, India still has a very large poor population. However, the rapid growth of the total GDP means that India is a fast-growing consumer goods market. And its companies are gaining confidence very fast as they grow into multinational powerhouses on the strength of an educated and entrepreneurial elite.

History

India's educational system is a heritage from British colonial rule, with advanced English-language instruction that is the envy of many other countries. In the past, a large portion of its elite could not find an outlet for their productive capability in the developing home country and found it necessary to emigrate to Western countries. In these Western countries the Indian immigrants still constitute a large ethnic minority at the upper end of the income scale. For example, in 1990 Indians were the ethnic segment of the U.S. population with the highest median income. As the socialist policies and government controls in India gave way to privatization and free markets, domestic opportunities for India's citizens multiplied, and the country's educated elite started to return.

Indian industry did not develop much under British colonialism, which exploited the country's raw materials, precious gems, textiles, tea, and exotic foodstuffs. When the British granted independence to India, the country split into predominantly Muslim Pakistan (East and West) and India. During the next three decades, both the public and private sectors developed considerable corruption and bureaucratic inefficiencies, remnants of which still plague the political and economic functioning of the country.

Domestic products were of poor quality with marketing activities aimed mainly to inform the customer of the products' existence. The Indian consumer had very little choice. What mattered most was that the products were durable. During those three decades most information coming to India about foreign goods was via the Indian emigrants abroad, who sent back gifts of higher-quality foreign goods. Consequently, in popular imagination, anything having a foreign-made label was seen as having high quality.

During this period there were restrictions not only on the flow of products but, more importantly, also on inbound **technology transfer into India.** The private companies advertised the fact that they had been in business for 30 years, and they often had regional monopolies. There was almost no research and development into new technology, with the exception of government-sponsored R&D into weaponry and nuclear power. Amazingly, products on the Indian market hardly changed from 1950 to 1980.[26]

The FDI Effect

From 1980 onward, India started to allow foreign investment, alliances, and technology transfers. Foreign firms were allowed to have a stake of up to—but no more than—26 percent in the equity of a joint venture. Among the first collaborators to enter India were Japanese motorcycle companies Yamaha, Kawasaki, and Honda, creating competition with domestic automakers. Later, Japanese electronic firms began to enter. To maintain market share, almost all domestic companies started collaborating with multinationals. Market success during this period depended directly on which company had

Getting the Picture

INDIA'S SOFTWARE—AND HARDHATS

India has always been a paradox of sorts. A poor country with a large population, it has some of the most highly educated managers and engineers in the world. Brimming with political turmoil and ethnic strife, it is also the world's largest free democracy. Part of Asia, its assertive and argumentative people seem a far cry from the serenity and softness associated with the East.

India's great new industry is computer software development. To be truthful, India has always been very adept at advanced technology, and only the fact that many of its most accomplished citizens have left for greener pastures in the West has kept India from realizing its true potential. But this is changing as India's gradual emergence into economic freedom and openness has enticed talented people to stay and, in not a few cases, come back home. The Bangalore area in southern India is one where the climate and living conditions are sufficiently similar to California's Silicon Valley for a software engineer to thrive and for a software industry to flower.

Many of the new software companies, to be sure, are funded by direct foreign investment from abroad. The typical firm is a supplier and possibly a subsidiary of large multinationals headquartered elsewhere. Still, there are enough indigenous entrepreneurs to proclaim Bangalore the Indian Silicon Valley. The industry has set its sights on expansion into the world's largest markets and, drawing on its past colonial history, has already become a strong presence in the United Kingdom. Its Electronics and Computer Software Exports Promotion Council is developing a pan-European strategy, and it organized an "Indiasoft" exhibition in Amsterdam in June 2001 to coincide with a European conference on outsourcing information technology.

The growing software industry also offers its own concrete examples of the paradox that is India. As a foundation is prepared for the construction of another wired high-tech office building in Bangalore, the rubble is cleared not by bulldozers but by sari-clad women who carry it away in baskets on their heads. Yet more striking to the foreign observer, the rubble bearers wear the yellow hardhats common on Western construction sites, and the hats are fitted with small platforms, on which the rubble baskets rest.

Sometimes, even in India, the West and the East do meet.

Source: "India: ESC Plans Wider Reach in Europe," *Business Line*, June 4, 2001; Brooke Unger, "The Plot Thickens," *The Economist*, May 31, 2001.

the best international collaboration. Goods were expensive, since the foreign firms wanted to make sure that their returns were sufficient, given the uncertain prospects in the Indian market. The technology offered, although advanced according to Indian standards, was internationally substandard.

The further **liberalization in India** in the early 1990s eliminated the ceiling on the share of foreign ownership. The return of Coca-Cola, General Electric, and other Western companies that had left during the socialist regime was a tremendous boost to the Indian economy. Although the **political risk in India** remains high because of ethnic and religious violence, the country is showing strong economic progress and revitalized domestic firms (see box, "India's Software—and Hardhats"). The annual growth rate of 7 to 9 percent, although lower than China's, is well above the average of mature economies.[27]

In the new millennium the Indian economy has gained significant traction from the outsourcing practices of Western multinationals. India has the advantage of an educated work force and a facility with the English language that has helped the country become a magnet for low-wage production of components, call centers, customer service, and so on. Many of the supply operations in India has been started by highly educated entrepreneurs who have guided their organizations gradually into more and more advanced manufacturing and design operations (see box "Outsourcing Entrepreneurs Help India Grow").

The same entrepreneurial spirit has also helped Indian companies expand their influence in other product categories as well. In early 2008, Tata Motors from India acquired luxury automakers Jaguar and Land Rover from faltering owner Ford Motor Company. This was the same Tata company that a few months earlier had announced the introduction of, if not the smallest (the Swatch-Mercedes Smart car might be that) at least the cheapest, car in the world, the Tata Nano. The cute, snub-nosed hatchback is 3-meters long, seats four comfortably or five at a squeeze, does 65 mph, and should revolutionize travel for millions. Called the "People's Car," it is also the cheapest in the world at 100,000 rupees (about US$2,500)—the same price as the DVD player in a Lexus.[28]

Getting the Picture

OUTSOURCING ENTREPRENEURS HELP INDIA GROW

What do the following companies have in common—and which one does not belong? Infosys, Infotech, Flextronics, MindTree Consulting, Tata Consultancy, and Wipro. These are all IT companies with operations in Bangalore (or Bengaluru, as it now wants to be called) in Southern India. How do they differ? Only one is not from India—Flextronics is headquartered in Singapore.

These companies are similar in many other respects. They got their start as suppliers of advanced electronic components and software for multinational corporations. They were created by entrepreneurs who realized the opportunities in providing outsourcing to large Western electronics makers that needed to cut costs to be competitive. They knew the strength of the well-educated local workforce and the discrepancy in wage levels between India and the West. In many ways these companies started the way Microsoft and Bill Gates started—with a contract to supply a large multinational with a crucial component (in the case of Gates, supplying the MS-DOS operating system to IBM). And like Bill Gates, these entrepreneurs have not stood still. These companies have grown by expanding overseas from their Indian (or Singaporean) location, opening plants in countries closer to the markets, and with low-cost wages and skilled workers.

Outsourcing to India by Western multinationals has spread much beyond the earliest effort in the early 1990s to place 24/7 call centers and customer service operations on the other side of the globe. Now, the local talent pool is strong and versatile enough to provide cost-saving opportunities in a variety of jobs and services—much to the chagrin of us in the home country labor force. By 2003, anywhere from one-half to two-thirds of all Fortune 500 companies were already outsourcing to India, and the amount of work done there for U.S. companies was expected to keep increasing.

One example is the outsourcing of the analysis of medical tests, including the interpretation of X-rays and getting a second opinion on a mammogram overnight. Another example is the outsourcing of legal work to India. In these cases, as in the medical cases, outsourcing vendors target the more mundane tasks. But as technology diffuses and competitive skill levels rise, the writing would seem to be on the wall. More advanced work will be outsourced until wage levels equalize and the Indian workers become too expensive. This seems to actually be happening already. According to one source, wages are forecast to rise by 14.4 percent during 2008, the fifth successive year of double-digit growth. This far outstrips wage inflation in China (8.6 percent in 2007).

Outsourcing does indeed seem to flatten the world, as Thomas Friedman suggests.

Sources: "Wages in India to Rise by 14.4 % in 2008: Report," **www.zeenews.com,** India edition, April 29, 2008; Stephanie Overby, "Inside Outsourcing in India," **www.cio.com,** June 1, 2003; Anthony Lin, "Legal Outsourcing to India Is Growing, but Still Confronts Fundamental Issues," *New York Law Journal,* January 23, 2008.

As for consumer products, with increased competition from entering multinational brand producers and retailers, local Indian companies are finally starting to deliver products to suit consumers' needs rather than expecting the consumer to adapt to their products. As competition has increased, domestic companies have become more aggressive in their marketing policies as well. Competition is increasingly on the basis of product features, quality, image, price, and so on (see box "The Indian Consumer is Here").

Market Segmentation

During the 1980s, the Indian market started to divide into two large segments: a still impoverished rural population and an increasingly well-off urban middle class. As the new opportunities pulled people away from the countryside, cities became huge metropolitan markets, and towns grew into cities. This trend was strengthened after further market-opening measures of the early 1990s. The disposable income of the Indian middle class has increased considerably. Not only has there been strong economic growth, but trends in family planning have changed, with households having fewer children. This has also meant that in many families the wives, often well educated, have started contributing to the family income. Traditional habits are changing, and the Indians are even starting to have cold cereal for breakfast (see box, "Basmati Flakes in the Morning").

Even though the majority of the purchasing power in India is in the urban areas, the 70 percent of the population residing in rural areas is increasing their demand for products and services. They are increasingly aware of brand names, and as products and services are adapted to their demands, they constitute a large segment not to be ignored. As

Getting the Picture

THE INDIAN CONSUMER IS HERE

Indian consumption is accelerating. Private consumption currently accounts for 64 percent of GDP—higher than in Europe (58 percent), Japan (55 percent), and especially China (42 percent). India's 7 percent growth path in recent years is partly a result of the emerging consumerism of one of the world's youngest populations. That provides a powerful leverage to the Indian economy that is different from other developing countries, where export success is the major force driving progress.

According to one observer, the increasing number of shopping malls in both India and China exhibit one difference: Although in both countries the malls are packed, in India the locals buy. Sales increases are solid in same-store sales comparisons—consumer spending is on the increase. One key component seems to be that most stores in India have sophisticated marketing and product development plans. This goes for both large domestic firms such as Reliance, the largest retailer in India, but also for the multinationals that are operating in India. Their business models are tailor-made to local markets and customs, not standardized. The Indian consumer market is large enough that it pays off to not only localize but also seriously adapt. Coca-Cola learned this the hard way, when Thums Up, a leading local cola, beat the world leader handily in the domestic Indian market.

The roads and airports are still terrible in India, but they are improving. New airports are built, low-price airlines are started up, mobile phones are as prevalent as elsewhere, and investment in infrastructure is increasing. The country's highly fragmented retail sector is being consolidated as restrictions on foreign direct investment are lifted. Wal-Mart has entered in a joint venture with Bharti Enterprises. The threat of foreign competition is spurring a big consolidation push and domestic players like Pantaloon and Reliance are scaling up in an effort to meet the coming Wal-Mart challenge head-on.

According to a McKinsey report, as Indian incomes rise, the shape of the country's income pyramid will also change dramatically. Over 291 million people will move from desperate poverty to a more sustainable life, and India's middle class will swell by more than ten times from its current size of 50 million to 583 million people. By 2025 over 23 million Indians—more than the population of Australia today—will number among the country's wealthiest citizens.

Marketing and advertising are gaining in importance as Indian consumers are becoming increasingly sophisticated and knowledgeable about products and brands. Media channels for advertising are becoming more available and growing in diversity and reach. The foreign brands remain very attractive and powerful in India, especially in clothing and personal care products, but increasingly brands have to be associated with value. Advertising is becoming a bigger part of the marketing mix as companies attempt to satisfy an increasingly fickle consumer.

Looks like the Indian consumer is becoming like one we all know already.

Source: Stephen Roach, "Here Comes the Indian Consumer," *The Wall Street Journal,* November 9, 2005; "The Bird of Gold: The Rise of India's Consumer Markets," Executive Summary, McKinsey Global Institute, May 2007; "Consumer Markets in India: The Next Big Thing?" KPMG International 2006; John Elliott, "India's Retail Revolution," *Fortune,* June 27, 2007.

for the urban population, according to reports, a wealthy class of people at the top has emerged, although its size is small. According to this research, the middle class includes families in the market for consumer durables, singles and younger people who want personal care products and nondurables, and professionals more interested in status and comfort. Indian consumers surely are beginning to look similar to their peers elsewhere.

Product Positioning

Exposure to new products and services has increased the appetite for further purchases. The Indian consumer who was earlier focusing on the durability of products has now started buying products as symbols of status and success. Consumers are becoming more demanding. Products that were earlier a luxury now have become necessities. Cable TV has entered Indian homes, and households have more than one car. Foreign automakers compete for the privilege of tying up with domestic automakers.

However, it should be emphasized that many Western companies in the past have been disappointed with the response to their products launched in India. The problem is partly an overestimate of the size and depth of the demand—the middle class might be large in numbers but incomes are not always sufficient. But the bigger problem has been to offer global brands at global prices without any attempt at localization. This is partly a matter adapting products (see below) but also a matter of positioning. Simply relying on the cachet brought by global presence and global brand has not been sufficient to entice customers to purchase. While it is likely that the status is higher for

Getting the Picture

BASMATI FLAKES IN THE MORNING

Kellogg, the American cereal company that made cornflakes a staple of many Western children's breakfasts, is scoring again. This time it is having success in India with corn, wheat, and basmati rice flakes, which are selling faster than hotcakes in Bombay. The key is an intensive advertising and promotional campaign designed to make Indian consumers change their breakfast eating habits.

A $450,000 multimedia campaign includes three 30-second TV spots featuring a family around the breakfast table addressing the problem of overeating as well as the effects of a bread-and-butter diet and skipping breakfast. The campaign "does leave behind a suggestion that current fried breakfasts are not the best you could provide for your family to begin the day," says Anil Bhatia, senior vice president-general manager at Hindustan-Thompson Associates.

Kellogg also sponsors a TV special featuring a panel of nutritionists, dieticians, and physicians on the government-run Doordarshan Network. The company is also sponsoring "Kellogg's Breakfast Show," a morning talk show that runs daily on radio. The first guest celebrity was Sushmita Sen, Miss Universe 1994.

Kellogg is also sponsoring two message boards on the main Bombay commuter thoroughfare featuring healthful advice from medical experts. Informative and copy-heavy ads are being placed in English and local-language newspapers as well as women's magazines and health periodicals.

"The Indian market is similar to the Mexican market because the Mexicans also used to consume a hot, savory breakfast," says Damindra Dias, Kellogg India's managing director. "We are saying, 'Take the right food. Don't fill yourself with fat the first thing in the morning.'"

Source: Dubey, 1994; *Advertising Age,* November 14, 1994, p. 60.

the foreign brand, especially given India's past history with domestic-only variants, not many middle-class Indians yet have the funds to indulge in such status-oriented consumption.

As the liberalization of the economy continues, Indian companies are being forced to become more efficient. Drawing on the large pool of talented and well-educated people, the domestic industry is now surging ahead. Foreign companies are also eager to utilize the local expertise. Motorola, the American cellular phone company, has been awarded a "plum" contract to provide cellular phone service to the Indian public and can easily find local engineers and MBAs who are familiar with both the technology and the market. But with its difficulties in coming up with a success to follow on its highly imitated Razr brand, Motorola has lost some cachet. In a twist that shows how far the Indian companies have come, Motorola is courted by the Videocon Group, India's largest consumer electronics maker, who is considering making a bid to buy Motorola Inc.'s mobile-phone business.

Marketing Tactics

Product Policies

Multinational firms entering India have gradually come to learn two things: one, the market demands a full line of adapted products; two, there is a significant first-mover effect at work. The full-line policy requirement derives from the increasing competitiveness of the local firms and from the long-time involvement in India by some large multinationals, including Matsushita, ABB, and Unilever. These companies have acquired first-mover advantages in the Indian market, and as new multinationals enter after liberalization, the newcomers face an uphill battle against the "old India hands." Procter & Gamble, which by default entered India with its 1986 purchase of Richardson-Vicks, has decided to gradually introduce all its brands into the market and is now helping Wal-Mart in its entry strategy. Philips, the European electronics company, introduced a product each month for 18 months from 1994 to 1995, and the company has now captured 13 percent of the Indian television market, in competition with strong Japanese and domestic joint ventures.[29]

As some companies have learned the hard way, to sell successfully to the Indian middle-class consumer, product adaptation is a must. Suitability and adaptation to Indian preferences are perceived as significant benefits for the emerging middle-class shopper, including packaging, distribution availability, and after-sales support. This is particularly necessary when marketing to the poorer consumers in rural areas, but adaptation is also a must in the urban population centers. The positive aspect of this is not to be missed: India is simply large enough that any scale and scope economies are still achievable with adaptation.

Pricing

Given the generally low incomes, price is a very significant factor in purchasing decisions. A simple conversion of Western prices to Indian rupees does not work. Lowering prices by reducing package sizes, simplifying designs, and offering less service is not always the best way, but often necessary to get a foothold. One problem is that if the product then can be imitated easily, local entrepreneurs will develop "me-too" versions. A better approach is to lower prices by shifting some assembly into the country, establishing a joint venture with a local business that can also help defend against imitations.

Even though global brands are very attractive to the emerging Indian middle class, they can no longer count on an automatic price premium when competing against strong local products. As in so many other markets, the majority of the consumers in the middle-income group are generally price-sensitive. Several multinational companies entering India, including Reebok, incurred losses before realizing this fact. Unilever, the large packaged goods company with a long and successful record in India, keeps overhead costs under strict control to allow prices to be lowered and still capture positive margins.

Price level is especially important when a brand name is less known. This also affects global companies whose brands might not be well known yet in India. For example, Procter & Gamble, a relative newcomer in India, struck up a short-lived but useful entry alliance with Godrej Soaps, a local company with a better-known name. P&G gained quick access to distribution and recognition through Godrej and could gradually introduce its global brands into the market at acceptable prices.[30]

Distribution

India is a subcontinent, geographically speaking, nearly 2,000 miles from north to south and 1,800 miles from east to west. Its coastline is 3,800 miles long and its area is 1.3 million square miles. The urban population centers are widely dispersed around the huge country and to reach them all with nationwide distribution requires a mammoth effort. For example, a leading manufacturer of cosmetics and personal care products sells through a network of 100,000 retail outlets across the country. Most Indian manufacturers use a standard three-tier selling and distribution structure: distributor, wholesaler, and retailer. But the number of contact points is anything but standard. A typical company may have between 400 to 2,300 distributors. The retailers served by the wholesalers might vary between 250,000 to 750,000. India is estimated to have about 12 million retail outlets, mostly family-owned.[31]

As one might expect (and as we saw in the box on "The Indian Consumer Is Here"), economic growth has also meant that this massive distribution network is gradually being consolidated and rationalized. Larger, integrated chains are being developed by different industry groups. For example, Dairy Farm of Hong Kong and RPG Enterprises of India are jointly promoting MusicWorld and FoodWorld chains in India. Retail chains from Europe are developing plans to enter the market (although India does not yet allow 100 percent ownership in retailing). Franchising already accounts for some 5 percent of the country's total GDP, and is still growing. The Bata shoe chain is one very successful example. Shopping malls are also being developed in the bigger population centers, partly targeting the returning expatriates who long for the Western-style weekend trip to the mall.

Overall, however, a weak infrastructure in a vast country is still one of the drawbacks to doing business in India, and companies need to assist with structural improvements. For example, Matsushita, the Japanese electronics giant, has invested heavily in building a viable distribution network for its products. Dividing the large country into geographical sales territories, Matsushita built large warehousing facilities at strategic points in the network to ensure adequate supply and inventory of finished products and parts for its Panasonic brand. Matsushita has also invested in training its Indian dealers in retail service, inventory management, and customer service programs.[32] Borrowing a page from its strategy at home in Japan, the company's dealers became exclusive Panasonic dealers by the year 2000.

Promotion

With the dismantling of the regulations hampering the economy, India has moved from a seller's market to a buyer's market. This has also meant an increased emphasis on brand awareness and a consequent need for advertising. Media availability has increased exponentially, companies' ad budgets are large, and domestic and foreign advertising agencies are competing freely. The advertising business is booming. Television commercials in India tend to be funny and upbeat, mixing British-style humor with Asian irreverence toward material possessions. One Indian spot from 2002 for French automaker Peugeot took first price in a global advertising competition.

Advertising in India does not include direct attacks on the competition (it is prohibited by law), though it is often implied. Many multinationals have to modify their global advertising campaigns to meet local Indian tastes and the various local dialects. For example, Motorola, the American mobile phone company, advertised its pagers with traditionally dressed commodity traders. The increased penetration of television has made TV advertising very popular, but in terms of cost-effectiveness other media such as print and outdoor ads will often be superior.

Corporate advertising also is on the upswing. Showing how marketing can help reposition previously protected companies, giant industrial conglomerates like Tatas and Birlas—companies that make and sell everything from candy to industrial machinery—advertise defensively what they do for local communities.

A leading industrialist, Rahul Bajaj of Bajaj Autos, proclaimed in the preliberalization period: "We are a Third World country; our consumers do not expect very high quality."[33] Unless political forces intervene, such sentiments are a thing of the past in India's marketplace. The Indian consumers have developed expectations similar to those in more advanced economies.

Summary

New growth markets in the NIE countries differ from the typical growth markets in mature economies. What is important is further market development, helping to increase the total market size. As the markets evolve, the global marketer needs to shift from infrastructure and distribution issues to developing product lines and communication strategies that are sensitive to local culture, language, and religion. It is also important to continue adaptation of packaging and pricing to accommodate smaller budgets. To take advantage of opportunities in the new growth markets of the NIEs, the local marketer needs to gradually shift from a basic localization strategy to a more mature market strategy involving product development and targeted communications. This effort will benefit from working closely with local partners.

In terms of economics there are many basic similarities among these new growth markets, but their cultural, ethnic, and political heritages differ considerably. Most of them share a basic pent-up demand for products and brands from mature markets, which global communications have revealed to them. At the same time the distinctions in terms of religion and culture make for important differences in means of communication. The disparity between the Buddhist Asian and the Catholic Latin American countries dealt with here reflects Kipling's words, "East is East, and West is West—and never the twain shall meet." The global marketer tries to prove Kipling wrong—and sometimes succeeds.

Key Terms

authoritarian political regimes, *273*
brand names, *274*
colonial domination, *273*
core middle class, *274*
full-line policies, *290*
global identification, *290*
"harmonious whole," *290*
labor costs, *273*
leading markets, *291*

liberalization in India, *297*
neocolonial, *275*
newly industrialized economies (NIEs), *273*
pan-regional Asian marketing, *294*
pan-regional Latin American marketing, *286*
penetration price, *291*

political risk in India, *297*
raw materials, *273*
religious influence, *278*
skimming price, *291*
technology transfer into India, *296*
trade blocs, *274*
urban versus rural population, *279*

Discussion Questions

1. For a product category of your choice (select one with which you might want to work, for example), search in news media and online data sources to generate a market evaluation for an Indian, Asian, or Latin American country (your choice again), in the new global financial situation.
2. Discuss the major factors that affect market acceptance of a new consumer product in a Latin American country. In an Asian country. In India. Any similarities?
3. Use the Web sites of PC manufacturers to do an analysis of the competitive situation facing Acer, the Taiwanese PC maker, when expanding into other Asian countries. Is Acer's Taiwanese origin an advantage or disadvantage?
4. What are the reasons why entry into the Korean market is so expensive?
5. Why might a successful North American marketer not be the best one to head the company's marketing effort in Latin America? What about in Asia? In India? What kind of person is needed, and how would he or she be trained?

Notes

1. Papadopoulos and Heslop, 1993, discuss many of these remnants of the past in Chapter 2 of their book.
2. This section draws on Garten, 1997, and on research assistance by Kerri Olson, Ernesto Priego, and Huyn Jung.
3. See the *Crossborder Monitor,* February 16, 1994.
4. See Kotabe and Arruda, 1998. In 2004, as Brazilian AmBev and Interbrew merged to become inBev, Brahma became a brand in the InBev product line-up
5. See Krauss, 1998.
6. From Krauss, 1998.
7. See Capell, 1998.
8. From Barks, 1994.
9. From "Tropicana Enters South American Juice Market," *PR Newswire* (PRN) on ProQuest Business Dataline, February 21, 1994.
10. See Sanchez, 1992.
11. See Schemo, 1998.
12. From *Crossborder Monitor,* November 24, 1993, p. 2. See also, Nicholls et al., 1999.
13. From Krauss, 1998.
14. See, for example, *Crossborder Monitor,* April 21, 1993.
15. See Turner and Karle, 1992.
16. See Rosenberg, 1993.
17. From Barks, 1994.
18. This section draws on Yip, 1998; Garten, 1997; and Lasserre and Schuette, 1995. Thanks are extended to Chong Lee and Stephen Gaull from whose research part of this section is also drawn.
19. See Landler, 1998.
20. From Steinhauer, 1997. See also, "Luxury Brands Target Asians' Desire to Show Off Wealth," www.AFP Google.com, January 13, 2008.
21. From Jun and Yip, 1998, p. 73.
22. From Steinhauer, 1997.
23. See Jun and Yip, 1998, p. 76.

24. See Fackler, 2008.
25. This section draws on Ramachandran and Yip, 1998. Thanks are offered to Ashwani Gujral for drafting the section and to Sachin Anand for reviewing and updating it. Unless otherwise noted, the country statistics are from United Nations and the U.S. Department of Commerce publications.
26. This is the popular imagination in India. There were changes: For example, already by 1980, India did have electronic word processors and some personal computers, brought in by expatriates from abroad. But the relative stagnation in, for example, automobiles, where the models remained unchanged over a 30-year period, is a striking testament to the power of trade barriers to retard economic growth.
27. See Ramachandran and Yip, 1998, and "India: Progress and Plans," 1998.
28. See O'Connor, 2008.
29. See Ramachandran and Yip, 1998.
30. Ibid.
31. These figures are from the FY 2004 Country Commercial Guide for India, published by the U.S. Commercial Service.
32. Ibid.
33. From "Foreign Car Makers," 1994.

Selected References

American Chamber of Commerce in Mexico. "Setting Up a Distribution Operation: How Amway Adapted Its Direct Sales System to Mexico." *Business Mexico* 2 (January–February 1992), pp. 22–23.

Barks, Joseph V. "Penetrating Latin America." *International Business,* February 1994, pp. 78–80.

Boddy, Clive. "The Challenge of Understanding the Dynamics of Consumers in Korea." In *Meeting the Challenges of Korea: The 1994 AMCHAM Marketing Seminar.* Seoul: American Chamber of Commerce in Korea, 1994, pp. 7–12.

Brooke, James. "More Open Latin Borders Mirror an Opening of Markets." *New York Times,* July 4, 1995, p. 47.

Capell, Kerry. "What a 'Euro' Could Do for the Latins." *BusinessWeek,* April 13, 1998, p. 46.

Dreifus, Shirley B., ed. *Business International's Global Management Desk Reference.* New York: McGraw-Hill, 1992.

Dubey, Suman. "Kellogg Invites India's Middle Class to Breakfast of Ready-to-Eat Cereal." *The Wall Street Journal,* August 29, 1994, p. 83B.

Fackler, Martin. "South Korea Questions the Corporate Status Quo." *New York Times,* April 24, 2008, pp.C1, 8.

Faiola, Anthony. "Harrods by the Si." *Washington Post,* June 8, 1998, pp. D1, D7.

"Foreign Car Makers Make Drive for India's Middle Class." *Washington Post,* September 17, 1994.

Garten, Jeffrey E. *The Big Ten: The Big Emerging Markets and How They Will Change Our Lives.* New York: Basic Books, 1997.

"India: Progress and Plans." *Washington Post,* October 6, 1998, p. A13.

Jun, Yongwook, and George S. Yip. "South Korea—New Prosperity and Agony." Chapter 3 in Yip, 1998.

Kotabe, Masaaki, and Maria Cecilia Coutinho de Arruda. "South America's Free Trade Gambit." *Marketing Management* 7, no. 1 (1998), p. 39.

Krauss, Clifford. "Despite Uncertain World Markets, a Big U.S. Retailer Bulls into Latin America." *New York Times,* September 6, 1998, sec. 3, pp. 1, 11.

Landler, Mark. "2 Asian Economies Seek to Keep Global Markets at Bay." *New York Times,* September 12, 1998, pp. C1, C2.

Lasserre, Philippe, and Hellmut Schuette. *Strategies for Asia Pacific.* London: Macmillan, 1995.

Nash, Nathaniel C. "Bunge & Born: More Mindful of Latin America," *New York Times,* January 3, 1994, p. C5.

Nicholls, J. A. F.; Tomislav Mandakovic; Fuan Li; Sydney Roslow; and Carl J. Kranendonk. "Are U.S. Shoppers Different from Chilean?" www.marketing.byu.edu, 1999.

O'Connor, Ashling. "Tata Nano—World's Cheapest New Car Is Unveiled in India." *The Times India,* January 11, 2008.

Papadopoulos, Nicolas, and Louise A. Heslop, eds. *Product-Country Images: Impact and Role in International Marketing.* New York: International Business Press, 1993.

Ramachandran, K., and George S. Yip. "India—Giving Multinationals a Chance." Chapter 12 in Yip, 1998.

Robinson, Eugene. "In Argentina, Private Firm a Power Player; Bunge & Born, a Multinational Wields Clout in Nation's Economy." *Washington Post,* December 6, 1989, p. G1.

Rosenberg, Sharon Harvey. "Burger King Maps Move into Latin America." *Miami Daily Business Review,* December 13, 1993, p. A1.

Sanchez, Jacqueline. "Some Approaches Better than Others When Targeting Hispanics." *Marketing News,* May 25, 1992, pp. 8, 11.

Schemo, Diana Jean. "In a Straitened Brazil, Talk of Pay in Goods." *New York Times,* October 22, 1998, p. C4.

Smith, Geri. "Why Wait For NAFTA?" *BusinessWeek,* December 5, 1994, pp. 52–54.

Steinhauer, Jennifer. "Design Houses Lament Asia's Faltering Economies." *New York Times,* December 23, 1997, p. A22.

Taylor, John. "The Critical Elements of Sales and Distribution." In *Meeting the Challenges of Korea: The 1994 AMCHAM Marketing Seminar.* Seoul: American Chamber of Commerce in Korea, 1994, pp. 23–28.

Turner, Rik, and Delinda Karle. "Shops See Unity of Latin America." *Advertising Age,* April 27, 1992, pp. I– 4, I–38.

Yip, George S. *Asian Advantage: Key Strategies for Winning in the Asia-Pacific Region.* Reading, MA: Addison-Wesley, 1998.

10

Local Marketing in Emerging Markets

"Sleeping giants wake up"

After reading this chapter, you will be able to:

1. Adapt the fundamentals of marketing in order for the firm to take advantage of the opportunities in emerging markets.

2. Recognize the differences between specific emerging markets, and to adjust for the different political regimes and how they affect strategic decisions, in particular foreign direct investment.

3. Help design an effective distribution system that takes into account the often weak infrastructure in many emerging countries and also helps to improve it.

4. Be an educator of local service providers, showing how free markets require customer service and how to overcome the ambivalent feeling about free markets that newly democratized nations still harbor.

5. Learn how to monitor the environmental trends in these markets, and track how they change as political, military, and economic realities change—by external forces, such as the rising oil prices in 2007–2008.

In this, the third of three chapters on different marketing environments, the challenges posed by emerging markets are discussed. *Emerging markets* include the newly democratized postcommunist nations, including Russia and Central Asia, China (still communist but with a more open economy), the Middle East, and other developing countries. Although some of the discussion will cover developing countries in general, the focus will be on "newly democratized countries" (NDCs). In these markets the heritage of a centralized planning economy means that marketing activities are suspect, marketers need to be legitimized, and there is a traditional supremacy of producers over consumers. Marketing becomes an act of rebellion against the old order and places people's mindsets under stress. The standard injunction of good marketing practice—satisfy the customers with good products and services—still applies. However, there is a lot of basic education about the workings of the free market system needed (among competing producers, middlemen, and customers) before marketing action can be effectively implemented. Marketing is a part of the free market system, and the marketing manager becomes its foot soldier and standard-bearer.

Is Marketing to Poor Countries Good or Bad?

While antiglobalization critics attack global companies for exploiting workers in the Third World and frustrating people there with unattainable aspirations and wrong or unfulfilled desires, global firms continue to explore new business opportunities in poor countries. Companies such as Hewlett-Packard, Unilever, and Citibank have opened a proverbial hornet's nest by targeting developing markets in Africa, Asia, central Europe, Latin America, and the Middle East.

Inspired by marketing consultants specializing in developing countries, these companies are going after hot new growth markets. Hard as it might be to believe, the markets experiencing rapid growth comprise the 4 billion people worldwide subsisting on less than $1,500 annually. The multinational firms and their consultants argue that they are providing affordable, high-quality products that can have a positive effect on the quality of life for people not normally considered potential customers. The companies are developing innovative ways of marketing their products. For example, they stretch out installment payments longer for larger purchases and pay attention to any opportunity for shared village access to, for example, telephones and televisions. They also change the packaging with the general idea that smaller is more beautiful. A typical illustration comes from Hindustan Lever Ltd., Unilever's Indian subsidiary, which sells detergents and personal care products in single-use sizes to low-income Indians. Since sales have been growing at a fast rate while percentage profit margins are the same as for larger packages, Unilever management is replicating the practice in Brazil.

Although the practice is not new—Gillette has long sold single razor blades in poor countries, for example—there is an increased focus on these markets as mature markets get saturated and more competitive. The effort is variously described as "selling to the bottom of the pyramid," or "selling to premarkets" (not yet developed enough to be considered a consumer market) or B2-4B (business to 4 billion). This is of course the point at which the globalization foes step up.

The antiglobalization argument is mainly that there are so many other things that are needed in these countries before consumer products such as personal care are introduced. For example, the mother of a child might find it tempting to spend on herself instead of caring for her offspring. Consumerism creates habits that are really not conducive to what the family or the individual needs. Many developing countries still lack even the most basic health and education standards. These 4 billion people earn less than $4 a day, live in remote areas, are illiterate, and may have their access and ability to use products seriously compromised by a lack of roads, electricity, and water. The increased communication access also has its negative side. People at the bottom of the pyramid did not aspire to the way of life shown on television until they were exposed to it by the marketers. Although economic growth rates for developing countries are about twice those of developed nations, the majority of these consumers are essentially destitute subsistence farmers without any discretionary income.

Not surprisingly, many inhabitants still treat foreigners and foreign firms with a great deal of mistrust and skepticism. This prompted Hewlett-Packard to partner in Senegal with a local firm, Joko, Inc., in its efforts to bring the Internet to that nation's poor. Since community members are allowed to own and manage the initiative's computer centers, the local response has been fairly positive.

As always, the way of the free market meets opposition among people who want to care for the poor. There is simply no avoiding the fact that trying to protect others involves a certain amount of patronizing, of suggesting that others are not quite able to choose for themselves, that these people need to have better education and information so that they can make informed decisions. The problem is that however objective one tries to be about judging other people's behavior, in the end one cannot get away from the projection of one's own preferences on others. Should they not choose for themselves? This is a real dilemma.

It is clear that everyone would like the poor mother to care for her little one—but also to be able to care for herself. It is also clear to everyone that people should be informed about their choices and the sacrifices they entail. The question is how one goes about accomplishing these things all at once and without interfering with the individual's rights. Antiglobalization forces would like at least a minimum of public oversight, while global marketers are likely to want the choices and the decisions to be left entirely to the individual consumer. In the end, one would hope that the two could come together at some balanced midpoint, which would help the individual choose really desirable and helpful products freely, responsibly, and without fear.

As so often, finding the best ethical way in the free market system involves trade-offs.

Sources: Dana James, "B2-4B Spells Profits," *Marketing News,* November 5, 2001, pp. 1, 11–12; Naomi Klein, *No Logo* (London: Flamingo, 2000). C. K. Prahalad, *The Fortune at the Bottom of the Pyramid* (Philadelphia: Wharton School Publishing, 2004).

Introduction

Emerging markets as defined here comprise Russia and the newly democratized post-communist nations, China (whose communist government has eased central control over the economy), the Middle East, and developing countries. Among typical **developing countries** are many of the poor nations in Africa (Nigeria, Zambia, Tanzania), Asia (Pakistan, Vietnam), and Central America (Nicaragua, Guatemala). They are defined primarily by *low per capita income levels* and are discussed here together with the newly democratized countries (NDCs) mainly because they share a severe *lack of marketing infrastructure.*

This chapter will first deal briefly with some general problems of marketing in developing countries and then concentrate on marketing in the newly democratized countries (NDCs), especially Russia and Central Asia. We then discuss the special cases of marketing in China and the Middle East.

Local Marketing in Developing Countries

Marketing in the typical developing country faces a number of special problems engendered by the poor economic conditions, the low educational levels and high illiteracy rate, and the general apathy of the populace. Western marketing activities tend to assume a substantial and economically strong middle class, something usually lacking in developing countries. Local marketing in such countries becomes a special challenge.

The macroenvironment in the typical developing market is characterized by *uncertainty*, and thus "environmental scanning" becomes part of the job for the local marketer. Radical political change can develop quickly, and financial risk tends to be great. Convertibility problems, black markets, and exchange rate fluctuations tend to lessen the value of revenues. The possibility of abrupt changes in tariff rates and other trade-impeding measures creates a need for constant vigilance. It becomes necessary for the local marketer to work with international lending agencies such as the World Bank and the International Monetary Fund (IMF) and to use insurance agencies such as the Overseas Private Investment Corporation (OPIC).[1]

Because developing markets have typically not had access to many consumer products in the past, consumer needs tend to be basic and easy to identify. However, the same lack of products has also made for a poorly advanced **marketing infrastructure.** Distribution channels are few and show low productivity, and communication media are limited in reach and coverage. Marketing research, therefore, rather than focusing on the buyer, is more usefully focused on the feasibility of various marketing activities. The well-known problems Nestlé faced with its baby formula products in African countries underscore this point. Although mothers were pleased with the product, the lack of clean water with which to mix the formula made it dangerous for the infants.[2]

Africa is a particularly difficult case, mostly because of political problems but also because of a very weak infrastructure. Rich in minerals and other raw materials,

EXHIBIT 10.1
GDP Per Capita in Africa
(2007, in U.S.$, PPP), Rank
in World, and Population

Source: Data from **www.worldbank.org;
www.imf.org**.

Nation	GDP Per Capita	GDP Rank in World	Population
Nigeria	2,035	137	148,093,000
Ethiopia	806	166	77,127,000
Congo	309	119	62,636,000
South Africa	9,761	76	47,850,700
Tanzania	1,256	156	40,454,000
Kenya	1,699	145	37,538,000
Uganda	939	163	30,884,000
Ghana	1,426	150	23,478,000
Mozambique	830	165	21,397,000
Zimbabwe	188	176	13,349,000
Egypt	5,491	97	75,498,000

Africa has to some extent been a victim of the early colonial intrusions and lack of strong market-based institutions. As political freedom was gained, many countries still did not have sufficiently strong political and economic institutions to prevail over the seemingly intractable tribal and ethnic divisions. This has meant that economic progress has been very weak (see Exhbit 10.1), and also, unfortunately, that the kind of trade blocs between neighboring countries that have been so successful elsewhere have not been formed. With the end of apartheid, however, it seems possible that South Africa with its relatively high per capita income could become a factor in the continent's revival.

Market Segmentation

In these markets *income level* represents the basic segmentation criterion, and the market for upper-end status products from the West is often potentially lucrative because of an uneven income distribution. But the effective income measure is not necessarily defined in terms of salary or wages per household but rather in terms of *access to foreign or convertible currency*. For example, government bureaucrats may not be paid much in Uganda, but they may have better access to convertible currency than a local small entrepreneur. On the other hand, the secondary (or black) market for foreign currency may offer the small entrepreneur access to hard currencies but at a price premium.

Once income level has been identified, the standard demographics may be used to segment the market. But the relatively low level of customer sophistication makes segmentation unnecessary on any other basis than geography. "Where" the customers are is the second question after income has been taken care of. And usually the most promising market is the urban population of big cities.

It is important not to be too casual about the emergence of more sophisticated tastes and preferences on the part of the customers. In most markets even relatively poor buyers have some aspirations concerning emotional satisfaction, a desire to get more than just functional performance from a product. In relatively low-priced items, for example, it pays to adapt to local tastes (see box, "African Romance").

Furthermore, contrary to popular belief, high prices may not be such an impediment to market success in these countries as one would expect. For example, by focusing their spending on a few items, consumers are able to afford some luxuries. In such instances, a low price can be a drawback, since high prices are automatically associated with a luxury image.

It is useful to recognize that upscale positioning—targeting an upper, more status-oriented niche of the market—can play an important role in newly democratized countries. But in *developing* markets such luxury desires tend to be exactly that, only developing. Gradually, as the markets shift into growth, the consumers will develop their individual preferences.

Getting the Picture

AFRICAN ROMANCE

"The sun was setting far, far away, casting a mysterious glow on Ebrie Lagoon. From her villa, Vanessa Toulay, a former hostess for Afrique Air, watched the sunset with sad, downcast eyes. . . . A gin and tonic in his hand, Christian Magou stood in front of a bay window in his bachelor pad in Deux-Plateaux. He gazed longingly at the stars twinkling in the sky, unable to get Vanessa's bewitching smile out of his mind."

Another Harlequin romance set in a far-off and mysterious land? Well, almost. It is a scene from "Un Bonheur Inattendu," or "Unexpected Happiness," one of six titles in *Adoras,* a new series of African romance novels published in the Ivory Coast and marketed in several of the countries of formerly French West Africa. The difference with Harlequin is small, but telling: The writers of the novels are African, as are the characters and the settings of the stories.

To be sure, the arrival of the typical Harlequin novels into stores and kiosks in Abidjan, the capital of Ivory Coast, jump-started the romance market. The Canadian publisher of romance novels sold 193 million books in 1991 on six continents and in 20 languages. But the enterprising direc-

tor of *Adoras,* Meliane Boguifo, spotted a weakness in the typical Harlequin offering: The Prince Charming was always blond and blue-eyed, and the Beauty Queen would blush. Neither description rings any bells for West African readers.

The writers for *Adoras* make sure that the love triangles depicted fit what its readers can identify with. For example, Vanessa and Christian exchange glances not over candlelit French dinners but over plenty of couscous and tchepdiene, a Senegalese dish. The backdrop is Abidjan, West Africa's most modern city with skyscrapers and highways built around Ebrie Lagoon.

But even with the drive to be truly African, the *Adoras* series makes one exception: The writers' pseudonyms are exotic and akin to the Harlequin style. As Ms. Boguifo explains: "Marketing research showed that names like Christopher Hill and Carmen P. Lopez had more credibility than purely African names." It seems that some country-specific advantages still accrue to the more established purveyors of romance.

Sources: Norimitsu Onishi, "The Africans Fall Heavily for Amour and All That," *New York Times,* December 11, 1998, p. A4; John A. Quelch, and Nathalie Ladler, *Harlequin Romances—Poland,* Harvard Business School, case no. 9-594-017, 1993.

Product Positioning

The developing market environment makes product policy a key issue. At the core of the market customer needs tend to be basic and domestic alternatives weak, and the initial offering usually consists of standardized simpler selections from the existing product lines. Limited features also make it possible to sell through low-service outlets; the reliability that comes with standardization alleviates the need for extensive after-sales service. General Motors uses this strategy. The company has developed a special automobile for use in rural areas in Southeast Asian countries such as the Philippines, where dirt roads are common. The chassis can be constructed from steel bars that come in a kit and require only simple tools for assembly. The engine and transmission are then mounted on the frame together with two seats and a canopy. The vehicle is cheap, runs high off the ground, and is easy to repair. It's perfect for the market (although with rising incomes and better roads, countries such as Malaysia have increasingly turned to more sophisticated Japanese cars assembled in neighboring Indonesia or Thailand, and to their domestic marquee and market leader, the Proton).[3]

Pricing

Price policies in developing markets are dominated by the balance between affordability and upper-end positioning. Thus, pricing often fluctuates between maintaining a *skimming price,* which will yield a high-end positioning and possibly quick payback, and a lower *penetration price,* which ensures affordability but also lowers margins and endangers the most desirable position. Striking a middle ground, many companies opt for a relatively high price that eliminates some buyers but offers the firm first-mover advantages in terms of image and brand loyalty.

The lack of purchasing power means that the marketer often must find ways of offering a simpler product paid for through innovative financing. A washing machine can be sold to a communal village, for example, with several families helping to foot the bill. Smaller and less expensive packages of shampoos sold by Unilever are popular in many of these markets. Soft drinks and packaged foods often come in smaller sizes as well, as do cigarettes (it is not unusual for someone to buy or sell one cigarette, for example), and beer cans are smaller. Store credit to customers is common, forcing manufacturers and distributors to offer liberal credit terms in turn.[4]

Distribution

Distribution is usually the most critical area facing the local marketer in the developing country. In fact, unless effective ways of distributing the product can be found or created, market entries might be thwarted and the economic growth of the developing countries will not take off. To reach small urban centers and the rural population one might have to rely on clusters of small stores or roadside kiosks that sell a variety of products. On the other hand, cheap labor and personal service are usually readily available in developing markets. Where established logistical systems are weak, one can often pursue alternative routes using cheap domestic labor.

For example, where telephone systems are unreliable, messengers on bicycles or Vespas are often able to carry on. Lack of fast road systems can be compensated for by slower river traffic and hand-carry services. Overcrowded mass transportation systems are avoided by taking taxis to faraway destinations. In developing markets personal service is a "convenience good" for many people and a necessity for the upper crust of society, including the expatriate manager in a multinational firm.[5]

Marketing organization and control are difficult management problems in overseas business, regardless of the environment. In developing markets things get particularly difficult, since the local professional skills tend to be lower than elsewhere.

Promotion

Promotion in developing markets is initially limited because of the lack of broadcast media. However, as such media become available, the effectiveness of promotional messages can be considerable because of the lack of other advertising: There is less clutter. Of course, this is not true for outdoor advertising, which is often an effective means of establishing brand awareness and image. It is important to keep in mind the level of literacy; in developing countries the notion that "a picture is worth a thousand words" should be taken literally. By the same token, product demonstrations and sampling become important ways of promoting products.

Close-Up: Marketing in Russia and the NDCs

After the fall of the Berlin Wall, the Soviet Union gradually dissolved. What developed in 1991 was a constellation of Russia and 11 independent countries (Estonia, Latvia, and Lithuania had already declared their independence). Three belong geographically to central Europe (Belarus, Moldova, and Ukraine), while eight are central Asian (Armenia, Azerbaijan, Georgia, Kazakhstan, Kyrgyzstan, Tajikistan, Turkmenistan, and Uzbekistan). These **newly democratized countries (NDCs)** are now learning to deal with the free market system and a globalized world economy. From a total Soviet population of 286,717,000 in January 1989, Russia emerged with 147 million people, a number that had been reduced to 142 million by 2007.

From a marketing perspective, there are three major features that set newly democratized countries markets apart from those of the typical developing country.

1. *Basic needs satisfied.* Although these countries may be poor in per capita income by Western standards, the most basic needs of the population have in the past been satisfied through the government planning system. The consumers in these countries have not been starving (except during years of drought or political repression), and they have been able to buy clothing, shoes, housing, soap and detergent, and lately, also televisions and automobiles. Since most of these products have been produced domestically, they may not be up to world standards, but the people had their needs met. This is especially significant considering that some of the NDCs have very large populations (Russia and China, for example).

2. *Education and social control.* These countries have usually offered their citizens a solid basic education, strong social control, and a secure life. At the same time, they have inculcated, intentionally or not, an aversion to the capitalist system and free markets. The people in these countries are not illiterate, many are very creative, and they have considerable pride in past accomplishments by their countries. They have some hope for a better future and can be energized by the new prospects for individual growth.

3. *No free market.* What these people don't have, on the other hand, is a clear understanding of what a free market system entails, and they have trouble appreciating the magnitude of the changes of mindset required. Placing the consumer ahead of the producer is inconceivable to someone reared on the Marxist theory of labor value. Teaching Russian retail clerks that customers are important takes a lot of patience. For consumers, making a choice between three alternative coffee brands is a new and sometimes disconcerting experience.

These factors make the marketing manager's task different in NDC economies. But these markets also share characteristics with other developing markets, adding further complexity. The marketing infrastructure is typically weak. Channels of distribution are few and provide few service functions. Communications media are often still controlled by the state, and advertising is frowned upon. Customers do not have much purchasing power, and foreign currency is difficult to come by except for a few privileged groups.

Market Environment

NDC economies share many of the typical problems of developing countries: underdeveloped legal and financial institutions, uncertain political leadership, generally low purchasing power for foreign products, and so on. As in the case of developing countries generally, assistance from **international agencies** plays an important (though sometimes controversial) role in economic progress.

International institutions such as the United Nations, the World Bank, and the International Monetary Fund (IMF) play important roles in many NDC markets. The functions of these international agencies—lending capital, technical assistance, and economic planning help—have been mobilized to support the transformation of many of the eastern European countries into free market economies. The European Bank for Reconstruction and Development (EBRD), created by the European Union, was developed expressly to support the central European countries. These international agencies are important facilitators and guarantors of foreign investments for improving the basic infrastructure (road construction, electric power, and telephone service) and factories. From a marketing perspective they can be seen to help create a favorable market environment. The markets for products and services in the construction and telecommunications industries, for example, depend directly on loans from international agencies such as the World Bank.

Still, what happens in these countries is very much dependent on what happens with "Mother Russia." Russia's economic performance in the 1990s was erratic but stabilized in the new millennium. Several years of strong economic growth in the 1990s, fueled by huge investments of foreign capital, abruptly came to a stop in 1998. Widespread corruption, a failure of the government to collect taxes, and the spread of the Asian financial crisis forced the devaluation of the Russian ruble. Foreign investors left in droves, as Russia defaulted on its external debt.

While the banking collapse and ruble devaluation played a role in bringing Vladimir Putin to power, the former KGB operative presided over stable and growing economic indicators. For instance, real GDP growth was more than 8 percent in 2000 and GDP per head was $4,970 for 2000, rising to $8,920 in 2003 and $14,692 in 2007 (US$ at PPP).[6] Still, the irony of these comparatively anemic numbers has not been lost on Russia's former satellite states in central Europe, which have all (save Romania) eclipsed their former ruler's economic performance. Decades of totalitarian control contributed to a Soviet command economy that skewed development in favor of heavy industry (especially the energy, raw material, and defense-related sectors) while neglecting consumer goods and

Getting the Picture

RUSSIAN GOODS ARE GOOD AGAIN

Throughout the 1990s, Russians flocked to consume food, movies, music, and any products that were made in the West. Multinational firms were able to sell almost anything provided it had English on the package. But lately it has become cool to be Russian again and now foreign firms are even trying to conceal their ownership of Russian brands.

A rise in political nationalism under the leadership of President Vladimir Putin has spurred a new era of consumer nationalism in Russia in which products with "made in Russia" labels are now much easier to sell. Russian bears are now selling beer and kerchiefed babushkas are starring in new music videos featuring Russian rock bands. Even the trademark onion domes of Russian churches are being used to decorate labels for chocolate bars and dumplings.

At a time when globalization is sweeping the business world, this Russification movement highlights how Russia is again swimming against the tide and returning to its isolationist roots. Market research confirms this dramatic turnaround in a country that recently embraced all things Western after 70 years of communist deprivation. According to the firm Comcon, before 1998 only 48 percent of Russians said they preferred to buy domestic goods when considering quality and not just price. By 1999, that figure jumped to 90 percent, no doubt fueled by the ruble devaluation that made many imported goods too expensive for Russians.

Clearly price has much to do with this desire for products that are *nasha,* Russian for "ours," since the rising incomes are not evenly distributed and many Russians cannot afford imported luxuries on average salaries of less than $100 a month. But Russian firms are not the only ones tapping this recent country-of-origin effect.

British American Tobacco aimed to capitalize on the lucrative market for inexpensive cigarettes in Russia by launching the Muzhik brand in 1995. Muzhik is a historic Russian name for a peasant but it more colloquially means a "man's man" or a "tough guy." Despite the Russian name, local advertisers frowned on the selection as demonstrating an unclear understanding of the Russian market. Muzhik is the kind of superficial Russian lingo that foreigners typically pick up, just like "vodka" and "balalaika." One creative agency manager laughed uncomfortably, imagining a Russian smoker requesting a "Muzhik Light."

Times have changed in Russia but its economic promise is still complicated by its enigmatic populace.

Sources: Susan B. Glasser, "Patriotism Selling like Hot Cakes," *Washington Post,* May 9, 2001, p. C1; Anatoly Tyomkin and Dina Vishnya, "What's in a Name Is Hit-and-Miss Game," *St. Petersburg Times,* August 14, 2001, p. A1.

---

agriculture. Central planning also resulted in inefficient resource use within most industries, since most production was not profitable at current market prices. The retail and services sectors expanded 36–55 percent in the decade ending in 2000, but industrial (particularly energy) production still dominates the economy.

The good news is that former President Putin, despite his preference for top-down control and authoritarian ways, brought a measure of stability to Russia's economy. Russia has averaged economic growth of 7 percent annually since the financial crisis of 1998. Although high oil prices and a relatively cheap ruble are responsible, consumer demand also played a role. Personal incomes have achieved real gains more than 12 percent per year, poverty has declined, and the middle class has continued to expand. Oil export earnings have allowed Russia to increase its foreign reserves from $12 billion in 1999 to some $470 billion at year-end 2007, the third largest reserves in the world. Foreign direct investment has risen from $14.6 billion in 2005 to approximately $45 billion in 2007, demonstrating investors' confidence in Mr. Putin. This is all the more important since the plants of the former state enterprises are old and dilapidated and seriously in need of updating.

Despite Russia's recent success, serious problems persist. Oil, natural gas, metals, and timber account for more than 80 percent of exports and 30 percent of government revenues, leaving the country vulnerable to swings in world commodity prices. The prospect of Russian membership in WTO, by some expected in 2006, has been put on hold. Exports to Russia have come with sharply increased ruble prices to counter the devaluation. Not surprisingly, many Western companies—from American Nabisco with its supermarket snack foods like Ritz crackers and Oreo cookies to Italy's Fiat with cars assembled in Russia—are recording sharp downturns in sales as Russian consumers can no longer afford the prices with their devalued rubles. But the domestic Russian producers are now learning the tools of marketing and adapting very quickly (see box, "Russian Goods Are Good Again").

The former Soviet Union's already shoddy infrastructure was crumbling, but with the rise in oil and gas prices, the government's coffers are full and new infrastructure and housing are now being constructed. But the results have yet to materialize and in the meantime the average Russian citizen is facing an abysmal housing and transportation situation, which, combined with a weak health network, have contributed to one of the dreariest and shortest life expectancies in the world. While women can expect to live to 73 years of age,[7] Russian men's life expectancy is a low 60 years. As of 2007, the Russian population was declining annually.

Political and Legal Risks

In NDC markets it is necessary to treat political and legal factors as part of the economic landscape. Since communism typically banned private property, a legal system required to create and sustain orderly free markets is often not in existence. The result is that some fundamental marketing activities have a loose legal basis.

For example, marketing usually involves the exchange of products and services for money (or other goods and services). When the transaction is completed, the ownership of a product passes from the seller to the buyer. Each has important rights—based on explicit and implicit contracts—concerning product use, fulfillment of payment obligations, delivery times, return rights, and so on. This legal machinery is often not yet in place in NDC economies, making binding transactions difficult to enforce.

Export controls are another political–legal problem area for the marketer. During the Cold War it was important to control trade with adversarial nations, especially in technology-intensive products. In the West, export controls became common for goods traded to any communist country, and even some nonaligned nations such as India.

The administration of the control regime was the task of COCOM, the coordinating committee for multilateral export controls. After the fall of the Berlin Wall, the importance of export controls diminished, and in the spring of 1994 COCOM was dissolved. This did not mean the end of export controls, however, since there continues to be a need to control the proliferation of various weapon systems to belligerent countries. A new international control regime is being developed by the United States and other countries, and the marketer of technology-intensive products should not expect an export license to be automatically granted for NDC markets.[8]

Even seasoned multinationals can run afoul of the export controls. For example, in 1998, IBM was found guilty and fined for selling supercomputers to Russia without federal approval. The deal took place in late 1996 and early 1997. Independent middlemen were used to first ship the computers from an IBM subsidiary in Germany to Amsterdam. They were then shipped back across Europe to Russia and ended up at Arzamas-16, a nuclear weapons laboratory. IBM American executives claimed ignorance, and Russian officials said they thought the deal was approved. The United States requested the return of the computers, but the Russians refused.

The **political risk** in these countries primarily involves the chance that the regime will dramatically change the foreign investment climate or private property regulations. Although commentators agree that such a reversal is unlikely, the local marketer needs to keep a close watch on these developments.[9] It is important that contacts with knowledgeable insiders be established so that developments can be monitored. This is not only the job of the general manager of a local subsidiary or branch. Since marketing is the function in the firm that consistently relates to the external world, it is incumbent on the marketer to demand that salespeople and distribution channel members track and report new developments.

Politics also influences NDC peoples' **attitudes toward the free market system.** Education in economics by its reliance on Marx has been effective in discrediting the free market system. In addition, the obvious successes of Soviet Russia—Sputnik, military weaponry, the achievements in high culture, the strong sports teams—have

Getting the Picture

WAS IT BETTER BEFORE?

The Soviet past left not only Russia but also several former Soviet republics in Asia unprepared for free markets. For example, Kazakhstan's industrial production seriously declined with the centrally planned system's collapse, but its oil exportation sector has played a major role in reversing that trend. Unfortunately, oil production employs few people, agriculture remains the country's largest employer, and the service sector is still in its infancy. Still, real GDP grew by almost 10 percent in Kazakhstan by the end of 2000 and continued efforts to diversify the economy should accelerate the transformation process.

Known as the traditional "breadbasket" of Mother Russia, Ukraine has been working to survive the shock independence dealt its collective farms. Dependence on antiquated technology and production methods left the country ill prepared to compete with the West. Although government officials have attempted to restructure the economy away from heavy industries, privatization and foreign investment have proceeded much more slowly than in the former communist countries of central Europe. A corresponding high level of overregulation, high taxes, and rampant corruption has further contributed to a business environment that is still uncompetitive on international markets. The result is that Ukraine's GDP per head in terms of purchasing power parity stood at around US$6,941 in 2007, decidedly worse than Kazakhstan's US$11,086.

Clearly, any country blessed with deep factory endowments can become globally competitive in selected areas. The challenge for Russia's struggling former Asian republics (Armenia, Georgia, Azerbaijan, Kazakhstan, Kyrgyzstan, Tajikistan, Turkmenistan, Uzbekistan) as well as its former European republics (Belarus, Ukraine, Moldova), is to institute the policies necessary to accelerate this process. Since hyperinflation and food shortages have now given way to a stable currency and strong economic growth there is cause for optimism. However, there are still too many old-guard well-connected people and organizations with power and wealth invested in the current system. Dismantling this cadre could prove even more difficult than shrinking a stockpile of nuclear warheads. But increased competition across all facets of economic life should bring down prices and improve the standard of living, once these governments are committed to capitalistic concepts such as private property and free entrepreneurship. Long-term and sustained growth will depend on luring the foreign investment necessary to permanently transform this part of the world.

This is a tall order, even for a patient person. Small wonder if some people there think it was better before.

Sources: Lucas, 2001; "Now for a Challenge or Two," *The Economist,* January 3, 2002; Susan B. Glasser, "Patriotism Selling like Hot Cakes," *Washington Post,* May 9, 2001, p. C1.

inspired justified pride in the communist system (see box, "Was It Better Before?"). The dismantling of the Berlin Wall was a result of economic failure—but for many of the people in these countries, economics is not everything. Marketing is not well understood by these people, and when they see it in action, they don't always like it. "Hard sell" promotions, for example, are likely to backfire, not only among older consumers.[10]

Market Segmentation

The local marketer in NDC economies may find it useful to define the market served in terms of **ethnic market segmentation** of subgroups among the population in each of the countries. For example, ethnic Hungarians in Slovakia may have consumer preferences similar to those in Hungary and Moldavia. Despite the breakaway of many countries from the former Soviet Union, Russia is still home to many ethnic minorities who are represented also in other central European countries.[11]

As the transition toward a market economy progresses, the NDC consumers will undoubtedly move closer to their Western counterparts. One study showed that they already have—among the teenage segment. Another market segmentation study of Russian consumers found that more than half of all men and women could be categorized as independent, ambitious, or self-reliant, all traits uncommon in communist days (see Exhibit 10.2).[12] As the exhibit shows, the then 147 million consumers in the Russian market could be grouped into five different segments. Apparently Western products are often preferred in some groups. As economic progress proceeds, one would expect actual sales to follow in the not too distant future as retailers upgrade their offerings. New evidence suggests that this is now underway (see box, "Finally on Track").

According to the Russian official statistics office Goscomstat, at the turn of the millennium 25 percent of the country's population lived in poverty, 35 percent were reaching a level of basic need satisfaction (food and simple clothing), another 35 percent

Getting the Picture

FINALLY ON TRACK: RUSSIA'S RETAIL MARKETS

After the fall of the Berlin Wall and the emergence of a new Russia in 1989, the expectations were that Russia's consumers would finally have a chance to indulge in some of the Western brand name products. Although some of this took place—Nike, Sony, Levi's, and other brands certainly became more easily available—many Russian consumers found themselves without the means to acquire the products. Especially after the devaluation of the ruble in 1998, many Russian consumers were forced to retreat back to the old days of scarcity and careful spending. Retail business fell off, and stores also looked like they did in the old days.

This situation has now finally changed, perhaps for good. Flush with the gains from high energy prices, Russia's population are now able to demand and pay for consumer goods. As a result, new investment in retailing has shot up. Hypermarkets and supermarkets are springing up all over the country. From 2003 to 2006 their number surged from 8,991 to 20,524. Modern commercial outlets' share of the market is expected to triple by 2010, reaching 50 percent.

Several smaller international retail chains are successful in Russia, including Auchan, AVA, Metro, Migros Turk, REWE, SPAR, and Tengelman. The Russian consumer market is becoming increasingly Westernized. Merchants are offering more and more luxury and premium goods and are implementing different discount programs. Yet the world's leading companies are still in no hurry to come to Russia: Such giants as Carrefour, Makro, Tesco, and Wal-Mart are not there yet.

Why is that? Some observers claim that one major factor is Russia's poor reputation. A country's general business conditions are very important, and investors look at the political risks before investing their money in a country.

There is another obstacle. The best markets in Russia were already occupied by local players, and the entry of international retail chains met with an immediate response from local players that were quick to upgrade their operations and increase scale. Wal-Mart explored the possibilities in Russia but decided against entering, perhaps mindful of its difficulties in Germany and England.

Russian retailers are expanding fast and even starting to look for new opportunities abroad. Today there are only three truly foreign firms among Russia's top ten retailers, and even they are at the bottom of the list. Auchan is ranked sixth, Ramstor ninth, and Germany's REWE tenth. Unlike in China, India, and Brazil, foreign companies have encountered tough competition in Russia, more typical for well-developed markets.

Sources: Alexander Yurov, "Russian consumer market becoming more westernized," RIA Novosti, October 25, 2006, **www.bilkent.edu.tr;** Polina Belkina, "Consumer Trends in Russia," U.S. Department of Commerce, International Trade Administration, #19 - JRL 7206, May 2003; "Johnson's Russia List," **www.cdi.org.**

belonged to the middle class with modest but steadily growing disposable income, and 5 percent were really "rich" with above-average luxury European consumption standards.

As other statistics suggest, the middle class in large Russian cities now already represents the fastest growing consumer segment in terms of buying power. For instance, in the capital city of Moscow the middle class comprises only 12.5 percent of the population but accounts for 60 to 70 percent of all consumer spending. Up to 94 percent of Moscow's middle-class people regularly eat out in fast-food restaurants (compared to

EXHIBIT 10.2 **A Psychographic Segmentation of the Russian Market**

Sources: *The Russian Consumer,* 1992; Elliot, 1992.

	Kuptsi (merchants)	Cossacks	Students	Business Executives	"Russian Souls"
Percent of all men	30%	10%	10%	25%	25%
Percent of all women	45%	10%	5%	10%	30%
Dominant traits	Reliant, nationalistic, practical, seeks value	Ambitious, independent, nationalistic, seeks status	Passive, scraping by, idealistic, practical	Ambitious, Western-oriented, busy, concerned with status	Passive, follows others, fears choices, hopeful
Likely preferences	*Car:* Volkswagen	BMW	2CV	Mercedes	Lada
	Cigarettes: Chesterfield	Dunhill	Marlboro	Winston	Marlboro
	Liquor: Stolichnaya	Rémy Martin	Local vodka in Smirnoff bottles	Johnnie Walker	Smirnoff

Getting the Picture

AMERICAN STANDARD IN RUSSIA

American Standard, the New Jersey–based multinational, is the world's largest manufacturer of bathroom furniture, with strong market presence in many countries. Its early entry into Russia was not so successful, however.

An initial market survey of demand in Russia in early 1991 suggested that the main market, new construction, would be slow and closed to outside vendors for the time being. The company decided to target reconstruction, the renovation and upgrading of old apartments in Moscow and St. Petersburg for office use by Western firms.

American Standard decided that the Russian private entrepreneurs who took on the renovations would mainly be interested in the low-end equipment, which would lower building costs. Accordingly, the company brought in its low-end product line, priced competitively. The products did not move. The entrepreneurs wanted the top of the line. They went to European competitors for their upscale products. Price was no object. The reason? The builders figured that the Western companies would be willing to pay top dollar for their offices. And they were right. In 1994 central Moscow was perhaps the world's most expensive business district, where prices of $15,000 to $20,000 per month for a small office were not unheard of.

Sources: Lloyd, 1994; Personal interview with Eric Crabtree, vice president and director, CMT Moscow, Construction Marketing and Trading, Inc., Washington, DC, October 20, 1994.

40 percent of the general population), 63 percent eat at upscale establishments (compared to 16 percent), and about 85 percent own a car (versus 31.8 percent).

Product Positioning

One question for the new local marketer in an NDC is whether to lead with the upper or lower end of the product line. Most indicators—income, usage conditions, needs—would suggest that these markets would be best served with a more basic product at the low end of the price scale. However, being the first company to offer a more advanced product can yield first-mover advantages. Furthermore, the lower end typically pits the entrant squarely against existing domestic brands. In addition, the few upscale customers may prefer the most advanced high-end product (see box, "American Standard in Russia").

Marketing Tactics

Product Policies

In NDC markets customers tend to feel ambivalent about their domestic products. On the one hand, they know that new offerings from outside are often superior. Still, they do not necessarily want to give up the old brands. The reasons are not only sentimental remembrances of things past or country-of-origin affections. They also realize that if the products are not bought, the domestic factories can't stay open and they will lose their jobs. But the best argument for choosing a domestic brand is the same in Russia as elsewhere—it's one that offers the right mix of functional and emotional satisfaction. And Russian firms are getting savvy enough with their branding efforts to offer something for foreign markets as well (see box, "The Russian Brands Are Coming!").[13]

Pricing

Entering global brands will typically be able to command a price premium over existing local brands. But for the typical Western firm the primary task is not to skim a small existing market but to develop the market generically with new and superior products from leading markets. This means that a better strategy will be to price at a lower penetration level, keeping it sufficiently affordable to induce trial and continued usage.

For most firms the long-term prospects of these markets matter much more than short-term payoffs, leading firms to establish a penetration price level. With the ruble's devaluation in 1998, however, many firms found it necessary to take a short-term view, raising prices on their exports to Russia to offset the fact that ruble earnings lost more than half of their value in U.S. dollars. Fortunately, many of the eastern European countries seem to weather the storm better, leading firms to stay in for the longer run rather than withdraw from these markets completely.

Getting the Picture

THE RUSSIAN BRANDS ARE COMING!

Russian consumer products are perhaps less well-known than their industrial counterparts. Closed borders, coupled with the well-known Soviet focus on production rather than consumption, means that top-of-mind awareness of Russian products naturally involve military hardware (the AK-47 semiautomatic rifle, for example, or Antonov aircraft troop carriers) and industrial products such as the Belarus tractor. Despite the isolation, we did learn about Stolichnaya vodka and caviar, and perhaps about fur coats and hats and Matryoshka nested dolls, but not much else.

This is now changing. Even though the current economic boom depends on the rising process on Russia's vast oil and gas resources, Russian firms are getting wise to the advantages of branded products, some of which are beginning to show on Western markets. Names such as MTS, Lukoil, and Baltika have started to appear on the international stage.

In its 2008 annual Brandz 100 listing, marketing analysis firm Millward Brown ranked MTS, Russia's top mobile phone operator, in 89th place, making it the first and only Russian brand to appear in the top 100. Lukoil came in eighth on the list of the top 10 international motor fuel brands, and Baltika beer was ranked 15th out of the top 20 beer brands worldwide.

The MTS ranking is the result of a successful rebranding effort by its parent company, Sistema. The company paid Omnicom Group's Wolff Olins consultancy $4 million to develop the brand, which consists of a white egg surrounded by a solid-colored square. The objective was to develop a recognizable look that would connect all its products—mobile phones, Internet, digital television, and land-line services. Initially the effort was considered a failure, but by conceiving of the rebranding in terms of a complete "make-over" of the company, the company turned the effort to success. "Rebranding is not a mere change of name or logo. It is a complete change of corporate values, promises, attitudes and feelings about brands and products," says Yelena Georgobiani, a rebranding consultant at media company SPN Ogilvy.

Other Russian brands are adopting the rebranding strategy. In fact, the successful MTS rebranding effort was done after competitive rival Beeline had a very successful rebranding effort, with a new brand featuring the black and yellow stripes of a bee. In another example, Dixy, a leading retailer of foodstuffs and household supplies, used parts of a public offering generating $360 million in a rebranding campaign. According to one spokesperson, "Russia is caught up in a rebranding fever. Now every company wants to put on a new face."

The authorities are suspicious of the idea of changing the brand name of a company's product, suspecting the company might be involved in tax evasion. Eldorado, a leading electronics retailer whose head office was raided, said it was doing all it could to keep its brand name intact, even as authorities press tax-evasion charges.

In Russia branding is used to help create a market-oriented culture within the organization—and perhaps it will also help to make authorities more customer-friendly.

Sources: Tai Adelaja, "Rebranding Puts Russian Firms on World Stage," *The Moscow Times*, **www.moscowtimes.com,** April 28, 2008; "BRANDZ Top 100 Most Powerful Brands, 2007," Millward Brown Optimor, **www.millwardbrown.com.**

Distribution

A big problem that the new local marketer faces in typical NDCs is a wasteful and dysfunctional distribution system. Because the economies were closed off to outside competition, ineffective systems for delivery of products and services have been left in operation. Marxist ideals hold that only production has value, and unfortunately distribution was seen as unworthy of serious attention. Furthermore, the priority was on industrial products over consumer goods, which means that the entire marketing infrastructure (the logistics of distribution, the media of communications, and the means of transferring payments) in consumer products is particularly weak.

Weak Infrastructure It is mostly the deficiencies of the marketing infrastructure that make it difficult for the local marketer to penetrate NDC markets. The functions provided by middlemen are weak or nonexistent, and the local marketer can't expect to rely very much on independent middlemen. This creates a need for localization by augmenting the product sold. For example, since electricity is often in short supply and rationed with frequent blackouts, electric appliances might need to be redesigned with a buffer battery that kicks in when cutoffs occur. Similarly, digital alarm clocks, radios with push-button station memory, coffeemakers with preset timers, and rice cookers with warming features are all products that might need to be redesigned. In some cases complete battery function is preferable; battery radios without a recharger are still bestsellers in many NDC markets.[14]

It is important to find out what functions the existing channel members can and can't perform, and to what degree it is necessary to create entirely new channels for

Getting the Picture

P&G GOES TO RUSSIA

When Russia opened up its borders to Western products, the giant multinationals in consumer packaged goods quickly started to reconnoiter the potentially huge market. But the initial delegations of top marketing executives soon came to realize the difficulty of selling through the existing distribution channels. Weak transportation systems, inferior storage facilities, and out-of-date warehousing operations created costly inefficiencies in the delivery of the products to the stores. And in the stores the limited shelf space, the dull gray atmospheres, and the sullen clerks made for a dreary shopping experience, even though the stores had been recently privatized.

Accordingly, the first tasks for a company such as P&G in Russia involved creating a much more efficient and modern distribution network. Investing in existing facilities and new warehouses, helping to improve transportation fleets and parking space, and training store employees were some of the measures taken. P&G even invested in improving port facilities in St. Petersburg and sent its products by ship rather than trucking through country border stops.

Sources: *New York Times,* July 23, 1994, pp. 1, 43; Lloyd, 1994.

products, services, and communications. Procter & Gamble's experience in Russia is instructive (see box, "P&G Goes to Russia").

To accomplish the job, the local marketer sometimes has to think about reconfiguring the firm's *value chain.* For example, in addition to localizing the product, services that at home are provided by independent operators may need to be added to the value chain. To service vacuum cleaners and other household appliances, Western firms at home often depend on small entrepreneurs who run their own independent operations and service several makes. In NDC markets, the required know-how may not yet be

With capitalism, outdoor advertising has come to Russia. A central Moscow subway entrance creates the kind of heavy pedestrian traffic pattern that entices outdoor advertisers to go all out. AP Photo/Ivan Sekretarev.

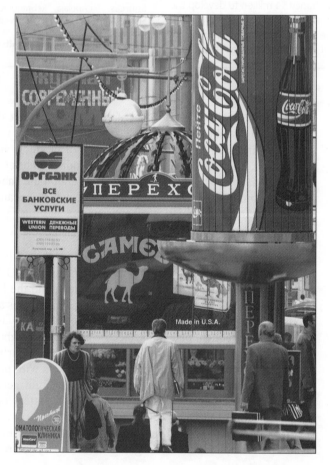

diffused enough to rely on independents. Instead, the Western entrant has to help create such a service network and train the staff.[15]

At the beginning of the new millennium, Russia is experiencing a boom in new Western-style shopping malls, restaurants, and supermarket openings. According to the Russian news agency Interfax, in the Ural city of Yekaterinburg with 1.4 million inhabitants, five shopping complexes were opened in the first six months of 2001. The Dutch Spar chain has now opened over 30 outlets throughout Russia. Turkish retailer Ramenka recently opened its fourth outlet in Moscow. German Metro AG and French Auchan have both identified sites for retail development and securing construction sites. Swedish IKEA enjoys enormous popularity from Muscovites actively shopping in the company's three stores. The major attraction, as always with IKEA, seems to be do-it-yourself reasonably priced items with some Western chic.[16]

Marketing Education   In NDCs the marketing manager must be prepared to do a lot of on-the-job training and **educating of middlemen** and others in basic marketing principles and practices, and in how to distribute, sell, and service the product effectively. There is also a secondary audience consisting of actual and potential customers, as well as domestic competitors. Finally, many government bureaucrats need to be informed about free markets, although this part of the educational process is usually handled during the initial negotiations before starting to do business in the country.

Broadly speaking, the aim of the education is to demonstrate the role of marketing in the free market system. It is necessary to elaborate on principles taken for granted and self-evident to the Westerner. Thus, before the marketer can serve as a teacher, he or she may have to study some of the basics of the system at home.

The marketer first of all has to explain the basic functioning of a product or service to the middlemen involved in the distribution chain. Many products have no counterpart in the NDC markets, or their advanced character requires explanation and instruction in use and service. Furthermore, how to listen to customer questions, how to offer product information, and how to give after-sales support are all "naturals" for the Western marketer to which he or she must now give some thought. The Japanese incursion into American and Western markets has served to educate even Western middlemen about these basic prerequisites of effective marketing.

The marketer in NDC economies needs to be able to explain how the roles in the distribution chain have changed with the emergence of free markets. Now the idea is to perform efficiently—to help move the products through the chain with speed, respond quickly to demand shifts, and be alert to competitors' moves. Gone are the days when the suppliers and the customers were captive: Now only the best can survive. The marketer needs to explain—"teach"—that in the free market system costs need to be controlled and revenues have to cover expenses. It is "Welcome, brave new world" for the middlemen.

Service Training   The new teaching will be heresy to many and will seem to go against many things in their past experience. The middlemen will have ingrained ideas about what is appropriate and may find it difficult to accept the new ways. It becomes important that the "teacher" explain why these changes are necessary. Of course, the market and competitors are the new "teachers," but the manager can't wait for mistakes to show up before taking action. Luckily, people are generally willing to try the changes, having seen how badly the previous system performed. For example, the successful Western cosmetics firms' marketers in eastern Europe train the in-store sales personnel, teaching them how to care for a customer and, in the process, teaching them how to take care of themselves.[17]

Practically speaking, the local marketer needs to:

1. Develop training programs for store personnel, focusing on how to treat customers.
2. Prepare manuals and pamphlets describing products and services and helping middlemen devise appropriate facilities and procedures for the transportation, storage, and shelving of the product.

Getting the Picture

MARKET RESEARCH REACHES RUSSIA

In a country where many families have had a relative deported to Siberia or simply vanish after being apprehended by the KGB, market research has arrived but not without some typically Russian twists. As recently as a few short years ago, young women with clipboards in downtown Moscow had difficulty getting any responses from skeptical Russian shoppers who questioned whether the data had a government purpose or why their opinions were relevant to anyone.

This Russian cult of suspicion has complicated the targeting of viable consumers for various products. Market research firms are realizing that personalized contact must be well prepared psychologically and linguistically to avoid antagonizing the target audience. Despite such concerns, by the end of 2000, 54 companies were involved in conducting market research in Russia with more than $2 million in revenue at stake. Although this may be minor revenue compared to developed markets, rapid growth and a largely undefined population are presenting great business opportunities. According to Yevgeniya Gromova, general director of Comcon SPb, localizing companies are particularly interested in concept testing, market segmentation/product positioning, pricing, brand evaluation and loyalty, and pre- and postcampaign ad effectiveness evaluation

research. "They are especially important when a firm wants to launch a new service or product on the market," he says. "Larger firms also order studies of the lifestyles of particular demographic or class segments in order to determine the preferences of their target consumers."

Direct marketing would seem a promising avenue to reach the Russian consumer. However, acquiring a reliable database poses its own problems. Since many Russians fail to declare private property and some register in another person's name to avoid taxes, car and property ownership lists are hardly reliable. Further, many with sufficient wealth wish to keep it private, so targeting the percentage of the population affluent enough to respond to a particular campaign is particularly vexing.

Russian market research firms are clearly facing a greater demand for their services and in time a more sophisticated and comprehensive understanding of the market is likely to result—provided, of course, that Russian respondents—and researchers—can learn to distinguish between interviews and interrogations.

Sources: Andrey Musatov, "Research Firms Arm Agencies with Facts," *St. Petersburg Times,* August 14, 2001; "The Secret Way of Russian Life," *Precision Marketing,* November 9, 2001, p. 9.

3. Help the middlemen develop a tracking and cost accounting system to make it possible to trace shipments and locate where in the chain there may be a problem, such as overstocking.

4. Make sure that product localization in terms of design and packaging also takes into account the needs of the middlemen. This often involves educating the home office about special requirements, such as different sizes and packaging of existing products.

5. Distribute instructional videotapes and other educational material to various members of the distribution channel, explaining why customers are so important in the free market system and why marketing is as important as manufacturing.

Promotion

Marketing communications often have to be revised in NDC markets. The common advertising media—television, magazines, and newspapers—are becoming widely available, although they may have limited reach. Also, because of the immaturity of the market, many products are new and any communication needs to stress simple, functional explanations. People who have not seen a 10-speed bike need some instructions and explanation of its advantages over the domestic clunker that has served so well for 30 years—and justification for the high price. The solid education of the people, however, will make the requisite advertising copy quite easy to develop. The average Russian is quite capable of processing information.

Lack of **credibility of advertising** claims is a problem. In previously totalitarian countries people maintain a healthy disrespect for public announcements and mass communication, which is also a problem for marketing research (see box, "Market Research Reaches Russia"). This naturally reduces the power of advertising, at least in the short run until its benefits in terms of new products and services materialize. By contrast, word-of-mouth is often considered more reliable and effective than mass media. This can have its own negative consequences. In Poland, for example, a rumor that P&G's Head and Shoulders shampoo made your hair fall out turned out to be particularly difficult to put down. In some of these markets, domestic companies sometimes resort to such "dirty" campaign tricks as they see their protected advantage dissipate.[18]

When the political, economic, and social fabric is undergoing the kind of revolution seen in newly democratized countries, old values are crumbling along with the political system. There is a need for the country and its people to learn what a free market system is about. To change the old order, communications have to be open and the old implicit understandings reexamined. The American insistence on transparency of transactions helps tear down the labyrinthine networks and closed systems that in many NDCs have made corruption and exploitation of the common man and woman prevalent. The American way with marketing is an agent for democracy.

Still, the hard-hitting approaches used in some American advertising could lead to a backlash when applied in an NDC market. On the one hand, cynicism and suspicion can be a problem. On the other hand, people are not used to the "puffery" associated with much of American promotion and may take assertions of "best" and "most" at face value. This potential downside risk of the free market experience will taper off in intensity as the people gradually become more insensitive to preposterous assertions and reap the benefits of new ideas and new products. In the meantime, the local marketer will do well to temper some of the more obvious excesses of American advertising.[19]

Close-Up: Marketing In China[20]

China is a large and important emerging market deserving special treatment. China can be viewed as a "new growth" market with features similar to NDCs. But China is not (yet) a democracy, and presents some very special problems for the local marketer. These problems have mostly to do with the political legacy of the country, and much of the discussion about the NDCs above is relevant for China. In what follows, only the additional peculiarities of the marketing environment in China will be highlighted.

Market Environment

China has 1.3 billion people, largest in the world. The gradual opening of the economy in the 1990s has led to an impressive export-led growth record. Throughout the 1990s its annual growth was in the double digits, although it has slowed somewhat in recent years toward roughly 8 percent per year. In 2003, China overtook Japan to become the second-largest economy in the world measured on a purchasing power parity (PPP) basis.[21] In 2007, its per capita GDP stood at US$5,292, almost double that of also fast-growing India (see Exhibit 9.2 in Chapter 9). While the Indian population keeps growing, China's policy of restricting families to one-child-per-household (more lenient in rural areas) has stopped population growth, and the rising economic output is not divided by a rising number of people.

The large population plus the growing economy make China a large importer of machinery, production equipment, technology, telecommunication equipment, aircraft, oil and raw materials for industrial production. The Chinese government has expanded its importation of agriculture-applied technology; fertilizers; industrial raw materials; and technologies and equipment for energy, transportation, telecommunication, and industrial renovation programs. Importation of consumer products is expected to grow because of recent tariff reductions as China became a member of the World Trade Organization in December 2001. In 2003, the annual bilateral trade surplus with the United States alone stood close to US$124 billion and by 2007 its total trade surplus stood at US$262.2 billion.[22] China's growth is export-based.

With its underlying strength in natural resources and able and disciplined workers, the strength of the Chinese economy has become the engine that drives growth elsewhere in Asia. Strong central leadership by its communist rulers combined with a "hands-off" policy toward Hong Kong, its new Special Administrative Region, has

Getting the Picture

GUESS WHO IS KNOCKING?

In April 1998, door-to-door selling was banned in China, putting an end to the successful market penetration of Amway, direct marketer of a wide variety of inexpensive household products, and cosmetics sellers Avon and Mary Kay. The Chinese government claimed that direct sales techniques worked like a religion, making people passionate about new ideas—something the government abhors.

For the American companies, one of their largest international markets was suddenly "off-limits." Amway alone had 80,000 distributors in China who sold $178 million worth of products in 1997, accounting for 21 percent of the company's total sales. All three companies stopped their door-to-door selling activities—including recruiting new salespeople—by the end of April. Throughout the summer, the companies negotiated with the Chinese government to work out new deals that would allow them to stay in China. Their basic argument was

that the law was aimed against fly-by-night direct selling companies, which had a shady past in China, and not against well-established companies selling reliable products. By early June, Avon had negotiated a deal with the government in which the company would operate as a wholesaler to Chinese retail stores, with plans to convert its 75 supply branches into actual retail outlets.

As China developed further and the leadership gained more confidence, the deal was renegotiated, and in 2006 Avon was permitted to start direct sales again. By July the company had employed 114,000 sales staff, and was planning to hire another 31,000 new recruits.

If you can't fight them, join them.

Sources: Ligos, 1998; "Penetrating the Great Wall," 1998; Simon Pitman, "Avon Goes Full Throttle in China," **www.cosmeticsdesign.com**, July 18, 2006.

made devaluation of the yuan unnecessary. But the country's rulers can be unpredictable (see box, "Guess Who Is Knocking?").

The size and potential of the Chinese market, coupled with its fast-growing purchasing power, make China a very attractive market. The per capita income in 1992 was equivalent to US$224, but by 2007 it stood at an estimated US$5,292. As economic progress continues, the huge market potential for Western products is coming closer to realization. One sign of this is the fact that the (interminable) Kodak–Fuji battle for supremacy of the world's photographic film market continues apace in China, as we saw in Chapter 2.

McDonald's arches near Beijing's 580-year-old Drum Tower. In 2002 the Beijing city government issued new regulations that required more than 30 McDonald's signs to come down. Officials said that many commercial signs, for both foreign and Chinese companies, do not fit with the traditional style of the buildings nearby. During China's Ming and Qing dynasties, the beat of the tower drums at sunset marked the end of the day. AP Photo/Greg Baker.

Getting the Picture

ANOTHER GREAT LEAP FOR CHINA?

To gain entry into the WTO, China has promised to gradually reduce its tariff and nontariff barriers to a level comparable to that of other WTO members. The effect promises to be profound, although it will take time according to experts. As the duty reductions kick in, import producers will be more competitive with previously protected domestic firms. This means, in turn, a likely shift to consolidation among local producers, and several product markets are likely to go from regional fragmentation to a national market. In beer, for example, Anheuser-Busch, the large American brewer, foresees the emergence of more national brands. Also, it anticipates a reduction of the power of the local governments inside China, which in the past could close access to distribution and stores. Rules such as trademark protection, commercial practices, tax administration, and labor management will be more uniform and transparent across the country, making local regulators much less susceptible to local political pressure to protect indigenous industries.

Also important for Anheuser-Busch and other beer importers is that the WTO rules break the monopoly of state-owned distributors and retailers. Not only will the distribution channels open up—it will also be much easier to pursue a push marketing strategy, getting the distribution channels to promote a branded product. Says Philip Davis, managing director of Anheuser-Busch Asia Pacific: "It's a lot easier to motivate and incentivize an owner than a government employee."

Sources: "Anheuser-Busch Sees China WTO Entry Benefits as a 'Very Long-Term Process,'" *AFX-Asia*, November 12, 2001; "Penetrating the Great Wall," 1998.

Foreign Entry

Although the WTO entry may one day change this, the Chinese government is still by most measures the greatest entry barrier into China. It controls importation through various measures: import license controls, protective tariffs, foreign exchange control, and government-controlled foreign trading companies. However, tariffs are coming down, foreign direct investment for the domestic market is now allowed within certain constraints, and the requirement that foreign entrants enter through joint ventures with Chinese firms has been loosened. General Motors still has eight joint ventures and but also two wholly owned subsidiaries in China, one of its most successful markets, with Buick a best-seller in the full-sized sedan class. Its Chery marquee from the joint venture with Shanghai Auto was China's top seller in 2007.[23]

Import License Controls

The Ministry of Foreign Trade and Economic Cooperation (MOFTEC) is the main regulatory organization governing the current import-licensing system. China has used a centralized system to restrict imports of consumer and luxury goods in order to conserve foreign exchange for other items. As foreign reserves have accumulated, the controls are loosened, but China's leaders still keep controls. Import license categories are slowly removed from the controls in an effort to meet World Trade Organization (WTO) requirements. Despite its exporting success, China still keeps a wary eye on the kind of goods that the country imports. Even if tariffs have come down, luxury products carry very steep taxes, raised again in 2006.[24]

Protective Tariffs

From 1986 to 1998, China adjusted tariff rates several times and continues to do so. However, its former rate of 20 percent was still much higher than the average 5 percent for the developed countries and the average 13 percent for the developing countries. With the entry into the WTO, the government has promised to continue tariff reduction until it meets the average level of the other WTO members (see box, "Another Great Leap for China?").[25]

Foreign Exchange Control

In April 2006, China implemented a new exchange rate system. China's central bank announced the relaxation of controls on foreign exchange accounts, simplifying approval procedures for foreign exchange payments in the service trade, and procedures for individuals to buy foreign currencies. Because of its successful export record, China was flush with foreign currencies, and needed to be able to invest in foreign

Getting the Picture

CHAIRMAN BILL?

For Bill Gates and Microsoft, China has become the next *big* market. Since arriving in 1992, the company has established a network of business operations in China, from sales and marketing, to customer support and even research and development. Its size is second only to the operations at home in Redmond, Washington. But this does not mean doing business in China is easy: Microsoft is still dogged by piracy of its software.

Microsoft estimates that 90 percent of its software used in China is pirated. Outside the company's $80 million research center in Beijing, young Chinese line the sidewalk attempting to steer potential customers away from the authorized seller, down alleys to run-down apartments where bootleg copies are sold. A typical price is $1 for software that regularly sells for $200. Sure, not all the accompanying booklets are available with the diskettes, backup service might be questionable, and later upgrades are impossible to get, but isn't it worth a try?

Microsoft has been battling back with a mix of government appeals and consumer bullying, but with little success. The Chinese government actively has been promoting the Linux alternative, and its bureaucrats also find it distasteful to punish their own citizens just to add more funds to Bill Gates's already full coffer. Even China's accession to the WTO seems to have done little to dent this attitude. So Microsoft has lately decided on a new strategy. Thinking positively, the company has started to offer its top customers in government and business upgraded customer support, dedicated account managers, and even more sharing of the technology. The strategic notion is that with the added value of these services, top customers will be reluctant to endorse—and use—pirated software. Then, in turn, they will be more sympathetic to pursuing the bootleggers.

Only time will tell if this "trickle-down" approach will work. China, after all, is still part of the mysterious East.

Sources: Sarah Schafer, "Microsoft's Cultural Revolution," *Newsweek*, June 28, 2004, pp. E10, 12; "Microsoft Makes New Effort to Expand in China," *SinoCast China IT Watch*, July 9, 2004.

countries. It also meant that foreign direct investment into China was significantly facilitated, including portfolio investments in Chinese stocks.

The change meant that qualified banks can accept capital in renminbi, the Chinese currency, from domestic institutions and individuals for overseas investment. The official exchange rate of the renminbi has been brought into line with the market-driven rate that applied on the foreign exchange swap market. The rate has stayed stable at around 7 yuan to the U.S. dollar.[26] The bank also allowed fund management firms and other securities institutions to invest in a combination of stocks and other overseas securities using foreign currencies gathered from domestic institutions and private sources.

Special Economic Zones

Several **Special Economic Zones** (SEZs) have been established by the Chinese government to attract foreign investment in production for export. The major ones are in Shenzhen, Zhuhai, Shantou (all in the Guangdong province in the South), Xiamen (in Fujian province), and Hainan (in Hainan province). Besides these five, the Pudong New Area in Shanghai and several other industrial zones are entitled to similar preferential policies as an SEZ. To attract investment, the corporate tax rate within SEZs is only 15 percent, compared with a national rate of 33 percent. Also, enterprises within the zones enjoy some tariff exemptions.[27]

The SEZs serve to bring in foreign manufacturing jobs, with Chinese workers staffing the assembly lines. The products are intended for reexport, helping the government to generate hard foreign currency. But it has also meant increased penetration by foreign products in China. Although the products imported into those areas are not allowed outside the zones' borders, many are smuggled into China, copied, and sold. The difficulty of controlling this black or gray trade and widespread **copyright infringement** practices mean that the authorized distributors find themselves competing with local **counterfeits and pirated copies.** Pirated computer software is a case in point (see box, "Chairman Bill?").

The WTO Effect

With the ongoing reform of China's foreign trade system and the WTO entry, the government-controlled trading companies have lost their monopoly to the mushrooming local trading companies and the industrial firms. The foreign-invested companies are

Getting the Picture

CHINA'S VIDEO AND AUDIO PIRATES: STILL GOING STRONG

Back in the spring of 1995, the U.S. Trade Representative's Office seemed to score a major diplomatic victory, convincing China's government to agree to strongly enforce a ban on copyright and trademark violations in that country. Chinese entrepreneurs had long copied popular videotapes and compact disks from the West for resale on the streets and in the small shops of Beijing and Shanghai. Other copies were trucked or shipped by boat into Hong Kong, Ho Chi Minh City, and other Southeast Asian cities.

But the effect was minimal, hardly making a dent in the flow of pirated goods. Even when China joined the WTO in 2001, many observers remained skeptical about the real effect of the agreement. For one thing, with regular prices many of the products would have a hard time making it against local competition: Mandarin and Cantonese artists are still more popular than Western performers, and their

CDs, many of them also pirated copies, cost a fraction of Western CDs at regular price. Another difficulty was the sheer number of small factories and outlets. New factories are easily established, and the manufacturers and the street salesmen are often entrepreneurial young people. Enforcing WTO rules against the many small Chinese entrepreneurs is not easy.

The naysayers have been proven right. In 2008 the U.S. government still listed China at the top of its "priority watch list" for pirated goods. The piracy has not been stopped, and any visitor tour to Shanghai or Saigon or Singapore still mandates a visit to the "open-air market"—whether it's for $2 DVDs and CDs, or for $25 Rolex watches, or fake Tiffany jewelry. Not buying, just watching, mind you!

Sources: *New York Times*, February 27, 1995, pp. D1, D6, and May 17, 1995, pp. D1, D5; "Business Beams on IPR Breakthrough," *South China Morning Post*, March 17, 1995, p. 7; "U.S. Chides China, Russia for Piracy in Annual List," **www.reuters.com**, April 25, 2008.

automatically granted foreign trade rights. In general, China's foreign trade system is undergoing a big reform and most of the effort is geared toward the goal of satisfying the requirements of the new WTO status.

Even with the accession to the WTO, the recommended entry mode into China is by a joint venture with a Chinese partner. This makes for easier market access and overcomes language and cultural barriers. Also, in support of the WTO requirements, government representatives in China are given incentives to attract foreign direct investments in manufacturing. Virtually all of the manufacturing subsidiaries of foreign companies have Chinese partners. One foreign company successful in China, Korean electronics maker Samsung, goes to great length to localize its operations. Being Korean, and thus a neighbor, is not sufficient. To profit in China, Samsung has established operations from research to design to sales in China. Even if design differences are minor between products in Korea and China, the labor costs are so much lower in China.

China is eager to attract foreign capital, and has now become very open to FDI, although most of it involves production for exports. China is still a difficult market to earn money in. Samsung might be one of the exceptions. Reflecting the sobering experiences of many Western companies, a major 2004 magazine feature on business in China was headlined "The China Trap."[28] And despite the WTO promises and some valiant efforts, the Chinese government has not been able to curb piracy (see box, "China's Video and Audio Pirates").

Hong Kong's Role

Of all the things that could have gone wrong and tripped up China's debut on the world stage, the Hong Kong takeover seemed the most likely. Fortunately, it didn't. The 1997 Hong Kong handover from British to Chinese rule has had surprisingly little impact on economic policy so far, since China has exercised restraint in dealing with the former British colony. Many European and American companies used to enter China from Hong Kong, where many sophisticated **Hong Kong trading companies** were familiar with both Western business practices and Chinese language and culture. Nowadays most entrants go straight to Shanghai or Beijing or Guangzhou—or Shenzen, just up the road from Hong Kong. Trade fairs, exhibitions, and technical seminars at the industrial zones around these locations are commonly used to promote awareness among trading middlemen and mainland customers.

With the opening of the access to China itself, Hong Kong's role has gradually changed. Initially, Hong Kong served as the natural point of entry to the mainland because of language, culture, and old ties. The task was to help foreign companies to establish a foothold in the Chinese market, but more importantly to assist in finding joint-venture partners and identifying opportunities for export-oriented manufacturing. These roles have now gradually been taken over by companies, traders, and intermediaries on the mainland—some managed by returning expatriates. Bypassing Hong Kong and going directly into China meant that Hong Kong's economy had to find other sources of income.

Resourceful as ever, the Hong Kong government quickly moved to make the city a magnet for incoming business. Hong Kong is today a big financial center, an educational center for Asia, a convention city, and a big transportation hub with a large modern airport. It has also established itself as a tourist destination, opening Disneyland Hong Kong in a joint venture with the Walt Disney Company.

Instead of becoming dominated by the Chinese mainland, Hong Kong has moved to become the destination for many of the emerging middle-class Chinese. The proximity and freedom of Hong Kong entices many Chinese mainlanders and their families to travel down to Hong Kong for their short vacation. And for the newly rich highrollers, there is also another attraction next door. Macau, the other Special Administrative Region island situated on the western side of the Pearl River delta, has become the gambling capital of the world, beating out Las Vegas by taking in about US$7.0 billion to Las Vegas's $6.5 billion in 2006.[29]

Market Segmentation

A natural first segmentation criterion in China is geographic region. Philips, for example, the Dutch electronics maker, subdivides the country into four regions: eastern China (with Shanghai as the center), northern China (with Beijing at the center), southern China (with Guangzhou as the center), and western China (with Chengdu as the center). These are also natural market groupings in that languages and dialects, food and drink preferences, and even ethnic roots vary across the regions.[30]

A second segmentation is the urban/rural split in the typical emerging market pattern. Mainly because of the weak infrastructure in these emerging countries, the urban population offers a much more accessible marketplace than the rural areas. Along the same lines is the income differential. If there is an emerging middle class, it will come in the cities first. The rise in per capita income is most rapid in Shanghai, Beijing, and Guangzhou: Here there are segments with enough funds to provide a market for some of the Western luxury products. In fact, China has become such a major market for luxury goods that many are now produced in the country (see box, " Chinese-Made Luxury Goods?").

The young-people segment, the teenagers and the college-age students of both sexes, represents the Chinese version of the global youth segment. Less affluent than many of their counterparts elsewhere, they do aspire to many of the same world-class branded products—and might resort to counterfeiting to satisfy their needs. The increasing number of expatriates, Chinese individuals returning from successful careers in the West, also constitutes a very promising niche market in the big cities.

Product Positioning

With exposure to Western communications and media via Hong Kong and from overseas Chinese, and despite the central government's insistence on controlling Internet access, the Chinese market is open for global brands and standardized campaigns. But for effective penetration, some localization is usually necessary. In particular, there is a need to revisit the company brand names and how they will translate into the Chinese kanji characters. Coca-Cola had to change its original transliteration from one meaning "dry mouth full of wax" to one signifying "happiness in the mouth" when read and spoken. Sprite was said

Getting the Picture

CHINESE-MADE LUXURY GOODS? YES!

In this day and age of copied luxury brand names and gray trade, nobody should be surprised to find that a fake Prada, Armani, or Burberry product they bought at a great price might be made in China. What is surprising is to realize that what they bought in the manufacturer's own boutique might also be made in China. According to a Chinese spokesperson for the World Luxury Association, luxury brands might claim all of their products are made at home, but as much as 60 percent of them might actually be made in China.

According to an association report, more and more brand-name luxury goods are shifting their production to China. Foreign luxury-goods manufacturers started to shift part of their production line to China in 2004, and products made in China with foreign labels have been common in the Chinese market since 2005. The association expects that 60 percent of the world's luxury brands will have their products made in the country by 2009.

Goods "Made in China" are no longer limited to cheap, low-end products. More and more brand-name luxury consumer goods are made in China, as more and more Chinese can afford them. Demand for luxury goods in China has already surpassed the manufacturing capacity of European makers by about 60 percent. In response, luxury makers have opened new production in China, where labor and other costs are relatively low and they are closer to the market.

Afraid of a negative consumer reaction, manufacturers are still relatively mum about the proportion of made-in-China products that finds their way onto overseas markets. But there is no doubt that some already do, and some firms are brave enough to admit it. They include Pierre Cardin, Burberry, Armani, and Prada. As globalization progresses, consumers will presumably not be surprised to see a "Made in China" label on their Burberry jacket—it's still a Burberry, no?

Sources: Olivia Chung, "China's Global Luxury Brand Workshop," *Asia Times Online*, April 14, 2007; Fallows, 2007.

to beat Seven-Up because its Chinese name came out as "Snow Jade," while Seven-Up had to fight against a transliteration that in Shanghai suggested "death from drinking." It is small wonder if a foreigner hears some familiar brand names with slightly out-of-the-ordinary sounds added to get the right touch for the Chinese consumer.[31]

Marketing Tactics

Product Policies

The quality gap between foreign and local products is disappearing quickly, with technology transfer in the joint ventures and imitation through reverse engineering. Chinese customers cite two reasons for buying a foreign product: (1) no availability of similar products on the domestic market and (2) the superior status of the foreign brand. Because of high tariffs, a foreign product can seldom compete with a Chinese product on a price basis.

For most Chinese acquiring foreign-made products is a novel experience. With very few choices for four decades, the Chinese are eager to see what is in the stores. Their limited experience leads them, predictably, to rely on famous brand names. In a wide range of goods surveyed, well-known brands accounted for as much as one-half of intentions to choose.[32] Like the Japanese, the Chinese consumers tend also to be brand loyal, making for a definite first-mover advantage among competing firms. With the emergence of very competitive domestic players, the first-mover may well be one of China's own (see box, "China Brands to Watch (out) For").

Reflecting the rise of a more affluent consumer, a new consensus has developed about the "four big things" (*shi da zen*), the four products everyone aspires to. In the 1970s, they were a bicycle, a black-and-white television set, a refrigerator, and a washing machine. In the 1990s, they became a video camera, a CD hi-fi system, a personal computer, and an air conditioner—soon followed, of course, by a cell phone and a car.[33]

Pricing

The relatively low per capita income makes China and the Chinese price-sensitive customers.[34] But low income is only half the story.

Although things are gradually changing, most Chinese customers are price-oriented out of habit. They are not willing to pay more for alleged superior quality because from experiences in the past they assume a uniformly low quality level for all products. This

CHINA BRANDS TO WATCH (OUT) FOR

As China opened up, it was first seen as a low-wage manufacturing location for outsourcing production. As its workers began to earn a living wage, it gradually emerged as one of the largest and fastest-growing markets in the world. Then, as workers raised their skill levels, and technology diffused (helped by voluntary spillover in joint ventures and involuntary diffusion via piracy), China became an OEM producer of higher-technology export products and also imitative domestic versions of brand-name products. By 2005, when China's Lenovo company bought IBM's PC business, China had moved to the next level, with domestic firms producing innovative products and starting to export under their own brand names. Haier appliances and Lenovo PCs can now be purchased in many Western markets, and the Chinese cars are not far behind.

Just to get a heads up, it might useful to check out what other brands are up-and-coming in China. The Chinese consumer electronics industry just finished their 2008 rankings of the top brands, and it brought out some new names that are likely to soon appear in Western markets. The top 10 brands were chosen for obtaining 3 million votes by Chinese consumers and retailers via the Internet, and selected by 50 experts of an evaluation board. The top 10 are, in order: Haier, Hisense, Changhong, TCL, Lenovo, Great Wall, Tongfang, BOE, Desai, and Asustek.

For single-subject prizes, Hisense won the prize for "most innovative brand" in flat-screen TVs, while Shinco won the award for Greatest Potential Brand. The theme of the award was "Brand Originated from Innovation" and placed particular weight on the R&D strength of the companies. The award press release emphasized that expenditure on R&D by leading consumer electronics enterprises has been increasing. Haier, for example, spent 6.7 billion yuan (US$920 million) on R&D in 2006, while Lenovo spent 2.8 billion yuan (US$380 million).

Predictably, the press release also suggested that the winning manufacturers are likely to establish overseas production bases and sales companies. The Chinese are coming!

Sources: Steve Lohr, "Lenovo Evolves With Its I.B.M. PC Unit in Tow," *New York Times*, September 30, 2005; "Top 10 Chinese Consumer Electronics Brands Revealed," *Xinhuanet*, January 10, 2008.

is not an entirely mistaken assumption either today. Many products are still in short supply, and some domestic companies are still in the "quantity, not quality" frame of mind nurtured during the central planning era.

Because of still relatively high taxes, and requirements for local content, prices are still high for products with imported content. For example, a Chinese-assembled Volkswagen Santana car costing around US$14,000 on world markets sold in China for 180,000 yuan ($20,000).[35] For pure imports at the high-end, the difference is even greater. Strikingly, however, still one of every two cars running on China's tough roads is imported.

Distribution

The infrastructure in China has been significantly improved in recent years. Even though the vast distances make "national roll-outs" a logistical impossibility, transportation around the big metropolitan areas is much improved. Rural roads are still unpaved, however, flooding is common, and railroads reliable but slow. Air transportation is a necessary option for many firms. And with the growth of mobile telephone communications, the lack of communication lines is partly overcome. It is small wonder that Motorola, Samsung, Sony-Ericsson, and Nokia all consider China an immense opportunity.

The improving physical distribution system has also helped the growth of online commerce. E-commerce suffers from other problems, however. China is still basically a cash-based economy. Internet access and privacy are problems considering the strong government oversight.

Many of the distribution channels are controlled by the government, again creating some obstacles to a focused distribution effort and affecting service levels negatively (see box, "Rude Service in China"). For example, department stores are typically state-owned, leaving little possibility for firms to offer individual achievement incentives. Multinationals therefore hire promotional staff to assist in store stocking, selling, and service, an expense that a company such as Philips finds worthwhile and necessary to generate acceptable sales levels of its electronics goods.

As in the past, personal contacts play an important role in sealing a transaction. The Chinese customers value the **guanxi,** or "mutual good feeling and trust" between old friends.[36] Personal selling is a necessary tool to establish good channel relationships.

Getting the Picture

RUDE SERVICE IN CHINA

By the mid-1990s, personal service in China was still below par. The past top-down, in-your-face attitude of service providers toward customers was alive and well. It went far enough that the Chinese government, true to its top-down style, banned 50 common phrases that the rude clerks were not to use when dealing with customers. The list is instructive as a reminder of the changes a market orientation imposes on a noncapitalist society. Selected items are:

1. If you don't like it, go somewhere else.
2. Ask someone else.
3. Take a taxi if you don't like the bus.
4. I don't care whom you complain to.
5. If you're not buying, what are you looking at?
6. Buy it if you can afford it; otherwise, get out of here.
7. Are you buying or not? Have you made up your mind?
8. Don't you see I'm busy? What's the hurry?
9. I just told you. Why are you asking again?
10. Why didn't you choose well when you bought it?
11. Go ask the person who sold it to you.
12. If you don't like it, talk to the manager.
13. The price is posted. Can't you see it yourself?
14. No exchanges; that's the rule.
15. If you're not buying, don't ask.
16. It's not my fault.
17. I'm not in charge. Don't ask so many questions.
18. Didn't I tell you? How come you don't get it?
19. If you want it, speak up; if you don't, get out of the way. Next!
20. Why don't you have the money ready?
21. What can I do? I didn't break it.

Past habits die slowly.

Sources: Faison, 1995; Engardio, 1996.

And this sentiment has been successfully exploited by new foreign entrants into China's insurance market (see box, "Selling Life Insurance in China").

Before China's accession to the WTO, China prohibited companies in the Foreign Trade Zones from distributing imported products or providing repair and maintenance services. This naturally made it difficult to provide the kind of in-store and after-sales service that many customers wanted. Now, under the WTO rules, foreign companies are allowed to establish offices outside of the trade zones. This enables the companies to establish distribution networks around the country, making it possible to improve their own customer service and also help upgrade the Chinese distribution infrastructure overall.

Getting the Picture

SELLING LIFE INSURANCE IN CHINA

It may come as a surprise in a country where communists are in power and food and housing are in principle guaranteed, but China has long had a viable life insurance industry. A traditional family focus has encouraged savings and risk sharing, and when the one-child-per-family policy was enacted by Chairman Mao, the demand for life insurance to protect the one offspring rose further.

Naturally, in the past, the industry has been a government monopoly. Not surprisingly, service was deficient. Each month, a person would have to stand in line to pay the premium, and if late, a penalty would be charged. Only a straight insurance policy was available, with no interest and no options to borrow against the policy.

Enter the American International Group, whose chairman had wooed the Chinese government officials since his first visit to China in 1975. American International, or "Friendly Nation" in its Chinese incarnation, is the only foreign insurance company allowed to market its product in China. In Shanghai it sells life insurance policies that pay interest after 5 years. The policies can be borrowed against after 3 years and are fully refundable after 20 years. The sales agents are young Chinese ladies who have adapted the now outlawed door-to-door sales techniques to the Chinese situation.

The "Friendly Nation" ladies visit offices, where underemployed workers do not mind being interrupted. They sell to the boss first, so the authority-conscious employees know it is acceptable to buy. They appeal to parents to buy insurance for their children. And they sell to women.

"I go for the women," says Lily Hua, an agent, flashing a mischievous smile. "You sell a policy to a man and the next day he may come back and ask for a refund because his wife objected. That never happens when I sell to a woman."

Sources: *New York Times*, April 4, 1995, pp. D1, D5; Yuen, 1995; Ligos, 1998.

Getting the Picture

MADE-IN-CHINA EFFECTS?

One of the reasons for international brands keeping a low profile when shifting their production to China is the negative image of goods "Made in China," which are often regarded as low-cost, low-quality products. To avoid the possible negative impact on the brand value of their products, foreign manufacturers proceed with caution even if they shift only part of their production to China. For instance, their Chinese partners are assigned to produce mid-end products, or products made in China are sold under other brand names.

Chief executives of the typical global brand manufacturer try to make sure that quality stays intact regardless of where the brand is produced. Their brand name value is easily eroded if quality is substandard. In addition to quality-control measures initiated by manufacturers themselves, China's authorities try to ensure that their policies help improve the average quality of the country's exports. The idea is to transform the "Made in China" image into something desirable.

It is not such an easy job. In an examination carried out by the Shanghai Administration of Industry and Commerce in 2006, one brand's dresses, suits, coats, and pants were found to be substandard with high levels of formaldehyde (a chemical that can cause cancer) unacceptable acid levels, and poor dyes. And it certainly does not help a nation's image when consumers in other countries find its pet food laced with melamine, a coal derivative that can kill pets, or find that its toy trains are painted with lead-based paints.

In addition, product quality is not the only thing that matters in country-of-origin effects. There are also historical and other factors that suggest it might take some time for consumers to change their perception of the "Made in China" label. The Japanese brands have shown the way, coming from a similar cheap and shoddy reputation to becoming leading quality manufacturers. Now Korea is following suit. But consumers of global brands also want higher self-esteem and peer approval, benefits still delivered better by the established brands from the old countries.

Sources: Fallows, 2007; Paul Mooney,"'Made in China' Label Spurs Global Concern," *YaleGlobal,* **http://yaleglobal.yale.edu,** August 23, 2007.

Promotion

Advertising is strictly controlled by the Chinese government, and censorship is severe. For instance, an advertisement that showed LeBron James against a dragon was deemed unacceptable, and so was one that featured the word *Hollywood,* apparently viewed as a subversive influence. Also, comparison advertising is not allowed in China, and one cannot use superlatives in the ads. No "Best in the World" claims, in other words. Still, television advertising accounts for the major part of promotional expenditures. An estimated 84 percent of Chinese people are television viewers, a staggering number considering China's 1.3 billion population. Because of the great demand, TV stations in the big cities require advertising to be booked up to ten months in advance. Entering multinationals such as Coca-Cola rely heavily on television advertising to create awareness and goodwill among consumers and the trade. And, not the least, the advertising serves to signal to the prospective buyers that the new product comes in fact from the advertised firm and is not a counterfeit![37]

Print and outdoor advertising also play a large role, as do in-store factors. The consumers have time to browse and search for brands in the stores. Their lack of experience with variety leads them to trust a brand they know, have tried, and found satisfactory, generating a strong first-mover advantage for foreign entrants. They will also look for a brand they have only heard of—especially if the information came through advertising on the commercial TV stations.

Continuous Change

Change brings fresh opportunities. The economic growth in China has opened up a vast potential market. Change also brings problems, as the Tiananmen Square events of 1989 and the Tibet uprising in 2008 demonstrated. Now, with the Olympic games in 2008 and as a member of the WTO, China has to enforce international rules not only in reducing tariffs but also in unifying and clarifying its foreign trade policies, laws, and regulations. There is already a latent tension between the central Beijing bureaucracy that wants to present a strong country image to the world and regional and local businesses, which have been operating with lax rules and less than stringent provisions (see box, "Made-in-China Effects?").

Getting the Picture

VIETNAM ON THE RISE

Vietnam is emerging as one of the new economies to reckon with. With the proclamation of the "Doi Moi" (New Changes) initiative in 1986, the Vietnamese communist leaders followed the pro-market economic path struck earlier by China. After several years of negotiations, a U.S. government trade embargo was lifted in 1994. From then on, the small nation with "only" 87 million people—less than one-tenth of China—has come back as a new low-wage manufacturing location for export production, and, gradually, as an emerging market in its own right.

With a low per capita income, at US$2,587 per capita in 2007, about the same as India's but less than half of China's, Vietnam reaps the benefits of a communist government's insistence on basic education for men and women, provision of necessities, and emphasis on group coherence. This means the workforce is well educated with strong discipline. With "Doi Moi" and, in particular, the trade opening in 1994, the one thing missing—individual incentives to work hard and achieve—has now been put in place. The Vietnamese are young and strong and ready to take their place in the world economy—and like China, with a central communist government keeping a careful eye on the speed of expansion.

The Vietnamese is now replacing China in some areas for lower wage production for exports in several product categories, including athletic shoes and sportswear. Nike has a large shoe factory in one of the industrial parks surrounding Ho Chi Minh City. Vietnam's educated workers are good learners whose labor skills increase rapidly, and the geographical location is advantageous for Southeast Asian markets. Because of these factors, a company such as Cargill, the agricultural products company, was induced to locate a new distribution center there. Roads and infrastructure is still a problem, but steadily improving.

As for trade, major Vietnamese exports to the United States are textiles and garments, seafood, crude oil, home furnishings, footwear, and coffee. U.S. exports to Vietnam in 2007 were mainly aircraft, fertilizer, steel, computers and parts, equipment and parts, leather goods and footwear, and pharmaceuticals and chemicals. The two-way trade between the two countries increased from US$220 million in 1994—the year the embargo was lifted—to over US$6.4 billion in 2004, and US$10.6 billion in 2007.

The Vietnam economic boom is most noticeable in the south around Ho Chi Minh City (formerly Saigon). The city is as bustling as ever, with many people holding down two or three jobs simultaneously in order to support their desires for the good life. Delivery trucks and Chinese and Indian scooters—and increasingly small China-made cars—jam the streets (and sometimes sidewalks), and outside the city the big construction projects bottle up all traffic. Vietnam is on the move, and there is a spring feeling in the air. As one expatriate American manager remarked: "Vietnam might have won the war, but America won the peace."

Sources: Foreign Trade Statistics, **www.census.gov**; U.S. Commerce Department, **www.export.gov/vietnammission.**

A mounting tension is also present between the centralized big cities and the countryside population, with farmers worried about the effects of lower tariffs on their economic survival. There is also massive emigration from the rural areas into the major cities. Most foreign marketers find it challenging to operate on such a moving stage, but the stakes may well be worth it.

Vietnam: Another China?

Vietnam is an interesting case, very poor and still communist, but rising very quickly. Less than one-tenth of China's size, it still has a potentially large, young, and dynamic market (the population in 2007 stood at 87 million, with more than half under 30 years of age). After a trade agreement with the United States in the 1990s, the country has become a formidable manufacturing site and exporter, not only to the United States but to the rest of Asia, including China. Nike produces athletic shoes there (using a Korean subcontracting firm to manage the workforce), and Intel is building a manufacturing plant to open in 2008 (see box, "Vietnam On the Rise").

Close-Up: Marketing in the Middle East[38]

The Middle East, as commonly defined, comprises the following countries: Egypt, Jordan, Saudi Arabia, Lebanon, Syria, Iraq, the UAE (United Arab Emirates, with seven small kingdoms, including Dubai and Abu Dhabi), Qatar, Bahrain, Kuwait, Oman and

Yemen (all Arabic-speaking), Iran, Turkey, Israel, and the occupied Palestinian territories. Adding the four North African countries of Algeria, Libya, Morocco, and Tunisia, the region is sometimes referred to as the Middle East North Africa (MENA).

The MENA region has over 300 million people, lead by Egypt (75 million) as the most populated nation followed by Iran (71 million) and Turkey (70.5 million). The majority of the Middle Easterners speaks variations of the Arabic dialects. The region is home to a combination of a culturally varied people. Iranians are Persians and speak Farsi, an Indo European language; Turks are non-Arabic speakers; and the official language of Israel is Hebrew. Apart from Israel, the dominant religion is Islam and the people are Muslim.

Governing Structures

The region is home to a variety of political and governmental structures. Oman, Morocco, Saudi Arabia, and Jordan are hereditary monarchies. Egypt, Syria, Algeria, Libya, Yemen, and Tunisia have an authoritarian military presidential structure. The smaller Persian Gulf states are mostly governed by emirs who are traditional tribal chiefs.

Iran, Israel, the Palestinian Authority, Lebanon, and Turkey represent various forms and degrees of democratic governance and political systems with greater political space and freedoms. They feature more market-oriented economies, with Turkey as the most privatized and most Westward looking.

The Islam Factor

Islam, the religion based on the Koran, is a system of thought that permeates all facets of life in these regions. It provides an inner compass to individuals and society as a whole, and affects everything from society's rituals to the business environment to daily life. With the exception of Turkey, in the Middle East there is virtually no separation between religion and the state. The traditional culture of the Middle East has strong characteristics of paternalistic authority and submergence of the individual to family and society, and much of Islamic religion and culture is incompatible with transparent markets, individual freedom, and "Western" life. And since religious rules and prohibitions are strictly enforced, doing business in the Middle East can be complicated.

The Middle Eastern countries have a centuries-long history of trading, and business is not in itself foreign in these lands. Nevertheless, Islamic religious teaching is not as conducive to capitalism as the Protestant ethic in the West. Property rights are respected and valued, but money does not have an intrinsic value, and nonmonetized values do count greatly. Goods and services must be made available to the needy, and corporate social responsibility must be observed. Productive wealth creation is encouraged and valued over consumption, and the customer is not king. Keeping ones word is crucial in maintaining trust and building mutual obligation, contracts are strongly enforced, but the pricing of a transaction is not always transparent.

There is obligatory and enforced observance of important national holidays, including

- The Mawlid—the birth of the Prophet Muhammad, March.*
- The Hijra—Prophet Muhammad's migration from Mecca to Medina, September.*
- The Hajj—the once-in-a-lifetime obligatory pilgrimage that brings more than 2 million Muslims from all over the world to Mecca, Saudi Arabia, December.*
- Iranian New Year—the first day of spring.

*Because the Islamic calendar is a lunar calendar, holidays cannot be exactly matched to the Gregorian calendar, whose solar year is eleven days longer.

Islam prohibits a few things outright:

- A general prohibition against drinking alcohol in most countries.
- Pork and pork-related products, including pigskin leather, cannot be marketed.
- Severe punishments for seemingly minor offenses to protect society from social vice.

- Physical contact with people one could potentially marry.
- Muslim women should dress so as to cover up their bodies when outside of the house, wearing the black full-length "chador" to avoid enticing men's imagination.

There are also some general "suggestions," useful when doing business in the Middle East:

- Dress well. In the Middle East, casual dress is a sign of disrespect.
- Small talk is very important to build trust.
- Refrain from slang;even casual profanity is unacceptable.
- Speak softer and slower. A loud voice is often perceived as offensive and aggressive.

So far, Islamic societies have refused to become post-Islamic in the manner in which the modern European West became post-Christian. With the exception of a few countries—Dubai, Abu Dhabi, Lebanon—secularization has not taken place. If anything, the efforts to democratize the Middle East and promote individual freedom have added legitimacy to some of the more strident religious orthodoxies. However, according to some observers, with increased globalization the conflict between modernization and Islam is no longer as salient as before. More and more Middle Easterners argue that it is possible to be Muslim and modern at the same time, and that technological progress and Islam are not contradictory, but can be complementary. Still, these are very recent stirrings among a few thought leaders, drawing on the success of the Arabs in countries such as Dubai and Abu Dhabi and the progress in Turkey. Overall, traditional Islam remains the primary organizing principle in the region and in these markets the need for adaptation is clear.

Market Environment

In the 1990s, Persian Gulf states began to recover from the last decade of the 1980s. Real per capita income, as measured by gross domestic product (GDP) per capita, still only grew at 1.5 percent annually, with economic growth counterbalanced by rapid population increase. Since 2003, the region has enjoyed an average growth rate of over 5 percent annually, led by Iran, Turkey, and UAE. High oil prices since the 2003 U.S. invasion of Iraq have boosted government revenue and thus spending, making for stronger real GDP growth in the oil-exporting states. At the going rate, by 2012, the region could have accumulated $500 billion in oil revenues. However, this must be set against continued security concerns across the region, which is affecting both investment and tourism.

One dominant characteristic of the region is the unequal distribution of wealth. The region includes countries with the highest GDP per capita in the world (Qatar is number one) and some of the poorest nations (see Exhibit 10.3).

Economically, the region can be broken down into three categories of countries:

1. The oil-producing economies of Saudi Arabia, Kuwait, Bahrain, Qatar, Oman, Libya, and the United Arab Emirates. These are some of the wealthiest and fastest-growing markets. For example, Dubai (in the UAE) has been growing more than 10 percent annually.
2. The emerging markets, including Iran, Iraq, Egypt, Turkey, Algeria, Israel, Lebanon, and Tunisia. Less wealthy, these countries have more diverse market economies.
3. The Lesser-developed economies of Jordan, Yemen, Morocco, Oman, Syria, and the Palestinian territories. These are some of the poorest markets in the world.

Trade Blocs

There are basically two major trade blocs in the region.

1. The Gulf Cooperation Council (GCC), with member-states Kuwait, Saudi Arabia, Bahrain, Qatar, and U.A.E. (United Arab Emirates). This is the club of "the rich and famous" in the region. GCC is moving toward currency unification by 2010 and a common market by 2008.

EXHIBIT 10.3
GDP Per Capita in the Middle
East (2007, in U.S.$, PPP),
GDP rank in World, and
Population

Source: Data from
www.worldbank.org; www.imf.org.

Nation	GDP Per Capita	GDP Rank in World	Population
Bahrain	32,064	26	760,168
Egypt	5,491	97	75,498,000
Iran	10,624	71	71,208,000
Iraq	N/A	—	28,993,000
Jordan	4,886	105	5,924,000
Kuwait	39,306	11	2,851,000
Lebanon	11,270	66	4,099,00
Oman	23,967	37	2,595,000
Qatar	80,870	1	841,000
Saudi-Arabia	23,243	38	24,735,000
Syria	4,488	111	19,929,000
Turkey	12,888	59	70,586,256
UAE	37,293	17	4,380,000
Yemen	2,335	132	22,389,000
Algeria	6,533	93	33,858,000
Libya	12,277	61	6,160,000
Morocco	4,076	115	31,224,000
Tunisia	7,473	87	10,327,000
Israel	25,799	33	7,262,600
Palestinian territories	N/A	—	4,017,000

2. The Arab Maghreb Union (AMU). This union includes Libya and Algeria (both resource-rich) and Morocco and Tunisia (more service-oriented).

Several countries have signed free trade agreements with EU Mediterranean countries. Also, Morocco, Jordan, and Bahrain have free trade agreements with the United States. In addition, any Arab state that no longer supports the Arab Boycott of Israel, imposed by the 21-member Arab League, can now have duty-free access to the U.S. market as long as the product has a minimum of 8 percent Israeli-made components. As a result, export of light-manufacturing products to the United States has increased.

Turkey has also initiated negotiations with EU representatives, but with the aim of becoming a full-fledged member of the EU. Turkey is in many ways different from other countries in the Middle East (see box, "Turkey: A Very Special Case").

Market Segmentation

The viable Middle East markets tend to be urban, with consumers that live in the large metropolises such as Cairo and Teheran and have the necessary buying power. The massive rural population in many of these countries is drawn to the cities in search of jobs and greater opportunities. Due to the various military conflicts in the region (the Iran–Iraq war, the U.S. invasion of Iraq, the Lebanese civil war, and the protracted Palestinian–Israeli conflict) women outnumber men by a wide margin. In addition, the population is very young, with nearly 70 percent of the population under the age of 30. While gender segregation is practiced in countries such as Saudi Arabia and Kuwait, in the rest of the region women have strong rights, and tend to dominate in universities and advanced professions. As elsewhere, women are typically the decision makers for consumer products.

Product Positioning

Most urban middle-class Middle East consumers are brand and status conscious, and are willing to pay for products that satisfy this desire. In many cases the consumers would rather wait and not buy rather than spend money on a perceived inferior brand. Foreign brands often carry a cachet, with higher prices, partly because of tariffs and high taxes. The unequal income distribution across countries means that there are a few markets with very wealthy consumers. Competition in luxury goods is very intense in these markets.

Getting the Picture

TURKEY: A VERY SPECIAL CASE

With a respectable GDP per capita of US$12,888 in 2007 and a population of 71 million, and with a geographic presence in Europe, Turkey is unusual in the Islamic world. It is still considered an emerging market, and despite being a member of the WTO Turkey still has some entry barriers in terms of customs regulations, procedures, and import licensing practices, as well as lax intellectual property rights protection. But in recent years Turkey has managed to grow at over 6 percent annually, with GDP per capita doubling since 2002.

The rising economy of Turkey has benefited from foreign investment by multinationals eager to tap into the new consumer markets. But existing Turkish manufacturers have also upgraded products and services, and in many cases are able to draw on past allegiance and prodomestic sentiments. When American and allied troops invaded Iraq in 2003, a wave of anti-Americanism swept Turkey, and a local company quickly introduced a Turca Cola, which soon captured 15 percent of the cola market.

Some of the more ambitious companies have bought foreign brands to establish a presence abroad. The biscuits company Ülker bought Belgian chocolatier Godiva in 2007, and also in 2007 the Eczacibasi Gruppe bought a controlling 51 percent interest in V&B Fliesen GmbH, the German-French fine tableware and crystal producer with the strong Villeroy&Boch international brand. And there are Turkish brands appearing in the West as well, including Arçelik in home appliances; Beko in television, DVDs, and personal computers; and Vestel, which already has 20 percent of Europe's color TV market. Beko is part of Koç holding, one of the strongest industrial groups in Turkey, and with Beko already in more than 100 countries under its own name, the vision is for Beko to be a "World Brand."

So where does religion and Islam come in the picture? Well, according to observers, Turkey's Westward looking attitude has long differentiated the country from the rest of the Middle East. Yes, the full-length black chador can still be spotted on perhaps less than 5 percent of the women, and the black headscarf is not uncommon. But in urban areas, and especially in cosmopolitan Istanbul, the consumer markets are like many European markets. Mobile phones are ubiquitous, as penetration has increased from 16.1 million in 2000 to 49.7 million in 2007. With a large and young population (median age was 27.1 years in 2006, much lower than Europe's 39.0 years), coupled with rapid growth rates, the consumer markets in Turkey look very attractive.

As always, politics can derail this rosy picture. The success of the economy has prompted Turkey to start negotiating for EU membership. The initial negotiations have proven rocky, however, as France and Germany balk at inviting a large Islamic country as a member. This has, not surprisingly, induced some stirring of pro-Islamic political forces inside Turkey, also fueled by unresolved questions about the Kurds' insurgence among the Iraq border in southeastern Turkey. The negotiations are now at a stalemate.

Turkey has looked Westward ever since Kemal Atatürk took over in 1923, changed the written language from Arabic to the Latin alphabet, and introduced a Western dress code. The next step is surely membership in a strong trade bloc—and perhaps a World Cup triumph in 2010.

Sources: Andrew Ross Sorkin, "Refocusing, Campbell Sells Godiva," *New York Times,* December 21, 2007; Olivier Hofmann, "Young Population Drives Turkey's Mobile Market," Euromonitor, August 7, 2007.

High-end standardized products are desired as they feed the perception of high quality. Middle East consumers tend to demand the same products that are used by their European and American counterparts. Well-known brands such as Benetton, IKEA, Sony, Nokia, and Coca-Cola are popular among the youth and young professionals.

The typical high-end consumer, whether man or woman, young or old, does not hesitate to pay top price for the newest products and brands in the market—assuming, of course, they are able to buy at all. Price is not an object—or, more precisely, high price can even be attractive. It is not uncommon for the buyer to simply demand the highest priced item—something that explains hotel room prices in Dubai at US$5,000 per night.

Distribution

Retailing has a very long history in the Middle East. International business activity goes back to the pre-Christian period. The Silk Road that linked China to Europe came through the Middle East. For a long time the infrastructure relied on the same camel roads and sailing sea-lanes. But today, distribution and retailing is modern.

Shopping malls in Abu Dhabi, Dubai, Kuwait, Saudi Arabia, Lebanon, Turkey, and Tehran carry the latest products. In the Iranian free port island of Kish, across from Dubai, luxury brands such as Gucci and others are easily available. The region is home to some of the busiest ports and airports in the world. Telephone density, road and transportation systems are good. Twenty-five years ago Abu Dhabi had no more than 100 kilometers (60 miles) of paved roads. Today it is the home to advanced six-lane highways.

Promotion

The extended family plays an important role in Middle Eastern society, and promotional messages need to conform to family values. In Hofstede terms, the culture is high in power distance and a high-context culture. This influences the persuasive power of claims made, as messages become filtered by family and peer group norms, Appeal to emotions and subjective feelings tend to be more powerful than specific arguments, since they play on the aspirations of the audiences and are less susceptible to counter-argumentation.

Western-style family oriented commercials may be seen in Abu Dhabi, Dubai, Bahrain, Egypt, Lebanon, Morocco, Qatar, Tunisia, or Turkey. In more conservative countries, such as Iran, Kuwait, Saudi Arabia, or Yemen, Western-style commercials are rare, and irreverent Western-style advertising is frowned upon. In general, women are not shown moving or with men, and commercials with women usually do not show physical contact. Muslim women are not shown without a head cover or with revealing, tight clothing.

As for media, newspapers and specialized magazines such as children, youth, sports, and women's magazines are popular. There is a mix of state-owned and privately owned electronic media available. Television stations such as Al Jazeera in Qatar, Al-Manara, the Hezbollah station in Lebanon, and Arabia, a Dubai station, are viewed regionally and frequently. Although satellite dishes are not allowed everywhere, many Middle Easterners are able to receive satellite TV programming from Europe, Asia, and the United States, and CNN and BBC are viewed by many. However, consumer access to electronic media and the Internet varies from the more limited strictures of Iran, Kuwait, and Saudi Arabia to the openness of Lebanon, Qatar, Turkey, and UAE.

Summary

Developing countries are characterized by low disposable incomes, low educational levels, and a general apathy among the people. Market potential in these countries is often low, and trading with these countries often involves intermediaries such as specialized trading companies and international financial institutions like the World Bank and the IMF. Also, the local marketer has to be prepared to evaluate and accept countertrade offers.

Internally, these countries have an overriding need to develop a more effective marketing infrastructure, in particular a functioning distribution network. But to accomplish this more is needed than a mere infusion of capital and know-how. The local marketer has to become a teacher of sorts, educating middlemen as well as consumers about how to do effective marketing.

The NDC markets differ from those in other developing countries in that the political systems have long attempted to provide the basic conditions of a decent life and good elementary education but have also emphasized production instead of consumption and have pursued a consistent strategy of hostility to capitalism. These background factors make these markets different and in some ways more difficult to penetrate. The idea of consumer sovereignty, so basic to the Western market systems, is foreign to people who have been taught that labor is the supreme value. The notion that consumers must be satisfied by producers is hard to accept, and a service orientation is difficult to inculcate in retail clerks. The local marketer in these nations becomes a foot soldier and a teacher in the struggle to bring the marketing concept to these budding free markets.

But consumer psychology in NDC economies is changing rapidly as economic progress continues. As new products appear, people change their attitudes and preferences, and traditional habits give way to new lifestyles. Over time, unless the political situation reverses itself, customers in the NDC markets can be expected to become more similar to their compatriots in more mature markets.

Key Terms

attitudes toward free markets in NDCs, *315*
copyright infringement, *326*
counterfeits and pirated products in China, *326*
credibility of advertising, *322*
developing countries, *309*
educating of middlemen, *321*

ethnic market segmentation, *316*
export controls, *315*
guanxi, *330*
Hong Kong trading companies, *327*
international agencies in NDCs, *313*

marketing infrastructure, *309*
newly democratized countries (NDCs), *312*
political risk in NDCs, *315*
Special Economic Zones in China, *326*

Discussion Questions

1. How strong would you say the evidence is that the emerging markets will sooner or later have the same kind of consumers as mature markets? What will the role of national differences and culture become? How do entry barriers stall the process toward similarity?

2. What are the basic functions of an effective distribution system in mature markets? As online shopping across country borders becomes feasible and accepted, what are the demands on the countries' distribution systems (including customs duties) that need to be handled? How well and by whom are these functions likely to be performed in an NDC market such as Russia?

3. Access one of the Web sites for Amway, Avon, or Mary Kay. What do they say about their operations in China and other emerging markets? Check out other direct marketers with pyramid-type sales organizations, such as Nu Skin, and see what they do in these markets. What are the pros and cons of being a distributor for such a company in an emerging country?

4. What factors would you think are particularly important for a marketer of cosmetics to teach retailers in the stores of NDC markets? For a marketer of automobiles?

5. What factors in your own country's typical consumer advertising do you think will not be the same in an NDC economy? How do consumers in your country and the NDC learn about new product features?

Notes

1. This is of course much too brief a discussion to do justice to the range of agencies and services available and what the firm can do to mobilize support for its overseas endeavor. The extent of support differs by region, country, and industry. More will be said below in the context of the newly democratized countries (NDCs), but this chapter can only scratch the surface. There are specialized books and directories available, and the interested reader can start by consulting, for example, the sources listed in Chapter 4.

2. See "Nestlé Alimentana S. A.—Infant Formula," Harvard Business School, case no. 9-590-070.

3. This example is from "General Motors' Asian Alliances," Harvard Business School, case no. 9-388-094.

4. See *The Russian Consumer,* 1992, and "A New Brand of Warfare," 1994.

5. For more on this perspective, see "Gillette Keys Sales," 1987.

6. See "Now for a Challenge or Two," *The Economist,* January 3, 2002.

7. See LaFraniere, 1998, and "The Secret Way of Russian Life," *Precision Marketing,* November 9, 2001, p. 9.

8. See Czinkota, 1994.

9. Events in Russia have created some anxiety. See, for example, Lucas, 2001.

10. See *The Russian Consumer,* 1992.

11. See, for example, "Cosmetics Companies," 1994.

12. From Elliott, 1992; *The Russian Consumer,* 1992; and Jagger, 1998.

13. See "A New Brand of Warfare," 1994.

14. See Yan, 1994, and also "What Clinton Won't Find," 1994.

15. See "A New Brand of Warfare," 1994.

16. See Yurov, 2006.

17. See "A New Brand of Warfare," 1994, and "Cosmetics Companies," 1994.

18. From "A New Brand of Warfare," 1994.

19. For an informative view on advertising strategy in the new Russia, see *The Russian Consumer,* 1992, and Jagger, 1998.

20. This section draws on Lee and Yip, 1998a. Thanks are offered to May Guo for drafting the section and to Mingxia Li for reviewing and updating it.

21. www.cia.gov/cia/publications/factbook/geos/ch.html$Econ
22. See "China: Special Report," 1995; Lee and Yip, 1998a; and www.cnn.com.
23. See "China's Low-Cost Loans in Doubt," 1995; Lee and Yip, 1998a; and "GM's Joint Venture Is China's Top-Selling Brand in 2007," www.edmunds.com, January 16, 2008.
24. See "China: Trade Regulation," 1995, and "Jewelry Next," 2006.
25. See "China Tariff Cut Seen," 1995, and "Peugeot Chief," 1995.
26. See "China Pledges," 1995.
27. See "No Holiday," 1995.
28. See *Newsweek,* July 28, 2004, pp. E1–E26.
29. Barboza, 2007.
30. See Lee and Yip, 1998a.
31. Ibid.
32. From Yan, 1994.
33. See note 30.
34. See note 20 above, and "Chinese Bikes," 1995.
35. See "China Expert," 1994.
36. Davies et al., 1995, are very informative about the role of "guanxi" in marketing relationships.
37. See note 30.
38. This special section was prepared by Professor Masoud Kavoossi of Howard University, author of *The Globalization of Business and the Middle East* (Westport, CT: Quorum Books, 2000).

Selected References

"Actel Signs Unique as New Distribution Partner for Hong Kong/China." *Business Wire,* September 3, 1998.

"A New Brand of Warfare." *Business Central Europe,* April 1994.

Babakian, Genine. "Smirnoff Pop Chart Causes Russian Flap." *Adweek* 36 (August 7, 1995), p. 14.

Barboza, David. "Macao Cashes In on Casinos, Apparently Catching Up with Las Vegas," *International Herald Tribune*, January 23, 2007.

Beck, Simon. "Trade Go-Ahead to Boost Ties, Says Clinton." *South China Morning Post,* July 24, 1998, p. 7.

"China Expert Sees 'A Car in Every Garage' by 2010." *Reuter European Business Report,* April 6, 1994.

"China Pledges Three-Stage Currency Convertibility." *Reuter Asia-Pacific Business Report,* February 11, 1995.

"China's Low-Cost Loans in Doubt." *The Age (Melbourne),* March 30, 1995.

"China: Special Report—The Long March to Market Economy Continues Unabated." *Lloyds List,* November 24, 1995.

"China Summit Opportunity." *Washington Times,* October 22, 1995.

"China Tariff Cut Seen to Slash Surplus by $10 Billion." *Reuters, Limited,* December 10, 1995.

"China: Trade Regulation." *EIU ViewsWire,* October 30, 1995.

"Chinese Accused of Pirating Disks." *New York Times,* August 18, 1994.

"Chinese Bikes Being Dumped in U.S." *Los Angeles Times,* May 20, 1995.

"Cosmetics Companies Stake Out Eastern Europe." *New York Times,* October 11, 1994.

Czinkota, Michael R. "Export Controls: Providing Security in a Volatile Environment." Working paper, MKTG-1777-13-994, School of Business Administration, Georgetown University, 1994.

Davies, Howard; Thomas K. P. Leung; Sheriff T. K. Luk; and Yiu-hung Wong. "The Benefits of 'Guanxi': The Value of Relationships in Developing the Chinese Market." *Industrial Marketing Management* 24 (1995), pp. 207–14.

Ecenbarger, William. "There's No Escaping Us: The Sun Never Sets on America's Pop-Culture Empire." *Chicago Tribune Sunday Magazine,* February 13, 1994, p. 16.

Elliott, Stuart. "Sampling Tastes of a Changing Russia." *New York Times,* April 1, 1992, p. D1.

Engardio, Pete. "Rethinking China," *BusinessWeek,* March 4, 1996, pp. 57–65.

Faison, Seth. "Service with Some Bile." *New York Times,* October 22, 1995, sec. 4, p. 4.

Fallows, James. "China Makes, the World Takes." *Atlantic Monthly,* July/August, 2007.

"Gauging the Consequences of Spurning China." *New York Times,* March 21, 1994.

"GE's Next Century: China, India, and Latin America." *BusinessWeek,* April 12, 1993.

"Gillette Keys Sales to Third World Tastes." *The Wall Street Journal,* April 2, 1987.

Hays, Constance L. "RJR Nabisco Braces for Drop in Russian Sales." *New York Times,* September 30, 1998, pp. C1, C19.

"In Polish Shipyard Signals of Eastern Europe's Revival." *New York Times,* July 4, 1995, pp. 1, 46.

Jagger, Steven. "Smells Like Teen Spirit." *Brand Strategy,* June 19, 1998, pp. 8–9.

"Jewelry Next on Luxury Tax Hit List," *The Standard (Hong Kong)*, November 16, 2006.

LaFraniere, Sharon. "'Every Day We Are Angry': Russian City Discovers the High Price of Free Market." *Washington Post,* September 13, 1998, pp. A1, A40.

Landler, Mark. "2 Asian Economies Seek to Keep Global Markets at Bay." *New York Times,* September 12, 1998, pp. C1, C2.

Layne, Rachel. "Kodak to Invest $1 Billion in China in Attempt to Slow Fuji's Advance." *San Diego Union-Tribune,* March 24, 1998, p. C–6.

Lee, Kam Hon, and George S. Yip. "China—Enter the Giant." Chapter 4 in Yip, 1998a.

———. "Hong Kong—A New Role." Chapter 6 in Yip, 1998b.

Ligos, Melinda. "Direct Sales Dies in China: Door-to-Door Sales Banned." *Sales & Marketing Management,* August 1998, p. 14.

Lloyd, John. "Survey of Russia." *Financial Times,* June 27, 1994, p. VIII.

Lucas, Edward. "Putin's Choice." *The Economist,* July 19, 2001.

Michaels, James W. "The Elephant Stirs." *Forbes,* April 24, 1995, pp. 158–59.

"Missing Out on a Glittering Market." *New York Times,* September 12, 1993.

"No Holiday for HK Pro-Labor Group." *United Press International,* December 16, 1995.

"Penetrating the Great Wall: Entry of Direct Marketers into the Chinese Market." *Target Marketing,* June 1998, p. 26.

"Peugeot Chief Urges China to Protect Car Market." *Reuters, Limited,* December 8, 1995.

"Radio Advertisers Tune In to Russia's Middle Class." *New York Times,* August 12, 1994.

Siegle, Candace. "Crap Shoot." *World Trade* 6, no. 10 (November 1993), pp. 64–66.

Tagliabue, John. "Tilting but Standing as a Big Domino Falls." *New York Times,* October 6, 1998, pp. C1, C4.

The Russian Consumer: A New Perspective and a Marketing Approach. New York: D'Arcy Masius Benton and Bowles, 1992.

"What Clinton Won't Find in Russia." *New York Times,* January 10, 1994.

Yan, Rick. "To Reach China's Consumers, Adapt to *Guo Qing*." *Harvard Business Review,* September–October 1994.

Yip, George S. *Asian Advantage: Key Strategies for Winning in the Asia-Pacific Region.* Reading, MA: Addison-Wesley, 1998.

Yuen, Darrel K. S. "China: The Next Life Insurance Frontier?" *National Underwriter* 99 (May 22, 1995), pp. 2, 17.

Yurov, Alexander. "Russian Consumer Market Becoming More Westernized," *RIA Novosti,* October 25, 2006.

Cases

Case 3-1

P&G's Pert Plus: A Pan-European Brand?

Procter & Gamble was one of the first packaged goods companies to go pan-European. Already in the early 1980s the American company had established a pan-European focus in its R&D-effort and a system of "lead countries" for pan-European product roll-outs.

The Pert Plus shampoo is a good example of the company's pan-European drive. Although the brand was sold by P&G in 2006 to another company, Innovative Brands, Inc., it is still a very successful brand. The case incorporates the market research information that typically is available for pan-European decision making and includes production cost data and competitive comparisons.

Procter & Gamble (P&G), the U.S. manufacturer of consumer packaged goods, was considering the introduction of a new hair care technology (BC-18) into the European market. The technology combined a shampoo and a conditioner in one product with the same effect as a shampoo and conditioner used separately. The product was launched in the U.S. hair care market in 1986 as Pert Plus and its success provided the impetus to consider a "roll-out" launch in Europe.

Company Background

Procter & Gamble was founded in the United States in 1837. Today it is the world's biggest manufacturer of packaged consumer goods and a global leader in health and beauty care products, detergents, diapers, and food. P&G products include Pampers, Ariel, Mr. Proper, Camay, and others. More than one-third of P&G's total profit is generated by its international operations, which are the fastest-growing part of its total business. To strengthen its health and beauty care division, P&G in 1985 bought the Richardson-Vicks Company (with brands like Vidal Sassoon and Pantene) and in 1987 bought the German Blendax Group (dental care products). These acquisitions resulted in a leading position in health and beauty care products in Europe.

Over its more than 150-year history, P&G has accumulated a broad base of industry experience and business knowledge. A great deal of it has been formalized and institutionalized as management principles and policies. One of the most basic principles is that P&G's products should provide "superior total value" and should meet "basic consumer needs." This has resulted in a strong commitment to research to create products that are demonstrably better than others. In contrast to the conventional product life cycle mentality, P&G believes that through continual product development, brands can remain healthy and profitable in the long term.

Perhaps the most widely known of P&G's organizational characteristics is its legendary brand management system. The brand management team, usually a group of three or four people, assumes general responsibility for its brand. They plan, develop, and direct their brand in its market. The group develops business objectives, strategies, and marketing plans. It selects advertising copy and media, develops sales promotion activities, manages package design and product improvement projects, and initiates cost savings. To carry out their responsibilities, members of the brand management team draw on the resources available to them. These include the other disciplines within and outside the organization (e.g., manufacturing, product development, market research, sales, advertising agencies). Summing up, it may be said that they know more about their product than anyone else, and they feel a real sense of ownership as they strive to develop business opportunities in their local market.

But in the early 1980s it became more and more obvious that greater coordination was needed between local markets in Europe. Increasingly, competitors had been able to imitate P&G's innovative products and marketing strategies and had preempted them in national markets where the local subsidiary was constrained by budget or organizational limitations. Therefore, closer coordination was important, particularly for new brands, to ensure they reached the marketplace first. Marketing strategies had to be thought through from a European perspective. This meant also the possibility of simultaneous or closely sequenced European product introductions. Furthermore, the European approach, through maximizing efficiency across countries, pooling know-how, and manufacturing with better economies of scale, could give a big advantage over the competition.

As a main forum for achieving this goal the Eurobrand team meetings were introduced, chaired by the brand management of the so-called "lead country." This European perspective did not necessarily mean Europewide standardization. Market conditions still varied widely within Europe. P&G's concept was that of "Eurobalancing," meaning as much standardization as possible, as little localization as necessary. A P&G senior manager commented: "It is occasionally better to allow some complexity to get a better overall result."

Pert Plus

The most important P&G shampoo brands lost U.S. market share in the years up to 1986. Therefore, it was decided to introduce a new technology, called BC-18, in the U.S. market at the beginning of 1986 by replacing the brand Pert with Pert Plus. The technology, "2-in-1" for shampoo and conditioner in one wash, was new to the market and had been developed in the P&G research lab.

The long-term marketing goal of Pert Plus was to take over the leading value position in the U.S. shampoo market, with a market share of at least 10 percent by the end of the fiscal year 1989–90. For the first year the specific target was a market share value of 5 percent.

In order to achieve this, Pert Plus was positioned as the shampoo that offered attractive hair in a convenient way. This was backed up by the unique Pert Plus formula, which combined a mild shampoo with a fully effective conditioner in one wash.

Because of the newness of the technology, the launch was viewed as the introduction of a new product and a target group was not specifically identified. Apart from previous Pert loyals, management expected sales also to come from people who had not used Pert or a conditioner before. Pert Plus was introduced with a price of US$3.20 for the 15 oz. size (US$ = 2.17DM; 15 oz. = 425 ml). Pert Plus was an instant success, doubling Pert's market share in one year, and growing steadily after that.

Market Development and Competitive Environment

In Europe, economic growth and increased living standards meant a steady growth of both the shampoo market and the conditioner market. There was ample evidence of increased frequency of hair-washing. However, compared with the United States, the conditioner market was still relatively undeveloped. The share of shampoo users who also used conditioner was still below the 44 percent that had been reached in the United States. This was particularly true for southern European countries. Therefore, the initial focus was on West Germany, Great Britain, France, Scandinavia, and Benelux. An underdeveloped conditioner market was, however, also evident in France (in terms of sales volume, only 10 percent of shampoo consumption). Among the European countries considered, Great Britain, with 42 percent, showed the strongest user share (see Exhibit 1).

EXHIBIT 1   Market Sizes, Shampoo/Conditioner, Europe, 1988

	West Germany	Great Britain	France	Scandinavia	Benelux
Shampoos					
Value (TDM)	650,000	485,000	700,000	250,000	200,000
Volume (MSU)	20,000	18,000	20,000	7,000	7,500
Use per head (SU/1,000 of population)	325	325	350	300	300
Conditioners					
Value (TDM)	230,000	250,000	100,000	85,000	60,000
Volume (MSU)	4,500	7,500	2,000	1,700	1,500
Use per head (SU/1,000 of population)	70	140	35	70	70

1 MSU = 1,000 SU (statistical units).
1 SU = 2.5 litres.
TDM = Thousand German marks.

EXHIBIT 2 Percentage of Market Shares, Shampoo, Key Brands, Europe 1988

	West Germany		Great Britain		France		Scandinavia		Benelux	
P&G brands	*Volume*	*Value*	*Volume*	*Value*	*Volume*	*Value*	*Volume*	*Value*	*Volume*	*Value*
Vidal Sassoon	0.5	1.3	1.1	3.6	N/A		1.0	2.4	N/A	
Pantene	N/A		N/A		1.0	2.1	N/A		N/A	
Petrole Hahn	N/A		N/A		3.0	2.1	N/A		0.6	
Shamtu	11.0	6.3	N/A		N/A		N/A		N/A	
Head & Shoulders	1.1	1.7	6.5	12.0	1.1	1.6	1.0	1.4	2.9	5.4
Competitor brands										
Timotei (Unilever)	5.0	5.7	8.5	11.8	4.9	5.2	7.5	7.8	3.8	5.3
Nivea (Beiersdorf)	9.0	9.2	N/A		N/A		2.5	2.3	4.4	5.5
Schauma (Schwarzkopf)	21.0	10.0	N/A		N/A		N/A		7.0	4.1
Palmolive (Colgate)	N/A		4.6	2.7	12.3	5.4	7.0	3.0	18.2	10.6
Elsève/El' Vital (L'Oréal)	3.3	4.6	N/A		4.5	5.8	6.5	8.2	5.0	8.4

N/A = product not on offer in this country.

With respect to the number of suppliers and brands, the European market was more fragmented than the U.S. market, undoubtedly a function of the different nationalities. The most important competitors for P&G were Unilever, Colgate, and L'Oréal. Some brands could be found in all countries, others only in their domestic markets (see Exhibit 2).

The gap between the top and bottom price classes was even bigger than in the U.S. market. Between brands there were price differences of over five times for the same quantity, which meant that the value-based market share of a shampoo brand was very important (see Exhibit 3).

In order to carry through the brand message, media spending and support would be a key driving force. Competitor brands, including P&G's own, were heavily advertised by European standards (see Exhibit 4), and the new launch needed not only to illustrate the quality of the product and the time-saving benefits, but also to educate the market in the use of conditioners.

EXHIBIT 3 Sizes and Shelf Prices, Shampoo, Europe 1988 *(in German marks)*

	West Germany	Great Britain	France	Scandinavia	Benelux
P&G brands					
Vidal Sassoon (200 ml)	6.99	6.99	N/A	6.99	N/A
Pantene (200 ml)	N/A	N/A	4.99	N/A	N/A
Petrole Hahn (300 ml)	N/A	N/A	2.99	N/A	2.99
Shamtu (400 ml)	2.99	N/A	N/A	N/A	N/A
Head & Shoulders (300 ml)	5.99	5.99	5.99	5.99	5.99
Competitor brands					
Timotei (Unilever) (200 ml)	2.99	2.99	2.99	2.99	2.99
Nivea (Beiersdorf) (300 ml)	3.99	N/A	N/A	3.99	3.99
Schauma (Schwarzkopf) (400 ml)	2.49	N/A	N/A	N/A	2.49
Palmolive (Colgate) (400 ml)	N/A	2.49	2.49	2.49	2.49
Elsève/El' Vital (L'Oréal) (250 ml)	4.49	N/A	4.49	4.49	4.49

N/A = product not on offer in this country.
To simplify matters, the retail prices have been rounded off to a European average. However, price relations within a country have been retained.

EXHIBIT 4 Media Spending, Shampoo, Europe 1988 *(in thousands of German marks)*

	West Germany	Great Britain	France	Scandinavia	Benelux
P&G brands					
Vidal Sassoon	1,000	3,000	N/A	1,000	N/A
Pantene	N/A	N/A	0	N/A	N/A
Petrole Hahn	N/A	N/A	3,000	N/A	0
Shamtu	4,000	N/A	N/A	N/A	N/A
Head & Shoulders	3,000	3,000	2,000	800	2,800
Competitor brands					
Timotei (Unilever)	6,500	6,500	3,000	3,000	1,500
Nivea (Beiersdorf)	8,000	N/A	N/A	2,000	1,000
Schauma (Schwarzkopf)	10,500	N/A	N/A	N/A	N/A
Palmolive (Colgate)	N/A	4,000	4,000	1,000	1,000
Elsève/El' Vital (L'Oréal)	5,000	N/A	7,000	2,000	2,000
TOTAL	80,000	80,000	60,000	60,000	50,000

N/A = product not on offer in this country.

The Go Decision

In 1988, Procter & Gamble decided to introduce BC-18 into the European market. The opportunity for easy, time-saving, and convenient everyday use of the product was a strong competitive advantage and essential when considering positioning. There was also no doubt about placing the new product in the premium-priced segment. As with Pert Plus, a premium price was necessary to be consistent with the high-quality product concept. The main question was still, however, under what brand name to introduce the product in the individual European markets. There was also the question of whether a 200 ml bottle, used in the United States, or possibly a larger bottle would be accepted by the European consumer and the question of price sensitivity at premium pricing.

Consumer Research

It was decided, therefore, to undertake some consumer research. Obviously, it was impossible to test all possible product concepts with respect to brand names, positioning alternatives, pack sizes, pack designs, and price alternatives, for all European countries. So, in a prescreening phase, the possible brand alternatives were reduced to

four. In each test combination, there was to be a brand that, already present in the United States and several European markets, had so far shown a certain European potential (Vidal Sassoon). The U.S. brand Pert Plus, unknown in the European market, was also to be tested. The two other alternatives were national brands firmly established in their domestic markets (Pantene and Shamtu). Price and packaging alternatives were tested on only two brands: one brand from the lower-price segment and another brand that had a high-quality product concept (i.e., product concepts where possible price sensitivity would be easily detected). An abridged version of the positioning statements can be found in Exhibit 5. The consumer tests were carried out in the relevant European countries (for average results, see Exhibit 6; there were no significant differences between countries).

Economics

The basis for cost planning for the BC-18 introduction in individual European countries was the cost structure of the existing P&G shampoo brands. This also gave an idea of the profitability of the brands tested in the consumer test, which might be one of the deciding factors in the choice of an introductory brand name for BC-18 (see Exhibit 7).

EXHIBIT 5 Consumer Test, Europe

Positioning Statement	Price/Pack Size
Vidal Sassoon Wash & Go—for great-looking hair in a convenient way	4.99 DM/200 ml
Shamtu 2 in 1—shampoo and conditioner in one—silkiness and bounce in one step	4.99 DM/200 ml
Shamtu 2 in 1—shampoo and conditioner in one—silkiness and bounce in one step	4.99 DM/250 ml
Pantene—shampoo with built-in vitamin conditioner—the perfect hair care in one step	4.99 DM/200 ml
Pantene—shampoo with built-in vitamin conditioner—the perfect hair care in one step	5.99 DM/200 ml
Pert Plus Wash & Go—for great-looking hair in a convenient way	4.99 DM/200 ml

EXHIBIT 6   Consumer Test, Europe, Results *(percent)*

Product Concepts	Vidal Sassoon Wash & Go 4.99DM/ 200ml	Shamtu 2 in 1 "silkiness and bounce" 4.99DM/ 200ml	Shamtu 2 in 1 "silkiness and bounce" 4.99DM/ 250ml	Pantene "perfect care" 4.99DM/ 200ml	Pantene "perfect care" 5.99DM/ 250ml	Pert Plus Wash & Go 4.99DM/ 200ml
"Would definitely buy"	29%	20%	27%	28%	17%	28%
"Is very new"	41	40	41	39	40	40
"Is very convincing and relevant"	70	73	72	73	72	70

The costs of producing the new product, including average transport costs, were relatively easy to estimate, since the decision had been made to limit production to one plant in the United Kingdom for the whole European market. However, it had still not been decided whether to use the available 200 ml bottle or a 250 ml bottle still in development. Two figures were therefore used in the plans: production costs would be roughly 22DM/SU for the small bottle and 20DM/SU for the larger bottle. (2DM = German mark; 1 SU, or statistical unit = 2.5 liters; 1,000 SU = 1 MSU.) These figures presumed a capacity utilization of 50 percent, and it was assumed that working at higher capacity would not generate lower costs because of the special production technology. To determine total costs it was necessary to consider also advertising and sales support budgets, which depended on the individual countries and their chosen introduction program (see Exhibit 8).

Decision Constraints

Management also faced some decision constraints. A main constraint arose in the available production capacity. For the first year a capacity of 2,000 MSU was available. This could potentially be increased to 4,000 MSU in the second year and to 8,000 in the third year. In case of shortages, with six months notice it would have been possible to add an extra 500 MSU capacity, but this would lead to 2DM/SU higher production costs.

Lead times for alternative pack sizes and designs were also a restriction. The development of a new 200 ml bottle would take a lead time of 12 months. Although development of a new bottle containing 250 ml was under way, it would still take six months before it could be used. By contrast, using the existing U.S. bottle for Pert Plus would not require any lead time.

EXHIBIT 7   Overview, Economics/Profits, Europe, 1988

		W. Germany VS 200 ml	W. Germany Shamtu 400 ml	Great Britain VS 200 ml	France Pantene 200 ml	Scandinavia VS 200 ml	Benelux H&S 300 ml
Volume	MSU	100	2000	300	200	100	400
Shelf price	DM/pack	6.99	2.99	6.99	4.99	6.99	5.99
Manufacturer's list price	DM/pack	4.50	2.40	4.50	3.20	4.50	4.80
Manufacturer's list price	DM/SU	56.25	15.00	56.25	40.00	56.25	40.00
Discount	DM/SU	5.60	1.50	5.60	4.00	5.60	4.00
Manufacturer's net price	DM/SU	50.65	13.50	50.65	36.00	50.65	36.00
Production costs (incl. transport)	DM/SU	30.00	8.00	28.00	22.00	30.00	18.00
Overheads (sales, R&D, etc.)	DM/SU	5.60	1.50	5.60	5.00	5.60	4.00
Advertising costs for trade	DM/SU	2.80	0.75	2.80	2.00	2.80	2.00
Budget for advertising and sales promotion	DM/SU	20.00	2.50	14.00	6.00	14.00	10.00
Profit	DM/SU	−7.75	0.75	0.25	1.00	−1.75	2.00

VS = Vidal Sassoon
H&S = Head & Shoulders
DM = German marks
MSU = 1,000 SU
SU = statistical unit

EXHIBIT 8 Media and Promotion Costs

	W. Germany	Great Britain	France	Scandinavia[2]	Benelux
Media (TDM per month)[1]					
TV normal advertising month	600	600	600	—	200
strong advertising month	800	800	800	—	250
Radio normal advertising month	400	400	400	—	130
strong advertising month	500	500	500	—	160
Print normal 3-month campaign	3,000	3,000	3,000	1,000	1,000
strong 3-month campaign	5,000	5,000	5,000	1,600	1,600
Sample distribution (DM per piece)					
Sample costs	0.40				
Distribution costs					
Door-to-door	0.10		(same as for West Germany)		
Hypermarkets	0.20				
Via other products	0.15				
Additional promotions (TDM)					
Hypermarket—display activities	500	600	500	200	200
Consumer competition	100	100	100	50	50
Wheel of Fortune competition	300	300	300	100	100
Additional Costs (TDM)					
Production TV	400	400	400	—	400
radio	30	30	30	—	30
print	50	50	50	50	50
Listing funds	1,000	1,000	1,000	400	300
Material for sales representatives	50	50	50	20	20
Number of households (millions)	26	22	21	10	10

[1]Strong advertising month means that the frequency (number of spots) is about one-third higher than in a normal advertising month.
[2]TV and radio advertising not possible for legal reasons.
DM = German marks.
TDM = 1,000 German marks.

Source: This case was written by Dr. Wolfgang Breuer and Professor Dr. Richard Köhler, University of Cologne (Germany). It was devised together with the German P&G office. It is based on real facts but the figures have been partly changed for teaching purposes. A more detailed version of the case was published by Sage Publications, Ltd., London, in the volume *Marketing in Europe: Case Studies,* ed. Jordi Montaña, 1994. Reprinted with permission.

Discussion Questions

1. How attractive is the pan-European market for Pert Plus in terms of demand potential? Competition? Any cannibalization problems?

2. What competitive advantages does Pert Plus have? Disadvantages? Any country-of-origin effect?

3. Which countries would be the leading markets in Europe? What are the advantages or disadvantages of entering a leading market first?

4. What does the marketing research tell about the price and positioning decision for Europe? Brand choice? Should the BC-18 technology be introduced with a pan-European name, or with local brand names, or even with a mixture of both approaches?

5. Given the economic data, what is your recommendation for launch strategy?

Case 3-2

Levi Strauss Japan K.K.: Selling Jeans in Japan

Levi Strauss, the original jeans-maker from San Francisco, has long had a global presence. Jeans provide a great example of a standardized product whose positioning differs across countries.

The case shows how the jeans-maker approached the Japanese market, where both foreign and domestic competition was strong and distribution was a key success factor. It focuses on how Levi's capitalized on its image

as the original and maintained growth with a premium image.

In May 1993, Mr. A. John Chappell, president and representative director, Levi Strauss Japan K.K. (LSJ), was contemplating a conversation he had just had with the national sales manager and managing director, Mr. Masafumi Ohki. They had been discussing the most recent information regarding the size of the jeans market in

Japan. It appeared that after two years of market shrinkage in 1990 and 1991, the market had contracted further in 1992. Although LSJ was still increasing its share of the market, Mr. Chappell was disturbed by this trend and wondered what new strategies, if any, LSJ should pursue.

Levi Strauss Associates

Levi Strauss invented jeans in San Francisco in the middle of the nineteenth century gold rush. At that time, Levi Strauss made pants for the gold miners that would not rip apart when miners filled their pockets with gold. Since then, the company bearing the founder's name had been faithful to the guiding principle—"Quality Never Goes Out of Style"—and had built a strong reputation and broad customer base.

Levi Strauss Associates (Levi Strauss) designed, manufactured, and marketed apparel for men, women, and children, including jeans, slacks, jackets, and skirts. Most of its products were marketed under the Levi's® and Dockers® trademarks and sold in the United States and throughout North and South America, Europe, Asia, and Australia. In 1992, Levi Strauss was the world's largest brand name apparel manufacturer. Sales of jeans-related products accounted for 73 percent of its revenues in 1991.

Levi Strauss International

Levi Strauss International (LSI), which marketed jeans and related apparel outside the United States, was organized along geographic lines consisting of the Europe, Asia Pacific, Canada, and Latin America divisions. In terms of sales and profits, Europe was the largest international division. Asia Pacific was the second largest, particularly due to the strong performance of its Japanese and Australian operations. Sales growth in LSI was faster than in the domestic division. The following table gives the breakdown of domestic and international sales for the recent years.

Levi Strauss—Domestic and International Sales (in millions of dollars)					
	1989		**1990**		**1991**
Domestic	$2,395 66.0%		$2,560 60.3%		$2,997 61.1%
LSI	$1,233 34.0%		$1,686 39.7%		$1,906 38.9%
Total	$3,628		$4,247		$4,903

In 1991, LSI was more profitable than the domestic operations on a per unit basis. LSI was generally organized by country. Each country's operations within the European division were generally responsible for sales, distribution, finance, and marketing activities. With few exceptions, Canada, Latin America, and the Asia Pacific divisions were staffed with their own merchandising, production, sales, and finance personnel.

The nature and strength of the jeans market varied from region to region and from country to country. Demand for jeans outside of the United States was affected by a variety of factors, each of varying importance in different countries, including general economic conditions such as unemployment, recession, inflation, and consumer spending rates. The non-U.S. jeans markets were more sensitive to fashion trends, as well as being more volatile than the U.S. market. In many countries, jeans were generally perceived as a fashion item rather than a basic functional product and were higher priced relative to the United States. Internationally, LSI maintained advertising programs similar to the domestic programs, modified as required by market conditions and applicable laws. Advertising expenditures for LSI were $108.4 million (5.7 percent of total sales) in 1991, a 21 percent increase from 1990.

Japanese Jeans Industry Environment and Trends: Jeans Market

Jeans were introduced into the Japanese market before World War II. Yet, the first market boom occurred right after the war, when U.S. forces brought a large supply of jeans into the country. The second growth spurt in the market for jeans was in the mid-1970s concurrent with the United States' bicentennial. During this time, "being American" was in vogue, greatly enhancing the demand for American culture and products. The third boom, in 1986, was fueled by the increasing popularity of the casual fashion look among Japanese youth. This fashion trend, along with more leisure time, greatly increased the market for jeans, resulting in a doubling of output from 26 million pairs in 1985, to more than 50 million pairs in 1990[1] (compound annual growth rate of 14 percent). However, the trend was toward slower growth, and the market actually shrunk in 1991. Later Japan had a revival in authentic, vintage (used) jeans, and a host of Japanese companies began to reproduce replica vintage lines. The growth in total production of jeans from 1987 to 1991 is given in Exhibit 1.

The financial results of major jeans manufacturers in 1992 indicated that the market continued to shrink following 1991. Yet, toward the end of 1992, some companies started to see the market revive. After the last couple of years of market contraction, the jeans industry seemed to be revitalized due to the development of new dying techniques (such as antique look jeans), as well as the development of jeans made of new fabrics such as light ounce denim and rayon. In addition, some of the smaller jeans manufacturers that targeted the women's market experienced double digit growth in sales.

---

[1]"Fashions Come and Go, But Blue Jeans Never Fade," *The Nikkei Weekly*, August 17, 1991.

EXHIBIT 1 Size of the Japanese Jeans Market

Source: Japanese Jeans Manufacturing Association (JJMA).

| | Units of Total Jeans Production | | | | | |
| | Blue Jeans | | Color Jeans | | Total Jeans | |
	Units	Growth	Units	Growth	Units	Growth
1987	36,924		15,186		52,110	
1988	43,274	17.2	12,904	(15.0)	56,178	7.8
1989	45,614	5.4	13,310	3.2	58,924	4.9
1990	45,401	(0.4)	13,238	(0.5)	58,639	(0.5)
1991	43,864	(3.4)	12,946	(2.2)	56,810	(3.1)

Notes: These numbers include imports, but not exports, thus are an appropriate proxy for market size. Also, these production quantities are more than LSJ estimates based on annual consumer surveys. For example, in 1991, LSJ estimates the total market size to be 45 million pairs, while the JJSM indicates 25% more. As JJMA's figure is based on self reporting by each of the jeans manufacturers, it is likely to be inflated over the actual sales quantity.

Source: Yano Institute.

| | Total Jeans Production in Yen (¥ millions) | | |
	Blue Jeans	Color Jeans	Total
1988	90,660	27,273	117,933
1989	95,562	28,124	123,686
1990	95,115	27,972	123,087
1991	86,992	24,774	111,766

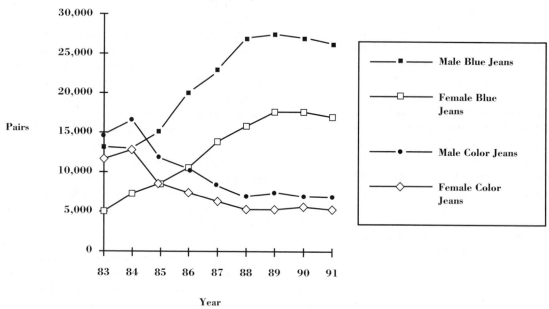

Jeans Production by Type

Competitive Environment

During this period of rapid expansion, LSJ grew 35 percent annually, more than twice as fast as the market.[2] As a result, LSJ enjoyed the highest share of any single brand at

[2]"Fundamentals Lend More-Than-Casual Look," *The Nikkei Weekly,* September 14, 1991.

16 percent of total market sales. Still, there was fierce competition for market share with the five other large brands in the jeans market: Lee, Wrangler, Edwin, Big John, and Bobson, due to the fact that all of the brands marketed similar product lines (emphasizing basic blue denim jeans, followed by other basic jeans, fashion jeans, and chino pants) targeted at essentially the same customer

segment. Also, all the American brands marketed their products by emphasizing the image of Americana.

Sales figures for the six largest jeans manufacturers are given in Exhibit 2. These figures show that the market shares of the three large domestic Japanese brands, Edwin, Big John, and Bobson were declining. LSJ, however, moved up from fifth position in 1986 to second position following Edwin in 1990 with a market share of almost 13 percent, and in 1991 LSJ became the top-selling brand with approximately 15 percent of total jeans sales.

Following is a brief description of each of LSJ's major competitors.

Edwin

In addition to marketing its own brand of jeans, Edwin, the largest domestic manufacturer, also marketed Lee jeans under a license agreement with VF Corporation, the U.S.

company that owns the Lee brand. Edwin wanted to increase market share of its original brand; however, Lee was important for them to compete with Levi's. This posed a dilemma for Edwin, since the Lee brand was cannibalizing the Edwin brand. In 1992, for the first time, LSJ exceeded Edwin in the total sales amount as shown in Exhibit 2. The figures for Edwin include revenues from Lee and Liberto brands. Edwin was also planning to sell a new Italian brand called Fiorucci beginning in the autumn of 1992.

Big John

Sales and net income were expected to increase after two consecutive years of decrease. This was due to the success of their new product line, the "antique collection." The company expected the blue jeans market to grow again in 1993. Since blue jeans was Big John's major product line, the company believed it was well

EXHIBIT 2 Sales and Income Data for Jeans Manufacturers

Source: Company Financial Statements. Yano Institute.

	Sales of Top Six Jeans Brands (¥ million)					
	1988	**1989**	**1990**	**1991**	**1992**	**1993E**
LEVI'S	15,425	21,508	28,855	35,056	37,626	38,600
Edwin (incl. Lee)	30,342	33,579	38,250	38,534	37,099	
Lee			5,000(e)	6,300(e)	6,500(e)	10,000
Wrangler	11,715	13,550	15,367	16,972	17,847	
Big John	13,939	16,472	18,163	17,674	17,421	18,400
Bobson	13,190	15,578	18,187	18,277	16,403	
Other	90,439	98,674	103,689	108,363	111,327	
Total	175,050	199,361	222,511	234,886	237,723	

	Net Income of Top Five Jeans Manufacturers (¥ million)					
	1988	**1989**	**1990**	**1991**	**1992**	**1993E**
LEVI'S	3,585	4,421	6,124	7,058	6,532	6,280
Edwin (incl. Lee)	2,592	3,445	3,365	3,045	3,039	
Wrangler	596	631	1,118	1,127	802	
Big John	881	1,358	827	781	346	1,250
Bobson	531	812	1,413	883	925	
Other	1,814	3,023	2,380	2,416	3,141	
Total	9,999	13,690	15,227	15,310	14,785	

	Return on Sales of Top Five Jeans Manufacturers (%)					
	1988	**1989**	**1990**	**1991**	**1992**	**1993E**
LEVI'S	23.2	20.6	21.2	20.1	17.4	16.3
Edwin (incl. Lee)	8.5	10.3	8.8	7.9	8.2	
Wrangler	5.1	4.7	7.3	6.6	4.5	
Big John	6.3	8.2	4.6	4.4	2.0	6.8
Bobson	4.0	5.2	7.8	4.8	5.6	
Other	2.0	3.1	2.3	2.2	2.8	
Total	5.7	6.9	6.8	6.5	6.2	

Notes: e, E = estimates by LSJ.

positioned for growth in 1993. In May 1993, the company was to begin construction of a new headquarters, which would enable it to effectively concentrate the cutting, distribution, trading, and kids clothes sections into one location.

Wrangler Japan

Wrangler, also a jeans brand of VF Corp., was produced and sold through a license agreement with Wrangler Japan, a joint venture between Mitsubishi and Toyo Boseki. Sales began to pick up in September 1992, especially in the women's jeans market which grew at double digit rates.

Bobson

Bobson's sales target for 1993 was ¥20,000 million. The company had been extremely successful in the women's jeans market. As a result, from October 1992 to January 1993, sales in that segment increased 40 percent over the same period of the previous year. The company expected 1993 to be a growth year.

Up to this point, Levi Strauss's U.S. competitor, VF Corporation, had chosen to operate in Japan solely under licensing arrangements. However, there was speculation that the VF Corporation was planning to shift its marketing strategy from licensing to direct sales. This could drastically change the competitive market in the near future. Market experts predicted that the Japanese jeans market would eventually be dominated by the three major American brands: Levi's, Lee, and Wrangler.

New Emerging Segments

In 1990, Wrangler Japan Inc. tried to reinforce its traditional image by marketing "revival jeans," which featured natural dye extracted from the indigo plant. These indigo blue jeans, named Vintage Wrangler, were made of 100 percent denim and hand dyed. They were priced at ¥30,000 (approx. $242.00), but were selling well.[3] LSJ also introduced reproductions of its 5033BSXX and 701SXX styles, popular in the 1950s and 1960s, which were priced at ¥48,000 ($384.00) in September 1991. Yet, it was reported that LSJ could not make these jeans fast enough to satisfy the demand.[4]

On the other hand, well-preserved secondhand jeans were in high demand, some selling for more than ¥500,000 ($4,000.00). About 30 to 40 stores had opened specializing in used jeans from the United States made in the 1940s, 1950s, and 1960s. One store owner indicated that the most popular items were priced slightly below ¥100,000 ($800.00).[5] However, the slowing growth in demand seemed to indicate that oversupply was becoming a problem and that the market was close to saturation. According to the national sales manager of LSJ, the secondhand trend was supported primarily by jeans enthusiasts and might not last long.

Sales of women's blue jeans registered a phenomenal 109 percent growth between 1985 and 1989, increasing from 8.5 million to 17.8 million pairs a year. With the forecast that the young men's market was stabilizing, all the companies were looking at the potential in the market for women's jeans, creating fierce competition in that category.[6]

Changing Distribution Channel

Unlike in the United States, Europe, and other countries in Southeast Asia, jeans sales in Japan were still predominantly through jeans specialty stores. In other countries, jeans specialty stores had already lost market share to large national chains (such as Sears and J.C. Penney's) and to discounters (such as Wal-Mart and Kmart). The successful specialty stores in the United States were those that had been able to develop their own brands, such as The Gap and The Limited.

Although there had not been a similar shift in the Japanese market (from speciality stores to national chains), the shift was occurring within the jeans specialty shop channel. The structure of this channel seemed to be changing with the emergence of a new type of jeans shop. Traditionally, jeans shops were located in urban areas and sold only jeans (both factors placing a constraint on store size). Recently, new chain stores had been built in the suburbs that were usually five to seven times larger and might carry other products besides jeans. These jeans stores had proliferated at the expense of the smaller jeans stores. Their success was partly a result of their emphasis on sales promotions, ability to stock a full line of products, and the unique store designs. Two such chains, Marutomi and Chiyoda (the two largest shoe store chains), entered the jeans retail market four to five years ago and now boasted retail stores in excess of 200 each. This emergence of jeans specialty store chains had saved this category from losing market share following those in other countries.

In 1992, approximately 250 new stores were opened, most of which were large-scale suburban stores of the type described above. Even though the peak was over, an additional 230 stores were likely to open in 1993. These consisted mainly of Chiyoda's 75 to 85 "Mac House" stores and Marutomi's 100 "From USA" stores. In some suburban areas, the increasing number of stores had started to stimulate competition for local market share. For example, in the city of Tsukuba, a growing suburban area outside of Tokyo, 10 jeans stores (including those under construction) ranging in size up to 4,500 square feet were clustered in 3.1 square miles. Many retailers,

[3]"Fashions Come and Go...," op. cit.
[4]"Vintage American Products Attract Japanese Rebels," *The Nikkei Weekly,* December 7, 1991
[5]Ibid.

[6]"Fashions Come and Go...," op. cit.

therefore, were attempting to differentiate themselves by increasing customer service and being more selective in what product lines they would carry. Yet, with the slowing down in the jeans market, compounded by the recession, the excessive increase in jeans retail space was worsening the inventory turnover leading to inventory surpluses.

Potential Impact on Pricing

Thus far, most of the distribution channels, including jeans specialty stores, department stores, and even national chain stores, had maintained the suggested retail price. National chain stores such as Daiei and Itoh Yokado had discount stores as their affiliates, yet these discount stores had different supply routes and sold different products. This enabled Daiei and Itoh Yokado to maintain the retail price suggested by jeans manufacturers.

A similar change in channel structure had occurred in the distribution of business suits, where sales by department stores and specialty stores in the cities had suffered due to the emergence of larger men's shops in the suburbs. In this case, price competition was increasing between the discount stores (the "category killer"), but not between the national chain stores as had occurred in past. National chain stores had not entered the price war but were stuck in the middle between the discount stores (at the low-end) and the specialty and department stores (at the high-end).

If this held true in the jeans industry, national chain stores would not likely begin competing on price. Also, department stores and traditional jeans specialty stores (with few stores) were unlikely to discount. However, the new jeans specialty stores with many outlets, giving them strong purchasing power against manufacturers, might begin competing on price. These stores, which had expanded rapidly, were experiencing increasing competition and inventory surpluses, creating a ripe environment for price competition. The eventual outcome depended somewhat on how jeans manufacturers would react to discounting, should it occur, and on the sales policies of traditional jeans specialty stores.

Levi Strauss Japan K.K.—Overview

Levi Strauss entered Japan with the opening of a branch office of Levi Strauss (Far East) Limited (Hong Kong) in April 1971. Prior to this, its presence was limited to a minimal level of sales generated by importers. The Hiratsuka Distribution Center was opened in November 1973, and in June 1974, Levi Strauss began domestic production of jeans products.

In December 1975, Levi Strauss began selling through wholesale agencies, in addition to its direct sales to retailers. Levi Strauss also began importing products from the United States in 1978. In the same year, the reporting line of the Japanese office was changed from Hong Kong to LSI headquarters in San Francisco.

In 1982, Levi Strauss Japan K.K. (LSJ) was established as an independent operating company. Another important milestone occurred in June 1989, when 4.1 million shares of LSJ were listed on the Tokyo OTC market in an initial public offering. This sale brought in $80 million, while still leaving Levi Strauss with an 85 percent share of the Japanese company's equity.

LSJ's strategy had been to maintain consistency and a long-term view. With a strong emphasis on advertising, constant new product introduction in addition to traditional styles, systems development, good relationships with suppliers, contractors, wholesalers, and retailers, and personnel training, LSJ had successfully built its position in Japan.

This position was largely due to LSJ's marketing strategy described below.

1. Target young male customers and advertise extensively through TV commercials and men's magazines, creating the image that Levi's jeans are cool American casual wear.
2. In order to have extensive accessibility, contract with various kinds of sales outlets from small specialty jeans shops, mainly located in urban areas, to national chain stores that have larger sales space, mainly located in suburbs.
3. Provide not only the traditional jeans imported from the United States, but also new jeans that are in line with current fashion and sewn to fit Japanese physical features.

Performance

LSJ experienced sluggish sales until around 1984. Since then, year-on-year sales increased by approximately 35 percent every year until slowing down to 20 percent in 1991. The company expected this slower level of growth to continue in the short term. In 1991, LSJ sales were ¥35.056 billion with profits of ¥7.058 billion. LSJ was planning to raise its market share to over 20 percent by fiscal 1995.

The company experienced a decrease in profit in 1992, due to an increase in indirect marketing costs, including depreciation from investment on the distribution center and system development. Yet, LSJ still posted an impressive 17.4 percent return on sales, far higher than its competitors, and nearly three times the industry average. In 1993, the company expected sales growth to be moderate, therefore expecting a further decrease in net income.

Employing the strategy described above, LSJ successfully increased sales volume through stimulating the jeans market. It enjoyed constant demand not subject to the whims of fashion or the changing season. LSJ was successful in establishing the reputation of high-quality products and brand image, allowing them to sell higher-end products than their competitors. This high quality, premium product strategy was successful since it capitalized on the Japanese economy (with one of the highest GNP per capita and significant growth).

On the cost side, LSJ was very efficient in the sense that it did not have a factory requiring huge capital expenditure, but instead, contracted out all its production in Japan. As a result, it did not have to worry about potential costs associated with downtime, equipment improvement, and workers compensation both in monetary and nonmonetary terms. Moreover, LSJ had a very small sales force to cover all of Japan. As a result, LSJ's sales-to-employee ratio was ¥180 million ($1.4 million), which was roughly three times the average of its rivals.[7] Another strength of LSJ was its no-debt strategy to alleviate risk due to interest rate fluctuations. Since its IPO on the Tokyo Stock Exchange, the stock price had been constantly increasing to a P/E ratio of 50.[8]

Products

Product lines sold by LSJ consisted of tops (shirts, jackets, and sweatshirts), men's and women's basic jeans, other basic jeans, and fashion jeans. There were approximately 18 kinds of men's basic jeans (excluding multiple colors), 10 kinds of women's basic jeans, 20 kinds of other basic jeans (including 5 for women), and several fashion jeans. Other jeans consisted of trendy jeans products and fashion jeans consisted of cotton (nondenim) pants. The sales breakdown was as follows: 20 percent from tops, 20 percent from women's jeans, 40 percent from basic men's jeans, and 20 percent from the remainder.

Belts, accessories, shoes, socks, bags, and kids' jeans were sold by another company under a license agreement. In addition, apart from traditional styles, product managers in LSJ designed new styles that were in line with the fashion at the time. New products were introduced twice a year in spring and in autumn. Occasionally, product innovations developed for the Japanese market were later introduced into other markets. This was the case for "stone-washed" denim jeans and the Dockers line, which were successfully introduced in the United States after being developed and introduced in Japan.[9]

While LSJ did not own its own production facilities in Japan, all its domestically produced clothing was made by contracted factories that produced only Levi Strauss products. These contractors sewed jeans products from denim purchased by LSJ from various domestic textile manufacturers and from trading companies. The domestic production accounted for 50 percent of the total products sold in Japan, while 30 percent was imported from the United States and 20 percent from Southeast Asia, mainly from factories in the Philippines.

Until 1978 the company sold only domestic- and Asian-made jeans products in Japan. Then realizing the importance of having the original U.S.-made jeans, the company started to sell some U.S.-made products (specifically the 501 product line) in Japan. According to Mr. Ohki, it was crucial to send customers a message that LSJ was selling "real" American products. Yet, the domestically made jeans products actually fit Japanese bodies better, which partially contributed to the company's success in the early years.

Distribution

The company first established its distribution center in Hiratsuka, Kanagawa, in November 1973, two years after establishing operations in Japan. However, LSJ later reconstructed its distribution center in order to enhance customer service by improving the quality and quantity of warehouse and shipping facilities. In October 1990, it completed the first stage of reconstruction, including installation of the computer-controlled warehouse system named AS/RS (Automated Storage and Retrieval System). Automation of picking and shipping areas, which were controlled along with the automated warehouse, was completed in May 1991. These renovations greatly improved the storage capacity and more than doubled the daily shipping capability. They also enabled the company to handle small quantity, frequent, short-term delivery orders. In addition, LSJ had installed automated ordering systems at some of the national chain stores, allowing for better inventory control and quicker response.

The company had two distribution channels—one was direct sales by sales personnel, and the other was wholesale by sales agencies. Fifty-three percent of total sales came from direct sales made by 40 LSJ sales personnel located in the four sales offices. Using 1991 sales data to calculate the revenue generated by the direct sales force, the average salesperson generated ¥464.5 million (approximately $3.7 million) of revenue in that year. This demonstrated the extraordinary productivity of LSJ's sales force. The remaining 43 percent came from 13 domestic sales agencies.

Sales of LSJ products occurred through four kinds of sales outlets. LSJ's sales personnel and sales agencies both had contact with these key outlets consisting of: (1) major nationwide jeans shops such as Big American and Eiko; (2) major nationwide department stores, from the prestigious Mitsukoshi Department Store to Marui, a department store specifically targeted to the younger generation; (3) national chain stores such as Daiei, Itoh Yokado, and Seiyu; and (4) nationwide men's shops such as Iseya. Most of LSJ's sales occur in jeans shops (70 percent), with the remaining sales fairly evenly split among department stores (12 percent), national chain stores (10 percent) and other stores (8 percent).

---

[7]"Fundamentals Lend More-Than-Casual Look," op. cit.
[8]Ibid.
[9]Geoffrey Duin, "Levi's Won't Fade in the Japanese Market," *Tokyo Business Today,* April 1990, p. 46.

Levi's were sold at fewer sales outlets than some of their domestic competitors. For example, 5,000 stores carried the Levi's brand, while more than 10,000 stores sold the Edwin brand. Although LSJ received a higher percentage of its sales through traditional jeans shops (70 percent) than the market overall (60 percent), there was very little difference between LSJ distribution patterns and those of the other top brands.

LSJ's effort to be a Japanese company could be observed from its strategy of building good relationships with its sales outlets. LSJ provided various services to each outlet store, from giving advice on product displays and in-store arrangements to organizing seminars and handing out sales manuals. Japanese department stores relied heavily on the manufacturers to provide sales staff, forcing LSJ to place 160 employees in department stores as sales clerks. However, this necessity allowed LSJ and other Japanese manufacturing companies to gather information regarding customer preferences.

Pricing

Historically, LSJ was positioned as a price leader, charging 15 to 20 percent higher than competitors for similar jeans products. However competitors raised their prices to match Levi's (pricing of Levi's remained flat), allowing LSJ to greatly increase their market share. By 1993, compared to competitive brands such as Edwin, Lee, and Wrangler, LSJ had a similar price range for its jeans products. Even so, the average product price which LSJ's customers paid (¥7,900 = approximately $63.20) was about 5 to 10 percent higher than the average price received by competitors. This was due to the fact that LSJ customers were willing to buy more expensive types of jeans.

Wholesale price varied by distributor due to the rebate scheme. However, the average price charged to sales outlets was 55 percent of retail, while sales agents paid about 50 percent of retail on average. LSJ charged a higher wholesale price to the department stores in order to offset the cost of LSJ employees who worked as sales personnel in those stores. However, there was no significant difference in retail price across the various distribution channels, since retail outlets maintained the suggested retail price.

Advertising and Promotion

Similar to the strategy employed by Levi Strauss in the United States, LSJ emphasized a pull strategy, spending heavily on advertising to increase demand. Since 1976, LSJ had been spending approximately 6 percent of total sales on advertising (TV and print) compared to an industry average of 4 percent.[10] It used James Dean as an advertising character in order to establish the image of the young, active American. Its target customer had traditionally been young men, aged 16 to 29, who had

grown up with, and maintained a good image of, American products.

When LSJ first launched its campaign in 1984 with the slogan "Heroes Wear LEVI'S," its main purpose was to increase the awareness of the Levi's brand. The ads showed movie scenes in which James Dean, John Wayne, Steve McQueen, and Marilyn Monroe wore jeans, while a famous movie announcer, Mr. Haruo Mizuno, read the slogan. In 1985, the slogan was changed to "My Mind, LEVI'S" and, in 1987, "The Original LEVI'S," both of which were intended to project traditional American values and a pioneering spirit with a more familiar nuance. The next slogan, "Re-Origin," was launched in 1989 to emphasize the revival of traditional jeans. Since the very beginning, the company had recognized the Japanese purchase mentality toward imported goods—Japanese were willing to choose imports and even pay more for these goods—and had been maximizing its marketing by appealing to this psychology.

LSJ focused on TV commercials and magazine advertisements, which accounted for 65 percent of the total promotional budget. Of this advertising expense, approximately 70 percent was used for TV commercials, and 30 percent for magazine advertisements. The company used mass media effectively based on differences in features. For TV commercials, LSJ used an advertising agency in order to maximize reach and communicate the company's image to a larger audience. In contrast, the company created its magazine advertisements mostly in-house, since the goal of the magazine ads was to increase consumers' understanding of its products and to appeal strongly to certain target customer segments (see Exhibit 3 for the audiences targeted). In terms of cooperative advertising with sales outlets, LSJ was consistent with other Japanese manufacturing companies, which tended not to use this method as much as U.S. companies.

LSJ also published seasonal product catalogs named "LEVI'S BOOK" and placed them in outlet stores in

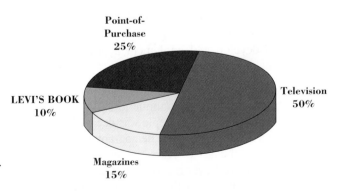

LSJ Promotional Expenditures

Point-of-Purchase 25%

Television 50%

LEVI'S BOOK 10%

Magazines 15%

[10]"Fundamentals Lend More-Than-Casual Look," op. cit.

EXHIBIT 3   LSJ Magazine Advertising 1991 and 1992

1991 LSJ Magazine Advertisements			
Magazine	**Type**	**Readership Profile**	**Number of LSJ Ads.1/91-12/91**
Popeye	Fashion	Young males,18–23	22
H D Press	Fashion	Young males,18–23	24
Men's Non No	Fashion	Young males,18–23	20
Fineboys	Fashion	Young males,18–23	15
1992 LSJ Magazine Advertisements			
Magazine	**Type**	**Readership Profile**	**Number of LSJ Ads.1/92-10/92**
Popeye	Fashion	Young males, 18–23	18
H D Press	Fashion	Young males, 18–23	17
Men's Non No	Fashion	Young males, 18–23	17
Fineboys	Fashion	Young males, 18–23	11
Asahi Weekly	News	White collar males, all ages	1
Shincho Weekly	News	White collar males, all ages	1
Bunshun Weekly	News	White collar males, all ages	1
Bart	News	Young, white collar males	1
Non No	Fashion	Young single females	1
Pia	Entertainment	Young males/females, <35	1
Dime	New Product Intro	Affluent males, 30–40	1
Sarai	Housekeeping	Married females, 25–35	1
Number	Sports	Males, all ages	1

order to introduce new products. Two million copies of this catalog were produced twice a year, accounting for 10 percent of LSJ's promotional expenditures. The remaining 25 percent of promotional expense was used for direct communication with customers at the point of purchase. By these consistent advertising and promotional activities, the company was trying to increase (1) awareness of the Levi's brand, (2) understanding of its products, and (3) the willingness to buy.

Future Challenges

LSJ's major challenges, resulting from the changing market and retail environment were:

1. How to continue to grow faced with a contracting market.
2. How to respond to the changing structure of the distribution channel.
3. How to develop and implement a pricing strategy given the current retail environment.

First, the traditional market for jeans in Japan had peaked and was likely to continue to shrink or remain flat. The number of young people was decreasing due to the lower birth rate, shifting the demographics to an older population. For the last 12 years, the birth rate each year had been the lowest ever recorded, a trend that was expected to continue.[11] Also, the average frequency of jeans purchased per person per year in Japan was a meager 0.5

compared to the 1.5 in the United States.[12] This was due to the fact that high schools in Japan required students to wear uniforms, so there was significantly less time and chance to wear jeans. These trends would further impact the market size of the young male segment, the traditional market that jeans manufacturers (including LSJ) had targeted.

In addition, Mr. Ohki brought up the issue of selection criteria for retailers and sales agents. The distribution channel was undergoing structural changes, and Mr. Ohki believed that LSJ needed to evaluate and possibly revise their distribution strategy. LSJ was very selective in choosing its retailers and historically focused their distribution on traditional urban jeans specialty shops. However, there were many new, large stores opening in the suburbs that were carrying jeans, amongst other items. Although LSJ did sell their jeans in some of these new stores, they had not pursued this new channel as aggressively as some of their competitors.

Mr. Chappell realized that increasing the number of stores would improve LSJ's reach and possibly help to stimulate the overall market. However, this could have a serious impact on LSJ's image. LSJ had spent years developing a premium product image that had catapulted them to market leader. Besides their product and advertising strategies, this

[11]1992 Statistics Handbook. Statistics Bureau, Management and Coordination Agency; Ministry of Health and Welfare.
[12]"Fundamentals Lend More-Than-Casual Look," op. cit.

image had also been cultivated by their selectivity in choosing retail outlets and sales agents. Not only did this ensure that Levi's would have a good image with the consumer, but it also was the only way LSJ could influence the retail price. Mr. Chappell feared that a decision to expand the number of retail outlets would have a negative impact on Levi's prices and might even result in discounting. This could seriously affect the premium product image LSJ had worked hard to foster over the years.

Discussion Questions

1. What are the key success factors (KSFs) in the Japanese marketplace?
2. To what extent do the Levi Strauss's FSAs and CSAs match the KSFs? How has Levi's been able to leverage its country-of-origin to become a leading brand? Can other American jeans do the same?
3. How would you explain the apparent success of LSJ's advertising campaign stressing American values in Japan?
4. List the pros and cons of the different distribution alternatives facing LSJ. Which one do you think has the best chance of succeeding?
5. Would you retain the premium positioning of Levi's in Japan? Why, or why not?

This case was prepared by Elizabeth Carducci and Akiko Horikawa, second-year MBA students, and Professor David B. Montgomery, Stanford University Graduate School of Business, as the basis for class discussion rather than to illustrate either effective or ineffective handing of an administrative situation. The authors gratefully acknowledge the cooperation and assistance of Mr. A. John Chappell and Mr. Masafumi Ohki of Levi Strauss Japan, and Mr. David Schmidt and Mr. S. Lindsay Webbe of Levi Strauss International. Copyright © 1994 by the Board of Trustees of the Leland Stanford Junior University. All rights reserved. Used with permission from the Stanford University Graduate School of Business.

Case 3-3
Colgate-Palmolive: Cleopatra in Quebec?

Colgate-Palmolive, one of the leading personal care product manufacturers, markets many brands (including Colgate toothpaste) globally. The Cleopatra facial soap, very successful in France, seemed a likely candidate for another global success, especially in Canada's French-speaking Quebec province. The case shows that cultural similarities don't ensure success.

The Canadian launch extravaganza in February 1986 began with cocktails served by hostesses dressed like Cleopatra, the queen of ancient Egypt. Then followed a gala dinner with a dramatic, multimedia presentation of the new brand, ending with the award-winning commercial and these words:

> Today the memory comes alive,
> a new shape rises up, a new texture,
> a new standard of beauty care
> worthy of the name it bears,
> Today the memory frozen in ancient stones comes
> alive . . .
> Cleopatra.

Each of the retailer guests had received an exclusive, golden, three-dimensional pyramid invitation to the launch, and expectations were high. The retailers were sick of discounted brands, all basically the same, and were looking for something different and exciting. Finally, the new soap Cleopatra was revealed to the audience of nearly 1,000—a huge turnout by Canadian standards—and the response was overwhelmingly positive.

So enthusiastic was the audience, that by the end of the evening the Colgate-Palmolive salespeople had received orders for 2,000 cases. Bill Graham, the divisional vice president of marketing for Canada, and Steve Boyd, group product manager, agreed that the night had been a grand success and that Cleopatra's future looked very rosy.

The French Experience with Cleopatra

Cleopatra soap was first introduced in France in November 1984. By May of the following year, the brand had reached an amazing market share of 10 percent, despite its 23 percent price premium compared with other brands. In fact, Colgate-Palmolive's biggest problem was keeping up with demand. By the end of 1985, market share shot up to 15 percent. Cleopatra had actually become the number one brand in France.

Cleopatra's success in France received a great deal of publicity within the organization. Encouraged by the experience, the Global Marketing Group, situated in New York, set out to find other markets for the product. They reasoned that if Cleopatra had worked well in France, it should do likewise elsewhere in the world.

Canada, especially French-speaking Quebec, seemed like an obvious choice to the Global Marketing Group. At the annual update meeting in New York, the group strongly recommended to the Canadian management that a test be done in Canada to see if Cleopatra was a proposition for them.

The Reaction of the Canadian Subsidiaries to Cleopatra

The idea of a market test for Cleopatra was greeted with mixed feelings by the Canadians. Some managers, such as Stan House, assistant product manager, were enthusiastic, especially because they knew that Steve Boyd, group product manager for Canada, was convinced it would work. In Boyd's opinion, Canada could show the people in New York that the same formula would do as well or even better than in France.

Other managers, like Ken Johnson, were more skeptical. They resented having a brand thrust on them. Johnson believed that what Canada really needed was a strong "national" brand, and he doubted that Cleopatra could ever be that.

Nonetheless, a decision was made to proceed and test the Canadian market. One fundamental question had to be answered: Was there reasonable certainty that Cleopatra would be accepted by consumers in Quebec? Two types of research, both conducted in Toronto, tried to answer that question. The first study was among a "super group" of articulate professional women, specially chosen and brought together for the event. They were introduced to the product, its price, and the advertising; then they were asked to discuss their likes and dislikes openly. On balance, the results were positive; the women seemed to like the soap and the concept.

The second research study used more-typical consumers; these people were exposed to the proposed advertising for Cleopatra and then were asked whether they would buy it. Fifty percent said they would. They were also given a bar of soap to try at home and were phoned a week later for their reactions. Sixty-four percent of the group who used the soap said they would buy Cleopatra as soon as it was available on the shelves.

The research confirmed the feelings of Boyd, and most of the marketing team in Toronto that Cleopatra could indeed be a winner. Immediately, plans were made for an early launch the following year.

The Canadian marketing team was determined not to allow Cleopatra to go to war with all the other brands. They felt something had to be done to reverse the negative profit trends that had been brewing in the industry for some time. This was the ideal opportunity. They would position Cleopatra as the premium-quality, premium-priced soap and differentiate it from all the others. They wanted to avoid having a price war at all costs.

Some Background on Colgate-Palmolive Canada

Colgate-Palmolive, a multinational consumer packaged goods corporation operating in 58 countries, marketed a variety of personal care and household products

worldwide. With annual sales of $5.7 billion, many of its brands were global leaders. For example, Colgate toothpaste was number one and Palmolive soap was number two in the world in their respective markets.

The Canadian subsidiary opened its doors in 1912, and since then had grown into a $250-million-a-year corporation. Together with two competitors, Procter & Gamble and Lever (both $1 billion subsidiaries of their parent companies), they dominated the aggressive and innovative personal care and household market sectors in Canada.

Colgate-Palmolive Canada manufactured and marketed a wide range of personal care and household products inside Canada and also supplied brands to the United States and Puerto Rico. The major products marketed in Canada were as follows:

Personal care products	Household products
Colgate toothpaste	Palmolive liquid soap
Colgate toothbrushes	Palmolive automatic dishwasher soap
Colgate mouth rinse	ABC detergent
Halo shampoo	Arctic Power detergent
Irish Spring soap	Fab detergent
Palmolive soap	Baggies food wrap
Cashmere Bouquet soap	Ajax cleanser
Cleopatra soap	Ajax all-purpose liquid cleanser

The Colgate-Palmolive head office and manufacturing facility were both located in a building in Toronto. Sales offices were in each of the six major regions across Canada, namely, the Maritimes, Quebec, Ontario, the Prairies, Alberta, and British Columbia.

Marketing was organized at the head office under a product management system, whereby each person was responsible for a brand or group of brands and reported to a group product manager who, in turn, was responsible to the vice president of marketing. The brand managers made decisions on all aspects of marketing planning and execution, from market research to consumer and trade promotion. The product managers made sure that their brands received the needed resources from the head office.

The State of the Canadian Soap Market

In 1986, the soap market in Canada was worth $105 million to manufacturers. This revenue figure was projected to grow by 4 to 5 percent in the years ahead. The Canadian soap market was probably one of the most competitive in which Colgate-Palmolive competed—a fact that even the average consumer could see each time he or she turned on a television set or opened a magazine.

The competition would continue at the store level, where limited shelf space was at a premium. Because of the intense competition, retailers were all-powerful. They literally could pick and choose with whom to do business. Inside the store, a brand's fate was in their hands; they decided what to promote, which prices to cut, and how to allocate shelf space.

Competition was extremely fierce for some of the following reasons:

1. Volume growth in the market had slowed and coincided with the growth of the Canadian population (1.0–1.5 percent annually). No further rapid expansion was expected.
2. The only method of survival for the many new brands and new variants of existing brands was to steal share from other products in the market.
3. Competition from no-name and private label products had increased.
4. Technological advances were slowing, and relaunches were increasingly "cosmetic" in nature (new color, new fragrance, etc.).
5. Consumers had a group of "acceptable" brands that they were willing to purchase (usually 3 or 4 in number). Buying decisions within this group were based on price. There were 15 mainstream brands, along with 20 to 25 minor ones, fighting to become one of these "acceptable" choices.
6. Trends toward larger bundle packs had developed (more than one bar of soap packaged and sold as a unit), reducing the number of purchases each consumer made during the year. For example, in the skin care segment, twin-packs (two bars sold together) were becoming the norm, whereas the refreshment segment was dominated by three- and four-packs, and the utility segment by four-, five-, and six-packs.
7. Competition was based on price, as there were no real competitive advantages or meaningful differences among most brands and because of increased pressure from the retail trade to meet competitive deals and prices.
8. Liquid soaps had entered the market and held an 8 percent share. Based on current consumer reaction, the maximum share was not expected to grow beyond 10 percent in the future.

For most consumers, "a soap is a soap is a soap," with few perceivable differences among brands. Bombarded by advertising in every conceivable type of media, consumers mainly bought the "acceptable brands" on price. Therefore, becoming and staying an "acceptable brand" was where the ongoing competitive battle among the various brands took place.

The soap market was divided into three distinct groups: the skin care segment, the refreshment segment, and the utility segment (see Exhibit 1). The skin care market was the largest of the three segments, which were split as follows:

EXHIBIT 1 Market Segments and Brand Advertising Claims, 1986

Source: Colgate-Palmolive Canada.

Segment	Brand	Advertising Copy Claim
Skin care	Dove	For softer, smoother skin, try Dove for 7 days
	Camay	Skin care as individual as you are
	Caress	The body bar with bath oil
	Cleopatra	New soap: rich as a cream, sensual as a perfume
	Aloe & Lanolin	Good for skin because it has natural ingredients
	Palmolive	Not advertised
Refreshment	Zest	Zest leaves you feeling cleaner than soap
	Coast	Coast picks you up and pulls you through the day
	Irish Spring	Fresh fragrance, double deodorancy
	Dial	You will feel clean and refreshed all day long
Utility (price)	Jergens	Not advertised
	Woodbury	Not advertised
	Cashmere Bouquet	Not advertised
	Lux	Not advertised
	Ivory*	Ivory is 99 44/100 pure soap

*Ivory competes with different creative executions in each of the three segments.

	1985 (%)	1986 (%)	1987 (%)
Skin care	37.3	38.4	38.8
Refreshment	34.9	33.4	32.3
Utility (price)	27.8	28.2	28.9

Exhibit 2 contains details of market share for each of the three large companies and their competitors. Although there were at least 15 mainstream brands (Exhibit 2), only 4 had managed to create a really distinctive niche.

In the skin care segment, Dove had been advertised for years as the facial soap. It had a loyal customer base, mainly because of its unique formulation and moisturizing capabilities. Low on additives and scent, it was seen as the "Cadillac" of this segment and was priced accordingly.

Ivory was an "institution" in the Canadian soap market, with its 100-year heritage and ever-powerful "I use it because my mother used it" pure soap positioning. The market leader, it successfully competed with all three markets.

Irish Spring, made especially for men, did well in the male market as a refreshment soap, although females used it as well. Consumers associated its strong scent and high lathering capability with cleaning strength.

EXHIBIT 2   Category Market Shares (Quebec)

Source: Colgate-Palmolive Canada.

	1985	1986	1987 YTD*
Colgate-Palmolive			
Irish Spring	6.2	6.0	6.5
Palmolive	3.7	3.6	6.4
Cashmere Bouquet	3.3	3.4	2.8
Cleopatra	0.0	0.9	1.1
Total:	13.2	13.9	16.8
Lever			
Lux	4.3	6.0	8.3
Dove	7.1	9.6	10.8
Caress	1.5	1.7	2.9
Other	3.9	2.7	1.2
Total:	16.8	20.0	23.2
Procter and Gamble			
Ivory	28.2	24.9	22.9
Zest	4.9	6.1	4.7
Coast	5.6	5.5	6.4
Camay	6.4	5.3	2.6
Other	0.1	0.1	0.1
Total:	45.2	41.9	36.7
Jergens			
Aloe & Lanolin	2.4	3.2	2.6
Woodbury	0.3	0.8	1.4
Jergens	5.4	5.4	5.4
Total:	8.1	9.4	9.4
Canada Packers			
Dial	2.4	2.4	3.2
Other	0.1	0.0	0.0
Total:	2.5	2.4	3.2
Other	14.2	12.4	10.7

Note: Market share is calculated on an equivalent case basis.
*Year end is the October/November share period. Therefore, 1987 YTD (year-to-date) is made up of two bimonthly share periods: December/January and February/March.

Zest was also positioned in the refreshment segment. Seen as the "family brand that gets you cleaner than soap," it was low in additives and perfume. It especially appealed to people in "hard water" areas of the country. Its detergent formulation allowed it to make special claims against other brands, such as "it rinses clean and doesn't leave a soapy film."

The Quebec Market

Quebec is Canada's second-largest province in population and the largest in geographical size. The 6.7 million people (or 26 percent of Canada's total population) are clustered throughout the southern portion of this immense region, which is 2.5 times the size of France.

Unlike the other nine provinces, whose populations are of British ancestry, Quebec has a population that came originally from France. In fact, over 80 percent of the 2.3 million households in Quebec list French as their mother tongue. Needless to say, with this unique culture,

marketing strategies sometimes differ from those used in the rest of the country.

Quebec accounts for 28 percent of the Canadian soap market volume and is, therefore, slightly overdeveloped in proportion to the country's total population. The major brands and their positions in the Quebec market are similar to those throughout the rest of Canada. The exceptions are Zest, which does poorly because Quebec is mainly the soft-water market, and Lux, which has done extremely well due to its strong European image.

The Canadian Cleopatra Marketing Strategy

Cleopatra looked like an excellent prospect for Canada. Not only was it a premium-quality product in all respects, but it complemented Colgate-Palmolive's Canadian product line and had a past history of success. If launched, the product line would include Irish Spring, well positioned and strongly niched in the refreshment segment; Cashmere Bouquet, performing well in the utility segment; Palmolive soap, positioned as the all-family skin care bar; and Cleopatra, the premium-quality skin care brand worthy of competing with the segment leader, Dove.

After considering these facts as well as the positive research results from the two analyses, Colgate-Palmolive decided to launch Cleopatra as the "premium-quality, premium-priced beauty soap." The marketing team, however, decided that it would not be financially feasible to launch Cleopatra like any other soap, where ultimately its success would be determined by its ability to compete on price. Although the marketing team knew the risks, they wanted to avoid having to rely on retailers and being forced to offer large trade allowances and discounts. They wanted the demand to come directly from the consumers, by generating their interest in Cleopatra through strong media and consumer promotions.

This approach was very different from the industry norm, where manufacturers traditionally paid large sums of money to retailers just to get the product listed in their "accounts order books." Then, manufacturers would have to pay even more in discounts and allowances to have a showing in the retailers' weekly advertising fliers. Once management decided to forgo these payments, it was critical for the company to make the best possible media and consumer promotion schedule for the launch.

The company set an ambitious objective: a 4.5 percent market share for 1986; 100 percent distribution of the product with retail accounts; maximum shelf presence, defined as the same number of facings as the current segment leader, Dove; proper shelf positioning, which meant being next to Dove; and, finally, maintaining Cleopatra's premium pricing strategy.

To make the strategy work, especially since targets were based on an 11-month first year, the company knew it had to get both consumers and salespeople enthusiastic about the brand. Therefore, it was essential to generate excitement from day one. The promotion had to be very powerful. In fact, it had to be so good that consumers would demand the brand and force retailers to stock it. That meant the emphasis would be on advertising. Television was chosen as the most obvious way to focus resources and create an impact and instant awareness among the target group—women between the ages of 18 and 49. The campaign, which the marketing team wanted to be "an event," began the first week in May.

The budget was set to make Cleopatra the number one spender in the entire soap market. The objective was clear to all: ensure that Cleopatra gets the most "share of voice" in its category in Quebec, which amounted to 15 percent. In other words, for every 100 minutes of advertising for soaps, 15 minutes would go to Cleopatra.

The Quebec TV commercial was the same one used in France, with one or two minor and hardly noticeable modifications. This commercial, shot in Rome on a very elaborate set, had been one of the most memorable aspects of the French marketing strategy. It showed the Egyptian Queen taking a perfumed bath. The feedback from consumer research in France had been particularly positive, and the commercial had received a number of awards for excellence.

Equally important in the marketing strategy was sales promotion, always popular with the average Canadian consumer. Since the team's research had established that 64 percent of the market would buy Cleopatra after trying it at home, the first and foremost aim was to be sure that people tried it. Thus the promotion campaign, scheduled to run from May to October, centered on the product being tried. Approximately 250,000 households in Quebec received free bar coupons that could be exchanged for a free bar of soap at the nearest store. All stores were fully informed.

There was also the "Cleopatra Gold Collection and Sweepstakes Promotion," which offered consumers a wide range of popular and fashionable costume jewelry at very reasonable prices. For example, one could send for a necklace and earrings that cost only $12.99. Consumers who bought the jewelry received forms and were automatically entered into the grand prize draw, a chance to win a Cleopatra-style, 14-karat gold necklace worth $3,500. Research among current brands on the market showed that mail-in offers and sweepstakes were very successful with consumers, and management had high hopes that this promotion would stimulate interest in the brand. The promotion began in August and ended with the draw in early January 1987.

Since Cleopatra had been positioned as the premium-quality brand in soap, no discounts were offered. Single cartons were packed 48 to a case, at a price of $41.71. Cleopatra's pricing strategy was to be higher than Dove, historically the most expensive brand. (Comparative prices are shown in Exhibit 3.)

EXHIBIT 3 Price and Trade Discount Structure

Source: Colgate-Palmolive Canada.

	Cleopatra	Dove
Case size*	48 × 140g	48 × 140g
Case price	$41.71	$39.72
Unit cost	0.87	0.83
Regular selling price	1.29	1.19
Off-invoice allowance	—	3.00
Deal unit cost	—	0.77
Feature price	—	0.99

Note: The average manufacturer's price for Cleopatra was 87 cents per single bar, compared with an average manufacturer's price of 31 cents per single bar for all toilet soaps.
*Dove is also available in a twinpack.
(24 × 2 × 140g case size)

The product itself had been developed in France, with no changes made for the Canadian market. As it turned out, Cleopatra was the finest-quality soap made by the company in Canada. Its unique formulation contained the best ingredients, including the equivalent of 15 percent beauty cream, which delivered a rich, creamy lather and was noticeably soft on the skin.

The perfume, blended in France, was said "to produce an unforgettable fragrance." The soap was also carved into a special shape to make it easy to hold and use. The Cleopatra logo was stamped on the ivory-colored bar—another differentiating feature intended to convey quality, luxury, and prestige. The bar was slightly larger than the French product, to conform to the other Canadian brands.

Each bar of soap came in its own gold-colored laminated carton, a difference from being wrapped in paper as in France. The laminated material was unique in that it not only reflected light, which made it stand out against the other brands on the shelves, but it also prevented the perfume from escaping.

The Results of the Canadian Launch

Due to the launch, sales had started off with a bang. On the first evening alone, 67 percent of the first month's objectives had been achieved. But from then on, the brand started missing its targets.

Steve Boyd had warned his team not to expect an instant miracle. After all, the Quebec soap market was one of the most competitive, and it took time to establish a brand. As the retail trade had been so positive at the launch, he felt sure that things would eventually pick up. The results, however, continued to be discouraging well into the first year. Cleopatra simply was not selling and could not seem to reach the explosive growth everyone was anticipating and expecting to be "just around the corner."

After 13 weeks, the advertising commercial had created an awareness of 63 percent, the highest in the skin care segment. At that time, Camay was at 49 percent;

EXHIBIT 5 Profit and Loss Statement (000)

Source: Colgate-Palmolive Canada.

		Actual 1986	Ist Quarter 1987
Sales	$	755	167
Margin[a]	$	477	108
	%	63.2	64.8
Trade[b]	$	53	12
	%	7.0	7.2
Consumer[c]	$	401	34
	%	53.1	20.3
Media[d]	$	465	94
	%	61.6	56.3
Total expenditures	$	919	140
	%	121.7	83.8
Contribution[e]	$	(442)	(32)
	%	(58.5)	(19.2)

[a]Includes direct product costs, freight/warehousing, etc.
[b]Includes all expenditures directed to the retail trade.
[c]Includes all consumer promotion expenditures.
[d]Includes cost of developing a commercial, plus air-time.
[e]Contribution toward allocated overheads and operating profit.

EXHIBIT 6 Consumer Research on Brands (Quebec)

Source: Tracking study, Colgate-Palmolive Canada.

	Brands (total random sample)[a]				
	Aloe & Lanolin	Camay	Cleopatra	Dove	Palmolive
Brand awareness (%)[b]	54.4	98.5	73.5	99.5	96.1
Brand in-home (%)[c]	3.5	15.2	6.9	23.9	7.4
Ever tried (%)[d]	12.3	86.3	14.2	83.5	65.2
Brand used[e]					
All of the time (%)	1.5	8.3	2.9	12.3	3.9
Most of the time (%)	0.5	3.9	1.5	5.4	3.9
Occasionally (%)	7.4	47.6	8.8	46.6	36.3
Stopped using (%)	2.9	26.5	1.0	19.2	21.1

[a]Total random sample —204 respondents.
[b]Question: Have you ever heard of _____?
[c]Question: What brands do you have in your home now?
[d]Question: Have you ever tried _____?
[e]Question: Do you use _____? If yes, would you say you use it all of the time, most of the time, or occasionally? If no, did you use _____ at some time in the past?

EXHIBIT 7 Consumer Research on Best Brands (*Quebec*)

Source: Tracking study, Colgate-Palmolive Canada.

Brands Best for . . .[a] Brand	Being Good Value for Money		Being Mild and Gentle		Having a Rich, Creamy Lather		Having a Pleasant Fragrance		Moisturizing Your Skin		Suitable for the Whole Family		Leaving Skin Soft and Smooth	
	Total Sample[b]	Cleo Triers[c]	Total Sample	Cleo Triers	Total Sample	Cleo Triers	Total Sample	Cleo Triers	Total Sample	Cleo Triers	Total Sample	Cleo Triers	Total Sample	Cleo Triers
Aloe & Lanolin	11	2	31	9	8	0	13	0	27	2	13	1	19	1
Camay	40	11	31	7	50	9	53	13	28	7	32	10	41	10
Cleopatra	10	30	8	33	27	51	21	53	15	31	6	23	20	49
Dove	26	13	53	29	63	31	51	16	39	20	49	21	68	24
Palmolive	36	18	20	5	12	5	19	9	9	3	43	19	19	4
All	26	10	5	5	19	2	29	5	2	4	6	5	5	8
None	22	7	28	8	8	0	6	2	38	19	25	12	15	2
Don't know	33	8	28	3	17	1	12	1	46	13	30	8	17	1

Note: The two sets of data are from separate panels (i.e., the 99 Cleopatra triers are not included in the total random sample of 204 respondents).

[a]Question: Which of these five brands—————, ————, or ————is best for "Being good value for the money" (for example).

[b]Total random sample = 204 respondents.

[c]Cleopatra trier sample (people who have tried Cleopatra in the last 6 months) = 99 respondents.

365

EXHIBIT 8 Consumer Research in Attitudes toward Cleopatra

Source: Tracking study, Cleopatra-Palmolive Canada.

	% of Triers[a]
Likes Cleopatra[b]	
The smell/good/nice/pleasant/perfume	29
Makes a lot of suds/foam/suds well	26
Mild perfume/light	22
Miscellaneous	21
Softens skin/soft for skin/leaves skin smooth	20
It's mild/good for skin/the mildness	19
The smell/perfume lasts/leaves nice smell on skin	12
It's creamy/creamier	11
The fresh smell/refreshing	10
It's soft/as silk/like satin/like milk	7
Dislikes Cleopatra:[c]	
Price too high	20
Too strong a smell/contains too much perfume/harsh	17
Too harsh a soap/not mild enough	12
It melts too fast	10
The smell/the smell left on skin	7
Irritates the skin/burns skin/too much perfume	6
Dries the skin	5
Miscellaneous	5
Doesn't suds enough/not enough foam	3
Doesn't moisturize skin	3

Note: Only the 10 most frequent responses are shown here.
Note: For many French Canadians, the level of perfume is perceived to vary directly with the cleaning strength and harshness of the product.
[a]Cleopatra trier sample (people who have tried Cleopatra in the last 6 months) = 99 respondents.
[b]Question: Given that you have tried Cleopatra, what are your likes and/or dislikes of the brand?
[c]42 respondents had no dislikes.

EXHIBIT 9 Consumer Research, Usage

Source: Tracking study, Colgate-Palmolive Canada.

Questions Asked of Users[a]	% of Respondents
Do you plan on buying Cleopatra again?	
Regularly	27
Occasionally	66
No intention to buy again	7
Do you use Cleopatra every day?[b]	
Yes	41
No	59
What part of the body do you use Cleopatra on?	
Face only	3
Body only	76
Face and body	21
Who uses Cleopatra in your household?	
Yourself only	65
Others	35
How often do you use Cleopatra?	
Regularly	33
Occasionally	67

[a]Questions asked of those who have tried Cleopatra in the last 6 months (Cleopatra trier sample = 99 respondents).
[b]Showers outnumber baths 4 to 1 in the province of Quebec.

EXHIBIT 10 Consumer Research, Advertising

Source: Tracking study, Cleopatra-Palmolive Canada.

	% of Respondents[b]
Main point recall[a]	
It's a beauty soap/soap for women	22
It's perfumed/contained perfume	18
It's mild/a mild soap/mild as milk	16
Contains cream/milk/oils	15
Cleopatra/beauty linked together	14
Cleopatra/Egyptians linked together	14
It suds well/lots of lather	10
Fresh smell/it's refreshing	8
Smells good/nice	5
Makes skin soft/smoother skin	5
Note: Only the top 10 responses are shown here.	
Reaction to Cleopatra after seeing advertising[c]	
Positive	41
Negative	13
No reaction	46
Intention to try Cleopatra after seeing advertising[d]	
Yes	37
No	63

Note: Questions c and d were asked of those in the total random sample who had seen the advertising but who had not tried Cleopatra at the time of the study.
[a]Question: Do you recall Cleopatra advertising? If yes, what were the main points of the ad?
[b]Number of respondents out of the total random sample who recalled Cleopatra advertising =128.
[c]Question: What is your reaction to Cleopatra?
[d]Question: Do you intend to try Cleopatra?

EXHIBIT 11 Consumer Research, Trial

Source: Tracking study, Colgate-Palmolive.

Reasons for not Trying Cleopatra?[*]	% of Respondents
Not available where I shop	29
Haven't needed any soap	21
Too expensive	19
Happy with my present brand	19
Has too much perfume in it	16
I don't think about it	10
Miscellaneous	9
Waiting to get a coupon	6
It's new	4
Don't know	4

Note: Only the top 10 responses are shown here.
*Question: Why haven't you tried Cleopatra soap? (Asked of those who have seen the advertising and had originally intended to try the brand.)

Discussion Questions

1. What are the similarities between the French and the Quebec markets that suggest acceptance for Cleopatra after the French success? Critically evaluate the market research prior to the launch. Are there any significant findings that would alert you to potential problems ahead of the launch?

2. How would you evaluate the positioning of Cleopatra in Canada? Are there any alternative options?

3. Evaluate the promotional launch and the advertising campaign. Were mistakes made that could have been anticipated?

4. On the basis of the consumer research data collected after launch, what is your diagnosis of what went wrong?

5. If you were Steve Boyd, which of the three options would you pursue? Justify your choice.

Source: This case was prepared by Professor Sandra Vandermerwe, with the assistance of J. Carter Powis (MBA, IMI 1988–89). Copyright © 1990 by the International Institute for Management Development (IMD), Lausanne, Switzerland. Not to be used or reproduced without permission.

Part 4

Global Management

After the company has expanded into foreign markets and become confident in several local markets, there is usually a need to integrate the global network and develop a global strategy. There are many reasons for this. On the cost side, unnecessary duplication (meaningless differences in product designs, separate advertising campaigns, different brand names) is wasteful. On the demand side, global communications make for homogeneous preferences and positive spillovers from global brand names. Global competitors often force other firms to go global as well.

Part Four deals with the globalization of marketing management, that is, how a firm coordinates and integrates its local marketing efforts globally. Chapter 11 deals with the corporate strategic framework and how firms develop global segmentation and positioning strategies within this framework. Chapter 12 focuses on global products and services, discussing the management of standardized product lines and how the management of global services differs from the management of products. Chapter 13 discusses global brand management. Chapter 14, which covers global pricing, shows how companies have tried to come to grips with price coordination across borders, including the problem of arbitrage opportunities because of fluctuating exchange rates. Global distribution is covered in Chapter 15, including the Internet channel and a discussion of the massive changes in global logistics technology.

Chapters 16 and 17 deal with global advertising and promotion. Chapter 16 gives the pros and cons of globally uniform ad campaigns and shows how the emergence of global agencies has facilitated global advertising. Chapter 17 covers alternative promotional tools including public relations, publicity, and e-commerce and also discusses personal selling and the increased importance of direct marketing for global commerce.

Chapter 18 treats the organizational problems that arise when global marketing is undertaken and the question of how to motivate local subsidiary managers.

Chapter

11

Global Marketing Strategy

"Think global, act local"

After reading this chapter, you should be able to:

1. Rethink the basic marketing orientation when implementing a global strategy, and know how to balance the local customer orientation against the unavoidable top-down coordination.

2. Map out the firm's global portfolio of markets and products and understand the resulting resource allocation between countries.

3. Interpret global segmentation data and develop clusters of similar countries for which standardized marketing is acceptable.

4. Do the necessary localization and adaptation of standardized products which overcome the unavoidable mispositioning in local markets.

5. Understand how target segments and brand position can be different in different countries even for universal products, depending on competitive situations and stage of the product life cycle.

Just as in marketing management at home, the global marketing strategy has to fit into the overall global strategy for the corporation. Given the overall resource allocation between countries and products, the first step in global marketing strategy is to define the segments to be targeted and the product positioning to pursue. But the task is much greater than at home. The global marketer needs to decide whether to target the same segments everywhere, and whether to use the same positioning in each country market. As one would expect, the answer hinges on the extent to which the markets are similar, whether the competitive situation is the same everywhere, and whether the customers are alike. To assess these factors properly takes a great deal of research and analysis. This chapter shows how to do it.

Which Companies Are Truly Global?

As we saw in Chapter 1 of this text, new research suggests that the great majority of the typical "global companies" are really not so global after all. When one looks at where they sell their products, very few have significant sales outside of one or two regions.

Defining as "global" a company that derives at least 20 percent of its revenues from each of the three so-called triad regions—North America, Europe, and Asia Pacific—and not more than 50 percent from any one region, a book-length study of 2001 data by Rugman (2005) finds that only nine of the Fortune Global 500 firms qualify as truly "global." These firms are:

From North America: IBM, Intel, Coca-Cola.

From Europe: Philips (the Dutch electronics company), Nokia (Finland), LVMH (French luxury goods).

From Asia: Sony, Canon, Flextronics (the Singaporean electronics component manufacturer).

You probably have your own favorite company that you thought was global. For example, how about Toyota? Well, says Rugman, Toyota is actually bi-regional-it gets 49.2 percent of its sales from Asia, 36.6 percent from North America, but only 7.7 percent from Europe. Unilever? Another bi-regional, with 38.7 percent of its revenues from Europe, 26.6 percent from North America, but only 15.4 percent from Asia. McDonald's story is the same, with a relatively low percentage from Asia (14.8 percent), similar to Nike's story, with 12.9 percent in Asia, but Nike is basically home-region based, with 58.2 percent of its sales in North America. And what about Procter & Gamble, the leading global advertiser? P&G, also, is actually a home-based company, with 55 percent of its sales from North America.

You can argue with this classification, of course. Why cut at 20 percent and at 50 percent? Why focus only on the triad regions? Seems quite arbitrary. Anyway, McDonald's getting 14.8 percent of its sales from Asia is still a good chunk of revenues—in fact, in 2001 it was US$2.21 billion—and McDonald's is surely a real presence in Asian markets. One could also argue that if P&G was slightly less successful at home, it would soon be a global company, or at least a bi-regional company, and if Toyota takes just a bit more of the market in Japan it will be relegated to the home-market focused category.

For local marketing purposes, a large presence in a local market is clearly what matters. It is worthwhile for P&G to figure out its optimal strategy in Asia even though it derives "only" 10.0 percent of its revenues there. That would be US$3.92 billion in 2001, enough to warrant serious strategic attention. But this is actually Rugman's point. When a company develops a "global strategy" it means that all the major markets are considered jointly and equally. But if the company has one market, say the home market, so much bigger than the rest, it is not clear how to strike a global balance. If the company is regionally organized, common among these large companies, it is likely that the region with the most sales will carry more weight and get more resources. This is not necessarily counterproductive per se, but when a new growing market opportunity appears—such as when the China market opened up, or the Indian market—one would suspect that firms with relatively lower sales in Asia would be slower to pick up on the opportunity. This is exactly what happened with P&G in India, where bi-regional Unilever entered very quickly, and locked up a first-mover position before home-region based P&G's entry. Even if Unilever did not have that much bigger a position in Asia than P&G, it was less tied to home.

Truly global companies are apparently rare—but for speed and flexibility "going global" beats staying home.

Sources: Alan M. Rugman, *The Regional Multinationals: MNEs and "Global" Strategic Management.* *Cambridge: Cambridge* University Press, 2005. Pankaj Ghemawat, *Redefining Global Strategy: Crossing Borders in a World Where Differences Still Matter.* Boston: Harvard Business School Press, 2007.

Introduction

To develop a coordinated global marketing strategy, the first step is typically to decide upon which countries and product lines should be involved. Since global coordination necessarily involves some managerial constraints on the marketing activities of local organizations, a global strategy cannot be completely localized to any one market. This means that in practice the global coordination should not be attempted for truly multidomestic products, that is, products for which the demand situation is unique in each market. But for intrinsically global products, such as hi-tech products, global coordination is a natural strategy with great benefits. There are additional instances where coordination can be beneficial. For example, there could be a region or a group of countries for which the demand is quite homogeneous. Then, coordination of marketing strategy for that particular region might be feasible. Furthermore, there may be pockets of similar customers in each of several otherwise different markets. Then, those pockets could be targeted with a coordinated cross-country niche strategy.

The purpose of this chapter is to discuss how the firm can develop standardized and coordinated segmentation and positioning strategies across countries that it has entered. To set the stage, a first section demonstrates how the mindset behind such strategies is fundamentally different from the domestic-only case. Then, the chapter shows how the corporate portfolio of products and markets is managed, and how the resulting resource allocation sets the framework within which the global marketer functions. A presentation of the basic principles of global market segmentation leads the reader to a two-step approach wherein the country-level macrosegmentation precedes the "within-country" microsegmentation (discussed in Chapter 7). The chapter continues with the clustering techniques for grouping similar markets and the procedures to identify segments across countries for which a standardized strategy might be successful. The targeting strategies are then discussed, with an analysis of the pros and cons of diversification versus focus strategies. The chapter then discusses how all three strategic components—segmentation, targeting, and positioning—need to be fully integrated for maximum benefit, and ends with a step-by-step guide for how to develop a global marketing plan.

The Global Marketer's Mindset

As we saw in Chapter 1, the antiglobalization movement focuses its attacks on global brands and products. As a response, many global companies have shifted their global marketing orientation to a more localized strategy. Still, as we will see in this and the following chapters, a global coordination of marketing strategies can yield substantial benefits to a company. Marketing costs come down because one campaign can be used in more places and because spillovers between countries will reinforce a uniform message. More than that, global marketing still brings the benefits of globalization to people around the world when implemented with attention to local sensitivity. But this requires some rethinking in many companies. Managers should get out of the mindset that what is good enough at home is good enough abroad. This is easy to see, but often not followed in practice. Global marketing can be—and has often been—"bad marketing."

Selling Orientation

Remember that "good" marketing should have a "customer orientation." This ought to be true for global marketers as well, but it just isn't. By and large, companies have a "selling orientation" when attempting to address international markets. The global marketer is intent on selling an existing product, not on finding out what the foreign consumer's true desires are. Of course, using some of the techniques discussed in Chapter 4 on country attractiveness, the global marketer usually has a projection of whether the market will like the product and how many units might be sold. But there is usually not effort to develop a new product for the foreign market. Typically, the global marketer sells what it makes, not makes what it can sell as the ideal marketer supposedly does.

The lack of customer orientation comes naturally. The introduction of a new product is always difficult and uncertain. Launching it into a foreign market only adds complexity and risks to the problem. Consequently, the global marketer will typically delay its plans until the product is successful at home or in a lead market. While much research might have been at home before the original launch, the research in foreign markets is usually not so deep.

There are cases where a global marketer has introduced completely new products in a foreign market, after assessing the preferences in that market. The Japanese show several examples of this. Toshiba, the first to introduce the laptop computer, designed it for the American market. Sony's sporty Walkman designs are targeted at consumers in the West. Western and even American companies have also done this. Ford and GM run strong operations in Europe with cars designed primarily for the European market. There are also companies today that develop products and services with an eye to the global market directly, attempting to satisfy everybody through one design (the Ford Focus car is a case in point, discussed in the next chapter).

But in global marketing of the past these cases are the exceptions. By and large the leading brands of global products and services—the Nikes, the Starbucks, the McDonalds, the Coca-Colas, the Wal-Marts, and so on—involve existing brands in pretty much unadulterated form expanding outward from their home country. Until very recently, this was the model used in globally coordinated marketing strategies. Strikingly as well, these are the brands that have been disparaged by antiglobalizers.

Standardization

For similar reasons, global marketers' mindset is to sell standardized products. In a very influential 1983 *Harvard Business Review* article, Theodore Levitt suggested that because of technology and communication advances global markets are becoming homogenized. People everywhere want the same thing. Multidomestic markets are transformed into global markets. This set the stage for globally standardized products, which, argued Levitt, would let companies provide products with state-of-the-art technology at low cost.

Even though Levitt's thesis was widely disputed, the implied global marketing strategy was gradually adopted. To gain the scale advantages associated with globalization, standardization has been the norm until recently challenged by antiglobalization. Standardization is the norm not only for global products and brands but also extends to advertising, pricing, and other elements of the marketing mix. For example, global TV commercials are shot in extravagant surroundings and at extraordinary expense only because they can be shown around the world. Shifting dialogue from speaking actors to voice-overs makes it possible to dub in different languages more easily. Using music-only with unintelligible words (not uncommon in pop and rock music) allows the use of the audio portion of TV commercials without modifications. To cut costs further, ad agencies use some ideal "average guy or gal,"—perhaps not surprisingly, one favored country is Australia where the heritage of mixed races has produced such archetypes, as also filmmakers have discovered.

Nowhere is standardization more prominent than in the strategic use of brands. Today, the choice and use of brand names are typically tightly controlled from the top. Global companies from Pepsi-Cola to Sony to Electrolux have strict guidelines for how the brand name should appear, in what color and font, the size of the logo, and so forth. Top management also decides which brand names to promote globally, which regionally, which to retain nationally, and which to drop altogether.

As many travelers have observed, global standardization makes foreign countries look like home—or at least more similar. Standardization also makes people's behavior, habits, and tastes more similar. When Starbucks offers coffee in large paper mugs, people no longer use cups. When products are designed for people "on the go," people will learn to eat while walking. When products are offered in package sizes bigger than before, shopping habits have to change. Car drivers all around the world now drink coffee and talk on the phone, forgetting that the light has changed. Levitt's 1983 thesis about standardization as the wave of the future might have seemed wrong at the time, but the marketing efforts of the global companies have surely made it come true. It has also, as we now have seen, created a blowback in the guise of antiglobalization.

Coordination

The global marketing mindset is naturally different from the typical "customer orientation" also for another reason. Global marketing effort is by definition a coordinated effort across countries. Coordination means that what happens in one country market is made to depend on actions in other countries. Standardization can in a way be seen as a prerequisite for effective coordination, since it is more difficult—and less needed—to coordinate across dissimilar products and marketing activities. The consequent dependence on other markets will not always be perceived as a gain for local customers who realize that what they are now offered depends on what other countries get.

Of course, in many cases the local consumers won't know any of this, although they may suspect it. The delays in the launch of Microsoft's Windows'98 release was due to the difficulty of coordinating 30 language versions for simultaneous launch. Thus, even though the company festivities accompanying the product's global launch were held as scheduled, and public announcements about the simultaneous launch were not retracted, the actual release dates depended on when sufficient resources were freed up from other launches. After the U.S. and European releases in mid-1998, the Chinese launch came on September 2 and the Thai version on October 28. And some countries did not get Windows'98 until'99.

Centralization

A final reason for a deficient customer orientation is the decidedly centralized character of most firms' global marketing efforts. The marketing is directed from the company's home country. To implement global marketing policies, headquarters has to reduce the local subsidiaries' authority. What headquarters decides will have to be followed abroad. Even under the best of circumstances, with cross-country product teams, strategic input from lead countries and global mandates for local subsidiaries, the global marketing effort is a top-down activity.

For example, the timing of software releases from Microsoft is carefully calibrated from headquarters in Redmond, Washington. Disney's release dates for films and videos is set down from its Orlando headquarters. The centralization involves not simply senior-level decision making. Volvo cars did not feature cup holders until recently despite appeals from their American dealers. Volvo engineers in Sweden were too busy with more serious design issues.

Global marketing almost always involves centralization of decision making. This in turn means less autonomy for local subsidiaries. Economic decisions affecting local customers, management, and employees are no longer made in the market country, but abroad. The managers who make these decisions come from a specific organizational culture with a particular tradition. Although the basic profit-and-loss calculations behind a chosen strategy might not be affected, it is foolish to expect them not to be influenced by this tradition. And it doesn't take a stretch of the imagination on the part of an activist already upset with the weakness of the local economy to infer that the global entrant in a way represents a neocolonial power.

The New Global Mindset

What this all means for the global marketer is that he or she really has to do some rethinking. Sure, in the 1980s and 1990s, Levitt's "global imperative" suggested that the world was waiting for the global products, and people everywhere were just eager to buy. With the renewed emphasis on localization in the new millennium, the benefits of global coordination of strategies need to be balanced against local sensitivity. Today, while globalization might still be the dominating factor driving international business, the balance is shifting toward a coordinated strategy that is adapted to local differences. How to strike the right balance is the challenge that the rest of this chapter will deal with.

Global Market Planning

Any global marketing strategy has to be formulated and implemented within the constraints set by the overall corporate market plans. The basic task in global market planning is the efficient allocation of resources across products and markets around the world. That is, how much of the total budget, including the marketing budget—for activities such as new product introductions, design adaptations, advertising expenditures, distribution support and promotional spending—should be allotted to each of the subsidiaries in different markets and to each product in their product lines. Not a simple task. The optimal allocation is where the marginal payoff is the same across all markets and all products. But this is easier said than done.

To determine an optimal allocation the multinational firm needs data on sales, costs, and projected profitability for each product by country market. This is too massive an effort for most companies (although one company that has tried this is Samsung, the Korean company discussed below). In the traditional multinational, the solution was to decentralize operations. The country subsidiaries were managed quite independently of headquarters, often on a stand-alone profit basis. This basically meant that the country managers could run their own operation, emphasizing products that brought in high sales and revenues in their particular market. The cost-of-goods-sold would be determined by the transfer prices set by headquarters on the basis of factory costs, which also reflected localization and adaptation charges when demanded by country managers. Since any one country subsidiary would sell a product line with products manufactured in many foreign locations, manufacturing and sales were also established as separate organizational units, further contributing to a fragmented and decentralized multinational organization.[1]

Because it simplifies management and helps preserve local motivation, even today many companies operate with a fairly high degree of decentralization. In particular, the split between manufacturing and marketing has continued and, if anything, widened. The increased access to China, India, and other low-cost manufacturing locations, coupled with lowering of tariff barriers and transportation costs, has made companies move quickly into new manufacturing locations. This has made for further separation between manufacturing and sales, and has also, incidentally, had the effect of lowering the role of "made-in labels" in consumer perceptions of products (although brands still tend to have a "home country").

But as the need for global coordination of marketing has increased, decentralized operations have given way to more top-down control. Whether it is to coordinate global product rollouts, match competitors' global ad campaigns, or provide global customers with the same service everywhere, the independence of the local subsidiary is an obstacle. Global marketing coordination requires more top-down centralization and a companywide resource planning tool. The typical solution is to adopt a version of what has come to be called a **portfolio approach**.

The Boston Consulting Group Portfolio Matrix

The earliest example of the portfolio approach is perhaps the Boston Consulting Group's (BCG) **growth-share matrix**.[2] It was used to allocate resources between products, not markets, but can easily be extended to markets as well. The matrix subdivided a company's products into four categories, based on market growth and market share (hence the growth-share name). The matrix has become perhaps best known for the evocative naming of the four categories into "Stars, Cash Cows, Dogs and Question Marks," depending on their prospects. A typical matrix is shown in Exhibit 11.1.

EXHIBIT 11.1
The BCG Growth-Share Matrix

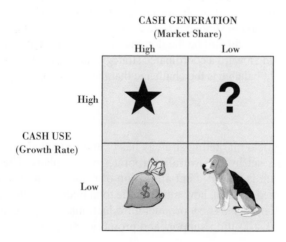

According to BCG, resource allocation between products flows naturally from this matrix. With Cash Cows in relatively slow-growing markets, the high market share of these products should be used ("milked") to cast off money to invest elsewhere-hence the name "Cash Cows." The advice is to allocate these funds to the Star products, where the market is growing and further investments can yield good returns. Whether the Question Mark products should be supported or not is an open question—hence the name. On the one hand, they are in fast-growing markets, a positive factor. On the other hand, their share is relatively weak, and possibly would require a great deal of support to become Stars in their own right. Finally, the Dogs are products with small shares in slow-growth markets and should get little or no support, perhaps dropped.

The GE/McKinsey Matrix

There have been several extensions of the BCG matrix. One of the most prominent is the GE/McKinsey version, developed jointly by the General Electric company and McKinsey, a consulting firm. Their extension involves an elaboration of what makes a market attractive beyond growth, and what determines competitive strength beyond market share. Of interest for global marketing purposes, the attractiveness of the market also includes measures of market size and entry barriers, such as high tariffs. Similarly, competitiveness includes measures of brand strength in the global marketplace. As in the original, the resource allocation involves allocating funds to products in attractive markets where the firm's competitive strength is high.[3]

Both the BCG and the GE/McKinsey matrixes focus primarily on allocation of funds between products. But the extension to allocation of funds between products and also markets—of special interest for global marketing purposes—is in principle straightforward. However, adding in different markets around the world adds a whole new level of complexity.

Ford's Country Matrix

One of the earliest and best-known examples of an application of the matrix to several country markets is the one developed by Ford Motor Company for its tractor division.[4] The resulting matrix for the European countries is shown in Exhibit 11.2.

EXHIBIT 11.2
The European Country Matrix for Ford Tractors

Source: *International Marketing*, 9e, by Philip Cateora. Copyright © 1996 by The McGraw-Hill Companies, Inc. Reprinted with permission.

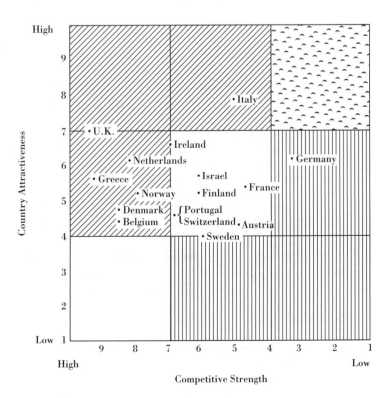

Basically, the matrix identifies "Star countries" in the upper left part of the matrix (UK, Ireland, possibly Greece) and "Cash Cow countries" (Belgium, Denmark) from which cash flows would be directed toward the star markets. Germany is clearly a "Question Mark country," with average attractiveness and relatively weak competitive strength, and Sweden may be a "Dog country" with low attractiveness and weak competitiveness. Both Germany and Sweden would likely receive less marketing support.

In the Ford tractor example, scoring a country's attractiveness and Ford's competitive strength in a country involved several factors. Exhibit 11.3 shows the indicators of market attractiveness, and Exhibit 11.4 shows the indicators of competitive strength.

As can be seen, the score on "market attractiveness" involves both regulation and political stability in addition to market size and growth rate. Similarly, "competitive strength" includes measures of service support capability and advertising strength in addition to market share and ranking. It should also be noted that several of these measures are based on subjective judgments. Ideally, competitive strength figures should include customer feedback, such as satisfaction scores.

Global Resource Allocation

Extending the analysis to different products and different country markets requires data on how a given product performs in a given market, across all products and markets. The question is, what is the market attractiveness and our competitive strength for each of the company products in each of the market countries? Given such data, the firm can then allocate funds to a given product-market combination, not just to one product

EXHIBIT 11.3
Country Attractiveness Scale Weights

Source: Harrell, G.D, Kiefer, R.O (1981), "Multinational Strategic Market Portfolios," MSU Business Topics, Vol. 21, No.1, pp.5–15.

1. Market Size		2. Market Growth	
Units	Rating	Amount (percent)	Rating
25,000	10	5+	10
22,500–24,999	9	4–4.9	9
20,000–22,499	8	3–3.9	8
—	—	—	—
—	—	—	—
—	—	—	—
5,000	1	Under 3	1

3. Government Regulation

a. Price Control		b. Homologation		c. Location Content/ Compensatory Exports	
Type	Rating	Type	Rating	Type	Rating
None	10	None	10	None	10
Easy to comply	6	Easy	6	Easy to comply	6
Moderately easy to comply	4	Moderate	4	Moderately easy to comply	4
Rigid controls	2	Tough	2	Tought	2

4. Economic and Political Stability

a. Inflation		b. Trade Balance		c. Political Stability	
Amount (percent)	Rating	Amount (percent)	Rating	Type	Rating
7 and under	10	5 and over	10	Stable market	10
—	—	0–4.9	9	Moderate	5
—	—	−5–0	8	Unstable	1
40 and over	1	—	—		
		—	—		
		—	—		
		−36	1		

Note: These measurements are indicative of what might be done, rather than concrete examples.

EXHIBIT 11.4
Competitive Strength Weights

Source: *International Marketing,* 5e, by Philip Cateora. Copyright © 1983 by The McGraw-Hill Companies, Inc. Reprinted with permission.

1. Market Share

a. Percentage of Market		b. Position	
Share	Rating	Rank	Rating
30+	10	1	10
27–21	9	2	8
—	—	3	6
—	—	4	4
—	—	5	2
4	1		

2. Product Fit

Because this scale suggests Ford's competitive product strategy, we decided not to publish it. In general, a 10-point subjective index was created to match product characteristics with key local product needs.

3. Contribution Margin

Again, this is proprietary, but it reflects two factors.

a. Profit per Unit		b. Profit Percentage of Net Dealer Cost	
Amount	Rating	Amount (percent)	Rating
$5,000	10	40+	10
(example)	—	—	—
—	—	—	—
—	—	—	—
1–400	1	5–	1

4. Market Support

a. Market Representation		b. Market Support	
Evaluation	Rating	Evaluation	Rating
Quantity and quality of Ford distributors and service are clearly "best in country"	10	Ford market support in advertising promotion is clearly "best in country"	10
Ford representation is equal to leading competitor's	8	Ford support is equal to leading competitor's	8
Ford representation is behind several leading competitors'	2	Ford support is behind several leading competitors'	2

Note: These measurements are indicative of what might be done, rather than concrete examples.

everywhere, or one country market in all products. A company such as Procter & Gamble might then allocate extra resources to its Head-and-Shoulders shampoo in China, but not elsewhere, and also allocate extra funds to the China subsidiary for shampoos and fragrances, but not for detergents. Such precise allocations require a considerable amount of data. Most companies make do with some basic indicators of past sales and rates of market growth—and then allocate a given percentage of last year's revenues to advertising and promotion, increasing the allocation where growth is stronger and reducing it in low-growth markets.

Because of the data requirements, very few companies attempt the complete analysis suggested by a global portfolio of countries and products. One exception is Samsung, the Korean electronics company. Samsung manufactures a number of products, from semiconductors and home appliances to cell phones and HDTV televisions. Its product divisions are represented in most major markets of the world, and Samsung is well known in Asia, Europe, and across the Americas. It's a global brand that downplays its Korean roots and has very strong engineering capabilities. The company's engineering-based culture is one reason why the complex global portfolio analysis, with its demand on numerical calculation of optimal allocation, is feasible and accepted by management.[5]

Samsung's approach to global market planning is based on a decision support model called the M-Net system.[6] The M-Net approach involves not only the major products and country markets, but also goes beyond a simple assessment of country attractiveness and competitive strength. For each product marketed in a country, future market sales of the product category are forecasted by trend analysis, analogy, or other established method. Then the approach assesses the role of country regulations, tariffs, and other entry barriers, political stability, and other factors, to develop a measure of the *potential* sales in the country. Competitive strength is a function of present market share and relative strength of domestic and foreign competition, but extended to incorporate the potential ease (or difficulty) of achieving an increase in market share. This means that data are collected also on price sensitivity, advertising response, and similar market characteristics, enabling Samsung to gauge the chances of capturing more market share. As a result, the resource allocation using the Samsung approach allows the company to give more support to products and countries that would otherwise be classified as "dogs" or "question marks."

To get from increased market share to profits, the model first multiplies the expected market share increase by forecasted country market sales to generate the potential revenue increase for a given product and market. Then, by assessing the costs of any specified marketing effort (advertising, promotion, etc.), the incremental costs can be subtracted from revenues to estimate the potential (marginal) profit increase. In addition, since this solution is only valid for a given marketing program (specific advertising and promotion levels, for example), alternative marketing mixes can then be tried out (simulated) against the potential profit increase for each product in each different country to find an ideal (optimal) allocation. The analysis is repeated for all country-product pairs.

The M-Net approach used by Samsung is an example of the economist's textbook solution brought into practice. In reality, of course, managerial judgment is also needed to put the solution into practice. For example, the possibility of spillover effects between countries (for example, the company's product placement of cell phones in *The Matrix* movie trilogy) necessitates a great deal of subjective assessment. Samsung's experience is also that a considerable amount of internal discussion and active participation by the affected managers and country subsidiaries are necessary to gain trust in the numbers and acceptance of the allocations.

Samsung has recently emerged as a new powerhouse in consumer electronics, dethroning Sony as the most valuable brand name in that category. In *Interbrand*'s 2007 rankings, Samsung was in 21st place and Sony in 25th place.[7] The in-depth M-Net analysis and the consequent resource allocation shift undoubtedly contributed positively to this achievement.

The differences between the traditional decentralized approach and the more data-based approach are summarized in Exhibit 11.5.[8]

EXHIBIT 11.5
Traditional and Fact-Based Resource Allocations

The traditional approach to budgeting and planning	The fact-based approach to budgeting and planning
1. Category managers campaign for incrementally larger annual marketing budgets.	1. Critical country- and product-category data are collected into M-Net, the company's Web-based marketing data repository.
2. HQ's marketing management responds based on incomplete information, tradition, and gut instinct.	2. Using M-Net's analytical engines, corporate marketers identify high-potential country-category combinations.
3. Outsized increases go to the biggest markets and the "squeaky wheels."	3. What-if scenarios are tested to determine the most effective allocation of marketing resources.
4. Over- and underinvestments are rampant—yet no one knows where or by how much.	4. The allocation is refined based on insights of field marketing managers, then finalized by HQ.
5. Marketing's total budget appears arbitrary and indefensible.	5. The fact-based case for the allocation is presented in meetings with field managers.
6. Top management grows increasingly uncomfortable with the overall marketing investment.	6. Senior management gains confidence in its level of marketing investment.

In sum:

- To reap the benefits of global marketing the firm has to coordinate and control its marketing across the globe. Resources have to be directed toward the most promising products and markets.

- Quantitative data on products and markets can be used to determine how marketing resources should be allocated. The basic data involve measures of country-market attractiveness and competitive strength, for each product in the company product line and for each market covered.

- The implementation of global marketing requires considerable people skills and managerial flexibility to accommodate local variations that require adaptation. The numerical allocations provide the starting point for the necessary adaptations.

Global Market Segmentation

As the Samsung example suggests, resource allocation is often done not just for specific country markets, but for larger regional markets. These regions are sometimes simply defined in terms of trade blocs—NAFTA, EU, Mercosur, and so forth. A better way is to group together countries that have similar characteristics in terms of markets and marketing, not just belonging to the same bloc. The semiglobalization approach proposed by Ghemawat also relies on the cultural, geographic, and general similarity between countries.[9] To identify these groupings of nations, companies rely on what is called macrosegmentation, the first stage of global market segmentation.

Global market segmentation typically involves a two-stage procedure. In the first stage countries are grouped using more general criteria, to identify clusters of countries that are similar in socioeconomic and cultural characteristics. This stage helps first of all in screening out countries that do not present good market opportunities for the firm. Secondly, it can be useful for the firm with multiple product lines, since it offers general insights applicable across all the firm's products. Most importantly, the clustering technique often called **macrosegmentation,** groups countries that are more homogeneous in general characteristics and thus might be responsive to a standardized and coordinated marketing strategy.[10]

In the second **microsegmentation** stage, market research is used to collect data on the potential customers in each of the countries belonging to the selected cluster or clusters. This stage resembles what is typically done in any local market segmentation analysis, but there are differences. The data collected involve variables related to product usage patterns, benefits desired, price sensitivity, media usage, and shopping behavior. Data are also collected on individual sociodemographics, income, and other background variables. The statistical analysis involves factoring out dimensions along which customers in a country market differ from each other and from customers in other countries. Then, the research assesses the size and sales potential for each group or segment of similar consumers. Finally, the data are analyzed to find the best ways to reach and communicate to each of the segments.

For example, in microsegmentation a typical segment that can be found in the beer market of most countries is the "heavy user" segment (defined as, say, those who consume more than three beers a day). For obvious reasons, this segment is often an attractive target segment for a beer brewer. However, the proportion of beer drinkers who belong to that segment can vary (a higher percentage in Germany and the United States, for example; much smaller in Italy and France). This reduces the incentive to coordinate strategies across countries. Also, the way to reach the heavy users of beer might seem the same in principle—sponsorship of sporting events, for example—but which sports are popular varies across countries. Thus, it might not be useful to coordinate the marketing communication mix either.

This type of analysis can be extended to other variables in the marketing mix. If, for example, the research shows that a price-sensitive segment exists across all the countries

A Bombay movie theater. The Bollywood film industry is the largest in the world. It long seemed without global potential because Indian religion and culture were different from the West. With globalization many Indians have emigrated abroad, in the process promoting interest in and understanding of Indian ways—and creating a fertile ground for Bollywood's global expansion. http://www.bitethemango.org.uk/2003/filmdetail.asp?ida=4013

in a cluster, the analysis can then assess the percentages of potential customers in that segment for each country. If these percentages are high everywhere, a coordinated low-price strategy might be called for. If the price-sensitive segment is large only in one or two countries, a coordinated strategy might not be advantageous since a low price everywhere would likely undercut quality perceptions and brand image in less price-sensitive markets.

We will next look at the macrosegmentation clustering process in more detail, and then discuss how the two-stage procedure has been implemented in one actual case.

Macrosegmentation

Macrosegmentation consists of grouping countries on the basis of common characteristics deemed to be important for marketing purposes. Actually, with more than 200 independent country markets to consider, many companies often start with the existing trade blocs or geographical regions when clustering countries. The EU, NAFTA, or ASEAN, or geographical regions such as Southeast Asia, Oceania, and the Middle East, are often already treated as relatively autonomous organizational units.[11] In addition, data for these regions tend to be readily available.

The variables typically used in macrosegmentation include sociodemographic data on population size and character, disposable income levels, educational background, and primary language(s), as well as indicators of level of development, infrastructure, rate of growth in GNP, and political affiliation. The choice of variables must take into account the possible lack of data comparability across many countries and will generally vary across products (for industrial products, a manufacturing intensity index is often used as an indicator of general level of economic activity, for example). The data sources used are the same as those used when evaluating individual country attractiveness (see Chapter 4).

To identify regional groupings (macrosegments) of countries, it is possible to use computerized techniques such as **cluster analysis.** Clustering maps show a picture of which countries are similar and which are far apart (recall Hofstede's similar approach to culture discussed in Chapter 3). To incorporate more than two criteria at a time, it is common to do an initial factor analysis before clustering the countries. The factor analysis helps combine all the criteria into a manageable few dimensions, although at the price of making interpretation of the dimensions less clear. The interested reader is referred to the many available statistical texts.[12]

An example of a country clustering map is provided in Exhibit 11.6. As can be seen, at this level the groupings usually turn out to be similar to the East–West and North–South categories typically employed in U.N. policy analyses. Although such groupings should not be mistaken for final market segments, these very broad indicators serve to indicate strength of markets and socioeconomic distance to the home market.

In one application, Cavusgil used six variables (population growth, median age, number of children per household, infant mortality, life expectancy, and GNP per

EXHIBIT 11.6

A Two-Dimensional Country Clustering Map

Source: Charles Ramond, "A Two-Dimensional Country Clustering Map," *The Art of Using Science in Marketing.* New York: Harper & Row, 1974. Copyright ©1974 by Charles Ramond. Reprinted by permission of HarperCollins Publishers, Inc.

Factor Number	Name and Number of Descriptors	Selected Descriptors
I.	Aggregate economic, of level of development (47)	Gross national product, radios in use, passenger kilometers flown
II.	Population size (31)	Total midyear population
III.	Personal economic, or standard of living (32)	Income per capita, newsprint consumption per capita, birth rate (negatively related)
IV.	Canada—conditions on which Canada ranks highest (12)	Newsprint production, visitor arrivals in the U.S., geographic area
V.	Linguistic affinity (10)	Adults who read English or speak it
VI.	YC—Code for private descriptors (11)	Brand and industry sales of a consumer product, number of Roman Catholics
VII.	International participation (22)	Membership in international organizations, foreign tourist arrivals, airfare to Tokyo
VIII.	Trade capacity (12)	Exports, number of Protestants
IX.	Climate or price stability (10)	Sunny days per year, temperature of key city, price index (negative)
X.	Mortality (5)	Infant death rate, number of Moslems

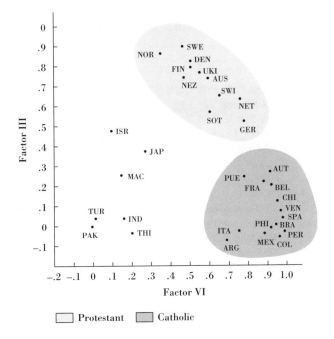

capita, all available in published U.N. data) to come up with market-based clusters of countries.[13] He then proceeded to name the clusters, and to describe their distinguishing features. Finally, he outlined the marketing implications. The results are presented in Exhibit 11.7. As can be seen, even these relatively crude measures are useful to judge country attractiveness, uncover market opportunities, and suggest interesting marketing implications.

The use of broad economic indicators in macrosegmentation has been challenged by marketers who argue that these indicators are too general to be really predictive of buyer behavior and market response. In an effort to test the predictive ability of the country groupings based on broad economic, social, and political criteria, one study examined the new product diffusion pattern for three products (color TVs, VCRs, and CD players) in different country clusters.[14] If the clusters are useful, one would expect the new product rate of penetration to be similar for countries within a cluster, and different across clusters. The study found little evidence of this. The new product diffusion patterns varied within clusters, and some countries from different clusters showed

EXHIBIT 11.7 **A Market-Oriented Clustering of World Markets**

Source: S. Tamer Cavusgil, 1990, pp. 206–7. Reprinted with permission of the author.

Cluster	Demographic Make-Up	Marketing Implications
Dependent societies Most countries in Africa, Asia, and a few in South America	Population growth: 3% Median age: 16 Children: 5+ Infant mortality: 100 per 1,000 births Life expectancy: 40 years GNP per capita: less than $300	Demand goods and services related to food, clothing, housing, education, and medical care. Investments related to extractive activities (agriculture and mining) are undertaken. Government/state economic enterprises are the major buying groups. Poor infrastructure and access to rural markets are major impediments.
Seekers Most countries in Latin America; some in Asia (Indonesia, Thailand, Philippines), and some in Africa (Morocco, Tunisia, Egypt)	Population growth: 1.5 to 2.5% Median age: 20 Children: 4+ Infant mortality: 50 per 100 per 1,000 births Life expectancy: 60 years GNP per capita: less than $900	Infrastructure-related projects are high priority (construction equipment, machinery, chemicals, etc.). Good opportunities for technology sales and turnkey projects. Independent trading groups and a few large holding companies have much influence. Increased urbanization but a "mass market" does not yet exist.
Climbers Brazil, Venezuela, Portugal, Mexico, Taiwan, Malaysia, Turkey, South Korea	Population growth: under 1.5% Median age: 30+ Children: 2 Reaching maximum longevity GNP per capita: greater than $8,000	Industrialization and service sector expenditures assume greater importance. Private enterprises have become more dominant than the state agencies. Good opportunities for joint ventures and technology agreements. Growing mass market.
Luxury and leisure societies United States, Canada, Japan, United Kingdom, Australia	Zero or very little population growth Median age 30+ Reaching maximum longevity GNP per capita greater than $8,000	Substantial discretionary income and availability of credit. Restructuring of economy. Maturing markets. Intense competition. Relocation away from large population centers.
The rocking chairs West Germany, Switzerland, Luxembourg, The Netherlands	Fertility rates below replacement level Median age: 37 Children: less than 2 Peak life expectancy GNP per capita: greater than $10,000	Dominance of service economy and high-technology sectors. Highly segmented markets. Ideal distribution and communications channels.

similar patterns. The study concluded with a caution, however. The clusters can still be useful in other ways. In particular, echoing other studies, the authors suggest that clusters of countries can be useful to gain scale economies in the execution of marketing research, uniformity of packaging, simplifying logistics, and similar promotions. Overall, managerial judgment is necessary to fully evaluate the benefits of these broadly defined clusters.

Less-general variables have been used for macrosegmentation, depending on the purpose of the segmentation. In an imaginative study for the purpose of developing reactions to a global advertising campaign, two researchers clustered countries on the basis of "think" and "feel" variables.[15] The "think" variables included cultural and

EXHIBIT 11.8
"Think" and "Feel" Country Clusters

Source: Fred Zandpour and Katrin R. Harich, "Think and Feel Country Clusters: A New Approach to International Advertising Standardization," *International Journal of Advertising* 15 (1996), p. 341. Reproduced with kind permission of the World Advertising Research Center (www.warc.com).

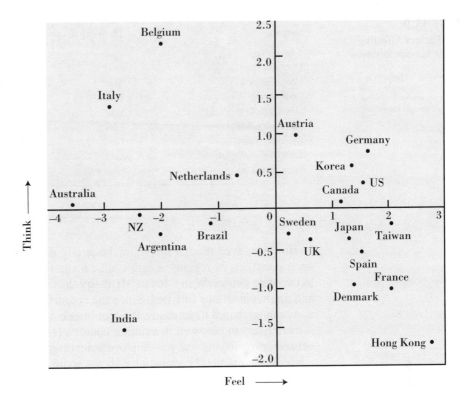

regulatory variables that suggested the population's inclination to approach communications on a "left-brain" critical reasoning basis. For example, countries with low tolerance for risk and with strong regulation of advertising content score high on the "think" dimension. The "feel" dimension captured the degree to which a country's population tend to be impulsive, want excitement, and become emotionally involved with products and people. Based on the resulting mapping of countries (see Exhibit 11.8), the authors were able to define clusters where the advertising appeals should use rational arguments and a lecture format, and other clusters where the appeal should be primarily emotional and dramatic. Again, however, the fact that these techniques need to be matched against managerial judgment is suggested by the fact that Italy is shown to prefer "high-think" and "low-feel" advertising, contrary to what most cultural analysts would suggest (see Gannon's metaphors in Chapter 3, for example).

Diversification versus Focus

The clustering approach to macrosegmentation leads generally to the identification of similar markets. However, some companies make a conscious effort to be a player in different markets and different clusters. This is done in order to balance market countries so that the international "portfolio" of countries provides diversification protection against the risk of large losses. This has become increasingly important since political risk remains high and financial turmoil spreads quickly through tightly integrated global markets.

Examples of **diversification strategies** are common. Volvo, the Swedish carmaker, limited its U.S. market involvement to 25 percent of total output for many years. In personal interviews with top management, Toyota executives reported feeling uneasy when their exports take more than 50 percent of their home market demand.[16] The recent tendency is for Japanese exporters to limit their unit shares going to the U.S. market, not only in autos but in electronics. The fear of too great a reliance on the U.S. market is palpable, especially at times when the United States seems to be vacillating in its adherence to free trade.

EXHIBIT 11.9
Market Factors Affecting Choice of Market Portfolio

Source: *Journal of Marketing* by Ayal and Zif. Copyright © 1979 by the American Marketing Association in the format Textbook via Copyright Clearance Center.

Factors	Diversity If:	Focus If:
Growth rate	Low	High
Demand stability	Low	High
Competitive lag	Short	Long
Spillover	High	Low
Need to adapt product	Low	High
Need to adapt promo	Low	High
Marginal sales	Diminishing	Increasing
Need for control	Low	High
Entry barriers	Low	High

However, even though there may be strong diversification benefits from entering several markets or regions, a case can be made for focusing on a few similar markets in the same cluster. With a **focus strategy** these markets can be given more attention and market positions fortified. Since the countries are relatively similar, spillover effects can be shared more easily. Product lines can be the same. Good advertising copy is more likely to play well in a similar country. How should a company strike a balance between diversifying and possibly overextending itself versus being too dependent on a few single markets? Exhibit 11.9 shows some of the market factors that need to be considered.[17]

As can be seen in the exhibit, high-growth markets require more marketing support for a brand, and a focused strategy tends to be desirable. On the other hand, instability and competitive rivalry in the market increase the benefits of diversification. When decisions have to be custom-tailored to the local market, there is greater need for focus. The "marginal sales" condition refers to the shape of the sales response curve to increased marketing expenditures. If the markets respond strongly to an increase in expenditures (the sales response curve shows a region of increasing returns), it will pay to focus and spend more, since every dollar spent brings in increasingly more sales.

Empirical research has shown that generally diversified strategies tend to lead to greater sales abroad, while concentrated or focused strategies tend to result in somewhat higher profitability.[18] One prime determinant of profitability is whether the firm can identify and track cost effectiveness, something that is easier in focused strategies. In firms aiming for diversification, sales objectives and market orientation tend to be more important than costs, leading to greater sales. In either case, global strategies proved more successful for companies whose objectives were clearly articulated than for companies with more diffuse objectives, where coordination was less effective.

A Case Illustration

To see how the two-stage segmentation procedure works in practice, a case study of a pan-European segmentation scheme for a consumer packaged goods company is instructive.[19] The company had initially used an unsegmented strategy in Europe, and had been disappointed by the performance of some its brands. Although successful in one or two countries, several new products were less successful when introduced in other European countries. The company had become aware that not all the receptive target segments were of equal size in each country, and decided to do in in-depth analysis of pan-European segmentation.

The company first clustered the EU countries using economic data on market size and demographics coupled with some product- and company-specific data (e.g. presence of the company in a country market). This stage resulted in two macrosegments, the largest five countries (Germany, United Kingdom, France, Italy, and Spain) and the "other" countries. Since the five largest countries accounted for 80 percent of the population, the company decided to focus on that cluster.

In the second stage, market research was conducted in the five countries to identify similarities and differences. Because the managerial problem involved new product acceptance rates, it was decided to focus the survey questions around the concept of "innovativeness." Following past research in the diffusion of innovation literature, the basic hypothesis was that each country would show some pioneers and early adopters, the kind of people important for the success of a new product (and the kind of people important in the early stage of the product life cycle introduced in Chapter 1). By identifying these "innovator" segments and measuring their size in the different countries, the company could then decide whether a coordinated introductory campaign would be likely to succeed in all five countries.

A key question facing the managers was where to make the cutoff for the "innovative" segments. There is no hard and fast rule that says that someone is an innovator if he or she scores higher than, say, a "5" on a 7-point innovation scale. But from past research it has been determined that the pioneers and early adopters constitute approximately 16 percent of any population. So, the researchers pooled the data for all five countries, and found the scale score above which 16 percent of the total number of respondents from all five countries was classified as "innovators." They then identified from which countries these innovative respondents came, and could then determine whether all countries had an equal portion of innovators.

What did the company find? It found that the innovativeness among consumers differed considerably between the five countries. Some countries had significantly more innovators than others. This meant that if "innovators" were targeted everywhere, the strategy would do well in some countries but not in others. Although disappointed, management uncovered the reason for lackluster sales of new products in some of the countries. Many of their initial new product introductions took place in one country (the United Kingdom) with a large proportion of innovators. When the product rollout then continued across Europe with a similar product formulation and marketing mix, the later countries did not respond as anticipated, simply because they had fewer innovators in the marketplace. A standardized pan-European strategy could not work. By using an adapted segmentation strategy the company estimated it was able to increase the effectiveness of its new product introductions by 50 percent on average.

Targeting Segments

Which countries and segments the company decides to target depends on several factors. First, if done correctly the segmentation scheme developed will already have taken certain feasibility factors into account. Thus, the potential countries and segments should be "reachable" and the segment members should be able and willing to buy the product. We have also seen that the microsegmentation stage has identified the size of the segments, making it possible to compute a sales potential for each candidate country and segment. To decide on the target, however, the firm needs also to develop a forecast of the market share the firm is likely to gain in each country and segment and the costs of achieving it. This means that targeting decisions need to be based on the competitive intensity in each country and the firm's competitive advantages and disadvantages in the segment. And it is important to recognize that the best target consumers might see other benefits in the product than marketers or consumers in the original country (see box, "Red Bull's Moving Target").

Competitive Analysis

The competitive analysis draws on the principles and tools presented in Chapters 2 and 4. To determine the level of competitive intensity, the firm has to go beyond the simple identification of which domestic and global competitors operate in each market and which segments they target. The firm also needs to assess the commitment of these firms to defending their market positions, and the resources they can marshal to sustain their local advantages in selected segments. When the Japanese carmakers attacked the

Getting the Picture

RED BULL'S MOVING TARGET

The Red Bull energy drink is recognized worldwide as being a trendy, stylish tonic drink for sports enthusiasts, over-worked urbanites, and clubgoers. Its home country is widely perceived to be Austria but its roots are in Thailand, where the brand was originated in 1981 by the Yoovidhya family. Dietrich Mateschitz, now said to be Austria's richest businessman, drank Red Bull on a trip to Asia, and decided to import the product into Europe.

In the 1980s and the early 1990s it was very common to see Red Bull and other energy drinks in Asia marketed toward machine operators and late-night workers. Its main target audience was the C and D market, which consisted mainly of laborers who needed that second wind or that extra pick-me-up to finish a long day's work. Thailand, the Philippines, Malaysia, and Indonesia aired television commercials for Red Bull featuring a sleepy truck driver. The ad emphasized Red Bull's ability to keep people awake, alert, and safe. Other commercials featured a boxer who needed a Red Bull just to get through another round.

Since the exodus from Asia into Europe, Red Bull's target market shifted dramatically. From blue-collar workers, the targeting first shifted to athletes, and then to the party crowd and bar-hoppers. When Red Bull was launched in Germany in the late 80s, it coincided with the all-night rave and party scene. This allowed Red Bull to become instantly "cool." At some point, Red Bull was actually banned in Germany. Red Bull's global tagline "Red Bull gives you wings!" has since shaped consumer perceptions of the product as more than an energy drink.

Gaining cult status, Red Bull shifted its target market from the blue-collar audience in Asia to the trendy youths and adults across Europe, and then America. And like any successful global brand, Red Bull trickled back into Asia with a newer target market in mind. Red Bull vodkas are now part of the drinks list in any stylish bar in Shanghai, Kuala Lumpur, Manila, and Bangkok.

Sources: Boonsong Kositchotethana, "Austrian Marketing Mogul Puts Stamp on Thailand's Original Red Bull Drink," *Bangkok Post Thailand,* August 29, 2003; Abram Sauer, "Red Bull all the Rage," *Brand Features–Brand Channel,* Online Internet, available from **http://www.brandchannel.com/features_profile.asp? pr_id=44 [2004];** www.epinions.com; *Speed-in-a-Can: The Red Bull Story,* Plan B—White Papers, Online Internet, available from **http://www.plan-b.biz/pdf/Speed_In_a_Can.pdf** [2004].

American auto market in the 1970s they targeted the small car segment, which was not a high priority among the American carmakers. By contrast, as the sports utility SUV segment emerged strongly in the latter half of the 1990s, the Japanese initially decided not to challenge the Americans. (Ironically, since the global auto market is a prime example of hypercompetition, in both cases the reluctance—by the Americans in the 1970s and by the Japanese in the 1990s—proved wrong in hindsight).

There are several other factors that need to be considered in the competitive analysis. One is the degree to which customers are loyal to home country brands. A domestic company that can count on local brand loyalty can be a much more formidable competitor than an analysis by numbers only might suggest. Thus, for example, the very fragmented German beer market, with most citizens favoring their own town beer, would seem a very easy conquest for a large global brewer such as Heineken. The fact is that the locals are very loyal. For example, the citizens of Cologne still favor "Kölsch," a fresh draft beer served in small juice-size glasses so it doesn't turn bad before the glass is emptied.

The firm also needs to do a very careful assessment of its own competitive advantages, the kind of firm-specific and country-specific advantages already discussed in Chapter 2, and how these advantages can be leveraged in each potential market segment. For example, even if Heineken might not have much competitive strength in the heavy user segment of the German beer market, it might stand a better chance in a more cosmopolitan segment where its prestige brand image would be appreciated more.

Profitability Analysis

Before doing a forecast of projected sales and revenues from each country and segment, competitive advantages need to be translated into market share estimates, using the tools and techniques discussed in Chapter 4. In global segmentation this needs to be done across all the countries in the selected cluster or clusters. Not a small task for any company, with strong need for combining managers' qualitative judgments with quantitative forecasts. A recent article suggests that managers should develop alternative strategy scenarios, which could then be evaluated using spreadsheet analysis. The advantage with this approach is that the outcomes of alternative strategies could be simulated on the spreadsheet, and the sensitivity of any solution to the assumptions made could be tested directly.[20]

The targeting decision needs, of course, to be based not only on forecasted revenues but also on costs of achieving those revenues. This brings back into focus the question of standardized versus adapted marketing strategies. Although there can be revenue payoffs to global coordination—the positive demand spillover from a global brand, for example—the major benefits from coordination are found on the cost side. Small and unnecessary design differences between local variants of the same product add to production cost and forgo scale economies. Advertising campaigns can be more cost-effective when usable for similar segments in different countries. Integrated distribution channels with reach into many markets can be used to cut shipping costs. Centralized purchasing for components of standardized products cut supplier costs. Global coordination of marketing strategy is often preferable from a cost perspective.

But such coordination also means that the product and the rest of the marketing mix are not adapted optimally to the local market. Where to strike the balance between complete standardization and local adaptation of the marketing is perhaps the major problem in global marketing. Deciding which segments to target in which countries and how to do it requires assessment of revenues and costs for a range of alternatives. Forecasted revenues and costs need to be tested against various levels of centralized coordination and standardization across countries, a big job. It is not surprising to find that the early multinationals allowed subsidiaries to localize strategies and treated them as freestanding profit centers. It is also true that many global companies still have trouble striking the right balance between global coordination and complete adaptation. Still, as technology and global communications have made global coordination increasingly feasible, global firms try to capture the cost efficiencies of coordination and to leverage their firm-specific advantages in countries and segments where at first glance they seem an ill fit.

A good illustration of the problem is Dell's entry into China. Dell is one of the leading PC makers in the world, well known for its reliance on a direct-sales business model. This means that even individual customers deal directly with Dell salespeople, over the phone or over the Internet. Dell has also been very successful in the business-to-business office equipment market, where the direct sales model is more natural because each transaction involves more money. However, in the mainland China market, the office segment involves sales to many government-owned businesses, for which high-level contacts and personal relationships were assumed important. Face-to-face contacts are not easily replaced by e-mail and Internet connections, the communication media employed in the Dell model. In addition, the direct-sales model assumes a certain technical sophistication on the part of the buyer to be willing to buy without actually seeing and touching the product. Going against local sensitivities, Dell reasoned that its competitive strength resided in the direct model, and proceeded to enter China by establishing an assembly plant and customer call center in Xiamen, which follows the same standardized sales model used by Dell elsewhere. The company was successful, with Chinese purchasing managers of information technology hardware willing and able to go along with less handholding and less personal interaction—and a better price.

Global Product Positioning

As with segmentation and targeting, a key question in global positioning is the degree to which the position should be identical in all countries. Many global brands attempt as much similarity as possible to reinforce their image, not always succeeding. Coca-Cola's is fun, refreshing, and young everywhere. Its "Always" slogan is omnipresent. Sony is "innovative" and higher priced everywhere, even at home in

Japan. But McDonald's has had to change its American fast-food image to a more localized "destination" position in several European countries by adapting menus, changing decor, and providing more comfortable chairs. And even if the same segment is targeted everywhere, it does not follow that the positioning need be the same. A classic example is Levi's jeans, targeting young people all over the globe, but positioned as fun and practical at home in the United States while overseas it is positioned on status as the original jeans.

Key Positioning Issues

Two major considerations play a role in the chosen positioning strategy: The degree to which the market is global and the stage of the product life cycle (the PLC).

In a global market, the product attributes and benefits customers look for are similar. As we saw in Chapter 1, technology markets tend to have these characteristics. In B2B technology markets in particular, the important attributes and customer preferences are often similar across markets (as we saw in the Dell in China case above). But also in consumer technology markets the similarities are often strong. In cell phones, for example, most consumers seem to look for the same attributes, even though the constant stream of new features changes what those features are, seemingly overnight. In these kinds of global markets, uniform positioning is feasible and desirable. **Uniform positioning** means that products, brand names, marketing communications, and distribution channels are similar across countries to provide demand spillovers and cost efficiencies.

In more multidomestic markets, such as food and clothing, consumers in different countries will be looking at products with different eyes. They will prefer more salt to more sugar, less to more butter, practicality and durability more than fashion, and so on. As we saw in the segmentation section, there could still be segments that are similar across countries, but their sizes vary. Uniform positioning in these kinds of multidomestic markets is less beneficial, as we saw in the McDonald's and Levi's examples above.

A second major factor in global positioning decisions is the stage of the PLC. Typically, different country markets are at different stages of the PLC, and this makes a uniform positioning less attractive.

As a rule, **product positioning** is particularly important in the mature stages of the PLC. In some sense positioning is not possible at too early a stage, because in the introductory stage customers have not yet learned enough about the product to understand the attributes and form preferences. This is why the first mover has a chance to educate potential customers and create an advantage as the original innovator. In global marketing this is a common case, with an entrant from a leading market—which has matured, and where sales growth is slowing down—expanding abroad to capture new markets. A typical case is America Online, now AOL, the company that became an early provider of home Internet access. By providing access at a low subscription price and offering features such as chat rooms, AOL not only educated people in Internet use but also tied

The Chevrolet Suburban has long been one of General Motors' most successful large vehicles, predating the SUV boom of the 1990s by more than 50 years. Its styling is unabashedly practical and utilitarian, with lots of space and a high ride for rough roads. The interior can be customized, however, with comfortable seats, high-performance audio and video systems—and bulletproof body and windows.

Getting the Picture

POSITIONING AN OLD GAS-GUZZLER: THE CHEVY SUBURBAN

The Chevy Suburban was one of Chevrolet's pickup truck offerings already back in 1936, and it is still one of the more popular brands of SUVs (Sport Utility Vehicles) in America. The Suburban features a powerful Vortec V8 engine, a new 2WD Z71 sporty model, and hauling capabilities unsurpassed in its class. It has 131.6 cu. ft. of space, which means there's room for all your stuff, but it gets less than 10 miles to the gallon with regular driving. At the turn of the millennium, the question was how it could survive against all the new competitors. The "Suburban" name tag seemed so old and boring when compared to its new SUV competitors: Amigo, Aviator, Sidekick, Hummer, Blazer, Discovery, Defender, Escape, Excursion, Expedition, Explorer, Forester, Freelander, Mountaineer, Navigator, Scout, Tracker, Trooper, Wrangler, Escalade, Sportage, Terracross. The Suburban did stand out from these other brands—but mainly because of its lack of aggressiveness and with no outdoorsy image.

Research uncovered a solution. Among dozens of SUV models from other automakers, the Chevy Suburban rated above all other brands (except Jeep) in terms of levels of engagement. "Engagement" referred to the amount of mental meaning (stories, associations, imagery, ideas) the Chevy Suburban name evoked, and how personally engaged consumers were in the brand name. The long history and

tradition of the Suburban had implanted the brand into the consciousness from the time when the now-adult Americans had been small children. This traditional theme was emphasized explicitly in the positioning statement and the promotional campaign, helping to differentiate the car from the newcomers.

But of course such an American traditional image—not to mention its gas-guzzling-is hard to market overseas. Consequently, while the sales of the Suburban continue to climb in America, its sales elsewhere are negligible—in terms of units sold, that is. But for special purposes, the Suburban has become a favorite. In the Middle East, for example, the journalists covering the Iraq war tracked across the desert terrain, followed military vehicles, and avoided grenade fire in Suburbans. In Latin America, the SUV is favored by VIPs, dignitaries, celebrities, or other important officials because of a customized feature: armored and bulletproof Suburbans. This custom Suburban is also a favored vehicle of the U.S. Central Intelligence Agency for their covert operations in foreign countries.

Mass market here becomes a niche market there.

Sources: Jeremy Cato, "Suburban is solid, stalwart and, surprisingly, nimble: Quadrasteer turns the new Suburban into a very nimble machine," *The Standard (Ontario)*, May 8, 2003, p. D1; **www.chevrolet.com;** "Taxonomy of Sport Utility Vehicle Names," Igor Naming and Branding Agency, Online Internet, Available from **http://www.igorinternational.com/suv-names-taxonomy. html** [2004].

up users to its own Web site. Going abroad, the company used its first-mover advantage from the leading U.S. market to strike alliances with local providers. The only positioning shift was to disguise the American connection by rebranding to AOL, on the premise that Internet users want local customer service (AOL's international expansion is discussed in Case 2.4).

In the later stages of the PLC, customers tend to understand product features well; they have established preferences and even loyalties to existing brands. Positioning becomes much more important, because the firm needs to communicate exactly what its brands' particular strengths are relative to competition. Because of the spillover benefits and cost savings of uniform positioning, where all countries in a selected cluster have markets at the maturity stage of the PLC, the firm needs to consider a uniform global positioning strategy. Of course, where usage conditions differ significantly, the fact that the markets are mature everywhere does not necessarily mean that consumers should be approached similarly (see box, "Positioning an Old Gas-Guzzler: The Chevy Suburban").

Global STP Strategies

What kind of segmentation-targeting-positioning (STP) strategies do global marketers employ and under what conditions? There are of course a number of alternative strategies depending on the level of similarity across segments targeted and the degree to which the positioning is uniform (see box, "Keegan's Positioning Strategies").

In broad terms, however, one can distinguish four generic situations: similar segments and similar positioning; similar segments but different positioning; different segments but similar positioning; and different segments and different positioning.

Getting the Picture

KEEGAN'S POSITIONING STRATEGIES

By focusing on two main aspects of the marketing mix, product and promotion, Keegan identified four basic positioning strategies that companies can use.

One strategy is *product-communications extension,* simply extending the existing product line and advertising appeals to the countries entered. This approach involves lower expenditures but naturally does not work in multidomestic markets. It fits a company such as Coca-Cola, since consumer preferences and competitive conditions for colas tend to be similar across countries.

A second alternative is *product extension-communications adaptation.* This involves repositioning a global product. The Minolta Maxxum, a leading automatic single-lens reflex (SLR) camera, is a good example. In Japan and Europe it is a camera for serious amateurs; young adults who are interested in the technology. In the United States, on the other hand, the camera's appeal is to a broader group of people, including families and older adults.

A third strategy, *product adaptation-communications extension,* can work well when product usage changes but the message can be the same. The well-known Exxon slogan "Put a Tiger in Your Tank" has been used successfully across the globe for many years. The gasoline itself, however, has been adapted by the use of additives to account for differences in climate, season, and performance requirements in various countries.

The fourth strategy alternative is *dual adaptation,* involving both product localization and communications adaptation. Benetton, the Italian apparel maker, has used this strategy in Southeast Asian markets. Because people's body proportions are not the same the world over, and because the preferred range and intensity of colors also differ, the designs have to be altered. Also, attempts to extend Benetton's politically charged European advertising have met with resistance from local retailers, whose customers are willing to buy the Italian design image but not Benetton's societal concern.

Source: Keegan, 1969.

The cross-classification in Exhibit 11.10 identifies the four alternatives and gives illustrative examples.

In the exhibit, two alternative market segmentation cases (similar and different) are crossed against two positioning appeals (similar, different). A *similar* segment refers to a segment that is basically universal, the same across countries— "teenagers," say, or "young professionals." A *different* segment is one that is unique in each country (for example, "college students" in country A, and "families with children" in country B). For the product positioning dimension, *similar* indicates a positioning that is uniform across countries, while *different* indicates that the positioning theme is adapted across countries.

Cell 1: *Similar segment, similar positioning.* A true global strategy. Exemplifying this cell, Nike's global brand appeals to young boys and aspiring athletes, whether they play on the streets of Buenos Aires, Philadelphia, Seoul, or Helsinki. The high-performance positioning is underscored by the use of well-known athletes.

Cell 2: *Similar segment, different positioning.* Here the positioning is adapted. As mentioned in several places in this book, Levi's jeans are a status symbol in many countries, while the American home market takes a more prosaic view of the

EXHIBIT 11.10

Segmentation and Positioning Examples for Global Products

Local Market Segment

		Similar	Different
Positioning	Similar	– Nike	– IKEA – Mobile phones
	Different	– Levi's – Pampers	– Volvo – Honda Prelude

denims. Similarly, as we saw in Chapter 1, the P&G Pampers' successful positioning message in Japan focused on happy babies rather than inconvenienced mothers.

Cell 3: *Different segments, similar positioning*. Here segments differ but the positioning appeals stay the same. Across the world IKEA offers largely the same selections and offers the same furniture as self-assembled kits, immediately available. But whereas the target segments everywhere include families with children, in the United States there is much greater stress on singles, while in Europe newly married couples are a prime target. In the case of mobile phones, this "must-have" product for young professionals in most places was in Scandinavia first used by delivery men.

Cell 4: *Different segments, different positioning*. A localized, nonglobal strategy. That target segment and positioning appeal can differ even though the product is standardized is easily seen in the case of Volvo cars, a car for the rugged individual in Europe. Volvo users in the U.S. market, families with small children, have traditionally been appealed to in terms of safety and upscale income. Another case in this cell is the Honda Prelude, a small sport coupe for singles, which has become a woman's car in the North American market, against the strategic intent of the company.

These cases go to show that with proper segmentation and positioning it is possible to standardize products—and positioning—even though the segments targeted are not universal or even very similar in different countries.

Many factors help determine which particular STP strategy is preferable. In an interesting empirical assessment of how companies' choice of strategy is impacted by country and market factors, the authors found that a few key factors influence company choice.[21] For the cell 1 strategy (similar segment, similar positioning) to be preferable, the countries should be similar in terms of macroeconomics (GDP per capita, economic growth rate). The consumers should be similar in terms of attitudes and product usage, and the local cultures and lifestyles should be similar.

For the cell 2 strategy (similar segment, different positioning) to be optimal, the macroeconomic factors and sociodemographics should be similar but the consumers should differ in terms of attitudes, product usage, and local culture, making an adapted positioning strategy necessary. The cell 3 strategy (different segments, similar positioning) is advantageous when product usage, attitudes, and demographics are similar, but local cultural and economic factors make it difficult to target the same segment everywhere. Finally, the cell 4 strategy (different segment, different positioning) is the best option when brand loyalty in the marketplace is high, regardless of other conditions. This is natural since this is the true localization option.

Global Marketing Planning

This section offers a step-by-step planning guide for the evaluation of the potential benefits and costs of global marketing strategies. It is best used in conjunction with other planning tools in corporate and marketing strategy and focuses primarily on the systematic assessment of a globally coordinated marketing strategy for a specified product or service.

The planning process involves a sequence of five steps. Each of these steps can be completed by following the worksheets presented below.

Step 1. The first step in globalizing the marketing for a given product or service involves the degree to which industry factors are conducive to globalization. The first worksheet evaluates the drivers involved, as specified in Chapter 1 (market, competition, cost, technology, and government). Once the systematic evaluation is done following the worksheet, management needs to use judgment to decide whether to pursue globalization further.

Step 2. If it is decided to pursue globalization, the next step is to evaluate the local situations in various countries. The goal is to see whether there are differences between local markets that may prohibit standardization and uniformity and whether the local marketing strategies need to be different. For start-up firms without presence in foreign markets, this step can be shortened, but several issues still need to be considered.

In step 2 the environmental differences across countries that affect marketing most are selected from the listing in Chapter 7, Exhibit 7.10. The key success factors of the industry in the particular country are matched against the company's country- and firm-specific advantages. The degree to which a particular country is a leading country is also factored in. For firms with subsidiaries overseas, this step also involves assessing whether the local subsidiaries can support a globalized strategy. This step is best completed with input directly from local managers.

Step 3. Given the input on the local market differences from step 2, the next step is to formulate the proposed global strategy. For firms with existing presence abroad, this is best done in terms of deviations from the current strategy in the local markets. The strategy formulated for each of the marketing activities will tend toward uniformity where there are only small differences between countries and toward adaptation where differences in step 2 are large.

Step 4. The next step is to get the proposed strategy evaluated at the local level to predict the likely effects of the strategy changes proposed. This again should be done with input from local managers. The entries here are necessarily estimates, possibly subjective, and an effort should be made to counter any particular local biases by relying on more than one source of information.

Step 5. The final step is to sum up the positive and negative benefits for each local market, and match the sum against the potential savings from centralized operations to arrive at a net benefit from the proposed global strategy.

The worksheet formats presented below should be viewed as a place to start, and typically will be in need of specific additions for any particular industry or business. Also, the strategic planning process in the typical multinational will need to fold the plan into the umbrella of the business unit and the corporate strategy overall. A good format for the corporate strategy assessment is offered in Chapter 10 of George S. Yip, *Total Global Strategy* (Englewood Cliffs, NJ: Prentice Hall, 1995). There can also be a need for more detailed marketing plans at the local level. The format for such a marketing plan is quite standardized—for one example, see Chapter 1 of Donald R. Lehmann and Russell S. Winer, *Analysis for Marketing Planning,* 2nd ed. (Homewood, IL: Irwin, 1991). For foreign entry strategies, see Chapters 4–6 of this book.

GLOBAL MARKETING PLANNING PROCESS

STEP 1.

INDUSTRY DRIVERS FAVORING GLOBALIZATION (Circle one number; 1 = very unfavorable, 5 = very favorable)					
Market Drivers					
Common needs	1	2	3	4	5
Global customers	1	2	3	4	5
Global channels	1	2	3	4	5
Transferable marketing	1	2	3	4	5
Competitive Drivers					
Global competitors	1	2	3	4	5
Product differentiation	1	2	3	4	5
Cost Drivers					
Production: Scale savings	1	2	3	4	5
Scope savings	1	2	3	4	5
Sourcing: Scale savings	1	2	3	4	5
Scope savings	1	2	3	4	5
Marketing: Scale savings	1	2	3	4	5
Scope savings	1	2	3	4	5

Technology Drivers					
Importance of technology	1	2	3	4	5
Rate of new technology	1	2	3	4	5
Rate of new products	1	2	3	4	5
Government Drivers					
Trade bloc preferences	1	2	3	4	5
Country tariffs	1	2	3	4	5
Nontariff barriers	1	2	3	4	5

STEP 2.

LOCAL SITUATION ANALYSIS (A)
PRODUCT/MARKET

Macro Environment	Country A (scale 1 = low . . . 5 = high)	Country B	Country C . . .	Degree of Difference (1, . . . , 5)
Development level				
(emerging, new-growth, mature)	＿＿	＿＿	＿＿ . . .	＿＿
Political risk				
(low, medium, high)	＿＿	＿＿	＿＿ . . .	＿＿
Financial institutions				
(weak, protected, strong)	＿＿	＿＿	＿＿ . . .	＿＿
Tariff barriers				
(low, medium, high)	＿＿	＿＿	＿＿ . . .	＿＿
Nontariff barriers				
(low, medium, high)	＿＿	＿＿	＿＿ . . .	＿＿
Consumer mkt development				
(low, medium, high)	＿＿	＿＿	＿＿ . . .	＿＿
Industrial mkt development				
(low, medium, high)	＿＿	＿＿	＿＿ . . .	＿＿
Market Environment				
Product life cycle stage				
(introduction, growth, maturity, decline)	＿＿	＿＿	＿＿ . .	＿＿
Domestic competition				
(weak, strong)	＿＿	＿＿	＿＿ . . .	＿＿
Foreign competitors				
(weak, strong)	＿＿	＿＿	＿＿ . . .	＿＿
Distribution infrastructure				
(weak, developed)	＿＿	＿＿	＿＿ . . .	＿＿
Advertising media				
(weak, developed)	＿＿	＿＿	＿＿ . . .	＿＿

LOCAL SITUATION ANALYSIS (B)
PRODUCT/MARKET

Entry Mode	Country A	Country B	Country C . . .	Degree of Difference (1, . . . , 5)
(exporting, licensing, alliance, FDI)	_____	_____	_____ . . .	_____
Marketing control	_____	_____	_____ . . .	_____
Level of independence	_____	_____	_____ . . .	_____
Key Success Factors				
KSF 1	_____	_____	_____ . . .	_____
KSF 2	_____	_____	_____ . . .	_____
KSF 3	_____	_____	_____ . . .	_____
Country-Specific Advantages				
CSA 1	_____	_____	_____ . . .	_____
CSA 2	_____	_____	_____ . . .	_____
CSA 3	_____	_____	_____ . . .	_____
Firm-Specific Advantages				
FSA 1	_____	_____	_____ . . .	_____
FSA 2	_____	_____	_____ . . .	_____
FSA 3	_____	_____	_____ . . .	_____
Strategic Importance				
Locally	_____	_____	_____ . . .	_____
Globally	_____	_____	_____ . . .	_____
Leading market	_____	_____	_____ . . .	_____

LOCAL SITUATION ANALYSIS (C)
PRODUCT/MARKET

Local Marketing Strategy	Country A	Country B	Country C . . .	Degree of Difference (1, . . . , 5)
Objectives	_____	_____	_____ . . .	_____
Target segment(s)	_____	_____	_____ . . .	_____
Intended positioning	_____	_____	_____ . . .	_____
Local Marketing Mix				
Product line(s)	_____	_____	_____ . . .	_____
New product(s)	_____	_____	_____ . . .	_____
Brand name	_____	_____	_____ . . .	_____
Packaging design	_____	_____	_____ . . .	_____
Package sizes	_____	_____	_____ . . .	_____
Local positioning price	_____	_____	_____ . . .	_____
Price competition	_____	_____	_____ . . .	_____
Main currency price	_____	_____	_____ . . .	_____
Advertising creative	_____	_____	_____ . . .	_____
Advertising media	_____	_____	_____ . . .	_____
In-store promotion	_____	_____	_____ . . .	_____
Events, publicity	_____	_____	_____ . . .	_____
Distribution channels	_____	_____	_____ . . .	_____
Selling process	_____	_____	_____ . . .	_____
Customer service	_____	_____	_____ . . .	_____
Profitability				
Selling price	_____	_____	_____ . . .	_____
Unit variable costs	_____	_____	_____ . . .	_____
Profit margin	_____	_____	_____ . . .	_____
Percent of local profits	_____	_____	_____ . . .	_____

STEP 3.

PROPOSED PRODUCT/MARKET STRATEGY
Levels of Standardization (current from Step 2 = 0, target = X)

Marketing Strategy	Locally Adapted	Globally Uniform
Marketing objectives	...............O...................X...................	
Target segment(s)	...................................O...X..............	
Intended positioning	...................................O..........X..............	

Marketing Mix

Product line(s)	.................O....................X..............	
New product(s)	........................O.........X..............	
Brand name	....OX....	
Packaging design	...........O....X....................................	
Package sizes	.....O..X..	
Local positioning price	.........................O....X..............	
Main currency price	...........O....X....................................	
Advertising creative	...........O...............................X.	
Advertising media	...........O........X................................	
Advertising execution	.....OX..	
In-store promotion	........X.........O.................................	
Events, publicity	.....O.................X.............................	
Distribution channels	.....O.................X.............................	
Selling process	.................OX.................................	
Customer service	...........OX..	

STEP 4.

LOCAL REVENUE-AND-COST ANALYSIS
(deviations from current performance)
PRODUCT/MARKET

Revenues	Country A	Country B	Country C	. . .	Aggregate effect (sum)
Losses:					
Local mispositioning	_____	_____	_____	. . .	_____
Lack of local support	_____	_____	_____	. . .	_____
Gains:					
Demand spillover	_____	_____	_____	. . .	_____
Media spillover	_____	_____	_____	. . .	_____
Cost					
Increased:					
Coordination costs	_____	_____	_____	. . .	_____
Reduced:					
Production savings	_____	_____	_____	. . .	_____
Sourcing savings	_____	_____	_____	. . .	_____
Marketing savings	_____	_____	_____	. . .	_____
Net Benefits	_____	_____	_____	. . .	_____

STEP 5.

HEADQUARTER'S COST/BENEFIT ANALYSIS (deviations from current performance)			
Revenues	Sum of local effects	HQ's cost reductions	Total effect
Losses:			
Local mispositioning	———	———	———
Lack of local support	———	———	———
Gains:			
Demand spillover	———	———	———
Media spillover	———	———	———
Cost			
Increased:			
Coordination costs	———	———	———
Reduced:			
Production savings	———	———	———
Sourcing savings	———	———	———
Marketing savings	———	———	———
Net Benefits	———	———	———

Summary

The first task for the marketer intent on developing a global marketing strategy is to recognize that this strategy has to fit with the overall corporate strategy, which allocates resources between countries and products. Global marketing naturally is a top-down activity, with a selling orientation rather than a customer orientation. The trick is really to strike the proper balance between centralized control and responsiveness to the local market.

When target segments within countries are identified, the increase in data availability is making it possible to use traditional marketing techniques to identify similar segments across countries. The typical approach to global segmentation involves a two-stage procedure. In the first macrosegmentation stage, some form of cluster analysis is used to form groups of similar countries on broad economic and social indicators. In a second stage, microsegmentation analysis is used to identify which segments are similar across the countries in a given cluster.

To select countries for targeting, the analysis has to be extended to competitive intensity and the firm's competitive advantages and disadvantages in each segment. This evaluation should result in a prediction of the market share that the company can be expected to capture in a given country with a standardized global strategy. Then sales can be forecasted for the target countries and the projected strategy. Because of the complexity of these computations, in practice most firms will be content with fairly rough estimates of projected sales, but it is still important to carry out the basic steps in the process so that any obvious weaknesses of a global strategy can be uncovered.

Global product positioning involves predicting how local markets abroad might react to the introduction of a standardized product with a global brand. Universal segments can often be approached with relatively uniform positioning. But the relationship is not that simple. Even universally similar segments (such as teenagers) might need some adaptation of product or positioning. In other cases, globally coordinated strategies, standardized products, and even uniform strategies can be employed even where the segments approached are different.

Key Terms

cluster analysis, *382*

diversification strategy, *385*

focus strategy, *386*

growth-share matrix, *376*

macrosegmentation, *381*

microsegmentation, *381*

portfolio approach, *376*

product positioning, *390*

uniform positioning, *390*

Discussion Questions

1. For what products would a "selling orientation" be more acceptable to the local consumer abroad? When would it seem an affront to local culture? How is B2B different, if at all?

2. Why is a high-tech product more likely to appeal to the same segment everywhere, compared with a frequently purchased packaged good? Any examples?

3. Would services be more or less likely to have universal segments than products? Is the success of global fast-food restaurants (a service category) an exception or typical of services?

4. What are the advantages of "similar segments, similar positioning" in a product such as digital cameras? In cell phones? In leisure clothing? In athletic shoes? Any disadvantages?

5. When discussing resource allocation between products and countries, the chapter used the example of Samsung's M-Net program. Using this framework, apply its logic to a current strategic situation by a multinational, such as Wal-Mart's positions in Asia and Europe. What would you recommend to Wal-Mart?

Notes

1. The organizational structure of the global company is a topic in Chapter 18.

2. For a good discussion of the BCG growth-share matrix and the portfolio approach, see Kotler, 2000, pp. 67–73.

3. Note that the two major dimensions of this kind of matrix can be seen as "Market Size" and "Market Share." As we saw in Chapter 4, the typical forecasting equation used is Company Sales = Market Size x Market Share. The underlying logic is the same, matching the total market against what the company can capture.

4. See Harrell and Kiefer, 1981.

5. The Samsung case is discussed fully in Quelch and Harrington, 2003.

6. The M-Net model is presented in Corstjens and Merrihue, 2003.

7. See "100 Best Global Brands," *Interbrand,* 2007.

8. From Corstjens and Merrihue, 2003, p.8.

9. Ghemawat, 2007, ch.1.

10. The term *macrosegmentation* was first proposed by Wind and Douglas, 1972.

11. As research on trade patterns has shown, the trade within such regions tends to dominate the trade between the regions (see, for example, Rugman, 2001).

12. A compact and accessible treatment of both factor and cluster analysis can be found in Churchill and Iacobucci, 2005.

13. See Cavusgil, 1990.

14. See Helsen et al., 1993.

15. See Zandpour and Harich, 1996.

16. From Johansson, 1982.

17. See Ayal and Zif, 1979.

18. See Piercy, 1982, and also Lee, 1987.

19. This case is adapted from Steenkamp and Ter Hofstede, 2002.

20. See Agarwal, 2003.

21. Hassan and Craft, 2005.

Selected References

Agarwal, Manoj K. "Developing Global Segments and Forecasting Market Shares: A Simultaneous Approach Using Survey Data." *Journal of International Marketing* 11, no. 4 (2003), pp. 56–80.

Amine, Lyn S., and S. Tamer Cavusgil. "Demand Estimation in a Developing Country Environment: Difficulties, Techniques, and Examples." *Journal of the Market Research Society* 28, no. 1 (1986) pp. 43–65.

Ayal, I., and J. Zif. "Market Expansion Strategies in Multinational Marketing." *Journal of Marketing* 43 (Spring 1979), pp. 84–94.

Cavusgil, S. Tamer. "A Market-Oriented Clustering of Countries." In Thorelli, Hans B., and S. Tamer Cavusgil, eds. *International Marketing Strategy*, 3rd ed. New York: Pergamon, 1990.

Churchill, Gilbert A., Jr., and Dawn Iacobucci. *Marketing Research: Methodological Foundations,* 9th ed. Mason, OH: South-Western, 2005.

Corstjens, Marcel, and Jeffrey Merrihue. "Optimal Marketing." *Harvard Business* Review, October 2003.

Du Preez, Johann P.; Adamantios Diamantopoulus; and Bodo B. Schlegelmilch. "Product Standardization and Attribute Saliency: A Three-Country Empirical Comparison." *Journal of International Marketing* 2, no. 1 (1994), pp. 7–28.

Ghemawat, Pankaj. *Redefining Global Strategy: Crossing Borders in a World Where Differences Still Matter.* Boston: Harvard Business School Press, 2007.

Harrell, G. D, and R. O. Kiefer. "Multinational Strategic Market Portfolios." *MSU Business Topics* 21, no. 1 (1981), pp. 5–15.

Hassan, Salah S., and Stephen H. Craft. "Linking Global Market Segmentation Decisions with Strategic Positioning Options." *Journal of Consumer Marketing* 22, no. 2 (2005), pp. 81–89.

Helsen, Kristiaan; Kamel Jedidi; and Wayne de Sarbo. "A New Approach: Country Segmentation Utilizing Multinational Diffusion Patterns." *Journal of Marketing* 57, no. 4 (October 1993), pp. 60–71.

Johansson, Johny K. "A Note on the Managerial Relevance of Interdependence." *Journal of International Business Studies* (Winter 1982), pp. 143–45.

———, and Hans B. Thorelli. "International Product Positioning." *Journal of International Business Studies* XVI, no. 3 (Fall 1985), pp. 57–76.

Keegan, Warren. "Multinational Product Planning: Strategic Alternatives." *Journal of Marketing* 33 (January 1969), pp. 58–62.

Koten, John. "Car Makers Use 'Image' Map as Tool to Position Products." *The Wall Street Journal,* March 22, 1984, p. 31.

Kotler, Philip. *Marketing Management,* The Millennium ed. Upper Saddle River, NJ: Prentice-Hall, 2000 .

Lee, Chong Suk. *Export Market Expansion Strategies and Export Performance: A Study of High Technology Manufacturing Firms.* Doctoral dissertation, University of Washington, 1987.

Piercy, Nigel. "Export Strategy: Concentration on Key Markets vs. Market Spreading." *Journal of International Marketing* 1, no. 1 (1982), pp. 56-67.

Quelch, John, and Anna Harrington. "Samsung Electronics Company: Global Marketing Operations." Harvard Business School case no. 9-504-051, rev. April 3, 2007.

Ries, Al, and Jack Trout. *Positioning: The Battle for Your Mind.* New York: Warner Books, 1982.

Rugman, Alan M. *The End of Globalization.* New York: Amacom, 2001.

———.*The Regional Multinationals: MNEs and "Global" Strategic Management.* Cambridge: Cambridge University Press, 2005.

Steenkamp, Jan-Benedict E.M., and Frankel Ter Hofstede. "International Market Segmentation: Issues and Perspectives." *International Journal of Research in Marketing* 19 (September 2002), pp. 185–213.

Szybillo, George J., and Jack Jacoby. "Intrinsic versus Extrinsic Cues as Determinants of Perceived Product Quality." *Journal of Applied Psychology* (February 1974), pp. 74–78.

Urban, Glen L., and John R. Hauser. *Design and Marketing of New Products.* Englewood Cliffs, NJ: Prentice Hall, 1980.

Urban, Glen L., and Steven H. Star. *Advanced Marketing Strategy.* Englewood Cliffs, NJ: Prentice Hall, 1991.

Wind, Jerry, and Susan Douglas. "International Market Segmentation." *European Journal of Marketing* 6, no. 1 (1972).

Zandpour, Fred, and Katrin R. Harich. "Think and Feel Country Clusters: A New Approach to International Advertising Standardization." *International Journal of Advertising* 15 (1996), pp. 325–44.

Chapter

12

Global Products and Services

"Best in the world"

After reading this chapter, you will be able to:

1. Understand the benefits and drawbacks of product and service standardization for global companies.
2. Assess which products and services in the line are the best candidates for global standardization.
3. Evaluate which features of a product or service can be standardized across markets, and which need to be adapted to local markets.
4. Judge the diffusion rate of a new product or service and whether it should follow a waterfall or sprinkler strategy.
5. Identify the entry mode for a global service expansion that will best preserve the FSAs of the service.

One of the first questions that arises in global product management is, "Can this product be standardized globally?" While a customized offering is closest to the marketing ideal, there are cost savings in large scale that make global standardization preferable. There are also demand spillover effects from a uniform approach—in brand name recognition, trade support, prestige, and word-of-mouth. This chapter discusses the management of global products and services, including standardization, new product development, the foreign entry of services, and how to preserve service quality when expanding abroad.

Ford's Global Car Drive

Ford Motor is a company that has long tried to develop a global car. About 50 years ago, of course, the idea of a global car was far-fetched. Europeans drove European cars, Americans drove American cars, and only the Japanese drove Japanese cars. Today automobiles are by and large standardized products. As more and better roads are built in many countries, as local safety and pollution regulations become more similar reducing the need for design changes, as countries' economies grow to where more and more people can afford cars, and as trade barriers remain low, the main obstacle to complete standardization tends to be widely different gasoline prices. But some fuel-efficient cars—as well as some gas-guzzlers—can be found in all countries, as worldwide segments regardless of nationality emerge based on economic affluence.

Ford's first big effort to develop a global car was the Ford Fiesta, a subcompact car. Built in Ford's German factory in Cologne, the Fiesta was conceived as a "world car" in the early 1980s, and gradually rolled out from Europe to Latin America and Asia and then to the United States. However, while successful outside North America, the Fiesta proved less than fit for driving conditions and climate in the United States. After years of tinkering with the car's design and components, by early 1990, allegedly the only common part between the European and the American Fiesta was the fuel-filler door. Although the Fiesta continued to be produced at the Cologne factory, by 1993 Ford had pinned its global hopes on another model, the Mondeo.

The name was chosen for its association with the world in several different languages. A compact-to-intermediate car larger than the Fiesta, the Mondeo was to be built in three locations: in Belgium for Europe, in Missouri for North America, and in Mexico mostly for Latin America but also for the United States. Ford spent $6 billion for the design and manufacturing of the car. In 1994 Ford reported that 614,000 cars had been ordered in 48 markets around the world and that it expected those numbers to grow to about 800,000 annual sales in 59 countries (in both right- and left-hand-drive markets). Learning from the Fiesta experience, Ford built the Mondeo on a common base platform for all markets, and the same model line of four-door sedan and station wagon was available everywhere. There were still some localizing features such as a revised front end to accommodate a larger air-conditioning unit in the United States, some differences in available engine sizes, and a five-door hatch design in Europe.

Its European launch in March 1993 was a "sprinkler" simultaneous launch in 15 countries, with a standardized advertising message: "Beauty with Inner Strength." A sporty car with individual style, the Mondeo was named European Car of the Year in 1994, and sold over half a million units in Europe before its September 1994 American launch date.

Despite these early positive results, the Mondeo encountered problems similar to the Fiesta's. It did not do well in the United States. One problem was its size classification. In Europe its compact-to-intermediate size placed it in competition with the Nissan Primera and Toyota Carina, neither available in the United States. However, in the United States it became the smallest of the mid-sized sedans, with a price positioning it against the Honda Accord, the Nissan Altima, and even the Toyota Camry. Another problem was a change in name. To accommodate its two divisions, the Mondeo became the Ford Contour and the Mercury Mystique, neither of which could capitalize on any Mondeo spillover. And a third mistake was that the promotional campaign, which included sponsoring a *Star Trek* documentary, targeted not the younger buyers as in Europe but more aged baby boomers. As dealer inventories grew, the cars became known in industry parlance as the "Detour" and the "Mistake."

Not giving up, Ford's third effort is the Focus. Introduced in Europe in October 1998, the Focus is a subcompact car meant to replace both the Fiesta and the Contour/Mystic. Actually, not quite. The Focus has the same wheel base as the Fiesta—so it's a subcompact—but the roof has been raised so that it has more space internally, in fact as much as the Mondeo's. And both the Fiesta and the Mondeo are still produced and sold in markets outside North America. But the Focus is intended as a potential world car and in contrast to both the Fiesta and the Mondeo it has garnered favorable reviews and sales both in North America and elsewhere.

In 2001 the Ford Focus sold 895,700 units worldwide, making it potentially the most popular car in the world. Of these, 568,000 units were sold in Europe where the Focus has garnered several awards, including the most reliable car in Germany in 2001. Its success is not only due to high quality and reliability, but also its styling, with one popular model available as a hatchback. The younger market has also responded well to its creative and entertaining advertising. In one TV spot designed to show the advantage of a hatchback, a woman shopper with an eye for a good-looking clerk lets him help her load the car. As he does, she pushes him in and quickly shuts the hatchback door, then drives off with her bounty. Unfortunately, an outraged male viewer in Toronto who successfully complained to Canada's Advertising Standards Council led Ford to pull the commercial off the air.

Despite such bumps in the road, the Focus still sells briskly in all its markets as it is gradually rolled out across the globe. Perhaps the third time is a charm.

Sources: Crapo et al., 2001; "New Model from Ford Stable," *The Statesman,* January 13, 2002; "Spoilt for Choice," *Business and Finance,* January 24, 2002; Bill Vance, "Focus Reduces Weight, Keeps Room," *Design Product News,* February 2000; David Rider, "Ford Fights Council to Reinstate 'Offensive' Ad," *The Ottawa Citizen,* January 16, 2002; "Ford Focus Considered Most Reliable Car in Germany," *Economic News,* February 7, 2002.

Introduction

As we saw in Chapter 1, globalizing marketing involves global *coordination* of marketing activities. It means taking a *global strategy* perspective on the marketing operations in any one country. It involves a certain degree of marketing *standardization,* maintaining a degree of *uniformity* in product, advertising, distribution, and other marketing mix elements across country markets. In this chapter we will deal with the implications of globalized products and services marketing.

First some definitions. Marketers generally make a distinction between "global" and "regional" products and brands. **Global products** are usually standardized with some uniform features in all countries. In particular, brand names are often the same across countries. **Global brand** examples include Gillette razor blades, Colgate toothpaste, Sony television sets, and Benetton sweaters. By contrast, **regional products** and brands are unique to a particular trading region, such as Honda's "European" car model Concerto, P&G's Ariel and Vizir in Europe, the Mexican beer brewer Corona's "pan-American" market, and Korea's ginseng tea makers covering the Asian market. These regional products are latently global, as global expansion occurs and customers learn more about the products. Also, the marketing issues raised by regional products are similar in *kind* to those raised by global products; only the *degree* of complexity and the magnitude of the task are different. Where the regional market is large enough to offer the cost savings associated with standardization—reaching a "minimum efficient scale"—the marketing issue is to what extent the local markets can accept one standardized product. "Pan-European standardization" essentially poses the same problems as "global standardization."

This chapter first discusses the pros and cons of standardization and how managers balance the demand for local adaptation against the benefits of uniformity. The important distinction between localization and adaptation is clarified. Then we discuss some pitfalls of companies that have practiced product standardization. Then a section on global product lines leads into a discussion of global new product development and the diffusion of new products across countries. The chapter then deals with global services, and discusses the differences and similarities with goods marketing. The potential for globalizing services is discussed and the role of the service product life cycle is stressed. The chapter ends with a section on foreign entry modes in services, and how to preserve service FSAs when going abroad.

The Pros and Cons of Standardization

For most companies some product standardization is unavoidable. Cost savings from longer product series often outweigh the disadvantages of not being perfectly adapted to customers' precise requirements. At the same time, the customer satisfaction advantages of a high level of adaptation are well understood by most companies. The point at which the combined costs are at a minimum (see Exhibit 12.1) is the optimal level of standardization. Finding this point in practice is often a delicate balancing act.

EXHIBIT 12.1
Optimal Level of
Standardization

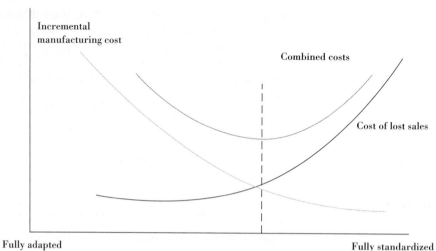

Incremental manufacturing cost

Combined costs

Cost of lost sales

Fully adapted

Fully standardized

Note that the minimum combined costs do not necessarily occur at the point of intersection—it depends on the actual slopes of the lines.

To evaluate the potential benefits of a standardized product or service strategy, it is useful to first summarize and review the advantages and drawbacks of standardized offerings. There are several pros and cons of standardization.[1]

The Advantages of Standardization

Cost Reduction

Cost reductions gained by **scale economies** constitute one major benefit from product standardization. Because of the longer production series there are considerable savings to be gained in manufacturing as well as purchasing. Product development costs can be spread over a larger number of units. Unnecessary duplication of effort, with minor variations in color or design of a product, can be avoided. Centralizing the purchase of media spots for advertising generates quantity rebates and other savings. When one global brand name is used in several countries, there are savings in media advertising and sales efforts. Furthermore, there are **scope economies** in marketing. The use of a globally standardized advertising campaign makes it possible to exploit good creative ideas to their fullest potential. Benetton's goodwill can be extended from apparel to sports gear. Advanced technology and new features can be used across a whole product line. New carbon material can be used for all tennis rackets, not just the upper end of the market.

Improved Quality

The standardized product or service is likely to offer improved quality in terms of functioning. Since additional resources can be focused on the product development effort and the design, the standardized product or service is likely to be more thoroughly tested. Investment in state-of-the-art production processes is justified. This leads to higher quality in terms of durability and reliability. The customized product may have more status and extra quality features—an expensive luxury car, for example, may have more expensive wood on the dashboard—but in terms of functionality, a standardized product is more likely to function well.

Enhanced Customer Preference

The firm can also enhance customer preferences by standardization. Positive experiences with a product in one country naturally encourage a consumer to buy the same brand elsewhere. One attractive feature of a camera can be that the same model is available in other countries, increasing the chance of getting service. Standardized advertising messages and slogans capitalize on spillover effects in marketing communications. Seeing attractive ads for the same camera at home and in a foreign country reinforces a customer's purchase decision. Tag Heuer, capitalizing on the recognition value of Tiger

Woods, the professional golfer, features him endorsing Tag Heuer watches in airport and magazine advertisements around the world.

Global Customers

There is also a special advantage to standardization because of global customers who demand uniform quality and services wherever they happen to be and buy. In consumer goods, global communications and the growth of international travel and tourism have helped spawn global markets for products as diverse as chocolate, watches, and apparel. In business-to-business markets, as firms grow more global and their purchasing function is centralized on a global basis, standardization of requirement specifications becomes necessary.

Global Segments

Finally, standardization has the advantage that it fits with the emergence of global customer segments. As we have seen, the customer segments in one market can often be similar to those in other markets. In technology-based product categories—computers, cameras, televisions—there are customer segments in various countries who all want similar products, and as these segments grow, the potential benefits of standardization grow as well.

The Drawbacks of Standardization

Off-Target

One drawback of standardized products or services is that they are likely to miss the exact target in terms of customer preferences in any one country. Where needs and wants across countries are homogeneous, this is not a problem. The problem is obvious in markets where customers in different countries have widely different tastes or needs. Offering only jumbo-sized packages of bathroom tissue makes no sense where storage capacity in the homes is limited.

Standardization may mean that some segments of the market are not targeted correctly, and the resulting positioning of many global products may be in the larger core segments of the market (the typical American and Japanese case) or in specialty niches (the more common approach for Europeans). Thus, IBM, Microsoft, Xerox, Sony, Panasonic, and Toyota tend to offer standardized products for core market segments in many countries, while Mercedes, Armani, Chanel, and Leica offer standardized products to upscale segments everywhere.

Lack of Uniqueness

There is also a drawback in the lack of uniqueness of standardized products. If customization or exclusivity is one of the overriding purchase considerations, a standardized

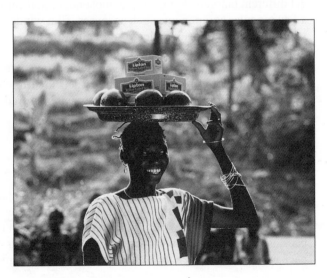

Lipton, the quintessentially British company now owned by Unilever, has long been a global player. Here it is sold in the Ivory Coast. Lipton's tea bags, packages, and labels might be the same everywhere, but its distribution is adapted to local conditions. Peter Hince.

offering is by definition in a weak position. As markets grow more affluent, uniqueness is likely to become increasingly salient. By contrast, in a period of recession, the luxury of being "special" might be forgone by the consumer.

Vulnerable to Trade Barriers

In order to reap the benefits of standardization, open trade regimes are necessary. The scale economies are difficult to realize unless production can take place in one or two countries, with plant capacity at least of the minimum efficient scale and with the standardized products exported globally. Where country markets are protected by trade barriers, local manufacturing may be necessary and the scale benefits from standardization can't be reaped. Then it may be better to target the local market specifically with an adapted product in order to avoid mispositioning.

Strong Local Competitors

Standardization can also fail simply because local competitors are capable and manage to mount a strong defense. By offering customized products, and working closely with local channel members and offering special services, the local competitor can hold off an attack from a global company. If, in addition, the global company is not able to execute effectively at the local level, the global strategy is likely to fail.

Which Features to Standardize?

In practice, 100 percent standardization is rare. Usually some features of a product need to be adapted.[2] For example, packaging should show information in the native language. Some global firms solve this problem by providing information in three or four languages on the same package. Personal care products in Europe typically come in packages with up to four languages (English, French, German, and Spanish, for example), making it possible to produce longer series and gain scale economies.

Standardization usually starts with a **core product** as the foundation. In automobiles this core is the "platform" chassis that forms the basic structure of the model. Then various features are added to the core product to complete the marketed product. These features may or may not be identical across countries. In the case of autos, for example, suspensions in Europe tend to be stiffer than in the United States to accommodate the more aggressive European driving habits. In the case of soft drinks, the adaptations may involve the development of smaller package sizes for some markets or a slight change in sugar levels. For example, Coca-Cola lowers the sugar content and uses smaller packages in Asian markets.

Standardization can also involve a **modular design.** Here the various features are prepackaged as modules that can then be assembled in different combinations to target different markets. For example, most nondigital cameras are now assembled from a few modular components such as lenses, film winder, body casing, flash unit, telescope motor, and various electronic chips for focus, aperture, and the like. These modular components can be produced in long series and then assembled to build a line of models at different prices. The flexibility created has also meant that companies are able to offer slightly different models in different countries, not only to adapt to demand differences but also to discourage gray trade—all at no loss of standardization advantages.

Localization Versus Adaptation

Successful companies often find that even the most standardized product or service usually requires some local changes. Every country has a few regulations not found elsewhere. For example, a country may demand certain product information on a package not needed in other markets. A case in point is the U.S. warning on cigarette packages about the health hazards associated with smoking, not required in many

Asian countries. Drivers in Sweden have to drive with their cars' parking lights on, and the lights are turned on automatically when the ignition key is turned. The United States is particularly confusing to foreign entrants since the individual states often feature separate requirements, such as the stricter pollution controls on cars registered in California compared with most other states.

Basic Requirements

But these differences do not mean "no standardization." Adhering to them involves localization more than true adaptation, an important difference in global marketing. **Localization** refers to the changes required for a product or service to function in a new country. For example, when a fax machine is fitted with a new type of telephone jack for a foreign country, it is "localized." When products are adapted, changes are made to match customer tastes or preferences. When the fax machine comes with a lighter handset for the Italian market, it is "adapted." Generally speaking, localization avoids having potential customers reject the product out of hand, while **adaptation** gives customers a positive reason for choosing it. Localization is a positive for all potential customers in the country, while adaptation aims to target some special segment or segments. Localization is necessary for consumers to even consider the product; adaptation tries to make them prefer it over other choices.[3]

In practice there is sometimes not a sharp and definite distinction between localization and adaptation. Disney's changes in its Disneyland Paris theme park is a mixture of both. Nevertheless, the distinction is very useful in analyzing the pros and cons of standardization. Even a "globally standardized" product needs to be localized. It would basically offer an unchanged core design and simply be refitted to a country's requirements.[4]

Compatibility Requirements

Localization is in many ways equivalent to compatibility. It represents the adjustments in the product specifications necessary for it to function in the foreign environment. With TV broadcast systems differing between European countries and the United States, VCRs need to be adapted. The sleeves of Western clothing need to be shortened for the Japanese market. Shampoos for the softer northern European hair are chemically different from those for southern Europeans' thicker hair. Effective skin care products need to be biogenetically different depending on the food of a nation's people. And so on.

Multisystem Compatibility

In many products today, localization is accomplished by building in compatibility with multiple systems at the outset. Thus, VCRs and TV sets are designed to operate in many system environments. Word processing software offers multiple formatting options, making it possible to transfer files between programs. Hardware developers offer built-in adapters and transformers that help make fax machines portable worldwide.

Multisystem compatibility ensures that localization requirements are satisfied. Products designed for easier construction are usually modularized, making the manufacturing more of an assembly task than before. Thus, building a camera or a motorcycle becomes something resembling the kit assembly of a model airplane. It is easy, then, to separate out those components requiring localization and to incorporate multiple options for those components alone. Laptop and notebook computers now come with adapters for various electric voltages. PCs offer expansion slots for floppy discs, sound cards, CD-ROM, and various other accessories, letting the buyer do the customization. IKEA, the furniture store chain, offers modular systems the customers can use to design different living environments in their homes. Multisystem compatibility makes it possible to generate the savings associated with long and standardized product series—even without the use of advanced robotics and flexible manufacturing systems.

Pitfalls of Global Standardization

Given the pros and cons of standardization, it is not surprising to find that companies do not always succeed with standardized product and service strategies. By systematically comparing the winners and losers, one researcher found that five factors explain why standardized products fail.[5]

1. Insufficient market research.
2. Overstandardization.
3. Poor follow-up.
4. Narrow vision.
5. Rigid implementation.

Insufficient Market Research

Good marketing research helps a standardized product strategy in two ways: (1) by correctly identifying commonalities and (2) by winning support from the local organizations involved in the research. In contrast, insufficient research means not only that similarities among customers are assumed rather than proved but also that the local subsidiaries feel stepped on. For example, when Polaroid introduced its pathbreaking SX-70 camera in Europe, the company employed the same advertising strategy—including TV commercials and print ads—it had used in its triumphant launch in the United States. When the local Polaroid executives protested that TV testimonials from unknown people would not be very useful for consumer perceptions in Europe and asked for a chance to do more research on possible replacements, headquarters refused. The subsequent lack of awareness and acceptance of the camera in Europe did not come as a surprise to the disenchanted local managers.

Overstandardization

Even though many technologically intensive products lend themselves to functional standardization, the same is not necessarily true of their positioning. The Canon AE-1 camera, the first automatic single-lens reflex introduced in the mid-1970s, was first positioned as an expert's choice in all markets. After a less than successful entry, the company decided to gamble and reposition it as a fun camera in the United States, taking on the then prevailing 110 standard Kodak camera. TV commercials were used, the first time ever for a single-lens reflex camera, using as a spokesman tennis player John Newcombe. The success of the new strategy led the company to reposition the camera in other markets as well, creating a much larger market for single-lens reflex cameras worldwide.

Poor Follow-Up

Impressive kickoff meetings, splashy presentations to country managers, and the personal appearance of the CEO are important attention-getters at the start of a global branding campaign. But these efforts need to be followed up diligently with communications, visits, and local effort if the campaign is to succeed. For example, after the German company Henkel to great fanfare launched a global campaign for its stick glue "Pritt" as an umbrella brand for related products, it failed to capitalize on the initial momentum. Instead of supplying extra resources and incentives to local units, the company left the implementation to be covered under the normal budget, forcing country managers to cut existing programs. Needless to say, as initial results proved weak, the resources were quickly reallocated to existing brands.[6]

Narrow Vision

There are two main approaches to organizing campaigns for standardized products. One is to direct the campaign from headquarters; the other is to designate a lead country, usually an important market for the product. Both approaches have their strengths, the main advantage of each being the clear focus of responsibility. However, the vision at the headquarters or in the lead country should not be narrow and inflexible. When Unilever introduced a new household cleaner Domestos, standardized for the pan-European market, the U.K. unit took on the lead role for global implementation. The problem was that the product was most successful in West Germany, where the local subsidiary had shifted the positioning from a "germ killer" to a "dirt remover." But this change in positioning was ignored by the U.K. unit, and its potential was lost, since other countries' organizations were not informed of it.

Rigid Implementation

When uniformity of marketing programs is dictated from headquarters, local units need to retain some flexibility in implementation. Not all local requests for deviations should be accepted, but shrewd managerial judgment is required to decide how far to go. When the U.S. subsidiary of Lego reported that an American competitor, Tyco, offered toys in a plastic bucket that could be easily used for storage and requested to be allowed to replace the globally standardized paperboard cartons with similar buckets, the Danish headquarters refused. After a two-year slide in market share, the headquarters finally relented. The Lego toys are now sold in plastic buckets worldwide.

Generally speaking, empirical research tends to show equivocal results as to the benefits of standardization. One study found that when standardized strategies were properly matched against homogeneous markets, sales growth improved but return on investment (ROI) did not.[7] Another study reported similar results, with sales growth affected positively by standardization strategies but with return on assets worse.[8] This study also found that the attractiveness of product standardization declined when market growth was slow; adaptation seems more beneficial in mature markets. In general, standardization seems to be associated with increased sales, while the effect on the bottom line is less clear.

Global Product Lines

Product lines in even the most global company are rarely identical across countries. Procter & Gamble has not introduced its detergents Ariel and Vizir in the United States. Coca-Cola sells its Georgia iced coffee and Aquarius isotonic drink in Japan but not at home. Honda's Concerto automobile is sold in Europe but not in North America.

There are varied reasons why product lines differ. Many are simply historical accidents.

- *History.* The different local products were well established before standardization and coordination were feasible and the benefits recognized. Several of P&G's brands in soaps and detergents fall into this category.
- *M&A.* If the product lines are formed through mergers and acquisitions, complete integration is usually difficult. Although the company has tried to sell off unrelated businesses, after acquiring Findus, Nestlé found itself in the canning business in Europe.
- *Preferences.* Differences in market preferences provide the fundamental strategic rationale for these product line differences. Many American sport utility vehicles are too big and gas-guzzling for Europeans, who have to pay very high prices for gasoline.
- *Capacity.* Global product lines need large production capacity, often through plant locations in several countries. A firm will take some time to develop that capacity, especially since forecasting demand is not without uncertainty. Because of strong demand in the North American target market, Toyota initially did not have enough capacity to sell its Lexus model in Japan.
- *Channels.* Differences in channel structure can make it difficult to support the same product lines. Coca-Cola's isotonic drink Aquarius is a "me-too" version of a popular Japanese drink, Pocari Sweat. By introducing Aquarius in addition to Georgia, the iced coffee, Coca-Cola made sure that its vending machines could be stocked with the variety demanded by the Japanese consumer.

Getting the Picture

MONTBLANC'S PRODUCT LINE EXTENSIONS

When is a pen not a pen? When it is an "art form." This is how Switzerland's Compagnie Financière Richemont positions its Montblanc pens. The fancy writing instruments boast individually numbered gold nibs and are topped with a white mark representing a bird's-eye view of snow-capped Mont Blanc, a mountain in the Alps. A single fountain pen will set you back $235 to $13,500 (for one made of platinum).

Apparently, the pen's style and quality have succeeded in making it more than just a status symbol. The upscale readers of *Robb Report,* a monthly magazine that rates products associated with an affluent lifestyle, voted Montblanc the best writing instrument in the world.

For Richemont subsidiary Montblanc North America, this reputation presents an opportunity to extend the product line. The company has opened stand-alone boutiques offering jewelry and leather accessories such as wallets, briefcases, organizers, and garment bags.

To support the brand extension, the company plans marketing communications reinforcing Montblanc's image of fine quality. This promotional effort includes magazine advertisements that link the Montblanc pen with the "art of writing." Newspaper ads announce the opening of the boutiques and the introduction of new products. Cultural events at the boutiques include displays of rare manuscripts, letters, and autographs. Together, such efforts are intended to convey, in the words of the ad agency's creative director, "an image that Montblanc isn't only a writing-instrument company but a European luxury brand. We hope that the Montblanc brand will stand not just for a pen, but for a certain lifestyle." In line with this extension strategy, the company now offers fragrances, eyewear, leather purses, and watches under the Montblanc name. Not forgetting its roots, a new Montblanc luxury pen titled "Prince Rainier III Limited Edition 81" was launched in Monaco at a VIP charity gala held to pay homage to Prince Rainier III of Monaco in 2007, two years after his death.

Sources: Glenn Collins, "Montblanc Expands on Gertrude Stein to Suggest That Sometimes a Pen Is More than a Pen," *New York Times,* July 27, 1995, p. D9; Reena Amos Dyes, "A Luxury Fountain Pen of Note," *Emirates Business,* March 30, 2008; **www.montblanc.com.**

As with all product line management, well-managed global lines also need to offer a certain rate of new product introductions (see box, "Montblanc's Product Line Extensions"). To be successful in globally competitive markets, a significant percentage of sales and profits should come from new products.

Developing New Global Products

In the past, most globally standardized products did not start out as global products. They were products that turned out to be successful in the home market and were then gradually introduced in markets abroad, following the waterfall strategy described in Chapter 5. A good example is the Ford Fiesta discussed in the opening vignette to this chapter. Other examples include P&G's Pampers diapers, Coca-Cola's overseas expansion spearheaded by the American soldiers in World War II, and Marlboro cigarettes.

Today, as in the case of the Ford Focus, new products are developed with an eye toward the global market. This is of course true for the companies characterized as "born global" in Chapter 6, whose products often involve computer software, peripherals, and other high-technology products. It is also true for new products whose home market is small and therefore the opportunity for success really lies abroad. Finland's Nokia cell phones are designed with the global market in mind. So are Switzerland's Swatch watch and Taiwan's Acer computer. But today more mainstream products also are designed for global appeal. The list includes not only hardware products such as automobiles, home appliances, consumer electronics, and cameras, but also movies, music CDs, and apparel. Design decisions about these products are no longer made with one local market in mind but with eyes firmly focused on the global marketplace.

The new product development process can be divided into five sequential stages: idea generation, preliminary screening, concept research, sales forecast, and test marketing. Most marketing texts will discuss these stages in detail.[9] Here we will focus on the way the global perspective changes what companies do.

Idea Generation

"Ideas are cheap?" Yes and no. In one way, ideas come easily. Brainstorming sessions, simple observations, or just an intuitive "Aha" experience can be counted on to yield a number of ideas. For example, when Lego, the Danish toy maker, needed some innovative thinking they employed a new session format where executives indulged in child's play to generate new product ideas and ways to combine their building blocks.[10] When the new minicopier task force at Canon looked for ways to lower cost and increase reliability, the leader of the group brought in an empty beer can as a stimulus for thinking about the kind of disposable aluminum cylinder that became the model for the copier.[11] The Mazda Miata small sports car was a proposed design by a British driver who convinced Mazda management that a more modern version of the old MG sports car would be a winner.

Other sources for new product ideas are more systematically used by multinationals. First of all, local subsidiaries are likely to have some ideas from their respective markets that can be used. Liquid Tide, one of P&G's top share leaders in detergents, came from the company's European operation, and compact Tide came from its Japanese subsidiary observing a product launch by Kao, its local competitor. Also, many companies involve employees via suggestion boxes and incentives for winning ideas. A well-known example is the 3M Post-it Notes, a real global product that emerged from a company engineer who needed a way of marking his choral songbook. Surveys and focus group sessions with customers are important, especially with modifications of existing products. Customers have user experience that can suggest new features and even completely new concepts. Snowboarding emerged out of downhill skiers' desires for extending the skateboard experience into the winter season.

New technology is perhaps the most common source of new product ideas, especially for global products. But not all new ideas are winners. Four-channel stereo, a "sure" winner, failed. Ski-sailing, adapting wind-surfing to snow, failed. Prepaid telephone cards, a winner in Europe and Asia, are slow getting accepted in the United States. High-definition TV took a long time to come, as were rectangular TV screens—although flat screens took off faster. Soccer is still in the embryonic stage in the United States. And so on. A typical quote is that it takes 64 new product ideas to generate one successful new product.[12] Even after launch, according to one 1997 count for the U.S. market, the success rate was less than 20 percent.

To reduce the chances of failure, most R&D undertaken for new products in multinational companies is still focused not so much on completely new products as on modifications and upgrading of existing products. Even an innovative company such as Sony, for example, estimates that over 80 percent of its new product activity is focused on improving and upgrading existing products.

Preliminary Screening

Once a promising idea has been identified, companies tend to assign the responsibility for new product development to cross-functional teams. There are typically engineering, design, and/or production representatives on the teams, as well as marketing executives, sales managers, and some financial control. In the case of global products, these teams also involve representatives from the major country markets. In particular, members are drawn from the lead countries for the product category. This team is responsible for taking the idea through the screening process to final decision.

At this stage the factors requiring localization of a global product are usually uncovered. For example, the size of parking spaces, the narrowness of streets, and the price of gasoline affect what size car is acceptable. Voltage levels, fire regulations, and circuit overloads affect what changes may be necessary in electrical products. Language, operating systems, and functions used affect what PC software applications may or may not be acceptable. When it comes to removing obstacles to convenient and proper local use, the local members of the development team will be particularly useful.

Concept Research

Even though a preliminary assessment of market acceptability can be done by members of the product development team, companies generally need more systematic data from the various markets. These data can come from standard marketing research tools, including focus groups and surveys, and from concept testing of alternative design features.

Focus Groups and Surveys

Using verbal and usually visual product descriptions, focus groups can be asked to react to the various alternative features of a new product. Focus groups offer the development team a chance to hear spontaneous reactions to a new concept, observe group interactions, and hear suggestions for improvement. Where a prototype is developed, focus groups also make it possible to see how potential users handle the product and to witness reactions to various design features and styling. For example, when Fuji photo entered the audio and videotape market, the development team decided that the differentiation factor would be packaging. Being a late-comer to the product category, a very competitive global market, the company's product involved basically a standardized technology, with well-defined quality standards and formats. Thus, the market research was focused on alternative packaging material, color designs, and logo, with prototypes tested through focus groups in the United States and several countries in Europe.

Concept Testing

A more formal approach to selecting product attributes is **concept testing,** using techniques such as trade-off analysis or conjoint analysis. Many marketing texts offer good introductions to these techniques, and we will highlight only the global aspects here.[13]

In concept testing, potential buyers rank specific product design alternatives in order of preference. The alternative product profiles include not only physical attributes and styling, but also price points. The preference ranking can be used to infer how much a particular feature is worth to the market. For example, a respondent who prefers paying $10 more for a set of blank CDs offering an erasable option clearly considers the option worth at least $10. By comparing similar trade-offs across product profiles and respondents, the concept testing analysis shows quite precisely how much the erasable option is worth in that segment.

This kind of analysis explains why standardized products are typically uniform not only where consumers have similar preferences but also in less critical features. Adaptation is required when local preferences differ sharply *and* the feature is important. Thus, a lot of cultural research would suggest that the preferred color of personal computers differs considerably between countries—but it is a less critical feature and we all get the same drab greyish noncolor (Apple and Acer are two players who try to make color more salient and important). By contrast, the PC keyboard "feel" is important and preferences differ. The smaller and lighter Asian PC keyboards have no market in the United States where, as always, the big and solid seems preferred.

Target Research

An alternative approach short-circuits the concept research process and speeds it up. It is called **target research.** By analyzing the leading brands and their attributes, they are able to understand what appeals to their consumers. Targeting one of the brands, that brand's customers can be questioned directly for possible improvements. By reverse engineering the brand and producing a new version incorporating the existing leader's strengths minus the weaknesses—a so-called me-too-plus product—the Japanese have been able to capture large market shares abroad. Examples include Toyota's Lexus, Camry, and Corona; the Canon Sureshot; and the VHS development by Matsushita.[14]

In developed countries with mature markets, the target research approach has the drawback that a striking innovation that completely changes market preferences will be missed. Targeting some leading brand and offering improvements is generally not enough to establish a sustainable advantage. The leading brand is likely to respond, and a cycle of actions and reactions will push prices down. This is a typical result of a Japanese entry in many markets. For the local marketer, it is important to recognize that establishing customer loyalty is as important in the foreign market as at home. The aim should not be the quick kill but the sustained satisfaction of the customer.

Sales Forecast

Even though rough sales projections are done throughout the development process, it is after the market research is done that a more precise forecast can be produced. By this time the product development team will know what design is preferable and, therefore, what the feasible product positions and target segments might be. This, in turn, suggests what the likely competition will be in the various markets.

As we saw in Chapter 4, the appropriate sales forecasting approach varies across the product life cycle. In mature markets unit sales can conveniently be broken up into two multiplicative components, product category sales and market share. The category sales depend on market segment targeted, and the market share depends on competitive factors. When forecasting sales of global products, each country can be handled separately and the results aggregated across countries.

Test Marketing

Once the sales forecast looks promising, the new product is usually placed in production and test marketed. Even though companies might prefer to simply launch the product, caution is often necessary. Whether the markets are emerging, developing, or developed, there are uncertainties that are difficult to erase simply by doing more research. The customers can't give reliable and valid responses without direct experience with the new product. Competitive reactions may be different from those expected. Local conditions may be quite different from those anticipated.

Although there are many similarities, the **test marketing** of a new global product candidate is different in scope from the domestic case. Usually several different country markets are used to ensure that potential problems are detected early. For example, in the case of Colgate's global introduction of Total toothpaste, six different markets were used: Australia, Colombia, Greece, New Zealand, the Philippines, and Portugal.[15] The positive results in all six markets indicated that the product's taste and unique positioning benefits—a long-lasting antibacterial formula that fought plaque, tartar, and cavities—could be the same throughout the world. Also, the tendency is to use leading markets, or smaller markets that are similar to the major target markets, much like musical shows are honed in smaller theaters before coming to the West End in London or Broadway in New York. Thus, Honda's Odyssey minivan was introduced in Canada before the United States, the Japanese use their home market as tests for consumer electronics products, and Nokia and Ericsson use Scandinavia for test marketing new designs.

Even though test marketing slows down the global rollout, there are other benefits. For one, there is more leeway in scheduling production capacity. Necessary product modifications can be uncovered and completed. The local sales force is given enough information and training for a successful rollout.

On the other hand, the delay can hurt because of competitive reaction and loss of first-mover advantage. Because of the cost and risk of competitive reaction, many companies find it useful to simply let customers use the product and offer feedback. Recruited subjects can be given the chance to try it in their homes for a period of time and then report their experiences. In software development, for example, test marketing is the so-called beta-testing stage in which selected users are asked to try the software for some period of time to help debug the program. A similar approach was used by Procter & Gamble when they introduced Pampers in European and Asian markets. It is done routinely by consumer goods companies going into emerging and developing markets, since it allows localization requirements to be uncovered. For example, when German electric irons were first introduced in Asia, their cords were too short. In

Europe there are usually several electric outlets in the wall, while in Asia at that time electric outlets connected to the one bulb in the ceiling.

Globalizing Successful New Products

We have already seen that new products fail at an alarming rate. Even following the most systematic and careful product development process does not ensure ultimate success. There is some research that shows which factors tend to make new product launches successful in different countries, however, and also research that uncovers how successful new products penetrate ("diffuse") into new country markets.

New Product Success Factors

According to research, the key success factors driving new product success for a company in a new market are the following (in order of importance):

1. New product superiority.
2. Technological synergy with company know-how.
3. Innovativeness of new product.
4. Company market orientation.
5. Marketing synergy with company know-how.

Not surprisingly, perhaps, the most important factor determining new product success is the new product superiority. That is, the greater the degree to which the new product possesses clear advantages over existing alternatives, the higher the chances of success. The second factor is the technological synergy with the company's existing products and processes. The higher the synergy, the more effectively the company can produce, service, and support the product. Also positive but less important factors are the degree to which the product is innovative, the level of market orientation in the company, and whether there is marketing synergy (using an existing brand name, for example). The main negative factor is the intensity of competitive reaction. The more competitors react, the less likely it is the new product will be successful.

These results are based on a wide variety of new product launches across a number of countries.[16] There are also some results that suggest that success factors are different between regions. Although not very much research has been published on this issue, the evidence we have is that Asia and North America show some significant differences. In particular, in Asia new product success is determined more strongly by technological sophistication, marketing synergies, market orientation, and senior management commitment. Although these factors have a positive influence also in North American markets, they are significantly stronger in Asia. For managers, the interpretation is that when launching a new product in Asia, there is a need for more technological sophistication and senior management involvement in the marketing effort.[17]

However, even these pro-success factors, positive though they may be, can explain only a little over 50 percent of the new product success rate. For academic purposes, 50 percent is a quite respectable figure. For the manager, however, it means that a lot of what determines success of a new product launch is as yet unknown.

Speed of Diffusion

The speed with which a new product diffuses across and into new countries depends on several factors. The major factors in **global diffusion** are product-related. Research has uncovered five specific product-related factors:[18]

1. *Relative advantage.* This is the same factor that is the leading cause of new product success. (Is a broadband connection much faster than a phone modem?)
2. *Compatibility.* Can the product be used locally without any problem, either in terms of infrastructure or customs? (Is cable available and does my computer have enough megabytes?)
3. *Complexity.* Is the new product easy to use? (How do I use broadband?)

4. *Trialability.* Is it easy to try the new product? (No wonder they gave me a free trial month—it takes that long to hook everything up.)

5. *Observability.* So, how much faster does it connect to the Internet?

Other potential factors include cultural differences (is the culture innovative?) and social factors (does the culture support a lot of word-of-mouth?). These two factors are reflected in an innovative and an imitative propensity, respectively, which together with the product factors determine the speed and depth of diffusion in a given country.[19]

Of special interest here, research has shown that diffusion rates for the same product differs between countries.[20] Three country-specific variables tend to influence both the innovative and the imitative propensities, and therefore make for different diffusion patterns across countries. One such variable is the level of cosmopolitanism. Cosmopolitanism refers to the degree to which a culture is open to outside influences. The more open it is, the more likely the speed of adoption will go up because the innovative propensity will increase. A second variable is geographic mobility, which influences the propensity of imitation (traveling gives you new ideas to bring home). A third variable is, unlikely though it may seem, the proportion of women in the workforce. The higher this proportion the less time there is for innovation, but the imitative propensity goes up since women will get exposed to outside influences.

These results are product-specific, and thus vary considerably across product categories. More robust results have been derived in further studies. In particular, it has been shown that cultures that are homogeneous and high context (such as some Asian countries) show higher propensities to imitate compared to low context countries with heterogeneous cultures. This means that penetration speed for a new product in a country such as Japan can be much faster than in the United States, where heterogeneity slows down the adoptions.[21] The research also shows that a new product introduced in a lagging country tends to show faster adoption and diffusion rates than in the original innovating country because potential buyers in the lagging country can observe the new product advantages in the original country.[22]

Several studies of new product takeoff in European and other countries have uncovered how diffusion rates vary by culture, innovativeness, and economic level. Some of the research focuses on how long it takes for a consumer durable product to reach the takeoff stage in the product life cycle in a country.[23] *Takeoff* is defined as the start of the growth stage of the PLC, and is identified in the country data as the threshold where growth rate in percentage market penetration shows a sudden jump that continues for several periods. The research shows that the time from when the new product is introduced to when it reaches that threshold depends on economic level, culture, and country innovativeness. New products diffuse faster in countries with higher economic level, countries low in uncertainty avoidance (Hofstede's measure of risk acceptance—see Chapter 3), and countries with open economies, high media intensity, and high mobility. In Europe, the smaller Scandinavian countries show faster diffusion rates than the mid-continental countries, with the Mediterranean countries last. By contrast, some research shows similarity among specific pan-European market segments. For example, acceptance rates of new consumer packaged goods were found to be similar in France, Germany, Spain, and the United Kingdom for three segments: Young consumers, large households, and consumer high in innovativeness.[24] Thus, new product market strategies can be similar across Europe when focused on these specific segments.

Differences in diffusion rates among countries suggest that waterfall strategies may be preferable to simultaneous sprinkler strategies. The logic of this hinges on the fact that research consistently has found that one strong factor in diffusion is the "demonstration effect" from seeing the new product in a foreign country. Thus, the strategy would be that new products first be introduced in countries with fast diffusion rates, to maximize first-mover advantages and create a platform for spillovers to countries with slower diffusion rates. These later countries would then show faster acceptance of the new product than otherwise, and the company would recoup its introductory marketing spending and investment faster.

Global Services

The service industries comprise a wide variety of businesses, including hotels and other lodging places; establishments providing personal, business, repair, and amusement services; health, legal, engineering, and other **professional services;** educational institutions; finance, insurance, and real estate; wholesale and retail trade; and general government, transportation, communication, and public utilities. Exhibit 12.2 gives a list of the many diverse businesses officially classified as service industries.[25] Although some of these services are not very significant globally, only few have no international involvement. Services are in fact traded internationally at an increasing rate. One task of this discussion is to explain how such trade is done.

Characteristics of Services

Although there is great variety among the industries, they tend to share four characteristics that make them different from physical goods and that affect their mode of entry.[26] Services are characterized by:

1. **Intangibility.** You cannot easily touch a service.
2. **Heterogeneity.** The service is not exactly the same each time.
3. **Inseparability.** Services are produced when they are consumed.
4. **Perishability.** You cannot store a service.

The different industries shown in Exhibit 12.2 possess these characteristics to a greater or lesser degree. For example, a restaurant visit exemplifies 2, 3, and 4 well, and even 1, although in a sense you can touch the food, the table, the hot plate, and so on. By contrast, a music CD or video can be touched, can be played again and again,

EXHIBIT 12.2
The Service Industries

Source: Saimee, 1999, p. 326.

Accounting	Funeral service
Advertising	Health care
Banking	Insurance
Broadcasting	Investment banking (brokerage)
Computer services	Leasing
Computer software	Legal services
Construction	Lodging
Consulting	Maintenance and repair
Contract research	Media:
Data entry	Cinema
Data processing	The Internet
Design and engineering	Radio
Distribution (including service distributors):	Still media
Agents, brokers, and representatives	Television
Franchising	Reservation systems
Freight forwarder, customs broker	Restaurants
Retailing	Royalties and licensing
Shopping malls	Security systems
Warehousing	Tourism
Wholesaling	Telecommunications:
Education:	Online services
Executive and management dev.	Mobile
Institutions of higher learning	Paging
Vocational and technical	Telephone
Entertainment:	Transportation (courier):
Music and other audio	Express delivery
Theme parks	Package delivery
TV productions, motion pictures	Transportation (merchandise)
Spectator sports	Transportation (passenger)
Theater, live performances	Utilities

Getting the Picture

WHEN LESS IS MORE

Commercial airlines constitute an industry where the differences between the core service, the basic service package, and the augmented service are very clear. The core service is rapid transportation between two or more points. The basic service package is what is included in the ticket price—first class, business class or coach, free meals, free drinks, baggage checks at the hotel, free limo service, and so on. The augmented service is in the personal touch, the attention from a stewardess, the willing accommodation of special seating requests, and so forth.

Since different segments of the traveler market desire different combinations of the complete service package, there is room for service differentiation. An interesting case is easyJet, a no-frills airline operating out of Luton, England. By focusing on the core service, minimizing the basic service package, and eliminating the augmented service altogether, easyJet is able to provide low-cost travel within the European Union. Its tickets are between one-half to one-third of the regularly scheduled airlines' prices.

easyJet is a "point-to-point" flyer, with no network of routes and no alliances. It simply offers short-haul flights between select destinations in Europe. Bookings can only be done via the Internet or the telephone. easyJet is basically a virtual enterprise, outsourcing functions such as check-in and baggage handling. Its paperless office in Luton also serves as a call center, taking orders over the phone—although Internet bookings are offered extra discounts. Their fleet consists only of Boeing 737s, minimizing demands on maintenance and repair crews. Flying to secondary airports—such as Orly in Paris instead of deGaulle, and Linate in Milano instead of Malpensa—not only cuts airport taxes but also puts travelers closer to the city centers. There are no onboard meals or frequent flyer programs.

Successful? You bet. easyJet flies over five million passengers annually, has an 80 percent utilization factor, high in a very competitive industry, and makes roughly $2 profit on each passenger. Thriving on the expansion of the European Union, in 2008 it opened service to the island of Malta. It established easyGroup as a unit to stretch the brand into new business, and has opened an easyEverything Internet cafe—"world's largest"—in London. And it has spawned imitators, British Airways with its "Go" subbrand and KLM with "Buzz."

Sources: Grönroos, 2000, pp. 200–202. Cynthia Busuttil,"Malta Welcomes First easyJet Flight," *Times of Malta*, March 30, 2008.

---

stored, and won't perish easily. Still, the audio and video sales of a Vienna Philharmonic New Year's concert are basically a service as classified here. For marketing strategy purposes services can sometimes be viewed as products (just like products can sometimes be viewed as a service—a car offers transportation, for example), and we will discuss this equivalence next.

A Product Equivalence

From a marketing viewpoint there are actually many similarities between physical goods and services. For example, one standard definition of a product is "a bundle of benefit-generating attributes." There is nothing inherently physical about this bundle. The same definition can be applied to an intangible service such as an insurance package. In fact, the similarities can be so strong that for some purposes there is no difference. In many ways the product is simply the packaging of a problem-solving service. For example, a book replaces the telling of a story, a car offers transportation, a cash machine replaces a teller, and so on.

Not surprisingly, perhaps, this equivalence means that services can be counterfeited too. A particularly intriguing case is that of software piracy, the duplication and sale of software programs for personal computers. The practice of copying diskettes is widespread, and it is very difficult to enforce the copyright limitations indicated on the packages. One research study, however, found that the quicker diffusion of the software programs made possible through pirating can actually help penetration. In England, where six of every seven adopters of popular spreadsheet and word processing programs utilize pirated copies, the pirates were responsible for generating more than 80 percent of new software buyers.[27]

The similarities and differences that affect the marketing management of services can be identified clearly with reference to the traditional product discussion in standard marketing texts. Adapting the product discussion of these texts, we distinguish between the "core service," the "basic service package," and the "augmented service."[28] Exhibit 12.3 demonstrates the relationships between these three concepts (See also box, "When Less Is More").

EXHIBIT 12.3
The Service "Product"

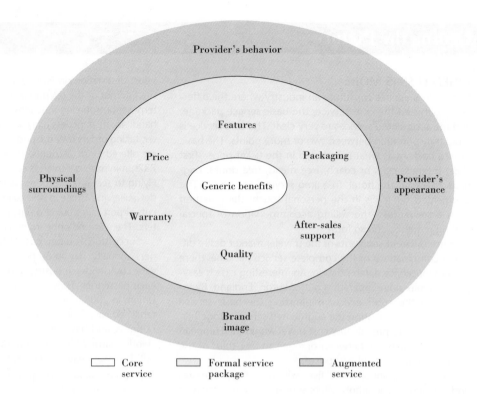

The **core service** is what the buyer is "really" buying. For instance, the person getting a tune-up for her car is really buying trouble-free operation and transportation. The individual checking into the Hilton in Manila is really buying a night's comfort and reliable service. The first job of the global services marketer is to make sure that these service benefits can be delivered in the foreign markets. While this task establishes a necessary condition for expansion, it is not sufficient by itself for success.

The **basic service package** refers to the specified services offered the customer, which include service features, the price, the packaging, and the guarantees offered. The basic service package of a bank involves the various "products" the bank offers and their features, including free checking, high-interest certificates of deposit, and so on. An airline provides a set of more or less tangible in-flight services (food, drink, duty-free sales, special baby care, movies). The second job of the global services marketer is to develop a service package that can be appropriately localized and replicated in the various markets around the world. Offering innovative and hard-to-duplicate service packages, such as the Club Med all-inclusive vacations in its own villages in different parts of the world, can help develop a loyal customer base and a sustained competitive advantage.

The **augmented service** is the totality of benefits that the individual receives or experiences when buying the product. These benefits revolve around the service delivery, the way the provider is dressed, the tone of voice and body language used, the confidence and credence imparted, and so on. These benefits also involve the brand image and status of the service provider, as well as the physical surroundings of the service. The third job of the global services marketer is to create a customer-oriented augmented service package.

Although they do play a role for physical products as well, these augmenting features can make a big difference in relatively standardized services. They can become the FSAs (firm-specific advantages). For example, the hair stylist's dress, the salon's furniture, the music played, and the other customers seen are all factors contributing to whether the hair styling itself will seem acceptable or not.[29] These augmenting benefits are often so inextricably linked to most services that without them the service can't be replicated properly elsewhere. Without such duplication, exporting to other

SERVICE STANDARDIZATION: IMPERSONAL PERSONAL SERVICE?

Just as with products, the standardization of services typically starts with a certain "core" service. Most fast-food restaurants, following McDonald's, focus on the basic principles of friendliness ("smile"), cleanliness of the premises, and quick service. But given the cultural diversity in the world, the human element can become an obstacle to **service standardization.** Thus, the consensus among many service marketers is that one can globally standardize the "backroom" aspects of the

service—quality control in fast-food restaurants, computerized bookings within a hotel chain, inventory control for retailers—but not necessarily the customer interactions, the "frontline" meeting of consumers with the service providers. The frontline personnel in even the most global service companies are usually natives, whose command of language and customs enables them to deliver the service appropriately—or, as some fast-food companies seem to aim for, standardize the personal service to make it impersonal.

Sources: Normann, 1992; Grönroos, 2000.

countries is less likely to succeed. One key factor in global services marketing is not whether the core benefit is desired or whether the basic service package can be replicated but whether the total **service delivery system**—the linked activities, hardware and software, which make the service delivery work—can be successfully transplanted abroad. If not, quality and customer satisfaction are jeopardized (see box, "Service Standardization").

Service Globalization Potential

Even if more and more services are going global, not all services have the same **globalization potential** or appropriate preconditions for globalization. The basic drivers of service expansion are the same as those for products: market drivers, competitive drivers, cost drivers, government drivers, and technology drivers. [30] These drivers define whether a particular service industry is ready for globalization. In particular, government factors in terms of regulations and other restrictions often constitute the main obstacles to global expansion.

Assuming that these drivers are relatively favorable, the feasibility of globalizing a particular service business depends on some factors that are unique to services as compared to products.

Stage of the Life Cycle

As with a product cycle, development of a business service over time follows a cycle from birth through growth and maturity to decline. In the typical marketing illustration, the product life cycle follows an S-curve, with the growth period corresponding to where the "S" has its steepest ascent. This is when a new product is often introduced in foreign markets to capture first-mover advantages. However, for services, it is in the maturity stage that the potential for global expansion of the service concept is the highest.

In the early and growth stage of the cycle, the "production process" employed by the service company is often still under development. The concept is still being created. In maturity, the software and hardware ingredients in the service have been fully developed, and the standardization of key components and features takes place. It is this standardization—whether it be in advertising, medical care, fast-food restaurants, accounting, or hotels—that is the basis for global expansion of the service. FSAs in services are often in innovative standardization—from McDonald's strict procedures for cleanliness and friendliness, to Hilton Hotels' training in how to greet guests, to Boston Consulting Group's growth-share matrix.

Infrastructure Barriers

The global applicability of a service depends on whether the **infrastructure** through which the service is offered exists in foreign markets. The availability of advanced telecommunications, a well-developed logistics infrastructure, and skilled local labor are typical requirements for many service businesses.

In brokerage firms, for example, a very sophisticated service concept that works well under a certain type of regulatory and economic environment might lose all relevance when the financial regulations and/or the institutional members change character. The buying and selling of call and put options or other derivatives, for example, is not feasible where there is no futures market.

Idiosyncratic Home Market

Another important inhibitor of services exporting is that many service systems exist as ingenious solutions to very special problems faced in the home country. The typical supermarket in the United States developed partly as a response to the growing availability of automobiles and parking lot space in many suburban areas of the nation. Similar idiosyncratic factors and other conditions in the local environment determine the specific shape of the service organizations found in many countries.

What is needed for services globalization is (1) a reasonable similarity to the home country situation, (2) a distillation of exactly what the key features of the service concept are, and (3) the localization of these to another environment while still maintaining the FSAs of the firm.

Foreign Entry of Services

Now we are ready to explain how the service characteristics influence mode of entry abroad. First we need to be clear on how foreign trade in services gets done.

Foreign Trade in Services

To understand mode of entry, it is useful to start with how trade in services actually occurs. Tourism exports provide one illustration. For example, as Japanese tourists descend upon Rome, their spending is done in local currency, bought by exchanging yen for euros. This means that hotel bills in Rome, food in the restaurants, payment for taxis, entrance tickets to the Coliseum, and similar expenditures are payments for services "exported" to Japan.

A Body Shop franchising expansion provides an illustration of a licensing mode of entry. As a potential Body Shop franchisee in, say, Mexico applies for a franchise, she will have to demonstrate appropriate business skills and access to sufficient financial resources and is likely to be interviewed by the founder Anita Roddick herself. Then, given support in how to establish and manage the business, the franchisee will be able to stock and sell the Body Shop product lines. From the revenues, the Body Shop will then be paid a certain percentage as a royalty payment. This payment needs to be made in pound sterling (unless some other arrangement has been agreed to). Thus, the franchisee has to buy pounds in a Mexican or multinational bank and transfer those funds to the United Kingdom. This will be recorded as a negative transfer from Mexico in the balance of payments account and becomes a service export for the United Kingdom.

In consulting services, foreign direct investment is sometimes necessary. A roving professor may do an executive seminar at a foreign company's headquarters and then return with a check drawn on a multinational bank and in the home country currency. This is exporting, in a sense just the opposite of tourism with the exporting occurring from the professor's home country (the tourist is buying services, the professor is selling them). But for sustained consulting to companies, it is typically necessary to have a local place of business to facilitate communication between the firm and its clients. Thus, consulting companies such as Accenture and McKinsey have branch offices in several large cities around the world, with local staff and some headquarters managers. This is an example of FDI in services, where the locals pay taxes to the host countries, but a share of the consulting fees is transferred back to headquarters, again recorded as service exports in the balance of payments.

Getting the Picture

PLAYBOY'S FOREIGN PLAYMATES

Although Playboy is still the world's best-selling men's magazine, profits are down and the firm has looked to international editions in local languages as one means to find revenue in less-developed and competitive markets. With a Russian edition released in 1995 and Croatia and Taiwan being investigated for entry, Playboy now has versions in more than 15 languages. Although Hungary and Hong Kong did not live up to the company's standards, Polish Playboy, South African Playboy, Dutch Playboy, German Playboy, and Japanese Playboy are merrily hopping along.

Starting small in 1995 with its first 100,000 copies sold at newsstands, the Russian-language edition is succeeding by following the same Playboy magazine format, albeit with less emphasis on politics and nudity and more focus on the cultural and entertainment scenes. Initially some articles and all cartoons were taken from various Western editions, but a host of Russian authors were hired to begin producing a local product. And while the first Playboy centerfold was packaged in the United States, because the Russian editor was unsatisfied with local photographers and models, Russian playmates are now exclusively featured. Surprisingly, Playboy is considered quite tasteful when compared to the more explicit images that are now pervasive in a country that once tightly regulated all facets of life.

This skill in leveraging a brand name would not have succeeded if Playboy's international edition editors had not localized the magazine in order to function in these different countries. Most female models come from the local culture. The rules for what is acceptable nudity vary and have to be observed. For example, censors make it necessary to airbrush away certain body parts in the American Playboy issues sold in Japan. The Japanese-language Playboy adheres to stricter limits in their playmate photos. Editorial content is also localized. About 75 percent of the articles are locally produced to be more attuned to the country's mindset. For example, the Russian edition focuses on topics such as consumerism, which is more compatible with a society experiencing the growth pangs of newly opened markets.

Sex apparently still sells, and it can be profitably sold in many markets around the globe provided that some measure of localization is reached.

Sources: Scott Allison, David Stephenson, Amy Venable, and John Whyte, "Playboy Enterprises, Inc.: Global Strategy," Team Project, McDonough School of Business, Georgetown University, December 14, 2001; Bernard Weinraub, "Reviving an Aging Playboy Is a Father–Daughter Project," *New York Times,* February 4, 2002, p. C1; Olivia Ward, "Russia's Playboy Sells Joy of Sex," *Toronto Star,* August 1, 1995; p. A2; Carmela Fonbuena, "Coming Soon: Playboy Philippine Edition," **abs-cbnNEWS.com/Newsbreak,** March 26, 2008.

Service Entry Modes

The background about how services are traded illuminates the way the four basic foreign entry modes apply to services.

Exporting

Services exporting is typical where services can be produced similarly to products and then simply shipped across to countries. This is typical for music and film, but today also with engineering services, software, architecture, and so on, where express mail and the Internet with its related technological advances have made global communication and transportation increasingly efficient.

Licensing

Where local involvement in the delivery is important and where the service can be standardized, licensing, including **franchising,** is very common. The fast-food restaurants, automobile rental firms, and hotel chains are typical examples.

In some ways licensing is the most obvious and visible mode of entry, because the firms that engage in it have built their competitive advantages on globally recognized brand names (KFC, Hertz, Hilton, etc.). A different but interesting example of licensing and localization is the way Playboy magazine has expanded globally (see box, "Playboy's Foreign Playmates").

Strategic Alliances

Where the service delivery requires local presence and the service is complex and standardization accordingly less feasible, the mode of entry involves either an alliance or FDI. In services where government regulations are restrictive, alliances are typically necessary. For example, accounting, legal, and medical services in most countries require local certification and are usually not open to foreign residents. If there are local

Getting the Picture

STARBUCKS'S JAPANESE ROAST

Starbucks distinctive green and circular logo can be found on busy street corners, in shopping malls, as well as at airports and train stations in an increasing number of countries around the world.

Although the company started out in the Pacific Northwest and is widely credited with changing the way Americans view coffee, its managers were always considering global expansion. Since Japan is the world's third-largest coffee consumer after the United States and Germany, Starbucks viewed the island nation as a huge challenge and opportunity for the firm.

Starbucks decided not to use franchising as an entry mode into foreign markets. The reason was the anticipated lack of control. The way to brew the best cup of coffee is not easily standardized, and the company wanted to make sure that its brand image was not hurt by uneven quality. Thus, entering Japan in October 1995, Starbucks entered into a joint venture with Tokyo-based Sazaby, Inc. This joint venture, amounting to 25 million yen ($2.33 million) in capitalization, helped Starbucks open 12 new stores in Japan by the end of 1997. Although the Japanese were not used to Italian-style coffees, Starbucks executives believed the Japanese consumers would embrace the Starbucks concept.

The positioning in Japan for Starbucks was between two contrasting coffee bars. One was the traditional coffee houses (*kissaten*) where couples and friends are likely to spend time away from their small apartments. The other was exemplified by Doutor Coffee Company, started in 1980. Doutor was Japan's leading coffee-bar chain with over 466 shops in and around Tokyo. Its focus was on speed of service and quick turnover of customers. The average customer stayed in a Doutor coffee shop about 10 minutes, about one-third the stay in a typical *kissaten*. Starbucks placed more emphasis on the coffee and store experience, with less stress on the social aspects and being targeted to single people.

Despite very strong competition from the established coffee houses, Starbucks's format proved successful and led to five years of uninterrupted growth. The only problem was that much of that growth accrued to competitive look-alikes.

In true Japanese fashion, the Japanese competitors quickly imitated the Starbucks formula, and created their own me-too versions of the Starbucks shops. The imitations were, also as usual, sometimes better than the original. If you enter a Doutor's me-too coffee house in Tokyo, named "Excelsior Caffe," you'll find the typical Starbucks menu of coffees posted behind the counter, the various brews are offered in the well-known paper and plastic cups, the coffeemaking procedure and serving is the same, the atmosphere with comfortable seating and Internet access is indistinguishable from a Starbucks, and the store front looks pretty much like a Starbucks, complete with logo and coloring. There is just enough of tweaking of the basic concept to make the stores avoid a legal challenge for copyright infringement.

Yes, even with tariffs down and entry barriers low, the Japanese market is still a tough one to crack.

Sources: Melissa Schilling and Suresh Kotha, *Starbucks Corporation: Going Global* (Kotha & Schilling, 1997); Michelle Gerenyi Jones, Cathy Kaboski, Michael Morpeth, and John Polevoy, "Global Marketing—Starbucks," Team Project, McDonough School of Business, Georgetown University, 2001; "Starbucks Celebrates Five Years of Unprecedented Growth in Japan," *Business Wire*, August 1, 2001.

---

prohibitions against foreign ownership, firms cannot just establish a branch office and hire local professionals but need a native partner. It can also help when the company has no experience in a mature market (see box, "Starbucks's Japanese Roast").

Foreign Direct Investment

Where foreign ownership is permitted, service firms with complex services tend to opt for FDI. The reason is that vertical integration improves the ability to control the quality of the service delivery.[31] Local employees are typically still needed as service providers, but training can be used to support high-quality performance. Banking offers an example. Government restrictions long prohibited the global expansion of retail banking, but deregulation and liberalization of financial markets have meant that one can now find a Citibank office in many foreign cities.

Entry and Exit Barriers

As with products, the mode of entry choice in services is affected by entry barriers and by the strategic objectives of the firm. Entry barriers in services are generally greater than for products. The reason is the uncertainty of control that comes with the intangibility of services, which induces governments to regulate services and causes firms to have problems with quality controls. One study of 384 service firms found the problems shown in Exhibit 12.4 to be the five most important barriers in foreign entry.[32]

An Excelsior Caffe storefront in Tokyo. The Japanese knockoff of the Starbucks formula reduces Starbucks's profitability—but it also helps market acceptance of the new format. The market growth entices other Japanese entries into the market as well, including Caffe Veloce with its "World Beans" and New Yorker Espresso. Still, Starbucks commands a 15–20 percent price premium even though its cups are slightly smaller.

In another study of the strategic constraints on entry mode, the author found that limited resources consistently accounted for a significant shift away from a vertically integrated mode of entry.[33] Interestingly, the reason was not limited access to capital, but limited availability of human resources. One reason is that, in contrast to products, services entry with FDI is relatively inexpensive. What is required is basically an office and some office equipment plus materials. This also means exit barriers are relatively low, and the risk exposure that always accompanies FDI is much lower than in products. However, the resources in short supply are managers from the home office who can be counted on to train the local employees and transfer the service effectively, with the quality intact.

EXHIBIT 12.4
Barriers to Service Expansion Abroad

Problem	Frequency with Which Cited
1. Host-country restrictions and regulations	21.6%
2. Quality delivery and customer service	19.5
3. Cultural differences	13.8
4. Staffing and Personnel	13.0
5. Logistics	8.3

Controlling Local Service Quality

Service quality is usually a matter of perceptions of the buyer at the moment of interaction with the service provider. For the marketing of a service it is therefore important to understand which service encounters the customer views as positive and which as negative. This is the basic rationale behind analyzing the "critical incident" when service is delivered and **service satisfaction** is registered or not.

Critical Incidents in Global Services

A "critical incident" or "moment of truth" is defined as "the period of time during which a consumer directly interacts with a service."[34] Once the pros and the cons in the critical incident are identified, the service encounter can be appropriately designed both in terms of a person's behavior and in terms of the physical surrounding or "servicescape."[35]

The quality of a service during a **critical incident** or **moment of truth** is typically measured in terms of a "gap" between the customer's expectations of the service and the perceived actual performance. If the latter is at or above the expected level, the customer is satisfied. If it's above the expected level, the customer is positively "surprised." If the perceived performance is below this level, the customer is dissatisfied and rates the quality low. Thus, according to this **"gap" model,** service "quality" really becomes a matter of whether the customer is satisfied or not (customer satisfaction in mature markets was discussed in Chapter 8).[36]

To apply the critical incident gap approach to the international case, it is useful to analyze the situation where the service provider and the service customer come from different cultures. The gap then involves expectations that are partly culture based, and the gap is likely to be greater than otherwise. There are likely to be three different levels of expectations at work:[37]

The **desired service** is the highest or ideal quality.

The **adequate service** forms the lower limit below which the service quality is unacceptable.

The **expected service** lies somewhere between the desired and the adequate service.

The relationships between these service quality levels are depicted in Exhibit 12.5. As long as the **perceived service** performance lies between the desired and the adequate

EXHIBIT 12.5
The Gap and the Zone of Tolerance

Source: Adapted from Stauss and Mang, 1999, p. 333.

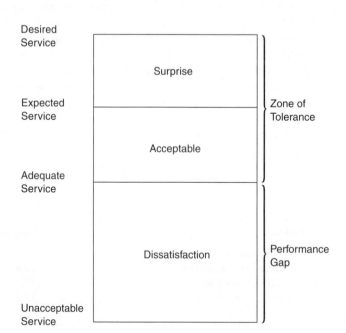

service levels there is no gap and the customer is satisfied. If the performance drops below the adequate level, there is a gap and dissatisfaction. Between the desired and the adequate service levels is the **zone of tolerance,** where the customer will be more or less satisfied. If the performance is above that expected, the customer is positively surprised.

It is probable that in intercultural service encounters the expectations are influenced by the home country culture. That is, the expectations on the part of the customers are formed partly by their cultural background and past experiences. The French know what they expect in a restaurant. However, when the same customer visits a McDonald's on Champs Elysees, he or she more or less adjusts these expectations according to the French image of the American fast-food chain. In the case of a McDonald's, the service expectations may shift downward, lowering the "expected" and the "adequate" service levels and increasing the zone of tolerance. However, they can also shift upward, as when a French multinational shifts from using the local post office to using FedEx. Then the "expected" and "adequate" service levels may rise, reducing the zone of tolerance.

This means that the foreign service firm entering a certain market is not necessarily judged by the same standards as a domestic firm. The standards may be higher or they may be lower. In the long run, as the entrant becomes more of an insider and an acceptable presence, these differences will not necessarily remain, and the businesses will compete on an even playing field. In the short run, however, there may be a period of grace for the incoming firm.

Research has demonstrated another effect from the intercultural factor in service encounters. When customers realize that there is a cultural difference between themselves and the service provider, they tend to question whether the performance gap, if any, is due to a simple misunderstanding. That is, perhaps the language barrier or other cultural differences are to blame for the perceived poor service. Furthermore, when the customer is the foreigner and the service provider is domestic, perhaps it is the customer who does not really know what should be expected? Most of us have been in situations like that. What the research shows is that in such cases the blame for the poor service might be accepted by the customer, who consequently drops the "adequate" service level and increases the zone of tolerance.[38] Needless to say, for the global marketer it is not advisable to count on such reactions for the long haul.

Summary

This chapter has discussed the emergence of standardized global products. It emphasized the distinction between localization to a country's infrastructure and adaptation to customer preferences. Localization is always necessary, but adaptation to customer preferences is more a matter of managerial judgment. The key is whether a product feature is important, and preferences vary across countries. If both conditions are fulfilled, there is no avoiding adaptation.

The chapter also examined the new product development process as it applies to global products. It showed how global products are today developed with an eye toward standardization across markets. The chapter then discussed the rate at which new products are diffused around the globe, stressing that lagging and culturally homogeneous countries might well show faster penetration rates than originating countries.

A global service is generally a more intricate and fragile export than a physical good. The intangibility and other characteristics that make services different from physical goods also make it difficult for the marketer to re-create the service and control the quality level abroad. In terms of marketing, however, many of the standard concepts and tools from product marketing are still applicable. The one major difference comes with distribution, where the inseparability of consumption and production of services makes the service delivery the "moment of truth" for quality and customer satisfaction. The necessary reliance on the customer's subjective judgment means that cultural factors play a very prominent role in determining quality and satisfaction levels.

Global service expansion is driven by the same factors that drive globalization of products. Issues that arise when going global involve defining what the service concept is "really about," how the same service delivery system can be reproduced abroad, whether the necessary localization to the new markets can be made without jeopardizing the firm-specific advantages, and how the necessary local personnel can be properly trained. Judging from the successes, many companies are up to the challenge.

Key Terms

adaptation, *407*	global brand, *403*	perishability, *416*
adequate service, *424*	global diffusion, *414*	professional services, *416*
augmented service, *418*	global products, *403*	regional products, *403*
basic service package, *418*	globalization potential, *419*	scale economies, *404*
concept testing, *412*	heterogeneity, *416*	scope economies, *404*
core product, *406*	infrastructure, *419*	service delivery system, *419*
core service, *418*	inseparability, *416*	service quality, *424*
critical incident, *424*	intangibility, *416*	service satisfaction, *424*
desired service, *424*	localization, *407*	service standardization, *419*
expected service, *424*	modular design, *406*	target research, *412*
franchising, *421*	moment of truth, *424*	test marketing, *413*
"gap" model, *424*	perceived service, *424*	zone of tolerance, *425*

Discussion Questions

1. Analyze the extent to which a particular multinational (such as Benetton, Procter & Gamble, or Nokia) offers the same product line in different countries by comparing the company Web site entries for different countries.

2. Access the Web site for one of the auto companies and see whether the company invites ideas for car design (by asking you to design your ideal car, for example). To what extent do they offer feedback? How will you know whether ideas were listened to?

3. Discuss how culture influences one's perception of what would be considered good service in a restaurant. Do the same for a store visit. (Use cultures with which you have some personal experience.)

4. Check out the Web sites of some service companies (for example hotels, brokerage firms, auto dealers), and analyze how they try to translate their offering to the new medium. Are services more or less adaptable to online shopping than products?

5. Why are most personal services not easily globalized? Give some examples that show how a service has to be standardized before going global—and how standardized personal service is almost always impersonal.

Notes

1. This section draws on Buzzell, 1968, and Yip, 1992.

2. Yavas et al., 1992, illustrate this point well with empirical data.

3. This difference is similar to the split between "practical" and "emotional" preferences cited by Du Preez et al., 1994. Practical preferences are desires associated with a country's infrastructure, climate, or physical environment (a desire for air-conditioning in a desert country, say). Emotional preferences involve more subjective taste, such as a preference for a certain color or designer name. Incorporating air-conditioning in an automobile is more of a localization strategy, while offering a pink Cabriolet version is more of an adaptive strategy to target some niche in the market.

4. In PC software, the word *localization* is commonly used, but the word *adaptation* is rare. Software is generally a globally standardized product. Adding umlauts and hyphens to word processing programs or changing from English to a native language in a spreadsheet are typical localization practices. Like changing the steering wheel of automobiles to the right side for countries where people drive on the left side of the road, such changes are not really a matter of preferences. There is always, of course, a "lunatic fringe" or "status at any price" part of every market who take pride in weird and dysfunctional features.

5. From Kashani, 1989.

6. From Robert J. Dolan, "Henkel Group: Umbrella Branding and Globalization Decisions," Harvard Business School case no. 585-185, 1985.

7. See Carpano and Chrisman, 1995.

8. See Samiee and Roth, 1992.

9. Kotler, 2000, Chapter 11, is a good start. For more in-depth treatment, see Thomas, 1993.

10. See Statler and Roos, 2000, for a discussion how the "play" approach works.

11. See Nonaka and Takeuchi, 1995, pp. 65–66.

12. See Kotler, 2000, p. 333.

13. Here, a text in marketing research will be most useful. See, for example, McDaniel and Gates, 2002, Chapter 17.

14. See Cooper, 1994, and Hanssens and Johansson, 1991.

15. See Kotabe and Helsen, 1998, p. 317.

16. See Henard and Szymanski, 2001, and Song and Parry, 1997. The critical factors have been used to develop a screening mechanism for new products called NewProd—see Cooper, 1985.

17. See Parry and Song, 1994, and Henard and Szymanski, 2001.

18. See Robertson, 1971.

19. See Ganesh and Kumar, 1996, and Ganesh et al., 1997.

20. Gatignon et al., 1989, and Ganesh et al., 1997.

21. See Takada and Jain, 1991.

22. See Ganesh et al., 1997, and Dekimpe et al., 2000.

23. See, for example, Tellis et al., 2003, and Stremersch and Tellis, 2004.

24. See Gielens and Steenkamp, 2007.

25. From Samiee, 1999, p. 326.

26. See, for example, Zeithamel and Bitner, 2000, p. 12.

27. See Givon et al., 1995.

28. In Kotler's version, the product definition now takes five levels: core benefits, generic product, expected product, augmented product, and potential product (Kotler, 2000, p. 395). For global services, the more standard three-level split is sufficient.

29. See, for example, Bitner, 1992.

30. See Lovelock and Yip, 1996. We discussed the drivers in Chapter 1 of this book.

31. Anderson and Coughlan (1981) first pointed out the (dis-)advantages of vertical integration for foreign entry.

32. From Reardon et al., 1996.

33. See Erramilli, 1992.

34. Shostack, 1985, p. 243.

35. See Bitner, 1992.

36. See Zeithaml and Bitner, 2000, Chapter 18.

37. The discussion here follows the interesting article by Stauss and Mang, 1999.

38. See Stauss and Mang, 1999. In these situations, of course, cultural factors really come to the fore. For example, individualistic people who are taught to be in control have trouble accepting blame and are likely to resist lowering the standards, while less assertive cultures are more prone to accept lower standards as inevitable.

Selected References

Albrecht, Karl. *The Only Thing That Matters*. New York: Harper Business, 1992.

Anderson, Erin, and Anne T. Coughlan. "International Market Entry and Expansion via Independent or Integrated Channels of Distribution." *Journal of Marketing* 51 (1981), pp. 71–82.

Bitner, Mary Jo. "Servicescapes: The Impact of Physical Surroundings on Customers and Employees." *Journal of Marketing*, April 1992, pp. 57–71.

Bobinski, Christopher. "Polish License for Deutsche Bank." *Financial Times,* July 4, 1995, p. 24.

Boddewyn, J. J.; Robin Soehl; and Jacques Picard. "Standardization in International Marketing: Is Ted Levitt in Fact Right?" *Business Horizons,* November–December 1986, pp. 69–75.

Buzzell, Robert D. "Can You Standardize Multinational Marketing?" *Harvard Business Review,* November–December 1968, pp. 102–13.

Carpano, Claudio, and James J. Chrisman. "Performance Implications of International Product Strategies and the Integration of Marketing Activities." *Journal of International Marketing* 3, no. 1 (1995), pp. 9–28.

Clark, Terry, and Daniel Rajaratnam. "International Services: Perspectives at Century's End." In Hult, 1999, pp. 298–310.

Cooper, Robert G. "Selecting New Product Projects: Using the NewProd System." *Journal of Product Innovation Management* 2, no. 1 (March 1985), pp. 34–44.

Cooper, Robin. *Cost Management in a Confrontation Strategy: Lessons from Japan.* Cambridge, MA: Harvard Business School Press, 1994.

Crapo, Arlee; Ginny Hallum; Shana Levitt; and Chris Priest. "Ford Mondeo in the United States: Mispositioning and Missed Opportunity." Team Project, McDonough School of Business, Georgetown University, December 14, 2001.

Czepiel, J. A. "Managing Customer Satisfaction in Consumer Service." Marketing Science Institute, working paper, September 1980, pp. 80–109.

Dekimpe, Marnik G.; Philip M. Parker; and Miklos Sarvary. "Global Diffusion of Technological Innovations: A Coupled-Hazard Approach." *Journal of Marketing Research* 37 (February 2000), pp. 47–59.

Du Preez, Johann P.; Adamantios Diamantopoulos; and Bodo B. Schlegelmilch. "Product Standardization and Attribute Saliency: A Three-Country Empirical Comparison." *Journal of International Marketing* 2, no. 1 (1994), pp. 7–28.

Elliott, Stuart. "Advertising." *New York Times,* June 21, 1995, p. D9.

Erramilli, M. Krishna. "Influence of Some External and Internal Environmental Factors on Foreign Market Entry Mode Choice in Service Firms." *Journal of Business Research* 25 (1992), pp. 263–76.

Ganesh, Jaishankar, and V. Kumar. "Capturing the Cross-National Learning Effect: An Analysis of Industrial Technology Diffusion." *Journal of the Academy of Marketing Science* 24 (Fall 1996), pp. 328–37.

Ganesh, Jaishankar; V. Kumar; and Velavan Subramaniam. "Learning Effects in Multinational Diffusion of Consumer Durables: An Exploratory Investigation." *Journal of the Academy of Marketing Science* 25 (Summer 1997), pp. 214–28.

Gatignon, Hubert; Jehoshua Eliashberg; and Thomas S. Robertson. "Modeling Multinational Diffusion Patterns: An Efficient Methodology." *Marketing Science* 8, no. 3 (Summer 1989), pp. 231–47.

Gielens, Katrijn, and Jan-Benedict E.M. Steenkamp. "Drivers of Consumer Acceptance of New Packaged Goods: An Investigation across Products and Countries," *International Journal of Research in Marketing* 24, no. 2 (2007), pp. 97–111.

Givon, Moshe; Vijay Mahajan; and Eitan Muller. "Software Piracy: Estimation of Lost Sales and the Impact on Software Diffusion." *Journal of Marketing* 59, no. 1 (January 1995), pp. 29–37.

Grönroos, Christian. *Service Management and Marketing,* 2nd ed. Chichester, U.K.: Wiley, 2000.

———. "Internationalization Strategies for Services." In Hult, 1999, pp. 290–97.

Hanssens, D. M., and J. K. Johansson. "Rivalry as Synergy? The Japanese Automobile Companies' Export Expansion." *Journal of International Business Studies* 22, no. 3 (1991), pp. 503–26.

Henard, David H., and David M. Szymanski. "Why Some New Products Are More Successful Than Others." *Journal of Marketing Research* 38 (2001), pp. 362–75.

Hult, G. Tomas M., ed. "International Services Marketing." *Journal of Services Marketing* 13, no. 4/5 (1999).

Hyun-Joo, Jin. "No Lack of Fake Luxuries," *The Korea Herald,* June 3, 2004.

Kashani, Kamran. "Beware the Pitfalls of Global Marketing." *Harvard Business Review,* September–October 1989, pp. 91–98.

———. *Managing Global Marketing.* Boston: PWS-Kent, 1992.

Keller, Kevin Lane. *Strategic Brand Management.* Upper Saddle River, NJ: Prentice Hall, 1998.

Knight, Gary. "International Services Marketing: Review of Research, 1980–1998." In Hult, 1999.

Kotabe, Masaaki, and Kristian Helsen. *Global Marketing Management.* New York: Wiley, 1998.

Kotler, Philip. *Marketing Management.* The Millennium Edition. Upper Saddle River, NJ: Prentice Hall, 2000.

LaBarre, Polly. "Quality's Silent Partner." *Industry Week* 243, no. 8 (April 18, 1994), pp. 47– 48.

Lovelock, C. H. *Services Marketing*. Englewood Cliffs, NJ: Prentice Hall, 1984.

———. "Developing Marketing Strategies for Transnational Service Operations." In Hult, 1999, pp. 278–89.

———, and George Yip. "Developing Global Strategies for Service Businesses." *California Management Review* 38, no. 2 (Winter 1996).

McDaniel, Carl, and Roger Gates. *Marketing Research,* 5th ed. Cincinnati, OH: South-Western, 2002.

Nonaka, Ikujiro, and Hirotaka Takeuchi. *The Knowledge-Creating Company.* New York: Oxford University Press, 1995.

Normann, R. *Service Management*, 2nd ed. New York: Wiley, 1992.

Normann, R., and Rafael Ramirez. "From Value Chain to Value Constellation." *Harvard Business Review,* July–August 1993, pp. 65–77.

Parry, Mark E., and X. Michael Song. "Identifying New Product Successes in China." *Journal of Product Innovation Management* 11, no. 1 (January 1994), pp. 15–30.

Reardon, James; M. Krishna Erramilli; and Derrick Dsouza. "International Expansion of Service Firms: Problems and Strategies." *Journal of Professional Services Marketing* 15, no. 1 (1996), pp. 31–46.

Robertson, Thomas S. *Innovative Behavior and Communication.* New York: Holt, Rinehart and Winston, 1971.

Rosen, Barry Nathan; Jean J. Boddewyn; and Ernst A. Louis. "U.S. Brands Abroad: An Empirical Study of Global Branding." *International Marketing Review* 6, no. 1 (1989), pp. 7–19.

Samiee, Saeed. "The Internationalization of Services: Trends, Obstacles and Issues." In Hult, 1999, pp. 319–28.

———, and Kendall Roth. "The Influence of Global Marketing Standardization on Performance." *Journal of Marketing* 56, no. 2 (April 1992), pp. 1–17.

Shelp, R. K. *Beyond Industrialization: Ascendancy of the Global Service Economy.* New York: Praeger, 1981.

Shostack, Lynn. "Planning the Service Encounter." In John A. Czepiel; Michael R. Solomon; and Carol F. Surprenant, eds. *The Service Encounter: Managing Employee/Customer Interaction in Service Businesses*. Lexington, MA: Lexington Books, 1985, pp. 243–54.

Simmons, Tim. "A Global Brand of Dialog." *Supermarket News* 40, no. 28 (July 9, 1990), p. 2.

Song, X. Michael, and Mark E. Parry. "The Determinants of Japanese New Product Successes." *Journal of Marketing Research* 34 (1997), pp. 64–76.

Sorenson, R. Z., and U. E. Wiechmann. "How Multinationals View Marketing Standardization." In D. N. Dickson, ed. *Managing Effectively in the World Marketplace.* New York: Wiley, 1983, pp. 301–16.

Statler, Matt, and Johan Roos. "A Place to Play: Redefining Strategy Research." Imagination Lab Working Paper 2001-8, December 11, 2001.

Stauss, Bernd, and Paul Mang. " 'Culture Shocks' in Inter-Cultural Service Encounters." In Hult, 1999, pp. 329–46.

Stremersch, Stefan, and Gerard J. Tellis. "Understanding and Managing International Growth of New Products." *International Journal of Research in Marketing* 21, no. 4 (December 2004), pp. 421–48.

Takada, Hirokazu, and Dipak Jain. "Cross-National Analysis of Diffusion of Consumer Durable Goods in Pacific Rim Countries." *Journal of Marketing* 55, no. 2 (April 1991), pp. 48–54.

Tellis, Gerard J.; Stefan Stremersch; and Eden Yin. "The International Takeoff of New Products: The Role of Economics, Culture, and Country Innovativeness." *Management Science* 22, no. 2 (Spring 2003), pp. 188–208.

Thomas, Robert J. *New Product Development.* New York: Wiley, 1993.

Urban, Glen L., and Steven H. Star. *Advanced Marketing Strategy.* Englewood Cliffs, NJ: Prentice Hall, 1991.

Yavas, Ugur; Bronislaw J. Verhage; and Robert T. Green. "Global Consumer Segmentation versus Local Market Orientation: Empirical Findings." *Management International Review* 32, no. 3 (1992), pp. 265–72.

Yip, George. *Total Global Strategy.* Englewood Cliffs, NJ: Prentice Hall, 1992.

Zeithaml, Valarie A. "How Consumer Evaluation Processes Differ between Goods and Services." In James H. Donnelly and William R. George, eds. Marketing of Services. Chicago: American Marketing Association, 1981.

Zeithaml, Valarie A., and Mary Jo Bitner. *Services Marketing: Integrating Customer Focus across the Firm*, 2nd ed. New York: McGraw-Hill/Irwin, 2000.

Chapter 13

Global Branding

"Your reputation precedes you"

After reading this chapter, you will be able to:

1. Understand why branding has become so important in today's competitive markets.
2. Evaluate what it takes to build a strong brand and why globalization helps build brand equity.
3. Identify which local brands would be good candidates for globalization and what strategy to use to globalize them.
4. Assess when an acquired local brand should be kept instead of converted to the global brand.
5. Help protect a global brand against counterfeits.

Global brands such as Nike, Sony, and Nokia have become household words in many countries around the world. By the same token, they have also lost some, but not all, of the association with their national origin. Consumers in different countries know they like Samsung cell phones, but might know only that they come from Asia, not necessarily that they come from South Korea. And where a product is made matters less. A Sony television is still perceived as Japanese even if made in San Diego, California. Adding to the confusion, a brand such as Nokia is allegedly misperceived by many as Japanese, although it comes from Finland. Global brands come from somewhere, but it is not always clear where that is.

At the same time, as globalization has proceeded nations and nationality have become more salient. Forces of antiglobalization, anti-Americanism, and ethnic identities have asserted themselves. Furthermore, national branding in the interest of attracting foreign investment, appealing to tourists, and gaining a strong international reputation has become a government preoccupation in many countries. As a result, global branding has become more prevalent and important. Managers attempt to get customers to focus on the positives and minimize the negatives. If "being global" is a positive brand benefit in the customer's eyes, stress it; if it is a negative factor, localize the brand. The meaning of "glocal" is that global brands try to combine the affinity and intimacy of a local name with the power and strength of global reach.

A Beer Is a Beer Is a Beer?

Beer seems to be a product for which consumers' subjective perceptions count for more than objective facts, and where taste preferences reveal astonishing country-of-origin effects. Two, um, cases come from Mexico and Europe.

In 1999, at 55 million cases, Corona beer from Mexico became the most popular imported beer in the United States, handily beating perennial leader Dutch Heineken's 42 million cases. For Mexicans, who regard Corona as a relatively

431

low-class beer, the U.S. success is a mystery. But Carlos Fernandez Gonzales, Corona's CEO, credits marketing smarts.

Entering the U.S. market in the 1970s, Corona's sales were initially sluggish. Then the company's distributors in the United States hit upon the idea of focusing on two niche segments. First came the more obvious notion of targeting the millions of Mexicans living in the United States. Then in an imaginative stroke, the company decided to target young American beer drinkers, many of whom had vacationed on Mexican beaches in Cancun, Mazatlan, and Acapulco.

Featuring ads of attractive college-age women and men enjoying spring break on a sun-drenched Mexican beach and positioning Corona at a premium price between domestic and expensive import beers, the company saw sales take off. A temporary slowdown occurred as a rumor was heard that Corona's light color reflected "urine content" (a rumor Corona managers believe was started by competitors), but sales soon recouped, helped by the clever "hook" of suggesting that Corona be drunk direct from the bottle with a slice of lime, appealing to the irreverent young.

Corona is going global, with sales rising in several new markets including Israel, Russia, and Japan. The company is targeting Europe, even making inroads at the holy shrine of beer lovers, Munich's traditional Oktoberfest. Validating the globalization of markets idea, the same tropical beach ads that worked in the United States seem to work also in other countries.

But even as it seems some beer brands are becoming global, it is sobering to learn that in terms of consumption patterns, beer is still one of the least global consumer goods of all. Heineken, available in 170 countries, claims to be the most international beer in the world, but 61 percent of its sales are inside the EU. Budweiser still gets a majority of its revenues from the American home market. And in the 2007 brand rankings, Budweiser is the only beer among Interbrand's 100 top global brands, well behind Coca-Cola, McDonald's, and Marlboro.

Even though beer drinkers everywhere would seem to constitute one large universal segment, the "global" beer market is in fact largely fragmented and multidomestic. Even with the consolidation of many European breweries that has created behemoths such as Belgian Interbrew, now InBev, the world's largest with its Stella Artois as the flagship global brand, and Denmark's Carlsberg, the global market shares of the largest brands are still small. The size of the home market tends to determine the rankings. By the turn of the new century, Budweiser, the leading brand, took 3.6 percent, with Bud Light adding another 2.6 percent. Third was Japan's Asahi Super Dry at 1.8 percent. Heineken placed sixth with 1.6 percent of global sales.

Why hasn't the market grown more truly global? Insiders blame lack of marketing effort—and Corona with its excellent marketing seems well poised to prove them right after all. But it could also just be that when it comes to consumers and beers, local tastes are just that—local.

Sources: Brian Bremner, " 'Made in America'—Isn't the Kiss of Death Anymore," *BusinessWeek*, November 13, 1995; James Sterngold, "The Awakening Chinese Consumer," *New York Times*, October 11, 1992, pp. D1, D4; Rick Wills, "The King of Imported Beers," *New York Times*, May 28, 1999, pp. C1, C2; "The Big Pitcher," *The Economist*, January 20, 2001, pp. 63–64.

Introduction

A company's principal brands are major assets, worth billions to their firms. In one study, the median value assigned by 153 senior managers to their principal brand was $5.3 billion.[1] Exhibit 13.1 shows what the London-based Interbrand consulting firm found to be the world's most valuable brands in 2007. Other surveys tally roughly the same set of brands, although the ranking varies by region. As can be seen, all of the brands on the list belong to companies that market globally standardized products.[2]

EXHIBIT 13.1
The World's Most Valuable Brands

Source: **Interbrand.com,** "Best Global Brands 2007."

	Brand Name	2007 Brand Value ($ billions)
1.	Coca-Cola	$65.3
2.	Microsoft	$58.7
3.	IBM	$57.1
4.	G.E. (General Electric)	$51.6
5.	Nokia	$33.7
6.	Toyota	$32.1
7.	Intel	$31.0
8.	McDonald's	$29.4
9.	Disney	$29.2
10.	Mercedes	$23.6

The growing impact of global brands makes **global brand management** of crucial importance. In a 1995 study senior managers ranked the 10 most effective global brand managers (see Exhibit 13.2). The results confirm Coca-Cola's preeminence as a global marketer. In fact, the most striking fact about Exhibit 13.2 is perhaps the sharp drop-off after the leader. Managing a global brand is not necessarily easy.

This chapter first defines what brands are and establishes the distinctions between several different types of brands, and also extends the discussion to nations as brands. The chapter then defines what distinguishes global brands from regional and local brands, and explains why brands have become so important in today's marketplace. This will help set the stage for understanding what brands can do, and, in particular, what *global* brands can do. This will lead up to a summary of the pros and cons of a global brand.

The chapter then focuses on global brand management and starts by explaining how the value of a brand can be calculated, and how brand equity is typically measured. This also helps demonstrate why a global brand can be so valuable to top management. The chapter then discusses how global brands are built, and shows why, typically, firms expand a strong local brand in a waterfall strategy rather than creating a global brand from scratch. The chapter also explains why, when acquiring a local brand, it is sometimes preferable to retain its brand name rather than imposing the global brand name. It then shows the typical brand portfolio of the multinational company and how the brands are organized. The chapter then discusses how firms choose a global brand name, and how they go about changing local brands to the global brand name where needed. The chapter ends with the problem of counterfeits, and how to protect a strong global brand against dilution by fake products.

EXHIBIT 13.2
The 10 Most Effective Global Brand Managers*

Source: Elliott, 1995, with data from the "Brands at the Crossroads" study by Bozell Worldwide and Fortune Marketing, New York, 1993.

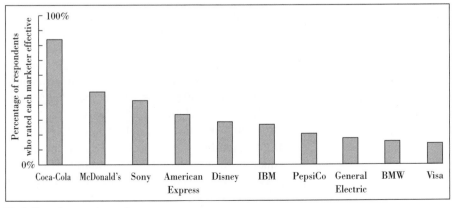

*Ranked by senior corporate executives.

Brands Defined

Brand names are basically symbols that identify the maker of a product or provider of a service. As such, they have been with us for centuries. They are the signatures of the Italian artists of the renaissance, the name of the four-star restaurant in Lyon, the royal faces on the old European banknotes. The tourist guides in Beijing's Forbidden City point to the signs on the stonework forming the Emperor's staircase: In case an imperfection was discovered, the culprit could be identified and properly punished, often decapitated.[3] Early on merchants discovered the added value of having a trustworthy and reliable name, and started claiming an old heritage ("Established in 1789," "Since 1864," etc.). With the long tradition came customer familiarity and loyalty, and the automatic expectation of consistent quality.

There are many types of brands:

- **Product brands**—Product brands represent the traditional meaning of brands. They are specific to a product or service, so that the name is clearly associated with a given product. Examples include Tide detergent, Nokia cell phones, Budweiser beer, Starbucks coffee, HSBC bank, BMW cars, and so on. Sometimes these brands are identical to the corporate brand, sometimes not. Much of the brand discussion in this chapter refers to such brands, whether stated explicitly or not.

- **Corporate brands**—Brands that stand for the corporation as a whole. An example is Boeing, the aircraft manufacturer. These brands are the ones that become the umbrella, endorsement, or family brands defined below. Very diversified companies tend not to place too much emphasis on the corporate brand, but manage their product brands more independently. Few consumers are likely to know that Swiss Nestlé sells Perrier or that Dutch-British Unilever owns Ben & Jerry's.

- **Family brands**—A family brand name is a name used for all products in a product line. Each product features the brand name prominently. Examples are common in food products, including Kellogg's cereals, Betty Crocker baking products, and Nivea skin care products.

- **Master brand**—A specific overarching brand name that serves as the main anchoring point on which all underlying products are based. One example is Intel with its Pentium and Centrino processors. Apple computers is another example, although it is arguable that the master brand is actually Steve Jobs himself, just as Bill Gates is the master brand at Microsoft.

- **Umbrella brands**—Brands that cover a diverse set of products that are still more or less related. An example is the electronics, music, and pictures offerings of Sony. Nation images are naturally used as umbrella brands, as in French wine and Italian suits.

- **Endorsement brands**—Well-known corporate brands that support a given product brand. They are typically identified using the word *by*. For example, Ralph Lauren uses this strategy in "Polo by Ralph Lauren." The iPod and iPhone are endorsed by Apple through the device of using the lowercase initial "i" established as the iMac. In B2B, Honeywell uses this to endorse its subsidiary products, as in "NexWatch by Honeywell."

- **Sub-brands**—The product brands that are "in the family" or endorsed or under an umbrella brand. Examples include Honda Accord, Chaps and Polo for Ralph Lauren, and Microsoft's Xbox. Sub-brands that are becoming brands in their own right are Sony's PlayStation, where Sony's name is downplayed, and Apple's similar efforts to make "the Mac" a free-standing brand.

- **Dual branding**—Dual branding is the practice of featuring two brands on an equal level. It is common in marketing of cell phones, where the distribution involves selling the product brand and the network simultaneously (for example, iPhone and AT&T).

- **Ingredient brand**—The branded components of a product made by other manufacturers, the ingredient brand manufacturers. Examples are Bosch components in Mercedes cars, and Intel components in personal computers.
- **Brand extensions**—A product with a well-developed image uses the same brand name in a different product category. An example is Virgin Group, which has extended its brand from stores to record labels and an airline. Not all succeed. BIC pens tried to market BIC pantyhose and failed. A typical example of a brand extension is the Montblanc revival, discussed in Chapter 12.

One reason why all these various types of brands have emerged is overseas expansion. When companies enter a new market, their brand name is new to many of the potential customers. Thus, it becomes natural to inform the potential customers about the company and assure customers that the company stands behind its brand. Corporate advertising to establish the corporate brand helps to do that. Procter & Gamble uses its corporate brand more in overseas markets than at home, where Tide, Head & Shoulders, and its other product brands are already well established. Similarly, for smaller companies in particular, it is tempting to associate themselves with an established local brand, and derive the endorsement and support from a combined branding strategy. Often this can be provided by a well-established partner in the distribution channel—the Italian coffee maker Lavazza is entering the U.S. market by distributing through Whole Foods supermarkets, gaining credibility from the strength of the Whole Foods brand.

Global, Regional, and Local Brands

A global brand is one that is available and recognized in most markets around the world. Strictly speaking, one should define a global brand as one that is available in absolutely all countries in the world. But since some country markets might not be reachable—Myanmar, for example, or North Korea—some researchers argue that a global brand should have significant sales in most major markets. For example, the AC-Nielsen market research company has defined a global brand as one that is available in the major regions of the world and is also a strong player in each market region.[4] The firm imposed the requirement that a region should account for at least 5 percent of the company sales. This is very strict. As a result, they were able to classify only 43 brands as "global" in the consumer packaged goods categories.

The consensus is that the main factor is simple availability and recognition in most markets in the world. These criteria can be based on consumer perceptions, as in, for example, some of the academic research (see Steenkamp et al., 2003), or on the actual geographic reach of the brand sales (as in Interbrand's 100 Best Global Brands). By contrast, a local brand is one that has only a limited reach in a few local markets, often domestic only, such as Karma Cola in India. Such a local brand might be well known and well liked by local consumers, but has no significant sales outside the local market.

It is also possible to identify *regional* brands. These brands are well-known product brands that have different names in different parts of the world. For example, P&G's Tide detergent is Ariel in Europe, and Toyota's luxury brand Lexus was introduced as Celsior in Japan, now changed to the global Lexus name.

The following list summarizes and exemplifies these points:

- **Global brands** *are brands that are available and well known in most markets of the world.* (Examples: Sony, Mercedes-Benz, Microsoft, Coca-Cola).
- **Regional brands** *are brands that are uniform across a region but different between regions.* (Examples: P&G'S Pert Plus in North America is Vidal Sassoon in Asia; Acura is Honda Legend in Asia).
- **Local brands** *are brands found in only one or two markets* (Examples: Jever Pilsener in Germany, Fortnum & Mason in the United Kingdom, A&W root beer in the United States, and Pocari Sweat in Japan).

Many large multinationals expand abroad by buying up local brands. An acquired brand name may be strong enough to stand on its own but it may also be desirable to add the entering brand logo to the local brand, at least during a time of transition. This will help the entering brand to gain awareness and familiarity, before changing to the global brand name. Lenovo's acquisition of the IBM personal computer business follows this strategy. Alternatively, the acquiring company may also provide support for the local brand by serving as an endorsement or master brand. Swedish appliance maker Electrolux uses this strategy when acquiring brands with strong local loyalty, to maintain local customer allegiance while providing state-of-the-art technology.

Extending The Brand Concept

In what follows we will mainly concentrate on the traditional notion of brands associated with the marketing of products and services. But it is important to recognize that the concept of a "brand" has been extended beyond the domain of products and services, and is now used in the popular press when discussing entertainment celebrities, sports teams and stars, institutions, and even nations. Some of these are truly global. Movie stars such as Leonardo DiCaprio and Nicole Kidman are global celebrities, now described and managed as global brands. BBC television is a global brand, but so is also TV's Oprah Winfrey. British footballer David Beckham is today one of the most famous global sports brands, and among teams, there is fierce global brand competition between soccer teams Real Madrid and Manchester United, with Barcelona and Liverpool close runners-up. Beckham's transfer to the Los Angeles Galaxy team in 2007 is akin to an acquisition of a global brand, the way Chinese Lenovo's purchase of the IBM Thinkpad brand was. "Forza Barca," the Barcelona motto, is a true brand slogan.

In other examples, politicians running for election are naturally brand conscious and, especially in the United States, use typical brand-building strategies such as television commercials and repeated "sound bites" as slogans to get their message through the media clutter. The anti-American sentiment in various countries after the U.S. invasion of Iraq in 2003 induced the Bush government to ramp-up public relations efforts and marketing communications aiming to improve the image of "Brand America."

Nation Branding

Many nations have now become aware of the impact a positive nation image has not only to attract tourists and gain a country-of-origin advantage for its products, but also to attract foreign direct investment, skilled immigrants from other countries, and political credibility. Emerging nations take out advertising pages in daily newspapers to acquaint readers with their resources, and most nations train their diplomats in sales and marketing techniques.

One of the first and best introductions to what is called "Nation Branding" is Simon Anholt's book *Brand New Justice: The Upside of Global Branding* (Anholt, 2003). As we saw in Chapter 4, Anholt has worked with GMI International, a market research firm, to develop national profiles (also of cities and regions), which can be used to identify strengths and weaknesses in the national image. The research identifies six dimensions that together summarize the image of a country. The dimensions are Culture & Heritage, Exports, Governance, Immigration & Investment, People, and Tourism.

The results are summarized in illustrative diagrams, which visually capture and contrast the images of different nations and how different peoples perceive the same country differently. See Exhibits 13.3 and 13.4 for examples of the differences in the perceptions of France represented as a jagged centerpiece of a hexagon.

In the diagrams, the further out a country's profile reaches on one of the six dimensions the more favorable is its rating. Thus, the profiles are useful in assessing each country's strength and weaknesses, as viewed by the citizens of another country. Since

EXHIBIT 13.3
How Americans See Brand France

Source: Copyright © 2002 Simon Anholt.

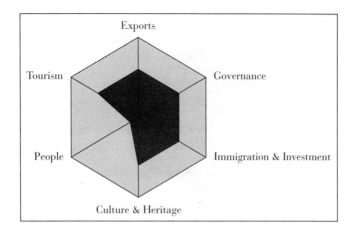

perceptions can differ between countries, the profiles are useful by pinpointing the extent to which those perceptions vary. As can be seen, the Japanese have a much more favorable view of the French people than the Americans, while the Americans are slightly higher on the culture and heritage dimension. Stressing the country-of-origin of a brand will make more sense for the French in Japan, where the image is overall very positive, than in the United States. By contrast, the Americans would be much more receptive to a British origin, as Exhibit 13.5 shows.

Place Branding

The nation branding approach has now been extended to a more general "place branding" concept. One application has been to cities around the world, rating 30 cities in six areas: Presence (contribution to culture/science and general status), Place (physical aspects), Potential (job/education opportunities), Pulse (urban lifestyle), People (welcome/diversity), and Prerequisites (basic services and amenities). The top 10 in 2005:

1. London
2. Paris
3. Sydney
4. Rome
5. Barcelona
6. Amsterdam
7. New York
8. Los Angeles
9. Madrid
10. Berlin

EXHIBIT 13.4
How Japanese See Brand France

Source: Copyright © 2002 Simon Anholt.

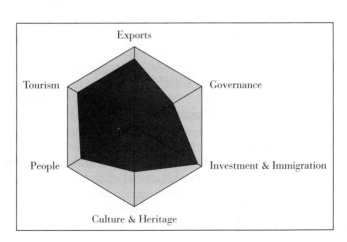

EXHIBIT 13.5
How Americans See Brand Britain

Source: Copyright © 2002 Simon Anholt.

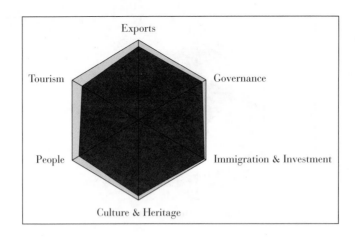

With globalization, it seems we cannot avoid branding—and we cannot avoid rankings either!

How Brands Function

There are several reasons why brands are important. Some reasons have been at work for a long time, others have emerged more recently with globalization and increased competition.

Risk Avoidance and Trust

The traditional explanation for why brands influence customers involves the consumers' desire to avoid risk and the consequent preference for a well-known brand. This is still a very powerful reason why strong brands tend to have an advantage and why consumers tend to trust and be loyal to their usual brand. The brand becomes a cue to the quality of a brand and the consumers learn what to expect from the brand. Consistency in a brand therefore becomes important—McDonald's offerings might not be perceived as high quality, but they must serve predictable quality so as not to cause consumer disappointment and dilute their brand.

Longevity and Familiarity

A related economic factor explaining the role of brands is that consumers understand that if a brand is able to remain in a market, it cannot be all bad. In the short run a weak brand can survive via strong promotion, but in the long run the actual product or service quality will win out. Thus, older brands can have an automatic advantage over new and unfamiliar brands. It is also one reason why a lack of familiarity is often a fundamental weakness in a brand. Research shows that consumers tend to stay with tried and true brands; one reason local brands often have an initial advantage over newly entered global brands.

Iconic and Experiential

But brands have taken on more importance than economics alone allows. Today, a brand is something more than just a familiar and trustworthy name that the customers can rely on. Brands have become icons in their own right, not simply signifying product quality or familiarity but offering excitement, peer group acceptance, and enhanced self-perceptions. They are **experiential brands,** meaning they provide a unique experience for the user. **Iconic brands** offer more than just the physical product, the way the experiential Harley-Davidson brand signifies more a lifestyle than just a motorcycle, or The Body Shop brand embodies environmental consciousness. Consumers develop affinity or intimacy with their favorite brands and use them to define their own special person, their identity.[5] Brands offer emotional satisfaction in addition to the functional satisfaction from a reliable product or service.

Branding managers try to position their brands as *iconic* since consumers then become even more attached to the brands—and iconic products are easier to extend into new product categories. A typical iconic brand-building strategy is the opening of company-owned stores. Disney, Sony, Virgin, and Apple were some the pioneers with this strategy, and others have followed and extended the idea. Harley-Davidson now sells apparel and has also opened a few cafes in addition to the special brand store common for iconic brands.

Emotional Drivers

The reason for the increased relevance of emotional factors in consumer choice is that today customers often choose between products and services on the basis of brand alone. Two factors in particular have made for this.

1. Many markets are often in the mature and saturation stages. This means that customers' needs are more emotional than physical. Brands can offer such emotional satisfaction over and above the functional requirements of a product or service. Beyond familiarity and trust, a strong brand can offer peer group approval, heightened self-esteem, and possibly status and prestige.
2. Benchmarking and "me-too" products have made functional product differentiation hard to sustain as a competitive advantage. We discussed this development in the preceding chapter. Many consumers cannot distinguish competing products without checking the brand logo. If you see a new car, a new motor bike, or a new purse, that looks great, what do you look for right away? The brand. You cannot decide whether you like it or not without seeing the logo. The brand naturally becomes a focus of attention.

Generally speaking, the importance of emotional drivers varies by hedonic versus utilitarian products. Utilitarian products include common household items—detergents, paper products, toothpaste, and so on—which are typically bought for their functional role alone. Here, brands tend to simply serve to identify the acceptable choices. Quality and value are basic determinants. Hedonic products, on the other hand, are those bought for their functional and emotional value, including social value, status, and so on. These include products such as apparel, cell phones, cars, and similar products. They are often conspicuous when used, and thus noticed and perhaps recognized by others.

Cultural Differences

The importance of brands also varies across cultures, especially for hedonic product categories. Since such products are very visible they tend to have a social and cultural impact. Hofstede's classification scheme of cultures (from Chapter 3) can be used to explain some of these differences. For example, the brand chosen in a collectivist culture is likely to be more influenced by social considerations than one in an individualistic culture. In societies with greater power distance, prestigious brands are more likely to be preferred. In cultures with greater risk avoidance, well-known brands would have more of an advantage. And so on.

To exemplify these distinctions, one can derive a few likely differences between collectivist Japan, individualistic United States, and the greater power-distance in the traditional European class societies (see Exhibit 13.6).

Exhibit 13.6 shows a listing of some of the major factors influencing choice of brand. In Japan, the brand has much emotional value and helps identify which group the individual belongs to. In the United States, on the other hand, the attraction of a brand is more economically based, and convenience and individual taste is much more prominent. The individual emphasis is also true in Europe, but here the social impact is very relevant as well, reflecting aspirations and status of the individual. It should be

EXHIBIT 13.6
Cultural Differences in the Role of Brands

Japan	United States	Europe
Consumer Benefits:		
Image	Risk Reduction	Recognition
"Feel good"	Time saver	Achievement
Emotional	Identity	High Aspirations
"Belonging"	Individual	Distinct
Selling Point:		
"Value added" affect	Convenient and sure	Calculated social value
Social Role:		
Peer acceptance	Peer domination	Status

stressed that these factors are all at play when consumers choose a brand, and the exhibit only suggests the likely differences in emphasis among the three cultures.

To summarize, brands typically serve three main functions for the customer in any market:

1. As a guide to evaluating the product or service. This is the traditional economic function.
2. As an icon in its own right, with emotional impact that affirms affinity and self-perception. This is the emotional aspect of a brand, creating an association between the consumers and "their own" brands.
3. As a social statement, offering recognition among peers. Brands are social statements, especially in terms of conspicuous consumption.

Brand Equity

The increased importance of brands has led to the development of the concept of brand equity, a customer-based measure of the strength of a brand. Managing brand equity has become a major concern not only for marketing managers but also for top management. **Brand equity** is basically the added value that a strong brand offers to the customer and to the firm. David Aaker, a branding guru, defines *brand equity* as "a set of assets linked to a brand's name and symbol that adds to the value provided by a product or service to a firm and/or that firm's customers.[6] The major asset categories are

1. Brand name awareness.
2. Brand loyalty.
3. Perceived quality.
4. Brand associations.

Brand equity involves benefits both to the customers and to the firm. The customer benefits involve what might be called "soft" benefits, relating to the comfortable feeling of choosing a familiar brand, the sense of security that comes from choosing a well-known brand, the affinity that comes from being loyal to "your own" brand, the approval from your peers when selecting a well-recognized brand, and so on. The benefits to the firm are closer to the bottom line, the revenue benefits from being able to count on a strong and loyal customer base. These benefits can be called the "hard" benefits of brand equity.

Soft equity is usually measured by a combination of measures of consumer awareness, knowledge, liking, affinity, and other measures of brand strength. A good example of such a customer-oriented measure of brand strength is one used by Landor Associates, a branding design and research firm affiliated with the Young & Rubicam advertising agency. Landor uses survey respondents' scores on brand awareness,

The global Coca-Cola name in eight different languages. Although the logo of most global brands are jealously guarded to ensure exact replication and consistency and prevent imitation, the original cursive writing of the Coca-Cola name is not easily rendered in some foreign versions. Reproduced with permission of The Coca-Cola Company.

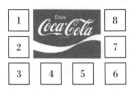

1. Arabic
2. French
3. Japanese
4. Thai
5. Spanish
6. Chinese
7. Hebrew
8. Polish

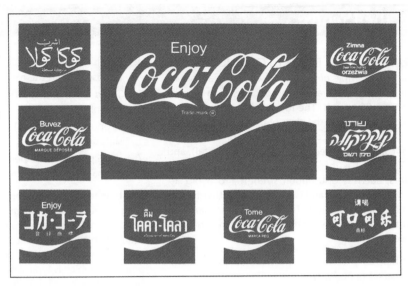

knowledge, and esteem to first develop a measure of brand *stature*. Respondents' perceptions of the brands in terms of "Differentiation" and "Relevance" are then combined to yield a measure of the leverage or *vitality* of a brand. The overall equity of a brand is assessed as a multiplication of stature with vitality.[7]

Brand Valuation

The development of the "hard" concept of brand value was spurred by the need to assess company value in acquisitions, mergers, and takeovers. In many cases the purchase price is mainly determined by the brand value or "brand equity." Gradually, what has emerged is a sense that a strong brand might be the most valuable asset a firm has. For example, in the 1998 sale of Rolls Royce by Vickers of England to German Volkswagen, the name itself ("Rolls Royce") was sold separately to BMW, a transaction that led some observers to claim that Volkswagen got cheated. Brand equity assets are still off the corporate balance sheets in most countries (although "goodwill" entries often include a good deal of brand value), the United Kingdom being one significant exception. Nevertheless, the creation of the brand equity concept has had a profound effect on global marketers and why there is a drive toward global brands.

Brand value is usually measured as a combination of these various elements. Although the exact formulas differ between analysts (see box, "Interbrand's Hard Equity Formula" for one example), the basic approach is similar. The basic idea is the same as in the valuation of stock shares, deriving expected future cash flows. First, the formulas attempt to identify that part of total earnings of a company that can be attributed to the brand. The brand equity is then computed as a discounted brand earnings flow into the future.

The basic steps involved in brand equity valuation are as follows:

1. Identify the relevant markets or market segments where the brand is sold.

2. Estimate intangible earnings in each market as brand revenue less operating costs, taxes, and cost of capital employed. These are the net earnings that could potentially be due to the brand itself.

3. Assess the role of the brand in intangible earnings to get a measure of "brand strength." To do this, identify first the true demand drivers (e.g., price, advertising), then what role the brand itself plays in the effectiveness of these drivers (e.g., a strong brand should lower the price elasticity and thus the brand should be less sensitive to price increases). This is typically a percentage measure, where 100 percent means that the brand accounts for all of the intangible earnings. This would be a very strong brand.

Getting the Picture

INTERBRAND'S HARD EQUITY FORMULA

One prominent example of how a dollar value can be assigned to a brand is Interbrand's approach used to identify the world's top 100 brands. The formula first deducts from total company earnings (1) the costs of brand sales, (2) marketing costs, (3) overhead costs, including depreciation, (4) a charge for capital employed (5–10 percent of capital), and (5) taxes. The result is then adjusted to account for non-brand factors, such as distribution strength, to avoid attributing revenues to the brand when in reality other factors are responsible for the earnings. The resulting *brand earnings* are then further adjusted by *brand strength*. Brand strength involves several factors:

1. Leadership (25 percent)—The brand's ability to dominate a market (a positive).
2. Stability (15 percent)—How long the brand has been established (a positive).
3. Market volatility (10 percent)—The risk of new technology, low entry barriers (a negative).

4. Reach (25 percent)—The geographic spread of the sales (a positive gain the more global the brand).
5. Trend (10 percent)—The upward (or downward) trajectory of the brand.
6. Support (10 percent)—The consistency of marketing support (a positive).
7. Legal protection (5 percent)—Problems with protecting the name in different markets (a negative).

These factors are combined according to the percentage weights into a *brand strength index,* which is used to derive a discount factor for the projected future earnings. A strong brand with a high index score will be sure to yield strong future earnings, and thus its discount rate is small, around the 5 percent, which is typical of a low-risk investment. A weaker brand will have a higher discount rate, reflecting the higher risk of its future earnings. The resulting brand value for each brand is the number used to derive the list of the top 100 brands.

Sources: **Interbrand.com;** Clifton et al., 2004.

4. Multiply the intangible earnings in step 2 by the branding percentage in step 3 to get a corrected value of brand earnings due to the brand itself.
5. Estimate the future potential of the brand by deriving a "viability score," which indicates the long-term competitiveness of the brand.
6. Calculate the appropriate discount rate as a function of the brand viability score—stronger brands have lower discount rates.
7. Compute the NPV (net present value) of the projected future earnings attributable to the brand, using adjusted earnings in step 4 and the applicable discount rate from step 6.
8. The total brand equity is the sum of brand value NPVs in each market.

As can be seen from the formulas, global brands have advantages. Their higher reach figures prominently in the brand strength computation. Furthermore, even though local brands may be stronger in a given market, a global brand will be a player in more markets. Thus, once the worldwide market is considered, a local champion's score is diluted by its weakness elsewhere. Since brand equity is basically a sum of brand earnings across markets, it is not surprising to find that virtually all of the top 100 brands can be considered "global."

The Advantages of Global Brands

The factors behind brand equity and brand value computations encourage the expansion of local brands into global brands. The strong brand becomes an asset that can be leveraged in many markets. A brand is not difficult to transfer abroad, allowing global expansion. Also, with the advent of global communications, the international promotion of a unique brand name is both feasible and desirable, because of the scale advantages. If the brand name is everywhere culturally acceptable and legally available, a global brand strategy is natural. And the firm-specific brand names can be legally protected.

Getting the Picture

BUILDING BRANDS ON THE INTERNET? YOU BET!

Commenting on Internet marketing, Steve Knox from Procter & Gamble admitted at the 2002 Ad:Tech in San Francisco that building brands on the Internet has now proven possible. One problem is that it only truly works if the product has some inherent "wow" factor that people are attracted to. If not, one has to turn to "viral" marketing.

One product that apparently has "wow" in it is the automobile, at least for the models targeting the "young and wild" ones in all of us. One very successful online ad campaign is from BMW, via their BMW Films project *The Hire.* The online film series premiered in 2001 with original short films directed by some of Hollywood's most noted directors, including John Frankenheimer, Ang Lee, Wong Kar-Wai, Guy Ritchie, and Alejandro Gonzales Inarritu. The constant in each short film is star Clive Owen, a mysterious, unnamed driver-for-hire around whom all the films revolve. Joining Owen is an illustrious supporting cast: *Hostage* features Maury Chaykin and Kathryn Morris; *Ticker* stars F. Murray Abraham and Don Cheadle, with special cameo appearances by Ray Liotta, Robert Patrick, and Dennis Haysbert; and *Beat the Devil* pits Gary Oldman against James Brown in a race between good and evil, with a special cameo appearance by Marilyn Manson.

The logic? Well, 85 percent of the kinds of people who buy a BMW use the Internet to conduct prepurchase research. They also like movies. "Never before (or since) had an automotive company taken such a strong stance to drive consumers to the Web, and the results are compelling," advertising analysts say. More than 10 million "hits" have been registered from people who actually then watch the movie. Nearly 2 million people have registered on the BMW site, with 60 percent of those opting to receive more information via e-mail.

When the product lacks the intrinsic "wow," Internet marketers have turned to "viral" marketing. Viral marketing is the new name for efforts made by marketers to get people to talk about their brand. Planting the "virus" can take many forms—an outrageous claim, an offensive remark, a striking event. This is when even bad news is good news—the "Janet Jackson baring a breast during the Superbowl" phenomenon. A typical Internet viral marketing effort to build a brand is the way home appliance manufacturers—those square white appliances—offer quizzes, intelligence tests, irrelevant historical tidbits, and cartoon figures on their home pages. Create buzz, make it fun, and make people talk is the name of the game. In some ways viral marketing is hardly new—but the Internet way to reach the consumer is. And to build the brand, make the visit memorable and exciting.

One successful example of using online viral marketing to deliver not only buzz but also tangible brand benefits is the auto maker Mazda's "parking" campaign (mazdamovies.com). The campaign film clip sparked global debate on blogs and forums about male and female parking capabilities, and even resulted in a threat of a lawsuit. Globally, the campaign generated over a million quantified clip views in less than a month and helped sell a staid product that is very similar to many others in its class. As Steve Jelliss, CRM manager for Mazda Motors (UK), stated, "Our online viral marketing campaigns have proven their value in providing high brand exposure to a wide-as-possible audience, and ultimately contributing to car sales."

Sources: Justin Kirby, "Getting the Bug," *Brand Strategy,* July 12, 2004, p. 33; Rodney Chester, "What's On," *Courier Mail (Queensland, Australia),* October 31, 2002, p. 16; "Microsoft, BMW and Artisan Debut BMW Films Digital Cinema Series with Premiere of 'Standing in the Shadows of Motown,'" *PR Newswire, Financial News,* October 30, 2002.

There are several equity gains for companies using global brands. The three major factors are:

- Demand spillover
- Global customers
- Scale economies

Demand spillover is an important factor favoring the global brand. Sales in one country market generate demand in another country. Media coverage spills over into new country markets, and the brand name becomes well known and easily recognized. What people in one country buy is what other people want; they know about it through news reports, television coverage, and magazines. To capitalize on spillovers the brand name needs to be the same everywhere, so a global brand has a clear advantage over local brands. A global brand name also makes a difference on the Internet, since research shows that well-known brands attract more hits (and the Internet may now be a good way to develop a great brand—see box, "Building Brands on the Internet: You Bet!").

Brand awareness tends to follow a cycle similar to the product life cycle: After introduction and growth in awareness, saturation is reached as the penetration of a market rises to a certain level (although a decline stage is not necessarily part of the **brand**

cycle, with many older brands doing well). It is much harder to raise awareness levels from 80 to 85 percent of the market than from 35 to 40 percent. Because of this "ceiling" effect, raising brand equity in a given market tends to be difficult for established brands. Instead, it is usually more effective to extend the brand in two ways: new products and new markets. Demand spillover helps in either case.

A second way that benefits are gained is through *global customers.* In business-to-business markets, where the consumers might be large multinational firms, global customers are common. But this is also the case in consumer goods markets. As people travel internationally for business or pleasure, airport shops become important distribution outlets for product categories such as cosmetics, cameras, and fashion goods. These global customers are naturally more attracted to global brands that they can find in many places.

Scale economies constitute a third reason favoring a global brand. The standardization of logo, packaging, and production lowers manufacturing costs. As for promotional expenses, the cost for producing a global TV commercial can easily run into more than US$1 million, much higher than a local campaign. Playtex's "Traumbuegel" commercial ran a good US$2.5 million. But when used as a prototype for campaigns all over the world, the production costs can be spread over a much larger volume, making global TV commercials very cost-effective. The same goes for the volume discounts in global media and global distribution. Creating brand awareness becomes much less costly.

According to the most recent research, people tend to judge global brands different from local brands.[8] Three dimensions stand out. The most important is an assumption of *quality,* global brands seen as providing higher quality than local brands. Second, global brands naturally elicit a sense of belonging to the larger cosmopolitan world, a sense of *global identity.* Third, global brands are held to higher standards in terms of *social responsibility.* A global brand is expected to do more about global warming than a local brand, for example. Strikingly, the research shows that these dimensions are quite similar among consumers in a diverse set of countries, including Brazil, China, Egypt, France, Japan, and the United States (although the salience of global identity is weaker in the United States than in the other countries).

The advantages of global brands are typically stronger in less-developed countries, where the aspirational aspects and pent-up demand create a status advantage to global brands. Most research showing the advantages of global brands has shown the increased prestige, cosmopolitanism, belonging to a global class of consumers, and so on—characteristics that are particularly attractive to disadvantaged consumers.

In brief, the perceptions of global brands add to their strength:

- Perceived *globality* of a brand is consistently associated with high *product quality*, across all countries, and across all product categories (Holt et al., 2004).
- Perceived *globality* of a brand also adds a cachet of *esteem* and *prestige* (Johansson and Ronkainen, 2005; Steenkamp et al., 2003).
- Global brands are associated strongly with *power* and social responsibility (Holt et al., 2004).

The Disadvantages of Global Brands

There are several disadvantages of global brands. Basically the disadvantages in the marketplace are advantages for local brands.

Disadvantages in the marketplace:

1. Global brands are not adapted to local conditions and preferences.
2. Global brands are perceived as dominating local brands and threatening local culture.
3. Global brands are less unique than local brands.

Of course, global brands are domestic in their home market, and the global-local distinction becomes less important. Since the United States harbors the majority—about two-thirds—of the top global brands, it is not surprising to find that many consumers in the United States do not distinguish much between global and local brands. By contrast, in many other countries, consumers are very aware of the fact that many of the global brands are in fact not domestic but "foreign," although they may not be able to pinpoint exactly what the country-of-origin is.[9]

The high brand awareness for a global product can have its drawbacks. Intel, the PC chipmaker, used a "piggybacking" approach to promote its name by inducing hardware manufacturers to indicate "Intel inside" on advertising materials. Consumer awareness, though, helped exacerbate the negative public relations damage when the company had problems with its Pentium chip.

Another problem for global brands is that they are the natural targets for antiglobalization actions. In fact, Klein (2000) suggests in her primer for activists that media coverage and thus effectiveness of any antiglobalization demonstrations requires a prominent global target. If a smaller brand is attacked, the public's sympathy will easily be swayed in favor of the underdog.

Disadvantages of global brands for the firm:

1. Capturing the scale economies require skillful top-down coordination.
2. Local subsidiary managers lose motivation.
3. A global brand is an easy target for antiglobalizers and other activists.

If the disadvantages are great, the multinational firm will have to consider whether entry with the global brand is still desirable, or, alternatively, whether it is better to consider acquiring a local brand. Where the expansion takes place via acquisition of a local brand, the decision of whether to keep the local brand name or not depends crucially on the strength and loyalty associated with the local brand. In recent years, with antiglobalization and rising nationalist sentiment, the tendency has been to keep the local name. For example, when Coca-Cola acquired French Orangina, a carbonated soft drink, the decision was easy. Orangina was a very strong name with high loyalty and had already expanded outside of France. On the other hand, when Coca-Cola acquired a major competitor in India, Thums Up, the plan was for gradually replacing it with the Coca-Cola brand. However, while the effort to make Coke the market leader failed, the acquired brand held on to its customers without much promotional support, and Thums Up became the market share leader.

Global versus Local Brands

Once the manager has gained an understanding of what drives the consumer brand choices in a given market, it is time to decide whether a global or a local brand is best. Some of the factors to consider are the following:

- Is the market/product category *global*? If it is, a global brand is likely to be preferable. By contrast, in multidomestic markets local fit and identity matter, favoring a local brand.
- Is the *competition* global? If yes, a global brand would be better equipped to handle competitive pressures. In markets with strong local competition, it might be better to attempt to acquire a local brand—or stay out of the market completely.
- Do other global competitors use global brands? Competitors may be global, but their brands are mainly local. This suggests a preference on the part of the customers for local brands, again favoring local brands.
- Antiglobalization and related sentiments (such as anti-Americanism) are also factors to consider. Where strong, a global brand strategy is less desirable.
- Pro-domestic sentiment, where strong, is also a factor that favors the use of a local brand.

- The branding strategy needs also to take into account the likely shift in the local marketplace when a new brand enters. This was also discussed in Chapter 11. Market research before entry might indicate a positive (or negative) reception for an entering global brand, but things can of course change after entry, either because consumer preferences change or because new competitors enter.
- Other factors to consider include the fact that consumers typically associate global brands with positive attributes, including higher esteem, good quality, and a sense of aspiration.[11]

Brand extensions into new product categories are a common but risky strategy that sometimes fails when the new product category is too different.[12] Coca-Cola's efforts in jeans and other apparel have not been very successful, and neither was Nike's excursion into brown leisure shoes. Expansion into new markets is often the simpler and safer alternative, especially when media spillovers have created a latent demand for the brand. Globalizing the brand by introducing the products in new markets overseas becomes the natural solution to growing brand equity.

Acquiring a Local Brand?

The decision whether to expand internationally via acquisition or with an existing brand name depends not simply on market reactions but also on the capabilities of the firm. Global brands require greater management skills at headquarters than simply using a decentralized organizational structure with a great deal of local autonomy. For multinationals whose managerial advantage lies in access to financial resources, acquiring leading brands in other markets and leaving them under local management offers a relatively simple avenue to growth. This helps explain strategies of companies such as InBev, the large Belgian brewer that is one of the top beer producers in the world. InBev's global expansion has been accomplished by the acquisition of leading beers around the world—the company owns Labatt's in Canada, Dos Equis in Mexico, and Rolling Rock in the United States, in addition to its flagship brand, Stella Artois. InBev is using the local subsidiaries to help establish Stella as its one global brand, to compete effectively with Heineken and Carlsberg, two brewers with much more of a one-brand strategy (although Heineken has bought Amstel, both Dutch, and Carlsberg has acquired its Danish compatriot Tuborg).

The beer market, as we saw in the opening vignette, is in fact a multidomestic market with global players. This affects the globalization strategy employed. The leader, Anheuser-Busch, has long been very active in globalizing its own Budweiser and Bud Light brands (including the sponsorship of the soccer World Cup in Germany in 2006), but has now also recognized the need to globalize by acquiring local breweries and keeping their brand names.

Anheuser-Busch became one of the first international beer makers in China when the company bought the Wuhan brewery in 1995. Since then, Wuhan's beer production has more than quadrupled to some 4 million barrels per year. Locally produced Budweiser and Harbin brands are distributed to clients in Hong Kong as well as in northern, eastern, and southern China. In 2004, Anheuser-Busch also acquired China's fifth-largest brewer, Harbin, in northern China, where per capita beer consumption is double China's national average. Not only has Anheuser-Busch made Harbin's brands available throughout most of mainland China, the company has launched Harbin as an imported brand in the United States starting in 2006. Anheuser-Busch also owns 27 percent of the Tsingtao Brewery, part of a key strategic alliance. The Tsingtao Brewery is China's largest domestic brewery and beer exporter.[13]

The Brand Portfolio

At any point in time, especially among companies with a history of growth through mergers and acquisitions, multinationals are likely to have a portfolio of a few global brands and several local brands. Exhibit 13.7 shows the **brand portfolio** of six major multinational companies across 67 countries. The exhibit shows that less than

EXHIBIT 13.7
Brands of Six Multinational Companies in 67 Countries

Source: Betsy V. Boze and Charles R. Patton, "The Future of Consumer Branding as Seen from the Picture Today," *Journal of Consumer Marketing* 12, no. 4 (1995), p. 22

Company	Total Number of Brands	Brands Found in 50% or More Countries (%)	Brands Marketed in Only One Country (%)
Colgate	163	6 (4%)	59 (36%)
Kraft GF	238	6 (3%)	104 (44%)
Nestlé	560	19 (4%)	250 (45%)
P&G	217	18 (8%)	80 (37%)
Quaker	143	2 (1%)	55 (38%)
Unilever	471	17 (4%)	236 (50%)
Total	1,792		

10 percent of the brands can be considered truly global. The fact is that there are relatively few brands that are truly global, if by global you mean available practically everywhere under the same name.

The brands are typically managed in a hierarchical fashion. The **brand hierarchy** can take several forms. In one, the most important global brands are at the top, followed by regional and local brands. This is the typical branding scheme of companies such as Nestlé and Sara Lee. Alternatively, the top can be the corporate brand, possibly global, followed by sub-branded model names, also possibly worldwide, and specific model designations, possibly worldwide. This is the typical hierarchy of auto companies such as Honda and Mercedes. In the case of Sony, the hierarchy starts with the corporate name and cascades down through the various divisions (consumer electronics, entertainment, business markets) to specific product lines and finally to models.

The hierarchies mirror the levels in the organization where brand responsibility is lodged, top management focusing on the global brands, often the corporate brand.[15] While brand managers in individual markets still manage the local execution of the marketing strategy, global brand management is necessarily a strategic function at headquarters.[16] In the senior management study mentioned, fully 91 percent of the 153 executives had a "definite plan or strategy" for enhancing their brand in the next two years. The basic thrust of these plans was similar across the companies. With quality and functional performance comparable across brands and therefore expected by the customers, differentiation would come from customer service and increased promotional support for the brand image—and global expansion.

Implementing a globalization strategy in such a multiproduct and multibrand company raises its own issues. A basic consideration is which local brands can and should be replaced:

1. Should one brand be globalized by simply changing other local brand names? If the corporation already has local brands in the product category, those might need to be changed to the globalizing name. In the drive to globalize the Nokia name, the Finnish company used its name for all the telecommunication products manufactured by its acquired foreign firms. By contrast, Nestlé opted to keep the old names for its bottled water products, including Vittel, Perrier, and Ramlosa. In 2006 Nestlé sold a number of its local water brands to concentrate on a few of the large international brands, and also introduce its own brands, Nestlé Pure Life and Nestlé Aquarel.

2. Which local brands should be chosen for the changeover? Can the local managers be persuaded to drop one or more of their brands? The local brand to be changed has to offer a product line that matches the globalizing brand's product line. Furthermore, it should preferably not be a very strong brand locally so as not to lose loyal customers and discourage local managers. Electrolux, the appliance maker intent on globalizing its name, has met resistance in India, where it owns Kelvinator, a locally strong brand. By contrast, Merrill Lynch has had little problems among either customers or employees in using its name in Japan after acquiring the local branch network of failed Yamaichi Securities.

Getting the Picture

WHAT'S IN A NAME? PLENTY!

Even though global brand managers would like to use the same brand name everywhere, there are numerous examples where this has failed because of difficulty of pronunciation, unfortunate associations, or ambiguous meaning—or simply because the name had already been taken. Mr. Clean is Mr. Propre in France, Toyo Kogyo became Mazda in the West (and then changed to the same name in Japan), and Philips became Norelco in the United States. But when the brand is introduced in a country such as China where the written characters are entirely different, the problems escalate dramatically.

A language such as English has a phonographic writing system, where the alphabet and the words represent the sound of the spoken language. By contrast, the Chinese writing system is logographic, with words and concepts represented by icons, or *kanji* characters, which were originally derived as pictures of the things described. There is no necessary link between the sound of the word and the *kanji* used to write it. To some extent the Chinese *kanji* ideographs

are in fact also well known to Koreans and Japanese, with the same meaning but with often completely different pronunciations.

This means that a western brand introduced into China might be "translated" in two different ways. The translation can be by sound, or by meaning. To get the sound right, the chosen *kanji* might well be meaningless or worse. Coca-Cola's first effort has become famous: The characters chosen as correct-sounding, said in fact, "Bite the wax tadpole," whatever that means. Shifting to a more meaningful set of characters, the Coca-Cola brand emerged as, "Tastes good and makes you happy," a much preferred suggestion. On the other hand, the pronunciation is slightly off, with a suggestive Hawaiian flavor, "Ko-kou-ko-le."

Since brands become symbols of people's lifestyles, it is important to match the name to what the consumers aspire to.

Sources: Shi Zhang and Bernd H. Schmitt,"Creating Local Brands in Multilingual International Markets," *Journal of Marketing Research* XXXVIII (August 2001), pp. 313–25; Bernd H. Schmitt and Alex Simonson, *Marketing Aesthetics* (New York: Free Press, 1997).

Globalizing A Local Brand

Global brands typically start out as strong brands in their domestic market. Having established themselves as leading shareholders domestically, they then expand in a waterfall type of strategy into foreign markets. This helps the brands capitalize on the brand-building experiences at home, especially useful when expanding from a leading market. It also allows the brand to benefit from media spillovers. A typical example is Starbucks, the coffee chain, whose success in the U.S. market has been the basis for its rapid expansion abroad. Although the American market cannot be viewed as a leading market for coffee, the American-style ambiance and service of Starbucks was finetuned at home before venturing abroad. Starbucks is now successful in London and Paris as well as Tokyo and Shanghai, having opened up a whole new coffee segment among the young and restless.

To evaluate the globalization potential of a local brand, it is useful to systematically go through a checklist of factors.[10] First are some questions about appropriateness or **brand fit:**

1. Does the brand name make sense outside of the source country? What does it mean? What associations are generated? Nokia from Finland, a leading company in mobile phones, is not unaware of the fact that its name sounds vaguely Japanese: The Finnish and Japanese languages come from the same roots. But often a simple translation of the brand name will not be sufficient (see box, "What's in a Name? Plenty!").

2. If the name suggests a country association, is the effect positive? Is the source country a leading market or a follower? The name of GM's German subsidiary ("Opel") may be preferable to "Chevrolet" with its American heritage.

3. Is the name available legally in many countries? Philips, the Dutch electronics giant, has been hampered continuously in the North American market because the Phillips oil company was the first to register its similar brand name there.

If the answers to these questions are positive, the strong local brand is a good candidate for globalization. Next, its place in the brand portfolio needs to be considered.

4. Does the brand complement other global brands in the portfolio or compete directly against them? Because of resource demands and the threat of cannibalization, it is seldom justifiable to keep two directly competing global brand names, which is one reason Sony decided to drop the Columbia record label after acquiring CBS's music business. On the other hand, Sony supports Aiwa—a subsidiary, a global brand with electronic goods at a lower price than the Sony parent—on the premise that cannibalization is minimal. And of course the brand may simply help extend the product line, as in the case of Campbell Soup's acquisition and globalization of Godiva, the Belgian chocolatier.

5. Should the growth be limited to the creation of a regional brand? Even if the brand portfolio has a direct global competitor, or if some local brands cannot be changed, the possibility of creating a regional brand should be considered. A regional brand can be a stiff competitor for the global brand in its region and will also help the company gain a larger and more defensible position in a region. For example, apart from its global "Kronenbourg" label, the Strasbourg-based beer maker also markets its "1664" label in southern Europe.

Changeover Tactics

Once the brand to be globalized has been identified, standard **brand changeover** tactics can be employed.[14]

The *fade-in/fade-out* gradual option is the most common. The global brand is linked to the local brand for a time, after which the local brand is dropped. The time involved varies from months to a couple of years. Frequently purchased products require less time because the exposure penetrates faster. The approach usually involves a dual branding tactic:

- "Endorsement branding," with one brand introducing the new brand. Messages such as "From the makers of…" or "From the folks who brought you…" or simply "From…" or "By…" establish the connection and the legitimacy of the new brand. Mars, the American-based confectionery maker, used "Pedigree by Pal" to prepare the way for global Pedigree to replace local Pal dog food.

- "Double-branding," in which both names are reproduced faithfully to their old logos and simply placed next to each other. This can be somewhat confusing but avoids losing loyal customers and channel members. Both the Whirlpool and Philips names appeared on appliances when Whirlpool took over Philips's white-goods division, and after a transition period the Philips name was dropped. Black and Decker used the same approach to put its name on the acquired G.E. product line of appliances.

A less gradual approach, sometimes called *summary axing*, simply drops the local brand name and introduces the new brand. Although simpler to manage, this approach can create problems. In 1986 Mars pulled its Treets brand off the European market and introduced the product as M&Ms, using the same Treets slogan: "Melts in your mouth, not in your hand." Reaction among adult customers was negative, and sales and profits suffered. Learning the lesson, when Mars changed its local Raider brand to global Twix, the company used extensive *forewarning,* another approach to name changeover. TV commercials explained, "Now Raider becomes Twix, for it is Twix everywhere in the world."

Defending Local Brands

The success of global brands of products does not mean that locally adapted products have no opportunity.

As the experiences of many travelers attest, even in open markets many local products survive and prosper next to global brands. In audio products, shoes, apparel, and other consumer goods, local products coexist with well-known world brands. In

Getting the Picture

THIS BUD IS NOT FOR YOU, ANHEUSER

Its market saturated in the United States, St. Louis–based beer maker Anheuser-Busch, the world's biggest brewer, is trying to market its leading Budweiser brand globally. But the rights to the Budweiser name in Europe belong to a much smaller beer maker, Budejovicky Budvar, the original Czech brewer of Budweiser. The Czech company has the leading market share at home and has a growing export business to other European countries as well.

Since beer marketing is very brand oriented, Anheuser-Busch has long made efforts to acquire the rights to the Budweiser name globally, all in vain as the government-owned company has always refused to negotiate. But after the fall of communism, when the Czechs started to privatize industry and sell off government-owned businesses, Anheuser-Busch figured it had another chance and decided to try again to buy the little beermaker and the trademark.

But the Czech managers and workers were not about to be bought up by the American giant. They did not want any part of a company that they suspected would only pull the plug on their operation, siphon the profits away, and try to take their beer off the market. And they did not like the idea of replacing their own great beer with the lightweight watery-tasting beer of the American namesake.

To soften up the folks, Anheuser-Busch opened up a $1 million cultural center in Ceske Budejovice, the town where the brewer is located, inaugurated baseball and basketball teams, opened a marble-floored cafe, and offered scholarships and English lessons. But to no avail. Listen to Frantisek Nedorost, a 52-year-old electrician: "I absolutely disagree with the Americans buying part of our company. I like Americans, their culture, their films. But I know American beer doesn't reach the quality of Czech beer. It's much poorer, much weaker."

In 2001, the fight was joined in the courts. While Anheuser-Busch gained the rights to the Budweiser and Bud brands in most of the European countries, Budejovicky Budvar won the rights to the Budweiser name in Denmark, Latvia, Finland, and South Korea. By 2004 there were about 40 lawsuits still pending in different countries.

What's in a name? Plenty!

Sources: Perlez, 1995; Koenig; 1995; "Czech brewer favored in 'Budweiser' fight," *Associated Press*, June 29, 2004.

business-to-business markets local vendors do well with custom software and supplies. Local beers are successful throughout North America and Europe, even though in some cases their market is directly targeted by global competitors (see box, "This Bud Is Not for You, Anheuser").

The defense of local brands often involve maintaining or even upgrading the product quality, and then expanding abroad from the local base. Today's ease of global communication and efficient transportation makes such a strategy increasingly feasible even for small local brands. A particularly strong option is to counterattack any entering global brand by expanding into that brand's home market. A typical case is the strategy employed by Illycaffe, the Italian espresso producer, when threatened by the Starbucks entry into Europe. Even though Starbucks has basically expanded the market for coffee in Europe and elsewhere, making its entry much less threatening, Illy has seen fit to respond by adopting a similar strategy of opening its own small coffee outlets. Given its limited resources, the family-owned company has concentrated its shops in trendsetting locations such as New York, London, and Tokyo, country capitals (Saigon, Beijing, Budapest), and several major airports (see also Cases 2-2 and 2-3).

The sameness of global products creates a potential for local products in special niche segments of the market. These niches comprise consumers who are looking for ethnic color, uniqueness, and local tradition. There are people who still like stick shifts, cigarettes without filters, and hair spray. Local products provide variety for consumers in special situations for which the global product is not suitable. Thus, while global brands may capture a large segment of the market, local variants can coexist underneath the global umbrella.

The Advantages of Local Brands

But local brands do not necessarily have to be on the defensive. There is research that shows how most of the top brands in a market tend to be local brands. In one study covering eight different countries (including the United States, the United Kingdom, and Japan) the authors found that about 75 percent of the top 150 brands were represented in only one of the countries, suggesting the majority of the brands were not very global.[17] Similarly, research focusing on the European markets shows that a similar majority of the preferred brands are in fact local. The authors even found that local brands are perceived as equal to global brands in quality, a surprising finding given that most previous research has shown a quality advantage to global brands.[18] Local brands tend to be more familiar to consumers, and familiarity with a brand is strongly correlated with a quality perception. Any brand that is not well known is at a serious disadvantage.

Familiar local brands can have several advantages. Four in particular can be identified:

1. Customization
2. Iconic status
3. Differing regulations
4. Trust

The typical reason for the success of local products is the **customization** involved. In consumer goods, the provision of adapted packaging, smaller units with lower prices, and special features such as easy repairs can make local brands very strong competitors. Customization can also involve special customer service, house calls, and the convenience that comes with proximity to the customer. In B2B markets in particular, personal attention, fast delivery, and prompt after-sales service are all factors tending to favor local products. In less-developed markets such as India, the ability to buy one cigarette, one small piece of soap, or one razor blade are things that global brands find hard to accommodate.

A local brand can also become *iconic,* an institution and representative of the local community in a way that global brands usually cannot. Mozart-kugels are a quintessential Viennese chocolate product, just as Kölsch beer is what one drinks in Cologne, while for soft drinks in India the preference is for Thums Up Cola. These local iconic brands usually have an allegiance that transcends mere brand loyalty and repeat purchases. Local consumers might also patronize other brands, but feel a certain emotional bond with the local brand, which enables the brand to survive when competitive global brands enter the market. In some cases the iconic brand starts global expansion. It is hard to believe that a company such as L.L. Bean, the original hunting and fishing equipment catalog retailer that is an emblematic New England brand, has now become a successful global brand.

Differing *regulations* across countries also play a role in supporting local brands. The differences raise barriers to entry and mean that scale economies are difficult to generate. For example, different countries tend to have different electrical norms, forcing companies to adapt their products and favor local smaller-scale manufacturers. Thus, in the electrical switches markets in Europe, the leaders are Elko in Norway, Elda in Poland, Esmi in Finland, Wibe in Sweden, and Stago in Holland. As one might have expected, in this case the global company Lexel Group has acquired the local producers, and kept their brand names.[19]

For many consumers the most important advantage of a local brand is the higher level of *trust* it inspires. This trust is mainly a result of the fact that most strong local brands have a longer history in the market than most global brands. Its long-standing presence means that the local brand has great awareness, comes easily to mind, and is automatically associated with the product category. It will take time for a new global brand to prove its value, especially since it is most likely not perceived as fully committed to the local market. One often quoted reason for a foreign company to establish local production in a country—as Dell has done in China, for example—is the notion that this will assure the consumers that the company is committed to the market, increasing the trust in its brand. By the same token, hearing that both Peugeot and Renault have withdrawn from the American automobile market can make the American consumer less sure about other French producers and brands.

Counterfeit Products

Counterfeits or **knockoffs** are fake products, imitations designed and branded so as to mislead the unwary customer into assuming that they are genuine. Counterfeit products should be distinguished from "gray trade" or parallel trade. **Gray trade** is parallel distribution of genuine goods by intermediaries other than authorized channel members. Gray trade as related to exchange rates and pricing will be discussed in Chapter 14, "Global Pricing," and gray trade in distribution will be discussed in Chapter 15, "Global Distribution."

Extent of Problem

Counterfeit products pose an ominous problem in the global marketplace. According to expert estimates, worldwide company losses due to counterfeit products are over $20 billion annually. The traditional cases of counterfeit products involve luxury goods with global brand names. Gucci wallets, Louis Vuitton bags, Cartier watches, and Porsche sunglasses are typical examples. But counterfeit products are no longer confined to designer jeans and watches. Items now routinely counterfeited include chemicals, computers, drugs, fertilizers, pesticides, medical devices, military hardware, and food—as well as parts for airplanes and automobiles.

Counterfeiting is truly a global phenomenon. For example, in Australia, two sea containers shipped to Melbourne from China in July 2004 were opened by officials uncovering 20,000 fake brand-name leather handbags and wallets, travel bags, hats, toys, and batteries.[20] This shipment included rip-offs of Nike, Burberry, Adidas, Calvin Klein, Hugo Boss, and Timberland. Ports in France and Italy receive shipments of counterfeit goods, too. Three-fourths of the counterfeit goods seized in these ports in 2003 originated in mainland China or Hong Kong, according to customs officials in Europe. In England, an estimated 6.4 billion pounds is lost to the economy every year—the U.K. government alone loses 1.7 billion pounds annually in value added tax (VAT) to counterfeiting and piracy. The clothing and footwear industries lose around 3.2 percent of their annual revenue; the toy and sportswear industries an amazing 11.5 percent.[21]

Meanwhile in the United States, in a June 3, 2004, raid, Federal officials busted a multimillion-dollar handbag counterfeiting operation in New York and arrested 14 people.[22] Agents from the U.S. Immigration and Customs Enforcement department seized $24 million in counterfeit handbags, $174,000 in cash, and 11 bank accounts containing an unknown amount of money. The counterfeiting ring imported the merchandise from China and distributed it to street vendors around the world. The counterfeiters imported two cargo containers a week, which averaged between 25,000 and 40,000 items. Each container had a profit margin ranging from $2 million to $4 million. The merchandise seized was mostly phony Prada, Louis Vuitton, and Coach bags that were manufactured in China. The items entered the port of Newark, New Jersey.

Counterfeiters operate at all levels of the economy. As foreign direct investment transfers technology and manufacturing to new countries, these countries acquire the skills to turn out bogus goods. But not all counterfeits come from developing countries. For example, experts estimate that perhaps 20 percent of all fakes are made in the United States by producers who can't make a profit otherwise or who see the opportunity of a quick kill.

Some knockoffs can be almost as good as the original and hard to detect, especially since counterfeiters now know how to faithfully reproduce the identical labels (see box, "Counterfeit Goes High Tech"). For the global marketer trying to build and sustain a global brand name's equity, such practices are naturally alarming. In Korea, knockoffs of designer clothes are sold in some stores with various designer labels offered separately so that the customer can stitch the desired label on at home.

Getting the Picture

COUNTERFEIT GOES HIGH TECH

As computerized CAD-CAM techniques become ever more sophisticated in design and manufacturing, the possibility of producing exact copies of apparel designs increases proportionately. This poses a headache for global brand names in particular, because of the price premium they fetch.

The counterfeit products from Hong Kong's and Taiwan's many small factories have long been a problem for global brands. But even in New York's Soho district, the heart of the city's large business in the fashion trade, high-tech machinery is used by some business operators to produce illegal copies of branded apparel. Given a specimen of a new Polo shirt, for example, the machinery has the capability to photographically analyze the material, the design, and the stitching, and then "reverse engineer" the process to produce an almost exact copy, including the logo stitching of a polo player and the label inside the collar.

Chinese counterfeiters have become so technically adept that the fakes they are putting out are hard to distinguish from the real thing in terms of both design and technology. Masayuki Hosokawa is the head of the Beijing office of motorcycle maker Yamaha Motor Co. His main job is promoting sales of Yamaha bikes in China, but he spends 60 percent of his time battling fakes. The fake makers clone motorcycles by using 3-D measuring instruments on a genuine Yamaha motorcycle to obtain exact design data, and then making slight alterations to the designs on a computer for their own metal molds. That way, it makes it harder for companies like Yamaha to sue them.

With annual output exceeding 10 million units, more motorcycles are manufactured in China than in any other place in the world, and nearly 90 percent of them are imitations of Japanese-brand bikes, according to the Japan Automobile Manufacturers Association. The problems with well-made imitations are not limited to motorcycles. The Hitachi Ltd. Group, another Japanese company, makes everything from home appliances to electric tools, and there are Chinese fakes for almost all of them. Hitachi estimates that imitation production costs the company 2 billion yen ($18.5 million) a year in lost profits.

Only a specialist will be able to spot the copy's minor differences from the original. Buyers from the stores usually can't tell the difference, nor can a regular customer. Of course, since there is no discernible difference, the consumer might well be satisfied. For the owner of the brand name, however, the sale of the counterfeit items means a considerable loss of revenues, and the companies pay to have guards go through merchandise and interrogate store owners to find the illegal makers, prosecute them, and destroy fake merchandise.

Sources: *New York Times,* December 13, 1994; *BusinessWeek,* December 16, 1985, pp. 48–53; Toru Miyazawa, "Bad Quality No Longer Mark of Counterfeit Products," *The Nikkei Weekly (Japan),* May 3, 2004.

Counterfeit Demand

Why do consumers buy counterfeit items? The original handbags designed by such houses as Louis Vuitton and Chanel, Prada and Hermes, command prices at several hundreds of dollars, at times even moving into the thousands. To own a Vuitton with its trademark LV monogram or a Hermes Birkin with its unmistakable lock is to own more than a purse: It is to broadcast your membership in an exclusive club, to tell the world you live the life that goes with your bag. Counterfeit is a cheap membership ticket—although with currency shifts, the prices of originals may also be quite within range (see box, "Counterfeits? No, Gray Trade in the Real Thing!"). In London, according to a recent survey by the U.K. Anti-Counterfeiting Group, one-third of consumers would knowingly purchase counterfeit goods if the price and quality were right, and 29 percent would see no harm in selling fake goods unless the purchaser was in some way at risk.[23] In Korea, two out of three students purchase imitations, according to a 2002 study by sociology professors of six universities including Seoul National University.[24] Thirty percent of the fake goods available in Korea are made in Korea, the rest are from China. Koreans churn out replicas that are considered to be of the highest quality.

Where can consumers buy fake goods? In the United Kingdom, there are markets such as Wembley Market and Portobello Road. In the United States, there's Canal Street in New York and almost any street corner in any major city. In Hong Kong and Taiwan, almost all the night markets have stalls that sell name brands. In Montreal, there are no public markets, no street-side stalls for counterfeit goods. What it does have is a thriving living room/dining room/backroom scene through which these fake goods are sold privately, by appointment or by word of mouth. Montrealers selling

Getting the Picture

COUNTERFEITS? NO, GRAY TRADE IN THE REAL THING!

When it comes to counterfeit products, one of the most common fake product categories is women's handbags. They are expensive, with U.S. dollar prices into four figures. They are relative easy to copy, and it takes a trained eye to detect the more detailed quality work in the authentic brands. They are very visible and the bestsellers are very recognizable and fashionable, making for high demand and a strong global market. Despite the efforts of the brand makers to prevent counterfeits, the Louis Vuittons, the Pradas, the Guccis, and the Kate Spades one sees on the shopping streets in major world cities are as often as not counterfeits.

In 2007, however, another threat to the brands emerged. As the value of the U.S. dollar sank precipitously against the euro and other currencies, branded handbags became a popular item in the "gray tourist trade." Individuals from countries with increasingly strong currencies found that the cost for a trip to the United States could be partly paid for by the savings in buying branded products priced much higher at home. In particular, luxury items like handbags whose prices at home might be out of reach, looked quite affordable in New York's designer boutiques.

Some of these enterprising tourists also talked to friends and relatives at home, offering to buy handbags also for them. Even further, with the Internet, eBay, and other online auction sites, it became tempting to buy several bags, reselling them online at a discount. Such tourist gray trade could be made to pay for the whole trip and even provide a tidy profit.

This game has been going on for a long time across borders, but in the past the volumes involved have been rather small. By the holiday season at the end of 2007, however, a large number of European visitors with luxury handbags on their minds—they make great Christmas gifts, of course—descended upon the United States. Under pressure from their European retailers whose sales were down significantly, the brand makers decided that things had spiraled out of control.

The solution? The manufacturers took a page from supermarkets, where it is common to limit the number of units of a highly discounted product sold to any one customer (partly done in order to enhance the attraction of the promotion, but also to prevent running out of stock). In an unusual move, the handbag manufacturers decided that no single buyer should be able to buy more than three bags in a store. Although a manufacturer cannot generally enforce such a rule against independent retailers, many of the handbag brand manufacturers run their own stores where a limit can be imposed. They were also helped by the fact that the majority of sales were through the manufacturers' own stores. If you travel from Europe to New York to buy your Louis Vuitton bag, you will not take a chance that it is counterfeit.

Sources: Julie Shapiro, "Fashion's Private Eye Targets Canal St.'s Counterfeit Bags," *Downtown Express* 20, no. 34, January 11–17, 2008; Eric Wilson, "No More Bags for You!" *The New York Times*, January 10, 2008, pp. E1, 6.

knockoffs are rarely the ones who bring them into Canada. They get them from travelers and suppliers who, in turn, bring the bags in via stops like New York or Toronto.[25]

As one might have expected, one particularly attractive channel for counterfeit trade is the Internet. Many Internet sites are now selling fake luxury goods. Sellers of fake goods thrive on the Internet because of the anonymity, the ease of transactions between individuals, and the safety of a virtual store. As long as the Internet expands it is hard to see any reduction in this trade.

Actions against Counterfeits

What can the global marketer do? For some, the counterattack has been a two-pronged "search and destroy" mission. Firms make an effort to find the factories that turn out the counterfeits, and they track down the fakes in the stores. Private investigation outfits have emerged to offer their services to multinational companies.

To help identify fakes, some firms have resorted to various coding devices. Levi Strauss, the jeans maker, weaves into its fabric a microscopic fiber pattern visible only under a special light. To deter pirates, Microsoft launched a $1.09 million print media campaign in Hong Kong, claiming that Windows 95 is coded so that counterfeits can be tracked. Many companies also appeal to their government for assistance, although the cases have to be well documented before most governments react.

Companies that rely mainly on their brand name are fighting back especially hard. Cartier is involved in 2,500 legal proceedings and devotes $3.8 million annually to its

With today's advanced technology, pirating products is nowadays almost as easy as photocopying. The labels can be the trickiest part. These Korean counterfeits allow the buyer to choose which label to stitch onto the new sports shirt. Mark Richards/Contact Press Images, Inc.

crusade; Louis Vuitton has more than 1,000 active cases each year. Tiffany has also sued eBay, claiming the Web site has aided violations of the Tiffany trademark by allowing individuals to auction off fake Tiffany jewelry.

Global counterfeit trade is cutting into profits of companies that are successful because of their brands. But no amount of effort will ever completely eradicate the copycats. For as long as there is consumer demand, companies will find that imitation is the "severest form of flattery."

Summary

In this chapter we have seen how globalized markets and increased competition has produced an unprecedented importance of branding, especially global branding. The concept of a brand has been extended beyond its traditional role as identifying the maker of a product, and now is asked to provide emotional satisfaction beyond the assurance of product quality and trustworthiness. At the same time, the brand concept has been extended to a wide variety of contexts, including institutions, nations, and individuals. The WTO is today a "brand," as is "Beckham."

The chapter explained the increased brand equity of a global brand and its measurement. It showed why globalizing a brand is often a top-management priority, and how companies go about building a global brand. The discussion also dealt with the question of whether an acquired local brand should be replaced by a global brand, and how this is done in companies. But it also cautioned that in many cases the strength of the local brand is such that it is preferable to keep the local name. The chapter also discussed the issue of which of the local brands would be good candidates for a global rollout.

The chapter also dealt with the management of the firm's brand portfolio, and how to allow local subsidiaries the management of their local brands. Finally, the chapter discussed the threat of counterfeit products and brands, and what companies do to avoid dilution of brand equity.

Key Terms

brand changeover, *449*
brand cycle, *443*
brand equity, *440*
brand extensions, *435*
brand fit, *448*
brand hierarchy, *447*
brand portfolio, *446*
corporate brands, *434*
counterfeits, *452*

customization, *451*
dual branding, *434*
endorsement brands, *434*
experiential brand, *438*
family brands, *434*
global brand, *435*
global brand management, *433*
gray trade, *452*
iconic brand, *438*

ingredient brand, *435*
knockoffs, *452*
local brands, *435*
master brand, *434*
product brands, *434*
regional brands, *435*
sub-brands, *434*
umbrella brands, *434*

Discussion Questions

1. Use store visits, the Internet, and so on to try to identify whether a particular brand that you like is global or local—or regional.
2. Are you or your peers influenced by brand names? For which products? Why, or why not?
3. Analyze the reasons why some local products (such as local beers) might have an enhanced potential when standardized global brands enter the market.
4. How can a global brand (such as McDonald's, for example) protect itself against antiglobalization forces?
5. Examine one or more of your branded possessions. How could you know that it is not a counterfeit? Could it be a gray good?

Notes

1. See "Brands at the Crossroads," a study by Bozell Worldwide and Fortune Marketing, as reported in Elliott, 1995.
2. This does not mean that all standardized products are sold under global brand names. For example, the Unilever fabric softener called Snuggle in the United States uses the same logo and packaging in most countries, but its brand name is different everywhere (Yip, 2002).
3. As cited by my colleague researching copyright protection, Michael Ryan.
4. See ACNielsen, 2001.
5. See Holt, 2004, and Schmitt, 1999. The identity appeal is perhaps most visible among teenagers, a typical global segment, but also prevalent among many other market segments (see Quart, 2004, Chapter 1).
6. Aaker, 1996, pp. 7–8, slightly adapted.
7. Keller (1998, pp. 162–63) discusses Landor's work in more detail.
8. See Holt et al., 2004.
9. See Batra et al., 2000, about global brand status in developing countries. Balabanis and Diamantopoulos, 2008, demonstrate the relative lack of country-of-origin knowledge among U.K. consumers.
10. From Kapferer, 1997, Chapter 12.
11. See Johansson and Ronkainen, 2005; Steenkamp et al., 2003; and Holt et al, 2004.
12. Keller (1998, Chapter 12) discusses brand extension problems in detail.
13. See Workman, 2007.
14. This section draws especially on Kapferer, 1997, Chapter 10.
15. The hierarchy has given rise to the notion of "brand architecture" to describe the task facing management; see, for example, Macrae, 1996, Chapter 11, and Douglas et al., 2001.
16. The value of global brands has not escaped potential global marketers. Although a 1989 study found that only about one-half of the top brands in the United States were used abroad (and some of them only in neighboring Canada), the strategic intent is for more global branding (Rosen et al., 1989).
17. See Johansson and Ronkainen, 2005.
18. See Schuiling and Kapferer, 2004.
19. This example is from Kapferer, 2002. Jean-Noel Kapferer is a French branding expert who has done considerable work showing the viability of local brands.
20. From "Customs Nab Chinese Fakes," *Gold Coast Bulletin (Australia),* July 10, 2004.
21. From "Imitating Property Is Theft," *The Economist,* May 17, 2003.

22. See Gray, 2004.
23. See Cooke, 2004.
24. See Hyun-Joo, 2004.
25. See Schwartz, 2004.

Selected References

Aaker, David A. *Building Strong Brands*. New York: Free Press, 1996.

Aaker, David A., and Alexander L. Biel, eds. *Brand Equity and Advertising*. Hillsdale, NJ: Lawrence Erlbaum Associates, 1993.

Aaker, David A., and Erich Joachimsthaler. *Brand Leadership*. New York: Free Press, 2000.

ACNielsen. *Reaching the Billion-Dollar Mark: A Review of Today's Global Brands*. Chicago: ACNielsen Inc., 2001.

Alden, Dana L.; Jan-Benedict E. M. Steenkamp; and Rajeev Batra. "Brand Positioning through Advertising in Asia, North America and Europe: The Role of Global Consumer Culture." *Journal of Marketing* 63 (January 1999), pp. 75–87.

Andrews, Edmund L. "AT&T Reaches Out (and Grabs Everyone)." *New York Times*, August 8, 1993, sec. 3, pp. 1, 6.

Anholt, Simon. *Brand New Justice. The Upside of Global Branding*. Oxford: Butterworth and Heinemann, 2003.

Balabanis, George, and Adamantios Diamantopoulos. "Brand Origin Identification by Consumers: A Classification Perspective." *Journal of International Marketing* 16, no. 1 (2008), pp. 39–71.

Batra, Rajeev. *Consumer Evaluation of Global Brands*. Presentation at the Conference on Global Branding, Georgetown University, May 4–6, 2001.

———; Venkatram Ramaswamy; Dana L. Alden; Jan-Benedict E.M. Steenkamp; and S. Ramachander. "Effects of Brand Local and Nonlocal Origin on Consumer Attitudes in Developing Countries." *Journal of Consumer Psychology* 9, no. 2 (2000), pp. 83–95.

Bobinski, Christopher. "Polish License for Deutsche Bank." *Financial Times*, July 4, 1995, p. 24.

Clifton, Rita; John Simmons; and Sameena Ahmad. *Brands and Branding. The Economist Series*. New York: The Bloomberg Press, 2004.

Cooke, Rachel. "Fake," *The Observer (London)*, July 18, 2004, p. 34.

DeMooij, Marieke. *Global Marketing and Advertising: Understanding Cultural Paradoxes*. Thousand Oaks, CA: Sage, 1998.

Douglas, Susan P.; C. Samuel Craig; and Edwin J. Nijssen. "Integrating Branding Strategy across Markets: Building International Brand Architecture." *Journal of International Marketing* 9, no. 2 (2001), pp. 97–114.

Du Preez, Johann P.; Adamantios Diamantopoulos; and Bodo B. Schlegelmilch. "Product Standardization and Attribute Saliency: A Three-Country Empirical Comparison." *Journal of International Marketing* 2, no. 1 (1994), pp. 7–28.

Elliott, Stuart. "Advertising." *New York Times*, June 21, 1995, p. D9.

Erdem, Tülin; Joffre Swait; and Ana Valenzuela. "Brands as Signals: A Cross-Country Validation Study." *Journal of Marketing* 70, no. 1 (2006), pp. 34–49.

Gray, Madison. "Feds Bust Fake Handbags Operation, Arrest 14." *Associated Press Worldstream*, June 3, 2004.

Holt, Douglas B. *How Brands Become Icons*. Boston: Harvard Business School Press, 2004.

———; John A. Quelch; and Earl L. Taylor. "How Global Brands Compete." *Harvard Business Review* 82, no. 9 (2004), pp. 68–81.

Hyun-Joo, Jin. "No Lack of Fake Luxuries." *The Korea Herald*, June 3, 2004.

"Imitating Property Is Theft," *The Economist*, May 17, 2003.

Joachimsthaler, Erich A. "Managing Brands in the Global Village." Presentation at Georgetown University, November 7, 1997.

Johansson, Johny K. *In Your Face: How American Marketing Excess Fuels Anti-Americanism*. Upper Saddle River, NJ: Financial Times/Prentice-Hall, 2004.

———, and Ilkka A. Ronkainen. "The Esteem of Global Brands." *The Journal of Brand Management* 12, no. 5 (2005), pp. 339–54.

Kapferer, Jean-Noel. *Strategic Brand Management*, 2nd ed. London: Kogan-Page, 1997.

————. "Is There Really No Hope for Local Brands?" *Journal of Brand Management* 9, no. 3 (January 2002), pp.163–67.

Keller, Kevin Lane. *Strategic Brand Management*. Upper Saddle River, NJ: Prentice Hall, 1998.

Kerner, Noah, and Gene Pressman. *Chasing Cool: Standing Out in Today's Cluttered Marketplace*. New York: Atria Books, 2007.

Klein, Naomi. *No Logo*. London: Flamingo, 2000.

Koenig, Robert L. "Bud War: 2 Budweisers Square Off in Czech Republic." *St. Louis Post Dispatch,* October 22, 1995, p. 1A.

Kotabe, Masaaki, and Kristian Helsen. *Global Marketing Management*. New York: Wiley, 1998.

Kotler, Philip. *Marketing Management, The Millennium Edition*. Upper Saddle River, NJ: Prentice Hall, 2000.

Macrae, Chris. *The Brand Chartering Handbook.* Harlow, England: Addison-Wesley, 1996.

Owen, Stewart. "The Landor ImagePower Survey: A Global Assessment of Brand Strength." In David A. Aaker, and Alexander L. Biel, eds. *Brand Equity and Advertising*. Hillsdale, NJ: Lawrence Erlbaum Associates, 1993.

Perlez, Jane. "This Bud's Not for You, Anheuser." *New York Times,* June 30, 1995, pp. D1, D4.

Quart, Alissa. *Branded: The Buying And Selling Of Teenagers*. New York, NY: Basic Books, 2004.

Robertson, Thomas S. *Innovative Behavior and Communication*. New York: Holt, Rinehart and Winston, 1971.

Rosen, Barry Nathan; Jean J. Boddewyn; and Ernst A. Louis. "U.S. Brands Abroad: An Empirical Study of Global Branding." *International Marketing Review* 6, no. 1 (1989), pp. 7–19.

Schmitt, Bernd. *Experiential Marketing*. New York: The Free Press, 1999.

————, and Alex Simonson. *Marketing Aesthetics: The Strategic Management of Brands, Identity, and Image*. New York: Free Press, 1997.

Schuiling, Isabelle, and Jean-Noel Kapferer. "Executive Insights: Real Differences Between Local and International Brands: Strategic Implications for International Marketers." *Journal of International Marketing* 12, no. 4 (2004), pp. 97–112.

Schwartz, Susan. "Fakes: Don't Ask, Don't Tell: Montreal Has a Secret Thriving Knockoff Scene." *The Gazette (Montreal, Quebec)*, March 20, 2004, p. G3.

Statler, Matt, and Johan Roos. "A Place to Play: Redefining Strategy Research." Imagination Lab Working Paper 2001-8, December 11, 2001.

Steenkamp, Jan-Benedict E.M.; Rajeev Batra; and Dana L. Alden. "How Perceived Brand Globalness Creates Brand Value." *Journal of International Business Studies* 34, no. 1 (2003), pp. 53–65.

Tanaka, Hiroshi. "Branding in Japan." In Aaker and Biel, 1993, pp. 51– 66.

"The Best Global Brands." *BusinessWeek*, August 6, 2001, pp. 50–57.

"The Counterfeit Trade." *BusinessWeek*, December 16, 1985, pp. 48–53.

Workman, Daniel. "Anheuser-Busch Global Sales: China Leads Growth in International Beer Revenues," March 14, 2007, http://international-trade-leaders.suite101.com.

Yip, George. *Total Global Strategy II*. Upper Saddle River, NJ: Prentice-Hall, 2002.

Chapter 14

Global Pricing

"There are limits"

After reading this chapter, you will be able to:

1. Help develop coordinated price policies by regions or trading areas, and know why it is necessary to do so.
2. Keep prices in different countries within a narrow band or "corridor" in order to discourage gray trade, which attempts to take advantage of currency exchange shifts and local price differentials.
3. Explain how transfer prices between a global company's plants in different countries can be used to motivate subsidiaries and measure performance, while remaining supportable to local tax authorities.
4. Evaluate whether countertrade, including barter, is an acceptable pricing option in countries with a lack of hard currency, especially when global financial turmoil puts domestic currencies under pressure.
5. Formulate a global pricing strategy that still pays attention to basic issues such as competition, price–quality relationships, and stage of the product life cycle.

Pricing globally is much trickier than pricing in the home market. In the domestic market, deciding on price levels, promotional rebates to middlemen, and consumer deals requires careful analysis; but once the decisions are made, the implementation is straightforward. The opposite generally holds true for markets abroad. The level of price is often a minor headache compared with the problems of currency fluctuations and devaluations, price escalation through tariffs, difficult-to-assess credit risks, FOB versus CIF quotations, dumping charges, transfer prices, and price controls—all common issues in global pricing. In global marketing, the actual height of the product price is sometimes less important than currencies quoted, methods of payment, and credit extended.

The Pricing Challenges of European Automakers

From the arrival of the integrated European market in 1992 to the euro currency in 2002 and afterwards, European automakers have been buffeted by strong pricing challenges. Thanks to an antitrust exemption granted to them, the automakers were able to control prices and maintain dealers' exclusive territories relatively well during the 1990s, but their antitrust protection has now been eliminated, setting the stage for intense price competition across the EU.

The problem has been that automobile prices for the same model in different EU countries can vary as much as 30 percent. Since there are no longer official tariff or trade barriers between the countries, and even though the euro has been in use since 1999 (for electronic transfers), the antitrust exemption has allowed companies to prohibit cross-border gray trade. The regulation allowed automakers to prohibit dealers from selling outside of their exclusive territories, and even though used cars and also some new car dealers have managed to engage in gray trade, the volume has been limited. In addition, the luxury carmakers such as Mercedes and BMW have been successful at maintaining comparatively level prices in recent years, reducing the incentives for gray trade.

If you live in the European Union, the differences in prices between dealers in your country and those in neighboring countries could easily be 20 percent. This is surprising since the euro is the same local currency, and one would expect that all countries in the Euro-zone would have the same or similar prices since the models are very much standardized.

But there are still forces keeping car prices at a huge differential, making it beneficial to the consumer to take the time to shop around. One issue is the difference in prosperity among different members of the EU. Some of the newly joined countries still have economies less developed than those of the senior members, forcing car companies to lower their prices to accommodate these poorer consumers. Taxes are also different, creating differences in car prices since a country's tax often gets figured into the price of the car.

Ironically, German automobile prices are the most expensive in Europe even though it is the home of many manufacturers and designers. A Volkswagen Passat can be priced as much as 40 percent higher in Germany than in Greece. The second most expensive country for automobile purchases in the EU is the United Kingdom, where cars are considered to be overpriced compared to other EU countries—the English Channel still seems to be something of a barrier to equal prices. Getting a good deal on automobiles in Europe might mean getting on a plane to Finland, where the deals are the best in the European Union.

Not so in the future for the carmakers. The proposed rule is that the antitrust exemption should be removed in countries where a single car company holds more than a certain percentage of the car market. Thresholds of 10 or 15 percent have been considered. Such a change would affect Volkswagen in Germany, Renault in France, and Fiat in Italy. These carmakers generally charge higher prices in their home countries than elsewhere, and their no-longer-captive customers at home will likely buy from a foreign dealer in a neighboring country unless prices come down. In fact, dealers will be free to sell to any customer, including independent retailers or even supermarket chains. In 2001, to block a German supermarket chain from buying its subcompact cars for resale, Fiat sued one of its dealers—something that would not be possible under the new rules.

But other types of gray trade are still legally questionable. In 2007, lawyers representing Nissan have reportedly written to a number of European businesses regarding their vehicle importation activities. The businesses are suspected of importing Nissan vehicles originating in Japan and intended for sale only in Japan. Such activities would infringe on Nissan's trademark rights.

As a first step, Nissan lawyers have warned the businesses not to engage in such activities and, if this is ignored, Nissan will seek the support of the courts. The basis of this action is well established and has been confirmed in decisions of the European and English courts over a number of years. To clarify, the action does not seek to prevent individual customers or businesses from buying Nissan vehicles intended for the United Kingdom or European markets. But Nissan has a right to protect its brand by designating products specifically for one country.

Gary Frigo, Nissan Motor (GB) Limited's Managing Director, says: "Nissan's number one priority is to ensure that the GT-R and its dealer network are in optimal condition to facilitate and support our customers. It will take until start of sales in March 2009 to do this. Until that time the UK will have no GT-R trained technicians, no established GT-R parts supply and, most crucial of all, the GT-R will not be covered by a manufacturer's warranty."

As someone said, global pricing and gray trade are two sides of the same management headache.

Sources: David Greising, "Weak Dollar, Strong Profits," *BusinessWeek,* July 11, 1994, p. 39; Robert Hanley, "Car Buyers Play a Game of Beating the Tariff," *New York Times,* May 18, 1995, pp. D1, D5; Edmund L. Andrews, "Europe to Seek Uniformity in Car Pricing," *New York Times,* February 5, 2002, p. W1; **www.autospies.com**, 12/21/07; **www.gocurrency.com**, 2006; **www.carpages.co.uk.**

Introduction

In theory, any student of microeconomics is well equipped to handle pricing problems. Given fixed and stable demand and cost curves, the derivation of optimal price allows the simultaneous identification of optimal quantity to produce. This is a wonderful situation, since other company functions become ancillary and the "firm's problem" is solved.

The "next generation" texts in applied areas such as marketing then go on to demonstrate that the basic price theory learned in normative economics is not very practical. Demand and cost curves are not easily estimated, they are not stable over time, the competitors influence the demand function unpredictably, the firm produces for more than one market, and prices and output can't be set simultaneously because of organizational constraints. Even though the economists are patching up some of these holes, their theories (if not their terminology) have been largely abandoned by pragmatic price makers in the firm's marketing function. Instead, new procedures much closer to heuristic "rules of thumb" have been devised for the job.

These practical heuristics are also prominent in global pricing. Here the conditions that limit the value of microeconomics are further magnified when new limitations stemming from cross-border transactions are encountered. As a result, the pragmatic guidelines for price setting that have been developed over the years for the home markets need to be revised and augmented. New approaches have evolved—and keep evolving—under pressure from legal and governmental forces in the various countries in addition to the traditional market forces. These approaches represent truly eclectic combinations of practical experience and more or less theoretical suggestions.

It is perhaps fair to say that it is in pricing that the existing know-how from domestic marketing is least valuable for global operations. Market segmentation and product positioning principles can be extended abroad. Advertising and sales campaigns can be standardized for foreign markets. But the practical and institutional know-how required for global pricing decisions is of a wholly different order of magnitude.

A Global Pricing Framework

Global pricing involves a number of complex issues. Exhibit 14.1 provides a framework for our discussion.

It is useful to distinguish at the outset between pricing considerations facing the company as an exporter and the pricing problems specific to global coordination and integration. As we saw in Chapter 5, "Export Expansion," among the export pricing concerns are the currency exchange risk exposure and the credit risks, which can combine to make customer-oriented easy credit terms in local currencies financially irresponsible. Problems also arise relating to such matters as whether all of the price escalation due to the tariff (and nontariff) barriers should be passed on to the customer, lowering competitiveness. As for positioning strategy, a high *skimming* price and an "import" status image necessitate niche targeting but also slow down market growth and leave windows of opportunity for the competition. On the other hand, choosing a low *penetration price,* the firm runs a risk of being accused of *dumping,* that is, selling its products below cost. Again, these issues were discussed in Chapter 5.

For the global company, there are additional problems of constraints on pricing strategy. The first strategic task is that of deciding in which *currency* to price and what

EXHIBIT 14.1
A Global Pricing Framework

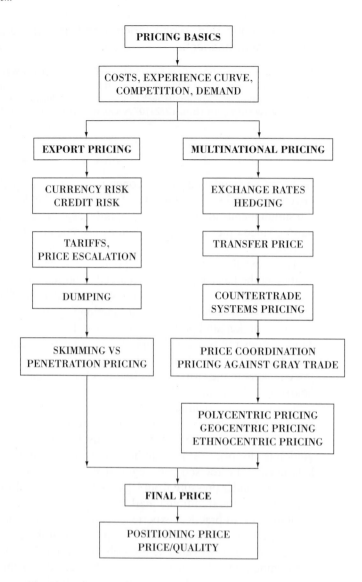

hedging tactics to employ. Next is the task of determining *transfer prices*—the prices charged country subsidiaries for products, components, and supplies—that are fair in terms of performance evaluation between country units and still optimal from the overall network perspective, including a desirable profit repatriation pattern. But foreign tax authorities have grown increasingly impatient with pricing schemes that rob a country of "fair" tax returns and, consequently, subject transfer prices to great scrutiny. Then there is the problem of coordinating pricing across countries, to satisfy multinational customers, without imposing a straitjacket on local subsidiaries and illegally fixing prices for independent distributors.

The manager might also have to face countertrade and getting paid in goods instead of hard currency. "Systems selling" and the questions that arise when pricing a complete system of hardware and software can also be an issue. In global markets there are many "turnkey projects," which pose their own peculiar kind of marketing problems. For instance, one typical headache for management is whether the components should be priced separately or whether one system price should be quoted.

These and related issues will be discussed in detail in this chapter. As always, it is in the end the "final" price of the product as viewed by the buyer that matters, regardless of what ingredients have come together to make it up. Differences in trade barriers make some prices escalate abnormally, and a great competitor in some markets might simply be priced out of other markets. Foreign cars have long been more or less shut out of the

Italian market by virtue of high tariffs and quotas to protect Fiat, Alfa Romeo, and the other domestic producers, a situation that is gradually changing as the European Union integration proceeds. Also complicating matters is that the stage of the product life cycle (PLC) will differ between countries for the same product. Furthermore, inflation and the selective price regulations imposed by governments will vary.

The chapter will start with the basics of pricing, then move to the financial issues of *currency exchange* and *hedging,* very salient problems in the turmoil at the beginning of the new millennium. The chapter will then turn to *transfer pricing, countertrade,* and *systems pricing.* The roles of the *price–quality* relationship and the product life cycle in positioning strategy are discussed next. This is followed by an assessment of the feasibility of a global or regional *price coordination* with particular emphasis on firms' "gray trade" experiences in the integrated European market.[1] The last section of the chapter deals with the relative merits of *polycentric, geocentric,* and *ethnocentric* pricing strategies in the global firm.

Pricing Basics

The basic principles of global pricing derive from the traditional pricing approaches in home markets. These revolve around production costs, competitive factors, and demand considerations.

The Role of Costs

The standard pricing procedure for exporting consists of a **cost-plus pricing** formula. The firm arrives at export prices by adding up the various costs involved in producing and shipping the product (cost-based pricing) and then adding a markup ("plus") to this figure to achieve a reasonable rate of return. The cost components include manufacturing costs, administrative costs, allocated R&D expenditures, selling costs, and the transport charges, customs duties, and requisite fees to various facilitating agencies (see Chapter 5 for the associated price escalation problems).

There is a long-standing argument about whether full costs should be used or whether only direct costs should burden the product or, the ideal case from a theoretical viewpoint, whether the firm should simply attempt to estimate marginal costs and then use those. In practice most firms seem to use all or a combination of these and other related methods. The emphasis varies with the company strategy and the market situation. For an existing product entering a new market, direct costs tend to be a natural choice, since overheads are already covered at home and investments have been recouped. If the product is new but relates directly to the firm-specific advantages (FSAs) of the company, marginal costs will be more important and the potential of grooming a "star" dominates the strategy. In the decentralized company where profit center accountability is featured, the tendency is to let the individual product carry itself and to load it down with its full share of overhead and contribution requirements.

The sole reliance on a cost-based pricing system is acceptable only in rare circumstances. It is frequently resorted to in the firm starting its exporting, since the know-how and the financial resources are not yet sufficient for market-oriented pricing. In most cases, however, it becomes absolutely necessary that competition and demand be factored into the decision process.

Experience Curve Pricing

The use of a cost-based price has become more common after the discovery of the "experience curve" effect. The **experience curve** shows how unit costs go down as successively more units of a product are produced. Through the "learning by doing" that comes from experience, the company's employees develop skills and capabilities that translate into lower costs.[2] Thus, a firm entering new foreign markets will gain in capabilities and scope economies from accumulated production and market experience.

Under this scenario, the entry into a new local market might well be accompanied by a lower price than that maintained in other markets, even at home. With the new market providing a chance for increased output and thus lower unit costs, the anticipated gains might be passed along to the customers in the form of low introductory prices ("penetration" prices in the early stage of the PLC). Whether the introductory price will be raised later or not depends directly on the correctness of the anticipated cost declines. If experience effects are smaller than anticipated, costs might certainly rise later; but a very low "cutthroat" entry price might stay down for a long time (because of competition) and still generate positive profits because of the experience curve decline.

Experience curve pricing has been adopted primarily by companies entering an existing market in the maturity stage. Many Japanese firms operate with this strategy, since it allows them to maintain a penetration price level in foreign markets.[3]

Competition

The competitive analysis might be as simple as finding out what global and domestic competitors in the particular country market charge for their products. These prices tend to set the "reservation" prices in the local market, that is, those limits beyond which the firm's product will not be considered and people will avoid buying. The analysis can go further and attempt to isolate the differential advantages that the firm's product might have over these existing offerings, so-called perceived value pricing.[4] One way to do this, developed by DuPont, the U.S.-based manufacturer of artificial fibers and related products, consists of dividing price into a "commodity" part and a "premium price differential" part. The commodity portion of price relates to underlying demand factors, while the premium differential focuses specifically on the competitive factors.

The **premium price differential** refers to the degree to which the firm might be granted a higher price by the market because of the particular strengths of its product. The size of this premium is directly related to the strength of the brand. For years, Sony's strong brand allowed the Japanese company a consistent premium of an approximately 10 percent higher price than its competition. With recent weaknesses and the rise of competing Samsung from Korea, this differential is in danger of elimination. To find the magnitude of the premium, the company needs to do market research in the local market, identify how important various product attributes are to customers, and assess how competition is perceived on the salient attributes. A company such as Caterpillar uses this approach to price its products in relation to those of Komatsu, its large Japanese competitor.[5] Although in domestic markets such research is typically done via comprehensive and in-depth marketing research, in foreign markets softer data from existing customers, distributors, and country experts can usually offer a preliminary guide.

Demand

Naturally, demand also needs to be considered when setting prices; and most firms do, however implicitly, pay attention to what the various local markets "will bear."

The **price elasticities** associated with the demand curve in economic theory identify the price sensitivity of consumers, that is, how many customers are willing to buy how much of the product at various price levels. This curve yields the "commodity" price in the DuPont approach, reflecting the underlying willingness to buy and ability to pay among the potential customers across the market. In many cases, the assessment of this "generic" demand can be done using statistical analysis; in other cases, especially when the product is new on the market, the analysis has to be judgmental (see Chapter 4 for some of these techniques).

The more seasoned manager will tend to base prices on an analysis of the costs involved and adjust the emerging prices in view of competitive and demand conditions in the market country. This naturally leads to an approach in which prices are set on the basis of costs plus a variable markup. Where demand is strong and the competitive differential large, the markup can be higher. In countries where the premium price differential is weaker because of strong competition, and especially where demand is relatively soft, the markup will come down correspondingly. This type of variable markup is common among companies with global strategies since it lends itself well to global coordination.

Financial Issues

Exchange Rates

Fluctuating exchange rates will routinely create problems with revenues and prices in a foreign market and can powerfully affect the performance of local subsidiaries. A particularly potent threat is the chance of a government **devaluation,** as happened in Argentina (see box, "Argentine Woes Pegged to the Peso").

In less severe cases, **exchange rate fluctuations** do not always affect prices in the manner postulated by economic theory. A rising currency does not necessarily mean higher prices, weakened competitiveness, and less exports. A simple example helps illustrate what might happen.

Take the case of trade between Germany and Japan. If the euro depreciates against the yen, theory says that German automobiles will be cheaper in Japan, while Japanese automobiles will be more expensive in Germany. Because of existing inventories and lags between ordering and delivery times, the effect may not be immediate, but gradually the trade balance will shift. German automobiles will sell better in Japan, while Japan's market shares in Germany will diminish. The extent of the shift depends on the price elasticities in the two countries for the automobiles traded and thus on available substitutes from domestic producers and other foreign producers.

From a managerial perspective, this scenario depends on prices being set by the headquarters in the home country currency—and staying unchanged. In other words, German exporters are assumed to quote prices to their Japanese importers in terms of the same euro price as before the currency depreciation. Similarly, the Japanese are assumed to stay with the same yen prices for their German subsidiaries as before. Neither case is necessarily realistic for the company with global operations.

First, the Japanese may decide that the German market is too important for them, and therefore they keep the euro prices in Germany unchanged in an attempt to maintain market share. Since the revenues from the automobiles sold in Germany will be lower than before, profits for the Japanese will tend to fall even as volume sales stay steady.

Second, the shrinking profitability will induce the Japanese to shift supply routes. Instead of shipping to Germany from Japan, which is now a more expensive producer, the Japanese companies will look for supplies from their manufacturing subsidiaries in a third country whose currency has moved with the euro. This was initially one reason why many Japanese companies started to supply Europe from their North American–based subsidiaries.

Third, when the shift in the exchange rate is judged to be more or less permanent, management will explore the option of investing in production in Germany (or in another euro country). Although currency rate fluctuations are notoriously difficult to forecast and rarely "permanent," the relatively small appreciation of the Japanese yen of about 10 percent at the beginning of the 1990s had this effect, since it coincided with long-term structural changes in the Japanese economy.

Today, German companies with an appreciating euro have become less price-competitive in Japan and their exports are depressed much in the way economic theory suggests. Their incentive to invest abroad is increased, and trade-substituting foreign direct investment (FDI) is likely to occur. Nevertheless, to the extent that the German automobiles rely on components produced abroad, perhaps in their own foreign subsidiaries, the cost of such components may decrease. The tendency will be for such components to replace German domestic supplies where feasible, and German value added will be decreased.

Getting the Picture

ARGENTINE WOES PEGGED TO THE PESO

With the dawn of 2002 Eduardo Duhalde, Argentina's fifth president in two weeks, was faced with whether or not to devalue the country's peso and avert the nation's largest financial crisis in history.

For a decade, Argentina had kept the peso pegged one-to-one to the U.S. dollar as a means of providing monetary stability in the face of hyperinflation in the late 1980s. While most Argentines earn pesos, an estimated 80 percent of debts, from home mortgages to corporate loans, were denominated in dollars. So a break of the currency peg was likely to result in widespread bankruptcies.

At the same time, there was broad agreement that the peso had been overvalued, making Argentine exports uncompetitive on world markets—and resulting in four years of recession. This was because the dollar's strength resulted in Argentine exports being more expensive than competitive offerings in many cases. For instance, Brazil's floating exchange rate made its currency 2.5 times weaker than the peso, which resulted in much cheaper Brazilian products. But not only did the pegged exchange rate make Argentine exports more expensive and imports cheaper, it also inflated the cost of doing business in Argentina and prompted many firms to consider manufacturing elsewhere to compete more effectively in Argentina.

Argentine businesses were scrambling to remain solvent. Many merchants in Buenos Aires were faced with looting or vandalism at the hands of panicked Argentines who had their bank accounts frozen or simply could no longer afford a dwindling supply of foreign imports or overpriced domestic goods. Some stores even went as far as selling merchandise at cost, as a means of quelling disgruntled consumers and recouping some investment. Given such a scenario Argentina had difficulty in raising the tax receipts and cutting government spending necessary to help pull the nation out of a recession. And businesses were unlikely to reinvest in a market with inflated production costs and declining discretionary incomes.

The decision? The peso's peg to the dollar was abandoned in January 2002, and the peso was floated in February. The medicine worked. The exchange rate plunged and inflation picked up rapidly, but by mid-2002 the economy had stabilized, albeit at a lower level. Led by record exports, the economy began to recover with output up 8 percent in 2003, unemployment falling, and inflation reduced to under 4 percent at year-end. Strong demand for the peso even compelled the Central Bank to intervene in foreign exchange markets to curb its appreciation in 2003.

Despite the success, Mr. Duhalde was not re-elected. On May 25, 2003, Nestor Kirchner was declared the winner of a runoff presidential election by default after Carlos Saul Menem withdrew his candidacy. And the new president, proud of his leftwing political past, has fought hard and with success against the IMF for forgiveness of Argentina's outstanding foreign debt. Argentina's continued economic upswing ensured an electoral win for his wife Cristina as the new president when his term ended in 2007.

Currency exchange issues not only complicate multinational pricing, but also have powerful political ramifications.

Sources: Anthony Faiola, "Devaluation Imminent in Argentina," *Washington Post*, January 3, 2002, p. A12; "Austerity, or Bust," *The Economist*, July 19, 2001; Dave Goldiner, "Cristina Fernandez de Kirchner wins Argentina presidency," *NY Daily News*, October 29, 2007.

A depreciating currency often leads to an increased ability to lower prices abroad and increased competitiveness for the exporter just as the theory predicts. By contrast, an appreciating currency does not necessarily lead to higher prices and lower competitiveness, since the company can often shift supply routes and invest in overseas manufacturing.

This asymmetrical pattern is even more pronounced for the company that has a global network of manufacturing locations and a presence in many markets. Not only can alternative supplier locations help limit the damage from currency fluctuations, but a presence in multiple markets makes it possible to shift emphasis from one country market to another. If their competitiveness in German markets decreases, Japanese companies can simply allow their shares to go down and instead focus on other markets where the currency rate against the yen is more favorable. This was happening in the late 1990s as the strong U.S. dollar made American markets more attractive and the then weaker euro made Germany a less attractive market.[6]

In the big picture, the effect of exchange rate fluctuations on the market prices of the products sold is limited not only by what managers can do but also by what they can't do. Prices can't be changed overnight, even if exchange rates do. Purchasing contracts for industrial products may be negotiated months in advance and remain in force for a prespecified period. Suppliers of high-quality components are sometimes asked to work closely with the company's designers and engineers and can't be easily dismissed.

There are considerable start-up costs in organizing and managing a distribution channel in a foreign country, and a shift in exchange rates will often be viewed as a "windfall" profit or loss to the channel members without any adjustment in prices and costs quoted. To avoid the risk of wide fluctuations in short-term profits, the global company will often turn to hedging.

Hedging

Hedging involves the purchase of insurance against losses because of currency fluctuations. Such insurance usually takes the form of buying or selling "forward contracts" or engaging in "currency swaps" with the help of financial intermediaries (banks and brokerage houses).

A **forward contract** refers to the sale or purchase of a specified amount of a foreign currency at a fixed exchange rate for delivery or settlement on an agreed date in the future or, under an options contract, between agreed upon dates in the future. A **swap** may be defined as the exchange of one currency for another for a fixed period of time. At the expiration of the swap each party returns the currency initially received. While the forward contract represents a simple insurance policy against downside risk—the firm buys today so as not to lose by deteriorating exchange rates—the cost of the contract reduces the gain from a favorable change in rates.

Various combinations of these contracts are possible, and hedging has become a major financial activity of the international division in many MNCs. From a marketing viewpoint, the most desirable arrangement would be for the seller to assume responsibility for currency fluctuations and quote prices in the local currency. This is not done very often by Western companies, however. Their prices, especially in commodities and industrial markets, tend to be quoted in the "hard" currencies, in particular the U.S.

Russians facing the new ruble rate at a currency exchange in Moscow, November 1998. The Russian ruble was devalued by 34 percent in August that year. While hedging can protect a company's bottom line, devaluation plays havoc with a company's global price coordination. This devaluation also helped bring in a new president, Vladimir Putin, who enjoyed a stronger currency courtesy of the rising oil prices. AP Wide World Photo.

dollar. A company such as Boeing, for example, quotes prices in U.S. dollars only and lets its customers worry about the exchange rate fluctuations and the conversion from the local currency.

Government Intervention

Different countries exhibit different rates of inflation, some like Israel and Argentina in the past showing hyperinflationary patterns. The currencies of such countries will continuously be losing their value against stronger currencies, while their governments will intervene in the workings of the financial system in order to bring some stability to prices. The standard solution is selective **price controls.** For the global marketer, price controls mean that prices can't be changed as frequently as might be desirable—in particular, inflationary erosion of revenues can't so easily be avoided.

Under price controls, increases in prices usually need to be officially sanctioned. To obtain such sanction it is typically required that price increases be directly related to costs. Accordingly, companies with exemplary accounting records tend to have a much better chance of getting their requests for increases in price sanctioned. But where inflation is very rapid, it is unlikely that cost increases alone are sufficient to justify price increases. In such a case, the company has to resort to the kind of currency management discussed above, getting involved in forward contracts and swap deals. Needless to say, such matters are best handled by financial, not marketing, officers of the firm.

There are other types of government intervention that affect pricing. Chief among these are the antitrust laws, in particular as they relate to price fixing and discrimination. Not much can be said here about these matters; the interested reader is referred to any international law book. The firm's legal counsel is the person most likely to be involved in these matters. In terms of price fixing it is important to point out that in certain countries price cartels are not forbidden per se as they are in the United States (there are several instances of cartels in Japan, for example). Under the current trend toward open markets and free international trade, however, cartels will be increasingly under attack.

In terms of **price discrimination,** there are very few laws of the American Robinson–Patman type that prohibit discrimination unless justified by cost savings. However, many laws do question discounts not tied to specific functions performed: The issue of bribery surfaces easily. The firm needs to get some legal advice on what is acceptable and what is not in the particular country. In Japan, for example, it is customary to give large functional rebates to the many middlemen handling the product in that country's complex network of distribution.[7] It is usually necessary to offer such rebates for any newcomer who wants to enter the market.

Transfer Pricing

With a considerable amount of some countries' trade accounted for by shipments between headquarters and subsidiaries, the question of what the value of these shipments is and what the prices mean naturally arises. This is the problem of "transfer" prices.

Definition

The basic reason for **transfer pricing** is simple: There has to be a price paid for the products shipped between units of the same organization when the shipment crosses national borders so that the correct duties and related fees can be paid. However, since the transfer prices directly affect the amount of purchases in the cost accounting of a foreign subsidiary, they have a direct influence on the subsidiary's financial performance. Because of this they have also become a mechanism for the multinational company to shift profits from one country to another. If the headquarters of a company sets a high price on the shipment to a subsidiary in an African country, say, this subsidiary will have trouble showing a profit; and if the (quite arbitrary) price is set low, the subsidiary will be very profitable.

Getting the Picture

HOW TO TRANSFER INCOME? CAREFULLY

Because of the tax and dumping implications of transfer prices and governments' insistence on transparent accounting rules, public accounting firms have developed guidelines for the transfer pricing process in large multinationals. The following 10 steps are typical of the recommended process:

1. Before the beginning of the annual business cycle, meet with outside advisers and agree on a game plan.
2. Compare third party (arm's-length) transactions with "related-party" transactions. Adjust prices.
3. Prepare a financial model to test the method agreed on.
4. Make sure senior management understands the transfer pricing audit process, issues, and exposure.
5. Prepare internal documentation.
6. Prepare external documentation.
7. Spot-check the process within the company.
8. Simulate a transfer pricing audit by outside advisers.
9. Evaluate year-end or cycle-end tax position against goals.
10. Prepare tax returns.

If convicted of cheating, the penalty can be severe. A 2008 ruling by an Administrative Appeals Tribunal in Australia against the Swiss pharmaceutical giant Roche is instructive. The ruling found that the foreign arm of Swiss pharmaceuticals company Roche, the makers of anxiety drug Valium, had charged the Australian arm of the company inflated prices, thereby reducing the tax paid by the Australian operation.

Roche's tax assessment has been increased by $59 million for the period being considered in the case, 1992 to 2002, under the preliminary ruling handed down by Justice Garry Downes. This represents the total amount by which the gross margin of Roche's Australian operation fell below 40 percent, a figure Justice Downes said was the margin expected were the transaction carried out at arm's length.

While the tribunal president upheld Roche's objection to the tax commissioner's assessment of its consumer and diagnostics division, the judge found against Roche in its prescription drug division.

Australian taxation law requires taxpayers to demonstrate that all cross-border-related entity transactions are undertaken on an arm's length basis.

If upheld in the final ruling, the finding will have far-reaching implications for international companies operating in Australia, potentially forcing other retrospective tax assessments, as well as putting pressure on companies to ensure all cross-border transactions with associated companies occur on an arm's-length basis.

Sources: Davis, 1994; Weekly, 1992; Ari Sharp, "Headache for Foreign Investment," **TheAge.com.au,** April 4, 2008.

The use of transfer prices for the purpose of profit repatriation has come under the close scrutiny of many governments whose tax revenues have diminished because of it (see box, "How to Transfer Income? Carefully").

Reputedly, the use of transfer prices for tax-shifting purposes is not as widespread as it once was because the governments have now caught on to past abuses. Transfer prices have taken on an additional role as control mechanisms, however.

The Arm's-Length Principle

From a theoretical point of view, the transfer prices set should reflect the prices the subsidiary might encounter in the open market—the so-called **arm's-length prices.**

The arm's-length principle is the international standard that the Organization for Economic Cooperation and Development (OECD) member countries and the United States have agreed should be used for determining the transfer price for tax purposes.[8] The arm's-length range is defined as a "range of reliable results" for determining the arm's-length price. Thus, the arm's-length price refers to the price at which trade takes place between "independent" enterprises. This definition as such presumes that companies operate at arm's length if they are independent in their commercial and financial relations.

When independent enterprises deal with each other, the conditions of their commercial and financial relations (for example, the price of goods transferred or services provided and the conditions of the transfer or provision) are ordinarily determined by market forces. However, when associated or related entities deal with each other, external market forces may not necessarily determine their commercial and financial relations.

The arm's-length principle follows the approach of treating associated enterprises as operating as separate entities, rather than inseparable parts of a single unified business.

The arm's-length theory is sound in that it provides the closest approximation of the workings of the "open market" in cases where goods and services are transferred between associated enterprises. But in practice, calculating an arm's-length price is not an exact science. In many cases any transfer pricing model will produce a range of possible results. If the results of the entity or firm under examination fall within an acceptable range of arm's-length prices, then no adjustment should be made. In addition, "there are a number of cases in which the arm's-length principle is difficult and complicated to apply. The arm's-length principle is difficult to apply in MNE groups dealing in the integrated production of highly specialized goods, in unique intangibles, and/or in the provision of specialized services."

The setting of arm's-length prices in the way outlined will mean that the costs of the goods to the subsidiary will give the right "signals" to the buyer about how much to buy, and the consequent operating criteria (such as return on investment and profits) will be valid indicators of the subsidiary's performance. In the practical world there are times when such market prices are difficult to identify, usually because there are no substitutes in the open market. The practice also goes against the use of transfer pricing to shift profits from one country to another.

Approaches to Transfer Pricing

In practice, the two main approaches to transfer pricing are market-based transfer pricing and cost-based transfer pricing.[9]

There is some variation in the transfer pricing policies used by multinational firms, with some preferring market-based prices while others use cost-based transfer prices. The choice can have a major impact on measures of financial performance of the foreign subsidiary. Changing a transfer price directly changes the bottom line of the subsidiary's income statement and thus profits and taxes paid in the host country.

Market price-based transfer price is the price for which the product or service could be purchased by the receiving subsidiary in the external marketplace. Generally, the market price is the most suitable transfer price because it cannot be manipulated as easily as the other types and reflects performance against independent benchmarks. However, the conditions for market price-based transfer prices are rarely found in practice. In the absence of the "perfect" market place, cost-based methods of transfer pricing are an option. Here, transfer prices are generally based upon cost, cost plus some mark-up, or some approximation of the market.

Judging from their public statements, many global American companies have given up trying to repatriate profits via transfer prices and do indeed attempt to set market-related transfer prices. This is also evident in the context of increasing transfer pricing aggressiveness by tax authorities and the growing sophistication of tax authorities to crackdown on profit repatriation. Several companies have even taken the logical step of introducing an option for the subsidiary to buy on the open market, should price and quality there be more favorable. Many of Ford Motor Company's subsidiaries around the world now have this option. To exercise it requires, however, a quite rigorous demonstration that the quality of components and parts is up to par.

To assist in determining the arm's-length transfer price, a functional analysis can be useful. A **functional analysis** is the process of decomposing the transactional price in order to determine the arm's-length price.[10]

A functional analysis is useful to the arm's-length principle because its purpose is to review and evaluate the functions performed, assets utilized, and risks assumed by the entity/subsidiary in question in the context of its dealings with international related parties. Importantly, however, by characterizing the nature of the company's operations, the functional analysis is also the starting point for identifying comparable companies used when applying a transfer pricing method.

Conflicting Objectives

There are other factors influencing the level of transfer prices, most related to the flow of funds between headquarters and the subsidiaries. Where the country suffers from rapid inflation, there is usually an attempt to keep the operating funds at a minimum. The shipments of intermediate goods going to the subsidiary in the country will be charged at a higher rate than otherwise, for example. A functional analysis will reflect this and will allow a company to support transfer prices that shift profits in this regard. If a country suffers from currency shortages (rationing of dollars, for example), this approach will not work since the payments are not convertible. Options then include currency swaps, forward contracts, countertrade, and so on. In the end, the global firm will attempt to reduce its dependence on the country, possibly pulling out its investments. This was why the Argentine devaluation in 2002 was making foreign investors wary. As it turned out, Argentina has done very well without them.

Generally, transfer prices are influenced by a range of conflicting objectives. For example, a corporation would aim to maximize worldwide profits after taxes, maintain flexibility in the repatriation of profits, encourage optimal decision-making by profit center management, provide profit data that are reliable indicators of managerial performance and entity profitability, build market share, and maintain competitiveness in foreign markets.

Transfer prices can also be used to support a subsidiary's competitive position in a local market. Where the market position is strategically important for the global position of the MNC, headquarters might well transfer more funds to the subsidiary by simply charging low prices for some key product components or parts. The approach is equivalent to government subsidies, but in this case it is carried out within a corporation. An example is the entry of many Japanese companies into the U.S. market. In the initial stages at least, the American offices are usually staffed by people paid directly from Japan without any attempt to make the subsidiary a profit center.

Finally, as transfer pricing affects various aspects of a subsidiary's business and it becomes a key influence on a corporation's worldwide tax burden, suitable tax planning strategies can be undertaken to reduce the overall tax burden and achieve long-term tax and strategic business benefits. In particular, as the levels of corporate income tax and tariffs vary considerably across different countries, transfer prices may be set in part to help minimize a firm's worldwide tax bill.

Countertrade

Countertrade is the term for transactions in which all or part of the payment is made in kind rather than cash. The practice has been known as *barter trade* throughout recorded history, but more recently new and ingenious wrinkles on the practice have emerged. The primary moving force has been the shortage of hard currencies available to developing countries, in particular those lacking a strong export sector to generate foreign earnings. In addition, the failure of the globally integrated financial markets to support the stability of domestic currencies has made countertrade again appear as a viable alternative payment.

It is useful to distinguish between five kinds of countertrade: barter, compensation deals, counterpurchase, product buy-back, and offset.

Barter is the oldest form of countertrade. It is the direct exchange of goods between two trading partners. A famous barter trade was the huge deal between Occidental Petroleum of the United States and the Soviet government back in the 1970s to exchange superphosphoric acid (from Occidental) for urea and potash (from the Soviet Union), an agreement valued at about $20 billion. No money changed hands and no third party was involved—a typical Armand Hammer transaction. (For a similar transaction involving consumer goods, see box, "Bartering Russian Vodka for American Cola.")

For barter to make economic sense, the seller must be able to dispose of the goods received in payment. In the case of Occidental, this was no problem since the company could use the urea and potash in its own manufacturing plants. To assist companies that

Getting the Picture

BARTERING RUSSIAN VODKA FOR AMERICAN COLA

One of the classic countertrade cases was Pepsi-Cola's entry into the Soviet Union back in 1972. At that time the Soviets did not have access to much hard currency since the Cold War was severely limiting trade outside the Soviet bloc and the oil that today accounts for much of Russia's foreign exchange was considered a strategic good and not exported. It so happened that then American president Richard Nixon had been an attorney at Pepsi-Cola and had maintained a close relationship with Donald Kendall, Pepsi's CEO. Kendall convinced Nixon that a trade relationship between Soviet Russia and the United States would help ease tensions, and what better symbol of this relationship than selling Pepsi-Cola to the Russians? For the opportunity to become the first Western consumer product sold in the Soviet Union, Pepsi would be willing to consider any countertrade offer.

Pepsi-Cola's relationship with the Soviet Union actually dated back to 1959 when then Soviet leader Nikita Khrushchev was photographed sipping Pepsi-Cola at an American national exhibition in Moscow. But it was on a visit to Soviet Russia in 1971 that President Nixon proposed to his Soviet counterpart President Leonid Brezhnev that Pepsi-Cola be allowed to build a bottling plant and sell its cola in the Russian market. The proposal was accepted and as a quid pro quo the Russians offered Pepsi the exclusive American distribution rights for the number one Russian drink, Stolichnaya vodka.

Exchanging cola for vodka was an offer that PepsiCo executives could not refuse. A $2 billion landmark countertrade agreement was reached in 1972 to exchange Pepsi-Cola concentrate for the rights to sell Stolichnaya vodka in the United States. Pepsi-Cola's first Soviet bottling plant opened in 1974 and soon 22 plants were turning out the concentrate.

At the time Pepsi managers had few alternatives for entering a closed market that lacked a fully convertible hard currency. Soviet officials were unwilling to part with any foreign exchange reserves, so a barter arrangement appealed to both sides. The difficulty, as in any other barter agreement, was being able to independently assess the value of the goods or services involved. Compounding this assessment was Pepsi's inability over the agreement's first 15 years to utilize any modern marketing techniques in the Russian market, since television advertisements, radio commercials, and supermarket promotions with entertainment celebrities or top athletes were all unavailable to the soft drink giant.

Fortunately for Pepsi, Stolichnaya became the best-selling imported vodka in the United States for the first 10 years of the agreement and is still near the top of the vodka market. Pepsi estimated having sold over 1 billion shots of vodka in the first decade after the first sales.

However, once the Berlin Wall fell in 1989 and the Russian market opened up, the Pepsi head start proved a handicap. Rather than gaining first-mover advantages, the brand seemed old and tainted by the old regime once world leader Coca-Cola entered. It did not help that another American president, Mr. Clinton, visited a Coke plant rather than a Pepsi plant on a trip to Russia in 1995. Although Coca-Cola took some time to develop its Russian distribution network, it seemed only a matter of time before Pepsi would be overtaken. By 1994, Pepsi still had 60 percent of the Russian market compared to Coke's 38 percent. However, an estimated $500 investment in Russia vaulted Coke to a 51 percent share in 1996 versus Pepsi's 44 percent, and Coke has been leading ever since.

With Stolichnaya having lost its leadership position to Absolut vodka of Sweden, Pepsi is looking for a new strategic recipe, mixing cola with vodka, and hoping for the next presidential endorsement.

Sources: Pamela Hollie, "Pepsico Renews Deal with Russians," *New York Times,* May 22, 1985, p. D5; Michael Lelyveld, "Innovation Is the Key to Keep Vodka Flowing to U.S. Shores," *Journal of Commerce,* July 29, 1993, p. 2C; Michael Parks, "For Pepsi, Road to Moscow Was a Trip Back in Time," *Washington Post,* July 6, 1988, p. A1.

engage in barter trading and cannot count on such arrangements, several barter houses have been established, primarily in Europe, where many of the exchanges are negotiated.

Compensation deals involve payment both in goods and in cash. In one case GM sold locomotives to the former Yugoslavia for $12 million and was paid in cash plus Yugoslavian machine tools valued at approximately $4 million. The introduction of the cash portion is to make the deal more attractive to the seller, and most companies faced with the possibility of a countertrade agreement will in fact insist that at least some portion of the bill be settled in cash. As in the case of barter, the goods portion of the payment has to be sold in a third market, and the additional transaction costs should logically be added to the original amount invoiced.

Counterpurchases represent the most typical version of the countertrade. Here, two contracts are usually negotiated: one to sell the product (the initial agreement) at an agreed upon cash price, and a second to buy goods from the purchaser at an amount equal to the bill in the initial agreement. This type of contract simply represents one way for the buyer to reuse valuable foreign currency and force exports and is usually introduced relatively late in the exchange negotiations. In practice the seller gets its money and then has a limited period of time (usually 6 to 12 months) before its purchases from the country must be completed. In some of these cases the second contract is sold (at a steep discount) to a third party (a barter house, for example), but this is not always easy. For a classic example, McDonnell Douglas, the American aircraft manufacturer now merged with Boeing, once had to buy and then resell ham from China in order to sell a few of its aircraft there.

Product buy-backs come in two types. Under one type of product buy-back agreement the seller accepts a certain amount of the output as full or partial payment for the goods sold. Alternatively, the seller can agree to buy back some of the output at a later date. Levi Strauss is accepting Hungarian-made jeans (bearing its brand name) in partial payment for setting up a jeans factory outside Budapest. Another Western company has established a tractor plant in Poland and agreed to buy back a certain number of Polish-built tractors as part of the deal.

In **offset** deals, the seller contracts to invest in local production or procurement to partially offset the sale price. In aircraft, for example, it is not uncommon for a national airline buying airplanes to demand that the manufacturer procure certain components, parts, or supplies in the buyer's country, or invest in some assembly operation there. This helps justify the purchase price paid to the manufacturer from cash-strapped nations.[11]

Business Evaluation

There are many multinational corporations and exporters that have found themselves in a situation where a countertrade represents the only feasible alternative for the buyer. In general, settlement in cash is preferable to the seller. Where there is no competition, the seller can insist on a cash settlement. But companies such as Coca-Cola and Ford have been forced to accept the "realities" of the international marketplace and will do countertrading if necessary. GM has even gone so far as to create its own in-house barter subsidiary, General Motors Trading Company. For Japanese companies, the close ties with the large trading houses have proved to be of vital importance for countertrade, giving the Japanese an edge in the marketplace.

Similarly, European companies rely on barter houses to provide the necessary expertise and contacts to sell the goods received. In the global marketplace of the 1990s, with Russia and the former Soviet republics suffering because of slow economic progress and currency problems, the acceptance of countertrade proposals were thought to be necessary in order to be able to compete at all. As it turned out, the rising oil prices have alleviated at least Russia's foreign currency problems.

A countertrade option means not only that the value of the offered goods must be assessed but also that the extra costs associated with the negotiations and future sale must be considered. It is usual, therefore, for the agreed upon price to rise considerably higher than the cash price. But for the buyer the gains are important; and in many situations the value to the buyer of the seller's products is much higher than the sacrifice in terms of domestic products, so the higher "price" is only a nominal figure.

For the seller evaluating a countertrade proposal, the following points are important to consider:

1. Is this the only way the order can be secured?
2. Can the received goods be sold?
3. How can we maximize the cash portion?
4. Does the invoiced price incorporate extra transaction costs?
5. Are there any import barriers to the received goods (so that we will have trouble disposing of the goods at home, say)?
6. Could there be currency exchange problems if we try to repatriate the earnings from sales in a third country?

If these issues receive a positive evaluation, countertrade might be a useful alternative. When the opposite happens, the firm might be better off curbing its appetite for foreign sales.

Systems Pricing

One pricing issue of frequent relevance in global markets is the question of systems pricing. **Systems selling** or **turnkey sales** refers to the notion that in many instances the firm not only is selling some particular physical product or offering a single service but also is providing the buyer with a complete "package." Examples include the turnkey plants being built by firms from developed countries in many less-developed countries (LDCs), for instance, the paper and pulp mill built in Japan and floated to the Manaus free trade zone on the Amazon river in Brazil.[12] Fiat's auto plant in Russia is another example. Many computerized office systems are sold as complete turnkey operations because of compatibility requirements. The German computer firm Nixdorf, now part of Siemens, has long specialized in complete information systems for banks in Europe. The driving force in these sales is not the hardware itself but the added value produced by wedding hardware and software into a functioning and complete system. The question is how such a system should be priced.

Exhibit 14.2 demonstrates how one firm has gone about analyzing this pricing problem.[13] The company deals with a varied set of customers in Southeast Asia in the telecommunications industry. The specific hardware sold is a mobile telephone, but the

EXHIBIT 14.2
Pricing a Turnkey Package

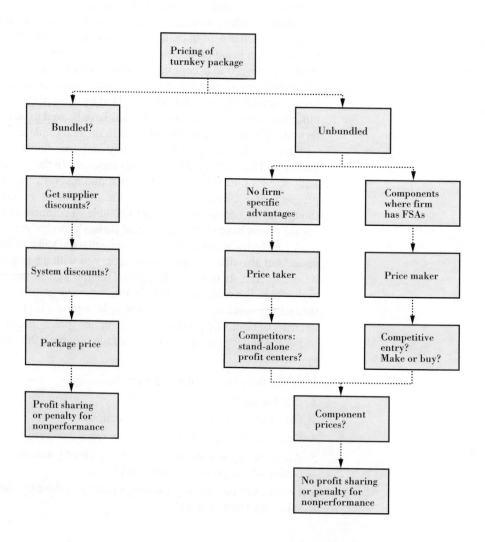

final sales to many customers also involve switching networks, computerized accounting and billing facilities, the construction of physical facilities, and the training of supervisors. The firm does not manufacture the switches or the telephones but serves basically as the prime contractor for the turnkey system, carries out the initial feasibility studies, develops the administrative software, and selects the hardware components and the construction subcontractor for the physical facilities. Its know-how and firm-specific advantage (FSA) lie in the experience accumulated in running these types of systems in the United States.

As Exhibit 14.2 demonstrates, an initial decision is made between offering an unbundled system and a complete turnkey operation. The unbundling option is less preferable from the seller's point of view and is resorted to only when the customer insists it has certain skills that can be used for parts of the project. The seller attempts to direct the participation of the buyer into areas where the seller has no FSAs, partly in order to protect against dissipation and also because alternative suppliers are available. This is done by pricing such components high, while areas where the firm's proprietary know-how and FSAs are lodged are priced more aggressively so as to discourage customers from going to outside firms or doing the work themselves. Thus, system design, an area in which the firm claims a great deal of expertise, tends to be sold aggressively, while the telephone hardware is less of a concern and accordingly priced higher.

In the preferred case the customer does not attempt to unbundle but allows the firm to become the supplier for the complete turnkey operation. In such a case the firm will identify the overall price by adding software and design charges as markups on hardware components. In addition, the seller will negotiate for possible supplier hardware discounts, using its previous connections with suppliers to obtain special rebates if possible. Where desirable, these discounts can then be passed on to the customer. The ability to obtain these special discounts is one argument used to convince the customer not to unbundle the package.

When the complete system is handled, the firm is in a position to guarantee its performance—a guarantee customarily not offered when unbundling has taken place (to accept responsibility the firm needs to be in complete control of the project). In its home market the firm has been willing to accept business risk on some projects, receiving full payment only after successful installation and marketing of the mobile telephone system. Such an exposure has not been deemed acceptable in foreign markets.

Price and Positioning

Before deciding on the final price, some basics of pricing and positioning need to be kept in mind. In the final analysis, price is important because it represents the sacrifice for the potential customer contemplating a purchase. As such, price is no different whether we think of a consumer in Tanzania, in Thailand, or in Turkey. Most of the pricing discussions in traditional marketing texts are relevant at this stage. A few issues, however, do not translate so directly from the domestic to the foreign, and global markets and need to be considered carefully when going abroad. They include the question of price–quality relationships in positioning of the product and the role of the product life cycle with its skimming versus penetration price.

Price–Quality Relationships

In many countries where the positioning objective of a product is for a high-quality niche in the market, it goes without saying that price has to be relatively high. What is assumed, often correctly, is that customers will attribute high quality to a product with high price. It would generally cost more to produce a high-quality product, and thus its price will be higher. Research has shown that this **price–quality relationship** varies in strength by products, standardized products being less affected. Also, a strong brand name or a strongly positive country-of-origin image can nullify the negative quality effect from a low price.[14]

The price–quality relationship is also weakened in markets protected by trade barriers. In such markets imported products will usually show an artificially high price (the price escalation phenomenon), and thus a high price signals an imported product, not only or even necessarily a high-quality product. In many cases such imports will be of higher quality (if they were not, why would they be imported?), so the high price is in a sense justified. In other cases, however, the escalated prices are simply too high to render a product competitive, and the imports will make no inroads against established domestic brands. An example is the situation in the Japanese market where high non-tariff barriers have made many markets "dualistic," with a domestic and an import segment.[15] The majority of the market falls to the domestic producers, between whom competition is intense, while the imports garner a small fringe segment of the market, whose primary buying appeal is "status." A typical case is cameras, where a Swiss Leica is priced at approximately 2.5 times the price of a Nikon, a high-priced Japanese rival; or autos, where a BMW is priced at double its American price. Perhaps not surprisingly, for both companies Japan is their most profitable market.[16]

In this type of distorted marketplace, the assumption that high prices necessarily imply higher functional quality no longer holds, and the consumers will by and large learn this fact. Status is what matters. A high-priced Western luxury car, such as a Cadillac, has only recently been built with right-hand drive, for example, to accommodate the Japanese market. In Japan, the customers can usually buy more functional quality products at relatively low prices by staying with domestic offerings.

The PLC Impact

It is generally agreed that in the introductory stage of the product life cycle (PLC) customers are relatively insensitive to price levels. The innovators and pioneers who venture to try the new product are not very much concerned with price but act out of a desire to experience new things. Thus, the firm entering a market in the early growth stage could possibly maintain a relatively high **skimming price,** charging what the market will bear.

This logic becomes much less clear in global markets. Even though a given local market might be new so that the product is in the introductory stage technically speaking, it might already have reached the maturity stage in other local markets and certainly in leading markets. If so, the existing producers in those countries will be potential entrants in the new market and thus serve to put a limit on prices. Furthermore, a **demonstration effect** serves to speed up the introductory phase of many products: Potential customers are prepared for the eventual arrival of the new product by exposure via television and related global media.

Consequently, the best entry pricing strategy in many markets will be a relatively low-priced **penetration price** approach. This is also the one followed in recent years by most companies, including those as diverse as Microsoft with its office products, Compaq in PC hardware, Mercedes's new model autos, Olympus cameras, and Xerox copiers. The competitive rivalry is potentially intense, the buyers in the global village already know much about the product, and the producers use the experience curve argument to justify very low prices based on marginal costs. If the competitors consider the new entry to be in the potential "star" category, they will price aggressively for global strategic reasons.[17] All in all, the role of a skimming strategy in the introductory stage in the PLC is severely limited, although in the mature stage of the cycle a well-protected position can possibly still be used to generate cash in the short term.

Global Coordination

When a company manufactures in several nations and sells its products in many countries, the same product might appear on the market in different countries at widely different prices. This can be due to **"parallel" imports,** unauthorized middlemen importing the identical products and brands from countries whose prices are lower

A Nike factory in Asia with working conditions upgraded after antiglobalization protests against the company. A pair of $65 shoes still requires just $2.40 in labor costs. The larger part of the costs in a pair of Nikes involves design and marketing. A well-known brand is a key asset—both for the firm and for the gray trader. Daniel Groshong/Tayo.

because of exchange rates. These imports are also called **"gray trade."** Regardless of the company's price policy, fluctuations in exchange rates tend to produce temporary misalignment in prices between countries. Entrepreneurial spirits in a country can exploit such arbitrage opportunities by purchasing the product abroad, shipping it to the market, and selling it at a discount. For example, it is estimated that as many as 20 percent of the Mercedes-Benz cars sold in Japan in 1992 were parallel imports from Europe and the United States.[18]

For many products there is a need to develop a formula for coordinating prices and avoiding confusion among customers and opportunities for gray trade. A global customer does not usually like to see a firm charge different prices for the same product in different parts of the world. If it does, the customer might simply concentrate purchases where the price is lowest, ship to subsidiaries elsewhere, and cut costs. Or the customer might opt to put pressure on the manufacturer. For example, a leading manufacturer of consumer products distributed through large local and pan-European retailers had its biggest retail customer request that all products be supplied at the lowest European price. The company had to comply, but the 20 percent price decline across Europe resulted in a profit disaster.[19]

A coordinated pricing policy is obviously desirable but not so easily implemented. Generally, one can identify a polycentric, a geocentric, and an ethnocentric approach. But first companies have to decide what to do about gray trade.

Usually, the problem relates to exchange rate fluctuations. A good example is the pricing of a McDonald's hamburger. Although the company attempts to position the products as affordable and targets broad-based segments in most local markets, the resulting prices vary a great deal. The 2007 Big Mac prices ranged from $1.54 in Hong Kong and $1.57 in the China mainland to $6.25 in Switzerland, and even between two relatively comparable countries such as Argentina and Brazil the range was from $2.61 to $4.02, respectively (here the differences in the two countries' currency regime show the Argentine peso devalued and floating while the Brazil real is tied to the dollar). Since a Big Mac is pretty much similar across the globe, the relative under- or overvaluation of the local prices against the U.S. dollar shows whether the local currency is generally undervalued or overvalued. To get to the real effect on consumer incomes, however, one needs to look at the purchasing power parity figures—$1.57 in China is still quite a lot of money. There is now also an iPod index attempting to capture these currency fluctuations (see box, "The iPod Index").

Getting the Picture

THE IPOD INDEX

One of Australia's biggest banks, the Commonwealth Bank, has used the latest version of Apple's music player—the slim-line Nano—to compare global currencies and purchasing power in 26 countries. Along the lines of the Big Mac index launched 20 years ago by *The Economist* magazine, the survey prices the iPod Nano in U.S. dollars and found Brazilians pay the most for an iPod, shelling out $327.71, well above second-placed India at $222.27.

The five high-price and five low-price countries in 2007 were:

1 Brazil $327.71
2 India $222.27
3 Sweden $213.03
4 Denmark $208.25
5 Belgium $205.81
22 Mexico $154.46
23 U.S. $149.00
24 Japan $147.63

25 Hong Kong $147.35
26 Canada $144.20

"However, the results could be influenced by different pricing policies that Apple might apply in different parts of the world," a spokesperson for the bank said.

By comparison, the Economist's Hamburger index stood at $4.02 for Brazil, the high-cost country, and $3.85 for Canada, the low-cost country; not much of a difference. But in other ways the two series match. For both series, a country like Sweden is a high-cost country, with hamburgers at $5.53—or, if you want, with an overvalued currency relative to the dollar—while Hong Kong is one the lowest-cost countries.

More than 21 million iPods had been sold in the last quarter of 2006, not quite as many as Big Macs, but still a very respectable amount, especially given the higher per-unit prices. The choice of index depends partly on whether you are interested in fast-food expenditures or thinking about purchasing a durable product.

Sources: **www.commsec.com.au; www.apple.com; www.usatoday.com;** *The Economist,* July 5, 2007.

Pricing Actions against Gray Trade

The problem of gray trade is particularly acute in trade areas where barriers have recently been dismantled and exchange rates fluctuate, the EU before the euro being one example. According to one report, for identical consumer products, prices typically deviated 30 to 150 percent, creating big **arbitrage** opportunities and **"consumer tourism,"** with people traveling to another country for the purpose of shopping.[20]

As will be seen in Chapter 15, "Global Distribution," controlling gray trade involves more than trying to set prices that eliminate price differentials between countries, an impossible task in a world of floating exchange rates. Nevertheless, some pricing actions can be taken to help reduce the gray trade problem (see box, "Checking Gray Trade the Hard Way").

Four approaches to coordinating prices under the threat of gray trade can be identified.[21] They are not mutually exclusive, since a company can pursue them in combination:

Economic Controls

The company can influence price setting in local markets by changing the prices at which the product is shipped to importers or by outright rationing of the product as in the German auto case (described in the box, "Checking Gray Trade the Hard Way"). This usually is most feasible in the case of transfer prices to wholly owned subsidiaries.

Centralization

The company can attempt to set limits for local prices. These usually involve so-called **price corridors,** a range between maximum and minimum prices within which all local prices in a trading area must fall. The corridor should consider market data for the individual countries, price elasticities in the countries, currency exchange rates, costs in countries and arbitrage costs between them, plus data on competition and distribution.[22]

Formalization

Headquarters can standardize the *process* of planning and implementing pricing decisions in order to direct the pricing at the local level.

Getting the Picture

CHECKING GRAY TRADE THE HARD WAY

With price differentials on automobiles within the Euro-zone still running in double digit percentages (see the opening vignette), gray trade in new cars is still a problem for manufacturers (the used car cross-border trade is flourishing, but out of company control). The legal avenues available to manufacturers are limited, since the EU is one marketplace and national exclusivity can no longer be enforced. The companies have to resort to other methods, some of which they are reluctant to talk openly about. One tried-and-true Mercedes approach suggests what might have to be done.

In 1994 some new Mercedes models cost 30 to 40 percent less in Italy than in Germany because of the recent devaluation of the lira. The flood of reimports prompted the German automaker to drastic action. To control reimports from Italy, the company bought back a number of reimported cars from the gray traders and offered them as a "special series model" to authorized German dealers at gray import prices. Next, headquarters limited the number of cars to the Italian dealers, who were no longer able to supply both local customers and gray trade demand. With a limited supply the prices in Italy moved up, and with the exception of a few gray reimports by private owners, the so-called pipeline control worked out well.

Sources: Assmus and Wiese, 1995; Simon, 1995; Edmund L. Andrews, "Europe to Seek Uniformity in Car Pricing," *New York Times*, February 5, 2002, p. W1; **www.autospies.com.**

Informal Coordination

The company can institute various informal coordination mechanisms, including explicit articulation of corporate values and culture, human resource exchanges, and frequent visits to share experiences in other markets.

The choice between these approaches is affected by many factors, but two have been identified as particularly important: level of marketing standardization and strength of local resources. Exhibit 14.3 helps identify how these factors affect choice of method.[23] Several different situations can be assessed from the exhibit:

1. When marketing standardization is high, target segments and the elements of the marketing mix are known well enough for headquarters to help set local prices.

2. If local resources are on a high level, *economic controls* tend to be preferable, since raising and lowering transfer prices or rationing will send clear signals to local representatives without imposing final prices.

3. But if local resources are weak, *centralization* of the pricing decisions may be necessary, creating limits beyond which prices may not deviate.

4. In the low standardization case, when marketing is multidomestic in orientation with locally adapted mix elements, headquarters' role will be less directive. Local managers are likely to be better informed about local conditions than headquarters.

5. When local representatives are less resourceful, *formalization* of procedures can be helpful in ensuring that the appropriate factors are taken into account when local prices are set.

EXHIBIT 14.3
Coordinated Pricing Strategies

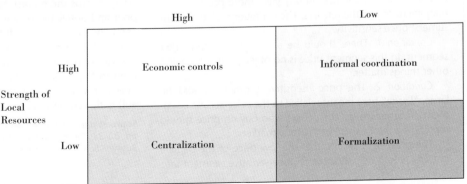

Level of Marketing Standardization

Strength of Local Resources	High	Low
High	Economic controls	Informal coordination
Low	Centralization	Formalization

Getting the Picture

PRICING COORDINATION: USING THE CARROT AND THE STICK

In global coordination of pricing, what is needed is a central point that sets a reference price. As Bryan Thompson of Oracle Consultant says: "This referenced price should take into consideration several factors such as the line of product being sold, the regional manufacturing and/or purchasing costs, expectations in margin, and selling conditions at a domestic and international level. It takes people to execute this philosophy. Essentially what is needed is a core 'pricing think tank.' The members of this committee should be representative of your organization across the globe and have long-term experience within the organization, a strong understanding of the organization at a regional and international level, and proven marketing and financial leadership."

An example is provided by a company in high-tech medical equipment that was faced with a sticky problem. In some countries, doctors needed extensive service support to operate the equipment, while in other countries hospitals had more trained staff. The transfer prices to these latter countries were set higher since sales costs for the subsidiaries were lower. But hospital purchasing managers in these countries were able to lower procurement costs by ordering equipment directly from subsidiaries in countries with lower transfer costs.

To solve the problem, headquarters first organized discussion groups with subsidiary managers to find an acceptable solution. After several meetings, the following strategy was adopted. First, the three most important markets were defined as lead countries. The main pricing authority was given to the local managers in the lead countries, who were to set prices so that gray trade would not be lucrative. Second, the country managers were trained and rotated between countries to better understand local competition and profit responsibility. Third, the reward system was changed by basing part of the local manager's annual bonuses on the success of the whole group. Managers who were uncooperative and hindered progress were laid off.

After one year, the problems were solved. Prices were coordinated, and profitability increased by more than 10 percent.

Sources: Assmus and Wiese, 1995; Bryan Thompson, "A Truly Global Pricing Strategy," Oracle Consultant, July 28, 2006.

6. With strong local resources, *informal coordination* is likely to be preferred, preserving local autonomy—but still using a stick if the carrot is not enough (see box, "Pricing Coordination").

In the end, it is useful to remember that in isolated instances, not all effects of gray trade might be negative. It is also possible to gain some advantages because gray trade tends to enlarge the market for a product through lower prices (see box, "The Silver Lining on Gray Trade").

Getting the Picture

THE SILVER LINING ON GRAY TRADE

Two academicians, Anne Coughlan at Northwestern University in the United States and David Soberman at INSEAD in France, set out to analyze the effects of gray trade on company and authorized resellers' sales and profits. The researchers were able to show that gray trade can actually be of benefit not only to the consumer but also to the firms.

Coughlan and Soberman demonstrated that under two conditions gray trade may in fact yield more profits to the manufacturer and the retailers. The conditions relate to consumers' price sensitivity.

Condition 1. There should be a *price-insensitive* market segment. In this segment price is no object, but service and other things matter.

Condition 2. The price-*in*sensitive segment should be large. "Large" here meant relative to the price-sensitive segment. In other words, the people who buy on price should represent a minor share of the total market.

The professors argued that the low price of the parallel imports would help attract the price-sensitive segment into the market. The authorized resellers could focus on the price-insensitive customers, providing value-adding items such as extra service, delivery, and special options. One caution from the professors to the authorized resellers: Don't let the extra service eat up all the profits.

Could this argument be extended to piracy? Of course, gray trade does not mean counterfeit trade. The gray traders still offer the real thing. In computer software, rampant piracy means the market gets a knockoff program, often a poor and unreliable version without backup service. Still, a company such as Microsoft has concluded that there is some value in the deep penetration of pirated Windows versions in the China market. Customers and content providers get used to the Windows interface, and as their incomes and needs grow and upgrades become available, a shift to the authentic version will come gradually.

Sources: *Harvard Business Review*, September–October 1998, pp. 22–23; Tarun Khanna, *Billions of Entrepreneurs* (Boston: Harvard Business School Press, 2008).

Global Pricing Policies

Apart from the global coordination of prices on specific products and services, firms usually adopt one of three alternative pricing policies that cuts across all their product lines. These pricing policies can be classified as *polycentric, geocentric,* and *ethnocentric.*

Polycentric Pricing

Polycentric organizations are those firms that leave a wide margin of discretion to local management. In these firms, prices are set at their appropriate levels in each local market separately, without constraints from headquarters. Naturally, prices might vary considerably between countries in **polycentric pricing** creating risk of gray trade. On the other hand, there is the undeniable advantage of really being able to adjust prices to the particular conditions facing the product in any one country.

Polycentric pricing is particularly useful when price sensitivity differs between markets and when the problem of gray trade is minimal. This can be the case in global service marketing (see box, "Pricing in Global Services").

Geocentric Pricing

The most common **geocentric pricing** scheme revolves around the use of a global or regional standard plus a markup that is variable across countries. The comparison price is derived for the home country or some other lead country for the world or a regional trading bloc. This base price is computed from a cost-plus formula. The markup is then adjusted for the particular situation the product faces in each country. When demand is strong and competition is weak (a "cash cow" situation), the added-on markup will be high; if competition is strong, the markup will come down. A Swedish pharmaceutical company with a successful ulcer drug uses this approach in its European markets.[24] The coordination is not easy, because the company has to take into account not only competition and demand but also regulatory factors and reimbursement formulas that differ between countries. Of course, the possibility of gray trade across country borders also needs to be taken into account, especially after the European Union (EU) integration. The overall consistency across EU countries is ensured by periodically reviewing the prices at headquarters and comparing them to the base price.

The biggest headache in geocentric pricing is the question of **product line pricing.** The markup deemed reasonable for one product in the line might not be very appropriate for another item in the line with a different competitive situation. Consequently, the assigned markup will differ across products in a local market.

Product line pricing is very much influenced by varying competitive conditions. When IBM competes with Sun microsystems in some particular country, only Internet servers might be involved. Accordingly, IBM could lower its prices on server units alone in the countries in question. The problem is that in terms of the overall product line, lower prices for the server units will make its large-scale multiuse computers seem overpriced. Furthermore, if the unit prices are lowered in some countries but not in others (where Sun does not have a sales office, for example), some large MNC might easily concentrate its computer purchases in the lowest-price country and do its own distribution to different countries--parallel trade again. The solution adopted by IBM is to avoid changing prices but rather increase the marketing (including service) support in the countries under competitive attack.

In contrast to IBM, Hewlett-Packard, another computer maker, has shifted from a "standard plus markup" approach to a more global system (see box, "Hewlett-Packard's New Global Pricing System").

Ethnocentric Pricing

In **ethnocentric pricing** the same price is charged to all customers regardless of nationality. It provides a standard worldwide price, usually derived on the basis of a full-cost formula to ensure that general overhead, selling expenses, and R&D expenditures will

Getting the Picture

PRICING IN GLOBAL SERVICES

Global service companies rarely face the problem of gray trade. The reason is that services are typically characterized by intangibility, perishability, and inseparability of production and consumption. This means polycentric pricing with different prices in different countries is more feasible for services than for physical products.

This does not mean, however, that prices cannot be usefully coordinated across countries. In an interesting article discussing global pricing by a provider of system support services for business customers in telecommunications, health care, and finance, Bolton and Myers show how global or regional prices can be coordinated. The key is whether the price elasticities differ by segment or by country. Rather than allowing each country subsidiary to set local prices, the company decided to explore the possibility of setting coordinated prices by segment. It identified the different price elasticities in different user segments (telecommunication firms versus hospitals, for example) and found that the different service levels required meant that price elasticities differed as well. But across countries in any region (such as Asia) there were similarities of price elasticities that made it possible to use coordinated pricing strategies for several of these segments.

In this kind of case, the centralized pricing strategies might be preferable to locally set prices not only for control purposes. The local subsidiary is likely to set a uniform price within the country to facilitate its control. This means the different price elasticities in the different segments are not adapted to, and the local price is likely to be suboptimal. By setting prices centrally, the local prices become more optimal.

Source: Ruth N. Bolton and Matthew B. Myers, "Price-Based Global Market Segmentation for Services," *Journal of Marketing* 67, no. 3 (July 2003), pp. 108–28.

---

be covered. This type of pricing approach is most useful when the company is producing a relatively standardized product with uniform usage patterns across many countries.

This is the typical pricing scheme for large-ticket items in industrial goods. Examples include aircraft and mainframe computers. IBM maintains this type of pricing policy, partly for the reasons stated above. Boeing, the aircraft company, is pricing its commercial aircraft in this fashion, only making adjustments because of special customization requirements and quantity discounts—as well as Airbus competition. Ethnocentric pricing is also a natural pricing procedure when the company is small and the international sales are few and far between. This is the kind of pricing scheme most acceptable to global customers since homogeneity of prices worldwide makes planning easier and concentrated purchases from central headquarters possible.

Managerial Trade-Offs

The ethnocentric approach to pricing in global companies has the great advantage of simplicity and allows headquarters to coordinate prices at the subsidiaries. But its drawbacks, primarily in terms of nonadaptation to the individual local markets, usually make it not useful to the multinational facing multidomestic markets and different competitive situations in each country. The polycentric approach is the one favored by most local managers of subsidiaries since it increases their control and allows complete attention to competing in the local market. Nevertheless, the lack of control and coordination from headquarters makes the polycentric strategy suboptimal in the global context, missing out on potential synergies and advantageous trade-offs. It also leaves the company open to the arbitrage possibilities of gray trade, with entrepreneurial middlemen buying up products in a low-price country, transporting the shipment back to a high-price country, and undercutting regular resellers at a profit. Many different product categories such as cameras, watches, jeans, and compact disks suffer from parallel imports. Even though these middlemen in a sense help markets become more efficient and equalize prices, they create a headache for multinationals trying to manage their regular distribution channels and motivate authorized resellers to support and service their products.

Geocentric pricing, especially as regionalized by trading blocs, emerges as a well-balanced compromise between global coordination and local adaptation. The variable markup, or the use of price corridors, allows the subsidiaries to adapt to the specific conditions within their particular local markets, including the threat of parallel imports

Getting the Picture

HEWLETT-PACKARD'S NEW GLOBAL PRICING SYSTEM

In 1992, faced with a globalizing marketplace, Hewlett-Packard, the computer maker based in Cupertino, California, realized that its international pricing system no longer worked. HP's old system relied on two parts. The first was a *base* price, quoted in U.S. dollars and derived on the basis of production costs at home and estimated price elasticities in the U.S. market. On top of the base price each country's sales organization would charge an "uplift," taking into account price escalation due to transportation, tariffs, and their own sales costs. There was little attempt to analyze the differences in demand between countries and across the various products (minis, PCs, notebooks, printers, and so on).

A spokesperson for HP also blamed the local compensation system. "A sales entity manager could drop the price of an extremely price-sensitive product and dramatically increase the volume [and his scorecard] by pulling in sales from neighboring countries. This is just a way of shifting business to make order performance look better."

In changing the global pricing system, the first move was to make each product division into a business unit responsible for pricing and profits worldwide. The base price was changed to reflect transfer costs to the various countries, and the local subsidiaries set final prices on the basis of their own sales costs, demand conditions, and competitive situations. But headquarters had final say in pricing, over possible protests by locals, in order to be able to optimize worldwide performance. Held responsible for worldwide performance, business unit managers at headquarters were expected to set transfer prices and sales incentives to local managers so as to maximize overall profits.

Sources: "The Price Is Right at Hewlett-Packard," *Financial Executive* 10, no. 1 (January–February 1994), pp. 22–25; Gates, 1995.

from a neighboring country. The markup adopted for a particular product and country can be based on both the demand conditions in the country and the role the subsidiary is supposed to play in the MNC's overall global strategy. In this way it allows synergies to emerge and a global perspective is naturally adopted by both headquarters management and managers at local subsidiaries.

Summary

This chapter has dealt with the many complex pricing issues facing the global marketer, showing how differences between countries constrain purely strategic considerations in global pricing. Building on the discussion in Chapter 5 on export expansion, this chapter placed the global pricing question in the context of pricing in economic theory and in marketing theory and practice, and then focused on issues and problems related to transfer prices and the global coordination of prices.

Many factors combine to determine what the actual price of a product will be when it finally appears on the market abroad. This final price might be quite different from the intended positioning: In global marketing it is not always easy to control what the final price will be because of regulatory limitations, exchange rate fluctuations, the number of independent middlemen and facilitating agents, and the need to motivate managers in local subsidiaries. Transfer prices to local subsidiaries have various functions over and above that of stimulating local sales, in particular a role in performance evaluations of the subsidiaries. Another complicating factor is the need to evaluate countertrade options and, in business-to-business settings especially, the possibility of bundling software and hardware together in larger systems.

As one ingredient of the product positioning mix, global pricing still has to take into account how customers in different countries evaluate high and low prices, as well as the stage of the PLC in the particular market. At the same time, the pressure from multinational customers to be quoted the same price anywhere in the world, along with the specter of gray trade, means that global coordination of prices is a necessary task of the global marketer. The chapter discussed the pricing aspect of the gray trade problem with special reference to the EU market, along with various schemes that companies use to counter gray trade. In the last section of the chapter we described the relative merits of polycentric, geocentric, and ethnocentric pricing strategies in the global firm.

Key Terms

arbitrage, *478*
arm's-length prices, *469*
barter, *471*
compensation deals, *472*
"consumer tourism," *478*
cost-plus pricing, *463*
counterpurchases, *472*
countertrade, *471*
demonstration effect, *476*
devaluation, *465*
ethnocentric pricing, *481*
exchange rate
fluctuations, *465*

experience curve
pricing, *463*
forward contract, *467*
functional analysis, *470*
geocentric pricing, *481*
"gray trade," *477*
hedging, *467*
offset, *473*
"parallel" imports, *476*
penetration price, *476*
polycentric pricing, *481*
premium price
differential, *464*

price controls, *468*
price corridor, *478*
price discrimination, *468*
price elasticities, *464*
price–quality
relationship, *475*
product buy-backs, *473*
product line pricing, *481*
skimming price, *476*
swap, *467*
systems selling, *474*
transfer pricing, *468*
turnkey sales, *474*

Discussion Questions

1. With the coming of the global marketplace on the Internet, will all prices be the same all over the globe? Why, or why not? What are the ways in which the prices in local markets can still be different?

2. Why are so many foreign-made products cheaper in the United States, while very few American-made products are cheaper abroad? How will global electronic commerce change this?

3. As a marketing manager for a non-European business, what obstacles would you face in attempting to coordinate prices between European countries? Why would you attempt it?

4. From a marketing viewpoint, what are the advantages and disadvantages of allowing local units to set their own prices?

5. What are the problems in implementing a coordinated pricing system to control gray trade?

Notes

1. The logistics aspects of the gray trade problem will be covered in Chapter 15, "Global Distribution."

2. See Abell and Hammond, 1979, Chapter 3.

3. Because the experience effect can't be documented in advance, companies that price on the basis of anticipated costs can be convicted of dumping based on historical costs.

4. See Anderson et al., 1993.

5. See Kotler, 1997, pp. 505–6.

6. See Johansson, 1989. The depreciating dollar in 2007-08 did of course change this picture dramatically. The trade conflict between the United States and Japan in mid-1995 concerning luxury cars again illustrated that exchange rate shifts alone will not necessarily change prices; see Pollack, 1995, and Tagliabue, 1995.

7. This practice lies behind the charges from foreign entrants that Japan's market is closed, as in, for example, the ongoing battle between Kodak and Fuji. See "Fuji Denies," 1995.

8. See Kapadia, 2001. Special thanks to Nick Matthews of KPMG, Melbourne, for transfer pricing sources.

9. This section draws on Livingstone and Grossman, 2002.

10. See Loughlin, 2003.

11. These are only highlights of the countertrade options. The book by Alexandrides and Bowers, 1987, can be suggested for further reading.

12. Because of the difficulty of transportation into an area such as Manaus and the standardized manufacturing processes involved, most of the plants built for this booming free trade zone are basically turnkey operations. See Brooke, 1995.

13. Adapted from Mattsson, 1975.

14. See Chao, 1993.

15. See Johansson and Erickson, 1986.

16. See Terry, 1994.

17. The pressure of aggressive competitive pricing at entry is perhaps most commonly observed in new electronics products. See, for example, "The Fight for Digital TV's Future," *New York Times,* January 22, 1995, section 3, pp. 1, 6; and "Digital Innovator Pays a Price for Being First," *New York Times,* February 1, 1995, p. D4.

18. Personal interview in Tokyo with Hans Olov Olsson on July 12, 1994. Mr. Olsson was then president of Volvo Japan.
19. From Simon, 1995.
20. The figures for the European Union come from Simon, 1995.
21. The following discussion draws on the excellent study by Assmus and Wiese, 1995.
22. See Simon, 1995.
23. Adapted from Assmus and Wiese, 1995.
24. See "Pharma Swede: Gastirup," case no. 14, in Kashani, 1992.

Selected References

Abell, D. F., and J. S. Hammond. *Strategic Market Planning.* Englewood Cliffs, NJ: Prentice Hall, 1979.

Alexandrides, C. G., and B. L. Bowers. *Countertrade: Practices, Strategies, and Tactics.* New York: Wiley, 1987.

Anderson, James C.; Dipak C. Jain; and Pradeep K. Chintagunta. "Customer Value Assessment in Business Markets: A State-of-Practice Study." *Journal of Business-to-Business Marketing* 1, no. 1 (1993), pp. 3–29.

Assmus, Gert, and Carsten Wiese. "How to Address the Gray Market Threat Using Price Coordination." *Sloan Management Review* 36, no. 3 (1995), pp. 31–42.

Bacher, Matthias Richard; Thomas Heger; and Richard Köhler. "Euro Pricing by Consumer Goods Manufacturers." Institut für Markt- und Distributionsforschung, Universität zu Köln, 1997.

Brooke, James. "Brazil Looks North from Trade Zone in Amazon." *New York Times,* August 9, 1995, p. D3.

Chao, Paul. "Partitioning Country of Origin Effects: Consumer Evaluations of a Hybrid Product." *Journal of International Business Studies* 24, no. 2 (Second Quarter 1993), pp. 291–306.

Davis, H. Thomas, Jr. "Transfer Prices in the Real World—10 Steps Companies Should Take Before It Is Too Late." *The CPA Journal* 64, no. 10 (October 1994), pp. 82–83.

"Fuji Denies Kodak's Contention of Unfair Trade." *New York Times,* August 1, 1995, p. D2.

Gates, Stephen. "The Changing Global Role of the Marketing Function: A Research Report." The Conference Board, report no. 1105-95-RR, 1995.

Hofmeister, Sallie. "Used American Jeans Power a Thriving Industry Abroad." *New York Times,* August 22, 1994, p. A1.

Iritani, Evelyn. "For Japanese, Hawaii's Hottest Spot May Be a Discount Mall." *Los Angeles Times,* September 25, 1995, p. D1.

Johansson, Johny K. "Stronger Yen and the United States—Japan Trade Balance: Marketing Policies of the Japanese Firms in the United States Market." In Tamir Agmon and Christine R. Hekman, eds. *Trade Policy and Corporate Business Decisions.* New York: Oxford University Press, 1989.

Johansson, Johny K., and Gary Erickson. "Price–Quality Relationships and Trade Barriers." *International Marketing Review* 3, no. 2 (Summer 1986).

Kapadia, Kaushal. "Arm's-Length Principle and Transfer Pricing Methodologies," *I.T.Review,* October 2001, pp. 36–40.

Kashani, Kamran. *Managing Global Marketing.* Boston: PWS-Kent, 1992.

Kotler, Philip. *Marketing Management,* 9th ed. Upper Saddle River, NJ: Prentice Hall, 1997.

Livingstone, John Leslie, and Theodore Grossman, eds. *The Portable MBA in Finance and Accounting,* 3rd ed. New York: John Wiley and Sons, Inc., 2002.

Loughlin, Peter J. "Transfer Pricing in the United States—A Primer." www.lawschoolbible.com, 2003.

Lustig, Nora. "The Outbreak of Pesophobia." *Brookings Review* 13, no. 2 (Spring 1995), p. 46.

Mattsson, L. G. *Systemforsaljning.* Stockholm: Marknadstekniskt Centrum, April 1975.

Pollack, Andrew. "U.S. and Japan Again Pull Back from the Brink." *New York Times,* June 22, 1995, pp. 31, 34.

Royal, Weld, and Allison Lucas. "Global Pricing and Other Hazards." *Sales & Marketing Management* 147, no. 8 (August 1995), pp. 80–83.

Rutenberg, D. P. *Multinational Management.* Boston: Little, Brown, 1982.

Shulman, J. S. "Transfer Pricing in the Multinational Firm." Reading no. 40 in Thorelli and Becker, *International Marketing Strategy,* pp. 316–24.

Simon, Hermann. "Pricing Problems in a Global Setting." *Marketing News,* October 9, 1995, p. 4.

Sims, Clive; Adam Phillips; and Trevor Richards. "Developing a Global Pricing Strategy." *Marketing & Research Today* 20, no. 1 (March 1992), pp. 3–14.

Tagliabue, John. "For Japan Auto Makers, It's Tougher in Europe." *New York Times,* June 28, 1995, p. D4.

Terry, Edith. "Japan: Where the Prices Are Insane!" *Fortune,* October 31, 1994, p. 21.

Thorelli, Hans B., and Helmut Becker, eds. *International Marketing Strategy.* Revised ed. New York: Pergamon, 1980.

Thurston, Charles W. "Surprise! It's Devaluation Time Again." *Global Finance* 9, no. 2 (February 1995), pp. 48–50.

Weekly, James K. "Pricing in Foreign Markets: Pitfalls and Opportunities." *Industrial Marketing Management* 21 (1992), pp. 173–79.

15

Global Distribution

"Here, there, everywhere"

After reading this chapter, you will be able to:

1. Understand not only how the wholesale and retail structure of a local market reflects the country's culture and economic progress, but also how new channel modes may be successful if timing and conditions are right.
2. Help design local distribution channels that account for the original mode of entry and allow local managers to play important roles in implementation.
3. Analyze globally coordinated channels by starting with a clear understanding of how the firm-specific advantages (FSAs) depend on distribution channel design.
4. Explain how global logistics and transportation are important determinants of financial performance, and their efficiency has been improving dramatically.
5. Defend a brand against parallel distribution and gray trade by close management and control of distribution channels.

The global marketer faces a complex problem in designing globally coordinated channels through which to market the product. The distributors and agents used for initial entry may not be suitable any longer when global expansion proceeds further, and new channels may have to be found. Which alternative intermediaries are available and what functions they perform vary across different local markets. The channel strategies successful at home might not be effective abroad—and might not even be feasible. The global logistics of transporting products between various countries increase in speed and flexibility but also become more difficult to manage, with diverted gray trade creating problems for manufacturers as well as local distributors. The global marketer attempting to create synergies and cost savings by rationalizing global distribution faces a formidable task.

European Retailers Challenge American Gap

Retailers, like producers, have been going global as never before. In the process they incite increased competitive rivalry with incumbent firms.

Successful entry into Europe of Gap involved offering American fashion not only in clothing but also in store design. The chain determined that the way products are presented to customers is even more important in Europe than in the United States, and Gap stores apply that knowledge. In London, Gap's interiors are white with light wood floors and chrome fixtures. This striking design, which is not typical of British retailers, has generated attention—and sales.

Now two European clothing retailers have decided to meet the enemy on its own turf and battle Gap for a share of the $182 billion annual U.S. apparel business.

H&M, a $3.9 billion Swedish chain with more than 700 stores in 12 European countries, hoped to have more than 85 outlets operating in the United States by the end of 2003. Spain's Zara opened its first U.S. location in 1998 and has planned on 40 more over the next few years. Some industry analysts are predicting an upcoming major price war.

Originally founded in Stockholm in 1947, the former Hennes & Mauritz began refining its version of low-price, high-volume, hip fashion retailing in Europe over the last 30 years. Just like Gap, Zara, and Benetton, H&M exclusively sells its own brand clothing, but unlike its competitors the focus is on young styles at prices difficult to match. In essence, H&M is a vertical retailer with its clothing designed by a team of 70 in-house designers who monitor global trends. Working with 1,600 suppliers throughout Europe and Asia, H&M bypasses the middleman to get items from the fashion runways to its stores within a few short weeks. "It is the world's best at controlling the supply chain and picking up on changes, with the possible exception of Zara," says Keith Wills, retail analyst at Goldman Sachs in London.

Dubbed "the poor man's Armani," Zara—with shops in more than 30 countries—owes its success to a vertically integrated business model spanning design, just-in-time production, marketing, and sales. Since Zara makes more than half its clothes in-house, rather than utilizing a network of disparate and slow-moving suppliers, it has more flexibility to respond to fickle fashion trends. The result is that Zara can make a new line from start to finish in three weeks, versus the industry average of nine months. This translates to 10,000 new designs a year with none remaining in the stores for more than a month. So while H&M's collection is committed six months in advance, Zara is able to quickly dump a production range that becomes unpopular and offer midmarket chic at down-market prices. "They produce it fast, read the feedback, and reproduce what's hot," says Candace Corlett, a partner with WSL Strategic Retail.

Both firms clearly have learned from Benetton's difficulties in penetrating the U.S. market in the 1980s. Benetton's experience revealed that customers willing to pay more for "made in Italy" only live in urban areas and that better quality and more fashionable content did not interest price-oriented U.S. customers. The lesson learned by both H&M and Zara is that if fashion is your strong suit, in the United States prices have to be low. Unlike the style- and status-conscious European consumers, Americans are more practical. Styles that are "in" will soon turn to styles that are "out," so you won't wear the item for long. So, why pay high prices?

Meanwhile Gap continues to lose brand value. According to Interbrand's rankings, it lost 22 percent in brand value between 2005 and 2006, and another 15 percent in the year up to 2007. It is not easy finding a new strategic formula.

Sources: Katherine Hobson, "Shop the Continent—at Your Local Mall," *U.S. News & World Report,* April 9, 2001, p. 47; Marianne Wilson, "Disposable Chic at H&M," *Chain Store Age,* May 1, 2000, p. 64; "About H&M," *Chain Store Age,* May 1, 2000, p. 75; Vlada Tkach, "International Feature: Retail Sans Frontiers," *Investors Chronicle,* June 15, 2001, pp. 80–81; **www.bwnt.businessweek.com.**

Introduction

In Chapter 5, "Export Expansion," the importance of finding good distributors for an exported product was emphasized. The capability of the distributor chosen is critical for two reasons. One, the distributor is the gateway to the new country market, the "face" of the exporter's firm, and the avenue through which the marketing effort is channeled. Two, because of contractual obligations it is often difficult to change distributors later when a global strategy favors an alternative.

In this chapter the issue of global distribution will be faced by the marketer who wants to impose some coordination on local distribution channels. The chapter shows how the attempt might involve reconfiguring channels by introducing new alternatives or by establishing parallel channels. Multiple distribution channels are often a fact of life anyway for the global marketer because of the growth of gray trade. As for the distribution of products between countries, technological development and competition have made independent global logistics companies crucial players in the firm's global strategy.

The chapter starts with a discussion of distribution as a competitive advantage. It continues with the question of how a company can rationalize local distribution. It then discusses wholesaling and retailing in different countries, and also covers the *globalization of retailing*. Then we shift our attention to *global logistics* and recent advances in global transportation. We then turn to the issue of gray trade and the threats and opportunities from multiple channels in *parallel distribution*. The chapter finishes with a discussion of the potential for coordinated *global channels*.

Distribution as a Competitive Advantage

As marketers well know, distribution is a major component of the marketing mix, a vital and necessary part of the so-called four Ps (where, besides product, price, and promotion, it stands for "place"). If the product is not available, it is difficult to buy it. As my old distribution professor liked to put it with some exaggeration: "When is a refrigerator not a refrigerator? When it is in Pittsburgh and the buyer is in Dallas." This can be put even stronger in global marketing—the refrigerator might be built in Korea and bought in France.

It is also important to remember that distribution can be a competitive advantage as well. That is, distribution is not simply a necessary component of marketing strategy, but it might be a decisive advantage for a firm. A dominant firm such as Coca-Cola in soft drinks attributes a large part of its success to intensive distribution coverage, including a variety of stores and vending machines and contractual arrangements to be the only vendor in colleges, schools, and so on. Starbucks covers city blocks with storefronts on every other corner. Apparel for teens sells partly on shopping experiences, with multiple store locations in shopping malls and city centers. Even in autos, where buyers could be expected to be willing to travel "that extra mile," there is a decided advantage in multiple-point availability, since it signals easy access to repairs.

The role of distribution in a firm's success needs to be evaluated very carefully by the global marketer. If intensive distribution is a key factor in the company's success, it becomes very important to assess whether foreign markets offer the same infrastructure opportunities. For example, when The Body Shop entered the United States, it was forced to open stores in shopping malls. Their stores in other countries were small, freestanding boutiques in downtown locations, where competition with other similar stores was limited. Would they be able to succeed in the malls where directly

A Zara store on Broadway in lower Manhattan in New York City. Zara's store location strategy is to put the large and often two-story stores at key pedestrian locations in the big cities. The H&M strategy is the same. Not surprisingly, this means the competitive stores are often close together. There is an H&M store just a block away from this store.

competing storefronts are close by? Or should The Body Shop attempt to pursue its customary strategy? These are difficult decisions; in this case the company did enter the malls, with some success, although less so than elsewhere.

The fact is that if distribution is a key success factor in a product category, global expansion can be difficult and expensive. The same successful distribution system might be hard to reproduce abroad. This makes global coordination and control more difficult. Even Coca-Cola has had trouble replicating some of its bottling and distribution systems abroad, although the company expanded after World War II when many countries were rebuilding. Today, in mature markets, the situation is decidedly different. The favored locations in retailing might already be occupied by strong domestic players. A good example is the way Fuji has been able to hold off Kodak in the Japanese film market (as we saw in Chapter 2). Starbucks has trouble using its saturation strategy where the number of store locations is limited by regulations as in many European countries. Toys "R" Us needs rezoning in many countries to make room for its large warehouse style stores. In this chapter, we will see that retailers often go global by acquiring domestic chains simply to get access to distribution points. But they often find that introducing a new way to do retailing into an existing foreign business is not always easy. Wal-Mart's purchase of ASDA in Britain initially proved successful, but its venture into Germany via Wertkauf and Interspar seemed doomed from the start.

The increased distance between manufacturing and point-of-sale that goes with global marketing makes the logistics part of distribution also more important than at home. This means that even when distribution is not a major success factor at home, it might be a major *dis*advantage abroad. For example, problems with lack of supplies, delivery delays, lost shipments, and access to spare parts can be magnified when shipping is across borders. Sony's PlayStation 3 has been difficult to find in American stores, although the problem seems to lie with chip manufacturing problems in Japan rather than with supply logistics. Fortunately, as this chapter will show, with the vastly enhanced global communications capability (not least through the Internet) and much improved technology, logistical problems are more manageable than ever. The global success of companies such as H&M and Zara owes much to their ability to manage logistics across many borders successfully. We have not yet reached "the death of distance" as some Internet writers claimed early on—physical products still need to be shipped, and the greater the distance the greater the chance that something may go wrong. But the logistical disadvantage of being far from the market and the ultimate buyer has been reduced considerably in recent years. That does not mean, of course, that being close to the customer is not important—the global marketer still has to learn the desires and preferences of the local customer. And in the new environment of high oil prices, global transportation is becoming more critical (see box, "Transportation and Energy Costs: A Global Threat?").

Rationalizing Local Channels

Channel networks, once designed, do not stay the same forever. It is in the very nature of the open market system that competitive and countervailing forces assert themselves and force change. The global marketer will want to try to rationalize distribution by introducing some uniformity across countries.

Changing Distributors

The distribution channel configuration created for entry into a foreign market is rarely optimal once the product is established on the market. In some cases the success of the distributor in selling the product contains the seeds of his or her undoing. Then the exporter may move aggressively to usurp some of the power of the distributor and grab some of the profits. But the traditional reason for termination of a distributor is the sense on the part of the exporting firm that the distributor is not doing a good enough job in the market.[1]

Getting the Picture

TRANSPORTATION AND ENERGY COSTS: A GLOBAL THREAT?

One of the major forces behind globalization has been the continuous improvement in global transportation. In the early days, geographic distances between countries and the associated transportation costs were a major international trade barrier, and figured prominently in the theory of comparative advantage of nations. As global communication became instantaneous, transportation technology improved, and consolidated shippers appeared, the cost of transportation became an almost negligible amount of the total product cost in any marketplace around the world.

With the steep rise in oil prices in recent years, this picture is no longer accurate. Transportation is now expensive, and a major new constraint on product sourcing for many markets. Supply chains between low-wage outsourcing countries and final assembly locations are strained, as ocean carriers quote higher shipping rates, trucks require increased mileage compensation, and air transportation costs have moved beyond the budgets allocated. Unable to raise prices sufficiently in a very competitive and price sensitive environment, airlines have curtailed service, limited flights, and gone bankrupt. If the trend continues—and most experts agree that it will, seeing no end to the energy crisis—international trade and with it globalization will slow down significantly.

Two areas particularly hard hit may be the fair trade items and green products designed to minimize global warming. There is an embedded energy cost in everything you produce or ship or use in the world. For fair trade products, once you add in the rising transportation costs from a distant producer, it is going to be harder for the Third World producer to be competitive in mature markets. And if you sacrifice and pay more for the fair trade item, are you not encouraging increased energy consumption? As for green products, evidence is accumulating that many green products can use up more energy in production than is saved by consumers changing their habits. We learn that converting corn to biofuels uses up almost as much energy as it produces—and also adds to a world food shortage. Even the highly praised Toyota Prius, the hybrid car, is being challenged. In a British test it gets slightly less miles per gallon than a BMW, and when the energy required to charge the Prius battery is added to the fuel equation, the net effect is not as green as one would have hoped.

In today's interrelated global economy, it is not easy to do good.

Sources: Mark Clayton, "As Global Food Costs Rise, Are Biofuels to Blame?" *The Christian Science Monitor*, January 28, 2008; "Toyota Prius Proves a Gas Guzzler in a Race with the BMW 520d," *The Sunday Times*, March 16, 2008.

Typically, the channel changes initiated by the manufacturer involve the termination of independent distributors' or authorized dealers' contracts and creating a wholly owned sales subsidiary. But termination often involves conflict.[2] As we saw in Chapter 5, it is useful to formulate the distribution contracts in such a fashion that conflicts are resolved in an orderly manner. And as we saw in Chapter 6, some joint venture distribution agreements even go so far as to include "divorce clauses" specifying how the dissolution of the "marriage" should take place if necessary.

When conflicts do arise, some painful and scarring experiences often result. One reason is the different view that people from different countries have of proper conflict resolution methods. In the United States, legal proceedings are resorted to rather quickly. By contrast, in many foreign countries such proceedings are invoked only as a last resort. Whereas certain cultures view the business relationship between manufacturer and middleman in terms of antagonism that readily engenders conflict, others view it in terms of cooperation and are willing to forgo immediate individual gratification for the benefit of a harmonious relationship in the longer run. When these two viewpoints clash, as they often do in global channel agreements, the whole channel design is in jeopardy.

Dual Distribution

The channel changes that occur do not necessarily involve termination of contracts. In some cases multiple channels emerge or are created.[3] For example, Lucky Goldstar's entry from Korea into the U.S. television market was made via original equipment manufacturing (OEM) agreements with retailers such as Sears; later a **dual distribution** system was initiated with sales under its own brand name, Goldstar and, more recently, the company has shifted to its new brand name, LG. Often the manufacturer tries to differentiate the offerings in different channels. Italian apparel maker Giorgio Armani has set up a number of stores in the West under a separate name, AX

Exchange, carrying more casual clothes and lower-priced items than the regular Armani's at his own specialty shops and department stores.

Changing to direct sales might solve the overseas distribution problem for the industrial goods multinational. The global marketer of consumer goods, however, also has to deal with the wholesalers and retailers that provide the link to the ultimate consumer.

Wholesaling

Wholesalers sell to retailers or industrial users. Their main functions involve making contact, negotiating, buying, selling, and warehousing; but they might also be involved in shipping, financing, and packaging as well as other middleman functions. Wholesaling is a major component of a country's infrastructure, and its structure reveals important clues as to the country's stage of development. The data presented in Exhibit 15.1 demonstrate how the number and size of wholesalers vary in different countries.

Perhaps the most striking fact in Exhibit 15.1 is the similarity between Germany and the United States. Both countries show a great consolidation at the wholesale level, with relatively few wholesale enterprises per capita population. By contrast, several of the other European countries as well as Australia and New Zealand show a larger number of wholesale enterprises, relatively speaking. The contrast between the Czech Republic and Slovakia is also striking, with Slovakia showing much less intensity, but here the reason is mainly a lack of economic development.[4]

Vertical Integration

Power and Competition

The size distribution of wholesalers in many countries approximates the well-known "80–20" rule: 80 percent of the transactions are handled by 20 percent of the firms. In Malaysia, for example, fewer than a dozen European merchant houses handle over half the import trade, while hundreds of small local trading companies handle the remaining volume. The giant Israeli wholesaler Hamashbir Hamerkazi handles all kinds of products and has full or partial ownership of 12 major industrial firms, representing approximately one-fifth of all Israeli wholesaling trade.[5]

The financial power of large wholesalers coupled with a good infrastructure and lack of government regulation has meant that in some countries they operate on a nationwide basis; Japan, Israel, and Australia are only a few examples among many. In other countries, however, the preponderance of small wholesalers means that in order to cover the whole country, more than one wholesaler is used: The smaller ones cover at most a regional portion of countries such as Italy, Turkey, and Egypt.

The U.S. trend toward **vertical integration** in channels—with large food wholesalers such as SuperValu and Associated Grocers controlling the production and

EXHIBIT 15.1
Number of Wholesale Enterprises in Selected Countries, 2004*

Country	No. of Wholesalers	Population (millions)	Wholesalers per capita (no. per thousand people)
Australia	82,184	19.91	4.13
New Zealand	15,516	3.99	3.91
France	183,341	60.42	3.03
Germany	93,543	82.42	1.13
Italy	406,790	58.06	7.01
Netherlands	57,190	16.32	3.50
Spain	201,763	40.28	5.01
Sweden	43,612	8.99	4.85
Czech Rep.	61,639	10.25	6.01
Slovakia	8,386	5.42	1.55
United Kingdom	111,018	60.27	1.84
United States	324,167	293.03	1.11

Source: OECD data,
http://epp.eurostat.ec.europa.eu.

*Excludes motor vehicles and motorcycles.

distribution of farm produce, for example—has now spread to other countries. There are cases in which wholesalers have organized retail chains (in Britain for soft goods, for example) and also cases in which wholesalers have integrated backward into manufacturing (as in Japan for certain food products).[6] This integration sometimes makes it difficult for an importer to gain access to a wholesaler. In India, the large wholesalers in several markets are entrenched "monopsonists," monopolistic buyers. If you don't deal through them, you don't deal.

Efficiency

The trend toward integration is based on the technological developments that have made large-scale economies and technical coordination feasible. It is an example of technological diffusion across the globe. The emergence of freezing equipment, automatic (and computerized) materials handling, models of optimal inventory control and large-quantity reordering, and reliable and fast communications (telecommunications and transportation) has made the growth of the large individual wholesaler possible and economically desirable. As the infrastructure in various countries has improved with economic development, the introduction of these technical innovations has become feasible. As entrepreneurial wholesalers adopt the new technology, they leave others behind; and if the wholesalers don't do it, there are always eager retailers and manufacturers who are keeping a watchful eye on possible cost savings or improved service in the middleman levels. In many countries the wholesalers have, in fact, been too slow to innovate and have been pushed aside by aggressive retailers integrating backward and manufacturers eager to simplify their distribution channels.[7] The functions carried out by the wholesalers still remain necessary for the movement of the product from producer to consumer: It is just that wholesalers are not always the most efficient at it, especially with the new direct importers providing stiff competition.

Types of Wholesalers

In most developed countries it is customary to identify a wide variety of wholesalers, and one can usually count on finding some wholesaler that will fill the bill when it comes to distributing the product. But this variety reflects more the aggressive nature of the entrepreneurial instinct and the particular nature of the market system in each of the countries rather than a homogeneous trend toward which all economies move. In general, the so-called **full-service wholesalers** can usually be counted on in most countries. But because of their size and tie-ins with existing brands and chains, they might not be willing, or the best ones, to distribute the firm's product. The full-service concept should be carefully assessed for each country entered. *Full-service* might mean "take title" (and thus ownership) to American sellers, but it might not prohibit a Middle Eastern wholesaler from returning a product that does not sell well in expectation of a full refund. Full service might not include service backup in European countries, but in India retailers expect to be able to hand over defective products to the wholesaler rather than the manufacturer.

Even practices in developed countries can vary considerably; see Exhibit 15.2. As can be seen, in a country such as Japan it is common that unsold goods can be returned to the manufacturer. This is in stark contrast to the practice in Western countries. While European countries offer some open and fixed rebates on purchases, and the United States allows functional discounts, Japan has a much more complex system of rebates, some of which are not open but only extended to favored customers. Suggested retail prices do not exist in principle in Europe (although price competition is usually less intense than in the United States), are allowed in the United States, and are not only common in Japan but quite vigorously enforced by some manufacturers (although the practice of cutting off supplies to uncooperative retailers has been successfully challenged in court). Manufacturers in Japan have also engaged in forward integration to a greater extent than elsewhere and tend to offer more sales support to the distribution channel members. Needless to say, complete standardization of channel design across these countries by a global marketer is not feasible without creating a new channel.

EXHIBIT 15.2 International Comparison of Wholesale Trade Practices

Source: "International Comparison of Wholesale Trade Practices," from Distribution Economics Institute, *Survey on International Comparison on the Distribution Industry*, May 1990.

Practice	Japan	United States	Britain	France	Germany
Returned goods	• Returning unsold goods is common	• Doesn't exist except for imperfect or damaged goods	• Doesn't exist except for imperfect or damaged goods	• Doesn't exist except for imperfect or damaged goods	• Doesn't exist except for imperfect or damaged goods
Rebate system	• Various and complicated structure (volume, fixed date, evaluation, promotion) • Long term in pay unit (yearly, half-year, etc) • Rebates are not necessarily open	• No rebates but discounts and allowances exist • Open rule • Pay unit depends	• Quantitative and date fixed rebates exist • Open rule • Pay unit depends	• Quantitative and date fixed rebates exist • Open rule • Pay unit depends	• Quantitative and date fixed rebates exist • Open rule • Pay unit depends
Quotations	• Manufacturer's suggested retail prices exist • Written materials and certain drugs and cosmetics are allowed to maintain resale prices	• Manufacturer's suggested retail prices exist	• Doesn't exist in principle • Books and drugs are allowed to maintain resale prices	• Doesn't exist in principle • Books and certain cosmetics, ski equipment, and some consumer electronics are allowed to maintain resale prices	• Doesn't exist in principle • Books, newspapers, and magazines are allowed to maintain resale prices
Forward integration	• Exists (consumer electronics, auto, cosmetics)	• Uncommon	• Exists (auto)	• Exists (auto)	• Exists (auto)
Others	• Loaned sales staff • Frequent and small-amount delivery • Perpetuates business relation • Unclear contracts	• Uncommon	• Uncommon	• Uncommon	• Uncommon

Between-country differences are perhaps even more common for the various limited-line wholesalers that specialize in one or two of the wholesaling functions. For example, a very unique institution in the U.S. economy is the rack jobber, the wholesaler that delivers the product to the retailer's shelf directly. Many supermarkets overseas do not have this system, and the chain drugstores (another semi-unique U.S. invention) where products such as compact disks and women's hosiery might be sold through displays rented to, and stocked by, the rack jobber are not yet common in many other countries. The reason a product such as L'eggs pantyhose has been accepted only slowly in overseas markets is not resistance to the product among buyers. A greater obstacle has been that the innovation (the firm-specific advantage) lies in the convenient packaging and the "front door" delivery system via rack jobbers through which the product is distributed.[8] Without the same channel linkage operating well in other countries, market penetration is difficult.

Retailing

Retailers are those middlemen who sell directly to the ultimate consumer. They fulfill similar functions as other middlemen, including ordering, creating assortments, presenting the merchandise, storing and packaging, and perhaps also shipping and financing. The variety in retailing across countries is, if anything, greater than in

EXHIBIT 15.3
Number of Retail Enterprises in Selected Countries, 2004*

Source: OECD data, http://epp.eurostat.ec.europa.eu.

Country	No. of Retailers	Population (millions)	Retailers per capita (no. per thousand people)
Australia	177,689	19.91	8.92
New Zealand	22,740	3.99	5.70
France	427,352	60.42	7.07
Germany	274,195	82.42	3.33
Italy	703,570	58.06	12.12
Netherlands	78,935	16.32	4.84
Spain	531,113	40.28	13.19
Sweden	57,494	8.99	6.40
Czech Rep.	134,025	10.25	13.08
Slovakia	4,522	5.42	0.83
United Kingdom	200,572	60.27	3.33
United States	618,042	293.03	2.11

*Excludes motor vehicle and motorcycle dealers, hotels, and restaurants.

wholesaling. In some countries such as Italy and Algiers, retailing is composed largely of small specialty houses carrying a narrow line of products. By contrast, in the northern European countries there are many stores with a broad assortment of products. The large Japanese chain of department stores, Mitsukoshi, maintains retail outlets around most major capitals in the world and attracts an average of 100,000 customers per day. The bazaars of the Middle East, on the other hand, contain as many shops as customers on some days.

Exhibit 15.3 presents a statistical picture of the number of retail enterprises in a selected number of countries. Just as in the case of wholesaling, the United States and Germany show strong patterns of consolidation into large enterprises. In Europe, the Italian and Spanish markets—and the Czech Republic—are apparently still served by a large number of independent retailers, while again the Slovakia lack of development shows a very low level of retailing, a possible heritage of its communist past. It should be noted that these are number of enterprises, not number of actual outlets. The United States actually has an unusually large number of people employed in retailing relative to the population.[9]

Retailing and Lifestyles

Because retailers cater to the individual consumer, it is hardly surprising that there are so many of them and such wide differences between countries. The retailing structure has to adapt to the varying living conditions and lifestyles of individual households. Shopping represents both a tiresome job and a leisure activity for individuals everywhere and is both a reflection of and a formative influence on the lifestyle of the people in a country. Where living standards differ between countries, one would therefore expect retailing structures to differ; and where lifestyles are similar, these similarities will be reflected in more homogeneity in the respective retailing structures. Retail stores are, in a sense, the most obvious indication of a country's economic achievement and thus are a most informative indicator of the lifestyles of a country's citizens. This also means that their habits are different, and one-size-fits-all kind of marketing is not going to work.

Thus, with globalization the number of retail outlets in most developing countries has increased consistently every year, reflecting increasing availability of consumer goods. At the same time, the number of retail stores in highly developed countries showed an equally consistent pattern of decline as scale economies of larger units led to industry consolidation.[10] Over time, economic progress is likely to lead to a convergence of the retail structures, as the large chains globalize their operations (a good example is Zara; see box, "Zara, the Spanish Fashion Retailer"). In the meanwhile, however, the global marketer has to face the differences and learn to work through them. For example, the standardized Gillette blades sold through drugstores in the United States are sold in tobacco shops in Italy, department stores in Germany, on the street in Moscow, at movie counters in Thailand, and from traveling vans in India.

Getting the Picture

ZARA, THE SPANISH FASHION RETAILER

Zara, the Spanish apparel chain, offers great fashion at cheap prices. It has become destination shopping for mothers and daughters, for fathers and sons, for children. The appeal of this unlikely Spanish retailing success is unisex and universal. And like Wal-Mart, it represents a new business model for successful retailing.

How did this come about? The start was not auspicious. Family-owned Zara began in 1963 as a supplier of women's lingerie in La Coruna, a city on the northwestern tip of Spain. The first Zara store did not open until 1975. The company now has 600 stores in 44 countries. Over the years Zara gradually learned to synchronize design, production, distribution, and sales with increasing precision and speed. Since fashion—what catches on and what does not—is notoriously difficult to predict, Zara managers realized that a solution would be to simply track closely the new designs from the fashion houses in Europe, America, and Japan and China, marry this information with consumer feedback from the market, and then quickly create new styles for the mass market. Then, with a flexible and fast production system, the factories could produce and distribute the new designs quickly and the stores would have new designs early. Over time, Zara learned to cut this design-to-production-to-store cycle down to weeks rather than the months that most competitors needed.

The process works as follows. As store managers feed back sales and market data from the field, creative teams in Spain of more than 200 professionals combine this information with the news from the fashion houses in Europe, America, and Asia. This interactive process helps suggest new designs and translate them into new Zara styles. The new designs are finished in about four to six weeks, but may be done in as little as two. The turnaround from styling design to finished product on the shop floor is about 15 days. Zara achieves this by holding fabric in stock and then cutting and dyeing it at the last minute. The result is new merchandise as often as

twice a week, and it is rare to have a style reordered. If you see a Zara top you like, better get it because it will likely not come back. This is different from a competitor like Benetton where a popular style is likely to be reordered and soon be back on the shelf.

Zara produces about 10,000 different styles annually, and store managers choose from that range twice a week. They receive information via handheld PCs, where they can see images of the product and then key in the orders for each style, including quantities, sizes, and colors. Orders have to be placed at predesignated times: stores in Spain and southern Europe on Wednesdays before 3:00 in the afternoon and Saturdays before 6:00 in the evening, in the rest of the world on Tuesdays by 3:00 in the afternoon and Fridays by 6:00 in the evening. Orders must be on time. If, for example, a store in Belgium misses the Wednesday deadline, then it would have to wait until Saturday for a shipment.

Zara produces approximately 50 percent of its products in its own network of 22 Spanish factories and uses subcontractors for all sewing operations. These factories work a single shift and are managed as freestanding profit centers. Another 50 percent of its products are procured from 400 outside suppliers, 70 percent of then in Europe, the rest mostly in Asia.

Zara is another illustration of the power of fast and flexible production systems. Its business model is based on the just-in-time methods of the automotive industry pioneered by Toyota. With the latest figures showing year-on-year growth of 25 percent in sales (fourth quarter of 2002–03) despite slowing consumer markets, Zara is beginning to look like an unstoppable global fashion force, just as Toyota has set the pace for automobile producers for the last ten or so years.

Sources: Kasra Ferdows, Jose Machuca, and Michael Lewis, *Zara*, European Case Clearing House, 2002; Robert Carruthers, "Trendy Euro Chains are Forcing the Pace of Fashion in the U.K." *Rapid Response Retail: Marketing*, April 3, 2003, p. 20; John Tagliabue, "A Rival to Gap that Operates Like Dell," *New York Times*, May 30, 2003, p. W-1.

Creating New Channels

But retailing is dynamic. As economic growth takes place and global trade expands, new alternatives emerge. Even the least developed countries experience dramatic changes in distribution channels as innovations such as self-service, discounting, vending machines, mail-order houses, and fast-food outlets are diffused globally.[11] Today, convenience stores such as 7-Eleven and its emulators, fast-food restaurants such as McDonald's and its similar offshoots, discount stores such as Tower Records and Virgin stores, and catalog merchandisers such as L. L. Bean and Eddie Bauer can be found in a number of countries around the globe.

The really new channels are of course the Internet-inspired e-commerce channels. The ability to quickly and inexpensively create a "storefront" on the World Wide Web and then start sales transactions online proved very tempting to many start-up dot-coms. One of the pioneers was Amazon.com, the bookseller whose name is now a globally recognized brand under whose umbrella a variety of products are offered. Despite the promise, however, many of the e-commerce transactions of products falter. While the more intangible services in finance, travel, lodging, and so forth, adapt well to the Web (as we saw in Chapter 13), products still

Getting the Picture

THE AMAZON.COM SYSTEM

Not very long ago, the Internet and e-commerce were touted as the new distribution channel that would make all "bricks-and-mortar" establishments extinct. Perhaps the most prominent example of the new cutting edge was Amazon.com, the online bookseller. Back in the early 90s, Jeff Bezos—Amazon.com's founder and CEO—had an epiphany: Selling books would be a perfect way to utilize the power of the World Wide Web and start up an e-commerce company. Since a large database of books in print already existed, uploading the titles electronically would make it possible to offer them to consumers everywhere. The logistics of getting the books to customers could be managed through outsourcing to independent express carriers. The fact that customers had to wait a couple of days for their books to arrive was no problem—to compensate for this Bezos simply offered the books at a discount. Within a couple of years the capitalized stock market value of Amazon.com stood at $3 billion, the company had 8,000 employees, and the 35-year-old Bezos was named *Time* magazine's 1999 Person of the Year.

But despite its visionary ideas and impressive performance, Amazon.com had trouble turning a profit. It turned out that the main beneficiaries of the operation were the consumers, who could buy books at a discount, and the express shippers who delivered the books. In 1998 the company decided to spend more than $300 million to build five distribution centers. Former Wal-Mart executive Jimmy Wright was hired to build a world-class logistics operation. The decision was made that rather than creating specialized distribution centers (DCs) for various products, each DC would handle

the full array of items. Amazon invested in the latest materials-handling technologies and even wrote its own warehouse management system software. By late 1998, a 93,000-square-foot building in Seattle and a 202,000-square-foot facility in New Castle, Delaware, were completed. A few months later a 322,560-square-foot highly mechanized distribution facility was opened in Fernley, Nevada, to serve the southern California market and a 750,000-square-foot facility began operating in southeast Kansas to serve the Chicago, St. Louis, Dallas, and Minneapolis areas. Soon two more facilities were opened in Campbellsville and Lexington, Kentucky, and a leased facility 20 miles south of Atlanta was chosen to serve the Southeast.

Amazon's warehouse operations handle fulfillment for all orders placed on the firm's Web site. "Amazon feels strongly about filling its own orders," says Paul Kruese, director of supply chain development. "We can control customer satisfaction when we fulfill the orders in-house." So it should come as no surprise that Amazon has invested in an even more modern facility in Bedfordshire to serve its United Kingdom customers.

And since the last quarter of 2001, Amazon.com has continuously registered a profit, as it has become a destination shopping center for millions of customers around the world.

Sources: "Q&A: Industrial Space Still Breathing Easy," *Business-Week,* May 21, 2001, p. 32B; James A. Cooke, "Clicks and Mortar," *Logistics Management & Distribution Report,* January 31, 2000, p. 36; Faith Keenan, "Logistics Gets a Little Respect," *BusinessWeek,* November 20, 2000, p. EB 112; Robert Hoff, "Suddenly Amazon's Books Look Better," *BusinessWeek,* February 21, 2000, p. 78. "Amazon.com Profit Surges," *Chicago Tribune,* January 31, 2008.

require shipment, an "old economy" kind of business (see box, "The Amazon.com system").

In a product such as PCs, the direct sales model pioneered by Dell has also shown its strength. Computers and related software are of course natural e-commerce items. Gradually, as ever more markets around the world reach a mature stage with savvy consumers, the Dell model of direct ordering, just-in-time inventory, customization, and direct delivery has been adopted by most major manufacturers. The conversion from actual store deliveries and service has been facilitated by the increased quality and reliability of the standardized components that make up the majority of today's computers.

Global Retailing

In spite of a not very impressive record, there is a consistent trend toward global retailing. In addition to increasing affluence in global markets, helping to spark this trend is the logistical and operational know-how of leading retailers around the world. Exhibit 15.4 shows the world's 10 largest retailers in terms of sales. The rapid deployment of **point-of-purchase information technology**—including bar coding, scanner data, and inventory controls—has shifted the power in the channel toward large retailers. Leading stores—such as Wal-Mart in the United States, Tesco in Britain, Carrefour in France, Delhaize in Belgium, and Ito-Yokado, owner of 7-Eleven, in Japan—have integrated upstream, established their own sourcing abroad, introduced point-of-purchase (p-o-p) technology, and created data banks on product and brand turnover that gave them power over both wholesalers and manufacturers. The sheer volume of product

EXHIBIT 15.4
World's 10 Largest Retailers (based on sales in the year 2005)

Rank	Company	Home Country	Basic type	Sales ($ U.S. Millions) 2005	2002	Countries
1	Wal-Mart Stores, Inc.	U.S.	Superstore	$312,427	$229,617	11
2	Carrefour Group	France	Hypermarket	$92,778	$64,762	31
3	The Home Depot, Inc.	U.S.	Home improv.	$81,511	$58,247	5
4	Metro AG	Germany	Dept. store	$69,134	$48,124	30
5	Tesco PLC	UK	Dept. store	$68,866	$39,517	13
6	The Kroger Co.	U.S.	Supermkt	$60,553	$51,760	1
7	Target Corporation	U.S.	Dept. store	$52,620	$42,722	1
8	Costco Companies	U.S.	Warehouse store	$51,862	$37,993	8
9	Sears/K-Mart	U.S.	Dept. store	$49,124	NA	5
10	Aldi	Germany	Disc. supermkt	$45,096	NA	14

Sources: **www.nxtbook.com**; Retail Forward, Inc: The Top 100 Retailers Worldwide 2002, October 6, 2003.

channeled through these large store chains, coupled with immediate access to sales data, give the retailers a strong hand in negotiating for functional discounts and preferential services. Global expansion has become the large retailer's avenue to growth.

The global expansion by retailers tends to follow a gradual "waterfall" kind of process. This allows managers in the firm to learn from experience, necessary because of the variety of retail regulations encountered in different countries and the economic, cultural, and lifestyle differences among consumers. The process at Wal-Mart shows how this gradual internationalization manifests itself in the mode of entry.

Wal-Mart's first foreign entry was into Canada in the early 1990s. It acquired a poorly performing chain store, Woolco (formerly the Woolworth company), available for purchase at a low price. Wal-Mart managers were confident about their knowledge of the market since many Canadian consumers had already crossed the border into the United States to patronize the stores. The acquisition was successful—the Wal-Mart business model was precisely what Woolco needed to transform itself into a viable and healthy organization. For its next entry (into Mexico), a more challenging entry, Wal-Mart chose to form a 50–50 joint venture with Cifra, Mexico's largest retailer, counting on Cifra to provide operational expertise in the Mexican market. The subsequent entry into Brazil was also accomplished through a joint venture—with Lojas Americana, a local retailer. Wal-Mart was now more confident and chose to establish a 60–40 joint venture in which it had the controlling stake. The entry into Brazil gave Wal-Mart even greater experience in Latin America, and so it chose to enter Argentina through a wholly owned subsidiary.

Wal-Mart's 1996 entry into China was facilitated by the fact that it already imported a vast amount of its products from Chinese suppliers. However, its first effort with a Thai joint venture partner was quickly dropped, in favor of a joint venture with representatives from the highest levels of China's central government. That meant that instead of negotiating for store approvals at the local level, Wal-Mart went directly to the State Council, China's cabinet, about building stores with a local joint venture partnership for each store, as Chinese law required. With the blessing of the top leadership, Wal-Mart was able to expand quickly into China's major metropolitan markets.

In 1997, Wal-Mart was ready for a German entry. It acquired the Wertkauf hypermarket chain of 21 stores, one of the most profitable hypermarket chains in the country. Wertkauf's stores, similar in format to Wal-Mart's, featured high-quality personnel and locations, and were larger than the average German hypermarket. In 1998 it went into South Korea through a joint venture and acquired four Makro stores; and in 1999 Wal-Mart acquired ASDA, a U.K. supermarket chain, for its entry into Britain, after two years of evaluating alternative entry modes. Finally, in 2002 Wal-Mart acquired a 37 percent interest in Japanese retailer Seiyu, still another mode of entry, to establish the retailer's first Japan entry.[12]

Of course, global expansion is not always successful. France's Carrefour has introduced the hypermarket concept to the east coast of the United States with little success so far. Japan's Takashimaya department store has established a branch on Fifth Avenue in New York City but has still to turn a profit. Its compatriot Isetan developed an even

Getting the Picture

WAL-MART'S STUMBLES ABROAD

Wal-Mart, the world's largest company in terms of revenues, has not exactly had an easy time going into foreign countries. Its firm-specific advantages of an efficient supply chain, huge stores with mass merchandise and groceries, and "everyday-low-prices" have not always translated easily into the various local markets. As of 2005, the company was in 11 countries: Argentina, Brazil, Mexico, and Puerto Rico in Latin America; China, Japan, and South Korea in Asia; and the United Kingdom and Germany in Europe, in addition to its presence in the United States and Canada. But in 2006 it pulled out of Germany and South Korea, and by 2007 was seriously considering leaving Japan and the United Kingdom.

What went wrong? Experts agree on a few issues. In Germany, the consumers did not take well to greeters at the entrance, nor to having anybody else bag—and thus touch—their groceries. Labor relations were poor. Wal-Mart has little or no patience with labor unions, mandated in Germany. German workers did not take well to an American boss who could not speak German. Competitors were very price competitive. The same issues dogged the company in Korea, where Wal-Mart encountered militant workers and demonstrators for the first time. In Korea, competitors

responded with more customized and upgraded store interiors making the Wal-Mart stores seem large and unwieldy.

In Japan, Wal-Mart decided against a pullout, despite lagging sales at its Seiyu-operated stores. In 2008 the company decided to take over the chain 100 percent, and formulate a new strategy. "Japan is quite different from Germany or South Korea. We realize they aren't going to sacrifice quality, and our goal is to provide the best value combined with the quality they expect," said Kevin Gardner, a Wal-Mart spokesman.

The problems in the United Kingdom are of yet another kind. The main competitor of Wal-Mart's ASDA chain is Tesco, with very competitive prices and reportedly better selection of merchandise mix. In addition, the concept of "Green Business" is more salient to U.K. consumers than in the United States. As a result people are shifting toward Organic foods, public transport systems, and eco-friendly products. Here ASDA's pseudo-American image is not helping against Tesco's U.K. origins.

Sources: Govindarajan and Gupta, 2001; **www.wal-martchina.com;** Kimberly Morrison, "Wal-Mart to Fully Acquire Japanese Supermarket," *The Morning News (Arkansas),* March 19, 2008; **http://arunkottolli.blogspot.com.**

less successful collaboration (joint venture, dissolved in 1997) with Barney's of New York for men's and women's upscale apparel and brought a Barney's store to Tokyo. Belgium's Delhaize, a successful top-of-the-line supermarket at home, has had trouble in the United States, where its Food Lion supermarkets have tried against odds to penetrate the market in the South. Marks & Spencer, which seemed a sure bet in Canada, encountered a lot of difficulties and has pulled out. And even for the careful Wal-Mart strategy, not all turned out well (see box, "Wal-Mart's Stumbles Abroad").

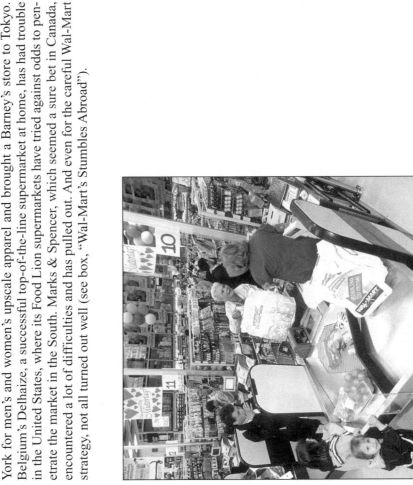

A Wal-Mart store in Germany. In 1997, the world's largest retailer brought its standardized retailing model with its streamlined supply chain to Europe and everyday low prices became "Jeden Tag Tiefpreise." But the German consumer did not acquiesce, and Wal-Mart pulled out in 2006. © Thomas Sandberg.

Global Logistics

Even though the emergence of **global retailers** would seem to offer global manufacturers a chance for central coordination of worldwide channel activities, it is important to remember that these retailers tend to become powerful units in the distribution channel between manufacturers and the ultimate customers. It is more than likely that the manufacturers (and wholesalers) will have to adapt to their needs; they want to be treated as customers. Selling through them will involve "relationship marketing"—offering special services, discounts, emergency supplies as necessary, and so on. To tilt the balance to a more even playing field, the manufacturer with a strong global brand has an advantage: The giant retailers need them as much as they need the retailers.[13]

Global logistics can be defined as the transportation and storage activities necessary to transfer the physical product from manufacturing plants and warehouses in different countries to the various local market countries. Global logistics is a subset of global distribution, which also involves the management of the channels within a country. It is a useful distinction for the global marketer, since the management of channels within a country requires a lot of interactions with local subsidiaries, distributors, and agents. By contrast, the distribution between countries is usually a matter for headquarters and the trading partners alone.

Supply chain management, that is, coordinating and rationalizing the global logistics function of the firm involved in many markets, is not a simple task. The number of independent suppliers is one factor that complicates matters. A typical automobile assembly might today contain 80 percent of parts from independent suppliers located in different countries. In addition, the company might have located manufacturing facilities in various countries, each specializing in only part of the complete product line, so that a particular local market needs to be supplied from a number of countries. The Nissan trucks sold in France might come from the company's U.S. plant in Tennessee, the Micras from its Sunderland plant in England, while the Maximas are imported from Japan by its European subsidiary located in Amsterdam. Furthermore, Nissan's engine plant in the United Kingdom might be supplying engines to its American and Spanish plants. From a marketing perspective this might seem quite irrelevant, but it means that parts for after-sales service and repairs have to be ordered from factories in several different countries. Global logistics in the heavily globalized automobile industry might be particularly complicated, but similar problems afflict most companies that attempt to implement a global strategy. Fortunately the arrival of the Internet and e-commerce has helped supply chain management considerably (see box, "E-Procurement Energizes Supply Chain Managers").

Competition and Technology

Considering the difficulties involved, many firms are reluctant to try to reengineer their global logistics. A decentralized solution, building on whatever localized solutions have gradually emerged during the global expansion, seems preferable, especially since the local managers know their customer requirements better anyway. But this goes counter to two external forces pushing the company: competition and technology.

As we have seen throughout this book, global competition requires more efficient operations, greater flexibility, and quicker response time. Global transportation is an area where considerable savings are often possible. Consolidating shipments, eliminating duplication in cross-border procedures, including shipping documents and customs declarations, and investing in specialized equipment at transfer points are only a few of the areas in which reengineering can help. Furthermore, inventory management can often be improved through rationalized global logistics, creating savings through just-in-time practices, and adding customer value by reducing delivery times.

Getting the Picture

E-PROCUREMENT ENERGIZES SUPPLY CHAIN MANAGERS

With business-to-business transactions (B2B) growing at a rapid pace, many firms are reinventing the physical value chains related to logistics and transport by focusing on electronic procurement, buying their supplies online.

Many U.S. and European firms are already reporting impressive savings from conducting some of their procurement over the Internet: 20–30 percent on the cost of indirect goods and 0.5–2 percent on the cost of direct materials. In Asia, B2B e-commerce transaction value is expected to exceed US$430 billion by 2003. General Electric announced projected savings of $1.6 billion a year through e-supply chain management.

Lower prices are the most immediate benefit from instituting an online supply chain management program but new levels of collaboration and the speed of delivery may eclipse even those gains. Just-in-time inventory management is enhanced considerably by e-procurement. All along the value chain, from product development through production, distribution, and managing customer relationships, e-commerce tools are allowing collaboration on many levels with suppliers, distributors, and customers.

General Motors is integrating its supply chain to link maintenance scheduling and needs with component suppliers. General Electric is conducting direct purchasing online by linking 1,500 corporate buyers and 16,000 suppliers. Hewlett-Packard cut its procurement costs by 17 percent and its automated purchase orders jumped from 20 percent to 70 percent of all orders.

E-commerce may never replace the need to shop in some traditional retail outlets, but the Internet has already translated into immediate B2B savings and improved corporate procurement performance.

Sources: "Don't Miss the Boat on E-Procurement," *Bangkok Post,* October 15, 2001; James Davidson, "A Logistics Solution," *Journal of Commerce,* November 5, 2001, p. 38; Penelope Ody, "E-Procurement," *Financial Times,* December 5, 2001, p. 10.

Also, because of new technology—global communication possibilities and computerized operations, in particular—more efficient logistics operations have become possible. Zara, the Spanish apparel company, is known for its fast market response. A competitor such as Levi's is now using point-of-sale terminals in some European locations, linked directly to regional headquarters in Brussels. Transactions and sales of its apparel can be traced quickly, and new and revised orders transmitted to factories as demand fluctuates and according to workloads. Order lead time is lowered, faster response is made possible, and inventories are reduced.[14]

The technology has spawned a number of new global distribution options available for the global marketer. Freight forwarders, ship lines, air express outfits, and airlines now offer more reliable and faster services than before and also offer services not available before, such as tracking of shipments and overnight delivery. In fact, the outsourcing of manufacturing and other business functions to low-wage countries is made possible largely through this new technology.

Air Express

Technical innovations in computerized inventory systems and numerically controlled machines for goods handling, including robotics, coupled with the speed and reliability of the jet aircraft, made possible the growth of air express systems exemplified by American-based Federal Express (now simply FedEx), DHL, UPS, and Airborne. Typically, the logistics involve shipment systems offering local pickups, the transportation of packages in the evening to a single transshipment point, sorting according to address during the night, and then shipping out to their destination by the early morning for local delivery.

These new **air express** freight services are growing rapidly. With the increased penetration of modern telecommunications and fax machines in developing and newly emerging markets, these shipping services have been very active in foreign markets. Overnight delivery is usually not available, since there is a need for a transshipment point in the country of destination. Typically, one or two more days are needed. For example, Atlanta to Frankfurt requires two days, while Detroit to Hiroshima takes three days. As technology is applied further, these limits have shortened, and competition among carriers with global reach has intensified (see box, "DHL Comes Home").

Getting the Picture

DHL COMES HOME

DHL is a global shipping giant now based in Brussels, Belgium, with more than 170,000 employees worldwide. It was founded in 1969 by three young Berkeley students (Adrian *Dalsey*, Larry *Hillblom*, and Robert *Lynn*—hence *DHL*) as an express carrier between San Francisco and Honolulu. Initially DHL focused on international shipping, leaving the U.S. domestic market to its competitors: Federal Express, United Parcel Service, and Airborne. But as these companies expanded abroad and into international shipping, DHL found it necessary to strike back. DHL decided it needed to have a presence in the U.S. domestic market.

The first step was to acquire Airborne, the smallest of the three American express carriers. Then in June 2004, DHL launched an ambitious $150 million advertising campaign to reestablish brand awareness in the United States, and go head-to-head with FedEx and UPS. The last consistent American ad campaign for DHL had been its flying truck TV spots in the late 80s and early 90s. The new advertisements showed FedEx and UPS truck drivers waiting at a railroad crossing somewhere in mid-America, stopped by a long train carrying DHL trucks. Message: DHL is going head-on against them in their own market.

The following month, July 2004, DHL announced that it had signed on as the official express carrier of the U.S.

Olympic team for the 2004 Olympic Games in Athens. Pointedly, it was not the official sponsor of the Olympics but only of the U.S. team. To capitalize on the sponsorship, the company launched a highly visible integrated marketing campaign emphasizing the company's commitment to the U.S. express delivery and ground parcel market. The success of the Athens games resulted in high impact for the sponsorship. The 2004 Olympic Games had a viewership equivalent to eight Super Bowl broadcasts, and gave DHL significant exposure in the U.S. market. Company executives judged this to be a big and very successful step in DHL's reintroduction into the American market.

The move into the Olympics may seem familiar to viewers. As part of its international expansion, UPS was a major Olympics sponsor in Atlanta 1996, Nagano 1998, and Sydney 2000. Total sponsorship spending by UPS for these three events amounted to about $100 million. The company used the Olympics to create global awareness of its brand. Doing the same, only opposite, DHL used the 2004 Athens Olympics to get back into the United States.

Sources: Sean Callahan, "*DHL's $150M Campaign Challenges Shipping Giants," " B to B*, July 19, 2004, p. 3; "DHL Agrees to Become the Official Express Delivery and Logistics Provider for the U.S. Olympic Team," *Business Wire*, July 6, 2004; Dave Hirschman, "UPS No Longer in Olympic Ring," *The Atlanta Journal-Constitution*, August 13, 2004, p. 1e.

computerized system makes it possible to track the packages, monitor the progress, and resolve obstacles or trouble.[15]

Ocean Carriers

The development of fast and efficient air transportation has opened up new international distribution channels, in particular for items high in value per unit weight. For shipments of bulky and low-value-per-unit products—such as automobiles, produce, dry goods, beer, and soft drinks—ocean-going vessels are still the most economical carrier alternative overseas. A few of these products—autos, oil, grain—are transported in specially designed ships owned by the producers, but the shipping is done largely by independent ship lines through containers, ship-to-truck, or rail. But even here global requirements have made for changes.

Because of the savings involved in sharing resources and the advantage in providing integrated one-stop services to the shipper, there have been a number of **global carrier alliances** in the shipping industry. American President Lines (APL), Orient Overseas Container Line from Hong Kong, and Mitsui O.S.K. Lines from Japan have joined in a global alliance consortium. APL and Matson Navigation Co., another American ship line, have shared vessels in a U.S.–Hawaii–Asia service since 1996. In another alliance, Sea-Land Service in Seattle and Maersk Line of Denmark have started a world partnership.[16]

Today, shipping computer software, cameras, many consumer electronic products, and even apparel overseas often starts with a call to the local express mail office for a pickup. Instead of taking one to two weeks or much more in the case of ocean shipping, the merchandise can arrive in a couple of days. The goods are cleared through customs faster by using the express carrier's dedicated access ports at the point of transshipment, usually away from crowded entry ports for general merchandise. The

The advantages of these alliances are similar to those in the airline industry. Sharing routes, vessels, and port facilities, better utilization of fixed assets is made possible, cargo destinations are expanded, and economies in documentation and customs clearing can be realized. The larger scale makes investment in specialized assets economically justified, reducing transfer costs further and offering lower prices to users.[17] These specialized assets—involving large-capacity lifting cranes, up-to-date storage facilities, and ever larger and faster ships—put pressure on competitors and ports as well. While competitors respond with alliances of their own, the future of ports is thought to depend on the building of **megaports,** which can accommodate huge ships, speed up container loading and unloading, and reduce the "dwell time" while the unloaded containers wait on the dock for further transportation via truck or rail.[18]

Overland Transportation

The increasing volume of international trade has put the system under pressure not only in ports but also inland. There is of course a direct link. For example, containers with tobacco products from Richmond, Virginia, are unloaded in Bremerhaven, put on trucks, and speeded overland to Poland on the German Autobahn—creating traffic problems, safety hazards, and long lines at the border. With so many new products entering the central European markets, the traffic problems are getting worse, and German authorities are contemplating placing a steep toll on trucks.[19]

One North American solution to this problem has been the **roll-on-roll-off (RORO)** system, in which a loaded container is simply rolled onto a railcar and shipped by rail for part of the way, avoiding congested freeways. Even quicker is the new RoadRailer system, in which a rail wheel carriage can be attached to the bottom of the trailer carrying the container on the road. Then the container can go directly on the rail and be hooked up to a train without the need for a railcar.

These North American solutions have not yet been introduced in many places elsewhere, mainly because of the costs involved in transferring from the existing systems. In Europe, the typical overland transportation involves trucking, and the changeover to rail requires a special truck/rail terminal with a capability of lifting the container off the trailer and then placing it on a railcar. The special equipment required and the time lost in the transfer mean that European roads are likely to be clogged by trucks for some time to come.[20]

Warehousing

The competitive need on the part of global companies to be "close to the customer" and provide fast and efficient service has placed increased demand not only on transportation but also on **warehousing** and **inventory management.** While increased speed on the part of independent carriers has made it possible to fill orders faster and cut response time for parts requests, increased competition has escalated customers' demands for service. SKF, the Swedish roller-bearing company, has centralized its European distribution system, reducing its distribution points in Europe from 24 to 5 and creating a new **distribution center** in Belgium, thereby cutting costs, increasing speed, and improving service.[21]

Thus, locating several warehouses close to customers is not necessary any longer for the customer-oriented firm. And if the company does not want to invest in its own distribution center, some of the middlemen in global logistics provide inventory services. For example, Federal Express, DHL, and also smaller outfits offer warehouse space for rent at their transshipment points.[22] Companies rent the space to store products in high demand. A company such as Eddie Bauer can stock some of the more popular catalog items in Memphis at the FedEx central location and ship directly from there, lowering the shipment time significantly.

Such options are useful for the company attempting to cut down the time required to respond to customer requests. In addition, companies attempt to speed up the manufacturing-to-market process further, not only by reengineering inventory management but by streamlining their own handling of shipments to multiple markets.

It is not surprising that senior managers from major manufacturing companies now consider logistics one of the key areas for company profitability.[23] The cost savings and the value added made possible by rationalized global logistics can be considerable.

Parallel Distribution

Developments in logistics coupled with floating exchange rates and widely different prices in different countries have led to the emergence of gray trade through **parallel distribution** channels.

Gray Trade

As opposed to the trade in counterfeit brands discussed in Chapter 13, **gray trade** is parallel distribution of *genuine* goods by intermediaries other than authorized channel members. Gray marketers are typically brokers who buy goods overseas either from the manufacturer or from authorized dealers at relatively low prices and import them into a country where prevailing prices are higher. The gray marketers sell the merchandise at discounted prices in direct competition with authorized local distributors, often advertising the lower prices openly in print media and direct mail. The practice is not illegal per se except under certain circumstances, but the activities tend to disturb existing trading relationships and are usually fought by manufacturers as well as authorized distributors.

As we saw in Chapter 14, gray trade tends to serve as an arbitrage mechanism, equalizing prices between markets in different countries. Three main factors motivate entrepreneurs to engage in gray trade:

1. *Wide price discrepancies.* There are substantial price differences between national markets, for example because of currency fluctuations (see Chapter 14).

2. *Limited availability.* There is limited availability of certain models or versions in one market. Demand outstrips supply and is likely to push local prices even higher relative to other markets. Certain Mercedes-Benz and Porsche models are unavailable in the United States, for example, as were originally some Lexus models in Japan, which stimulated gray trade. Localization requirements, such as local certification of emissions controls on cars, have a dampening effect, but with sufficient margins gray traders will invest in conversion equipment (although sometimes the buyer gets stuck with the job).

3. *Inexpensive logistics.* Transportation and importation can be accomplished with relative ease. The increased availability of global modes of transportation and the added services offered by carriers and freight forwarders have meant that the logistics problems are usually few. Gray traders can use the independent middlemen as well as any manufacturer.

Exhibit 15.5 shows some of the ways in which gray traders infiltrate the global distribution of Japanese watches. The Japanese companies export watches to the importer, often a sales subsidiary, in the various countries. From there the watches are shipped to the distributors and on to retailers. These are the authorized channels where the company offers merchandising support and sales training and, in turn, demands service support.

As can be seen in the exhibit, the gray trade arises from several sources. Some of the distributors in price-competitive markets, such as Hong Kong, will divert part of their shipment to more lucrative markets. They may sell directly to unauthorized (or even authorized) European or American distributors or retailers, getting higher prices that more than offset any transportation charges. Alternatively, Japanese distributors and retailers backed by a strong yen can go abroad to get watches from overseas distributors or retailers for sale at home. And for new models in great demand, a Hong Kong distributor may send people to Tokyo to buy at retail, sometimes in duty-free shops, and bring back watches that fetch premium prices.

The company's control over distribution is lost when gray trade proliferates. Sales statistics for individual country markets are misleading or meaningless. The Japanese watch,

EXHIBIT 15.5
**Seiko's Authorized and
Unauthorized Channels
of Distribution**

Source: Jack Kaikati, "Parallel Importation:
A Growing Conflict in International Channels
of Distribution," Symposium on Export-
Import Interrelationships, Georgetown
University, November 14–15, 1985.
Unauthorized channels depicted by
dotted lines.

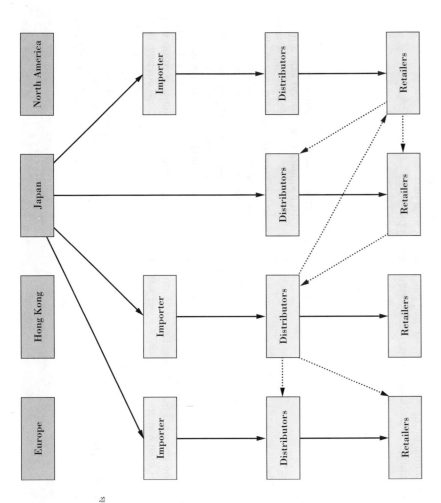

camera, and electronics makers try to do something about it. Apart from monitoring their independent importers and authorized distributors more closely, they also change model names, mix features differently, and generally make the styles for different regions (Europe, North America, Asia) slightly different. Such a solution represents "cosmetic" localization, since it does not involve adaptation to consumer preferences or needs.

Gray trade is extensive for global brands in certain product categories. Pharmaceuticals in particular are vulnerable, since drug prices vary considerably across countries, depending on the reimbursement policies of governments and insurance companies. Another category is cameras, a notorious gray trade product category since value per unit is high and brands are well recognized. Exact figures are hard to come by, since identification of gray goods is uncertain and the volume varies annually by exchange rate changes. Experts estimate the total volume to be easily over $10 billion.[24] However, firms are reluctant to discuss gray trade since the legal recourse is uncertain, and the fear is that as the general public learns more, the practice may become more widespread. In recent years the differences in drug prices across borders—as between the United States and Canada, for example—have made gray trade a more acceptable activity by consumers, to the chagrin of brand manufacturers. The average manufacturer might have recently lost sales of about $7.4 million annually. The volume is increasing as the opening of the communist blocs has further stimulated gray trade (as well as piracy).

Effects of Gray Trade

The damage from gray imports falls into four categories. Gray trade threatens to:

Erode brand equity.

Strain relationships with authorized channel members.

Lead to legal liabilities.

Complicate global marketing strategies.

Getting the Picture

The eroding of brand equity can happen if the gray goods do not perform to the level expected. For example, products with date marks, such as film and batteries, may be resold in gray markets with dates changed or obliterated, and the unwary buyer will find photos ruined and batteries dead. The strain with channel members arises from the fact that they will face intrabrand competition, the identical brand sold at lower prices elsewhere, and they will be asked to do service and repairs for gray imports. They may not have a legal basis for refusal and will have to be inventive (see box, "Do Gray Goods Get Serviced?").

The legal liabilities problem usually involves warranties that can't be honored and performance criteria that can't be fulfilled. These problems are especially acute for pharmaceutical products because of the potential injuries involved. Taking medication that has expired or whose dosages are meant for adults can severely harm children.

Gray trade affects global marketing management in a number of ways. Forecasted sales in a market may not be realized when there is a sudden influx of gray goods. Roll-out campaign plans for new product introductions might have to be changed if gray traders introduce the product prematurely, as happens frequently in film videos and popular music. And as was seen in Chapter 14, "Global Pricing," while gray trade means that the need for uniform pricing across countries grows, exchange rates need to be monitored and fluctuations may force a realignment.

Channel Actions against Gray Trade

What can global marketers do in the distribution channels about gray trade? There are a number of actions available to help reduce the volume of gray trade and limit the damage done.

Supply Interference

Most companies engage in some interchange and relationship building with their distributors in various countries, asking them to help stop gray trade at the source by screening orders carefully and being careful how they dispose of surplus inventory. Software makers, in an effort to stop dealers from ordering large quantities of popular programs at volume discounts and then selling the excess to gray traders, have been known to announce their determination to terminate any distributor that supplies the product to unauthorized dealers. These practices have to be done with care, since putting pressure on suppliers can easily turn into an illegal restriction of trade.

DO GRAY GOODS GET SERVICED?

Japan's notoriously tight distribution system was jolted throughout the 1990s by the appearance of gray goods in several product categories. Taking advantage of a strong yen, which had cheapened imports, a reduction in tariff rates, and the reluctance of existing distributors to pass savings on to consumers, Japanese entrepreneurs set up purchasing offices overseas and established direct import channels that sold products at savings as high as 50 percent.

One example was Steinway grand pianos directly imported from New York and Hamburg. The ensuing surge in sales of Steinways created problems for Steinway's sole authorized distributor in Japan. Rather than reducing prices to compete with the direct imports, the distributor opted for a more subtle strategy.

The gray pianos, easily identified because of their serial numbers, were the last to be serviced. Generally, a grand piano requires comparatively little service except for tuning. But there are some localization matters to take care of. The high humidity of Japan's summers requires expensive reconditioning of brands prepared for European or American conditions. In severe cases the entire soundboard, the key to the grand's sound, may have to be refinished. Also, tuning the pianos during the initial one to two break-in years requires specialists trained by Steinway, and they were suddenly in "short supply."

Disgruntled Steinway owners in Japan kept taking the distributor to court. But since service was not denied, only delayed, the legal outcome was always in doubt. Japan's "impenetrable" distribution system won the case.

Sources: *New York Times*, June 23, 1995, p. D1; Assmus and Wiese, 1995.

Getting the Picture

WHY GRAY MARKETS MAY TURN BLACK

Despite the borderless economic zone envisioned by the creation of the European Union, the borders with nonmembers are still intact. In fact, these borders have become more prominent than ever in a landmark ruling by the European Union's Supreme Court of Justice. The ruling is that the importation and sales of gray goods can constitute a trademark infringement.

In a suit that has lingered several years in the courts, Levi Strauss, the maker of Levi's jeans, tried to prevent England's Tesco from selling Levi's jeans imported from the United States, Mexico, or Canada at discount prices in the EU market. Tesco had sourced the product in the lower-priced North American market, and then resold them at home for prices up to 30 percent below regular prices for Levi's in Europe. In its suit, Levi's argued that their global distribution system has been developed to safeguard the quality of their products and that products destined for different continents may be significantly different. The company claimed the right to control distribution, although not necessarily prices per se, a more difficult case to win.

In November 2001, the European Court of Justice ruled that Tesco could not sell Levi's jeans imported from outside the European Economic Area. This area was defined as consisting of the EU member states, Norway, Iceland, and Lichtenstein.

The judges ruled that a retailer must be able to prove that its goods were obtained from legitimate sources within the EU or could be prevented from selling them. Thus, this ruling now places the onus on a vendor to prove that cheap designer goods were not obtained on the gray market but through legitimate wholesalers approved by the manufacturer.

Activists have argued that the ruling smacks of being anticonsumer, since higher prices for branded goods will result from tighter curbs on gray goods. Trademark holders, like Levi Strauss, hail the decision as the dawn of a new era. In the past, gray goods have never been illegal as such. That is, even if a shipment of a branded product was intended for a particular market, once a distributor had paid for the shipment, the right of ultimate disposal of the product was its alone. Of course, a reseller who consistently undercut other retailers would be cajoled into proper behavior or else could have trouble getting its orders filled, but in the law very little could ultimately be done.

The Levi's–Tesco ruling seems to have changed all that. Perhaps under the influence of the newly discovered importance of global branding, the judges have established a precedence of the trademark holder being able to control in what market a particular shipment of its branded product should be sold. From now on, gray markets may be as illegal as black markets are.

Sources: Craig Smith, "Leader-Parallel Importers Punish Brands for Distribution," *Marketing,* July 19, 2001, p. 21; Kieron Wood, "Levi's to Continue Tesco Legal Action over Jeans," *Sunday Business Post,* November 25, 2001.

Dealer Interference

A more drastic measure is to search for gray imports at the gray traders' outlets in the importing country and then ask the dealers—or help them—to get rid of their inventory. Companies sometimes attempt to simply destroy gray merchandise in the stores. This kind of "search and destroy" action requires a substantiated legal justification, such as an illegal change in the valid dates or improper packaging, and is more common for counterfeit goods (see Chapter 13).

Demand Interference

Some firms use advertising and other promotional means to educate potential customers about the drawbacks of gray goods and the limitations on warranties, returns, and service. Companies such as Rolex, Seiko, Mercedes, Microsoft, and IBM have engaged in these practices. There are two problems. One is the legal problem of threatening to limit service to products sold through authorized dealers only, not an acceptable practice in most countries. Second, firms are reluctant to call attention to the gray trade phenomenon and create hesitation on the part of potential buyers of the brand.

Strategic Attack

A more constructive solution is to go on the attack and create stronger reasons for customers to patronize authorized dealers. As we saw in Chapter 14, this might involve aggressive price cutting, but other measures should be considered as well. Supporting authorized dealers in offering innovative credit plans, improved service, and other customer-oriented initiatives is a possible tactic. Caterpillar, the heavy machinery company, helped authorized dealers develop customized warranties the individual buyer could tailor to his or her own special needs. More drastic actions may be necessary in the future if a new legal ruling will have the impact that some observers expect (see box, "Why Gray Markets May Turn Black").

Getting the Picture

YIN AND YANG: DUTY FREE IN MANILA AND THE EU

In the early 1990s, Philippine authorities changed the standard duty-free shopping regulations, which make duty-free alcohol, tobacco, and perfume available only to departing airline passengers. Recognizing that a large portion of the more than 4 million Filipinos working overseas returned home on vacations and holidays with food and household appliances for relatives, the government decided to get some of that business for itself. Now, at the airport in Manila, *incoming* passengers can spend up to $1,000 ($2,000 for returning Filipinos) at the duty-free stores and bring the goods duty-free into the country.

Most travelers would have trouble recognizing the duty-free scene that has grown up around the Manila airport. Much of the merchandise would never fit into an aircraft cabin's overhead storage bin: motorcycles, big-screen TV sets, brass beds, freezers, washing machines, air conditioners, even farm equipment. The grocery section includes large packages of Kellogg's Rice Krispies, Kool-Aid, Cheez-Whiz, Budweiser beer, and other mainstream American brands.

While it makes a lot of consumers happy, the new system has infuriated Philippine manufacturers and retailers who are crying unfair competition. "We're getting battered by duty-free," says Roberto S. Claudio, vice president of the Philippine Retailers Association. "It makes a mockery of retailing."

Whether viewed as a boon for consumers or a bust for local retailers, duty-free sales are soaring. Duty-free has

passed the Shoe Mart chain as the Philippines' number one retailer.

The duty-free story in Europe is decidedly different. When the European Union abolished border controls between member countries and created a single currency, duty-free shopping was no longer a viable option for travelers within EU. When duty-free shopping was officially abolished in 1999 (duty free is still available when traveling in or out of the EU), many sellers of cosmetics and liquor expected that retail sales would decline at the countries' international terminals. But sales quickly rebounded as field marketers discovered that the duty-free stores can be used effectively for product sampling and demonstrations and sales at regular prices. A busy airport such as Heathrow outside of London turns out to be an excellent location to reach travelers that are heavy shoppers, buying gifts for friends and relatives, stocking up on items that are scarce abroad, or simply killing time. So even though marketers can no longer promise duty-free savings, an opportunity to deal one-to-one with a large number of consumers with time on their hands and money in their pockets is one that many firms continue to exploit.

Now, this is turning problems into opportunities.

Sources: Lambert, 1995; Foster, 1995; Laura L. Myers, "Duty-free Developments," *Travel Age West*, June 5, 2000, p. 42; Robert McLuhan, "Promoting Sales in Departure Lounges," *Marketing*, December 7, 2000, p. 39; **www.dutyfree.com.**

Manufacturers also support their dealers by regionalizing their offerings, differentiating model features and numbers between trade areas to make it possible to spot gray imports and restrict servicing liability. Most Japanese camera makers use different model numbers and introduce slight differences in features between their Asian, North American, and European markets. By stressing features and model numbers in the advertising, their global advertising copy can remain uniform with the same brand name (Minolta, Canon, Nikon) while at the same time alerting buyers when a gray import does not correspond to an "authentic" model.

Multiple Distribution Channels

Given the increased speed and service in global logistics, the breakdown of single-channel distribution regimes, and the prevalence of gray trade, it is not surprising to find that multiple distribution channels are now common. The initiators are sometimes middlemen who decide that attack is the best defense. While authorized intermediaries appeal to the manufacturer to help block parallel importing, they also attempt to bypass some middlemen on their own. Local distributors, wholesalers, or retailers can now order directly from overseas distributors, bypassing one or more of the levels in the local link between the manufacturer and the ultimate consumer. In fact, these options are available not only to middlemen but often to ultimate consumers as well. There is an increase in **direct buying**, with consumers in different countries ordering directly from overseas stores and catalog houses, which ship the products through independent carriers.[25]

Some of these alternative channels, which may seem minor and of limited potential in the larger picture, can become important under special circumstances. An example is **duty-free shopping** as done in the Philippines (see box, "Yin and Yang: Duty Free in Manila and the EU").

Global Channel Design

Despite the idiosyncrasies of each individual country's channel structure, it is still possible to identify what middlemen should be used in a country to ensure that the strategic objectives of the marketing mix—the target segmentation and the desired product positioning—are reached. To do this requires an analysis of what the important functions in the channel network are (identification of what the key success factors are as they relate to channel choice) and then ensuring that the chosen intermediaries in each country measure up on those criteria.

The FSAs Revisited

To identify the channel requirements, the natural first step is to decide whether any of the firm-specific advantages are uniquely lodged in the distribution channels to be used. In the case of fast-food franchising, the answer is clearly yes: Without control over the outlets afforded by the franchising contracts, there would be little point in expanding globally. The product sold is a homogeneous (and therefore reliable) meal located at a convenient place. A less obvious example is automobile sales. Without a strong dealer network providing after-sales service, some auto manufacturers find it difficult to export. Part of the problem that British cars like MG, Triumph, and Rover faced in the United States was the weak service network available. Companies recognizing that such drawbacks will make sales difficult and might give the product a bad reputation sometimes refuse delivery into the countries where no service network exists. Toyota avoided Algiers as a market for its trucks until a sufficiently strong service network was built (in the meantime the Mitsubishi trading company sold its trucks in the country in a kind of gray import market).

Key success factors and FSAs may vary across countries. For example, many of the convenience products in Western markets (packaged foods, cigarettes, soft drinks, and so on) require intensive distribution coverage, precisely because customers want them to be conveniently available. One might infer, therefore, that the absence of such intensive convenience channels in some countries would lower the sales of these products there. But as has been mentioned, what constitutes a convenience good in one country might be a shopping good (or even a specialty good) somewhere else. Consequently, there might really be people who would be willing to "walk a mile" just to buy a Camel cigarette.

Availability of Channels

Once the critical features of the channel network have been identified, the question is whether the country market analyzed possesses channels that will provide the necessary service. Are there financially strong franchisees available if they are needed? Can dealers provide after-sales service? Are there boutiques where designer apparel is sold to an upscale market niche? Are there middlemen that can store frozen juice in sufficient quantities?

Where the answer is no, the firm needs to consider whether such outlets can be created, that is, whether the firm might invest in a dedicated network in order to supply the market. This is usually a big investment question, and as we have seen, there is no certainty of success. When the market is sufficiently large, as the U.S. market almost always is, it might pay for the company to develop its own distribution network, as Honda has done for its motorcycles. But where the market is smaller and the gains consequently less, the investment might not be worth the risks involved.

Channel Tie-Up

Where channel members are available to provide the functions necessary, they still might be unwilling to sign on with the new product unless special trade allowances bigger than those offered by the competition are made. There are reasons for making sure at this stage that the best units available are tied into, and it is customary for new entrants to pay a premium to established dealers to get them to accept the new product.

One reason for the resistance on the part of auto dealers in the United States to small cars was the lower margins offered on them. Cognizant of this fact, the Japanese small carmakers entered with higher dealer margins than customary for that size of auto. The thrust behind signing up good distributors and dealers is not only that sales will be high but that they are the ones most likely to sustain the FSAs identified as necessary for the competitive success of the company.

Coordination and Control

With a good distribution network established, coordination and control from a centralized headquarters location might now be feasible. The task is large even in small firms, making sure that shipments arrive on time, that the distributors are notified, that a standardized advertising campaign to middlemen across a number of countries is on schedule, that the sales reports for the last quarter have all been received, that the required reporting format is followed so that comparisons between budgeted and actual sales can be made, and so on. It is quite clear that before the advent of global telecommunications and LAN computer networks the control and coordination of distribution across different countries were very difficult tasks.

Summary

In this chapter, various aspects of a global distribution strategy have been discussed: first some of the differences in wholesaling and retailing in various countries, the feasibility of rationalization and creation of new channels, and the emergence of global retailing; then the independent organizations that facilitate global logistics between countries, emphasizing how competition and technology have pressured them to increase speed, reliability, and service; next problems with parallel distribution, especially gray trade, showing how multiple channels into a country have become a fact of life; and, finally, issues of coordinated global channel strategies.

In the end, the degree to which channel policy in different countries should be made consistent through a global strategy hinges on the degree to which FSAs are explicitly lodged in distribution channels and the degree to which the channel members' activities can be coordinated and controlled. If channels are very important because of FSAs, the company has to evaluate the alternatives very carefully and decide whether the available channels provide sufficient support. If they do not, the firm might have to establish its own distribution network, or else forgo entry. The channel strategy is only part of the overall business strategy of the global firm, and where the costs of control and coordination are too high, the global approach might have to yield to a polycentric approach in which the company takes a different angle on distribution in each local market.

Key Terms

air express, *501*
channel captains, *500*
direct buying, *508*
distribution center, *503*
dual distribution, *491*
duty-free shopping, *508*
full-service wholesalers, *493*

global carrier alliances, *502*
global retailers, *500*
gray trade, *504*
inventory management, *503*
megaports, *503*
parallel distribution, *504*

point-of-purchase information technology, *497*
roll-on-roll-off (RORO), *503*
supply chain management, *500*
vertical integration, *492*
warehousing, *503*

Discussion Questions

1. Compare and contrast the food retailing systems in two countries you are familiar with. Why have the differences occurred? Is a convergence under way?
2. Why is coordination of global logistics so complex? What technological innovations have made coordination easier?
3. Discuss how the phenomenon of gray trade affects the ability of the global marketer to control distribution. How can the difficulties be overcome? How will the emergence of the Internet spawn more gray trade, or will it?

4. Use the Web sites of FedEx, DHL, and UPS to analyze how the service is marketed. What are the competitive advantages of each? How do the firms attempt to keep air freight distribution from becoming a commodity?

5. Using library and Internet resources, investigate one of the successful cases of an introduction of a new approach to channels in foreign countries (Avon, 7-Eleven, Toys "R" Us, or L. L. Bean, for example). What customer factors were important determinants of the success? What did competition do? What are some lessons for other companies?

Notes

1. See Rosson, 1987.

2. Rosson, 1987, demonstrates some of the conflicts that can arise between manufacturers and independent distributors and how they lead to termination of contracts.

3. As the empirical study by Bello et al., 1991, demonstrates, where the multiple channels are not in direct competition, independent distributors can still provide strong benefits to the manufacturers in terms of market knowledge and specialized services.

4. Because of a lack of comparable data, the exhibit does not show the large number of people employed in wholesaling in Japan. While most European countries are on par, relative to the population, and the United States has relatively few establishments, each of larger scale, the Japanese have many units and a large number of people in wholesaling. This system is gradually being streamlined under pressure from direct imports and new technology, and also from entrepreneurial Japanese firms. Some observers claim that because of high value added relative to low wage rates, Japan's complex and multilayered distribution system is not particularly inefficient by international standards; see Maruyama, 1993.

5. Although this consolidation has perhaps gone furthest in the United States, even Japan with its notoriously large numbers and levels of wholesalers is moving toward larger units; see Czinkota and Kotabe, 1993.

6. See Munns, 1994.

7. Typical examples include, from the retailing end, Sears in the United States, Virgin stores in Britain, and the FNAC chain in France. Manufacturers moving forward include Compaq and Dell in personal computers, both selling their products mainly through telemarketing; and many luxury goods makers such as Cartier, Louis Vuitton, and Dunhill with their boutiques (see also the global retailing section below).

8. See "L'eggs Products, Inc," Harvard Business School case no. 9-575-090, 1979.

9. Alexander, 1990, discusses the variety among national retailers in more detail.

10. Data from International Marketing Data and Statistics, 2001.

11. For a striking example, see "Dell," 1992.

12. From Govindarajan and Gupta, 2001, and www.wal-martchina.com.

13. This power advantage has become one reason why manufacturers aim to develop more global brands; see, for example, Simmons, 1990.

14. See "How Levi's Works," 1993.

15. The emphasis on speed has made even small savings important. For example, in mid-1995 Federal Express induced the U.S. Trade Representative to pressure Japanese authorities for landing rights at Kobe's New International Airport even though other Japanese airports were available and landing in Japan was no longer a necessity on Far Eastern routes from FedEx's hub in Memphis. Rather, Federal Express, which got access, plans to use Kobe from its new hub in Subic Bay in the Philippines. See Pollack, 1995.

16. See Tirschwell, 1995.

17. Price competition among ocean carriers is guided by "conferences," loose agreements between industry participants, sometimes aided by governments, which attempt to regulate competition. These conferences have at times lost power as individual carrier lines refused to go along, but deregulation is not as far-reaching as in the airline industry, and there are still successful attempts to control prices. See, for example, Fabey, 1995.

18. These megaports may have to be built away from existing port sites because of a lack of land area, and they may also be built by the global alliance partners rather than the port authorities since the latter are limited in their actions by local governments. See DiBenedetto, 1995.

19. See Koenig, 1995. As was discussed in Chapter 10, when P&G found its truck shipments delayed at the border, the company helped invest in improved port facilities in St. Petersburg and shipped products to Russia from Germany by boat across the Baltic.

20. Change is under way, however. As of 1995, the RoadRailer system was in operation in Bayern in the south of Germany, with the first trains going from Munich across the Alps through the Brenner Pass with BMW cars destined for Milano and Verona in Italy, a trip of eight hours (see Barnard, 1995a).

21. See "SKF," 1993.

22. The smaller companies can be competitive by focusing on certain key routes and terminals and offering specialized services, a niche strategy; see Barnard, 1995b.

23. From a study reported in *The Journal of Commerce*; see Johnson, 1995c.

24. This section draws on Cavusgil and Sikora, 1988, Danzon, 1998, and Kyle, 2007.

25. Direct marketing will be discussed in more detail in Chapter 17.

Selected References

Alexander, Nicholas. "Retailers and International Markets." *International Marketing Review* 7, no. 4 (1990), pp. 75–85.

Assmus, Gert, and Carsten Wiese. "How to Address the Gray Market Threat Using Price Coordination." *Sloan Management Review* 36, no. 3 (1995), pp. 31–42.

Barnard, Bruce. "RoadRailer Trailer to Make European Intermodal Debut." *Journal of Commerce*, May 18, 1995a, pp. 1A, 2A.

——. "Jan Jansen Leading Ogden's 'Ground Troops' into Europe." *Journal of Commerce*, June 19, 1995b, p. 14A.

Bello, Daniel C.; David J. Urban; and Bronislaw J. Verhage. "Evaluating Export Middlemen in Alternative Channel Structures." *International Marketing Review* 8, no. 5 (1991), pp. 49–64.

Cavusgil, S. Tamer, and Ed Sikora. "How Multinationals Can Counter Gray Market Imports." *Columbia Journal of World Business*, Winter 1988, pp. 75–85.

Corben, Ron. "Thailand Megamerger Is Expected to Shake Up Retail Trade in Asia." *Journal of Commerce*, May 22, 1995, p. 5A.

Czinkota, Michael R., and Masaaki Kotabe. *The Japanese Distribution System*. Chicago: Probus, 1993.

Danzon, P. M. "The Economics of Parallel Trade." *PharmacoEconomics* 13 (March 1998), pp. 293–304.

"Dell: Mail Order Was Supposed to Fail." *BusinessWeek*, January 20, 1992, p. 89.

DiBenedetto, William. "Giant Ship Terminals Are Coming; The Question Is: Who'll Build Them?" *Journal of Commerce*, June 21, 1995, pp. 1A, 2A.

Fabey, Michael. "TACA Finds Cargo Surge Making Up for Rollback." *Journal of Commerce*, June 19, 1995, pp. 1A, 8A.

Foster, Peter. "The Capital of Duty-Free." *The Times*, September 28, 1995, Features, p. 1.

"How Levi's Works with Retailers." *Business Europe*, July 19, 1993.

Govindarajan, Vijay and Anil K. Gupta. The Quest for Global Dominance. San Francisco: Jossey-Bass, 2001.

Johansson, Johny K., and Ikujiro Nonaka. "Marketing Research: The Japanese Way." *Harvard Business Review*, March–April 1986.

Johnson, Gregory S. "Eastman Kodak Forms Own Air Freight Hub." *Journal of Commerce*, May 17, 1995a, pp. 1A, 7A.

——. "UPS Leaps Ahead with Next-Flight-Out International Service." *Journal of Commerce*, May 25, 1995b, p. 3A.

——. "Survey: Companies Consider Logistics a Key to Profits." *Journal of Commerce*, May 31, 1995c, p. 2B.

Kale, Sudhir H., and Roger P. McIntyre. "Distribution Channel Relationships in Diverse Cultures." *International Marketing Review* 8 (1991), pp. 31–45.

Kim, Jai Ok; Mary Barry; and Carol Warfield. "Gaining Ground in a Globalized Market: U.S. Clothing Industry." *Bobbin* 35, no. 9 (1994), p. 60.

Koenig, Robert. "Tenfold Increase in Truck Traffic Fuels German Plans for Toll Hike." *Journal of Commerce*, June 7, 1995, p. 1A.

Kyle, Margaret. "Strategic Responses to Parallel Trade," NBER Working Paper no. 12968, March 2007.

Lambert, Bruce. "In Philippines, Duty-Free with a Difference (or Two)." *New York Times*, June 24, 1995, p. 34.

Lyons, Nick. The Sony Vision. New York: Crown, 1976.

Markowitz, Arthur. "Wal-Mart Zones In on Foreign Trade." Discount Store News 32, no. 8 (April 19, 1993), p. 1.

Maruyama, Masayoshi. "The Structure and Performance of the Japanese Distribution System." In Czinkota and Kotabe, The Japanese Distribution System, pp. 23–42.

Morita, Akio. Made in Japan. New York: NAL Penguin, 1986.

Munns, Peter J. S. Marketing and Distribution in Japan Today. Master's thesis, Graduate School of Management, International University of Japan, 1994.

Pollack, Andrew. "U.S. and Japan Again Pull Back from the Brink." New York Times, June 22, 1995, pp. 31, 34.

Rapoport, Carla, with Justin Martin. "Retailers Go Global." Fortune, February 20, 1995, pp. 102–8.

Rosson, Philip. "The Overseas Distributor Method." In P. Rosson, and S. Reid, eds. Market Entry and Expansion Mode. New York: Praeger, 1987.

Simmons, Tim. "A Global Brand of Dialog; Food Products Manufacturers Moving to Market Products Globally." Supermarket News 40, no. 28 (July 9, 1990), p. 2.

"SKF to Centralize Distribution." Business Europe, April 12, 1993, p. 7.

Tirschwell, Peter M. "APL Seeks Shift to Terminal Adjacent to Partners." Journal of Commerce, June 23, 1995, p. 1A.

"What's Holding Back Computer Chains in Europe?" BusinessWeek, November 12, 1984, p. 120.

Chapter 16

Global Advertising

"One voice, many languages"

After reading this chapter, you will be able to:

1. Understand how spending on advertising increases as countries grow more affluent because new products and services appear and customers need more information.

2. Help design pan-regional advertising campaigns that are cost-efficient and more effective than multidomestic advertising as markets integrate.

3. Avoid the pitfalls of standardized and translated messages by following a pattern-standardization approach with unified slogan, visualization, and image but with local execution in terms of language, spokespersons, and copy.

4. Evaluate when a global advertising agency is at an advantage over local rivals and when independent local advertising agencies in multinational networks can offer stronger local talent.

5. Develop a global campaign that involves headquarters and ad agency managers but also local representatives whose knowledge will help formulate and implement the strategy.

Global promotion involves a variety of activities, ranging from in-store point-of-purchase displays and Sunday newspaper coupons to satellite TV advertising and sponsorship of symphony orchestras, athletic events such as the Olympics, soccer's World Cup, and major tennis tournaments.

All of these various tools need to be integrated and project a consistent message and image for maximum effectiveness. This is a stiff challenge for global marketers since the tools are not equally effective everywhere and some are not even available in certain country markets.

The most visible promotional activity is perhaps *global advertising*, the topic of this chapter. *Global sales promotion*, *public relations*, and *publicity* have also become powerful promotional tools because of developments in global communications and the opening up of new markets. Then there is participation in *international trade fairs*, *direct marketing*, and *personal selling*, the last typically much more localized but still important. These other promotional tools will be discussed in Chapter 17.

This chapter will start by discussing promotion as a competitive advantage. It then covers the extent of advertising and media spending that exists in various countries before focusing on global advertising issues. It will discuss the pros and cons of global versus multidomestic advertising, what is involved in doing global advertising, the role of the advertising agency, and the problems of global advertising management. The chapter concludes with an illustration of how one company has gone about developing a pan-regional advertising campaign.

Antiglobalization: Provocative Ads Give Benetton Edge

"Do you play safe?" asks an advertisement for Benetton Sportsystem, picturing Ektelon eyeguards on one page and a condom on the other. A different ad juxtaposes an Asolo climbing boot with a picture of Jesus's crucifixion ("Do you play alone?"), while another combines Kastle skis with photos of German and American Olympic athletes giving Nazi and black power salutes in 1936 and 1968 ("Do you play race?").

These global ads touching on seemingly universal values are undeniably provocative; many people find them offensive. They build on Benetton's experience that controversial images give the retailer worldwide recognition despite modest advertising budgets. These benefits convinced Benetton to stick with the provocative ad campaigns, even though some consumers bristled, and many critics doubted the messages could stimulate sales. Benetton's ads became more hard-edged. One showed a man dying of AIDS, another a priest and nun kissing. As it turned out, their realism and antiestablishment stance were well attuned to the antiglobalization movement—but not to the new business climate in the aftermath of the September 11 terrorist attacks.

Not blind to the new environment, Benetton changed its strategy in 2002. In a new \$15 million campaign called "Food for Life," the clothier, in partnership with the World Food Program of the United Nations, put a face on hunger in ads appearing in Europe, Asia, and the United States. Only a few advertisements were edgy, including one that showed a man with a mutilated arm, whose metal prosthesis ends in a spoon.

Some consumers still bristled, and many critics doubted the messages could stimulate sales. In the United States, where sales slipped, Benetton began using more conventional advertising to ensure that consumers knew what its stores offered: A television ad described a minidress as "your best dress . . . the one you sometimes think you love more than your boyfriend." "Provocative as that message is, it's a lot more like other fashion ads than the earlier Benetton billboards. Its advertising in Europe still took on controversial subjects such as domestic violence and anorexia by using arresting images in the advertisements, but elsewhere the advertising was less controversial. Still, with the added competitive pressure from H&M and Zara, Benetton encountered sales problems. Sales did not recover until the company changed its merchandising strategy, developing a product line for men and one for babies, and emphasizing its high-end Sisley brand.

Social and political effects of globalization are clearly on the minds of consumers and advertisers in the new millennium. Advertising has to reflect and relate to people's frame of mind. As a result, the walls between information, entertainment, and advertising are becoming blurred as cause-related advertising for AIDS, gays, women, and minorities is used by companies to demonstrate social awareness and responsibility. And Benetton was there before anyone else.

Sources: Stuart Elliott, "Benetton's Unrepentant Adman Vows to Keep Pushing the Envelope," *New York Times,* July 21, 1995, p. D4; Marshall Blonsky and Contardo Calligaris, "At Benetton, a Retreat from Revolution," *Washington Post,* April 30, 1995, pp. H1, H7; Stuart Elliott, "Creative Agencies That Feel at Home in the Global Village Are Writing Their Own Tickets," *New York Times,* September 30, 1994, p. D17; Normandy Madden, "World Congress Ends on Guardedly Optimistic Note," *AdAge Global,* February 1, 2002; **www.fashionunited.co.uk**, February 26, 2008.

Promotion as a Competitive Advantage

Promotion, including advertising, in-store promotions, and personal selling, is one of the four Ps in the traditional marketing mix. For many companies, it can also be a key competitive advantage, an FSA. As we saw in Chapter 2, Gillette and Unilever are two companies that view their advertising scale and strength as competitive advantages.

Procter & Gamble has limited its expansion into countries where advertising media exclude access to television advertising, on the premise that the P&G television commercials represent a key competitive advantage. Another example comes from the Xerox company. The sales force strength at Xerox is legendary, based on a unique sales training program for novices; the company has even leveraged this strength to help train other companies' sales forces as well.

As always in globalization, an early question is whether the firm-specific advantages (FSAs) are transferable. This is sometimes not an easy thing to assess. Especially when promotional strength is considered such an FSA, it is necessary to identify exactly what it is that is so good. Which parts of the firm's promotional efforts are more effective than the competition? To answer this question, it is helpful to distinguish between at least four different components of promotional strength.

1. Is the promotional advantage lodged in superior in-store merchandising and sales promotions rather than media advertising? Are we better at working with store managers, for example? If yes, the company should realize that regulations of promotional schemes and store access vary considerably across countries. It might not be possible to replicate successful in-store and shelf-space dealer promotions abroad.

2. Do we have an FSA because our creative advertising concept and execution is superior to competition, as in the "Put a tiger in the tank" slogan of Exxon? If yes, does the concept have universal appeal? The tiger in the tank might be a great concept, but what about the alleged superiority of the Budweiser frogs' "Bud-Wei-Ser" commercials in the United States? Hard to believe they will translate well abroad. Or Diesel jeans' sexually explicit print ads in Europe, credited with the jeans maker's success—unlikely to play as well in Asian countries. Of course, these kinds of subjective judgments should be tested in focus groups before entry, but the point is, one cannot take transferability of the concept for granted.

3. Are the advertising media we need available and do we have access to them? This is usually not a problem in the United States where media are plentiful and legally independent of advertisers and ad agencies. It is more likely to occur in other countries where some media have much less penetration and where there might be barriers against outsiders. For example, in many poor countries in Africa and elsewhere television reach is still limited. Television access can also be very expensive, as in Russia. Access can also be restricted. For example, in Japan certain media vehicles are only available through Dentsu, the largest ad agency. In many countries there is a limit on the amount of advertising slots available because of a limited number of channels, favoring already established incumbents. In yet other cases, government control over channels can limit access and favor government-controlled firms. China's efforts to control Internet access and content is one example.

4. Do we have a promotional advantage simply because of more promotional spending overall? For example, the advantage of a firm's brand might reside in saturation levels of advertising, not achievable by competitors with less financial resources. Nike has often been accused of this tactic because of the visibility and "in-your-face" character of its campaigns. Size is one advantage that is likely to transfer fairly well abroad. Especially when competitors are primarily domestic firms, global firms tend to have more promotional clout. Large multinationals often have better access to media buying discounts because of larger investments, making cost-per-audience-member-reached lower than otherwise. Their global advertising also generates spillover effects from neighboring countries. On the other hand, there is a negative factor to consider: It is often the sheer size of the global corporation that threatens the domestic firms and kindles antiglobalization sentiments, a problem most acute for American multinationals.

To sum up, the shift from domestic-oriented promotion to global promotion needs to be carefully considered, especially when promotion is a key advantage. As for any competitive advantage, the successful globalizing firm needs to make sure that these advantages can be transferred and controlled abroad. Promotional strength might or

The Global Advertising Task

The global advertiser faces a complex task. The communication has to be appropriate for each local market, while at the same time there is a need to coordinate campaigns and control expenditures across the globe. Because of the varying media availability in different countries and differing effectiveness of global media, the feasible channels for advertising will differ. Furthermore, the variations across country markets in customer behavior make for variable receptivity to advertising and message construction. But customizing the advertising to each individual country leads to increased costs and unwieldy control procedures. This chapter deals with these managerial issues in-depth and attempts to show how the optimal balance between the two extremes of ethnocentrically global and polycentrically multidomestic advertising can be achieved.

Global advertising can be defined as advertising more or less uniform across many countries, often, but not necessarily, in media vehicles with global reach. In many cases complete uniformity is unobtainable because of linguistic and regulatory differences between nations or differences in media availability, but as with products, **localized advertising** can still be basically global. In contrast, **multidomestic advertising** is international advertising deliberately adapted to particular markets and audiences in message and/or creative execution.[1]

There are several traditional problems facing the decision maker in global advertising. One is how to allocate a given *advertising budget* among several market countries. Another is what *media* to use in these various markets. A third is what *media* to select.

But even before tackling these management decisions, the advertiser needs to define the *objectives* of the advertising in the different countries. And before doing that it is imperative that the decision maker identify what can conceivably be expected from the global advertising effort. Thus, the logical starting point in global advertising management is the assessment of the *role of advertising* in the country markets and the availability of alternative advertising media.

The International World of Advertising

Advertising Volume

Judging from most published figures, there is a role for advertising to play in all economies, socialist as well as capitalist. At the same time, there is little doubt that the role of advertising in the United States is considerably greater than in many other places. The advertising per capita figures in Exhibit 16.1 illustrate this.

- Advertising intensity varies a great deal between countries. Advertising is simply not a very common form of communication in some countries and may not be an effective promotional tool there.
- Generally the higher the GDP, the more is spent on advertising in per capita terms. The more developed the country, the more money is allocated to advertising.

might not be transferable in unchanged form to countries elsewhere. This means that pursuing similar advertising and promotional activities everywhere—doing global promotions—might or might not be advisable. On the plus side, media costs for audience exposures and reach are likely to come down with global campaigns, and the sheer size effect associated with uniform saturation campaigns can be positives for global promotions. But people in different countries are unlikely to respond the same way to any one advertising slogan, and critical in-store promotional activities might simply not be allowed in certain countries.

As this chapter will show, when promotion is an important strength, the best strategy is often to start with a basic creative concept that has proved successful in a leading market, but then allow local managers to adapt the theme to local markets and local media.

EXHIBIT 16.1
Advertising Expenditures (US$) Per Capita

Sources: Euromonitor; World Association of Newspapers, 2008.

	2002	2003	2004	2005	2006	2007
World	49.5	53.4	59.7	62.6	65.8	72
Asia Pacific	15.8	17.2	18.8	19.6	20.2	21.9
China	4.8	6	6.5	7.5	8.9	11.4
Hong Kong, China	272.2	268.5	321.1	357.2	400.4	426.1
India	1.7	1.9	2.6	3.3	3.7	4.4
Japan	262.9	283.7	315.5	315.3	305.7	312.5
Singapore	225.5	242.2	283.9	259	271	275.9
South Korea	133.3	144.9	144.4	162.2	182	195.7
Taiwan	84.4	92.1	77.1	82.7	84.9	89
Australasia	206.4	270.1	340.8	379.5	382.9	455.4
Australia	210.9	272.7	343.2	380.6	389	397.6
New Zealand	183.7	257.3	328.8	374.3	352.5	356.1
Eastern Europe	25.8	35.1	45.7	57.7	70.9	95.5
Czech Republic	97	121.4	146.7	177.8	210.7	238.1
Poland	64.2	75	89.1	104	129.8	154.9
Russia	15.2	19.9	26.7	34.7	45.6	61.3
Latin America	22.5	22.9	25.6	30.4	34.2	39.4
Argentina	13.8	22.3	26	33.7	36.5	44
Brazil	18.8	20.5	25.3	34.7	43.6	50.8
Chile	30.6	31.7	37.6	44	51	55.7
Mexico	34.1	31	33.1	35.1	36.9	39.4
Middle East and Africa	5.2	6	7.4	8.5	10	11.4
Egypt	6.4	4.7	6	7.9	11.5	16.4
Israel	115.8	106.5	113	116	115.1	122
Saudi Arabia	73.1	82.9	104.3	116.5	157.9	174.1
South Africa	23.9	37.2	50	55.3	56.7	55.6
United Arab Emirates	93.9	114.2	153.1	221.7	289.5	330.1
North America	468.4	474.3	516.6	529.7	554.1	589
Canada	163.7	183.9	210.2	243.1	273.9	283.4
USA	501.6	505.8	549.9	560.8	584.5	619.7
Western Europe	158	185.8	215.3	222.7	231.4	251.6
France	166	199	227.5	233.8	239.3	245.8
Germany	192.1	218.7	243.7	246.9	254.1	264.5
Italy	124.8	154.2	179.8	183.4	188.9	198.8
Spain	124.8	151	180.5	192.2	201.7	214.8
Sweden	182.2	220.6	248.1	267.4	294.3	299.8
United Kingdom	256.9	288.3	345.8	359.9	365.8	376

- Advertising is an unusually important medium in the United States, partly a result of the cultural diversity that makes social norms and interpersonal communication (word-of-mouth) relatively less reliable. This has now been recognized by many foreign companies, which find that they have to spend much more on advertising in the United States than elsewhere. To illustrate, for German BASF and Siemens, both makers of industrial products, corporate advertising in the United States far outstrips that done by the two companies elsewhere.[2]

The global advertising manager also needs to remember that different cultures and target segments have different receptivity to advertising. This affects the desirability of having a job in advertising as well. In parts of Asia and the Middle East, advertising agencies have difficulty hiring the best people.[3] But things are changing over time; free

EXHIBIT 16.2
Global and Selected Regional Advertising, 2005–2009

Source: *Marketing News*, July 15, 2007, p. 28.

Year	$ billion	Percent in Central/Eastern Europe	Percent in Asia Pacific	Percent in Middle East, Africa
2005	406.25	4.7 %	21.1 %	2.6 %
2006	431.56	5.2 %	20.9 %	3.0 %
2007	453.93	6.1 %	21.1 %	3.3 %
2008	482.14	6.2 %	21.4 %	3.7 %
2009	506.12	6.6 %	21.4 %	4.2 %

market advertising crowds out traditional norms and inefficient ways of communicating. Even Italians are taking to voice mail. But differences persist.

The point is one can't assume that global market receptivity to advertising is already the same everywhere, because it isn't. Global advertising allocated equally across countries will lead to misallocated resources. Allocating so that the last dollar spent yields equal returns everywhere, a good rule of thumb, means that there will be widely different levels of coverage across markets, with countries like Singapore and the United Kingdom getting more than their share, and Italy and India less (using the figures in Exhibit 16.1). At the same time, the global marketer has to judge whether historical data for a country such as India are a good guide for the future; there might be a good opportunity for an expanded advertising effort there.

Global advertising is expected to grow strongly over the next few years. The data projections up through 2009 are given in Exhibit 16.2, which also shows the percentage for the new emerging markets.

As we can see in Exhibit 16.2, global ad spending is expected to grow from $406 billion in 2005 to $506 billion in 2009. While North American spending will continue to increase, its share of the advertising expenditures will decline from 42.9 percent to 40.3 percent. In the same period, advertising share for Western Europe will decline from 24.2 percent to 22.7 percent. As the exhibit shows, the increase will be greatest in Central and Eastern Europe and in the Middle East and Africa, albeit from a lower base. The relatively slow growth in share for Asia Pacific reflects the weakness of Japan, which counterbalances the increases in China and elsewhere.

Media Usage

It is important to know which media are important in different countries. In Exhibit 16.3 expenditure shares in six basic media types (TV, print, radio, cinema, and outdoor, and online) are shown for selected countries. Some differences stand out:

- *Television* advertising is strong in Eastern Europe, Latin America, and Saudi Arabia, but not very prominent in most of Europe compared to print media. The limitations of commercial time available in Europe undoubtedly contribute to the low percentages for television. The Eastern European figure is impressive, probably reflecting not only increased television penetration but also the efforts of new firms to build brand awareness and status.

- *Radio*, although not big, is still a viable media, with strong presence in Canada, Mexico, New Zealand, South Africa, and even the United States. The government monopoly control that used to limit commercial radio in Europe and elsewhere has now been eased and there are a number of commercial stations available.

- *Print* media are strong in countries such as France, Germany, and Sweden, mostly attributable to relatively limited availability of commercial broadcasting.

- *Cinema* advertising used to be strong in countries such as Argentina and Singapore, where films are popular pastimes and advertisers have good access to theaters. The relatively insignificant role of cinema is mostly a reflection of increased TV penetration.

EXHIBIT 16.3
Media Usage in Selected Countries, 2007 (% of advertising expenditures)

Source: Euromonitor; World Association of Newspapers, 2008.

	TV	Radio	Print	Cinema	Outdoor	Online
World	37.5	8.0	41.0	0.6	6.1	6.9
Asia Pacific	43.0	4.2	35.7	0.8	9.7	6.5
China	44.0	5.0	35.2	3.6	11.0	1.2
Hong Kong, China	35.9	3.5	51.7	0.0	8.1	0.7
India	43.5	2.6	45.7	1.5	5.6	1.2
Japan	44.1	3.8	30.7	0.0	11.1	10.4
Singapore	37.8	9.8	44.5	0.7	7.2	0.0
South Korea	33.6	2.8	45.2	0.0	9.1	9.2
Taiwan	40.5	5.5	40.1	0.0	8.5	5.4
Australasia	33.2	8.9	43.6	0.8	4.0	9.6
Australia	33.8	8.5	42.6	0.9	3.9	10.4
New Zealand	30.0	11.0	49.0	0.5	4.5	5.0
Eastern Europe	58.6	5.6	23.3	0.5	10.6	1.5
Czech Republic	49.0	5.3	38.8	0.3	3.8	2.6
Poland	51.1	8.9	29.6	1.5	7.3	1.6
Russia	49.5	5.4	23.5	0.3	19.7	1.7
Latin America	59.6	6.8	28.8	0.4	3.4	1.0
Argentina	47.3	2.9	41.2	1.5	6.3	0.9
Brazil	64.4	4.4	25.0	0.0	4.4	1.8
Chile	49.4	7.5	33.0	0.4	8.8	1.0
Mexico	60.7	12.4	26.9	0.0	0.0	0.0
Middle East and Africa	42.0	4.9	46.5	0.5	4.2	1.9
Egypt	37.5	4.6	57.6	0.3	0.1	0.0
Israel	29.4	6.5	47.4	0.5	6.4	9.8
Saudi Arabia	62.1	0.7	31.4	0.0	3.3	2.6
South Africa	46.3	12.2	36.3	1.1	3.5	0.6
United Arab Emirates	1.9	0.2	90.4	0.8	4.7	1.9
North America	32.1	11.8	43.1	0.3	3.9	8.9
Canada	30.6	14.2	41.6	0.0	3.7	9.8
United States	32.2	11.6	43.1	0.3	3.9	8.8
Western Europe	32.6	5.6	47.3	0.9	6.9	6.6
France	35.5	8.7	38.2	1.1	12.2	4.4
Germany	23.9	4.0	63.6	0.8	4.7	3.1
Italy	53.4	6.4	33.0	0.8	3.6	2.8
Spain	46.3	8.8	35.0	0.6	6.4	2.8
Sweden	22.5	2.9	55.5	0.4	5.6	13.1
United Kingdom	26.4	3.5	44.6	1.3	7.8	16.3

- *Outdoor* media show a seemingly random pattern, being high in Japan, France, and Russia. The likely explanation for the randomness is different regulations and local laws for outdoor advertising.

- *Online* advertising is higher in countries where Internet penetration is high, as one would expect (penetration figures are given in Chapter 17). The United Kingdom and Sweden show significantly higher numbers, as do Australia, Japan, Israel, and South Korea. Overall, the online advertising percentage is small in most countries, even the United States, but likely to rise as Internet penetration goes up.

Global Media

The figures in Exhibit 16.3 do not show the emergence of truly global media. Global media vehicles are increasingly available.

- In *television*, for example, Cable News Network (CNN) reaches into many of the globe's remote corners. The British Skychannel can be seen in most of the EU countries.

- In *magazines* such as U.S.-based *Time, Newsweek, Cosmopolitan,* and *Playboy,* overseas editions in the English language have editorial content adapted to the local

A Russian language advertisement for Colgate toothpaste. This ad is typical of multinationals' introductory advertising campaigns when emerging markets open up. It plays on the global leadership theme, and suggests that now also you can be part of the global community. Source: G. E. Belch and M. A. Belch, *Advertising and Promotion*, 5th ed. (New York: McGraw-Hill/Irwin, 2001).

© 1991 Colgate-Palmolive Co.

МИР ГОВОРИТ «КОЛГЕЙТ»—
ПОДРАЗУМЕВАЕТ ЗУБНАЯ ПАСТА.
МИР ГОВОРИТ ЗУБНАЯ ПАСТА–
ПОДРАЗУМЕВАЕТ «КОЛГЕЙТ».

Для людей в более чем 160 странах мира зубная паста «Колгейт» вот уже 100 лет является синонимом высочайшего качества. Люди больше доверяют пасте «Колгейт», чем другим пастам, потому что она содержит кальций и фтор, которые способствуют укреплению зубов и защищают их от кариеса.

С помощью пасты «Колгейт» вы и ваша семья смогут сохранить зубы здоровыми. Вашей семье также понравится освежающий вкус ментола. Чистите зубы пастой «Колгейт» и вы убедитесь сами, что «Колгейт» означает качество.

ЗУБНАЯ ПАСТА НОМЕР ОДИН В МИРЕ.

Translation:

COLGATE. WHAT THE WORLD CALLS TOOTHPASTE.

THE WORLD SAYS COLGATE, THE WORLD MEANS TOOTHPASTE.
THE WORLD SAYS TOOTHPASTE, THE WORLD MEANS COLGATE.

In the 100 years since it was first introduced, Colgate toothpaste has come to mean superior quality to people in over 160 countries. In fact, more families trust Colgate than any other toothpaste in the world because it contains calcium and fluoride for stronger teeth and unsurpassed cavity protection. Colgate will also help keep your family's teeth healthy. And it has a fresh, minty taste they'll love. Brush with Colgate. And see for yourself that, when the world says "Colgate," they mean quality.

THE NUMBER ONE TOOTHPASTE IN THE WORLD.

country. For major markets they also have more completely localized editions and offer, for example, Japanese-language editions.

- In *newspapers*, *The Financial Times* and *The Wall Street Journal* have global reach; *The Wall Street Journal* has an Asian and a European edition.

- The arrival of the *Internet* and the *World Wide Web* heralds further developments in global media. Publishing houses and broadcast networks are teaming up with online services to create a global multimedia environment. And we consumers are exposed to a wide variety of Web advertisements.

Web advertisements are those boxed "inserts" on the screen that pop up as you arrive on the Internet or at a Web site. They are *interactive* in the sense that you can point to them with the mouse and click to get more information about the product or service advertised. You are typically whisked electronically to the company home page.

There are several kinds of Web ads:

- *Banner ads* are the most common and simplest types of ads. The largest appear as elongated boxes on the top or the bottom of the screen, covering about two-thirds of the screen width—hence the name. They actually come in various sizes (measured in pixels) with the smaller ones placed at the sides as square boxes or "buttons."

- *"Tickers"* are banner ads that move across the screen.

- *Interstitial ads* are the ads that flash on the screen during the time your request is being handled. Loading a site can take several seconds, and these ads fill up the void. Again, clicking on it will shift your request to the advertised site.

- *Pop-up ads* are the ads that appear once a site has been loaded but before you get access. They usually contain messages from the site company but are increasingly sold to independent entrepreneurs who want to take advantage of a popular site. Amazon.com appears in many pop-up ads.

- *Transactional ads* let you order or request something without leaving the Web page you are on. They are getting increasingly popular as advertisers realize that users typically want to stay on the site requested but still explore the advertised offer.

- *"Roadblocks"* are full-screen ads that users must pass through to get to the other screens they wish to view.

- *"Rich media" ads* are any Web ads that move, talk, beep, or flash. As communication lines improve and desktop computers get more powerful, transmission times shorten and become less of an issue with users. This opens the door for these kinds of ads that require more processing capability—and provide the first glimpse of what filmed commercials on the Web would be like.

It may be too early to tell whether the cost-per-thousand figures for Web ads make online ads competitive with more traditional media. But so far the amount spent is increasing (see box, "Web Advertisements? Click Here!").

A relatively new force in global media is the emergence of giant media conglomerates. Often starting from relatively minor countrywide operations in publishing or broadcasting, these conglomerates have been assembled by strong entrepreneurs who have used mergers and acquisitions to expand their operations beyond the home country, into regional strength and ultimately global reach. Although several are U.S.-based, the media giants also come from Europe and Australia. Exhibit 16.4 shows a listing of the top five and their top brands.

It should be noted that these conglomerates do not stay the same for long. For example, in 2008, News Corp. acquired *The Wall Street Journal*, while Bertelsmann was unloading Random House.

How much effect this consolidation will have on the advertising business is not yet clear. Generally, global advertising should gain. These huge enterprises own or control global media channels that may be localized to a specific country or region, but the negotiations for media discounts and access can be handled centrally. This would cut costs of global campaigns. But global advertising does not rely exclusively on global media. Even the most global advertising campaigns have to be scheduled in local media vehicles with the help of media planners in the local ad agencies. A global 30-second television commercial for British Airways, which may run unchanged in a dozen or so countries (with some voice-over translation), still needs to be scheduled in the local media in these countries. This may change. With the growth of global multimedia giants, it is clear that

EXHIBIT 16.4
Global Media Conglomerates, 2006

Source: http://adage.com/datacenter.

1. Time Warner (U.S., Global Revenues: $31.8 billion; CNN, Cartoon Network)
2. Disney (U.S., Global Revenues: $23.4 billion; Disney, ABC, ESPN)
3. Bertelsmann (Germany, Global Revenues: $16.3 billion; BMG Music, Random House)
4. News Corp. (Australia, Global Revenues: $13.5 billion; *Times* (London), Star TV, Fox News)
5. Viacom (U.S., Global Revenues: $12.86 billion; MTV, Nickelodeon, Paramount Pictures)

Getting the Picture

WEB ADVERTISEMENTS? CLICK HERE!

In addition to its other revolutionary effects, the Internet has been hailed as the true communication medium of the new millennium. Online advertising has become one additional medium for reaching the global consumer.

Web advertising is increasing and marketers have devised a variety of vehicles to utilize it, such as banner ads, pop-up windows, "tickers," and "roadblocks." For example, a Web user investigating airline fares might find a flashing banner on the screen exclaiming, "Rent a car from Alamo and get up to 2 days free!" To attract viewers to its own Web site, Toyota pays for banner ads on other sites, such as ESPN SportsZone (**www.espn.com**). Another avenue being utilized is content sponsorship: Advil sponsors ESPN Sport-Zone's "Injury Report."

Despite the popularity of Internet advertising, some marketers (and consumers) question its overall value. Although costs are often less than other advertising media, its effectiveness remains a subject of debate. For example, a banner ad on ESPN SportsZone, which attracts more than 500,000 Web surfers and 20 million "hits" (the number of times the site is accessed) per week, costs about $300,000 per year. But a Web surfer can easily ignore these banner ads. Developing valid and reliable measures of Internet ad effectiveness will likely contribute to more widespread use in the future. Nielsen Media Research, the television ratings company, has begun monitoring Internet users by equipping

9,000 consumers with software that tracks their every online move. By tracking which Web sites consumers visit, the ads they look at, and what they do when they see those ads, Nielsen is developing some of the first online consumer behavior data sources and selling this research to clients. In 2008 Nielsen paid **$225** million to buy IAG, another audience research company. Using a panel of about 200,000 participants, IAG measures how well consumers remember TV and online ads and how much they like particular shows. On top of providing raw television or online audience numbers, Nielsen will now have data on how consumers respond to ads on television shows and online.

As recently as 1998, U.S. firms spent only $1.5 billion on online advertising, compared with **$40** billion each for newspapers and television. Internet ad revenues that were expected to reach $9 billion in 2002 fell far short. But by 2004 the dot-com collapse was over, and Internet ads started coming back in force. In 2005 spending was up again to $12.5 billion and projected to keep growing. Internet advertising is here to stay.

Viewer reactions? From "clever and fun" to "very annoying."

Sources: "Advertising Age Teams with e-Marketer for Research Report," *Advertising Age*, May 3, 1999, p. 24; Louis E. Boone and David L. Kurtz, *Contemporary Marketing*, 10th ed. (New York: Harcourt College Publishers, 2001); John Simon, "Nielsen's New Web Play," *Fortune 500*, April 8, 2008; **http://www.amazon.com.**

local subsidiaries and their ad agencies in the future might have to limit their choices to local media vehicles owned by the same global media conglomerate.

Strategic Implications

The global statistics are indicators of important differences between country markets. They have some important strategic implications:

1. Advertising expenditures create barriers to entry into an industry. A new firm bent on entering a market usually needs to match the advertising expenditures of existing firms in order to enter successfully. A global firm with established presence can use high advertising spending to "raise the ante" and make competitive entry difficult.

2. There are some countries where a scarcity of available media has made advertising a competitive weapon of limited usefulness. Since advertising represents mass communication and thus requires mass media, successful advertising campaigns are very dependent on a well-developed and functioning infrastructure.

3. The communication objectives realistically achieved through various media differ among countries. The so-called **hierarchy of effects**—which traces the effects of advertising through brand awareness to knowledge, attitude, liking, trial, and adoption (see Exhibit 16.5)—can be used to illustrate this fact as the following examples show.

Television

Whereas television is a true mass medium in Latin America and Asia and thus a reasonable avenue for creating *awareness* for a new product, in many other markets (including some European countries with limited time availability) it provides a status association for the brand and is thus better as an *attitude change* agent.

EXHIBIT 16.5
The Hierarchy of Effects

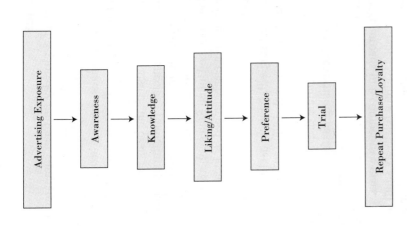

Radio

Similarly, radio is a true mass medium in many countries and thus useful for awareness campaigns, but it is very focused on specific segments (such as teenagers) in the United States and Canada and aimed at the direct action or *trial stage* rather than more general objectives.

Newspapers

Newspapers are the only available medium in some countries and will thus have to fulfill their standard role of a direct action influence as well as establishing more general *knowledge* and *liking* of the brand.

Outdoor

Where literacy levels are low (such as in Bangladesh), broadcast and outdoor advertising plus relatively odd media such as cinema advertising will outweigh print media in importance regardless of objectives of the campaign.

Online

Online advertising is close to sales promotion, and thus likely to be more effective in later stages of the hierarchy. In emerging markets, as Internet access opens up, some consumers are likely to surf and look for new products and brands. Judging from the experience in mature markets, however, very soon this effort gives way to a more targeted search, consumers having already decided what to buy, or deciding between a few brands. At that stage a pop-up Web ad serves very much like a point-of-purchase deal in a store. Some consumers might change their decision and try the advertised brand.

Pros and Cons of Global Advertising

There are several reasons why global advertising might be beneficial for a company—and why it might not be. The most immediate benefit usually centers around the cost advantages of unified campaigns.

Cost Advantages

From a cost viewpoint a globally uniform campaign is usually advantageous.[4] The creative ideas once developed can be used globally; the illustrations and messages can be developed once and for all or employed with only minor modifications. Media availability forces some changes, since a broadcast approach might not be directly translatable into print, but generally costs can be held down below those generated by original work for the local market.

Globalized campaigns can also be the basis for savings in media buying. Several media provide global services, especially print, through their international editions. Because media ownership is becoming multinational (so that newspaper owners in one country control newspapers in others—for example, Murdoch's string of newspapers in Australia, the United Kingdom, and the United States), there are sources of scale returns available to a globalized campaign not easily tapped by local buyers.

Global Markets

In general, global advertising will be most useful when the market itself is global. Air travel is a case in point. International airlines offer a typically standardized "product"— or service—and compete for passengers in a global marketplace. The various international airlines attempt to differentiate themselves by superior preflight, in-flight, and postflight service. Global advertising has become an important competitive weapon and a prime source of differentiation. British Airways' famous "Manhattan Landing" TV commercial from 1982 has become a landmark in global strategy.

Desperate to make inroads in a competitive market, airlines have pushed the limits of what can be accomplished within a relatively small range of possibilities. Singapore Airlines offers unparalleled in-flight service based on an extensive customer satisfaction program and uses global ads in business magazines to emphasize the attractiveness of its stewardesses.

Global Products and Brands

It might be assumed that global products and brands need global advertising. This is often true. The campaigns for Swatch watches, Club Med, Benetton, and Reebok are very similar across continents. But there is often a need to do some local adaptation of global campaigns. For example, a global product and brand such as Levi's jeans targets specific segments with different appeals in each local market, since the positioning of the product and brand varies as the target markets differ. Sometimes a brand's global campaign has misfired and the company has retreated to a more multidomestic adaptation. Parker Pen, a globally recognized American brand name, shifted to global advertising in the mid-1980s only to return to multidomestic advertising (and renewed success) after sales slumped badly. The cause of failure was the lack of cooperation on the part of the company's country subsidiaries, whose previously successful campaigns were discontinued.[5]

Drawbacks

Global advertising faces drawbacks that are the counterparts of the advantages.

Cost savings may not materialize because the necessary coordination between local subsidiaries is often complicated and requires management attention and takes time. Also, the local ad agencies lack motivation to participate because the creative initiative is no longer theirs. It can be necessary to gain their cooperation by offering incentives, raising costs.

Even *global markets* may still need localization and some adaptation to be competitive against strong domestic competitors. And what seems similar from a distance becomes more unique on closer inspection. The stage of the product life cycle may be different, for example. Differences between car buyers in Austria and Hungary might seem negligible—not necessarily so when you are on the ground.

Global advertising might also be problematic for global products and brands. The attributes desired differ, and the usage conditions are not necessarily the same. The needs of PC buyers in Korea may be far from the needs of the Japanese, who are unlikely to use the PC at home. And while both use some kanji characters, the characters are not always or even usually the same.

In summary, globally uniform advertising is most powerful if four conditions are satisfied:

- *Image*: The image of the brand (for example, its country-of-origin) communicated can be identical across countries.
- *Symbols*: The symbols used (especially the logo) carry the same meaning across countries.
- *Features*: The product features desired are the same.
- *Usage*: The usage conditions are similar across markets.

If all these four conditions hold, as they might do in the case of, say, airlines, global advertising is a natural. When one or more are not fulfilled—as in the case of Levi's—even standardized products may need adapted multidomestic advertising. If the conditions are not right, global advertising will fail, which helps explain why there is still so much controversy about global versus multidomestic advertising.[6]

Globalization Examples

There are many examples of successful campaigns based on global advertising. For many of its cola brands, Coca-Cola develops prototypes of advertising messages and layouts in the United States and ships them to its representatives abroad. The local offices are allowed to make changes so as to accommodate language differences and possible differences in regulations, but they are generally expected to follow the main script for the campaign. The result is a congruent presentation of the product throughout the world in a manner that is judged to yield the best payoffs. The synergy is naturally high, and unless the slogans are totally inappropriate for the target market, the possible loss due to lack of local adaptation is more than counterbalanced by the instant recognition of the brand name and the slogans (sometimes in English, even in non–English language countries). Added to that are the savings from the use of similar materials across the globe and the scale returns to globalization. It is easy to see that globalization might well pay off (see box, "Philips's Global Advertising Push").

Other companies (and products) that are practitioners of global standardization of advertising are the Revlon company (cosmetics), Philip Morris Altria (tobacco) with its Marlboro brand, the Ralph Lauren Polo and Chaps brands (men's clothing and accessories), Kodak film products, most high-fashion companies such as Yves Saint-Laurent and Dior, and home electronics companies such as Sony. There are others from which one might expect globalized campaigns but that do not use them. The Canon AE-1, a "world camera," employs different campaign material in Japan, Europe, and the United States, as do the Japanese automobile companies. The European car manufacturers develop special campaigns for their North American markets even though many of the selling propositions remain the same.

Investigating a cross-section of 30 print campaigns and 16 television campaigns from ad agencies in the United States, Germany, and Japan, one researcher found that standardization is more common for advertisements transferred between Western markets than for messages transferred between Western and Eastern markets.[7] Interestingly, the product type played a much smaller role than the market distance. Message standardization was much more common for television commercials than for print ads, regardless of country, probably because of the relatively higher cost of producing TV commercials.

Naturally, global advertising is not always the correct strategy. By far the most advertising spending in the world is for ads adapted to the local marketplace. In a recent study of 38 European and U.S. multinationals, it was found that only three practice complete standardization of advertising.[8] Another three reject any attempts at standardization. The majority of the companies practice some degree of standardization, from "standardizing strategy but not execution" (23.5 percent) to "limited standardization" (31.5 percent) to

Getting the Picture

PHILIPS'S GLOBAL ADVERTISING PUSH

The Dutch multinational Royal Philips Electronics (Philips, for short) has traditionally been more of a multinational than a truly global company. Its national subsidiaries were long run as independent fiefdoms under the country managers, especially in the United States where the Philips name was unavailable for certain products, replaced by Norelco and Magnavox. Recently, with restrictions on the use of the brand name eased, however, the company has made a big push into globally coordinated advertising for its flagship brand and its expanded product line.

The Philips product line includes not only consumer electronics, but also medical instruments, Norelco electric shavers, lightbulbs, computer chips, and coffee makers. To establish the Philips name as an umbrella brand for this product line, the company developed a new campaign with a new tag-line ("Sense and Simplicity") to replace the company's old slogan of "Let's make things better." The new tag-line supposedly represents a common thread among all these disparate products. It was developed from focus group research that showed that one common complaint among consumers was the complexity of technology products. "Consumers think the world is too complex," says Andrea Ragnetti, the company's chief marketing officer. "The relationship they have with products and with companies is overwhelmingly complex."

"standardize in most cases" (29.5 percent). The most common approach was that of "pattern standardization," employing a unified positioning theme but allowing local variation.

The global campaign involves a series of print and TV commercials around the "Sense and Simplicity" theme. The first commercial shows a white box opened by several off-screen hands, with a voice-over intoning things such as "I see technology as humanity" and "I see technology as simple as the box it comes in." Other ads focus on specific products in the line, helping to establish that Philips is more than a consumer electronics company. The dual approach is intended to help the company establish its Philips brand in the United States where its awareness and reputation is much lower than in Europe and Asia. The company has decided to relegate the Magnavox brand to low-end electronics and use Philips for higher-end products.

Can "Sense and Simplicity" work in today's tense and complicated global environment? Philips is hedging its bet. The company contracted to become the "official technology supplier" to the movie *Ocean's Twelve* filmed in Europe, starring George Clooney, Brad Pitt, Matt Damon, Catherine Zeta-Jones, and Julia Roberts, and not likely to inspire thoughts of sense and simplicity.

Source: Nat Ives, "Philips Widens its Product Range and Wants Consumers to Know," *New York Times*, September 17, 2004, p. C4; "Philips Electronics Named 'Official Consumer Electronics Supplier' to New Film," *Business Wire*, May 24, 2004.

The Global Advertiser's Decisions

Advertising, being so close to the cultural traditions of a country, was long one of the more decentralized decisions in the multinational company. Headquarters would perhaps be setting the budget, but the basic positioning strategy would be determined by the local subsidiary and approved by headquarters. When it came to execution, including message creation and especially media selection, the advertising agency and its local branch were the prime movers.

The global advertiser, aiming to gain some benefits from a unified approach, has to take charge of this process more effectively. Positioning strategy has to be unified across countries and the unique selling propositions of the brand made clear—and the same—everywhere. That is the strategy part. As for execution, the global advertising manager needs to work closely with local personnel in the subsidiaries and in the agency network to get consensus on a message that transcends borders, reflects the brand accurately, and has punch everywhere. As for media, although the agency still must be the main actor, the global advertiser will want to make sure that cost factors such as media discounts are properly taken into account. While doing all this, the global advertiser also needs to keep an open eye and open mind to suggestions from the local people, to quickly diffuse information through the various local affiliates, and to be flexible enough to change when new information and market research suggest so. In fact, with localization pressures increasing it is today common to have local campaigns run under the umbrella of the global campaign, and managed separately by each country subsidiary.

Getting the Picture

WHO ARE THE BIG SPENDERS?

The amount of money spent on advertising differs a great deal between industries. Companies in cosmetics and personal care products tend to show the highest advertising-to-sales expenditures, sometimes as high as 30 percent. Consumer packaged goods are also big spenders, as are automobile companies, although advertising-to-sales ratios are in the 5–10 percent range. The 15 biggest global advertisers are shown in Exhibit 16.6.

The rankings in the exhibit are based on worldwide advertising spending. The leaders Procter & Gamble and Unilever are fierce competitors in a wide range of household products. They are both in most major markets (68 and 66 countries in 1999), and while P&G is strong in the United States, Unilever tends to have a more even global spread,

and is very active in Europe. Nestlé, the Swiss food company, is similar to Unilever in its global reach. The list also includes other advertisers with strong global brands, such as Coca-Cola, L'Oreal, and several automobile companies.

According to the World Bank, there are some 208 countries in the world. Even with the multinationals' impressive coverage, no advertiser is in even half of those. Nevertheless, these advertisers reach most of the major markets and more. For one thing, the media spillover from satellite TV and other communications is likely to help spread the message to most peoples of the world. The ads may be broadcast from less than 50 percent of the countries, but they are likely to diffuse into the remotest corners of the globe. On this, the antiglobalization activists and the proglobalization forces can probably agree.

It is helpful to distinguish between four components of global advertising:

1. *Strategy.* Global advertising often involves products and services that are positioned similarly across markets, that is, those whose advertised benefits can be the same. As we saw in Chapter 7, it is not necessary that market segments or usage conditions be identical, but the product's appeal should be the same. The positive spillover won't happen unless certain elements of the product are standardized. Brand name should be identical or recognizably similar.

2. *Budgeting and Organization.* Global advertising is typically directed from headquarters with the help of advertising agencies with a global network. The overall budget and its allocation between markets and products needs to be determined. The need for central control of the global advertising campaigns has been one of the driving forces behind the ad agencies' expansion abroad, and this in turn has stimulated agencies to promote the use of more global advertising, as we have seen.

3. *Message and creative.* The copy and visualization go to the heart of the global campaigns. Global advertising is basically uniform in copy and visualization across markets. Three levels of gradually decreasing uniformity can be distinguished: identical ads, prototype advertising, and pattern standardization.

4. *Media.* Global advertising draws on media with global reach such as satellite TV and international editions of magazines and newspapers to reach customers in different countries and (b) following traveling customers around the globe.

Basically, the first two components are managed by the global advertiser, while the last two are managed by the appointed global advertising agency. Let's first discuss the advertiser's work, then the agency's tasks.

Strategy

Most managers approach global advertising with the intention of using the global reach of media and the similarity of message to enhance the awareness and unique positioning of the brand or product. The boost to the **brand image** and global brand equity is usually the most immediate benefit. When the target market involves global consumers, the ability to reach these customers in many places on the globe helps sustain a positive image of the brand. The traveler who recognizes a brand advertised in a foreign resort location may pay more attention to it there than at home. Global advertising helps create goodwill (see box, "Who Are the Big Spenders?").

EXHIBIT 16.6   Top 15 Global Advertisers

Source: *Ad Age Global*, November 10, 2003.

Rank 2002	Rank 2001	Advertiser	Headquarters	Worldwide Advertising Spending 2002	2001	% Chg	U.S. Measured Media Spending 2002	2001	% Chg	Spending by Region in 2002 Asia	Europe	Latin America
1	1	Procter & Gamble Co.	Cincinnati	$4,479	$3,675	21.9	$2,032	$1,679	21.0	$539	$1,647	$120
2	3	Unilever	London/Rotterdam	3,315	2,782	19.2	689	581	18.6	1,713	705	145
3	2	General Motors Corp.	Detroit	3,218	2,953	9.0	2,447	2,202	11.1		522	103
4	6	Toyota Motor Corp.	Toyota City, Japan	2,405	2,162	11.2	885	770	14.9	1,063	347	28
5	5	Ford Motor Co.	Dearborn, Mich.	2,387	2,226	7.2	1,407	1,273	10.6	89	746	92
6	4	Time Warner	New York	2,349	2,295	2.4	1,812	1,726	5.0	40	413	53
7	7	DaimlerChrysler	Auburn Hills, Mich./Stuttgart, Germany	1,800	1,791	0.5	1,341	1,398	-4.1	21	356	31
8	10	L'Oreal	Paris	1,683	1,458	15.4	545	502	8.6	65	1,001	38
9	9	Nestlé	Vevey, Switzerland	1,547	1,615	-4.2	494	520	-5.0	138	819	67
10	16	Sony Corp.	Tokyo	1,513	1,238	22.2	875	656	33.4	135	417	38
11	17	Johnson & Johnson	New Brunswick, N.J.	1,453	1,226	18.5	1,079	890	21.3	83	232	30
12	14	Walt Disney Co.	Burbank, Calif.	1,428	1,315	8.6	1,154	1,103	4.6	32	191	14
13	8	Altria Group	New York	1,425	1,639	-13.1	892	1,082	-17.5	29	436	37
14	11	Honda Motor Co.	Tokyo	1,383	1,393	-0.7	710	682	4.0	522	108	16
15	12	Volkswagen	Wolfsburg, Germany	1,349	1,390	-3.0	440	460	-4.4	39	756	83

Notes: Spending in millions of U.S. dollars. The table only lists parent companies. Figures for subsidiaries and brands are merged into those of the parent. The marketers are ranked by the amount of money they spent on advertising worldwide. To qualify for the Top 15 ranking, a company's 2002 ad spending had to be reported in more than three markets outside the U.S. Data from most countries is tabulated at rate card rates. In a few countries where ad discounting is known to be extremely deep, *Ad Age Global* adjusts ad totals to reflect more realistic spending.

But the effect of global advertising can also be more direct and come closer to **buyer action.** Global customers, such as businesses with a multinational spread, will usually be able to act on buying intentions even when away from the purchasing center. The manager visiting a plant in Malaysia can still place purchase orders through the head office in Honolulu, New York, or London. Global communications—telephone, fax, e-mail—makes this possible and even likely, considering the global manager's typical traveling schedule. In fact, the effect of advertising might be enhanced when the manager encounters it overseas, simply because of the pleasant surprise of recognition. For global customers, global advertising can be a trigger to action, not just goodwill. And in all likelihood, the consumer exposed to a global ad will see something more impressive than in a local effort (see box, "Global Ads Taking Flight").

Furthermore, as we saw in Chapter 15, people in many parts of the world are starting to buy more items over the phone or from catalogs, using credit cards and avoiding stores. This means the advantage of localized advertising will diminish. Chinese customers in Hong Kong call—or fax or e-mail—L. L. Bean in the state of Maine to place orders for outdoor boots using their Visa cards. They learn about L. L. Bean (and Eddie Bauer and REI) from travel in the United States, from Hong Kong media reports, and from advertising in international editions of English-language magazines. Global sources of information are available everywhere, in airplanes, dentists' offices, stores, and homes.

Getting the Picture

GLOBAL ADS TAKING FLIGHT

One of the first examples of global advertising, the "Manhattan Landing" TV commercial by Saatchi & Saatchi for British Airways, has achieved legendary status in the ad world. The commercial, developed in 1982, was inspired by the success of the Steven Spielberg film *Close Encounters of the Third Kind.* The long 90-second commercial showed Manhattan, with its well-known skyscraper skyline, landing slowly in an English village, lights blinding astonished onlookers, engines decelerating, and no voice-over during the first 40 seconds. As the island spaceship descends, the announcer intones, "Every year, we fly more people across the Atlantic than the entire population of Manhattan."

Although British Airways attempted to induce all its country managers to run the commercial, not all cooperated. In India, there were questions about the relevance of

Manhattan to Indian customers. Japan rejected the commercial as inappropriate because the challenge for advertising was first to make Britain attractive as a destination, then turn to British Airways as the best choice. In South Africa, 90 seconds were not available for commercial time.

In the end, the commercial was launched in 20 countries. The results showed positive improvement in most local markets. In the United States, especially, awareness of the company rose significantly and unaided recall of the advertising was high. Most important for the advertising industry, the campaign showed that the extra money spent on superior execution of global TV commercials could produce strong effects in local markets even without adaptation.

Sources: Quelch, 1984; Stuart Elliott," British Air Joins a Flight to New Saatchi," *New York Times,* May 3, 1995, pp. D1, D9.

Budgeting and Organization

In *domestic* markets, a common method for advertising budgets is **percentage-of-sales,** setting a certain percentage of last year's sales as next year's budget. The figure arrived at can be adjusted by considering a changing competitive situation, increasing growth objectives, or a squeeze on company profits; but percentage-of-sales has the advantage of establishing a stable and predictable expenditure level tied to revenues. The percentage chosen can be calibrated against the industry average ratio of advertising-to-sales, making for easy comparisons with competitors.

Although percentage-of-sales is popular among firms from most countries, it is not a very useful method for setting *global* advertising budgets. Even if total worldwide revenues can be used as a base, it is not clear what the appropriate percentage would be. Which country's industry average should be used as a starting point, for example? Different countries show widely different levels of advertising-to-sales ratios for the same industry, depending on media availability, competitive situation, and so on. Since the percentage-of-sales approach sets advertising on the basis of past sales, it is of little use when a shift from multidomestic to global advertising is contemplated. **Competitive parity** approaches, where advertising budgets are set on the basis of what competitors spend, are also of less relevance in global advertising. The main difficulty is to identify the appropriate parity to actual and potential competitors from different countries, many of which have very different FSAs and market presence. Competitive parity is most appropriate when the major global competitors are from the same countries, as with Coca-Cola and Pepsi-Cola, or with Sony, Matsushita, Sharp, and other Japanese players in consumer electronics.

Budgeting for global advertising typically involves some version of the so-called **objective-task method** favored domestically by more sophisticated marketers. In this method the objectives of the advertising are first made explicit and quantified, after which the requisite media spending to reach the required exposure levels is specified. Although precise calibration of spending is difficult because of the uncertainty in gauging worldwide audiences of media vehicles, the basic logic is sound. After the initial specification of the job to be done by advertising (target percentages for awareness, for example, or certain reach and frequency figures), the creative solutions and the media schedules likely to attain the levels desired are developed.

This is work requiring the expertise of an ad agency with a global network. The budgeting done for global advertising involves an unusually large amount of agency input, since assessing the feasibility and cost of global campaigns requires input from the

The Global Advertising Agency

The drive toward global advertising has to a large extent been supported by **global advertising agencies** that have developed worldwide networks of subsidiaries or affiliates.

Agency Globalization

Most large agencies in the United States and Europe today have more or less global reach (by contrast, the Japanese agencies, including large Dentsu, are very minor players outside of Asia), but the ability to execute a global campaign can vary because of uneven local capability. A more established and tightly knit network of branches and joint ventures around the globe has paid off very well for large integrated agencies in the new global environment. This meant that a firm such as McCann-Erickson, the largest global player before the mergers, gained business in the early 1990s from independent local agencies in Europe and Asia. In 1994, IBM centralized all its advertising to the global network of Ogilvy & Mather Worldwide, one of the large New York–based agencies.[10] However, as always, the trend can turn back (see box, "Coca-Cola's Global Agency Network").

As ad agencies expanded their global reach, many advertisers started to centralize their advertising spending and appointed a single firm as the global agency. This meant that many smaller agencies lost accounts as large firms consolidated their ad spending. As a result, smaller agencies merged and became part of larger global networks. Soon, even large agencies were gobbled up as consolidation continued. But the individual agency names tend to remain, partly because of the brand equity vested in the name. This makes for some confusion, since most if not all of the creative aspects of the business is still with the individual agencies, and the competition for a client can be between agencies under the same umbrella holding company. Exhibit 16.7 shows the "Big Four" agency conglomerates and their main agency brands.

With the members of the groups being large agencies in their own right and often with a proud history, most mergers have retained the independence of the individual units as far as possible. This strategy has been all the more important as many mergers placed accounts from competitors under the same roof. But it also means that the combined units, although large and well represented in many countries, tend to have some difficulty in making the parts work together (see box, "Ad Agencies' Acquisition Pains").

The Agency's Task

The global advertising agency will generally develop the message and media schedule working intimately with the advertiser and using its local representation in the various markets. The creative development and the production of a prototype ad or standardized commercial are usually centralized at an agency with headquarters in the company's home country and branch offices in the relevant market countries. The top 10 worldwide agency brands are shown in Exhibit 16.8.

The large multinational with entries in many country markets will generally find it advantageous from a control and coordination perspective to rely on a worldwide

---

EXHIBIT 16.7
The "Big Four" and Their
Main Agencies (*2006 revenues,
US$ in billions*)

1. Omnicom Group (U.S., Revenues $11.4); BBD&O, DDB, and TBWA.
2. WPP Group (U.K., Revenues $10.82); J. Walter Thompson, Young & Rubicam, Grey.
3. Interpublic (U.S., Revenues $6.1); McCann-Erickson, FCB, Lowe.
4. Publicis (France, Revenues $5.87); Leo Burnett, Saatchi & Saatchi, Fallon, Kaplan, Thaler Group.

Source: http://adage.com/datacenter.

Getting the Picture

COCA-COLA'S GLOBAL AGENCY NETWORK

In the early 1990s, the Coca-Cola Company radically changed its relationships with Madison Avenue. Following a "think global, act local" strategy, Coca-Cola shifted several assignments from McCann-Erickson, its main worldwide agency for 30 years, and instead relied on local talent to create exciting and trendy advertising under the overall tag line of "Always Coca-Cola."

Freely reshuffling the agency roster throughout the 1990s, Coke kept the pressure on creative talent. The advertising successes included Classic Coke from Edge Creative in Los Angeles and Diet Coke from Fallon McElligott of Minneapolis and Lintas Paris. Both brands were global leaders in their categories, Diet Coke marketed in many countries as Coca-Cola Light.

However, the dawn of the new millennium brought another change in Coca-Cola's global advertising strategy. With Coke's sharply lower stock price and tarnished image in several markets, a change was mandatory. The new mantra became "think local, act local." A new ad campaign "Life Tastes Good" was devised to focus on Coke's distinctive contour bottle and the product's effervescence in an attempt to embody a connection between Coke and life's happy moments.

The new strategy involved giving agencies responsibility for countries and regions first (an area organizational form). The logic was that an agency can then specialize in their particular market regions, promoting several of Coke's brands in those areas.

The account shakeup resulted in six agencies being given responsibility for the Coca-Cola brand and all its products in 139 countries around the world. Under the new organization plan the following agencies shared the worldwide advertising for Coke:

McCann-Erickson Worldwide was still the largest Coke agency with 49 countries, including Japan, Malaysia,

Mexico, the Middle East, the Netherlands, and South Africa.

Leo Burnett Worldwide was the agency of record for 26 countries including Argentina, Brazil, France, Germany, the United States, and Venezuela.

Publicis Worldwide was the agency of record for 25 countries including Australia, Sweden, Switzerland, Thailand, Turkey, and the United Kingdom.

D'Arcy Masius Benton & Bowles was awarded 20 countries, including Argentina, Australia, China, the United Kingdom, the United States, and Yugoslavia.

Lowe Lintas & Partners Worldwide managed brands in 11 countries, including Austria, Brazil, and Canada.

Bates Worldwide had responsibility for 8 mainly emerging countries, including Indochina, the Philippines, Romania, and South Africa.

Not only did the allocation of countries cut across all the common regional borders, but there was also duplication of country assignments. It was simply not possible for Coke to structure the agency responsibilities strictly along country lines.

Of course, nothing stays the same for long in advertising. By 2005, McCann had been given a reduced assignment while a new agency, Weiden+Kennedy, had been brought in. Who said global advertising is simple?

Sources: Stefano Hatfield, "Coke Ads Need Extra Fizz," *The Times,* January 28, 2000; Karen Benezra and Eleftheria Parpis, "Chasing Coca-Cola. As He Exits, How Does Zyman's Performance Rate?" *Brandweek,* March 30, 1998, pp. 1, 5–6; Mickey Gramig, "Coca-Cola to Release New Ads, but Retain Multi-Agency Approach," *The Atlanta Journal-Constitution,* May 14, 1998, p. 5F; Melanie Wells, "Coke Classic Ads Have Life," *USA Today,* October 19, 1998, p. 8B; Scott Leith, "Coke Ads Mark Return to Tradition," *The Atlanta Journal-Constitution,* April 20, 2001, p. 1D; Jane Bainbridge, "Coke's New Ad Focuses on Capturing Real-Life Moments," *Marketing,* May 31, 2001, p. 26; **adage.com.**

agency. Unilever, the large packaged goods company headquartered in London, employed J. Walter Thompson, part of the WPP Group, to handle most of its products and markets. Volkswagen was so impressed by Doyle Dane and Bernbach, an American agency, in its handling of Volkswagen's U.S. account that it gave the agency responsibility for its other country markets, including the home market in Germany. It deserves to be emphasized, however, that many of these arrangements are volatile. When expected sales and market share increases don't materialize, an agency shake-up is common. Coca Cola has changed its global agency line-up at least five times since the early 1990s. Nike changed its agency in 2007 to Crispin Porter & Bogusky to inject new creativity in the brand's advertising. Long term relationships and loyalty do matter, however. McCann-Erickson has long had at least part of the Coke business, and continues to do so. Nike stayed faithful to its Oregonian neighbor agency Wieden & Kennedy for 24 years before switching.

It is also common for companies to allot their advertising money to agencies in the local market when conditions in a country are particularly difficult or unique. Thus, Japanese multinational companies rely on the giant Dentsu or Hakuhodo agencies of

Getting the Picture

AD AGENCIES' ACQUISITION PAINS

Jockeying for position as world agency number one, McCann-Erickson Worldwide has set its sights firmly on the top spot by seeking to expand its international reach and capability farther. In the world of advertising this usually means building up the client base by acquiring agencies in foreign countries.

The lead agency within the Interpublic group, McCann was the first agency to embark on a deliberate policy of international development, and also the first to acquire foreign agencies. With 25 member agencies in its fold, McCann has the global size to offer a high level of expertise in integrated marketing communications across the world's cultures.

Growing by acquisition has its own problems. One is the possibility of conflict between the existing and the new clients. For example, in July 2001 a conflict arose when Interpublic acquired Foote, Cone & Belding. F,C&B handled S. C. Johnson, a multinational household cleaning products company. McCann already handled the account of a big competitor to Johnson, Reckitt Benckiser. The Benckiser management decided to part ways with McCann and take its $300 million account elsewhere. Similarly, Interpublic's acquisition also precipitated Foote, Cone & Belding's losing the Pepsi account since Interpublic agencies had long worked for Coca-Cola Co.

Interpublic is public, that is, its shares are listed and sold on the stock market. This means that the managers at head-

quarters have to be responsive to stock analysts and investors and not only pay attention to the agency work of creating ads. A prominent example of what this can do to creative talent is the fate of Saatchi & Saatchi, a London-based agency often credited with inventing global advertising (see the earlier box in this chapter, "Global Ads Taking Flight").

In early 1995 Saatchi & Saatchi, part of the Cordiant group and then one of the world's largest advertising agencies, was in trouble. Three years of recessionary economies around the world had led to lowered billings. The expansion of the agency business into marketing consulting had to be cut short. The acquisitions of several large agencies had placed a heavy debt burden on the London-based home office. And the bondholders and stockholders of the publicly listed company included professional money managers of pension funds who demanded high returns on their portfolios. In a coup engineered by American shareholders, chairman Maurice Saatchi, an advertising wizard who had founded the agency in 1970, and his brother Charles were ousted.

As analysts tried to diagnose Saatchi & Saatchi's problems, one thing stood out: A large multinational agency might need strong financial managers, but can it still allow enough freedom for the creative people to be a successful ad agency?

Sources: *Washington Post*, January 4, 1995; *New York Times*, January 12, 1995; Jane L. Levere, "Conflict Ends a Relationship," *New York Times*, November 27, 2001, p. C8.

EXHIBIT 16.8
Top 10 Core Agencies Worldwide

Source: Copyright © *Advertising Age* Data Center. Reprinted with permission.

Rank		Agency	Headquarters	Worldwide Revenue		
2006	2005			2006	2006	% Change
1	1	Dentsu [Dentsu Inc.]	Tokyo	$2,213.00	$2,165.90	2.2
2	3	BBDO Worldwide* [Omnicom]	New York	1,539.90	1,425.80	8
3	2	McCann Erickson Worldwide* [Interpublic]	New York	1,479.20	1,461.10	1.2
4	4	JWT* [WPP]	New York	1,286.50	1,245.00	3.3
5	5	DDB Worldwide Communications* [Omnicom]	New York	1,263.90	1,190.60	6.2
6	6	Publicis* [Publicis]	Paris, N.Y./ France	1,177.80	1,154.20	2
7	7	TBWA Worldwide* [Omnicom]	New York	1,135.00	950.2	19.4
8	8	Leo Burnett Worldwide* [Publicis]	Chicago	909	889.1	2.2
9	10	Y&R* [WPP]	New York	820	788	4.1
10	9	Hakuhodo [Hakuhodo DY Holdings]	Tokyo	780	788	-10

Notes: U.S. Dollars are in millions. (*Revenue is *Advertising Age* estimate and represents worldwide core-level returns from advertising only for the global network. Figures exclude revenue from nonadvertising operations such as direct marketing, sales promotion, interactive, media buying and planning.

Tokyo to handle many of their markets in Asia, but not the American market. Most of the personnel in a particular branch office (even a wholly owned subsidiary) of a multinational agency will be natives of the branch country. Even so, the avoidance of the home country agency by the Japanese is simply a step to ensure that the campaign will have no ethnocentric overtones. At the same time, the tendency for the U.S. multinationals is to prefer dealing with American agencies abroad. This practice might be questioned, since in the annual Clio awards given by an international jury to well-crafted and imaginative advertising, American ads tend to fare less well. But then, American-based advertising agencies rely largely on local talent in their offices abroad.

Research shows that the extent to which local branches focus on global advertising is relatively limited. By contrast, regionally coordinated advertising campaigns were more common. In a survey of 347 foreign branches of U.S. agencies it was found that about two-thirds (232) had at some time participated in multicountry advertising initiated by the home office.[11] Of these multicountry campaigns, most were regional in scope, followed by major-markets-only campaigns, with less than 10 percent truly global. According to the researchers, the emphasis on **pan-regional advertising** campaigns is mainly due to the emergence of regional groupings and trading blocs.

Local agencies are often preferable (and sometimes the only ones willing to accept the assignment) when the account is small. The reason is that global agencies, owing to their sheer size, tend to neglect smaller accounts. Even though payment agreements differing from the standard commission fee of 15 percent can be negotiated, the multinational agencies still tend to concentrate on the more important large accounts. This drawback for small local campaigns can be eliminated with the help of globalized campaigns directed from headquarters and managed through the local branch office of a multinational agency. Even though a particular country shows a small account size, the globally pooled advertising budget can be substantial.

One particular headache of agency–advertiser relations is the across-country variability in financial arrangements and payments. Advertisers in some countries insist on paying for the agency services with the product advertised or some other type of "countertrade." The agency then has to arrange the media payments. It is not surprising that some of the highly leveraged global agencies exhibit rather low levels of profitability, creating pressure from irate bondholders and shareholders, as the Saatchi & Saatchi experience demonstrates.

Message and Creative

For good reasons, message, visuals, and language translation are the aspects most consistently and thoroughly discussed in the literature on global advertising. Even experienced ad people commit mistakes with ease. And once committed, the faux pas are painfully obvious. The examples are legion (see box, "Translated Messages Have Their Pitfalls").

Message translation is complicated because of the cultural diversity among the various countries of the world. Language difference is only the most obvious manifestation of this diversity. Other factors, more subtle and therefore treacherous, include the use of idiomatic expressions to signify other matters than the ones literally expressed. An example is the slogan "Avoid embarrassment—use Quink" for an ink product, which translated into Spanish became "Avoid pregnancy—use Quink." Cultural symbolism makes darkened teeth very attractive among some Asian people, creates difficulties in employing an animal as a trademark across cultures (even the tiger had to be given up by Exxon in some countries, such as India), and forces close scrutiny of numbers and colors (4 is the number of death in Japan, as is 3 in the Philippines; 13 is not acceptable in the United States and Western Europe; black *and* white are funerary colors in Asia; white is happiness in Europe; red is a masculine color in Italy and feminine in northern Europe; and so on).[12]

Identical Ads

In the most extreme form of global advertising, the messages and visuals are identical, usually with localization only in terms of language voice-over changes and simple

Getting the Picture

TRANSLATED MESSAGES HAVE THEIR PITFALLS

Small nuances in words sometimes matter a lot. An American manufacturer in the auto industry advertised its batteries as "highly rated." In Venezuela the translation made it "highly overrated." A shirt manufacturer advertising in Mexico also had trouble with the Spanish language. Instead of declaring, "When I used this shirt I felt good," the character in the advertisement asserted, "Until I used this shirt I felt good."

Sexual connotations under the surface of day-to-day language create pitfalls. Chrysler tried to use its American slogan "Dart Is Power" in Latin American markets only to find that the message implied that drivers of the car lacked sexual vigor. An airline advertising its "rendezvous lounges" on its flights did not realize that to many Europeans a rendezvous carries the distinct connotation of meeting a lover for an illicit affair. Otis Elevators promoted parts of its line in

Russia as "completion equipment," which in Russian became "tools for orgasms."

Brand names are well-known stumbling blocks. Chevrolet's Nova car meant "won't go" in Spanish markets (fortunately, the company discovered this before entry). In Mexico, "Fresca" is slang for "lesbian." "Pinto," the Ford car, had to be renamed "Corcel" in Brazil after it was discovered that pinto was slang for the male appendage. The Japanese, on the other hand, have maintained several of their domestic names (in order to keep the Japanese connection) even though experts warned them that names such as "Facom" and "Datsun" ("That soon?") elicit snide remarks among English speakers. Such examples demonstrate why it is desirable to employ local agencies rather than rely on a home country agency that works at a distance from the market.

Sources: Ricks, 1993; and personal interviews.

copy translations. Pan-European advertising featuring Exxon gasoline's tiger in the tank and Marlboro cigarettes' cowboy is an example. In some cases the **identical ads** or commercials can be used without any translation at all. Levi's, the jeans manufacturer, uses cartoons with rock music and unintelligible, vaguely Esperanto-sounding vocals in one commercial where the Levi's-wearing hero rescues a beautiful woman from a burning building, an easily comprehended message. In other cases the commercials simply carry subtitles. IBM shows Italian-speaking nuns discussing the pros and cons of Internet surfing with subtitles translating the conversation: global ad, with a local touch.

Prototype Advertising

Then there are **global prototypes** in which the voice-over and the visual may be changed to avoid language and cultural problems; the ad may also be reshot with local spokespeople but using the same visualization. Drakkar Noir, a man's fragrance, in an Arab print ad shows a woman's hand caressing a man's hand holding the product; in the United States the same hand grasps the man's wrist. Colgate-Palmolive and Coca-Cola often use prototypes of actual commercial and advertisement samples that demonstrate what headquarters wants in the ads with specific written guidelines for acceptable deviations from the prototypes in terms of story and message (usually limited flexibility) and creative aspects (layout, color, symbols—usually more flexibility), with suggestions for appropriate media.

Pattern Standardization

A similar but less-structured global approach involves **pattern standardization,** in which the positioning theme is unified and some alternative creative concepts supporting the positioning are spelled out but the actual execution of the ads differs between markets. This has become perhaps the most common approach, since it allows creative flexibility at the local level. In particular, it allows the local execution to reflect differences in the use of copy versus visuals. The European ads for Xerox, the copier maker, often carry more copy than their corresponding ads in the United States, for example. To ensure the desired degree of uniformity, companies might send along photos showing the manner in which the product line should be illustrated. Electrolux, the European white goods manufacturer, sends CD-ROMs to its various subsidiaries from which the product displays can be downloaded and printed by each subsidiary's local agency.

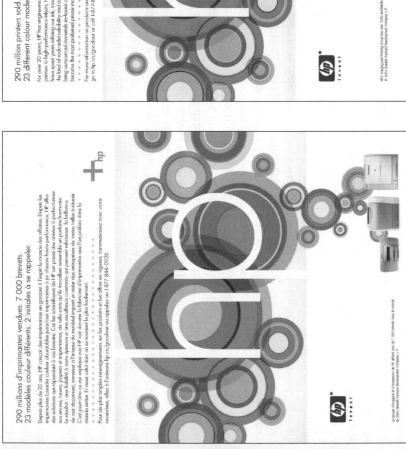

Two identical advertisements for Hewlett-Packard color printers, in French and English. The brand name, the theme, the positioning, the layout, the visual, and the copy are the same. The only difference is the language translation. Source: G. E. Belch and M. A. Belch, *Advertising and Promotion*, 5th ed. (New York: McGraw-Hill/Irwin, 2001), p. 689.

The two alternative strategies, prototype advertising and pattern standardization, are compared and contrasted in Exhibit 16.9. As the exhibit shows, in most respects the two are similar. The differences are in the choice of actors and the actual words spoken, which are chosen locally in pattern standardization. The types of media used are also a matter of local choice in pattern standardization, although the actual vehicles chosen will vary locally also in prototype advertising. The pattern-standardization strategy allows more freedom in reshooting a commercial or developing an advertisement.

Media Selection

If message creation needs the collaboration of the agency and the advertiser (to ensure a unified positioning theme), **media selection** is one area where the agency and its local representative rule. The reason is primarily expertise. Local knowledge of the

EXHIBIT 16.9
A Comparison of Which Features Two Global Advertising Strategies Keep the Same.

Prototype Advertising	Pattern Standardization
Brand name	Brand name
Theme	Theme
Visual	Visual
Positioning	Positioning
Actors	No, different actors
Words	No, different words
Language (local)	Language (local)
Media	No, localized
Materials	Some
Slogan	Slogan

availability of media alternatives is absolutely necessary so that the optimal media, given the constraints, are chosen. It might be possible to direct an advertising campaign from overseas insofar as budgeting, message creation, and general direction go, but the media choices must be made locally.

However, with the growth of global communications conglomerates, the negotiations involved in setting media costs are increasingly centralized. Buying media for many countries in one package from a global communications giant such as News Corporation, lead by Australian Rupert Murdoch, is best done from the center where the appropriate quantity discounts can be applied. Thus, while the particular program or newspaper used for the advertising can still be decided locally, the TV station or the newspaper would best belong to one conglomerate so that the lowest price can be obtained.

Varying media usage across regions was shown in Exhibit 16.3. As noted earlier, rates of media usage are determined by a number of factors—such as availability of commercial TV and radio, level of economic development, literacy rates, religion, and so forth—and reflect directly, of course, the actual media selection decisions made by the advertisers and agencies for the country in question.

What type of media to select hinges (within the availability constraints) very much on the objectives and target segment(s) of the campaign.

For *awareness*, television serves well in many countries where it is generally available. In markets with lower rates of TV penetration, radio can often be used to supplement television advertising. Television in most cases has the advantage of a high-attention value, especially in countries where it is relatively rare.

Effective communication of knowledge about a product usually requires the use of words, whether spoken or written. If illiteracy is a problem, knowledge will have to be transmitted through the spoken word and radio would be a logical candidate. Where literacy is high but the number of appropriate magazines low, newspapers might have to serve. In most Western nations the best medium for knowledge creation is the magazine, where specific selling points about the product can be well communicated. It is no coincidence, as noted earlier, that it is in these same countries that "rational," multiattributed product evaluations seem to be most applicable.

For *attitude* change and *image* building, newspapers and radio advertising are generally inferior to television and magazines. Cinema and outdoor advertising are important in certain countries. In Argentina, cinema is an important medium precisely because of the affective spillover from the movie's context and, of course, because of the captive audience (Argentines, unlike Americans, don't seem to mind). In most countries television is the most important medium for emotional communication, since it combines visual and verbal stimuli.

To affect *behavior* directly, the media chosen have to be timely; that is, they have to reach the audience near the time of purchase. Newspapers fulfill this function well in most cultures. Magazines (and TV) tend to be less useful here, unless the product can be sold through the special direct marketing channels opened up in some countries. An example of the latter is the United States, where credit cards are used to pay by telephone for goods advertised on TV. It is also at this stage that online ads seem to be more powerful. A presence on the Internet is good for a brand, and will generate some positive affinity, but the real impact of Web ads is in the way they can intervene in a consumer's decision process, and point to an alternative choice.

Once the media types have been decided upon, the particular vehicles to be used within each type are usually selected on the basis of some efficiency criterion, such as "cost per thousand" (CPM). The use of an efficiency criterion requires information about how much advertising in a vehicle costs and how many people (in the target market) will be reached. Here a major problem is encountered in many markets. The available audience measurements are either incomplete (lacking audience demographics, for example) or unreliable or even nonexistent. Even in developed countries it is sometimes hard to find accurate figures properly validated by independent agencies. As a result, it is often very difficult to be precise about the computation of an index such as the CPM. Again, local people with in-depth knowledge of the various media vehicles should be consulted before choices are made.

On the cost side, the rate schedules for advertising may provide great discounts for large quantity and special rebates, often to domestic agencies over foreign agencies. Again, the local connection becomes important in negotiations about proper pricing and payment procedures.

The Digitalization of Advertising

Digital communication, whether it is via television, the Internet, e-mails, or via cell phones or some other medium, poses both a threat and an opportunity to global advertisers and ad agencies.[13]

There is a big shift to digital in the way all existing media (TV, radio, outdoor, and print) deliver their messages. According to *Advertising Age*, in 2006 U.S. ad agencies collectively generated less than half of their revenue—46.4 percent—from traditional advertising and media planning/buying, with the rest coming from a range of marketing services including digital/interactive, direct marketing, and sales promotion. Marketing services grabbed 53.6 percent of U.S. marketing-communications agency revenue, up from 51.5 percent in 2005. A lot of the online spending is more or less automatically global—and although precise data are hard to come by, the pattern is similar or even stronger in other countries. The Internet might not have changed "everything," but it has changed a lot of things.

Total online ad spending worldwide was at $18.7 billion in 2005, and is projected to grow to $42.7 billion in 2009. U.S. online advertising alone grew from $12.5 billion in 2005 to $16.8 billion in 2006, or 34 percent in one year. It is projected to keep growing, although at a slower pace, up to $36.5 billion by 2011. Exhibit 16.10 shows how global online advertising is still a relatively small share of total advertising, but keeps growing at a faster rate. As can be seen, online advertising on search is projected to take an increasing share of the increased Internet spending.

The digitalization of advertising is having an effect on the industry. In 2006 the large French-based ad agency conglomerate Publicis paid $1.3 billion for an interactive agency, Digitas, to get up to speed with digital services. Since January 2006, the four biggest conglomerates (Omnicom, WPP, Interpublic, and Publicis) bought, or made investments in, more than 20 interactive ventures. The fact is that the traditional advertising business lacks the skills necessary to compete in the fast-growing digital arena, and therefore pay high prices to acquire young start-ups with specialists in the online business.

The advantage of the online medium is not simply its interactivity and targeting ability. It speaks more directly to the attractive younger market segments. It is also cost-effective in that the communications are virtually costless. As always with the Internet, barring government interference and blocking of access, the reach is inherently global. There are also intermediaries that can help with the necessary promotion and links. One way is to pay Google or some other search engine to place your Web address in a sidebar ad, appearing when certain terms are searched for. In fact, in a kind of reverse arrangement, Google even offers a program called AdSense that helps any one Web site to generate funds by allowing other businesses to place ads on the Web site in question. The AdSense program identifies appropriate ads from Google's own AdWords advertising base and helps place them on the Web site. The owner of the Web site gets paid when a visitor to its site clicks on the ad placed there by Google.

But the digitalization of advertising is also facilitating more traditional tasks. Media selection, the monitoring of campaign progress, and scheduling of insertions (the

EXHIBIT 16.10
Global Online Advertising, 2005–2009

Source: *Marketing News*, July 15, 2007, p.28.

Year	US$ Billion	% of Total	% of Online Ad Spending	
			Display	Search
2005	18.7	4.6 %	37.6 %	41.9 %
2006	24.5	5.7 %	35.2 %	43.4 %
2007	31.3	6.9 %	33.4 %	44.6 %
2008	36.9	7.7 %	32.1 %	45.5 %
2009	42.7	8.4 %	31.1 %	46.2 %

traditional domain of the agency's "traffic" department) are much facilitated by online access. The pattern standardization strategy for advertising message and creative discussed in this chapter gains immeasurably from digitalization. For example, the original advertisement or commercial film can be digitally transmitted to any one subsidiary around the world, and easily localized and adapted to each market. There is no need to spend time or effort on specifying exactly what each country can and cannot do. Instead, basic instructions for localization can be given and any necessary or desired local deviation can easily be sent back to headquarters for approval.

Digitalization also poses some threats. As more and more media are delivered via Internet Protocol (IP), they will be subject to what is called *disintermediation*. Disintermediation means that the audience will take control away from the channel intermediary. A good example is television, where TiVo and other DVRs not only can eliminate commercials but also shift the time of the program. Viewers actively avoid commercials and rearrange broadcasts into chunks that are time-shifted to correspond with their own schedules. The same thing will happen with radio and print as all media become increasingly interactive.

But these threats are also opportunities. Many observers claim that the ensuing empowering of the consumer will mean that there is more need than before to be communicating directly or indirectly with the consumer. This is why global advertising spending is projected to keep rising, as we saw in Exhibit 16.2.

Close-Up: Goodyear in Latin America

The way in which the headquarters managers, the local subsidiaries, and the ad agency work together to generate a global advertising campaign can be illustrated through Goodyear's development of a pan-regional campaign for Latin America.

Goodyear, the large American tire company headquartered in Akron, Ohio, has long taken a standardized approach to its advertising. Under the assumption that customer needs and wants in tires are largely dependent on basic factors such as climate and road conditions, the company has centrally coordinated its international advertising since the early 1970s. Goodyear's present regional approach has evolved into a prototype standardization program that involves the local subsidiaries in decision making more than previously. Its Latin American market advertising gains global scale advantages while remaining responsive to local conditions.[14]

Planning for a unified regional advertising strategy that properly involves local subsidiaries needs to start early. For Goodyear, prompted by a reorganization in 1992, the process began about 12 months before the new campaign rolled out. The planning process involved six stages (see Exhibit 16.11).

1. Preliminary Orientation (September)

The beginning stage was an educational one, allowing both headquarters and local subsidiary staff to understand each other's perspectives. Headquarters informed the subsidiaries of the benefits expected from a pan-regional approach, and the subsidiaries were asked to provide information about their current and planned communication strategies. To emphasize the pan-regional benefits, the regional director of Latin American sales and marketing described the cost reductions from lower trade barriers for advertising materials and the advantage of having available a bank of high-quality standardized commercials. Each national sales director was asked to provide answers to several strategic business questions, including brand image perceptions in their respective markets.

2. Regional Meeting to Define Communications Strategy (October)

An informal two-day working conference was organized in Miami where the communications strategy could be developed. From headquarters came the regional vice president for Latin America, the director of sales and marketing communications, and the

EXHIBIT 16.11
Goodyear's Latin American Campaign Development Stages

Source: David A. Hanni, John K. Ryans, Jr., and Ivan R. Vernon (1995), "Executive Insights: Coordinating International Advertising—The Goodyear Case Revisited for Latin America," *Journal of International Marketing* 3, no. 2, p. 88. Reprinted by permission of Michigan State University Press.

---

1. Preliminary orientation, September 1992

Subsidiary strategic information input on business and communications strategy on country-by-country basis. Home office review.

2. Regional communications strategy definition meeting, October 1992

Outputs: Regional positioning objective, communication objectives, and creative assignment for advertising agency.

3. Advertising creative review meeting, November 12, 1992

Outputs: Six creative concepts (storyboards). Research questions regarding real consumer concerns to guide research.

4. Qualitative research stage, November–December 1992

Consistent research results across five countries on purchase intentions and consumer perceptions of safety.

5. Research review meeting, January 15, 1993

Sharply defined "consumer proposition" identified and agreed upon with new creative assignment for agency.

6. Final creative review meeting, March 12, 1993

Campaign adoption.

---

manager of marketing research. From the subsidiaries came the sales director and the advertising manager for each country. Also participating were regional account executives and creative directors from Leo Burnett Worldwide, the recently appointed global ad agency based in Chicago with offices in Latin America.

The purpose was to develop an "umbrella" campaign theme that would fit all countries but with subsidiary autonomy to prepare retail, promotional, and product advertising to meet local requirements. The umbrella theme would make sure that local creative concepts reinforced common positioning and would make possible centralized (and thus cost-effective) production of a pan-regional pool of television commercials and print advertisements.

Everyone involved at the October meeting was requested to look at tire advertising afresh, disregarding previous regional campaigns to the extent possible. The various participants were happy to discover that no one country's problems were in fact unique, a common base soon emerged, and participants were able to agree on a unified positioning strategy to build brand equity throughout the region. At the same time, needs for local adaptation were uncovered. For example, even though Spanish is a common language among all the countries except Brazil, national differences in word choice and pronunciations made localized voice-over necessary (see box, "Smile and Say 'Tires'").

Using local talent would enable the country units to employ spokespeople with regional appeal. On the basis of the subsidiaries' input, a pattern standardization solution of the regional advertising campaign seemed logical.

Involving the ad agency at this early stage facilitated development of the creative brief for the pan-regional ads. To follow up on the development of creative alternatives, a task force was organized, consisting of advertising managers and sales directors from each country, the regional sales and communications directors from headquarters, and agency people (including creative teams from five countries).

3. Advertising Creative Meeting (November)

The task force met to consider six alternative concepts or storyboards developed by the creative teams. Each of the five creative teams explained and defended its particular concept or storyboard, and lengthy discussions ensued. The outcome was a decision to collect more data on the concepts from customers in the respective countries. Specifically, more marketing research was judged necessary to identify the extent to which the campaigns were targeted correctly at real consumer concerns.

Getting the Picture

"SMILE AND SAY 'TIRES' "

Goodyear has identified four different ways to say "tires" in Latin America, and a fifth way to say it in Puerto Rico. In some of these countries one of the expressions occurs less frequently, while in other countries expressions other than the main one either will not be understood or may convey an entirely different meaning. It's important to pick the right word for each local market.

Spanish word for tires	Countries using each word
Cauchos	Venezuela
Cubiertas	Argentina
Gomas	Puerto Rico
Llantas	Mexico, Peru, Guatemala, Colombia, and elsewhere in Central America
Neumaticos	Chile

Source: David A. Hanni, John K. Ryans, Jr., and Ivan R. Vernon (1995), "Executive Insights: Coordinating International Advertising—The Goodyear Case Revisited for Latin America," *Journal of International Marketing* 3, no. 2, p. 96. Reprinted by permission of Michigan State University Press.

4. Qualitative Research Stage (November–December)

The research on the proposed concept storyboards focused on two main issues. One was customers' degree of concern about safety and security of the tires. The second issue involved consumer reactions to four different creative themes:

a. Authority based on an emotional appeal.
b. Leadership positioning.
c. Technology transfer.
d. Advanced technology with rational appeal.

Using focus groups in five countries (Brazil, Chile, Colombia, Mexico, and Venezuela) to test the alternatives, the company found that the results were consistent throughout the region, with safety and security a strong theme everywhere, and with support for an emotional authority-based approach. It was also found that the typical "We are not the same" local sentiments were overstated: The respondents in each country rated their roads "the worst in Latin America."

5. Research Review Meeting (January)

The task force met to consider the research results. The aim was to reach a consensus on one unique selling proposition, a convincing argument why consumers should change their beliefs about tires and choose Goodyear. This theme would be the recurring motto serving to unify the various local executions.

The outcome of the meeting was a succinctly worded "consumer proposition," a theme that was assigned to the ad agency for the development of a full pan-regional campaign. In a subsequent meeting, the task force reviewed the creative proposals from the agency and its local creative teams, and further directions for the work were issued.

6. Final Creative Review (March)

At this final decision-making meeting of the task force, each team's concept was presented without indicating the team identity or the country in which the campaign originated. A regionwide creative team presented all the proposals, with the supporting material reflecting an entire campaign from print to outdoor media. This was done to avoid the "not invented here" syndrome and reduce the inclination to defend one's own particular proposal at all cost.

The process worked smoothly, as one of the campaigns was judged clearly superior in capturing the positional theme and creative concept. This campaign was adopted, and the agency and its local offices were instructed to proceed with full-fledged development of the campaign material and local executions. The production of the commercials, advertisements, and other support material took place through the summer months, and media buys were completed by the start of the campaign at the end of August.

Lessons

There are several points to emphasize about this illustration of an effective approach to pattern standardization in pan-regional advertising.

First, by focusing on regions it may be possible to reap the scale benefits and cost efficiencies of global advertising without sacrificing too much on the side of local adaptation. The recent emergence of new trading blocs suggests that this perspective can be generally useful.

Second, the early involvement of country subsidiaries and agency professionals not only facilitates later acceptance of unified themes but helps broaden the sources of powerful campaign concepts. This is especially useful since in most cases the local subsidiaries can be expected to have greater market knowledge than headquarters.

Third, and very important, the process by which pattern standardization is arrived at needs to allow open and free exchange. In the Goodyear case, it is striking how local differences seemed to be based on misperceptions that vanished once participants interacted without pressure to defend the home turf. By the same token, headquarters can't assume to know more about the markets involved than its local units but should focus on explaining carefully why standardization might be beneficial. The way the local operation fits into the whole needs to be clarified, and headquarters should not expect local units to sacrifice for the common good without a compelling rationale. Then, headquarters should be flexible when the local units suggest alternative options.

Fourth, even when the company has operated for years in a market, research is still necessary, especially when conditions are changing. Yesterday's solutions were perhaps good for yesterday's problems, but new times need new information and new solutions. A planning process that is systematic, thorough, and flexible—such as the one implemented by Goodyear—is far more likely to generate successful advertising campaigns than one based on a static and unchanging perception of the environment.

Summary

Despite the pitfalls of standardized and translated messages, global ads have become an important alternative to adapted multidomestic advertising. The technological advances in global communications, the growth of global media, and the strength of global advertising agencies have combined to make global advertising possible. And the positive spillovers from unified messages and the increasing homogeneity of many markets have made global advertising desirable.

As the affluence of countries grows, new products and services appear and customers need more information. Advertising becomes more important, and advertising expenditures as a percentage of the GDP increase. For the global marketer, faced with increasing spending needs in all markets, a coordinated effort with synchronized campaigns, pattern standardization, and unified image across trade regions is usually more effective and cost-efficient than multidomestic campaigns. We took note of the advantages, problems, and pitfalls of global advertising and discussed how the advertiser and ad agency can jointly develop a regional or global campaign, using as illustration a case study of one company, Goodyear.

Key Terms

brand image, 529
buyer action, 530
competitive parity, 531
global advertising, 518
global advertising agencies, 532
global prototypes, 536

hierarchy of effects, 524
identical ads, 536
localized advertising, 518
media selection, 537
message translation, 535
multidomestic advertising, 518

objective-task method, 531
pan-regional advertising, 535
pattern standardization, 536
percentage-of-sales, 531
Web advertisements, 522

Discussion Questions

1. Using library sources and the Internet, find three examples of global advertising. What characteristics make these campaigns global?

2. Using the same sources, can you find examples of global advertising for which the markets are not global but "multidomestic"?

3. Discuss what an advertiser may do to avoid conflicts with country managers when a global advertising campaign is contemplated.

4. How can an advertiser use the company Web site to create global advertising? How can the message be localized?

5. Rather than enforcing complete uniformity, global advertising tends to follow a "pattern standardization approach." What does this mean? How does this help avoid the pitfalls of standardized and translated messages?

Notes

1. These definitions are necessarily crude. Some "global" advertising, such as the pan-European ads done by Pioneer car audio products, is perhaps better seen as "regional." Even the most multidomestic advertising, such as that done for Budweiser beer in many countries, retains a certain similarity across markets, with the featured packaging and brand name remaining constant. As in the case of product standardization, global advertising is a matter of degree.

2. From Greyser, 1992.

3. See DeMooij and Keegan, 1991.

4. Although not always as advantageous as one would initially assume. In one case an American company wanted to use the same TV commercials abroad as the ones used at home, without any dubbing or change of language. But the actors employed for the U.S. commercials demanded so high a compensation for the world rights that reshooting the commercial with local talent became the cheaper option.

5. From Lippman, 1988.

6. See, for example, the contrasts between Banerjee, 1994, and Elliott, 1995a.

7. See Mueller, 1991.

8. From Harris, 1994.

9. See, for example, the role of Saatchi & Saatchi in the British Airways' decision to use global advertising.

10. See Johnson, 1994.

11. From Hill and Shao, 1994.

12. Many of these culturally based idiosyncrasies are documented by Ricks, 1993.

13. My colleague Gary Bamossy was very helpful with the material on digitalization of advertising.

14. The following account draws on the excellent article by Hanni et al., 1995.

Selected References

"Advertisers Seek Global Messages." *New York Times*, November 18, 1991.

Banerjee, Ashish. "Global Campaigns Don't Work: Multinationals Do." *Advertising Age* 65, no. 17 (April 18, 1994), p. 23.

Belch, George E., and Michael A. Belch. *Advertising and Promotion*, 5th ed. New York: McGraw-Hill/Irwin, 2001.

DeMooij, M. K., and Warren Keegan. *Advertising Worldwide*. London: Prentice Hall International, 1991.

Elliott, Stuart. "What's in a Name? Perhaps Billions." *New York Times*, August 12, 1992, p. D6.
———. "At Coke, a Shift to Many Voices." *New York Times*, January 20, 1995a, pp. D1, D6.
———. "Creative Agencies That Feel at Home in the Global Village Are Writing Their Own Tickets." *New York Times*, September 30, 1995b, p. D10.

"Firms Opt for Pan-Regional Marketing Strategies in EC." *Business International*, October 29, 1990.

Freeman, Laurie. "Colgate Axes Global Ads; Thinks Local." *Advertising Age*, November 26, 1990, sec. 1, pp. 1, 59.

Greyser, Stephen A. *Siemens: Corporate Advertising.* Harvard Business School case 593–022, 1992.

Greyser, Stephen A., and W. S. Schille. *British Airways: The World's Biggest Offer.* Harvard Business School case 592–051, 1993.

Hanni, David A.; John K. Ryans; and Ivan R. Vernon. "Coordinating International Advertising—The Goodyear Case Revisited for Latin America." *Journal of International Marketing* 3, no. 2 (1995), pp. 83–98.

Harris, Greg. "International Advertising Standardization: What Do the Multinationals Actually Standardize?" *Journal of International Marketing* 2, no. 4 (1994), pp. 13–30.

Hill, John S., and Alan T. Shao. "Agency Participants in Multicountry Advertising: A Preliminary Examination of Affiliate Characteristics and Environments." *Journal of International Marketing* 2, no. 2 (1994), pp. 29–48.

Johnson, Bradley. "Tumult Ahead for IBM, Ogilvy." *Advertising Age* 65, no. 23 (May 30, 1994), pp. 36–37.

Lippman, Joanne. "Marketers Turn Sour on Global Sales Pitch Harvard Guru Makes." *The Wall Street Journal*, May 12, 1988, p. 1.

Marketing News, July 15, 2007.

Mårtensson, Rita. *Innovations in Retailing.* Lund, Sweden: Liber, 1983.

Mueller, Barbara. "Multinational Advertising: Factors Influencing the Standardised versus Specialised Approach." *International Marketing Review* 8, no. 1 (1991), pp. 7–18.

Quelch, John. *British Airways.* Harvard Business School case 585–014, 1984.

Ricks, D. A. *Blunders in International Business.* Cambridge, MA: Blackwell, 1993.

Solomon, Michael R. *Consumer Behavior,* 2nd ed. Needham Heights, MA: Allyn & Bacon, 1992.

Sorenson, R. Z., and U. E. Wiechmann. "How Multinationals View Marketing Standardization." In D. N. Dickson, ed. *Managing Effectively in the World Marketplace.* New York: Wiley, 1983, pp. 301–16.

Wentz, Laurel. "Global Village." *Advertising Age*, November 21, 1994, p. 13.

———. "Global Marketers: Who Spends the Most Worldwide?" *Advertising Age*, November 19, 2007.

Wylie, Kenneth. "How and Why Marketing Services are Going Digital." Agency Profiles Yearbook, *Advertising Age*, April 30, 2007

Chapter

17

Global Promotion, E-Commerce, and Personal Selling

"In your face"

After reading this chapter, you will be able to:

1. See how to integrate global advertising with other promotional tools so a unified image and message is communicated.

2. Engage local representatives to find out exactly what local regulations are so that the constraints can be adjusted for implementation of the global promotion strategy.

3. Use the advances in the Internet, telecommunications, and express mail—as well as the development of address lists and the availability of credit cards—to transform direct mail from a simple promotional tool to a viable global marketing option, especially for small businesses.

4. Implement an e-commerce solution as a new medium that combines one-to-one communication and sales transactions— especially in services and in B2B.

5. Help design a field sales staff that can be the front-line service providers for global customers and be part of the localization of global strategies.

The main components of the promotional mix besides advertising are sales promotion, public relations, and publicity, as well as personal selling. This chapter will cover these plus some special international promotions, including international trade fairs and the use of direct marketing and e-commerce in a global setting.

Because of widely different local trade regulations and the obstacles of local customs and culture, at first sight many of these promotional activities don't seem good candidates for globalization. Global coordination of promotion is complicated by the fact that implementation and execution are in the hands of local employees. Local salespeople are necessary for running promotional schemes such as in-store displays, free samples, and contests. But globalized promotional activities have become very important in global marketing. The main reasons involve the globalization of markets, the growth of global media reach, and the resulting emergence of megastars and megabrands. Globally recognized endorsers and brand names are opening doors for global promotions.

Blowin' Your Own Horn

Bill Gates of Microsoft might not have been the first one—Anita Roddick of the Body Shop, Lee Iacocca when he was at Chrysler, and Richard Branson of Virgin Airlines were perhaps there before him—but he is surely one of the more visible ones. We are talking about CEOs who have taken on the role as their company's main spokesperson in advertising, publicity, and public relations.

Although the monopoly court case against Microsoft muted Bill Gates's public persona at the beginning of the new millennium, the launch of Windows 95 remains one of the more audacious uses ever of event marketing, publicity, and paid advertising. And in the middle of it all was the bespectacled face of Bill himself, managing to look like a freckled little kid although he has no freckles and was no longer a kid.

What the New York Times called "the splashiest, most frenzied, most expensive introduction of a computer product in the industry's history" started in New Zealand. Microsoft had announced it would release Windows 95 on August 24, 1995, and it kept that promise to the minute. Windows 95 went on sale at midnight in the first English-speaking country to greet the new day. As midnight arrived in one time zone after another, stores joined the hoopla with late-night hours, balloons, and special sales.

In New York, the company arranged for the Empire State Building to be lit with spotlights in colors from the Windows logo. In Toronto, the landmark CN Tower bore a Windows 95 banner. And in a move that dismayed some, Microsoft underwrote the cost of distributing the Times of London. A box at the top of the first page read, "Windows 95 Launch—Today The Times Is Free Courtesy of Microsoft." At the bottom of the first page was this ad: "Windows 95. So Good Even The Times Is Complimentary." The paper also carried an editorial supplement sponsored by Microsoft.

Meanwhile, in the Redmond, Washington, home of Microsoft, Bill Gates was throwing a party. Jay Leno hosted the introductory ceremonies, the product's theme song ("Start Me Up" by the Rolling Stones) was played, and commemorative T-shirts sold briskly. Those who didn't get an invitation could attend electronically. Microsoft made the party's sights and sounds available over the Internet (thereby promoting the product's easy-to-use Internet connection, known as the Microsoft Network). Forty-five Microsoft employees wielded digital cameras, sound digitizers, and other electronic equipment to record the festivities for anyone able to navigate the World Wide Web. And though the real-world party was a day long, the online version lasted over two weeks.

Such hoopla is also not foreign to the mind of Richard Branson, the founder and CEO of Virgin Atlantic Airways in London. Although he has paid such luminaries as Mike Myer's movie alter ego Austin Powers to promote Virgin, he, the founder, remains its corporate face and identity. Branson has continually worked to keep his outdoorsy features and unkempt hair in the public's collective consciousness, with stunts such as circling the globe in a hot air balloon (which crashed, unfortunately—or fortunately?—anything for publicity). Branson's entrepreneurial style has made Virgin Records a top music publishing label and established Virgin Atlantic as Britain's second largest long-haul airline. A similarly intrepid Brit, Anita Roddick, has taken her fights for the environment and against animal testing public, netting lots of free publicity for her Body Shop stores around the globe.

Another convert to the cause is Steve Jobs. Since the original co-founder returned to power at Apple Inc. in 1997, he has been on an almost religious mission to court the press and speak to the technocrats that are shaping the next generation of computer products. In a 2001 Time magazine cover story, Apple and Jobs were pointedly identified as the vehicles to unite disparate technology and simplify our home lives. Taking a cue from Bill Gates's use of the London Times, Time magazine's online edition even included a sales link to Apple, creating some questions of where the line between editorial content and advertising should be drawn. The enthusiasm is hardly unprecedented, but for many it remained a bit surprising that a niche product with around 10 percent of the market could receive such unswerving and purportedly objective publicity. The quid pro quo was an exclusive interview with Jobs, now apparently another corporate megastar.

Do these intense personal efforts pay off? Well, yes, judging from the companies' scorecards. To illustrate, many would not have predicted that while relatively faceless Compaq reported an 80 percent decline in the last quarter of 2001, Apple would post $1.4 billion in revenue, up 37 percent from a year ago. And that was before the i-Pod and the iPhone.

Sources: Carey Goldberg, "Midnight Sales Frenzy Ushers in Windows 95," *New York Times,* August 24, 1995, pp. A1, D6; Richard W. Stevenson, "Software Makes Strange Bedfellows in Britain as Microsoft and Murdoch Team to Push Windows 95," *New York Times,* August 24, 1995, p. D6; Peter H. Lewis, "Microsoft Has Windows 95 Party; the Internet Shows Up," *New York Times,* August 25, 1995, p. D4; Stuart Elliott, "So Much Stock, but So Little Liquidity," *New York Times,* August 25, 1995, p. D4; Amy Cortese, "The Software Resolution," *BusinessWeek,* December 4, 1995, pp. 78–90; Jean-Claude Larreche and Pantea Denoyelle, *Virgin Atlantic Airways: Ten Years After* (INSEAD: June 1994); "Apple's New Cider House Rules," *Business and Finance,* January 24, 2002.

Introduction

While global advertising has been around for a few years, other global promotions have only recently come into their own. Although businesses have long sponsored sports and arts events—including World Cup soccer, tennis tournaments, auto racing, and painting exhibitions—companies have recently taken to creating events and news with the promotions being the main purpose. Disney's gala film openings or video releases, Swatch's parties when launching new lines, Benetton's ultrahip advertisements, and Microsoft's launch of each new Windows releases are global events created for the purpose of maximum visibility for products. In the beginning they may have reflected the 1980s unabashed hedonism, but their continuation in the new millennium suggests that they reflect a structural change in the way promotions will be done in the future. With the emergence of the Internet as a genuine global and accessible communications medium, one can only assume that these promotional stunts will continue over the next few years.

But global promotions also involve more mundane and traditional tools, such as point-of-purchase merchandising, public relations, and personal selling. There is also the new development of global direct marketing and e-commerce, emerging from the old direct mail campaigns, and, of course, the "tried and true" international trade fairs where prospective buyers and sellers get together to check out new products and establish ties. It is the purpose of this chapter to discuss these various promotional tools and give the global marketer a sense of where they can be most useful.

The chapter will start by discussing global *sales promotion,* covering in-store promotions, events and sponsorship, and cross-marketing. Then the discussion will shift to *publicity,* recently emerging strongly in global marketing communications, and global *public relations.* The role of international *trade fairs* will be dealt with briefly before we discuss *direct marketing* and *e-commerce,* tools enabling even the smallest firm to go global. The last part of the chapter will focus on *personal selling* and the problems and opportunities in a global sales effort.

Global Sales Promotion

Sales promotion involves a variety of activities, ranging from point-of-purchase displays and trade promotions to Sunday newspaper coupons and the sponsorship of symphony orchestras and athletic events such as the Olympics, soccer's World Cup, and major tennis tournaments.

In-Store and Trade Promotions

In-store or point-of-purchase (p-o-p) **promotions** refer to promotional activities inside the store; **trade promotions** are targeted at channel intermediaries ("the trade"). Both are important in the U.S. market and are becoming more important in many other markets as well.

Typically, in-store sales promotion is a much more localized activity than advertising, which uses global media such as cable television and international magazines. Sales promotion needs to be localized because its use is often more rigidly regulated than advertising. Cents-off coupons, free samples, and two-for-one offers can be prohibited in some countries where regulation is aimed at ensuring orderly markets and steady margins for local retailers. Premiums, gifts, and competitions are sometimes allowed but with major restrictions. Outright prohibition is unusual, but most countries impose limits on what can be done. These restrictions vary between countries. In France, for example, a gift can't be worth more than 4 percent of the retail value of the product. In Germany, requiring proof of purchase for participation in a competition used to be illegal.[1]

Apart from constraining regulations in many countries, several other factors influence the effectiveness of in-store promotions:

Cooperation from the Trade

In-store promotions to the consumer need to be supported by trade promotions, that is, promotions to channel intermediaries. The aim of in-store promotion is to "move product," and retailers and upstream wholesalers need to be induced to cooperate and increase the product flow. This is usually done through trade discounts, cooperative advertising, and sales support. If the trade is not compensated, middlemen may not cooperate. For example, ACNielsen tried to introduce cents-off coupons in Chile, but the nation's supermarket union opposed the project and asked its members not to accept them.

Attitudes toward Coupons

The retailers need to handle promotions such as coupons professionally and not embarrass the consumers, often difficult in countries with a history of producers dominating the customers.

Limited Capability

Since distribution infrastructure is often different between countries, some promotions may simply not be feasible. Procter & Gamble tried to introduce its Cheer detergent in Japan using the type of trade promotion employed in the United States, including coupons, cents off, and trade discounts. The stores in Japan, however, were too small to handle the necessary volume and quickly ran out of stock. Consumers were disappointed, retailers were frustrated, and the introductory campaign was a failure.

Presold Customers

In-store promotions work best when the consumer expects to make choices in the store. In some cases the choice is already made before entering the store: Preselling a product through advertising or newspaper coupons, for example, often means that no in-store choice is necessary. Brand loyalty has the same effect. But when channels are dominated by manufacturers (as used to be the case in Japan), stores may feature only one brand and the store choice dictates which brand will be bought.

Trade promotions have their own problems. When General Electric broke into the air-conditioning market in Japan, the company offered overseas trips to outstanding dealers and a free color TV set to purchasers of high-end models. The successful campaign drew complaints from the trade association, and new rules to limit promotions were approved by the Japanese Fair Trade Commission. A limit was set on the size of the premium that could be offered, and no overseas trips were allowed as dealer incentives for any home appliances.[2]

Calculating the cost of a promotion relative to its revenue-raising potential is not always easy. It involves not only the actual cost of the promotional material and the

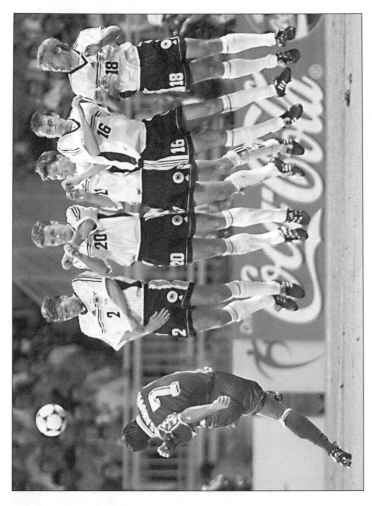

Most eyes are probably on the ball, but Coca-Cola gets some subliminal exposure as the free kick makes the players jump. In this 1998 World Cup match in France, great soccer power Germany was trounced 3–0 by a newcomer, Croatia. Germany again lost to Croatia in the Euro 2008 Cup, 2-1, but still went to the final in the tournament, won by Spain. © Corbis.

accompanying marketing communications as well as a forecast of anticipated sales but also an estimate of the amount of sales that would have been made without the promotion. Simple mistakes can ruin the projections. One British firm created a very successful promotion by offering free airline tickets to buyers of its home appliances. However, the firm neglected to eliminate some longer routes from the offer and found that most customers opted for an expensive trip from London to New York. Once the losses started to mount, the promotion had to be broken off, leading to legal entanglement and the promotional manager losing his job.

Sponsorships

With the advent of global media the possibilities for global **sponsorships** are opening up. Sponsoring a World Cup match by plastering the brand name on the bleachers and piggybacking on the television broadcasts has helped companies such as Hitachi, Kodak, Siemens, and Volvo establish a strong identity in the global marketplace.[3] More direct spending involves sponsoring tennis tournaments (Volvo, Virginia Slims), Formula One race cars (Coca-Cola, Marlboro), single-man treks to the South Pole (NordicTrack), and athletic team wear (Nike, Reebok). The Olympics sponsorship, which started seriously in Los Angeles in 1984, and crested at new heights (or depths, for some purists) in Salt Lake City in 2002, has spilled over into promotional sponsorship of Russian hockey players (Visa) and Italian basketball teams (Sony). It is somewhat unsettling to see newspaper pictures of the star-studded national soccer team of Brazil and find it sponsored by Nike. Global promotion knows no boundaries.

The global reach of sporting events, which has created possibilities for products to become associated with globally recognized sports figures, has made the sports figures rich in addition to famous. Kobe Bryant, the basketball player, receives more money from his endorsements than from his playing. The use of well-known athletes has its downside. When the superhuman perfection of the stars is in doubt, the sponsorship can be a liability rather than an asset. And athletes don't last forever. As part of its efforts to streamline marketing costs in order to compete more effectively in the athletic footwear industry Nike ceased sponsoring a number of star athletes, including former number one tennis player Pete Sampras. Although Nike's Beaverton, Oregon, global corporate facilities still include the "Pete Sampras building," Nike officials later decided that Andre Agassi's

Getting the Picture

WORLD CUP PROMOTION KICKS INTO HIGHER GEAR

The 2006 FIFA World Cup held in Germany set a new record of sponsorship money. FIFA raised an estimated €700 million from sponsorships alone. The World Cup had fifteen "Official Partners," each thought to have paid about €40 million for the privilege.

Corporate sponsorships are nothing new in the area of event marketing, but once again technology has created a new means for advertisers to pitch their products. Budweiser and Mastercard International were the first two to sign up to become sponsors of the official World Cup Web site, FIFAworldcup.com. The two American giants were not new to sports, and Mastercard had a long-standing sponsorship with the Cup dating back to 1994 in the United States. But it was strange and somehow comforting to see Americans as prime sponsors of a world event where their team ranked at the second or third level. This meant Bud was going to be the only beer served at the tournament sites, upsetting many Germans who consider their beers infinitely superior to the "watered down" American beers. The German beers attempted a variation of "ambush" marketing by threatening to sell their beers outside the stadiums, but Bud prevailed upon FIFA not to allow any beer on stadium grounds.

The fifteen official sponsors were: Adidas, Budweiser, Avaya, Coca-Cola, Continental, Deutsche Telekom, Emirates, Fujifilm, Gillette, Hyundai, MasterCard, McDonald's, Philips, Toshiba, and Yahoo!. The large number of sponsors led to complaints, and the number was cut down to six for future World Cups. Adidas, Hyundai, Coca-Cola, Sony, Visa, and Emirates have already paid more than €100m each to secure their places for the 2010 World Cup in South Africa. The replacement of Mastercard with Visa occurred after Mastercard questioned the steep price increase,

The sponsors tried some imaginative promotions. Hyundai Motor Company supplied team buses for each of the thirty-two finalists, and held a contest to decide the team bus slogans. Adidas supplied the match balls for every match of the tournament. Each "Teamgeist" ball had the name of the stadium, the national teams, the date of the match and the kickoff time printed. The balls used for the final match were gold, rather than the normal white. The official match song, in case you did not hear it, was "Time of Our Lives," sung by Il Divo and Toni Braxton.

It will be interesting to see what South Africa can come up with. Perhaps something more intrinsic, like an African team in the finals?

Sources: Hannah Cleaver, "Beer Deal Chokes Fans," *The Daily Telegraph*, April 21, 2004, p. 14; Marianne Arens, "Football World Cup 2006—A Multibillion-euro Business," **www.wsws.org,** May 31, 2006; Paul Maidment, ed., "The FIFA World Cup 2006," **www.Forbes.com,** June 5, 2006.

image is more in line with their corporate goals, particularly striking since Agassi had earlier been a Reebok spokesman. Today Nike relies more on Federer and Nadal.

As markets have become more saturated and many products have reached maturity, more companies have been turning to sponsorships to more effectively segment the market. Technology has also changed the nature of sponsorships. World Cup 2006 was one of the most watched events ever in the history of sports, and companies signed lucrative sponsorships for the matches and even for various teams involved in the competition. However, the promise of the Internet has resulted in firms also sponsoring the official World Cup Web page (see box, "World Cup Promotion Kicks into Higher Gear").

Event Marketing

Companies also help arrange **events** at which their brands can be promoted. An extreme example of creating an "event" associated with a brand was the launch of Microsoft's Windows 95 computer operating system as described at the beginning of this chapter. Similar strategies, although perhaps less extravagant, are used by other companies. The Swiss watchmaker Swatch relies extensively on sponsorship of special events. The company has a policy of spending a major share of its promotional budget on special events promotion. Some events, such as hanging a large Swatch on a Frankfurt building, are simply "happenings" created to draw attention to Swatch and generate free publicity for the brand. The company organizes "launch parties" in various countries, when a new collection of Swatches is introduced. The company has positioned its watches as fashion products, and its product policy is to keep the Swatch designs fresh by introducing new styles twice a year, in the spring and in the fall. [4]

Cause Marketing

A special tool of public relations management involves what has come to be called **cause marketing.** The term refers to the activities by which a company will try to

Getting the Picture

CAUSE MARKETING? AUTOMAKERS EMBRACE GAYS

After decades of ignoring gay consumers, automakers are now courting them in advertisements and through sponsoring gay events, awards, and causes. In 1994, Saab became the first to advertise in the national gay press, but Subaru has certainly taken the biggest step by hiring Martina Navratilova, the world's best-known lesbian athlete, to star in televisions spots.

This is nothing new for Subaru, which was a founding sponsor of the Rainbow card, an affinity card program that has raised more than $1 million for gay causes. Back in 1994 Subaru management identified gays as one of its core groups of buyers and gay publications have demographics that are very appealing to advertisers. For instance, *Out* and *The Advocate* have an average reader that is a 39-year-old white-collar professional man with a college degree and a "household" income of $95,000.

These kinds of numbers prompted Daimler-Chrysler, Ford, and General Motors to sponsor the annual show of the Lambda Car Club, a group of 2,000 gay collectors. Jaguar has sponsored media awards given by the Gay and Lesbian Alliance Against Defamation, and Volvo provided cars for the Los Angeles gay pride parade. In addition to sponsoring the L.A. gay pride parade, Subaru is also involved in underwriting events organized by the Human Rights Campaign, an advocacy group.

Sponsorships and advertisements are expected to keep increasing, since advertisers calculate that less than half the estimated 15–23 million gays and lesbians in America read gay publications. With that in mind, Subaru chose to advertise on billboards in public spaces in Washington and other cities during gay pride month and in gay-popular neighborhoods.

Many corporate boards may still not be ready to embrace the gay market in an overt manner. But it seems likely that this niche group will continue to be aggressively targeted by more and more companies in the United States and abroad, regardless of what happens to the question of gay marriages.

Sources: Cliff Rothman, "A Welcome Mat for Gay Customers," *New York Times*, August 17, 2001, p. F1; Stuart Elliott, "Martina Navratilova Enters the National Mainstream Market," *New York Times*, March 13, 2000, p. C14; Kimberly Shearer Palmer, "Gay Consumers in the Driver's Seat," *Washington Post*, July 4, 2000, p. C1; David Osborne, "Pink Smoke and Secret Codes in the Battle for the Gay Dollar," *The Independent*, July 9, 2000, p. 23.

associate itself with a worthy societal cause. In the name of good corporate citizenship, companies may sponsor a drive for aid to a disaster-stricken area, print and distribute informational booklets about illnesses such as AIDS, or fund activist environmental groups or local symphony orchestras. Generally, such efforts are not easily measured in terms of bottom-line payoffs, but companies find them worthwhile for the goodwill and positive image created. But in some cases such PR efforts can go against the bottom-line interests of the company. For example, big multinational Unilever found itself sponsoring antiglobalization groups after its purchase of Ben and Jerry's ice creams, a firm with a long-standing commitment to antiglobalization causes. By contrast, in other cases, the support of a cause is clearly aimed at getting sales (see box, "Cause Marketing?").

Cross-Marketing

As markets have globalized and regulations have been harmonized, cross-promotions have become a very active area of competition. The promotional tactics in the globally successful American entertainment industry are illustrative. The **cross-marketing** of related products from successful events and stars represents one of many tactics. There is a big global business in selling products associated with Elvis Presley, James Dean, various successful films (*Hunchback of Notre Dame*, *Titanic*), and TV shows (*Star Trek*, *Sesame Street*). It is possible to buy T-shirts, lunch boxes, pencils, hats, bags, puzzles, music tapes, and a CD-ROM game featuring Disney's film *Monsters, Inc.* The leveraging of a strong brand name by product-line extension has been done for a long time by luxury brands such as Dunhill, Gucci, and Burberry. Other brands are getting into the act, combining global advertising to sustain the brand name with product-line extensions that make it economically feasible to open separate boutiques.

The practice of using popular success for promotion has spilled over into media advertising and has been adopted by non-U.S. companies. Honda, the Japanese auto firm, introduced its new minivan Odyssey using characters based on the work of Keith Haring, the New York artist—and sold more units than forecast despite a premium price.[5] Japan Air Lines, a most staid organization, has painted two of its 747s used on the Hawaii route in bright and irregular patches of color. The sky is the limit—once regulation opens up.

EXHIBIT 17.1
Product Placement in Three Popular Movies

The Departed (starring Jack Nicolson and Leonardo DiCaprio)	Warner Bros. (Time Warner)	52 brands, including Adidas, Bayer, Beck's, Budweiser, Buick, Coca-Cola, Coors, Dell, Ford, Ford Mustang, Mountain Dew, Samsung, Sennheiser, Sprint, TAG Heuer
The Da Vinci Code (starring Tom Hanks)	Sony	25 brands, including Belstaff, BMW, Gillette, Heinz, Land Rover, Louvre, Mercedes, Peugeot, Renault, Rolex, Sony, Sony Ericsson, Sony Vaio, Volkswagen
Mission: Impossible III (starring Tom Cruise)	Paramount (Sony)	35 brands, including 7-Eleven, Acura, BMW, Budweiser, Coca-Cola, Dell, DHL, Dodge, Lamborghini, L'Oreal, Mazda, Mercedes, Volkswagen Beetle, Volvo

Source: www.brandchannel.com.

Product Placement

The last few years have seen an increase in the use of **product placement** for promotional purposes. Product placement refers to the use of branded products in films and television. For example, in the movie ET: The Extraterrestrial, an alien creature was seen eating Reese's Pieces, a peanut-flavored candy; sales of the product subsequently increased by 70 percent. Sales of Ray-Ban Wayfarer sunglasses tripled after Tom Cruise wore them in the movie Risky Business.[6] The very successful introduction of BMW's Z3 roadster was credited partly to its use by James Bond in the GoldenEye movie.

Product placement involves contracting with producers about using the branded product as a natural prop in the film or TV program. In many cases the product is offered free, and no guarantees about its use are made by the producers. Partly because of this, the impact can be negative as well as positive. A Mercedes car used as a prop in one film was set on fire, not a particularly successful product placement.

The use of product placement has been stimulated largely by the global success of American entertainment vehicles, ensuring wide exposure across the world. One might judge the drawing power of film stars by the number of placements his or her film attracts. See Exhibit 17.1 for three examples.[7]

Even though some of these product placements may be minor and simply offer "free publicity," in some categories, such as automobiles, paid presence in a film is apparently getting to be a "must" promotional coup.

Nike, the athletic shoe maker, has managed to place its swoosh logo on many athletes around the world, resulting in a lot of almost-free publicity. But again the results can veer out of control, and have, especially as the financial crises have raised anti-American sentiments in various countries. When a 1997 demonstrator in Mexico City burned the American flag, the photograph transmitted over the newswires showed him in a Nike cap. The stone-throwing Korean rebel in a 1998 wirephoto similarly sported the Nike swoosh in big print on his bloodied T-shirt. And when the 39 members of the Heaven's Gate religious cult in southern California committed joint suicide in March 1997, they were equipped with new Nike shoes "for the life beyond." This is more like product misplacement—and Nike sales predictably dipped, as we saw in the opening vignette to Chapter 2.

Publicity

Publicity, the publishing of news about the company and its products, is an increasingly important part of global companies' promotion function.

"Good News . . ."

Publicity is more credible than paid advertising, and since a global expansion effort is inherently more newsworthy than expansion at home, global companies often get featured in news media. The press coverage can even be orchestrated by the firm, as we saw in the opening vignette about Windows 95. Many of the products and services involved represent high technology, of importance for security reasons or for national

Getting the Picture

TOTAL COMMUNICATION INC.

In the world of high technology, global publicity counts as a major promotional medium. The introduction of the Macintosh personal computer was accompanied by a "full-court" media blitz with Apple press conferences, customer contests, educational "giveaways," appearances of software producers (Microsoft, Lotus) giving assurances of program designs, and of course personal interviews with *Time's* "Man of the Year," Steve Jobs, Apple's chairman. The international press duly reported on the American developments, in fact preparing an entry mat for Apple into many European and Asian countries.

High-tech companies often create news as a matter of course in their daily business, and the press is a ready channel to tell the world about it. The release of a new product occasions a press conference, where pictures, models, technical summaries, and prototypes are available for publicity purposes. The hoopla and excitement are orchestrated to create an event and atmosphere worthy of Hollywood—and of news coverage. Charismatic business leaders are company

assets, and the worldwide media help give well-recognized public persona a global impact.

Consulting firms help companies manage this important function. The large PR firms, such as Hill & Knowlton in the United States, have global reach, following their customers around the world. Smaller companies that specialize in certain countries and industries offer unique services.

San Francisco–based Autodesk, which sells LAN software for networked PCs, uses smaller publicity consultants extensively in its global markets in addition to the large global media relations firms. By releasing newsworthy items about its products, the company aims to create curiosity among potential customers. Using local consultants, the company is able to draw on people with intimate ties to local journalists who can adapt the global press releases to the needs of the local media. Through frequent travels and personal appearances at conferences and industry seminars, executives at Autodesk make themselves available for local interviews.

Sources: Smith, 1994; *New York Times*, June 14, 1994; Jan Segerfeldt, personal communication; **www.autodesk.com.**

competitiveness, which also enhances potential reader interest. And managing publicity—including coordination with the public relations function—is important when foreign direct investments or trade barriers become news, as they often do.

Publicity has the obvious advantage that there is no need to pay for airtime or press coverage. But it is not always without cost. Publicity requires some management and can be labor-intensive. Media contacts need to be created, nurtured, and maintained. Press coverage of the opening of a plant or warehouse in a new market involves travel, food, and sometimes lodging for journalists. The preparation of **press releases,** copy written for immediate news publication, requires skill, especially when the information is about a technical breakthrough. Making top managers available for personal interviews takes their time and diverts their attention. Still, the payoff in goodwill and free advertising can be considerable and the investment well worth it (see box, "Total Communication Inc.").

". . . and Bad News"

Even "negative" publicity can have its rewards since it serves to keep the brand name in the public eye. Benetton, the Italian apparel maker, is one example. Through its famous (or infamous, depending on one's views) realistic TV commercials and large full-page magazine ads of a man dying from AIDS, a priest kissing a nun, an automobile ablaze after a car bomb, and a boatload of refugees without copy but with the brand logo displayed after the commercial or below the picture, Benetton has garnered plenty of publicity, mainly negative. The ads seem to be in bad taste, and Benetton has been accused of exploiting human suffering to sell its products. In Germany, irate store owners refused to stock Benetton products unless the advertisements were withdrawn, claiming that the ads kept customers away. But the company argues that it is doing a positive thing—and to help prove it, it opened a new store in war-torn Sarajevo.[8]

Global Public Relations

Similar to publicity, **global public relations** is a form of indirect promotion of products and services that focuses on creating goodwill toward the corporation as a whole. The corporate communications staff at headquarters and its counterpart in the various host countries serve as promoters of the corporation to various stakeholders interested in the company's foreign expansion. These stakeholders can include a wide variety of groups:

Stockholders
Employees
Customers
Distributors
Suppliers
Financial community
Media
Activist groups
General public
Government

These groups can lay some legitimate claim on a company to conduct itself ethically and to operate with a certain level of transparency in accordance with the free market system. However, because of the many countries in which a global company is likely to do business, ethical standards and customary business secrecy can vary considerably. This easily creates conflicts between host country stakeholders' claims and headquarters' policy guidelines. One job of the public relations staff is to make sure that such potential conflicts do not erupt and, when they do, to carry out "damage control."

Conflicts typically arise when a firm enters a new country by acquiring a local company or by investing in manufacturing. When American companies such as Ford, GM, IBM, Xerox, Honeywell, and General Electric became big investors in Europe in the 1950s and 60s, Europeans became alarmed by the "American challenge." As Japanese companies like Nissan (trucks), Mitsubishi (real estate), Matsushita (electronics), and Honda (automobiles) established presence in the United States by large investments, many Americans voiced misgivings.[10] Even though the economic justifications of these and other FDI entries are usually sound, and the host countries also benefit, the companies' PR departments have to work hard to establish the "good local citizen" image among stakeholders such as the general public. This involves compiling statistics about the number of natives employed, the local content of the products, and the tax contribution made to the local municipality—and publicizing this information.

From the global marketing perspective, the critical issue is whether alarm or misgivings about corporate strategy spill over into a negative brand evaluation and lower sales. According to company research, the negative evaluation against Japanese investments in the United States did lead to some temporary loss of American market share for Honda in the early 1990s.

Effective **damage control,** actions taken to limit the spillover into a negative public opinion, requires both public relations and timing. When a Volvo TV commercial in the United States was found deceptive because the car used in a demonstration of Volvo's body integrity was reinforced, the company first publicly admitted the mistake, retracted the advertising, and then moved to dismiss the advertising agency.[11] The German automaker Audi, by contrast, stood firm in defending its Audi 4000 model design against repeated accusations of malfunctioning. Several accidents had happened because drivers mistakenly (as the courts found) stepped on the gas pedal instead of the brakes. The Audi engineers won their court case, but consumer PR damage was not contained, and Audi market share slipped badly.

Another example of how a company can mishandle public relations was the problem Intel had with its Pentium chip at the end of 1994. At first belittling the importance of the flaw, which led to miscalculated long divisions, the company rallied after a week and offered apologies to the public, explanations to media, and free replacements to users.[12] This quick about-face in a relatively straightforward case can be contrasted with the much more complicated PR problem of Nestlé's infant formula in the Third World (see box, "Nestlé and Babies").

Getting the Picture

NESTLÉ AND BABIES: WHO IS RIGHT?

The Large Swiss multinational Nestlé is a major global company in the food industry. Its Nestlé instant tea, Nescafé coffee, Libby's juices, and Carnation milk products are household names all over the world.

The company got its baptism by fire in global PR in the latter half of the 1970s. Having developed a superior infant formula that could effectively supplant a breast-feeding mother, the company saw great potential among malnourished Third World children. Distributing the formula through clinics and wet-nurses, the company was able to tap into the market effectively. There was only one problem. Some mothers, partly to offset the relatively high cost of the formula, took to diluting it with water. As a consequence, many babies on formula did not get the requisite nourishment, and in a few cases, the water used for the dilution was infected and there were some deaths.

Through various sources, activist groups in Europe and North America soon learned about the situation. As initial appeals to the company in Vevy, Switzerland, were rebuffed, the groups started a massive international campaign against Nestlé and its products.

Through press conferences and media releases as well as in direct meetings with activist leaders, Nestlé argued that withdrawing a beneficial product would do more harm than good. The company undertook scientific research projects designed to establish the superiority of the product against weak mothers' milk and projected the expected death rates should the product be withdrawn.

In the end, the activists were fought to a standstill and the company succeeded in maintaining its product in the Third World markets and reducing the damage to its brands. But the process is still ongoing, with various monitoring activities coordinated by IBFAN, the International Baby Food Action Network. Their argument is that according to the World Health Organization (WHO) 1.5 million infants die every year because they are not adequately breastfed. While Nestlé claims that it is in full compliance with International Codes, many European universities, colleges and schools have banned the sale of Nestlé products from their shops and vending machines. In the United Kingdom, many businesses, consumer groups, labor unions, politicians, and celebrities still support a boycott. In a 2005 online opinion poll that surveyed 15,500 consumers in 17 countries, GMI research found that Nestlé was the one of the four most boycotted brands (beside Nike, Coca-Cola, and McDonald's) because of what respondents consider its "unethical use and promotion of formula feed for babies in third world countries."

Sources: Shirk, 1991; C. B. Malone and N. Harrison, "Nestlé Alimentana S.A.—Infant Formula," Harvard Business School case no. 9-580-118; **www.nestle.com; www.ibfan.org; www.gmi-mr.com.**

International Trade Fairs

As we saw in Chapter 5, participation in **international trade fairs** is an important way of identifying potential distributors in a new local market. Although these industry gatherings can seem quaint and old-fashioned, they are in fact more vibrant than ever. The reason is that when it comes to introducing new products, establish trust and confidence in a partner, or simply keeping track of what competition is up to, there is no better way than walking around the worldwide industry fairs.

This is a list of some of the traditionally most important international fairs:

- The Consumer Electronics Show (CES), Las Vegas, U.S., in January
- Hannover Messe's Industrial Fair, Germany, in April
- North American International Auto Show, Detroit, U.S., in January.
- Paris Airshow, Paris, France, in June (every other year)
- CeBIT Trade Fair, Hanover, Germany, in March (largest IT trade fair)
- The IFA electronics exhibition, Berlin, Germany, in August-September.
- Frankfurt Book Fair, Frankfurt, Germany, in October
- Hong Kong Jewelry and Watch Fair, Hong Kong, in September.

Because of the boost to the local economy and even more because of the international exposure and enhanced global image, many cities now actively compete for the hosting of trade fairs. Relative newcomers include China's Shanghai, Russia's St. Petersburg, Bangalore (now Bengaluru) in India, and Dubai of the United Arab Emirates.

For the global marketer, fairs are an excellent promotional avenue. Participation enhances and sustains visibility and local presence. The fairs' attraction is the chance to introduce a company's latest products and models, to discover industry trends, and to spot new competitive developments.

Direct Marketing

Direct marketing is defined by the Direct Marketing Association as "an interactive marketing system that uses one or more advertising media to effect a measurable response and/or transaction at any location." The traditional direct marketing medium is **mail order,** with catalogs and sales offers sent directly to individual households, which then order via mail. The names and addresses are drawn from various lists—in the beginning often from subscription lists of newspapers and magazines but today more often from commercial data banks that can screen for key words and develop lists of qualified prospects. In recent years **telemarketing,** selling via the telephone, has grown fast in the United States, and so has **direct response television (DRTV),** where TV commercials will list telephone numbers to let viewers call for purchases. With the growing presence of the World Wide Web, direct marketing has become a very important channel.

Direct marketing is growing rapidly because it is fast, safe, convenient, low-cost—and eliminates the job of going to the store. Express mail delivery means that most goods can arrive within one or two days. Return privileges are generous. Payment can be made by simply giving a credit card number. The liability for improper use of a card number is limited. Toll-free 800 numbers make it possible to use the telephone free of charge.

Can direct marketing be globalized? The answer, despite the need for fast delivery and efficient communications, is an emphatic "Yes, absolutely!" First of all, the postal systems of many countries, despite otherwise weak infrastructures, seem to function quite well. Second, countries' telephone systems are growing increasingly reliable and have in many cases penetrated into remote rural areas. This has not escaped the attention of international long-distance carriers. AT&T International Service 800 S.A. now offers toll-free dialing to more than 50 countries on five continents. Third, credit cards have gone global, and people pay by American Express, MasterCard, or Visa all over the world. Finally, as we saw in Chapter 15, the express carriers have globalized their operations and now reach most places on the globe.

The increase in coverage of global communications has meant not only that customers almost everywhere can be reached but that the marketer can be located in any small place on the map, not needing a major metropolitan location for its headquarters or a large staff (see box, "In Global Direct Marketing, Small Is Beautiful").

Global Strategy

Although direct marketing is relatively new, early experiences suggest that there are basically three alternative ways of implementing a global strategy.[13]

- *"Do it yourself."* The most obvious method is the company developing the market and the necessary contacts on its own. This involves time, travel, and expense. At some point when volume justifies it, it also involves developing a relationship with a local company to handle "fulfillment," that is, dealing with customs as necessary, some delivery, lost goods, and other incidental services. This is a labor-intensive and costly method for a small company, with a typical overseas business trip lasting two to three weeks and costing easily $5,000.

- *Marketing intermediary.* A second way to go is to turn the product over to a direct marketing company specializing in international marketing and to let it act as a general contractor (akin to an export management company). The intermediary will be responsible for establishing infrastructure and setting up local representatives to handle inventory as needed, order taking, and fulfillment. These intermediaries often work through a global network of local entrepreneurs. Going this route, the company will need to establish a consistent global pricing structure, to prohibit reexporting, yet offer the intermediary sufficient margin to realize a profit.

Getting the Picture

IN GLOBAL DIRECT MARKETING, SMALL IS BEAUTIFUL

To get a grip on how global direct marketing works, have a look at Acton Ltd. for an object lesson. A typical company in global direct marketing, Acton is a small (48 employees) direct marketer in the publishing and financial services industries. The firm is located in Lincoln, Nebraska, in the heart of Buffalo Bill and Wild Bill Hickok country.

Acton's direct marketing operation started by marketing U.S. client banks' checking accounts and related services across the country and gradually developed or acquired address lists of prospects and leads at home and overseas. One of the lists it has exclusive rights to includes 14 million households in Japan, developed from client contacts over a few years. The address files are digitalized and can be transferred

back and forth on the Internet. For any particular direct marketing campaign, the company will work with a local agent who is part of Acton's emerging global network.

About 70 percent of the company's clients are large banks on the East and West Coasts of the United States that are primarily interested in expanding their credit card customer bases overseas. Says Cheri Pettet, vice president of international sales: "Our marketing programs for credit cards work so well we can almost guarantee the client will gain customers."

Being able to locate the operation in a low-cost rural area of a country had another advantage: It makes employees less worried about outsourcing, boosting worker morale.

Sources: Kelly, 1994; Egol, 1994a; Dregner, 2004.

- *Strategic alliance.* A third option is to develop a strategic alliance with a direct marketing company in the local market. Such a company will have better knowledge of the local market and may be able to help with neighboring country markets. It will also have the required infrastructure capabilities in place.

To date, the second option seems to be the one chosen most often by smaller companies. It enables the direct marketer to get into foreign markets quickly and without major expense. It is the natural alternative when the company is starting out and learning how global direct marketing works. Established catalog houses, such as L. L. Bean and Eddie Bauer, prefer the first option since it offers more control over the local marketing effort. The three options are likely to vary in attractiveness across local markets, and most companies find it useful to examine all three alternatives for any one market. In Europe, a relatively difficult direct marketing region because of fragmentation of languages and cultures, alliances tend to be common. One American publisher tackled the U.K. market by partnering with Direct Marketing Services, a British firm, which adapted the American promotional material and address list characteristics to those in Britain with good success.

Direct marketing is emerging as a new global option for many companies. It is an option capitalizing directly on the technological advances in global communications and transportation during the last two decades, opening up global opportunities for even the smallest companies.

Electronic Commerce

Electronic commerce or e-commerce refers to buying and selling goods and services on the Internet. It is sometimes simply called **online marketing.** Actually, electronic commerce defined broadly includes more than just buying and selling on the Internet. It can also refer to simple informational or service exchanges, such as those between a government agency and its constituents, teacher-student relationships, and fund-raising. As in marketing generally, electronic commerce refers to the "exchange" between a provider and a customer, this time using electronic communications.

All indications are that the World Wide Web marketplace will continue to grow by leaps and bounds. Although the collapse of scores of dot-com companies caused a major reevaluation of the high-tech industry, the Internet still has enormous potential for a range of global products and services. Many established global firms have committed themselves to electronic commerce as a means of directly selling products or

Getting the Picture

THE WEB 2.0 OPPORTUNITY

The New Media are often seen as a key component of the "new" Internet, or "Web 2.0." Web 2.0 refers to a second generation of Web-based communities and hosted services which facilitate collaboration and sharing between users. Examples of New Media include interactive television, podcasts, blogs, social bookmarking, social networks, wikis, and video games. They also include chat rooms, bulletin boards, and interlinked Web pages. All of these venues provide new opportunities for marketers to advertise and interact in new ways with customers and other stakeholders.

Web 2.0 has attracted a great deal of attention and speculation in the business and advertising press regarding its impact on promotional mixes. Marketing managers continue to shift larger portions of their budgets to online media sites (Bughin and Manyika, 2007), and as we saw in Chapter 16, all forms of online advertising expenditures are expected to increase dramatically in the next few years.

In a recent large-scale global survey of companies' intentions to further invest in Web 2.0 platforms, technology executives felt that Web 2.0's opportunities in collective intelligence (systems to tap the expertise of a group rather than an individual for gathering information and making decisions), P2P (peer-to-peer networking to efficiently share files of any format), social networking (systems that allow member of a specific site to learn about other members' expertise, skills, talents, knowledge, and preferences), podcasts (audio or video recordings, typically posted in a multimedia blog), and mashups (an aggregation of content from different online sources to create a new message or service) were all important investments. What all these technologies have in common is the ability to communicate in new, economically efficient, engaging, and meaningful ways with customers and business partners everywhere, and to encourage collaboration within a company. Apart from the added channels to reach an elusive consumer, the relative ease of tracking the impact of digital messages allows for precise measurement of message effectiveness, an added attraction.

Sources: Jacques Bughin and James Manyika, "How Businesses Are Using Web 2.0: A McKinsey Global Survey," *McKinsey Quarterly:* The Online Journal of McKinsey & Co., March 2007; Marketing Science Institute, "Creating and Cultivating Brand Connections," Carlson School of Management, University of Minnesota, June 6–8, 2007. Accessed March 31, 2007 at **www.msi.org.**

---

services or simply promoting their corporate and noncorporate activities. The second-generation Web 2.0 promises to drive the movement to new heights (see box, "The Web 2.0 Opportunity").

The driver and key factor is access to the Internet. Exhibit 17.2 gives some of the projections for the first few years of the new millennium.

Internet penetration is clearly not yet uniform across the world. As Exhibit 17.2 shows, less than one in five people in the world have access to the Internet. The so-called digital divide is most clearly seen in the differences between mature market economies and emerging market economies.

E-tailing Growth

Online retail, so-called **e-tailing,** is growing rapidly around the world. The research firms expect most of the consumer sales growth to come in just five categories, all of them already established on the Internet: computers, software, entertainment, books, and travel (see box, "The Internet Global Promise").

EXHIBIT 17.2

World Internet Usage and Population Statistics

Source: Accessed at **www.internet-worldstats.com/stats.htm**, December 31, 2007.

World Region	Population % of World	% Population of Internet Users (Region Penetration)	Internet Usage as % of World Usage	Usage Growth 2000–2007
Africa	14.20%	4.70%	3.40%	882%
Asia	56.50%	13.70%	38.70%	347%
Europe	12.10%	43.40%	26.40%	231%
Middle East	2.90%	17.40%	2.50%	920%
North America	5.10%	71.10%	18%	120%
Latin America & Caribbean	8.60%	22.20%	9.60%	598%
Oceania & Australia	0.50%	57.10%	1.50%	152%
World Total	100%	20%	100%	266%

Getting the Picture

THE INTERNET GLOBAL PROMISE

Although *global* electronic commerce is still in its infancy, its rapid rise in advanced economies gives some hints of what is to come. Not surprisingly, perhaps, most transactions so far have involved *services* rather than products. While products need to be shipped to the buyer's location, services can often be transmitted electronically to any destination. Some promising high-potential examples include:

Airline tickets. Buy online and pick up at the airport ticket counter.

Tourist packages. Compare prices and features, then order for express delivery of tickets to the home.

Banking services. Transfer money, check credit card balances, pay bills.

Brokerage services. Buy and sell shares.

Rental cars. Reserve a car at the airport upon arrival.

Hotel reservations. Get lodgings anywhere in the world.

Because of the need for shipment, global online *product* purchases involve the usual logistics costs—from warehousing and transportation to customs clearing and home delivery (see Chapter 15). Still, there are many successful examples:

Personal computers. Dell's customized direct sales have been very successful.

Books. Amazon.com is perhaps *the* best example of online product marketing.

Computer software. A natural!

Cameras. Catalog sales of cameras were a forerunner of online selling.

Leisure apparel. L. L. Bean, Lands' End, and Eddie Bauer are well established through catalogs and are now online as well.

Sports equipment. Another natural, although the category faces obstacles in the form of stiff tariff barriers and exclusive distributorships in many countries.

Compact discs. The global Internet music business is fighting against old and well-established local price cartels in many countries. It is also threatening the music industry itself through new technology that allows digital downloading of CDs from the Web.

According to the Interactive Media Retail Group (IMRG) in the United Kingdom, in 2003 one in 24 retail purchases around the world were made online. By 2009, this ratio will have risen to one in four retail purchases.[14] IMRG estimates that online sales worldwide will reach US$145 billion in 2009 out of a total of US$574 billion. The United Kingdom appears to be ahead of continental Europe in Internet shopping. While 27 percent of British consumers have shopped online, for the EU as a whole the figure is 16 percent, still a respectable figure. The Internet is finally becoming a mass market channel. Lack of trust in payment systems and low consumer confidence in buying online, once threats to e-commerce, are no longer big concerns, and the fact that products cannot be touched is apparently not much of a problem anymore (see box, "E-Commerce Goes Personal").

U.S. data also suggest strong growth for e-tailers. Forrester, a U.S.-based research firm, projects that online retail sales in the United States will rise to $316 billion in 2010 and account for about 10 percent of total retails sales.[15] In North America, where shoppers tend to be loyal to specific retailers, in an August 2004 study, research firm Vividence found that customers prefer Amazon.com over all other retail Web sites.[16] Amazon was followed by Barnes & Noble, Circuit City, and eBay. The world's largest retailer, Wal-Mart was ranked number 14 on the list, despite its power in the overall marketplace.

On mainland China—and Asia as a whole—net-shopping is also becoming popular. The official China Internet Network Information Center says the number of Internet users in the country hit 87 million by the end of June 2004, up nearly 28 percent from a year earlier. In China, service to urban customers still relies heavily on payment on delivery to bicycle couriers (versus online credit card transactions). Announced on August 20, 2004, Amazon.com, the world's biggest online retailer, was to buy 100 percent of Chinese rival Joyo.com for about $75 million in a deal that would give it substantial presence in China's growing Internet market.[17] The acquisition is one in a series of moves into China by international companies. U.S. auction site eBay paid $180 million for Chinese counterpart EachNet in a deal completed in 2003. Other e-commerce firms

Getting the Picture

E-COMMERCE GOES PERSONAL

Two persistent drawbacks of e-tailing compared to traditional retailing are that the product cannot be touched and there is no real face-to-face interaction with a salesperson. This has not stopped the Internet from becoming a major avenue for that most personal of exchanges: finding a suitable mate.

For a fee, online dating sites ask members to post snapshots of themselves, give a description of their vital statistics and interests, and spell out what their ideal mate would be like. The members are then able to scroll through "the database" of all the members and identify potential mates. In true online fashion, there are also "matchmaking agents," search engine software that uses the ideal specification to find the best fits in the database in seconds. A quick call or e-mail message is sufficient to set up a rendezvous and find a partner for life. For the harried young man or woman executive—or, for that matter, the divorced man or woman with two teenage kids at home—the time savings can be a godsend. Online dating takes segmentation, positioning, and targeting to new heights. No more time wasted on blind dates.

At least that is the promise. And despite early misgivings in traditional cultures and some continued problems with misinformation and sex-related crime, Internet dating has become a global success phenomenon. One reason is the relative privacy. John Suler, a pioneering American researcher into cyberspace behavior, has suggested that "an online disinhibition effect" helps people be who they really are.

In North America, the biggest site, MatchNet's AmericanSingles.com, has 11 million members who each pay a $24.95 monthly fee. Ethnic groups have their own Web sites. For example, one site, Jdate.com, holds a virtual monopoly on Jewish internet dating, with more than 600,000 members—including 100,000 Israelis—signed on with color photos and descriptive essays with personal details such as

synagogue attendance and annual income. One of the most successful Web sites in Canada is Mehndi.com, a "matrimonial" Web site tailored to traditional Pakistanis. The site features numerous personals posted by eligible Muslim young people—and their parents. By pursuing the process together, families retain Islam's traditional parental oversight of the matchmaking process.

Since January 2003, there has been a 17 percent rise in the use of British dating Web sites, according to figures from the Internet tracking company Hitwise. Despite membership fees of about 15 pounds a month, one site says it has up to 100,000 new hopefuls joining every month and up to 200,000 members logging on every weekday evening. As for other European nations, Internet giant Yahoo announced on June 11, 2003, that it was launching online dating services for three of its European portals. And Internet project manager Valery Bocharov says his Moscow-based speed-dating company Flirtanica is only one of many Internet dating firms on the rise in Russia.

Internet dating is also gaining momentum in Asia. In Singapore, Yahoo.com launched their Yahoo Personals dating service in February 2003, recording 50 percent monthly rises in new members. In Japan more than a third of the males and almost a third of females in the 15-to-20-age bracket said they have accessed Internet dating sites. Internet dating sites have become popular in Japan due to ease of access via mobile phones and anonymity provided to users, but related crimes have also increased, with some users becoming victims of rape, extortion, robbery, and even murder.

What happened to "All you need is love"?

Sources: Clare Jones, "Tangled Web: Looking for Love in the 21st Century," *The Daily Telegraph (London)*, August 2, 2003; Carl Schreck, "Life Moves Fast, and Dating Finally Catches Up," *The Moscow Times*, February 18, 2004; Robbie Hudson, "E-dating Sheds Its Stigma," *Sunday Times (London)*, June 29, 2003; "Devout Pakistanis Use Internet to Marry," *United Press International*, July 7, 2004.

---

have since followed suit, including Yahoo and Google. The results have been less than glorious. As we saw in Chapter 10, the Chinese market—consumers and domestic competitors—"grew up" in sophistication much faster than anybody expected, and especially in technology-related product categories where the government keeps a close watch, success for foreigners has been slow.

As always with new ways of doing business, external events can affect the growth rate greatly. For example, in early 2003, with the SARS disease scare, shopping online enabled the Chinese to buy things in the safety of their own homes. Cosmetic company Sa Sa International's online sales in March 2003 rose 25 percent compared with earlier months.[18] Park 'N Shop, Hong Kong's largest supermarket chain, is reporting a 40 percent rise in online sales since March 2003.

One looming threat to e-tailing is increased attention from tax authorities. Value added taxes (VAT) often are not applied to online sales since products are shipped directly to homes and across borders. This has made online sales especially popular in Europe, where sales taxes can be as high as 25 percent. But in July 2003, a new EU directive warned companies that they will have to charge VAT on certain online sales to avoid unfair advantages over traditional retailers. The European Union Directive on the Taxation of Digital Sales says that Internet companies operating in Europe must charge VAT on all services and products sold from their Web sites, adding a 15 percent to 25 percent levy on transactions involving software and music downloads, as well as subscriptions to online services, and items bought through online auctions.[19] This is likely to slow down the growth of e-tailing in Europe, but is unlikely to stop it.

Marketing Strengths and Weaknesses

When properly implemented, there are several **marketing strengths** of electronic commerce. Online marketing:

- Makes it easy and convenient for the customer to do business with a vendor.
- Creates a natural one-to-one relationship between buyer and seller, with customization of products and services.
- Fosters customer loyalty and increases customer retention rates.
- Helps the company focus on providing customer value.
- Lowers costs for buyers and sellers in the whole process from prepurchase stage to postpurchase stage.
- Facilitates price comparisons. In fact, proponents of electronic marketing argue that the Internet will make for more efficient markets. Probably so: Preliminary research findings suggest that price competition is heating up for goods on the Web.

At the same time, electronic commerce has some **marketing weaknesses:**

- It can reach only a certain segment of the total market, those with computers and Internet access. Globally, this is still a severe limitation, although in many countries this drawback is getting to be minimal. Exhibit 17.3 shows the leading countries in Internet penetration.
- It cannot (yet) provide the full tactile experience with the product or the personal interaction in services. This limitation is not a drawback for many of the services already successful on the Internet, such as banking and airline travel.

EXHIBIT 17.3
Top 20 Countries in Broadband Penetration, 2007

Source: **www.internetworldstats.com.**

Rank	Country or Region	Broadband Penetration Rate	Broadband Subscribers	Population
1	Bermuda	36.5 %	23,600	64,574
2	Netherlands	32.8 %	5,388,000	16,447,682
3	Denmark	31.8 %	1,728,359	5,438,698
4	Iceland	29.3 %	87,738	299,076
5	Switzerland	28.5 %	2,140,309	7,523,024
6	Liechtenstein	28.1 %	10,000	35,622
7	Monaco	28.1 %	9,400	33,443
8	Finland	28.0 %	1,474,605	5,275,491
9	Korea, South	27.4 %	14,042,728	51,300,989
10	Norway	27.4 %	1,278,346	4,657,321
11	Sweden	27.2 %	2,478,003	9,107,795
12	Hong Kong	25.1 %	1,796,200	7,150,254
13	Luxembourg	23.8 %	110,317	463,273
14	Canada	23.7 %	7,675,533	32,440,970
15	United Kingdom	23.1 %	13,957,111	60,363,602
16	Belgium	22.4 %	2,353,956	10,516,112
17	France	22.3 %	13,677,000	61,350,009
18	Singapore	21.8 %	796,500	3,654,103
19	United States	21.4 %	64,614,000	301,967,681
20	Faroe Islands	20.3 %	10,100	49,760
TOP 20 Countries		23.1 %	133,651,805	578,139,479
Rest of the World		2.7 %	160,454,692	5,996,526,938
Total World - Users		4.5 %	294,106,497	6,574,666,417

Note: Broadband corresponds to fast Internet, and includes several technologies (ADSL, Cable, Dedicated Lines, etc.).

- For effective implementation, electronic commerce needs good electronic communication links. Faulty technology will ruin customer relationships.
- Many customers are put off by computers and technology. The degree of aversion varies across cultures, but online customers will constitute only a minority in many markets for years to come.
- The perceived risks involved can be great. Who can buy a car simply on the basis of a picture on the Web? (Some apparently can, though even the typical Internet car shopper will visit a dealer before committing to a purchase.)
- Without credit cards, electronic commerce would be unthinkable. Many purchases now on the Internet are as routine as paying with a credit card in a shop or in a restaurant. The card-issuing banks by and large extend the standard limits and exposure rules to their global customers. Still, many individuals balk at putting their card numbers into cyberspace. The security procedures put in place by different companies seem to be working, although some level of credit card fraud will probably always be with us.

Promoting the Site

The **Web home page** is the first screen image that pops up when a user accesses a particular company site. It typically shows the company name, logo, and representative product line. On the home page the user can then usually point and click to get further information about company products, to request information to be mailed, to fill out a research questionnaire, or sometimes to play a game. Some car companies (Honda, BMW, Volkswagen) allow the users to design their own version of a car. The new VW Beetle was in fact designed using suggestions from a large number of online amateur car designers—and presumably potential buyers.

Specialized software developers can design the home page for companies and also maintain and update the site for a fee. Once the store is "open for business," advertising will be necessary to let potential users know about it and request it. This is usually done by adding the **URL** (Universal Resource Locator) address to all of the company communications. The address is also added to traditional media advertisements and placed on product packages. In addition, however, to reach the online target segment, it is useful to advertise online. For users, a good start to finding a company's URL is to use a search engine such as google.com.

E-commerce on the Internet is necessarily a global effort. As communication links with all countries, and offices and homes around the world get access to the "information superhighway," anyone anywhere can log onto a computer and "go shopping" in any "country." In fact, e-commerce sites that don't accommodate international shoppers may be "throwing away half their potential sales," says Jakob Nielsen, co-founder of Web site usability design consultancy Nielsen Norman Group in Fremont, California. Accommodation goes beyond shipping internationally. Questions such as whether a product works with the electrical connections in countries outside the United States or what a price is in another currency can stymie international shoppers, Nielsen says.[20]

Globalizing the Web site, one can choose between an internationalized and a localized site. An internationalized site uses basic English and international symbols and avoids metaphors that might be unfamiliar in another country. A localized site is a version of the site design translated and adapted for a specific locale. For example, Lands' End Inc.'s U.S. site features the many colors that the company's mesh polo shirts come in. Its localized U.K. site instead features conventional men's shirts and exclaims, "Lands' End summer shirts are pukka!" The French version warns that summer will be hot (L'ete sera chaud!).

Today it is very easy to imagine a consumer in Japan ordering a polo shirt online from Lands' End in Wisconsin or a Finnish customer buying a video camcorder from Hong Kong. Of course, the availability of terminals and required investments in infrastructure—such as fiberoptic cable—can still limit access for many countries and individuals. As important, transport costs and tariff barriers will still make some transactions prohibitively expensive. The point here, however, is that a globalized Web site can prove very beneficial for the company. To see which option to choose, first check the server logs to see whether there are enough users from a particular country to warrant localization and a translation.

Global Personal Selling

As we saw in Chapter 3, culture affects the "people skills" of the global marketer. Because of the importance of personal factors in selling, it is not surprising to find that good **salesmanship** varies across countries. Personal selling is usually the least global of all the marketing activities. As Percy Barnevik, former CEO of ABB puts it: "When you are selling in Germany, your salesmen have to be German."[21]

Managing a Sales Force

When the company is simply an exporter using independent distributors, management of the **sales force** is not an issue. However, when more control over local marketing is desired, the local company agent needs to work with the distributor's salespeople, help train them, and offer incentives to push the company's products. When the company takes over distribution in the country, it will usually end up establishing its own sales force.

Establishing the company's own sales force in a foreign country requires faith in the market and considerable resources. But some companies, especially those for which the selling function is a key success factor, have decided to take the plunge and have done it successfully. As we've mentioned, firms such as Avon and Mary Kay (cosmetics), Amway (miscellaneous products), and Electrolux (vacuum cleaners) have managed to create viable direct sales forces in various countries by following the selling practices back home. This has typically meant that the sales force has been started from scratch, with the company hiring people whom it can train from the beginning.

In the more general case, where personal selling is used primarily to sell to middlemen and large customers, the practice is often to hire some of the people who used to work for the distributor in order to avoid high start-up costs as well as interruptions in service. When Microsoft decided to open its own sales subsidiary in Japan, the people who previously had worked at ASCII, its distributor, were given the chance to interview for positions in the new outfit. Since switching jobs in Japan is a sensitive matter, following Japanese tradition, these interviews were kept secret so as not to jeopardize the person's status in his or her current position.

The major question facing the manager trying to coordinate the global sales effort is the transferability of the selling strategies and techniques used in the home market. Interviews with multinational managers and reviews of published literature have shown that there are basically four factors that affect transferability:[22]

1. *Geographic and physical dimensions.* The geographical spread of a country, its climate and terrain, as well as roadways and transportation conditions are obvious factors in determining the size of the territories that can be economically covered by one salesperson and the expense of individual calls. In cases such as rural India, for example, a single salesperson will rarely be able to cover more than a village area. Advanced techniques for optimizing territorial limits need considerable adaptation to provide guidance in such countries.

2. *Degree of market development.* In countries where customers are sophisticated and demanding, with high potential, in-depth training and specialization of the sales force are both necessary and possible. By contrast, where the life cycle is at an early stage, customers are less knowledgeable and require more information and education. Products tend to be less advanced, and the salesperson has to be more broadly trained and sell a wider product line. In the EDP industry, for example, Unisys compresses its sales territories in smaller markets and each salesperson carries a broader line and assumes servicing tasks in addition to sales tasks.

Much of a salesperson's activities fall under the rubric of "relationship marketing." Here Nestlé salespeople from the Thailand subsidiary explain new products and help check the stocking levels for retailers in Bangkok. Peter Charlesworth/SABA.

3. *Differing regulatory environments.* In some countries where fringe benefits—such as medical coverage, severance pay, and pension funding—may be high, the cost for a salesperson will escalate. Since such benefits are usually accompanied by a high tax rate on individuals, offering high commission rates to a salesperson may be ineffective in comparison with special gifts, a free car, or housing, all of which offer opportunities for tax avoidance.

4. *Differing human relations.* In many societies the job of a salesperson is looked down on as relatively unworthy. Hierarchical cultures such as Hindu India, Muslim Iran, and the Shinto culture in Japan tend historically to be aristocratic, favoring military castes, the priesthood, and feudal landowners over businesspeople or "merchants." Even in more democratic societies there may be some remnant of this pattern, and there is often a subtle ranking that puts a salesperson below engineers and the professions. The effect is to make it difficult to attract the best people to a sales job, and for those who accept the challenge it is often difficult to remove a certain aura of defensiveness in them that can mar the sales presentation. Commissions, contests, and bonuses are less effective since they make obvious the extrinsic monetary motivation behind salespeople's behavior.

These fundamental factors affect sales force recruiting, hiring, training, compensation schemes, and territorial allocation. The global marketer also needs to understand more specifically what can be realistically expected from the salespeople in different countries. What constitutes good salesmanship?

Personal Salesmanship

Salesmanship is the art of making a sale to another person. There are a few key personal characteristics of good salesmanship. One is enthusiasm, another self-confidence, still another appearance. These and other related factors all refer to the **salesman as a person.**[23]

There is no doubt that appearance is a very important factor in international business dealings, perhaps more so than domestically. But the important features of a person's appearance are not the same everywhere: Even those features that are relevant are often given a different interpretation. Asian nationals tend to be much less preoccupied with "good looks" and more concerned about appropriate clothing for the occasion than Westerners, whose individualism is usually given much more play. There are naturally a great many such small differences of style (which might make a large difference to the business relationship), and the astute salesperson will learn in-depth about the host country's particular customs.

As for enthusiasm and self-confidence, these factors are always important abroad but tend to go over best in "hard sell" situations of the kind typically encountered in

New York, Mumbai, or Tel Aviv. To the extent that enthusiasm reflects an interest in showing one's company and product in a positive light, it is certainly an asset in most countries. But excited delivery, loud voice, and fast talking do not sit well in many cultures. The same is true for self-confidence, that great asset of Western individualists. In cultures where group decisions are the norm, the role of self-confidence is appropriately reduced. In many high-context cultures the objectives of the business transaction go beyond the immediate business proposition. In such cultures, the relationship is so important that the "personal worth" of the salesperson becomes a much bigger issue than it is customarily in the American tradition.

In salesmanship books one is usually told that "the salesperson is the company." Yes, the person traveling abroad is, in a sense, the company and the person who localizes the global strategy. But to the customer in foreign markets he or she is so much more. Precisely because this salesperson is from another country, the individual implicitly becomes associated with many of the ideas, facts, stories, and images that the customer has of that country. The standard approach to preparing for a sales call by focusing on (1) the product, (2) the customer's needs, and (3) the competition, is still necessary but not sufficient. More broadly, the person sent abroad should show some genuine interest in nonbusiness matters that could be of interest to the customer. In many countries such "human worth" needs to be established first before more serious, focused business discussions can take place.[24]

The Western type of salesmanship, enthusiastic and confident individuals asserting themselves as the "face" of their companies, is successful in Western cultures, in particular the United States. The opposite type of salesperson—a simple conduit when it comes to business, an interesting human being outside of business—is more successful in Eastern cultures, in which individualism is subdued and the ultimate objectives of the business transaction are more than just economic. But, as always, there are exceptions (see box, "Going against the Grain: Dell in China").

The Presentation

The presentation made during a sales visit in domestic markets is typically viewed as consisting of five distinct stages:

Stage 1—Attention. Get the customer to listen to you.

Stage 2—Interest. Get the customer interested in what you have to say.

Stage 3—Desire. Get the customer to desire what you are selling.

Stage 4—Conviction. Get the buyer convinced that the offer is a good deal.

Stage 5—*Action.* Get the customer's signature on the contract.

In global marketing these stages are still valid, but their relative importance and the way an individual salesperson goes about moving the customer through them deviate considerably from the home market.

First of all, the attention and interest stages are often less critical when making sales calls abroad. The obvious investment in time and travel plus the "exotic" flavor of the visitor naturally arouses the curiosity of the prospect. The exception to this rule is the salesperson representing a country not too well known for the particular product sold, such as a Brazilian visitor to France selling loudspeakers, a new export product from Brazil. In general, however, the first two stages are easier to surmount in global markets.

By contrast, the next three stages are for the same reasons less easily traversed in global transactions. The distances involved, geographically and psychologically, and the consequent difficulties in establishing reliable supply and payment systems, not to mention future service support, all combine into obstacles for a successful agreement. These global factors create an environment in which the traditional salesmanship virtues of "preparedness," "handling objections," and "closing tactics" take on new and deeper meanings.

Getting the Picture

GOING AGAINST THE GRAIN: DELL IN CHINA

By 2001 Dell was the number one PC brand in the world, with revenues for the last four quarters totaling $31.8 billion. Its road to the number one spot involved an innovative production and distribution strategy. Instead of being a technological leader, Dell operated as an assembler of computer components bought from independent vendors. Its assembly operation was fast and flexible, allowing the company to customize configurations for different buyer needs. The distribution system involved direct sales to customers, using catalogs, telephone, and online sales via the Internet, the shipping handled by independent express services such as UPS. Although initially focused on the consumer market, Dell's approach turned out to be particularly useful in the office and B2B markets where sophisticated corporate IT buyers were able to get computers to their exact specifications.

One market where the Dell approach seemed less appropriate was China, where the consumer market was embryonic at best, and where B2B sales often involved dealing with government bureaucrats rather than knowledgeable IT engineers. From intermittent Internet sales, Dell so far ranked only number seven in China's PC market. Management realized that the firm could not rely on Internet sales alone to succeed.

Deciding to go with an adapted strategy playing to its strengths, in August 1998 Dell opened a component warehouse and assembly and service center in Xiamen, an industrial center and transportation hub in the southern part of China. Since the average Chinese consumer could not afford a PC and very few had bank accounts or credit cards, Dell decided to focus on the B2B market.

Taking a gamble, Dell's sales strategy avoided the customary use of go-between contacts when approaching corporate prospects. Instead, the salespeople bypassed the government-appointed officials in the companies, going directly to the IT managers and the technical staff. The notion was that in the new open atmosphere in China, the old way of doing business would no longer be needed. The salespeople would come as a team with aggressive American-style presentations and upbeat promises of what Dell could do for their business. They were not shy to point out the success of Dell elsewhere in the world and how the flexible customization and service support from Xiamen were more than competitors could offer.

The gamble paid off, as the technical directors enjoyed the entrepreneurial spirit of the Dell salespeople and the straight talk on technical matters. And, in contrast to the tradition, the bureaucrats stayed out of much of the purchase decision making, content as long as budgetary limits were observed.

By the second quarter of 1999, Dell recorded year-on-year unit growth of 561 percent. By 2001 its ranking in the Chinese market had catapulted from seventh to third, and Dell was the fastest-growing PC brand in China.

A later incursion into the consumer market did not go so well, however. Meeting fierce resistance and sharply reduced prices from its main domestic competitors Lenovo (formerly Legend) and Founder, Dell opted to withdraw from the lower-end consumer market and focus on higher-priced models for consumers and expand its B2B market share.

Sources: Pauline Ng, "Dell: Selling Directly, Globally," Centre for Asian Business Cases, University of Hong Kong, 2000; "Dell Paves the Way for a New Level of Direct Economics and Customer Benefits," April 14, 1997; "Dell Computer Retreats from China's Low-End PC Market," *AFX.COM*, August 17, 2004; **www.dell.com.**

Be Prepared!

There is no shortcut to effective sales presentations abroad, and the most fundamental building block in this process is preparation. The visitor must be knowledgeable with respect to her or his product and the competition, as well as the customer's situation and needs, but must also be able to handle questions concerning tariff and nontariff barriers and other trade complications affecting shipments. In many cases the requirements for an effective sales call are such that a single individual simply can't be expected to handle all the questions alone. Teams of visitors are therefore dispatched (at consequently higher expense), or a representative of the consulate in the country may be asked to join. The important fact here is usually not that specific information can be instantaneously accessed and questions answered right away but that the salesperson demonstrates that he or she has paid close attention to the customer's specific situation and the special requirements for doing business in the country. Such a demonstration, again, comes down to not only specific knowledge about the "strictly business" aspects of the transactions but also the "nonbusiness" aspects of the relationship. Learning about Subhas Chandra Bose ("Netaji") and his role in Bengal during the first half of the twentieth century is "good for business" in India in the broadest sense. For the visitor, it generates an understanding of the complex social and political forces at work in the country that in turn leads to a deeper appreciation of similar anticolonial movements and postcolonial societies elsewhere. It tends to make the individual a more compassionate and less prejudiced human being, and that is always useful.

Handling Objections

Handling objections is a difficult task in any sales presentation, and it is more so in global settings where communications are more easily garbled. In fact, there is perhaps no other area of the sales presentation in which the cultural differences are more pronounced. The best procedures for handling objections vary considerably from country to country.

Generally speaking, some pointers can be suggested. It is important that the objections not be escalated into an argument. Even in very contentious societies—as in Israel, for example—it is better to allow for the fact that most objections do have merit. Rather than attempting outright refutation and persuasion based on facts and figures, it is more effective to suggest the direction in which the answer lies and lead the customer toward it rather than pushing.

The best way to handle objections is to avoid having them raised in the first place. Whether this can be done hinges very much on the amount of "ego" that the salesperson presents. The self-confident salesperson so highly praised in American textbooks is told to "keep standing so that the prospect can be dominated," or at least be equal to the customer: "I know you are busy. I am busy myself." [25] It goes without saying that such tactics might be inappropriate in countries where the "customer is the king" and where the use of confrontation and intimidation is highly counterproductive. Even though in many such countries the presentation will meet no overt objections, it is likely to fail miserably. In such cases the unfortunate salesperson is often back in the hotel room before long wondering, "What hit me?"

Closing Tactics

The **closing tactics** also vary considerably between countries. Most infuriating for foreigners, it is not always easy to discern when exactly the "decision to buy" is made or when a felicitous moment for closing is at hand. There are times when the senior manager on the customer's side leaves a meeting without any particular agreement with the salesperson, who is expected to continue the presentation without his presence. Some quietly whispered words in the native tongue not understood by the salesperson can easily be misinterpreted as a polite way of saying "no" when in fact they mean "yes." A direct question from the salesperson to gauge interest and reaction of the customer may be given an evasive answer, again yielding mixed and exasperating signals.

When closing is seemingly within reach, some person with intimate knowledge of the country's customs should be present to assist the salesperson. It is in these later stages that the particular cultural norms have been set down most precisely. Generally, cultural norms can be suspended more easily in matters of low importance. Since the signing of the contract is the most serious action to be taken during the whole of the negotiations, most customers (and salespeople) tend to lean on standard, formal procedures when committing themselves and their company. The presence of a knowledgeable person (often with legal expertise) to assist in the final stages therefore becomes very important.

But this same person might be useful throughout in indicating to the salesperson what is going on among the customer's people by listening in on their discussions and also interpreting what their nonspeaking, their silences, mean. Silence has a particularly strong effect in international presentations as a closing technique. Sometimes the "final offer" is modified when the customer remains silent, although the offer would have been quite acceptable. This is common in Japan when American salespeople get impatient and give unnecessary concessions, but it occurs often enough in Europe and even in the United States. A salesman for industrial products related how he had closed a sale to the U.S. manufacturing operation of a European ski producer: "I had made all my points, laid out the whole situation, answered the questions. I saw he was thinking, thinking hard, so I shut up and just sat there. Seconds stretched into minutes. I sensed that the first man to speak would lose, so I let it ride. We sat there for perhaps 15 minutes, not saying a thing. Suddenly he said, 'Let's do it,' and I had a sale."

Global personal selling has to be localized and adapted; but with sensitivity, persistence, preparation, and a good product, most cultural obstacles can be overcome.

Integrated Marketing Communications

Any one customer, whether global or local, receives information about a brand from a number of sources. It is naturally important that the message coming through be consistent. The promotional tools discussed in this chapter need to be integrated with each other and also with the media advertising covered in Chapter 16. This is the task of **integrated marketing communications,** or IMC for short.

The IMC concept stresses the need to combine the various communication disciplines—for example, media advertising, direct marketing, sales promotion, Internet advertising, and public relations—to ensure clarity, consistency, and maximum communications impact. It argues for a broad perspective that takes into account all sources of brand or company contacts that a customer has with a product or service. Instead of seeing media advertising or in-store promotion as the major promotional vehicle, with other communication tools ancillary, IMC says that all tools need to be managed jointly to achieve maximum impact.[26]

The IMC concept is difficult to implement globally since it enlarges the number of communication functions that need to be coordinated. It also runs up against the problem that, as we have seen in this chapter, different rules and regulations govern the use of promotional tools in different countries. Nevertheless, the IMC concept is valuable globally since it forces the company to define the brand identities and communication platforms more clearly. It may not be possible to use the same promotional tools in different countries, but the message put across can be uniform and consistent.

In fact, IMC forces advertising and promotional specialists to "think outside the box," that is, to take a broader view of their communication means and goals. This can be particularly useful when entering new markets where communication media are different. Intel, the chipmaker from Silicon Valley, placed television and billboard ads throughout China to establish brand awareness for its microprocessors. The company also distributed nearly 1 million bike reflectors—which glow in the dark with the words "Intel Inside Pentium Processor"—in China's biggest cities. Taiwan-based Yonex Corporation pays $2 million annually to be the exclusive equipment sponsor for Indonesia's powerful national badminton team. Nike sponsors four teams in China's new professional soccer league, including one owned by the People's Liberation Army. Citibank captured 40 percent of Thailand's credit card market relying on a sales force of 600 part-timers who are paid a fee for each applicant approved.[27]

The same realization that there are usually several means of reaching a given objective pervades the global marketing function at Levi Strauss, the jeans maker. Robert Holloway, then vice president, was moving the company toward a "think globally, act locally" approach with campaigns that carried a unified message but with looks that mirrored their individual markets. He said global marketing brings very powerful benefits to the brand and is also important to the bottom line, since global images can be more cost-efficient than local ones. Using the same campaign in multiple markets saved production costs of $100,000 to $1 million for a 30-second commercial. But local managers were allowed to select their own ad agencies with no pressure from headquarters. "How can I possibly know all the local markets?" Holloway said.

As part of its IMC strategy, Levi Strauss is also examining its worldwide media mix, 75 percent of which goes to television. It plans on spending fewer TV ad dollars in mature markets (where TV is losing share) and allocating more in emerging markets (where TV is more efficient). In mature markets the stress is shifting to newer media, in particular the Internet. Levi's Web sites feature brand history, fashion tips, games, and youth trends. The American-style, pioneer brand identity of Levi's fits well with the new media, and plans are to expand the Web spending as the Internet reach increases.[28]

Summary

Although much of the execution of promotional strategies needs to be localized because of varying regulations in different countries, the growth of global communications, global media, and global events in sports and other areas has made global promotion feasible. Sponsorship and creation of global events, participation in international trade fairs, and a global public relations perspective, including global publicity, are promotional tools for the company's global marketing effort. The increasing feasibility of direct marketing and e-commerce helps even smaller companies capitalize on global opportunities.

As for the promotional regulations that often force localization, the growth of integrated trading blocs is gradually forcing harmonization of regulations. Challenges from global companies to arcane legislation designed to protect local businesses have been successful. The trend has been toward increasing importance of global recognition and reputation, as evidenced by the growth of global brand names. The various promotional tools discussed in this chapter play an important role in developing and sustaining the equity in such global brand names. This is accomplished by globally integrated marketing communications, with all promotions based on a unified brand identity and global copy platforms, but with room for local implementation taking into account differing promotion regulations and availability of promotional tools.

Many people around the world do not like the way promotional hoopla seems to have become more important than what is promoted—the game or the product itself. However, with open global markets, democracy, and capitalism, promotion is unavoidably part of the game.

Key Terms

cause marketing, *552*
closing tactics, *569*
cross-marketing, *553*
damage control, *556*
direct marketing, *558*
direct response television
(DRTV), *558*
electronic commerce, *559*
electronic marketing
strengths, *563*
electronic marketing
weaknesses, *563*

e-tailing, *560*
events, *552*
global public relations, *555*
handling objections, *569*
in-store promotion, *550*
integrated marketing
communications, *570*
international trade fairs, *557*
mail order, *558*
online marketing, *559*
press releases, *555*
product placement, *554*

publicity, *554*
sales force, *565*
salesman as a person, *566*
salesmanship, *565*
sponsorship, *551*
telemarketing, *558*
trade promotions, *550*
URL, *564*
Web home page, *564*

Discussion Questions

1. What is it that makes a created media event such as a Hollywood movie opening a powerful promotional tool? What does this tell you about when such events should (or should not) be attempted by the global marketer?

2. Analyze how some companies' Web sites serve as both a source of information and a point-of-purchase promotional site. What do the companies do in order to create an interactive, highly involved encounter? How do they try to induce "action"?

3. As we saw in the opening vignette to Chapter 2, Nike's high visibility and publicity have had some negative effects. Use the Internet and other media sources to find out what they are. What can Nike do to counter the product "misplacement" effects?

4. What are the forces that have led to the success of direct marketing? What are the threats against its continued success? What has helped the globalization of direct marketing? Do you see any obstacles now or in the future?

5. Drawing on the cultural discussion in Chapter 3 and your own cultural background, compare the salesmanship skills needed to sell an automobile in Germany, in the United States, and in Japan (or some other countries of your own choice). What skills would be most advantageous? Which ones could land you in trouble?

Notes

1. See Boddewyn, 1988.
2. From Terpstra and Sarathy, 1994, p. 508.
3. Such "serendipitous" advertising, broadcasting of brand names through TV coverage of the events, is coming under scrutiny, at least in the United States. The rental rates for stadium advertising space have risen to reflect the TV coverage, at the same time that broadcasters are starting to complain about the "free ride" they are giving to nonpaying advertisers. But although cigarette advertising such as Marlboro's has been curtailed (see McKinley, Jr., 1995), it will probably be a long time before the Nike swoosh disappears from view.
4. The Swatch material is drawn from two case studies, Pinson and Kimball, 1987, and Jeannet et al., 1985, and from www.swatch.com.
5. See Bennet, 1995.
6. These figures are from Belch and Belch, in their 1998 edition, p. 431.
7. Thanks to Gary Bamossy for ideas and data here and in the e-commerce section of this chapter.
8. See Levin, 1994, and Case 4-3.
9. Jean-Jacques Servan-Schreiber's *The American Challenge* became a great bestseller in the late 1960s.
10. Many of the negative attitudes have been documented and shown to be based on a one-sided view of Japanese management as all-powerful; see Sullivan, 1992.
11. See Stephen A. Greyser and N. Langford, "Volvo and the Monster Mash," Harvard Business School case no. 9-593-024.
12. See Markoff, 1994.
13. This section draws on Sacks, 1995, and www.the-dma.org.
14. See Nuttall, 2004.
15. See "Forrester Projects," 2004; www.forrester.com.
16. See "Amazon.com," 2004; www.imediaconnection.com.
17. See Dickie, 2004.
18. See Lau and Pesola, 2003.
19. See Neal, 2003.
20. From www.computerworld.com, June 17, 2002.
21. From an interview in *Harvard Business Review* (Taylor, 1992).
22. This section draws on Hill et al., 1991, and Futrell, 2003.
23. Much of the noninternational material in this section comes from Buskirk and Buskirk, 1992, a leading text on salesmanship, and from Futrell, 2003.
24. Hall, 1960, has an extended example of a telecommunications deal in a Latin American country that is fun reading as well as instructive.
25. From Buskirk and Buskirk, 1992, pp. 266 and 331.
26. As defined by the American Association of Advertising Agencies; see Belch and Belch, 2007, pp. 9–10.
27. These examples come from Warner and Hsu, 1996, and "Sticky Wickets," 1995.
28. The Levi Strauss example is from Fannin, 1996. See also www.levistrauss.com.

Selected References

"Amazon.com Leads Web Site Retailers." *iMedia Connection,* August 24, 2004.

Belch, George E., and Michael A. Belch. *Advertising and Promotion,* 6th ed. New York: McGraw-Hill/Irwin, 2007.

Bennet, James. "An Auto Maker Uses a Cult Artist's Colorful Images to Make Its Minivans Stand Out from the Pack." *New York Times,* January 19, 1995, p. D23.

Boddewyn, Jean J. *Premiums, Gifts, and Competitions.* New York: International Advertising Association, 1988.

Buskirk, R. H., and B. Buskirk. *Selling: Principles and Practice,* 13th ed. New York: McGraw-Hill, 1992.

Dickie, Mure. "Amazon Buys into Growing Chinese Online Retail Market." *Financial Times (London),* August 20, 2004, p. 20.

Dregner, Daniel W. "The Outsourcing Bogeyman," *Foreign Affairs,* May/June 2004.

Egol, Len. "Europe: Uncommon Market." *Direct* 6, no. 10 (October 1994a), p. 83.

_____. "Is China Ready for U.S. Mail, U.S. Direct Marketers?" *Direct* 6, no. 12 (December 1994b), p. 55.

Fannin, Rebecca A. "Levi's Global Guru Shakes Up Culture." *Advertising Age International,* November 1996, pp. 120, 123.

Farhi, Paul. "Selling Is as Selling Does." *Washington Post,* April 30, 1995, pp. H1, H6.

"Forrester Projects Booming Online Retail Sales by 2010." *Media Daily News,* August 24, 2004.

Futrell, Charles. *Fundamentals of Selling: Customers for Life Through Service*, 8th ed. New York: McGraw-Hill/Irwin, 2003.

Goldberg, Carey. "Midnight Sales Frenzy Ushers in Windows 95." *New York Times,* August 24, 1995, pp. A1, D6.

Hall, Edward T. "The Silent Language in Overseas Business." *Harvard Business Review,* May–June 1960, pp. 87–96.

Hill, John S.; Richard R. Still; and Unal O. Boya. "Managing the Multinational Sales Force." *International Marketing Review* 8, no. 1 (1991), pp. 19–31.

Jeannet, Jean-Pierre; Susan W. Nye; and Barbara Priovolos. "The Swatch Project." Imede, 1985.

Kelly, Gene. "Direct Marketing Going Overseas." *Lincoln Evening Journal,* June 1, 1994, business sec.

Lau, Justine, and Maija Pesola. "Hong Kong's Shoppers Seek Online Refuge." *Financial Times (London),* May 6, 2003, p. 13.

Levin, Gary. "Benetton Ad Lays Bare the Bloody Toll of War." *Advertising Age,* February 21, 1994, p. 38.

Markoff, John. "In About-Face, Intel Will Swap Its Flawed Chips." *New York Times,* December 21, 1994, pp. A1, D6.

Mårtenson, Rita. *Innovations in Retailing.* Lund, Sweden: Liber, 1983.

McKinley, James C., Jr. "The Garden Agrees to Curb Cigarette Ads." *New York Times,* April 5, 1995, p. C2.

Neal, David. "EU Imposes Online Tax." *VNU NET,* June 16, 2003, p. 21.

Nuttall, Chris. "Quarter of Purchases to Be Over the Web by 2009." *Financial Times (London),* March 22, 2004, p. 5.

Parke, Jo Anne. "The Case for Going Global: Globalization in Direct Marketing." *Target Marketing* 17, no. 11 (November 1994), p. 8.

Pinson, Christian, and Helen Chase Kimball. "Swatch." INSEAD-CEDEP, 1987, case no. 589-005-IN.

Sacks, Douglas. "Entering the Asian Living Room: Direct Response Television." *Target Marketing* 18, no. 2 (1995), p. 12.

Segal, David. "With Windows 95's Debut, Microsoft Scales Heights of Hype." *Washington Post,* August 24, 1995, p. A14.

Servan-Schreiber, Jean-Jacques. *The American Challenge.* New York: Atheneum, 1968.

Shirk, Martha. "Simple Formula No Answer for Hungry Children." *St. Louis Post-Dispatch,* September 23, 1991, p. 18.

Smith, Dawn. "Putting Soul into the Machine." *Marketing Computers* 14, no. 7 (July 1994), p. 38.

"Sticky Wickets, but What a Future." *BusinessWeek,* August 7, 1995, pp. 72–73.

Sullivan, Jeremiah J. *Invasion of the Salarymen.* Westport, CT: Praeger, 1992.

Taylor, William. "The Logic of Global Business: An Interview with ABB's Percy Barnevik." In Christopher A. Bartlett and Sumantra Ghoshal, *Transnational Management,* Homewood, IL: Irwin, 1992, pp. 892–908.

Terpstra, Vern, and Ravi Sarathy. *International Marketing,* 6th ed. Fort Worth, TX: Dryden, 1994.

"Thais and Indonesians Are Good Direct Mail Targets." *Market Asia Pacific,* February 1, 1995.

Warner, Fara, and Karen Hsu. "Intel Gets a Free Ride in China by Sticking Its Name on Bicycles." *Wall Street Journal,* August 7, 1996, p. B5.

18

Organizing for Global Marketing

"Making it all work"

After finishing this chapter, you will be able to:

1. See how to leverage the global network of the multinational firm with a global strategy by creating the appropriate organizational linkages to the local market.
2. Understand why local managers are consulted early in a global strategy formulation process so that local motivation is not diminished.
3. Recognize that local managers can assume a more global view and that local subsidiaries can be given global responsibilities for a particular product line—local globalization.
4. Help institute coordination mechanisms that range from creating a common global culture, sharing information, and establishing personal relations to the creation of new organizational units such as global account managers and global teams.
5. Realize how the organizational structure and systems can be designed to serve one common purpose: to bring the global company closer to the local customer—global localization.

To implement a global marketing strategy, the organization's structure—the solid and dotted lines connecting management positions, departmental staff, divisional units, and subsidiaries on the organizational chart—often needs to be changed. The typical multinational organization with an international division and semi-independent country subsidiaries can work well in the multidomestic case when coordination across local markets is of less importance. As markets globalize, the central coordination requirements grow stronger, and country subsidiaries' autonomy must be reined in. In matrixed organizations, where coordination across product divisions and countries is explicit, global marketing can be implemented more easily. However, since a global marketing strategy tends to limit the role of local adaptation, in global companies the product dimension of a matrix tends to dominate the country dimension. It is the global counterpart of "product management." Needless to say, this creates conflicts at the local country level, and firms have to find a way to tilt the balance, for example, by placing strong managers at regional centers.

This chapter deals with the organizational aspects of global marketing. It explains how to structure centralized coordination and integration and how to manage the potential conflicts at the local level. As in all organizations, the *organizational structure,* the *management systems* installed, and the *people* in the organization are the critical ingredients in the successful implementation of global marketing strategies.

Nestlé's Shift to Global Centralization

The multinational company Nestlé, based in Vevey, Switzerland, is the world's largest food and drink company, employing approximately 253,000 people around the globe. The company's main lines of business are water, ice cream, pet food, and confectionery (chocolate and candy). The company is best known for its instant coffee—yes, Nescafé—but it also owns Perrier, Vittel, San Pellegrino, and Contrex waters, and the world's favorite candy bar, Kit Kat. On a less upbeat note, the company has for the last 30 years or so been engaged in a on-again, off-again conflict over its sales of baby-milk formula to poor countries in Africa (where clean water to mix with the formula tends to be in short supply).

During the 15 years before the new millennium, Nestlé, already a big global company, expanded greatly through mergers and acquisitions. In 1988 it bought Rowntree, an English chocolate maker (acquiring Kit Kat in the process). Perrier was acquired in 1992; San Pellegrino in 1997. Four years later the company bought Ralston Purina, a leading American pet-food maker. Although some businesses were also sold off, Nestlé's brands number in the hundreds, most of them local.

How is such a global corporation organized? How can it be managed? Initially, Nestlé followed its own traditional model, allowing local subsidiaries maximum independence and flexibility. This was a deviation for the more centralized, top-down and focused strategies adopted by its main competitors, including Unilever and Cadbury Schweppes. The Nestlé company had always prided itself on being a good local citizen, and the general managers of the different national subsidiaries had become "kings in their kingdoms," according to Nestlé Chief Executive Peter Brabeck. The strategy had a solid marketing foundation. There is no global consumer, according to Mr. Brabeck. For example, Nescafé, the flag brand, comes in 200 different varieties. Russians want a thick, strong, and sweet coffee with milk, very different from continental Europeans. But the local variations come at a price. Centralized purchasing becomes impossible, not only across countries but even within countries. In the case of the United States alone, for example, the company found that the vanilla ordered by its American plants was paid for at 20 different prices. Supply chain management was clearly inefficient.

So Nestlé decided to do away with two of its most heralded principles. First, local independence had to be reined in. Decentralization was replaced by a globally centralized structure, consolidating the management of factories in individual countries into regions, and combining similar products into "strategic business units" with global reach. To implement the change, accounting, administration, sales, and payroll records were consolidated on a regional basis, not a popular move among the country general managers. Some senior managers were sent elsewhere in the global organization, others simply quit.

The second move was to accept the inevitability of introducing an improved supply chain management system. Tradition at Nestlé had been to avoid using IT (information technology) in the day-to-day running of the company, with the idea that a focus on people, products, and brands would be superior to managing "by the numbers" on a spreadsheet. But the inefficiencies had become too great, and Nestlé's supply and distribution costs were much higher than the competition. So, with the help of the German IT-firm SAP, in 2000 Nestlé launched a worldwide conversion to managing suppliers, inventory, and ordering routines via computer. Known as "GLOBE" (for "Global Business Excellence") inside the firm, the project aims to establish a single resource-planning technology platform for the global (or at least regional) operations, standardize packaging codes, and provide real-time data about prices of raw materials and stock levels in inventory, all in the same units. The vast project, which requires recasting almost all administrative routines and position descriptions across all the local and national units in the organization, was completed in 2007.

How do you run a global operation? Some centralization is apparently necessary, and people skills are useful but not enough. You need up-to-date information technology as well. Of course, it helps if everybody speaks the same language and uses the same units. For American companies, the English language and the U.S. dollar are natural, but it is probably time to give up inches, ounces, gallons, and miles and start thinking in terms of meters, liters, and kilometers. It would surely make it easier to compare numbers across countries.

Sources: Robert Gottliebsen, "Nestlé's Tastes Change," *The Weekend Australian,* July 31, 2004, p. 39; "Daring, Defying, to Grow," *The Economist*, Special Report Nestlé, August 7, 2004, pp. 55–58; **www.nestle.com.**

Introduction

The *formulation* of a global marketing strategy for a product line is primarily an intellectual challenge for managers. The *implementation* of the strategy, by contrast, involves much more interpersonal discussion and persuasion. The global marketing manager needs to become an internal salesperson and champion. And the global organization needs to be structured carefully to be able to respond to the challenge. The local units have to be motivated to *execute* the global strategy effectively.

The focus of this chapter is the organizational problems of global marketing. It starts by establishing the *context* in which the organizational decisions are made, then spells out the *job* that needs to be done, along with the tools that exist to do it. It discusses some common organizational *structures* found in multinational firms and looks at the global *network* as a firm-specific advantage. A section on *globalizing management* leads into a discussion of management *systems* and the role of *people and culture* in global marketing management. The chapter then deals with the special case of organizing to serve *global customers,* and presents techniques for *resolving conflicts* between headquarters and local units. The final section discusses what it takes to be a good global marketer today.

The Context

To see why implementing global marketing is generally difficult, it is important to first understand the managerial context. The typical situation is one where:

1. The company is already present in many markets.
2. The company is successful in at least some of the major markets (global marketing is usually *not* a crisis solution).
3. There is a history of quite successful operations with local autonomy.
4. The country managers have experience and status at home and in the organization. For administrative and control reasons the subsidiaries may be run by expatriates, but the local marketing effort is run by a local marketing manager (and/or by the country manager, when a native).
5. The *legitimacy* of the global marketing "imperative" is not all that obvious in the organization—unless successful competitors have forced the issue.
6. The global advantage derives from (*a*) cost savings, (*b*) demand spillover effects, and (*c*) serving global customers. Only in the last category will the benefits be unequivocal.
7. One obvious effect of a global strategy will be less autonomy for the local subsidiary.
8. The initiative for the global strategy comes from the top.

Given this context, it is not surprising if local country managers have to be dragged into globalization against their will.

The Task

There are essentially three main organizational requirements when a global marketing strategy is implemented. The organization needs to provide:

1. *Communication.* An effective *multiple-way communication system* needs to be set up to carry directives from the center to the local markets and to feed back information to headquarters and other subsidiaries.
2. *Motivation.* The local country managers need to be given *incentives* to implement the global strategy even though it often involves a reduction in local autonomy and resources.
3. *Flexibility.* The organization structure and/or systems need to be *flexible* so that changing conditions and new developments can be responded to and capitalized on as they arise.

The typical organization has several *organizational* tools to accomplish these tasks:

- *Creating new organizational units.* The most common new units are perhaps *global teams,* drawing members from headquarters and country subsidiaries, with the team leader from a major lead country.
- *Creating new positions* (or reformulating existing position descriptions) that emphasize global responsibilities. A typical example is the creation of a *global marketing director.*
- *Changing the reporting lines.* The organization can change the existing *structure,* that is, the formal lines of reporting and authority. This is in some ways the most clear-cut change toward centralization and the most far-reaching and dramatic change in the local organization. For example, one company wanting to create a pan-European marketing strategy directed its local marketing managers to report to European headquarters instead of the country managers, who saw themselves as losers.
- *Creating new systems.* The organization can create *new systems* and procedures within the given structure. Generally, this means that local managers retain formal authority and reporting lines but are forced to work harder and/or differently. For example, among globalizing firms it is very common to initiate periodic global meetings among country managers to explain and reinforce the global strategy.
- *People adapting.* The organization can rely on *people* to change their behavior and accommodate the changes. In one technology-intensive firm, the global "change agent" was the marketing manager at headquarters who spent most of his time on the road explaining the global strategy and sharing information from other subsidiaries.

Organizational Structure

There is no single best way to organize for global marketing. There is simply too much variety in product lines, customers, and country environments. Even companies with similar product lines and global reach will organize differently. The diversity and flexibility of people and existing systems differ between firms, and the global organization is a product of the historical evolution of the company. Naturally, it is easier to implement global marketing when people and systems in the company have previous experience with marketing in foreign countries.

The key issue for **organizational design** tends to be how to strike an appropriate balance between headquarters' need for central coordination and the local subsidiary's motivation for implementing the global strategy.

The firm can organize its international coverage in different ways. Most have gone through a sequence of these stages as they change their structure to expand overseas.

- *Export department.* The creation of an **export department structure** is usually the first step in the functional organization toward entry into foreign markets. Export departments are typically cost centers without independent authority in product and marketing mix decisions. The typical export department structure is given in Exhibit 18.1.

EXHIBIT 18.1
The Export Department
Structure

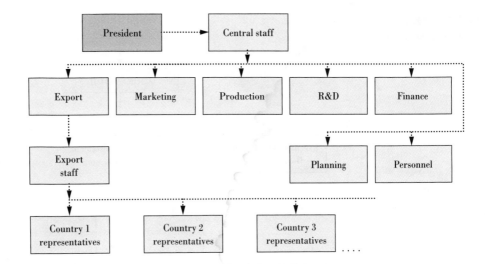

- *International division.* As the export revenue share increases (a common threshold value is around 10 percent of total revenues) and there are several countries in the strategic portfolio, the firm changes to a full-fledged **international division structure,** where the general manager has profit-and-loss responsibilities. The international division is often a **strategic business unit** (SBU), an operating unit functioning basically as a freestanding business. It competes with the domestic units for resource allocations, buying services from the central headquarters' staff and demanding a say on product design, product positioning, and other decisions affecting its effectiveness abroad. Exhibit 18.2 shows the typical structure with an international division.
- *Geographical/regional structure.* As overseas sales expand and the management of the countries takes more time and resources, the firm usually subdivides the international division into country groups or trade regions. Typical areas are western Europe, Latin America, Africa and the Middle East, east Asia and the Pacific, and eastern Europe and Russia. The international division is still usually intact, and a

EXHIBIT 18.2
The International Division
Structure

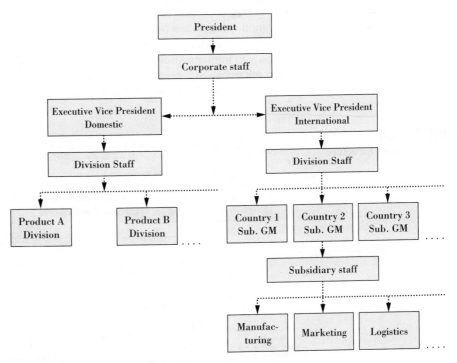

Note: Sub.GM = subsidiary general manager.

EXHIBIT 18.3
The Regional Structure

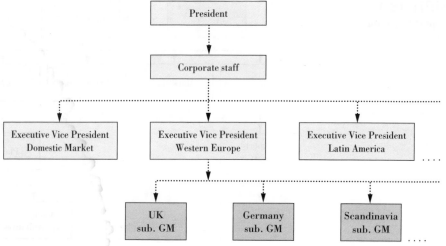

Note: Sub.GM = subsidiary general manager.

new organizational level is introduced to coordinate within the newly established regions. This **regional organization** is common among Japanese companies, whose home market is large and structured separately. When the home market is minor compared with the overseas sales, as in many European companies, the home market is simply subordinated in the area and there is no domestic division as such. A regional structure is shown in Exhibit 18.3.

- *Global product divisions.* The attempt to develop a truly global strategy for a firm's product line tends to force a rejection of the international-versus-domestic split. The solution is often a **global product division,** where regional and local managers' authority is subordinated to that of the global division chief, who approves and directs. Although the structure has a strong logic behind it and the implementation of global marketing is facilitated, this structure demands a lot from the division manager.[1] The reason is simple. The division manager's staff is often too far away from the local market to have a very secure understanding of the local issues and differences. Furthermore, the need for speed and responsiveness to local competitive moves and customer requests makes central direction of operations difficult. One common solution has been for the division chief to set only broad policy goals and formulate the global strategy and then allow the local managers a great deal of autonomy in implementing the strategies. Even though global uniformity might be less than otherwise, the positive effect on the motivation of the local country managers often makes up for it. The global product structure is displayed in Exhibit 18.4.

EXHIBIT 18.4
The Global Product Structure

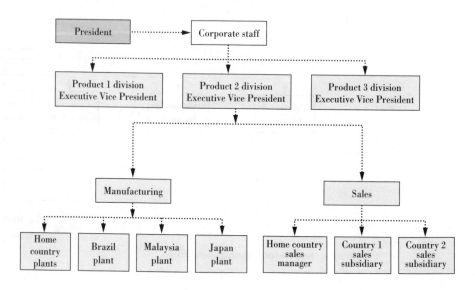

EXHIBIT 18.5
The Global Matrix Structure: Honda's Global Organization

Source: Osamu Iida, executive vice president, Honda North America.

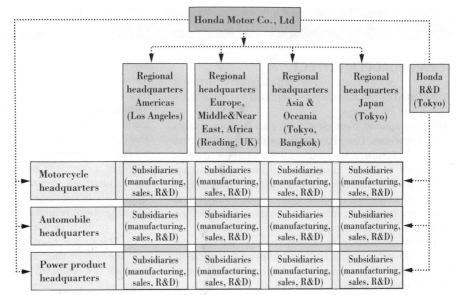

- *Matrix organizations.* Matrix structures are those in which both country and product receive equal emphasis. Marketing of one product in a given country has to report to both the global product manager, who oversees all the countries for that product, and the country manager, who is responsible for all the products in the country. The local marketer has to respond to two bosses, an undesirable feature but often workable if the people are experienced and the management systems are handled flexibly. This is the essence of coordination and integration, and the **matrix organization,** whether formally established or not, is a natural structure for the global marketer. The global matrix structure at Honda Motor Company is shown in Exhibit 18.5.

- *Transnational organizations.* As globalization requirements increase in reach and scope, global strategies involve not only manufacturing and marketing but also R&D, design, and engineering. This has led especially technology-intensive companies to develop organizational structures in which different parts of the firm's value chain are located in different parts of the world. These are called **transnational organizations** to emphasize their cross-country network character.[2]

For example, companies such as Ericsson from Sweden in telecommunications can place its R&D for certain products in one country, manufacturing of the product somewhere else, and then do global sales and marketing from a third location. Other firms have gone even further, splitting up country subsidiaries into specialized units. Honeywell, the U.S.-based multinational in electronic measurement, has distributed its functions for design, engineering, sales, and marketing throughout Europe, allowing each country subsidiary to specialize. The reorganization of former full-fledged country subsidiaries into "special resource centers" is not particularly easy on the people displaced because their specialty is now in a new country location. Nevertheless, given some flexibility in the implementation of the new structure, many firms have succeeded in developing global networks with the country units drawing on the particular strengths of the local economy. How the transnational structure involves all units of the global network is shown in Exhibit 18.6.

- *Horizontal networks.* The natural result of the recent emergence of transnational expertise, effective global communications, and the drive toward "lean" organizations, **horizontal networks** have become the new "ideal" type of organizational structure. In these networks, the traditional hierarchical arrangement—with a decision maker at the top of the international division or global product division, directives flowing out to the various country subsidiaries, and performance results fed back up—has been replaced by a much less pyramidal structure. In horizontal networks,

Getting the Picture

THE PAN-EUROPEAN EFFECT

The effect of global marketing on organization structure is well illustrated by the attempts of companies to capitalize on the European integration.

Many companies have developed pan-European structures and processes. Lever Europe, the regional headquarters of Unilever in Europe, added a general manager for strategic development to whom Europewide product group managers report. The strategic European group complements the existing geographic structure with country managers responsible for operating profits. The company is developing Euro-brands for which Europewide product managers have responsibility to develop marketing strategy, package design, and advertising. The Europewide product managers have their own budgets, operate as cost centers, and have to "sell" the country managers on the introduction of the Euro-brands through the existing channels in each country. Additional reporting lines represent a simple coordinating device.

Dell Computer is asking its product marketing managers in the various European countries to report to the pan-European

head office in addition to the country managers. Going halfway is sometimes not enough. 3M, the Minnesota-based maker of videodisks and tapes and related products, tried to develop Euro-products by creating small European product teams that had to draw on functional expertise in local units. This structure became too weak, and the company shifted to full-fledged Europewide business units.

When a company dominates its markets and products are standardized, centralized direction is facilitated. Since 1994 Gillette's international headquarters in the United States has been responsible for all marketing in Europe, including product positioning, advertising, and public relations. The former head man at Gillette spent a long time with the firm in Germany, so the European market conditions are not unknown at headquarters. Gillette's effort in Japan, which is managed with much more local autonomy, is unfortunately less successful, Schick being the market leader there.

Sources: Gates, 1995; Uchitelle, 1994; Gillette, *Annual Report*, 2003.

not only do local managers implement global strategies but the local subsidiaries are also involved in the formulation of the strategy, often in fact initiating the global approach. In the horizontal network structure local and central managers are virtually indistinguishable, as flows are generally horizontal from the periphery into the home country center and directly between country subsidiaries. In practice, the picture is not quite so simple, of course (see box, "The Pan-European Effect").

Although very few corporations have yet attained the perfect equality implied between all parts of the network, the structure itself is enabling the emergence of such horizontal or "democratic" relationships. In actual organizational life, even if the *structural* reporting lines are horizontal and management *systems* encourage free participation, *people* do not always respond to the implied equality. Leadership and charisma still matter. An organization has a tradition and a culture, which enable certain behaviors and discourage others. It is not surprising to find the horizontal organization working in new

EXHIBIT 18.6
Integrated Network: The Transnational Structure

Source: Reprinted by permission of Harvard Business School Press. From "Integrated Network: The Transnational Structure," *Managing Across Borders: The Transnational Solution,* by Christopher A. Bartlett and Sumatra Ghoshal (Boston, MA: Harvard Business School Press), p. 89. Copyright © 1989 by the President and Fellows of Harvard College.

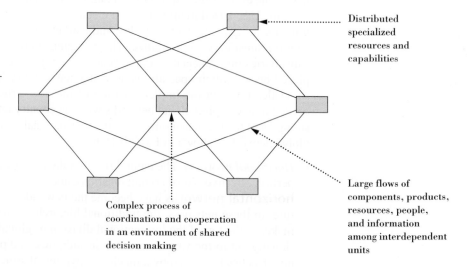

Distributed specialized resources and capabilities

Complex process of coordination and cooperation in an environment of shared decision making

Large flows of components, products, resources, people, and information among interdependent units

start-up companies, such as in computers and software, but not very far advanced even in such high-tech industries as telecommunications, where old and established companies still dominate.

A Dominant Regional Structure?

In Chapter 1, we explored the fact that for the most part the multinational firm is not truly global but regional. While Rugman argued that "globalization" should be replaced by "regionalization," in Ghemawat's terminology, "globalization" should best be termed "semi-globalization."[3] Terminology aside, the notion is that when trade data are examined, by far the majority of multinationals are really focused on one or two regions of the world, not really covering all regions. For example, one recent study found that only 9 of the world's 380 largest firms are truly global, with 320 being home-region based, that is, doing the majority of trading with neighboring countries.[4] Their strategies are not really "global" but "regional."[5]

Ever since Chandler's seminal work on large American corporations, the received wisdom has been that organizational structure follows strategy.[6] Only after the corporation has specified its objectives and goals and formulated its strategy can the appropriate organizational structure be devised. This means that, given the regional strategy adopted by so many multinationals, few firms are potential candidates for the truly global transnational solution. They need a regional, rather than a transnational, solution to organizational structure.

This dominance of regional structure is particularly evident in Ghemawat's discussion of the strategies of several large multinationals. Most of the examples in his book reinforce and support the need for the regional solution to organizational structure. For example, the discussion of Toyota's strategy and structure demonstrates how such a "global" company in fact is better described as "bi-regional," with a vast majority of its operations (and revenues) in Asia and North America (about 85 percent of sales according to Rugman, 2005, p.15). According to Ghemawat, the Toyota organization is moving toward a full global network, especially in terms of production. However, the regional organization is the current design, with a strong Toyota Motor North America hub from 1996 in tandem with the Asia region, and a fledgling Toyota Motor Europe established in 2002. A similar pattern is found at General Electric, which in 2001 established a regional headquarters in Europe and one in Asia (in 2003), each with their own CEO.

While Toyota and GE are moving via regional headquarters to a more truly global organization, several other companies have moved back home with a "de-globalization" strategy and structure. Examples include Bayer, the German pharmaceutical company, and Whirlpool, the Michigan-based home appliance firm. Other companies with a home-centered strategy retain a regional portfolio structure with the home region in the lead. Examples include Korean Samsung in semiconductors (low transportation costs and low trade barriers help keep manufacturing in Korea) and Zara, the Spanish fast-supplier of apparel.

The typical argument from globalization advocates is that the regional organizational form is a stepping-stone toward a more global structure. Although the plans by companies such as Toyota and General Electric seem to bear them out, so far the record gives little support. A truly global organization is difficult to implement and manage. A particularly illuminating case comes from Procter & Gamble, the American consumer packaged goods producer that successfully markets its many products and brands in most countries of the world. Its original country-by-country structure with mini-P&Gs in most markets was consolidated into a matrix structure in the 1990s. But the matrix structure proved unwieldy, and slowed down innovation. In 1999 the company designed global business units (GBUs), and coupled them with a geographic sales organization, shared by all GBUs. Subordinating the sales organization to the global units (a truly global structure) proved difficult to implement, however, with confusing profit responsibilities and a de-motivated sales force. After a new CEO was installed, P&G decided to decentralize. Market development operations in emerging markets, a task needing local initiatives, were given freestanding profit responsibilities, and product categories such as pharmaceuticals, a relatively recent acquisition by P&G with unique distribution channels, were kept out of the regular sales organization.

The advantage of a regional structure is perhaps not simply one of organizational manageability. Given the size of the typical regions, most scope and scale economies can be reaped within a region. And in terms of people and culture and language, odds are that countries within a region are more similar than across regions.[7] Distance still matters.

The Global Network as an Asset

Many companies think of their global network of country subsidiaries as an "invisible resource" or "hidden asset." The network is one of their FSAs. After the years it has taken to develop a presence in the many separate country markets, the companies start contemplating how to further leverage the investment. This is a natural development for entrepreneurial managers. For example, as we saw in Chapter 16, advertising agencies that develop global reach to follow their clients abroad start attracting new business because of their network. Procter & Gamble used its global network to be the first to introduce condensed detergents in major countries, beating the innovator, Japan's Kao, to the market.

The strategic view of the **global network as an asset,** as an FSA, is doubly useful since it tends to make local units more important, helping to counter the problem when country managers feel their local authority is being compromised by a shift to global strategy. Treating the network itself as an asset means that the global strategy becomes more of a "win–win" proposition for both headquarters and subsidiaries.[8]

Painful History

To understand how companies may leverage network resources, we can learn from the past history of multinational expansion. It teaches some painful lessons.

The increased need for an integrated global strategy has come about partly because of the successful attacks on world markets by newly emerging multinationals, especially the Japanese. A key ingredient in their success has been their lack of existing foreign subsidiaries, allowing their global expansion to take place through well-coordinated exporting from Japan and other home countries. As Western companies have tried to emulate the Japanese successes, their efforts at globalized strategies have been hampered rather than helped by their traditionally independent country subsidiaries. The European multinationals, in particular, had long allowed local subsidiaries to run their own operations, a historical accident partly due to Europeans' bent for respecting different local customs.

American companies have traditionally operated with stronger central authority than the Europeans, which means that many American brand names are well recognized globally while European brand names differ between countries. But even American companies have had trouble coordinating global marketing, involving as it does more limited independence for local subsidiaries. As late as the early 1990s, Western companies still lagged behind Japanese firms in their level of global marketing integration.[9] Subsidiary managers balk and refuse to cooperate, citing differences in customer preferences and the lowered motivation among local personnel as impenetrable barriers to coordination with headquarters. Norelco, the American subsidiary of Dutch Philips, is still largely run as an independent company; the head of Ford's operation in Germany resigned; and even Procter & Gamble's decade-long struggle for pan-European product teams has encountered some fierce resistance.

The Win–Win View

Perhaps not surprisingly given this history, the win–win solution to the problems involved in implementing a global strategy against local resistance has come primarily from companies and researchers in Europe. Scandinavian academicians in particular

Getting the Picture

RESEARCHING THE POWER OF NETWORKS

Since the network approach places the key competitive advantages in the linkages between players rather than in individual companies, it is natural to replace the topic of organizational behavior with that of network behavior, an approach suggested primarily by Swedish researchers. Network researchers study how networks are created, grow, and change over time. For example, researchers have dealt with how companies get new trade contacts (often quite haphazardly, as through random encounters while traveling), how often and for what purposes face-to-face meetings are necessary (common when a subsidiary adopts an innovation), and how "sleeping" relationships can be activated by new opportunities (such as when the Berlin Wall's dismantling allowed Swedish companies to reactivate past contacts in eastern Europe).

In the same stream of research, there is relatively little discussion of leadership. The reason is that traditional leadership is typically a top-down activity with followers being motivated by leaders. The network view is much more egalitarian and fits nicely into the newer organizational frameworks of empowerment and decentralized authority. The businesses that have shown themselves particularly adept at global networking involve high-technology products or services with skills distributed throughout the network, and many of them can be quite small. Size is no object in networks—quite the contrary. The so-called virtual corporation is one extreme form of the network approach, with company employees attached to the center by virtue of only a computerized communications link. It remains to be seen whether such communication links can be strong enough to completely replace face-to-face encounters. But the fact remains that the computer-linked global network competitor is here to stay.

Sources: Forsgren and Johanson, 1992; Hakansson, 1989; Hertz and Mattsson, 1998.

have been active in promoting what has become known as "the network theory" of global enterprise.[10]

The central tenet of the **network theory** is that the linkages between actors in the global network—not only between headquarters and subsidiaries but also between company and suppliers, marketers and channel members, and company and loyal customers—constitute the true source of competitive advantage for the firm. Rather than thinking of the firm as "we" and the other actors as "they," the approach is inclusive. The best way to gain advantages is for the network to be strong, not only the individual participants. "What is good for them is good for us."

In this view, *competition occurs mainly between networks of businesses.* Analyzing Japanese competitors, for example, the network approach suggests that Nissan and Toyota compete not only directly but also through their related *keiretsu* (or network) suppliers. This view is shared among many businesspeople inside and outside Japan. Another factor of importance in the network view is the enlarged role of a country subsidiary in communicating and supporting other subsidiaries—and not only reporting to headquarters. The role of headquarters, in the network view, becomes one of sharing knowledge, disseminating innovations, and facilitating communication among network members rather than giving orders and directing from the center (see box, "Researching the Power of Networks").

From a global marketing viewpoint, the most striking benefit derived from the network approach is the fresh recognition of *what* the firm's resources and FSAs are and *where* new ideas and innovation might emerge. Remember, knowledge assets are a critical resource in competitive markets. The existence of the network opens up new possibilities, rather than constraining solutions. The so-called core competencies of the corporation involve not simply what the company can do but what the network can do. The network can do more things than the individual company; and, conversely, an absence of a global network reduces management strategy options.

The ideas for expansion and growth can come from anywhere in a network, which is why communication is so important. By sharing information, news, and knowledge via the firm's e-mail system—and even via the public Internet—managers inside the network learn about the capabilities of other members; new visions open up, and imaginative innovations emerge. It is small wonder that most multinational companies today spend huge amounts to create internal communication links through so-called **intranets**, protected communication systems that help tie together a global firm's network.

As global competition heats up, the global network is a key source of competitive advantage and new possibilities. Rather than viewing the network members as out-of-date and obstacles to progress, their local know-how and motivation need to be allowed to impact the member companies and the network as a whole. This takes much less "leadership" from the center but requires facilitation and sharing of knowledge. The marketing manager whose organization operates with a "network as an asset" not only uses the most up-to-date telecommunications and videoconferencing equipment but also spends considerable time on the road, cajoling and persuading and sharing. Global integration is not a matter of centralized command over an army of exporters, as in the Japanese system, but rather a matter of inspiring individual network members to share in the win–win philosophy.

Globalizing Management[11]

Because of the large home market, many American companies come to global marketing with an international division structure separating domestic and overseas markets. This structure tends to prohibit global integration of marketing effort, since the home country occupies a special position. For integrated marketing, the home country needs to be viewed as part of the global market. To accomplish this, companies are shifting to global marketing directors. A typical position description for a global marketing director is shown in Exhibit 18.7.

EXHIBIT 18.7
Position Description for Global Marketing Director, XYZ Corporation

Responsibilities
- Lead the development and implementation of global marketing strategies to ensure maximization of the XYZ product line's growth and long-term profitability. The strategies must be commercially viable, customer focused, innovative, and market driven to ensure commercial success.
- Lead the strategic market process to develop global product positioning, global product pricing strategies, global brand development, and global communication strategies.
- Responsible for unifying marketing and nonmarketing strategies, coordinating sales and marketing functions between countries and regions.
- Responsible for setting and achieving annual sales and marketing objectives.
- Lead the development of life-cycle management strategies.
- Ensure optimal communication, collaboration, and synergies with all other business units.
- Develop global strategic brand plans in collaboration with other business units.
- Allocate resources across the functions that contribute to global strategic brand development.
- Manage the salary, expense, and budget for all team members.
- Lead the economic evaluation process for the strategic global brands, including new indications and line extensions. Consolidate global forecasts and develop priorities and recommendations.
- Lead the team through the development of a clear vision and common goals. Motivate team members to reach goals through sound decision making and effective conflict resolution.
- Manage the team's recruitment, objective setting, issue resolution, and appraisals in line with the overall global strategy.
- Identify present and future hiring needs and make primary selection of team members.
- Motivate the team, maintain a positive work environment, and secure team member commitment and shared ownership to the project's success. Reward team and individual performance.

Requirements
- Bachelor's degree or equivalent, MBA preferred.
- Extensive sales and marketing experience.
- Excellent written and oral communication skills.
- Knowledge of the XYZ market.
- International experience; lived, worked, or studied abroad; general understanding of cultural differences, country markets, and multicultural environments.
- Foreign language ability strongly preferred.

Global Marketing Directors

In companies organized along the lines of global product divisions or separate business units, the **global marketing director** naturally becomes the head of marketing for both the home country and overseas. At the end of Chapter 17, for example, we met Levi Strauss's former global marketing director, Robert Holloway. Each product division will then have a global marketing manager reporting to the director. Even without a global product structure, global marketing directors may be appointed to operate in a matrix fashion across a geographic structure. In either case, the global marketing director is generally given the following responsibilities:

- *Strategy.* Strategic planning, budgeting, and implementation with functions and regions.
- *Systems.* Design, creation, and maintenance of global marketing systems.
- *Coordination.* Coordination of all functions affecting business and major product lines.
- *Performance evaluation.* Participation in performance evaluation of functional and regional managers.
- *Profitability.* Profit accountability for individual lines of business and major product lines.

These are major tasks and may demand that national marketing managers in the main markets report directly to the global marketing director. New product specifications, positioning, advertising, and distribution choices may become centralized decisions, while lower-level execution questions such as local sales and logistics remain a national responsibility. All major accounts are handled centrally.

Even without such a dramatic change in the reporting lines of the organization, global marketing directors can still exert considerable influence as staff members by sheer force of personality and access to information. They can bring vast experience to bear on a particular situation. For example, one manager exerted strong influence over the country managers simply by explaining why their advertising ideas had failed in other countries and by sharing where they had succeeded. Arguments about the particular tastes of a local market and the need for special advertising often dissolve when the success of a campaign in a neighboring country is demonstrated.

Global Teams

One of the commonest organizational changes for global marketing is to create **global teams.** The responsibilities can vary from specific programs or activities, such as the advertising campaign for a new product, to more wide-ranging responsibilities, including the whole marketing mix. The European integration has spawned many examples of global teams. For example, a French manufacturer of security devices uses a team of country managers, with the different countries playing the lead role for different products. While this approach is time-consuming, the company has found that the reliance on line managers makes it easier for various countries to accept input from other countries.

Similarly responding to the European integration, Minnesota-based multinational 3M initially used "European Management Action Teams," one for each of its 50 product lines. Each team had eight to fourteen members representing several functions and different countries, and each was chaired by a Brussels-based product manager. As the integration proceeded and customers demanded more extensive pan-European sales and services, the teams eventually were succeeded by "European Business Centers" (EBCs). A 3M EBC has responsibility and accountability for managing a business throughout Europe, from planning and manufacturing to selling and delivering the product to the customer. One such business center is the "Consumer and Office Markets EBC." The center's six product lines (home care, consumer stationery, do-it-yourself/paint and drywall products, commercial care, visual systems, and commercial office supply) are managed by separate European Business Units (EBUs) with pan-European responsibility. These six product lines are coordinated in each of 3M's eight European regions, with a local organization that

A transnational product development team in 3M's European Business Center for medical products in Brussels. From left: Valori Seltz, a U.S. citizen; Philippe Husson, French; Kurt Wiethoff, German; Inge Thulin, Swedish; and Stig Eriksson, Finnish. © Steve Niedorf.

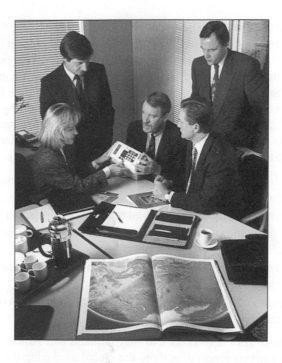

mirrors that of the pan-European structure. For example, the German consumer and office markets EBC manager coordinates sales and marketing for six EBUs in that region.[12]

Management Systems

Companies can also implement global marketing within their existing organizational structure by instituting new **management systems** as integrating mechanisms. Global budgeting, global performance reviews, and global accounting are some of the general systems that create a basis for globalized strategies. Companies can also achieve greater global emphasis with integration mechanisms such as meetings and informal networks, committees and task forces, and coordinating staff groups and information sharing on a global basis. The advent of electronic communication media such as videoconferencing and electronic mail has also helped develop a global culture in companies.

The choice of integration mechanism depends on the intensity of the global marketing activity.

Informal Coordination

Information sharing about similar experiences in different markets is a first step in achieving integrated strategies. Most companies today are involved in these types of informal exchanges, and they are one reason why the global marketer has to travel so often and so far. Experiences are rarely the stuff of formal reporting, and it usually takes some time spent in mutual discussion before the relevance of a particular experience is recognized.

This type of informal management interaction is difficult to systematize. It is akin to MBWA (management by walking around) on a global scale. The outsider has to come to the country subsidiary as a consultant and friend rather than as a boss on an inspection tour. Such informal cooperation can't be achieved through telecommunications or through written memos. In one study of managers in Swedish multinational firms traveling to subsidiaries abroad, it was found that as many as 44 percent of the managers traveled without specific problem or action objectives, but in order to "cultivate the network."[13]

Coordinating Committees

A number of companies attempt to achieve more effective implementation systems by creating joint committees of regional or country managers that meet on a regular basis.

These high-level meetings serve to reinforce ties at the top levels, creating umbrellas for operational coordination and integration between units. Many large multinationals have used such committees for a long time. IBM, GE, and ITT are some of the well-known examples of this; but so are Philips, Siemens, and Volvo in Europe, and well as Sony, Honda, and Matsushita of Japan. Swapping new-product information and competitive data, sharing market research, selecting which brands to promote as regional or global, setting international standards for sales performance, and synchronizing product launches—it is from these joint committees that more permanent organizational fixtures such as Euro-brand groups or global advertising units develop.

In many cases the higher-level committee efforts are followed up by regular meetings between functional managers or task forces with professionals at various levels. Temporary personnel transfers are also used, although not so commonly. In one study of 35 European multinationals, only 5 sent their head office marketing managers for a stint in a foreign subsidiary, and only 9 transferred their local marketing managers to the head office.

Coordinating Staff

As the global strategy is endorsed at top-management levels, its implementation usually leads to temporary arrangements of meetings between the various country subsidiary managers. The coordination will initially consist of simple consultation, exchange of information, and informal cooperation, but soon the need for a more systematic approach will be clear.

The emergence of permanent coordinating mechanisms from initial temporary management processes is typical of the incremental character of much of the global integration efforts in companies. For example, product design may require a unified task force of designers and engineers from various countries, drawn together in some central location. In automobiles, many companies from various countries have a design office in southern California, where many of the new design ideas originate. Similarly, they have engineering offices in Germany, where technology is strong.

The need for global marketing thus often leads to the creation of a new staff group with global integration responsibilities but without line authority. The group may facilitate shared new-product development in lead countries, an approach now common in companies such as Procter & Gamble, Nissan, and Nestlé. The group may also facilitate the wedding of global brands to the existing lineup of brands in local campaigns, such as adding Euro-Vizir to P&G's detergents in Britain. The staff may also help develop a more coordinated campaign across the globe, such as when the Sony Walkman was rechristened replacing the "Soundabout" name already launched in Europe. The global staff group can be responsible for organizing the many global meetings that oil the mechanism of the global management effort. There is a need for travel arrangements, hotel accommodations, alignment of schedules, and simple caretaking that can tax the energies of many organizations. The visits from headquarters are expensive distractions unless real business can be transacted—with global marketing and business decisions made at the meetings.[14]

People and Organizational Culture

In the end, the implementation of global marketing stands or falls with the capability of the people involved. Because of the complexity of the task and the inherent conflict with local management, **people skills** matter a lot.

If the organizational *structure* is the body and the chassis that hold the car together and the management *systems* are the engine and the gearbox, *people* provide the necessary lubrication that makes the pistons pump and the car run smoothly. And "people" means everybody in the organization, from top management down.[15]

Local Acceptance

Global marketing strategies almost always require a leap of faith on the part of local managers, because local conditions are almost always different from other places.[16] A

Getting the Picture

P&G'S VIZIR EXPERIENCE

The 1983 successful launch of Vizir, Procter & Gamble's liquid detergent, in Germany, Holland, and France was spearheaded by a novel organizational innovation, a Euro-team. In order to develop and test the new product, the company had appointed one manager from Germany as the head of a Europewide team of experts and managers. With Germany the largest market in Europe and since the new product development had originated there, Germany became a natural lead country in the product development effort.

Even though the product launch was a success, there were some setbacks in the organization of the team. The local country managers were reluctant to participate, since the periodic meetings were time-consuming. As a result, the team members were not always given adequate support in their home countries, participation in the Euro-team changed frequently, and attendance at meetings fluctuated. The solution was to distribute Euro-team responsibilities among the various countries to motivate their participation and to make local managers more sensitive to the difficulties involved in the integrated effort.

Procter & Gamble is pursuing the global team further, and the company is instilling a global perspective in all product managers by regular meetings to share ideas of potential value elsewhere. For example, the product modifications to the Pampers diapers originating in Japan have been introduced globally. The new condensed detergents, also from Japan, have been quickly expanded elsewhere. The global perspective has been further strengthened by the appointment of CEOs with extensive experience abroad.

Sources: Bartlett, 1983; Bartlett and Ghoshal, 1989, pp. 93–94; Yoshino, 1990; Procter & Gamble, *Annual Report,* 2003.

skilled manager must persuade the local managers and motivate them to work for the success of the global strategy. Simply forcing the strategy on the local office leads to surreptitious efforts to undermine the global brand, as Henkel found with its Pritt product line (as we saw in Chapter 12). While paying lip service to the global branding concept, the local subsidiary manager went about supporting the existing brands in direct competition with the new global brand.

Research on the acceptance of global strategies demonstrates the importance of allowing country managers to participate in the global strategy formulation process. The acceptability of a global directive from headquarters is directly related to the perceived fairness of the process.[17] Where local managers have been involved in formulating global marketing strategies, they have been much more likely to accept and to implement them. Regardless of the management incentives and penalties adopted to promote local implementation, the major factor in acceptance was what managers call "due process." If a global strategy did not have sufficient local input, managers felt ignored—and acted accordingly. The "people" factor is important.

Another factor is the level of agreement with the "global imperative" at the local level. In many globalized firms, the local managers are well aware of their dependency on the global network of the organization and are quite willing and able to assume a global perspective.[18] Giving more global responsibility to local managers, however, requires some organizational changes. The headquarters role is not so much that of pushing a global strategy as facilitating interaction between various local managers who will be directly dependent on each other. The Euro-brand managers at Procter & Gamble provide one example of this process (see box, "P&G's Vizir Experience").

People skills and country cultures do not always work in predictable ways. As BBD&O, the advertising agency, expanded its Brussels office in anticipation of the European Union, the intent was to draw in talent from several continental countries. Instead, the agency found that British and American employees were much more effective, partly because of the language facility but also because the continental Europeans tended to remain close to their home culture. Southern Europeans, in particular, with their high context cultures, tend to be less flexible when asked to jettison preconceived and culture-bound ideas.[19] The French and Italians' attention to dress, for example, tended to blur their appreciation of easygoing, casual spokespersons.

The people factor directly affects the execution of global advertising strategies. Telling the local marketing manager to work with the branch office of a global agency rather than with a longtime friend in a local agency is not a pleasant job. If handled badly, the local manager will leave the company, as happened when Pioneer, the consumer electronics company, centralized its European marketing in Antwerp with advertising given to BBD&O's expanded Brussels office.

Many of these personnel losses are motivated by personal as well as professional reasons. Ford Werke AG in Cologne lost its top marketing manager in Germany when it instituted pan-European product development strategies and pulled in design responsibilities from Germany and gave them to the European headquarters in Dagenham, England, even though a promotion to England was offered. The head of market research at Brown Boveri, the Swiss electrical machinery manufacturer, left when Swedish Asea took over to create ABB, not wanting to work for a company dominated by Swedes.

Corporate Culture

The fact is that since global strategies often involve centralization, they are also prone to make a company's culture ethnocentric. While the old-style multinationals—companies like Philips of Holland, Nestlé of Switzerland, Beiersdorf (Nivea) of Germany, and Singer (sewing machines) of the United States—offered products that many consumers around the world vaguely thought were local brands, the new global emphasis has placed nationality in the forefront. The global marketer who carries the orders from the home office needs a lot of interpersonal skill to get the necessary cooperation. While 20 years ago the local manager for an American multinational in Germany had credibility as a local figure, today the position is undermined by the home office's insistence on direct control. It is hardly surprising when the experienced local managers quit as global strategies get implemented.

Many coordination and integration activities involve communication. Firms use people and **organizational culture** to enhance communication in different ways, such as to:

- *Build a strong corporate culture internationally.* IKEA, the furniture retailer, does this by fostering its Swedish values of egalitarianism, frugality, hard work, and simplicity among its employees worldwide (and IKEA has had more problems doing this in the United States than in western Europe and Canada).
- *Build a common technical or professional culture.* Elf-Aquitaine, the French oil company, sets high standards for professionalism and technical knowledge to create group affiliation.
- *Build strong financial and planning systems.* Emerson Electric promotes careful planning, financial reporting, and cost reduction as company values.

The key notion is that managers in different countries should be induced to communicate and interact more in line with company values than to rely on their different national cultures. Honda's way is a good example (see box, "Honda's Global Management by Culture").

The Expatriate Manager

The discussion so far has treated the local manager as a native of the country. This is the usual case if the manager in question has the marketing responsibility. But for control and communication purposes, many country subsidiaries are run by **expatriates** from the home country, typically executives who have been sent to the foreign subsidiary after several years with the firm at home. What is their role in the implementation of the global strategy and the local marketing effort?

Apart from being the headquarters' "envoy," the expatriate country managers in a global company have three typical marketing *leadership* roles to fill.[20]

Role 1. Customer representative. The expatriate manager must serve as a high-level contact with existing customers, prospects, and suppliers *in the local market.* The local marketing effort can then be carried out by locals, who can follow up at operating levels on contacts provided by the expatriate. This part of the job relates directly to the "relationship marketing" function so prominent in today's customer-oriented firm.

Role 2. Local champion. The expatriate manager must be a champion for the local office at *headquarters.* Local requests such as product modifications, advertising

Getting the Picture

HONDA'S GLOBAL MANAGEMENT BY CULTURE

Honda is a company with a strong global vision. The impetus derives partly from its founder, Soichiro Honda, who was blocked out of the Japanese home market by powerful and well-established competitors. This pushed the company overseas, and the United States became its primary market. Recognizing its dependence on foreign countries, the company has attempted to create a corporate culture of "three world headquarters": Japan, the United States, and Europe.

The company attempts to be an "insider" in all three areas by assembling cars in several different locations (Swinton, United Kingdom, and Marysville, Ohio, are the major sites) and hiring local workers as well as local managers.

There is little or no "selling" of the global strategy necessary because the company avoids being "Japanese." Products are standardized but often designed outside Japan; some are developed for specific non-Japanese markets (such as the Concerto for Europe), and cars built abroad are exported back to Japan (such as the Accord from Ohio). The company also takes workers and supervisors (the "associates," as the company calls its employees) from its plants abroad for stints in factories in Japan—and sends many Japanese workers and managers abroad.

Sources: Sakiya, 1987; Pearson and Ehrlich, 1989; **www.honda.com**

approvals, and additional resources need to be explained and justified back home by the manager.

Role 3. Network coordinator. The expatriate manager must provide *linkages* with the firm's other offices in the *worldwide network* of the firm. Coordinating product launches in different countries, production scheduling, and exchange of market information are examples of the kinds of issues that require close communication links between the various country managers.

The last two tasks are critical when implementing global marketing strategy. While the local representative task is often similar to the task of marketers anywhere, it is the linkage with headquarters and other country offices that provides the added sources of advantage for the global marketer. The strength of these linkages depends on the expatriate as much as on the native people.

When strategies are globalized, the expatriate manager is often put in a delicate position, since the strategy often reduces the autonomy of the local subsidiary. Being the connecting link with headquarters, it is natural that the expatriate must be the one to explain and implement the strategy locally. This usually involves limiting the local marketing manager's authority and may force a change of ad agency, new directions in sales efforts, and termination of distribution contracts. Since in many cases certain parts of the business are consolidated and placed with other country units or at headquarters, the strategy may involve layoffs and voluntary retirements. Often these measures are a threat to an expatriate's authority in the firm and to the existing network of contacts outside. In one fairly typical case in which the expatriate manager was asked to fire 20 percent of the local workforce, the manager decided to quit since his standing in the local business community, as well as in the firm, was jeopardized.

When strategies are globalized, expatriate managers may need (or want) to be replaced, rotated to another country, or promoted. It is often more difficult to transfer the native marketing manager or the country manager if a native. In these cases, the companies have options available, discussed below, that can help avoid the low morale that globalization often incurs.

Global Customers

As we have seen repeatedly throughout Part Four of this book, a very clear-cut rationale for the introduction of a globalized marketing strategy is the emergence of global customers. It is easiest to recognize the advantages of a coordinated offering to multinational buyers that can choose in what country to make their purchases. A consistent image; well-recognized brand; assurance of parts, supplies, and service; and coordinated pricing—all are obvious benefits to a company selling to global customers. With the emergence of global purchasing on the part of individual customers as well, the benefits of coordination are increased further. When an individual buyer of a personal computer in Toronto, say, can choose between the local stores, buying through a direct import house, shopping at home via catalog from New York, or a duty-free purchase at Tokyo's Akihabara district or Frankfurt's airport, the need for the computer company to coordinate product specifications, pricing, warranties, and parts distribution is quite clear.

Global Account Management

In practice, however, the coordination is not that easy. The typical solution for the multinational buyer is for companies to organize **global account managers** or account groups whose sole responsibility is to serve that customer globally. The account managers serve primarily a coordinative function, usually without direct line responsibility over functions. Their tasks involve the coordination of orders from the customer's various locations, the negotiations for uniform prices, the coordination of communications from various sources inside the firm (R&D, manufacturing, parts) to the various customer locations, and, above all, the provision of consistent after-sales service and follow-up from the seller in all countries. The account managers are the global counterparts to the account groups serving similar functions with domestic customers, such as P&G's large account group (over 60 people strong) focused on Wal-Mart.

Global customers naturally force a coordinated marketing approach, with the marketer's local subsidiaries asked to execute similar strategies as elsewhere. These coordinated strategies involve **relationship marketing,** with the account managers and their groups providing special services. Instead of treating the customer as one among many, relationship marketing increases customer satisfaction by treating the customer as a special client.

This means that extra services can be offered on demand and that the SOPs (standard operating procedures) may be altered for this customer. Banks change opening hours for their corporate customers, packaged good manufacturers help manage inventories for their top wholesalers, and auto companies offer vacation trips for their largest dealers. For some large and favored customers, the global account manager at the head office is the guy they can squeeze to get the lowest global price.[21] (See box, "Global Accounts: I Win, You Lose.")

Needless to say, some of these "relationship marketing" tools can be demoralizing for the local subsidiaries, as the buyer actively tries to play headquarters against local sellers. To carry these activities out on a global scale is a challenge, requiring a lot of information sharing and coordination across the seller's subsidiaries. The global account manager needs to have people skills in dealing not only with the customer but also with the managers in the local subsidiaries (see also Case 4-5, "Hewlett-Packard's Global Account Management," at the end of Part Four).

Coordination of marketing activities for smaller customers and individual buyers who purchase globally is usually more narrowly focused on avoiding the pricing arbitrage possibilities we discussed in Chapter 14. As for distribution control, rather than relying on innovations in organizational structure, firms tend to attempt coordination via more ad hoc measures and specific interventions in the channels as discussed in Chapter 15. Global account clients can be selected on the basis of several criteria. They are often industry leaders, in terms of both technology and sales. This creates a competitive advantage where it counts and spreads the awareness of the program throughout the industry. The global accounts, including manufacturing and design, should have active operations in several countries. This is the source of the advantage of cross-country coordination. There should be an expressed desire for worldwide procurement, price, service, and support agreements. The global buyer, in effect, needs to be organized for centralized buying.

Getting the Picture

GLOBAL ACCOUNTS: I WIN, YOU LOSE

Recent research shows how power differences between the customer and the vendor can make global accounts vehicles for exerting bargaining pressure. There can certainly be benefits for both parties, as relationship marketing converts would suggest. However, the increased information exchange and transparency involved in global account management means it can work to the disadvantage of the multinational seller as buyers try to take advantage of the account manager and ask for increased service. According to the research this is especially likely to happen when the power balance is unequal. In fact, the research shows that where the buyer is the stronger, the "partnership" envisioned by the relationship marketing advocates turns into a forum where the buyer will bargain for further advantages.

From the seller perspective, the research also suggests that it is unlikely that a multinational vendor will gain from creating global accounts unless they are able to exert pressure on the buyers. That is, from the sellers' viewpoint, global accounts work better when they are in control. Rather distressingly, but perhaps not surprisingly, the research suggests that the "win–win" situation envisioned by proponents of relationship marketing does not seem to fit many relationships in B2B. Indeed, it seems to be the inequality that makes these relationships more successful, in that it at least brings a clarity to the table. "Who's got the power will call the shots" seems still to be the winning paradigm.

Sources: Royal and Lucas, 1995; Birkinshaw et al., 2001.

Retail Trade Groups

Retailers who are resellers of the manufacturer's product lines are a special type of global customer. As we saw in Chapter 15, they are also becoming globalized.

In most developed countries, the leading five or six retailing chains control well over 50 percent of the total food and drink volume. French Carrefour is the leading retailer in Spain and Brazil; Tesco in Britain and Aldi in Germany are other dominant chains, as is Wal-Mart in North America. The heavy investments in computer equipment needed for scanners to streamline inventory control and stock the shelves have required these retailers to hire highly qualified staff people who do not hesitate to make strong demands for service from suppliers. For example, the Wal-Mart success (and failures overseas) is partly the result of its managers' insistence that manufacturers supply just-in-time inventory. The success of high-quality private labels and store brands is helping fuel the retail chain's expansion. In some European countries store brands account for more than 30 percent of the total market.

In response, consumer goods manufacturers are creating a special form of **retail trade marketing groups.** These groups attempt to meet the powerful retailers' need for customized product design, advertising, direct marketing, and sales promotions. Trade marketing groups learn which of their company's services and products are most needed by a customer, spot opportunities, and detect problems. Members of these groups include personnel from sales, service, manufacturing, logistics, management information systems, and other business activities. Nestlé's cooperation with French retailer Casino and the 7-Eleven experience in Japan illustrate these points (see box, "Manufacturers Pay Attention to Retailers").

Conflict Resolution

Coordinating the marketing function on a global basis usually means consolidation of local staff, reduced budgets at subsidiaries, and less local autonomy. This naturally threatens to demoralize country managers, who typically lose control first over manufacturing and then gradually over strategic marketing decisions. What remains are usually tactical decisions about sales, promotions, and local advertising.

The local units are crucial for effective execution of global programs. This is where the middlemen are contacted, advertising media are bought, customers are encountered, and sales are made. Even in the case of global customers, whose negotiations may be with a

Getting the Picture

MANUFACTURERS PAY ATTENTION TO RETAILERS

A consumer goods company such as Nestlé has unique contributions to bring to its partnerships with retailers. Its leading global brands offer strong appeal. The products offer high quality at competitive prices. The company's market research provides detailed knowledge of consumer habits and requirements, and R&D generates a stream of improvements and new products.

When Nestlé encountered some conflict about shipments and service with Casino, a large French retailer, the company decided to leverage these resources by establishing a retail trade group focused on Casino. The trade group initiated a series of cooperative meetings to develop joint marketing, logistics, and sales efforts. For example, the partners agreed to test a joint breakfast promotion, with 10 Nestlé brands matched against 10 store brands to help determine which products sell well. The companies jointly analyzed bar code information and scanner data to create a database of how to build customer loyalty for brands and stores while reducing

costs. Casino got help to find out which products needed to be stocked more (and which less), while Nestlé got help to reduce supply channel delays (in France goods-to-market time for breakfast cereals is 11 weeks compared with 3 weeks in the United States).

A similar type of alignment that helps manufacturers offer low prices without jeopardizing their clout in regular channels is represented by the various tie-ins arranged by 7-Eleven in Japan. Companies such as Philip Morris, Hershey, and Häagen-Dazs make specially designed products available for sale in 7-Eleven stores only. For example, under one arrangement, the Kraft division of Philip Morris sells smaller-sized cheesecakes through the convenience store chain. These practices have migrated from Japan to other markets. For example, the 7-Eleven stores in the United States have become major outlets for some of the more popular EA Sports' electronic games, including Madden NFL.

Sources: Gates, 1995; Johansson and Hirano, 1995; Simmons, 1990; McClatchy-Tribune News Service, "EA Sports' NCAA Football 09," August 11, 2008.

---

headquarters global account group, the deliveries of the goods or services are usually local. To counter the threat of lowered morale and to resolve actual or potential conflicts, companies have introduced some or all of the following **conflict resolution** practices:

1. *Let country managers retain local brands and marketing budgets.* In many companies country managers maintain a local product and brand portfolio. While they may have little control over global or regional brands, they have full responsibility for the marketing programs of their local brands. They control promotional budget allocations between the brands and the amount allocated to specific tactics such as sales contests and in-store couponing. Also, they have a role to play in global brands. Even though the ad agency choice may be made higher up, they can choose the agency for sales promotions and for direct marketing efforts.

2. *Solicit country managers' input for new-product development.* Country managers, especially in leading markets, are well positioned to develop and test new products. Especially where new products are market rather than technology driven, the local managers' inputs become crucial. Companies in which the local product manager reports to the country manager rather than to a global product manager tend to have a higher success rate for new products.[22]

   Bausch & Lomb, the optics and glassmaker, improved its new-product development success by switching from a global to a regional substructure. Each region has its own product development team, and each local manager participates in the regional level's decisions about priorities for new-product development. New-product ideas from local markets are encouraged, and after the idea is presented and evaluated at the regional level, it passes to a global product coordinating committee for worldwide sharing.

3. *Give country managers lead roles in global teams.* To create mutual dependence and improve implementation, it is important that over time different country managers take responsibility for a global brand or at least one component of the global marketing. As in the Vizir case, the country managers are often at the receiving end of the stick, so to speak, when they have to persuade other country managers to participate in a global program, and this helps make them sympathetic in turn to the requests of other global team leaders. It is important that the country managers

assume responsibilities in the global teams, so that the local subsidiary's role is endorsed by the boss. Lower-level managers, such as the local product manager and advertising manager, will then have the requisite support and legitimacy to implement the local part of the global campaigns.

4. *Provide international transfers for country managers.* A clear perspective on foreign local markets helps when making global marketing decisions. Consequently, global marketing groups at the head office would benefit from foreign national marketing team members. Unfortunately, frequent international transfers of marketing managers are still rare. There is even less exchange between subsidiaries in different countries. In one study, only 4 of 35 companies reported any regular transfers of marketing people between country subsidiaries.[23]

    Foreign marketing managers are caught in a double bind.[24] A lack of experience at corporate headquarters limits the foreign managers from reaching the upper echelons where their different perspective could be very valuable. However, since most global companies do not offer the marketing managers the opportunity to work at the home office, there is no way to accumulate the required corporate experience.

    If neither marketing nor country managers rotate, their experiences remain parochial. This can be a disadvantage since the implementation of global strategies requires local sacrifices for the benefit of the entire company. Creating alternative career opportunities for country managers outside their home market can broaden their perspectives and lessen conflict with global or regional managers.

5. *Involve the country managers in the formulation of the global marketing strategy.* In the end, the best medicine against local subversion of global marketing is to co-opt the country managers by inviting them to help design the global marketing strategy. The impetus for a globalized strategy is almost always from the top, since headquarters marketers are the ones who most easily notice the potential savings and gains. But once the start has been made, country managers from, at the least, the leading countries and the markets most directly affected should be directly involved in the strategy formulation. The implementation success of global strategies tends to be directly proportional to the level of local involvement in strategy formulation.[25]

    There are, of course, obvious problems associated with having managers from several countries involved in the strategy formulation:

- Local managers propose strategies without a full understanding of the global situation.
- Country managers feel forced to put their local interests first.
- Communication between managers of different nationalities is not always easy.

These obstacles have made many companies reluctant to involve too many country managers in their global strategy development. Instead of relying on foreign managers, many companies rely on home office nationals with experience abroad. This is the common style in Japanese corporations, with the global strategies developed in Japan and disseminated to local subsidiaries. The local perspectives are mainly represented through Japanese managers with experience in the various countries, a solution made possible because Japanese multinationals consistently try to develop top career paths that include rotations to overseas sites. Unfortunately, the local perspectives brought to the home office for the formulation of the global strategies are sometimes quite biased and unreliable, especially when based on only one or two individual experiences.

Japanese companies are doing well in the Americas where most of the Japanese corporations can draw on a number of senior internal advisers with direct country experience for the strategy formulations. By contrast, in the European market most Japanese companies are dependent on a few individuals with direct experience in any one country. But the language and cultural barriers—and the Japanese consensus-style decision making—make such relative outsiders' advice difficult to assimilate. Not surprisingly, the Japanese are baffled by the fragmented European markets, and the EU integration has been warmly welcomed by them.

The **ethnocentricity** of the Japanese corporations is paralleled in some global European companies: Mercedes and Siemens have strong German identities, Philips is Dutch at the core, and IKEA is Swedish, while Marks & Spencer is English, and Benetton is Italian. This situation arises from the desire not only to avoid conflict in strategy formulation but also to draw strength from the cultural heritage of the country.

American companies sometimes, though not always, show less ethnocentricity in the handling of their country managers. This is commonly attributed to the openness and multiculturalism of the American society. Regardless, a lack of ethnocentricity becomes desirable and beneficial because the American multinationals do have such a large share of their resources located overseas. As data show, both in absolute value and in terms of proportions, the American global companies have more assets abroad than any other country. About one-fifth of the output of American firms is produced offshore, and about a quarter of all U.S. imports and exports represent intrafirm transfers. There is an accompanying cadre of foreign nationals in management positions in the local subsidiaries, providing a rich source of local market information and know-how. Some observers argue that future American competitive strength will come increasingly from the judicious use of these national managers inside the global organizations, and that the absence of promising global careers in European and Japanese companies will make it impossible for them to attract the best local managerial talent.[26]

Involving the country managers in the formulation of global marketing strategies not only is good for the quality of the strategy designed and the collaboration that makes local implementation easier but also makes the country manager's job more interesting, attracting the best local talents.

The Good Global Marketer

In today's tense global environment, keeping the national subsidiaries happy and productive is not the only task to be accomplished locally. The good global marketer will also have to deal with potential antiglobalization sentiments. Antiglobalization and anti-Americanism are latent in many countries and can flare up easily. The global marketer must try to avoid stoking the fires.

The strength of the antiglobalization sentiment has major implications for managerial action in the multinationals. First, as always, the global marketer has to stand behind the product fully, warranting its functional and emotional satisfaction. To do this, the marketer needs to take the potential customer's situation into account, presenting products and services that have a clear need to fulfill and are adapted to the consumer's situation. These should be self-evident propositions for any marketer. They imply, for example, that the promotional communication—and promises—accompanying the offer need to be sensitive and framed appropriately for the consumer's situation. Local adaptation is not simply the best strategy to overcome any latent antiglobalization sentiment, it is often the *only* strategy.

Local adaptation is helped considerably by the advances in modular designs and flexible manufacturing. But with the scale economies in platform designs, standardized components, operating manuals, and single brand names, there is still a strong degree of uniformity in many a company's product and service across different countries. A McDonald's restaurant in Beijing, run by a Chinese franchisee, is still at its core the American hamburger icon—the company makes sure of that. If not up to its (American) standards, the contract will be voided. A Honda built in Ohio is still up to the quality of Honda's from Japan, the company marquee guarantees that. The same is true for all well-run global companies. But more can be done.

For most managers the question of global localization is a matter of where to strike the optimal balance between localization and standardization. Now this calculation needs to consider not only demand factors and cost efficiencies. In the bigger picture, potential antiglobalization sentiments also play a role. The audience of stakeholders goes beyond the immediate customers. The most visible global marketers are necessarily noticed outside their immediate market segments, and as we have seen the antiglobalization spillover effect on public opinion can easily turn negative. The solution lies in finding a broader kind of balance, between local responsiveness to the society at large and the branding imperative for global marketers to always communicate the same message. Integrated marketing communications might seem like an ideal from a marketing perspective, but it is counterproductive when it means a mind-numbing oversell of foreign brands—fueling antiglobalization and anti-American sentiment from a populace sick of commercialization.

A marketing strategy that avoids stirring antiglobalization fervor needs to have two things. First, the products need to be localized, including changes in the design of products, ingredients and formulation, size and style of packaging, pricing, and so on. Second, the promotional communication needs to be adapted not only in terms of language and benefit explanations, but also in terms of usage suggestions. The product changes involved can be major for developing countries; selling to the "bottom of the pyramid" often involves rethinking the product and packaging.[27] By contrast, the communications changes are likely to be more important for many developed countries.[28]

Clearly, many of the scale returns involved in going global will be lost with this approach. But this places the critical entry decision precisely where it belongs. Where these adaptations are deemed too costly because scale economies are lost, the brand should not be introduced. If it is introduced anyway, unchanged and with a standardized promotional campaign emphasizing brand meaning and identity, it not only creates frustrations among some people and helps divide the society into haves and have-nots, it also kindles emotional resentment against the foreign elements. This is a recipe for how to get antiglobalization feelings aroused, something future global marketers, especially from the United States, need to consider carefully. Remember, the global marketer is a guest in the foreign country, and might, in today's tense and belligerent global environment, easily be disinvited.

Summary

The inherent conflict between local country managers and the top-down imposition of global marketing needs to be recognized and handled very candidly throughout the organization. The limits of the resources allocated to the local marketing budgets need to be justified to the local managers, and appropriate compensating measures in terms of new global team responsibilities should be considered. In addition it is important that local managers be consulted early in the global strategy formulation process to get their input and stimulate acceptance of the globalization as well as to encourage cooperation with the local implementation of the strategy. Not many companies can go as far as GE and ABB, whose strong and single-minded CEOs virtually force local implementation of the global strategy, but any globalizing effort involves a certain overcoming of local resistance.

Of the various organization structures that the large multinational firm can operate with, a split between a domestic and an international division is consistently a negative factor in implementing globalized marketing. Having global product divisions without a division between the domestic and the foreign markets is more conducive to a global strategy, but there is almost always a need to consider a strengthening of the foreign market perspective. This has led many globalizing companies into a matrix structure with a geographic dimension cutting across the product divisions, which has meant that local country managers are charged with coordination of the firm's involvement in the country while global product managers are responsible for the global marketing program for each particular product line.

While a firm may globalize marketing strategy, marketing tactics usually need to be adapted to local conditions. Thus, the implementation of a global strategy involves a considerable amount of local activity, and it is important that the local subsidiary manager is motivated to support the global brand. This is often accomplished by the creation of global teams focusing on specific brands, on specific tactical measures, or even special global campaigns. These teams can take the temporary form of task forces rather than becoming permanent fixtures in the organizational structure. However, over time the success of such teams has tended to make them the prime vehicle for global marketing implementation, and companies have come to institutionalize them. The added advantage is that serving on a global team is a good way for a country manager to become familiar with corporate headquarters and other country managers, creating a basis for future promotions up the corporate ladder.

The role of people and organizational culture in the implementation of global marketing is also crucial. Regardless of how globalized the organizational structure and the management systems are, there is always need for people skills to lubricate the relationships and make the organization function. Global communications require the telephone, faxes, and perhaps multimedia, but in the end the global marketer needs to travel and meet with people face to face. This also has the advantage that the marketer can stay closer to the customer, a particularly important factor when organizing for global consumers. It also helps the global marketer adapt to local conditions, often a prerequisite for success in today's tense antiglobal environment.

Key Terms

conflict resolution, *595*
ethnocentricity, *597*
expatriates, *591*
export department
structure, *578*
global account managers, *593*
global marketing director, *587*
global network as an asset, *584*
global product divisions, *580*

global teams, *587*
horizontal networks, *581*
international division
structure, *579*
intranets, *585*
management systems, *588*
matrix organization, *581*
network theory, *585*
organizational culture, *591*

organizational design, *578*
people skills, *589*
regional organization, *580*
relationship marketing, *593*
retail trade marketing
groups, *594*
strategic business unit, *579*
transnational organization, *581*

Discussion Questions

1. Discuss how a global team would work to create the kind of pricing "corridor" to control gray trade mentioned in Chapter 14. How would it work with the local subsidiaries to create and implement the kind of global advertising campaign created by Goodyear in Chapter 16?

2. "Global managers are made, not born. This is not a natural process. We are herd animals. We like people who are like us. But there are many things you can do. Obviously, you rotate people around the world. There is no substitute for line experience in three or four countries to create a global perspective. You also encourage people to work in mixed-nationality teams. You *force* them to create personal alliances across borders. This is why we put so much emphasis on teams." So says Percy Barnevik, former CEO of Asea Brown Boveri (ABB), the large Swedish–Swiss multinational in electrical machinery.[29] Discuss what is gained by such rotation and forced personal alliances. Are there any risks involved? What alternatives to the team concept are there?

3. Discuss how a multinational can use its Web site home page to share information with its employees around the world. Try to identify several ways in which the emergence of electronic communication links make it less difficult to implement a global strategy? Any negatives?

4. Why are people skills so important in the implementation of global marketing? Will the emergence of electronic communications over the various networks (Internet, intranets) make people skills more or less important than before?

5. What are the pros and cons for a native country manager to drop a strong local brand in favor of a global brand? How would you go about presenting the need for the global brand to your local staff?

Notes

1. The burdensome tasks are well documented by Davidson and Haspeslagh, 1982.
2. This is the terminology proposed by Bartlett and Ghoshal, 1989.
3. See Rugman, 2005, and Ghemawat, 2007. Much of this section draws on these two sources.
4. See Rugman and Verbeke, 2004.

5. In this text we have not made a very sharp distinction between regional and global. Many of the global problems and issues discussed also arise with regional strategies.

6. See Chandler, 1969.

7. Lasserre and Schutte (2006) offer evidence that supports a regional structure in the case of Asia.

8. Harvey et al., 2000, and Griffith and Harvey, 2001, show evidence on how power in a network depends on unique market knowledge and the degree to which a firm is invested in the relationship.

9. There is some evidence that the Japanese managers' people skills and company commitment help motivate subsidiaries to adopt a global strategy; see Yip and Johansson, 1993.

10. See Forsgren and Johanson, 1992.

11. Much of this and the following section draw on Gates's review (Gates, 1995), on Griffith and Harvey, 2001, and on McDonough et al., 2001.

12. These examples are taken from the review by Gates, 1995, from Marquardt and Horvath, 2001, and from **www.3m.com**.

13. From Axelsson et al., 1992.

14. Huddleston, 1990, shows vividly why visits from headquarters can be a real distraction for local management.

15. Griffith and Harvey, 2004, describe the ways in which a marketing manager's ability to develop social capital within the firm's global network is a crucial ingredient in company success.

16. It is useful to remember that a uniform global strategy more or less explicitly assumes that headquarters has better information than locals. In specific instances, such as the degree of price sensitivity on the part of local customers, the notion that headquarters "knows better" than the locals is debatable; see Assmus and Wiese, 1995.

17. The importance of local "ownership" of the strategy formulation process for fairness evaluations was empirically demonstrated by Kim and Mauborgne, 1993.

18. See Hanni et al., 1995.

19. The example of Goodyear's development process of pan-regional advertising in Latin America discussed in Chapter 16 shows how a global mindset can be instilled—and how local knowledge can be integrated into the strategy formulation—by repeated interactions between local subsidiary managers and headquarters personnel (Hanni et al., 1995).

20. Thanks to Norio Nishi of Canada's Commonwealth Bank in Tokyo for suggesting the three roles.

21. See Royal and Lucas, 1995, for a rather cynical view of global account management.

22. This was one of the empirical findings of Theuerkauf et al., 1993.

23. This surprising finding is reported by Gates, 1995. Despite the many reasons why experiences in different countries are good for management development, especially in marketing, relatively few companies seem to be able to create effective programs to induce people to take a stint abroad.

24. This dilemma is well illustrated in the *Business International* 1990 report.

25. From Kim and Mauborgne's 1993 findings.

26. This point is forcefully made by Ferdows, 1993.

27. See Prahalad, 2004.

28. See Johansson, 2004.

29. See Taylor, 1992.

Selected References

Assmus, Gert, and Carsten Wiese. "How to Address the Gray Market Threat Using Price Coordination." *Sloan Management Review* 36, no. 3 (1995), pp. 31–42.

Axelsson, Bjorn, Jan Johanson, and Johan Sundberg. "Managing by International Traveling." Chapter 7 in Forsgren and Johanson, 1992.

Bartlett, Christopher. "Procter & Gamble Europe: Vizir Launch." Harvard Business School case 384–139, 1983.

Bartlett, Christopher, and Sumantra Ghoshal. *Managing across Borders: The Transnational Solution.* Boston: Harvard Business School Press, 1989.

Birkinshaw, Julian, Omar Toulan, and David Arnold. "Global Account Management in Multinational Corporations: Theory and Evidence." *Journal of International Business Studies* 32, no. 2 (Second Quarter 2001), pp. 231–48.

Chandler, Alfred. *Strategy and Structure: Chapters in the History of the American Industrial Enterprise.* Cambridge: MIT Press, 1969.

Business International. "Marketing Strategies for Global Growth and Competitiveness." October 1990.

D'Aveni, Richard. *Hypercompetition.* New York: Free Press, 1994.

Davidson, William H., and Philippe Haspeslagh. "Shaping a Global Product Organization." *Harvard Business Review,* July–August 1982, pp. 125–32.

Ferdows, Kasra. "Leveraging America's Foreign Production Assets." Working paper, Georgetown University, School of Business Administration, OPMT-1977-01-293, 1993.

Forsgren, Mats, and Jan Johanson, eds. *Managing Networks in International Business.* Philadelphia: Gordon and Breach, 1992.

Gates, Stephen. "The Changing Global Role of the Marketing Function: A Research Report." *The Conference Board,* report no. 1105-95-RR, 1995.

Ghemawat, Pankaj. *Redefining Global Strategy.* Boston: Harvard Business School Press, 2007.

Griffith, David A., and Michael G. Harvey. "A Resource Perspective of Global Dynamic Capabilities." *Journal of International Business Studies* 32, no. 3 (September 2001), pp. 597–606.

_____. "The Influence of Individual and Firm Level Social Capital of Marketing Managers in a Firm's Global Network." *Journal of World Business* 39, no. 3 (August 2004), pp. 244–54.

Hakansson, Hakan. *Corporate Technological Behavior: Cooperation and Networks.* London: Routledge, 1989.

Halliburton, Chris, and Reinhard Huenerberg. "Pan-European Marketing—Myth or Reality?" *Journal of International Marketing* 1, no. 3 (1993), pp. 77–92.

_____. and Ian Jones. "Global Individualism—Reconciling Global Marketing and Global Manufacturing." *Journal of International Marketing* 2, no. 4 (1994), pp. 79–88.

Hanni, David A.; John K. Ryans; and Ivan R. Vernon. "Coordinating International Advertising—The Goodyear Case Revisited for Latin America." *Journal of International Marketing* 3, no. 2 (1995), pp. 83–98.

Harvey, Michael, David Griffith, and Milorad Novicevic. "Development of 'Timescapes' to Effectively Manage Global Interorganizational Relational Communications." *European Journal of Management,* online November 29, 2000.

Hertz, Susanne, and Lars-Gunnar Mattsson. *Mindre foretag blir internationella: Marknadsforing i natverk* (Smaller Firms Go International: Marketing in a Network). Lund, Sweden: Liber Ekonomi, 1998. (In Swedish.)

Huddleston, Jackson N., Jr. *Gaijin Kaisha: Running a Foreign Business in Japan.* Tokyo: Charles E. Tuttle, 1990.

Johansson, Johny K. *In Your Face: How American Marketing Excess Fuels Anti-Americanism.* Upper Saddle River, NJ: Financial Times/Prentice Hall, 2004.

_____, and Masaaki Hirano. "The Recession and Japanese Marketing." *International Executive,* 1995.

Kim, W. Chan, and Renee A. Mauborgne. "Making Global Strategies Work." *Sloan Management Review,* Spring 1993, pp. 11–27.

Lasserre, Philippe, and Hellmut Schutte. *Strategies for Asia Pacific: Building the Business in Asia,* 3rd ed. Basingstoke, UK: Palgrave Macmillan, 2006.

Marquardt, Michael J., and Lisa Horvath. *Global Teams: How Top Multinationals Span Boundaries and Cultures with High-Speed Teamwork.* Mountain View, CA: Davies-Black Publishing, 2001.

Mazur, Laura, and Judie Lannon. "Crossborder Marketing: Lessons from 25 European Success Stories." *Economist Intelligence Unit,* February 1994.

McDonough, Edward F. III, Kenneth B. Kahnb, and Gloria Barczaka. "An Investigation of the Use of Global, Virtual, and Colocated New Product Development Teams." *Journal of Product Innovation Management* 18, no. 2 (2001), pp. 110–20.

Pearson, A. E., and S. P. Ehrlich. "Honda Motor Co. and Honda of America (A)." Harvard Business School case no. 9-390-111, 1989.

Prahalad, C. K. *The Fortune at the Bottom of the Pyramid.* New York: Wharton School Publishing, 2004.

Royal, Weld, and Allison Lucas. "Global Pricing and Other Hazards." *Sales & Marketing Management* 147, no. 8 (August 1995), pp. 80–83.

Rugman, Alan M. *The Regional Multinationals.* Cambridge, UK: Cambridge University Press, 2005.

_____ and Alain Verbeke. "A Perspective on Regional and Global Strategies of Multinational Enterprises." *Journal of International Business Studies* 35, no. 1 (2004), pp. 3–18.

Sakiya, Tetsuo. *Honda Motor: The Men, the Management, and the Machines.* Tokyo: Kodansha, 1987.

Simmons, Tim. "A Global Brand of Dialog." *Supermarket News* 40, no. 28 (July 9, 1990), p. 2.

Taylor, William. "The Logic of Global Business: An Interview with ABB's Percy Barnevik." Reprinted in Christopher A. Bartlett, and Sumantra Ghoshal. *Transnational Management.* Homewood, IL: Irwin, 1992, pp. 892–908.

Theuerkauf, Ingo; David Ernst; and A. Mahini. "Think Local, Organize . . ." *McKinsey Quarterly,* no. 1 (1993), pp. 107–14.

Uchitelle, Louis. "Gillette's World View: One Blade Fits All." *New York Times,* January 3, 1994, p. C3.

Yip, George, and Johny K. Johansson. "Global Market Strategies of U.S. and Japanese Business." Working paper, Marketing Science Institute, Cambridge, MA, 1993, pp. 93–102.

Yoshino, Michael. "Procter & Gamble Japan (A)(B)(C)." Harvard Business School case nos. 9-391-003, 004, 005, 1990.

Case 4-1

Banyan Tree Hotels and Resorts: Building an International Brand from an Asian Base

Banyan Tree Hotels and Resorts is an interesting case about the issues management faces when building a small but strong local brand into a regional and potentially global brand. It shows how an imaginative entrepreneur can create a strong brand with a clear and well-defined image, but then poses the dilemma of how to grow the brand beyond its market niche. As is typical in brand building, one choice is whether to introduce brand extensions under the same brand name or whether to introduce a second brand.

"I felt that Asian business would never get anywhere if it didn't own brands. Partly this reflected the earlier experience in our family business of putting in the energy to build a brand as agent for an overseas principal, only to lose it when they eventually took the brand in house. I also knew the problems of competing in commodity markets where the business disappears as soon as a cheaper supplier comes onto the scene," reflected Ho Kwon Ping (KP), chairman of Banyan Tree Hotels and Resorts (BTHR), a subsidiary of his family-controlled Wah Chang Group, which he also chaired, in 2001. He had certainly acted on this belief: from a standing start, in just five years Banyan Tree had joined the list of Asia's top 50 brands independently ranked by the consultancy Interbrand, coming in at number 18 against established marques like Sony and Canon, and well ahead of its closest competitors such as Aman Resorts. In 2005 Banyan Tree tied up with Dubai Properties to manage a luxurious resort and spa at the prestigious Jumeirah Beach Residence project in Dubai.

As KP pondered the future of BTHR, he asked himself how far the brand could be extended into new regions such as the Caribbean, across new channels such as e-travel, and into other aspects of travel, leisure, and lifestyle. "Try to stretch it like Richard Branson's Virgin brand, and I'm sure it would break" said KP. The Banyan Tree brand was now a valuable asset that should be fully utilized. Yet, it also needed to be protected and nurtured so as not to lose the distinctive values that had made it successful.

Company History

It was 1916 when KP's grandfather founded Wah Chang Corporation in New York. The business expanded into Thailand and diversified from trading in minerals and tungsten to production of tapioca starch, mung-bean vermicelli, and wheat flour in the 1950s when KP's father, a Singaporean diplomat, was sent there to serve as ambassador. Its business in Thailand, under the name of Thai Wah Group, was listed on the Stock Exchange of Thailand in 1985. When the family moved back home to Singapore, they established Wah Chang International. KP joined the family business as chairman of the group in the early 1980s. Prior to that, he had been a journalist with the Far Eastern Economic

Review in Hong Kong. He was educated at Tunghai University, Taiwan; Stanford University, California; and the University of Singapore, majoring in development economics.

While searching for a plot of land to build a summerhouse for his family, KP came across a disused tin mine in Phuket, Thailand. A United Nations team had written it off as impossible to rehabilitate when it surveyed Phuket's tourism potential in 1977, pointing out that all nutrients had been stripped from the soil, the lagoons were acidic, and the beaches were rapidly eroding. But where others saw a wasteland, KP saw a potential luxury resort. He bought the 1,000 acres of land and established Thai Wah Resorts Development Company Limited to undertake the project.

The "Laguna Phuket" Project

KP launched the project together with his younger brother, Ho Kwon Cjan (KC) and transformed the ravaged area into Asia's first integrated resort—a destination in its own right named "Laguna Phuket"—with an investment of US$200 million. KC, an architect, established Architrave Design and Planning (ADP) under the umbrella of Wah Chang to design and manage the construction of the area. It started with a 232-room Dusit Laguna Resort in 1987, followed by a 256-room Laguna Beach Resort in 1992, and a 292-room Sheraton Grande Laguna Beach Resort in 1993. In 1993, Allamanda Laguna Phuket, an apartment-style resort of 235 rooms, was also added. In 1994, Banyan Tree Phuket, offering 109 exc-lusive villas, was opened together with the luxury Banyan Tree Spa. The project also included an 18-hole golf course—Banyan Tree Laguna Phuket Golf Club—which had opened in 1992.

Lacking experience in hotel management at that time, Thai Wah contracted the management to established hoteliers, including the Thai company, Dusit Laguna Dusit Hotels & Resorts, Sheraton (owned by the U.S. Starwood Hotels and Resorts), and the Pacific Islands Club Group. But serendipity intervened in the case of Banyan Tree: "We were about to build the complex's last hotel and wanted something totally different—a really beautiful, unique, small property. We couldn't find anyone to manage it as we wanted, so we decided to do it ourselves," recalled KP. In fact, by then Laguna Phuket had already acquired significant experience both from developing the other hotel properties and through interaction with the operators it had hired to manage the other parts of the resort.

The Luxury Resort Market in Phuket in the Early 1990s

In the early 1990s, Aman Resorts occupied the high-end resort market in Phuket with its award-winning resort, Amanpuri, which had opened in January 1988. The luxurious resort was built on a coconut plantation and had 40 private pavilions and 30 Thai villa homes. The pavilions were 115 sq.m each, including a private outdoor sundeck and dining terrace. The villas consisted of two to six bedrooms, a private pool, as well as living and dining salas. Each villa came with a live-in maid and cook. Pavilion and villa rates ranged from about US$400 to US$4,000 per night. Amanpuri was not only well-known for its magnificent architectural design and interior décor, but also for its guest profile of Hollywood movie stars, singers, and supermodels. Guests could engage in beach activities, golf, or sail to nearby islands. Other facilities and services included dining options at the restaurant or in-villa dining, swimming pool, gymnasium, health and beauty treatments, a library, and so on.

The other main competitors at the luxury end of the market were Le Royal Meridien Phuket Yacht Club and the resorts within Laguna Phuket. These resorts offered room and suite-type accommodation, mostly situated near a beach. Room rates started at about US$150 per night. Guests could enjoy a variety of facilities including water sports and golf, various dining options, day trips and excursions, and health and beauty treatments. Since a significant proportion of their guests were families, some of these resorts offered special facilities for children such as a kids' club with day programs and staff to take care of them.

KP saw a gap in the luxury resort market. In terms of pricing, there seemed to be a huge gap between Amanpuri and the rest of the resorts. There was a market segment for room rates that ranged from US$250–US$500. In terms of value proposition, he felt that there was a demand for luxury accommodation that emphasized romance, intimacy, privacy, and rejuvenation. He believed that "a resort is not a hotel, it's an experience" and envisaged building a resort based on the concept of individual villas designed as love nests for couples. None of the top-class hotel chains had yet embraced this approach.

Making The Idea a Reality

Banyan Tree Phuket had 109 private villas of three types depending on their centerpiece: the Garden Villa, the Jacuzzi Villa, the Pool Villa, as well as a two-bedroom Pool Villa. In addition to a spacious villa interior that ranged from 170 sq.m to 450 sq.m, every villa had a private landscaped garden and an open-air sunken bathtub. The Jacuzzi Villas came with an outdoor Jacuzzi while the Pool Villas had a private swimming pool and a

---

[1] Aman Resorts operated 11 resorts and hotels around the world including Phuket, Bali, Java, Moyo, and Manila in the Asian region.

traditional Thai sala for al fresco villa dining. These were launched at rates from US$200 per night upwards.

Besides engaging in water sports, golfing at Banyan Tree's own golf course, and taking boat trips to outlying islands, guests could also indulge themselves at the Banyan Tree Spa, a signature service of the resort. To differentiate its offering from leading western spas, BTHR adopted the concept of a "nonclinical" tropical garden spa with an oriental feel, the first of its kind in Asia. The spa was not air-conditioned and the masseuses were barefoot. It offered a variety of luxurious face and body beauty treatments, and aromatic oil massages based on both Asian and European techniques. Guests could select from a wide range of spa packages with names like "Oasis of Peace" or opt for a customized treatment program. Treatment rates ranged from US$33 to US$289. The spas also offered specially formulated spa cuisine, since food was considered an integral part of the renewal process.

"We promise our guests a haven for the body, mind, and spirit where they can indulge and rejuvenate themselves. We seek to deliver luxury without excessive indulgence. In whatever we offer, we must 'live' this concept," explained Abid Butt, general manager of Banyan Tree Phuket and vice president of operations. KP continued, "The question I always ask when creating a hotel is: What effect will it have on the couple using it? Since most of our hotels are resorts, the key question is: Will it make our guests feel romantic and intimate? The complete privacy of the villas is one of the signature features of Banyan Tree resorts, and we have had a lot of feedback from guests who have said that they particularly appreciate the seclusion of the pool villas."

Dharmali Kusumadi, general manager, ADP, added, "Many hotels and resorts tend to spend lavishly on their common areas, especially the lobby, to make it look very grand. For us, the common areas are less crucial compared to the interior décor and facilities of the villas because the 'Banyan Tree experience' focuses on what's happening inside them. For instance, our beds are specially chosen and we place a lot of emphasis on the ambience created by our bathroom designs."

Explaining how the initial set of ideas for the resort came about, KP said, "My wife and I thought about what app-ealed to us, looked at their potential, and then tried them out to see whether they worked." In terms of resort design, ins-piration for new ideas came from brainstorming sessions, architectural design magazines, and other hotels and resorts.

Asked how the Banyan Tree brand name was conceived, KP recalled: "When my wife and I first sat down to think of a brand name, we wanted something that evoked both an Asian feel and the environment. We wanted a brand that we could identify with and had a passion for. We chose 'Banyan Tree' because it was the name of the place where we lived in Hong Kong for four years and had one of the best times in our lives." To complete the picture, a logo was designed together with a tag line, "Sanctuary for the Senses," developed by Batey Advertising, BTHR's agency in its initial years.

Key Strategies and Capability Building

With its initial Banyan Tree resort in Phuket up and running, BTHR turned its attention to expanding the business. Deciding on the right strategies, ensuring that its capabilities grew, and then keeping up the pace to support an international business would be key to future success. Among these would be BTHR's ability to zero-in on the right target market, select the right sites, effectively manage design and construction, manage relations with local governments and communities, develop and staff a suitable international organization capable of sharing best practices while adapting the formula sensitively to local conditions, and to build and manage the Banyan Tree brand.

Targeting the Right Market Segment

Describing his guests at Banyan Tree Phuket, Abid Butt said, "Our target is the luxury, premium market. Eighty-four percent of our guests are couples looking for romance and intimacy. Most of them are in their mid-30s and 40s. They are rich, but not necessarily famous. For an average stay of four nights, each person spends about US$2,500. Our guests are people who want the finer things in life and a high level of service without an astronomic price tag."

Edwin Yeow, senior vice president of marketing and joint managing director added, "Besides romance and intimacy, there is also a trend towards a new age lifestyle where people go on a holiday to explore their inner self. We provide our guests with a place to relax and rejuvenate—an escape from their hectic and pressured life."

Other categories of Banyan Tree guests included corporate clients (10 percent) and families (6 percent). The resorts were equipped to hold corporate meetings and retreats and targeted companies with high spending power such as those in the financial sector, IT, and aerospace industries. Banyan Tree Phuket also had a corporate training facility called "Quest Laguna Phuket Adventure" that offered customized outdoor team-building training programs.

Site Selection

"Branding is very important to our success, but it is only a part of it. Location also plays a strong strategic role," said Bernold Schroeder, general manager of Banyan Tree Maldives and vice president of business development.

When evaluating a site, BTHR managers developed a matrix based on the following criteria: "Is there a strong market potential for BTHR?"; "Does it have a unique view or direct access to a good beach?"; "Does the site appeal to BTHR's target market as a resort destination?"; "What is the competition in the vicinity—existing resorts, room rates charged, and occupancy rates?"; and "Can the local conditions support BTHR's operations—operating costs and staff availability?" Other considerations included air access to the destination and reasonably easy access to the site in terms of distance and mode of transport because BTHR preferred sites in exotic and secluded areas.

Design and Construction Management Capabilities

Unlike most hotel owners who engaged various external companies, such as hotel operators, architects, and construction management companies, to develop and manage their hotels, KP felt that it was advantageous for BTHR as the owner to have all these capabilities and resources in-house. One reason was that BTHR could open a resort built from scratch within two years compared to the industry norm of about five years. All those involved shared BTHR's corporate culture and were familiar with one another, allowing flexible, informal, and rapid decision making. Changes were implemented immediately without contractual concerns. BTHR regarded its resort development capabilities as strategic and ensured that they remained proprietary within the company. While ADP designed properties for other hotel groups, it agreed not to accept assignments for competing hotels with villas, pools, and spas.

Managing a project team was complicated by potential conflicts between the requirements of key contributors. Commenting on the future challenge of managing projects, KC pointed out the trend toward increasing specialization of skills, which meant that more people would be involved, would make it harder to manage team dynamics and find solutions that satisfied everyone. To manage these situations, KC would hold full-day meetings with all parties involved to sort out the problems and find solutions together.

The project management challenge was heightened by the fact that most of BTHR's sites were in remote areas where local contractors were often small and with limited capabilities. Without tight management, building would proceed at a slow pace. To speed things up, BTHR usually deployed prefabrication methods or engaged more than one contractor to work on different areas simultaneously. Progress was tracked against weekly targets so that problems could be rectified quickly. Recounting how BTHR had encouraged contractors to complete the project on time, KC said, "We would select a realistic date to hold a black tie dinner and request a list of things to be ready. This worked very well. The contractors usually delivered about 80 percent–90 percent of the desired requirements on time."

BTHR's decision-making process during resort development and construction was hastened by the creation of a GX group,[2] usually consisting of the project manager, project architect, spa manager, general manager, and a purchasing manager. The group met regularly and had the authority to make overall project decisions within a certain financial limit, with the exception of decisions that had aesthetic implications. This concept was pioneered during the Laguna Beach Resort project and adopted in subsequent projects.

Sensitive Management of Government and Local Community Relations

As BTHR expanded across different countries, it had to familiarize itself with local bylaws and manage its relationship with the local government. In Phuket, BTHR had a full-time government liaison staff. Based on this experience, it engaged a local law firm to handle community relations when it entered the Maldives and planned to liaise closely with the government on its proposed development on Bintan through Bintan Resort Management Pte Ltd., the master developer on the island.

One of the criticisms of beach resort developments is that they tended to disturb the surrounding ecological balance and create disparities between locals and foreigners. KP, a long-time major critic of environmental destruction, resolved to ensure that BTHR was an environmentally and socially responsible resort company. Although BTHR resorts generally targeted locations in countries with limited awareness of environmental issues, BTHR set its own demanding standards, which always exceeded local regulations and environmental standards. It insisted on not using wood as a structural element in constructing its resorts. It also minimized air-conditioning in the public areas through special architectural design to avoid the use of CFC-based air-conditioning and to reduce energy consumption. When it entered the Maldives, it sought to rely on sea breezes to ventilate the villas, which were specially designed to maximize air flow. However, after many complaints about discomfort, especially from Asian guests, BTHR installed standard air-conditioning in some of the villas.

BTHR learned to work with the local communities in various ways. It set up a free school in Phuket and procured its merchandise locally to help conserve traditional craft skills in the declining Asian cottage industries. The merchandise ranged from an assortment of indigenous handicrafts and artifacts for display in the villas to spa products like essential oils, massage oils, and incense

[2] G represented Group and X represented an arbitrary number, depending on the size of the group.

sticks and burners. These were also sold at the Banyan Tree Gallery, BTHR's retail boutique that would become part of each BTHR resort so that guests could recreate the "Banyan Tree ambience" at home. It also gave artisans from the region a chance to showcase their work to guests from all over the world.

Building and Managing the Banyan Tree Brand

Contrary to the industry norm of having general managers oversee the marketing and sales activities of their respective hotels, BTHR's marketing and sales function, employing about 25 staff, was centralized at its Singapore corporate headquarters. Edwin Yeow explained, "General managers at the resort level usually come and go in a few years, and we believe that they should focus on delivering a positive guest experience. To ensure consistency and continuity in brand building, we feel that it is better to centralize our long-term marketing strategy."

The centralized marketing budget represented 7 percent of total revenue. Marketing expenditure was split 60 percent aimed at trade and 40 percent directly at consumers. BTHR focused on its wholesaler network because this generated more than 50 percent of its sales. BTHR had a number of sales offices worldwide, and worked with only three to five wholesalers in each country so that the wholesalers were able to generate higher returns (see Exhibit 1). Wholesalers visited the properties at least once a year to establish close relationships and to get feedback. When BTR Phuket was first launched, the individual villa concept was new to the industry and seemed intimidating to some potential customers. BTHR spent a lot of time explaining its offering and the individual villa concept to the wholesalers so that they would know how to sell the villas.

EXHIBIT 1   Banyan Tree Hotels and Resorts Worldwide Sales Offices

Banyan Tree Hotels & Resorts Worldwide Sales Offices	
Australia	South Korea
Germany	Taiwan
Hong Kong	Thailand
Japan	United Kingdom
Singapore	United States

Small Luxury Hotels GDS: LX	
Australia	Netherlands
Canada	New Zealand
France	Spain
Germany	Switzerland
Hong Kong	United Kingdom
Italy	United States
Japan	

In terms of consumer marketing communication, BTHR engaged an agency, Batey Advertising, during its first two years. As a new resort group, BTHR needed consistent brand exposure. But after gaining initial recognition in the industry, it cut back on extensive advertising to keep costs down and built the brand more around public relations and direct marketing programs. BTHR advertised mainly in prominent travel magazines such as Condé Nast Traveler and Premier Hotels & Resorts. Edwin Yeow believed that editorial coverage was more effective in conveying the "holistic Banyan Tree experience." To encourage this, he regularly invited travel magazine writers to visit the resorts. Collaboration with magazines for model photo shoots was another way for the resorts to gain exposure. One example was with a popular Korean bridal magazine whose target market fitted well with BTHR's targeting of honeymooners. BTHR also participated in specific event-related advertising and engaged extensively in collaborative advertisements with business partners all over the world, such as airline magazines and Citibank's Credit Cards Division, to offer special deals.

In a *Fortune* magazine article on Asian brands where Banyan Tree was praised for its success in creating a strong pan-Asian brand, it was described as being "meticulous about preserving its refined and upscale image through tastefully done low-key ads." Explaining how BTHR projected itself in its advertisements and collateral materials, Edwin Yeow said, "We place a lot of stress on photographs that are very evocative. We make sure that the brand logo is always projected powerfully. There are usually very few words so that the advertisement will not look cluttered. We focus on endorsement of the brand rather than hard-sell as it gives more mileage to the brand. That's why we always capitalize on the awards and accolades that we win. It gives people who do not know us an idea of where we stand compared to the more established resorts in our market segment." KP believed that creative advertisements and collateral were crucial to BTHR's brand building efforts and in projecting the desired image. He participated actively in the production process, especially the creative part: every item had to be endorsed by him before it could be released publicly.

Another major factor in the rapid development of the Banyan Tree brand was the fact that it targeted a niche market and word tended to spread very quickly. A word-of-mouth recommendation by guests to their friends was one of the most effective ways of getting people interested in the "Banyan Tree experience." Limiting the rate of expansion, which created some difficulty in getting bookings for a particular date given BTHR's high occupancy rates, also reinforced people's desire to visit its resorts.

One of BTHR's major concerns was consistency in delivering its brand promise. Since both the physical product and quality of service were equally important to this, BTHR preferred to build its own resorts rather than

EXHIBIT 3   Banyan Tree Group Financial Performance 1996–1999 (All Figures in SGD '000)

Source: Company Data, BTHR.

	1996	1997	1998	1999
Banyan Tree Hotels				
Occupancy	73%	71%	73%	77%
Average Room Rate	308	416	373	434
Revenue	25,794	27,326	37,524	45,255
Gross Operating Profit	9,909	9,172	17,553	22,625
Banyan Tree Spas				
Revenue	370	1,348	3,775	6,147
Gross Operating Profit	57	375	2,417	4,404
Banyan Tree Golf Club				
Revenue	2,953	2,543	4,002	3,745
Gross Operating Profit	1,171	683	1,605	1,211
Banyan Tree Gallery				
Revenue	1,674	1,845	2,983	3,419
Gross Operating Profit	(71)	59	541	795
Banyan Tree Management Co				
Revenue	3,077	6,269	9,126	11,332
Gross Operating Profit	457	2,118	4,863	6,145
Combined Banyan Tree Group				
Revenue	33,868	39,331	57,410	69,898
Gross Operating Profit	11,523	12,407	26,979	35,180
GOP as % of Revenue	34%	32%	47%	50%
Exchange rates:				
THB: SDG	17.99	20.68	24.60	22.34
USD: SGD	1.4	1.48	1.67	1.69

respectively. In January 2002, BTHR assumed management of Banyan Tree Bangkok from Westin Hotels and Resorts after the expiry of a five-year management contract. Other new destinations under consideration included Mexico, the Napa Valley in California, and Tuscany in Italy.

Despite the downturn in the luxury travel market due to the social and economical uncertainty faced by Asia from 1997, BTHR continued to experience an overall average occupancy rate of above 70 percent and an increasing stream of total revenue and gross operating profits between 1996 and 1999 (see Exhibit 3). Overall average room rates increased from US$219 in 1996 to US$256 in 1999 based on "rack rates" (the price to the general public) of between US$265–$2,150 depending on location of the property, villa type, and season. To keep close track of performance, BTHR benchmarked each resort against its main competitors in the vicinity by conducting a monthly "Fair Share Analysis" (see Exhibits 4a, 4b and 4c).

Evolving The BTHR Organization

BTHR now viewed itself as an international company that identified more with a distinctive positioning in the global hospitality industry rather than with any one nationality or national culture. Its vision was to be a global

niche player. It now had more than 15 nationalities represented within its middle and senior management ranks. At the corporate headquarters, there was about 80 staff. The fact that its headquarters was in Singapore was more coincidental than precipitated. KP recognized that BTHR's Asian origin was a positive factor in positioning its existing resorts but he was quick to point out that it was not something that would limit the places where the resorts could be located. He was also determined that it would not influence the people he hired nor their progression within the company. Rather, the emphasis was on its corporate culture: the BTHR culture.

BTHR had a flat organizational structure. The executive committee was led by KP, chairman and president. Other members consisted of Ariel Vera, senior vice president of finance and joint managing director; H. L. Tee, general manager, Wah Chang Group; and Edwin Yeow, senior vice president of marketing and joint managing director. Resort general managers reported directly to the executive committee. They were given the autonomy to run their respective resorts as long as they were profitable.

BTHR's management team at the resort level was made up of relatively young and ambitious people who saw BTHR as a valuable stepping-stone to help them jump the system of slow career progression offered at

EXHIBIT 4a   Fair Share Analysis of Banyan Tree Phuket (Year End December 1999)

Source: Company Data, BTHR.

Main Competitors							
Hotel	Keys	Potential Room Nights	Occupancy % Fair Share	Room Nights Sold	Paid Occupancy %	Occupancy % Market Share	Occupancy % Fair Share Achievement*
Banyan Tree	108	39,432	22.6	31,117	78.9	24.6	109
Amanpuri	40	14,880	8.5	8,707	58.5	6.9	81
Sheraton	323	120,156	68.9	86,432	71.9	68.5	99
Total	467	174,468	100	126,256	72.4	100	
Average Rate (Thai Baht)							
Hotel	Actual Average Rate	Potential Room Revenue	Room Revenue—Fair Share %	Occupancy %	Actual Room Revenue	Revenue Market Share %	
Banyan Tree	11,887	468,728,184	32.1	78.9	369,887,779	35.6	
Amanpuri	22,308	331,943,040	22.7	58.5	194,235,756	18.7	
Sheraton	5,490	659,656,440	45.2	71.9	474,511,680	45.7	
Total	8,226	1,460,327,664	100	72.4	1,038,635,215	100	

*Occupancy fairshare achievement = Occupancy market share/Occupancy fairshare.

the big hotel chains where they had been trained. Although these people were perhaps less "loyal" to the company, their ambition and drive complemented KP's style of getting things done fast. BTHR was keen on "double-hatting" which was KP's way of developing his staff. Bernold Schroeder, for example, was appointed as both general manager of Banyan Tree Maldives and vice president of business development, while Abid Butt was both general manager of BTR Phuket and vice president of operations.

Consistency and Local Adaptation

Understanding that resort general managers faced different circumstances in different countries, the company adopted a flexible approach to providing consistent adherence to its key customer propositions delivered with a local flavor to enhance the experience. Service standards were set primarily in terms of customer satisfaction rather than specified in technical terms like times and quantities. The process of service delivery could

EXHIBIT 4b   Fair Share Analysis of Banyan Tree Maldives (Year End December 1999)

Source: Company Data, BTHR.

Main Competitors							
Hotel	Keys	Potential Room Nights	Occupancy % Fair Share	Room Nights Sold	Paid Occupancy %	Occupancy % Market Share	Occupancy % Fair share Achievement*
Banyan Tree	48	17,856	14	13,492	76	17	109
Sonevafushi	62	23,064	18	12,666	55	16	79
Four Seasons	106	39,432	31	22,107	56	27	81
Hilton Maldives	130	48,360	38	32,959	68	41	98
Total	346	128,712	100	81,224	63	100	
Average Rate (US$)							
Hotel	Actual Average Rate	Potential Room Revenue	Room Revenue % Fair Share	Occupancy %	Actual Room Revenue	Revenue Market Share %	
Banyan Tree	262	4,678,272	14	76	3,534,904	15	
Sonevafushi	301	6,942,264	21	55	3,812,466	23	
Four Seasons	341	13,446,312	41	56	7,538,487	35	
Hilton Maldives	158	7,640,880	23	68	5,207,522	27	
Total	247	32,707,728	100	63	20,093,379	100	

in the semiconductor industry, in part because it was the only American company that continued to manufacture dynamic random access memory chips in the face of fierce Japanese competition in the 1980s. The company had manufacturing sites spread throughout North America, Asia, and Europe, and was pursuing its strategy of increasing manufacturing capacity and developing manufacturing excellence.

The Semiconductor Group

In 1958, Texas Instruments engineer Jack Kilby developed the first integrated circuit, a pivotal innovation in the electronics industry. Made of a single semiconductor material, the integrated circuit eliminated the need to solder circuit components together. Without wiring and soldering, components could be miniaturized and crowded together on a single chip. Only a few years after Kilby's invention, electronics manufacturers were demanding these integrated circuits, or chips, in smaller sizes and at lower costs, a move that led to unprecedented innovation in the electronics industry. Soon chips became a commodity, and chip manufacturers relied on high-volume, low-cost production of reliable chips for success. Only a few manufacturers had strong positions in the production of differentiated semiconductors.

Forty years after its discovery, Texas Instruments still remained dependent on its semiconductors sales, which fell primarily in integrated circuits. The Semiconductor Group, a part of the Components Division, had total sales of $2 billion in 1994, the third consecutive year in which Texas Instruments' semiconductor revenues grew faster than the industry. The company's return to financial success in the early 1990s was based on its strong performance in semiconductor sales and profits, both of which were at record levels in 1994. Management in the company expected semiconductor sales to continue to grow strongly and was planning heavy capital expenditures on new or expanded plants in the United States, Malaysia, and Italy to increase the company's capacity.

The Semiconductor Group divided its business into two segments: standard products and differentiated products. Standard semiconductors, which accounted for 90 percent of the group's sales, included products that could be substituted by competitors. Standard semiconductors performed in the market much like other products for which substitutes were readily available. Texas Instruments, like its competitors, competed for market share in these commodity products based primarily on the price it offered to original equipment manufacturers and distributors. The remaining 10 percent of the company's semiconductor business came from differentiated products, of which Texas Instruments was the sole supplier. Because substitutes for these products were not available in the marketplace, differentiated products commanded higher margins than their standard counterparts and were receiving greater strategic emphasis on the part of group management. While the company continued to hold a strong position in standard semiconductors, it was searching for a strategy that would allow it to achieve a higher return on development and manufacturing investments. Managers at Texas Instruments believed that higher returns were possible only by developing more successful differentiated semiconductors.

Electronics Distribution Market

Texas Instruments sold its semiconductors through two channels: directly to original equipment manufacturers and through a network of electronics distributors. Szczsponik estimated that 70 percent of the group's U.S. customers dealt directly with Texas Instruments. The remainder bought their semiconductors through one or more of the seven major semiconductor distributors that served the North American market (refer to Exhibit 4 for information on the top electronics distributors). Whether an original equipment manufacturer dealt directly with Texas Instruments or bought from a distributor depended on the manufacturer's size. The largest original equipment manufacturers were able to negotiate better prices from semiconductor manufacturers than were the distributors and therefore bought directly from the manufacturers. Because mid-sized and small original equipment manufacturers were fragmented, and thus more difficult to serve, these customers were served more efficiently through the distribution channel. Szczsponik explained:

> The semiconductor market can be divided into three tiers. Fifty percent of our sales in semiconductors go to the top tier of perhaps 100 large electronics manufacturers who deal with us directly. The next 46 percent of sales come from 1,400 medium-sized companies at the next level, half of whom deal directly with us and half of whom buy through distributors. The remaining 4 percent of sales are to 150,000 smaller companies at the bottom tier in the market, who deal only through distributors. Distributors have a clearly defined role in servicing mid-sized and small buyers.

Distributors were considered to be clearinghouses for the semiconductor industry. Each distributor dealt with products from all the major semiconductor manufacturers. For example, Arrow Electronics sold semiconductors manufactured by Motorola and Intel as well as those made by Texas Instruments. The distributors specialized in handling logistics, material flows, sales, and servicing for electronics manufacturers who were either too small to negotiate directly with the major semiconductor manufacturers or lacked sufficient expertise in logistics management. In addition, the distributors sometimes knitted packages of different products together for the smaller original electronics manufacturers as an added service. Some also performed varying scales of assembly operation.

The electronics distribution network had originally consisted of a large group of smaller companies. By 1995,

EXHIBIT 4   Top Electronic Distributors

Source: Lehman Brothers, "Electronic Distribution Market," December 22, 1994.

Company		1994	1993	1992	1991	1990
Arrow Electronics	Sales ($ billions)	3.973	2.536	1.622	1.044	971
	Share (%)	21.5	17.4	14.8	11.0	10.2
Avnet	Sales ($ billions)	3.350	2.537	1.690	1.400	1.429
	Share (%)	18.1	17.4	15.4	14.8	15.0
Marshall Industries	Sales ($ billions)	.899	.747	.605	.563	.582
	Share (%)	4.8	5.1	5.5	6.0	6.1
Wyle Laboratories	Sales ($ billions)	.773	.606	.447	.360	.359
	Share (%)	4.2	4.2	4.1	3.8	3.8
Pioneer Standard	Sales ($ billions)	.747	.540	.405	.360	.343
	Share (%)	4.0	3.7	3.7	3.8	3.6
Anthem	Sales ($ billions)	.507	.663	.538	.420	.408
	Share (%)	2.7	4.6	4.9	4.4	4.3
Bell Industries	Sales ($ billions)	.395	.308	.282	.257	.239
	Share (%)	2.1	2.1	2.6	2.7	2.5

however, industry consolidation had left almost 40 percent of the distribution market in the hands of its two largest competitors, Arrow Electronics and Avnet. The seven largest distributors captured 58 percent of sales in the market (refer to Exhibit 5 for the sales and market shares of the top distributors). This trend toward consolidation had had a major impact on the nature of the relationships among semiconductor manufacturers and the distributors through which they sold their products. According to Szczsponik:

> Fifteen years ago, 30 distributors were active in the industry and it was clear that the semiconductor manufacturers controlled the distribution network. With the consolidation of the distribution network into only 7 or 8 powerful players, however, power is shifting. It's hard to say if we are more important to them or they are more important to us.

Price Negotiations and Global Pricing Issues

Since the vast majority of semiconductors were considered commodity products, the buying decisions of distributors were based almost entirely on price. Distributors forecast the demand for the various semiconductor products they carried and negotiated with vendors for their prices. Since semiconductor prices were notoriously volatile, the price levels negotiated between manufacturers and distributors played a vital role in the distributors' profitability. The Semiconductor Group at Texas Instruments combined the practices of forward pricing and continuous price negotiations to set prices with its distributors.

Forward Pricing. The cost of semiconductor manufacturing followed a generally predictable learning curve. When a manufacturer first began producing a new type of chip, it could expect only a small percentage of the chips it produced to function properly. As the manufacturer increased the volume of its production, it both decreased the costs of production and increased the percentage of functioning chips it could produce. This percentage, termed "yield" in the industry, and the standard learning curve of semiconductor manufacturing together had a large impact on the prices semiconductor manufacturers set for their products (refer to Exhibit 6 for the price curve of semiconductor products). This yield was important to TI; a 7 percent increase in overall yield was equivalent to the production of an entire Water Fab plant, an investment of $500 million.

EXHIBIT 5   Total Sales and Market Share of Top Distributors

Source: Lehman Brothers, "Electronic Distribution Market," December 22, 1994

		1994	1993	1992	1991	1990
Industry Total	Sales ($ billions)	16.22	12.95	10.18	9.06	9.17
Top 25	Sales ($ billions)	13.41	10.69	8.11	7.10	7.20
	Share (%)	82.7	82.5	79.7	78.4	78.5
Top 7	Sales ($ billions)	10.75	8.42	6.36	5.05	5.00
	Share (%)	58.0	57.9	57.9	53.5	52.5
Top 2	Sales ($ billions)	7.32	5.07	3.31	2.44	2.40
	Share (%)	39.6	34.8	30.2	25.8	25.2

EXHIBIT 6   **Forward Pricing Curve**

Forward Pricing Curve

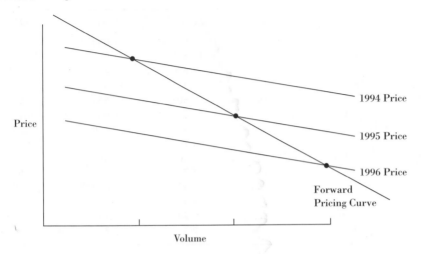

According to Jim Huffhines, manager of DSP Business Development in the Semiconductor Group, managers could predict with considerable accuracy the production cost decreases and yield improvements they would experience as their production volumes increased:

> We know the manufacturing costs for any given volume of production. We also know that these costs will decrease a certain percentage and our yields will increase a certain percentage each year. These predictions are the basis of the forward prices we set with both original equipment manufacturers and distributors.

Continuous Price Adjustments. Production costs and yield rates were not the only contributing factors to price levels for standard semiconductors: market supply and demand also played a powerful role in establishing prices. As a result of volatile prices caused by shifts in supply and demand, distributors often held inventories of semiconductors that did not accurately reflect current market rates. To protect distributors from price fluctuations, most semiconductor manufacturers offered to reimburse distributors for their overvalued inventories. Szczsponik explained:

> Semiconductor prices have fallen by 15 percent over the past nine months. If Arrow bought semiconductors from me for $1.00, nine months ago, they are worth only 85¢ now. Arrow is carrying a 15 percent "phantom" inventory. If Arrow sells those semiconductors now, we give it price protection by agreeing to reimburse it the 15¢ it has lost per semiconductor over the past three quarters.

At the same time, distributors had at their disposal sophisticated systems for monitoring semiconductor prices from each of the major manufacturers, and were constantly in search of price adjustments from vendors when placing their orders. Szczsponik continued:

> Distributors have access to the prices of products from all the semiconductor manufacturers at any given time, and

some anywhere in the world. The largest distributors have a staff of 20 to 30 people shopping around continuously for the best prices available for different types of semiconductors; add to this group a staff of accountants managing the price adjustment transactions. For example, they may call us to say that Motorola has quoted them a certain price for a semiconductor, and ask us if we can beat their price. In total, we get close to 150,000 of these calls requesting adjustments from distributors a year, and do over 10 percent of our sales through price adjustments. I have 10 people on my staff who negotiate price adjustments for distributors: 5 answer their calls, and 5 work with our product managers to make pricing decisions. These decisions are critical: if we make a mistake in our pricing, we lose market share in a day that can take us 3 months to recapture. At the same time, through our negotiations with distributors, we capture masses of data regarding the pricing levels of our competitors and the market performance of our different products. These data are critical to our ability to set prices.

As the distribution network consolidated into a small number of powerful companies, Szczsponik had begun to notice that his price negotiations were increasingly focused not only on beating the competition in North America, but on beating prices available around the world, including those of TI in other regions. With distributors becoming more active in the global market, they were more often exposed to semiconductor price levels from Europe and Asia. Industry analysts expected North American distributors to become more active in global markets as they pursued aggressive expansion campaigns in Europe and Asia. Although Texas Instruments' current contracts with its distributors prevented them from selling semiconductors outside of the region in which they were purchased, distributors were becoming insistent on access to freer global supplies and markets. While the concept may have appeared reasonable to the distributors, it was somewhat more complicated for Texas Instruments. Kevin McGarity elaborated:

Because business is different everywhere in the world, our international distribution channels have evolved independently. They aren't subjected to the same costs, and don't operate under the same methods and calculation models. In the United States, for example, we offer a 30-day payment schedule for our customers. If they don't pay us within 30 days, we cut off their supply, no matter who they are. Italy operates under a 60-day schedule. Europeans include freight in their prices; we don't in North America. Finally, the cost of producing semiconductors varies by country. Europe tends to be more expensive than North America or Asia, simply because their infrastructure is more costly. So when one of our large distributors phones with the Singapore price for semiconductors manufactured in Düsseldorf, he is crossing boundaries that may be invisible to him but are very real to us.

Preparing for the Meeting with Arrow

With sales of almost $4 billion in 1994, Arrow Electronics was the largest semiconductor distributor in North America, of which TI products accounted for approximately 14 percent. Its aggressive growth had taken the company into global markets and had given it increased exposure to fluctuating price and exchange levels in different international markets. Seeking to minimize its costs, Arrow had begun to pressure semiconductor manufacturers to set standard global prices for each of their products. Motorola, one of Texas Instruments' largest competitors in the semiconductor industry, was rumored to be preparing for global pricing. Management at Texas Instruments, however, was unsure of the wisdom of moving toward global pricing. According to Szczsponik, the pros and cons of global pricing seem unevenly balanced:

> The large distributors want global pricing to reduce their costs and simplify their planning. But does it make sense for us? Right now our organization's calculation systems and costs in each country are too different for us to offer standard global prices. There are other things to consider

as well. If we set global prices, we will no longer continue our price adjustment negotiations with the distributors. This may save us the cost of staffing our negotiations team, but it also takes away from us a powerful tool for gathering information on our customers' prices and our product performance. As soon as we stop negotiating price adjustments, we lose our visibility in the market.

To prepare for his discussion with McGarity and the forthcoming meeting with Arrow Electronics, Szczsponik knew TI had to make some fundamental decisions regarding global pricing. Who held the power in the relationships Texas Instruments had with its distributors? What was the source of the negotiating strength each party would bring to the meeting? Finally, what position should the Semiconductor Group take with its distributors regarding global pricing? And what organizational implications would such a decision imply?

Discussion Questions

1. What are the reasons the semiconductor market is global? Why is it so difficult to create an FSA or CSA? Are there any differential advantages?
2. What drives the need for global pricing? Is there any risk of gray markets? Are there any options apart from global pricing?
3. Who has most power in the value chain from manufacturers through distributors to customers?
4. How would you try to manage the global pricing process—by formalization of the pricing process, economic controls, centralization, or informal persuasion? Are there any other options?

Source: This case was developed by Professors Per V. Jenster, CIMID; B. Jaworski, USC; and Michael Stanford as a basis for classroom discussion rather than to highlight effective or ineffective management of an administrative situation. Copyright © 1995 Center for International Management and Industrial Development (CIMID). Not to be reproduced without the permission of CIMID. Used with permission.

Case 4-3

United Colors of Benetton

Benetton is the well-known Italian apparel maker and retailer whose "United Colors" clothes are sold worldwide. This case deals with the firm's global promotional strategy. In particular, it focuses on the role of the controversial advertisements by Oliviero Toscani, and the ensuing uproar among Benetton's independent retailers who claim the ads alienate customers. The case raises interesting questions about universal ethics and cross-cultural differences—and about how a limited promotion budget can still create global brand awareness.

It was October 1995. Luciano Benetton, chairman of Benetton Group S.p.A, prepared to address yet another

audience of business leaders. This tall, smiling yet reserved man with very blue eyes and longish hair was the guest speaker at a dinner held by the Italian Chamber of Commerce for France in Paris. Over the past 40 years, Benetton had become famous for its technological advances and novel approach to retailing. By 1995, it had become one of the world's best-known brands, with 8,000 shops worldwide, and a successful winning Formula One racing team (key financial data can be found in Exhibit 1). For most people, however, Benetton was synonymous with its communication strategy—one of the world's most visible and controversial,

EXHIBIT 1 Benetton Group SpA: Financial Highlights 1986–1995 (millions of lire)[1]

	Italy	Other Europe	The Americas	Other Countries	Consolidated
1986 Revenues	388,872	470,530	173,322	19,558	1,089,983
Operating profits	99,680	86,160	16,180	4,030	206,050
Net Income					113,029
Share price/MIB[2]					15,900/104.8
1987 Revenues	437,101	609,973	222,780	12,050	1,261,077
Operating profits	108,426	117,071	8,928	(2,526)	249,839
Net Income					130,291
Share price/MIB					10,460/99.6
1988 Revenues	641,633	702,462	236,372	35,266	1,475,282
Operating profits	111,937	115,196	16,134	(2,361)	239,673
Net Income					130,171
Share price/MIB					10,560/80.3
1989 Revenues	665,530	672,635	222,874	96,460	1,657,519
Operating profits	120,986	99,462	(637)	5,560	225,307
Net Income					115,412
Share price/MIB					8,720/99.3
1990 Revenues	749,930	819,825	220,463	268,830	2,059,048
Operating profits	147,477	142,820	(8,265)	9,952	266,180
Net Income					133,271
Share price/MIB					8,580/100.0

	Italy	Other Europe	The Americas	Other Countries	Consolidated
1991 Revenues	790,339	933,751	215,409	364,265	2,303,764
Operating profits	150,374	151,368	(12,255)	35,123	311,757
Net Income					164,783
Share price/MIB					10,320/84.7
1992 Revenues	862,495	987,603	237,798	424,745	2,512,641
Operating profits	170,770	172,533	(12,029)	43,106	356,639
Net Income					184,709
Share price/MIB					13,870/70.5
1993 Revenues	850,609	1,062,823	270,021	568,005	2,751,458
Operating profits	165,003	204,150	(22,418)	74,490	407,926
Net Income					208,038
Share price/MIB					26,730/83.5
1994 Revenues[3]	882,744	1,019,478	227,302	658,148	2,787,672
Operating Profits	151,153	175,040	(19,138)	93,841	388,740
Net Income					210,200
Share price/MIB					12,038/104.1

Note: Results for 1995: revenues of L2,940 billion with net income of L220 billion.
Share price on 31.12.95: 18,890 lire

[1]Exchange rate Lire/US$: 1986 = 1,358; 1987 = 1,169; 1988 = 1,306; 1989 = 1,271; 1990 = 1,130; 1991 = 1,151; 1992 = 1,471; 1993 = 1,704; 1994 = 1,626

[2]MIB = MIB Index, calculated by the Milan Stock Exchange and based on the average of all stocks traded on that exchange, 1990 = 100.

[3]On 1 February 1994, Benetton had a capital issue of 10 million shares at L26,500/share

almost always provoking reactions of outrage or praise and, quite often, both.

Rather than advertising its products, Benetton used its communications budget to provoke debate on broad social issues such as racism, AIDS, war, and poverty. A number of observers had criticized its "use of social problems to sell knitwear." Luciano knew that he would have to explain one more time why he spent Benetton's L115 billion[1] communication budget on "penetrating the barriers of apathy," and that, inevitably, some of his audience would remain unconvinced.

The Benetton Group

Benetton Group S.p.A. was the world's biggest consumer of wool and Europe's largest clothing concern, with 1994 sales of L2,788 billion and net income of L210 billion. Its largest markets were Italy (34 percent of sales), Germany (12 percent), Japan (11 percent), and France (9 percent). Sixty-four million items were sold worldwide in 1994, up 12.7 percent on 1993. Outside the EU, the increase was 36 percent. Aided by several devaluations of the lira, Benetton had cut prices by up to 40 percent over the previous two years.

In 1995 Benetton had three main brands:

- United Colors of Benetton (clothing for men and women), which also included Blue Family (with an emphasis on denim) and Benetton Undercolors (underwear and beachwear): 60.8 percent of sales.
- 012 United Colors of Benetton (clothing for children under 12), including Zerotondo (clothing and accessories for babies): 18.5 percent of sales.
- Sisley (higher-fashion clothing): 11.8 percent of sales.

Over two-thirds of their clothing was for women, who represented 80 percent of Benetton's shoppers. Fabrizio Servente, head of product development, commented:

> The "objective" target for the adult Benetton stores is the 18–24 year old, but of course there is no age ceiling. Our product takes into account quality and price. It's clean, international, with a lot of attention to design. It can be worn just as easily by Princess Diana and by her maid, or her maid's daughter. The way young people dress is becoming more and more "uniform," but there are differences from one region to another. Benetton must still be Italian in Italy, Brazilian in Brazil, Indian in India.

The Benetton System

Benetton operated through a complex system of over 500 subcontractors and several joint ventures specializing in design, cutting, assembling, ironing, or packaging, plus thousands of independent retail outlets. Benetton's success was largely attributed to this ability to combine fashion with industry.

[1] On 16 October 1995, US$ 1 = L1602.10.

Benetton's unique distribution philosophy was an important reason for its success. "We didn't want to become directly involved in the selling side," Luciano Benetton said, "so in the beginning it was friends with financial resources who moved into this part of the business." By 1995, from over 8,000 retail outlets Benetton owned and operated fewer than 50 "flagship stores" in cities such as Milan, New York, Paris, and Dôsseldorf. The rest were owned by independent retailers who typically ran five or six outlets.

The company dealt with these retailers through a network of 83 agents, controlled by seven area managers reporting to Benetton's commercial director. The agents, who were independent entrepreneurs, had exclusive rights over a territory; they selected store owners and received a 4 percent commission on orders placed with them. They supervised operations in their territory, kept an eye on the market, and offered guidance to store owners on product selection, merchandising, and the location of new stores, making sure that Benetton's policies were respected. Another important responsibility of the agents was to find new retailers who "fit" the Benetton culture. They were themselves encouraged to reinvest their earnings in new stores of their own.

Benetton's Communications

Benetton's early advertisements were rather conventional, focusing on the product and stressing the quality of wool.

The logo, a stylised knot of yarn and the word "Benetton," were later united within a green rectangle with rounded corners. During the 1970s, the company reduced its advertising consistent with its decision to adopt a low profile in Italy. The first U.S. advertising campaigns, handled by a small agency (Kathy Travis), stressed the European origins and international success of Benetton. "Last year we made 8,041,753 sweaters sold through 1,573 Benetton stores internationally." These campaigns contributed less to Benetton's breakthrough in the United States than the runaway success among students of a simple model (the rugby polo) and the awakening of Americans to fashion "Made in Italy."[2]

In 1982 Luciano Benetton met Oliviero Toscani, a well-known fashion and advertising photographer who lived in Tuscany and had studios in Paris and New York. His clients included, among others, Jesus Jeans, Valentino, Esprit, Club Med, and Bata. Toscani convinced Luciano that Benetton ought to promote itself as a lifestyle, not a clothing business. At Toscani's suggestion, Benetton retained Eldorado, a small Paris agency with which Toscani had often worked as a photographer.

[2] Benetton's sales have always relied upon a few highly successful models. For example, in 1994, the crew-neck navy blue pullover accounted for 40% of the winter sales in France.

All the Colors in the World

The first campaigns were conventional in style, stressing social status and conformism, and featuring groups of young people wearing Benetton clothing. The real departure came in 1984 with a new concept, "All the Colors in the World." This campaign showed groups of teenagers from different countries and ethnic groups dressed in colorful knitwear. The print and billboard campaign was distributed by J. Walter Thompson (JWT) in 14 countries.

The campaign was greeted with enthusiasm and Benetton received hundreds of letters of praise. But it prompted shocked reactions in South Africa, where the ads were carried only by magazines catering to the black community. A few letters from England and the United States reflected hysterical racism. "Shame on you!" wrote one correspondent from Manchester in the north of England, "You have mixed races that God wants to keep apart!"

United Colors of Benetton

In 1985, a UNESCO official visited the studio where Toscani was photographing a multiracial group of children and exclaimed: "This is fantastic, it's the United Colors here!" This became the new slogan: "United Colors of Benetton." The posters reconciled instantly recognizable "enemies": a German and an Israeli, a Greek and a Turk, and an Argentinean and a Briton. Another poster showed two small black children bearing the U.S. and Soviet flags.

The multiracial message was made clearer still with the theme chosen for the 1986 and 1987 campaigns: "the globe." One ad showed a white adolescent dressed as an Hassidic Jew holding a moneybox full of dollar bills, next to a black teenager dressed as an American Indian. "In the eyes of Eldorado's directors, all of them Jewish, the picture was humorous enough to make it clear that we were taking aim at the stereotype [of the money-grabbing Jew]," wrote Luciano Benetton.[3] Benetton was flooded with protests, mostly from France and Italy. In New York, Jewish groups threatened to boycott Benetton shops. Benetton replaced the ad with a picture of a Palestinian and a Jew, which was also criticized. Luciano commented:

> I was a bit discouraged, but I had learned a fundamental lesson. We had chosen to promote an image that touched very deep feelings, identities for which millions of people had fought and died. We had reached the limits and felt the responsibilities of commercial art. Everybody was now watching us, and even a small dose of ingenuity could hurt us and irritate others. I promised myself I would control our image even more rigorously.[4]

The 1987 autumn/winter campaign, "United Fashions of Benetton," showed models wearing Benetton clothes with accessories that evoked the great names in fashion. "United Superstars of Benetton" was the slogan for the 1988 campaign, featuring pairs dressed up as Joan of Arc and Marilyn Monroe, Leonardo da Vinci and Julius Caesar, or Adam and Eve—two-long haired teenagers dressed in denim.

A Message of Racial Equality

1989 marked a turning point in Benetton's communication activities. The company terminated its relationship with Eldorado.[5] "From the beginning, Luciano Benetton wanted image to be an in-house product, so that it would reflect the company's soul," Toscani explained later. United Colors Communication would soon handle all aspects of Benetton's communication including production and media buying. The entire process was managed by less than 10 people; Toscani's visuals would be discussed by the advertising team, then shown to Luciano for final approval. This allowed Benetton to produce advertisements which cost about one-third of those of its competitors.[6] Benetton did not usually advertise on television because of the high costs but used print and outdoor media extensively. It limited itself to two series of campaigns (spring and fall). Each campaign would typically last a couple of weeks, and consist of a small number of visuals shown in an increasing number of countries. By 1995, Benetton spent about 4 percent of turnover on communication, which included campaigns for United Colors of Benetton and Sisley, sports sponsorship, a quarterly magazine, Colors,[7] and funding for its communications school, Fabrica.

This shift to in-house communications was accompanied by a radical change in approach. The 1989 ads no longer showed the product, didn't use a slogan, and replaced the knot logo with a small green rectangle that was to become the company's trademark. Hard-hitting images began to deliver an unambiguously political message championing racial equality. One ad showing a black woman nursing a white baby generated controversy in South Africa and in the United States, where it was seen as a throwback to the era of slavery. Benetton withdrew the ad in the United States, explaining that "the campaign is intended to promote equality, not friction."

This became Benetton's most praised visual ever, winning awards in five European countries. Another ad, showing a black man and a white man handcuffed together, offended British blacks, who thought it showed a

---

[3] Luciano Benetton and Andrea Lee, *Io e i miei fratelli,* Sperling e Kupfer Editori, 1990 (translated by the authors).
[4] *Io e i miei Fratelli.*

[5] Two years later, Benetton fired JWT and set up United Colors Communication as a full-service agency.
[6] *Financial World,* 17 September 1991, p. 41.
[7] In 1993, spending amounted to 5.7% to finance the TV launch of Tribù, a line of scents and cosmetics. The complete Benetton fragrance business was restructured in 1995.

white policeman arresting a black. London Transport refused to show the poster in its network.

The 1990 campaign continued the theme, with softer images: the hand of a black child resting in a white man's hand; a white wolf and a black lamb; a small black child asleep amid white stuffed bears; the hand of a white relay runner passing a baton to a black teammate.

Benetton's attempt to show two babies on their potties on a 770-square-meter billboard opposite Milan's cathedral was banned by the city authorities and the Roman Catholic cardinal. That year, Benetton won its first advertising award in the U.S.A.

Social Issues

By 1991 Benetton's campaigns, which now tackled issues beyond racism, were reaching audiences in more than 100 countries. A picture showing a military cemetery, released at the start of the Gulf war, was turned down by all but one newspaper, Il Sole 24 Ore in Italy. An ad displaying brightly colored condoms ("a call for social responsibility in the face of overpopulation and sexually transmitted disease") was intended to "demystify condoms by displaying them in a playful and colorful way, like fashion items."

Simultaneously, condoms were distributed in Benetton's shops worldwide. Benetton also distributed HIV guides in the shantytowns of Rio "because it was important that even people who could never buy a Benetton sweater should get the basic communication."

Other ads included a white boy kissing a black girl, a group of Pinocchio puppets in different hues of wood, and a multiethnic trio of children playfully sticking out their tongues.

While this last ad won awards in Britain and Germany, it was withdrawn from display in Arabic countries, where it was considered offensive.

Later that year, Toscani chose to focus on: "love, the underlying reason for all life." The campaign photo featured, among others, a priest and a nun kissing; and Giusy, a screaming newborn baby with her umbilical cord still attached.

In the United States, the Anti-Defamation League condemned the priest-and-nun ad for "trivializing, mocking, profaning and offending religious values," and several magazines rejected it.

In France, the Bureau de Vérification de la Publicité (BVP), a self-regulating advertising body, recommended the removal of the priest-and-nun ad in the name of "decency and self-discipline," while in England, it won the Eurobest Award. Others were also positive: Sister Barbara Becker Schroeder from Alzey, Germany, wrote to Benetton: "I feel the photo expresses great tenderness, security and peace. I would be grateful if you would let me have one or more posters, preferably in different sizes."[8] In November 1991, Benetton won a court case initiated by AGRIF (L'Alliance générale contre le

Courtesy Benetton Group, S.p.A. Reprinted with permission.

racisme et pour le respect de la famille française) where it was accepted that the nun and priest poster was not racist or anti-Christian.

In Britain, Benetton ignored a warning issued by the Advertising Standards Authority (ASA) concerning the Giusy ad and within days, the authority received some 800 complaints. The offending posters were withdrawn—and replaced with an ad showing an angelic blond-haired child next to a black child whose hair was styled to evoke horns, which the ASA also criticized.

In the U.S.A., Giusy elicited some negative reactions but was accepted by Parenting, Self, and Vogue. It was rejected by Child, Cosmopolitan, and Elle. The posters were not displayed in Milan where the city officials complained of "the excessive impact and vulgarity of the subject." The local High Court ruled that "the picture offended public order and general morality." Giusy was also banned in France, Germany, and Ireland, where the advertising space was donated to the Association for the Fight Against Cancer. These reactions surprised Benetton, as well as a number of others:

> We should ask ourselves the question of why such a natural, vital and basic image as that of a baby being born, offends the public. Every day we are confronted with pictures of death, often meaningless, and we put up with them in silence, or very nearly. Yet we are afraid to see an image of life. (*L'Unita,* 10/9/91)
>
> Why must beer be drunk topless on the deck of a sailing boat and the smiling, happy mum always be half-naked as she swaddles the baby in a nappy like a scented pastry? Isn't all this rather ridiculous? (*Il Giornale Nuovo,* 26/10/91)

According to Benetton, "Once the period of rejection was over, the picture began to be understood and appreciated." Giusy won an award from the Société Générale d'Affichage in Switzerland and Bologna's General Clinic asked for a copy to decorate its labor room.

[8] This is one of 100 letters (positive and negative) published at Benetton's initiative in P. Landi and L. Pollini, eds. *Cosa C'entra L"Aids Con i Maglioni?,* A. Mondadori Editore, 1993.

Courtesy Benetton Group, S.p.A. Reprinted with permission.

The "Reality" Campaigns

In 1992, Benetton broke new ground with two series of news photographs on issues such as AIDS, immigration, terrorism, violence, and political refugees. The use of real-life pictures showing, for example, a bombed car, Albanian refugees, a Mafia-style killing, and a soldier holding a human bone provoked controversy around the world, despite Benetton's repeated claim that it was trying to prompt debate of serious social issues.

This claim was supported by Patrick Robert, a photographer with the Sygma agency, some of whose pictures had been used in the campaigns: "the absence of an explanatory caption on my photographs [soldier with human bone, truck bulging with refugees] does not bother me . . . for me the objective of the campaign is reached to draw the public's attention to these victims.[9]

A picture showing David Kirby,[10] an AIDS patient, surrounded by his family on his deathbed, stirred particularly strong emotions.

In Britain, the ASA described the ad as "obscene" and "a despicable exploitation of a tragic situation" and asked magazines to reject it. Benetton donated the use of 500 paid U.K. poster sites to the charity Trading. Maggie Alderson, the editor of the U.K. edition of Elle, which ran a statement on two blank pages instead of the ad, commented:

> It is an incredibly moving image in the right context, but to use it as an advertisement for a fashion store selling jumpers is incredibly insulting. They have stepped out of the bounds of what is acceptable and what makes this so sickening is that they have touched up the photograph to make it look biblical because the AIDS victim resembles Jesus Christ. (The Guardian, 24/1/92).

In France, the BVP took an unprecedented step: without even waiting for the ad to be printed, it threatened to exclude any publication that dared carry it. Only one publication ignored the ban: Max, a magazine for young people. Its editor, Nicolas Finet, commented, "Our readers, those between 15 and 30 years old, are directly affected by this topic. This campaign is one way of approaching the AIDS problem whilst avoiding the socio-medical aspect. Our readers' letters have shown that we were not wrong" (quoted in the French advertising weekly Stratégies, 18/2/92). In Switzerland, Schweizer Illustrierte decided to accept the ad saying that it did not hurt mass sensitivity but "wounded only one thing: the rules of the games according to which the message must be dull, stale even."

Many organizations and advocacy groups for homosexuals charged Benetton with callous exploitation, saying it offered no information about prevention. However, some AIDS activists felt it gave the issue a higher public profile, an opinion that others shared:

> For the large majority of the population which thinks that AIDS is not their business, Benetton's ads will be a slap in their face and I am sure it will be more effective than every campaign to date by any public or private body. (*L'Unita*, 25/1/92).
>
> The company estimates that between 500 million and one billion people have seen the AIDS image, far more than ever saw it when it came out in Life. A public that is reading fewer newspapers and believing fewer broadcasts might begin to swallow tiny doses of information between the ads for liqueur and lingerie. (Vicky Goldbert in the *New York Times*, 3/5/92).
>
> The picture . . . has done more to soften people's heart on the AIDS issue than any other I have ever seen. You can't look at that picture and hate a person with AIDS. As far as the comment that it was "touched up to look like Jesus Christ" I know that at Pater Noster [hospital], several times, with several patients through the years, nurses have made the same comment, "he looks like Jesus" (Barb Cordle, David Kirby's nurse in Interview, 4/92).

The Economist (1/2/92) felt that the ads targeted the young and,

> what better means to appeal to them than by offending their elders . . . expect no repentance, or tamer ads, from Benetton unless its sales start to drop.

Asked about the campaign's impact on sales, Peter Fressola, Director of Communications, Benetton Services New York, emphasized that individual ads were not geared to boost sales and that Benetton was aware that

> people are not going to look at an image of a burning car, and then make a best-seller out of our fuschia sweater. (*The Wall Street Journal*, 28/5/92).

Reacting to the charges of exploitation, Benetton argued that the David Kirby visual increased awareness of the need for collective and personal solidarity with AIDS patients, created a media tribune for HIV organizations and others involved in the issue, and encouraged a debate

[9] In *Benetton par Toscani,* Musée d' Art Conetmporain, Lausanne, 1995.
[10] The photographer, Therese Frare, won the World Photo Award for this picture.

on how best to communicate on AIDS.[11] They also stressed that David's family was in favor of the photo being used. In support of the ad, the Kirby family went on the record:

> It is what he would have wanted. We don't feel used. Rather it is we who are using Benetton. David is speaking louder now that he is dead than when he was alive. (Il Mattino, 22/3/92).

The second 1992 campaign once more used hard-hitting news pictures: an oil-covered bird from the Gulf; an albino Zulu woman ostracised by other Zulus; a grime-smeared Salvadoran child carrying a white doll; pigs in a trash heap in Peru; children building a brick wall; KGB agents arresting a suspect; an empty electric chair in a U.S. jail.

The *Financial Times* commented:

> Like its previous campaign, Benetton has again focused on the downbeat and the unhappy, this time selecting a set of apparent outcasts to sell its colourful jumpers. (17/9/92)

The Clothing Redistribution Project

The spring 1993 campaign showed Luciano Benetton, newly elected to the Italian Senate and named as Italy's leading entrepreneur, stark naked, modestly screened by a caption reading, "I want my clothes back." A second ad followed: "Empty your closets."

People were invited to donate clothes of any brand at Benetton stores. The campaign, which ran in about 1,000 magazines and 150 dailies, was widely welcomed: "It is a clear break from Benetton's self-serious attitude of the past. It also marks the first time the company has engaged in direct action to support a cause." (The Wall Street Journal, 27/1/93).[12]

Some 460 tons of clothes were collected in 83 countries and redistributed worldwide with the help of charities such as Caritas, the International Red Cross, and the Red Crescent.

The Venice Triptych

In June 1993, Toscani exhibited a 400-square-meter triptych at the Venice Biennial art show. A specially restored chapel housed the work, which showed 56 close-up photos of male and female genitals—blacks and whites, adults and children. Benetton added its logo and published the picture as an ad in *Libération*.

That day the newspaper sold an extra 40,000 copies. The BVP threatened to sue. Two days later, French men's underwear-maker Eminence published a double page in *Libération* showing as many (male) crotches with the same layout and the slogan: "We like dressing them."

The HIV-positive Campaign

A near-unanimous outcry greeted the Fall 1993 campaign, which consisted of three stark photographs showing an arm, buttock, and crotch, each branded with the words "HIV Positive."

Benetton explained that the pictures referred to the three main avenues for infection, as well as to the ostracism of AIDS victims. In Singapore, Danny Chow (president, ASA) dismissed the ads as "easily another ploy to get free publicity" (*Straits Times*, 27/9/93). The Italian advertising watchdog, the Giuri della Pubblicità, condemned the campaign for "not respecting the dignity of human beings."

The AIDS association LILA (*Lega Italiana per la Lotta control l'AIDS*) didn't approve of it but took a pragmatic approach and decided to use it in its fight against AIDS. In the U.S.A., reactions were mostly negative. David Eng (Gay Men's Health Crisis, New York) felt that "the ad can fuel hatred and disempowerment . . . people can get the message that this [i.e., branding] is what we should be doing to people who are HIV positive." (*New York Times*, 19/9/93). The *National Review* refused the ad without seeing it. The British ACET (AIDS Care Education and Training) demanded the ad's withdrawal.

The *Association Française de la Lutte contre le Sida* (AFLS), a French government-sponsored AIDS group, sued Benetton for "hijacking a humanitarian cause for commercial ends." Four HIV sufferers joined in the lawsuit, with charges of "humiliation" and "debasement." According to their lawyers, the brandings were an implicit call to discriminate against patients, and evoked the Nazi death camps.[13] A representative of AIDES, another French association, felt the ad could be misinterpreted: "It is clearly stated that sodomy or intravenous drug abuse are the [major] causes of AIDS. Such short cuts are misleading and stupid." (*CB News*, 20/9/93).

The brother of one sufferer bought a full page ad in *Libération*, and published a picture of his brother's emaciated face with the caption: "During the agony, the selling continues. For the attention of Luciano Benetton, from Olivier Besnard-Rousseau, AIDS sufferer, terminal phase." There were increasingly strident calls to boycott the firm, including one from a former cabinet minister. Arcat Sida, a French AIDS support group headed by Pierre Bergé, CEO of Yves Saint Laurent, sponsored a

---

[11] Around this time, Benetton started advertising in gay magazines, which were generally ignored by major corporations.

[12] Pascal Sommariba, Benetton's International Advertising Director, countered charges of a lack of charitable giving, saying "If a company makes 10% profits and takes 20% of it for charity, this is 2% of its turnover. If you take just 1/3rd of a communication budget of, say 5% of turnover, you are already there and it does not look like a charitable company, it is fairer."

[13] On 1 February 1995, a Paris court rules against Benetton and awarded damages of about US$32,000. On 6 July 1995, a German court ruled that these pictures offended the dignity of HIV-infected people.

poster showing a condom stuffed with bank notes next to a "United Boycott" logo in Benetton's signature typeface and green color. Stores were vandalized and sprayed with graffiti, leading some store owners to complain that "Mr. Benetton listens to nobody." (Le *Nouvel Observateur*, 20/12/93).

Luciano Benetton was himself surprised and hurt by the violence of these reactions. In the group's defense, its long-standing commitment to the fight against AIDS and the extent of its actions were cited. On December 1, 1993 (World AIDS Day), Benetton in cooperation with the association Actup had a 22-meter pink condom placed over the obelisk in the Place de la Concorde in Paris. In early 1994 Luciano received an award given by the president of South Korea in recognition of the consciousness-raising role played by the company.

The Known Soldier

In February 1994, a Benetton ad showing bloodied battle fatigues appeared on billboards and in newspapers across 110 countries.

The clothes had belonged to a Croatian soldier killed in Bosnia, as a caption in Serbo-Croat indicated:

> I, Gojko Gagro, father of the deceased Marinko Gagro, born in 1963 in the province of Citluk, would like that my son's name and all that remains of him be used in the name of peace against war.

The advertisement was greeted by an immediate uproar. While it became an instant success in Sarajevo, where the Oslobodenje newspaper printed it, leading dailies such as the *Los Angeles Times, Le Monde*, and the *Frankfurter Allgemeine Zeitung* refused to carry it, and the Vatican denounced Benetton for "image terrorism." Reactions among the combatants and people in the war zones depended on whether Gagro was seen as a victim or an aggressor and whose cause the ad was perceived as helping. Indignation reached a climax in France, where the minister for human rights and humanitarian action urged consumers to stop buying Benetton clothes and to "rip them off the backs of those who wear them." Once again, several Benetton stores were vandalized, causing a growing sense of unease among some retailers.

The French advertising weekly *Stratégies* announced it would not write about Benetton's advertising as long as it remained in the same vein: "Besides the disgust it causes, this [latest] ad raises the issue of the responsibility of advertisers. Can one do anything, use anything, to attract attention?" (25/2/94). Marina Galanti, Benetton's spokeswoman, reacted to the outcry: ". . . If we were trying to sell T-shirts, there probably would not be a worse way of doing it. We are not that naïve. It's meant to question the notion of institutionalized violence and the role of advertising." (*The Guardian*, 16/2/94). The autumn 1994 worldwide campaign featured in print media and billboards showed a mosaic of 1,000 faces arranged to softly highlight the word AIDS at its center. This campaign attracted little attention.

The Alienation Campaign

The spring 1995 campaign featured two visuals based on the theme of "alienation." One showed lines of barbed wire, coming from a variety of troubled countries such as Bosnia, Lebanon, and Israel as well as from private gardens.

The other showed a jungle of TV antennae symbolizing the "invisible barriers erected by the overcrowding of video images, which not only affect interpersonal relationships, but also people's perception of reality." Billed as "an invitation to an open discussion on real and virtual prisons, on the mental and televisual dictatorships which restrict freedom," the campaign did not elicit strong reactions. Benetton denied that the ads reflected a softer, toned-down communications strategy.

Around the same time, Benetton's U.S. retailers launched a campaign developed by Chiat/Day of New York, designed to appeal to more conservative audiences. The new U.S. campaign focused on clothing and included TV spots as well as eight-page magazine inserts. Luciano explained that this initiative was not an alternative to their international campaign, but an additional support to its U.S. store owners.

The German Lawsuits

The furor over the recent Benetton campaigns reached a peak in Germany. Here 12 retailers being sued by Benetton for nonpayment[14] defended their case by accusing Benetton of provoking adverse reaction in consumers through their ads, with a consequent drop in sales. Benetton stated that ". . . total sales in Germany have remained stable in 1994 . . . 1992 was a record year . . . 8 million items were sold in 1993 and 1994 versus 4 million in 1985." While the group of retailers claimed that the number of Benetton stores had dropped from 650 to 500, with 100 more dropouts expected, Benetton maintained that it had 613 stores in Germany in 1994 as opposed to 650 in 1993. Marina Galanti explained that, "What we are talking about is a lawyer's trick to use a cause célèbre as a peg on which to hang every kind of grievance. . . these store owners may not like the ads, but the Frankfurt Museum of Modern Art has them on permanent exhibition." (*The Independent*, 6/2/95).

Threats of legal action in France and other European countries had also been made. A body called The Benetton Retailers Interest Group had been formed to coordinate the various actions against Benetton. However, other

---

[14] Ulfert Engels, the lawyer co-ordinating the 12 cases said: '. . . Our tactic was to get Benetton to sue, otherwise we would have had to fight in an Italian court and we prefer to fight in Germany.' *Marketing Week*, 3/2/95

retailers formed the "Pro-Benetton" group in Germany to "fight the discredit done to Benetton by the disgruntled retailers."

In October 1995 Luciano indicated that all 12 cases had been won by Benetton and that "the affair was now over."[15] Financial analysts were generally optimistic about Benetton's prospects as they felt the markets had

[15] Germany: Benetton ends dispute with retailers'. *Handelsblat,* 12 October 1995.

already discounted any possible negative impact due to the controversies. Salomon Brothers issued a "Buy" recommendation on Benetton stock on October 17, 1995.

The visibility and uniqueness of Benetton's communications had prompted a number of advertising agencies and publishing and market research companies to conduct independent studies of their effectiveness, very often without Benetton's knowledge. These studies evaluated specific Benetton campaigns (Exhibit 2)

EXHIBIT 2   Ipsos Tests of Benetton Campaigns in France (billboards, Paris and suburbs), 1985–1993

Source: Ipsos Publicité, Paris, France.

	Recognition[2]	Attribution[3]	Confusion[4]	Liked	Disliked
Overall sample (N = 300)	57	29	3	73	23
18–34 year olds (N = 150)	63	36	3	73	21

Date of Campaign: 1–20/3/85
Date of Test: 20/9/85
Cost[1]: 2,000,000 FF and 4,000,000 FF ($223,000 and $446,000)

N = 301	Recognition	Attribution	Confusion	Liked	Disliked	Indifferent
Overall sample	75	64	2	79	20	1
Gender						
Men	75	60	3	77	23	1
Women	75	68	1	81	17	2
Age group						
18–24	81	77	1	83	16	1
25–34	81	76	1	83	15	3
35–55	69	53	3	75	25	—
Income group						
Higher	83	72	3	81	18	1
Medium	72	60	2	77	22	1
Lower	65	58	2	77	20	3
Ipsos standards[5]	43	18	—	60	35	5

Date of Campaign: 1989
Date of Test: 28/9 to 3/10/89
Cost: 2,396,000 FF ($375,543)

N = 302	Recognition	Attribution	Confusion	Liked	Disliked	Indifferent
Overall sample	79	72	1	32	66	2
Gender						
Men	76	67	1	34	64	2
Women	83	77	—	30	69	1
Age group						
18–24	84	75	1	34	64	2
25–34	80	77	1	38	62	—
35–55	79	67	1	26	70	3
Income group						
Higher	80	71	—	44	56	1
Medium	82	78	1	23	75	3
Lower	75	63	2	27	71	2
Ipsos standards	43	18	—	59	35	6

Date of Campaign: 2/9 to 11/9/91
Date of Test: 19/9/91
Cost: 2,440,000 FF ($432,463)

(Cont.)

[1] Estimated cost of the campaign in French Francs (US$). This refers only to billboards and does not include print.
[2] Respondents were shown a folder containing several ads with the brand name blocked out. As they leafed through, they were asked which ads they remembered seeing. The recognition score is the percent of respondents remembering having seen (at least one of) the ads listed.
[3] For each ad recognized, respondents were asked whether they remembered the name of the brand blocked out.
[4] Percentage of respondents who incorrectly identified the brand.
[5] Average score of all other billboard campaigns tested by Ipsos within the same industry and with similar budgets.

EXHIBIT 2   Ipsos Tests of Benetton Campaigns in France (billboards, Paris and suburbs), 1985–1993 (*Continued*)

N = 193	Recognition	Attribution	Confusion	Liked	Disliked	Indifferent
Overall sample	64	59	1	59	38	3
Gender						
Men	67	60	1	60	38	2
Women	60	58	—	58	39	3
Age group						
18–24	65	63	—	65	29	6
25–34	67	65	—	60	36	4
35–55	60	53	1	58	41	1
Income group						
Higher	67	63	1	56	43	1
Medium	60	53	—	66	30	4
Lower	66	62	—	48	48	3
Ipsos standards	43	18	—	59	35	6

Date of Campaign: 2/9 to 11/9/91 and 14/10 to 21/10/91
Date of Test: 24/10/91
Cost: 2,440,000 FF ($432,463) and 1,097,000 FF ($194,431)

N = 301	Recognition	Attribution	Confusion	Liked	Disliked	Indifferent
Overall sample	81	77	2	23	70	7
Gender						
Men	78	72	3	22	70	8
Women	85	81	1	24	70	6
Age group						
18–24	86	84	—	21	69	10
25–34	82	79	1	22	71	7
35–55	81	75	3	24	68	7
Income group						
Higher	86	85	1	20	75	6
Medium	82	75	4	25	68	7
Lower	69	60	—	28	62	10
Ipsos standards	44	21	—	61	31	8

Date of Campaign: 14/9 to 21/9/93
Date of Test: 23/9/93
Cost: 2,200,000 FF ($338,473)

together with the image of Benetton and other leading brands across a variety of countries (Exhibit 3).

After Toscani

The last campaign with Toscani, photographed in 2000 in a number of American jails, focused on the death penalty and had strong impact in the media. TV stations throughout the world devoted part of their news programs to the subject. The photos of the condemned prisoners were printed in the international press while the debate on the death penalty was enriched.

From 2000, Oliviero Toscani handed over responsibility for creativity to Fabrica, the communication research center that he himself helped to establish. Fabrica is called a "true workshop for research," which is open to youngsters under 25 from all over the world. Since 2001, the brand has alternated every three seasons between

conventional product campaigns and wide-ranging institutional campaigns. They include " Volunteers in Colors" (2001), "Food for Life" (2003), and "James & Other Apes" (2004).

The 2001 "Volunteers in Colors" campaign included a special issue of COLORS and a concert, in collaboration with U.N. volunteers to celebrate the "International Year of Voluntary Work." With this campaign, Benetton tackled a theme typical of its advertising and spoke, once again, about "real people," touching on society's real problems. Voluntary work was depicted not as it usually is, associated with emergencies and pain, but rather as a way of finding fulfillment in helping others; a personal choice and a way of enriching one's own life.

The endorsement of these institutions marked the beginning of Benetton's current phase of communication. The United Nations, SOS Racisme, associations fighting AIDS and the death penalty, pacifist groups, the U.N.

EXHIBIT 3 Overall Awareness and Use of Some Clothing Brands in 21 Countries, 1994 (*A Young & Rubicam Brand Asset™ Valuator Study*)

Source: A Young & Rubicam Europe, Brand Asset™ Valuator Study, 1994.

	Benetton		Chanel		Dior		Esprit		Gap		Armani		Lacoste		YSL	
	Aware[1]	Use[2]	Aware	Use	Aware	Use	Aware	Use	Aware	Use	Aware	Use	Aware	Use	Aware	Use
Australia	59	2/81	93	4/84	94	11/73	87	7/63	12	1/93	43	2/95	74	4/65	82	16/76
Brazil	54	3/81	51	1/93	42	4/86	30	0/98	9	0/98	20	1/97	29	6/85	34	5/88
Canada	61	2/78	97	11/69	89	2/89	83	22/58	57	5/79	60	2/92	41	2/78	84	15/64
Czech Rep	69	1/77	92	3/38	91	6/36	32	1/45	23	1/70	22	0/47	51	1/57	37	2/44
France	91	8/53	98	16/64	98	14/65	21	1/96	25	2/91	37	3/91	97	24/30	99	19/58
Germany	71	8/51	80	5/66	83	3/70	68	8/54	19	1/79	44	4/72	66	4/54	63	2/71
Hungary	73	3/87	78	3/90	75	7/87	31	2/95	13	1/95	35	2/93	60	4/67	45	4/91
Italy	94	21/35	85	15/67	83	13/68	25	1/97	16	1/96	93	25/49	86	19/37	73	14/70
Japan	75	3/64	98	21/63	93	27/50	47	3/93	28	1/90	75	6/85	88	6/36	93	29/49
Mexico	66	8/74	90	13/63	79	17/59	73	5/86	22	4/86	33	7/82	60	7/57	47	14/69
Netherlands	74	1/53	93	10/70	86	5/73	66	3/41	11	0/10	36	3/31	78	2/54	78	6/64
P.R. China	19	2/95	15	1/97	23	1/98	6	0/99	12	0/99	7	0/100	9	0/99	13	1/98
Poland	40	0/81	69	2/50	58	4/52	13	0/59	9	0/76	31	2/57	27	1/70	32	2/55
Russia	17	0/99	53	4/91	67	4/91	5	1/99	11	1/98	22	1/98	22	0/93	12	1/98
S. Africa	25	3/88	29	3/91	49	13/72	56	3/89	25	1/89	12	1/97	29	2/86	22	5/88
Spain	73	9/48	85	6/69	86	7/65	28	1/79	12	2/77	55	5/72	87	18/36	59	7/66
Sweden	74	0/62	93	1/65	92	1/61	54	1/74	14	1/91	58	1/74	89	18/42	83	2/63
Switzerland	89	11/50	91	14/56	93	14/63	69	11/55	19	2/92	65	12/68	89	10/50	87	14/61
Thailand	55	3/18	51	3/25	64	5/37	14	1/6	37	2/12	23	0/12	49	6/20	39	2/17
U.K.	88	2/65	96	7/78	94	7/77	35	1/93	27	1/87	70	5/85	55	2/78	87	8/77
U.S.	53	1/30	90	11/51	86	15/51	76	16/58	77	12/24	61	5/51	51	2/23	70	12/51

The database consists of a survey of 30,000 consumers in 21 countries across 6,000 global and local brands and 120 product categories.

[1] Awareness: respondents were asked to rate on a 7-point scale (1 = never heard of, 7 = extremely familiar) their "overall awareness of the brand as well as their understanding of what kind of product or service the brand represents." The figures correspond to the percent of respondents answering 2 or above.

[2] First figure: percent of respondents indicating that they "use or buy regularly/often"; 2nd figure: percent of respondents indicating that they have "never used or bought."

High Commission for Refugees (UNHCR), and many volunteer associations now take advantage of the power and fame of the Benetton logo to communicate about issues they take to heart but for which they would never have had adequate budgets. The old charge that "Benetton exploits pain to sell sweaters" has been turned on its head. It is the U.N. and humanitarian groups that are taking advantage of the power and recognizability of the Benetton logo and its sweaters to give voice to the "rest of the world."

This puts the logo at the threshold of a new, more advanced phase of value creation. Benetton is still talking about consumption and communications. The company has neither the desire nor, of course, the means to solve the world's problems. The label is geared not to a specific target but to a collective one: Shoppers whom Benetton considers intellectually sophisticated enough to stop assailing them with "buy now"-type advertisements.

Discussion Questions

1. What are the explanations for the global success of Benetton?

2. What is the marketing logic behind the "United Colors of Benetton" campaign? Do the Toscani photographs "add value" to the Benetton brand name or dilute it?

3. Why do some people (including Benetton's own distributors) react so negatively to some of the advertising? Judging from the research, some of the ads score high on "Liking" while others are clearly "Disliked." What is it in the ads that makes for this?

4. To what extent is the communicated message universal? To the extent the message is universal, one would expect a uniform global ad campaign to be successful. Would this be the case here? Why, or why not?

5. Discuss the ethical aspects of using human suffering in ads. Does your answer influence how likely you would be to buy a Benetton product? Why, or why not?

Source: This case was developed by Christian Pinson, Professor, and Vikas Tibrewala, Associate Professor of INSEAD, with the assistance of Francesca Gee. It is intended to be used as a basis for class discussion rather than to illustrate either effective or ineffective handling of an administrative situation. Copyright © 1996 INSEAD-CEDEP, Fontainebleau, France.

Case 4-4

Cathay Pacific Airways: China or the World?

Cathay Pacific is Hong Kong's privately owned international airline. As for most Hong Kong businesses, the 1997 takeover of Hong Kong by China created uncertainties that were difficult to anticipate and manage. The case details the situation before and after the takeover and shows the two basic strategic options available: going global through alliances or focusing on the China market. It is a good case for studying how political factors enter into strategic decisions.

On July 1, 1997, the British government relinquished sovereignty over Hong Kong to the Chinese government. The Joint Declaration and the Basic Law of the Hong Kong Special Administrative Region (SAR) provided for Hong Kong to maintain a high degree of autonomy in aviation matters and "for the maintenance of the status of Hong Kong as a center for international regional aviation." Since the airline industry was characterized by a high degree of governmental regulation, mainland Chinese support was critical to the solvency and growth of any flag-carrier airline. Could Cathay Pacific, a division of Britain's Swire Pacific, still have allies in the SAR government? Would its ownership interests now endanger its ability to penetrate the lucrative Chinese mainland market? Should Cathay aim to become a truly global carrier or another regional player?

Company Background

Cathay Pacific was founded in 1946 by an American, Roy C. Farrell, and an Australian, Sydney H. de Kantzow. Although initially based in Shanghai, it soon relocated its airline business in Hong Kong. Legend has it that Farrell and a group of foreign correspondents thought up the airline's unique name in the bar at the Manila Hotel. In 1948, the company was incorporated, and the Swire Group became its largest shareholder. In 1959, Cathay acquired Hong Kong Airways and became Hong Kong's flag carrier.

Over five decades Cathay had flown through numerous major political and economic crises in the region. Cathay had managed to thrive on each of these crises and grow bigger and stronger. By the mid-1990s, it had a fleet of aircraft that were among the youngest in the world, while its replacement program involved orders and options for US$9 billion in new aircraft. Cathay was now providing scheduled passenger and cargo services to 50 destinations around the world.

Marriage of Convenience

Despite these promising developments, the situation close to home was not nearly as encouraging for Cathay. With the Chinese takeover, Chinese airline operators were likely to move into Hong Kong to compete head-on with Cathay. The China National Aviation Corporation (CNAC), the commercial arm of the regulatory Civil Aviation Administration of China, had carried on business operations in Hong Kong since 1978, the year when China began its phenomenal economic reform.

To address this potential threat, Swire made a series of strategic moves. Cathay was initially floated on the stock exchange in 1986, but prior to that the carrier was owned 70 percent by Swire and 30 percent by Hong Kong's largest bank, The Hong Kong Bank (HSBC). After the flotation, their respective holdings were diluted to 54.25 percent and 23.25 percent.

Maintaining a good relationship with key officials in China also remained of strategic importance for the future. So, in February 1987, China International Trust & Investment Corporation Hong Kong Limited (CITIC HK) sold a 12.5 percent stake in Cathay Pacific and thus became its second-largest shareholder. CITIC HK was a leading "red chip" company[1] controlled by Beijing's China International Trust & Investment Corporation. This marked the beginning of a closer relationship between Swire and the Chinese.

In the following decade, CITIC HK actively invested in strategic industries in Hong Kong. For instance, CITIC HK acquired Tylfull Company Limited in 1990 and later renamed it CITIC Pacific Limited, and it subsequently became the major holding and investment vehicle for CITIC HK. Over the next five years, CITIC Pacific acquired a major trading company, a 12 percent interest in Hong Kong's largest telecommunications company, a 10 percent interest in Hong Kong Air Cargo Terminals Limited, and 10–25 percent interests in Hong Kong's three cross-harbor tunnels.

Dragonair and the China Market

Since the inauguration of its Open Door policy in 1979, a rapid growth in economic activities has led to great demand for air travel throughout China. The outbound travel potential of 1.25 billion people and several hundred thousand foreign businessmen presented a huge potential windfall for the industry.

To capitalize on this opportunity, the Hong Kong Dragon Airlines (Dragonair, www.dragonair.com) was founded in 1986 by Hong Kong Macau International Investment Ltd., a company controlled by K. P. Chao. Mr. Chao was later joined by Y. K. Pao, but after Dragonair's initially disappointing performance, the Pao family withdrew from Dragonair in 1989 and sold its shares back to the Chao family.

Realizing the need to acquire industry expertise in order to obtain better access to the Chinese market, Chao

decided to invite the Swire Group and CITIC HK to become partners. In January 1990, Cathay Pacific and Swire Pacific acquired 30 percent and 5 percent respectively of Dragonair's issued capital. The cost to Cathay was approximately US$38 million. The Chao family retained a 22 percent stake, while CITIC HK became the largest shareholder with 38 percent (increased to 46 percent in 1992). In 1992 Dragonair's shareholders were CITIC Pacific (46.15 percent), Cathay (30 percent), Swire Pacific (13.16 percent), and the Chao family (5.57 percent).

Cathay also entered into a management service agreement with Dragonair. As part of this move, some senior executives were transferred to Dragonair. Cathay transferred its China routes, consisting of Shanghai and Beijing services, to Dragonair on April 1, 1990.

Because of the booming Chinese market, the first half of the 1990s was great for Dragonair—in contrast to Cathay and the global airline industry. By 1992, Dragonair was serving 13 cities in China and 4 cities in north and south Asia. It established itself as the preferred carrier for passengers traveling to and from China. With expanding services and high load factors, Dragonair reported record profits in 1993. By 1994, it was providing services to 14 cities in China and 8 cities elsewhere in Asia by a fleet of nine aircraft.

Of course, the mainland market was not without competition. Since the early 1990s, the Civil Aviation Administration of China (CAAC) had gradually decentralized the civil aviation rights to established regional airlines in order to stimulate air travel. In addition to Air China, the flagship carrier, new airlines included China Eastern (Shanghai based), China Southern (in Guangzhou), and China Northwest (based in Xian).

With China's entry into the WTO in 2002, air traffic between the mainland and other parts of the world was expected to increase even further. Given the comparatively weaker Japanese and Southeast Asian economies, mainland destinations could become even more important. Apart from passenger service, the mainland was also expected to become more and more important on the cargo side.

Troubled Skies

Cathay's strategy of using Dragonair to crack the mainland market proved successful for a few years. Yet amidst such healthy progress, the potential of a threat was never far away. In 1992, CNAC had issued a warning by establishing a wholly owned subsidiary, CNAC HK, to act as its commercial vehicle in Hong Kong. To strengthen its ties to Chinese interests, CNAC and China Travel Service Hong Kong Limited each became 5 percent shareholders of Cathay in 1992.

Furthermore, in March 1995 CNAC announced that it had applied for licenses with a new airline company to fly between China and Hong Kong, and Hong Kong and

[1] "Red chip company" is the popular terminology for a company with strong ties to China.

Taiwan (a very profitable route for Cathay). Sensing that its worst nightmare might come true, Cathay protested by claiming a potential conflict existed if a Hong Kong airline regulator was allowed to operate a carrier in Hong Kong. For instance, CNAC could easily promulgate rulings that favored itself while penalizing Cathay, or even rescind its primary landing slots in the new Hong Kong airport. Unfortunately, Cathay could not rely on Chris Patten, the colony's last British governor of the colony, to negotiate with China. In addition to being a "lame duck" ruler, his relationship with the Beijing government was strained due to some last-minute democratic reform measures he had introduced.

In July 1995, Cathay announced a preliminary deal with the Taipei Airlines Association to license a second carrier in both Taiwan and Hong Kong. The additional carriers were expected to be Dragonair and Taiwan's EVA Airways. The Chinese were not happy. The general manager of CNAC, Wang Guixiang, stated that Cathay was not authorized to negotiate the deal, and that laws were violated. No specific action was taken, however.

During early 1995 a great deal of speculation focused on Cathay's future and its shareholders' intentions. In September 1995, CITIC reduced its holdings in Cathay from 12.5 percent to 10 percent. Then in March 1996, CNAC was rumored to have sold its 5 percent stake in Cathay. Many investors considered these moves to indicate a vote of no confidence in Cathay and anticipated that a powerful Chinese company would soon replace Cathay as Hong Kong's flagship carrier.

On April 3, 1996, one of the most influential financial newspapers in Hong Kong reported that the Swire Group planned to sell its stake in Cathay. The report claimed that the Swire family had approached five potential buyers, among them United Airlines, Northwest, and Lufthansa. Although Peter Sutch—the Swire Group and Cathay's chairman—categorically denied the report, the rumor persisted.

In May 1996 these rumors were put to rest when the various parties announced a series of transactions that resulted in the following shareholder changes in the different companies:

- CITIC Pacific increased its holdings in Cathay to 25 percent.
- Swire Pacifics' was diluted from 52.6 percent to 43.9 percent.

[2] "Beijing Is Buying Hong Kong—But at Its Own Price," *Business Week*, May 13, 1996, p. 24; "Changing of the Guard," *Asiaweek*, May 10, 1996, p. 53.
[3] China National Aviation Company Limited (CNACL) was incorporated in February 1997 to be the listing vehicle of CNAC Group. CNAC Group's 35.86 percent of Dragonair was injected into CNACL and an additional 7.43 percent was acquired from the Chao family and Peregrine International in a share swap agreement in October 1997 prior to its listing.

- The CNAC Group (a holding company formed in 1995 by CNAC to control CNAC HK) acquired a 35.86 percent interest in Dragonair from CITIC Pacific, Cathay Pacific, and Swire Pacific.
- After these transactions Dragonair's stakeholders were CNAC Group (35.86 percent), CITIC Pacific (28.49 percent), Cathay Pacific (17.79 percent), Swire Pacific (7.71 percent), and the Chao family (5.02 percent).

Industry insiders proclaimed the CNAC Group the deal's winner,[2] since it gained control of Dragonair at only 7 times its estimated earnings for 1996. Also CITIC Pacific was able to acquire additional shares of Cathay at HK$11, 15 percent less than Cathay's share price before the announcement, without having to reduce its holding in Dragonair.

Shortly after the deal, Dragonair was granted the right to fly scheduled flights to Chengdu, Xian, Qingdao, Urumqi, and Chongqing. Swire Pacific expanded its aircraft engineering, airport cargo services, and car dealership business in the mainland over the next couple of years.

Post-1997 Calm

Shareholdings in Cathay and Dragonair had been stable since the deal. By year-end 2001, CITIC Pacific held 25.6 percent in Cathay and 28.5 percent in Dragonair; Cathay held 19 percent in Dragonair; Swire held 45.6 percent in Cathay and 7.7 percent in Dragonair; and the listed subsidiary of CNAC Group held 43.3 percent[3] in Dragonair.

By June 2001 Cathay was employing over 14,700 people in 30 countries and territories around the world, which helped position the carrier as "the Heart of Asia." The airline carrier owned 7 aircraft and leased 62 more, while its average passenger fleet age was 5.9 years, amongst the lowest of any major airline.

Exhibits 1A, B, and C show the mainland passenger traffic and commensurate share of the major carriers in recent years. Exhibit 2 shows passenger counts and Cathay's market share outside mainland China. By 2001 mainland traffic accounted for around 17 percent of all passenger traffic in and out of Hong Kong, and Dragonair was able to maintain an impressive 31–36 percent of all mainland traffic. While Cathay's cargo volume dropped 9 percent during the first 11 months of 2001, Dragonair's cargo volume showed a 27 percent increase.[4]

Overall, mainland traffic was responsible for about 70 percent of Dragonair's business. In fact, this figure actually understated its share since a large number of Dragonair's Kaohsiung–Hong Kong passengers were in transit

[4] "Dragonair Flies in Face of Recession," *South China Morning Post*, January 17, 2002.

EXHIBIT 1a   **Mainland China Passenger Statistics 2000/2001** *(Passenger Arrival and Departure, 4/2000 to 3/2001)*

Source: *2000/01 Annual Report* of the Director of Civil Aviation, Hong Kong SAR Government.

	Total	Dragonair	Air China	China E.	China N.	China N.W.	China S.	China S.W.	Errata
Behai	23,856						23,856		0
Beijing	1,030,254	467,828	460,309				102,114		−3
Changchun	8,523				8,523				0
Changsha	59,141	25,521					33,620		0
Chengdu	142,834	68,359						74,475	0
Chongqing	67,782	17,316						50,466	0
Dalian	78,477	21,098	40,227		17,152				0
Dayong	20,914						20,914		0
Fuzhou	291,992	62,014		229,978					0
Ganzhou									
Guangzhou	326,829						326,829		0
Guilin	189,905	90,774					99,131		0
Guiyang	18,588							18,588	0
Haikou	135,061	43,089					91,972		0
Hangzhou	243,682	118,613		125,069					0
Harbin	13,802				13,802				0
Hefei	16,198			16,198					0
Jinan	29,618			29,618					0
Kunming	126,982	42,321					84,661		0
Lanzhou									
Meixian	15,258						15,258		0
Nanchang	22,186			22,186					0
Nanjing	192,981	95,577		97,404					0
Nanning	28,230						28,230		0
Ningbo	81,988			81,988					0
Qingdao	120,207	42,406		77,801					0
Sanya	135,957	18,143			60,299		57,515		0
Shanghai-H	1,507,430	768,756		738,335					−339
Shanghai-P	285			285					0
Shantou	99,696						99,696		0
Shenyang	23,095				23,095				0
Shenzhen	54		54						0
Shijiazhuang	21,496		21,496						0
Taiyuan	5,506			5,506					0
Tianjin	50,089		50,089						0
Tunxi	14,485			14,485					0
Wenzhou	19,494			19,494					0
Wuhan	70,640	6,704					63,936		0
Wuyishan									
Xiamen	294,665	107,632					187,027		−6
Xian	91,451	23,480				67,971			0
Xuzhou									
Yantai	23,610			23,610					0
Zhanjiang	8,290						8,290		0
Zhengzhou	22,588						22,588		0
Mainland Total	5,674,119	2,019,631	572,175	1,481,957	122,871	67,971	1,265,637	143,529	−348
All destination	32,612,363	2,815,705	572,175	1,481,967	122,871	67,971	1,287,632	143,487	
Transit	1,206,611	0	0	0	0	0	54,532	0	
Transfer	9,909,596	1,124,053	173,146	643,665	27,952	33,784	633,806	70,714	
Mainland/All%	17.40	71.73	100.00	100.00	100.00	100.00	98.29	100.03	
Mainland %		35.59	10.08	26.12	2.17	1.20	22.31	2.53	

EXHIBIT 1b   **Mainland China Passenger Statistics 1999/2000** *(Passenger Arrival and Departure, 4/1999 to 3/2000)*

Source: *1999/2000 Annual Report* of the Director of Civil Aviation, Hong Kong SAR Government.

	Total	Dragonair	Air China	China E.	China N.	China N.W.	China S.	China S.W.	Errata
Behai	23,643						23,643		0
Beijing	919,543	375,012	423,092				121,439		0
Changchun	8,382				8,382				0
Changsha	52,908	25,734					27,174		0
Chengdu	114,331	45,379						68,952	0
Chongqing	47,165	13,723						33,442	0
Dalian	67,613	21,451	32,802		13,360				0
Dayong	15,729						15,729		0
Fuzhou	269,057	38,066		230,858					−133
Ganzhou									
Guangzhou	331,692						331,689		−3
Guilin	211,884	105,700					106,184		0
Guiyang	15,157							15,157	0
Haikou	159,745	72,020					87,725		0
Hangzhou	227,776	107,403	45	120,328					0
Harbin	14,561				14,561				0
Hefei	14,621			14,621					0
Jinan	24,079			24,079					0
Kunming	154,140	60,097	47				93,996		0
Lanzhou									
Meixian	15,546						15,546		0
Nanchang	19,935			19,935					0
Nanjing	160,886	93,149		67,737					0
Nanning	19,852						19,852		0
Ningbo	73,895	1,604		72,291					0
Qingdao	99,370	30,684		68,686					0
Sanya	105,743				48,658		57,085		0
Shanghai-H	1,242,657	559,703		682,954					0
Shanghai-P									
Shantou	107,391						107,391		0
Shenyang	26,809				26,809				0
Shenzhen	127	127							0
Shijiazhuang	12,118		12,118						0
Taiyuan									0
Tianjin	47,987		47,887						−100
Tunxi	12,551			12,551					0
Wenzhou	17,804			17,804					0
Wuhan	59,970	5,661					54,309		0
Wuyishan	15,972						15,972		0
Xiamen	276,779	107,026					169,753		0
Xian	71,648	19,289				52,359			0
Xuzhou									
Yantai	21,792			21,792					0
Zhanjiang	14,850						14,850		0
Zhengzhou	19,440						19,440		0
Mainland Total	5,115,148	1,681,828	515,991	1,353,636	111,770	52,359	1,281,777	117,551	−236
All destination	29,598,732	2,413,449	515,991	1,353,636	111,770	52,359	1,294,594	117,551	
Transit	1,306,099	0	0	0	0	0	19,000	0	
Transfer	8,547,449	830,486	146,087	557,677	21,163	22,544	633,006	58,643	
Mainland/All %	17.28	69.69	100.00	100.00	100.00	100.00	99.01	100.00	
Mainland %		32.88	10.09	26.46	2.19	1.02	25.06	2.30	

EXHIBIT 1c   Mainland China Passenger Statistics 1998/1999 *(Passenger Arrival and Departure, 4/1998 to 3/1999)*

Source: *Annual Report (1998/99, 1999/2000, 2000/01)* of the Director of Civil Aviation, Hong Kong SAR Government.

	Total	Dragonair	Air China	China E.	China N.	China N.W.	China S.	China S.W.	Errata
Behai	12,237						12,237		0
Beijing	888,762	328,957	417,096				142,709		0
Changchun	5,640				5,640				0
Changsha	40,931	25,468					15,463		0
Chengdu	93,568	35,661						57,907	0
Chongqing	38,244	11,974						26,270	0
Dalian	69,440	24,355	35,276		9,809				0
Dayong									0
Fuzhou	197,826	19,946		177,880					0
Ganzhou	50							50	
Guangzhou	327,594						327,594		0
Guilin	174,596	95,750					78,846		0
Guiyang	10,763							10,763	0
Haikou	175,843	70,504					105,339		0
Hangzhou	209,456	89,964		119,492					0
Harbin	7,941				7,941				0
Hefei	12,540			12,540					0
Jinan	17,780			17,780					0
Kunming	97,081	21,591					75,490		0
Lanzhou	155					155			
Meixian	14,077						14,077		0
Nanchang	13,771			13,711					0
Nanjing	138,220	84,938		53,282					0
Nanning	17,144						17,144		0
Ningbo	71,580	10,599		60,981					0
Qingdao	79,387	22,369		57,018					0
Sanya	62,827				38,123		24,704		0
Shanghai-H	1,086,773	453,642		632,915					−216
Shanghai-P									0
Shantou	112,363						112,363		0
Shenyang	26,121				26,121				0
Shenzhen									0
Shijiazhuang	4,119		4,119						0
Taiyuan									0
Tianjin	55,263	5,322	49,752						−189
Tunxi	6,684			6,684					0
Wenzhou	15,704			15,704					0
Wuhan	50,283	9,872					40,411		0
Wuyishan	6,289						6,289		0
Xiamen	274,557	100,220					174,337		0
Xian	58,986	22,894				36,092			0
Xuzhou	70						70		0
Yantai	16,652			16,652					0
Zhanjiang	20,872						20,872		0
Zhengzhou	21,949						21,949		0
Mainland Total	4,534,078	1,434,026	506,243	1,184,639	87,634	36,247	1,189,894	94,990	−405
All destination	27,595,960	2,047,504	507,704	1,184,639	87,634	36,247	1,207,320	94,990	
Transit	1,443,564	0	192	188	0	0	14,610	0	
Transfer	7,236,781	656,403	125,719	436,468	14,219	12,988	542,435	37,392	
Mainland/All %	16.43	70.04	99.71	100.00	100.00	100.00	98.56	100.00	
Mainland %		31.63	11.17	26.13	1.93	0.80	26.24	2.10	

EXHIBIT 2 Passenger Statistics and Market Share of Cathay outside China (*Top 20 Arrivals and Departures Destination, excluding Mainland*)

Source: *1998–2001 Annual Reports* of the Director of Civil Aviation, Hong Kong SAR Government.

	2000–01							1999–00							1998–99				
	Total-Ar	Cathay	%	Total-Dp	Cathay	%	Overall %	Total-Ar	Cathay	%	Total-Dp	Cathay	%	Overall %	Total-Ar	Cathay	%	Total-Dp	Cathay
Amsterdam															106,070	37,898		110,481	43,592
Bangkok	1,345,684	420,444	31.24	1,319,170	431,730	32.73	31.98	1,299,522	407,658	31.52	1,274,008	407,049	31.95	31.73	1,215,237	383,644	31.6	1,159,801	367,575
Frankfurt	250,065	111,138	44.44	262,551	119,387	45.47	44.97	236,697	105,510	44.58	243,528	113,371	46.55	45.58	218,089	107,665	49.4	219,026	113,088
Jakarta	161,405	89,732	55.59	152,220	72,777	47.81	51.82	103,215	6,103	65.01	96,274	55,499	57.65	61.46					
Kaohsiung	513,787	0	0.00	516,696	0	0.00	0.00	469,518	0	0.00	470,330	0	0.00	0.00	392,958	0	0.0	399,215	0
Kuala Lumpur	435,516	189,980	43.62	371,474	161,793	43.55	43.59	385,368	167,398	43.44	322,920	141,139	43.71	43.56	335,643	145,377	43.3	276,060	115,976
London-Heathrow	494,465	226,573	45.82	487,363	224,271	46.02	45.92	475,658	205,523	43.21	466,240	210,445	43.21	43.21	465,421	192,747	41.4	450,577	184,559
Los Angeles	245,266	168,665	68.77	270,406	183,909	68.01	68.37	214,922	142,048	66.09	236,103	156,274	66.19	66.14	261,029	171,537	65.7	275,990	182,356
Manila	776,505	430,693	55.47	769,373	427,195	55.53	55.50	810,450	419,990	51.82	806,732	421,352	52.23	52.03	745,508	422,730	56.7	747,140	418,403
Melbourne	142,336	72,488	50.93	128,418	70,923	55.23	52.97	117,500	62,684	53.35	106,742	64,709	60.62	56.81	106,346	65,053	61.2	106,829	66,770
Nagoya															117,501	75,871	64.6	124,734	78,977
New York-JFK	149,085	68,737	46.11	156,729	59,894	38.22	42.06	145,235	64,332	44.30	153,084	53,789	35.14	39.60	149,269	69,317	46.4	143,696	63,961
Osaka	351,712	151,518	43.08	372,402	162,389	43.61	43.35	317,411	120,484	37.96	333,599	129,710	38.88	38.43	322,543	127,328	39.5	353,231	142,796
Paris	189,381	111,443	58.85	190,528	108,219	56.80	57.82	184,750	103,142	55.83	185,360	102,092	55.08	55.45	177,085	103,496	58.4	178,966	103,003
San Francisco	249,511	79,728	31.95	260,580	78,277	30.04	30.98	238,112	72,451	30.43	243,095	71,595	29.45	29.93	188,825	21,854	11.6	191,708	20,091
Seoul	699,209	263,287	37.65	679,596	255,341	37.57	37.61	691,889	255,761	36.97	665,739	249,079	37.41	37.19	609,839	231,304	37.9	588,998	221,326
Singapore	1,002,700	274,861	27.41	989,294	277,760	28.08	27.74	868,703	251,902	29.00	856,370	250,166	29.21	29.10	851,249	221,300	26.0	813,193	225,880
Sydney	353,064	152,599	43.22	359,807	156,678	43.55	43.38	312,794	117,564	37.59	320,571	127,691	39.83	38.72	312,306	125,736	40.3	315,799	133,409
Taipei	2,750,185	1,103,747	40.13	2,753,021	1,079,719	39.22	39.68	2,409,636	965,592	40.07	2,417,417	969,515	40.11	40.09	2,085,455	946,686	45.4	2,133,184	954,707
Tokyo	954,541	333,706	34.96	920,085	317,923	34.55	34.76	865,889	280,051	32.34	822,980	263,365	32.00	32.18	834,800	287,447	34.4	791,283	262,761
Vancouver	287,090	146,912	51.17	301,246	158,067	52.47	51.84	260,951	130,572	50.04	274,331	141,473	51.57	50.82	271,624	137,756	50.7	262,662	137,969
Total Top 20	11,351,507	4,396,251	38.73	11,260,959	4,346,252	38.60	38.66	10,408,220	3,941,765	37.87	10,295,423	3,919,313	38.07	37.97	9,766,797	3,874,746	39.7	9,652,583	3,837,199
Top 20/All %	69.47	80.31	80.07	69.20	80.07	80.07	69.34	70.09	80.55	80.55	69.80	80.53	80.53	69.95	70.67	80.88	80.88	70.07	81.08
All destination Direct and transfer	16,340,279	5,474,187	33.50	16,272,084	5,428,191	33.36	33.43	14,849,826	4,893,361	32.95	14,748,906	4,867,138	33.00	32.98	13,820,909	4,790,816	34.7	13,775,051	4,732,659
Transit	603,265	0	0.00	603,346	0	0.00	0.00	653,090	0	0.00	653,009	0	0.00	0.00	721,753	0	0.0	721,811	0
Transfer	4,952,754	2,444,437	49.36	4,956,842	2,445,984	49.35	49.35	4,257,412	2,161,747	50.78	4,290,037	2,190,622	51.06	50.92	3,610,150	1,916,144	53.1	3,626,631	1,945,710

on their way to and from the mainland and Taiwan. This was the second most popular route in Dragonair's schedule and accounted for 19–20 percent of its total passengers. Shanghai–Hong Kong was the most popular route while Beijing–Hong Kong was third.

Global Opportunities and Challenges

Airline industry experts forecasted that by 2020, global airlines would purchase 16,000 aircraft worth US$1,200 billion. It was estimated that infrastructure providers—airports and air traffic services—around the world would spend US$350 billion to accommodate the growth in air traffic. Global aviation was the prime engine of travel and tourism that at the beginning of the millennium contributed more than US$3,500 billion to the world economy, or 12 percent of the total. More than 190 million jobs were generated by the global aviation industry, or 8 percent of the world total. Capital investment for travel and tourism was at US$733 billion a year, more than 11 percent of the world total. This truly represented an enormous potential market for all the global airlines.

Whether Cathay could repeat its winning formula that had proven successful in the Asian region depended not only on the developments in the China market, but also on how effectively the company could address two major challenges: capitalizing on the benefits of globalization and growth without losing Cathay's local/Asian identity and individuality; and forging rewarding relationships with strong global partners without cannibalizing Cathay's own market shares.

The first challenge was essentially a "think global and act local" issue. Through networks with global partners, Cathay could become connected with a number of major markets around the world. However, it remained important for Cathay to reinforce "the Heart of Asia" brand image, anchored at Hong Kong city and conveniently linked with all major Asian cities. That image would provide a distinct advantage over other national flag carriers in Asia, even more than being known as Hong Kong's flag carrier.

The second challenge related to leveraging the relationships with Cathay's allied partners. Cathay joined with American Airlines, British Airways, and Qantas to found Oneworld in February 1999, and soon the new alliance had doubled in size with the additions of Iberia, Aer Lingus, and LanChile. By 2002 Oneworld airlines served 574 destinations in 134 countries and territories, with more than 8,500 flights every day. Further, the eight member airlines were expected to benefit by almost US$1 billion in 2002 by virtue of the various relationships amongst them: revenue generation, protection and feed, and savings from joint purchasing and shared airport and city facilities.

More Turbulence?

After a few quiet years, there were signs that the status quo might be changing again. It was reported that CNAC might merge with Air China and China Southwest Airlines.[5] The resulting group would have total assets of approximately HK$52.9 billion and a fleet of 118 aircraft. Also, the listed arm of CNAC Group swapped its rental property portfolio for a 51 percent stake in Air Macau, which principally provided a transit point for mainland–Taiwan traffic until direct cross-strait flights would be permitted.

The extent to which this would affect Dragonair's position in the merged group was of strategic importance to Cathay and Swire. Should Cathay strike out on its own? Complicating the picture further, in 2001 China Eastern Airline joined the Asia Mile Travel Reward Programme, which also includes Dragonair, Swissair, Japan Airlines, Japan Asia Airways, Asiana Airlines, and Qantas Airways.

In March 2002 Cathay announced that its net profit for 2001 fell 87 percent from the preceding year. According to its chairman, James Hughes-Hallett, Cathay's traffic had already been affected by the economic slowdown in 2001 and with the sudden drop after September 11, 2001, the carrier was forced to cut back several routes. To attract customers back to flying, the airline then discounted its fares severely. The reported net profit for 2001 was $84.7 million, down from $645 million the previous year.[6]

Adding salt to the wounds, the 2003 SARS (Severe Acute Respiratory Syndrome) epidemic also hit the Hong Kong tourist traffic and Cathay Pacific hard. In May, with international travel to the mainland restricted and SARS having spread to Taiwan, the airline recorded a loss of US$5 million a day.

Once the epidemic was under control toward the second half of 2003, travel resumed as China's rapid economic expansion continued apace. While high fuel prices increased costs and reduced profitability, by March 2004 the airline reported net earnings of US$167 million for the year, higher than analyst expectations.[7]

During 2003 Cathay Pacific negotiated intensively with Chinese authorities about getting direct access to three mainland destinations: Beijing, Shanghai, and Xiamen. Strong opposition came from Dragonair, where Cathay held a minority stake, and from government-controlled airlines including China Eastern Air.[8] In October 2003 Cathay was finally granted a permit for takeoffs

[5] "CNAC Looks for Boom after Merger," *South China Morning Post*, March 1, 2002.
[6] "Hong Kong: Loss at Airline," *New York Times*, March 7, 2002, p. W1.
[7] Ien Cheng, "Cathay Pacific rebounds, after SARS Outbreak," *Financial Times*, March 11, 2004, p. 1.
[8] Nicholas Ionides, "Dragonair Fights Cathay Pacific China License," *Flight International*, April 29, 2003, p. 10.

and landings in Beijing, and in December flights began, three times weekly. Access to Shanghai and Xiamen was still denied, however.

In September 2004, with important democratic elections in Hong Kong upcoming, the Chinese government further liberalized access to mainland cities from Hong Kong, although not directly to Cathay. The main question involved the role of a large new airport outside of Guangzhou, just north of Hong Kong. The giant Baiyun International Airport had opened in August about 80 miles up the Pearl River from Hong Kong, in direct competition with the huge new Chek Lap Kok airport outside Hong Kong, which had opened in July 1998. The move to preserve Hong Kong's status as the entry hub into China was seen as a political move by the Chinese authorities to reduce the pressure for greater democracy in the former British colony.[9] The pact also reaffirmed the limits on international access to Hong Kong destinations, limiting foreign competition and solidifying Cathay Pacific's status as the Hong Kong flag carrier.

In 2007 Cathay Pacific posted a 71.8 percent increase in profit, taking advantage of booming growth in Asia and defying the impact of historically high oil prices. The sharp jump in Cathay's profit during the year, well beyond the expectations of analysts of more than HK$7 billion, or US$900 million, followed similar performances from other major regional carriers including Qantas and Singapore Airlines. Driving the good times of the airline industry was a leap in passenger volume, in particular business travelers, as Asian economies enjoyed robust economic growth. Demand from business and first-class passengers was particularly strong.

But industry executives and analysts were concerned about dark clouds on the horizon from a softening U.S.

economy and a weaker performance in cargo traffic. While the growing business Cathay had in the aviation powerhouse of China was a significant plus, some 60 percent of its business comes from outside China, exposing it to a global slowdown. Still, the results confirmed the benefits of Cathay's acquisitions in China—the 2006 takeover of Dragon Air, which had an extensive network of connections between Hong and the mainland, and a stake in Air China.[10] Those acquisitions, which had now produced their first full-year contribution to the results, were already having a positive impact on the business of the Cathay Pacific Group.

Discussion Questions

1. Given the political complications, how attractive is the China mainland market? How would you evaluate the threat from Baiyun? What if China's economic expansion slows down?

2. What strategic alternatives are there for Cathay to develop the mainland market? Should it rely on Dragonair, develop new alliances, or continue to go it alone?

3. How should Cathay develop and market its global image without diminishing its local/regional identity as *the* Hong Kong (and China) carrier?

4. Should Cathay focus on China by attempting to develop it further or instead focus on the overall global market?

[9] Keith Bradsher, "Deal Preserves Hong Kong's Hub Status," *New York Times,* September 9, 2004, p. W1,7.

Source: This case was prepared by Eddie Yu, associate professor at the City University of Hong Kong, and Anthony Ko, associate professor at the Open University of Hong Kong, and revised by Paul Kolesa.

Case 4-5

Hewlett-Packard's Global Account Management

Hewlett-Packard, one of the Silicon Valley pioneers, was one of the first B2B companies to create a global account management structure for their major multinational customers. This case shows the pros and cons of such a structure, and demonstrates the kind of organizational effort needed to create it.

In a November 1989 interview, John Young, president and chief executive officer, Hewlett-Packard, summarized the situation in the computer and electronics industry that was the mainstay of this $11.9 billion multinational corporation:

"Customers no longer want a box, they want solutions."

In Young's view, the industry was moving from an era in which the product defined the solution, to one in which the customer defined the solution. A pure techno-

logical focus was no longer appropriate as customers were demanding more standardization and support. In addition, industry growth was slowing in the United States, which represented just less than half of the global market for computers and electronics. Challenges were particularly evident in H-P's largest division, the computer systems organization (CSO).

One CSO executive, Greg Mihran, manager, industry marketing, and a 14-year H-P veteran, summarized H-P's position as follows:

"H-P has a long history of success with a product-oriented, country-based sales and support organization. While considerable progress had been made during the past two years toward an account focus, ongoing efforts to adjust the balance between account and geographic strategies continued. It seemed evident, however, that the right answer was somewhere in between these two extremes. Both strategies must coexist to ensure success and respond to the complex mix of country and global account priorities."

Company Background

H-P, incorporated in 1947 as successor to a partnership formed in 1939, designed, manufactured, and serviced electronic products and systems for measurements and computation. The company was committed to a set of core values: leadership in technology, quality and customer service, financial stability, and uncompromising integrity in all business dealings. H-P sold nearly all of its products to businesses, research institutes, and educational and health care institutions and was one of the United States' largest exporters. H-P's basic business purpose was to provide the capabilities and support needed to help customers worldwide improve their personal and business effectiveness. In 1990, the company employed over 92,000 people and operated product divisions in 53 cities and 19 countries, with over 600 sales and support offices in 110 countries, and generated revenues of $13.2 billion. In 1990, net revenue grew by 11 percent following a 21 percent increase in 1989. In 1990, H-P experienced a slower net revenue growth in most of its product areas and declines in operating profit and net earnings when compared to amounts reported in 1989. H-P maintained manufacturing plants, research and development facilities, warehouses, and administrative offices in the United States, Canada, West Germany, France, Spain, Italy, Switzerland, the Netherlands, Australia, Singapore, China, Japan, Hong Kong, Malaysia, Mexico, and Brazil. H-P had a strong market presence in Europe with net revenue for European operations equal to approximately 5 billion dollars. H-P's market participation was weaker in Latin America but strong in Asia. The geographic distribution of H-P's orders was as follows: 46 percent—United States; 35 percent—Europe; and 19 percent—Asia Pacific (includes Latin America).

Industry Trends

In 1990 the computer industry was moving away from a geographic focus to more of a customer focus with an emphasis on global strategy. As customers demanded more standardization, hardware producers were being driven into complex and occasionally secret alliances. For example, AT&T, creator and owner of the Unix operating system, teamed up with Sun Microsystems to promote its standard. On the other side of the fence, IBM, Digital Equipment, and a few others were trying to promote another version of Unix, possibly the one used by Steve Jobs, Apple Computer founder, in his new workstation. These two groups then began to discuss working together on a common version of the operating system.

In addition, customers also wanted to work with vendors that provided consistent service and support across geographic regions and industries. Multinational customers demanded that vendors be strategic partners who could demonstrate an understanding of specific international needs and deploy solutions to these needs on a global basis. H-P executives increasingly saw the need for "one platform common across vendors and across many industries." While competitors appeared to be interested in taking a more global approach to the business, one of H-P's senior executives indicated that "the industry looked at 'global' as a buzzword." Many at H-P saw the need to integrate the current geographic approach with a global strategy.

Alternative sales channels such as dealers, two-tier suppliers, systems integrators, or resellers had become prevalent throughout the industry. Thus, companies in the industry needed to identify strategies to maximize these alternative channels and the opportunities presented by them. In H-P's case, the organization needed to couple industry/customer focus with an all-channel strategy as well as develop ways to measure and develop alternative channels.

Account Management Program

In 1990, H-P's account and sales management program was product focused, organized on geographic lines, and supported approximately one thousand accounts worldwide. Under this structure, sales responsibility did not extend beyond geographic boundaries and according to one executive, the amount of business tended to shift up and down from year to year.

The organization structure consisted of four levels. First, there were field operations managers for each of the three worldwide sectors: Europe, Asia Pacific, and the Americas. Second, each sector was divided by countries and/or regions, and managers were identified for each country or region. The number of country/region managers was a function of country size and business. For example, the United States was divided into four regions: the West, South, Midwest, and East. Each country or region manager reported to the field operations manager.

Third, the regions or countries, depending on size, were further divided into areas. Area sales managers reported to the country or region managers. Fourth, district sales and account managers reported to the area sales managers. Just as area sales manager responsibility did not extend beyond the area geographic lines, district manager responsibility did not extend beyond district lines. District managers were designated as the major account managers for the largest accounts in their districts but were also responsible for the entire geographic area. In addition, there were approximately eight sales representatives per district manager. Distinct geographic boundaries existed within this framework such that sales activity did not cross boundaries. Minimal interaction occurred between regions and districts and there were no mechanisms in the system to encourage interaction across areas, districts, or regions. In addition to the field operations sales and account structure, headquarters account managers were located at corporate headquarters. Headquarters account managers reported to the product divisions while the rest of the sales staff reported to the geographic operations. Account managers utilized these contacts to gather information and determine if H-P had sufficient resources to support their customers. One of the executives interviewed indicated that since the headquarters account managers reported directly to the different product divisions they did not always act in the interests of the district or region managers. As a result, many of the geographic account managers were not sure if they could trust or would benefit from the use of a headquarters account manager.

Performance Measures

Under the geographic structure, performance measures were based on product quotas. Managers focused on meeting product line targets within their designated region, area, or district. For many years H-P had set sales quotas and tracked performance by product lines solely within geographies. This was an important metric to quantify product performance but lacked clear differentiation of account quotas and expenses. Expenses and account quotas were reported and managed together within all other product quotas and costs in each country and region. As a result, within the product focus structure, it was difficult to differentiate individual account performance at any level and there was a lack of a complete measure of global account performance. In 1990, when H-P began to shift more to a customer focus, one senior executive indicated that it was very difficult to get the sales team to shift to an account focus while they still were required to satisfy product line targets.

The organization structure and the performance measures did not facilitate the development of new accounts outside regional boundaries. Area and district managers had no incentive to provide information to other district or area sales managers regarding new account development, as their primary focus was meeting product quotas in their own designated region or district. In many ways, different regions, areas, and districts competed with each other. Ken Fairbanks, district sales manager, indicated that if managers wanted to help develop business for a customer in another region, the manager was forced to use a "tin cup approach." For example, if an account manager for the Northwest region of the United States needed to coordinate activities for his customer in another region in the United States, he or she had to provide an incentive to the account manager in the other region if

they wanted any assistance. Mr. Fairbanks indicated that he had to approach managers in other regions with a "tin cup" or "beg" for support. Managers often spent considerable amounts of time trying to convince managers in other regions of the benefits that would result from their support. Managers in different regions had no incentive to coordinate activities of major customers across regions because their performance was measured only on product quotas for their region and was not differentiated for particular major accounts. Under this system new account development was lacking and product sales fluctuated from year to year.

Global Account Management

In January 1991, Franz Nawratil, vice president and manager, worldwide marketing and sales, computer systems organization (CSO), Hewlett-Packard, received approval to implement a pilot program based on a proposal for global account management. At this time, Mr. Nawratil asked Alan Nonnenberg, director of sales, Asia-Pacific, to help head the pilot program and appointed Greg Mihran as the new director of sales, global account management, CSO.

The program proposal envisioned a critical role for the global account manager (GAM). Accordingly, the pilot program focused on providing the GAM with the authority, power, and tools to manage the global account. GAMs were responsible for defining the global account sales and support needs and budget, developing an account plan, and identifying the goals and objectives for the account and the strategies and resources necessary to achieve those goals and objectives.

Trying to define the GAM requirements more completely, Mr. Nawratil asked Greg Mihran to draft a typical position description for a GAM. After some discussions a prototype position description was developed:

> *GAM Desired Skills:* Five years hardware and software sales experience minimum. Experience selling one of the following required: FPM, ERP, CRM, SCN, Security, Integration/Middleware, Business Intelligence, Data Analysis Applications, Database Systems, and/or data warehousing and mining solutions. Background in accounting, finance, and corporate finance solutions required.

The Pilot Program

The first step of the pilot program involved selection of the global accounts based on various criteria. Good executive relationships between the customer and H-P were required to exist and H-P had to hold a strong defensible position in the account. The global customer needed to be interested in developing a global account program and to also be demanding more global consistency and support than were other customers. From a financial perspective, global accounts were required to have greater than $10 million in current annual sales and support. The first six major global accounts identified were four American companies—AT&T, Ford, General Motors, and General Electric; one Canadian company—Northern Telecom; and one European company—Unilever. Within five of the six accounts, 5–10 percent of each customer's total spending on information technology was allocated to H-P. In the sixth account, H-P was heavily installed with 70 percent of that customer's business.

The dual structure defined in the proposal empowered the GAM to manage his or her sales team to meet the global needs of the customer. The GAM jointly reported to the country manager of the customer's HQ country and to the field operations manager, but was empowered to make decisions independent of geography. In addition, the GAMs were evaluated on worldwide performance of a single account while a country manager was evaluated on sales performance in a single geography.

To facilitate visibility of the program, a quarterly report, the Global Account Profile, documented by the headquarters account managers (HAMs), summarized the status of the global accounts. This report diffused information about the global accounts throughout the entire organization and worked as an internal awareness document. The Global Accounts Profile was not a problem-solving tool but informed executives of the opportunities and strategic issues related to each global account. It provided the GAMs with a vehicle to communicate the status of the account to the rest of the organization. In addition, GAMs held quarterly meetings to bring district sales managers together to share best practices.

The Ham Program

The headquarters account management (HAM) program was redefined during the first year of the pilot program and provided a point of contact at H-P headquarters for the customer. The HAMs represented the global account at headquarters, assumed global responsibility and ownership, and were the link between account-assigned executives and the global account. In this role, HAMs were seen as an investment by the global sales team to maximize success of the account. HAMs were selected during the development of the pilot program and two were identified by the end of fiscal 1991. Mr. Mihran, Mr. Nawratil, and Mr. Nonnenberg all agreed that sales and field experience was a requirement for all HAMs.

The HAMs worked closely with the GAMs to address technical, pricing, and strategy issues and basically to do whatever was necessary to support the customer. While the HAMs' role was to provide a point of contact at headquarters, they also traveled to customer locations about 30–50 percent of the time depending on the account. Mr. Mihran indicated that initially they did not realize how important it was to keep the HAMs together. But he soon found that locating the HAMs at H-P's

headquarters facilitated the sharing of knowledge as well as the development of an important network of resources across industries.

While representing the GAM at H-P headquarters, HAMs also supported business development opportunities presented by the global account and shared H-P best practices with the global account. One headquarters account manager, Teresa Clock, emphasized that the program provided business development opportunities that otherwise might have been missed. For example, Ms. Clock developed an alliance with a third party in Singapore to support the global account with Shell. This would not have been possible without the global account program structure because the country managers previously had no incentive to extend sales operations outside their region. Another HAM, Ann Johnson, on the Northern Telecom account, believed that a main benefit of the program was the sharing of best practices with the customer. In this case, Northern Telecom's operations were organized similarly to H-P's, and the sharing of best practices provided value-added support to the global account.

Internal Acceptance of HAMs

HAMs as well as the entire sales staff for each global account were funded by the global account. During the pilot program, not all accounts funded HAMs and several GAMs were skeptical of the value added by the HAMs' role. Initially many GAMs hesitated to invest in a HAM because of negative experiences with headquarters account managers and sales personnel prior to the GAM program. Within the previous account management organization, headquarters account managers had reported directly to individual product divisions and did not always represent the best interests of the major accounts they supported. As the global account program evolved, most GAMs came to see the value added by the HAMs' role in the new structure, and began utilizing HAMs where funding allowed. HAMs' value-added activities included the development of new business opportunities, sharing of best practices, account visibility at headquarters, and being the eyes and ears of the GAM. Some customers began to recognize the value of having a presence at H-P headquarters.

Other product divisions within H-P also questioned the HAMs' role. Many product division managers initially saw the HAMs as just another layer of management to deal with. Even after the pilot program, many product marketing managers were still not thinking along global lines. But most changed their view once the organization began to better understand the GAM program and the HAMs' role, and product marketing managers began to change their internal approach, emphasizing a more global strategy.

In fiscal 1992, 50 percent of the global accounts funded half a HAM, 20 percent funded a full HAM, and

30 percent did not use a HAM. In contrast, by fiscal 1993, 57 percent of GAMs funded half a HAM while 31 percent funded a full HAM.

Country Reactions to the GAMS

Within the first year, many managers at H-P saw the program as a fad and this presented a large challenge to the GAM team. But by 1993, approximately 80 percent of the people who viewed the program as a fad or did not believe in it were no longer in their positions with H-P. Upper management did not tolerate anyone who did not support the program. Further, individuals in key country management positions that were seen as obstacles to the success of the program were encouraged to pursue other opportunities. H-P did not expect automatic buy-in from everyone, and gave senior management two or three opportunities to buy into the program.

During the first two years of the program, the difference in performance measurements often created conflict between GAMs and country managers. Country managers continued to focus on their geographic regions and felt threatened by the GAMs. Field operations managers often had to step in to resolve conflicts or assist in negotiations between the GAMs and country managers. Many executives considered this as one of the problems with the performance measurement system. As a result, the global account performance measurements were revised in fiscal 1993. The new system linked the country managers' evaluation to the worldwide performance of global accounts headquartered in his or her country in addition to the geographic regions. This change reduced conflicts and provided country managers with an incentive to coordinate and collaborate with the GAMs.

Beyond the performance measurement system, country managers felt threatened by the GAM program as a whole. Outside the United States, the country managers controlled all accounts within their geographic regions. With the initiation of the pilot program, some of the country managers' largest and most profitable accounts were now under the control of a global account manager. While GAMs dually reported to country managers, the GAM was empowered to manage the global account to satisfy the account goals. In addition, because the program received a large amount of top-down support and visibility, GAMs were seen as having an advantage over the country managers. Country managers felt their territory was being encroached upon and this adversely impacted coordination between country managers and GAMs. Country managers that did not buy into the GAM program were given several opportunities to accept the program and work with the GAMs. If managers did not eventually buy into the program they were encouraged to pursue opportunities elsewhere in the organization or outside H-P.

Overall, H-P's senior management felt the program was successful, although during the first two years of the

pilot program a few global accounts changed. In one case, the customer had funded the account, then pulled the funding out, and the global account manager was no longer needed. In other cases, the global account manager was not the right person for the job. For example, an area sales manager was successful at managing several accounts in one geography but was not effective at managing one account across multiple geographies.

The GAM program had a high profile at H-P and as the program evolved and diffused to more accounts, its success became highly visible. While Mr. Nawratil's proposal was designed to use the current sales force, he did not intend to create an elite group or autonomous division, but this occurred to some extent. During 1992 and in early 1993, the success of the program was heavily promoted and in mid-1993, Mr. Mihran was requested to "tone down" the promotion to avoid conflicts within H-P. As the program received more visibility there was a concern that the success of the program might create tension between the CSO and other product divisions.

Customer Reaction

The initial response from customers was positive. Some customers identified the Global Account Program as a strong differentiator between H-P and its main competitors, IBM, Sun, and Digital. Ms. Clock, headquarters account manager, commented that the global account program positioned H-P as more than just a first-tier or second-tier supplier: "The customers feel value in the linkage with product groups and headquarters executives."

The HAM for Northern Telecom, Ms. Johnson, believed that her customer encouraged the global account concept and wondered why it had taken so long for H-P to develop the program. Ms. Johnson indicated that the program made a significant impact by breaking down barriers between regions and field operations. She emphasized that the strength of the program stemmed from the program promotion and visibility to other levels at H-P, and stated that Mr. Mihran had played a critical role in championing the program with executives. Ms. Johnson commented that this type of headquarters presence was an essential feature of the program.

Overall, H-P believed the program was extremely effective. The pilot program began with 6 accounts, evolved to 20 accounts in fiscal 1992, and 26 accounts in fiscal 1993. Mr. Mihran believed that customers were extremely happy with the program. H-P saw the program as a competitive differentiator and this was reinforced by the company's inclusion in Fortune's 1993 ranking of America's most admired corporations. In the category of computers and office equipment, H-P was identified as the organization with the best managers: "Apple is judged more innovative, IBM a better corporate citizen, but H-P's managers are tops."[1]

[1] *Fortune,* February 8, 1993.

Discussion Questions

1. What obstacles to global synergy do you see in the current sales organization?
2. How does the GAM program solve some of the global synergy problems of H-P?
3. What is the role of the HAMs? Why are they necessary? How do GAMs and HAMs collaborate? Is there any conflict?
4. How did H-P try to make the GAM program acceptable to the current sales managers? Are there any other options?
5. Would you say that the program was a success? Are there any negatives? Where should H-P go from here?

Source: This case was developed by George S. Yip and Tammy L. Madsen, Anderson Graduate School of Management, University of California at Los Angeles (UCLA). Copyright George S. Yip.

Name Index

Organization Index